Fodor's upCLOSE

GERMANY

the complete guide, thoroughly up-to-date

SAVVY TRAVELING: WHERE TO SPEND, HOW TO SAVE

packed with details that will make your trip

CULTURAL TIPS: ESSENTIAL LOCAL DO'S AND TABOOS

must-see sights, on and off the beaten path

INSIDER SECRETS: WHAT'S HIP AND WHAT TO SKIP

the buzz on restaurants, the lowdown on lodgings

FIND YOUR WAY WITH CLEAR AND EASY-TO-USE MAPS

Previously published as *The Berkeley Guide to Germany & Austria*

FODOR'S TRAVEL PUBLICATIONS, INC.

NEW YORK • TORONTO • LONDON • SYDNEY • AUCKLAND

www.fodors.com

ISBN 0-679-00442-4

FODOR'S UPCLOSE™ GERMANY

EDITOR: Tania Inowlocki

Editorial Contributors: Stacy Corless, Garrett Hering, Barbara Hui, Charles Mondry, Benny M'tudela, Deike Peters, Stephan von Pohl, Peggy Salz-Trautman, Vikram Singh, Sarah Sloat, Helen Sommerville, Michael Woodhead

Editorial Production: Tom Holton

Maps: David Lindroth Inc., Eureka Cartography, *cartographers*; Robert Blake, *map editor*

Design: Fabrizio La Rocca, *creative director*; Allison Saltzman, *cover and text design*; Jolie Novak, *photo editor*

Production/Manufacturing: Robert B. Shields

Cover Art: Elizabeth Opalenik/The Stock Market

SPECIAL SALES

Fodor's upCLOSE™ Guides and all Fodor's Travel Publications are available at special discounts for bulk purchases for sales promotions or premiums. Special editions, including personalized covers, excerpts of existing guides, and corporate imprints, can be created in large quantities for special needs. For more information, contact your local bookseller or write to Special Markets, Fodor's Travel Publications, 201 East 50th Street, New York, NY 10022. Inquiries from Canada should be directed to your local Canadian bookseller or sent to Random House of Canada, Ltd., Marketing Department, 2775 Matheson Blvd East, Mississauga, Ontario L4W 4P7. Inquiries from the United Kingdom should be sent to Fodor's Travel Publications, 20 Vauxhall Bridge Road, London SW1V 2SA, England.

IMPORTANT TIP

Although all prices, opening times, and other details in this book are based on information supplied to us at press time, changes occur all the time in the travel world, and Fodor's cannot accept responsibility for facts that become outdated or for inadvertent errors or omissions. **So always confirm information when it matters,** especially if you're making a detour to visit a specific place.

PRINTED IN THE UNITED STATES OF AMERICA

10 9 8 7 6 5 4 3 2 1

CONTENTS

2. FRANKFURT AND HESSEN 39

3. HEIDELBERG AND BADEN-WÜRTTEMBERG 65

4. THE BLACK FOREST 100

5. MUNICH 118

6. BAVARIA 151

7. NUREMBERG AND FRANCONIA 181

8. THURINGIA 212

9. SAXONY 238

10. SAXONY-ANHALT 263

11. BERLIN 279

12. BRANDENBURG AND THE BALTIC COAST 319

13. HAMBURG AND SCHLESWIG-HOLSTEIN 343

14. LOWER SAXONY 376

15. NORTH RHINE-WESTPHALIA 412

16. THE RHINE AND MOSEL VALLEYS 446

GERMAN GLOSSARY 465

INDEX 471

TRAVELING UPCLOSE

Grab a beer and find a shady spot in a Biergarten. Commune with Nature on the trails of the Harz mountains. Treat your ears to a Bach festival. Stay in a hay loft and wake up to a generous farmer's breakfast. Bike past half-timbered houses in the Tauber valley. Probe the underbelly of German art in Berlin's Scheunenviertel. Watch the sun set slowly from a windswept Baltic beach. Peruse Goethe's correspondence. Go castle-hopping on the Rhein. Dip into the Bodensee on a sunny afternoon. In other words, if you want to experience the heart and soul of Germany, whatever you do, don't spend too much money.

The deep and rich experience of Germany that every true traveler yearns for is one of the things in life that money can't buy. In fact, if you have money, try not to use it. Traveling lavishly is the surest way to turn yourself into a sideline traveler. Restaurants with white-glove service are great—sometimes—but they're usually not the best place to find the perfect *Sauerbraten mit Knödel* (marinated roast beef with dumplings). Doormen at plush hotels have their place, but not when your look-alike room could be anywhere from Dover to Detroit. Better to stay in a more intimate place that truly gives you the atmosphere you traveled so far to experience. Don't just stand and watch—jump into the spirit of what's around you.

If you want to see Germany up close and savor the essence of the country and its people, this book is for you. We'll show you the local culture, the offbeat sights, the bars and cafés where tourists rarely tread, and the B&Bs and other hostelries where you'll meet fellow travelers—places where the locals would send their friends. And because you'll probably want to see the famous places if you haven't already been there, we give you tips on losing the crowds, plus the quirky and obscure facts you want as well as the basics everyone needs.

OUR GANG

Who are we? We're artists and poets, slackers and straight arrows, and travel writers and journalists, who in our less hedonistic moments report on local news and spin out an occasional opinion piece. What we share is a certain footloose spirit and a passion for Germany, which we celebrate in this guidebook. Shamelessly, we've revealed all of our favorite places and our deepest, darkest travel secrets, all so that you can learn from our past mistakes and experience the best part of the 16 *Länder* (states) to the fullest. If you can't take your best friend on the road, or if your best friend is hopeless with directions, stick with us.

Garrett Hering is a native of the Pacific Northwest. He has a master's degree in Germanics from Portland State University in Oregon, and has lived and traveled in Europe for more than three years. He currently lives in Frankfurt am Main, where he works as a freelance travel writer, restaurant critic, and translator. He has also written for *German Brief*, an English-language newsletter owned by the German daily newspaper *Frankfurter Allgemeine Zeitung*.

Charles Mondry and **Deike Peters** currently reside in New York City, undertaking frequent expeditions in their ongoing quest to explore the earth's great mysteries as cheaply as possible. No strangers to Germany (Deike was born and raised in Dortmund), the couple grabbed pen and paper and headed east—to the majestic hills and valleys of Saxony and Thuringia. Their experiences in these recently Westernized, ex-communist regions made them keenly aware of the link between political ideology and big, air-conditioned shopping malls with fake plants and ATMs. Until not so long ago, the couple thought their hectic and unstable lifestyle to be just a "phase" after which they'd eventually settle down and buy a dog; they've since willingly succumbed to their voyager nature and their passion for learning from other peoples and traditions. In addition to writing, Charles teaches English and Literature at Borough of Manhattan Community College. Deike is completing her doctorate in Urban Planning at Rutgers University; her work on gender issues and sustainable transportation regularly takes her to far-flung regions of Europe, Latin America, and Africa.

Peggy Salz-Trautman arrived in Germany over 15 years ago to study abroad, but somehow she forgot to return to her native Pittsburgh. The time has been well spent, however. In addition to keeping her finger on Germany's pulse as a freelance contributor to *Time* and other U.S. magazines, she has consistently explored the country's less traveled roads. She winds up discovering family-run businesses and restaurants and frequenting beer gardens where only the locals congregate. Peggy has a passion for the so-called New German States—a misnomer for the former East German states, many of which are older than their western counterparts. Steeped in history and secrecy, these states are a real challenge to charter—but that's probably what she'll spend the next 15 years doing.

Sarah Sloat landed in Germany in 1992 to work for a couple years as a language book editor. Four apartments, a husband, and two children later, she is still there. She has since become a convert to German wines and, after holding out for five years, gave up vegetarianism in 1997 to finally experience real German food. Her favorite destinations include the little towns of the Rhineland region, the city of Bamberg, and rural Franconia. Originally from Plainfield, New Jersey, Sarah is now a resident of Frankfurt, where she works as a journalist for Dow Jones.

Since moving to Germany 12 years ago, **Helen Sommerville** has discovered the Teutoburger Forest and spa towns of East-Westphalia, and regions as far north as Bremen and Lower Saxony and as far-flung as the East Frisian Islands. As writer and editor of a series of Frankfurt lifestyle titles, including a visitors' guide and a food and drink guide published by the German daily newspaper *Frankfurter Allgemeine Zeitung*, Helen has explored the sights of the Rhine-Main region, as well as its culinary and cultural highlights.

Michael Woodhead often thinks his upbringing has given him a nomadic outlook on life. He was only six weeks old when he took his first long-distance trip, leaving his native England to go to India with his mother. She had decided that his father was having far too good a time on his own working for Shell. As a family they moved around the vast Indian subcontinent for sixteen years. After that kind of start to life, Michael tends to see those who stay put as a little parochial, and he himself has worked and traveled in Russia, the United States, Australia, and most of Europe. He's been based in Germany for four years, working as a journalist for the *Sunday Times* and contributing regularly to BBC programs about life in Europe.

A SEND-OFF

Always call ahead. We knock ourselves out to check all the facts, but everything changes all the time, in ways that none of us can ever fully anticipate. Whenever you're making a special trip to a special place, as opposed to merely wandering, always call ahead. Trust us on this.

And then, if something doesn't go quite right, as inevitably happens with even the best-laid plans, stay cool. Missed your train? Stuck in the airport? Use the time to study the people. Strike up a conversation with a stranger. Study the newsstands or flip through the local press. Take a walk. Find the silver lining in the clouds, whatever it is. And do send us a postcard to tell us what went wrong and what went right. You can E-mail us at: editors@fodors.com (specify the name of the book on the subject line) or write the Germany editor at Fodor's upCLOSE, 201 East 50th Street, New York, NY 10022. We'll put your ideas to good use and let other travelers benefit from your experiences. In the meantime, *gute Reise*!

INTRODUCTION

BY PEGGY SALZ-TRAUTMAN

Like a model pupil after graduation, Germany is both full of promise and anxious about its future. While it still rates among Europe's richest countries, Germany has trouble accepting that it is no longer at the top of its class. Despite what politicians say, Germans have only grudgingly given up their strong DM currency for the euro—whose value has reflected an eruptive socio-political climate. As a result, Germans, traditionally risk-averse, are worried about what will become of their hard-won *Wirtschaftswunder* (economic miracle) and their beloved political and economic stability. To further complicate matters, both the champagne and the economic boom that marked the first euphoric years following unification have long gone flat. For the first time in over a decade Germany is in a recession. Pessimism and self-pity run like a leitmotiv throughout daily life. Ask a German how things are, and chances are the answer will be "Bad, and probably worse tomorrow."

Indeed, Germany is at a critical crossroads in its development. Stuck in the middle is the country's new Social Democrat government, the first wind of change to sweep across Germany after 16 years of the Christian Democrats. Chancellor Gerhard Schröder, who many say takes lessons in smiling from President Bill Clinton, is having a tough time convincing the country that prosperity is just around the corner. His rhetoric can't hide the cracks that threaten to split Germany into a country of haves and have-nots. After Schröder formed a coalition with the minority Green Party in fall 1998, near chaos ensued when a rack of tax changes upset everybody except the unions, and fuel prices rose as the Greens forged a deal to hike fuel prices each year until 2002. All the while, political transformations have not been able to assuage the struggling people in eastern Germany—one reason why the former Communist Party there is making such gains. In search of a scapegoat, Germans in East and West are voting for their homegrown extremist parties, a lunatic fringe that covers the spectrum from left-wing radicals to right-wing fascists. It's a loud minority—but it's also a scary one.

To escape this gray reality Germans have adopted many of the bad habits socially-conscious Americans have been trying to break. Conspicuous consumption is the trend; traditional German modesty has been replaced by a fetish for status symbols. Even the corner bakeries advertise special offers on 14-karat gold chains and platinum rings. German youth, in particular, seems obsessed with sun, fun, and the pursuit of the perfect tan. Don't expect to run into them when you're on vacation; chances are they will spend all their free time in Spain or Italy and as far away from Germany as they can get. It's not without good reason that Majorca is considered Germany's 17th *Land* (state). Back in Germany mediocrity flourishes as television belches out a mix of old American reruns (*Married . . . with Children* has cult status) and daytime talk shows that would make even Jerry Springer blush. Some visitors may enjoy the similarities between Germany and the United States, but many on both sides of the Atlantic are waiting for the fad to pass.

It's not that Germans are shallow by nature. They are merely insecure and unaccustomed to being residents of a country that must accept responsibility and choose its identity. Gone are the cold-war days when Germany could hide in obedient silence behind its allies. That privilege dissolved with the Berlin Wall in 1989, and was permanently withdrawn when the Soviet Union ceased to exist in 1991. Today, like it or not, Germans must lend a hand in NATO missions, represent national interests before the European Commission, and generally grow up. Normally a country would embrace a chance to stand on its own two feet and take responsibility for its actions—but not every country is Germany. Without its allies to take the lead, Germany is temporarily lost and anxious not to make waves—hence the new popularity of third-person references and use of the verbs in the passive mood. Even the pacifist Greens, who adamantly rejected the establishment and ruled out compromise on issues such as nuclear energy and dual citizenship for German-born foreigners, are losing both their steam and their membership. Rather than create, take risks, and try to build a new Germany for the new millennium, Germans from all political parties are anxious to preserve the status quo. This wouldn't be so bad—except that globalization won't allow it.

Against this backdrop it's easy to see why Germans appear mixed up. Case in point is the Germans' sensitivity about their role in this globalizing world: To avoid the grave insult of being called "typically German," many simply refer to themselves as "Europeans." Despite occasional shows of nationalism, Germany never wanted to become a country in the first place. Crisscrossed by conquerors from Caesar to Napoleon and divided into dozens of fractious kingdoms and duchies, Germany finally united in 1871 on the basis of aggressive militarism. Allied with Austria, Germany went on to wage two world wars during the 20th century, sending millions to their deaths in concentration camps in the World War II. Germans have been trying to figure out how to deal with this past ever since, in a process termed *Vergangenheitsbewältigung*. While the scar of World War II and the collective guilt for the atrocities that were committed in the name of the Third Reich are a heavy burden to bear for many Germans, citizens of the former East German states, who were the least educated about the horrors of the Holocaust, are relatively eager to follow right-wing radicals and demagogues. The rise in social unrest and neo-Nazi riots has thus been most pronounced in the East, yet many sociologists are convinced that it is a mood that will pass. Many more are crossing their fingers. Recent government reports show a decrease in the number of right-wing and racist attacks—but this is not to say that the danger is over. Keep your wits about you as you travel through Germany: Avoid—as you would anywhere—dangerous-looking neighborhoods and angry demonstrations.

German society has undergone other profound transformations during the past half century. Postwar reconstruction in West Germany drove an economic boom that reached its peak in the 1960s. Facing an ensuing labor shortage, West Germany imported workers from southern Europe and Turkey with the expectation that they would leave when the boom ended. Meanwhile, these *Gastarbeiter* ("guest workers") married, bore children, and put down roots, and when recession hit in the '70s and '80s, they didn't just conveniently disappear. Today the German government can no longer ignore the touchy issue of dual-citizenship and hopes to achieve a compromise that will satisfy the demands of both the communists and the conservatives. For the most part, Germany has developed into a country that celebrates other cultures and tolerates all forms of alternative lifestyles. The German media are not afraid to give prime-time or front-page coverage to people involved in interracial marriages, homosexual relationships, or extreme sexual practices. The annual Love Parade in Berlin is just one of a long list of public displays of approval for nonconformism in its purest form. Germans are also learning to accept and applaud the renaissance of Jewish culture after decades of darkness and silence. Across Germany Jewish neighborhoods, schools, and synagogues in large city centers and small towns are finally rising from the ashes—it's a touching and inspiring rebirth to witness.

As always, generalizations fail to capture Germany's complexity. The same country that gave the world Adolf Hitler and crimes of hate is also synonymous with great thinkers and artists, from Goethe to Bertolt Brecht, Albrecht Dürer to Käthe Kollwitz, Bach to Beethoven, and Martin Luther to Karl Marx, to name a very few. Germany also offers a spectacular variety of landscapes and landmarks. The most finicky travelers are bound to find something for them, from the Rhine Valley favored by so many Romantic poets, to the beaches and Baltic vistas of Rügen Island, to Europe's new premier capital: a vibrant Berlin that flaunts a restored Brandenburg Gate, a rebuilt Potsdamer Platz, and the nearby Babelsberg film studios, completely revived and revitalized. Undiscovered expanses of former East German states invite you to step into a Germany of 60 years ago, where somber Gothic spires stand in stark contrast to structures inspired by the *Einheit* (unity) craze for glass and concrete elsewhere in the country. You'll find that many eastern towns reveal a startling juxtaposition of medieval castles, 19th-century palaces, and ugly "Bolshevik" concrete apartment blocks (now gaudily painted to hide their former drabness). Wherever you turn you'll discover a Germany coming of age; take advantage of this climate by exploring and trying to understand Germany's many, often conflicting facets.

GERMANY

BELGIUM
LUX.
FRANCE
SWITZERLAND
AUSTRIA
CZECH REPUBLIC

RHINELAND-PALATINATE
SAARLAND
HESSEN
THURINGIA
SAXONY
BADEN-WÜRTTEMBERG
BAVARIA
BAVARIAN ALPS

Cologne
Aachen
Bonn
Siegen
Marburg
Koblenz
Alsfeld
Fulda
Bad Hersfeld
Eisenach
Ilmenau
Weimar
Gera
Zwickau
Chemnitz
Plauen
Meiningen
Thüringer Wald
Hof
Coburg
Münchberg
Bayreuth
Bamberg
Wiesbaden
Mainz
Frankfurt-am-Main
Darmstadt
Würzburg
Trier
Mosel
Rhine
Main
Mannheim
Ludwigshafen
Heidelberg
Rothenburg-o-d-Tauber
Fürth
Nuremberg
Saarbrücken
Heilbronn
Karlsruhe
Stuttgart
Baden-Baden
Regensburg
Deggendorf
Ingolstadt
Passau
Danube
Danube (Donau)
Isar
Rhine (Rhein)
Tübingen
Offenburg
Ulm
Augsburg
Munich
Inn
Black Forest
Biberach
Memmingen
Freiburg
Tuttlingen
Ravensburg
Wangen
Rheinfelden
Konstanz
Bodensee
Friedrichshafen
Füssen
Garmisch-Partenkirchen
Mittenwald
Berchtesgaden

GERMANY

0 100 miles
0 150 km
KEY
Major Rail Lines
Ferry Lines
N
North Sea
East Frisian Islands
Baltic Sea
DENMARK
POLAND
THE NETHERLANDS
Sylt
Niebüll
Flensburg
Husum
Fehmarn
Rügen
Stralsund
Kiel
SCHLESWIG-HOLSTEIN
Rendsburg
Neustadt
Rostock
Greifswald
Usedom
MECKLENBURG-VORPOMMERN
Wismar
Güstrow
Teterow
Anklam
Cuxhaven
Elbe
Lübeck
HAMBURG
Hamburg
Schwerin
Neubrandenburg
Norden
Wilhelmshaven
Emden
Bremerhaven
Waren
Neustrelitz
Ludwigslust
Oder
Bremen
Oldenburg
BREMEN
FORMER BORDER BETWEEN EAST AND WEST GERMANY
Elbe
Wittenberge
Oranienburg
Ems
LOWER SAXONY
Stendal
Berlin
Potsdam
Brandenburg
Hanover
Osnabrück
Braunschweig
BRANDENBURG
Frankfurt-an-der-Oder
Odra
Magdeburg
Bielefeld
Hildesheim
Lübben
Münster
Halberstadt
Dessau
Wittenberg
Cottbus
NORTH RHINE-WESTPHALIA
SAXONY-ANHALT
Saale
Essen
Göttingen
HARZ MOUNTAINS
Nordhausen
Neisse
Dortmund
Halle
Elbe
Hagen
Kassel
Leipzig
Görlitz
Düsseldorf
Meißen
Buchenwald
Dresden
Erfurt
Weimar
SAXONY

BASICS

Basic Information on Traveling in Germany, Savvy Tips to Make Your Trip a Breeze, and Companies and Organizations to Contact

If you've ever traveled with anyone before, you know the two types of people in the world: the planners and the nonplanners. You also know that travel brings out the very worst in both groups: Left to their own devices, the planners will keep a grueling schedule and rush you in and out of Germany's once-in-a-lifetime attractions, while the nonplanners will invariably miss the flight, the bus, and the point. This Basics chapter offers you a middle ground: It provides enough information to help plan your trip without saddling you with an itinerary. Keep in mind that companies go out of business, prices inevitably go up, and sooner or later you're going to miss a train connection.

AIR TRAVEL

Thanks to the fact that the air routes between North America and Germany are heavily traveled, you'll have a choice of many airlines and fares. But remember, fares can change quickly, so always consult your travel agent before booking a flight.

BOOKING YOUR FLIGHT

When you book **look for nonstop flights** and **remember that "direct" flights stop at least once.** Try to avoid connecting flights, which require a change of plane. Frankfurt is the most common hub for flights to Germany; flights to Berlin usually require a connecting flight and roundtrip fares will be more expensive.

CARRIERS

MAJOR AIRLINES • The U.S. airlines that serve Germany are **American Airlines** (tel. 800/433–7300), which flies to Frankfurt and Düsseldorf; **Continental** (tel. 800/525–0280), which flies to Düsseldorf, Frankfurt, and Munich; **Delta** (tel. 800/241–4141), which flies to Frankfurt, Stuttgart, Hamburg, Berlin, and Munich; **Northwest Airlines** (tel. 800/447–4747), which flies direct to Frankfurt, with service to a slew of other cities by its European partner, **KLM**; **TWA** (800/221–2000), which flies to Frankfurt; **United** (800/241–6522), which flies to Düsseldorf, Frankfurt, and Munich.; and **US Airways** (800/428–4322), which flies to Frankfurt and Munich. **Lufthansa** (tel. 800/645–3880), the German national airline, flies direct to Berlin, Düsseldorf, Frankfurt, Bonn/Cologne, Hamburg, Munich, Stuttgart, and Hanover.

SMALLER AIRLINES • A German carrier called **LTU International Airways** (tel. 800/888–0200) flies from New York, Miami, Orlando, Atlanta, San Francisco, and Los Angeles to Frankfurt, Munich, and Düsseldorf.

FROM THE UNITED KINGDOM • **British Airways** (tel. 020/8745–7321 or 0020/8897–4000) and **Lufthansa** (tel. 020/8750–3300 or 020/8897–4000) each have up to two flights a day into Cologne, with a minimum round-trip fare of £90. British Airways has up to seven flights and Lufthansa six flights to Frankfurt from London, with a minimum fare of £95. Each airline has three flights to Munich, with a minimum fare of £135. British Airways has up to three nonstop and three one-stop flights to Berlin each day, with a minimum fare of £135. Lufthansa also flies to Berlin. Both airlines fly to Bremen, Hanover, and Stuttgart as well; Lufthansa has one flight daily to Nuremberg. **Air UK** (tel. 01345/666777) flies from London Stansted to Frankfurt and Düsseldorf, while **RFG Regional Flug** (tel. 01293/567977) flies every second day from Gatwick to Münster.

FROM DOWN UNDER • The only airline that offers direct flights from Sydney and Melbourne to Frankfurt is **Lufthansa** (tel. 02/367–3888). Otherwise, **Qantas** (tel. 02/957–0111) has flights from Sydney, Cairns, Melbourne, and Brisbane to Frankfurt via Bangkok. **British Airways** (tel. 02/258–3300 in Sydney or 03/367–7500 in Auckland) operates flights from Auckland, Sydney, Melbourne, and Perth to Frankfurt, Bonn, Berlin, Düsseldorf, Hamburg, Munich, and Stuttgart via London. Finally, **Cathay Pacific** (tel. 02/131–7477) has flights from Melbourne and Brisbane to Frankfurt via Hong Kong.

CARRIERS WITHIN GERMANY

Germany's internal air network is excellent, with frequent flights linking all major cities in little more than an hour. Services are operated by **Deutsche BA**, a British Airways subsidiary, **Lufthansa**, and **LTU**. In addition, small airlines operate services between a limited number of northern cities and the East and North Frisian islands, though many of these flights operate only in the summer.

German Rail operates a "Rail and Fly" service under which persons with a valid round-trip air ticket can buy a heavily-discounted rail ticket to an airport. Some trains that stop in Frankfurt also stop at Frankfurt airport.

DOMESTIC AIRLINES • **Deutsche BA** is headquartered at Munich's Franz-Josef-Strauss International Airport (089/9759–1500); **Lufthansa** has counters at any German airport; **LTU** is based in Düsseldorf (0211/941–8888).

CHECK-IN & BOARDING

Assuming that not everyone with a ticket will show up, airlines routinely overbook planes. When that happens, airlines ask for volunteers to give up their seats. In return these volunteers usually get a certificate for a free flight and are rebooked on the next flight out. If there are not enough volunteers, the airline must choose who will be denied boarding. The first to get bumped are passengers who checked in late and those flying on discounted tickets, so **get to the gate and check in as early as possible,** especially during peak periods.

Always **bring a government-issued photo I.D. to the airport.** You may be asked to show it before you are allowed to check in.

CUTTING COSTS

The least-expensive airfares to Germany must usually be purchased in advance and are nonrefundable. It's smart to **call a number of airlines, and when you are quoted a good price, book it on the spot**—the same fare may not be available the next day. Always **check different routings** and look into using different airports. Travel agents, especially low-fare specialists (*see* Discounts & Deals, *below*), are helpful.

Consolidators are another good source. They buy tickets for scheduled international flights at reduced rates from the airlines, then sell them at prices that beat the best fare available directly from the airlines, usually without restrictions. Sometimes you can even get your money back if you need to return the ticket. Carefully read the fine print detailing penalties for changes and cancellations, and **confirm your consolidator reservation with the airline.**

When you **fly as a courier** you trade your checked-luggage space for a ticket deeply subsidized by a courier service. There are restrictions on when you can book and how long you can stay. Look in your yellow pages for courier company listings.

CONSOLIDATORS • **Cheap Tickets** (tel. 800/377–1000). **Up & Away Travel** (tel. 212/889–2345). **Discount Airline Ticket Service** (tel. 800/576–1600). **Unitravel** (tel. 800/325–2222). **World Travel Network** (tel. 800/409–6753).

ENJOYING THE FLIGHT

For more legroom **request an emergency-aisle seat.** Don't sit in the row in front of the emergency aisle or in front of a bulkhead, where seats may not recline. If you have dietary concerns, **ask for special meals when booking.** These can be vegetarian, low-cholesterol, or kosher, for example. On long flights, try to maintain a normal routine, to help fight jetlag. At night **get some sleep.** By day **eat light meals, drink water** (not alcohol), and **move around the cabin** to stretch your legs.

FLYING TIMES

From New York, the flight to Frankfurt takes 7½ hours; from Chicago, 9–10 hours; from Los Angeles, 11–12 hours.

HOW TO COMPLAIN

If your baggage goes astray or your flight goes awry, complain right away. Most carriers require that you **file a claim immediately.**

AIRLINE COMPLAINTS • U.S. Department of Transportation **Aviation Consumer Protection Division** (C-75, Room 4107, Washington, DC 20590, tel. 202/366–2220). **Federal Aviation Administration Consumer Hotline** (tel. 800/322–7873).

AIRPORTS

AIRPORT INFORMATION • Berlin: **Flughafen Tegel Tempelhof** (011–49–30/41011). Düsseldorf: **Flughafen Düsseldorf** (011–49–211/421–2223). Frankfurt: **Flughafen Frankfurt Main** (011-49–69/6903–0511). Köln: **Flughafen Köln/Bonn** (011–49– 2203/404001). Munich: **Flughafen München** (011–49–89/97500), also known as the Franz- Josef-Strauss International Airport.

BIKES IN FLIGHT

Most airlines accommodate bikes as luggage, provided they are dismantled and boxed. For bike boxes, often free at bike shops, you'll pay about $5 (at least $100 for bike bags) from airlines. International travelers can sometimes substitute a bike for a piece of checked luggage at no charge; otherwise, the cost is about $100. Domestic and Canadian airlines charge $25–$50.

BOAT & FERRY TRAVEL

The quickest routes from the United Kingdom to Germany, via ferry, are through Calais, France, and Hoek van Holland, the Netherlands. The major ferry carriers are: **P&O European Ferries** (tel. 0990/980980) with Dover–Calais (1½ hrs) service for £25 one-way (£50 with a car) and **Sealink** (tel. 0990/707070), with Harwich–Hoek van Holland service (6½ hrs) for £36 one-way (£82 with a car). If you're coming from the north of England, consider **North Sea Ferries** (tel. 01482/795141) with Hull–Rotterdam service (14 hrs) with prices starting at £44 one-way (£114 with car), depending on overnight accommodation. If you're headed for Hamburg or northern Germany, you may also want to consider the direct overnight Harwich–Hamburg boats (20 hrs) operated by **Scandinavian Seaways** (tel. 01255/240240) with fares starting at £82 one-way (£136 with car), depending on overnight accommodation. If you're coming from Scandinavia, you can also get direct ferries from Gedser, Denmark, to Rostock (2 hrs), with good train connections on to Berlin, and from Helsinki, Finland, to Travemünde (near Lübeck; 38 hrs).

DISCOUNT PASSES

Ferries in Germany tend to be expensive, but the KD-line (Köln-Düsseldorf) accepts Eurail and InterRail passes, even on trips along the Rhine, as does the DB-run Bodensee-Verkehrsdienst, the main ferry operator on Lake Constance. In many cases, a rail pass will get you a discount on ferries, if nothing else.

BUS TRAVEL

Eurolines U.K., a subsidiary of National Express, provides direct service from London's Victoria Coach Station to some 50 German cities. Some buses run daily, others three times a week. All now go via the Channel Tunnel through France, Belgium, and Holland to Cologne (14½ hours), Frankfurt (15 hours), Stuttgart/Nuremberg (17 hours), Munich (20 hours), and other cities.

FROM THE U.K. • **Deutsche Touring** (Am Römerhof 17, 60486 Frankfurt/Main, tel. 01805/250254). **Eurolines U.K.** (tel. in the U.K. 0990/143219).

CUTTING COSTS

In Germany, all buses run by Deutsche Bahn will let you ride for free if you have a DB rail pass; some lines also accept Eurail and InterRail passes (read the fine print on your pass). Always ask about student discounts before hopping aboard, too. Many buses, however, are operated by local or private organizations, which have their own discount plans.

BUSINESS HOURS

Germany has laws dictating when businesses can be open (24-hour shopping is unheard of in these parts). Until very recently legal business hours were laughably short, yet now new laws permit stores to stay open until 8 PM weekdays and 4 PM Saturday. Bakeries are even open on Sunday (be prepared to stand in line). Gas station convenience shops, tiny versions of American supermarkets, are often open around the clock and stock a variety of items ranging from frozen pizza to corn flakes. Some after-hours shops in major train stations can meet your needs at somewhat inflated prices. Business hours vary regionally, with longer hours in the big cities and shorter hours in small towns. These restrictions don't affect restaurants and bars, which can stay open quite late seven days a week.

BANKS & OFFICES

Banks have always kept shorter hours than the law permitted, and so banking hours seem unlikely to change much. Most banks are open weekdays 8:30 or 9 until 3 or 4. Banks, as well as many other businesses in Germany, frequently shut their doors for 1–1½ hours between noon and 2. Banks in train stations and airports often keep longer hours; some open as early as 6 and close as late as 11:30.

MUSEUMS & SIGHTS

Museums are generally open Tuesday–Sunday 9–6. Some close 1–1½ hours for lunch, and a few are open Monday.

CAMERAS & PHOTOGRAPHY

EQUIPMENT PRECAUTIONS

Always **keep your film and tape out of the sun.** Carry an extra supply of batteries, and **be prepared to turn on your camera or camcorder** to prove to security personnel that the device is real. Always **ask for hand inspection of film,** which becomes clouded after successive exposures to airport X-ray machines, and **keep videotapes away from metal detectors.**

PHOTO HELP • Kodak Information Center (tel. 800/242–2424). *Kodak Guide to Shooting Great Travel Pictures,* available in bookstores or from Fodor's Travel Publications (tel. 800/533–6478; $16.50 plus $4 shipping).

CAR RENTAL

Rates with the major car rental companies begin at about $55 per day and $165 per week for an economy car with a manual transmission, and unlimited mileage. You will be charged an additional tax of 16% on car rentals. Volkswagen, Opel, and Mercedes are some standard brands of rentals; most rentals are manual, so if you want an automatic, be sure to request one in advance. If you're traveling with children, don't forget to arrange for a car seat when you reserve.

MAJOR AGENCIES • Alamo (tel. 800/522–9696; 020/8759–6200 in the U.K.). **Avis** (tel. 800/331–1084; 800/879–2847 in Canada; 02/9353–9000 in Australia; 09/525–1982 in New Zealand). **Budget** (tel. 800/527–0700; 0144/227–6266 in the U.K.). **Dollar** (tel. 800/800–6000; 020/8897–0811 in the U.K., where it is known as Eurodollar; 02/9223–1444 in Australia). **Hertz** (tel. 800/654–3001; 800/263–0600 in Canada; 0990/90–60–90 in the U.K.; 02/9669–2444 in Australia; 03/358–6777 in New Zealand). **National InterRent** (tel. 800/227–3876; 0345/222525 in the U.K., where it is known as Europcar InterRent).

CUTTING COSTS

To get the best deal **book through a travel agent who will shop around.** Also **price local car-rental companies,** although the service and maintenance may not be as good as those of a major player. Remember to ask about required deposits, cancellation penalties, and drop-off charges if you're planning to pick up the car in one city and leave it in another. If you're traveling during a holiday period, also make sure that a confirmed reservation guarantees you a car.

Do **look into wholesalers,** companies that do not own fleets but rent in bulk from those that do and often offer better rates than traditional car-rental operations. Payment must be made before you leave home.

WHOLESALERS • Auto Europe (tel. 207/842–2000 or 800/223–5555, fax 800–235–6321). **Europe by Car** (tel. 212/581–3040 or 800/223–1516, fax 212/246–1458). **DER Travel Services** (9501 W. Devon Ave., Rosemont, IL 60018, tel. 800/782–2424, fax 800/282–7474 for information; 800/860–9944 for brochures). Kemwel **Holiday Autos** (tel. 914/825–3000 or 800/678–0678, fax 914/381–8847).

INSURANCE

When driving a rented car you are generally responsible for any damage to or loss of the vehicle. Before you rent see what coverage your personal auto-insurance policy and credit cards already provide.

Collision policies that car-rental companies sell for European rentals usually do not include stolen-vehicle coverage. Before you buy it, check your existing policies—you may already be covered.

SURCHARGES

Before you pick up a car in one city and leave it in another **ask about drop-off charges or one-way service fees,** which can be substantial. Note, too, that some rental agencies charge extra if you return the car before the time specified in your contract. To avoid a hefty refueling fee **fill the tank just before you turn in the car,** but be aware that gas stations near the rental outlet may overcharge.

CAR TRAVEL

Entry formalities for motorists in Germany are few: All you need is proof of insurance, an international car-registration document, and a U.S. or Canadian driver's license (an international license is helpful, but not a must). You should probably get an International Driver's Permit (IDP) before leaving home. If you're over 18, your driver's license is valid in Germany for 12 months, but the IDP reduces confusion and complications. It's available from the **American Automobile Association** (AAA) for $10 if you bring two passport-size photos. Some offices can take photos for you; fees vary and nonmembers must pay cash. Some offices can issue an IDP in about 15 minutes, but be sure to call ahead; during the busy season IDPs can take a week or more. Stop by your local AAA branch and ask for the list "Offices to Serve You Abroad," or send a S.A.S.E. to the head office (1000 AAA Drive, Heathrow, FL 32746).

If you or your car are from an EU country, Norway, or Switzerland, all you need is your domestic license and proof of insurance. All foreign cars must have a country sticker.

Motorists have a choice of either the Channel Tunnel or the ferry services when traveling to the continent. Reservations are essential at peak times and always a good idea, especially when going via the Chunnel. Cars don't actually drive in the Chunnel, but are loaded onto trains. Cars without reservations, if they can get on at all, are charged 20 percent extra.

It's recommended that drivers **get a green card** from their insurance companies, which extends insurance coverage to driving in continental Europe. Extra breakdown insurance and vehicle and personal security coverage is also advisable.

FERRIES FROM THE U.K. • Operating car ferries between the United Kingdom and ports in the Netherlands, Belgium, France and Germany are **P&O European Ferries** (tel. 0990/980–555), **P&O North Sea Ferries** (tel. 01482/795141), **P&O Stena** (tel. 087/0600–0600), **Scandinavian Seaways** (tel. 01255/240–240), **Seafrance-Sealink** (tel. 0990/711–711), and **Hoverspeed** (tel. 0134/240–241).

AUTO CLUBS

IN AUSTRALIA • Australian Automobile Association (tel. 02/6247–7311).

IN CANADA • Canadian Automobile Association (CAA, tel. 613/247–0117).

IN NEW ZEALAND • New Zealand Automobile Association (tel. 09/377–4660).

IN THE U.K. • Automobile Association (AA, tel. 0990/500–600). **Royal Automobile Club** (RAC, tel. 0990/722–722 for membership; 0345/121–345 for insurance).

IN THE UNITED STATES • American Automobile Association (tel. 800/564–6222).

CHILDREN IN GERMANY

DRIVING

If you are renting a car don't forget to **arrange for a car seat** when you reserve.

FLYING

If your children are two or older **ask about children's airfares.** As a general rule, infants under two not occupying a seat fly at greatly reduced fares or even for free. When booking **confirm carry-on allowances** if you're traveling with infants. In general, for babies charged 10% of the adult fare, you are allowed one carry-on bag and a collapsible stroller; if the flight is full the stroller may have to be checked or you may be limited to less.

Experts agree that it's a good idea to use safety seats aloft for children weighing less than 40 pounds. Airlines set their own policies: U.S. carriers usually require that the child be ticketed, even if he or she is young enough to ride free, since the seats must be strapped into regular seats. Do **check your airline's policy about using safety seats during takeoff and landing.** And since safety seats are not allowed just everywhere in the plane, get your seat assignments early.

If you need them, **request children's meals or a freestanding bassinet** when you make reservations. Note that bulkhead seats, where you must sit to use the bassinet, may lack an overhead bin or storage space on the floor.

LODGING

Most hotels in Germany allow children under a certain age to stay in their parents' room at no extra charge, but others charge for them as extra adults; be sure to **find out the cutoff age for children's discounts.**

COMPUTERS ON THE ROAD

Checking your e-mail in Germany takes a little planning. First off, you need a local access number (AOL and CompuServe have numbers in Germany). Then you need to find a place to hook up. If you brought a modemized laptop, you will need to stop by a German electronics store to get an adapter for your phone jack (about DM 4). Then find a phone socket and dial away. If you don't have your laptop/modem with you, there are still a few places where you can plug in. Internet cafés, though few and far between, are popping up in larger cities, and you can, in effect, rent an account from which to telnet to your account back home.

CONCIERGES

Concierges, found in many hotels, can help you with theater tickets and dinner reservations: a good one with connections may be able to get you seats for a hot show or prime-time dinner reservations at the restaurant of the moment. You can also turn to your hotel's concierge for help with travel arrangements, sightseeing plans, services ranging from aromatherapy to zipper repair, and emergencies. Always, **always tip** a concierge who has been of assistance (*see* Tipping, *below*).

CONSUMER PROTECTION

Whenever shopping or buying travel services in Germany, **pay with a major credit card** so you can cancel payment or get reimbursed if there's a problem. If you're doing business with a particular travel agency or other company for the first time, **contact your local Better Business Bureau and the attorney general's offices** in your state and the company's home state, as well. Have any complaints been filed? Finally, if you're buying a package or tour, always **consider travel insurance** that includes default coverage (*see* Insurance, *below*).

LOCAL BBBS • Council of Better Business Bureaus (4200 Wilson Blvd., Suite 800, Arlington, VA 22203, tel. 703/276–0100, fax 703/525–8277).

CRIME AND PUNISHMENT

Germany has fairly rigid and well-enforced legal codes. While here, you are expected to carry some form of ID on your person, and small infractions (e.g., fare jumping on public transit, jaywalking) are dealt with quickly and efficiently with on-the-spot fines. As a foreigner (with ID) you can expect courtesy but not leniency, and pleading ignorance rarely helps. If you are actually arrested, call the nearest consulate or embassy. The police must let you make a call and take you before a judge by the end of the next day. The judge then decides whether to proceed with the investigation against you; if so, you can be held indefinitely—bail for someone without a registered residence is unlikely except for minor crimes. There are no jury trials in Germany; instead, verdicts are rendered by a panel of judges. Be forewarned that your status as a foreigner is rarely like having a get-out-of-jail-free card, and you'd be wise to plan your Crime of the Century somewhere else. If you are over 18, you may carry mace, pepper spray, or a stun gun without a permit.

Be advised that the possession of marijuana and hashish—even in small amounts for personal use—is still illegal and you'd be smart never to buy, sell, or smuggle any controlled substance. Though some German states (notably Schleswig-Holstein and Hessen) do not currently make arrests for small-time possession, purchase and sale is another matter. The legal situation is subject to change and it doesn't appear that Germany will declare the substances completely legal. Keep in mind that big cities tend to be more tolerant than smaller towns. As for alcohol, beer and wine are part of a German's culture from birth. With meals, particularly, it is rare not to have alcohol. If you look over 15, you will probably have no trouble getting served in bars (assuming you don't break the dress code!). Of course, public drunkenness is frowned upon, and you'd be utterly irresponsible to have even one drink before driving a car on a German highway. The penalties here are harsh.

Nudity is quite accepted in Germany—at appropriate times in appropriate places. Signs that read FREIKÖRPER or FKK tell you whether the park or beach you're at approves of nudity.

CRUISE TRAVEL

KD Rhine Line (Köln-Düsseldorfer Rheinschifffahrt) offers a program of luxury cruises along the Rhine, Main, Mosel, Neckar, Saar, Elbe, and Danube rivers. The cruises include four-day trips from Frankfurt to Trier from DM 720, five-day journeys from Amsterdam to Basel in Switzerland (from DM 1,456), and eight-day holidays from German Danube ports to Budapest (from DM 2,072). Prices include all meals. The cruises are supplemented by trips of one day or less on the Rhine and Mosel. During the summer there is good service between Bonn and Koblenz and between Koblenz and Bingen; both trips take around five hours. The cruises, especially for the newer Elbe routes, are in great demand, so reservations are necessary several months in advance.

CRUISE LINES • Köln-Düsseldorfer Rheinschifffahrt (Frankenwerft 15, D–50667 Köln, tel. 0221/208–8288); in the United States, **JFO CruiseService Corp.** (2500 Westchester Ave., Purchase, NY 10577, tel. 914/696–3600 or 800/346–6525) and **KD River Cruises of Europe** (323 Geary St., Suite 603, San Francisco, CA 94102, tel. 415/392–8817 or 800/858–8587).

CUSTOMS & DUTIES

When shopping, **keep receipts** for all purchases. Upon reentering the country, **be ready to show customs officials what you've bought.** If you feel a duty is incorrect or object to the way your clearance was handled, note the inspector's badge number and ask to see a supervisor. If the problem isn't resolved, write to the appropriate authorities, beginning with the port director at your point of entry.

IN AUSTRALIA

Australia residents who are 18 or older may bring home $A400 worth of souvenirs and gifts (including jewelry), 250 cigarettes or 250 grams of tobacco, and 1,125 ml of alcohol (including wine, beer, and spirits). Residents under 18 may bring back $A200 worth of goods. Prohibited items include meat products. Seeds, plants, and fruits need to be declared upon arrival.

INFORMATION • Australian Customs Service (Regional Director, Box 8, Sydney, NSW 2001, tel. 02/9213–2000, fax 02/9213–4000).

IN CANADA

Canadian residents who have been out of Canada for at least 7 days may bring home C$500 worth of goods duty-free. If you've been away less than 7 days but more than 48 hours, the duty-free allowance drops to C$200; if your trip lasts 24–48 hours, the allowance is C$50. You may not pool allowances with family members. Goods claimed under the C$500 exemption may follow you by mail; those claimed under the lesser exemptions must accompany you. Alcohol and tobacco products may be included in the 7-day and 48-hour exemptions but not in the 24-hour exemption. If you meet the age requirements of the province or territory through which you reenter Canada, you may bring in, duty-free, 1.14 liters (40 imperial ounces) of wine or liquor *or* 24 12-ounce cans or bottles of beer or ale. If you are 16 or older you may bring in, duty-free, 200 cigarettes and 50 cigars. Check ahead of time with Revenue Canada or the Department of Agriculture for policies regarding meat products, seeds, plants, and fruits.

You may send an unlimited number of gifts worth up to C$60 each duty-free to Canada. Label the package UNSOLICITED GIFT—VALUE UNDER $60. Alcohol and tobacco are excluded.

INFORMATION • Revenue Canada (2265 St. Laurent Blvd. S, Ottawa, Ontario K1G 4K3, tel. 613/993–0534; 800/461–9999 in Canada).

IN GERMANY

When going through customs, looking composed and presentable expedites the process. If you're bringing any foreign-made equipment with you from home, such as cameras or video gear, it's wise to carry the original receipt or register it with customs before leaving the United States (ask for U.S. Customs Form 4457). Otherwise, you may end up paying duty on your return.

Travelers age 17 or over may bring into Germany the following duty-free goods: 200 cigarettes or 100 cigarillos or 50 cigars or 250 grams of tobacco (half that if you are an EU resident); 1 liter of alcohol over 22% volume or 2 liters of alcohol under 22% volume; 2 liters of still table wine; 50 grams of perfume and 250 ml of toilet water; and other goods worth up to DM 350. If you're arriving from another EU country, you can import what you please as long as you can prove that your goods are for your own personal use and not for commercial purposes. Note that customs officials have agreed to an unofficial limit of 800 cigarettes and will stop you if your baggage consists of liquor alone; if you plan on exceeding these limits, you can count on a tax of 5%–30% of your goods' total value.

German goods carry a 16% value added tax (VAT). You can claim the tax back either when you leave the country or once you've returned home. When you make a purchase, ask the shopkeeper for a form known as an *Ausfuhr-Abnehmerbescheinigung*; he or she will help you fill it out. As you leave the country present the form, the goods, and the receipts to the German customs officials; they will give you an official export certificate or stamp and point you in the direction of a refund point where you can recover the tax in cash. Alternatively, send the form back to the shop, and it will send the refund.

IN NEW ZEALAND

Homeward-bound residents 17 or older may bring back $700 worth of souvenirs and gifts. Your duty-free allowance also includes 4.5 liters of wine or beer; one 1,125-ml bottle of spirits; and either 200 cigarettes, 250 grams of tobacco, 50 cigars, or a combination of the three up to 250 grams. Prohibited items include meat products, seeds, plants, and fruits.

INFORMATION • New Zealand Customs (Custom House, 50 Anzac Ave., Box 29, Auckland, New Zealand, tel. 09/359–6655, fax 09/359–6732).

IN THE U.K.

If you are a U.K. resident and your journey was wholly within the European Union (EU), you won't have to pass through customs when you return to the United Kingdom. If you plan to bring back large quantities of alcohol or tobacco, check EU limits beforehand.

INFORMATION • HM Customs and Excise (Dorset House, Stamford St., Bromley Kent BR1 1XX, tel. 020/7202–4227).

IN THE UNITED STATES

Non-U.S. residents ages 21 and older may import into the United States 200 cigarettes or 50 cigars or 2 kilograms of tobacco, 1 liter of alcohol, and gifts worth $100. Meat products, seeds, plants, and fruits are prohibited.

U.S. residents who have been out of the country for at least 48 hours (and who have not used the $400 allowance or any part of it in the past 30 days)may bring home $400 worth of foreign goods duty-free. U.S. residents who have been out of the country for at least 48 hours and who have not used the $600 allowance or any part of it in the past 30 days may bring home $600 worth of foreign goods duty-free.

U.S. residents 21 and older may bring back 1 liter of alcohol duty-free. In addition, regardless of your age, you are allowed 200 cigarettes and 100 non-Cuban cigars. Antiques, which the U.S. Customs Service defines as objects more than 100 years old, enter duty-free, as do original works of art done entirely by hand, including paintings, drawings, and sculptures.

You may also send packages home duty-free: up to $200 worth of goods for personal use, with a limit of one parcel per addressee per day (and no alcohol or tobacco products or perfume worth more than $5); label the package PERSONAL USE and attach a list of its contents and their retail value. Do not label the package UNSOLICITED GIFT or your duty-free exemption will drop to $100. Mailed items do not affect your duty-free allowance on your return.

INFORMATION • U.S. Customs Service (inquiries, 1300 Pennsylvania Ave. NW, Washington, DC 20229, tel. 202/927–6724; complaints, Office of Regulations and Rulings, 1300 Pennsylvania Ave. NW, Washington, DC 20229; registration of equipment, Registration Information, 1300 Pennsylvania Ave. NW, Washington, DC 20229, tel. 202/927–0540).

DINING

If you're watching your fat intake and your cholesterol level, then most cheap German food is not for you. Consider spending a bit more money and time in the country's better restaurants. You'll find that light pasta dishes and salads no longer play second fiddle to national pork and potato dishes; after all, Germans have become rather health-conscious over recent years. If you can find authentic German food (which may prove difficult outside of Bavaria), try **specialties** like *Sauerbraten* (marinated roast beef), *Karpfen Blau* (a regional fish dish), or *Schweinshaxe* (leg of roasted pork). Side dishes not to miss are *Knödel* (dumplings), *Spätzle* (noodles), and sweet-and-sour *Rotkohl* (pickled red cabbage). North German cuisine features treats like *Matjes* (marinated fresh herring filets) and *Häring Hausfrauen Art* (housewife's herring in cream sauce); both are made with sweet, marinated fish fresh from the docks. Place that diet on the back burner because desserts may be the high point of German cuisine. Do not leave German soil unless you've savored *Apfelstrudel* (apple pastry), *Lebkuchen* (gingerbread), *Erdbeertorte* (strawberry tart), *Rote Grütze* (vanilla pudding topped with red berry compote), or the heavenly *Schwarzwälder Kirschtorte* (Black Forest cherry cake).

BUDGET EATING TIPS

A *Metzgerei* (butcher shop) is likely to serve warm snacks. The Vinzenz-Murr chain in Munich and throughout Bavaria has particularly good-value food. Try *Warmer Leberkäs mit Kartoffelsalat*, a typical Bavarian specialty, which is a sort of baked meat loaf with sweet mustard and potato salad. In north Germany, try *Bouletten*, small hamburgers, or *Currywurst*, sausages in a piquant curry sauce.

For lunch, restaurants in local *Kaufhäuser* (department stores) are especially recommended for wholesome, appetizing, and inexpensive food. Kaufhof, Karstadt, Horton, and Hertie are names to note.

A number of fast-food chains exist all over the country. The best are Wienerwald, McDonald's, Pizza Hut, and Burger King. Nordsee (North Sea) fish bars serve hot and cold fish dishes.

To save money, **consider dining in restaurants serving non-German cuisine.** Germany has a vast selection of moderately priced Turkish, Italian, Greek, Chinese, and Balkan restaurants. All offer good value. Italian restaurants are about the most popular of all specialty restaurants in Germany—the pizza-to-go is as much a part of the average German's diet as the *Bratwurst* or a hamburger.

Imbiß stands—readily found on almost every busy shopping street, in parking lots, and in train stations—serve anything from traditional *Wurst* and stuffed rolls to *Döner Kebab* (spit-roasted lamb on Turkish bread) or Indian snacks. Prices range from DM 5 to DM 8 per portion. Wash it down with a German fast-food favorite, a Spezi (Fanta with cola), or stick to the excellent local beer. Also widely available, affordable, and greasy are the pizzas sold at stands and restaurants all over. Cafeterias at department stores like Hertie and Kaufhof serve cheap, mediocre food. One last note: The price categories in this book are loosely based on the assumption that you are going to order a main course, a soft drink, and a cup of coffee.

To turn lunch into a picnic, **buy some wine or beer and some cold cuts and rolls** (called *Brötchen* in the north and *Semmel* in the south) from a market, department store, supermarket, or delicatessen. Excellent bakeries offering fresh-baked, hearty German bread can be found in every neighborhood. Take your pick among wheat, rye, or *Mischbrot* (a mix of rye and wheat flour), dark or light, *Vollkorn* (whole grain) or not, with *Kerne* (seeds) or without. Local butchers and supermarkets offer an array of yummy cheeses and cold cuts, like *Schwarzwälder Schinken* (Black Forest ham). Together with sliced cheese or cold cuts, a loaf of bread makes a filling meal for two. Consider taking your fixings to a beer garden, where you can order a *Mass* (liter) of beer.

ETIQUETTE & BEHAVIOR

Unless you are dining in elegant restaurants, you will usually seat yourself and wait to be served. Smoking in restaurants, bars, and cafés is acceptable and no-smoking sections are rare.

WINE, BEER & SPIRITS

Germany is known for its beers, which come in an amazing variety, from *Alt*, a kind of ale favored in Düsseldorf (like English bitter), to the ubiquitous *Pils* (lager), brewed in subtle variety in nearly every German city (including the light, almost effervescent Kölsch of Cologne), to the heavier beers of Bavaria, like *Bockbier* (a kind of malt liquor), *Dunkelbock* (a darker variety of the same), and *Hefeweizen* (a yeast-brewed wheat beer, often called Weißbier or Hefeweiß). These brews themselves are nearly worth the trip.

While Germany is famous for its beer, German white wines, often made with the Riesling grape, are also worth a sample or two. Look for the labels *Qualitätswein mit Prädikat* or *Auslese*, which indicate wines of special quality. The best vintages tend to come from the Mosel valley, the Rheingau west of Frankfurt, or Rhineland-Palatinate. A unique and wonderful wine, little known outside Germany, is *Frankenwein*, made in the Main valley around Würzburg in Franconia. Be sure to have a glass (or two, or three . . .) if you pass through that region, or even if you don't. Germany also produces some competent red wines, particularly in Baden in the upper Rhine valley.

DISABILITIES & ACCESSIBILITY

The best advice is to call ahead to find out whether facilities are wheelchair-accessible; many regional tourist offices in Germany have lists of wheelchair-accessible restaurants and hotels. Plan your trip and make reservations far in advance. Always ask if discounts are available, either for you or for a companion; you may be pleasantly surprised.

LODGING

When discussing accessibility with an operator or reservations agent **ask hard questions.** Are there any stairs, inside *or* out? Are there grab bars next to the toilet *and* in the shower/tub? How wide is the doorway to the room? To the bathroom? For the most extensive facilities meeting the latest legal specifications **opt for newer accommodations.**

TRANSPORTATION

In Germany, express trains (InterCity, EuroCity, and InterRegio trains) are wheelchair accessible, while local trains frequently are not. Train stations in major cities are generally accessible, though even major stations may have only one or two accessible platforms. For access to trains on other platforms, travelers in wheelchairs will need to request assistance from the **Deutsche Bahn** (call the 24-hour hotline 01805/996633) three working days before their trip. Call **Rail Europe** (tel. 800/438–7245) for more information about accessibility where you will be traveling.

COMPLAINTS • Disability Rights Section (U.S. Department of Justice, Civil Rights Division, Box 66738, Washington, DC 20035-6738, tel. 202/514–0301; 800/514–0301; 202/514–0301 TTY; 800/514–0301 TTY, fax 202/307–1198) for general complaints. **Aviation Consumer Protection Division** (*see* Air Travel, *above*) for airline-related problems. **Civil Rights Office** (U.S. Department of Transportation, Departmental Office of Civil Rights, S-30, 400 7th St. SW, Room 10215, Washington, DC 20590, tel. 202/366–4648, fax 202/366–9371) for problems with surface transportation.

TRAVEL AGENCIES

In the United States, although the Americans with Disabilities Act requires that travel firms serve the needs of all travelers, some agencies specialize in working with people with disabilities.

TRAVELERS WITH MOBILITY PROBLEMS • Access Adventures (206 Chestnut Ridge Rd., Rochester, NY 14624, tel. 716/889–9096), run by a former physical-rehabilitation counselor. **Accessible Journeys** (35 W. Sellers Ave. Ridley Park, PA19078, tel. 610/521–0339 or 800/846–4537, fax 610/521–6959). **Accessible Vans of the Rockies, Activity and Travel Agency** (2040 W. Hamilton Pl., Sheridan, CO 80110, tel. 303/806–5047 or 888/837–0065, fax 303/781–2329). **Accessible Vans of Hawaii, Activity and Travel Agency** (186 Mehani Circle, Kihei, HI 96753, tel. 808/879–5521 or 800/303–3750, fax 808/879–0649). **CareVacations** (5-5110 50th Ave., Leduc, Alberta T9E 6V4, tel. 780/986–6404 or 877/478–7827, fax 780/986–8332) has group tours and is especially helpful with cruise vacations. **Flying Wheels Travel** (143 W. Bridge St., Box 382, Owatonna, MN 55060, tel. 507/451–5005 or 800/535–6790, fax 507/451–1685). **Hinsdale Travel Service** (201 E. Ogden Ave., Suite 100, Hinsdale, IL 60521, tel. 630/325–1335,fax 630/325–1342). **Tomorrow's Level of Care** (Box 470299, Brooklyn, NY 11247, tel. 718/756–0794 or 800/932–2012), for nursing services and medical equipment.

TRAVELERS WITH DEVELOPMENTAL DISABILITIES • New Directions (5276 Hollister Ave., Suite 207, Santa Barbara, CA 93111, tel. 805/967–2841 or 888/967–2841, fax 805/964–7344). **Sprout** (893 Amsterdam Ave., New York, NY 10025, tel. 212/222–9575 or 888/222–9575, fax 212/222–9768).

DISCOUNTS & DEALS

Be a smart shopper and **compare all your options** before making decisions. A plane ticket bought with a promotional coupon from travel clubs, coupon books, and direct-mail offers may not be cheaper than the least expensive fare from a discount ticket agency. And always keep in mind that what you get is just as important as what you save.

DISCOUNT RESERVATIONS

To save money **look into discount-reservations services** with toll-free numbers, which use their buying power to get a better price on hotels, airline tickets, even car rentals. When booking a room, always **call the hotel's local toll-free number** (if one is available) rather than the central reservations number—you'll often get a better price. Always ask about special packages or corporate rates.

When shopping for the best deal on hotels and car rentals **look for guaranteed exchange rates,** which protect you against a falling dollar. With your rate locked in, you won't pay more, even if the price goes up in the local currency.

AIRLINE TICKETS • 800/FLY–4–LESS; **800/FLY–ASAP**.

HOTEL ROOMS • Accommodations Express (tel. 800/444–7666). **Central Reservation Service (CRS)** (tel. 800/548–3311). **Hotel Reservations Network** (tel. 800/964–6835). **International Marketing & Travel Concepts** (tel. 800/790–4682). **Players Express Vacations** (tel. 800/458–6161). **Quickbook** (tel. 800/789–9887). **Room Finders USA** (tel. 800/473–7829). **RMC Travel** (tel. 800/245–5738). **Steigenberger Reservation Service** (tel. 800/223–5652). **Travel Interlink** (tel. 800/888–5898). **VacationLand** (tel. 800/245–0050).

PACKAGE DEALS

Don't confuse packages and guided tours. When you buy a package, you travel on your own, just as though you had planned the trip yourself. Fly/drive packages, which combine airfare and car rental, are often a good deal. In cities, ask the local visitor's bureau about hotel packages that include tickets to major museum exhibits or other special events. If you **buy a rail/drive pass** you may save on train tickets and car rentals. All Eurail- and Europass holders get a discount on Eurostar fares through the Channel Tunnel. A German Rail Pass is also good for travel aboard some KD River Steamers and some Deutsche Touring/Europabus routes.

DUTY-FREE SHOPPING

Duty-free shopping is no longer available on journeys within the European Union (EU), but you can still purchase duty-free goods (sometimes called tax-free goods or travel value goods) when traveling between an EU country and a country outside the EU.

The new regulation on duty-free shopping went into effect on July 1, 1999, and affects the following countries: Austria, Belgium, Denmark, Ireland, Finland, France, Germany, Greece, Italy, Luxembourg, the Netherlands, Portugal, Spain (but not the Canary Islands), Sweden, and the United Kingdom (but not the Channel Islands or Gibraltar). You may thus purchase duty-free goods when traveling between Germany and Gibraltar, but not between Germany and France.

ELECTRICITY

To use your U.S.-purchased electric-powered equipment **bring a converter and adapter.** The electrical current in Germany is 220 volts, 50 cycles alternating current (AC); wall outlets take Continental-type plugs, with two round prongs.

If your appliances are dual-voltage you'll need only an adapter. Most laptops operate equally well on 110 and 220 volts and so require only an adapter.

EMBASSIES

AUSTRALIA • Uhlandstr. 181–183, Berlin, tel. 030/880–0880.

CANADA • Friedrichstr. 95, Berlin, tel. 030/261–1161.

NEW ZEALAND • Bundeskanzlerpl. 2, Bonn, tel. 0228/228070, fax 0228/221687.

UNITED KINGDOM • Unter den Linden 32–34, Berlin, tel. 030/201840.

UNITED STATES • Embassy: Neustädtische Kirchstr. 4, Berlin, tel. 030/238–5174; Consulate: Clayallee 170, Berlin, tel. 030/832–9233.

EMERGENCIES

For aspirin, prescriptions, and the like, head to your neighborhood *Apotheke* (pharmacy). Posted on every pharmacy's door is the address of the nearest all-night pharmacy. For an ambulance, call 112. The police number is 110 in Germany. Someone at these numbers usually speaks English.

GAY & LESBIAN TRAVEL

Homophobia is no more rampant in Germany than anywhere else in the western world. As could be expected, it's generally less widespread in larger cities than in small towns. If confronted with homophobia, your best bet is simply to turn around and walk away. On a more positive note, gay nightclubs and other gathering spots can be found in most large cities in Germany. Refer to individual chapters in this book for specific listings.

GAY- AND LESBIAN-FRIENDLY TRAVEL AGENCIES • **Different Roads Travel** (8383 Wilshire Blvd., Suite 902, Beverly Hills, CA 90211, tel. 323/651–5557 or 800/429–8747, fax 323/651–3678). **Kennedy Travel** (314 Jericho Turnpike, Floral Park, NY 11001, tel. 516/352–4888 or 800/237–7433, fax 516/354–8849). **Now Voyager** (4406 18th St., San Francisco, CA 94114, tel. 415/626–1169 or 800/255–6951, fax 415/626–8626). **Skylink Travel and Tour** (1006 Mendocino Ave., Santa Rosa, CA 95401, tel. 707/546–9888 or 800/225–5759, fax 707/546–9891), serving lesbian travelers.

PUBLICATIONS

Are You Two . . . Together?, written by Lindsy Van Gelder and published by Random House, provides insight into issues facing same-sex pairs on the road. It's fairly anecdotal and skimps on practical details like phone numbers and addresses, but it still makes an excellent read at $18. *Spartacus International Gay Guide* ($32.95) bills itself as the guide for the gay male traveler, with practical tips and reviews of hotels and agencies in over 160 countries. This book is available at gay and lesbian bookstores or by mail through the Damron Company (Box 422458, San Francisco, CA 94142, tel. 800/462–6654). Another excellent resource for gay men is the bilingual "Von Hinten/From Behind" (e.g., *Berlin von Hinten*) series of guides to big German cities, with listings for every need, from outdoor cruising zones to health services. They are available at gay and lesbian bookstores. One of the better gay and lesbian travel newsletters is *Out and About*, with listings of gay-friendly hotels and travel agencies, plus health cautions for travelers with HIV. A 10-issue subscription costs $49; single issues cost about $5; call 800/929–2268. Once in Germany, lesbians should buy a copy of *UK2*; *Männer Aktuell* and *Magnus* are for the guys.

HEALTH

AIDS and other sexually transmitted diseases (STDs) do not respect national boundaries, and protection when you travel takes the same form as it does at home. The best form of protection is condoms (*Kondome* in German), readily available throughout Germany. Avoid buying them from machines: They could be ancient or only for "novelty" use. Pharmacies and large grocery stores have the most reliable goods. Council Travel distributes a free "AIDS and International Travel" brochure containing information on safe sex, HIV testing, and hotline numbers. Women should bring any birth-control gear from home because it is often not readily available abroad (birth-control pills require a prescription in Germany).

MEDICAL PLANS

No one plans to get sick while traveling, but it happens, so **consider signing up with a medical-assistance company.** Members get doctor referrals, emergency evacuation or repatriation, hot lines for medical consultation, cash for emergencies, and other assistance.

MEDICAL-ASSISTANCE COMPANIES • AEA International SOS (8 Neshaminy Interplex, Suite 207, Trevose, PA 19053, tel. 215/245–4707 or 800/523–6586, fax 215/244–9617; 12 Chemin Riantbosson, 1217 Meyrin 1, Geneva, Switzerland, tel. 4122/785–6464, fax 4122/785–6424; 331 N. Bridge Rd., 17-00, Odeon Towers, Singapore 188720, tel. 65/338–7800, fax 65/338–7611).

MEDICAL ASSISTANCE

A list of English-speaking doctors is usually available from your embassy and often at local tourist offices. Although most doctors in Germany speak some English, having a phrase book on hand never hurts. To be better informed before you go, or to just have an emergency number handy, contact the organizations below.

International Association for Medical Assistance to Travellers (IAMAT) is a nonprofit travelers' health organization that provides a worldwide directory of qualified English-speaking physicians who are on 24-hour call and who have agreed to a fixed-fee schedule. Membership is free; donations are appreciated. United States: 417 Center St., Lewiston, NY 14092, tel. 716/754–4883. Canada: 40 Regal Rd., Guelph, Ont. N1K 1B5, tel. 519/836–0102. Switzerland: 57 Voirets, 1212 Grand-Lancy-Geneva. New Zealand: Box 5049, Christchurch 5.

British travelers can join **Europe Assistance Worldwide Services** (252 High St., Croyden, Surrey CR0 1NF, tel. 0181/680–1234) to gain access to a 24-hour, 365-day-a-year telephone hotline that can help in a medical emergency. The American branch of this organization is **Worldwide Assistance Incorporated** (1133 15th St. NW, Suite 400, Washington, DC 20005, tel. 800/821–2828), which offers emergency evacuation services and 24-hour medical referrals. An individual membership costs $62 for up to 15 days, $164 for 60 days. Families may purchase coverage for $92 for 15 days, $234 for 60 days.

Diabetic travelers should contact one of the following organizations for resources and medical referrals: **American Diabetes Association** (1660 Duke St., Alexandria, VA 22314, tel. 703/549–1500 or 800/232–3472) or **Canadian Diabetes Association** (15 Toronto St., Suite 1001, Toronto, Ont. M5C 2E3, tel. 416/363–3373). The **Diabetic Traveler** (Box 8223, Stamford, CT 06905, tel. 203/327–5832), published four times a year, lists vacations geared toward diabetics and offers travel and medical advice. Subscriptions are $18.95. An informative article entitled "Management of Diabetes During Intercontinental Travel" and an insulin adjustment card are available for free.

PRESCRIPTIONS

If you take prescription drugs, prior to your trip ask your doctor to type an extra prescription including the following information: dosage, the drug's generic name, and the manufacturer's name. To avoid problems clearing customs, diabetic travelers carrying syringes should have handy a letter from their physician confirming their need for insulin injections. If you need to fill a prescription after regular business hours (9–6:30 in most cities), each German town has a system of rotating after-hours pharmacies. Every *Apotheke* (pharmacy) posts the name, address, and telephone number of that night's late-night pharmacy on its front door.

HOLIDAYS

To avoid being caught without cash on bank holidays or going hungry when stores close, keep in mind the following holidays in Germany: New Year's Day; January 6 (Epiphany, only in parts of southern Germany); Good Friday, Easter Sunday, and Easter Monday; May 1 (Workers' Day); the Thursday 40 days after Easter (Ascension Day, or *Himmelfahrt*); the seventh Sunday and Monday after Easter (Pentecost, or *Pfingsten*); the following Thursday (Corpus Christi, or *Fronleichnam*, only in parts of southern Germany); August 15 (St. Mary's Ascension, only in parts of southern Germany); October 3 (Unification Day); November 1 (All Saints' Day); Day of Repentance and Prayer (a Wednesday in mid-November, observed only in some German states); and December 25–26 (Christmas). Certain other regional holidays exist to catch you off guard.

INSURANCE

The most useful travel insurance plan is a comprehensive policy that includes coverage for trip cancellation and interruption, default, trip delay, and medical expenses (with a waiver for preexisting conditions).

Without insurance you will lose all or most of your money if you cancel your trip, regardless of the reason. Default insurance covers you if your tour operator, airline, or cruise line goes out of business. Trip-delay covers expenses that arise because of bad weather or mechanical delays. Study the fine print when comparing policies.

If you're traveling internationally, a key component of travel insurance is coverage for medical bills incurred if you get sick on the road. Such expenses are not generally covered by Medicare or private policies. U.K. residents can buy a travel-insurance policy valid for most vacations taken during the year in which it's purchased (but check preexisting-condition coverage). British and Australian citizens need extra medical coverage when traveling overseas. British and Australian citizens need extra medical coverage when traveling abroad.

Always **buy travel policies directly from the insurance company**; if you buy it from a cruise line, airline, or tour operator that goes out of business you probably will not be covered for the agency or operator's default, a major risk. Before you make any purchase **review your existing health and home-owner's policies** to find what they cover away from home.

TRAVEL INSURERS • In the U.S. **Access America** (6600 W. Broad St., Richmond, VA 23230, tel. 804/285–3300 or 800/284–8300), **Travel Guard International** (1145 Clark St., Stevens Point, WI 54481, tel. 715/345–0505 or 800/826–1300). In Canada **Voyager Insurance** (44 Peel Center Dr., Brampton, Ontario L6T 4M8, tel. 905/791–8700; 800/668–4342 in Canada).

INSURANCE INFORMATION • In the U.K. the **Association of British Insurers** (51–55 Gresham St., London EC2V 7HQ, tel. 020/7600–3333, fax 020/7696–8999). In Australia the **Insurance Council of Australia** (tel. 03/9614–1077, fax 03/9614–7924).

LANGUAGE

You'll find that English is spoken in most hotels, restaurants, airports, stations, museums, and other places of interest, especially in urban regions of western Germany. English is not widely spoken in rural areas and in the eastern part of Germany.

Although most Germans can speak High, or standard, German, you may hear regional dialects throughout the country. Unless you're fluent in German, these dialects may be hard to follow, particularly in Bavaria.

ADDRESSES

The following abbreviations are used within italicized service information in this book: *Gasse* (alley) is shortened to G., as in Breite G. or Haseng.; *Platz* is abbreviated Pl., as in Max-Joseph- Pl. or Marktpl.; *Strasse* (street) is abbreviated Str., as in Budapester Str. or Theaterstr.; *Weg* (road) is shortened to W., as in St.-Peters-W. or Hornburgw.

LANGUAGES FOR TRAVELERS

A phrase book and language-tape set can help get you started.

PHRASE BOOKS & LANGUAGE-TAPE SETS • *Fodor's German for Travelers* (tel. 800/733–3000 in the U.S.; 800/668–4247 in Canada; $7 for phrasebook, $16.95 for audio set).

LODGING

During summer, hostels and cheap pensions are filled to the brim, especially in the big cities and popular outdoors areas like the Black Forest or the coastal resorts. Even in the off-season, conventions or festivals can clog accommodations and raise prices. Calling in advance may save you a headache.

APARTMENT RENTALS

If you want a home base that's roomy enough for a family and comes with cooking facilities **consider a furnished rental.** These can save you money, especially if you're traveling with a group. Home-exchange directories sometimes list rentals as well as exchanges.

INTERNATIONAL AGENTS • At Home Abroad (405 E. 56th St., Suite 6H, New York, NY 10022, tel. 212/421–9165, fax 212/752–1591). **Drawbridge to Europe** (5456 Adams Rd., Talent, OR 97540, tel. 541/512–8927 or 888/268–1148, fax 541/512–0978). **Europa-Let/Tropical Inn-Let** (92 N. Main St., Ashland, OR 97520, tel. 541/482–5806 or 800/462–4486, fax 541/482–0660). **Hometours International** (Box 11503, Knoxville, TN 37939, tel. 423/690–8484 or 800/367–4668). **Interhome** (1990 N.E. 163rd St., Suite 110, N. Miami Beach, FL 33162, tel. 305/940–2299 or 800/882–6864, fax 305/940–2911). **Rental Directories International** (2044 Rittenhouse Sq., Philadelphia, PA 19103, tel. 215/985–

4001, fax 215/985–0323). **Rent-a-Home International** (7200 34th Ave. NW, Seattle, WA 98117, tel. 206/789–9377 or 800/964–1891, fax 206/789–9379). **Vacation Home Rentals Worldwide** (235 Kensington Ave., Norwood, NJ 07648, tel. 201/767–9393 or 800/633–3284, fax 201/767–5510). **Villas and Apartments Abroad** (1270 Avenue of the Americas, 15th Floor, New York, NY 10020, tel. 212/759–1025 or 800/433–3020, fax 212/897–5039). **Villas International** (950 Northgate Dr., Suite 206, San Rafael, CA 94903, tel. 415/499–9490 or 800/221–2260, fax 415/499–9491). **Hideaways International** (767 Islington St., Portsmouth, NH 03801, tel. 603/430–4433 or 800/843–4433, fax 603/430–4444; membership $99).

CAMPING

Germany is loaded with campsites. Campgrounds around urban centers tend to be on the outskirts of town but are usually accessible by public transport. Most campgrounds have modern facilities such as toilets, showers, running water, and even kitchens. Some sites, especially those around beaches, may also have shops, restaurants, and the occasional minigolf course. The trade-off is that these sites are often overcrowded with rowdy youth groups and RV-driving tourists, particularly in summer. Prices are fairly standard: about DM 6–DM 8 per person per night and an additional DM 5 for each tent.

HAY HOTELS

Though there are relatively few *Heuhotels* (hay hotels) throughout Germany, their popularity is growing, prompting more and more farmers to convert their own hay lofts to accommodate budget travelers. Chances are you'll stay in the attic of a farmhouse and be served a generous farm-style breakfast—replete with homemade cheeses, sausages, and breads and homegrown vegetables. Dinner may also be served, along with homemade schnapps, if you're lucky. If you're not biking to the hay hotel, call to arrange for shuttle service from the nearest town. The whole package won't cost you more than DM 35. Remember to flatten out the hay under your sleeping bag; otherwise you'll wake up with a tremendous backache. (If you're allergic to the hay, the farmers will let you sleep in a guest room.) Tourist offices in Lower Saxony and Baden-Württemberg are likely to have information on hay hotels and "hay tours."

Farmers around the Black Forest are known for their hospitality toward backpackers and cyclists. If you ask permission to camp in a field, they may invite you to sleep in a warm bed or join the family for a traditional meal.

HAY HOTELS • Bi'Wilhelm (Wietzetzer Hofwirtschaft, W.Grimmel, Doerpstraat 8, 29456 Hitzacker, tel. 05858/292). **Eichenhof, Familie Lehnen** (OT Bellahn 4, 29499 Zernien, tel. 05863/1858). **Ferienbauernhof/Heuhotel Stahl** (Weidenhof 1, 97993 Creglingen, tel. 07933/378, fax 07933/7515, e-mail: ferien-heuhotel@t-online.de).

HOME EXCHANGES

If you would like to exchange your home for someone else's **join a home-exchange organization,** which will send you its updated listings of available exchanges for a year and will include your own listing in at least one of them. It's up to you to make specific arrangements.

EXCHANGE CLUBS • HomeLink International (Box 650, Key West, FL 33041, tel. 305/294–7766 or 800/638–3841, fax 305/294–1448; $93 per year). **Intervac U.S.** (Box 590504, San Francisco, CA 94159, tel. 800/756–4663, fax 415/435–7440; $83 for catalogues.

HOSTELS

No matter what your age you can **save on lodging costs by staying at Jugendherbergen** (hostels). With more than 700 locations around the country, the German youth-hostel network—overseen by Deutsches Jugendherbergswerk (DJH)—is one of the most extensive in Europe. Almost without exception, Jugendherbergen (hostels) are affiliated with Hostelling International (HI), which means there is a shopping list of rules and regulations: single-sex dorm rooms, no smoking, no noise after 10, curfews that range from 10 to 1 AM depending on the specific hostel, and, officially, no sleeping on beds without sleep sheets or the hostel's own linen (which you can rent for DM 7 per night).

Hostels affiliated with HI also require that you have an HI membership card, which can be bought at student travel agencies around the world. If you space out, you can get a card from the first hostel you visit. You'll then receive a stamp (DM 5) for every night you sleep in an HI hostel, and once you collect six stamps you're an official HI member. All HI hostels provide you with a simple breakfast, and most serve lunch and dinner for DM 6–DM 8 by prior arrangement (let them know when you check in). Check-in time is usually about 4 or 5 PM. Many hostels have a lockout from 9 or 10 AM until anywhere between noon and 5 PM for cleaning. Nearly all hostels close for a week to a month around Christmas. For putting up with all these rules and regulations you'll be rewarded with the cheapest beds in Germany. Prices are DM 18–DM 38. For more info in Germany, contact **DJH** directly (tel. 05231/74010, fax 05231/740194).

ORGANIZATIONS • Australian Youth Hostel Association (10 Mallett St., Camperdown, NSW 2050, tel. 02/9565–1699, fax 02/9565–1325). **Hostelling International—American Youth Hostels** (733 15th St. NW, Suite 840, Washington, DC 20005, tel. 202/783–6161, fax 202/783–6171). **Hostelling International—Canad** (400–205 Catherine St., Ottawa, Ontario K2P 1C3, tel. 613/237–7884, fax 613/237–7868). **Youth Hostel Association of England and Wales** (Trevelyan House, 8 St. Stephen's Hill, St. Albans, Hertfordshire AL1 2DY, tel. 01727/855215 or 01727/845047, fax 01727/844126). **Youth Hostels Association of New Zealand** (Box 436, Christchurch, New Zealand, tel. 03/379–9970, fax 03/365–4476). Membership in the U.S. $25, in Canada C$26.75, in the U.K. £9.30, in Australia $44, in New Zealand $24.

HOTELS

Hotel prices in Germany vary widely as you travel from big cities to rural villages. Although most hotel prices include breakfast, the primary factor affecting rates is whether the room has a shower or private bathroom. In the cities, prices for the most spartan rooms usually start at DM 45–DM 55 for singles and DM 70–DM 85 for doubles without a shower. But don't fret; virtually all hotels have bathing facilities off the hallway. If you insist on a private bath, the price of a room will usually go up at least DM 10 for singles and DM 10–DM 20 for doubles. In smaller towns not yet saturated with tourists, single rooms at pensions and low-end hotels can start as low as DM 35, with doubles at DM 50.

PENSIONS

As far as the budget traveler is concerned, a pension is just a cheap hotel. Breakfasts tend to be a bit simpler—usually two pieces of bread, butter, jam, cheese, a slice of meat, and tea or coffee—and there are typically fewer rooms than in a hotel (sometimes less than ten), but otherwise the differences are minimal to nonexistent. Prices are basically the same as at low-end hotels, but sometimes you can find pensions for a few marks less. In more popular destinations, reservations are strongly recommended, especially during the high season.

PRIVATZIMMER

If you're looking to save a little money and would like to meet a German family, renting a room in a private home is a great option. Most local tourist offices list available *Privatzimmer* and book rooms for a small fee. Prices for rooms—often every bit as nice if not nicer than rooms in pensions or cheap hotels—run DM 25–DM 50 per person, usually including breakfast. They can, however, skyrocket during certain festivals and events. One drawback is that most of these rooms require minimum stays of two or three nights, especially on weekends; if you're only looking for an overnight stay, try phoning anyway, as many families are flexible. Another possible negative is location: Before you book a certain room, check a map—many are far away from city centers and bus lines. Lists of Privatzimmer are available at most tourist offices.

MAIL & SHIPPING

The easiest way to send mail from Germany is simply to drop by the local *Postamt* (post office), hand your postcard, letter, or package to the clerk, and leave the rest to him or her. If you're feeling confident, you can buy extra postage and mail your next batch from any postal box (found in front of all post offices as well as on urban street corners). From Germany, airmail letters cost DM 3, airmail postcards DM 2. Letters to the United Kingdom or Ireland run DM 1.10 postcards DM 1. If you're sending mail across an ocean, don't mess with surface post—it could take months. Stick to airmail, and remember to ask for airmail stickers (*Luftpost* in German), without which your postcard could end up lost in the bottom of some slow-moving container ship.

RECEIVING MAIL

You can receive mail at any German post office free of charge. Simply have the letter marked with your name, the address of the post office (Postamt, city name, zip code), and the words **"Postlagernde Briefe,"** (equivalent to poste restante). Pick it up within 30 days by showing some ID. Another option is to have your mail sent to any AmEx office. Just make sure the sender writes the words "Client Mail" somewhere on the envelope (packages are not accepted). Your mail will be held for 30 days, unless it says otherwise on the letter. This service is free for AmEx members; just show the clerk your card or an AmEx traveler's check and some sort of identification. Others pay DM 2 per collection.

MONEY MATTERS

While Europe on $20 a day is a thing of the past, how much you actually spend depends upon your travel style. It also depends on fluctuating exchange rates. Check the business pages of the newspaper when you're planning your trip. If the U.S. dollar is worth more (in marks) than the rate listed below (*see* Currency), prices will be lower (in U.S. dollars) than those listed in the book; if the U.S. dollar is worth less than DM 1.98 during your trip, your U.S. dollar cost will be higher.

If you buy food at markets, camp, and go easy on bars and cafés, it's possible to travel on DM 60 a day. On the other hand, if you don't have a rail/bus pass, take most of your meals in restaurants, and stay in hotel rooms with private showers, you will certainly spend over DM 150 a day. Thrifty hostelers who indulge themselves on occasion should be fine with DM 90 per day. Prices are higher in the larger cities (Munich, Frankfurt, Hamburg, and Berlin), where you should add 20% to the above prices. Traveling during the off-season can save you a little money in resort towns and large cities, but otherwise prices in Germany stay nearly constant year-round.

LODGING

The cheapest way to bed down in most German towns is to head directly to a youth hostel. Beds in hostel dorm rooms go for DM 19–DM 35, DM 23–DM 44 if you're over 26. Those without HI membership can expect to pay DM 6 more for a bed. A significant step up in price, hotels and pensions offer more privacy and fewer rules. Cheap hotels or pensions run DM 38–DM 62 for singles and DM 65–DM 100 for doubles, depending on the size of the city and whether you want a private shower. Renting a *Privatzimmer* (a room in a private home) will set you back anywhere from DM 35 to DM 65 per person. For those who come prepared, the cheapest option are the campgrounds found in most rural towns and in many big cities. A night's stay at a Campingplatz *usually runs about DM 6–DM 10 per person and per tent, and DM 7–DM 12 per car.*

FOOD

One of the best ways to save money in Germany is to shop at local markets. While it is handy to grab a bite at one of the numerous take-out stands, known as *Imbiß* stands; be advised that this greasy cusine—rarely more than a *Bratwurst* and fries—can cost as much as DM 12 without a drink. Assembling a meal from various markets and shops is cheaper and by far more nutritious. A restaurant meal of traditional German fare, including salad, entrée, and drink, starts at DM 18. More affordable ethnic eateries, especially Middle Eastern restaurants, are growing in popularity. For more information, *see* Budget Eating Tips *under* Dining, *above.*

TRAVELING WITH MONEY

Cash never goes out of style, but traveler's checks and a major credit card are usually the safest and most convenient ways to pay for goods and services on the road. Strike a balance among these three forms of currency, and protect yourself by carrying cash in a money belt or "necklace" pouch (available at luggage or camping stores), and by keeping accurate records of traveler's checks' serial numbers, credit card numbers, and an emergency number for reporting the cards' loss or theft. Carrying at least some cash is wise, since most budget establishments accept cash only, and changing traveler's checks outside urban areas can prove difficult. Bring about $100 (in as many single bills as possible) in cash; changing dollars will be easier than cashing traveler's checks.

ATMS

Virtually all U.S. banks belong to networks of ATMs (Automated Teller Machines), which gobble up bank cards and spit out cash 24 hours a day in cities throughout Germany. Most German banks are connected to the Cirrus and/or Plus systems; other U.S. networks such as Star and NYCE won't do you any good. Cirrus is by far the most common; Plus outlets tend to exist only in the largest cities and resorts. *Geldautomaten* (ATMs), however, are better in theory than practice; they may not always function or even exist outside big cities. Some German banks may charge fees of DM 4–DM 10 for the use of their ATMs: You may want to check with a given bank before putting your card in its machine. To find out if there are any cash machines in a given city, call your bank's department of international banking. Or call **Cirrus** (tel. 800/424–7787 in the U.S.) for a list of worldwide locations. Since you pay a flat fee for each ATM transaction, you may want to withdraw a sizable amount. On the upside, the exchange rate will be based on the bank, so ATMs are often better than the local exchange office. If the transaction cannot be completed, chances are that the computer lines are busy (try to avoid Friday afternoons), and you'll have to try again later.

To receive a card for an ATM system, you must apply at a bank and select a Personal Identification Number (PIN). In many European machines, including those in Germany, this must be a four-digit code; if your PIN is longer, ask your bank about changing it. If you know your PIN number as a word, learn the numerical equivalent before you leave, since some ATM keypads show no letters, only numbers. Even if you have a four-digit code, check with your bank to see whether your card will give you access to banks in Germany.

A Visa or MasterCard can also be used to access cash through certain ATMs (provided you have a PIN for it), but the fees for this service are usually higher than bank-card fees. Also, a daily interest charge usually begins to accrue immediately on these credit card "loans," even if monthly bills are paid up. Check with your bank for info on fees and on the daily limit for cash withdrawals.

Express Cash allows American Express cardholders to withdraw up to $1,000 in a 21-day period from their personal checking accounts via ATMs worldwide. If you have a Gold Card, you can receive up to $2,500 in a 21-day period. Each transaction carries a 2% fee, with a minimum charge of $2.50 and a maximum of $20. Apply for a PIN and set up the linking of your accounts at least two weeks before departure. Call 800/528–4800 for an application.

CREDIT CARDS

They're definitely bourgeois, probably environmentally unsound, and possibly the most convenient invention since sliced bread. They can also be lifesavers in financial emergencies and allow you to rent a car, reserve a flight, or keep a roof over your head when your pockets are empty. Though you might not want to rely on the plastic too heavily while traveling (accrued interest on that wild night out in Berlin could put a dent in your student loans), it never hurts to have a card tucked in your pocket. Visa and MasterCard (but not AmEx) are accepted at many banks in Germany for withdrawing cash. Visa is the more widely accepted of the two. Each bank seems to set its own limits on the amount of money you can withdraw and which cards it accepts; policies may even vary from branch to branch. Typically, the daily withdrawal limit is about $400. A small commission—no more than if you were exchanging traveler's checks—is charged by the bank, though most credit card companies charge a horrifying (often 20% annual) interest rate immediately on cash advances. In other words, you don't get a 25-day grace period as you do on purchases. Avoid the interest charges by having a credit balance on your credit card ahead of time; credit card companies hate this and promise chaos to those who try it—but don't listen to them. On the other hand, rates are generally more favorable on credit card charges than on cash or traveler's check exchanges. Expensive restaurants and hotels accept credit cards, most commonly Visa or MasterCard, as do car-rental agencies. If you get a PIN number for your card before you leave home, you can also use your credit card at German ATMs (*see* ATMs, *above*).

REPORTING LOST CARDS • American Express (call collect 301/214–8228). **Diners Club** (05921/ 861234 or call collect 303/799–1504). **Mastercard** (0130/819104). **Visa** (0800/811– 8440).

CURRENCY

The German currency is the deutsche Mark (DM), which is broken into 100 Pfennige. Bills come in DM 10, DM 20, DM 50, DM 100, DM 500, and DM 1,000 denominations. Germans also use plenty of coins, in denominations of 1 Pf, 2 Pf, 5 Pf, 10 Pf, 50 Pf, DM 1, DM 2, and DM 5 (yep, that's a coin worth over $2—don't throw it in a fountain).

At press time, the mark stood at DM 1.87 to the U.S. dollar, DM 1.27 to the Canadian dollar, and DM 3 to the pound sterling. Although you may see prices listed in German marks and euros, the European currency won't be physically replacing national currencies of the European Union until 2002.

CURRENCY EXCHANGE

For the most favorable rates, change money through banks. Although ATM transaction fees may be higher abroad than at home, ATM rates are excellent because they are based on wholesale rates offered only by major banks. You won't do as well at exchange booths in airports or rail and bus stations, in hotels, in restaurants, or in stores. To avoid lines at airport exchange booths **get a bit of local currency before you leave home.**

If you can't get to a bank, you may find that hunting down the best exchange rate can be time consuming and, in the end, not all that profitable. Still, it's important to check the commission charge to avoid being gypped out of 8% of your capital. If you have traveler's checks, local offices of the issuer (such as American Express) often cash checks without charging a commission. Post offices charge DM 6 per check, which is painful if you have small denominations. Hotel exchange rates are generally a rip-off.

If you are **exchanging a currency from another European Union country** into German marks, do so free of charge at any branch of Germany's central bank, the **Deutsche Bundesbank** (Wilhelm-Epstein-Str. 14–16, Frankfurt am Main, tel. 069/9566–3511 or 069/9566–3512, fax 069/9566–3077). You may exchange any EU currency into the currency of the EU country you are in free of charge at any EU central bank. (It doesn't work the other way around, though: You cannot get Italian lire or French francs free of charge at the Deutsche Bundesbank. You can only exchange another currency into marks free of charge.) To locate another central bank or for information about the European System of Central Banks, go to the web site www.ecb.int.

EXCHANGE SERVICES • International Currency Express (tel. 888/842–0880 on East Coast; 888/278–6628 on West Coast). **Thomas Cook Currency Services** (tel. 800/287–7362 for telephone orders and retail locations).

GETTING MONEY FROM HOME

Provided there is money at home to be had, there are at least seven ways to get it:

Have it sent through a large **commercial bank** that has a branch in the town where you're staying. Unless you have an account with that large bank, though, you'll have to go through your own bank, and the process will be slower and more expensive.

If you're an AmEx cardholder, you can cash a **personal check** or a substitute counter check (as long as you know your personal bank account details) at any AmEx office in Germany for up to $1,000 ($5,000 for holders of a Gold Card) every 21 days. There is a 1% commission on traveler's checks.

The **MoneyGram™** service is a dream come true if you can convince someone back home to go to a MoneyGram agent and fill out the necessary forms. The sender pays up to $1,000 with a credit card or cash (and anything over that in cash) and, as quick as 10 minutes later, it's ready to be picked up. Fees vary according to the amount of money sent, but average about 3%–10% to send money from the United States to Europe. You have to show ID when picking up the money. For locations of MoneyGram agents call 800/926–9400 in the United States.

MasterCard and **Visa**: *See* Credit Cards, *above*.

Western Union offers two ways to feed your hungry wallet, both of them requiring a beneficent angel with deep pockets on the other side of the wire. Said angel can transfer funds from a MasterCard, Visa, or Discover card (up to the card's limit, or $10,000) by calling from a home or business (credit card transfers cannot be done at a Western Union office). Alternatively, your friend can trot some cash or a certified cashier's check over to the nearest office. The money can be sent to any post office in Germany and will be available in as little as two business days. Fees range from about 5% to 15% depending on the amount sent.

If you plan on staying for a while in Germany, you can set up a **Konto** (account) with a German bank, though it is impossible for most travelers to get a German ATM card. Contact a German bank (such as Deutsche Bank or Dresdner Bank) with a branch in your own country and get the address of a German branch to apply. The entire process takes about six weeks. In Germany, a Kontonummer (account number) can be a lifesaver, as many hotels and ride-share services accept them as guarantees.

In extreme emergencies (hospitalization, arrest, or worse) there is one more way American citizens can receive money: by setting up a **Department of State Trust Fund** (this does not require adoption by the State Department). This service is available only in emergencies and involves a friend or family member sending money to the Department of State, which then transfers the money to the U.S. embassy or consulate in the German city in which you're stranded. Once this account is established, you can send and receive money through Western Union, bank wire, or mail, all payable to the Department of State. For information, talk to the Department of State's Citizens' Emergency Center (tel. 202/647–5225).

TRAVELER'S CHECKS

Traveler's checks may look like play money, but they work a lot better. They can be used for purchases in the same way as personal checks (always ask first), or they can be exchanged for cash at banks, some hotels, tourist offices, AmEx offices, and currency-exchange offices. AmEx checks are the most widely accepted; small hotels and hostels are likely not to accept other brands. Some banks and credit unions issue checks free to customers, but most charge a 1%–2% commission. American Automobile

Association (AAA) members can purchase AmEx traveler's checks from AAA commission-free. By purchasing large denominations of traveler's checks ($100, for example) you will diminish the commissions most financial institutions in Germany charge to exchange them. On the other hand, many establishments won't accept large-denomination checks, and, even when they do, breaking a large check for small purchases may leave you carrying too much cash. Getting traveler's checks in marks before you leave enables you to avoid the currency-exchange fee at most bureaux de change; inquire at your bank's international banking department.

American Express (tel. 800/221–7282 in the U.S. or toll-free 0130/853100 from Germany) cardholders can order traveler's checks in U.S. dollars or German marks by phone, free of charge (with a Gold Card) or for a 1% commission (with your basic green card). In three to five business days you'll receive your checks; up to $1,000 can be ordered in a seven-day period. If you lose your checks or are ripped off, American Express can provide you with a speedy refund—often within 24 hours. At their Travel Services offices (about 1,500 around the world) you can usually buy and cash traveler's checks, write a personal check in exchange for traveler's checks or cash, report lost or stolen checks, exchange foreign currency, and pick up mail. Ask for the American Express Traveler's Companion, a handy directory of their offices, to find out more about services at different locations.

Traveler's checks are available from **Citibank** (tel. 800/645–6556; outside U.S., call collect 813/623–1709) and other banks worldwide in U.S. dollars and some foreign currencies. Plan at least five days ahead if you want checks in marks, since they must be special-ordered. For 45 days from date of check purchase, purchasers have access to the 24-hour International S.O.S. Assistance Hotline, which provides referrals to English-speaking doctors, lawyers, and interpreters; assistance after loss or theft of travel documents; traveler's-check refund assistance; and an emergency message center.

MasterCard International (tel. 800/223–7373 in U.S.; or toll-free 0130/859930 from Germany) traveler's checks, issued in U.S. dollars only, are offered through banks, credit unions, and foreign-exchange booths. Call for information about acceptance of their checks at your destination and for the local number to call in case of loss or theft.

Thomas Cook brand of MasterCard traveler's checks are available in U.S. dollars and foreign currencies. If purchased through a Thomas Cook Foreign Exchange office (formerly Deak International), there is no commission. For more info, contact MasterCard (*see above*).

Visa (tel. 800/227–6811; outside U.S., call collect 410/581–5353) boosted its name recognition and acceptance worldwide. Visa traveler's checks are available in various currencies.

Do you need traveler's checks? It depends on where you're headed. If you're going to rural areas and small towns, go with cash; traveler's checks are best used in cities. Lost or stolen checks can usually be replaced within 24 hours. To ensure a speedy refund, buy your own traveler's checks—don't let someone else pay for them: irregularities like this can cause delays. The person who bought the checks should make the call to request a refund.

OUTDOORS & SPORTS

BIKING

Bicycles are an extremely popular mode of transportation; well-connected, well-marked bike trails crisscross Germany's nature preserves and recreation areas. Mountain biking is becoming increasingly accepted, although bike-only mountain trails are scarce and hikers may sniff and cast the mountain biker an icy glance. For general biking information—where to go, how to arrange a tour, etc.—contact the **National German Cycling Association** (ADFC) in Bremen (Postfach 1077740, 28077 Bremen, tel. 0421/346290, fax 0421/346–2950).

HIKING

Germans are undeniably among the world's enthusiastic nature-lovers. Germany alone has thousands of kilometers of marked hiking and mountain-walking tracks. These Wanderwege are administered by regional hiking clubs and, where appropriate, mountaineering groups, all of which are affiliated with the **Verband Deutscher Gebirgs- und Wandervereine e.V.** (Wilhelm-Höher-Allee 157–159, 34121 Kassel, tel.0561/938730). This hiking and mountaineering society can provide information on routes, hiking paths, overnight accommodations, and mountain huts in western Germany. Local tourist offices in eastern and western Germany can provide info about trails and regional hiking clubs. For more advanced backpacking and mountaineering options, contact the **Deutscher Alpenverein** (Von-Kahr-Str. 2–4,

80997 Munich, tel. 089/140030). The club administers more than 50 mountain huts and about 15,000 kilometers of Alpine paths. In addition, it provides courses in mountaineering and touring suggestions. Foreign members are admitted, and it has a cooperative agreement with its counterparts whereby members of one organization can use the others' facilities. Various mountaineering schools offer week-long courses ranging from basic techniques for beginners to advanced mountaineering. Contact the **Verband Deutscher Ski- und Bergführer** (Lindenstr. 16, 87561 Oberstdorf).

WINTER SPORTS

Southern Bavaria is a big winter-sports region. There are also winter-sports resorts in the Black Forest, the Harz region, the Bavarian Forest, the Rhön Mountains, the Fichtelgebirge, and the Schwäbische Alb. The ski season generally runs from mid-December to the end of March, though at higher altitudes you can ski from as early as November to as late as May. Unless you're really serious, there's no need to bring skis with you—you can rent them on the spot.

For *Langlauf* (cross-country skiing), there are *Loipen* (prepared tracks) in the valleys and foothills of most winter-sports centers, as well as in the suburbs of larger towns. *Alpin* (downhill) skiing is less popular and less challenging in the northern (flatter) German mountain ranges than in ski resorts in the Bavarian Alps and the Black Forest. In the Alps, schools and runs can be found at Berchtesgaden, Garmisch-Partenkirchen, Füssen, and Oberstdorf. Black Forest skiing is centered in and around Feldberg.

Swimming in rivers, especially larger ones, is not recommended and in some cases is positively forbidden—either due to shipping, pollution, or both. BADEN VERBOTEN signs mean "no way."

PACKING

What you pack depends on what you plan to do while you're here. While Germany has its share of backpackers and students, it isn't a country that glorifies this kind of lifestyle. Be advised that better quality shops, hotels, and restaurants tend to wait on you last and with little interest if you don't look as if you are one of the world's affluent. For this reason, you should consider packing a few casual but sporty outfits and keep in mind that jeans are definitely out in many social settings. Sneakers are also forbidden in some discos and restaurants—so remember to pack a pair of walking shoes or dress shoes if there's enough space in your luggage. If you're a teenager you can still get away with dresing like a throwback to the 1970s, but if you're in your early 20s your casual attire is certain to raise eyebrows. After all, Germany is one of the richest countries in Europe and likes to show it. Check heavy, cumbersome bags at train or bus stations and just carry the essentials with you while you hunt for lodging. Germany gets plenty of rain year-round, so don't forget to bring something to protect yourself and your luggage. If you plan on traveling in winter or in the high Alps, pack plenty of warm, woolen, and waterproof things to combat the often subfreezing temperatures and slush.

BEDDING

If you're planning to stay primarily in hotels or pensions, you won't need to bring any bedding. On the other hand, hostels require that you use a sleep sheet; you can bring your own or pay DM 4.50–DM 6 per night to rent one. Since some hostels strictly enforce the HI rule that guests use a sleep sheet and not a sleeping bag or regular sheet, it may pay to invest in one.

CAMPING GEAR

Sleeping bags are a first concern. Synthetic bags run $60 and up and provide good protection against damp weather. Down bags start at around $175, are much warmer, and can be scrunched into a tiny sack, but they're useless when wet. For further protection against the cold ground and to provide soft padding, pick up a thin foam pad or air mattress that can be rolled up and tied to your pack.

Tents come in many breeds, built to handle the wilderness challenges posed by anything from the Alps to your backyard. Most crucial is the weight of the tent. A two-person, 3½ pounder is the lightest you're likely to find; a 7- or 8-pound tent is probably the heaviest tent comfortable to carry. For camping in damp areas, make sure your tent has edges that can be turned up off the ground to prevent water from seeping in, or bring a plastic tarp along. Also check the tent's windows and front flaps for mosquitoproof netting, and make sure the front flap can be completely zipped shut during rain. Expect to pay about $100–$150 for a low-end two-person tent, $200 and up for one of its more upper-crust cousins.

You can buy a white-gas-burning ministove that provides one amazingly powerful flame and folds up into a little bag, all for about $35. A kerosene-burning lantern costs about $40. Other odds and ends include matches in a waterproof container, a Swiss army knife, something for banging in tent pegs (your shoe can work if it's sturdy enough), mosquito repellent, and a mess kit ($15).

CLOTHING

Smart—and not terribly fashion-conscious—travelers will only bring a few outfits and learn to wash their clothes by hand. At the very least, bring comfortable, easy-to-clean clothes. Black hides dirt but also absorbs heat. Artificial fabrics don't breathe and will make you hotter than you'd thought possible, so go with light cotton instead. Bring several T-shirts and one sweatshirt or sweater for cooler nights. Socks and underwear don't take up too much room, so throw in a few extra pairs.

Packing light does not mean relying on a pair of cut-off shorts and a tank top to get you through any situation. In general, you may find that Germans dress a little more formally than Americans.While they won't throw you out for wearing jeans, you won't be welcomed with open arms. If you must wear them, make certain they are clean, not torn and by no means baggy. Whatever you pack will have to stand up to a lot of wear and tear in the washing machines. The machines and the detergent in Germany are generally stronger than in the U.S. and whites are literally cooked in the 90°C "Kochwäsche."

LAUNDRY

Consider taking along all the ingredients necessary to set up your very own launderette in any hotel or campground bathroom: a small plastic bottle (available in Germany) of liquid detergent or soap (powder doesn't break down as well), about 6 feet of clothesline (enough to tie to two stable objects), and some plastic clips (bobby pins or paper clips can substitute). Be sure to bring an extra plastic bag or two for damp laundry and dirty clothes. If this just isn't your style, you can find a Waschsalon (laundromat) in most German towns. A load in a coin-op will cost DM 8–DM 13 and an additional DM 2–DM 3 for 10 minutes in the dryer.

TOILETRIES

Toiletries are heavy and bulky, so leave as many of them at home as possible. What you do bring, seal tightly in a separate, waterproof bag; the pressure on airplanes can cause lids to pop off and create instant moisturizer slicks inside your luggage. Shaving cream is particularly apt to explode on the airplane. Use soap and water instead, or pick up a can of German shaving cream when you get there. Besides, German shops are chock-full of interesting and environmetally friendly soaps, lotions, and deodorants. You may also want to bring prescription drugs with you. Condoms and birth control are also important, although you can purchase condoms in any supermarket.

In your carry-on luggage **bring an extra pair of eyeglasses or contact lenses** and **enough of any medication you take** to last the entire trip. You may also want your doctor to write a spare prescription using the drug's generic name, since brand names may vary from country to country. In luggage to be checked, **never pack prescription drugs or valuables.** To avoid customs delays, carry medications in their original packaging. And don't forget to copy down and carry addresses of offices that handle refunds of lost traveler's checks.

CHECKING LUGGAGE

How many carry-on bags you can bring with you is up to the airline. Most allow two, but not always, so make sure that everything you carry aboard will fit under your seat, and get to the gate early. Note that if you have a seat at the back of the plane, you'll probably board first, while the overhead bins are still empty.

If you are flying internationally, note that baggage allowances may be determined not by piece but by weight—generally 88 pounds (40 kg) in first class, 66 pounds (30 kg) in business class, and 44 pounds (20 kg) in economy.

Airline liability for baggage is limited to $1,250 per person on flights within the United States. On international flights it amounts to $9.07 per pound or $20 per kilogram for checked baggage (roughly $640 per 70-lb bag) and $400 per passenger for unchecked baggage. You can buy additional coverage at check-in for about $10 per $1,000 of coverage, but it excludes a rather extensive list of items, shown on your airline ticket.

Before departure **itemize your bags' contents** and their worth, and label the bags with your name, address, and phone number. (If you use your home address, cover it so that potential thieves can't see it readily.) Inside each bag **pack a copy of your itinerary.** At check-in **make sure that each bag is correctly tagged** with the destination airport's three-letter code. If your bags arrive damaged or fail to arrive at all, file a written report with the airline before leaving the airport.

PASSPORTS & VISAS

When traveling internationally **carry a passport even if you don't need one** (it's always the best form of ID), and **make two photocopies of the data page** (one for someone at home and another for you, carried separately from your passport). If you lose your passport promptly call the nearest embassy or consulate and the local police.

ENTERING GERMANY

Visas are not required for U.S., Canadian, British, Australian, or New Zealand citizens for stays in Germany of up to three months. For information on longer stays, see Working Abroad, below. However, all travelers need a valid passport. Hang onto your passport for dear life, because you can't do anything—cross the border, check into accommodations, change money, et cetera—without it.

PASSPORT OFFICES

The best time to apply for a passport or to renew is during the fall and winter. Before any trip, check your passport's expiration date, and, if necessary, renew it as soon as possible.

AUSTRALIAN CITIZENS • Australian Passport Office (tel. 131–232).

CANADIAN CITIZENS • Canadian Passport Office (tel. 819/994–3500 or 800/567–6868).

NEW ZEALAND CITIZENS • New Zealand Passport Office (tel. 04/494–0700 for information on how to apply; 04/474–8000 or 0800/225–050 in New Zealand for information on applications already submitted).

U.K. CITIZENS • London Passport Office (tel. 0990/210–410) for fees and documentation requirements and to request an emergency passport.

U.S. CITIZENS • National Passport Information Center (tel. 900/225–5674; calls are 35per minute for automated service, $1.05 per minute for operator service).

RESOURCES FOR PEOPLE OF COLOR

Racial hate crimes, in both city centers and rural districts throughout western and eastern Germany, are on the decline, but that doesn't mean they don't happen. Note that German racism is subtly different from what you know from home: The term "people of color" isn't as useful here. *Ausländer* (literally meaning "foreigners" but in practice usually meaning "visible foreigners," i.e., those with darker skin or Asian features) is the relevant term, and English speakers with Mediterranean ancestry may need to exercise as much caution as those of African, Asian, or Native American descent. On the other hand, many ethnic Germans are committed to accommodating those of other backgrounds in their country, and there is a growing population of German descendants of immigrants; as a result, resources have grown, especially in larger cities.

For a list of resources for foreigners throughout Europe, contact **UNITED for Intercultural Action** (Postbus 413, 1000 AK Amsterdam, Netherlands, tel. 020/683–4778, fax 020/683–4582, united@antenna.nl). In Germany, university student groups are a good resource for cultural events and support groups. If you have questions about safety, discrimination, or want to connect with people of color in Berlin, contact **ARiC** (Chaussee Str. 29, 10115 Berlin-Mitte, tel. 030/280–7590, fax 030/280–7591, ARIC-BERLIN@IPN-B.comlink.apc.org). The **Regionale Arbeitsstelle für Ausländerfragen in Berlin** (Chaussee Str. 29, 10115 Berlin-Mitte, tel. 030/308–7990, fax 030/3087–9912) is part of a network of support organizations for foreigners throughout eastern Germany, with offices in most larger cities, including Leipzig, Erfurt, and Rostock. If you need legal help, contact **Foreigner Legal Service** (Cremon 11, tel. 040/366534) in Hamburg, which has information on German laws and is ready to help foreigners in need. Another useful resource is the **Foreigner Commission** (Washingtonerallee 42, tel. 040/6555791) in Hamburg, an antidiscrimination organization; they can direct you to organizations in other parts of Germany. Their phones are open weekdays 8:30–4. All of the organizations listed should have an English-speaker on hand.

SENIOR-CITIZEN TRAVEL

To qualify for age-related discounts **mention your senior-citizen status up front** when booking hotel reservations (not when checking out) and before you're seated in restaurants (not when paying the bill). When renting a car ask about promotional car-rental discounts, which can be cheaper than senior-citizen rates.

EDUCATIONAL PROGRAMS • Elderhostel (75 Federal St., 3rd fl., Boston, MA 02110, tel. 877/426–8056, fax 877/426–2166). **Interhostel** (University of New Hampshire, 6 Garrison Ave., Durham, NH 03824, tel. 603/862–1147 or 800/733–9753, fax 603/862–1113). **Folkways Institute** (14600 Southeast Aldridge Rd., Portland, OR 97236-6518, tel. 503/658–6600 or 800/225–4666, fax 503/658–8672).

STUDENTS IN GERMANY

The **International Student Identity Card** (ISIC), the universally recognized student ID, entitles students to discount student airfares; special fares on local transportation; and discounts at museums, theaters, sports events, and many other attractions. If purchased in the United States, the $19 cost for the popular card also buys you $3,000 in emergency medical coverage; limited hospital coverage; and access to a 24-hour international, toll-free hot line for assistance in medical, legal, and financial emergencies. In the United States, apply to Council Travel or STA; in Canada, the ISIC is available for C$15 from Travel CUTS. In the United Kingdom, students with valid university IDs can purchase the ISIC at any student union or student-travel company. Applicants must submit a photo as well as proof of current full-time student status, age, and nationality.

The **Go 25: International Youth Travel Card** (GO25) is issued to travelers between the ages of 12 and 25 and provides services and benefits similar to those given by the ISIC card. Get the $19 card from the same organizations that sell the ISIC. When applying, bring a passport-size photo and your passport as proof of your age.

The **International Student Exchange Card** (ISE) is available to students and faculty members. You pay $18 and receive a $10 discount on flights within the United States and a $50 discount on certain flights to Europe. Write or call for more information or to enroll over the phone. 5010 E. Shea Blvd., Suite A104, Scottsdale, AZ 85254, tel. 602/951–1177 or 800/255–8000, fax 602/951–1216.

The $20 **International Teacher Identity Card** (ITIC), sponsored by the International Student Travel Confederation, is available to teachers of all grade levels, from kindergarten to graduate school. The ITIC procures benefits similar to those you get with the student cards. The International Teacher Identity Card Handbook, available when you buy the card, has all the details.

STUDENT IDS & SERVICES • Council on International Educational Exchange (CIEE, 205 E. 42nd St., 14th fl., New York, NY 10017, tel. 212/822–2600 or 888/268–6245, fax 212/822–2699) for mail orders only, in the U.S. **Travel Cuts** (187 College St., Toronto, Ontario M5T 1P7, tel. 416/979–2406 or 800/667–2887) in Canada.

STUDYING ABROAD

Studying in Germany is the perfect way to scope out the culture, meet locals, and learn or improve language skills. You may choose to study through a U.S.-sponsored program, usually through an American university, or enroll directly in a European program. Do your homework: Programs vary greatly in expense, academic quality, exposure to language, amount of contact with local students, and living conditions. Working through your local university is usually the easiest way to find out about exchange programs in Europe.

Students thinking about enrolling in a German program are in luck: German universities generally reserve 8% of their available places for foreign students. Those considering entering the world of German academia should realize that the cost of living in Germany is high, especially in university towns; though rent varies, you will probably need DM 13,000–DM 16,000 for a year of modest student living in Germany. Although German universities do not charge tuition, there are mandatory "contributions" to student organizations (DM 50–DM 100), compulsory health insurance fees (DM 600 per semester), books and study materials to be purchased (DM 450–DM 600), and other small expenditures.

ORGANIZATIONS

A good resource for people who want to study in Germany is the **Deutscher Akademischer Austauschdienst** (Kennedyallee 50, 53175 Bonn, Germany, tel. 0228/8820), which has an office in New York (950 Third Ave., New York, NY 10022, tel. 212/758–3223, fax 212/755–5780, daadny@acf2.nyu.edu). This organization can provide you with a comprehensive booklet including general info about the German university system and addresses of more than 80 universities throughout Germany that have foreign-student programs; it also lists the courses they offer. The **American Institute for Foreign Study** and the **American Council of International Studies** (102 Greenwich Ave., Greenwich, CT 06830, tel. 800/727–2437) arrange semester- and year-long study-abroad programs in universities throughout the world for full- or part-time students. Fees vary according to the country and length of stay. Council's College and University Programs Division administers summer-, semester-, and year-long study-abroad programs at various universities worldwide. To navigate the maze of programs, contact **Council** (*see* Students in Germany, *above*), or purchase their excellent *Work, Study, Travel Abroad: The Whole World Handbook* ($13.95). The **Institute of International Education** (IIE; 809 U.N. Plaza, New York, NY 10017, tel. 212/984–5413) publishes the helpful *Academic Year Abroad* ($42.95), which lists over 1,900 study-abroad programs for undergrads and grads. If you're more interested in summer-abroad and living-abroad programs, check out IIE's *Vacation Study Abroad* ($36.95). **World Learning** (Kipling Rd., Box 676, Brattleboro, VT 05302, tel. 800/451–4465, fax 802/258–3248) offers more than 100 semester-abroad programs, many structured around homestays.

TAXES

VALUE-ADDED TAX (VAT)

The price of German goods includes a value added tax (V.A.T.); you are entitled to receive a refund on the V.A.T. dollar amount embedded in the price. Global Refund is a V.A.T. refund service that makes getting your money back hassle-free. Global Refund services are offered in more than 125,000 shops worldwide. In participating stores, **ask for the Global Refund Cheque;** in other stores, request an *Ausfuhr-Abnehmerbescheinigung,* which can be processed by Global Refund at a higher fee. As is true for all customs forms, when leaving the European Union you get them stamped by the customs official. If you have made purchases in countries within the EU, only declare them when you leave the EU. Then cash your Cheque at any Cash Refund Office. Alternatively, you can mail your validated Cheque to Global Refund and your credit card account will automatically be credited. A 3–4% service fee is deducted from the total amount you paid for your goods.

VAT REFUNDS • Global Refund (707 Summer St., Stamford, CT 06901, tel. 800/566–9828, www.globalrefund.com).

TELEPHONES

COUNTRY & AREA CODES

Germany's country code is 49. Germany's phone system is modern, efficient, easy to use, and relatively inexpensive now that price wars have pushed rates for long distance calls down to a record low. If you're calling German numbers from abroad, first dial your country's international access code (in the U.S., 011), then dial these codes, and leave the initial "0" off the city code before dialing it and the local number.

INTERNATIONAL CALLS

International information: 11834. International calls can be made from phone booths marked with the silhouette of a receiver and the word INTERNATIONAL. International phones generally accept 10 Pf, DM 1, and DM 5 coins or (more often) phone cards. DM 5 will give you up to ten minutes' worth of conversation to the United States. You can also place calls from post offices with a telephone center. Simply get a booth number from the attendant at the FERNGESPRÄCHE counter and pay when you complete your call. Because the German rates are so low it may not make sense to use a credit card or call-back service. Check on current prices before making your decision.

LOCAL CALLS

Information: 11833 is the main number in Germany and belongs to the nation's carrier Deutsche Telekom. Keep in mind, however, that the government regulatory authority has recently ruled that another 15 companies can offer directory assistance services—and that's just the beginning. A popular competitor is Telegate, a company that is a bit cheaper the longer you use it. If it's only one number you're looking for, use Telekom since the price is basically the same. The best way to save money is to use one of the country's mobile providers. The rates are cheap and you can purchase a prepaid card (usually DM 50) make certain you don't exceed your budget. The phones are usually part of the package. Most German phone booths have instructions in several languages, including English. When calling within the city you're in, drop the city code. Making a local connection costs 30 Pf and most coin-operated phones take 10 Pf and DM 1 coins. A series of beeps signals that you have 10 seconds to insert more money. Save yourself the hassle and buy a phone card.

LONG-DISTANCE CALLS

AT&T, MCI, and **Sprint** access codes make calling long distance relatively convenient, but you may find the local access number blocked in many hotel rooms. First ask the hotel operator to connect you. If the hotel operator balks ask for an international operator, or dial the international operator yourself. One way to improve your odds of getting connected to your long-distance carrier is to travel with more than one company's calling card (a hotel may block Sprint, for example, but not MCI). If all else fails call from a pay phone.

ACCESS CODES • In Germany: **AT&T Direct** (0130–0010). **MCI WorldPhone** (0130–0012). **Sprint International Access** (800/888–0013). In the United States: **AT&T Direct** (800/435–0812). **MCI WorldPhone** (800/444–4141). **Sprint International Access** (800/877–4646).

PHONE CARDS

The vast majority of German pay phones don't accept coins—so it is imperative to have a phone card (known as a *Telefonwertkarte* or simply *Telefonkarte*). Cards come in amounts of DM 12 and up, and are available at tobacco stores, post offices, newsstands, and many currency-exchange agencies. A DM 50 phone card gives you DM 60 worth of calls. Don't be confused if one phone number in a city has seven digits while another has three or eight—that's just the way it is.

TIPPING

Even though the bill at a German restaurant includes tax and service, it is common to round up to the nearest mark or two and keep in mind that record unemployment and high taxes in Germany have put people in a bad and desperate mood. Don't tip under a mark—unless you enjoy being stared at. However, German waitstaff earn more per hour than their American counterparts, so they are not counting on a 15% tip. When your waiter or waitress tells you what you owe, instead of leaving the tip on the table (considered rude), tell him or her how much you want to pay including the tip; for example, if your meal costs DM 12.40, say "14 Mark." For hairdressers, taxi drivers, and the like, round up a couple of marks, or tack on about 5%.

TOURS & PACKAGES

On a prepackaged tour or independent vacation everything is prearranged so you'll spend less time planning—and often get it all at a good price.

BOOKING WITH AN AGENT

Travel agents are excellent resources. But it's a good idea to collect brochures from several agencies because some agents' suggestions may be influenced by relationships with tour and package firms that reward them for volume sales. If you have a special interest **find an agent with expertise in that area**; ASTA has a database of specialists worldwide.

Make sure your travel agent knows the accommodations and other services of the place he or she is recommending. Ask about the hotel's location, room size, beds, and whether it has a pool, room service, or programs for children, if you care about these. Has your agent been there in person or sent others whom you can contact?

Do some homework on your own, too: Local tourism boards can provide information about lesser-known and small-niche operators, some of which may sell only direct.

BUYER BEWARE

Each year consumers are stranded or lose their money when tour operators—even large ones with excellent reputations—go out of business. So **check out the operator.** Ask several travel agents about its reputation, and try to **book with a company that has a consumer-protection program.** (Look for information in the company's brochure.) In the United States, members of the National Tour Association and United States Tour Operators Association are required to set aside funds to cover your payments and travel arrangements in case the company defaults. It's also a good idea to choose a company that participates in the American Society of Travel Agent's Tour Operator Program (TOP); ASTA will act as mediator in any disputes between you and your tour operator.

Remember that the more your package or tour includes the better you can predict the ultimate cost of your vacation. Make sure you know exactly what is covered, and **beware of hidden costs.** Are taxes, tips, and transfers included? Entertainment and excursions? These can add up.

TOUR-OPERATOR RECOMMENDATIONS • American Society of Travel Agents (*see* Travel Agencies, *below*). **National Tour Association** (NTA, 546 E. Main St., Lexington, KY 40508, tel. 606/226–4444 or 800/682–8886). **United States Tour Operators Association** (USTOA, 342 Madison Ave., Suite 1522, New York, NY 10173, tel. 212/599–6599 or 800/468–7862, fax 212/599–6744).

TRAIN TRAVEL

FROM THE UNITED KINGDOM

Most people traveling from the British Isles to Germany will want to follow one of two major routes: either London–Hamburg or London–Cologne. To reach Hamburg or Berlin or elsewhere in northern Germany, catch a train at London's Liverpool Street Station to Harwich and take the boat to Hoek van Holland. From here you can get a train into Germany via Amsterdam or Amersfoort; you may have to change in Osnabrück for your final destination. The entire drawn-out journey to Hamburg takes 20 hours and will set you back £99 (£75 for students under 26).

To get from London to Cologne, start at Victoria Station and head to Dover, where a ferry will carry you to Oostende, Belgium. From Oostende regular trains run to Cologne, where connections are available to Bonn, Frankfurt, Stuttgart, Munich, Düsseldorf, Hanover, and Berlin—heck, just about anywhere you want to go in Germany. The trip from London to Cologne can take anywhere from nine to 11 hours and runs about £60 (£43 for students under 26). Book through any **British Rail Travel Centre** (tel. 020/7834–2345) or **Deutsche Bahn Passenger Service** (tel. 020/8390–8833).

FROM CONTINENTAL EUROPE

There are as many different routes into Germany as there are travelers. What follows is a partial list of some of the quickest and cheapest ways to reach Germany from around Europe.

Direct trains from Paris run to Frankfurt and Cologne. Though both journeys take 5½–7 hours, the ride to Cologne from Paris Nord costs about 375F, while the ride to Frankfurt from Paris Est runs 556F. If you're coming from Italy, you can take a six-hour train from Milan to Basel, Switzerland, where connections can be made to most major German cities. If you're coming from Venice or headed to Bavaria, however, you're better off crossing the Alps via Trento and Innsbruck. Trains from Copenhagen to Hamburg (via Puttgarden) take approximately five hours and cost 400kr. Trains from Oslo or Stockholm to Berlin require transfers at Malmö. The 16-hour ride from Stockholm via Trelleborg and Saßnitz costs about 1,250kr.

One of the best rail lines to know about if you're coming from Eastern Europe is one that runs from Budapest to Berlin via Vienna or Bratislava and Prague. The full 13-hour ride from Budapest to Berlin will set you back DM 176; the 10-hour ride from Vienna to Berlin goes for 906 AS; the short five-hour journey from Prague to Berlin costs 1500 Kč. From Warsaw, direct trains to Berlin take 6½ hours and cost 120 zł—easy on your wallet but infamously risky overnight. To get to southern Germany, you'll need to first travel to Munich or Regensburg. Eight-hour trains from Budapest to Regensburg via Salzburg run DM 187. The six-hour trip from Prague to Munich costs roughly 1600 Kč.

CUTTING COSTS

To save money **look into rail passes.** But be aware that if you don't plan to cover many miles, you may come out ahead by buying individual tickets.

Rail passes are a great deal if you're planning to cover a lot of ground in a short period, and they save you time standing in line to buy tickets, though for most long-distance trains in Germany, you'll still have to stand in line for supplements and/or reservations. But there's something very gratifying about arriving at a train station, looking up at the departure board, and just picking any promising-looking destination.

Choose your pass carefully to avoid spending more on rail travel than you did to fly to Frankfurt or Berlin in the first place.

Before plunking down hundreds of dollars on a pass there are several issues to consider. First, add up the prices of the rail trips you plan to make; some travel agents have a manual that lists ticket prices, or you can call **Rail Europe** (tel. 800/438–7245), **Railpass Express** (tel. 800/722–7151), or **DER Tours** (tel. 800/782–2424), three agencies that sell rail passes over the phone. If you're under 26, subtract about 30% from the prices quoted by Rail Europe or your travel agent; that's how much you can save by purchasing a **TwenTicket** (*see below*) in Europe.

If you decide that you'll save money with a rail pass, ask yourself whether you want a EurailPass, an InterRail pass, or a pass issued by the **Deutsche Bahn** (DB)—Germany's national rail company. **InterRail** (*see below*) costs about 25% less than Eurail, but it's available only to those under 26 who are either European residents or have lived in an EU country for longer than six months. Eurail passes are a good deal only if you plan to tackle at least a few countries.

Last warnings: Don't assume that your rail pass guarantees you a seat on every train. Seat reservations are required on some express and overnight trains. Also note that many rail passes entitle you to free or reduced fares on some ferries (though you should still make seat reservations in advance) and some buses run by the national rail companies.

GERMAN RAIL PASSES

If you're under 26, one option is to get a **DBYouth Flexipass**, which is good for second-class travel on five to ten days within a one-month period: five days ($156), seven days ($174), 10 days ($210). The pass is good for second-class travel on all DB trains; on most buses run by Europabus and Deutsche Touring (under the DB umbrella); and on KD Rhine ferries operating on segments of the Rhine, Mosel, and Main rivers. Travelers over 26 can buy a second-class **Flexipass** for five to ten days: five days ($196), seven days ($240), 10 days ($306). Take a date across the country with the **Twinpass**; a second-class ticket for two (no youth rate) runs $294 (five days) to $459 (10 days). Be sure to buy any of the above before you leave home; comparable passes bought in Germany are much more expensive.

There are also a number of passes that can only be purchased in Germany. If you are planning on doing a lot of traveling in the country, consider the DB BahnCard, available at any train station. The pass costs DM 260 (DM 130 for students under 27, anyone under 23 or over 60) and gets you half off all tickets for the next year (so it's worth your while if you are planning on spending more than twice the price of the pass in a year). The Guten Abend ticket lets you take any regular train anywhere as long as you travel between 7 PM and 2 AM. It costs DM 59, DM 74 on Friday and Sunday. Add DM 10 when traveling ICE. Another option is the TramperTicket (DM 370), which lets anyone under 27 travel 10 days within a 30-day period June 15–October 15. Travelers under 26 can purchase a TwenTicket (a.k.a. Billet International Jeune, or BIJ) at train stations throughout Germany. TwenTickets allow you to travel round-trip between two major European cities (e.g., London–Vienna–London or Paris–Hamburg–Paris), making as many stops as you like along the way over a two-month period, with the caveat that you may only travel four days within Germany (or the country where you purchase the ticket) in each direction. BIJ tickets cost 20% less than what you'd pay for standard second-class fare between the two cities, and the fact that you can make unlimited stops along the way means big savings.

If you're under 26, the **Eurail Youthpass** is a better deal. One or two months of unlimited second-class train travel costs $623 and $882, respectively. For 15 consecutive days of travel you pay $388. A more free-form option for those under 26 is the second-class Eurail Youth Flexipass. Within a two-month period it entitles you to 10 days ($458) or 15 days ($599) of unlimited travel. Remember that these passes only save you money if you plan to spend a lot of your time on trains.

The **Europass** (first-class) and **Europass Youth** (second-class) are the latest things to hit the market, and allow travel in Germany, Italy, France, Switzerland, and Spain, or any combination thereof, as long as the countries are contiguous. Five days of unlimited travel in three countries cost $348 (first-class) or $233 (second-class); eight days in four countries cost $448 (first-class) or $313 (second-class). For 10 days in all five countries you'll pay $528 (first-class) or $363 (second-class). In all cases, the days of travel can be spread out over two calendar months. Another bonus is that with the three-country and four-country passes you can add up to two extra travel days, and up to four extra days with the five-country pass; you can also expand the reach of your pass to Austria, Belgium, Greece, Luxembourg, and Portugal.

If you decide on a EurailPass, be sure to buy it before leaving home. Eurail passes are not available in Europe. Also, if you have firm plans to visit Europe next year, consider buying your pass this year. Prices for Eurail passes generally rise on December 31, and your pass is valid as long as you start traveling within six months of the purchase date. The upshot is that a pass bought on December 30, 1999, can be activated as late as June 30, 2000. Prices listed above may have changed since press time (summer 1999).

PASS VALIDATION & INSURANCE • The first time you use any EurailPass you must have it validated. Before getting on the train, go to a ticket window and have the agent fill out the necessary forms—a painless but important procedure that could save you being asked to get off the train, or being fined. Another pitfall to avoid is having your pass stolen or lost. The only real safeguard is Eurail's "Pass Protection Plan," which costs $10 and must be arranged at the time of purchase. If you bought the protection plan and your pass mysteriously disappears, file a police report within 24 hours and keep the receipts for any train tickets you purchase. When you get home, send a copy of the report and receipts to Eurail; you'll get a 100% refund on the unused portion of the pass.

INTERRAIL

European citizens and anyone else under 26 who has lived in the EU for at least six months can purchase an InterRail Pass (DM 650), valid for one month's travel in Austria, Belgium, Britain, Bulgaria, Croatia, the Czech Republic, Denmark, Finland, France, Germany, Greece, Hungary, Ireland, Italy, Luxembourg, Morocco, the Netherlands, Northern Ireland, Norway, Poland, Portugal, Romania, Slovakia, Slovenia, Spain, Sweden, Switzerland, and Turkey. The InterRail pass works much like Eurail, except that you only get a 50% reduction on train travel in the country where the pass was purchased. Keep in mind that there are a number of additional offers to make travel even cheaper—part of the German railways recent efforts to streamline and attract more customers. The list is changing all the time—so it's best to simply ask at one of its many information counters or call its 24-hour hotline at 01805/996633. Be prepared to prove EU citizenship or six months of continuous residency. In most cases you'll have to show your passport for proof of age and residency, but sometimes they'll accept a European university ID. Be forewarned that each time passes are presented, the ticket controller has the option of looking at passports and confiscating "illegitimate" passes. InterRail can only be purchased in Europe at rail stations and some budget travel agencies; try the European branches of STA or Council Travel.

In Germany, young people under 26 get a 25% discount off regular train fares listed throughout this book.

TRANSPORTATION AROUND GERMANY

Advice on traveling in Germany boils down to one deliciously succinct statement: When in doubt, jump on a train. Buses may reach the obscure nooks and crannies, but they are generally much slower, less comfortable, and nearly as expensive as trains. Furthermore, train stations are more likely to have services such as currency exchange, luggage storage, after-hours shops, or tourist info. A better way to salvage your budget is by contacting the local *Mitfahrzentrale* (ride-share office), which will hook up riders and drivers heading to the same destination for a small fee.

BY TRAIN

Germany's rail systems are nearly perfect: fast, convenient, clean, comfortable, notoriously punctual, and just as affordable as any other form of public transportation. The two separate rail networks of East and West Germany merged in 1994 into **Deutsche Bahn** (DB, or German Rail), bringing Berlin and the cities of the old German Democratic Republic much closer to the main railheads of the west. The electrification and renovation of the ancient tracks in eastern Germany also made big strides forward, allowing the extension there of the high-speed InterCity Express (ICE) service. InterCity (IC) and EuroCity services have been improved and expanded, and the regional InterRegio network now extends nationwide. All overnight InterCity services and the slower D-class trains have sleepers, with a first-class service that includes breakfast in bed.

Deluxe "Hotel Trains" have been introduced with success on the Berlin–Munich and Berlin–Bonn lines. All InterCity and InterCity Express trains have restaurant cars or trolley service, and InterRegio services have bright bistro cars. All meals and snacks are catered by Mitropa—the company that sends a cart out to sell passengers traveling in second class cookies, snacks, hot Bockwurst with mustard, and an assortment of beverages. To avoid theft, take all valuables with you whenever you go to the bathroom.

A DM 7 surcharge is added to the ticket price on all InterCity and EuroCity journeys irrespective of distance (DM 14 return). The charge is DM 9 if paid on board the train. InterCity Express fares are about

20% more expensive than normal ones. Seat reservations on all trains cost DM 3. Bikes cannot be transported on InterCity Express services, but InterCity, EuroCity, and some D-class trains and all local trains have special storage facilities, and InterRegio trains even have compartments where cyclists can travel next to their bikes. Bikes cost DM 6 on local trains (for journeys up to 100 km) and DM 12 on all other trains.

Changing trains couldn't be easier. You often only have to cross to the other side of the platform. Special train maps on platform notice boards give details of the layout of trains arriving on that track, showing where first- and second-class cars and the restaurant car are, as well as where they will stop along the length of the platform.

Rail passengers with a valid round-trip air ticket can **buy a heavily discounted "Rail and Fly" ticket for DB trains** connecting with 14 German airports (Berlin's Schönefeld and Tegel airports, Bremen, Dresden, Düsseldorf, Frankfurt/Main, Hamburg, Hanover, Cologne-Bonn, Leipzig/Halle, Munich, Münster/Osnabrück, Nuremberg, Stuttgart) and two airports outside Germany (Basel and Amsterdam).

Note that in high season you will frequently encounter lines at ticket offices for seat reservations. Unless you are prepared to board the train without a reserved seat, taking the chance of a seat being available, the only way to avoid these lines is to **make an advance reservation by phone**. Call the ticket office (*Fahrkarten-Schalter*) of the rail station from which you plan to depart. Here again, you will probably have to make several attempts before you get through to the reservations section (*Reservierungen/Platzkarten*), but you will then be able to collect your seat ticket from a special counter without having to wait in line.

Train stations—called either *Hauptbahnhof* (main train station) or *Bahnhof* (train station)—and tourist offices can provide local, regional, and national railway timetables. The yellow *Abfahrt* (departures) and white *Ankunft* (arrivals) signs show train times and *Gleis* (track) or *Bahnsteig* (platform) numbers. Reservations for long trips are a good idea, especially if you want to take an overnight train, and reservations are required for most InterCity express trains. For trips of less than four hours, getting a seat is usually not a problem. Before you grab one, look above the seat you desire or on the door outside: A slip of paper indicates for which leg of the trip, if any, a seat is *reserviert* (reserved).

DEUTSCHE BAHN • 24-hour hotline (01805/996633). **Flughafen Berlin-Schönefeld** (tel. 030/2972–9528). **Berlin Zoologischer Garten** (tel. 030/2974–9277). **Dresden Hauptbahnhof** (tel. 0351/461–3508). **Düsseldorf Hauptbahnhof** (tel.: 0211/368–0466). **Düsseldorf Flughafen** (tel. 0211/368–0596). **Frankfurt (M) Flughafen Rhein-Main** (tel. 069/691844). **Frankfurt (M) Hauptbahnhof** (tel. 069/2653–4581). **Hamburg Hauptbahnhof** (tel. 040/3918- -4313). **Hanover Hauptbahnhof** (tel. 0511/286–5465). **Heidelberg Hauptbahnhof** (tel. 06221/52348). **Leipzig Hauptbahnhof** (tel. 0341/968–3275). **Köln (Cologne) Hauptbahnhof** (tel. 0221/19419). **Lahr** (Schwarzwald, tel. 07821/43278). **München Hauptbahnhof** (tel. 089/1308–5890 or 089/593889). **Stuttgart Hauptbahnhof** (tel. 0711/2092–2464).

BY BUS

Germany has good local bus services, but no proper nationwide network. A large portion of services are operated by **Deutsche Touring**, a subsidiary of the Deutsche Bahn. Rail tickets are valid on these services. There are also numerous regional lines that coordinate with the railroad to reach remote places. Most cities have a *Busbahnhof* (central bus depot), sometimes labeled *ZOB* (*Zentralomnibusbahnhof*), with an information booth, and train stations usually offer bus info (some train stations also function as bus terminals). Long-distance buses connect large cities as a supplement or alternative to train travel. Europabus honors Eurail passes and, within Germany, DB rail passes (read the fine print on your pass). Most companies also offer their own daily and monthly passes.

One of the best services is the Romantic Road bus between Würzburg (with connections to and from Frankfurt and Wiesbaden) and Füssen (with connections to and from Munich, Augsburg, and Garmisch-Partenkirchen). Buses with an attendant on board, offer one- or two-day tours in each direction in summer, leaving in the morning and arriving in the evening. Eurailpasses and German Rail Passes (*see* Train Travel, *below*) are good for 75 percent reductions on this and other Deutsche Touring scenic routes. For details and reservations, contact Deutsche Touring (*see* Intercity Buses, *below*).

All towns of any size operate their own local buses. For the most part, those link up with local trams (*Straßenbahn*), electric railway (S-bahn), and subway (U-bahn) services. Fares vary according to distance, but a ticket usually allows you to transfer freely between the various forms of transportation. Most cities issue 24-hour tickets at special rates.

INTERCITY BUSES • Deutsche Touring (Am Römerhof 17, D–60426 Frankfurt/Main, tel. 069/79030) or big city tourist offices.

BY CAR

Driving is a great way to enjoy Germany's beautiful countryside. It's also a challenge since Germany's superhighway, the Autobahn, has no speed limit. If it isn't a BMW barreling down on your tail at 200 km per hour, it's the fact that, at those speeds, any distraction or hazard—potholes, crosswinds, windshield grime—becomes 10,000 times more distracting and hazardous. Most deadly, however, are the legendary fogs that roll in and cover the highways. Randomly placed cameras capture your license plate and mug, should you exceed the speed limit (unless otherwise posted, **50 kph within cities and towns, 100 kph on country roads; no speed limit on the German Autobahn**). In the city, leave your car at the hotel—downtown parking costs up to DM 5 per hour. Americans should remember that gas is sold in liters and for about three times the U.S. price. In Germany, you drive on the right, and seat belts are mandatory for all passengers including those traveling in the backseat.

Alcohol limits on drivers are equivalent to two small beers or a quarter of a liter of wine (blood-alcohol level .08 percent). Passing is permitted on the left side only. Headlights, not parking lights, are required at night and during inclement weather.

Many cyclists swear that the best bike tour in Germany is along the scenic Rhine and Mosel rivers, especially between Koblenz and Mainz or Trier.

Allgemeiner Deutscher Automobilclub (ADAC; Am Westpark 8, 81373 Munich, tel. 089/76760, fax 089/7676–2500), Germany's principal motoring club, has offices in most German cities and provides free towing (up to 50 km), emergency roadside service and free accommodation referrals. On minor roads, **go to the nearest call box and dial 01802/222–222.** (If you have a mobile phone, just dial 222–222 without the prefix.) Ask, in English, for road service assistance. Help is free (with the exception of all materials) if the work is carried out by the ADAC. If the ADAC has to use a subcontactor for the work, charges are made for time, mileage, and materials.

Gasoline (petrol) costs are between DM 1.20 and DM 1.70 per liter. As part of antipollution efforts, most German cars now run on lead-free fuel. Some models use diesel fuel, so if you are renting a car, **find out which fuel the car takes**. Some older vehicles cannot take unleaded fuel. German filling stations are highly competitive and bargains are often available if you shop around, but *not* at Autobahn filling stations. Self-service, or *SB-Tanken*, stations are cheapest. Pumps marked *Bleifrei* contain unleaded gas.

A word of warning on German garages: you must **pay immediately on returning to retrieve your car**, not when you are driving out. Put the ticket you got on arrival into the machine and pay the amount displayed. Retrieve the ticket, go to your car and, on driving out, insert the ticket in a slot to get the barrier raised. Once you get in your car it's too late to pay. The barrier won't go up and the furious drivers behind you will quickly begin honking.

Roads in both the western and eastern part of the country are generally excellent. The best known road maps of Germany are put out by the automobile club ADAC and by Shell. They're available at gas stations and bookstores.

Germany has many specially designated tourist roads, all covering areas of particular scenic and historic interest. The longest is the *Deutsche Ferienstrasse*, the German Holiday Road, which runs from the Baltic to the Alps, a distance of around 1,720 km (1,070 mi). The most famous, however, and also the oldest, is the *Romantische Strasse*, the Romantic Road, which runs from Würzburg in Franconia to Füssen in the Alps, covering around 355 km (220 mi).

Among other notable touring routes—all with expressive and descriptive names—are the *Grüne Küstenstrasse* (Green Coast Road), running along the North Sea coast from Denmark to Emden; the *Burgenstrasse* (Castle Road), running from Mannheim to Nuremberg; the *Deutsche Weinstrasse* (German Wine Road), running through the heartland of the German wine country; and the *Deutsche Alpenstrasse* (German Alpine Road), running the length of the country's Alpine southern border to Bodensee. Less well known routes include the *Märchenstrasse* (Fairy-tale Road), the *Schwarzwälder Hochstrasse* (Black Forest High Road), and the *Deutsche Edelsteinstrasse* (GERMAN GEM ROAD).

BY MITFAHRGELEGENHEIT

Germany has an abundance of *Mitfahrzentralen* (ride-share offices) that connect drivers and riders heading in the same direction. These offices have an extensive computer file of names, driver's-license numbers, and vehicle-registration numbers, so if something goes wrong you can report it easily. As a rider, all you pay is a small commission to the agency that arranges the ride, plus your portion of fuel costs. To avoid being scammed, make sure to ask agents at the Mitfahrzentrale the approximate cost of fuel to your destination. Some drivers take advantage of the fact that carpooling agencies don't ask how long the trip will take, or what other detours the driver plans. In other words, your driver may want to go shopping in a junkyard, stop by a friend's house, or do some sightseeing. If language isn't a barrier, call your driver before accepting the ride; ask about detours and agree on a route. The addresses and telephone numbers of local Mitfahrzentralen can be found in the Coming and Going sections of cities in this book.

BY BIKE

Germany is a virtual paradise for those looking to pedal around town or between cities. Almost all cities have bike paths, and the countryside is laced with a network of quiet roads from one village to the next so that you can avoid the major highways. Particularly scenic (and relatively easy) are bike tours down Germany many river valleys. If you start upstream, you'll be heading downhill all the way. Tourist offices usually sell *Radwegkarten* (biking maps), as does the **Allgemeiner Deutscher Fahrrad-Club** (ADFC), which has offices in major cities. You can usually rent a bike for DM 12–DM 17 per day, mountain bikes for DM 20–DM 30 per day. Many trains have space for bikes, so that you can travel by rail through the steep or mundane areas and hop right back on your bike for the scenic and more moderately sloped routes. Check ahead: Not all trains allow bikes, and taking your bike on most forms of public transit involves an extra fee.

TRAVEL AGENCIES

A good travel agent puts your needs first. Look for an agency that has been in business at least five years, emphasizes customer service, and has someone on staff who specializes in your destination. In addition **make sure the agency belongs to a professional trade organization.** The American Society of Travel Agents (ASTA), with 27,000 agents in some 170 countries, is the largest and most influential in the field. Operating under the motto "Integrity in Travel," it maintains and enforces a strict code of ethics and will step in to help mediate any agent-client disputes if necessary. ASTA also maintains a Web site that includes a directory of agents. (Note that if a travel agency is also acting as your tour operator, *see* Buyer Beware *in* Tours & Packages, *above.*)

LOCAL AGENT REFERRALS • American Society of Travel Agents (ASTA, tel. 800/965–2782 24-hr hot line, fax 703/684–8319, www.astanet.com). **Association of British Travel Agents** (68–271 Newman St., London W1P 4AH, tel. 020/7637–2444, fax 020/7637–0713). **Association of Canadian Travel Agents** (1729 Bank St., Suite 201, Ottawa, Ontario K1V 7Z5, tel. 613/521–0474, fax 613/521–0805). **Australian Federation of Travel Agents** (Level 3, 309 Pitt St., Sydney 2000, tel. 02/9264–3299, fax 02/9264–1085). **Travel Agents' Association of New Zealand** (Box 1888, Wellington 10033, tel. 04/499–0104, fax 04/499–0786).

BUDGET TRAVEL ORGANIZATIONS

Council on International Educational Exchange (Council) is a private, nonprofit organization that administers work, volunteer, academic, and professional programs worldwide. Its travel division, Council Travel, is a full-service travel agency specializing in student, youth, and budget travel. They offer discounted airfares, rail passes, accommodations, guidebooks, budget tours, and travel gear. They also issue the ISIC, GO25, and ITIC identity cards (see Student ID Cards, below), as well as Hostelling International cards. Forty-six Council Travel offices serve the budget traveler in the United States, and there are about a dozen overseas, including Munich (tel. 089/395022) and London (tel. 020/7437–7767). Council also puts out a variety of publications, including the free Student Travels magazine, a gold mine of travel tips (including information on work-abroad, study-abroad, and international volunteer opportunities). 205 E. 42nd St., New York, NY 10017, tel. toll-free 888/COUNCIL, http://www.ciee.org.

COUNCIL TRAVEL OFFICES IN THE UNITED STATES • ARIZONA: Tempe (tel. 602/966–3544). **CALIFORNIA**: Berkeley (tel. 510/848–8604), Davis (tel. 916/752–2285), La Jolla (tel. 619/452–0630), Long Beach (tel. 310/598–3338), Los Angeles (tel. 310/208–3551), Palo Alto (tel. 415/325–3888), San Diego (tel. 619/270–6401), San Francisco (tel. 415/421–3473 or 415/566–6222), Santa Barbara (tel. 805/562–8080). **COLORADO**: Boulder (tel. 303/447–8101), Denver (tel. 303/571–0630). **CONNECTICUT**: New Haven (tel. 203/562–5335). **FLORIDA**: Miami (tel. 305/670–9261). **GEORGIA**: Atlanta (tel. 404/377–9997). **ILLINOIS**: Chicago (tel. 312/951-0585), Evanston (tel. 847/475–5070).

INDIANA: Bloomington (tel. 812/330–1600). **IOWA**: Ames (tel. 515/296–2326). KANSAS: Lawrence (tel. 913/749–3900). **LOUISIANA**: New Orleans (tel. 504/866–1767). **MARYLAND**: College Park (tel. 301/779–1172). **MASSACHUSETTS**: Amherst (tel. 413/256–1261), Boston (tel. 617/266–1926), Cambridge (tel. 617/497–1497 or 617/225–2555). **MICHIGAN**: Ann Arbor (tel. 313/998–0200). **MINNESOTA**: Minneapolis (tel. 612/379–2323). **NEW YORK**: New York (tel. 212/822–2700, 212/666–4177, or 212/254–2525). **NORTH CAROLINA**: Chapel Hill (tel. 919/942–2334). **OHIO**: Columbus (tel. 614/294–8696). **OREGON**: Portland (tel. 503/228–1900). **PENNSYLVANIA**: Philadelphia (tel. 215/382–0343), Pittsburgh (tel. 412/683–1881). **RHODE ISLAND**: Providence (tel. 401/331–5810). **TENNESSEE**: Knoxville (tel. 423/523–9900). **TEXAS**: Austin (tel. 512/472-4931), Dallas (tel. 214/363–9941). **UTAH**: Salt Lake City (tel. 801/582–5840). **WASHINGTON**: Seattle (tel. 206/632–2448 or 206/329–4567). **WASHINGTON, DC** (tel. 202/337–6464). For U.S. cities not listed, dial 800/2–COUNCIL.

Educational Travel Center (ETC) books low-cost flights to destinations within the continental United States and around the world. Their best deals are on flights leaving the Midwest, especially Chicago. ETC also issues Hostelling International cards. For more details request their free brochure, Taking Off. 438 N. Frances St., Madison, WI 53703, tel. 608/256–5551.

STA Travel, the world's largest travel organization catering to students and young people, has over 100 offices worldwide and offers low-price airfares to destinations around the globe, as well as rail passes, car rentals, tours, you name it. STA issues the ISIC and the GO25 youth cards, both of which prove eligibility for student airfares and other travel discounts. For more information, call 800/777–0112 or the nearest STA office, or look them up at http://www.sta-travel.com/.

INTERNATIONAL STA OFFICES • AUSTRALIA: Adelaide (tel. 08/223–2426), Brisbane (tel. 07/221–9388), Cairns (tel. 070/314199), Darwin (tel. 089/412955), Melbourne (tel. 03/349–2411), Perth (tel. 09/227–7569), Sydney (tel. 02/212–1255). **AUSTRIA**: Graz (tel. 0316/32482), Innsbruck (tel. 0512/588997), Linz (tel. 0732/775893), Salzburg (tel. 0662/883252), Vienna (tel. 0222/401480 or 0222/5050–1280). **DENMARK**: Copenhagen (tel. 031/358844). **FRANCE**: Paris (tel. 01/4325–0076). **GERMANY**: Berlin (tel. 030/281–6741), Frankfurt (tel. 069/430191 or 069/703035), Hamburg (tel. 040/442363). **GREECE**: Athens (tel. 01/322–1267). **ITALY**: Bologna (tel. 051/261802), Florence (tel. 055/289721), Genoa (tel. 010/564366), Milan (tel. 02/5830–4121), Naples (tel. 081/552–7960), Rome (tel. 06/467–9291), Venice (tel. 041/520–5660). **NETHERLANDS**: Amsterdam (tel. 020/626–2557). **NEW ZEALAND**: Auckland (tel. 09/309–9995), Christchurch (tel. 03/379–9098), Wellington (tel. 04/385–0561). **SPAIN**: Barcelona (tel. 03/487–9546), Madrid (tel. 01/541–7372). **SWEDEN**: Göteborg (tel. 031/774–0025). **SWITZERLAND**: Lausanne (tel. 0121/617–5811), Zurich (tel. 01/297–1111). **TURKEY**: Istanbul (tel. 01/252–5921). **UNITED KINGDOM**: London (tel. 0171/937–9962).

STA OFFICES IN THE UNITED STATES • CALIFORNIA: Berkeley (tel. 510/642–3000), Los Angeles (tel. 213/934–8722), San Francisco (tel. 415/391–8407), Santa Monica (tel. 310/394–5126), Westwood (tel. 310/824–1574). **FLORIDA**: Miami (tel. 305/461–3444), University of Florida (tel. 352/338–0068). **ILLINOIS**: Chicago (tel. 312/786–9050). **MASSACHUSETTS**: Boston (tel. 617/266–6014), Cambridge (tel. 617/576–4623). **NEW YORK**: Columbia University (tel. 212/865–2700), West Village (tel. 212/627–3111). **PENNSYLVANIA**: Philadelphia (tel. 215/382–2928). **WASHINGTON**: Seattle (tel. 206/633–5000). **WASHINGTON, DC** (tel. 202/887–0912).

Student Flights, Inc. specializes in student and faculty airfares and sells rail passes, ISE cards, and travel guidebooks. 5010 E. Shea Blvd., Suite A104, Scottsdale, AZ 85254, tel. 602/951–1177 or 800/255–8000.

Travel CUTS is a full-service travel agency that sells discounted airline tickets to Canadian students and issues the ISIC, GO25, ITIC, and HI cards. Their 25 offices are on or near college campuses. Call weekdays 9–5 for information and reservations. 187 College St., Toronto, Ont. M5T 1P7, tel. 416/979–2406.

Hostelling International (HI), also known as IYHF, is the grandmammy of hostel associations, offering single-sex dorm beds ("couples" rooms and family accommodations are available at certain HI hostels) and kitchen facilities at over 700 locations in Germany and over 100 in Austria. Membership in any HI national hostel association (see below), open to travelers of all ages, allows you to crash in HI-affiliated hostels at member rates (about $10–$25 a night). Members also have priority if the hostel is full and are eligible for discounts around the world, including rail and bus travel in some countries.

A one-year membership is $25 for adults (renewal $20) and $10 for those under 18. A lifetime membership, regardless of age, will set you back $250; a one-night guest membership is about $3. Handbooks listing all current hostels and special discount opportunities (like budget cycling and hiking tours) are available from some national associations. There are two international hostel directories: One covers

Europe and the Mediterranean, while another covers Africa, the Americas, Asia, and the Pacific ($13.95 each). The HI web site (http://www.gnn.com/gnn/bus/ayh/index.html) gives addresses and phone numbers for hostels all over the world and notes which ones will let you reserve in advance. 733 15th St. NW, Suite 840, Washington, DC 20005, tel. 202/783–6161.

Other associations aiding and abetting hostelers include **Hostelling International–American Youth Hostels** (HI–AYH; 733 15th St., Suite 840, Washington, DC 20005, tel. 202/783–6161); **Hostelling International–Canada** (HI–C; 400-205 Catherine St., Ottawa, Ont. K2P 1C3, tel. 613/237–7884 or 800/663-5777); **Youth Hostel Association of England and Wales** (YHA; Trevelyan House, 8 St. Stephen's Hill, St. Albans, Herts. AL1 2DY, England, tel. 01727/855–215); **Australian Youth Hostels Association** (YHA; Level 3, 10 Mallett St., Camperdown, New South Wales 2050, tel. 02/565–1699); and **Youth Hostels Association of New Zealand** (YHA; Box 436, Christchurch 1, tel. 03/379–9970).

VISITOR INFORMATION

TOURIST INFORMATION

Aside from offering the usual glossy tourist brochures, the **German National Tourist Office** (DZT) can answer general questions about travel in their respective countries or refer you to other organizations for more info. DZT offices are open to the public and easy to contact via the Internet at www.germany-tourism.de. Be as specific as possible when writing to request information, or you may just end up with a stack of glossy brochures on cruises or shopping expeditions. If you can get someone to answer questions over the phone, so much the better—the offices are usually staffed by natives.

IN THE UNITED STATES • DZT: 122 E. 42nd St., New York, NY 10168, tel. 212/661–7200, fax 212/661–7174; 11766 Wilshire Blvd., Suite 750, Los Angeles, CA 90025, tel. 310/575–9799, fax 310/575–1565.

IN CANADA • DZT: 175 Bloor St. E, North Tower, Suite 604, Toronto, Ont. M4W 3R8, tel. 416/968–1570, fax 416/968–1986.

IN THE UNITED KINGDOM • DZT: Nightingale House, 65 Curzon St., London W1Y 8NE, tel. 020/7495–0081, fax 020/7495–6129.

IN AUSTRALIA • DZT: Lufthansa House, 9th floor, 143 Macquarie St., Sydney 2000, tel. 02/367–3890, fax 02/367–3898.

U.S. GOVERNMENT ADVISORIES • U.S. Department of State (Overseas Citizens Services Office, Room 4811 N.S., 2201 C St. NW, Washington, DC 20520; tel. 202/647–5225 for interactive hot line; 301/946–4400 for computer bulletin board; fax 202/647–3000 for interactive hot line); enclose a self-addressed, stamped, business-size envelope.

VOLUNTEER PROGRAMS

PUBLICATIONS

Bill McMillon's *Volunteer Vacations* ($13.95) lists hundreds of organizations and volunteer opportunities in the United States and abroad. Pick up a copy at your local bookstore.

ORGANIZATIONS

Council's **Voluntary Services Department** offers two- to four-week environmental or community service projects in Germany and other countries. Participants must be 18 or older and pay a $195 placement fee. Council also publishes Volunteer! *The Comprehensive Guide to Voluntary Service in the U.S. and Abroad* ($12.95, plus $1.50 postage), which describes nearly 200 organizations around the world that offer volunteer positions.

Service Civil International (SCI) and **International Voluntary Service** (IVS; 5474 Walnut Level Rd., Crozet, VA 22932, tel. 804/823–1826) work for peace and international understanding through two- to three-week workcamps in Europe for those 18 or older (fee $100–$150). **Volunteers for Peace** (*VFP; 43 Tiffany Rd., Belmont, VT 05730, tel. 802/259–2759, fax 802/259–2922) sponsors two- to three-week international workcamps in the United States, Europe, Africa, Asia, and Central America. Registration is $175. Send for their International Workcamp Directory ($12); it lists over 800 volunteer opportunities in 60 countries around the world.

WEB SITES

Do **check out the World Wide Web** when you're planning. You'll find everything from up-to-date weather forecasts to virtual tours of famous cities. Fodor's Web site www.fodors.com, is a great place to start your online travels. Most official German city web site addresses consist of the city name followed by ".de"; for example, Hamburg's site may be found at www.hamburg.de. Many German have English pages with useful information for tourists.

WHEN TO GO

The summer months bring crowds of foreign travelers to Germany, not to mention monumental traffic jams that accompany the exodus of German tourists as they move from north to south and east to west. Summer here often means long lines, harried tourist offices, and crowds of youngsters filling the youth hostels. In winter, prices for food and lodging drop slightly, but then again, many places close for at least part of the season, while transportation in some areas, such as the Black Forest, becomes much more difficult. If you can, swing some free time in autumn or spring, the best seasons to explore. In particular, traveling in May or October allows you to cash in on off-season prices while the weather is still pleasant and the streets are relatively free from camera-toting tourists and school groups.

FESTIVALS

Heaps of local festivals provide travelers with one of the most enjoyable ways to experience German culture. Outdoor theater festivals abound in town centers and castles in summer, wine festivals take place in spring and late summer, and endless varieties of local fairs are held throughout the year. To find out more about these local festivals, contact the national tourist offices or local branches in cities you're visiting. Also see the individual chapters in this book. What follows is a list of some of Germany's largest festivals:

JANUARY • Sports enthusiasts head for the German Alps in droves to catch crowd-pleasers such as the **Snowboarding World Championship** in the Götschen ski region and the **Bobsleigh World Championship** at the track in Königssee of the Berchtesgadener Land.

FEBRUARY • **Fasching**, or Karneval, is one of the most important festivals in Catholic Germany. It starts in January and runs through Fasching Dienstag (Shrove Tuesday) in February, 48 days before Easter. Cologne's Karneval is especially lively; raucous carnivals, parades, masked balls, street fairs, and other events turn the city into one ongoing party for the duration of the event. The **Berliner Filmfestspiele**, Germany's version of the Cannes Film Festival, brings movies and movie stars from around the world to Berlin.

MARCH • Spring fairs bring revelry and major parties to towns across Germany from March through April, including Augsburg, Hamburg, Münster, Nuremberg, and Stuttgart. Hamburg's **Frühlingsdom** is one of Germany's liveliest spring fairs.

APRIL • The **Wine and Blossom** festival comes to Koblenz, the **May Fair** to Mannheim. Both are fairly bacchanalian events. Spring fairs continue in many cities. In the Harz region April 30 reminds of Halloween with the celebration of **Walpurgis Nacht**, an evening when witches gather on the Brocken mountain to act out ancient rites. Today the locals and an increasing number of tourists meet on the same spot to dance, sing, play medieval instruments, and wait for demons to appear.

MAY • Hamburg's harbor is filled with boats and musicians during **Hafengeburtstag** (Harbor Birthday). Across the rest of Germany cities celebrate the pleasant weather with a variety of outdoor markets and May festivals.

JUNE • In early June, Munich hosts **castle concerts** as well the **Munich Film Festival**. Berlin's **Jazz in the Garden** livens up the Neue Nationalgalerie, and Leipzig hosts its **Street Music** and **Jazz Festivals**. In mid-June, towns in the Danube Valley celebrate the **Danube Festival**. Dresden's extremely popular **Elbhangfest**, centered along the Elbe River, begins in late June, as does Kiel's renowned **Kieler Woche** sailing regatta.

JULY • The biggest and perhaps loudest event is Berlin's massive techno and house party, the **Love Parade**, usually on the first or second Sunday of the month. A variety of folk festivals grace German towns such as Würzburg and Munich. Kulmbach hosts a heady **Beer Festival**. In Bayreuth, the **Richard Wagner Festival** begins.

THE HIGHS AND THE LOWS

Average daily high and low temperatures stack up as follows:

CITY	JANUARY: HIGH/LOW	JULY: HIGH/LOW
BERLIN	36°F/27°F 2°C/-3°C	76°F/58°F 24°C/14°C
BONN	40°F/32°F 4°C/0°C	74°F/57°F 23°C/14°C
DRESDEN	36°F/25°F 2°C/-4°C	76°F/56°F 24°C/13°C
FRANKFURT	39°F/29°F 4°C/-2°C	77°F/59°F 25°C/15°C
FREIBURG	40°F/29°F 4°C/-2°C	76°F/58°F 24°C/14°C
HAMBURG	36°F/29°F 2°C/-2°C	72°F/56°F 22°C/13°C
MUNICH	35°F/23°F 1°C/-5°C	74°F/55°F 23°C/13°C

AUGUST • Heidelberger celebrates its **Schloßfestspiele**, one of Germany's many open-air music-and-theater festivals. Wine festivals flood the Rhineland, much of southwest Germany, Franconia, and many other wine-producing regions.

SEPTEMBER • **Oktoberfest**, Munich's famous beer and merriment marathon, is the largest party in Germany—period. Würzburg puts on its own week-long fête, the **Winzerfest**.

OCTOBER • October 3 marks Germany's **unification**, with celebrations throughout the country. Munich hosts yet another Volksfest, the **Herbst Dult**.

NOVEMBER • **St. Martin's Festival**, with children's lantern processions, takes place throughout the Rhineland and Bavaria.

DECEMBER • Christmas markets featuring local foods and handicrafts are held in many towns across Germany, including Berlin, Cologne, and Nuremberg, home to the largest and most famous market, the **Christkindlmarkt**. In Berchtesgaden the market is accompanied by a shooting contest.

CLIMATE

The climate in Germany defies generalization, as the seasons' duration and severity vary widely. Summers are usually warm and often unbearably humid in large cities such as Frankfurt, Cologne, and Berlin. Weather in Germany has been tough to predict and many recent summers have been either too hot or too wet with no in-betweens. Nearly all of Germany, except for much of the Rheinland, sees snow in winter, and winters in northern Germany are especially gray and dreary. The average daily highs and lows stack up as follows.

FORECASTS • **Weather Channel Connection** (tel. 900/932–8437), 95per minute from a Touch-Tone phone.

WOMEN IN GERMANY

Women traveling in Germany should use common sense when it comes to safety, especially when traveling alone. Harassment may seem minimal, especially during the daytime or in public at night, but this doesn't mean problems don't exist. Most larger cities have a *Frauenzentrum* (women's center) that can lend a helping hand in solving any problems. As always, keep your wits about you, and try not to end up alone with a strange man in a train compartment (or anywhere else, for that matter).

PUBLICATIONS

Aside from the lesbian-oriented *Women's Traveller* and *Are You Two . . . Together?* (*see* Gay & Lesbian Travel, *above*), check out *Women Travel: Adventures, Advice, and Experience* ($12.95), published by Prentice Hall. While the book covers more than 70 countries by way of women's journal entries and short articles, it offers few details on prices, phone numbers, and addresses. The *Handbook for Women Travelers* ($14.95), by Maggie and Gemma Moss, has some very good tips on women's health and personal safety on the road. For a nice companion book, look for *Maiden Voyages* ($14), edited by Mary Morris and published by Vintage Books. This collection of travel writing by women includes everyone from Mary Wollstonecraft to Joan Didion. Women traveling alone might check out *Traveling Solo* ($14) by Jennifer Cecil or *Connecting—News For Solo Travelers*, which is available by writing Box 29088, 1996 W. Broadway, Vancouver, BC V6J 5C2, Canada, or calling 604/737–7791. Resources for women in Germany can be found in Emma Kolpingsplatz's *Frauen Kalender* (Women's Calendar), a calendar of events and guide to traveling in Germany. Write or call Box 1a, 50482 Cologne, tel. 0221/49221. Another option is *Frauen Unterwegs* (Women on the Move), available at Potsdamer Straße 139, 10783 Berlin, tel. 030/215–1022.

ORGANIZATIONS

Women Welcome Women (WWW; 10 Greenwood Ln., Westport, CT 06880, tel. 203/259–7832; 88 Easton St., High Wycombe, Buckinghamshire HP11 1LT, England) is a nonprofit organization aimed at bringing together women of all nationalities, ages and interests. Membership can put you in touch with women around the globe.

WORKING ABROAD

As the economic and financial superpower of the new European Union—and as the continent's leader in all things high-tech and pharmaceutical—Germany attracts many foreigners in search of work. Generally, you'll have the best chance of setting up a decent job if you speak German and have some documented, specialized skill and a good contact in the area where you want to work. On the other hand, some people arrive in Germany and stumble upon a job, generally off the books and under the table. If you're in the latter group, be aware that this sort of work arrangement is illegal and that you are subject to deportation if you're caught. Furthermore, since Germany's new Social Democrat government has committed itself to deporting illegals, your chances of being caught are higher than ever. To complicate matters, the influx of people from eastern Europe looking for a job means it will even be harder for you to find one.

LEGAL REQUIREMENTS

If you're planning to work in Germany and wish to do so legally, you'll need to jump through some bureaucratic hoops. To obtain a work permit, which can be done before you leave home through your local German consulate or once you arrive at the local *Ausländerbehörde* (foreigners office), you must present proof of employment, preferably in the form of a written job offer from your prospective employer. You'll also need two passport-size photos, proof of citizenship, and up to DM 75. Work permits must be obtained before starting work and are officially required for employment of any duration.

PUBLICATIONS

Council (*see* Students in Germany, *above*) publishes two excellent resource books detailing work/travel opportunities. The most valuable is *Work, Study, Travel Abroad: The Whole World Handbook* ($13.95), which gives the lowdown on scholarships, grants, fellowships, study-abroad programs, and work exchanges. Also worthwhile is Council's *The High School Student's Guide to Study, Travel, and Adventure Abroad* ($13.95). Both books can be shipped to you at book rate ($1.50) or first-class ($3). The U.K.-based Vacation Work Press publishes two first-rate guides to working abroad: *Directory of Overseas Summer Jobs* ($14.95) and Susan Griffith's *Work Your Way Around the World* ($17.95). The first lists over

45,000 jobs worldwide; the latter has fewer listings but makes a more interesting read. Look for them at bookstores, or contact the American distributor, Peterson's (202 Carnegie Center, Princeton, NJ 05843).

ORGANIZATIONS

The easiest way to arrange work in Germany or elsewhere in Europe is through Council's Work Abroad Department. Through this program, U.S. citizens or permanent residents over 18 who were full-time students for the semester preceding their stay overseas can work in Germany for three to six months. Past participants have worked at all types of jobs from hotel and retail work to the occasional career-related internship. A good working knowledge of German is required. The cost of the program is $200, which includes legal work, permission documents, orientation and program materials, access to job and housing listings, and ongoing support services overseas. Contact Council (*see* Students in Germany, *above*) for their free "Work Abroad" brochure. Canadians are not eligible for the Council Work Abroad program, and should contact **Travel CUTS** (187 College St., Toronto, Ont. M5T 1P7, tel. 416/979–2406), which has similar programs for Canadian students who want to work abroad for up to six months.

Au Pair Abroad (1015 15th St. NW, Suite 750, Washington, DC 20005, tel. 202/408–5380, fax 202/480–5397, 708439@mcimail.com) arranges board and lodging for people between the ages of 18 and 26 who want to work as nannies for three to 18 months in a foreign country. Basic language skills are required for some countries, and all applicants must go through a somewhat lengthy interview process.

IAESTE (10 Corporate Center, Suite 250, 10400 Little Patuxent Pkwy., Columbia, MD 21044, tel. 410/997–2200, fax 410/997–5186) sends full-time students to practice their engineering, mathematics, and computer skills in Germany, among other countries. You don't get paid much, though the program is designed to cover day-to-day expenses. Applications are due between September and December for travel the following summer, so get going.

FRANKFURT AND HESSEN

2

UPDATED BY MICHAEL WOODHEAD

Most travelers' experience of Hessen (Hesse) begins and ends with the Frankfurt airport and train station, portals to Germany's cosmopolitan rat race. But if you venture into Hessen's less frenzied cities and towns, you'll find that this *Land* (state) devotes considerable resources to preserving a rich cultural heritage. The noble families that ruled the region from the Middle Ages to modern times left behind architectural gems, many of which can be seen today. Remote villages like Büdingen have never shed their medieval skin, and former *Residenzstädte* (cities of residence for regional nobles) like Weilburg are dotted with Baroque palaces and mansions that demonstrate the region's former wealth and power. In fact, some of the best parts of Hessen are the most unspoiled, including the Taunus mountains north of Frankfurt, and the Rhön uplands south of Fulda, protected as a UNESCO wildlife preserve. The Lahn Valley, though not as dramatic or famous as the Rhine and Mosel valleys, is calm, beautiful, and home to Marburg—a small university town virtually untouched by war and graced by one of the finest Gothic churches in Germany; the valley also harbors handsome, quiet towns like Wetzlar, with its Gothic cathedral. The underrated region between Frankfurt and Heidelberg known as the Odenwald includes towns like Darmstadt, with unique architectural and cultural treasures. Hessen's landscape isn't as dramatic as the mountainous regions to the south, but it somehow embodies more of the essence of Germany—even-keeled, orderly, and brimming with culture.

FRANKFURT

Frankfurt am Main comes at you from all sides; its skyscrapers jut out from the flat Hessen landscape like a cluster of giant needles. The tallest, naturally a bank in this banking city, reaches 900 feet—Europe's highest building. Frankfurters do not mind the jibes of their more traditional-minded neighbors on the Rhine or in Bavaria, who deride Frankfurt as a cosmopolitan blot on the map. Indeed, the city authorities plan to build 18 more skyscrapers. With a population of only 600,000, Frankfurt has assumed an importance far greater than its size; it is the seat of Europe's most influential bankers, professionals who are steering the European Union toward Economic and Monetary Union (expected by mid-2002, when the euro is supposed to replace national currencies as the EU's sole legal tender).

HESSEN

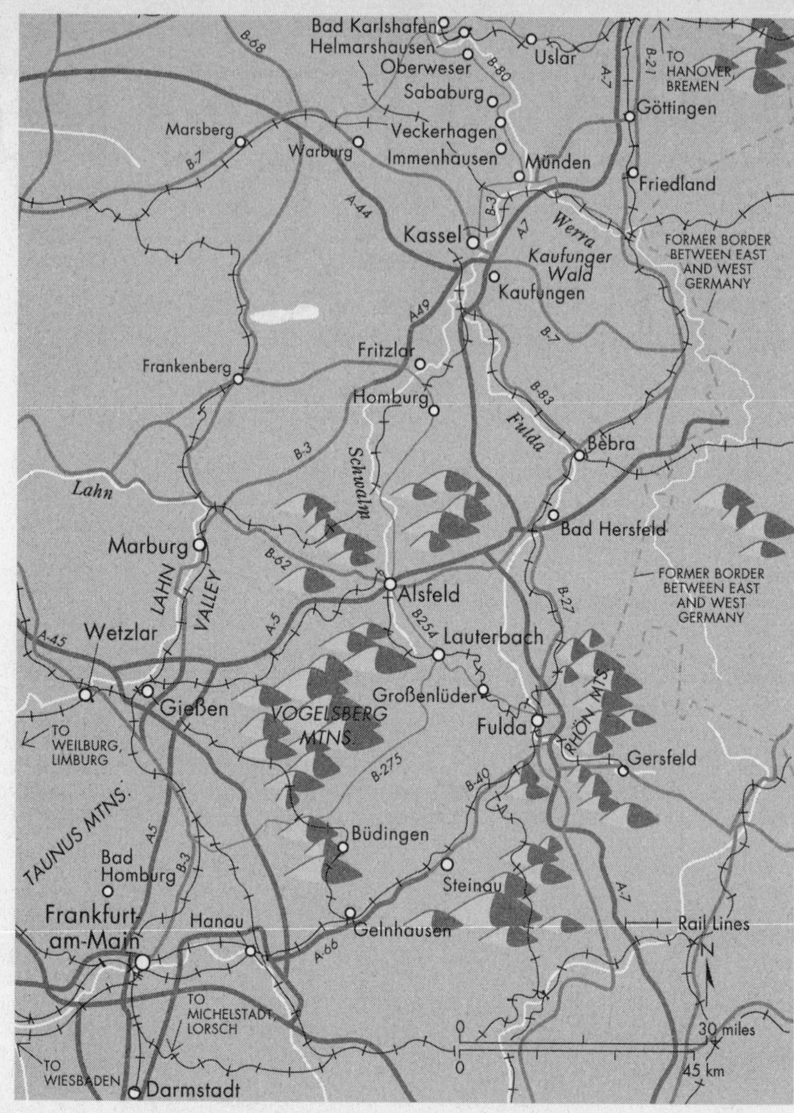

While Frankfurters sometimes refer to their home as Mainhatten, or their Autobahn route A 66 as "Route 66," this most American of German cities manages to remain thoroughly Teutonic. Spanning 700 years, its rich and varied past has been integrally tied to the development and role of money, regionally and internationally. The major trading capital was the seat of the Holy Roman Emperors, the capital of the German Federation from 1815 to 1866, and the birthplace of the "Frankfurt School" of critical theory. Although its crime rate is high within Germany, Frankfurt is relatively tame compared with any American city of similar size; nevertheless, if you'd like to steer clear of the seedier sights of Frankfurt, try to avoid the area around the Hauptbahnhof (central train station), even in daylight. Head instead to the city's many good museums, cafés, and bars.

BASICS

AMERICAN EXPRESS

This office offers the usual AmEx services. *Kaiserstr. 8, tel. 069/21050. Open weekdays 9:30–5:30, Sat. 9–noon.*

BIKE RENTAL

Holger's Radladen-Fahrradverleih rents two-wheelers for DM 15 per day. Call first for availability, especially on weekends. *Eschenheimer Landstr. 470, tel. 069/522004. U1, U2, or U3 to Lindenbaum. Open weekdays 9–1 and 3–6:30, Sat. 9–1.*

CHANGING MONEY

Volksbank and **DVB** charge only DM 3 per exchange. DVB has branches in the post office (*see* Mail and Phones, *below*), train station, and airport (Arrival Hall B), open daily until 10 or 11 PM. The wacky little **Wechselstube** (Römerberg 28, tel. 069/929–1320) on the Römer has good rates, charges DM 4 per exchange, and gives away postcards and other little surprise gifts with each transaction. Any bank will change money and traveler's checks and offer far better rates than hotels.

CONSULATES

Australia. *Gutleutstr. 85, tel. 069/273–9090. From Hauptbahnhof, right on Baseler Str., left on Gutleutstr.*

United Kingdom. *Bockenheimer Landstr. 42, tel. 069/170–0020. U6 or U7 to Westend.*

United States. *Siesmayerstr. 21, tel. 069/75350. After-hours emergency number: 069/7535–3700. U6 or U7 to Westend; exit at Palmengarten, right on Siesmayerstr.*

DISCOUNT TRAVEL

For discount international plane tickets and ISIC cards (DM 15), head to **STA Travel,** which also has info on discount car, bus, and train travel. *Bockenheimer Landstr. 133, tel. 069/703035, fax 069/777014. U6, U7, or Tram 19 to Bockenheimer Warte. Open weekdays 10–6.*

ENGLISH-LANGUAGE BOOKSTORES

For your literary needs, try the **British Bookshop** (Börsenstr. 17, tel. 069/280492), one block from Hauptwache.

INTERNET RESOURCES

CybeRyder (Töngesg. 31, tel. 069/9208–4010, fax 069/287929, www.cyberyder.de) is a cozy electronic café open daily until 11 PM.

LAUNDRY

Two blocks south of the hostel, **Wasch Center** (Wallstr. 8, tel. 069/628333; open daily 6 AM–10 PM) charges DM 6 to wash and DM 1 for 15 min of drying.

MAIL AND PHONES

The post office at the Hauptbahnhof is open daily until 9 PM. The airport branch is open 24 hours. The **main post office,** on the Zeil by Hauptwache, has fax and poste restante services. All offices exchange money for a painful DM 6 per traveler's check. *Zeil 110. Postal code: 60313.*

PHARMACIES AND MEDICAL AID

The **pharmacy** in the Hauptbahnhof is open weekdays 6:30 AM–9 PM, Saturday 8 AM–9 PM, and Sunday 9–8. No one speaks English at the **emergency prescription service** (tel. 069/19292), so have a German speaker call.

VISITOR INFORMATION

Tourist Information Römer. The friendly staff provides maps, hotel listings, museum brochures, and info on upcoming events. They also book rooms for DM 5. *Römerberg 27, next to Römer, tel. 069/2123–8708. Open weekdays 9–7, weekends and holidays 9:30–6.*

Tourist Information Hauptbahnhof. This office is busier than the Römer office but has the same services. *Opposite Track 23, tel. 069/2123–8849. Open Mon.–Sat. 8 AM–10 PM.*

FRANKFURT

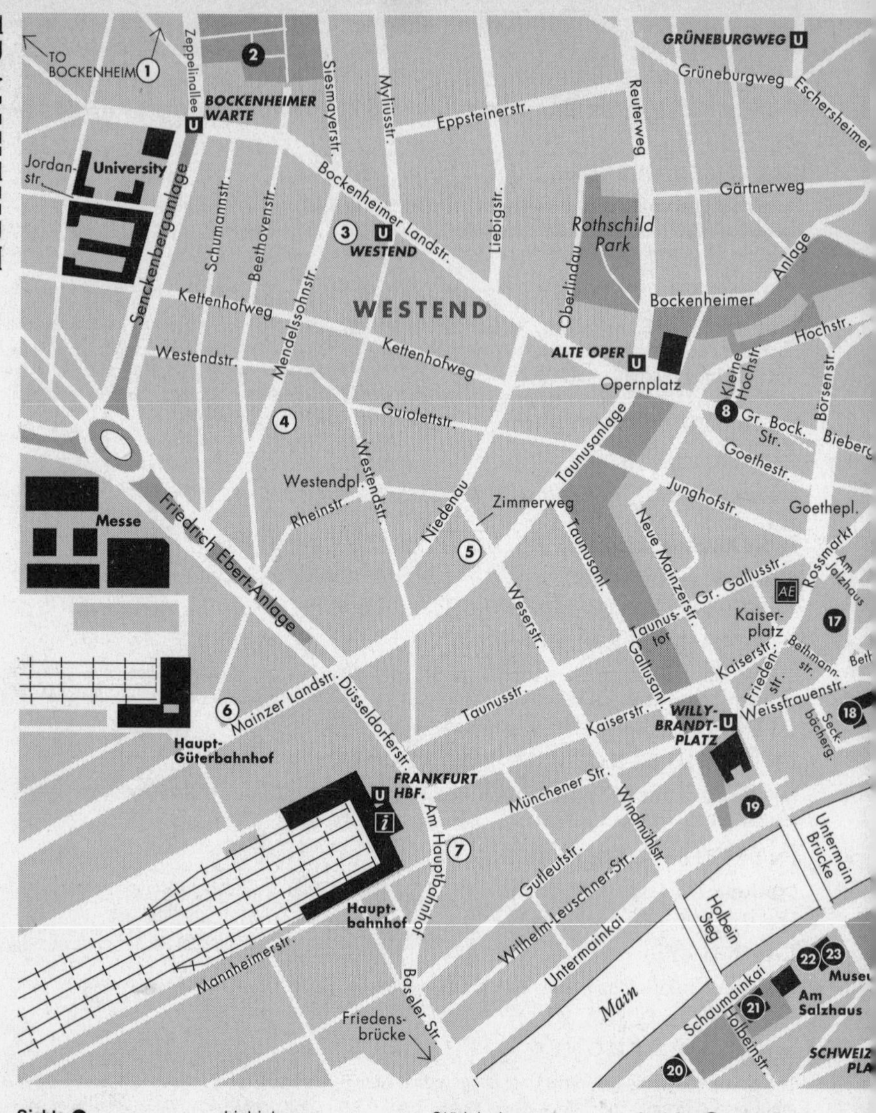

Sights ●

Architektur Museum, **22**

Dom St. Bartholomäus, **14**

Filmmuseum, **23**

Freßgasse, **8**

Goethehaus, **17**

Hauptwache, **9**

Jüdisches Museum, **19**

Karmeliterkloster, **18**

Liebighaus-Museum alter Plastik, **20**

Museum Judengasse, **12**

Museum für Kunsthandwerk, **24**

Museum für moderne Kunst, **13**

Palmengarten, **2**

Römerberg, **16**

Schirn Kunsthalle, **15**

Städelsches Kunstinstitut und Städtische Galerie, **21**

Zoo, **11**

Lodging ○

Haus der Jugend (HI), **25**

Hotel Atlas, **5**

Hotel Glockshuber, **6**

Hotel Terminus, **7**

Hotel Zur Rose, **10**

Pension Backer, **3**

Pension Bruns, **4**

Sophien Hotel, **1**

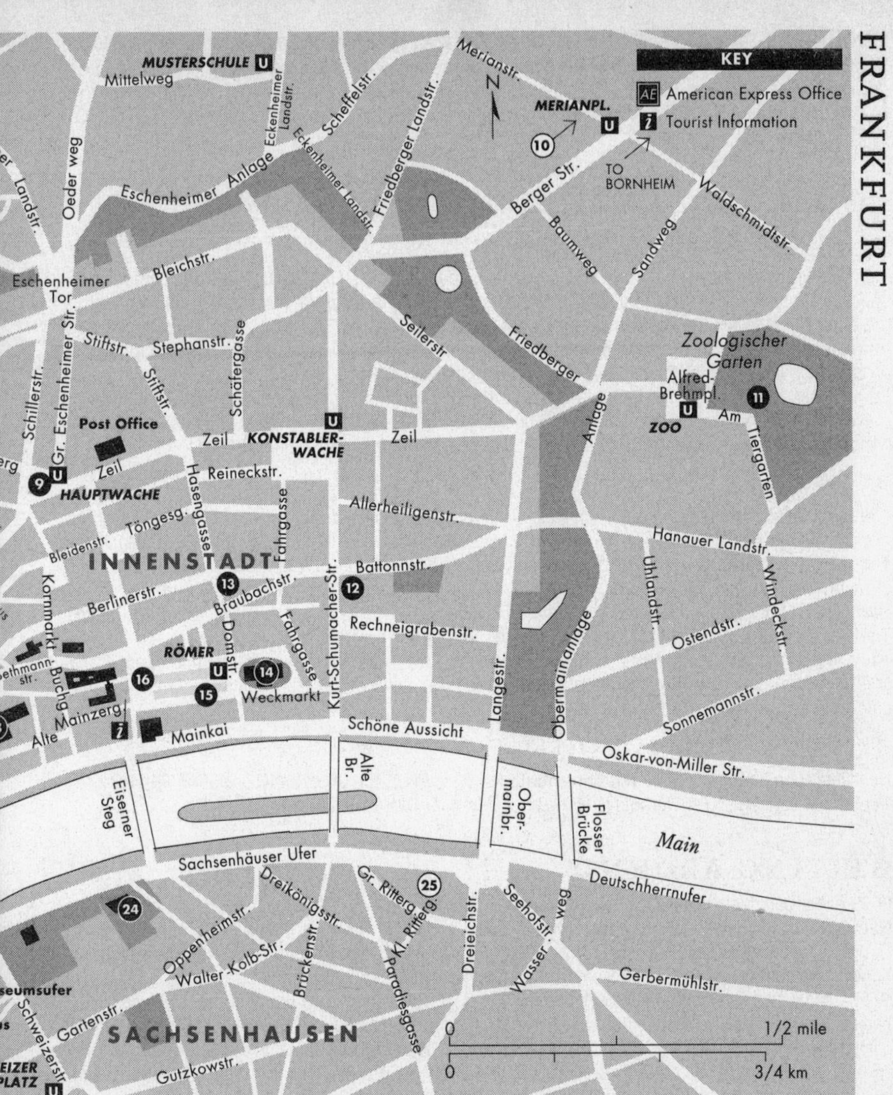
KEY
American Express Office
Tourist Information
N
MUSTERSCHULE
Mittelweg
Eckenheimer Landstr.
Scheffelstr.
Merianstr.
MERIANPL.
TO BORNHEIM
Oeder weg
Landstr.
Eschenheimer Anlage
Eckenheimer Landstr.
Friedberger Landstr.
Berger Str.
Waldschmidtstr.
Baumweg
Sandweg
Eschenheimer Tor
Bleichstr.
Gr. Eschenheimer Str.
Stiftstr.
Stephanstr.
Schäfergasse
Seilerstr.
Friedberger
Zoologischer Garten
Alfred-Brehmpl.
ZOO
Am Tiergarten
Schillerstr.
Post Office
Zeil
KONSTABLER-WACHE
Anlage
HAUPTWACHE
Reineckstr.
Hasengasse
Fahrgasse
Allerheiligenstr.
Töngesg.
Bleidenstr.
INNENSTADT
Hanauer Landstr.
Uhlandstr.
Windeckstr.
Battonnstr.
Berlinerstr.
Braubachstr.
Kornmarkt
Buchg.
Domstr.
Fahrgasse
Rechneigrabenstr.
Ostendstr.
RÖMER
Obermainanlage
Langestr.
Kurt-Schumacher-Str.
Weckmarkt
Mainzerg.
Alte
Mainkai
Schöne Aussicht
Sonnemannstr.
Oskar-von-Miller Str.
Eiserner Steg
Alte Br.
Ober-mainbr.
Flosser Brücke
Main
Sachsenhäuser Ufer
Dreikönigsstr.
Gr. Ritterg.
Kl. Ritterg.
Dreieichstr.
Seehofstr.
Wasserweg
Deutschherrnufer
Oppenheimstr.
Walter-Kolb-Str.
Brückenstr.
Paradiesgasse
Gerbermühlstr.
Schweizerstr.
Gartenstr.
SACHSENHAUSEN
Gutzkowstr.
0
1/2 mile
0
3/4 km

RESOURCES FOR GAYS AND LESBIANS • Lesben Informations- und Beratungsstelle (LIBS) (tel. 069/499–0008) provides counseling and info on lesbian activities. Unfortunately, the phone line is staffed infrequently. **Switchboard** (Alte Gasse 36, tel. 069/283535; open Tues.–Sat. 7 PM–1 AM, Sun. 4–1), a café and phone hot line, provides info in German and English. They mostly serve gay men but also welcome calls from lesbians.

COMING AND GOING

BY PLANE

All major European cities and many U.S. cities have direct flights to **Flughafen Frankfurt,** Europe's second-busiest airport. For flight info, call 069/690305. To reach the *S-Bahn* (commuter rail) station from the airport, just follow the signs (a big green dot with an "S" inside). Buy a ticket for "Frankfurt a. M." from the ticket machine and take the S8 to Hauptbahnhof or Hauptwache (where you can transfer to other transit lines). It's about 15 min to either stop and costs DM 1.90 (DM 2.60 during rush hour). Eurail passes are good on the S-Bahn. To reach the bus stop, follow the signs with bus icons; Bus 61 makes the half-hour trip to Sachsenhausen (home of the youth hostel) every 15 min. A taxi ride from the airport to the city center costs about DM 40 and takes 20–40 min, depending on traffic.

BY TRAIN

Frankfurt's **Hauptbahnhof,** about 1 km west of the city center, sits at the center of Germany's rail network. Frankfurt has direct trains leaving at least once per hour for Berlin (5½ hrs, DM 207), Cologne (2½ hrs, DM 68), Hamburg (4 hrs, DM 191), Heidelberg (1½ hrs, DM 29.40), Leipzig (3½ hrs, DM 111), and Munich (4½ hrs, DM 130), as well as several S-Bahn trains that depart hourly for nearby cities like Darmstadt, Mainz, and Wiesbaden. For train info, call 069/19419 or ask at the office opposite Track 8. The station is like a little indoor city, with restaurants, cafés, two banks, a shopping passage, a post office, a pharmacy, a tourist office, and luggage lockers (DM 2–DM 4). If you are tired of burgers, Coke, and lukewarm coffee, grab a snack and read a free newspaper at Deutsche Bahn's modern Intercity café, perched above the main ticket hall.

BY MITFAHRGELEGENHEIT

Near the Hauptbahnhof, **ADM Mitfahrzentrale** (Baseler Pl. 1, tel. 069/19440 or 069/236444; closed weekends) can get you to Hamburg, Munich, or Berlin for DM 40–DM 50.

GETTING AROUND

Frankfurt's many neighborhoods reach out like the tentacles of an octopus, with the creature's head at **Hauptwache,** a busy square in the center of town, about 15 min east of the Hauptbahnhof. From Hauptwache, transit lines run to all of Frankfurt's neighborhoods. South of the Main River lies **Sachsenhausen,** which has quite a few museums, and even more bars and clubs sprinkled along its cobblestone streets. Next to the Hauptbahnhof is **Westend,** the financial district, with many of the city's affordable hotels. Just northwest is **Bockenheim,** a lively low-income and university district dotted with sidewalk cafés, *Imbiß* (snack food) stands, and produce markets. **Nordend** is a quiet, tree-lined residential area spotted with hip corner cafés and restaurants. In the northeast, **Bornheim** is an ethnically diverse neighborhood with a cluster of *Ebbelwoi* (apple wine) taverns and cozy pubs. Don't limit yourself to Sachsenhausen or downtown; most of Frankfurt's local color is found in its outlying neighborhoods.

BY PUBLIC TRANSIT

The four modes of transport—**U-Bahn** (subway), **S-Bahn** (commuter rail), **Straßenbahn** (tram), and **bus**—all use the same tickets and operate 4 AM–1 AM. You can buy **short-trip tickets** (DM 3–DM 4) and **24-hour tickets** (DM 8.80) from bus drivers or at blue machines labeled FAHRSCHEINE. The newer machines even have instructions in English; just push the button by the flag icons. On weekends, *Nachtbusse* (night buses) operate midnight–5 AM. On request, bus drivers will arrange for a taxi to pick you up from your stop. Most of these lines stop at Hauptwache and Hauptbahnhof. Pick up a *Gesamtlinienplan,* which combines a map with all lines and stops labeled, an S- and U-Bahn map, and a night bus map, from the tourist office or info booth at the train station. *Stadtwerke Frankfurt am Main, tel. 069/2132–2236 or 069/2132–2295. S-Bahn info: tel. 069/19419.*

BY TAXI

Taxis (tel. 069/230033, 069/542003, or 069/250001) are expensive, but they can be lifesavers after dark. The initial fee is DM 3.80. The rate per km depends on the time of day: From 10 AM to 4 PM you pay DM 2.15 per km, evenings and nights it's DM 2.35, and weekends the rate climbs to DM 2.55. Some cabs charge an additional fee when requested by phone; some accept credit cards.

WHERE TO SLEEP

Hotel prices soar during Frankfurt's many *Messen* (trade fairs), which tap expense accounts from April to September. Call and reserve a spot before showing up, as rooms fill quickly throughout the year. If you're stuck, consider a youth hostel in nearby Wiesbaden or Bad Homburg, a 20–40-min S-Bahn ride from the Hauptbahnhof. Do not sleep at the Hauptbahnhof. If you are considering it, here's a little test: Look at the various specters floating around the station, then look in a mirror. If they look scarier than you do, get thee to the airport; the guards will usually leave you alone if you look harmless or have a plane ticket.

UNDER DM 80 • Pension Backer. In a safe and quiet part of Westend, Backer is the best deal in town aside from the hostel. It's friendly and clean, though rooms are smaller and darker than at pricier places. Singles DM 40–DM 70, doubles DM 60–DM 80. *Mendelssohnstr. 92, tel. 069/747992 or 069/747900. U6 or U7 to Westend. 35 rooms, none with bath. Breakfast included, showers (DM 3). No credit cards.*

For a view of the whole metropolis, head to the Europaturm (U-Bahn to Dornbusch, then Bus 34 to Fernmeldeturm), where the hourly elevator will rocket you to the 220th floor in 45 seconds.

Pension Bruns. The spacious and airy (but slightly run-down) rooms here have hardwood floors and comfortable beds. The management isn't the friendliest, but it's near the station and the rooms are a deal at DM 56 singles, DM 86 doubles, breakfast included. *Mendelssohnstr. 42, tel. 069/748896. 7 rooms, only one with bath. Showers (DM 2). Reservations advised. No credit cards.*

UNDER DM 100 • Hotel Atlas. This small, friendly, clean hotel has singles (DM 66) and doubles (DM 96) overlooking a sketchy but central street. *Zimmerw. 1, at Mainzer Landstr., tel. 069/723946, fax 069/723946. 8 rooms, none with bath. No credit cards.*

Hotel Glockshuber. Near the Hauptbahnhof, this friendly hotel has spacious, bright rooms (singles DM 55, doubles DM 90 and up), but it is also located on a busy, rather seedy street. *Mainzer Landstr. 120, at Hafenstr., tel. 0691/742629, fax 069/742629. From Bahnhof, Tram 11 or 21 to Güterpl. 20 rooms, none with bath. No credit cards.*

Hotel Zur Rose. If your nerves are easily frayed, you may want to opt for this hotel in quiet, green Bornheim. Singles start at DM 60, doubles at DM 80. *Berger Str. 283, tel. 069/451762. U4 to Bornheim Mitte, then NE on Berger Str. 24 rooms, none with bath. Breakfast included. No credit cards.*

UNDER DM 130 • Hotel Terminus. Directly across from the train station, this modern, sparkling-clean hotel has singles for DM 90 and up, doubles for DM 100 and up, all with shower/bath, TV, and telephone. Book ahead. *Münchener Str. 59, tel. 069/242320, fax 069/237411. 107 rooms. Reception open 7 AM–2 AM. No credit cards.*

Sophien Hotel. The rooms at this hotel (singles DM 75 and up, doubles DM 120 and up), in a quiet neighborhood near the university, are spotless and modern, yet homey. *Sophienstr. 36, tel. 069/702034, fax 069/777370. U6, U7, or Tram 19 to Bockenheimer Warte, up Zepellinallee, left on Sophienstr. 50 rooms, all with bath. Reception open 7 AM–1 AM.*

HOSTELS

Haus der Jugend (HI). This clean but harsh (the radio starts blaring at 7:30 AM) Sachsenhausen hostel is in a modern building near museums and *Apfelwein* taverns, 15 min on foot from downtown. The midnight curfew is not enforced: If you'll be coming in late, ask the staff, and they'll make sure someone is around to let you in. Dorm beds DM 23 (DM 28 over 20), doubles DM 77, and quads DM 33 per person, plus a mandatory DM 10 deposit. *Deutschherrnufer 12, tel. 069/619058, fax 069/618257. From Hauptbahnhof, Bus 46 to Frankensteiner Pl., then backtrack on Deutschherrnufer. 500 beds. Lockout 9 AM–1 PM. Breakfast included, luggage storage. No credit cards.*

FREẞING IN FRANKFURT

Frankfurters love rowdy eating and drinking. Join them in the Freßgass' ("pig-out alley"), a popular eating quarter on Große Bockenheimer Straße between Alte Oper and Hauptwache. During spring or summer, sample Grüne Soße, *a 14-herb sauce poured over hard-boiled eggs and boiled potatoes, sometimes with a piece of meat thrown in. Also try* Handkäse mit Musik, *a hunk of cheese served with onions, herbs, and vinegar dressing. Accompany both with Apfelwein (in Hessisch, Ebbelwoi), the local apple wine. Get it* süß *(sweet-spritzed with lemon-lime),* sauer *(sour-spritzed with soda), or* pur *(pure). The latest thing is* Bio-Ebbelwoi *(organic). Pine wreaths above doors in Sachsenhausen mean they serve apple wine on tap.*

FOOD

Frankfurt is, of course, the home of a famous sausage, but there's more to the city's culinary scene than pork-stuffed intestine linings. As everywhere in Germany, Turkish Imbiß stands offer filling stand-up meals for DM 4–DM 6. There are stands galore along the Zeil between Hauptwache and Konstablerwache. The **Freßgass'** (*see box, below*) is loaded with restaurants, and in **Sachsenhausen,** the Rittergasse triangle (behind the hostel) is one big chow-a-rama. In Bockenheim, **Ristorante da Nico** (Leipziger Str. 50, tel. 069/771356) has melt-in-your-mouth pizzas for DM 7–DM 14. The **Kaufhof** department store at the Hauptwache has a huge basement market with relatively cheap prices. Gräfstraße and Adalbertstraße in **Bockenheim,** the university district, are dotted with affordable restaurants and cafés bustling with students on weekdays. Berger Straße in **Bornheim** teems with ice cream parlors, beer gardens, and somewhat pricier Asian eateries. **Nordend**'s mellow bars and café/restaurants are popular evening haunts, good for conversation and drawn-out eating and drinking. The new **Commerzbank Plaza** tower (Taunus Str. 46, tel. 069/13620) has an ultra-modern café and restaurant open to the public on the ground floor. Rub shoulders with Frankfurt's elite and pay an average of 15 DM a meal. The best guide in Frankfurt for every restaurant and bar is *Journal,* a weighty guide (in German) that costs DM 8.80 at newsstands.

UNDER DM 15 • Café Albatros. University students pack this hole-in-the-wall at lunchtime. Funky local art adorns the walls, and locals meditate over espresso in the quiet garden in back. Choose from breakfasts and baguette sandwiches (around DM 5) or pasta and main dishes like lentil casserole (DM 7.50). *Kiesstr. 27, tel. 069/707–2769. U6, U7, or Tram 19 to Bockenheimer Warte, west on Bockenheimer Landstr., left on Kiesstr.*

Klaane Sachsenhäuser. They've been serving typical Frankfurt cuisine here since 1886. On warm summer nights, grab a couple of frankfurters (the sausage, not the people) with potato salad (DM 10.80) and relax in the large beer garden under an enormous tree. Larger entrées cost up to DM 20. *Neuer Wall 11, tel. 069/615983. From hostel, through Ritterg. Triangle to Paradiesg., walk 1 block south. Closed Sun.*

UNDER DM 20 • Café Größenwahn. This cozy Nordend restaurant and bar is filled with a laid-back, thirtyish crowd enjoying good conversation. Try spaghetti al pesto (DM 12), Greek spinach pie with feta (DM 10), or a pricier seafood dish (from DM 15). *Lenaustr. 79, tel. 069/599356. U5 to Glauburgstr., walk 3 blocks east to Lenaustr.*

Suspect. This mellow, candlelit restaurant in Nordend is filled with student types eating dishes like chili con carne (DM 7.50) or tortellini (DM 10.50). Sip on a walnut shake (DM 6.50) and enjoy the wall art and warm, friendly atmosphere. *Rotlintstr. 32, no phone. From Konstablerwache, Tram 12 to Friedberger Pl., walk up Rotlintstr.*

CAFÉS

If you venture into Nordend and Bornheim, you'll find corner cafés scattered along Berger Straße and its tributaries. **Café Klatsch** (Mainkurstr. 29, tel. 069/490–9709; U4 to Höhenstr.) has filling salads and pastas (DM 11–DM 15). Relax with an Apfelwein (DM 4.80) or a huge bowl of *Milchkaffee* (café au lait; DM 3.80) along with the young, artsy-fartsy crowd. Right on the Nordend/Bornheim border is **Café Curios** (Schopenhauerstr. 5, tel. 069/443582; U4 to Höhenstr.), a popular daytime hangout for locals gay and straight. Enjoy a huge bowl of chili (DM 6) and daily specials like broccoli cream soup (DM 7). In Bockenheim, **Café Bauer** (Jordanstr. 1, tel. 069/777967; U6, U7, or Tram 19 to Bockenheimer Warte) is *packed* with students from the university. Salads (DM 6.80), pasta dishes (DM 5.90), and shakes (DM 3.50) can be devoured on the busy patio.

WORTH SEEING

Most of Frankfurt's attractions lie on or near the Main, in a 1-km belt south of Hauptwache. Get the two-day **Frankfurt Card** (DM 13) at the tourist office for discounts on admission to all museums listed below, the Palmengarten, and the zoo, as well as unlimited rides on all public transportation within the city, including the S-Bahn to the Frankfurt airport. Entrance to all museums is free on Wednesdays.

Among Frankfurt's unique attractions is the beautiful **Palmengarten** (Siesmayerstr. 61, tel. 069/2123–3939; admission DM 7, DM 3 students), where you can wander with peacocks past flower beds, fountains, and sculptures. In the elaborate arboretums, you'll hear and see tropical birds and may even get caught in an indoor storm. Rent a rowboat on the lake (Mar.–Oct.) and play battleship with the ducks (beware the stealthy regiment of attack geese). Take the U6 or U7 to Frankfurt's **zoo** (Alfred-Brehm-Pl. 16, tel. 069/2123–3731; admission DM 11, DM 9 with transit ticket, DM 5 students), which is famous for its preservation of rare species, especially nocturnal animals. The highlight is the huge bat cage, with jillions of flying, hanging, screeching bats. The critters are particularly active around feeding time (4 PM). Overall, though, the zoo has known better days; you may come across an empty cage or two.

RÖMERBERG

Frankfurt's few rebuilt historical buildings lie in and around the Römerberg (U4 to Römer), the square that has been the center of the city for centuries. The Gothic, three-building **Römer** has overlooked the square since 1405 and houses Frankfurt's *Rathaus* (City Hall). Newly coronated Holy Roman emperors celebrated in the **Kaisersaal** (admission DM 3, DM 1 students; closed Mon.) in the Römer's upper story. Renovated in 1994, the **Dom** (open daily 9–noon and 2:30–6) looks so new that you fear the paint might rub off on you. The grand cleanup also removed some of the church's 700-year-old character—a shame, since more than a dozen Holy Roman emperors were crowned here. The most interesting aspect of the Dom is its **tower** (open Apr.–Oct.), which you can climb for DM 3. Even if you're not into contemporary art, check out the postmodern architecture of the **Schirn Kunsthalle,** next to the Dom (tel. 069/299–8820; closed Mon.). A rotunda with a spiral glass ceiling forms the entrance, and long exterior hallways lead like a rifle barrel to the Dom. The exhibits rotate every few months, and admission varies but can be steep.

MUSEUMS

Unless otherwise noted, all museums below are open Tuesday–Sunday 10–5; all have 50% reduced admission with the Frankfurt Card, and all are free on Wednesdays, when they have extended hours (until 8 PM). You'll find the most concentrated collection of museums at the **Museumsufer** (*see below*).

In his autobiography, *Poetry and Truth,* Johann Wolfgang von Goethe describes his childhood home, now part of the **Goethehaus und Goethemuseum** (Großer Hirschgraben 23–25, tel. 069/282824; open Mon.–Sat. 9–6, Sun. 10–1). The museum annex contains portraits and letters from people who influenced this German genius. Admission is DM 4 (DM 3 students). From Hauptwache, head down Roßmarkt, left on Am Salzhaus, right on Großer Hirschgraben, and enter through the adjacent Volkstheater. Three blocks south, the late-Gothic **Karmeliterkloster** (Karmeliterg. 1, tel. 069/2123–5896), with beautifully renovated 16th-century frescoes, is the official art exhibit space for the city, with shows rotating every few months. Also in the cloister, the **Museum für Vor- und Frühgeschichte** has archaeological finds donated by local scholars. Combined admission to the cloister, gallery, and museum is DM 5 (DM 2.50 students). The nearest U-Bahn stop is Willy-Brandt-Platz (formerly Theaterplatz). Just north of the Römerberg, the **Museum für moderne Kunst** (Domstr. 10, tel. 069/2123–0447), whose postmodern triangular wedge design was the talk of the town after it opened in 1991, houses an in-your-face presentation of big names (Johns, Warhol, Rauschenberg) in airy, angular rooms between Escheresque staircases. Admission is DM 8 (DM 4 students).

Near Willy-Brandt-Platz along the Main, the **Jüdisches Museum** (Untermainkai 14–15, tel. 069/2123–5000; admission DM 5, DM 2.50 students) documents eight centuries of Jewish life in Germany. Almost all of the text is in German, but the lists of Jews the Nazis deported from Frankfurt to ghettos or concentration camps don't need much explanation. On the other side of the *Innenstadt* (city center), the somber **Museum Judengasse** (Kurt-Schumacher-Str. 10, at Börnepl., tel. 069/297–7419) houses what was left of the old Jewish Quarter and synagogue after the Nazis demolished them. Actual excavations of five homes, a *mikveh* (ritual bath), and parts of the ancient sewer network are the core pieces, along with photos and artifacts from 19th- and early 20th-century Jewish life on *Judengasse* (Jews' Lane). Admission to the museum is DM 3 (DM 1.50 students), except on Saturday, when it's free. Behind the museum is the city's oldest Jewish cemetery.

MUSEUMSUFER • Along the Schaumainkai, the street running along the south side of the Main River, stretches the Museumsufer, a string of varied museums. To reach it from the Hauptbahnhof, take Bus 46 across the river; or simply walk across either the Eiserner Steg or Untermainbrücke bridges from the Innenstadt. For the **Museumsuferfest,** in late August, the Museumsufer sets up outdoor exhibition tents, and the theater puts on outdoor plays. The **Museum für Kunsthandwerk** (Schaumainkai 17, tel. 069/2123–4037; admission DM 6, DM 3 students) is the first museum you encounter after crossing the Eiserner Steg. It displays an impressive collection of ceramic, glass, metal, and wood works, as well as some ancient illustrations and tapestries. Definitely worthwhile is the **Deutsches Filmmuseum** (Schaumainkai 41, tel. 069/2123–3369), which shows famous and not-so-famous films from all over. In the permanent exhibit, hands-on machines explore the use of light and depth in projection. Admission only to the museum is DM 5 (DM 2.50 students); for both museum and cinema, DM 9 (DM 4.50 students), and admission to the cinema alone, DM 8 (DM 4 students). Saturday hours are 2–8. Across Schweizer Straße and next to the Filmmuseum, the **Deutsches Architekturmuseum** (tel. 069/2123–8844; admission DM 8, DM 4 students) depicts the history of architecture from primitive concepts to contemporary metropolises, all in modern, glaringly white exhibition rooms.

The huge **Deutsches Städelsches Kunstinstitut und Städtische Galerie** (Schaumainkai 63, tel. 069/605098), also called the Städel, has one of the top art collections in Europe, including medieval German painting, Dutch masters, early Italian Renaissance painting, 17th- to 19th-century painting, and 19th- and 20th-century sculpture and painting. Admission is DM 8, DM 4 students. The **Liebighaus-Museum alter Plastik** (Schaumainkai 71, tel. 069/2123–8612) houses sculptures from various periods (medieval, Renaissance, Baroque) and ancient civilizations (Egyptian, East Asian, Roman). Admission is DM 5 (DM 2.50 students).

CHEAP THRILLS

During the summer, the Römerberg and Alte Oper host free jazz concerts, plays, and nighttime art showings. The monthly magazine *Prinz* (DM 3.50) has a column in the back called "Freies Theater," which lists free comedy shows, dance performances, and plays. The Frankfurt **flea market** (open Sat. 8–2) is considered one of the best in Germany, and once you see it you'll understand why. Tons of people crowd the streets looking through the new, used, and stolen stuff for sale, stopping at food stands to pick up almost every cuisine imaginable. If you're in town on a Saturday, don't miss this animated scene on the south bank of the Main. From Hauptbahnhof, take Bus 46 to Eiserner Steg, or cross it on foot from the Innenstadt.

AFTER DARK

Anything from highbrow culture to lowlife beer-swigging can be cheap in Frankfurt, so get over your jet lag and check out *Fritz* for tonight's offerings. If you're in Westend or Bockenheim, check out the café scene typified by **diesseits** (Konrad-Broswitz-Str. 1, near Kirchpl. U-Bahn, tel. 069/704364).

BARS

Sachsenhausen is well known for its Apfelwein taverns and beer gardens. **Balalaika** (Dreikönigsstr. 30, tel. 069/612226) is a cozy, wood-paneled pub around the corner from the hostel. A youngish crowd gathers here to hear live blues singers and other vocalists on weekends and sip beer in the candlelight. Just down the street is **Dreikönigskeller** (Färberstr. 71, tel. 069/629273; open after 8 PM), another cozy, hobbit-hole of a bar where a late-20's crowd gathers to hear live bands and DJs. Pick up a flyer there or at the tourist office to see what's coming up. **Club Voltaire** (Kleine Hochstr. 5, off Freßgass', tel. 069/

292408) is a low-ceilinged, cellarlike pub filled with young student types. Come to hear poetry or read it yourself. Light meals cost under DM 10.

In the gray area between Bornheim and Nordend, you'll find chic watering holes where post-university trendies and gay men wind down after work. Deep in Bornheim, **Harvey's Café Bar** (Bornheimer Landstr. 64, tel. 069/497303) takes full advantage of its expansive corner sidewalk. You'll see yuppies, Sinéad O'Connor wanna-bes, and lots of gay couples. For DM 5.50 you can get a beer big enough to take a bath in. Take U4 to Höhenstraße; backtrack on Berger Straße, and turn right on Bornheimer Landstraße. In Nordend, **Café 5 Bar** (Am Glauburgpl., tel. 069/558830), a smoky, hip joint with sponge-painted, pastel green walls, hosts live music by local musicians and has a mellow, mixed crowd. A *Pils* (lager) goes for DM 4, and there's also food (like chili, DM 8) for those evening hunger pangs. From Konstablerwache, take Tram 12 to Rohrbachstraße and walk up Glauburgstraße.

CLUBS

Frankfurt is one of Germany's techno centers, but many clubs open only one or two nights a week. **Dorian Gray** (Airport C, Level 0, tel. 069/690–2212) is a famous four-club complex playing different styles of music for anyone who passes the fashion police at the door. The cover is DM 12 and they're closed on Monday. **Cooky's** (Am Salzhaus 4, tel. 069/287662; open daily after 10 PM), around the corner from Hauptwache, plays hip-hop, techno, funk, and soul to a lively, youngish crowd. It'll cost you DM 12 on weekends, DM 8 during the week (cover includes one drink) to boogie. Locals claim **Nacht Leben** (Kurt-Schumacher-Str. 45, near Konstablerwache, tel. 069/20650) is THE place to go; it's also one of the few clubs with no cover that's open daily. Occasional live gigs break up the usual diet of soul, funk, and house music.

Batschkapp (Maybachstr. 24, tel. 069/531037; cover DM 5) is a serious haunt for punks and alternative rockers—not for the meek. The guy at the door doesn't give a rat's ass what you wear. It's open weekends for dancing and some weeknights for live music 10 PM–2 AM; U1, U2, or U3 to Weisser Stein, head northwest on Am Weissen Stein, and right on Maybachstraße. The **Kulturcentrum Brotfabrik** (Bachmannstr. 2–4, tel. 069/789–5513), housed in an old bread factory, comes complete with a Spanish restaurant, a café, a beer garden, and a concert/dance hall. The concert hall hosts jazz, Indian, South African, and other international bands and has a salsa party every Wednesday. Hop on the U6 or U7 to Fischstein, and then walk up Am Fischstein onto Bachmannstraße.

The gay club scene clusters in the area bordered by the Zeil, Stiftstraße, Bleichstraße, and Seilerstraße. **Plastik** (Seilerstr. 34, tel. 069/285055) has a gay disco on Tuesdays (DM 5). **Blue Angel** (Brönnerstr. 17, tel. 069/282772) is another well-known gay dance spot.

LIVE MUSIC

You can listen to live performances, especially jazz, all over Frankfurt. The best jazz clubs in town are on **Kleine Bockenheimer Straße** (parallel to Freßgass'), fondly called *Jazzgasse* (Jazz Lane). Jazz masters from all over the world play Wednesdays 9 PM–3 AM at **Jazzkeller** (Kleine Bockenheimer Str. 76, tel. 069/288537), to the tune of a DM 10–DM 35 cover. **Alte Oper** (Opernpl., tel. 069/134–0400; U6 or U7 to Alte Oper) hosts classical concerts, musicals, and even pop concerts. Student and rush tickets cost DM 16.50 and are only available for selected shows—it's best to show up about a half hour before shows to snatch up leftovers. The **box office** (Opernpl. 8) takes credit cards and is open weekdays 10–2 (Thurs. also 4–6).

MOVIE THEATERS

Two cinemas in Frankfurt show English-language films on a regular basis. **Turm 4** (Am Eschenheimer Turm, tel. 069/281787; U1, U2, or U3 to Eschenheimer Tor) plays recent flicks as well as some cult classics like *The Rocky Horror Picture Show* and *A Clockwork Orange.* In Bockenheim, **Orfeo** (Hamburger Allee 45, tel. 069/702218; Tram 19 to Varrentrappstr.) shows more obscure films. Tickets for either cost DM 11–DM 13.

THEATER AND DANCE

The small **English Theatre** (Kaiserstr. 52, tel. 069/2423–1620) has produced English and American plays and musicals for the last 15 years; it's quite good, even though the accents tend to be mixed up. Tickets run DM 42–DM 50, DM 20 for students. If you have any interest in modern dance, try to catch a **Ballett Frankfurt** performance in the opera house (Willy-Brandt-Pl., tel. 069/2123–7999). As befits European standards of public decency, some "experimental" ballets are all nude shows. Student and rush tickets (when available) cost DM 16.50 and can be used for a one-way trip on Frankfurt public transit. The box office opens at 7 PM on performance nights, and it's the only place you can buy discount tickets.

NEAR FRANKFURT

Frankfurt's location at the center of a culturally rich region and at the hub of its rail network makes it an ideal base for day trips to nearby towns and cities. **Wiesbaden** is half an hour away by train, and smaller, more isolated towns such as **Gelnhausen** and **Bad Homburg,** with their natural beauty and clean air, are also just a short train ride away. Outside the immediate area, but also within an hour by train, are **Darmstadt, Marburg** (*see* Hessen, *below*), **Mainz** (*see* Chapter 16), and **Aschaffenburg** (*see* Chapter 7). Leave your pack of bricks behind, pack a picnic, don your walking shoes, and have a daylong adventure.

WIESBADEN

Frankfurters consider Hessen's capital, Wiesbaden, a provincial, spoiled-rich cousin. They may be right, but then again, they may just be jealous because hardly a stone was scratched in Wiesbaden during World War II. (Wiesbaden was, in fact, being saved by the Allies to take out à la Dresden if the Germans didn't say "uncle" in time.) What survived is a spa town now full of wealthy people driving BMWs or walking neatly groomed dogs. Ignore the pomp, check the place out, and then hop on S1 or S8 for the 40-min ride back to Frankfurt.

BASICS

Both the **tourist office** inside the Hauptbahnhof (tel. 0611/172–9781) and the downtown branch (Rheinstr. 15, tel. 0611/172–9780; closed weekends) have city maps (DM 1) and book rooms for a DM 6 fee. The **American Express** office (Weberg. 8, tel. 0611/39144) is open weekdays 9–5, Saturday 9–noon. The main **post office** (Kaiser-Friedrich-Ring 81) is just west of the Hauptbahnhof.

COMING AND GOING

Both the S-Bahn and long-distance trains connect Wiesbaden to Mainz (S8; 11 min, DM 4) and Frankfurt (S1 or S8; 40 min, DM 10). Within Wiesbaden a bus ride will cost you DM 3.20, or purchase a 24-hour pass for DM 8.50. Pick up a bus map at one of the tourist offices. To get to the center of town from the station (15 min on foot), cross the busy street and head down Bahnhofstraße, turn left on Rheinstraße, and right on Kirchgasse, the main drag of the pedestrian zone.

WHERE TO SLEEP

Lodging in Wiesbaden is expensive, so consider visiting on a day trip from Frankfurt. If you're determined to stay, your only budget option apart from the hostel is the no-frills **Hotel Jägerhof** (Bahnhofstr. 6, near Luisenstr., tel. 0611/302797). All rooms (singles DM 60, doubles DM 80) have showers, and breakfast is included. From the Hauptbahnhof, walk 10 min up Bahnhofstraße. The clean, modern **Jugendherberge (HI)** (Blücherstr. 66, tel. 0611/48657, fax 0611/441119) is a 15-min walk west of the city center. Beds are DM 24 (DM 29 over 26) including breakfast, and curfew is at midnight. From the Hauptbahnhof, take Bus 14 to Gneisenaustraße, then continue up Blücherstraße.

FOOD

The pedestrian zone and *Altstadt* (old town) abound with cafés, beer gardens, and refined restaurants. Vegetarians and those sick to death of Wurst will be thrilled to find **Viva** (Schützenhofstr. 3, tel. 0611/301077), tucked off the pedestrian zone. Load up on roughage at the salad bar (DM 2.35 per 100 grams) or sample the selection of soups, casseroles, and fish dishes (DM 4.50–DM 11). For picnic food, try **Tengelmann** (Luisenstr. 23, east of St.-Bonifatius-Kirche), which even has a salad bar (DM 1 per 100 grams). If you're here after dark, head for the rowdy bars on Nerostraße north of the pedestrian zone, or the more stylish scam scene in the "Schiffchen" area of the Altstadt, between Goldgasse and Bärenstraße.

WORTH SEEING

Wiesbaden has been a spa town since Roman times: You can see the excavation site of an ancient temple supposedly used by Mithraists—members of a cult very similar to early Christianity. But the majority of Wiesbaden's sights were built in the 19th century, during the city's heyday as a playground for the elite. The **Kurhaus** (Kurhauspl. 1) is a former spa that now hosts conventions in its ornate interior, and the casino inside caters to people who aren't reading this book. But don't let the grand facade keep you from venturing inside, into one of the most beautiful old-style cafés in Hessen. The waiters dress in traditional black, wear long white linen aprons, and serve you at old wooden tables covered with white cloths. Everything about the place—from the polished wooden floor to the fin-de-siècle pictures on the walls—will conjure up an Impressionist painting. An entrée runs about DM 15 and the menu changes frequently. The north end of the pedestrian zone, called *Quellenmeile* (Hot Springs Mile), is full of spas frequented by naked, aging Germans. If you really want to laze in warm, soothing waters, head instead to the more plebeian **Thermalbad** (Leibnizstr. 7, tel. 0611/172–9880; admission DM 10). From the Kurhaus, walk up Parkstraße and turn right on Leibnizstraße.

One of the hills north of the city is **Neroberg,** from which you can gaze down upon the church spires of Wiesbaden. The *Nerobergbahn,* a 100-year-old, water-powered cable car (the only one of its kind in Europe), climbs up and down the mountain every 15 min April–October (DM 3 round-trip). There are two cars on opposite ends of the line, and the uphill car's ballast is filled with enough water to send it down the hill and pull the other car up. On Neroberg is the **Russian Chapel,** sometimes incorrectly referred to as the Greek Chapel. The Duke of Nassau built it in 1848 as a tomb for his Russian bride, who died in childbirth. To reach the Neroberg, take Bus 1 from the Hauptbahnhof to the last stop.

A traditional song sung at Wiesbaden's Weinfest claims that if you drink the local Neroberger wine, you'll be on intimate terms with your neighbor before the night is out.

BAD HOMBURG

Bad Homburg is only 20 min away from Frankfurt's Hauptbahnhof via S5 (DM 5), and it makes an easy day trip (the last train to Frankfurt leaves at around 11 PM) or a convenient base for the **Taunus,** a gentle range that rises above the Main River basin. The Bad is best known for its spas and casino; Dostoyevsky's novel *The Player* was supposedly inspired by his experience in here, though the casino in Wiesbaden makes the same claim. Like Wiesbaden, Bad Homburg is filled with geriatric spa-goers; the only reason to stay is to hike through the hills. The tourist office (*see below*) has info and maps (DM 7.50) on hiking in the Taunus; from town there are several 5–10-km loops of varying difficulty including one to Saalburg (*see below*), offering fresh, clean air and views of sprawling Frankfurt below.

BASICS

The **tourist office** (Louisenstr. 58, tel. 06172/675110; open weekdays 8:30–6, Sat. 9–1) in Bad Homburg's Kurhaus has info on exploring the Taunus. From the station, walk up Marienbader Platz and Ferdinandstraße and turn left on Louisenstraße.

WHERE TO SLEEP

The tourist office has lists of private rooms and hotels, but the least expensive option is the spartan but convenient and beautifully situated **Jugendherberge (HI),** just next to the stately Schloßgarten. It's a good place to stay if you want to do some hiking in the Taunus or can't find accommodations in Frankfurt. Beds with breakfast cost DM 21.50 (DM 26.50 over 26). *Meiereiberg 1, tel. 06172/23950, fax 06172/22312. From Bahnhof, up Marienbader Pl. onto Ferdinandstr., left on Schöne Aussicht (which becomes Dorotheenstr.), left on Löweng. 96 beds. Curfew 11:30. Reception open 7 AM–midnight.*

FOOD

As Bad Homburg is a rich man and woman's playground, you won't be surprised to hear that there are only two **Imbiß** stands: Hermann Horst Imbiß (Urseler Str. 30, tel. 06172/302589) and Hugo Nordmann Imbiß (Langemeile 9, tel. 06172/44235). Although you have a choice of 150 restuarants, none of them square with budget travel and most will cause credit card meltdown. Your best bet is **Amigos Mexicana** (Kirdorfer Str. 52, tel. 06172/867619), which offers a wide range of meals around DM 12 each.

WORTH SEEING

The **Kurpark,** outside of the Altstadt, is good for a stroll and a sip or two of Bad Homburg's curative waters. Most of the town's other sights are along Louisenstraße. At the top of the hill are the Altstadt and the 17th-century **Schloß Homburg** (open Tues.–Sun. 10–5). The 57-m **Weißer Turm** (White

Tower) is all that remains of the 14th-century castle that stood here previously. Unfortunately, to see the former summer haunt of Prussia's kings and Germany's Kaisers, you have to take the hourly German-language tour (DM 4, DM 2 students, last tour 4 PM). If you skip the tour, check out the castle from the outside and take a stroll around the beautiful **Schloßgarten** (palace gardens). Even if you absolutely can't stomach another church, make an effort to visit **Erlöserkirche** (Dorotheenstr., at entrance to Schloß Homburg), which will astound you with its Escheresque floor patterns, marble arches, and intricate gold, turquoise, and onyx mosaics. Look carefully at the mosaic pattern in the aisles along the sides and you'll notice some very pagan-looking figures. Kaiser Wilhelm II used Byzantine and Romantic architectural models in the design of this eccentric art nouveau church in the early 20th century.

Since you're already in Bad Homburg, take the short train ride (2 per hr, 20 min, DM 5) to **Saalburg** (open daily 8–5; admission DM 4, DM 3 students). This reconstructed Roman fort was once a bulwark against truculent tribes of Teutonic warriors and has an interesting exhibit on Roman culture and fortress life, including such artifacts as shoes, cookware, weapons, and writing utensils. Although the reconstruction is too pristine to be mistaken for the original, it's still interesting to use a bit of imagination and transport yourself back to Roman times.

GELNHAUSEN

Gelnhausen, 30 min east of Frankfurt, is a well-preserved medieval city with quite a few sights up its sleeve. On an island in the Kinzig River southeast of downtown is the 12th-century **Kaiserpfalz** (admission DM 2, DM 1 students; closed Mon.), also called Barbarossaburg after its red-bearded founder, Emperor Friedrich I (Barbarossa). Barbarossa lived here off and on until he led the Third Crusade and gloriously drowned in a swamp in Romania. Crusades themselves were bloody affairs blessed by successive Popes who decreed that anyone who killed a Jew before marching on Jerusalem had his sins forgiven for life. Consequently entire Jewish quarters in cities like Frankfurt were eradicated with impunity by zealots. Gelnhausen is also known as the proud home of Hans Jakob Christoph von Grimmelshausen (1622?–1676), who wrote *Simplicissimus,* the first great German novel, whose hero contends with complex adversities during the Thirty Years' War.

The three black-tiled steeples of the Protestant **Marienkirche** jut above the rooftops of the medieval buildings lining the **Obermarkt** and **Untermarkt.** If you walk toward what was once the city wall, you'll notice the oddly shaped **Hexenturm** (Witches' Tower), where persecuted "witches" were tried in the 16th century. In the tower garden is a memorial to the women executed during that particular hysteria. A more recent tragedy is evoked by the early 17th-century **synagogue** (Brentanostr., at Ohmgasse; open weekdays 10–5), the center of one of Germany's oldest Jewish communities until the Nazis annihilated it. At the **Halbmond** (Half Moon), an ancient fortification above the Hexenturm, check out the view of the city, the Odenwald and Spessart mountains to the south, and the Vogelsberg to the north.

BASICS

The **tourist office** (Obermarkt 7, tel. 06051/830300; open Mon.–Sat. 9–noon and 2–4:30, Sun. 2–4:30) can arrange a tour (DM 20) of the Hexenturm's dungeon and torture instruments, and has maps (DM 1.50) of local hiking trails. Trains run to Gelnhausen from Frankfurt once an hour (45 min, DM 10). To get to the Altstadt and Obermarkt from the station, head right on Bahnhofstraße, left on Altenhaßlauer Straße to Untermarkt, and left on Langgasse; the Obermarkt will be on your right.

WHERE TO SLEEP

The weathered **Jugendherberge (HI)** is in a funky old house with great views of the countryside. Call ahead to make sure the reception is open. Beds DM 21.50 (DM 24.50 over 26), including breakfast. *Schützengraben 5, tel. 06051/4424, fax 06051/13072. From the train station, right on Bahnhofstr., left on Altenhaßlauer Str. until you reach Untermarkt, down Langg., right on Schützengraben. 80 beds. Curfew 10 PM.*

BÜDINGEN

With so many towns making a production of their medieval past, Büdingen's genuineness makes it unique. You can actually feel how the craftsmen and peasants lived, huddled inside a protective wall under the imposing castle. And once inside Büdingen's perfectly intact medieval walls, you may want to stay the night. The **Schloßpark,** with its ponds, old stone walls, and surrounding forest, is an excellent place to spend an afternoon, even if you don't actually go inside the 12th-century **Schloß** (tel. 06042/889212; admission DM 6.50, DM 4 students) to check out the alchemy lab and Romanesque and Gothic rooms. The castle has beautiful, rustic courtyards that feel like something out of Robin Hood, and has been home to counts and countesses for centuries. Tours of the Schloß (in German) are given mid-March–December 23, Tuesday–Sunday at 11:30, 2, 3, and 4. The **Schloßcafé** (Schloßpl. 1, tel. 06042/68262) has a garden patio and is a great place to breathe in that fresh Vogelsberg air.

Büdingen is situated at the mouth of a mountain gorge, where the Vogelsberg mountains ease into the Wetterau plains. Hiking and biking trails abound where you can check out huge basalt outcroppings and old church ruins. The tourist office has trail maps for DM 1.50.

BASICS

Hourly trains make the 20-min trip from Gelnhausen (DM 7.50); to get here from Frankfurt (DM 29), change at Gelnhausen. There's a direct line from Gießen (hourly, 1½ hrs, DM 18.50) in the Lahn Valley (*see below*). To reach the Altstadt from the train station, turn right on Bahnhofstraße and follow it for about 10 min (through the medieval gates), turn right on Neustadt, and left on Marktplatz. At the **tourist office** (Marktpl. 7, tel. 06042/8840), a cheery gentleman hands out maps and historical info. The spartan, but clean and restful **Jugendherberge (HI)** (Am Pfaffenwald, tel. 06042/3687, fax 06042/68178) sits on a hill overlooking the Vogelsberg—a 30-min walk from the station. Beds cost DM 23 (DM 26 over 26), including breakfast. From Bahnhofstraße, turn left on Pferdsbacher Weg, right on Am Rosenkränzchen, a quick left on Auf der Beude, and right on Am Pfaffenwald.

Accused witches were tied up and tossed into the Kinzig River—if they floated, they were judged guilty and burned; if they drowned . . . well, tough luck.

HESSEN

As you leave the industrial Frankfurt region, you'll enter Hessen's pristine hinterlands. The Brothers Grimm lived and worked here, and Goethe was inspired by his wanderings through the countryside. Go for a hike in the quiet **Vogelsberg** or **Rhön** mountains, or explore the **Lahn Valley,** whose green, softly undulating hills have a sturdiness and simplicity that reflect the character of this German heartland. Its string of small towns, including *Residenzstädte* (seats of ruling dukes and princes) and the college town **Marburg,** offers a refreshing break from big cities and touristic hype. Don't miss the cultural and architectural treasures of stately **Darmstadt** or nearby **Michelstadt** and **Lorsch** if you're headed south. Friendly **Fulda** harbors even more architectural and cultural goodies and even big, overwhelmingly concrete **Kassel** redeems its harsh exterior with cultural offerings.

DARMSTADT

On the northwest edge of the tranquil Odenwald, Darmstadt is a modern, prosperous city between Frankfurt and Heidelberg. The city was capital of an independent grand duchy until the late 19th century, and abundant cultural funds, originating first from the dukes and later from private citizens and the generous German state, have left the city with more than a few artistic and architectural gems. Artists invited here by Grand Duke Ernst-Ludwig at the end of the 19th century designed **Mathildenhöhe,** which features a fabulous collection of *Jugendstil* (art nouveau) houses, buildings, and *objets d'art*. The **Landesmuseum** has a collection of works by the German and Dutch masters, as well as more modern pieces. Today, students from the prestigious Technical University liven up Darmstadt's gentility with hipness and a decent nightlife.

BASICS

A branch of the **tourist office** is located just outside the train station in a round kiosk (tel. 0615/132783) whose friendly, English-speaking staff gives out maps, hotel lists, and sightseeing info weekdays 8–6 and Saturday 8–1. They also book hotel rooms at no charge, but only in person. The main office in the city center (Luisenpl. 5, tel. 0615/132780) offers the same services and is open weekdays 7 AM–8 PM, Saturday 7–noon. The main **post office** is directly to the left when you exit the station (Poststr. 6, tel. 0615/9070). You can rent two-wheelers from **Schlößchen im Prinz-Emil-Garten** (Heidelberger Str. 56, in the minigolf center, tel. 0615/664890) for DM 7 per day plus ID as deposit.

COMING AND GOING

Trains arrive from Frankfurt every half hour (30 min, DM 7.60), and hourly trains run to Mainz (30 min, DM 10.80), Heidelberg (30 min, DM 14.80), and Michelstadt (1 hr, DM 14.80). To get to the city center from the station, take Bus D or Bus F to Luisenplatz. A trip within Darmstadt on the bus costs DM 2, a day pass DM 7. Bus maps and schedules are available at the tourist office for DM 2.

WHERE TO SLEEP

The friendly, homey **Hotel zum Rosengarten** (Frankfurter Str. 79, tel. 06151/77000, fax 06151/716644) has lots of warm, brown wood decor and (you guessed it) a rose garden in back, along with a beer garden. The ample rooms (singles DM 75 and up, doubles DM 98 and up) all come with bath and TV. Book ahead. From Luisenplatz, Tram 7 or 8 to Rhönring, and backtrack on Frankfurter Straße. **Zentral Hotel** (Schuchardstr. 6, tel. 06151/26411, fax 06151/26858), centrally located (surprise) just a block south of Luisenplatz off Luisenstraße, has clean, cozy rooms starting at DM 60 for singles, DM 100 for doubles without private bath.

HOSTELS • Jugendherberge (HI). The perk at this otherwise out-of-the-way hostel is its location next to the Großer Woog (an artificial lake) and an open-air pool available to hostelers for free. Beds DM 23 (DM 27 over 26). *Landgraf-Georg-Str. 119, tel. 06151/45293, fax 06151/422535. From Bahnhof, Bus D to Woog/Beckstr. 126 beds. Curfew 1 AM. Reception open 24 hours.*

FOOD

A few blocks north of Mathildenhöhe, **Havana** (Kranichsteinerstr. 8, tel. 06151/784263) serves up Cuban fare in a colorfully furnished restaurant. They have *bocadillo con pollo* (chicken sandwich; DM 12.50), broccoli casserole (DM 14), and a host of other entrées, including good veggie options for DM 11–DM 15. What's more, the menu's in English. Chow on Greek food at **Pitta-Gyros** (Elisabethenstr. 50, tel. 06151/22753), southwest of Luisenplatz. You can get a juicy gyro with *tzatziki* (yogurt sauce) for DM 6, a gyros plate for DM 9, and a pita feta for DM 5. Vegetarians will be in their element at **Kulturcafé** (Hermannstr. 7, tel. 06151/25832), where you can sip tea (DM 3) while checking out German environmentalist mags, graze from the well-stocked salad bar (DM 2.60 per 100 grams), or try the veggie lasagna (DM 12.80). Tram 1 from the station or Tram 3 from Luisenplatz to Hermannstraße.

WORTH SEEING

One block east of Luisenplatz, Darmstadt's rust-red Baroque **Schloß,** built in 1727 with Versailles as a model, was home for centuries to Hessen-Darmstadt's ruling grand dukes. Destroyed in the war and subsequently reconstructed, the Schloß now houses various public offices, departments of the university, and the **Schloßmuseum** (tel. 06151/24035). On a mandatory tour you'll see various knickknacks attesting to the affluence of the grand duchy, as well as Hans Holbein the Younger's *Darmstadt Madonna,* a Renaissance masterpiece. Tours (DM 3.50, DM 2 students) are given Monday–Thursday 10–1 and 2–5, weekends 10–1. Just across from the entrance to the Schloß stands the smart, red-trimmed **Rathaus,** a reconstruction of the original 16th-century Renaissance building; across from its southwestern corner stands the **Weißer Turm** (White Tower), a corner tower of the former 14th-century town wall. North of the Schloß is the **Landesmuseum** (Friedenspl. 1, tel. 06151/165703; closed Mon.), which houses a dizzying variety of exhibits (DM 5, DM 2.50 students). Don't let the cluttered natural history display on the ground floor put you off; venture upstairs to see Flemish, Dutch, and German works of art dating from medieval times to the 20th century, including works by Rembrandt and the largest display of Joseph Beuys's works anywhere. In the basement you can gaze at stained glass works spanning the years from 800 to 1980.

Be sure to check out the **Mathildenhöhe,** where, at the turn of the century, a subsidized community of artists engaged in a project to "merge art and life." The result is a collection of houses funkily yet gracefully designed in then avant-garde Jugendstil. The front doors alone on Joseph Maria Olbrich's and Peter Behren's houses are satisfying pieces of eye candy; take the time to wander around and look at all of the houses, each uniquely designed and crafted. The **Museum Künstlerkolonie** (Art Colony Museum; Olbrichw. 13, tel. 06151/132778; admission DM 5, DM 2 students), housed in the impressive Ernst-Ludwig-Haus, has a sumptuous display of the artists' work, including furniture, jewelry, and other items. The museum is open Tuesday–Sunday 10–5. The climb to the top of the five-fingered **Hochzeitsturm** (Wedding Tower; Lucasw., at Olbrichw., admission DM 3, DM 1 students) is worth it for the panoramic view. To reach Mathildenhöhe from Luisenplatz (20 min), walk one block up Luisenstraße, turn right on Zeughausstraße (which turns into Alexanderstraße), and then Dieburger Straße, then take a right on Lucasweg to Olbrichweg. Or take Bus F to Lucasweg and then walk up Lucasweg to the right.

AFTER DARK

Pick up a free copy of *Fritz* from the tourist office for monthly listings of cultural happenings. In the basement of the Schloß is the student-run **Schloßkeller** (tel. 06151/163117; open daily 9 PM onwards), which has everything from beer nights, lesbian and gay parties (Sundays), and films, to smoke-free dance nights. Pick up a program outside. **Goldene Krone** (Schusterg. 18, tel. 06151/21352; open daily 1–1) also hosts a variety of dance parties and bands (cover charge around DM 5) and attracts a young, mixed crowd. Right across from the train station, **Café Kesselhaus** (Rheinstr. 95, 06151/84492; open 11 AM–1 AM, until 3 AM Thurs.–Sat.) is a bar/club/beer garden that attracts "alternative," studenty types and offers up a mixed platter of live music, DJs, and theatrical performances. Call for the program and possible cover charge.

NEAR DARMSTADT

MICHELSTADT AND ERBACH

Deep in the lush, green Odenwald, Michelstadt boasts a picture-perfect Altstadt with a 13th-century castle, a 9th-century church, and many a half-timbered house. Though Michelstadt's architectural treasures, fresh air, and relaxed atmosphere definitely merit a visit, its treasures also attract swarms of camera-wielding tourists, and you get the feeling that everything is somewhat self-consciously on display. The focus of the Altstadt is the 15th-century Gothic **Rathaus** on the *Marktplatz* (market square), complete with pointy turrets. A 10-min walk northwest of the Altstadt, in the Steinbach district, is the crusty 14th-century **Schloß Fürstenau.** You can't go inside, but you're welcome to wander around the grounds and look at its stately, aging exterior. Just west is the ancient, simple **Einhardsbasilika** (Schloßstr. 23, tel. 06061/2447), a church dating back to 827 and a rare example of Carolingian architecture. To reach Steinbach from the Altstadt, head up Bahnhofstraße past the station where it becomes Kutschenweg, and take a right on Einhardstraße. From the corner of Schloßstraße, the basilica is to your left and the castle to your right.

A 20-min walk south of Michelstadt lies **Erbach,** with a grandiose Baroque **Schloß** (tel. 06061/3700) in the center of town. Skip the museum inside, whose collection of hunting trophies and antlers is far less interesting than the palace's groovy exterior. To get to Erbach from Michelstadt's Altstadt, follow Braunstraße out of the Altstadt and turn right on Erbacher Straße, left on Michelstädter Straße, and right on Hauptstraße to the center of town.

BASICS • The helpful **tourist office** in Michelstadt (Marktpl. 1, tel. 06061/74146; open weekdays 9–noon and 2–4) has maps, lists of hotels and private rooms, and info on hiking in the Odenwald. It also rents out **bikes,** all three-speed, for DM 8 per day. From the train station, walk right on Hulster Straße, left on Bahnhofstraße, and right on Große Gasse. Trains run from Michelstadt to Darmstadt hourly (1 hr, DM 14), and six times daily via Eberbach to Heidelberg (1½ hrs, DM 16). All trains also serve the station in Erbach, where you might want to go if you're staying at the hostel.

WHERE TO SLEEP AND EAT • Your best budget bet for lodging is **Pension zum Rosengarten** (Am Rosengarten 3, tel. and fax 06061/72793), with a gorgeous view over the trees and fields. The clean, homey rooms are DM 38 for a single, DM 70 for a double, and DM 96 for a triple. From the station it's a 15-min walk: Head down Hulserstraße onto Contistraße, then turn right over the brook and under the tracks on Hammerweg, which becomes Mossauer Straße. Am Rosengarten is to the left. **Campingplatz Odenwaldparadies** (Am Stadion, tel. 06061/3256; closed Oct.–Apr.) is a km or so out of town in the midst of trees and meadows. It'll cost you DM 4 per person, DM 3 per car, and DM 6 per tent to spend the night (showers DM 1). From the station, head towards the Altstadt on Bahnhofstraße, and turn left on Waldstraße, which becomes Am Stadion. Erbach's tidy **HI hostel** (Eulbacher Str. 33, tel. 06062/3515) has basic wooden bunks that cost DM 23 (DM 27 over 26); call before coming to make sure the reception is open. From Erbach's train station, head left down Bahnhofsplatz, and right on Sophienstraße, which becomes Brückenstraße. Turn left on Hauptstraße, left on Michelstädter Straße, and right on Eulbacher Straße.

In Michelstadt, the Altstadt has numerous bakeries, grocery stores, and Imbiß stands. For a hearty German meal, try **Zum Grünen Baum** (Große Gasse 17, tel. 06061/2409), which has been in business for 300 years and has three-course veggie meals for DM 11, carnivorous ones for DM 15—*richtig gemütlich* (real atmospheric).

LORSCH

Now a sleepy little town that's easily accessible on a day trip from Darmstadt, Worms (*see* Chapter 16), or even Heidelberg (*see* Chapter 3) or Frankfurt, Lorsch features a monastery founded in 764 whose abbot wielded heavy political clout in the Holy Roman Empire. All that now remains are the impressive **Königshalle** and **Vorkirche** (front section) of the old church, both located just across from Lorsch's Marktplatz. The Königshalle itself is reason enough to pay a visit, however. Built in 880, this red-and-white checkered structure, with its three archways and pointed, black-tiled roof (the original was flat), is a UNESCO World Heritage site and one of the best surviving examples of Carolingian (early medieval) architecture. The interior can be seen only on guided tours, available (in English) through the otherwise unremarkable **museum** (Niebelungenstr. 35, tel. 06251/596773; open Tues.–Sun. 10–5). DM 6 (DM 4 students) gets you admission to the museum, interesting historical tidbits, and a chance to climb into the Königshalle and see its very faded frescoes.

BASICS • The **tourist office,** located in the half-timbered Rathaus (Marktpl. 1, tel. 06251/596570; open Mon.–Thurs. 9–noon and 2–4, Fri. 9–noon), has the usual maps, hotel lists, and brochures. From the **train station,** take Bahnhofstraße straight to the center of town; the tourist office will be on your right. Trains shuttle to Bensheim once or twice hourly; the last leaves Lorsch at 6:30 PM. Via Bensheim, trains connect several times per hour to Darmstadt (25 min, DM 10 from Lorsch) and once an hour to Heidelberg (30 min, DM 12 from Lorsch). Direct trains also leave Lorsch for Worms, across the Rhine, once an hour (30 min, DM 5).

WHERE TO SLEEP AND EAT • The tourist office gives out a list of people with private rooms whom you can call. Otherwise, the only budget option is **Gasthof Schillereck** (Schillerstr. 27, tel. 06251/52301), a small, homey, family-run establishment in a quiet residential area. Clean, pleasant singles go for DM 55, doubles for DM 90, including breakfast. From the station, walk right on Lindenstraße, left on Klarastraße, right on Rheinstraße, left on Moltkestraße, and right on Schillerstraße. For bakeries, grocery stores, and ice cream, walk up Bahnhofstraße (which becomes Römerstraße) past the Marktplatz.

FULDA

Fulda grew around the 8th-century Benedictine abbey that first brought Christianity to central Germany. The abbey was founded atop the tomb of the English monk St. Boniface, the "Apostle of Germany," and from 969 on, its abbot was directly responsible for all the Benedictines in France and Germany. In 1720 the Benedictines built themselves a grand castle; a university followed and ensured Fulda's continued growth and prosperity. Today Fulda has a welcoming small-town feel and a carefully restored Baroque quarter that preserves a strong 18th-century flavor.

The enormous Renaissance-era **Stadtschloß** was baroqued between 1706 and 1721 to match the rest of the city. Originally erected as home to the Prince Abbots, the castle mostly houses Fulda's city offices today, though there is a **Schloßmuseum** (Entrance D-1) with rooms decorated in extravagant 18th-century style. Don't leave without climbing the 14th-century **Schloßturm** (admission DM 4, DM 2 students), a round tower with sweeping views of the pristine castle gardens and surrounding towns and hills. Just west of the Schloß, around Bonifatiusplatz, are a series of Baroque palaces. *Schloßstr. 1. Admission: DM 4, DM 3 students. Open Sat.–Thurs. 10–6, Fri. 2–6. Guided tour at 2:30 daily.*

The 9th-century **Michaelskirche,** across Pauluspromenade from the Stadtschloß's northern exit, is a must for fans of the Middle Ages. The altar feels strangely cultish rather than Christian, and there's an eerie crypt downstairs where bodies were prepared for burial. Next door is the grandiose 18th-century **Dom,** the third cathedral built over St. Boniface's tomb. By the main altar, Christ's right foot has been buffed to a shine by the devout, who rub it for blessings. From the altar, look up at the dome to spot four fat cherubs peeking over a wall at you. Go down the steps behind the altar, and you'll find what's left of St. Boniface's skull and a ghastly relief depicting the circumstances of his death (pagans in Friesland dispatched him with a dagger to the head). A nasty little cherub sticks its fingers in Boniface's skull ventilation. The **Dommuseum** (admission DM 4, DM 3 students) displays the church's treasures.

BASICS

Located in the Stadtschloß (Entrance D-2), the **tourist office** (Schloßstr. 1, tel. 0661/102345; closed Sat. afternoon and all day Sun.) has maps and a friendly, English-speaking staff that books rooms for no fee. From the station, walk up Bahnhofstraße, right on Rabbanusstraße, and left on Schloßstraße. For nature-oriented info, go right from the station, under the tracks on Magdeburger Straße, and left on

Wörthstraße to **Fremdenverkehrsverband Rhön** (Landratsamt, Wörthstr. 15, Entrance G, Room 338, tel. 0661/600–6305). Make sure to specify what you want, or the staff will just sit and blink at you. The office is closed weekends. The **post office** (Heinrich-von-Bibra-Pl. 5) is at the east end of the Stadtschloß. If you want to canoe the Fulda River, **Kanu Club Fulda** (Bootshaus in der Gartenau, tel. 0661/72667) rents boats for DM 18 per day.

COMING AND GOING

Every hour, express trains leave for Frankfurt (1 hr, DM 36) and Kassel (30 min, DM 30), and trains to Eisenach (1 hr, DM 27.20) leave once an hour or so from Fulda's **Hauptbahnhof,** which is equipped with luggage lockers. The town center is three blocks down Bahnhofstraße, past Rabanusstraße. City bus lines begin and end at the **Omnibusbahnhof,** down Rabanusstraße to the right, at the corner of Schloßstraße. The *Umweltkarte* (environmental ticket; DM 5) allows you as many bus trips as you can stomach for any two days in one week. Inner-city bus fare is DM 2.

WHERE TO SLEEP

In the Altstadt, **Pension Hodes** (Peterstor 14, at Rabanusstr., tel. 0661/72862) has eight rooms that fill up fast. Avocado and mustard are the colors of choice, and the walls are hung with jigsaw puzzles. Singles start at DM 40, doubles at DM 90, none with bath. The homey **Zum Kronhof** (Am Kronhof 2, tel. 0661/74147) also vies for "Funkiest Decor." Here it's an array of clashing colors and patterns in every room, but it's clean and friendly. You're right behind the Dom, so you won't need an alarm clock. Singles cost DM 35, doubles DM 65–DM 90, some with bath. They usually have space, but call ahead just to be safe.

HOSTELS • Jugendherberge (HI). The yellowing pillows and mattresses in this cramped hostel are hardly welcoming, and you're an infrequent bus ride or a 35-min trek on foot from town; however, breakfast is huge, delicious, and included in the DM 24 price (DM 28 over 26). *Schirrmannstr. 31, tel. 0661/73389, fax 0661/74811. From Omnibusbahnhof, Bus 1B to Stadion, then uphill (buses run until 6 PM weekdays, 2 PM Sat., and not at all on Sun.). Or, from station, walk down Bahnhofstr., diagonally cross Universitätspl. onto Floreng., turn right on Karlstr. (which becomes Loherstr.), right on Bardostr., quick left on Johannisstr., which leads up to hostel. 125 beds. Curfew 11:30. Reception open 7 AM–10 PM.*

FOOD

For Greek cuisine, head to **Südpfanne** (Am Stockhaus 1a, tel. 0661/71900), which serves up dishes like Greek farmer's salad (DM 13) and *spanakorizo* (spinach rice with sheep's cheese and lemon; DM 11) in a homey setting. Bakeries, butchers, and small cafés fill **Friedrichstraße** (southwest of the Schloß) and the surrounding streets. A rowdy evening crowd gathers at **Altstadt** (Kanalstr. 53, tel. 0661/79322), near the southwest end of the pedestrian zone, where beer and bites are cheap, the music is loud, and the lights dim. For groceries, head to **Okay** (Rabannusstr. 3), just opposite the bus station.

NEAR FULDA

Fulda lies between the 750-sq-km **Rhön-Naturpark** and the **Vogelsberg** mountains. Both are punctuated with picturesque rural towns and crisscrossed by hiking and biking trails. The Vogelsberg will make you want to go skipping tra-la-la through the lavender-and-yellow meadows. **Alsfeld** in the Vogelsberg and **Gersfeld** in the Rhön make excellent starting points.

ALSFELD

The Hessian government chose Alsfeld as the center for preserving old Hessian culture. Along the **Marktplatz** you'll find many old-style houses, once home to the craftsmen who built this town. The **Regionalmuseum** (Ritterg. 3–5, tel. 06631/4300; admission DM 2, DM 1 students) documents Hessian life. Among the collection of traditional artifacts is a frightening time capsule of Nazi-era leaflets and posters—including a Gestapo death-sentence announcement. In the same building, the **Städtisches Verkehrsbüro** (tel. 06631/182165) has a friendly staff that hands out city and hiking maps and provides info on *Wandervereine* (hiking clubs) that organize group hikes. Hourly trains leave from Fulda (50 min, DM 9) and Gießen in the Lahn Valley (1½ hrs, DM 14) for Alsfeld. From the station, walk down Bahnhofstraße (which turns into Am Lieden) and make a left at Mainzer Tor for the Altstadt.

WHERE TO SLEEP AND EAT • The verkehrsbüro books rooms free of charge; or try **Hotel Zur Alten Schmiede** (Unterg. 12, tel. 06631/2465), a cozy, family-run place with clean singles for DM 28, doubles from DM 55, breakfast included. It's best to reserve ahead, since their nine rooms fill up fast.

From Mainzer Tor, go right along Roßmarkt to Untergasse. Over on Marktplatz, **Kartoffelsack** (Marktpl. 16, tel. 06631/2057) has potato pizza, potato lasagna, potato roast beef casserole . . . and so on (DM 10–DM 14). **Aldi,** just around the corner from the tourist office on Alicestraße, is a good place to stock up on hiking fuel, or try one of the bakeries and delis scattered throughout the Altstadt.

GERSFELD

Gersfeld, a short train ride from Fulda (45 min, DM 7.50), is hardly worth mentioning as a town, but it's a perfect base for exploring the **Rhön.** The forest here is protected by UNESCO as a "biosphere reserve," so pick up a trail map from the **tourist office** (Am Rathaus, tel. 06654/1780), a mountain bike (DM 25 per day) from **Fahrradverleih** (Hauptbahnhof, tel. 06654/7595), and get outta town. In winter, **Sporthaus Friedrich** (Ebersberger Pl., tel. 06654/233) rents skis; call 06654/1211 for weather reports and the latest slope conditions.

If you're planning to backpack into the Rhön, the tourist office has a list of hostels and farms where you can pitch a tent. The big draw, though, is the **Wasserkuppe,** Hessen's tallest peak. In summer the main ski slope becomes a hair-raising toboggan run; contact **Wiegand Riesenrutschbahn** (tel. 06651/9800).

WHERE TO SLEEP • You're here to relax, so head west on bahnhofstraße to frau Anna Weber's **Pension Panorama** (Auf der Wacht 21, tel. 06654/1436) with its views of the valley. Singles cost DM 28–DM 35, doubles DM 52. For the **Jugendherberge (HI)** (Jahnstr. 6, tel. 06654/340, fax 06654/8877), walk down Bahnhofstraße, then turn right on Peter-Seifert-Straße and left on Jahnstraße. Beds cost DM 20.20 (DM 27 over 26), including breakfast. Reception is open 5 PM–11 PM.

KASSEL

The Brothers Grimm lived and studied here for a long time, but you won't find Old World charm in Kassel. After wartime bombing destroyed nearly 75% of the city, Kassel adopted a pragmatic "out-with-the-old, in-with-the-new" approach. It was the first city in Germany to create a pedestrian zone and still reserves 60% of its downtown for trees and lawns, punctuated by utilitarian modern architecture. Kassel's other nod to things modern is **documenta,** a massive, contemporary art festival that fills Kassel with art and art lovers, and artists and their lovers, every five years. The last documenta took place in '97 and incorporated the whole city of Kassel in an extensive display of modern art from around the world. Book a room *way* ahead of time or you'll be left out in the cold. For more info, contact **Museum Fridericianum** (Friedrichspl. 18, tel. 0561/707270, fax 0561/774276; closed Mon.), with exhibits on modern art and past documentae. Traces of past documentae decorate otherwise boring grassy splotches around town—there's even an entire documenta neighborhood designed by various architects (Tram 4 or 6 to Helleböhn). Other than documenta, check out Kassel's quirky museums and **Wilhelmshöhe,** a showy 600-acre "mountain scenery park" complete with museums, two castles, and outlandish water displays.

BASICS

There's a **tourist office** (tel. 0561/34054; open weekdays 9–1 and 2–6, Sat. 9–1) at Bahnhof Wilhelmshöhe, with brochures, a city map (50 Pf), a list of hotels (50 Pf), a free bus map, and a not-so-knowledgeable staff. The main branch of the tourist office has a few more brochures (Königspl. 53, tel. 0561/787–8008, fax 0561/103838; open Mon.–Thurs. 9:15–6, Fri. 9:15–4:30). Both offices have a list of private rooms (DM 35 and up) and book rooms for a DM 5 fee. Change money at the **Deutsche Verkehrsbank** (open weekdays 9–1 and 1:30–4:15) inside the Hauptbahnhof. Bahnhof Wilhelmshöhe has a **post office,** but the main office (Untere Königsstr. at Bremer Str.) has the whole buffet of services—phones, money change, and fax. Just outside Bahnhof Wilhelmshöhe, the **Fahrradhof** (tel. 0561/313083) rents bikes for DM 20–DM 50 per day.

COMING AND GOING

Hourly trains from Berlin (3½ hrs, DM 133), Munich (5 hrs, DM 174), and Eisenach (1 hr, DM 27) and twice-hourly trains from Frankfurt (2 hrs, DM 54), Fulda (30 min, DM 30), Marburg (1 hr, DM 27), and Göttingen (30 min, DM 27) arrive at **Bahnhof Wilhelmshöhe,** a huge, modern station built especially for express trains. To get downtown, hop Trams 1, 3, 4, or 6 and exit anywhere between the Rathaus and Königsplatz. Frequent local trains also connect the station with the seedy **Hauptbahnhof,** in the center of town, which serves nearby rail destinations. The **info office** (open weekdays 7:15–4:45) inside has bus schedules and route info.

One ticket (DM 3.30–DM 5) buys one hour of travel on Kassel's trams and buses. Purchase tickets at the kiosk at the Hauptbahnhof, from machines inside the trams, or directly from the driver/conductor. The **24-hour ticket** (DM 8) gets you one weekday or an entire weekend of transit fun. Validate tickets when you get on the tram or bus by sticking them in the clunky orange boxes. Kassel's **Mitfahrzentrale** (Friedrichstr. 18, tel. 0561/19440) has service to many German cities; you can get to Frankfurt for DM 21.

WHERE TO SLEEP

Accommodations in Kassel aren't cheap. **Hotel Lenz** (Frankfurter Str. 176, tel. 0561/43373, fax 0561/41188) is clean and quiet, but somewhat out of the way. Singles cost DM 49.50 with shower and DM 90 with bath, doubles DM 90 with shower and DM 130 with bath. To reach Lenz, take Tram 5 or 7 to Güterbahnhof Niederzwehren, then walk down Frankfurter Straße. **Hotel Palmenbad** (Kurhausstr. 27, tel. and fax 0561/32691) has a friendly management, with singles for DM 50, doubles start at DM 88. From Bahnhof Wilhelmshöhe, hop on Tram 3 or 4 to Brabanter Straße.

HOSTELS • The comfortable, renovated **Jugendherberge (HI)** is definitely one of the friendliest in Europe. There's a café downstairs where you may meet students waiting to get into university housing. It's also a short walk from the city center. Beds DM 24.50 (DM 29.50 over 26), including breakfast. *Schenkendorfstr. 18, tel. 0561/776455, fax 0561/776832. From Bahnhof Wilhelmshöhe, Tram 4 or 6 (direction: Lindenberg or Wolfsanger) to Annastr.; backtrack on Friedrich-Ebert-Str., right on Querallee (which becomes Schenkendorfstr.). 191 beds. Reception open 24 hrs; ask for door code after hours. Luggage storage.*

What is it about Germans and the Irish? A puzzling question when you consider the massive popularity of the Kelly Family—a huge singing family dressed like flower-power beatniks. They are hardly known in Ireland, let alone Britain.

FOOD

Friedrich-Ebert-Straße, southwest of the Hauptbahnhof, has the highest concentration of cafés, bars, and restaurants. **Fernando Póo** (Friedrich-Ebert-Str. 78, tel. 0561/103626) attracts a young crowd for their unique *Rollos,* a homemade *Fladenbrot* (crusty, floppy Turkish bread) filled with anything you can imagine and then tossed in the oven. Roll one to your pal for only DM 11–DM 13.50. Ponder the Kassel student scene at candlelit **Podium** (Kölnische Str. 34, tel. 0561/104693), an affordable bar and restaurant near the Hauptbahnhof. The Greek salad (served with Fladenbrot) goes for DM 10.40.

WORTH SEEING

Conveniently, most of Kassel's sights are in Wilhelmshöhe Park, reached via Tram 1 or 4 (to Wilhelmshöhe). Kassel's museums cluster downtown near the Rathaus. If you plan on visiting more than two museums, the **Kassel Service Card** (DM 12 for one day, DM 19 for 3 days) gets you unlimited free rides on city buses and trams, free city bus and walking tours, free entry to the city's casino, and discounts on admissions to all major sights.

WILHELMSHÖHE • On the western edge of Kassel stretches the biggest city park in Europe. If you're not the hiking type, Bus 23 circles the park and stops at the major sights. The park's highlights are its two castles and the *Wasserkünste* (fountain and cascade display). The stately 18th-century **Schloß Wilhelmshöhe** (tel. 0561/36011; admission DM 4, DM 2 students; closed Mon.), near the park entrance, is one of the best examples of neoclassical architecture in Germany. In one wing of the Schloß, the **Gemäldegalerie** (tel. 0561/36011; admission DM 3, DM 2 students; closed Mon.) includes such famous pieces as Rembrandt's *Blessing of Jacob.* To tour the palace, you must join an hour-long, German-language tour (English handbook available). Then there's the *faux* Scottish castle, **Löwenburg,** built around 1800 to look like a medieval ruin. Wander through the labyrinth and then head to the **armory,** which displays 16th- and 17th-century weapons and armor (including the impressive armor of the "Black Knight"). From Schloß Wilhelmshöhe, it's a hefty one-hour hike up to the **Temple of Herkules** (tel. 0561/36011). For DM 2 (DM 1 students) you can climb to the observation deck of the enormous octagonal structure. This is also the starting point for the Wasserkünste—the park's pièce de résistance. On Wednesday and Sunday at 2:30 PM, and at dusk on the first Saturday of each month (June–Sept.), the fountain grotto at the base of the temple shoots a torrent of water over the Poseidon waterfall at the bottom of the steps. This sets off a chain reaction in the other fountains all the way down to the Schloß, timed so that everyone can stampede to the next segment in time. Bus 43 connects Herkules to Tram 3 if you don't want to hike back.

MUSEUMS • The Brothers Grimm worked as librarians in Kassel for most of their lives and got more than 30 of their fairy tales from a local woman named Dorothea Viehmann. The **Brüder-Grimm-Museum** (Schöne Aussicht 2, tel. 0561/787–2033), in the Bellvue Schlößchen, documents the lives of Wilhelm and Jakob with family artifacts, period drawings of Kassel, and various editions of their (i.e., Dorothea's) stories, including nifty pop-up books. Across the way at the **Neue Galerie** (Schöne Aussicht 1, tel. 0561/15266; closed Mon.), you'll find a collection of more or less modern art. Cross the footbridge over Frankfurter Straße to Weinbergstraße for the one-of-a-kind **Museum für Sepulkralkultur** (Weinbergstr. 25, tel. 0561/918930; admission DM 4, DM 2 students). This museum devoted to the culture of death contains a permanent collection on the history of coffin and gravestone design, from medieval knights' tombs to contemporary gravestones. If it's open, the **crypt** in the basement includes such morbid goodies as simulated rotting skulls.

FESTIVALS

Besides the documenta, Kassel hosts a number of smaller annual festivals. **Zissel,** a folk festival held in early August on the Fulda River, features jousting, folk costumes, boat displays, and lots of booze. On the first Saturday of September, Wilhelmshöhe Park is illuminated by fireworks for **Lichtfest,** which peaks around 10 PM. In November Kassel celebrates **Musiktage,** one of Europe's oldest festivals of classical music.

AFTER DARK

Check the free *Info Tip* magazine for shows, concerts, and performances. If you understand German and feel goofy, check out the theater troupe **Komödie** (Friedrich-Ebert-Str. 39, tel. 0561/18383). Performances, held Thursday–Sunday, start at 8 PM. Get tickets (DM 10–DM 15) at the door or at the box office Monday–Saturday 10–1. The **Irish Pub** is the only place in town with free, nightly live music. (*See* blurb on Irish Pubs in Germany.) An older twentysomething crowd flocks to **Kulturbahnhof Gleis 1** (Hauptbahnhof, tel. 0561/78060; closed Mon.), inside the station, for jazz concerts, other live music, DJs (house, soul, funk), and artsy films.

NEAR KASSEL

FRITZLAR

Fritzlar has the look and feel of a quiet medieval town, forgotten but prosperous. The town was founded more than 1,200 years ago by St. Boniface, who, so the story goes, chopped down the local pagans' sacred oak tree and, feeling fairly righteous, built a church out of the wood. The result can be seen by crossing the Eder River from the Bahnhof and walking for 10 min down Gießener Straße to Fritzlar's Gothic **Dom.** Along the way you'll pass Fritzlar's well-preserved medieval wall (punctuated with 14 turrets) and a crooked collection of colorful 15th-century buildings. Inside the Dom, check out the **Domschätze** (cathedral treasury; admission DM 4, DM 2 students), which houses relics, old manuscripts, and a jewel-encrusted cross from 1020. The **Pferdemarktplatz** is the site of a huge annual horse auction and fair that draws about a quarter of a million visitors to this tiny town from the second Thursday in July through the following Sunday. The largest medieval sentry tower still standing in Germany, the **Grauer Turm** guards the old city wall; for DM 1 you can wind your way up its 39-m core to a view over Fritzlar's rooftops. Just look up for the tallest tower—the one with three points. Recover from the climb in one of the cafés on the **Marktplatz.**

The quickest route to Fritzlar from Kassel is on Bus 50 (30 min, DM 9) from the Hauptbahnhof. When coming by train from Kassel, Frankfurt, or the Lahn Valley, you'll have to transfer at Wabern. The **tourist office** has maps and brochures and can book you into a private room for a DM 3 fee. *Im Rathaus, next to Dom, tel. 05622/988643. Open Mon.–Thurs. 10–1 and 2–4:30, Fri. 10–11:30.*

THE LAHN VALLEY

The Lahn River flows through the Hessian heartland, past small towns and a bucolic countryside that undulates down toward the Rhine like a voluptuous woman in a green velvet pantsuit. The highlight of the Lahn Valley is **Marburg,** a small university town that has seen Hessian dynasties come and go. The even smaller towns of **Wetzlar, Weilburg,** and **Limburg** offer beautiful riverside locations and royal history.

COMING AND GOING

Gießen, a modern, industrial city at the center of the valley, serves as a regional rail hub but has little to offer beyond transit connections. Make your transfer here and move on. Trains leave Gießen hourly for Fulda (2 hrs, DM 29), Frankfurt (40 min, DM 16.40), and Kassel (1½ hrs, DM 36), and twice hourly for Cologne (2½ hrs, DM 47). Frankfurt–Kassel trains continue from Gießen to Marburg (20 min, DM 7 from Gießen; 1 hr, DM 18 from Frankfurt) every hour. From Gießen, the *Lahntalbahn* runs every hour down the Lahn to Koblenz (2½ hrs, DM 32), with stops in Wetzlar (10 min, DM 5), Weilburg (30 min, DM 10), and Limburg (1½ hrs, DM 14). You can also reach Limburg directly from Wiesbaden/Mainz (1 hr, DM 11) or from Frankfurt (1 hr, DM 14) by hourly train via Niedernhausen. Take an express (DM 6.50 extra) unless you want to stop in every podunk town along the way.

OUTDOOR ACTIVITIES

Because of its slow, almost oozing current, the Lahn is a waterway beloved by canoeists, and its banks are dotted with campgrounds for paddlers on longer trips. **Lahn Tours** (Lahntalstr. 45, Roth, tel. 06426/855, fax 06426/1819), in a suburb of Marburg, leads tours and rents boats (DM 45 per day, discounts for longer rentals). Boats can be dropped off downstream. Tourist offices hand out a map titled "Fahrradwege in Hessen" that describes the various bike routes (all signposted) and their lengths. You can rent bikes at **Velociped** (Auf dem Wehr 3, Marburg, tel. 06421/24511, fax 06421/161627) for DM 15–DM 50 per day, and you can arrange to drop the bike off at your destination. Reservations for bike and canoe rentals are a good idea.

The Marktfrühschoppen is a huge festival held the first Sunday in July on Marburg's Marktplatz. Alumni return to enjoy the game booths, carnival attractions, and lots of food and drink.

MARBURG

In a conversion frenzy, Philip the Magnanimous established the first Protestant university here in 1527, and student life has flavored the town ever since. The Grimm brothers studied here, as did many Romantic writers. Gently tucked into a valley about 70 km north of Frankfurt, Marburg's narrow cobblestone alleyways, medieval buildings, and hilltop castle escaped destruction in World War II. They've also escaped the blight of large-scale tourism. Instead, students fill the narrow streets, and Marburg has a tolerant, lively, and colorful atmosphere rarely found in small historic towns.

BASICS

You can stash your stuff at the luggage lockers in the Hauptbahnhof at DM 2–DM 4 for 72 hours. From the Hauptbahnhof, it's a 20-min walk (down Bahnhofstraße, and left on Elisabethstraße, which becomes Pilgrimstein) or a short ride on Buses 1–6 to **Rudolphplatz** and Marburg's historic Oberstadt. **Volksbank** (Bahnhofstr. 23, tel. 06421/2920) has good exchange rates and gives cash advances. If they're closed, change money (DM 6 per check) at the main **post office** (Zimmermannstr. 2; postal code 35034), right by the station. Also outside the Bahnhof, the **tourist office** (Neue Kasseler Str. 1, tel. 06421/201249, fax 06421/681526) sells maps for 50 Pf, has a list of hotels and private rooms, and organizes free city tours every Saturday. They're open weekdays 8–12:30 and 2–5, Saturdays (Apr.–Oct. only) 9:30–noon; a machine outside dispenses city maps and lists of hotels and museums for DM 1.

WHERE TO SLEEP

This university town's hotels cater mostly to well-paid parents and professors. The tourist office has a list of private rooms for as little as DM 25 per person, though many require a minimum stay of three nights or more. Be sure to ask. The cheapest option is **Campingplatz Lahnaue** (tel. 06421/21331), along the river behind the hostel. It's often filled with locals having picnics and barbecues. Campsites cost DM 6 per person, DM 3 per car, and DM 6 per site. If you're looking for a real bed, try **Gästehaus Tusculum** (Gutenbergstr. 25, tel. 06421/22778, fax 06421/15304), a clean and central hotel with a decor inspired by the proprietor's love of Miró. Singles are DM 55–DM 65, doubles DM 95–DM 125. From the Hauptbahnhof, take Bus 1, 3, 5, or 6 to Gutenbergstraße.

HOSTELS • Marburg's bright, spanking clean **HI hostel** is located on the tree-lined riverbank just 10 min from the Oberstadt. Comfortable beds cost DM 24 (DM 29 over 26), including a breakfast buffet. *Jahnstr. 1, tel. 06421/23461, fax 06421/12191. From Rudolphspl., cross the bridge and follow the path* *to the right down the opposite riverbank to Jahnstr. 158 beds. Curfew 11:30. Luggage storage. Reception open 7 AM–11 PM.*

FOOD

Every Saturday and Wednesday until 2 PM, a **market** is held behind Elisabethkirche (*see below*); otherwise, stock up on staples at Plus (Bahnhofstr. 20). The collective **Café am Grün** (Am Grün 28, tel. 06421/14260; closed Mon.) has tables on the grass right next to the Lahn River. Munch down a sizeable breakfast (DM 7) or an open-faced sandwich (DM 4.50), or slurp down a spiked mocha (DM 6) with the amiable student clientele as canoeists and ducks drift by. One block west, **Quodlibet** (Gutenbergstr. 35, tel. 06421/22803) is a popular beer garden and pub with pool and darts. It serves breakfast from 9 AM, lunch noon–2:30, and dinner 5–11. Sandwiches and Wurst cost DM 2.50–DM 7.50. In the Oberstadt, **Café 1900** (Barfüßerstr. 27, tel. 06421/27167) is a rough version of a Vienna coffeehouse. The menu includes everything from grilled eggplant (DM 6.50) to *Auflauf* (huge potato casseroles; DM 8–DM 12). The cozy **Brasserie** (Reitg. 8, tel. 06421/21992) offers a wide variety of salads and German entrées for DM 8–DM 14.

WORTH SEEING

The Elisabethkirche, with its striking 88-m-tall Gothic spires, was built in 1235 for Saint Elizabeth. Her husband, Count Ludwig of Thuringia, died when she was only 20, and she was then banished. She came to Marburg, became a nun, set up a hospital, and led an ascetic life that killed her in four years. Instant sainthood followed, an honor scorned by her Protestant descendant Philip (founder of Marburg's university), who not-so-magnanimously disposed of Elisabeth's Catholic remains. Her humble bones were recovered and are now on display in a bejeweled golden shrine. In a dark alcove to the left of the entrance are the remains of a completely different character: Hindenburg, the Reich president who appointed Hitler as chancellor in 1933. Dumped here by the Americans after the war, his remains have incited both neo-Nazi pilgrimages and left-wing protests. *Elisabethstr., at Deutschhausstr. Admission to shrine DM 3 (DM 2 students). Open weekdays 9–6, Sat. 9–5:30, Sun. 11:15–5:30.*

The rest of Marburg's sights are in the Oberstadt (Upper Town), which edges its way up a hill over the Lahn River. Most of the Oberstadt's tiny alleys converge on Barfüßerstraße (Barefoot Street), which leads to the Marktplatz. The winding, *steep* climb from the Marktplatz to the 14th-century **Landgrafenschloß,** an enormous castle overlooking the city, takes about 10 sweaty min. The castle's **Museum für Kulturgeschichte** (tel. 06421/285871; closed Mon.) is worth the visit, especially if you like early Christian treasures, Renaissance furniture, and beautiful medieval costumes. Admission is DM 3 (DM 2 students).

AFTER DARK

Thanks to the university, Marburg has a lively, largely bohemian scene with lots of live music venues. Pick up a free *Express* or *Kultur News* at the tourist office or any kiosk to see what's up. Among **Café Trauma**'s (Robert Koch Str. 15a, off Bahnhofstr., tel. 06421/66317) multiple offerings are punk shows, art films, French performance artists, and live bands. Most interesting (or frightening) are the psycho-sociological evenings, when psych and sociology students offer free analysis to the overstressed and overpaid. Now popular in Germany and neighboring France, these cultish evenings have their roots in gatherings at literary cafés, where discussions quickly turned into therapy sessions when clients ended up talking about themselves rather than Existentialism or Tom Clancy. Cover is DM 5–DM 10, but you save a Mark if you come before 9. **KFZ** (Schulstr. 6, tel. 06421/13898) is THE live music venue, and people come from as far away as Frankfurt for the eclectic mix of jazz, blues, rock, and country artists from all over the world. Another live-music nook is **Molly Malone's** (Wehrdaer Weg 16a, tel. 06421/66363), north of the Elisabethkirche, where a cozier, calmer crowd gathers to hear Irish folk music and contemporary jazz. Another popular student hangout is **Café News** (Reitg. 5, tel. 06421/21205; no cover), where you can sip beer and watch live bands perform on weekends. Want to dance? Take a disco nap and head to **Kult/Lager** (Temmlerstr. 7, tel. 06421/947015; open Tues., Fri., and Sat., with special events on other nights), a newly opened dance club where you can strut your stuff with a twentysomething crowd. People already flock to this joint from all over the Lahn Valley. The club is located south of the city, accessible by Bus 2 or 3.

WETZLAR

Tidy and tranquil Wetzlar is a *Goethestadt* (Goethe town), and it was along these cobblestone streets and in the funky, multi-hued Dom that young Johann received inspiration for his first novel. During his summer in Wetzlar, Goethe met Charlotte Buff and instantly fell in love, but Lotte was a heartbreaker and ended up marrying someone else. When a similarly brokenhearted friend committed suicide with a pistol he borrowed from Charlotte's fiancé, Goethe combined their stories, and *Die Leiden des jungen Werthers* (1774, *The Sorrows of Young Werther*) was an instant hit. You can visit Charlotte's home, **Lottehaus** (Lottestr. 8–10, tel. 06441/99221; open Tues.–Sun. 10–1 and 2–5), and see original editions of *Werther* in many languages. On the south side of town is Jerusalemhaus (Schillerpl. 5, tel. 06441/99269; open Tues.–Sun. 2–5), where Goethe's troubled friend lived and died. Admission to both houses is free. The enormous Dom, begun in the 12th century, is the focal point of Wetzlar. Bombed to bits during World War II, it was later restored to its original unfinished state, with a beautiful, airy interior, colorful ceilings, and fading frescoes on the walls. Check out the floating angels in the Baroque chandelier over the pews. Wetzlar's pristine Altstadt, now a pedestrian zone and shopping area downhill from the Dom, also merits a stroll.

BASICS

The friendly staff at the **tourist office** (Dompl. 8, tel. 0641/405338; closed Sun.) have city maps and other info. They'll also book hotel rooms free of charge. Mail postcards at the main **post office** (Sophienstr. 7). To reach the Altstadt from the station, walk down the pedestrian zone (Bahnhofstraße), cross the Lahn River, veer left, and follow the signs.

Though the surrounding countryside was pelted with bombs, Limburg's oddly cartoonish Dom went completely unscathed in the war. Locals like to say that it is God's favorite cathedral, so he put his hand over it to deflect the bombs.

WHERE TO SLEEP

Wetzlar's **Jugendherberge (HI)** (Richard-Schirrmann-Str. 3, tel. 06441/71068, fax 06441/75826) is close to several hiking trails—pick up maps at the tourist office. There is no curfew (ask for the front door code), and the reception is open all day. Beds cost DM 26.50 (DM 32.50 over 27), including breakfast. From the Bahnhof, Bus 12 or 13 to Sturzkopf, then follow the signs. You can also hike (or swim) at the riverside **Campingplatz Wetzlar** (tel. 06441/34103; open year-round) for DM 4.50 per person, DM 4.50 per tent, and DM 2.50 per car; walk (20 min total) along the overpass next to the Bahnhof, follow the GIEßEN-NAUNHEIM signs, then turn right toward the Lahn River.

FOOD

Cafés aplenty infest the plazas and streets of the Altstadt, including **Café Dom** (Am Fischmarkt 13, across from Dom, tel. 06441/42290), in what was the high court building in the late 17th century. A cheaper option is **Max und Moritz** (Bahnhofstr. 5), a trashy-looking storefront on the Fußgängerzone that fills the air with the luscious smell of roasted chicken (DM 6). Inside the Herkules Center, at the Bahnhof end of the pedestrian zone, are two **grocery stores**. On Wednesdays and Sundays a market is held on Domplatz, and on Thursdays locals sell their wares on Bahnhofstraße.

WEILBURG

Thirty min downstream from Gießen is the town of Weilburg. In its glory days, Weilburg was a Baroque Residenzstadt, home to generations of Nassau dukes as well as princes from Russia and Luxembourg. Little Weilburg makes a good day trip from Limburg, or a good rest stop if you're biking or canoeing downriver. If you didn't arrive in a canoe, rent one and paddle through the only ship tunnel in Germany, constructed in 1841 to connect the shipping enterprises on the Rhine with the Lahn Valley. It's now closed off to larger craft and safe for canoers.

The elegant **Renaissance Schloß** (tel. 06471/2236; closed Mon.), on a cliff overlooking the river, gives the city a majestic air. It's definitely worth visiting, not least for its period furnishings and decor. From the train station, walk up Bahnhofstraße, cross **Steinerne Brücke,** an elegant stone bridge built in 1768, and continue up toward the castle and the Altstadt. Admission and the mandatory German-language tour of the castle (every half hour 10–3:30; hourly in the off-season) is DM 4 (DM 2 students). In June and July, the **Weilburger Schloßkonzerte** bring Baroque music to the courtyard. Concerts are also held in the **Schloßkirche** (open weekdays 9:30–5, Sat. 9:30–noon, Sun. 1–5), a small Protestant chapel with goopy gilding, and in the **Schloßgarten,** the Versailles-like grounds on the edge of the cliff. You can get concert tickets for as little as DM 10.

BASICS

Weilburg's **tourist office** (Mauerstr. 6, tel. 06471/7671; open weekdays 9–noon and 2–4:30, Sat. 10–noon) has maps and hotel lists (including private rooms, about DM 35 per person) and rents bikes (DM 12 per day), boats, and canoes (DM 40–DM 50). The **Jugendherberge (HI)** (Am Steinbühl 1, tel. 06471/7116, fax 06471/1542) is clean, modern, friendly, and worth the 40-min climb for its views of the countryside. Just dump your pack in the Hauptbahnhof's lockers (DM 2–DM 4 for 24 hrs), walk down Bahnhofstraße, turn right on Limburger Straße, left on Spielmannstraße (which becomes Am Steinbühl), and follow the signs. Beds are DM 23.50 (DM 28.50 over 26), breakfast included. The reception is open daily 5–11:30, and the hostel is closed mid-November–December.

LIMBURG

The sock-scented cheese comes from another Limburg, so don't shy away on that account or you'll miss one of the most charming Altstädte in Hessen. Follow the Altstadt map that the tourist office sells (*see below*) and pick out the oldest houses, dating from the 13th century. The town is best known for its eclectic (some would say gaudy) **proto-Gothic Dom,** with seven towers, orange and black paint, and a big stained-glass front that looks like an old telephone dial. Friendly, soft-spoken nuns give free tours of the Dom at 11 and 3, and after mass (11:30-ish) on Sunday. Free organ concerts every Saturday at 5 PM offer an eerie experience. The best views of the Dom are from across the **Lahnbrücke** to the north. The bridge was built in 1315 for toll collection, and for years it served as the city's primary source of revenue. Limburg is also famous for its stoneware, still handmade and fired as it was hundreds of years ago. The sturdy gray and cobalt-blue crockery is as useful as it is pretty, since the salt glaze and the clay give it thermos-like qualities. There are artisans' studios at **Am Fischmarkt** in the Altstadt, just downhill from the Dom.

BASICS

When you get off the train, walk up Bahnhofstraße, turn left on Werner-Senger-Straße, and right on Hospitalstraße for the **tourist office** (Hospitalstr. 2, tel. 06431/203222), which hands over maps and brochures weekdays 8–12:30 and 2–6 (until 4 in off-season). Be sure to get the self-guided tour pamphlet for the Altstadt (DM 1). Rent **bikes** (DM 2.50 per hour, DM 18 per day) at the campground (*see below*) and **boats** at Bootsverleih an der Lahn (Eschhofer Weg, tel. 06431/22610) for DM 15 per hour, on the Dom side of the Lahn between the Dom and the Autobahn bridge.

WHERE TO SLEEP AND EAT

Gasthaus Schwarzer Adler (Barfüßerstr. 14, tel. 06431/6387) has clean, simple singles for DM 30, doubles DM 60, including breakfast. From the Bahnhof, walk down Bahnhofstraße, cross Kornmarkt, and turn right on Barfüßerstraße. The **Jugendherberge (HI)** (Auf dem Kuckucksberg, tel. 06431/41493) is a 25-min uphill walk south of the Altstadt, or take Bus 3 or 4 (direction: Limburg Süd) to Hannaberg Meilenstein from the Hauptbahnhof. Beds cost DM 15 (DM 19.50 over 26), including breakfast. Camp on the Lahn in the shadow of the Dom at **Campingplatz an der Lahn** (Scheusenw. 16, tel. 06431/22610; closed Nov.–Easter), for DM 5.50 per person and DM 5 per tent. On the Lahn below the Dom, enjoy pizza, schnitzel, or fish for under DM 15 at **Zum Schwan** (Eschhöfer Weg 12, tel. 06431/3135) as you watch the birds on the island sanctuary in the middle of the river.

HEIDELBERG AND BADEN-WÜRTTEMBERG

3

UPDATED BY SARAH SLOAT

Baden-Württemberg covers much of the territory that epitomizes Germany in the eyes of the world, from Heidelberg's castle and Black Forest kitsch to the Mercedes-Benz star. Both geographically and economically one of the most important German states, Baden-Württemberg also boasts a rich historical tradition (the oldest university in Germany *and* one of the world's tallest church spires are found here) and diverse natural beauty: the **Neckar Valley** in the north; the Schwarzwald (*see* Chapter 4) in the west; Germany's largest lake, the **Bodensee,** in the south; and the vast, rural **Schwäbische Alb** region in the east. Striking a balance between the rural and the industrial are ancient university towns like **Heidelberg** and **Tübingen,** both of which deserve a few days' exploration.

By creating Baden-Württemberg from the three small provinces of Baden, Württemberg, and Hohenzollern in 1952, occupying Allied forces hoped to create a bastion of conservatism to balance the left-leaning, socialist-oriented Ruhrgebiet region (*see* Chapter 15). Today, the state still has a reputation for right-of-center politics. The Swabian half of the state—home to Baden-Württemberg's capital city, **Stuttgart**—is strongly associated with hard-working, thrifty Calvinists, and bears the brunt of the conservative stereotype. The mostly Catholic residents of Baden, in the west, are considered easygoing—partly because of Baden's historic links with France and other more decadent Catholic countries.

HEIDELBERG

Surrounded by mountains, forests, vineyards, and the Neckar River, Heidelberg has long been considered by travelers the embodiment of the spirit of Germany. Established in 1196, Heidelberg was a wealthy town by the 17th century, celebrated throughout Europe for its castle and university (Germany's oldest). Deflated by the Thirty Years' War and ransacked by Louis XIV in 1689 and 1693, Heidelberg stagnated until the advent of Romanticism in the early 19th century, when crumbling, overgrown castles became fashionable. Eventually, Heidelberg's charms were celebrated by virtually the entire German Romantic movement: Scores of poets, writers, and composers from Goethe to Schumann praised the town and its natural beauty.

BADEN-WÜRTTEMBERG

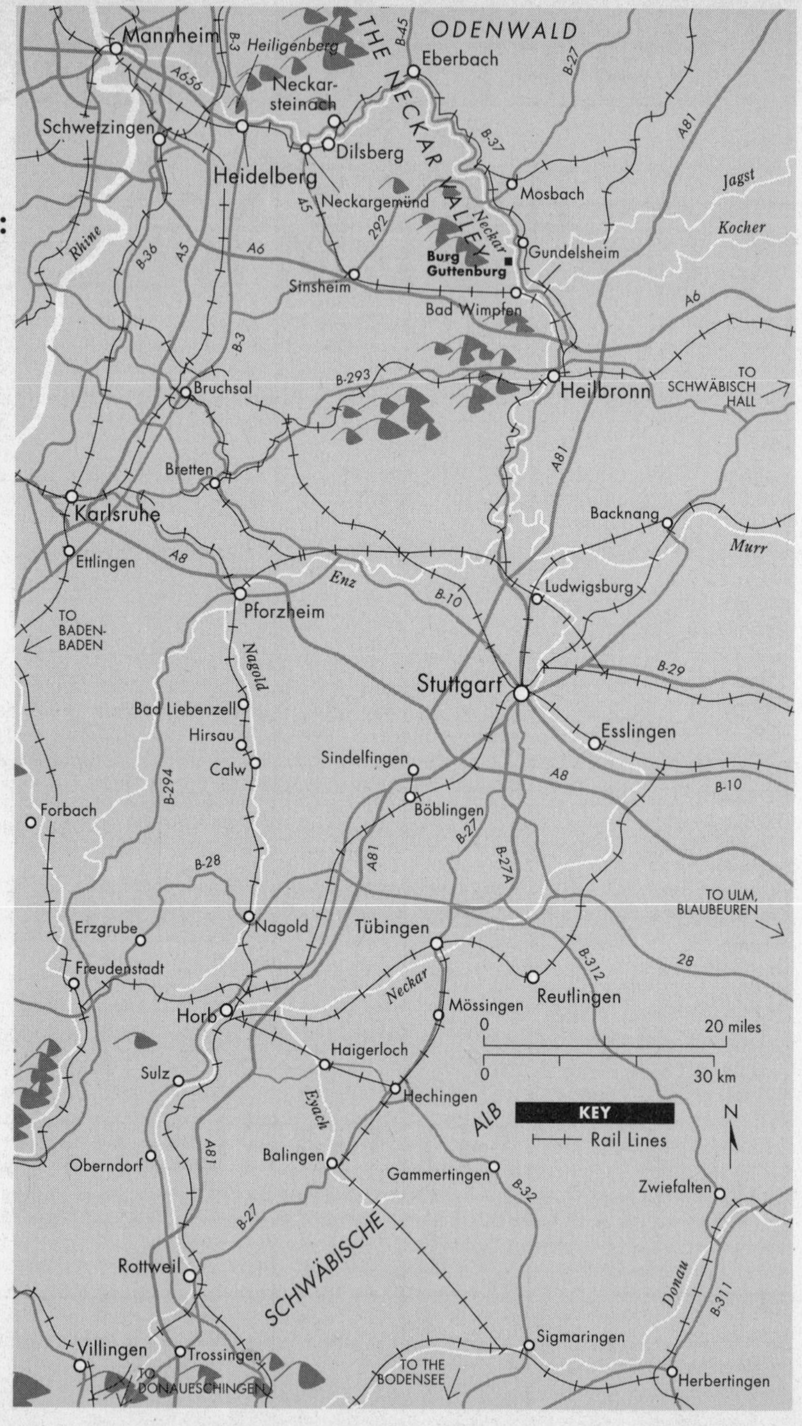

The city's venerable academic tradition has continued unbroken, ensuring that Heidelberg is far more than merely a museum piece. Heidelberg possesses a definite "college town" feel, and its popularity as both a tourist destination and a commuter suburb has given rise to an inordinate number of bars, cafés, and shops. As you might imagine, summer in town is jam-packed and stifling. Try to visit in late fall or early spring, when the pace is more peaceful.

BASICS

CHANGING MONEY • **American Express** (Brückenkopfstr. 1–2, tel. 06221/45050, fax 06221/410333) doesn't charge a commission and holds client mail for 30 days; the office at Theodor-Heuss-Brücke is open weekdays 10–6 and Saturday 10–1. The post office tends to take a slightly lower cut than Heidelberg's banks. The 24-hour ATM at **Dresdner Bank** (Rohrbacher Str. 5, tel. 06221/5270) accepts Cirrus and Plus cards. If you only have greenbacks, **H & G Bank** (Hauptstr. 46, tel. 06221/909295) has a 24-hour machine that will exchange bills for marks at a below-average rate.

LAUNDRY • Take your washables to the central but tricky-to-find **Wasch Salon SB,** where a cycle runs DM 7, including soap. It costs DM 1 for 20 min in a dryer. *Poststr. 49. From Bismarckpl., south on Rohrbacher Str., right on Poststr. Open Mon.–Sat. 7 AM–11 PM, Sun. and holidays 9–8.*

MAIL AND PHONES • The **main post office** (Belfortstr. 2), near the train station, handles poste restante and all regular postal services. Other post offices are at Sofienstraße 6–10, just off Bismarckplatz, and on Grabengasse near Universitätsplatz.

MEDICAL AID • For after-hours **medical assistance,** call 06221/19292. A convenient pharmacy in the city center is **Universitäts Apotheke** (Hauptstr. 114, 2 blocks west of Universitätspl., tel. 06221/22514).

VISITOR INFORMATION • The overworked but surprisingly patient staff at the **main tourist office,** in front of the train station, answers questions and finds rooms for DM 4 plus a 5% deposit. They can give you info about rooms outside of town, but won't book one. *Am Hauptbahnhof, tel. 06221/19433, fax 06221/167318. Open Mon.–Sat. 9–7, Sun. 10–6; closed Sun. in winter.*

Two smaller, private tourist offices provide roughly the same services, but don't ask them anything too difficult—they actually just want to sell you maps and postcards. The branch on **Neckarmünzplatz,** by the water on the eastern edge of the Altstadt, is open March–October, Monday–Saturday 9–6:30. The other, at the **Schloß** (Neue Schloßstr. 54), is open daily 10–5.

COMING AND GOING

BY TRAIN • From Heidelberg, you can reach any major city in Germany, including Frankfurt (50 min, DM 22), Stuttgart (1¼ hrs, DM 38), Karlsruhe (30 min, DM 14.60), and Mannheim (10 min, DM 5.60), all several times a day. The **Hauptbahnhof** (main train station) is about 3 km west of the city center and has lockers, a left-luggage desk, a bank, a small market, and even a McDonald's.

BY BUS • Buses are the best way to reach some of the smaller towns near Heidelberg, including Schwetzingen (Bus 7007, 30 min, DM 5) and Neckargemünd (Bus 35, 15 min, DM 5), with hourly departures from the Hauptbahnhof and Bismarckplatz. If you're headed for Dilsberg, Bus 35 leaves four times daily from the Hauptbahnhof. The tourist office has current schedules.

BY FERRY • Between June and early September, from 9:30 to 4, hourly ferries head south from Heidelberg along the Neckar River, stopping in Neckar Valley towns like Neckargemünd (1 hr, DM 8.50) and Neckarsteinach (1½ hrs, DM 9.50). Ferries also run north down the Neckar to Mannheim (2 hrs, DM 12) and on to the Rhine on Wednesday and Sunday. For schedules, call **Rhein-Neckar-Fahrgastschifffahrt GmbH** (tel. 06221/20181) or pick up a brochure at the tourist office. Since this is a private company, rail passes won't get you a discount. All ferries leave from below the **Stadthalle,** between Bismarckplatz and Universitätsplatz.

BY MITFAHRGELEGENHEIT • The **Citynetz Mitfahrgelegenheit** (ride-share) office can sometimes arrange a ride immediately, but it's always advisable to call as soon as you know your plans. Most of the staff members speak English. Popular destinations include Berlin (DM 56), Hamburg (DM 54), and Cologne (DM 28). *Bergheimerstr. 125, tel. 06221/19444. Open weekdays 9–6, Sat. 9–1, Sun. and holidays 11–2.*

GETTING AROUND

Heidelberg stretches for several km along both sides of the Neckar River, but its heart is the *Altstadt* (Old Town), bisected by the 3-km-long, pedestrian-only Hauptstraße. Most of the major attractions, as well

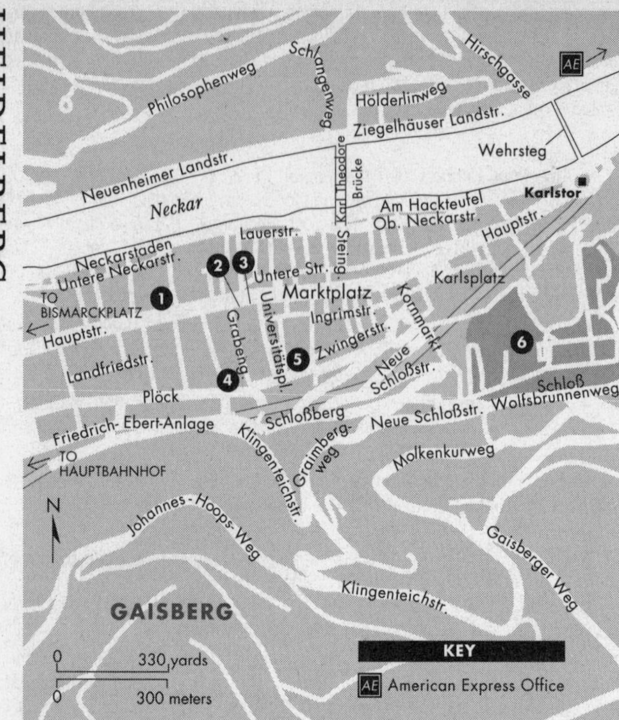

Alte Universität, **2**
Heidelberger Schloß, **6**
Kurpfälzisches Museum, **1**
Neue Universität, **5**
Studentenkarzer, **3**
Universitätsbibliothek, **4**

as many restaurants, pubs, and shops, lie on or near the street. To get here from the Hauptbahnhof, just take any public transport (except S4) going to Bismarckplatz. Bus 11 or 33 will whisk you all the way across the Altstadt to Kornmarkt or Karlstor. Single rides on any bus or tram cost DM 3, but if you plan to use public transit a lot, buy a **Tageskarte** (Day Card; DM 8.50) from a driver or a ticket machine. The card is valid for 24 hours, or the entire weekend if bought on Saturday. If you're out late, call 06221/302030 for a **taxi.** Take advantage of the beautiful bike paths in the surrounding countryside with a **bike** (DM 25 per day) from Fahrrad Per Bike (Bergheimer Str. 125, tel. 06221/161148).

WHERE TO SLEEP

Trying to find a cheap room in Heidelberg—especially during the summer—is a major headache. Reserve ahead if you can; otherwise, call ahead, even from the station, to see if there is a vacancy. You can get a free list of hotels and *Privatzimmer* (private rooms) from the tourist office. The latter are in the nearby suburb of Ziegelhausen, serviced by Bus 34, which runs until midnight from Bismarckplatz and the Hauptbahnhof. Unfortunately, Privatzimmer often require multi-night stays. If you're going the hotel route, you can call most of them for free from outside the main tourist office.

In summer, consider staying in a suburb like Ziegelhausen or nearby Neckar Valley town like Neckargemünd (*see below*). If you're staying for a week or more, contact the **Mitwohnzentrale,** a roommate referral service that will try to find you a room in an apartment or private home. *Zwingerstr. 14–16, 2 blocks south of Marktpl., tel. 06221/19445. Open Mon. and Wed. 4–6, Fri. 2–4.*

UNDER DM 50 • Hotel Jeske. Surprisingly, the cheapest place in town is in the heart of the Altstadt. Not surprisingly, it's usually full. Reservations are not accepted, so call the moment you arrive. If you're given the green light, you must check-in by 11:30 AM and look presentable—Erika Jeske, the sprightly proprietress, screens all prospective guests from a window above the front door. Beds in adequate doubles, triples, or quads are DM 24 each, not including shower or breakfast. *Mittelbadgasse 2, off Marktpl., tel. 06221/23733. From Hauptbahnhof, Bus 33 to Kornmarkt. 14 beds. Showers (DM 2). Closed late Nov.–early Jan.*

UNDER DM 100 • Astoria. This ivy-covered hotel might be a stretch for budget travelers and the rooms are rather plain, but the jovial proprietors, cozy ambience, and tranquil neighborhood merit the splurge. The Altstadt is across the river, and the Universitätsplatz is a pleasant 20-min walk from the hotel. Singles cost DM 65, doubles run DM 90–DM 110, including a bigger-than-usual breakfast. *Rahmengasse 30, btw Ladenburger Str. and Schröderstr., tel. 06221/402929. Take Theodor-Heuss-Brücke across river, left on Rahmengasse; or, from Hauptbahnhof, S1 (direction: HD-Handschuhheim) to Ladenburger Str. 12 rooms, some with bath.*

Hotel Elite. An elegant 19th-century house and a quiet, attractive neighborhood make the Elite the best value in Heidelberg. Each of the 14 airy and quaint rooms has two large double beds and a private bath. The friendly English-speaking proprietor throws in a generous buffet breakfast, which you can eat in the garden. A single costs between DM 75 and DM 85; doubles start at DM 95. Each extra person in a double is just DM 15. *Bunsenstr. 15, 4 blocks south of Bismarckpl., tel. 06221/25734, fax 06221/163949. From Hauptbahnhof, Bus 21 to Hans-Böckler-Str., right on Bunsenstr.*

Hotel Garni Ballman. Around the corner from the Elite, this three-building complex has drab but clean rooms with TVs, refrigerators, and a mediocre breakfast. Singles cost DM 70 to DM 90, doubles DM 90 to DM 120. *Rohrbacher Str. 28, south of Kurfürsten-Anlage, tel. 06221/25320, fax 06221/182035. From Hauptbahnhof, Bus 21 to Hans-Böckler-Str.; continue past Bunsenstr., hotel on right. 50 rooms, all with bath.*

HOSTELS • HI-Jugendherberge Heidelberg. Schoolchildren frequently inundate the hostel during the summer—make your reservations ASAP; reserve by fax or letter only. There's usually someone around to let you in if you come back after the mignight curfew. Beds cost DM 23 (DM 28 over 27). *Tiergartenstr. 5, tel. 06221/412066, fax 06221/402559. From Hauptbahnhof, Bus 33 (direction: Sportzentrum Nord) to Jugendherberge stop (last bus 11:50 PM). 451 beds. Lockout 9–1. Reception 7:30–9 and 3–11:30. Laundry (DM 2–DM 3).*

CAMPING • Camping Haide. Haide is the roomier of the two campgrounds on either side of the Neckar, and more trees give it a somewhat private feel. There are bathrooms, showers, and laundry facilities. Sites cost DM 8 per person, DM 6 per tent, and DM 2 per car. Bare-bones huts will keep you out of the rain for DM 14.50 per person, but you'll need your own bedding. *Ziegelhausen Landstr., where it becomes Kleingemünd Landstr., tel. 06223/2111. From Bismarckpl., Bus 35 (direction: Neckargemünd) to Orthopädische Klinik (last bus 12:40 AM); walk behind water break across pedestrian bridge, turn right, and follow signs. Closed Nov.–Mar.*

Camping Heidelberg-Schlierbach. Offering scenic views of Heidelberg and the Neckar Valley, this clean, safe campground on the banks of the Neckar River is about 5 km east of the city center. If you don't mind sharing your roadside campground with lots of RVs and cars, you can sleep here for DM 10 per person, DM 4 per tent, and DM 2 per car, hot showers included. *Schlierbacher Landstr. 151, tel. 06221/802506. From Bismarckpl., Bus 35 (direction: Neckargemünd), ask driver for bus stop Im Grund; follow signs under pedestrian underpass. Closed Nov.–Apr.*

FOOD

Hundreds of diverse restaurants blanket the area on and around Hauptstraße, where you'll probably pay at least DM 8–DM 15 for a decent meal. Keep an eye out for *Mittagstische,* lunch specials of dinner-size proportions. Bistros offer lighter fare for lighter prices. For cheaper food, try a supermarket chain like **Nanz** (Hauptstr. 17 and 116) or the **open-air market** (Marktpl., Wed., Sat. 7–noon; Friedrich-Ebert-Pl., Tues., Fri. 7–noon).

Goldener Stern. This candlelit Greek restaurant on a narrow street near the Neckar is a favorite among locals. The souvlaki and moussaka won't disappoint; both come with a crisp green salad. *Lauerstr. 16, west of Alte Brücke, tel. 06221/23937. Open daily.*

Vetters Brauhaus. Just as much bar as restaurant, Vetters serves delicious and filling German meals like Schnitzel or their famous fried potatoes for under DM 15. The house-brewed Bock is the strongest in the region and draws a crowd of students, locals, and tourists alike. *Steing. 9, off Marktpl., tel. 06221/165850. Open daily.*

Zum Roten Ochsen. This traditional student meeting place, run by the same family for over 160 years, offers meals for DM 15–DM 30, plus four kinds of beer. The food is regional German and portions are plentiful. *Hauptstr. 217, tel. 06221/20977. Closed Sun.*

CAFÉS • The Altstadt, especially Hauptstraße and Untere Straße, is loaded with hopping cafés. One of the more interesting is **Café Journal** (Hauptstr. 162, tel. 06221/161712), where the walls are covered with framed newspapers and magazine covers. The hip local crowd enjoys the view and the shaded patio at **Hemingway's** (Fahrtg. 1, near Theodor-Heuss-Brücke, tel. 06221/165033), a comfortable café-bar on the Neckar. On the north side of the Marktplatz is **Max Bar** (Marktpl. 5, tel. 06221/24419), which feels like a small Paris café. Heidelberg's version of the **Hard Rock Café** (Hauptstr. 142, tel. 06221/22819) serves breakfast until 5 PM. All of the above are open daily 8 or 9 AM to midnight or 1 AM.

WORTH SEEING

ALTSTADT • Heading east on Hauptstraße toward the castle, you'll find the **Kurpfälzisches Museum** (Hauptstr. 97, tel. 06221/583402), Heidelberg's leading museum. Housed in a Baroque palace with a beautiful garden courtyard, the museum contains a great selection of paintings, sculptures, furniture, and engravings of Heidelberg's cityscape through the ages. The archaeology wing has a cast of the lower jawbone of *Homo Heidelbergensis,* one of the oldest human skeletons discovered in Europe. Most of the exhibits are labeled in German, but you don't need complete explanations to appreciate them (there's a DM 1.50 English brochure for the archaeology section). The museum is open Tuesday–Sunday 10–5 (Wed. until 9 PM); tickets cost DM 5, DM 3 students (Sunday DM 3, DM 2 students).

Farther down Hauptstraße to the right is **Universitätsplatz,** where you'll find the oldest surviving building of Germany's oldest university, the **Alte Universität,** established 1386. Part of the new university is here as well. Behind the university is the **Studentenkarzer** (Augustinergasse 2, tel. 06221/542334), the former students' prison. Between 1712 and 1914, university administrators incarcerated students here for offenses ranging from drunkenness to political pamphlet distribution (it was actually quite cool among students to get thrown in the slammer). Take a gander at the graffiti Tuesday–Saturday 9–5 for a mere DM 1.50, DM 1 students. West of and behind the new university building is the **Universitätsbibliothek** (Plöck 107–109, tel. 06221/542380; open 8:30 AM–10 PM), where you can cast an eye on the beautifully gilt and floriated Manesse Manuscript, a one-of-a-kind collection of medieval German poetry and Heidelberg's prize possession—the pictures alone are worth a visit, and it's free. The building's effusive Renaissance facade in red sandstone and gold makes up for the rather plain exteriors of the other university structures.

More of the Renaissance red can be seen at Hauptstraße 178 on the **Marktplatz.** The 16th-century **Haus zum Ritter** is the only building to have survived all of Heidelberg's uninvited guests. Across the Platz, **Herkules Brunnen** (Hercules's Fountain) marks the spot where, until 1740, petty criminals were caged and whirled around in front of a taunting public. Think twice before jaywalking. Also on the square is the **Heiliggeistkirche,** open Monday–Saturday 10–5, Sunday 1–5. Originally a richly decorated Catholic church (1400), the Heiliggeistkirche's stern interior is the product of fires, war, and the Reformation. In the 15th century, when the church and university were so joined at the hip that Heidelberg's professors were required to obey holy orders, Kurfürst Ludwig III brought his own library here for the school's use. This *Biblioteca Palatina* is now in Rome, commandeered by the Pope during the Thirty Years' War. Although the move was bitterly challenged at the time, it ended up saving the collection from the ravages of war.

North of the Marktplatz, the landmark stone bridge, **Karl-Theodor-Brücke** (a.k.a. Alte Brücke), is dwarfed by its own twin-towered gate. It was built around 1788, after eight wooden predecessors fell to various hazards. The bridge leads to Philosophenweg (*see below*) and **Hirschgasse,** where *Burschenschafter,* Germany's version of fraternity brothers, traditionally dueled as part of their initiation ceremony. When not playing with swords, the brothers would waste time in bars like **Zum Sepp'l** (Hauptstr. 213) and **Roter Ochsen** (Hauptstr. 217). You can waste time there, too, and see Heidelberg's present-day, colored-sash-sporting Burschenschafter quaffing a pint on the house in exchange for their "authentic" (read: tourist-drawing) presence.

HEIDELBERGER SCHLOß • Perched on a ridge above Heidelberg, the grandiose, well-preserved ruins of Heidelberg's castle dominate the rest of the city. The oldest remains date from the late 15th century, though most of the complex was built during the Renaissance. You'll also see evidence of the Baroque styles of the late 16th–mid-17th centuries, when Heidelberg's Palatinate electors had their heyday, before the castle was burned and cannon-bombed during the rest of the 17th century.

Housed in a corner of the Schloß is the quirky **Deutsches Apothekenmuseum** (German Pharmaceutical Museum). Check out medications and instruments used by doctors and pharmacists from the 16th to 19th centuries, and try to imagine what might be cured by dried horse testicles and Egyptian mummy hair. Another titillating feature of the castle is the **Faß,** an enormous wine barrel made from 130 oak trees with a holding capacity of 55,000 gallons. The Faß, once the world's largest functioning wine barrel, is the subject of some whimsical legends. The most popular story concerns a dwarf named Perkeo, who was guardian of the Faß in the 18th century. In an attempt to empty the great barrel, little Perkeo, a court jester with a big thirst for wine, drank 18 bottles a day for 50 years. One day he substituted a glass of water for wine—and instantly died.

To reach the Schloß, either walk up one of the two steep paths that begin south of the Kornmarkt, or ride up the **Bergbahn** funicular (DM 4.70 round-trip) that begins in the basement of Hotel am Schloß (22 Zwingerstr., at Burgweg). The funicular runs every 10 min, daily 9–8 . For an even better view of the valley, ride the funicular to Königstuhl (DM 7.40 round-trip) at the top of the hill. Meandering around the beautiful castle grounds is free, but admission to the courtyard and wine cellar runs DM 3 (DM 1.50 students) and it's an additional DM 4 (DM 2 students) to get you into the castle proper for one of the required (and highly recommended) English-language tours. *Schloß: tel. 06221/538414. Open daily 9–5.*

PHILOSOPHENWEG • This age-old path—affording great views of the Schloß, the Neckar River, and the valley's green hills—has been trodden by the likes of Georg Hegel and Max Weber. Wander to the end of the Philosophenweg on the top of the Heiligenberg, and you'll find the ruins of the **Michaelskloster** (St. Michael's Basilica) **and the Stefanskloster** (St. Stephen Cloister), as well as a Nazi-era amphitheater, now used for rock concerts and picnicking. To reach the trail, cross the Alte Brücke to the north side of the Neckar and climb Schlangenweg.

Heidelberg's castle has become a popular wedding venue for Japanese tourists. A local travel agency makes all the arrangements for a "fairy-tale" wedding—the blushing couple just shows up and foots the hefty bill.

FESTIVALS

If your travel plans bring you to Heidelberg in late summer, contact the tourist office for details and tickets for the annual **Schloßfestspiele.** This renowned series of concerts, plays, and operas—all held in Heidelberg's Schloß—takes place from late July until the end of August. As with most high art, tickets are pricey, though some DM 19 seats are available on the day of performance. Karlsplatz is the site of two small but intoxicating (literally) festivals, the **Heidelberger Frühling** in early June and the **Heidelberger Herbst** in late September. Heidelberg also hosts a large **Weihnachtsmarkt** (Christmas Market), where locals and tourists gather on the Marktplatz and Universitätsplatz to buy Christmas tree ornaments, sip mulled wine, do last-minute shopping, and stuff themselves with potato pancakes and sausages.

AFTER DARK

The magazine *Meier* (DM 2), which you can pick up at the tourist office, magazine stands, and tobacco shops, lists all the bars, restaurants, and goings-on in the Ludwigsburg–Mannheim–Heidelberg triangle. There's also the less complete but free *Fritz,* found at record shops and cafés. When looking for nightlife in Heidelberg, it's hard to go wrong—just head for Untere Straße, Hauptstraße, and the Marktplatz.

BARS • The happening spots in the center of town close early, so if you don't want the night to end, try the following. **Sonder Bar** (Untere Str. 13, tel. 06221/25200) is a small, sweaty, smoky bar with 100 brands of whiskey and music in the Santana/Floyd vein. There's also **Vater Rhein** (Untere Neckarstr. 20–22, tel. 06221/21371), between Hauptstraße and the river, with late hours (nightly 8 PM–3 AM) and cheap late-night food.

LIVE MUSIC • For local live music, your best bet is to read the posters splattered around the city or peruse *Meier.* To get tickets for the bigger-name acts that occasionally play in or near Heidelberg, head to the tobacco shop, **Zigarren Grimm** (Sofienstr. 11, tel. 06221/20909), on the east side of Bismarckplatz. **Ziegler-Bräu** (Bergheimer Str. 1b, tel. 06221/25333) hosts bands in its back room (cover DM 15–DM 30) every Friday or Saturday, with top-of-the-charts dancing the other weekend night. The trendy bar in the front room offers delicious Tex-Mex with beers to wash it down. Ziegler-Bräu is open Sunday–Thursday 5 PM–1 AM, Friday and Saturday 5 PM–2:30 AM. A more charming after-hours choice is **Cave 54** (Krämergasse 2, tel. 06221/27840), the oldest student jazz club in Germany. Doors open at 9 PM, and after the show ends at 12:30 there's dancing until 3 AM. The **Schwimmbad Music Club** (Tiergartenstr. 13, near youth hostel, tel. 06221/470201) is known for underground bands that play everything that now is or soon will be cool. The cover is DM 10 and the club is open Wednesday and Thursday 8 PM–1 AM, Friday and Saturday 8 PM–3 AM.

MOVIE THEATERS • The **Harmonie-Kino Center** (Hauptstr. 110, tel. 06221/22000) shows mostly American films with German subtitles (DM 11–DM 13). The hip but seedy **Gloria** (Hauptstr. 149, tel.

06221/25319) lets you swig beers and whiskey while you watch artsy European and American flicks, most in their original language (DM 8–DM 9).

NEAR HEIDELBERG

MANNHEIM

One of Germany's youngest cities (founded in 1606), the large river-port town of Mannheim is an underrated destination just 15 km northwest of Heidelberg. In 1720, Elector Karl Philipp moved his residence from war-torn Heidelberg castle to Mannheim, and the city has been growing ever since. Despite heavy wartime bombing, Mannheim reshaped itself into a modern metropolis, now the second-largest city in Baden-Württemberg. If you look beyond Mannheim's concrete-block architecture, you might be pleasantly surprised by its elegant, carefully reconstructed Altstadt. Historic buildings, world-class museums, parks, fountains, a university, and a castle await you—making Mannheim a great detour on the usual Heidelberg tourist route.

Mannheim bills itself as a "theater around which the city is built." Along with the opera house and playhouse, the famed **National Theater** offers over 900 performances each year, with everything from Shakespeare to Schiller, who got his big break here when the theater produced his first drama, *Die Räuber* (The Robbers). For info on plays and operas, ask at the tourist office or call 06221/168–0203. The office also sells tix, but with a student ID you can get them at a 20%–30% discount directly from the daytime box office (Collinistr. 26, tel. 06221/24844) or, a few hours before curtain, at the theater (Goethepl., tel. 06221/168–0252).

COMING AND GOING • Mannheim's layout came from a dream Prince Friedrich IV had, in which he envisioned a city laid out like a chessboard. It consists of a series of squares designated by numbered and lettered coordinates rather than street names; grab a free map at the **tourist office** (Willy-Brandt-Pl. 3, tel. 0190770020 [no area code needed]; weekdays 9–7, Sat. 9–12) to navigate the city. Mannheim has exceptionally good service to major German cities and hourly **trains** to Heidelberg (10 min, DM 5.60). From Mannheim's Hauptbahnhof (just off L15), Trams S3 and S7 go straight to the Marktplatz in the center of town. **Citynetz Mitfahrzentrale** is run by the tourist office (*see above*), so if you can't get through by calling 06221/19444, call the tourist office directly. Within Mannheim you can walk to every sight of interest, though there is an extensive system of electric streetcars and buses that cost DM 3 per ride.

WHERE TO SLEEP • Mannheim doesn't have Privatzimmer, and most of its hotels are well out of the budget traveler's range. The exception is the centrally located, fake-flower-adorned **Arabella Pension** (M2, 12, tel. 06221/23050, fax 06221/156–4527), which has clean rooms and shared showers for DM 45 per single and DM 80 per double; breakfast is DM 7.50 extra. The place is usually full, so reserve in advance. A long shot during high season is **Hotel Rosenstock** (N3, 5, tel. 06221/27343, fax 06221/25097), where singles with showers are DM 50, doubles DM 80, breakfast not included. In summer, reservations are recommended at least two weeks in advance. For a complete list of hotels, or to have a booking made for you for DM 3, talk to the tourist office.

HOSTELS • The cheapest option in Mannheim is the **HI-Jugendherberge,** with 112 beds in clean, standard dorms for DM 23 (DM 28 over 26), including breakfast. Curfew is 12:30 AM in summer and 11:30 PM in winter, but ask about getting a key. Closed over Christmas. *Rheinpromenade 21, tel. 06221/822718, fax 06221/824073. From back entrance of Hauptbahnhof, turn right, cross tracks (stay left); walk right down Rennershofstr., left on Rheinpromenade. Reception open 1–2, 4–6, and 7–10.*

CAMPING • To the east of the city along the Neckar River is the less than idyllic **Campingfreunde Neuostheim,** which charges DM 5 for small tents, DM 8 for large ones, and DM 8 per person. Trams out here stop running early; check the schedule. *Seckheimer Landstr. 191, tel. 06221/416840. From Hauptbahnhof, S6 to end station Neuostheim, then follow the signs. Closed Oct.–Mar.*

FOOD • The *Fußgängerzone* (pedestrian zone) teems with traditional German restaurants and has several bars. For something a bit different, try **Merhaba** (K1, 7, tel. 06221/291469; open daily), with an astounding variety of Turkish treats, belly dancing on Wednesday and Friday nights, and live music on Thursdays. The cheapest bistro beers and grub can be found at the crowded and lively **Uni-Club** (L4, 11, tel. 06221/155214; open daily), just north of the university; pizza and pasta go for around DM 8. The most convenient **grocery store** is in the train station.

WORTH SEEING • A few blocks north of the tourist office and east of N7 is **Friedrichsplatz,** home to Mannheim's official landmark, the monstrous, sandstone Jugendstil **Wasserturm** (Water Tower), mercifully surrounded by a pleasant grassy park. Drink the potable water spurting from the evil shell-men's mouths if you dare.

A short walk away is the foremost of Mannheim's hidden treasures, the **Städtische Kunsthalle,** which boasts an impressive collection of 19th- and 20th-century paintings and sculpture. The big names, from Manet to Warhol, Beckmann to Kandinsky, are all here. *Moltkestr. 9, tel. 06221/293–6413. Admission: DM 4, DM 2 students. Open Tues., Wed, and Fri.–Sun. 10–5, Thurs. noon–5.*

The **Reiss Museum** houses two vastly different collections in two different buildings. The original museum building, the 18th-century *Zeughaus* (arsenal), contains a somewhat boring collection of art, handicrafts, and furniture from the 18th and 19th centuries. The stylish modern addition across from the Zeughaus on D5 has outstanding anthropological exhibits on African and Asian cultures, as well as rooms full of Greek and Roman archaeological finds. *C5, at D5, tel. 06221/293–3150. Admission: DM 4, DM 2 students; free Thurs. Open Tues., Wed., and Fri.–Sun. 10–5, Thurs. noon–5.*

Walk through the ornate, wrought-iron entrance gates of the **Jesuitenkirche** (Jesuit Church) on A4 and you'll find one of Germany's largest and most significant Baroque churches. Take the time to examine its massive classical facade, graceful domed spires, and heavy dome (look up into the dome once you're inside).

Mannheim's other grandiose landmark is the **Residenzschloß,** the largest Baroque palace in Germany. The prince electors who authorized its construction—between 1720 and 1760—seem to have put a premium on quantity rather than quality. Five architects produced an enormous, symmetrical structure with more than 500 rooms, now owned by Mannheim's university. Most impressive is the view down Kurpfalzstraße from the main staircase. *South of grid, btw A4 and L3. Admission: DM 4, DM 2.50 students. Open Apr.–Oct., Tues.–Sun. 10–1 and 2–5; Nov.–Mar., weekends 10–1 and 2–5.*

SCHWETZINGEN

In the mid-18th century, Elector Karl Theodor of the Palatinate decided that everyone who was anyone had a summer retreat, so he planned a small Baroque castle and garden here for himself. The result was the imposing, rose-colored **Schwetzinger Schloß,** which defines and dominates this tiny town, along with asparagus. Unless you have or want a Ph.D. in Palatinate history, skip the castle's Xylon Museum and head instead to the immense and amazing **Schloßgarten,** a successful combination of the formal French and "natural" English styles. The castle itself may be seen by guided tour only (English tours available). Admission to the castle and gardens is DM 9 (DM 5 students) in summer, DM 8 (DM 4 students) in winter. The castle is open from April through October, Tuesday through Friday 10–4; weekends and holidays 10–5. From Nov. to March, there's a tour every Friday at 2 and on weekends and holidays at 11, 2, and 3. If you just want to see the gardens (open daily 8–8 in summer, 9–5 in winter), admission is DM 4.50 (DM 3 students) in summer and DM 3.50 (DM 2 students) in winter; bring a picnic and spend the afternoon in 18th-century aristocratic style, admiring the prospect from various vantage points, skipping merrily from fountain to fountain. Don't forget to pack some asparagus: Schwetzingen is famous for its high-quality *Spargel.* The advent of asparagus season (Apr.–June) is joyously proclaimed around town by numerous posters reading DER SPARGEL IST GEKOMMEN (THE ASPARAGUS HAS ARRIVED).

To tour the spectacular rococo **Schloßtheater** on the Schloßgarten's grounds, you must join one of the DM 2 guided tours that includes classical music soundbites and a visual display. Tours leave July–September at 11:30, 2, 3, and 3:30. Once inside the theater, look up at the painted ceiling—the young boy playing piano is Wolfgang Amadeus Mozart (at age seven he performed here with his older sister). The theater continues to attract some of the world's finest young classical musicians during the annual **Schwetzinger Fest,** which runs from the end of April to the middle of June. Tickets cost DM 10 (nosebleed seats) to DM 250 (stylish private boxes). The other annual music fête is the September **Mozartfest,** with tickets running DM 25–DM 95. For schedules and tickets, call 06202/4933. Remember: Half-price tickets are usually available to students one hour before showtime at the box office.

COMING AND GOING • Bus 7007 (30 min, DM 5) leaves Heidelberg's Hauptbahnhof for Schwetzingen every half hour, dropping you off right on Schloßplatz. The last bus from here back to Heidelberg leaves weekdays around 10 PM, weekends around 11 PM. Trains on the short Karlsruhe–Mannheim rail line also serve Schwetzingen 5–6 times per day. To reach the castle and gardens from Schwetzingen's Hauptbahnhof, head north on Bahnhofanlage to Karl-Theodor-Straße.

BADEN IN BADEN-BADEN

So you're tired of dragging your travel-weary self from sight to sight and wrestling preteens for a hostel bed, and you're beginning to wonder if that chafing backpack imprint is permanent. You need a little luxury, and the spas are calling. Treat yourself to a day in Baden-Baden, located on the Karlsruhe–Freiburg rail line. The town itself nestles in the verdant foothills of the Black Forest and is the definitive old bath town. Immerse yourself in the healing waters at the neoclassical Friedrichsbad (Römerpl. 1, tel. 07221/275920), where DM 36 buys three hours, and for a mere DM 12 more you get another half hour of rejuvenating massage. Mark Twain extolled the virtues of the baths but complained about the snobby locals; today, it's overcrowding and high prices that make Baden-Baden less attractive for a longer visit. Steer clear of casinos and evening wear, and return to your lodgings a poorer but happier, smoother-skinned you.

KARLSRUHE

When the margrave of Baden-Durlach, Karl Wilhelm, decided that his wife's chronic complaints concerning his mistresses were unbearable, he did what any self-respecting aristocrat would do—he built a castle away from home where he could conduct his affairs with a little privacy. After becoming capital of the state of Baden in 1771, Karlsruhe (literally "Karl's rest") prospered and grew into one of the largest cities in southwest Germany. With the formation of Baden-Württemberg after World War II, Karlsruhe lost its designation as a capital city but received the consolation prize of Germany's two most important courts: the *Bundesgerichtshof* (Federal Supreme Court) and the *Bundesverfassungsgericht* (Federal Constitutional Court). Today, Karlsruhe is a dull modern city and major rail hub; if you travel through the region for any amount of time, you'll probably end up here at some point. History and art buffs will want to check out Karlsruhe's fine museums; everyone else should grab a beer at the station and wait for the next train.

Karlsruhe's two most important squares, the **Marktplatz** and the **Europaplatz,** lie along Kaiserstraße, the city's commercial lifeline. The Marktplatz is adorned with a series of structures by Friedrich Weinbrenner, the architect who gave Karlsruhe its neoclassical appearance. On the north side of the square is a red-sandstone **pyramid,** the tomb of the city's eccentric founder. Karl was quite an Orientalist and an avid collector of things Near Eastern, hence the atypical monument. The western side is home to the pink, neoclassical **Rathaus** (city hall).

At the axis of Karlsruhe's fan-shaped plan sits the yellow **Schloß,** an uninspired piece of Baroque architecture with a tower that can be climbed for DM 3. More interesting is the Schloß's **Badisches Landesmuseum** (tel. 0721/92655; open Tues.–Sun. 10–5, Wed. until 7). The prized display of an otherwise typical German-noble-family collection is the *Türkenbeute* (Turkish booty), an array of 17th-century Turkish goodies, including military equipment and rugs, looted by Baden's dukes and brought to Germany between 1683 and 1692. Admission is free. On sunny days, Karlsruhe's university students mellow out in the Schloßgarten. West of the Schloß is the impressive **Kunsthalle** (Hans-Thomas-Str. 2–6, tel. 0721/926–3355), with a collection of paintings by European artists from the 15th to 19th centuries. Its adjunct, the **Kunsthalle Orangerie,** has a smaller but equally impressive collection of 20th-century art, from Braque and Ernst to Marc, Beckmann, and Miró. Admission to both is DM 5 (DM 3 students); the collections are open Tuesday–Friday 10–5, weekends 10–6.

BASICS

Across the street from the Hauptbahnhof, the **tourist office** (Bahnhofpl. 6, tel. 0721/35530; open weekdays 9–6, Sat. 9–1) has maps and a room-booking service, both free. One block south of the Marktplatz, **Stadtinformation** (Karl-Friedrich-Str. 22, tel. 0721/3553–4376) also gives advice and sells tickets for local events weekdays 9–6, Saturday 9–12:30. Change cash and traveler's checks at the **main post office** next to the train station; it's open weekdays 8–7:30 and Saturday 8–1. You can also change money at **DVB** in the train station.

COMING AND GOING

Regular trains run to all major German cities and many destinations around Europe. The most frequent trains run to Heidelberg (30 min, DM 14.60), Baden-Baden (15 min, DM 12.80), Frankfurt (1½ hrs, DM 49), and Stuttgart (50 min, DM 24.20). To reach the city center, about 2 km north of the Hauptbahnhof, catch Tram S3 or S4 west to Europaplatz, or S1, S3, S4, or S11 to Marktplatz (DM 3, DM 8 for a 24-hour ticket). Karlsruhe's main north–south streets are Karlstraße and Ettlinger Straße; the major shopping and pedestrian zone extends east from Europaplatz past Marktplatz along Kaiserstraße.

WHERE TO SLEEP

The price of lodging in the city center is astronomical. A five-min walk north of the station, the quirky, homey **Pension Am Zoo** (Ettlinger Str. 33, tel. 0721/33678) is actually a large apartment with '70s-style rooms (DM 65 singles, DM 100 doubles without shower, but with breakfast. Add DM 20 if you want a private bath and shower). The nearest campground is **Campingplatz Turmbergblick** (Tiengerer Str. 40, tel. 0721/497236, fax 0721/497237), in the neighboring village of Durlach. Campsites are DM 9.50, plus DM 6.50 per person. From the Hauptbahnhof, take S3 to Durlacher Tor and transfer to S1 or S2 (direction: Durlach) to Turmberg; cross the street and follow the signs down the cobblestone Alte Weingartenstraße to the campground.

The centrally located **HI-Jugendherberge** has clean rooms, buffet breakfasts, and beds for DM 23 (DM 28 over 26)—easily the best deal in town. Be tucked in by the 11:30 curfew. *Moltkestr. 24, tel. 0721/28248, fax 0721/27647. From Europapl., up Karlstr., left on Stephanienstr., right on Seminarstr., left on Moltkestr. Reception open 5 PM and from 7 PM (try to be there at those times).*

FOOD

For Middle Eastern food with a twist, **Ararat Imbiß** (Akademiestr. 43, north of Europapl., tel. 0721/24801), open daily, offers excellent Kurdish specialties (veggie and meaty) for under DM 10. Or you might head to the Rathauspassage, home of the vegetarian restaurant **Viva** (Lammstr. 7a, tel. 0721/23293). If that's not to your taste, you'll find plenty of traditional meaty German fare on Ludwigplatz, also the center of Karlsruhe nightlife. Nearby **Krokodil** (Waldstr. 63, tel. 0721/27331) is the trendiest evening spot, with sidewalk tables and a beer garden.

THE NECKAR VALLEY

The Neckar Valley once offered travelers a winding river, densely forested hills, rustic villages, and relatively few tourists. Unfortunately, things have changed: In some towns the cobblestones have given way to parking lots and postcard shops, while parts of the valley have been heavily deforested. Still, the valley is guarded by ancient castles that recall the area's colorful and illustrious past. Bad Wimpfen especially retains the sort of medieval charm and historic atmosphere that originally inspired travelers to come here. The towns worth exploring generally offer homier and more affordable lodging choices than Heidelberg and Heilbronn, the two biggest cities at either end of the valley.

GETTING AROUND

Because many of the valley's castles are separate from the towns and atop large hills, the easiest way to see the valley is by car. Otherwise, you must rely on infrequent trains, buses, and ferries—and expect to do some major hiking.

BY TRAIN • The Heidelberg–Heilbronn train line (2 hrs total) runs approximately hourly from 5 AM to 11 PM and connects Heidelberg with Neckargemünd (DM 4.60), Neckarsteinach (DM 5.60), and Heilbronn (DM 19.40). On a different rail line that joins Heidelberg with Heilbronn via Sinsheim, south of the river, is Bad Wimpfen (1¼ hrs); the last train runs around 7 PM. Don't expect to find luggage storage at valley "stations"; many are only a bench and a timetable. Erbach is the exception, with four available lockers. Sometimes attendants will keep packs behind the counter if you ask politely.

BY FERRY • The most pleasant way to travel the Neckar Valley is by boat. Between June and September, ships regularly connect Heidelberg, Neckargemünd, Neckarsteinach, and Eberbach. For prime castle-viewing, don't miss the short stretch between Neckargemünd and Neckarsteinach. Of the three ferry companies on the Neckar, the largest is **Rhein-Neckar-Fahrgastschifffahrt GmbH** (*see* Coming and Going *in* Heidelberg, *above*). **Stumpf OHG** (Friedrich-Ebert-Brücke, tel. 07131/85430) is based in Heilbronn and runs boats between there and Bad Wimpfen twice daily (1½ hrs, DM 10). **Kappes** (Binetzg. 1, tel. 06271/3768), out of Eberbach, runs one boat every Tuesday and Thursday between Eberbach and Heidelberg, stopping in Neckarsteinach (3½ hrs, DM 19). All three ferry lines are private, so don't expect to use your rail pass.

BY BUS • Public buses service the Neckar towns. For general bus info, call the **Busvehrkehr Rhein-Neckar GmbH** (tel. 06221/596–0726) or pick up a schedule at the tourist office in Heidelberg.

BY BIKE • There are several bike routes in the area, including the popular, 85-km-long **Burgenstraße** route, which runs from Heidelberg along the Neckar to Bad Wimpfen. You can rent bikes for about DM 10 per day at train stations or through private companies. Stop by any local tourist office for route maps.

NECKARGEMÜND

If you arrive in Neckargemünd by boat, you'll see a peaceful half-timbered marketplace and inviting riverside cafés. Unfortunately, the rest of town is spoiled by two busy roads intersecting its center, but Neckargemünd still manages to retain a bit of its Old World charm. From the Bahnhof, turn right and walk about 15 min to the **Marktplatz,** graced by several beautiful houses, notably the colorful **Haus Illenburg** at No. 14. Another well-preserved sight is the **Haus zum Ritter,** nestled among several more 16th-century dwellings near the Marktplatz on Neckarstraße. You can obtain more info on the sights in English, along with a free map, at the **tourist office** (Hauptstr. 25, in Altes Rathaus, tel. 06223/3553), open summer weekdays 9–noon and 2–5, Saturday 10–noon. They also provide info on hiking trails and the nearby historic town of Dilsberg (*see below*). After a couple of hours in Neckargemünd, think about hopping on the hourly Bus 7021 to Dilsberg (10 min, DM 2.50), or take the riverside path.

WHERE TO SLEEP • Neckargemünd is a good alternative to Heidelberg's high prices and crowds. If you want to stay overnight, get a list of hotels and Privatzimmer from the tourist office. A convenient choice is **Gasthaus Griechische Taverne** (Hauptstr. 57, tel. 06223/2252), with singles for DM 50, doubles for DM 80. For camping, try **Friedensbrücke** (Falltorstr. 4, tel. 06223/2178; closed Nov.–Mar.), right on the water and packed with car-camping types. Sites cost DM 9 per person and DM 6 per tent.

DILSBERG

High on a hill above the Neckar Valley and across from Neckarsteinach, the walled city of Dilsberg overlooks the twisting river and green countryside. In 1150 **Schloß Dilsberg** was built on this strategic hilltop so that residents could see approaching enemies, and for hundreds of years the castle stood its ground against all challengers. Unfortunately (and ironically), it couldn't defend itself against its owners. In 1826 they deemed it worthless and decided to tear it down to build new houses; thanks to such foresight, Dilsberg is now an official suburb of Neckargemünd. Still, the town remains neatly contained on its hilltop perch, and you can play around on the ruins and walk sentrylike on the wall, taking in the beautiful panorama. There's also a mysterious passage through a rock that leads to the town's one-time water source. To this day nobody is sure why it was hewn.

WHERE TO SLEEP • Housed inside the gate tower of the old city wall is **HI-Jugendherberge Dilsberg** (Untere Straße 1, tel. 06223/2133, fax 06223/74871), with typical dorm beds for DM 21 (DM 26 over 26). The doors are locked at 10 PM but you can get a key; reception is open between 5 and 7. Down the hill, **Unterm Dilsberg** (tel. 06223/72585) has campsites for DM 6 per person, DM 6 per tent, and DM 2 per car. A small motorboat crosses from the campground to Neckarsteinach and back "on demand" for DM 1 per person.

NECKARSTEINACH

The only reason to come to Neckarsteinach is to leave—four hilltop castles beckon. From the train station, walk west on Bahnhofstraße until it becomes Hauptstraße and then look for the path on your right marked ZU DEN VIER BURGEN (TO THE FOUR CASTLES). On the way you'll pass the **tourist office** (Hauptstr. 7, tel. 06229/920022; open Mon.–Wed. 8–noon and 1:30–3:30, Thurs. until 5, Fri. mornings only), which will load you down with free maps, brochures, and a list of affordable private rooms.

Neckarsteinach's four castles were built between 1100 and 1230 by four members of the same family. The first castles you reach on the woodsy 2-km hike—**Vorderburg** and **Mittelburg**—are still inhabited. The first is strictly off-limits (unless you've been invited to dinner), but the second has a climbable tower with sweeping views over the valley. If you still have the energy, continue to the ruins of the westernmost castles, **Hinterburg** and **Schwalbennest.** If you happen to be around the last Saturday in July, check out the **Vierburgenbeleuchtung,** a small festival with fireworks highlighting the castles.

BAD WIMPFEN

The undisputed star of the Neckar Valley, Bad Wimpfen is one of the best preserved and most romantic medieval towns in Germany. This tiny village is divided into two distinct parts, **Wimpfen am Berg** (Wimpfen on the Hill) and **Wimpfen im Tal** (Wimpfen in the Valley), collectively home to a mere 6,000 people. The town's buildings, monuments, and museums attest to the variety of rulers who have held sway here: Roman emperors, Franconian kings, the bishops of Worms, and, starting in AD 1180, the emperors and kings of the Staufen family line.

If you have the time, hike down to Wimpfen im Tal and visit the Ritter Stiftskirche. The church is especially atmospheric at 6 PM weekdays, 7 AM and 9:15 AM Sundays, when the resident Benedictine monks hold services, complete with Gregorian chants.

Like most medieval holdovers, Bad Wimpfen's prime attraction is the town itself, which is best explored on aimless rambles. Start near the Bahnhof at the top of the hill in the Burgviertel, where you'll find the remains of the 12th-century **Pfalz,** one of the Staufian royalty's many palaces. This, like other Pfälze (Palatinates), consisted of a castle and its surrounding lands, ruled over by a noble who had bucked the feudal system enough to be responsible only to the emperor. The emperor (along with his court) would then eat and drink his way around his Pfälze under the guise of keeping order. Originally Bad Wimpfen's massive Pfalz filled the entire quarter, but then fell into disuse. Starting in the 14th century, rows of half-timbered houses were built in, on, and around the palace, leaving the photogenic hodgepodge of buildings you see today. Among the palace remains is the village's most obvious landmark, the **Blauer Turm** (Blue Tower), one of the three original watchtowers. The foundations date from roughly 1200, though your experience will be limited to the 19th-century tower top (open Easter–Oct., Tues.–Sun. 10–noon and 2–4:30), which you can ascend for DM 2.

If the Blauer Turm's 169 steps don't turn you on, a few meters east down Burgviertel, at No. 19, is the mostly Romanesque **Steinhaus** (admission DM 2, DM 1 students), which now houses the local medieval history museum (after all, the town's glory days were in the 12th and 13th centuries), open Easter–October, Tuesday–Sunday 10–noon and 2–4:30. Every summer, the Altstadt hosts a **medieval fair and market**; get info at the tourist office. Further east of the Burgviertel stands the **Pfalzkapelle** (admission DM 1), home to a small museum of church history and religious art; it's open April–October, daily 10–noon and 2–4:30. Continuing east you come to the edge of the town wall and the other extant watchtower, the **Roter Turm** (Red Tower), used as a hiding place for the emperor himself in times of danger. Note the roundish protuberance on the tower's east side—this tiny chamber was once used as a toilet by the tower's keeper. Heading southwest from the Roter Turm is **Schwibbogengasse,** a narrow medieval street. The building at No. 16 is the oldest house in Bad Wimpfen, and No. 5 was the town's synagogue (note the Hebrew inscription above the stairway). German pop culturologists should bring their cameras and notebooks to the **Glücksschweinmuseum** (Kronengäßchen 2, tel. 07063/6689), where there are over 3,000 examples of "lucky pigs" to snuffle over and wonder at and lots of porcine postcards to send home. The museum is open daily 10–5; admission is DM 4.99, DM 2.49 for students—you get one Pfennig back for your piggy bank.

BASICS • The **tourist office** (tel. 07063/97200, fax 07063/972020), right in the train station, can hook you up with info and a map for DM 1. The office is open weekdays 9–1 and 2–5, weekends 10–noon and 2–4 (closed weekends Nov.–Mar.). Although they don't book rooms, they do have lists of hotels and

GARAGE WINE

All over Baden-Württemberg, and especially in little wine towns around Heilbronn, vintners take turns transforming their homes or garages into Besenwirtschaften, or broom pubs. This offers the vintners a chance to advertise their wine and get rid of excess bottles. It also gives travelers a chance to do lots of cheap wine drinking in a fun atmosphere. Broom pubs are marked by a broom hung outside the door, but since they're set up in private dwellings, the best way to track them down is to ask at the tourist office or follow the local lushes.

Privatzimmer. They can help visitors find lodgings starting at DM 25 per night in a private room, although it can be difficult to find something for just one night. To reach the Altstadt on foot from the Bahnhof, turn right and follow the cobblestone road uphill.

WHERE TO SLEEP • Bad Wimpfen has about 10 hotels, only two of which are even close to cheap. For convenience, ambience and price, you can't beat **Pension Traube** (Hauptstr. 1, tel. 07063/950521), just two blocks from the Bahnhof. Lace-curtained singles are DM 55, doubles DM 105, both with bath; a restaurant/beer garden serves light meals. Farther afield is the shiny, modern **Hotel Neckarblick** (Erich-Sailor-Str. 48, tel. 07063/7002, fax 07063/8548), along the river 10 min from the Altstadt. The cheapest singles here cost DM 80, doubles DM 130. The hotel also rents bicycles for DM 10 per day.

BURG GUTTENBURG

Without a car, the only way to reach enormous Burg Guttenburg, one of the few Neckar Valley castles to escape the Middle Ages unscathed, is to catch a train from Heidelberg (1 hr, DM 15) or Heilbronn (20 min, DM 8) to the town of Gundelsheim, cross the bridge, and hike 2 km up that darn hill. Spread out over four floors of the castle's **tower** (the views up here are superb) is an excellent **museum** filled with old documents, weapons, suits of armor, and items depicting the everyday life of the castle's medieval inhabitants (the famous Staufens again). Today, you can't enter the actual castle because the family von Gemming-Guttenburg, who purchased the castle in the 14th century, still lives there. *Tel. 06266/228. Museum admission: DM 4. Open Mar.–Oct., daily 9:30–5.*

Besides the stellar views, what really makes this expedition worthwhile is the castle's **wildlife preserve and aviary** for endangered birds of prey—the birds are bred and trained here and then released into the wild. Every day at 11 and 3, ornithologist Claus Fentzloff takes some of the hawks and vultures out of their cages and demonstrates the hunting skills he's taught them. *Tel. 06266/388. Admission (including bird show): DM 10. Open Mar.–Oct., daily 9–6.*

HEILBRONN

Heilbronn is, unfortunately, one of those German cities whose prewar splendor and rich medieval character are barely traceable in the modern version. Founded in 741 under the name Helibrunna, Heilbronn was dubbed a free city in 1281, almost 50 years after it had obtained the right to control the Neckar's course. The Industrial Revolution made the town the region's largest industrial powerhouse and, later, a target of intense Allied bombing. Miraculously, the Gothic **Kilianskirche** (Church of St. Kilian) survived devastation. The exterior is dominated by an enormous, exquisitely adorned belfry, while the church's interior contains an equally intricate carved-wood altarpiece. Across the street is the **Marktplatz,** home to the friendly **tourist office** (tel. 07131/562270; closed Sun.); they provide hotel listings, brochures, and loads of info about the Neckar Valley and the Burgenstraße. On the north side of the Marktplatz is the 15th-century **Rathaus** (city hall), notable for its complex and beautiful 16th-century ornamental clock. To reach the Marktplatz from the Hauptbahnhof, turn left out of the station, continue along Bahnhofstraße, and cross Friedrich-Ebert-Brücke to Kaiserstraße; the Marktplatz is ahead on your left.

The **Städtisches Museum,** south of Kilianskirche, is easily one of the best local history and art museums around—and admission is free. *Deutschhofstr. 6–8, tel. 07131/562295. Open Mon., Wed., and Fri.–Sun. 10–5, Tues. and Thurs. 10–7.*

Although Heilbronn is one of Germany's major wine producers, the industry is more a part of the city's economy than a part of its culture, probably due to the lack of *Gemütlichkeit* (coziness). The tourist office has info on wine tasting, wine lectures, and wine walks through the vineyards. Local *Weinstuben* (wine taverns) also offer tastings, but are usually frighteningly stuffy. A better bet is a *Besenwirtschaft* (*see box,* Garage Wine, *above*). If you're traveling in September, stick around for the nine-day-long **Weindorf** (Wine Village) festival, when booths near the Rathaus have inexpensive samples of hundreds of different wines.

WHERE TO SLEEP AND EAT • For such a straightforward town, Heilbronn has surprisingly expensive hotels. The cheapest option near the town center is **Hotel Schlachthof** (Frankfurter Str. 83, 2 blocks south of the train station, tel. 07131/81413), where singles with breakfast start at DM 40, doubles at DM 80. If staying in "Hotel Slaughterhouse" has whet your appetite, there's a small **market** held on the Marktplatz Tuesday, Thursday, and Saturday 7–1. The cheapest supermarket is **Norma** (Sulmerstr. 41, at Schellengasse), on the north side of the pedestrian zone.

Heilbronn's **HI-Jugendherberge** may not be attractive or convenient but it has the cheapest beds in town (DM 23, DM 28 over 26). *Schirrmannstr. 9, tel. 07131/172961, fax 07131/164345. Bus 1 from Bahnhof to Trappensee; walk 100 m up steep hill, left at sign. Curfew 10. Reception open daily 5 PM–7 PM and 9:30 PM–10 PM. Closed mid-Dec.–early Jan.*

STUTTGART

It's fitting that one of the first things you see when arriving in this hypermodern city is the three-pointed Mercedes-Benz star high above the train station. Stuttgart's star began to rise when Gottlieb Daimler (Benz's partner—Mercedes was his daughter) invented the gas-powered engine in a nearby suburb in 1883. The city was a stuffy residence of the Württemberg dukes, somewhat provincial and reactionary, until the Industrial Revolution pushed it into the machine age, through two world wars and utter destruction, and, over the past 30 years, back to prominence. Stuttgart remains one of Germany's top industrial and technological centers—rich and conservative. To its credit, the capital of Baden-Württemberg has used its wealth to become a center of the graphic and performing arts, compensating for its lack of historical sights with a host of excellent museums and galleries.

BASICS

AMERICAN EXPRESS • This office cashes traveler's checks commission-free. *Lautenschlagerstr. 3, in front of Hauptbahnhof, tel. 0711/18750. Open weekdays 9:30–5:30, Sat. 9:30–12:30.*

CHANGING MONEY • Deutsche Verkehrs Bank in the Hauptbahnhof has long hours: Monday–Saturday 8 AM–8:30 PM, Sunday 9–8, as well as an ATM that takes Cirrus and Plus cards; however, American Express has better rates.

CONSULATES • United Kingdom. For visa information, call the Düsseldorf consulate at 0211/94480. *Breite Str. 2, SW of Rathaus, tel. 0711/162690. Open weekdays 8:30–noon, 2–4.*

United States. *Urbanstr. 7, near Charlottenpl., tel. 0711/210080. Open weekdays 8–5.*

LAUNDRY • Waschsalon Rausch (Teckstr. 8, tel. 0711/261191; U4 to Ostendpl.) isn't exactly central, but it's the closest laundromat to downtown. A wash costs DM 13, DM 3 to dry.

MAIL AND PHONES • The **Hauptpost** performs all postal services, holds poste restante (postal code 70173), has international phone facilities, and changes money. The branch inside the Hauptbahnhof (open weekdays 8–7, Sat. 8–2) has the same services but will not mail large packages. *Hauptpost: Bolzstr. 3, at Lautenschlagerstr., tel. 0711/12950.*

MEDICAL AID • Apotheke am Eugensplatz (Haußmannstr. 1, tel. 0711/240575) is near both hostels. For English-speaking medical help, call the **Red Cross** at 0711/280211.

VISITOR INFORMATION • Stuttgart's **tourist office,** in front of the Hauptbahnhof, is one of the most efficient in Germany. The friendly staff provides maps, books rooms for free, sells theater tickets, and quickly answers even the most esoteric question with a smile. *Königstr. 1a, tel. 0711/222–8240, fax 0711/222–8253. Open May–Oct., weekdays 9:30–8:30, Sat. 9:30–6, Sun. 11–6; Nov.–Apr., weekdays 9:30–8:30, Sat. 9:30–6, Sun. 1–6.*

WHERE'S SWABIA?

Traveling through what appears to be the eastern half of Baden-Württemberg, you'll hear Swabian and see Swabians, but you won't find Swabia on a map. Today, it's less of a state than a state of mind. The Swabians were a Germanic tribe that settled 1,500 or so years ago in what is now Württemberg; their modern-day descendants are defined culturally by what they eat and the way they talk. Erudite-sounding phrases like "naigugga, nahogga" may have come into use from early attempts to converse over a plate of Käsespätzle. While the Swabian dialect may be too much to tackle, definitely dig into regional specialties like the aforementioned cheese and noodle dish and Maultaschen, meat-filled dumplings similar to ravioli. You can find these treats all the way from the Bodensee (also known as the Schwäbisches Meer, or Swabian Sea) in the south, well into Bavaria to the east, on the Schwäbische Alb and into the Black Forest to the west, and as far north as Heilbronn. Confused? Take a look at an old map of southwestern Germany—the dizzying number of political boundaries will make you want to drink a Weizenbier toast to the end of feudalism.

For info on the gay and lesbian scenes, call **Rosa Telefon** at 0711/19446. Youth-oriented **Tips 'n' Trips,** in the Rotebuhlpassage, has the scoop on cheap places to eat and sleep, plus the lowdown on cool clubs. They have a number of publications, mostly in German, but the friendly staff speaks English. *Rotebuhlplatz 26/1, tel. 0711/222–2730. Open Mon.–Fri. 12–7 and Sat. 10–2.*

COMING AND GOING

BY TRAIN • Stuttgart has regular train connections to every major city in Germany. The most frequent service runs to Frankfurt (1½ hrs, DM 83), Heidelberg (1 hr, DM 38), Karlsruhe (45 min, DM 24.20), Munich (2 hrs, DM 82), and Ulm (1 hr, DM 24.20). The **Hauptbahnhof,** in the city center, has a bureau de change, a post office, markets, shops and restaurants, three hallways full of lockers, and long-term storage facilities (DM 7 per day). The **Busbahnhof** next door only serves small nearby towns.

BY MITFAHRGELEGENHEIT • You can arrange a ride through one of Stuttgart's two equally capable, equally English-speaking, equally priced ride-share offices. *Lerchenstr. 65, tel. 0711/19448. Open weekdays 9–6, Sat. 9–1, Sun. 11–1. Also: Hauptstätterstr. 154, tel. 0711/603606. Open weekdays 9–6, Sat. 10–1, Sun. 10–1.*

BY PLANE • Stuttgart's large **Flughafen** (airport) has service to every major German city as well as international flights to London's Heathrow, New York, and Los Angeles. For flight info, call 0711/948–3388. S-Bahn lines S2 and S3 leave about every 15 min (5 AM–midnight) from beneath Terminal 1, making the 30-min trip (DM 4.50) to the city center and Hauptbahnhof.

GETTING AROUND

Exit the underground passage from the Hauptbahnhof and you'll practically be in Stuttgart's center. Ahead of you to the right lies the city's thriving business and financial district. Beginning at the tourist office and running southwest for a few km is **Königstraße,** the city's main commercial artery. This wide pedestrian zone and its offshoots offer rows of department stores and sidewalk cafés, and plenty of street performers and strolling couples. Roughly halfway down Königstraße lies Stuttgart's main square, the **Schloßplatz.**

BY PUBLIC TRANSPORT • Many sites are scattered around the city, so you're bound to become intimate with the more or less user-friendly public transit system. The inner city is crisscrossed by an extensive network of buses and **Straßenbahn** (tram), **S-Bahn** (commuter train), and **U-Bahn** (subway, partially above ground) lines, all of which use the same tickets. If you have coins, you can buy tickets from the orange machines at most stops or from the driver. Be sure to validate your ticket in the orange boxes found onboard. Rides within the city center, indicated by a blue ring on the public transit maps, cost DM 2.70. A **four-ride ticket** costs DM 9.80 and a **Tageskarte** (day card) is DM 17.50. A **three-day ticket** for DM 10 (city center) or DM 18 (city center and beyond) is available at the tourist office upon presentation of a hotel or hostel receipt. Eurail and DB passes are valid on all S-Bahn lines. For prowling between midnight and 5 AM (when other transportation shuts down) watch for the purple-and-yellow signs marking **Nachtbus** (Night Bus) stops. A night bus map and schedule, along with colorful transit line maps, can be had for a smile at the tourist office. For a **taxi,** dial 0711/566061.

WHERE TO SLEEP

Cheap lodgings in the center of Stuttgart are extremely scarce, so be prepared to travel a little. If all the places below are booked, get a list of budget accommodations from Tips 'n' Trips or the tourist office (*see* Visitor Information, *above*). For stays of five nights or more, call **Mitwohnzentrale Korn** (Lerchenstr. 72, tel. 0711/221392) for a possible short-term sublet. The office is open weekdays 10–6, Saturday 10–noon.

Gästehaus Garni Eckel. The rooms here are not aesthetically appealing, but at least they're clean, and the surrounding neighborhood is pleasantly quiet. Singles are DM 65–DM 71, doubles DM 81–DM 101. *Vorsteigstr. 10, tel. 0711/290995, fax 0711/223–8123. Tram 2 or Bus 40 to Hölderlinpl., walk up Zeppelinstr., left on Vorsteigstr. 15 rooms, some with bath.*

Hotel-Restaurant Lamm. Simply put: basic, clean, and nicely located near a U-Bahn station and Rosensteinpark. Singles start at DM 65, doubles at DM 110. *Karl-Schurz-Str. 7, tel. 0711/262–2354, fax 0711/262–2374. U14 to Mineralbäder; follow path to Karl-Schurz-Str. 15 rooms, none with bath.*

Museumstube. This small hotel a few blocks west of Schloßplatz is one of the best values in town. The amiable proprietors can set you up in a clean, simply decorated single starting at DM 63; doubles are DM 98. *Hospitalstr. 9, tel. 0711/296810. From Hauptbahnhof, walk up Lautenschlagerstr. (which turns into Theodor-Heuss-Str.), right on Büchsenstr., left on Hospitalstr. 11 rooms, some with bath.*

HOSTELS • **Jugendgästehaus Stuttgart.** This pretty, older building with a shady garden should be your first choice. The impeccable rooms, pleasant atmosphere, and convenient location make this the best budget lodging in Stuttgart. The rules here are relaxed, and the staff is amazingly friendly. Beds in singles, doubles, and three-bed rooms cost DM 40 (DM 45 for single-night stays). *Richard-Wagner-Str. 2, tel. 0711/241132, fax 0711/236–1110. Tram 15 (direction: Heumaden) to Bubenbad; hotel is on corner in front of stop. 100 beds, some rooms with bath. No curfew. Best to call ahead to ask about availability. Checkout 10 AM. Key deposit (DM 20), laundry (DM 2).*

Jugendherberge (HI). This typical youth hostel has a great view over the city. Dorm beds go for DM 23 in a six-bed room, DM 28 for those over 26. *Haußmannstr. 27 (enter at Werastr. and Kernerstr.), tel. 0711/241583, fax 0711/236–1041. Tram 15 (direction: Heumaden) to Eugenspl.; down Kernerstr., right onto Werastr., up stairs on right. 240 beds. Curfew 11:30 (though they open the door for slowpokes again at 1 AM), lockout 9–noon. Reception open noon–11.*

CAMPING • **Cannstatter Wasen.** The closest campground to Stuttgart is along the Neckar River in the suburb of Bad Cannstatt, about 15 min east of the city center. This is definitely city camping—you'll share space with loads of RVs and groups of homeless permacampers. Women staying alone should be on the alert. Campsites are DM 8 per person, DM 6–DM 8 per tent, depending on size, and DM 4 per car. *Mercedesstr. 40, tel. 0711/556696. S1, S2, or S3 to Bad Cannstatt Bahnhof; walk across parking lot toward Neckar, follow signs to Cannstatter Wasen. Free showers. Laundry DM 8 per load, DM 5 for a spin in the dryer.*

Tramper Point. The brainchild of Stuttgart's tourist board, this canopied shelter is meant to help young international travelers (you must be 16–27 to stay here) meet one another. The site, a 15-min tram ride from central Stuttgart to suburban Feuerbach, has a great reputation as a safe and fun place. A spot on the floor, an insulated pad, and a shower cost DM 10 (add DM 1 for a wool blanket), and there's a three-night maximum stay. Make use of the cooking facilities and cafeteria. *Wiener Str. 317, tel. 0711/817–7476. U6 (direction: Gerlingen) to Sportpark Feuerbach. Check-in 5 PM–11 PM. Closed Sept.–late June.*

FOOD

Many cafés and bars in Stuttgart offer reasonably priced fare. If you're looking for something quick and cheap, head to the **Königstraße** pedestrian zone and keep your eyes peeled for Imbiß stands. For a more diverse selection, wander a block or two off Königstraße. If you're going the bread-and-cheese route, check out the enormous **Markthalle** (btw. Marktpl. and Karlspl.), an indoor market with vendors hawking everything from fruits and vegetables to prepared salads, exotic meats, and freshly baked bread. It's open weekdays 7–6, Saturday 7–2, and the streets around it teem with restaurants offering lunch specials. Sing the joys of groceries in the basement of the **Kaufhalle** department store, at Königstraße 19.

König X. This bakery-café prides itself on serving fresh, delicious food made from organic produce. It's best to come for lunch, when specials run DM 13–DM 18. The salads are great, the pastries divine. *Esslinger Str. 22, tel. 0711/232364. Open daily.*

Litfass bei Ali. Try Swabian or Turkish dishes while jammin' to a reggae beat at this student hangout. Word has it that the *Käsespätzle* (cheese noodles) are the best in town. Food is served until 4 AM, but after 11 most people come for the drinks. On weekends local bands play everything but the kitchen sink. *Eberhardstr. 37, in Schwaben-Zentrum, tel. 0711/243031. Open daily.*

Max and Moritz. M&M is one of the many good, cheap pizzerias in Stuttgart. Grab a cheesy pie for DM 10–DM 15 or sit outside and display your pasta twirling techniques to admiring pedestrians. *Geißstr. 3–5, tel. 0711/2364875. From Schloßpl., south on Königstr., left on Fritz-Elsas-Str., left on Steinstr., right on Geißstr. Open daily.*

CAFÉS • Café Stella (Hauptstätterstr. 57, tel. 0711/640–2583) is a comfortable and popular joint that serves bistro munchies. **Bei Jan** (Am Schloßpl. 2, tel. 0711/226–4149) makes coffee for the artsy musician set. Germany's largest gay magazine, *Magnus,* named **Café Jenseitz** (Bebelstr. 25, tel. 0711/631303) the second-best gay café in all of Germany. Jenseitz is also well known for its breakfasts (DM 5.50–DM 14.50).

WORTH SEEING

SCHLOßPLATZ • Postwar plans to turn Stuttgart into an ultramodern German city were countered with more conservative calls to rebuild from the blueprints of the past. The area around the Schloßplatz—crowned by the **Jubiläumssäule** tower and bordered by the enormous Baroque government offices of the **Neues Schloß**—is an excellent example of concessions made to both sides. Squaring off from across Königstraße is the modern, neoclassical-style stock exchange and shopping arcade, Königsbau, along with its brand-new neighbor, the modern Kleiner Schloßplatz. To the north, two contemporary art museums, the **Württembergischer Kunstverein** and the **Galerie der Stadt Stuttgart** (tel. 0711/216–2188; DM 8), are housed in the 20th-century Kunstgebäude. To the south is the bastion of Stuttgart's past, the **Altes Schloß,** which stonily guards the Württemberg crown jewels and other historical artifacts within the Württembergisches Landesmuseum (tel. 0711/279–3400; admission free). Next door is the late-Gothic **Stiftskirche,** home to a fabulous Renaissance sculpture of the Württemberg nobility, and **Schillerplatz,** dedicated to the famous poet-dramatist-philosopher Friedrich Schiller, who was born in nearby Marbach. Classical music concerts are held here every summer, competing with the modern music of buskers on the **Freie Treppe** (Open Stairs) on nearby Kleiner Schloßplatz.

LINDEN-MUSEUM • This surprisingly good anthropology museum has displays on many non-European cultures. Highlights include collections of African and Islamic art and artifacts. *Hegelpl. 1, near university, tel. 0711/202–2456. Bus 40, 42, or 43 to Hegelpl. Admission free. Open Tues., Thurs., weekends 10–5, Wed. 10–8, Fri. 10–1.*

MERCEDES-BENZ MUSEUM • On the factory grounds east of the city center, this homage to Mercedes-Benz (read: car propaganda) traces the history of the automobile as well as the development of ship and plane engines. Benz classics are also on display. Don't leave without the "You Need a Mercedes" promotional brochure. *Mercedesstr. 136, tel. 0711/172–2578. S1 (direction: Plochingen) to Neckarstadion. Admission free. Open Tues.–Sun. 9–5.*

PORSCHE MUSEUM • Porsche offers a car-museum experience similar to that of Mercedes-Benz, focusing on their sports models. It's for true, devoted auto buffs only, or those broke enough to appreciate a freebie. *Porschestr. 42, tel. 0711/9110. S6 (direction: Weil der Stadt) to Zuffenhausen. Admission free. Open weekdays 9–4, weekends 9–5.*

SCHWÄBISCHES BRAUEREIMUSEUM • This is a mellow spot to learn about the history of beer from Mesopotamian times to the present. You'll also find displays on the production of beer from the hop-and-malt harvest to bottling, plus a German-language exhibit on the religious aspects of beer.

Unfortunately, tastings aren't free, but you can stop in for a quaff at the brewery's *Lokal* (bar). *Robert-Koch-Str. 12, tel. 0711/737–7899. U1, U3, U6, or S1 to Vaihingen; walk down Vollmoellerstr., left on Robert-Koch-Str. Admission free. Open Thurs.–Sat. 10:30–5:30.*

STAATSGALERIE • Don't miss this impressive art museum, one of Germany's finest, housed in two connected buildings. The old wing contains paintings from the Middle Ages to the 19th century, including works by Rembrandt, Cézanne, and Manet. The new building, designed by famed British architect James Stirling, will make you feel like you're in a Lego fantasy world. Its galleries hold the largest Picasso collection in Germany and display creations by artists like Dalí, Dix, Kandinsky, Klee, and Mondrian. *Konrad-Adenauer-Str. 30–32, tel. 0711/212–4050. S- or U-Bahn to Staatsgalerie. Admission to the permanent collection free; special exhibition prices vary. Open Tues.–Sun 11–7.*

CHEAP THRILLS

For a beautiful view of the city, bring your binoculars and DM 5 (DM 3 students) to Stuttgart's pride and joy, the **Fernsehturm** (TV tower). Take Tram 15 (direction: Heumaden) to Ruhbank. Every Saturday, Karlsplatz (just east of the Altes Schloß) is overrun by a fun, colorful flea market—great for gawking and impulse buys. The "Grüne U" (green U) is a stretch of Schloßplatz full of beautiful lakes, sniffable flowers, and frolic-able lawns as well as museums, a planetarium, a zoo, and a botanical garden. Safety tip: Get your grass-stained self out of the park's southern section by sundown. A better bet on hot summer nights is to join the loafers who gather on the Freie Treppe of Kleiner Schloßplatz to drink beer, talk, and watch street performers.

FESTIVALS

From late September to early October, Stuttgart hosts its annual **Volksfest** in the Cannstatter Wasen fairgrounds (S1, S2, or S3 to Bad Cannstatt) along the Neckar River. You'll find rides, carnival games, cheap food, and gallons upon gallons of beer. Wine drinkers should head to the **Stuttgarter Weindorf,** a nationally famous wine festival held from the last Friday in August until the first Sunday in September. Stuttgart's **Weihnachtsmarkt,** held between the Marktplatz and Schillerplatz, is one of the country's oldest and largest Christmas fairs. In the spring it starts all over again with the **Frühlingsfest,** at the fairgrounds. The festival features an extensive and varied music program and, of course, plenty to drink.

AFTER DARK

Across the street from the Staatsgalerie (*see* Worth Seeing, *above*) is Stuttgart's famous **Staatstheater** (Oberer Schloßgarten, tel. 0711/221795), a complex of theaters that host ballet, opera, and plays. Listings and tickets are available at the tourist office, where you can also get info about the city's smaller theaters. For info in German about events and nightlife, pick up a copy of *Lift* magazine (DM 4.50) at any newsstand. Stuttgart doesn't get really interesting until 11 PM or so, but the impatient can start pub-crawling early at restaurant/bars like Litfass bei Ali (*see* Food, *above*). On summer evenings, sidewalk cafés and restaurants on Calwer Straße and around Steinstraße buzz with activity.

BARS • Amadeus. This ever-popular café-bar occupies a former orphanage, but you'll feel right at home inside or in the courtyard beer garden, where you can kick back and relax amongst an incongruous mix of button-downs and T-shirts. They also serve good affordable grub. *Charlottenpl. 17, tel. 0711/292678. From Schloßpl., follow Planie SE to Charlottenpl. Open daily.*

Octave. This slightly upscale, beige-and-black bar welcomes visitors to join in on mellow jam sessions—instruments provided by the house. *Eberhardstr. 49, tel. 0711/245545. Open Mon.–Sat. 6 PM–3 AM.*

Palast der Republik. This is the "in" meeting place for the artsy, black-and-leather-clad set, who crowd around the small bar and the few outside tables until the wee hours. Grab a brew or head next door to **Zum Zum Imbiß** for cheap eats. *Friedrichstr. 27, tel. 0711/226–4887. From Bahnhof, south on Lautenschlagerstr. to Friedrichstr. Open daily.*

CLUBS • Altes Schützenhaus. Out in the woodsy suburb of Heslach is Stuttgart's best beer garden (on weekdays); on weekends it also hosts a club beloved by a slightly wild twentysomething crowd. *Burgstallstr. 99, tel. 0711/649–8157. U14 to Heslach. Club cover: DM 5. Open daily. Club opens 9 PM.*

King's Club plays techno-pop and dance-floor hits for a predominantly gay male clientele. Sundays are women-only. *Calwer Str. 21, at Lange Str., tel. 0711/224558. Open Mon.–Sat.*

Perkin's Park. Stuttgart's young, well-heeled set boogies here on weekends, though anyone who's someone comes on Thursday. Groove through two big dance rooms or grab a seat for some late-night food. *Stresemannstr. 39, tel. 0711/256–0062. U7 to Killesberg Messe, back to Stresemannstr., left into park. Cover: DM 8–DM 10. Open Wed.–Sun.*

NEAR STUTTGART

ESSLINGEN

Esslingen's rich history dates from Roman times, and until the late 19th century it rivaled Stuttgart as an industrial powerhouse. Modern-day Esslingen, however, is simply an extension of Stuttgart's industrial sprawl. Luckily, the town's historic Altstadt is bordered by steep, vineyard-carpeted hills that block out the high-tech production facilities, creating a medieval oasis that sharply contrasts with Stuttgart's metropolitan wasteland. Consider a stay if you're looking for some peace and quiet, or a quick detour out of the city. To reach Esslingen from Stuttgart's Hauptbahnhof, take S1 (20 min, DM 4.20).

From the Hauptbahnhof, head northeast on Bahnhofstraße, cross the canal via the Agnesbrücke, and veer right to the **Marktplatz.** Dominating the square is the **Stadtkirche St. Dionys,** a Romanesque church whose two towers were connected so that lookouts could better detect approaching enemies. The **tourist office** (Marktpl. 16, tel. 0711/351–23177; open weekdays) can book you a room and give you a list of local Besenwirtschaften (*see box,* Garage Wine, *above*). They'll also outfit you with a map and a *Wanderkarte* (trail map) of the surrounding countryside. During the first weekend of August, the Marktplatz is also the site of Esslingen's annual **Zwiebelfest,** an onion extravaganza where you can savor every oniony entrée imaginable and still be socially acceptable. Maybe the wine makes everyone immune. On the square adjacent to the Marktplatz is the **Altes Rathaus** (old city hall), whose peach-colored Renaissance facade is adorned with an astronomical clock and a Glockenspiel. Try to be here at the top of the hour, when the Glockenspiel plays a groovy tune from its repertoire of over 200 melodies. A small alley on the east side of the Altes Rathaus leads to the café-lined **Hafenmarkt**; its most infamous building is a medieval brothel known as the **Gelbes Haus** (Yellow House), closed since 1701.

North of the Marktplatz across Augustinerstraße is the Gothic **Frauenkirche,** which contains some beautiful 14th-century stained-glass windows. East of the church, a covered pathway leads up to the ruins of the **Burg,** which once served as part of Esslingen's defenses. The fortress walls protect a grassy courtyard used for festivals and as an outdoor cinema in summer; the view of the town, the Neckar Valley, and the Schwäbische Alb (*see* Near Tübingen, *below*) in the distance make the steep climb worthwhile.

WHERE TO SLEEP AND EAT

The boxy **HI-Jugendherberge** (Neuffenstr. 65, tel. 0711/381848) has beds for DM 20 (DM 25 over 26) as well as views of the town below. From the Bahnhof, take Bus 118 to Zollbergstraße, turn around and head up Zollbergstraße, and turn left onto Neuffenstraße. Reception is open from 3:30 to 5, from 6:30 to 7:30, and again from 8:30 to 9:45. For a DM 20 deposit you'll get a key that lets you come home after the 10 PM curfew. Esslingen's best lodging options are the eight private rooms—some with castle views—offered by the very friendly **Herr Daniel Jaklitsch** (Untere Beutau 29, tel. 0711/352083). Spotless rooms with TV, plus nice bathrooms and kitchen access on every floor, go for DM 35–DM 40 per person. Dark, cozy **Weinstube Einhorn** (Heug. 17, tel. 0711/353590), east of the Altes Rathaus, is a good choice for hearty Swabian fare; open daily. Don't miss **Burgschenke** (Auf der Burg, tel. 0711/355558), a bar and beer garden tucked away behind the main section of the fortress.

SCHWÄBISCH HALL

Hall means "place of salt" in German, a fitting description of the town that dominated southern Germany's salt trade for about 700 years. The moniker does not, however, belie the town's sylvan setting, nestled amidst rolling hills in the Schwäbisch-Fränkischer Wald (Swabian-Franconian forest). Salt money did build the picture-perfect town and its magnificent Marktplatz, lined with stately facades. The architecture itself draws many a day-tripper, but in summer, guests stay past sunset to see the famous **Freilichtspiele,** a series of usually classic plays (Goethe, Shakespeare) performed on the steps of **St. Michael's,** the church that dominates the square. Ask about student tickets at the ticket office in the Markt's Rathaus.

If you follow the path along the Kocher River toward Steinbach and through the city park (about 3 km), you'll be rewarded not only by the lovely surroundings but also by an excellent view of the imposing **Klosterburg Gross Comburg.** You can climb to this awesome fortress-monastery via a statue-lined trail starting at the south end of the river path. Allow at least six hours for the excursion.

BASICS

Trains arrive frequently from Stuttgart (2 hrs, DM 27) and Heilbronn (45 min, DM 13.50). From the Hauptbahnhof, head down the steps of the path marked FUßGÄNGER ZUR INNENSTADT to Bahnhofstraße, cross the two bridges (Theatersteg and Epinalbrücke) over the Kocher River, and walk north toward the Marktplatz. You're on the right track as long as you're heading toward the **clock tower** that dominates the skyline. Pick up a detailed city map for DM 1 at the **tourist office** (Marktpl. 9, tel. 0791/751246), on the north side of the square. They'll also help you find lodging (no fee) weekdays 9–6, Saturday 10–3 (shorter hrs off-season).

WHERE TO SLEEP

Gästehaus Sölch (Hauffstr. 14, tel. 0791/51807), a friendly hotel with its own bakery, has singles for DM 65 and doubles for DM 105. It's south of the train station; from the back of the station, head south on Tullauer Straße, right on Hagerweg, left on Laccornweg, right on Hauffstraße. In the hills above town, the spotless **HI-Jugendherberge** (Langenfelder Weg 5, tel. 0791/41050, fax 0791/0791–47998; reception open 5 PM–9 PM) charges DM 23 (DM 28 over 26), plus DM 5.50 for clean sheets. It's a 20-min hike from the Hauptbahnhof—call ahead. From behind the Marktplatz, turn right up Crailsheimer Straße, left on Ziegeleiweg, and left on Langenfelder Weg. On the banks of the Kocher about 3 km south of town, **Camping Steinbach** (tel. 0791/2984; closed mid-Oct.–Mar.) has spots for DM 7 per person, DM 9 per tent. From the train station, head south down Steinbacher Straße, cross the Steinbacher Brücke, and go right between the arms of the river.

TÜBINGEN

Tübingen, on a stretch of the Neckar River lined with weeping willows, has enough beautiful old buildings to make you feel like you've been transported back in time. Tübingen's history is proudly linked with its place in German letters: Three of the city's most famous residents, philosophers Hegel and Schelling and poet Hölderlin, were roommates while studying at the Protestant *Stift.* Today, the dress and speech of the current university students (one third of Tübingen's 75,000 residents) will jolt you back to the 20th century. Add a thriving nightlife and a great setting for outdoor adventures and you've got the recipe for one of the most inviting university towns in Germany.

BASICS

CHANGING MONEY • Citibank (tel. 07071/91750) has a 24-hour ATM that accepts Cirrus, Visa, and MasterCard. They also change money here, but after 4 PM try the main tourist office (*see below*) instead.

MAIL AND PHONES • The **main post office** (Europapl. 2), around the corner from the train station, holds poste restante, changes money, has international phone facilities, and performs the usual postal services.

VISITOR INFORMATION • On the south side of the bridge between the train station and the Altstadt, the **main tourist office** exchanges money, books rooms (fee according to price of room), and sells city maps (DM 1) in English that outline a walking tour. A branch office at Haaggasse 1, off the Marktplatz, can help you Sundays 2–5. *Main office: An der Neckarbrücke, tel. 07071/91360, fax 07071/35070. Open weekdays 9–7, Sat. 9–5. In summer, Sun. 2–5.*

COMING AND GOING

Trains connect Tübingen with Stuttgart (1 hr, DM 16.20), the Nagold Valley (via Horb, 25 min, DM 9.80), and most Black Forest destinations. The Hauptbahnhof has plenty of lockers. **Buses** to the Schwäbische Alb and Nagold Valley towns like Haigerloch (daily, 1 hr, DM 8.80), Horb (4–5 per day, 1¼ hrs, DM 7.80), and Freudenstadt (twice daily, 2 hrs, DM 15.40) depart from the **Busbahnhof,** in front of the Hauptbahnhof. Obtain necessary bus info weekdays 7 AM–8 PM at the customer service office (tel. 07071/19449) in the western corner of the train station.

The official **Mitfahrzentrale** (Münzgasse 6, tel. 07071/26789 or 07071/5081) is about five blocks west of the Marktplatz and is open weekdays 9–7, Saturday and Sunday 11–5.

GETTING AROUND

From the Hauptbahnhof, veer right to Karlstraße, then left across the bridge—to your left is the old section of town, where you'll find most of the action. Two km farther ahead is the university. You can get around the Altstadt by sneaker, but the bus system is a necessity if you're staying outside the city. Single rides cost DM 2.80. You can also buy a book of 10 tickets for DM 21. Saturday nights and Sunday mornings the buses are tricky; you have to call the bus company 30 min in advance. If you see the word *Anmeldefahrt* printed on the schedule, call the number posted on the schedule. For night owls, there's also **Night-SAM** (tel. 07071/360808), a group taxi/bus with eight different routes around the city from midnight to 3 AM.

WHERE TO SLEEP

Lodging in Tübingen is scarce and expensive, and the cheap options in the suburbs are inconvenient, but be prepared to stay on the outskirts if you're not hosteling it. The fairly upscale and romantic **Hotel Am Schloß** (Burgsteige 18, tel. 07071/92940, fax 07071/929410), in the Altstadt just below the gates of the Schloß, has singles starting at DM 45 and doubles for DM 95. Visa and MasterCard are accepted. A mere five-min bus ride from the train station, **Gasthaus zum Löwen** (Kingersheimer Str. 18, tel. 07071/791085, fax 07071/78630) is a friendly neighborhood inn in Hirschau. Aesthetically pleasing and comfortable rooms (no linoleum in sight, great showers) start at DM 45 single, DM 70 double. Take Bus 18 (from Stand 2) from the Omnibusbahnhof to Hirschau; the hotel is just ahead on the right. On the north bank of the river, west of the Altstadt, is **Camping am Neckar** (Rappenberghalde 61, tel. 07071/43145, fax 07071/35070; closed Nov.–Apr.), which charges DM 9.50 per person, DM 5.50 per tent and DM 4 per car. Be prepared for the "environmental fee" of DM 3. From the Hauptbahnhof, take Bus 9 (direction: Spitzberg) to the end of the line, or walk 20 min from the town center.

HOSTELS • Along the Neckar and a five-min walk from the Altstadt, the ancient and often full **HI-Jugendherberge** offers creaky beds for DM 23 (DM 28 over 26) along with lockers and laundry facilities. Not just anyone can get a door key (deposit DM 30) to circumnavigate the 11 PM curfew; impress them by calling ahead for your bunk. *Gartenstr. 22/2, tel. 07071/23002, fax 07071/25061. From Hauptbahnhof, cross bridge and take first right, or catch Bus 11 to Jugendherberge. 211 beds. Reception open 5 PM–8 PM.*

FOOD

If you've had one too many wieners lately, don't worry—Tübingen is a vegetarian heaven. A refreshing twist on meat-free meals comes from **Maharaja Imbiß** (Schleifmühlew. 15, tel. 07071/45428), housed in an Indian store west of Haagtor. They serve authentic South Asian dishes at low prices Monday–Saturday 11–6:30 (until 4 in summer). For cheap groceries head to the **Plus** market on Lange Gasse, just north of the Stiftskirche.

Marquadtei. At this student-run hangout north of the Altstadt, the music is loud, the staff smokes, and the food—pizza for DM 8–DM 14.50 along with a wide array of meat and veggie dishes—is generally tasty. *Herrenberger Str. 34, tel. 07071/43386. Open daily.*

Neckarmüllerei. This microbrewery serves southern German food and meter-long beers (gulp!). The attached beer garden sits on the banks of the Neckar, making it a popular summer hangout. Occassionally there's live music. *Gartenstr. 4, at Eberhardsbrücke, tel. 07071/27848. Open daily.*

CAFÉS • Like any self-respecting university town, Tübingen has a plethora of groovy cafés. Two prime student hangouts are the mellow **La Bohème** (Nauklerstr. 22, tel. 07071/27440), open weekdays 10 AM–midnight, weekends 7 PM–midnight, and the see-and-be-seen **Piccolo Sole d'Oro** (Metzgergasse 39, tel. 07071/52837), open daily in summer 8 AM–10 PM, until 8 in winter. You can dig the neoclassical-ish interior at **Tangente Jour** (Münzgasse 17, tel. 07071/24572) Monday–Saturday 9 AM–1 AM, Sundays 11 AM–1 AM. The hippest café award goes to **Café Haag** (Am Haagtor 1, tel. 07071/21225), which attracts a large, lively crowd with its tasty food and drinks. It's open weekdays 4 PM–1 AM, weekends noon–1 AM.

WORTH SEEING

HOLZMARKT • On the eastern end of the Altstadt, Holzmarkt is dominated by the late-Gothic **Stiftskirche** (open daily 9–5ish). Inside you can browse around the choir, decorated with stone statues of Württemberg's rulers. Climb the tower for a view of the city's red-tiled roofs and the murky brown waters of the Neckar. Admission to the church is free, but you'll pay DM 2 (DM 1 students) to see the choir and tower.

The original buildings of the university, founded in 1477, are on Münzgasse, just off Holzmarkt. You can visit that amusing relic found in any old German university town, the **Studentenkarzer,** at Münzgasse

20. Tours (DM 1) happen weekends at 2 PM. The **Hölderlinturm,** on the bank of the river behind Holzmarkt, was home to underappreciated local poet Friedrich Hölderlin during his last 36 years of mental illness; it now houses a museum dedicated to him. To get every last gory detail, take the guided tour (DM 3, DM 2 students) weekends at 5 PM; call ahead to arrange for a tour in English. *Bursag. 6, tel. 07071/22040. Admission: DM 3, DM 2 students. Open Tues.–Fri. 10–noon and 3–5, weekends 2–5.*

MARKTPLATZ • Connected to Holzmarkt by Kirchgasse, Tübingen's central square is filled with half-timbered buildings and anchored by a fountain of Neptune. The real eye-catcher on the Marktplatz is the gabled **Rathaus,** built in 1435. The building is decorated with late-19th–century murals depicting various allegorical figures; university founder Duke Eberhard is the large, bearded guy off-center on the third story. From behind the Rathaus, follow the SCHLOß signs to the **Burgsteig,** one of the oldest and steepest streets in town. At the top, you get a good view of the Neckar Valley. Pass through the gate (open 7:30 AM–8 PM) for a peek at the 16th-century **Schloß Hohentübingen,** now used by the university. The fortress's overgrown walls make a great spot for a bottle of wine at sunset.

North of the Marktplatz is the giant half-timbered Kornhaus, home to the **Stadtmuseum.** The best display here is the pictorial history of Tübingen, which concentrates on the rise of the Nazis and the student uprisings in the late 1960s. *Kornhausstr. 10, tel. 07071/945460. Admission: DM 3. Open Tues.–Sat. 3–6, Sun. 11–1 and 3–6.*

NATURPARK SCHÖNBUCH • One of Tübingen's most unique and appealing attractions, the well-preserved **Bebenhausen Kloster und Jagdschloß** is set in the rolling green hills of Naturpark Schönbuch, about 5 km north of the city center—be sure to include a picnic and hike in your visit. Occupied by Cistercian monks from 1190 until the Reformation, the cloister is now a mix of Gothic, Romanesque, and Baroque styles. The Jagdschloß (Hunting Castle), originally part of the monastery, was the retreat of the dukes of Württemberg and offers a glimpse into their private world. Admission is by guided tour only and costs DM 4; DM 6 gets you into the cloister and the castle. *Tel. 07071/602180. From Hauptbahnhof, Bus 7955 or 7600 to Waldhorn. Kloster open Tues.–Fri. 8:30–noon and 1:30–5, weekends 9:30–noon and 1:30–5; Jagdschloß tours at 10, 11, 2, 3, and 4.*

AFTER DARK

The Altstadt is speckled with bars and cafés—you can't go wrong on or near the Marktplatz. For traditional Tübingen, relax under the wood beams in **Boulanger** (Collegiumsgasse 2, tel. 07071/23345), one of the oldest establishments in town. Legend holds that Hegel has an unpaid bar tab here. Another spot to check out is the bar/café **H A U P T Bahnhof** (in the train station, tel 07071/31816). Though Bahnhof bars are usually strictly for *Penner* (you know, those lurkers/bums who seem to have one hand permanently attached to a Pils), Tübingen's is the hip exception.

Arsenal. On Thursday nights this always cool film house and café/bar is popular with the gay male crowd, but everyone is welcome. Films sometimes play here in their original language. *Hintere-Grabenstr. 33, tel. 07071/51073. From St. Johannes Kirche, north on Lange Gasse, right on Hintere-Grabenstr. Open daily.*

Blauer Salon. Technically only for residents of this co-op and their guests, this quirky, punky place has five house bands that play when the mood strikes. The beer is all in bottles, but what do you want for DM 3? *Münzgasse 13, no phone. From Am Markt, Wienergasse south, left on Münzg. Open Sun.–Fri.*

Pfauen. This lively, packed bar is a Tübingen favorite. The noise from the spirited crowd may deafen, but this is the place to mingle with locals. *Kornhausstr. 1, tel. 07071/23095. From Am Markt, down Marktgasse, left on Kornhausstr. Open daily.*

Zentrum Zoo. Tübingen's best-known disco plays a variety of danceable tunes and has regular theme nights featuring African, funk, and '70s/'80s. *Schleifmühleweg 86, tel. 07071/42048. From Markt, take Haagg. through Vor dem Haagtor to Schleifmühlew. Cover: DM 8. Open Tues., Thurs.–Sat. 9 PM–2 AM, Sun. 8:30 PM–1 AM.*

OUTDOOR ACTIVITIES

On sunny days students gather in the grassy park between the Altstadt and the university to read, study, chat, picnic, and tan. Rent a bike at the **Radlager** (Lazerettgasse 19, tel. 07071/551651) for about DM 15 per day, and ride east along the bike path on the south side of the Neckar 10 km downstream to Lake Kirchentellinsfurt. Another typical Tübingen activity is **boating** on the Neckar; if you're a do-it-yourselfer, you can rent a rowboat from April 15 to September at the booth marked BOOTSVERMIETUNG (tel. 07071/31529) next to the tourist office. For a more relaxing and unique experience, take a ride in a **Stocherkahn** (similar to a Venetian gondola) for about DM 6 per person per hour (Hölderlinturm, tel. 07071/35011).

NEAR TÜBINGEN

SCHWÄBISCHE ALB

East of the Black Forest and north of the Bodensee lies the vast, sparsely populated region known as the Schwäbische Alb (Swabian Jura). Characterized by forested limestone plateaus and grassy flatlands, the region is frequently denigrated as aesthetically inferior to other, much more heavily touristed areas nearby. But the Schwäbische Alb's small towns and peaceful walking trails, along with the lack of tourists, make for a mellow off-the-beaten-track adventure. The main drawback is the lack of transportation. Major rail lines connecting Stuttgart to Konstanz and Friedrichshafen run along the border of the Schwäbische Alb, but only a few smaller lines run through the heart of the region. Buses pick up some of the slack but aren't always that frequent. If you've got the time and energy, grab a trail map at any decent-sized bookshop or tourist office and explore the area on foot.

HAIGERLOCH

It's worth the trouble it takes to reach the tiny, tranquil town of Haigerloch, nestled on and around a steep ridge beside the Eyach River. If communing with nature is what you have in mind, Haigerloch makes a great base for exploring the surrounding countryside. Don't overlook the town itself, though: It's the kind of untouched medieval German village visitors long for. From the central **Marktplatz,** look up across the river to the **Römerturm,** the sole remains of the first fortress built here around 1100. Its title is a misnomer, but only in the 19th century did someone finally figure out that it wasn't truly left over from the Romans. Just to the right of the Marktplatz, **St. Nikolaus** plays Gothic grandfather to the **Schloßkirche,** reached via the long staircase that climbs from the Marktplatz to the **Schloß.** The Schloßkirche's sugar daddy, Joseph Friedrich von Hohenzollern, gave the church a Baroque makeover in 1750 and (literally) left his heart here when he passed on.

In the Oberstadt, across the Eyach and to the right of the Römerturm, is the rococo **St. Anna Wallfahrtskirche,** also built by Joseph Friedrich. Through the old Jewish ghetto near the Römerturm lies the **Jüdischer Friedhof** (Jewish Cemetery). Hidden away in an old *Bierkeller* hewn from the rock beneath the Schloß is the **Atomkeller Museum** (tel. 07474/697–2627; open May–Sept., daily 10–noon and 2–5), on the site where members of Dr. Heisenberg's Berlin group worked feverishly on atomic research during the final years of World War II.

BASICS • The only direct **bus** between Haigerloch and Tübingen (1 hr, DM 9) leaves in the early afternoon. Otherwise, Bus 7623 runs about twice daily to Rottenburg with connections to Tübingen (1 hr, DM 10). Bus 10 runs several times a day to Horb (1½ hrs, DM 8) with connections to Rottweil, Tübingen, and Stuttgart. Buses leave from the Marktplatz, Schulzentrum/Unterstadt, and several stops on Oberstadtstraße. The **tourist office** (Oberstadtstr. 11, in the Rathaus, tel. 07474/69726), open Monday–Thursday 8–noon and 2–4, Friday 8–noon, has the scoop on transportation and outdoor fun. Lay your aching bones in one of **Gasthof Krone**'s (Oberstadtstr. 47, tel. 07474/95440) immaculate rooms for DM 55–DM 65 (singles) or DM 100–DM 120 (doubles), including breakfast.

ROTTWEIL

Rottweil perches above the Neckar Valley, marking the transition from Black Forest to Alb. The oldest town in Baden-Württemberg and the origin of that loveable pooch, Rottweil has been one of southern Germany's most important crossroads since the 1st century AD. Rottweil is definitely a place for the history buff, if not the dog lover, but once a year, any fool will feel at home here during **Fastnet** (late February or early March), when residents don garish wooden masks, parade through the streets, and generally whoop it up as part of an age-old Allemanic ritual to scare away winter. The Rottweil version is famous and quite worth a stop. To reach town from the **Hauptbahnhof,** turn right, gather your strength, and trudge up steep Bahnhofstraße for about 20 min. At the top, turn right and cross the 12th-century **Hochbrücke** (High Bridge). You'll find yourself on Rottweil's main east–west thoroughfare, Hochbrücktorstraße, which leads to Hauptstraße, the major north–south road. Late-Renaissance and Baroque houses—marked by colorful carvings and occasional murals—cram both streets.

The Gothic **Kapellenkirche,** at the south end of Hauptstraße, was meant to provide the Altstadt with a central monument, but the results were less than impressive, largely because plans to heighten the tower were never realized. For a look at the carvings that once adorned the Kapellenkirche's tower, as well as other stone statues and Renaissance fountains, head down Hauptstraße and turn left on Lorenzgasse to the **Lorenzkapelle** (Lorenzgasse 17; admission DM 1; closed Mon.). For a nice view of the valley, head to the left of the Lorenzkapelle into the adjacent park, home to a section of the city wall and the **Pulverturm,** one of its original lookout towers. The **Dominikaner Museum** (Am Kriegsdamm, tel. 0741/7862; admission DM 3), in a modern building directly uphill from the Pulverturm, holds treasures from excavations of the town's original Roman settlement, known as Arae Flaviae. The displays give a fascinating glimpse into life in the imperial outpost. One highlight is a colorful mosaic, with what's ostensibly a Rottweil doggie depicted in the right corner.

The Romans had impressive salt-water baths here in their day; the visitor to Rottweil today can partake of that tradition, as long as she doesn't mind seeing lots of flabby German skin. **Aquasol,** Rottweil's awesome indoor-outdoor (in summer) swimming complex, offers hot, cold, and salt-water pools, a water slide, a Jacuzzi, and a sauna. It's the perfect antidote to church-and-museum overload. *Brugger Str. 11, tel. 0741/27070. From Marktbrunnen on Hauptstr., go west on Hochbrücktorstr., right on Stadionstr., right on Brugger Str. (20 min total). Admission: DM 4.50 for one hour; DM 13 for the day. Open Mon. 1–10, Tues.–Sun. 10–10.*

Rottweil's **Stadtmuseum** (Hauptstr. 20, tel. 0741/494256; closed Mon., admission DM 1), housed in the Baroque Herder'sches Haus on the upper half of Hauptstraße, is worth a look for a model of the city in all its glory circa 1560. There's also a room containing some outlandish masks that locals wear every year during Fastnet.

Once upon a time, when much of Europe was covered by the sea, the elevated Alb was home to corals and other creatures. Their remains helped form the region's unique, limestone-laden karst topography you'll see today.

BASICS

Rottweil is a frequent stop on the rail line between Stuttgart (1½ hrs, DM 28) and Konstanz (1¼ hrs, DM 28). **Trains** to Horb (30 min, DM 12), Neustadt (1¼ hrs, DM 20), and Villingen (25 min, DM 8) allow easy access to the Black Forest. Your friendly neighborhood **tourist office** (Hauptstr. 21, tel. 0741/494280; open weekdays 10–6, Sat. and Sun. 10-12; shorter hours and no weekends in winter) has free maps and a guide to the sights in English. If you're spending the night, the cheapest hotel is **Gasthof Goldenes Rad** (Hauptstr. 38, tel. 0741/7412), with singles for DM 37.50 and doubles for DM 70. But the DM 22 beds (DM 27 over 26) at the small and appropriately antique-looking **HI-Jugendherberge** (Lorenzgasse 8, tel. 0741/7664) are the truly budget option. From November 15 to March 15 you can only stay if you've called ahead to arrange it; otherwise, reception is open 5 PM–10 PM, and there's no curfew.

ULM

Back in the Middle Ages, any town that aspired to greatness had a bishop. Unable to muster that wielder of power, Ulmers turned their sights toward heaven, pooled their funds, and built one of Europe's largest Gothic cathedrals. Still dissatisfied, they attached the world's tallest cathedral spire (161 m), thus ensuring inclusion in travel guides for centuries to come. The city's more modern claim to fame is none other than genius, scientist, Nobel Prize winner, and native Ulmer Albert Einstein. The face of Ulm was redefined by Napoleon's declaration that the Danube River would mark the administrative boundary between Bavaria and Württemberg, splitting the city into western and eastern halves. The older and more interesting part of the city, on the Württemberg side of the river, retained the name Ulm. The younger section, officially in Bavaria, took the name of Neu-Ulm.

During World War II, Ulm suffered severe damage from a crushing air raid, but enough historical structures were spared or rebuilt to preserve the architectural charm that so excited the author Hermann Hesse. If you're into churches and historic architecture, then the extravagant *Münster* (cathedral), the *Fischer- und Gerberviertel* (old Fisherman's and Tanner's Quarter), and the many half-timbered houses near the river should invite you to spend a day in this city. Or head off to the spectacularly scenic and uncrowded Danube Valley, just west of Ulm and easily accessible by rail. If you hit town in July, consider sticking around for the **Nabada** festival, held on *Schwörmontag* (Oath Monday), the second to last Monday of the month. The festival commemorates the signing of Ulm's 14th-century constitution and the mayor's oath to be fair to everyone, listen to their concerns, etc., etc. It's a kind of Mardi Gras on water, complete with parade floats on the river and lots of wet revelers.

BASICS

Housed in a disturbingly modern building next to the Münster, the **tourist office** (Münsterpl. 50, tel. 0731/161–2830; open weekdays 9–6, Sat. 9–12:30) provides travel tips, sells phone cards, and books rooms for free. After hours you can buy city maps from the machine outside for DM 1. The **post office,** adjacent to the Hauptbahnhof, has international phone booths and changes money. If you're in the center of town, change money at **Citibank** (Münsterpl. 42, tel. 0731/60999), which has a 24-hour ATM that accepts Visa, MasterCard, and Cirrus.

COMING AND GOING

By **train,** Ulm lies between Munich (1¼ hrs, DM 46) and Stuttgart (1¼ hrs, DM 24). Regular service also runs to Augsburg (1½ hrs, DM 22), Hamburg (7 hrs, DM 245), and Karlsruhe (2 hrs, DM 50). **Buses** leave from the south side of the Hauptbahnhof for all sorts of small nearby towns.

GETTING AROUND

All of Ulm's sights, as well as most of its hotels and restaurants, are near the city center. From the Hauptbahnhof, cross under Friedrich-Ebert-Straße to the main drag, first called Bahnhofstraße and then Hirschstraße, which eventually leads to Münsterplatz, the heart of Ulm. City **buses** and Stadtbahn **trams,** both of which cost DM 2.70 per ride, crisscross the city. You can buy tickets at machines near the stops or onboard the bus or tram. **Mountain bikes** can be rented at Ralf Reich's Fahrradhandlung (Frauenstr. 34, tel. 0731/21179) for DM 15 per day.

WHERE TO SLEEP

Gasthof Rose. Call ahead to get a room in the cheapest guest house near Ulm's center. Singles cost DM 40, doubles DM 80, without shower but with breakfast. *Kasernstr. 42a, tel. 0731/77803. Cross Danube at Herdbrücke into Neu-Ulm, left on Augsburger Str., right on Blumenstr. Reception open 7 AM–10 PM.*

Ulmer Stuben. This hotel-restaurant, decorated in about 18 shades of brown, has clean and spacious rooms. You're not too far from the most attractive part of the city, the Fischer- und Gerberviertel. Singles will run you DM 79, doubles DM 130, triples DM 180, all with shower and bath. *Zinglerstr. 11, tel. 0731/962200, fax 0731/962–2055. From Hauptbahnhof, south on Friedrich-Ebert-Str. and cross Zinglerbrücke. 25 rooms. Reception open 8 AM–11 PM.*

HOSTELS • Geschwister-Scholl-Jugendherberge (HI). Characterless but clean, this hostel is up on a hill and not easily reached. Beds DM 23 (DM 28 over 26). Reception is open 5 PM–9:30 PM. Curfew is 10 PM weeknights but guest keys are available. *Grimmelfinger Weg 45, tel. 0731/384455, fax 0731/384511. From Hauptbahnhof, S1 to Ehinger Tor, then Bus 4 or 9 to Schulzentrum Kuhberg and follow the signs. 144 beds. Lockout 9–noon.*

FOOD

For quick, cheap, and greasy meals, head to Hirschstraße, the main drag, which is lined with fast-food stands. Open-air **markets** are held on Wednesday and Saturday mornings on Münsterplatz, where you'll find the convenient **Kaisers** grocery store (Münsterpl. 43). For tasty (though pricey) traditional grub, try **Eulenspiegel** (Kornhauspl. 2, tel. 0731/66708; closed Sun.), three blocks northeast of the Münster. The **Ulmer Weizenbierhaus** (Kroneng. 22, on Rathauspl., tel. 0731/62496) has been turned inside out: Street signs, facades, and rooftops fill this beer garden and restaurant, open daily. The small menu of inexpensive eats takes a back seat to the beer selection—choose from 45 different brews.

WORTH SEEING

Undoubtedly the most gripping sight in Ulm is the mighty **Münster,** begun in 1377 and not finished until 1890. The cathedral's spire is not only the tallest in the world, but also one of the most intricately carved and beautifully adorned. You can climb the 768 winding steps of the steeple for a good view over Ulm; on a clear day you can see all the way to the Alps. Most people take 30–40 min to reach the apex of the tower, but the record stands at nine min. *Münsterpl. Church admission free; steeple admission DM 4, DM 2.50 students. Open summer, daily 8–7:45; winter, 9–4:45. Tower closes 1 hr before cathedral.*

After you've done the worthwhile tour of the Münster, proceed to Ulm's other treasure, the cobblestone-lined, romantic **Fisher- und Gerberviertel.** Bordered by the Danube and bisected by the much smaller

Blau River, this quarter was traditionally the home of Ulm's many fishermen and tanners; wandering through the narrow streets, you can get a sense of Ulm's rich medieval civic tradition. The crooked narrow lanes are lined with cafés and restaurants, making it the best place to spend an evening.

The **Metzgerturm,** a brick tower with a multicolor tile roof, lies south of the Marktplatz. Although it has been dubbed the "Leaning Tower of Ulm," the tilt is hardly discernible unless you've had a few drinks. Beyond the tower, a stretch of grass along the Danube allows for a good view of some of the remnants of the old city wall. A couple of winding streets west of the Marktplatz, you'll find the dainty pink-and-yellow facade of the **Schwörhaus,** where part of the Schwörmontag festivities take place.

South of the Münster, right on the Marktplatz, is the **Rathaus,** which is decorated with brightly colored frescoes of biblical scenes, medieval battles, and allegorical tales. The eastern facade has a 16th-century astronomical clock. The **Ulmer Museum** (Marktpl. 9, tel. 0731/161–4300) exhibits art from prehistoric to modern times but concentrates on Gothic and Baroque art from Ulm and Upper Swabia. Part of the museum also serves as a large gallery for temporary art exhibits. *Admission: DM 5, DM 3 students. Open Tues.–Sun. 11–5, Thurs. until 8.*

A few blocks northwest of the Münster, the **Deutsches Brotmuseum** details—that's right, folks—the history of bread. It's an interesting museum (honest) and displays are labeled in English. *Salzstadelgasse 10, tel. 0731/69955. Admission: DM 5, DM 3.50 students. Open Tues.–Sun. 10–5.*

After a visit to Haigerloch's atomic museum and the Jewish cemetery, take your pensive self up to "Kapf," a jagged crag adorned with a large wooden cross—just follow the signs from the Schloß.

NEAR ULM

BLAUBEUREN

Tucked into the southern edge of the Schwäbische Alb in a narrow green river valley, the small town of Blaubeuren is known primarily for its geological wonders. First and foremost of these is the **Blautopf,** a rocky pool of achingly clear blue water. The Blautopf is actually the surfacing point of the underground Blau River, filled with trout lively enough to have inspired Schubert's quintet. Unfortunately, swimming is strictly *verboten.* There is something truly enchanting about the Blautopf and its mysterious river; not surprisingly, it has been the subject of reverence and legend for centuries. The Blautopf inspired 19th-century author Eduard Mörike to write a fairy tale about the Lau, a beautiful but bored and lonely water nymph who lived in the spring. She couldn't leave the Blautopf and join her husband in the Danube (her fondest wish) until she laughed five times. The jovial women of Blaubeuren taught her to chuckle, thanks in part to the sometimes silly-sounding Swabian dialect.

Across from the Blautopf is Blaubeuren's other major sight, the **Benediktinerkloster,** an expansive 11th-century cloister that now holds the **Heimatmuseum** (open Apr.–Oct., Tues.–Sun. 10–5). In the cloister's bathhouse, the museum demonstrates what life, or at least living quarters, were like for medieval monks, from the bedroom to the bathing hall. Prosperous artisans built the Altstadt's fine half-timbered houses, hence the similarities to their quarters in Ulm. Pick up a brochure at the tourist office listing the architectural highlights.

BASICS

The **tourist office** (Auf dem Graben 15, tel. 07344/921025) keeps strange hours: They're open Friday 2–5, Saturday 1–5, and Sunday 11–5. In winter, they're open just on Sunday. Luckily the office in Ulm has plenty of info on Blaubeuren. **Trains** from Ulm run hourly and take only 10 min. To reach the Altstadt from the Bahnhof, walk straight down Karlstraße for about 15 min and you'll hit the Marktplatz. Blaubeuren's above average **HI-Jugendherberge** (Auf dem Rucken 69, tel. 07344/6444, fax 07344/21416; closed Nov.) has beds for DM 17 (DM 19 over 26), plus DM 6.50 for breakfast. The hostel perches on the Rucken, the hill to the right between the train station and town. **Gasthof zum Waldhorn** (Klosterstr. 21, tel. 07344/6342, fax 07344/3918) has single rooms for DM 45 per person (DM 70 with private shower and bath) and double rooms for DM 90 (or DM 100 with shower and bath) and a Swabian-style restaurant serving plenty of local specialties.

THE BODENSEE

Spanning some 80 km in length and 14 km in width, the Bodensee (Lake Constance) is the largest lake in the German-speaking world. It was formed thousands of years ago by a glacier that rolled through the area, leaving a gaping hole that the Rhine eventually filled, creating a natural border between modern Germany, Austria, and Switzerland.

The Bodensee offers warm weather, cool waters, busy resorts, and ancient cities encircled by gentle hills. Biking, hiking, swimming, sailing, and other get-wet activities are available just about everywhere, and there's plenty of grass for weary travelers looking to bask in the sun. Although outdoor activities dominate the region, the Bodensee is home to some quirky towns, of which **Konstanz** is the liveliest and **Lindau** and **Meersburg** the most picturesque. A fair number of youth hostels and numerous campgrounds provide cheap places to crash, but during the high season (mid-June–August), these fill up quickly. Do yourself a favor and call ahead. Otherwise, have the tourist offices book you a room (DM 5 fee) or be prepared to spend a lot of cash at expensive hotels.

GETTING AROUND

Ships are the most scenic and, owing to the lake's long, lanky line, sometimes the most efficient way to travel here. Deutsche Bahn's **Bodensee-Verkehrsdienst** (tel. 07531/281389) has regular ferry service between the Bodensee's worthwhile towns, and if you flash a EurailPass or DB pass, you get 50% off the regular ticket price; with InterRail you ride free. One major rail line runs from Radolfzell in the west to Lindau in the east, connecting all the towns on the northern shore. On the Swiss side, a rail line connects Kreuzlingen and Romanshorn with Bregenz, Austria. One great option is to rent a bike (DM 10–DM 15 per day) and zoom around the lake on the paved bike paths. Biking maps are available from the tourist offices, and you can throw your pack in the long-term storage available at the train stations in Konstanz, Überlingen, and Lindau.

KONSTANZ

Divided by the Rhine as it exits the western end of the Bodensee, the city of Konstanz consists of two parts: the large medieval Altstadt, on the Swiss shore of the lake, and the primarily residential section of town on the narrow German peninsula, dotted with scenic grassy beaches and mansions. Konstanz was the seat of a powerful bishop in the Middle Ages, and the location of more than one important diet in Church history, including the 15th-century sentencing of Czech revolutionary reformer Jan Hus. This university city is now the lake's most popular vacation destination and by far the most hip and happenin' one, thanks to its students—come here if you're looking for more action after a day in the sun. The Altstadt is well preserved and ideal for wandering. Konstanz's central monument, the 11th-century **Münster,** on the north side of the Altstadt, is topped by a spire (open Mon.–Sat. 10–6, Sun. 1–6; closed on rainy days) that affords dizzying views of the city and the Bodensee area.

The Romanesque **Stephanskirche,** a block south of the Münster, received a late-Gothic facelift and contains a rococo choir and a series of early 20th-century paintings depicting the 14 Stations of the Cross. On the peninsula side of town, east of the main bridge connecting Konstanz's two halves, runs **Seestraße,** where the wealthy wander and the young hang out on a stately promenade of neoclassical mansions with views of the Bodensee.

BASICS

You can change money, place international calls, and pick up poste restante mail at the **post office** (Bahnhofpl. 2) across the street from the tourist office. Near the Münster, do a load of laundry for DM 8 at **Waschsalon und mehr** (Hofhalde 3, tel. 07531/16027); a spin in the dryer costs DM 6.

The **tourist office,** in the city center, books rooms for DM 5 and sells nifty city maps (50 Pf) with a highlighted walking tour. The office also has ferry schedules and DM 2 maps of local hiking trails. *Fischmarkt 2, tel. 07531/133030, fax 07531/133060. Open Apr.–Oct., weekdays 9–6:30, Sat. 9–4, Sun. 10–1. Nov.–Mar. weekdays 9:30–12:30 and 2–6.*

THE BODENSEE

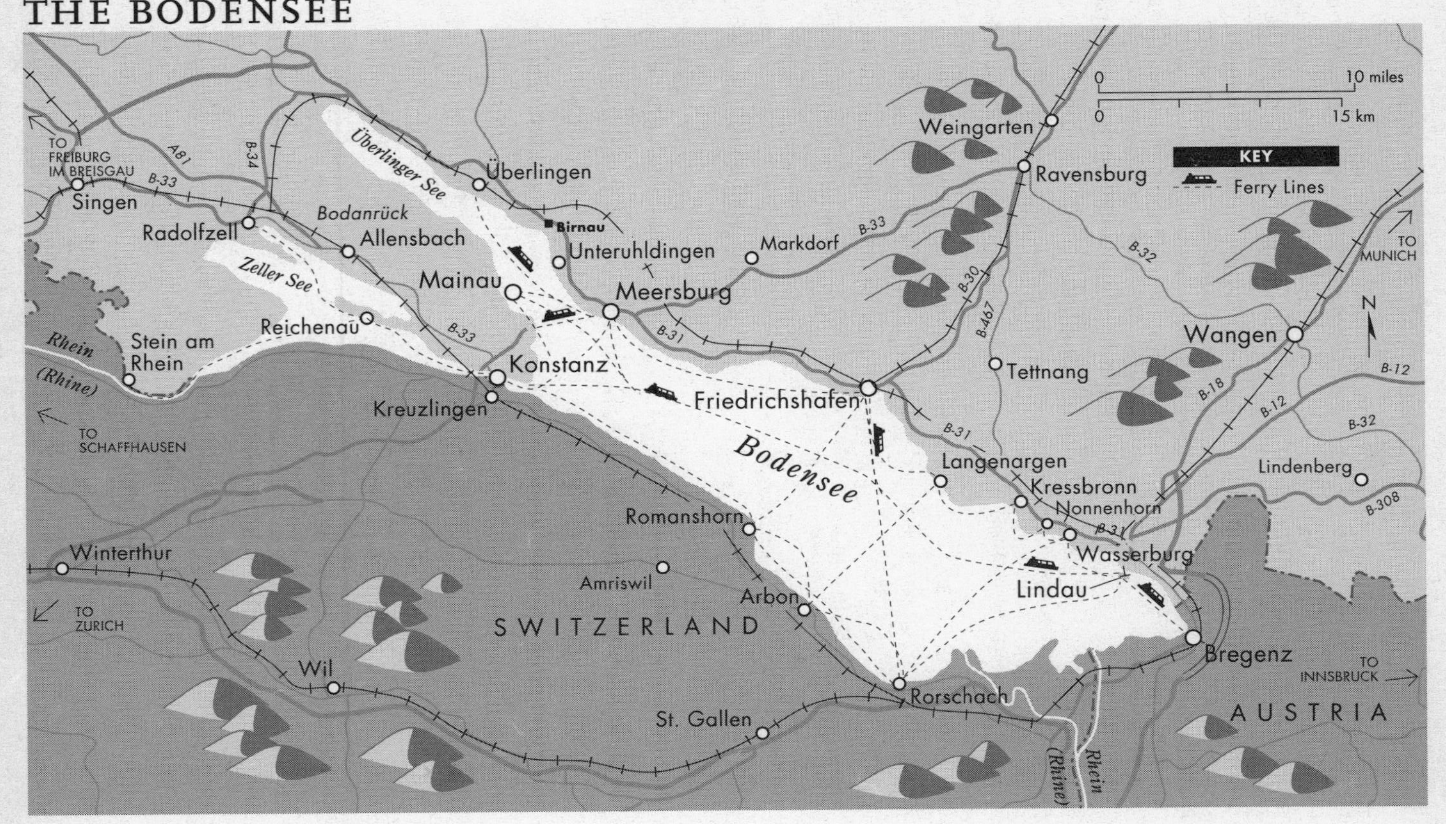

DIP INTO SWITZERLAND

Say Grüezi to Germany's neighbors in the south and see a bit of Switzerland on the DB cruise down the Rhine from Konstanz to Schaffhausen on the other side of the border. Boats make the three-hour trip three times a day in summer; for those without a rail pass, the DM 34 price includes return rail fare on the Swiss line. This is probably the most scenic journey of all the Bodensee lines; the ride includes stops at a number of towns along both sides of the river's densely forested banks. One highlight is the medieval Swiss town of Stein am Rhein, complete with hikeable castle on a hill. If it's hot out, jump off the Rhine bridge into the clear, fast-flowing river (don't worry, the water doesn't get toxic until much farther north). Once in Schaffhausen, hop on the bus waiting at the boat landing and head for the dramatic Rheinfall, one of Europe's highest waterfalls. Walk the 4 km back to town along the river and amble through Schaffhausen's stately Altstadt. From the train station, you can head back to Konstanz or to points north and west in Germany via Singen.

COMING AND GOING

Ships operated by Deutsche Bahn (Hafenstr. 6, tel. 07531/281398) run from the harbor behind the train station to Bregenz, Austria (3½ hrs, DM 26.20), Friedrichshafen (1½ hrs, DM 19.40), Lindau (3¼ hrs, DM 28) and Überlingen (1–1½ hrs, DM 12). Considering that Konstanz is a decent-sized city on an international border, rail traffic here is light, with only a few direct **trains** each day to Frankfurt (4–5 hrs, DM 107), Stuttgart (3 hrs, DM 55), and Radolfzell (15 min, DM 5.60); connect in Radolfzell for other towns on the German side of the Bodensee. To find a ride headed in your direction, contact the **Mitfahrzentrale** (Münzg. 22, tel. 07531/21444); from the Hauptbahnhof, walk up Konzilstraße (past the tourist office) and take the second left.

GETTING AROUND

To reach the Altstadt from the Hauptbahnhof, walk past the post office and tourist office and turn left on Marktstätte. A few blocks farther is Obermarkt, which bisects the Altstadt's main drag: To the south it's called Hussenstraße, to the north (where you'll find the Münster) it's called Wessenberg Straße. Your *Kurkarte* (guest card; *see below*) is good for free bus transportation.

WHERE TO SLEEP

Wherever you stay, get a **Kurkarte** (guest card) from the proprietor. If none of the following have vacancies, you can inquire at the tourist office about private rooms (DM 30–DM 35 per person), which usually require that you stay more than one night. **Pension Gretel** (Zollernstr. 6, tel. 07531/23283) is in a cute house near the train station where singles start at DM 55 and doubles at DM 90. Take Bus 1 (DM 2.50) to Staad/Fähre and follow the pedestrian path up the shoreline to the city's only campground, **Campingplatz Bruderhofer** (Fohrenbühlweg 50, tel. 07531/31388). Bruderhofer has 180 tightly packed sites north of Freibad Horn (*see* Outdoor Activities, *below*) at DM 6.50 per person, DM 6 per tent, and DM 5 per car. It's closed in winter.

HI-Jugendherberge "Hörnliberg" Kreuzlingen is quiet, clean, and close to the beach, but it's also a 25-min hike from Konstanz in the Swiss town of Kreuzlingen. Walk to the southern side of Konstanz's Hauptbahnhof, cross the footbridge, walk to the lake and follow it east over the Swiss border. From here continue along the path past the sporting greens, walk through the waterfront park, and follow the signs.

Beds are DM 26.50 (the hostel accepts DM), including breakfast. Reception is open 5–9 PM, reservations are held till 6 PM, and curfew is 11 PM. *Promenadestr. 7, tel. 0041/71/688–2663; once in Switzerland, tel. 071/688–2663. 99 beds. Closed Dec.–Feb.*

HI-Jugendherberge Otto-Moericke-Turm is a decaying, 10-story tower north of the city center whose top-floor common room has an unbeatable view of the Bodensee. Beds DM 23 (DM 28 over 26); curfew is 10 PM. *Allmanshöhe 18, tel. 07531/32260. From Bahnhofstr. (just outside train station), Bus 4 to Jugendherberge. 185 beds. Closed Nov.–Feb.*

FOOD

Konstanz's ethnic restaurants dish up delectable, inexpensive fare. **Radieschen** (Hohenhausg. 1, tel. 07531/22887) serves delicious Turkish vegetarian and meaty entrées (DM 8–DM 15), including a crisp mixed salad. A bit more upscale, **Allegro** (Emmishofer Str. 1, tel. 07531/17932) offers regional favorites and Italian cuisine. Assemble your next picnic at **Hensler** (Wessenberg Str. 2), north of the Obermarkt.

AFTER DARK

Because of its size and student population, Konstanz is the only lake town with a real nightlife. An absolute must is **Seekuh** (Konzilstr. 1, tel. 07531/27232), cozy and crowded with a terrace and, on occasion, jazzy live music. Next door, the very popular **Theatercafé** (tel. 07531/20243) draws a more stylish crowd that's not too hip to dance when the mood strikes. For tasty beer hit **Brauhaus J. Albrecht** (Konradig. 2, tel. 07531/25045), Konstanz's 475-year-old microbrewery. When the weather's hot, **Rheinterrasse** (Spanierstr. 5, tel. 07531/56093), along the water next to the Rheinbad, is the place to see and be seen. Another great warm-weather place on the water is **Hafenhalle** (Hafenstr. 10, tel. 07531/21126), on the boat landing in front of the train station. This stylish café/bar/disco serves delicious salads and bistro fare.

OUTDOOR ACTIVITIES

Freibad Horn (Eichhornstr. 89, tel. 07531/63550), the largest and most popular beach in Konstanz (due in no small part to its nude area), is at the tip of the peninsula. Take Bus 5, which runs every half hour, from the post office to the last stop. At a shack just north of the beach you can rent Windsurfers for DM 10 per hour or DM 35 per day.

ÜBERLINGEN

Überlingen draws crowds of spa-loving folks year-round, giving this *Kurort* a slightly slower-paced feel than other lake towns. If you're not looking for a steam bath, Überlingen's well-preserved Altstadt is another of the city's main draws. Remnants of the medieval **Stadtmauer** (Town Wall), with seven surviving towers, fill the Stadtgarten, a grassy park that encircles the city wall. The late-16th-century **St.-Nikolaus-Münster,** in the center of town, contains a lofty vaulted ceiling and a massive Renaissance altar. The Münster is open daily 9–noon and 2–6. Beside the Münster is the gabled Rathaus, housing the 500-year-old **Renaissance Rathaussaal** (open weekdays 9–noon and 2:30–5, Sat. 9–noon; shorter hrs off-season), an ornate meeting hall with a timbered ceiling and a carved frieze whose 41 statuettes represent the orders of the Holy Roman Empire. Uphill from the Münster is the **Stadt Heimatmuseum** (Krummebergstr. 30, tel. 07551/991079), whose purpose of documenting the history of Überlingen is overshadowed by its quiet garden and great view. Admission is DM 4 (DM 2 students), and it's open Tuesday–Saturday 9–12:30 and 2–5, Sunday 10–3 (shorter hrs off-season).

Überlingen's other draw is its range of sporting opportunities. Beach bums can choose between **Strandbad-West** and **Strandbad-Ost** on either end of the lengthy promenade. For windsurfing, head straight for Strandbad-West, directly across from Bahnhof-West. Rent Windsurfers at the **Windsurfschule** (tel. 07551/4277), in front of the Haus des Gastes. Fourteen-foot sailboats are available for about DM 20 per hour (two-hour minimum) from **Segelschule Überlingen** (tel. 07551/4718). Landlubbers can rent bicycles from Bahnhof-West and can pick up bike and hiking trail maps at the **tourist office** (Landungspl. 14, tel. 07551/991122), on the promenade at the harbor. The office is open weekdays 9–6, Saturday 9–2 (shorter hrs and closed Sat. off-season).

COMING AND GOING

Überlingen is a two-station town, though Bahnhof-West, on the west side of the Altstadt, is the main station. From here **buses** regularly run to Meersburg (30 min, DM 5), and **trains** chug to towns like Lindau (1 hr, DM 14.60) and Radolfzell (20 min, DM 7.40), where you can connect to major cities like Karlsruhe, Heidelberg, Frankfurt, and Stuttgart. To reach the Altstadt from Bahnhof-West, turn left on Bahnhofstraße. **Ferries** sail from the harbor for Konstanz (2 hrs, DM 10), Mainau (40 min, DM 7), and Meersburg (1 hr, DM 9).

WHERE TO SLEEP AND EAT

Get a lodging list at the tourist office; options under DM 50 are scarce, but do exist. Überlingen has four campgrounds, all of which lie along the lake not far from major roads. None are particularly designed for the backpacker, but **Camping-Park Überlingen** (tel. 07551/64583), min west of Bahnhof-West, is the closest and charges DM 10 per person, DM 7 per tent site. It's closed from mid-October until Easter. Pick up groceries at **Tengelmann** (Christofstr. 29).

HOSTELS • Jugendherberge Martin Buber (HI). With an indoor swimming pool, laundry facilities, and a bathroom for every two dorm rooms, this hostel, 2 km from the town center, is the best place to sleep in Überlingen. Try to call ahead or fax a reservation. Beds DM 20.50 (DM 24.70 over 26). The hostel sometimes closes in December and January. *Alte Nußdorfer Str. 26, tel. 07551/4204, fax 07551/1277. From Bahnhof-West, take any bus (direction: Friedrichshafen) to Jugendherberge stop and follow the signs uphill.*

MEERSBURG

Across the water from Konstanz and nestled on steep, vineyard bedecked shores, the 1,000-year-old town of Meersburg falls firmly into the "enchantingly medieval" category. Despite the fact that many of its finest half-timbered houses contain cheesy souvenir shops and overpriced restaurants, Meersburg exudes charm. In the center of the Oberstadt (Upper City) is the **Marktplatz,** surrounded by vine-clad Renaissance houses. From here, Kirchstraße leads west to the **tourist office** (Kirchstr. 4, tel. 07532/431110), open weekdays in summer 9–6:30 and Sat. 10–2 (shorter hrs off-season). They can help you with finding a room and your way around.

On a bluff overlooking the lake is the 7th-century **Altes Schloß,** the oldest inhabited castle in Germany and Meersburg's most famous sight. Inside is the worthwhile **Burgmuseum** (tel. 07532/8000; admission DM 9, DM 8 students), whose 28 furnished rooms offer a peek into the past. The museum is open daily 10–6:30. Next door, the pink Baroque **Neues Schloß** (tel. 07532/414071; admission DM 5, DM 4 students) contains the 17th-century living quarters of the *Fürstbischöfe* of Konstanz, replete with beautiful frescoes and a hall of mirrors where concerts are still held. On the second floor is the **Städtische Gemäldesammlung,** the municipal art collection. The Schloß and art collection are open April–Oct., daily 10–1 and 2–6.

If fine print and the bottom line fascinate you, head to the **Deutsches Zeitungsmuseum** (Schloßpl. 13, tel. 07532/7158; admission DM 3.50, DM 3 students), an excellent private museum of German newspaper production, located in the medieval Rotes Haus. Note the odd opening hours: 12–4 Apr. 1–Apr. 11, May 1–Jun. 6, and Jun. 19–Oct. 3.

To find out about Meersburg's historical and political roots, head to the **Stadtmuseum,** housed in a former Dominican cloister. *Kirchstr. 4, tel. 07532/431125. Admission free. Open Sun. only Apr.–Oct., 10–6.*

COMING AND GOING

Meersburg is not on the main rail line, but a few **ferries** run daily from the harbor to Friedrichshafen (1 hr, DM 10), Konstanz (30 min, DM 5), Lindau (2½ hrs, DM 16), Mainau (30 min, DM 6), and Überlingen (1 hr, DM 9). Much cheaper is the **car ferry** (pedestrians welcome), which runs every few minutes from a dock on the west side of the Unterstadt to the northern part of Konstanz (15 min, DM 2.20). Across the street from the ferry dock, or on Himmelbergweg near the tourist office, you can catch **Bus 7395** to Überlingen (via Birnau, 30 min, DM 5) or Friedrichshafen (35 min, DM 6).

WHERE TO SLEEP AND EAT

The centrally located **Gästehaus am Hafen** (Spitalg. 3–4, tel. 07532/7069), housed in a quaint half-timbered building, has tiny, clean doubles starting at DM 85. From the harbor, walk along Unterstadtstraße toward the center of town and take the first left. Unfortunately, you'll have to go to Friedrichshafen or Meersburg to get your hostel and camping fix. For groceries try **Oma's Kaufhaus** (Kirchstr. 1), on the Marktplatz. Imbiß-style food thrives at the **Tor Grill** (Unterstadtstr. 8). Every Friday until noon, a **produce market** is held on Schloßplatz.

OUTDOOR ACTIVITIES

There are some nice rocky beaches just west of town where you can swim and sunbathe for free. In the harbor, you can rent rowboats, paddle boats, electric boats, and motorboats from the kiosk marked BOOTSVERLEIH. The heavenly **Beheiztes Freibad** (tel. 07532/414060), east of the harbor on Uferpromenade, has lots of grass, a little sand, three pools, a thermal bath (33°C or 91.4°F), a sauna, minigolf, and a volleyball court. In summer you get all of the above until 8 PM for a mere DM 6 (DM 4 students). You can rent bikes and in-line skates at **Sport Pfau** (Unterstadtstr. 7, tel. 07532/48873). Pedal (or hike) to Birnau, just a few km west along a beachside path.

FRIEDRICHSHAFEN

Friedrichshafen has the dubious distinction of being the least cute and charming and most industrial-looking of all the Bodensee towns. Still, being on the lakeshore, it does draw plenty of sun-seeking vacationers. Aviation buffs will know that Friedrichshafen's real claim to fame is the Zeppelin: The first successful flight of a hydrogen-filled blimp took place here in 1900. The city became an aviation center and consequently was a target of Allied bombing in World War II—over 70% of Friedrichshafen was destroyed, hence the characterless nature of the place today. To experience Friedrichshafen's aviation history, visit the newly opened **Zeppelin Museum** (Seestr. 22, tel. 07541/380133; admission, including exhibits, DM 12, DM 6 students) in the old Hafenbahnhof. The museum's theme is "technology and art"—not only do you get everything you ever wanted to know about cigar-shaped balloons (including a full-scale reproduction of the *Hindenburg*), but there are also exhibits on local artists. The museum is open Tues.–Sun. 10–6 (shorter hrs in winter).

Even if you don't speak German, don't miss Friedrichshafen's **Schulmuseum** (Friedrichstr. 14, tel. 07541/32622), near the Graf Zeppelin Haus. Housed in a 19th-century mansion, the museum offers reconstructed classrooms and other displays evoking unique periods in German history, including a fascinating room on German education during the Third Reich. The museum is open daily 10–5 (2–5 in winter) and admission is DM 2. After visiting the Schulmuseum, walk west along Klosterstraße toward the water for a glimpse inside the reconstructed Baroque **Schloßkirche.**

BASICS

Get a map and sporting brochures or book a private room (DM 25–DM 30) at the **tourist office** (Bahnhofpl. 2, tel. 07541/30010) in front of the Hauptbahnhof. The office opens its doors May–Sept., weekdays 8–noon and 2–6, Sat. 10–1 (shorter hrs off-season). You can catch hourly **trains** to Lindau (25 min, DM 8), Radolfzell (1 hr, DM 14), and Ulm (1¼ hrs, DM 27), and rent **bikes** at the Hauptbahnhof (tel. 07541/201385). Otherwise hop aboard a **ship** bound for Konstanz or another Bodensee town. For ship info call 07541/923–8389.

WHERE TO SLEEP

HI-Jugendherberge Graf Zeppelin (Lindauer Str. 3, tel. 07541/72404, fax 07541/74986), about 3 km from the Hauptbahnhof, is a typical German youth hostel, offering beds with breakfast for DM 25 (DM 30 over 26). If you want to stay longer than two nights, the prices go up since another meal will be included. The bus out here is so infrequent that you should either take the DM 10 taxi ride or hoof it for 25 min. From the Hauptbahnhof, go straight to the water, turn left, and follow the signs. Zeppelin's curfew is 11 PM and reservations are held until 6 PM. Near the hostel, **Camping Dimmler** (Lindauer Str. 2, tel. 07541/73421), open Easter–Sept., offers lakeside campsites for DM 7–DM 10 per person, DM 5 per tent, and DM 5 per car. The other, larger campground is **Campingplatz Fischbach** in the Meersburgerstr. It's open May–Sept. Call 07541/42059 for prices.

LINDAU

This Bavarian island town in the *Schwäbisches Meer* (Swabian Sea) is the loveliest and possibly most romantic of any Bodensee settlement, partly due to its ideal location near the Austrian and Swiss borders. On clear days, the view from this 2½-sq-km island in the eastern end of the Bodensee stretches as far south as the Austrian and Swiss Alps. Three monuments mark Lindau's harbor: Standing guard over the harbor entrance is a massive marble statue of a seated lion, the symbol of the state to which Lindau belongs, Bavaria. Opposite the statue is the **Neuer Leuchtturm** (New Lighthouse), which you

GERMANY'S SEMITROPICAL PARADISE

The small island of Mainau—only about 45 hectares—offers an unusual and refreshing detour for the weary traveler. Lying in the Überlinger See, the island is home to a plethora of rare and tropical plants, including citrus and palm trees, bougainvillea, hibiscus, and hundreds more, which are nurtured by the mild, moist climate. In the spring and summer, you'll be overwhelmed by the perfume of the colorful flowers that blanket the island. Be sure to take a peek at the butterfly collection and stroll around the palm tree house. Mainau once belonged to the Teutonic Knights, who arrived in the 13th century; today, the island's Baroque castle is occupied by the Swedish Count Bernadotte and is closed to the public. A visit to Mainau, at DM 18 (DM 9 students) mid-March to mid-Oct., is a little pricey, but it is a unique experience (07531/3030; open mid-March–mid-Oct. daily 7–7. Admission free from mid-Oct.–mid-March). No cars are allowed on the island. Ships leave several times per day from Konstanz and other Bodensee towns. If you're in a hurry, take the bus from the Konstanz train station to the ferry.

can climb for DM 1. The **Alter Leuchtturm** (Old Lighthouse) stands on the ruins of Lindau's 13th-century city walls.

Many of Lindau's visitors never seem to leave the harbor promenade—there are even rows of chairs set up where these vacationing lurkers can sit and enjoy the view without having to order a drink (you can bring your own). The island's Altstadt is worth a meander, though; from the harbor, walk away from the water to plunge into the heart of the old town. Most of the north–south streets eventually hit Maximilianstraße, the Altstadt's main drag. Occupying the southern end of a large square off Maximilianstraße is the 15th-century **Altes Rathaus,** with its vibrant murals, covered stairwell, and gaily adorned gables. A few blocks northwest is the large stone **Diebsturm,** where lawbreakers were locked up. Next door, the bulky, 10th-century **St. Peterskirche** contains unique murals by Hans Holbein the Elder, and is now used as a war-memorial chapel. On the west end of the **Marktplatz** sits the elaborate Baroque **Haus Zum Cavazzen,** which houses the city's fascinating art and history museum. It's open Tues.–Sun. 10–noon and 2–5, with shorter hours in winter and a DM 4 (DM 3 students) admission price.

BASICS

You can make international phone calls and change money at the **post office** (Maximillianstr. 52). Across the street from the train station, the **tourist office** (Am Bahnhofpl., tel. 08382/26000; open Mon.–Sat. 9–7 in summer; in winter, weekdays 9–noon and 2–5) has free maps and brochures and books rooms. Everything on the island is accessible by foot, and two 200-m causeways link Lindau with the mainland.

COMING AND GOING

Lindau is a transfer point for international **trains** running to Austria through the border town of Bregenz (10 min, DM 5.60) and also has service to Swiss cities such as Bern (3¼ hrs, DM 87.60) and Zürich (2 hrs, DM 51). Several times a day, rail lines link Lindau to Munich (2¾ hrs, DM 54) and Ulm (1¾ hrs, DM 34) as well as to other Bodensee towns. Storage lockers and long-term storage are available. The **Busbahnhof** (tel. 08382/3038), a half-block north of the train station, has service to neighboring towns, including Friedrichshafen (Bus 7587). **Ships** travel between Lindau and Bregenz, Wasserburg, Friedrichshafen, and Meersburg and less frequently to Mainau and Konstanz; buy tickets onboard or at ticket counters at the dock.

WHERE TO SLEEP

With all the families that flock to Lindau in summer, reservations are strongly recommended. Request a list of Lindau's accommodations from the tourist office, or read it on their display board outside. **Campingplatz Lindau-Zech** (Fraunhoferstr. 20, tel. 08382/72236; closed Nov.), along the lake, is backpacker-friendly but a 4-km walk from town. Sites cost DM 10.60 per person plus a *Kur* fee of DM 1.50, DM 5.50 per tent, and DM 4 per car. Prices are lower in the off-season. Lindau also has a brand-new **Jugendherberge** (Herbergsweg 11; tel. 08382/96710), which is clean and comfortable. A bed here costs between DM 29 and DM 36 and a single room between DM 39 and DM 41. Unfortunately, you can only stay here if you're under 27. Curfew is midnight. Elsewhere, the extremely friendly Frau Weber welcomes young travelers at **Gästehaus Lädine** (In der Grub 25, tel. 08382/5326). Airy, bright rooms go for DM 40–DM 50 per person, depending on where your shower is. To get there from the Hauptbahnhof, walk down Bahnhofstraße, head right on Maximilianstraße, left on Schafgasse, and right on In der Grub.

FOOD

For Italian food there's **Il Mulino** (In der Grub 30, tel. 08382/6704), with pizza, pasta, and fish and meat dishes under DM 15. From the Rathaus, walk up Schneeberggasse and turn right on In der Grub. If you're looking for Swabian and Bavarian fare, visit the wood-beamed **Stube** at Hotel Goldenes Lamm (Paradiespl., tel. 08382/5732); you can sample traditional specialties for under DM 20. Across Paradiesplatz, you'll find **Taverna** (Paradiespl. 14–16, tel. 08382/23702), with scrumptious gyros (DM 6 to go) and other Greek treats. Stock up next door at the small Greek deli, or at **Plus** (Marktpl. 5). On Tuesday and Saturday mornings, the Marktplatz hosts a small **produce market.**

OUTDOOR ACTIVITIES

On a warm day consider renting a bike from the train station (open Mon.–Sat. 9–9, Sun. 9–noon) and heading out along the water to **Lindenhofpark,** a large, quiet park on the mainland. Along the water on the small dock beside Lindau's rail bridge, several boat rental companies such as **Bootsvermietung Hodrius** (tel. 08382/4285) can rent you a paddle boat (DM 15) or motorboat (DM 45) and handle your waterskiing needs. Beautiful hour-long cruises (about DM 15) that sail around the eastern side of the Bodensee leave from the harbor regularly during summer. If you want to swim, either join the locals at a tiny rock beach hidden beyond the seawall, across from a grassy park behind the train station, or pay DM 4 (DM 2.80 students) for the privilege of swimming at the temperature-controlled, outdoor **Strandbad Eichwald** (Eichwaldstr. 16, tel. 08382/5539), about 2 km east of town. This is also the spot for renting Windsurfers (DM 10–DM 20).

4 THE BLACK FOREST

UPDATED BY GARRETT HERING

Looking like something out of J. R. R. Tolkien's *Lord of the Rings,* the Black Forest (*Schwarzwald*) is a region of steep hills and deep valleys blanketed with fir and oak. Tourists and locals flock to the forest for its exceptional hiking and skiing opportunities and for a taste of the jovial friendliness, or *Gemütlichkeit,* of the Alpine villages. And why not? The residents of the Black Forest are some of the friendliest and most colorful characters in Germany: They speak a dialect even Germans no more than 35 km away have difficulty understanding, and many still live in the sloping, thatched homes associated with the region. These are also the folks who gave the world cuckoo clocks, some of the wackiest traditional clothing on the planet, and many of the fairy tales made famous by the brothers Grimm. Like Bavaria, though, much of the forest has gone full-tilt oompah, particularly in the central Black Forest, where Teutonic kitsch translates into major tourist dollars.

The Black Forest stretches some 165 km from Karlsruhe, in the north, to Switzerland in the south, and is flanked by the Rhine to the west. Until the 20th century, the Black Forest was largely inaccessible to the outside world. Today, getting around is a snap: Trains from all over Germany stop in **Freiburg im Breisgau,** a hip university town in the southern High Black Forest; if you're coming from Stuttgart, trains stop frequently in **Donaueschingen** on the forest's eastern fringe. Although traveling by train *through* the Black Forest is spectacular, many towns and villages are not actually served by rail. Fortunately, buses pick up the slack, though service can be slow and infrequent, especially during winter. Rail pass holders rejoice: Eurail passes are accepted on the regional buses, and Interail and German rail passes get you a 50% discount on fares, none of which exceed DM 12.50.

More than 20,000 marked trails make hiking and biking in the warmer months—and cross-country skiing in winter—the best ways to see the forest. Three excellent trails start in **Pforzheim** in the north and meander through the forest all the way to Switzerland. Get general Black Forest hiking info at the larger regional tourist offices in Freiburg and Pforzheim; for shorter treks and skiing ask at any local tourist office.

FREIBURG IM BREISGAU

Amidst all the German kitsch that floods the Black Forest, Freiburg emerges as a hip, sophisticated, and thoroughly entertaining city. Though Freiburg has a population of only about 220,000, it supports a remarkably lively cultural scene: Talented street musicians, thriving theater, and first-rate concerts are a fact of life in Freiburg. Blown to bits in World War II, Freiburg has reconstructed many of its most impressive buildings and preserved the historical atmosphere of its *Altstadt* (Old Town)—what you'll find today is a pedestrian-friendly, medieval-meets-modern city center. Located just outside the Black Forest, Freiburg is the largest, most accessible city in the region. It's also the perfect base for exploring the villages and hills of the southern Black Forest (the area around Freiburg) and the High Black Forest. The vineyards of the Breisach-Kaiserstuhl also make great day trips and hikes from town.

Aside from the surrounding forest, Freiburg takes much of its character from the centuries-old university in its center. The citizens of Freiburg have a reputation for being tolerant, politically engaged, and supportive of environmental concerns. At the same time, parts of Freiburg have been known to support the far-right politics of the *Republikaner* party. Freiburg's student population, however, remains strongly leftist and bohemian.

Let your palate go native. Käsespätzle (cheese-covered noodles), sometimes sprinkled with lentils, will do the trick as an entrée or side dish. For dessert, enjoy a slice of luscious Schwarzwälder Kirschtorte (Black Forest cherry cake)—served in any self-respecting café—with a Schluck of Schwarzwälder Kirschwasser (Black Forest cherry brandy).

BASICS

BIKE RENTAL • Geco Bikes rents mountainbikes for DM 50 per day, and city cruisers for DM 12–DM 20. You can sign up for a tour or go out on your own. Cross the Dreisam River to Turnseestr. *Turnseestr. 51, tel. 0761/71122. Closed Sun.*

CHANGING MONEY • You'll find currency exchange and an ATM in the train station at **Deutsche Verkehrs Bank.** The **Deutsche Bank** across from the tourist office has two ATMs—one regular, one that spits out German marks and Swiss and French francs. Both accept credit cards and Cirrus and Plus bank cards. *Hauptbahnhof. Open weekdays 7:30–7, Sat. 8–5, Sun. 9–1.*

LAUNDRY • For a wash with your cappuccino, head to **Café Fleck** (open weekdays 7–6:30, Sat. 8–2), a clean, modern laundromat attached to a similarly clean and modern café. A wash costs DM 7, 10 min in a dryer is DM 1, and soap costs 20 Pf. *Predigerstr. 3, tel. 0761/26829. Open weekdays 7 AM–1 AM. From tourist office, north on Rotteckring, right on Unterlinden, left on Predigerstr.*

MAIL AND PHONES • Make international calls, pick up mail, and change money at the **main post office** (Eisenbahnstr. 58–60), located between the train station and the tourist office. Freiburg's postal code is 79098.

PHARMACIES • Visit your local pharmacist at **Berthold-Apotheke,** just behind Martinstor. *Kaiser-Joseph-Str. 258, tel. 0761/36981. Open weekdays 9–6:30, Sat. 9:30–1:30.*

VISITOR INFORMATION

Freiburg's excellent **tourist office** has free city and Black Forest maps, books rooms free of charge, and sells tickets to cultural events. One counter is devoted to regional information—the staff can tell you almost anything you need to know about planning a Black Forest adventure, even in English. The *Freiburg Official Guide* (DM 6) is full of information about the city's sights, eateries, and accommodations. Pick up free copies of *Freizeit und Kultur* and *Freiburg Aktuell* for monthly listings of cultural events. An adjoining travel agency offers special youth fares on trains and flights. *Rotteckring 14, tel. 0761/388101. From Hauptbahnhof, 2 blocks down Eisenbahnstr. to Rotteckring (office is on left). Open June–Sept., weekdays 9:30–8, Sat. 9:30–5, Sun. 10–noon; Oct.–May, weekdays 9:30–6, Sat. 9:30–2, Sun. 10–noon.*

COMING AND GOING

Freiburg lies on the Basel–Karlsruhe rail line, so it's easy to connect to most major cities in Germany; **trains** head several times a day to Karlsruhe (1 hr, DM 20–DM 37), Frankfurt (2¼–3 hrs, DM 49–DM 72), and Hamburg (6–7 hrs, DM 84–DM 211). The *hauptbahnhof* (main train station) has scads of luggage lockers, but it closes 12:45 AM–5 AM. **Buses** to most Black Forest towns leave from the Omnibusbahnhof (tel. 0761/36172), next to the train station. Arrange ride shares at **Citynetz Mitfahrzentrale** (Belfortstr. 55, tel. 0761/19444; open weekdays 9–7, Sat. 9–1, Sun. 10–1), near the university.

To reach the city center from the Hauptbahnhof, walk two blocks up Eisenbahnstraße and continue straight across Rotteckring (Freiburg's busiest north–south street); within 10 min you'll bump into the town *Münster* (cathedral). You can see almost everything in town on foot, but if you're headed to the suburbs there's always the extensive **bus** and **tram** systems. Rides to most parts of the city cost DM 3, and public transit stops running about 1 AM. If you need a **taxi** call 0761/37777. Freiburg also has a women's taxi service (tel. 0761/24040).

WHERE TO SLEEP

Aside from the hostel, your cheapest bet is a private room (DM 25–DM 40), but they usually require a three-night minimum stay. The tourist office lists these and other lodging options.

Hotel Dionysos. Attached to a Greek restaurant, this 16-room hotel sits in a quiet, woodsy neighborhood south of the city center. Clean, very adequate doubles start at DM 70, singles at DM 48. *Hirschstr. 2, tel. 0761/29353. From overpass beside train station, Tram 4 to Klosterpl.; then double back 20 m and turn left on Hirschstr.*

Hotel Löwen. Even though it's the cheapest hotel in the Altstadt, the Löwen has an upscale feel with spring-fresh, dainty rooms that feel like grandma's. Doubles without showers start at DM 90, singles at DM 65. *Herrenstr. 47, just north of Schwabentor, tel. 0761/33161. From Hauptbahnhof, walk up Eisenbahnstr. (which becomes Rathausg. and Schusterstr.), right on Herrenstr.*

Hotel Schemmer. This small hotel in a working-class neighborhood behind the Hauptbahnhof has large, if linoleum-lined and noisy, doubles starting at DM 85 (DM 95 with shower); singles start at DM 55. *Eschholzstr. 63, tel. 0761/207490. From Hauptbahnhof, take overpass across tracks, walk straight on Wannerstr. (past Herz-Jesu church), left 2 blocks on Eschholzstr.*

Hotel Stadt Wien. You're only a 15-minute walk north of the Altstadt at this small hotel. Roomy and elegant doubles without showers start at DM 81, singles at DM 54. Be warned that a room without private shower means no shower at all, just a shared toilet in the hall and a sink in the room. The great breakfast buffet makes it all worthwhile, though. *Habsburgerstr. 48, tel. 0761/36560 or 0761/39898. From Altstadt, head north on Kaiser-Joseph-Str. (which becomes Habsburgerstr.).*

HOSTELS • Jugendherberge (HI). In a characterless modern building on the outskirts of town, Freiburg's hostel epitomizes dorm living. Still, it's the cheapest bed in town at DM 26 (DM 32 over 26), breakfast included. During summer the 380 beds fill up quickly, so call ahead. *Kartäuserstr. 151, tel. 0761/67656, fax 0761/60367. Tram 1 (direction: Littenweiler) to Römerhof; double back ½ block, take first right on Fritz-Geiges-Str., cross small river, turn right again. Curfew 11:30 PM.*

CAMPING • Get a list of Freiburg's five campgrounds at the tourist office. The best of the bunch is also closest to the Altstadt: **Camping Hirzberg,** halfway between the youth hostel and Schwabentor, on the edge of Schloßberg Park. The rates are DM 5–DM 7 per tent, DM 8 per person, and DM 3.50 per car. *Kartäuserstr. 99, tel. 0761/35054. Tram 1 (direction: Littenweiler) to Messpl.; left on Heimatstr., right along river, and cross bridge. Closed mid-Oct.–Mar.*

FOOD

As a center of liberal feel-good vibes, Freiburg has plenty of veggie options on top of the usual Wurst and Pommes. Inside the tacky but cheap **Freiburger Markthalle** (Kaiser-Joseph-Str., SW of Münsterpl.), you can get all kinds of ethnic food for less than DM 10. The area north of **Schwabentor** (Swabian Gate) is loaded with an eclectic selection of restaurants popular with a diverse crowd. There's a **Plus market** on Eisenbahnstraße just west of Rotteckring, complete with bakery for all your grocery needs.

Brennessel. If you find yourself in Stühlinger, a blue-collar neighborhood behind the Bahnhof, head straight to the friendly "stinging nettle" a few blocks from Hotel Schemmer (*see above*). Among the many veggie options are eggplant casserole (DM 15) and spaghetti with pesto (DM 14). There's also your stan-

THE BLACK FOREST

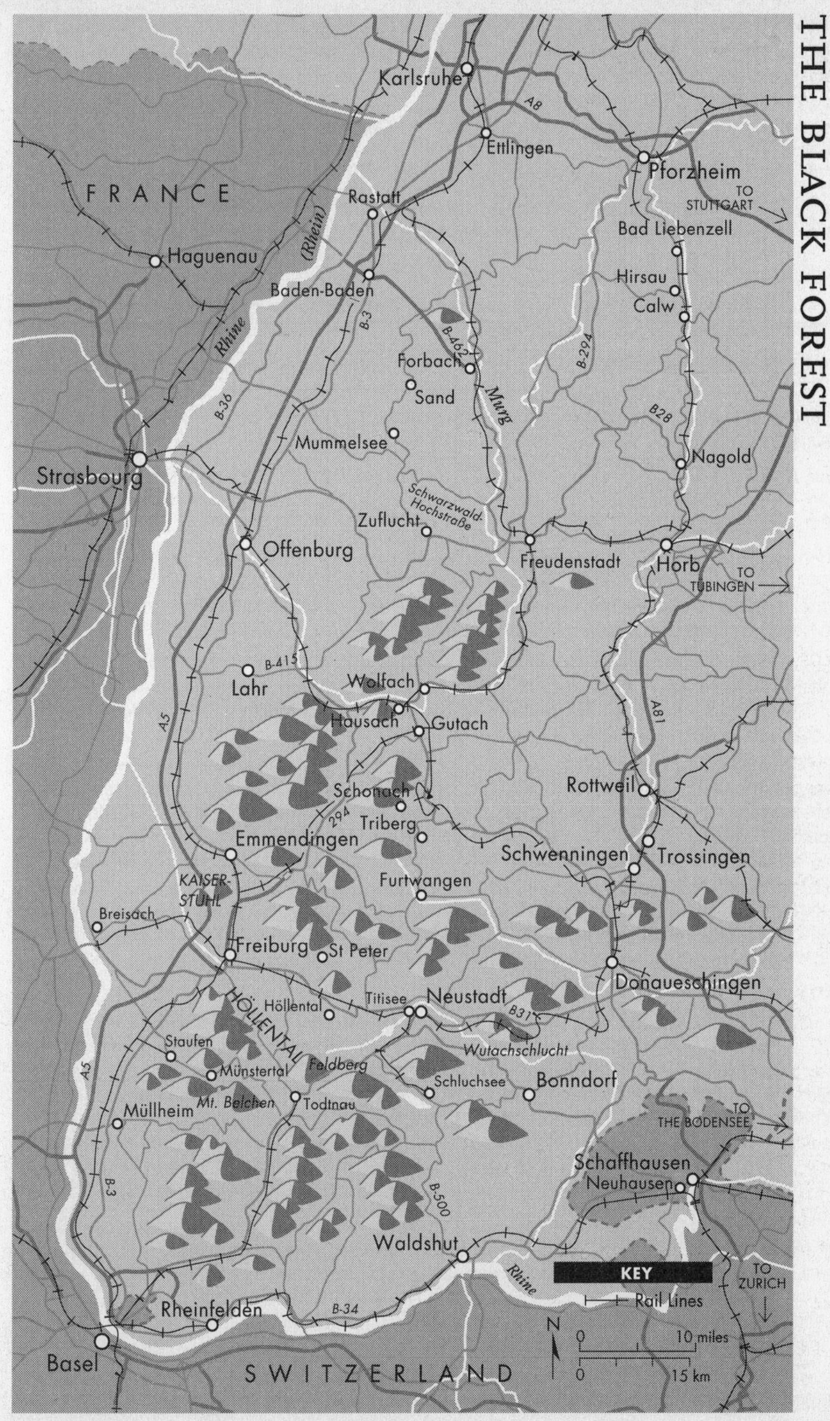

Karlsruhe
A8
Ettlingen
Pforzheim
TO STUTTGART
FRANCE
Rastatt
(Rhein)
Bad Liebenzell
Haguenau
Baden-Baden
Hirsau
Calw
B-3
Rhine
B-462
Forbach
B-294
Sand
Murg
B-36
B28
Mummelsee
Nagold
Strasbourg
Schwarzwald-Hochstraße
Zuflucht
Offenburg
Freudenstadt
Horb
TO TÜBINGEN
B-415
Lahr
Wolfach
Hausach
Gutach
A5
A81
Rottweil
Schonach
294
Triberg
Emmendingen
Schwenningen
Trossingen
KAISER-STUHL
Furtwangen
Breisach
Freiburg
St Peter
Donaueschingen
HÖLLENTAL
Höllental
Titisee
Neustadt
B31
Staufen
Wutachschlucht
Feldberg
Münstertal
Schluchsee
Bonndorf
A5
Mt. Belchen
Todtnau
Müllheim
TO THE BODENSEE
Schaffhausen
Neuhausen
B-3
B-500
Waldshut
KEY
Rhine
TO ZURICH
Rail Lines
Rheinfelden
B-34
N
0
10 miles
0
15 km
Basel
SWITZERLAND

Alte Universität, **2**
Augustiner Museum, **7**
Haus zum Walfisch, **4**
Kaufhaus, **6**
Münster, **5**
Museum für Neue Kunst, **8**
Museum für Ur- und Frühgeschichte, **1**
Neues Rathaus, **3**

dard German fare. Occasionally, student specials are offered for under DM 5. *Eschholzstr. 17, tel. 0761/281187.*

Café Atlantic. A funky place for beer or a filling meal for under DM 15, the Atlantic serves mostly Italian food; several vegetarian options always grace the menu. After 11 PM it fills with a hip, young crowd of all inclinations and persuasions. *Schwabentorringstr. 7, 1 block south of Schwabentor, tel. 0761/33033.*

Firenze. Inexpensive, well-prepared Italian food awaits you here. Choose from 26 pizza options (DM 5–DM 15), various soups and salad plates (DM 5–DM 15), pasta dishes (DM 7–DM 15), and meaty entrées. They even bring you a free glass of warm brandy with your check. *Friedrichring 5, northern border of city center, tel. 07.61/273370.*

Martin's Bräu. In an alley just off Martinstor is the self-proclaimed original Freiburg brew pub. Don't just come for beer—they serve excellent and reasonably priced regional cuisine. Huge entrées run DM 12.50–DM 22, like *Badisches Zwiebelfleisch mit Knöpfle,* a delicious take on pot roast, served with egg noodles. Smaller meals and daily specials start at DM 7.80. *Kaiser-Joseph-Str. 237, tel. 0761/387–0018.*

CAFÉS • Cafés in Freiburg range from co-op anarchist coffeehouses to sleek modern joints where everyone wears fabulous shoes. **Uni-Café** (Niemensstr. 7, tel. 0761/383355) is a fairly mainstream student hangout in the middle of the bustling, café-filled university quarter. For a quieter experience go to **Domino** (Konviktstr. 21, tel. 0761/35060), in a pretty street two blocks east of the Münster. The local gay and lesbian community meets on Fridays at the modern bohemian café **Jos Fritz** (Wilhelmstr. 15, tel. 0761/30019). The café sits in the courtyard behind a very intellectual bookstore of the same name (stemming from a fictional character who was the subject of a '60s ballad by the German Bob Dylan—Franz Josef Degenhardt). This is the place to see and be seen on warm nights—just look for the massive number of bikes lining the street outside the entrance.

WORTH SEEING

Freiburg's salient cathedral, affectionately called **Münster,** throws a long shadow upon the city with its 127-m tower. Originally begun in around 1200 as a burial site for the Zähringen monarchs, the Münster truly began taking shape after the death of the last Zähringen in 1218. Its consecration in 1513 also signified the completion of this late-Romanesque and Gothic structure. Aside from masses of tourists, the dark interior of the cathedral contains marvelously bright stained-glass windows from the 15th and 16th centuries. You'll have to catch a guided tour to see the 10 richly decorated side chapels; check signs for times. For a view over town and—better yet—a close-up of the cathedral's intricately fashioned, perforated spire, grit your teeth and climb the tower's 329 steps. *Münsterpl. Admission to tower: DM 2, DM 1.50 students. Tower open Mon.–Sat. 9:30–5, Sun. 1–5.*

On **Münsterplatz,** which surrounds the cathedral, a daily outdoor **market** offers the best in fresh produce, Black Forest meats and cheeses, flowers, and local arts and crafts; the market is widely regarded as the finest in southwestern Germany. The maroon **Kaufhaus** on the south side of the square is the old market hall, decorated with coats of arms and statues of the Hapsburgs, who ruled Freiburg, a free imperial city, for more than 400 years.

Between the tourist office and the Münster sits Freiburg's **Neues Rathaus** (New Town Hall), recast this century from a pair of Renaissance buildings. Be sure to peek through the arched doors at the photogenic inner courtyard. From the square in front of the Rathaus, Franziskanerstraße leads to the **Haus zum Walfisch** (House of the Whale), a beautiful gold-trimmed building reconstructed after World War II. The scholar Erasmus of Rotterdam lived here for two years when he was booted from Basel after the Reformation in 1529.

From the **Station der Schlossbergseilbahn** in the Stadtgarten, where Leopoldring and Schloßbergring meet, you can take a cable car up the 1,284-m-high **Schauinsland.** Freiburgers have sought the fresh air of these heights since the 12th century. Pack a lunch or eat at a restaurant at the valley station or at the top. Once the cable car reaches its highest point, you can walk to the final 200 m to the peak or take the path to Schniederlihof, a well-preserved mountain farmhouse built in 1592. The cable car runs year-round.

MUSEUMS • Except where noted, all museums are free to visit and open Tuesday–Friday 9:30–5, weekends 10:30–5. The **Augustiner Museum** (Augustinerpl., tel. 0761/201–2531; admission DM 4, DM 2 students), the largest in Freiburg, is housed in an old Baroque monastery between Schwabentor and Martinstor. Inside is a vast collection of medieval religious art from the monastery and the Münster, as well as 14th- to 20th-century paintings, sculpture, glassware, and furniture by artists from the upper Rhine region. If you'd rather check out modern art, try the nearby **Museum für Neue Kunst** (Marienstr. 10a, tel. 0761/201–2581), with emphasis on work from southwestern Germany.

A series of narrow streams, known as the Bächle, run through Freiburg's cobblestone streets. Used for watering cattle and as protection against fire in medieval times, they now help keep the air cool and provide a perfect place for uninhibited travelers to splash their feet.

Freiburg's **Museum für Ur- und Frühgeschichte** (Museum of Pre- and Early History, Rotteckring 5, tel. 0761/201–2571; open Tues.–Sun. 9–7) has a moderate collection of archaeological artifacts from the Rhine area, and its location in the gorgeous neo-Gothic Colombi Palace makes it worth a visit. The smallest and quirkiest museum in town is the **Zinnfigurenklause** (Tin Figure Collection, tel. 0761/24321; open Tues.–Thurs. 2:30–5, Fri. 5:30–7:30, weekends noon–2), located in the 13th-century Schwabentor. Shell out DM 2 (50 Pf students) to see the fascinating collection of tin figures. While you're here, cross the overpass and walk up **Schloßberg** for excellent views of the Münster and the Altstadt.

FESTIVALS

Starting in mid-June, the two-week **Zeltmusikfestival** (Tent Music Festival) brings world-class classical, jazz, and rock musicians to town. May and October host two different 10-day fairs: **Frühjahrsmesse** and **Herbstmesse,** both featuring lots of amusement park rides. During the four-day **Weintagen** (Wine Days), around the last weekend of June, you are encouraged to "sip" wines but not "consume in quantity." This hardly stops visitors and locals alike from becoming enchanted by a dionysian spirit and forgetting all moderation. The same goes for the nine-day **Weinkost** (Wine Tasting), a similar event in mid-August that features wines produced within Freiburg's city limits.

AFTER DARK

A number of bars, discos, and cafés grace the streets of the university quarter in the southwest corner of the Altstadt; Bertoldstraße west of Werderring is littered with colorful cafés and student-filled pubs. Freiburg also has loads of theaters and classical-music venues; check current listings in one of the free guides available at the tourist office.

Cafe Colonial–Hemingway. Have cocktails and a cigar at this Ernest Hemingway tribute pub. As you sip your mai tai, you may be compelled to compare your exhaustion (from climbing the Schauinsland) to that of Hemingway's (from fighting Franco's fascist thugs, or jungle beasts on safari in Africa). On Thursdays you'll sip to live music. *In Hotel Victoria at Eisenbahnstr. 54, tel. 0761/2073–4501.*

Café Légère. This is probably the most inviting of Freiburg's several gay/mixed bars. An unpretentious yet hip young crowd gathers here for drinks and light meals (served until 11 PM). *Niemensstr. 8, 1 block west of Martinstor, tel. 0761/32800.*

Club Parabel. Different DJs spin distinctive moods every night at this very hip venue. The club is connected to **Café Journal,** a bright and sophisticated place to have an espresso. *Universitätstr. 3, tel. 0761/30634. Cover varies. Closed Mon.–Wed. Opens at 11 PM.*

Freiburger Jazzhaus. A Freiburg institution, the Jazzhaus has been graced in the past by performers as diverse as the late Miles Davis and the still-living Kool and the Gang. It features a wide selection of live

WALDSTERBEN

Since the late 1970s, the Schwarzwald has become synonymous with Waldsterben (Forest Death), a term that describes the rapidly decaying health of Germany's forests as a result of airborne pollutants. Although evidence of Waldsterben can be seen throughout Germany, it's here in the Schwarzwald, the mother of all forests, that the disease has become a major issue. The exact cause of the problem remains unclear and is the subject of much controversy, but the results couldn't be clearer: Throughout the Schwarzwald trees are losing their leaves, saplings are failing to mature, pine needles are yellowing, and centuries-old trees are dying before their time. Huge sections of the Schwarzwald are already dead or dying, and Waldsterben shows no sign of slowing.

blues, folk, Latin, rock, and jazz nearly every night. Get listings and buy tickets at the tourist office. *Schnewlinstr. 1, tel. 0761/34973. From Hauptbahnhof, walk along tracks past Omnibusbahnhof. Cover: DM 10–DM 40.*

Hausbrauerei Feierling. This brewery serves sweet, tasty beer that's brewed on the premises—try the scrumptious, *very* wheaty Weißbier. The crowd can lean toward the yuppie side, but the place is always packed. To mingle with students, head across the street to Feierling's beer garden. *Gerberau 46, on Augustinerpl., tel. 0761/26678.*

NEAR FREIBURG

BREISACH

Breisach sits on the banks of the Rhine on the French border. Not surprisingly, the town has had the stuffing kicked out of it on numerous occasions during the many wars between France and Germany. The oldest part of town, strategically placed on a small hill beside the river and surrounded by tiered walls, testifies to this violent history. Two bulky towers, **Gutgesellentor** and **Hagenbachtor,** guard the south side of the hill. On the brow of the hill is **St. Stephans Münster,** the town's pride and joy. This cathedral, a blend of Romanesque and Gothic architecture, brims with late-15th- and early 16th-century artwork.

Between Breisach and Freiburg sits a vineyard-covered volcanic hill known as the **Kaiserstuhl,** or emperor's seat. The name probably derives from a Hapsburg into whose possession many of the area's villages came; today, the name is synonymous with wine. The Kaiserstuhl has great hiking, biking, and, of course, drinking. Spend a day here village and vineyard hopping, using either Breisach or Freiburg as a base. Consider staying in a Kaiserstuhl town like Sasbach, Jechtingen, or Königschaffhausen, where rooms cost as little as DM 25 a night. Just pick up a Kaiserstuhl map and *Unterkunftverzeichnis* at the Breisach or Freiburg tourist office and hop on the bus (rail pass holders get a major discount) or take the privately run *Kaiserstuhlbahn* that circles the hill. Either way, the journey won't cost more than DM 8, and a bottle of wine from a local *Winzer* (vintner) won't be any more expensive.

BASICS • Breisach has regular train service to Freiburg (30 min, DM 7). The main station is also where you can hop on the privately operated Kaiserstuhlbahn to nearby towns or catch a regional bus. From Breisach's station walk left along Neutorplatz (which becomes Rheinstraße) to Marktplatz, where you'll find the extremely helpful **tourist office** (Marktpl. 9, tel. 07667/83227; open weekdays 9–12:30 and 2–5, Sat. 9:30–noon). The English-competent staff offers trail maps (DM 10) and is happy to give tips to trekkers. Across the square is **Breisacher Fahrgast-Schifffahrt** (Rheinuferstr., tel. 07667/942010), which runs two-hour cruises (DM 15) up the Rhine to Basel and back from April to October.

WHERE TO SLEEP • The tourist office has a list of hotels and pensions in town. The friendly **HI-Jugendherberge** (Rheinuferstr. 12, tel. 07667/7665), along the Rhine about 1 km south of the town center, has comfy beds in a spotless environment for DM 23 (DM 28 over 26), including breakfast. To get here from Marktplatz, continue up the main drag, turn left on Rheinuferstraße, and continue along the river for about 10 min. Otherwise, you can camp in the green at **Campingplatz Münsterblick** (tel. 07667/93930), 2 km southeast of town in Breisach-Hochstetten. Spaces cost DM 7, plus DM 8 per person. To get here from behind the station, follow Ihringer Landstraße for about 15 min and hang a right on Hochstetten Straße.

MT. BELCHEN

Shaped more like an overgrown molehill than a mountain, Mt. Belchen is nevertheless the second-highest peak (1,414 m) in the southern Black Forest. What makes it such a popular attraction for visitors, though, are the tiny villages and deep valleys that surround it, as well as the views stretching to the Bodensee, the Rhine Valley, and even the Swiss Alps. The easiest way to reach Belchen, about 17 km south of Freiburg, is via the small village of **Münstertal,** which has regular train connections to Freiburg (40 min, DM 21 round-trip). From the Untermünstertal train station, it takes two to three hours of walking along a well-marked trail to cover the 10 km to the top. If you can't hack the trek, or the trek leaves you hacking, take one of the two daily buses that make the trip from the train station to the top. The local **tourist office** (Wasenstr. 47, Room 7, tel. 07636/70730), in the Rathaus, has lists of private rooms in the DM 25–DM 45 range. The office can also set you up with hiking maps and cross-country skiing maps.

Wine lovers can experience their own personal Allemanic bacchanalia at the Winzergenossenschaft in almost any of the villages nestled among vineyard-covered hills near Breisach. Try the rich Sylvaner, the tartish Müller-Thurgau, the sweet Riesling, and the sweeter Gewürztraminer.

ST. PETER

A nice half-day excursion from Freiburg, St. Peter is a tiny village well-known (and frequented) because of its landmark monastery, founded in the 11th century, and its huge Baroque church, designed by Peter Thumb (whose other Baroque works you're bound to stumble across somewhere in southern Germany). Ogle the gilt splendor, then hightail it out of town for a scenic 4-km hike to the nearby village of St. Märgen—just follow the frequent trail markers out of town. From Freiburg, Bus 7216 makes the one-hour trip to St. Peter (and on to St. Märgen) six–eight times per day (DM 8.50), and Bus 7205 (hourly) travels via Glottertal, a scenic village where Baden vineyards meet Black Forest pines.

HIGH BLACK FOREST

In the Hochschwarzwald (High Black Forest), thick forests and rolling hills reach their highest peak, the Feldberg, with some of the forest's best skiing and hiking. Pristine but resort-ified villages dot the area, marring the countryside with tackiness. Fortunately, the opportunities for hiking and biking in the forest still outnumber visitors, and isolation is easy to find. Major towns have rail connections (and tiny train stations with no luggage storage), but most of the Hochschwarzwald is traversed only by infrequent buses (and tinted-window tourist-mobiles). If you're planning on getting around by foot, pick up maps and advice at Freiburg's tourist office (*see above*).

TITISEE

A small lake sealed off from the rest of the world by a series of pine-covered hills, Titisee possesses the type of natural beauty that makes you want to wander through the trees wearing nothing but a well-worn pair of hiking boots. Unfortunately, never-never land has a problem with tourists—in summer swarms of foreigners indulge in a souvenir-grubbing feeding frenzy of frightening proportions. The main town, Titisee-Neustadt, offers little more than overpriced food and some of the tackiest souvenir shops in Germany; Seestraße, the main promenade, is ground zero. To join the maddening crowd, rent a paddle boat or rowboat from one of the innumerable stands along the shore, or jump on a ship for a short cruise around the lake. To get away from it all, follow any of the excellent hiking and biking trails that circle the lake; in winter escape on countless well-marked Nordic ski trails and groomed walking trails.

If you're in the mood for a dip, saunter over to the lake (just south of the tourist office) and jump right in. There are a couple short patches of beach to the right of the boat rental area, and there's a larger stretch of the west shore reserved for *Kurkarten* holders (get one from your lodgers). Take a walk or bike ride around the lake and find a secluded spot, or paddle your way across—if you want to fish, get equipment and a license at the boat rental. In winter, the focus shifts to the miles of surrounding skiing trails; although a few dinky downhill slopes exist, cross-country skiing is king. Pick up trail maps, lists of ski-rental outlets, and schedules for the Feldberg "Skibus" at the tourist office.

BASICS

From the Bahnhof, go right (west) for about 300 m to the Kurhaus (the big building with all the flags) and the **tourist office** (btw Seestr. and Strandbadstr., tel. 07651/980421), open weekdays 8–7, Saturday 10–noon and 3–6, Sunday 10–noon. Here you can pick up trail maps and three-speed **bikes** (DM 8 per day). Serious cyclists can rent **mountain bikes** from Sporthaus (Am Postpl., tel. 07651/7494), by the lakeside *Boothaus* (boat house) about 50 m past the tourist office. Going rates are DM 15 for three hours, DM 25 per day. Rent **skis** at Sport Lais (Hauptstr. 14, tel. 0765/5004) in Neustadt.

COMING AND GOING

Trains travel twice per hour to Titisee from Freiburg (40 min, DM 10), passing through Höllental (Hell's Valley). Despite the satanic name, the ride is one of the most beautiful in Germany. Hourly trains leave the Titisee station for Schluchsee and Seebrugg (20 min, DM 6.50). From the nearby Neustadt station, you can catch the main rail line to Donaueschingen (1 hr, DM 14).

WHERE TO SLEEP AND EAT

Titisee, not surprisingly, has few budget lodging options. The tourist office has lists of private rooms and smaller inns and pensions (DM 50–DM 80 for a double). If you're list-less, try the quaint, central **Gästehaus Wald und See** (Alte Poststr. 14, tel. 07651/8389). The friendly, English-speaking owner charges DM 48 for singles, DM 85 for doubles. From the Kurhaus, walk west on Strandbadstraße and right on Alte Poststraße. Avoid paying grossly inflated prices on food by steering clear of Titisee's tourist-trap sidewalk restaurants. Instead, assemble a picnic at the market **Gutscher** (Seestr., at Strandbadstr.), which features a variety of Black Forest meats and cheeses.

HOSTELS • Jugendherberge Veltishof (HI). With an idyllic setting just two min from the lake, this far-flung hostel is worth the trek. Comfy beds in spotless rooms go for DM 24 (DM 28 over 26), including breakfast, which you can eat outside at picnic tables. *Bruderhalde 27, tel. 07652/238. From Bahnhof, take infrequent bus (direction: Todtnau) to Feuerwehrheim; or, from Kurhaus, walk SW on Strandbadstr. onto Bruderhalde and continue for 3 km (about 30 min) along shore. 133 beds. Curfew 10:30 PM.*

CAMPING • Easy-to-reach **Campingplatz Bühlhof** (tel. 07652/1600) is a huge (220 spots), well-organized site overlooking the lake. Choose your own spot on the Bühlberg hillside for about DM 10 plus DM 8.50 per person. Hot showers cost 50 Pf, and laundry runs DM 10. Follow the directions for the hostel, but head up the hill when you see the sign (15 min total). You'll find a market, an Imbiß with a beer garden, *and* you'll pass a herd of billy goats on the way up. Farther along the lake, near the hostel, **Naturcamping Weilerhof** (tel. 07652/228) charges DM 20 for tent sites (DM 30 for two) and DM 18.50 for car sites, but notice all the people camping for free in the pine grove right above the campground. Both camping grounds are closed mid-April to mid-May.

NEAR TITISEE

FELDBERG

At 1,493 m, the Feldberg is the Black Forest's tallest peak. In the 18th and 19th centuries its rounded top received a serious crewcut from a group of farmers determined to turn the forested mountain into pastureland. To add insult to injury, the 20th century brought the addition of a TV tower and numerous radio dishes. Despite all this, Feldberg is still a center for outdoors enthusiasts. In summer, hiking and biking dominate the scene, and in winter Feldberg is the Black Forest's most popular downhill ski area. Get maps and info about rentals (about DM 25 a day) and Feldberg's 26 ski lifts at the hostel, at **Tourist-Information Feldberg** (Paßhöhe, tel. 07676/250), at tourist offices in Titisee or Schluchsee, or by calling **Skitelefon** (07676/1214) and busting out your German. The best hiking maps (DM 6) come in English versions and are available at the Titisee and Schluchsee tourist offices.

If you intend to hike or ski, your best bet is to base yourself at the mountain's only youth hostel, **HI-Jugendherberge Hebelhof** (Paßhöhe 14, tel. 07676/221), which charges DM 21 (DM 28 over 26). It lies within walking distance of the ski lifts (DM 6) and trails, including an ugly gravel path to the top of the mountain. Be sure to make reservations in winter. To get here from Titisee you can either hop on a bus (direction: Todtnau) to Hebelhof, or catch a train to Feldberg-Bärental (the highest train station in Germany) and then a bus to Hebelhof.

SCHLUCHSEE

About 10 km south of Titisee is Schluchsee, a larger lake with a smaller, sleepier town, far fewer tourists, and the same intense beauty as Titisee. Plenty of narrow beaches line the shores, and boats can be rented by the hour for excursions on the lake—not a bad way to spend a sunny afternoon. Rent a motorboat at the shore near the Wolfsgrund hostel for DM 13–DM 30. Pick up a detailed hiking guide in English (DM 6), or maps of skiing trails at the **Kurverwaltung** (Fischbacherstr., at Lindenstr., tel. 07656/7732), in the town center. Between April and October they rent clunky bikes for DM 10, mountain bikes for DM 20. The office is open Monday–Saturday 8–6, Sunday 10–noon (shorter hrs off-season). You can reach Schluchsee by hourly train from Titisee (20 min, DM 8).

WHERE TO SLEEP AND EAT

Schluchsee has a number of inexpensive pensions (DM 30–DM 46 per person); get a complete list at the Kurverwaltung. **Gästehaus Faller** (Lindenstr. 11, tel. 07656/644) has the cheapest rooms in town, with plenty of carved wood and lace for that Old World charm. Doubles with bath start at DM 30. From the Kurhaus, walk west down Lindenstraße. Foodwise, the town has fewer budget options. Stock up on groceries at **Isele Markt,** on Kirchplatz across from Hotel Schiff, or sample the standard German versions of pizza and pasta at **Pizzeria Ristorante da Franco** (Kirchsteige 4, tel. 07656/1261).

HOSTELS • Jugendherberge Schluchsee-Seebrugg. At the very end of the lake and the rail line lurks Seebrugg, which consists of little more than a hostel and a train depot. You'd think Seebrugg's isolation would make it ideal, but a well-traveled road and the DM 4 admission to the beach spoil the tranquility. Beds go for DM 23 (DM 26 over 26). *Seebrugg 9, tel. 07656/494. 134 beds.*

Jugendherberge Schluchsee-Wolfsgrund. This hostel beats the Schluchsee-Seebrugg all around, if only because a stairway leads from the hostel to one of the lake's nicer beaches. The DM 23 price (DM 28 over 26) includes breakfast. Call ahead. *Im Wolfsgrund 21, tel. 07656/329. With your back to water, walk left from the Bahnhof; at end of lakeside parking lot, turn left onto dirt trail, pass small bay on right, climb up railroad overpass, and continue for 100 m. 133 beds. Curfew 11 PM.*

CAMPING • Campingplatz Wolfsgrund. This campground has modern luxuries like hot running water, laundry facilities, and real toilets. Rates are DM 9.50 per person, DM 11.50 per tent, and DM 3.50 per car. *Tel. 07656/7739. From entrance to Schluchsee-Wolfsgrund hostel, walk to lake and continue along shore for ¾ km.*

WUTACHSCHLUCHT

On the eastern fringes of the Black Forest, the Wutachschlucht, named for the Wutach River that runs through a *Schlucht* (gorge), is a fine example of the deep, dark gorges from which the Black Forest gets its name (densely packed trees block out the sun and make the forest, well, sort of black). Most of the 25-km gorge is a protected nature reserve, cut by a narrow and swift river. A marked trail, characterized by steep drops and many tiny wooden bridges, runs the gorge's entire length—prime for hiking.

Bonndorf is the town closest to the gorge's dramatic eastern end. You can reach Bonndorf by bus only twice per day from Schluchsee-Seebrugg (25 min, DM 10.50), more frequently from Donaueschingen (45 min, DM 9) and Titisee-Neustadt (45 min, DM 8). The bus stops in front of the post office and within spitting distance of **Tourist-Information-Zentrum** (Schloßstr. 1, tel. 07703/7607), which has maps of the gorge. To reach said gorge from the post office, walk up Martinstraße and follow the signs to **Philosophenweg,** a dirt hiking path that leads 4 km through the one-tractor town of Boll to Wutachschlucht. If you want to get to the gorge itself ASAP, hop on a bus right to the entrance (the Schattenmühle Wanderparkplatz stop is a good place to start). From here you can walk as far as you like in either direction and double back when you run out of steam; or take the highly recommended hike to the town of **Wutachmühle,** at the eastern end of the gorge, where you can catch a bus back to Bonndorf (last bus at 5 PM).

At **HI-Jugendherberge Bonndorf** (Waldallee 27, tel. 07703/359, fax 07703/1686) you can cool off in the indoor pool before catching some Zs. Beds are DM 23 (DM 28 over 26). In winter the hostel rents cross-country ski equipment. To get here from the tourist office, walk down Schloßstraße and Mühlenstraße, turn left on Rothausstraße, right on Waldallee, and walk for about 10 min.

CENTRAL BLACK FOREST

The heart of the Schwarzwald holds the darkest valleys, the most thatched roofs, and the most cuckoo clocks. Many tour-bus travelers go cuckoo for the clocks, though, so if you eschew souvenir-buying frenzies, skip these towns and their famous timepieces. From tourist meccas like **Triberg,** take advantage of the region's efficient bus and rail lines to escape the hordes and discover the woods. Hiking and skiing trails abound, and there are plenty of hostels and hostel-type *Naturfreundehäuser* to take you in along the way. Get complete lists at local and regional tourist offices.

DONAUESCHINGEN

Sitting on a sparsely vegetated plateau between the Black Forest and the Schwäbische Alb (*see* Chapter 3), tiny Donaueschingen may just send you into paroxysms of sleepiness. However, many hikers and bikers stop here on their way to and from the Black Forest. The town is also where the Breg and Brigach rivers join to form the official source of the 2,840-km-long Danube River. While the Danube is the second-longest river in Europe (after the Volga), the source itself is less than awe-inspiring, and the 19th-century stone monument built around it, the **Donauquelle,** adds little zest. The **Fürstliches Schloß,** next to the Donauquelle, looks as if it has seen better days (it has), but don't head back to the train station yet. The von Fürstenberg family, whose residence forms the only "there" in Donaueschingen, has collected some strange and wonderful things over the centuries. Visit the **Fürstenbergsammlung** (Karlspl., 1 block uphill from the Schloß). To gain admittance, pull the bell next to the massive doors and hand over DM 4 (DM 2 students); for this, you'll get German masters, a facsimile of the original *Nibelungenlied* manuscript (the original is hidden in a vault beneath the town), and two scary rooms full of creatures killed and labeled by various von Fürstenbergs. The other reason to pay homage to the royal family? Beer. Work on your beer belly at the **Fürstenberg Brewery** (tel. 0771/86232), just west of the Donauquelle. Call about free tours or just head to their bar for a pint at the source.

BASICS

Many bookstores in town, including **Mory's Hofbuchhandlung** (Karlstr. 53–55, tel. 0771/2530), carry trail maps to supplement the rather spartan selection at the **tourist office** (Verkehrsamt; Karlstr. 58, tel. 0771/857221), which is open weekdays 8–noon and 1:15–5, Saturdays 9–noon (shorter hrs in winter). The tourist office also has lists of private rooms. If you want to explore the central Black Forest luggage-free, leave your stuff at the station here—there's no storage in Triberg.

COMING AND GOING

Donaueschingen lies on the rail line between Karlsruhe (7 per day, 1½ hrs, DM 46) and Konstanz (hourly, 1 hr, DM 22) and is regularly connected by trains to the Black Forest towns of Titisee-Neustadt (hourly, 45 min, DM 12) and Villingen (hourly, 10 min, DM 5), as well as Rottweil (via Tuttlingen, 45 min, DM 12) in the Schwäbische Alb. Josefstraße runs from the train station to the main drag, Karlstraße.

WHERE TO SLEEP AND EAT

Lakeside camping is available 5 km east of town at **Riedsee-Camping** (Am Riedsee 11, tel. 0771/5511), which has a tennis court, sauna, and a restaurant—all for DM 8 per tent plus DM 8 per person. You shouldn't have trouble snagging one of the 500 spots despite the camper-vans. From the train station, take Bus 7282 (DM 3) about 3 km toward Immendingen to Pfohren Riedsee. **Hotel Bären** (Josefstr. 7–9, tel. 0771/0518) is the cheapest place to sleep in town at DM 35–DM 50 for doubles. You can also contact the tourist office about private rooms.

Ristorante Gran Sasso (Karlstr. 63, near An der Stadtkirche, tel. 0771/7421) serves tasty Italian food like pizza (DM 8.50–DM 13) and 27 different pasta dishes (DM 9.50–DM 13). For bulk groceries head to the **Krone** supermarket on Mühlenstraße.

TRIBERG

Deep, thickly forested valleys surround the town of Triberg, boasting some of the best hiking and biking (and cross-country skiing) in southwest Germany. Built on a steep hillside, the town itself offers enough cuckoo-clock attractions to draw busloads of camera-toting tourists: Be prepared for a sickening overdose of German kitsch. For many, the biggest draw is Germany's highest **waterfall,** which drops 163 m in seven rocky steps. Spectacular as the falls are, you have to pay DM 2.80 to reach the crowded viewing area (open Apr.–Sept., daily 9–6). You can reach the waterfall via a path at the top of Triberg's main drag, Hauptstraße; there are also four well-marked trails that wind around the falls, each about 4 km long. These lead to longer trails through the forest. The **Westweg** passes through the central Black Forest nearby, and great hikes to less accessible villages like Schonach (*see box,* Be Very Afraid, *below*) and Nußbach will make you forget the din of the clocks. Get info about hiking as well as lodging along the trails at the tourist office.

The **Schwarzwaldmuseum,** one block from the waterfall, has one of the quirkiest and most interesting collections of Black Forest culture. Marvel at hundreds of cuckoo clocks, models of traditional artisans' workshops, and a room designed to look like a mine shaft, full of minerals from the surrounding hills. *Wallfahrtstr. 4, off Hauptstr., tel. 07722/4434. Admission: DM 4, DM 2 students. Open May–Oct., daily 9–6; shorter hrs off-season.*

BASICS

Triberg's **tourist office** (Luisenstr. 10, tel. 07722/953230), in the Kurhaus two blocks from the entrance to the waterfall, has maps of town and surrounding hiking trails. It's open weekdays 8–noon and 2–5 (May–Oct., also Sat. 10–noon). Rent a **mountain bike** at Trans-Alp (Hauptstr. 6, tel. 0772/21120) for DM 18–DM 25 per day.

COMING AND GOING

You can reach Triberg hourly by rail from Hausach (20 min, DM 7) and Donaueschingen (40 min, DM 12). To reach the town center from the station, cross the overpass, go down the stairs, and walk left uphill for about 15 min. Otherwise, hop on the bus (there's only one), which drops you in the center of town.

WHERE TO SLEEP AND EAT

With impressive views of the area, Triberg's **HI-Jugendherberge** (Rohrbacher Str. 35, tel. 07722/4110, fax 07722/6662) is a steep 20-min hike up Friedrichstraße from the waterfall (or you can take the bus toward Schwimmbad before 8 PM). The DM 23 price (DM 28 over 26) includes breakfast. Central **Krone** (Schulstr. 37, tel. 07722/4524) has rooms with creaky but comfortable beds starting at DM 38 per person, plus a restaurant with hearty Black Forest meals for under DM 20. From the waterfall, walk two blocks down Hauptstraße and turn right on Schulstraße. For tasty pizza or pasta (DM 8–DM 15), head to **Pinnochio** (Hauptstr. 64, tel. 07722/4424), near the top of the hill. Thanks to tourism, Triberg also has more Turkish fast food than one would expect in a mountain town.

NEAR TRIBERG

FURTWANGEN

About 15 km south of Triberg, Furtwangen attracts many visitors solely because of its **Deutsches Uhrenmuseum** (German Clock Museum), with more than 1,000 timepieces from around the planet. German-speakers can take advantage of tours and detailed explanations of the history of clock production; everybody else just looks at display cases of everything from simple wristwatches to enormous, beautiful grandfather clocks. *Gerwigstr. 11, tel. 07723/920117. Admission: DM 4, DM 2 students. Open Apr.–Oct., daily 9–5; Nov.–May, daily 10–5.*

BASICS • For a list of places to crash and a map of local hiking trails, pop into Furtwangen's **tourist office** (Marktpl. 4, tel. 07723/939111), in the Rathaus between the bus stop and the museum. Buses regularly make the scenic 45-minute trek from Triberg's train station to Furtwangen. To reach the clock museum, get off at the Friedrichstraße stop, walk straight one block, cross the street, and continue on Gerwigstraße. If you've had enough clocks and would rather ponder the meaning of time itself, Furtwangen offers great hiking and skiing; get tips at the tourist office.

BE VERY AFRAID

The origins of the Black Forest cuckoo clock are murky. Some say a nature-loving clock maker rescued a hapless cuckoo chick and brought it back to his workshop. The birdie learned to cluck to the ticking of the clocks and thus inspired the artisan to carve a clock with a bird chime. Be that as it may, it's still difficult to take Triberg's cuckoo mania seriously. Shops with names like House of 1,000 Clocks and Big Ben proliferate, creating a sort of warped Disneyland effect. But that ain't nothing: Nearby Schonach is home to the world's largest cuckoo clock, a massive contraption with huge swinging doors, a mammoth cuckoo bird, and plenty of troubling implications for the German psyche. Walk or take a bus a few km northwest from Triberg. On the outskirts of Schonach you'll find a small house with an unbelievably big clock face. You need to be seriously giddy to appreciate this place fully.

GUTACH

Sitting in a wide valley 13 km north of Triberg, the village of Gutach boldly asserts itself as the true home of *Bollenhüte,* women's hats decorated with bright red or black fuzzy balls. (The color of your balls, it seems, tells all—red balls mean you're single, black balls mean you've settled down.)

On the outskirts of town, the excellent **Schwarzwälder Freilichtmuseum** (Black Forest Open-Air Museum) provides a glimpse of the everyday life of the region's inhabitants. Housed in a number of traditional dwellings, most of which were brought to Gutach from other areas of the Black Forest, the Freilichtmuseum features live demonstrations of crafts practiced in the region for hundreds of years. Catch Bus 7160 in front of Triberg's post office to Gutach's Vogtsbauernhof stop. Only a few buses make the trip each day, and the last returns between 3 and 5:30 PM, so plan ahead if you don't want to hike back to Triberg. *Tel. 07831/230. Open Apr.–Oct., daily 8:30–6.*

NORTHERN BLACK FOREST

The northern fingers of the Black Forest are mostly unfamiliar to foreigners, and the region's river valleys and forests are unsullied by the commercialism that permeates so much of the southern Schwarzwald. Though it's possible to explore the northern forest by public transit—often on journeys with spectacular views—your best bets are hiking and biking, modes of transport that lead to the region's most interesting and undiscovered spots.

FREUDENSTADT

Despite its name, Freudenstadt (literally, "city of joy") is not necessarily the cheeriest place in the Black Forest, but it is a good base from which to take off for wilder parts of the region. The city's more modern demeanor stems from the fact that it is a newer settlement, a 19th-century planned community whose arcade-lined Marktplatz is Germany's largest. It owes its size to the unfulfilled plans of Duke Friedrich I of Württemberg, who wanted to build a Schloß on the site. Take a few moments to check out the **Stadtkirche,** in the square's southwest corner, which was built in the shape of an "L" so that men seated on one side and women on the other couldn't scope each other out during services. Then hit the trails. Although there is some downhill skiing, cross-country is by far the most popular and considerably more affordable option. Rental prices run DM 16.50–DM 28 a day—get a list at the tourist office.

BASICS

From the Marktplatz, Loßburgerstraße leads to Promenadeplatz, where you'll find the Kurhaus (Lauterbadstr. 5, tel. 07441/8640), which rents **bikes** for DM 13–DM 25 a day—bring your *Kurkarte* (a pass available at your hostel or hotel) for a discount. Next door, the **tourist office** (Promenadepl. 1, tel. 07441/86428; open weekdays 10–6, Sat. 10–1) sells trail maps of the surrounding area.

COMING AND GOING

Freudenstadt sits on a rail line between Karlsruhe (12 per day, 2 hrs, DM 21) and the Black Forest town of Hausach (8 per day, 45 min, DM 10.50), where you can connect to Donaueschingen or Offenburg. Get off the train at the **Stadtbahnhof**—not the Hauptbahnhof. From here, it's only a two-minute walk on Martin-Luther-Straße to the Marktplatz.

WHERE TO SLEEP

The most exciting thing about the local **HI-Jugendherberge** (Eugen-Nägele-Str. 69, tel. 07441/7720) is the washing machine downstairs. Beds cost DM 23 (DM 29 over 26), including breakfast. To get here from the Stadtbahnhof, turn left on Ringstraße, left on Ludwig-Jahn-Straße, and right on Gottlieb-Daimler-Straße. Right on the Marktplatz, **Gasthof Traube** (Marktpl. 41, tel. 07441/2880) is a cute, geranium-bedecked pension with rooms for DM 50 per person. To camp, take one of the 10 daily buses (Bus 12; weekends and holidays, Bus F2) from the Stadtbahnhof to **Campingplatz Langenwald** (tel. 07441/2862; closed Nov.–Apr.), in the woods about 3 km west of town. A spot for one costs DM 13.50, plus DM 8 for each extra person. They also rent bikes.

Forbach makes a most pleasant base for the "Tour de Murg," a bike path along the Murg River. Rent wheels in Freudenstadt, take the train one stop to Baiersbronn, and then pedal down to Forbach (unless you're a masochist and want to ride uphill).

NEAR FREUDENSTADT

SCHWARZWALD-HOCHSTRAßE

Covering 57 km between Freudenstadt and the chichi resort of Baden-Baden, the Schwarzwald-Hochstraße (Black Forest Highway) runs along a series of mountain ridges, offering outstanding views of Germany's Rhine Valley and France's Vosges Mountains. If you're here to hike, catch the **Westweg** trail, which parallels the road starting at **Zuflucht,** about 14 km out of Freudenstadt. The trail continues past the **Mummelsee,** a small lake that is sadly blemished by a hotel, a large parking lot, and a number of tacky souvenir shops, and on to the town of **Sand,** where it leaves the road and heads northeast for Pforzheim (*see* The Nagold Valley, *below*). Bus 12 (2 per weekday) and Bus F2 (5 per day on weekends) run from Freudenstadt's Stadtbahnhof to Zuflucht and Mummelsee, where Bus 7106 (2 per day) continues on to Sand and Baden-Baden.

HI-Jugendherberge Zuflucht (tel. 07804/611, fax 07804/1323), conveniently located halfway between Freudenstadt and Mummelsee, makes an excellent base for hiking or biking in summer and skiing in winter, and they rent equipment. Beds run DM 23 (DM 28 over 26), including breakfast. Farther along the trail, crash at the cheap **Naturfreundehaus Badener Höhe** (tel. 07226/238; closed Tues. and Dec.), about 2 km east of the Westweg and the Sand bus stop. Beds here cost a mere DM 8.50; breakfast is an extra DM 7.50.

FORBACH

Forbach, also along the Westweg hiking trail, is sprinkled with half-timbered houses and red sandstone fountains. It lies in the spectacular, pristine **Murg River Valley,** an area less populated by bus tourists than by hikers. Forbach's striking **St. Johanneskirche** (St. John's Church) sits on a small hill overlooking the center of town, flanked by a pair of thin towers. The colorfully painted interior looks more like that of a mosque than a church, except for the large sculpture of the crucifixion hanging from the vaulted ceiling. Definitely worth a look is the 16th-century **Alte Holzbrücke,** the largest single-span covered

PRESCRIPTION: VACATION

So you've seen the word "Kurort" (spa) and noticed the large number of towns in Germany that start with the letters B-A-D (bath), and you wonder what it all could mean. The answer is in the water (and the air). Sulphury spring water, mineral-rich mud, and cool, dry mountain air are believed to have healing properties. The bathing ("baden") tradition has been popular since Roman times, but the spa phenomenon hit its zenith in the 19th century, when resorts like Baden-Baden were playgrounds for Europe's aristocracy. Black Forest and other somewhat high-altitude resorts also became popular during this time as tuberculosis sanatoria (see Thomas Mann's "The Magic Mountain" for a glimpse into this world). Thanks to this tradition and a liberal health care system, the average German today can avail him- or herself of the healing waters a couple weeks every few years and have costs covered largely by health insurance. As they say at the spas: "Morgens Fango, abends Tango!" (loosely translated, "Mud in the morning, dance in the evening!").

wood bridge in Europe, traversing the Murg on the north side of town. Just north of the bridge in the Kurhaus, the **tourist office** (Striedstr., tel. 07228/2340) can outfit you with a map of hiking trails and campgrounds in the area. Forbach lies on the scenic Murgtalbahn rail line, which covers the 60 km between Freudenstadt (45 min, DM 8.50) and Rastatt (40 min, DM 7.50), where you can connect to Karlsruhe (1¼ hrs, DM 15).

WHERE TO SLEEP

The **HI-Jugendherberge** (Birket 1, tel. 07228/2427), in the hills above town, charges DM 23 (DM 28 over 26), including breakfast. To get here from the station, cross the bridge, turn right on Friedrichstraße, veer left onto Hauptstraße, and follow the signs up Braidstraße for about 2 km. There are quite a few reasonably priced (average DM 30 per person) pensions in Forbach; get a list at the tourist office or check the display across the street from the train station.

THE NAGOLD VALLEY

The serene waters of the Nagold River flow from the town of Nagold through a narrow, densely forested valley to Pforzheim. Tiny towns like adorable Calw and Hirsau remain refreshingly kitsch-free, but Pforzheim's proximity to Stuttgart has transformed it into a suburb of white-collar workers zooming back and forth on the Autobahn. Be aware that Nagold also exudes a somewhat upscale, yuppie atmosphere. If you're planning some serious hiking, stop by the excellent tourist office in Pforzheim. Armed with hiking maps and lists of accommodations (including a complete list of campgrounds), you can set out to discover the Nagold Valley's more pristine towns.

COMING AND GOING

Pforzheim, the valley's main northern transportation hub, has rail connections to most major German cities, with hourly trains to Karlsruhe (20 min, DM 9), Stuttgart (30 min, DM 13), and Heidelberg (via Karlsruhe, 1 hr, DM 25). Southern German cities like Konstanz (3¾ hrs, DM 49–DM 53) are accessible via Horb, a small town at the valley's southern end. A single rail line runs along the Nagold River from Pforzheim to Horb, along which trains run about once an hour from either end on weekdays (weekend service is sketchier). Buses also run through the valley, but with less frequency than trains and at a much slower pace.

PFORZHEIM

The modern city of Pforzheim, the northeastern gateway to the Black Forest, bears little relation to the densely wooded hills surrounding the city. Despite attempts by the tourism board to attract visitors, Pforzheim holds little allure for budget travelers—except as a starting point for three great hiking trails through the forest. The most challenging, the 280-km **Westweg** (*see* Near Freudenstadt, *above*), runs to Basel via Forbach, Mummelsee, and Titisee; it's recommended as a 12-day hike. The 220-km **Mittelweg** is a nine-day hike that runs to Waldshut via Wildbad, Freudenstadt, and Titisee. Also pegged as a nine-day hike is the 240-km **Ostweg,** which runs to Schaffhausen in Switzerland via the Nagold Valley, Freudenstadt, Alpirsbach, and Villingen. Stop by the tourist office for brochures (DM 2–DM 4) that describe each hike and list backpacker-friendly accommodations, detailed maps (DM 6–DM 10), and lists of people who will transport your baggage from one destination to the next.

Historically, Pforzheim is most famous for its jewelry, which explains the town's moniker, Goldstadt (City of Gold).

In the 16th century, Pforzheim became known for its jewelry- and watchmaking. See the gleaming products of that industry in the city's three museums; admission to all is free. The **Edelsteinausstellung Schütt** (Goldschmiedeschulstr. 6, tel. 07231/22001; open weekdays 9–noon and 1:30–5, Sat. 9–noon) displays minerals, gems, and precious stones, along with a gem-studded Burmese tapestry. The **Reuchlinhaus** (Jahnstr. 42, tel. 07231/392126; open Tues.–Sun. 10–5) houses a collection of jewelry through the ages. If you're in town on a Wednesday (or the second or fourth Sunday of the month), the **Technisches Museum** (tel. 07231/392869) details the production of local jewelry and timepieces. All three museums lie across the river, southeast of the Rathaus.

Back in the center, the **Schloßkirche St. Michael** is one of the few prewar buildings to be found in Pforzheim. Inside are the tombs of some of Baden's favorite rulers, including Duke Karl and his French bride Stephanie. They were the disputed parents of foundling Kaspar Hauser, Germany's favorite 19th-century "boy raised by wolves." Kaspar wasn't really raised by wolves but was found on the Nuremberg Marktplatz in 1828, unable to walk or talk. The current royal family is not fond of the spurious connection between their house and Kaspar, but some historians insist that Kaspar was kidnapped by Duke Karl's own brother and hidden in a cellar his entire childhood, only to be dumped in Franconia when things got out of hand. Let director Werner Herzog's 1974 film *Jeder für sich und Gott gegen alle* (usually translated as *Every Man for Himself and God Against All*) be your artsy primer of Kaspar's life.

BASICS

Pforzheim's tourist office (Marktpl. 1, tel. 07231/1442442; open weekdays 9–1 and 2–6, Sat. 9–noon), in the new Rathaus, can set you up with maps and all kinds of trail info. If you're just beginning a Schwarzwald hiking adventure, get complete regional information here, including lists of campgrounds and trailside Naturfreundehäuser where you can crash for around DM 10. To get here from the train station, walk down Schloßberg. You can rent a bike at Fahrrad-Fachgeschäft Schneider (Gymnasiumstr. 76, tel. 07231/12386), one block south of Östliche Karl-Friedrich-Straße, east of Schloßberg.

WHERE TO SLEEP AND EAT

Lodging in Pforzheim is generally not cheap. The newly renovated hostel, **Jugendherberge "Burg Rabeneck"** (Kräneckstr. 4, tel. 07231/972660), is a real find; take a dive in the pool on a warm day and enjoy a complimentary breakfast. Rooms go for DM 22 (DM 27 over 26). Otherwise, the cheapest option in the city center is **Pension Morlock** (Rudolfstr. 11, tel. 07231/351475), with doubles for DM 98 and singles for DM 55–DM 65. From the northern side of the Hauptbahnhof (away from downtown), turn left on Guterstraße and right on Rudolfstraße. Reservations are a good idea. If you want to escape the southern German sunshine, flee the dumpy station and head one block south to the dark and funky **Wun-**

derbar (Schloßbergstr. 23, tel. 07231/356700). If it's before 2 PM you can order breakfast for under DM 9. Otherwise grab a beer and hang out with Pforzheim's small collection of hipsters. For a more substantial meal, head to **i-Dipfele Café** (Östliche 1a, tel. 07231/357535), across from the tourist office.

CALW

Worn-out, tired clichés aside, the true gem of the Nagold Valley is Calw (pronounced something like an easy-on-the-a "calve") and its Baroque Altstadt. Nobel Prize–winning writer Hermann Hesse (born here in 1877) once remarked that "between Bremen and Naples, between Vienna and Singapore, I have had the opportunity to see many charming towns . . . but the most beautiful town of all is Calw on the Nagold." Hesse, an avowed pacifist, moved to Switzerland during World War I and later took on Swiss citizenship, earning him much disfavor among conservative Germans. His hometown, however, honors him with the **Hermann Hesse Museum** (Marktpl. 30, tel. 07051/7522), which depicts his life through original manuscripts, documents, and photographs. If your German is good, look for Hesse's budget-travel inspirational message in the display on his Italian journey. In the same building—and included in the DM 3 (DM 2 students) entrance fee—is the small **Galerie der Stadt Calw,** with 20th-century works by a handful of local artists. Both are open Tuesday–Saturday 2–5, Sunday 11–5.

Calw was a medieval textile town largely destroyed by fire in the 17th century, yet the modern town is hardly a bland reconstruction—especially if you like weathered facades and a mellow pace. The **Museum der Stadt Calw** (Bischofstr. 48, tel. 07051/167260; admission DM 4, DM 2 students) puts Calw into historical perspective, but you'll get a better sense of this small village on foot. In the center of it all lies the expansive, cobblestone **Marktplatz,** a small square lined with photogenic half-timbered houses. About 100 m south is the 15th-century **Nikolausbrücke,** a stone bridge with a small votive chapel tucked away on its span. Meander through the Altstadt until you find yourself before the austere, towering, red-sandstone **Stadtkirche Peter und Paul** (Church of Sts. Peter and Paul).

BASICS

Calw is perfect for aimless hikes through the surrounding hills on easy-to-find trails. Get detailed maps at a local bookstore, head out on your own, or visit Calw's **tourist office** (in nearby Hirsau, Aureliuspl. 10, tel. 07051/1670; open weekdays 8:30 AM–11:30 AM) for maps, trail maps, and brochures. If you don't make it to Hirsau in time, the information desk in the Rathaus, also open weekday mornings (and Thurs. until 4:30), has city maps and guides.

WHERE TO SLEEP

The 88-bed **HI-Jugendherberge** (Im Zwinger 4, tel. 07051/12614), in a green half-timbered house in the city center, is a great base for exploring the valley. A comfortable bed and standard breakfast cost DM 23 (DM 28 over 26), reception is open 5 PM–8 PM, and there's a strict 10 PM curfew. From the station, cross Nikolausbrücke and continue down Metzgergasse until it dead ends; to your right is Im Zwinger. Creaky but comfortable **Hotel Garni Alte Post** (Bahnhofstr. 1, tel. 07051/2196) has roomy rooms with TV for DM 48–DM 65 per person. The nearest campground is **Campingplatz Weidensteige** (tel. 07051/12845; closed winter), just east of Calw in Eiselstätt. From the station, head left on Bischofstraße, turn left under the train overpass onto Lange Steige, and veer right onto Weidensteige. Tent spots cost DM 7 plus DM 7 per person.

FOOD

A **produce market** is held Wednesday and Saturday mornings on the Marktplatz. **Restaurant Alt Calw** (Im Calwer Markt, tel. 0705/40933), between Marktplatz and the bridge leading to the train station, serves excellent Swabian and Italian meals under DM 15. For reasonable pizza and pasta (DM 8–DM 14), head south on Bischofstraße from the train station and walk under the train overpass to **Pizzeria Linde** (Lange Steige 2, tel. 0705/30347).

NEAR CALW

HIRSAU

From Calw it's a five-minute train ride or a pleasant 40-minute walk to the smaller village of Hirsau, home to one of the most influential monasteries in Germany, the Benedictine **Kloster.** Built in the 9th century and added to intermittently over the centuries, the cloister now stands in ruins, with two notable exceptions: the 12th-century **Eulenturm** (Owl Tower) and the beautifully restored, 16th-century **Marienkapelle** (Mary's Chapel). In the **Klostermuseum** you can view the remains of the cloister's decorations and learn the history of this once-powerful monastery, which launched a reform movement freeing religious institutions from secular rulers and placing them under the pope. If you end up staying a little too late at the ruins, Hirsau's **Gasthaus Zum Löwen** (Wildbaderstr. 20, tel. 07051/58576) has basic rooms starting at DM 55 per person, including breakfast.

NAGOLD

The town of Nagold lies south of Calw, where the Nagold Valley widens into a small forested plain. If your train approaches from the south, you probably won't be inspired to disembark; from the north, however, Nagold's setting will resemble the rest of the valley—steep, narrow, and green. Despite the town's modern, suburban demeanor, its Altstadt retains several fascinating buildings: the massive, late-17th-century **Hotel Post** (cnr Herrenbergstr. and Bahnhofstr.), the 18th-century **Altes Schulhaus** (Old Schoolhouse), and the unnamed, crooked affair at Marktstraße 15. You can't miss the two tallest structures in town: the early 15th-century **Alter Turm,** once part of the town's defenses, and the handsome, red-sandstone **Stadtkirche,** built between 1870 and 1874. On a hill above town, the meager ruins of a 17th-century castle offer a great view of Nagold and the river valley. To reach the ruins, cross the river behind Nagold's nondescript **Rathaus,** on Marktstraße at Badgasse, walk across the park, and follow one of the many paths up the hill. On your way, stop by the **tourist office** (Marktstr. 27, 2nd floor, tel. 07452/6810; open weekdays 7:30–5:30), just behind the Rathaus, but don't expect them to roll out the red carpet for you.

WHERE TO SLEEP AND EAT

South of Nagold's Altstadt, friendly **Gasthof Schwarzwald** (Hohenbergerstr. 50, tel. 07452/2976) has clean if characterless rooms from DM 37 to DM 54 per person. Nagold also has a **campground** (Calwer Str. 119, tel. 07452/2608), 2 km south of town. From the Bahnhof, turn right onto Calwer Straße. Rates are DM 8.50 per person, DM 4.50 per spot. The numerous Imbiß stands near the Busbahnhof are your best bet for food in Nagold, unless you choose to stock up on groceries at the **Edeka** supermarket across from the Busbahnhof. Also check out the **outdoor market** that lines the streets around Marktstraße on Saturday mornings.

5 MUNICH

BY PEGGY SALZ-TRAUTMAN

In the midst of provincial Bavaria, Munich (München) towers as a beacon of serene, liberal urbanity. "A German heaven on earth" is what the American author Thomas Wolfe called the unofficial capital of southern Germany. Proud of its reputation, Munich spends tens of millions each year to pack the city full of art, music, culture, and excitement—a spending spree the city can afford because it lies in the richest state in Germany. Munich is also fast emerging as a new mecca for high-tech corporations and entrepreneurs: Microsoft and CompuServe top the list of companies located in and around the city. The word is spreading among savvy executives and cosmopolitan artists alike that Munich is "the place to be." Fortunately, you can experience Munich without having to endure the impersonal hustle and bustle typical of a big city: Munich has kept its small town flair. Known for their helpfulness, Müncheners often converse in *Bayerisch* (Bavarian), a relaxed, lilting dialect suffused with farmer's wisdom and references to beer, the city's pride and patrimony. It's difficult not to feel at home in Munich—particularly since *Gemütlichkeit* (good-naturedness) is second nature to most of the city's inhabitants. But there is a certain seriousness about the city as well; locals make no effort to hide the uncomfortable recent history that lurks behind the city's majestic facades, awesome cultural cachet, and traditional mirth and merrymaking. Just outside Munich is Dachau (*see* Near Munich, *below*), a dreary, gray city that saw the erection of the concentration camp of the same name and carries the scar to this day.

Heinrich der Löwe, the Lion King, effectively established the Munich in 1158 when he spanned the River Isar in an effort to buttress his hold on the region's salt trade. Twenty years later began the dynastic rule of the House of Wittelsbach, whose formal authority endured up through World War I. In the utter chaos that ensued, worker's councils seized control of the city and established a short-lived Bavarian Soviet Republic, promptly crushed by revanchist generals and right-wing mercenaries. Soon after, Hitler trod the streets in search of recruits, and in 1923 declared his intent to seize municipal power and march on Berlin. The Beer Hall Putsch, as it came to be known, was quashed, yet Hitler would return to lead Germany and much of the world into unparalleled ruin. Following the war, Munich quickly rose from the rubble—a prime example of Germany's spectacular *Wirtschaftswunder* (economic miracle)—with the help of companies like Bayerische Motoren Werke (BMW). With Berlin isolated in the East, and Bonn little more than a glorified *Bundesdorf* (federal village), Munich became as much a center of cultural and financial power as was possible in the decentralized West.

In these postunification days, Munich has shifted its attention to high-tech, for which it has earned the nickname "Silicon Valley of the South," and high-profile industries such as fashion design, film, and photographic special effects. Munich also remains the main attraction for beer-lovers and American tourists, who target the city for a chance to taste-test the city's over 100 brands of beer and lose all inhibitions at Munich's Oktoberfest. If by some cruel twist of nature you detest beer, worry not. Munich has much more to offer. Under the spell of the classical statues in the Louvre in Paris and the Parthenon sculptures in London, King Ludwig I made up his mind during his regency in the early 1800s to transform Munich into "a cultural work of such sheer perfection as only few Germans have experienced." He made good on his promise—as a simple walk through the city will prove. But don't settle for the ancient Greek and Roman architectural splendor hidden among the common streets and parks—pay a visit to one of the city's many museums so you can truly see and understand why Munich is the attraction it is. Should you crave escape from the city walls, excursions to the Bavarian Alps, the glacial lakes of Starnberger See and Ammersee, loony King Ludwig's own Versailles on the Chiemsee, and the medieval town of Landshut (*see* Near Munich, *below*) all offer welcome, easily accessible relief.

BASICS

AMERICAN EXPRESS

The currency exchange rates here are poor, but they change AmEx traveler's checks commission-free. *Promenadepl. 6, tel. 089/290900. Open weekdays 9–5:30, Sat. 9:30–12:30.*

CHANGING MONEY

Reisebank AG, in the Hauptbahnhof (main train station), has the best hours and deals for credit card advances and currency exchange. Keep in mind that the bank fees depend on the amount of currency you want to exchange and in what form you want it. The rate can range between a minimum fee of DM 7.50 to 1.5% of the total you want to exchange. To change as many traveler's checks as you want for half the fee, flash a copy of *The Inside Track,* EurAide's monthly English-language travel newsletter (pick one up at the Hauptbahnhof's Reisezentrum, across from Tracks 21–22). *Hauptbahnhof, tel. 089/551–0837. Open daily 6 AM–11PM.*

Of the smaller private exchanges, try **Schmidt Wechselstube** (Bahnhofpl. 5, enter at Dachauer Str., tel. 089/557870), open weekdays 9–6, Saturday 9–noon, or **Wechselstube Schvarcz** (Schillerstr. 3a, tel. 089/598236), open Monday–Thursday 8:30–6, Friday 8:30–4. There are **ATMs** outside banks all over the city, including the DVB bank in the Hauptbahnhof. If you're really desperate and don't mind a laughable exchange rate, try one of the **automatic change machines** in the airport or at the end of Tal (near Marienpl.).

CONSULATES

Canada. *Tal 29, tel. 089/219–9570. Open Mon.–Thurs. 9–noon and 2–5, Fri. 9–noon, 2–3:30.*

Ireland. *Mauerkircherstr. 1a, tel. 089/985723. Open weekdays 9–noon and 1–4.*

United Kingdom. *Bürkleinstr. 10, tel. 089/211090. Open Mon.–Thurs. 8:30–noon and 1–5, Fri. 8:30–noon and 1–3:30.*

United States. *Königinstr. 5, tel. 089/28880. Open weekdays 8 AM–11 AM.*

DISCOUNT TRAVEL AGENCIES

Both branches of **Studiosus Studienreisen** offer discount plane tickets for all ages to the United States and Europe. Only the Oberanger office sells ISIC cards, which you can get between 9:30 and 11 AM if you bring a photo, dated proof of student status, and DM 12. *Riesstr. 25, tel. 089/5006–0544, fax 089/5006–0100. Open weekdays 9–7. Oberanger 6, tel. 089/235–0520. Open weekdays 9:30–7, Sat. 10–2.*

EMERGENCIES

Ambulance (tel. 19222); **police** (tel. 110); **fire** (tel. 112); **medical-emergency service** (tel. 557755); **pharmacy-emergency service** (tel. 594475); **rape hot line** (tel. 763737). For **lost and found** on the street, the U-Bahn, buses, or trams, call 089/124080; on German Federal Railways call 089/128–6664; on all S-Bahnen except S6 try 089/1288–4409. If you're going to lose something, make sure it's not your English–German dictionary: The lost-and-found staff speaks little or no English.

Sights ●

Alte Pinakothek, **14**
Altes Rathaus, **48**
Asamkirche, **45**
Bayerisches National-museum, **23**
BMW Museum, **3**
Bürgersaal, **42**
Deutsches Museum, **59**
Frauenkirche, **46**
Glyptothek, **11**
Jüdisches Museum, **30**
Kunsthalle der Hypo-Kulturstiftung, **28**
Ludwigskirche, **20**
Michaelskirche, **43**
Nationaltheater, **29**
Neue Pinakothek, **13**
Neues Rathaus, **47**
Olympic Spirit and Olympiapark, **4**
Paläontologisches Museum, **7**
Peterskirche, **49**
Pinakothek der Moderne, **15**
Prähistorische Staats-sammlung, **22**
Schloß Nymphenburg, **25**
Staatliche Antikensamm-lungen, **10**
Staatliche Graphische Sammlung, **12**
Staatsgalerie Moderner Kunst/ Haus der Kunst, **21**
Städtische Galerie im Lenbachhaus, **9**
Theatinerkirche, **27**
Tierpark Hellabrunn, **58**
Viktualienmarkt, **51**
Z.A.M., **53**

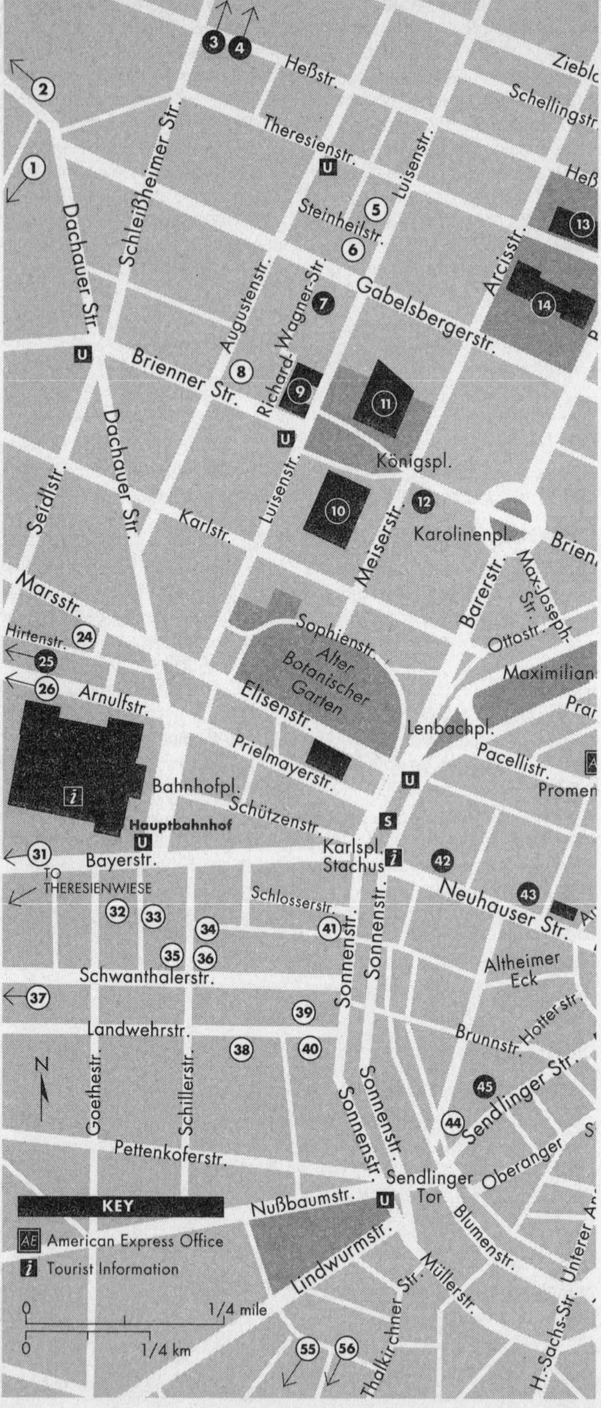

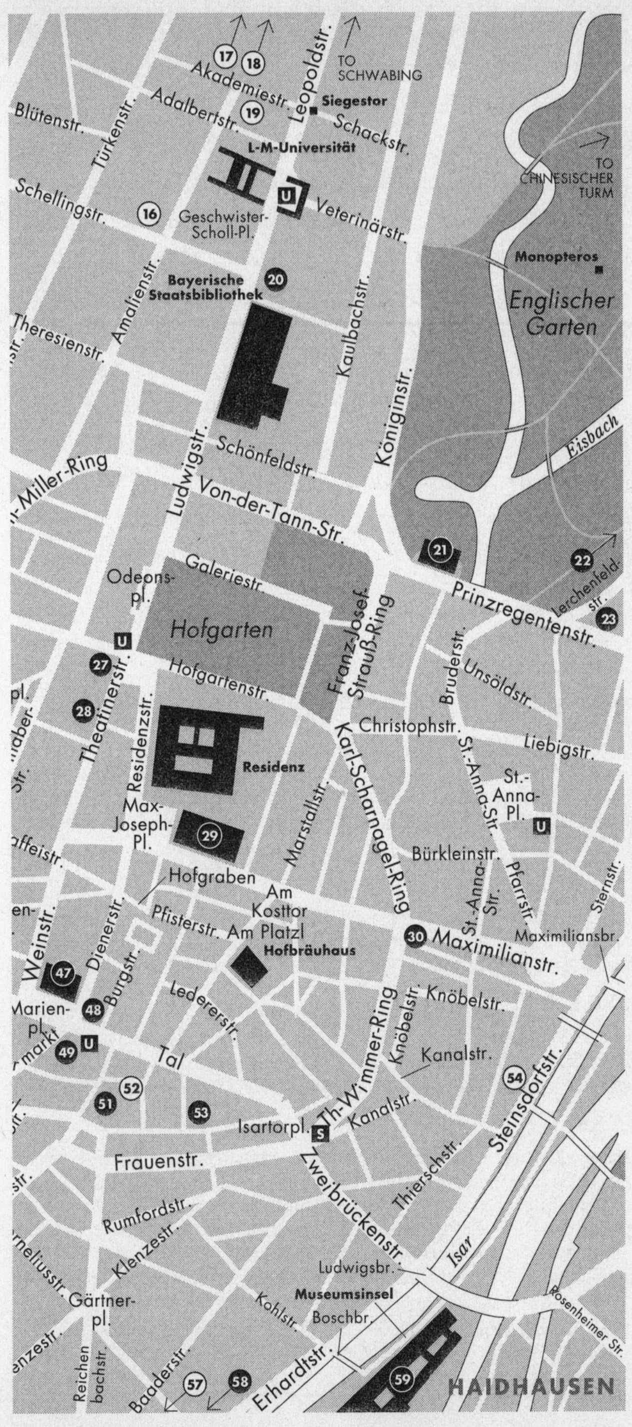

Lodgings ○

4 you münchen, **24**
Camping München Thalkirchen, **55**
Campingplatz München Obermenzing, **26**
CVJM Jugendgästehaus, **38**
Euro Youth Hotel, **33**
Hotel Atlanta, **44**
Hotel Blauer Bock, **50**
Hotel Erbprinz, **41**
Hotel Jedermann, **31**
Hotel Kurpfalz, **37**
Hotel Monaco, **34**
Hotel-Pension am Markt, **52**
Hotel-Pension am Siegestor, **19**
Hotel-Pension Beck, **54**
Hotel-Pension Erika, **39**
Jugendherberge, **1**
Jugendherberge Pullach, **56**
Jugendherberge Thalkirchen, **57**
Jugendlager am Kapuzinerhözl, **2**
Marienherberge, **32**
Pension am Kaiserplatz, **17**
Pension Augsburg, **35**
Pension Doria, **18**
Pension Frank, **16**
Pension Geiger, **6**
Pension Hungaria, **8**
Pension Luna, **40**
Pension Schillerhof, **36**
Pension Theresia, **5**

OKTOBERFEST

The world's largest party began as a wedding celebration in 1810, when Crown Prince Ludwig (later King Ludwig I) married Princess Therese of Sachsen-Hildburghausen. The royal family invited the commoners to celebrate in a meadow near the village of Sendling; the meadow was subsequently named Theresienwiese (Therese's Meadow) in the bride's honor. At that time the celebration consisted of a horse race, free beer, and snacks. Knowing a good party when they saw one, Munich's citizens decided to make it an annual tradition, wedding or no. The result—Oktoberfest, or "Wies'n," as the locals call it. Despite its name, the 16-day celebration starts in late September and ends on the first Sunday of October. Attend the bash nowadays and you'll find seven riotous tents, traditional Bavarian bands, a roller coaster (a real treat when you've had a few), and six million tourists of all ages and nationalities cavorting drunkenly and struggling to lift their huge Bierkrüge (beer mugs).

ENGLISH BOOKS AND NEWSPAPERS

Anglia English Bookshop (Schellingstr. 3, tel. 089/283642; open weekdays 9–6:30, Sat. 10–2) is jammed with new and used books, but don't expect any bargains. Take U3 or U6 to Universität. Opposite Track 24 in the Hauptbahnhof, **Sussmann's International Press** (tel. 089/551–1717; open daily 7 AM–10:45 PM) sells all sorts of foreign-language books, magazines, and newspapers, including the handy monthly English-language publication *Munich Found* (DM 4). **Hugendubel am Stachus** (Karlspl. 11–12; tel. 089/552–2530) sells English-language literature, novels, travel guides, and newspapers, as does its larger cousin on Marienplatz.

LAUNDRY

Ask at the reception desk where you're staying for the closest Waschsalon (laundromat). **Waschsalon,** near the Hauptbahnhof, charges DM 10 to wash and dry a load. *Paul-Heyse-Str. 21. From Hauptbahnhof, exit to Bayerstr. and head west, then left on Paul-Heyse-Str. Open daily 6 AM–10 PM.*

LUGGAGE STORAGE

The **Hauptbahnhof** has several banks of lockers; look upstairs opposite Track 26 and near the station's front entrance (by the erotic movie theater). Both are open 4:30 AM–12:45 AM. Otherwise, leave your stuff at the *Gepäckaufbewahrung* (luggage-storage; DM 4 per piece per day) at Counter 32, open 6 AM–11 PM daily.

MAIL AND PHONES

The main post office is **Postamt 32,** across from the Hauptbahnhof. Come to buy stamps, pick up and send *Telebriefen* (faxes), exchange traveler's checks (DM 6 fee per check), buy *Telefonkarten* (telephone cards), and pick up poste restante. Counter 1 offers more extensive telephone services (open weekdays 7 AM–7:45 PM, weekends 8–7:45). Pay DM 2 and a deposit, then make your call. If you're having trouble, some English is spoken at the **Postinformation** counter, at the far right as you enter the office. Mail to anywhere outside Munich goes in the boxes marked ANDERE ORTE. *Bahnhofpl. 1, tel. 089/5990–8716. Open weekdays 7 AM–10 PM, weekends 8 AM–10 PM. Postal code: 80074.*

Other post offices are located at **Residenzstraße 2,** (tel. 089/290–3870; open weekdays 8–6, Sat. 8–1) and at the **airport** (tel. 089/9705–8921; open weekdays 8–7, Sat. 8–noon, Sun. 10–noon). **EurAide** (*see* Visitor Information, *below*) also has a message service called Overseas Access. Mom can mail, phone, or e-mail a note, and it will be waiting for you at EurAide's office.

MEDICAL AID

The **international pharmacies** at Schleißheimer Straße 201 (tel. 089/308–6731), Schützenstraße 5 (tel. 089/557661), and in the Hauptbahnhof (tel. 089/594119) can set you up with American medicines. If you need an English-speaking **doctor** or **dentist,** the American and British consulates (*see* Consulates, *above*) can make recommendations.

VISITOR INFORMATION

Upon arrival at the Hauptbahnhof, make a beeline for the **EurAide** office to pick up a free city map, book a room (DM 6), organize a trip to Dachau or the Bavarian castles, or use the office's convenient message and mail service. While the office's ostensible purpose is to provide train info, owner Alan Wissenberg (who speaks fluent English) is extremely helpful in answering questions of all kinds. Access the Eurail timetable at EurAide's website (www.cube.net/kmu/euraide.html). *Hauptbahnhof, at Track 11, tel. 089/593889. Open May–Oct., daily 7:30–noon and 1–6.*

When you arrive you should also hit the **tourist office** (Fremdenverkehrsamt; Sendlinger Straße 1, tel. 089/233–0300), where you can pick up a free city map, make room reservations (DM 5 fee), and purchase helpful publications like the *Monatsprogramm* (DM 2.50), which lists everything from hotels, restaurants, and post offices to concerts, sports events, and art exhibits. Although the listings are in German, English translations of the headings are given, so you at least know what you're looking at. The *Beliebtes München* (50 Pf) brochure lists every pension, hotel, and hostel in the city and has a huge city map pinpointing each lodging. The staff does not provide train information, but does speak some English. *Open Mon.–Sat. 9–9, Sun. 11–7.*

The Franz Josef Strauß **airport** has a tourist information office (tel. 089/233–0300; open Mon.–Sat. 8:30 AM–10 PM, Sun. 1–9) that books rooms for a DM 5 fee. Flash the staff a smile and they'll toss you a "Walks through Europe—Munich" brochure gratis.

RESOURCES FOR GAYS AND LESBIANS • For lesbian-specific information, call **Lesbeninformation** (tel. 089/725–4272) Tuesday 10:30 AM–1 PM, Thursday 7 PM–10 PM. The **Zentrum Schwuler Männer** (Gay Men's Center; tel. 089/19446) gives advice and help via telephone daily 7 PM–10 PM. For listings of all the gay bars in Munich, along with a horribly inaccurate map, grab the **Rosa Seiten** (pink pages) at any gay bar.

COMING AND GOING

BY PLANE

Munich's new, ultra-sleek **Franz Josef Strauß Flughafen** (airport) is so cutting edge it could double as a set for *Star Trek Voyager.* It's served by several major airlines including **Lufthansa** (tel. 089/5456–0200); for all other general flight info call 089/9752–1313. Inside the terminal is 24-hour luggage storage, a tourist information office (*see above*), and a Reisebank (open daily 6:15 AM–10 PM; money exchange 7 AM–9:30 PM), which charges DM 5 to exchange currency and traveler's checks.

AIRPORT TRANSIT • Two S-Bahn lines link the airport with Munich's Hauptbahnhof; trains run about every 10 min, 4:06 AM–1:06 AM. Single fare to the airport is DM 14 (for discount tickets, *see* Getting Around, *below*). The trip into town takes about 40 min. To reach the S-Bahn, follow the green "S" signs through the airport. Option two is the Lufthansa Airport Bus (DM 15), which runs every 20 min to (6:50 AM–8 PM) and from (8 AM–9 PM) the airport and is available to passengers on all airlines. The bus departs from Arnulfstraße, just outside the train station, and from the M.-Schwabing/Nordfriedhof bus stop on Isarring, just east of the U6 Nordfriedhof station. If you want a **taxi,** set aside about DM 92.

BY TRAIN

The **Hauptbahnhof** (labeled HBF on many signs) is a shopping mall and train station in one. Here you'll find fast-food joints, restaurants, cafés, book and magazine shops, a travel center, tourist offices, lockers, clothing stores, bakeries . . . oh, and trains. If you get lost in the Hauptbahnhof's underground S- and U-Bahn stations, follow the overhead "DB" signs to the tracks. To reach the city center from the main entrance at Bahnhofplatz (just outside the DVB bank), cross the street to Schützenstraße, which leads to both the main pedestrian zone and to Marienplatz, Munich's main square.

For train info and reservations, try the friendly **EurAide** office (*see* Visitor Information, *above*) or the **Reisezentrum** office across from Tracks 21–22 (open daily 6 AM–10:30 PM). For general info in English, call the nationwide hot line at 01805/996633. Destinations and one-way fares from Munich include

Amsterdam (9 hrs, DM 240), Berlin (7 hrs, DM 265), Budapest (9 hrs, DM 148), Copenhagen (12 hrs, DM 340), Frankfurt (4 hrs, DM 129), London (12 hrs, DM 330), Paris (9 hrs, DM 195), Prague (6¾ hrs, DM 96. 40), and Vienna (5 hrs, DM 104).

BY BUS

Europabus, also called **Deutsche Touring,** serves destinations throughout Europe, including Greece, Scandinavia, and Turkey (but not Switzerland—go figure). Munich doesn't have a bus terminal, but most buses stop on the Arnulfstraße side of the Hauptbahnhof. One-way fares: Berlin (daily, 8½ hrs, DM 129), Paris (4 per week, 9 hrs, DM 118), and Budapest (3 per week, 8 hrs, DM 105). For schedules and info call 089/545–8700, or visit the **bus information** office in the Hauptbahnhof, open weekdays 9–8, Saturday 9–12:30, closed Sundays and holidays.

ROMANTIC ROAD BUSES • Munich is the hub of Europabus's **Romantic Road** service, which runs from April 11 through October 21 (*see* Romantische Straße, *in* Chapter 7). Romantic Road buses usually stop on the Arnulfstraße side of the Hauptbahnhof.

BY MITFAHRGELEGENHEIT

Munich has a number of ride-share organizations that arrange rides throughout Europe. Call at least a day or two ahead for information and availability, especially during summer. Most of the staff speaks English.

Känguruh. Sample fares: Berlin (DM 54), Frankfurt (DM 39), Regensburg (DM 18). *Amalienstr. 87, tel. 089/19444. U3 or U6 to Universität, exit to Schellingstr., right on Amalienstr., left on Amalienpassage. Open weekdays 9–4:30, Sat. 9–2, Sun. and holidays 10–2.*

Mitfahrzentrale. Sample fares: Berlin (DM 54), Frankfurt (DM 41), Cologne (DM 54), Regensburg (DM 16). *Lämmerstr. 4, tel. 089/19440. From Hauptbahnhof, exit to Arnulfstr., cross street and walk down Pfefferstr., left on Hirtenstr., right on Lämmerstr. Open daily 8–8.*

GETTING AROUND

Since downtown Munich is only one mile square, it's easy to explore on foot. Pedestrian streets link **Karlsplatz,** by the Hauptbahnhof, to **Marienplatz** and the **Viktualienmarkt,** and extend north around the Frauenkirche and up to **Odeonsplatz.** To the north of the city center university students, young bohemians, and image-conscious yuppies roam the bar-packed streets of **Schwabing,** a former artists' quarter. Along the edge of Schwabing stretches the **Englischer Garten,** where the whole city turns out to drink beer and let it all hang out. The frequently overlooked southeast corner of Munich is called **Haidhausen,** a quiet area that contains a multicultural menu of restaurants as well as the lion's share of Munich's funk. On the other side of town is **Nymphenburg,** where you'll find the famous palace and a gorgeous park behind it.

BY PUBLIC TRANSIT

Sights outside the city center can easily be reached on Munich's excellent transit system, which includes the **U-Bahn** (the subway), **S-Bahn** (suburban rail system), **Straßenbahn** (tram), and **buses.** Together, the U-Bahn and S-Bahn cover the inner city well; the S-Bahn also covers outlying destinations like the airport, Dachau, Starnberger See, and Herrsching (Ammersee). Trams and buses tend to get bogged down in traffic, but they do serve more stops. Despite the apparent lack of law enforcement, you really should invest in a valid ticket. Plainclothes officers do make the rounds (though you can usually pick them out by their little mustaches), and they make no exceptions—not even for tourists. In general, anyone caught riding without a valid ticket, or riding *schwarz,* is fined DM 60 on the spot; if you don't pay, your next free ride may be to a German jail.

OPERATING HOURS • Check the schedules posted at station platforms for specific arrival and departure times; trains generally run every 10 min. The **U-Bahn** runs Monday–Thursday and Sunday 4:30 AM–1 AM, Friday and Saturday 4:30 AM–2 AM. The **S-Bahn** runs daily from 5 or 6 AM until midnight or 1 AM (S8 to the airport runs daily 3:13 AM–12:30 PM). **Bus** and **tram** hours vary widely, but most run from 5 AM to 1 AM. There are some all-night buses on the main thoroughfares; check the schedules for exact times.

TICKETS • EurailPass, InterRail, and Deutsche Bahn (DB) rail pass holders may ride the S-Bahn free, but not the U-Bahn, trams, or buses. Munich's public transit uses a fare system based on two zones: the *Innenraum* (inner zone), indicated on the transport map by a blue ring, and the *Außenraum* (outer

MUNICH PUBLIC TRANSIT

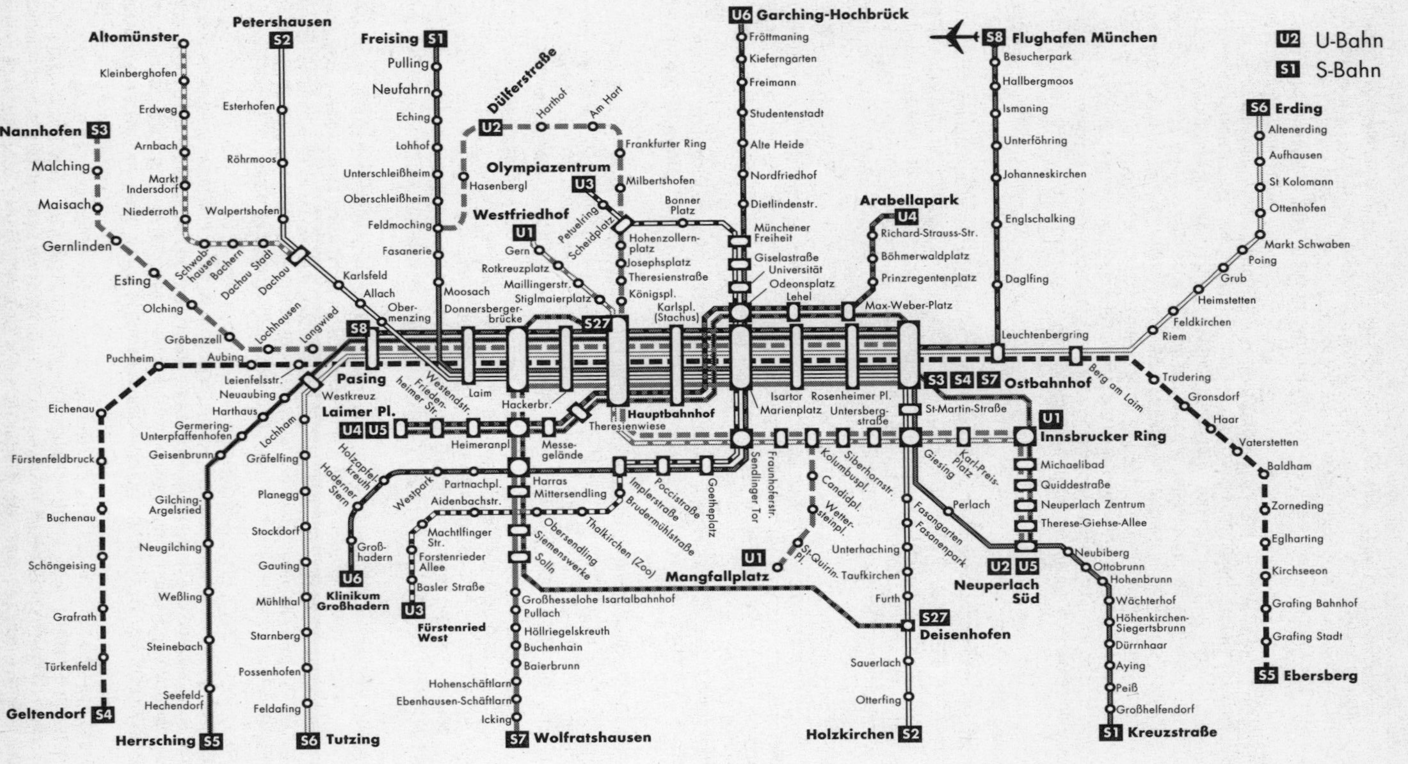

zone), anything outside the blue ring. Tickets are sold from vending machines, by tram and bus drivers, at some tourist offices, and at kiosks with a white "K" on the window. Whatever ticket you buy, be sure to validate it before you board by punching it in the blue machines marked "E" by U-Bahn and S-Bahn stops and at platforms for trams and buses. If none of this makes sense, pick up a copy of "Tickets and Fares" at the tourist information center.

Your fabulous ticket options begin with the **Einzelfahrkarte** (DM 3.50), good for one journey on all modes of transport (S-Bahn, U-Bahn, buses, and trams) as long as you're traveling in one direction, within a two-hour period, and within one zone. If you take a Kurzstrecke (short trip), defined as a maximum of four stops (only two of which can be on the U-Bahn or S-Bahn) within one hour, a ticket costs DM 1.70.

Usually the best deal is to get a **Tageskarte** (day ticket), which costs DM 8.50 for one adult and DM 12.50 for two. The day ticket allows you access to one of the zones and is valid until 6 AM the next day no matter when you activate it. Since all of Munich's sights are within the *Innenraum,* the only reason you would need a **Gesamtnetz Karte** (valid for both zones) is if you plan a day trip to Dachau, Starnberger See, or Ammersee. Gesamtnetz Karten are twice the price of the single-zone Tageskarten (DM 17 or DM 25).

Your third option is to buy **Streifenkarten** (strip tickets) that cost DM 14 for 10 strips. Use these if you're traveling alone or not using public transportation that often. The number of strips canceled depends on how many zones you cross. If you're making a short trip à la the Kurzstrecke detailed above, you only need to cancel one strip. If you're going more than two U- or S-Bahn stops, cancel two for the first zone and two more for each additional zone.

If you plan to stay in Munich for a longer period of time, the month-long **Grüne Karte** (green ticket) works out to be really cheap. It covers one adult, three children, and a dog, and is valid weekdays beginning at 9 AM and all day on weekends and holidays. Prices range from DM 62 to DM 84, depending on the number of zones you want to travel through. The Grüne Karte is available at all MVV ticket sales points.

The **München Welcome Card** is best if you want to combine travel costs with reduced admission (up to 50%) to museums, tours, palaces, towers, and movies. You'll travel free of charge on trams, buses, and the U-Bahn within the city boundaries (blue area of the fare zones), to the Flugwerft (Hangar), and to palaces at Oberschleissheim. You can purchase one of three tickets: a day ticket (DM 12), a three-day ticket (DM 29), or a three-day partner ticket (DM 42, good for 5 people: two over and three under age 18). Buy them at the tourist office or wherever you see the München Welcome Card display.

BY TAXI

While taxis aren't cheap, they may be your only option if you're out after public transportation stops running. You can find cream-colored Mercedes cabs in front of the Hauptbahnhof and large hotels, or just hail them from the street. Fares start at DM 3.90, with an additional DM 2.10 per km, regardless of how many people share the ride; standard tip is 10% of the fare. Call 089/19410 or 089/21611 to reserve a cab at no charge. Women who prefer women taxi drivers should call **Angelika's Hexenbesen** (tel. 089/755–8537).

BY BIKE

Environmentally conscious Munich has tons of bike paths; even major streets like Leopoldstraße have narrowed the lanes available for automobile traffic in favor of more bike lanes. Pick up a copy of "Radl-Touren" (50 Pf), a booklet with suggested biking tours, at the tourist office. It's in German, but the routes are clearly marked and easy to follow. You can rent bikes for DM 10 per 2 hours, or DM 20 per day, from **Radius Touristik** (Arnulfstr. 3, tel. 089/596113; open daily10–6), in the Hauptbahnhof across from Track 31. Also try the stand in the **Englischer Garten** (entrance at Veterinärstr. and Königinstr., tel. 089/282500), open Wednesday–Sunday 10:30–6, weather permitting. You can also rent bikes at S-Bahn stations like Dachau, Herrsching, and Starnberg (half price with valid rail ticket). The good news: The bikes may be returned to any other bike-renting S-Bahn station. The bad news: If you're expecting a slick racing machine, think again.

Another option is to join **Mike's Bike Tours of Munich** (DM 30), a three-hour guided cycling tour (in English). The price includes bike rental, an entertaining look at several of Munich's blockbuster sights, and a group dip in the Eisbach (a tributary of the Isar). Tours leave at 11:30 AM and 4 PM from the Spielzeugmuseum on Marienplatz. Book in advance by calling 089/651–4275 or just show up.

WHERE TO SLEEP

Munich offers a variety of budget lodging options, but reservations for pensions and the popular hostels are very, very important if you like sleeping indoors. Call at least a day in advance, pray to the pension gods, and hopefully fate will smile upon you. If your patron lodging saint deserts you, the **Fremdenverkehrsamt** (tourist office) books rooms for DM 5 and a refundable DM 5–DM 8 deposit, as does **EurAide** (*see* Visitor Information, *above*) for DM 6. And don't be late, because hotels will give your room away if you don't show by the stipulated time. At pensions expect to pay at least DM 50 for a single, DM 90 for a double, and DM 45 per person for triples and quads; add DM 5–DM 15 per person during Oktoberfest.

As in all large cities the area around the **Hauptbahnhof** is a convenient base for exploring the city and has a large concentration of inexpensive pensions, but it is also one of the seediest parts of town. Both **Schwabing** and the university district, one km north of the city center, are great neighborhoods for young people and for nightlife. If you stay in the **Stadtzentrum** (city center), you'll have easy access to some of Munich's top attractions.

Too broke to phone, too cheap for postcards? No problem! Now you can e-mail Mum with the 24-hour on-line service at Hotel Kurpfalz. The cost? Absolutely nothing!

NEAR THE HAUPTBAHNHOF

UNDER DM 50 • Euro Youth Hotel. If you can get a room here, don't even think of looking elsewhere. The hotel is just 50 m from the train station, the huge renovated rooms come with a phone and TV, and the wicker-chair lounge area is the perfect spot to wind down with an Augustiner Bier (sold by the friendly reception staff) after a night out dancing at the Kunstpark Ost (*see* box, Microcosmic Munich, *below*). Singles go for DM 50–DM 59, doubles with bath run DM 40–DM 49, including a generous breakfast; a night in a four-bed room starts at DM 30. There are no age restrictions. *Senefelderstr. 5, tel. 089/599–0880, fax 089/5990–8877, e-mail info@euro-youth-hotel.de, www.euro-youth-hotel.de. From Hauptbahnhof, walk left on Bayerstr., turn right onto Seenefelderstr. Reception open 24 hours.*

UNDER DM 90 • Hotel Kurpfalz. The Kurpfalz offers just about everything: a central location just minutes from the Hauptbahnhof, a sports bar with ESPN, a bountiful breakfast buffet, a young, amiable, English-speaking staff, laundry service . . . even room service! They also have rooms, all equipped with private bath, cable TV, and phone, and decked out in artful, hypoallergenic Venetian tile. Singles cost DM 89–DM 169, doubles DM 109–DM 259. Reserve in advance. *Schwanthalerstr. 121, tel. 089/540–9860, fax 089/5409–8811, e-mail Hotel-Kurpfalz@Munich-Online.de. From Hauptbahnhof, Tram 18 or 19 to Holzapfelstr., left on Holzapfelstr., right on Schwanthalerstr. 44 rooms. Reception open 24 hrs, flexible checkout 10:30 AM. Luggage storage.*

Pension Augsburg. Reception is on the third floor and there's no elevator, but this cheap pension is only three min from the train station. Singles cost DM 44 without shower, doubles DM 66 (DM 78 with shower), triples DM 96 (DM 114 with shower). If you need 'em, hall showers cost DM 3.50, breakfast DM 6. *Schillerstr. 18, tel. 089/597673. 31 rooms, some with bath, all with sinks. Reception open 7 AM–9 PM, checkout 11 AM. Closed Christmas–Jan. 10.*

Pension Hungaria. In an unintimidating neighborhood north of the Hauptbahnhof, the Hungaria offers sunny rooms at reasonable rates. Including breakfast, singles are DM 55, doubles DM 85, triples DM 105, quads DM 120–DM 130. Hall showers cost DM 3. *Brienner Str. 42, near Augustenstr., tel. 089/521558. U2 to Königspl. 15 rooms, none with bath. Reception open 7:30 AM–10 PM, checkout 11 AM.*

Pension Schillerhof. Operated by a pleasant woman, this small pension is only a three-min walk from the Hauptbahnhof. Rooms are clean and simple, but passing traffic can get a little noisy. You'll get no breakfast for these prices: singles DM 45–DM 50, doubles DM 75–DM 80, triples DM 100, quads DM 140. Showers are down the hall. *Schillerstr. 11, tel. 089/594270. 11 rooms. Reception open 9–9, checkout 11 AM. Closed Christmas–Jan. 6.*

UNDER DM 100 • Hotel Monaco. Spacious, spotless, modern rooms, almost all equipped with private shower, TV, radio, and phone, await you only one minute from the Hauptbahnhof. Singles cost DM 55–DM 90, doubles DM 90–DM 118, triples and quads DM 50–DM 45 per person, breakfast buffet included. *Schillerstr. 9, tel. 089/545–9940, fax 089/550–3709. 23 rooms. Reception open 24 hrs, checkout 11 AM. No credit cards.*

Hotel-Pension Erika. Moderately priced, spacious, well-decorated rooms make up for the curt management. Including breakfast, singles cost DM 70 (DM 100 with shower), doubles DM 100 (DM 130 with shower). Triples cost DM 125–DM 140, shower included. *Landwehrstr. 8, tel. 089/554327. 27 rooms, some with bath. Reception open 6 AM–10 PM, checkout 11 AM.*

Pension Luna. The large rooms have carpets and polished wood furniture. Prices include breakfast and hall showers; singles DM 55, doubles DM 99 (DM 110 with shower), triples DM 135 (none available with a shower). *Landwehrstr. 5, tel. 089/597833, fax 089/550–3761. 16 rooms. Reception open 7 AM–10 PM, checkout 10:30 AM.*

SCHWABING

UNDER DM 85 • Pension am Kaiserplatz. Frau Jakobi (possibly the sweetest woman in Bavaria) presides over this quiet pension with gorgeous baroque and modern rooms. Including breakfast and one shower, singles are DM 49–DM 59, doubles DM 79–DM 95, triples DM 105. Doubles and triples transform into a four- to six-person room for DM 35 more per extra person. Call to reserve. *Kaiserpl. 12, tel. 089/349190. From Marienpl., U3 or U6 to Münchner Freiheit; exit to Herzogstr., left on Viktoriastr. (becomes Kaiserpl.). 10 rooms, some with shower. Reception open 8 AM–8 PM, checkout 11 AM.*

Pension Doria. Newly renovated, this welcoming pension in the heart of Schwabing has received a badly needed face-lift. Singles cost DM 54–DM 59, doubles DM 89–DM 99, triples DM 110. Prices include hall showers but not breakfast (DM 5 per person). Call to reserve. *Hohenstaufenstr. 12, tel. 089/333872. U3 or U6 to Giselastr.; walk south on Leopoldstr., right on Georgenstr., right on Friedrichstr., left on Hohenstaufenstr. 7 rooms, none with bath. Reception open 7 AM–10 PM, noon checkout.*

UNDER DM 100 • Hotel-Pension am Siegestor. Comfortable, carpeted rooms and a prime location translate into relatively steep prices. Including breakfast and hall showers, singles are DM 75, doubles DM 98, triples DM 145. The pleasant woman who runs the place speaks fluent English. *Akademiestr. 5, tel. 089/399550, fax 089/343050. U3 or U6 to Universität. 20 rooms, none with bath. Reception open 7 AM–9 PM, checkout 11 AM.*

CITY CENTER

UNDER DM 85 • Pension Frank. You'll have to compete with fashion models, student groups, and backpackers to get a room here, so call or fax ahead. The lucky few get a cheap, dorm-style room in a happening part of town. Including breakfast and hall showers, singles are DM 65, DM 95, three- to five-person rooms DM 40 per head. *Schellingstr. 24, tel. 089/281451, fax 089/280–0910. U3 or U6 to Universität. 20 rooms, none with bath. Reception open 7:30 AM—10 PM, checkout 11 AM.*

Pension Theresia. Including breakfast, spacious, pleasant singles cost DM 58–DM 70, doubles DM 88–DM 108, triples DM 135, quads DM 140–160. Add DM 3 per person for one-night stays. At press time the owner was about to begin renovations, so call first to see if the hotel is open and if the prices are still accurate. *Luisenstr. 51, tel. 089/521250, fax 089/542–0633. U2 to Therèsienstr. 26 rooms. Reception open 7 AM–10 PM, checkout 10:30 AM.*

UNDER DM 100 • Hotel Atlanta. The friendly staff here actually likes backpackers. With breakfast (in an exceptionally cute breakfast room) and hall showers, singles cost DM 60–DM 98, doubles DM 118–DM 148. Prices may go up during trade show season. Singles have large beds, and two people may share a room at no extra charge. Rooms for three to six are available for DM 60—but there are discounts depending on the season. *Sendlinger Str. 58, tel. 089/263605, fax 089/260–9027. U1 or U2 to Sendlinger Tor, enter through Raab Schuhhaus shoe store. 20 rooms. Reception open 7 AM–10 PM, checkout 11 AM.*

Hotel Erbprinz. Across the street from the Altstadt near Karlsplatz, the Erbprinz offers clean, pension-style rooms at competitive prices. Singles cost DM 66–DM 72 (up to DM 96 with private shower), doubles DM 86–DM 110 (DM 110–DM 148 with shower), triples DM 123–DM 144; all prices include breakfast. *Sonnenstr. 2, tel. 089/594521, fax 089/558673. Reception open 24 hrs, checkout 11 AM.*

Hotel Jedermann. Only 5 min from the central train station, this family-run hotel has newly renovated rooms, a cosy breakfast room with buffet, and a well-kept bar. Singles cost DM 65–DM 110, doubles DM

95–DM 150, triples DM 180, quads DM 200, all including breakfast. *Bayerstr. 95, tel. 089/533617, fax 089/536506, e-mail hotel-jedermann@cube.net. 21 rooms. Reception open 7 AM–10 PM, checkout 11 AM.*

Hotel-Pension Beck. Everyone who comes through seems to love this place, both for its amenities and location (near the Deutsches Museum, Hofbräuhaus, and Haidhausen). With breakfast, singles are DM 52–DM 60, doubles DM 84–DM 108 (with showers); triples, quads, and quints cost DM 40–DM 50 per person. *Thierschstr. 36, tel. 089/220708, fax 089/220925, e-mail pension.beck@bst-online.de. S-Bahn to Isartor. 44 rooms, some with bath. Reception open 7 AM–10:30 PM, checkout 11 AM.*

Pension Geiger. Its modest but comfortable rooms are within walking distance of the Neue Pinakothek. Prices include breakfast but not hall showers (DM 2); singles DM 50–DM 70, doubles DM 90–DM 98, triples (all with bath) DM 130. *Steinheilstr. 1, tel. 089/521556. U2 to Theresienstr. 17 rooms, some with bath. Reception open 7 AM–9 PM, checkout 11 AM. Closed Christmas.*

UNDER DM 130 • Hotel Blauer Bock. Rooms here aren't anything special, but the location—300 m south of Marienplatz, between the Viktualienmarkt and the Stadtmuseum—is a major plus. Prices include breakfast and hall showers, and the more expensive rooms have either a shower, toilet, or both. Singles run DM 65–DM 110, doubles DM 100–DM 165, triples DM 185–DM 200. *Sebastianpl. 9, at Prälat-Zistl-Str., tel. 089/231780, fax 089/2317-8200. 75 rooms. Reception open 24 hrs, checkout 11 AM.*

Hotel-Pension am Markt. Right next to the Viktualienmarkt, this busy hotel has a beautiful, old-fashioned breakfast area and clean, medium-sized rooms. Including breakfast, singles are DM 62 (DM 110 with shower), doubles DM 110–DM 116 (DM 150–DM 160 with shower), triples DM 165 (DM 205 with shower). Reservations are a fine idea. *Heiliggeiststr. 6, tel. 089/225014. 32 rooms, most with bath. Reception open 24 hrs.*

HOSTELS

4 you münchen. Two min from the Hauptbahnhof, Germany's first and only "ecological youth hostel" sports cork floors, unfinished wood furnishings, organic grub, and even transparent toilet flushers. Beds in brand-new, dorm-style rooms cost DM 24 per person, DM 38 in a double, DM 54 for a single. Add DM 7.50 for breakfast, DM 5 for organic cotton sheets. Part of the hostel functions as a hotel and offers single rooms with all the amenities for DM 79 and doubles for DM 119. The hostel also organizes bike tours (starting at DM 19) of Munich, focusing on historical and green themes. *Hirtenstr. 18, tel. 089/552-1660, fax 089/5521-6666. No curfew. Reception open 24 hrs, checkout 10 AM.*

CVJM (YMCA) Jugendgästehaus. Call a week in advance unless you feel lucky. Youth groups and independent backpackers pack the clean, sex-segregated rooms; showers and toilets are down the hall. Singles DM 50, doubles DM 86, triples DM 40 per person. Breakfast is included. Hostel cards are not required, but guests over 26 pay a 16% surcharge. *Landwehrstr. 13, tel. 089/552-1410, fax 089/550-4282, e-mail info@cvjm-muenchen.org. 79 beds. Curfew 12:30 AM. Reception open 8 AM–12:30 AM, checkout 10 AM. Closed Easter and Christmas–Jan. 6.*

Jugendherberge (HI). Inexpensive and convenient, this hostel lies only three short U-Bahn stops from the Hauptbahnhof. A bed in a dorm costs DM 29, including an all-you-can-eat breakfast featuring the extremely important all-you-can-drink coffee. You must be under 27 and have an HI card to stay here. Only fax reservations are accepted. *Wendl-Dietrich-Str. 20, tel. 089/131156, fax 089/167-8745. U1 to Rotkreuzpl.; exit to Rotkreuzpl. (which becomes Wendl-Dietrich-Str.). 360 beds. No curfew. Reception open 24 hrs, checkout 9 AM. Key deposit DM 20. Closed Dec.*

Jugendherberge Pullach/Burg Schwaneck (HI). This castle–turned–youth hostel is worth a try if you can't get into one of the more central hostels. Per-person rates are DM 22.50, including breakfast. You must be under 27 and have a youth hostel card to stay here. *Burgw. 4–6, tel. 089/793-0643. S7 to Pullach (20-min ride); walk up Margarethenstr., left on Heilmannstr., right on Charlottenweg. Curfew 1 AM. Reception open 5 PM–11 PM. Closed Christmas–Jan. 1.*

Jugendherberge Thalkirchen (HI). Nestled in a quiet wooded neighborhood, this hostel fills its rooms with plenty of German schoolchildren. Leave stuff in the storage room, or in the lockers (DM 5). Only 26-year-olds and their juniors are welcome. Singles cost DM 36.50, doubles DM 31.50, triples and quads and dorms up to 15 beds are DM 31.50. Add DM 8 for dinner. *Meisingstr. 4, tel. 089/723-6560, fax 089/724-2567. U1 or U2 to Sendlinger Tor, then U3 to Thalkirchen; exit to Maria-Einsiedel-Str., continue down Maria-Einsiedel-Str., right on Frauenbergstr., left on Münchner Str. Curfew is 1 AM. Reception open 7 AM–1 AM, checkout 9 AM. Key deposit (DM 20), laundry facilities.*

Marienherberge. A minute's walk from the Hauptbahnhof, this church-run, women-only hostel is safe, clean, and cheap. Singles are DM 40, doubles and triples DM 35 per person, six-person rooms DM 30 a head. Prices include hall showers and breakfast. No student ID is required, but under 26-year-olds are preferred. The nuns may go on vacation for Christmas and Easter, but they make certain someone is always there to run the hostel. *Goethestr. 9, tel. 089/555805. 25–50 beds. Midnight curfew (strictly enforced). Reception open 8 AM–midnight, checkout 9 AM. Laundry facilities.*

CAMPING

Camping München-Thalkirchen. Munich's most centrally located (and most crowded) campground is 4 km from the city center. Tent sites cost DM 7, plus DM 7.80 per person. Tent rental is DM 22. On-site facilities include a rec room with a pool table and TV, a supermarket, laundry (DM 6.50 wash and dry), and showers (DM 2). *Zentralländstr. 49, tel. 089/723–1707, fax 089/724–3177. U3 to Thalkirchen, then Bus 57 to last stop (last bus midnight). Sites for 2,500 people. Reception open 7 AM–1 AM. Closed Nov.–early Mar.*

Campingplatz München-Obermenzing. This campsite is situated in a huge park some 900 m from the beginning of the Stuttgart-bound Autobahn. Sites cost DM 7 per person, DM 7.50 per tent, and it costs DM 2 for six min of hot water in the shower. For DM 6 you can also do a load of laundry (drying 50 Pf). *Lochhausener Str. 59, tel. 089/811–2235, fax 089/814–4807. S-Bahn to Pasing, then Bus 76 to Lochhausener Str. (last bus 1 AM). Reception open 7:30 AM–10 PM. Closed Nov.–mid-Mar.*

Jugendlager am Kapuzinerhölzl. This oversized circus tent, which enthusiasts call "Germany's Biggest Slumber Party," is open from mid-June through August. A camping spot—with blankets, mats, and a hot shower—costs DM 14, with a bed DM 18 per night. Lock your stuff up at the train station, but bring your passport with you. *Franz-Schrank-Str. 8, tel. 089/141–4300. From Hauptbahnhof, Tram 17 (direction: Amalienburg) to Botanischer Garten. 420 sites. Reception open 24 hrs.*

ROUGHING IT

If you're short on cash or arrive on an extra-congested weekend, try camping along the Isar River; some stragglers even pitch tents and barbecue on the grassy bank in front of the Volksbad (public bath) by Ludwigsbrücke (Ludwig's Bridge). Other desperate adventurers have slept in the Englischer Garten (*see* Exploring Munich, *below*), but police do patrol the area. Though it's more likely you'll get a slap on the wrist than a hefty fine, there's no lack of freaks and thieves in the rural fringe of urban Munich. If you have a train ticket, you can spend the night in the Hauptbahnhof without being hassled—at least by the police; there's no guarantee the locals won't decide you're their new best friend. During Oktoberfest the station is packed and totally chaotic, so lock up your valuables.

FOOD

In a pricey city like Munich, eating out can quickly empty your wallet. Avoid the touristy restaurants and head to an Imbiß (a stand-up snack bar) to feed on cheap Bavarian specialties like wurst and Leberkäs (warm beef, bacon, and pork slabs served with sweet mustard); take-out Turkish Döner kebabs cost DM 5–DM 6. Imbiß stands cluster on the **Viktualienmarkt** (*see* Exploring Munich, *below*), as do numerous if expensive fruit-and-veggie stalls. Metzgereien (butcher shops) like the ubiquitous **Vinzenz Murr** sell an array of cheeses, breads, and premade sandwiches for DM 3–DM 5.50; some have salad bars as well. Another spot for cheap snacks is the U-Bahn, where stands sell pizza (DM 3.60), cheeseburgers (DM 3.30), and chop suey (DM 7–DM 8) at **Danmark,** beneath Karlsplatz. Outside the city center, **Da Enzo Trattoria** (Wendl-Dietrich-Str. 4, near Rotkreuzpl.) sells big take-out pizzas for DM 6. For groceries hit **Aldi** (Schwanthalerstr. 12) near the train station. For a much better selection, vastly superior produce, and a salad bar, stop by **HL Markt** either in the city center (Tal 13, near Marienpl.) or in Schwabing (Hohenzollnerstr. 30, near Leopldstr.). If you're willing to splurge and put up with pushy throngs, head to **Dallmayr** (Dienerstr. 14–15, tel. 089/21350), off Marienplatz: This gourmet specialty food store proffers the best of coffee, cigars, exotic fruits and jams, breads, salmon, sausages . . . you name it.

The university district (U3 or U6 to Universität) wallows in smoky, cheap, restaurant-pubs (called Gaststätten). **Gaststätte Engelsburg** (Türkenstr. 51, tel. 089/272–4097) serves pizza and Bavarian fare for DM 9–DM 15 and a daily three-course lunch (DM 10–DM 13). Türkenhof (*see* After Dark, *below*) and **Atzinger** (Schellingstr. 9, tel. 089/282880) are also worth a look. All are open daily from around 10 AM to 1 AM.

CITY CENTER

UNDER DM 15 • Augustiner Bierhalle. This is an excellent alternative to the Hofbräuhaus (*see* After Dark, *below*), especially during the dog days of summer, when you can sit out front, drink beer and watch people pass by. Top-rated is the homemade *Gulasch* (soup; DM 6.50). It washes down well with an Augustiner Weißbier (DM 5.60 per ½ liter). Make sure you're at the Bierhalle and not the slightly more expensive restaurant next door. *Neuhauserstr. 27, btw Karlspl. and Marienpl., tel. 089/5519–9257. Closed Sun.*

Augustiner Bräustuben. You just can't go wrong with a juicy meal of *Schweinebraten* (roast pork; DM 11.50) and an Augustiner Weißbier (DM 4.20 per ½ liter) at this cozy beer hall frequented mostly by Müncheners. Daily Bavarian specialties run about DM 12. *Landsbergerstr. 19, at Holzapfelstr., tel. 089/507047. Tram 18 or 19 to Holzapfelstr.*

Bux am Viktualienmarkt. This place is a vegetarian's godsend in the heart of Porkland. Sure they have meat, but the soup, salad, dessert, and juice selection in this self-service café is huge. All food is sold by weight (roughly DM 15 for a full meal). *Frauenstr. 9, by Viktualienmarkt, tel. 089/293684. Closed Sun.*

Dar Sivestro. Tucked behind Marienplatz, this intimate Italian eatery has a wide variety of dishes that are both reasonably priced and delicious. Pasta dishes begin at DM 10; you can choose from a whole list of speciality sauces—try the spiced tomato sauce for DM 12.50 or the Bolognese-style meat sauce for DM 13. *Ledererstr. 11, tel. 089/224271. Closed weekends.*

If you do eat in a restaurant, one of the best deals for a quick and hearty meal is the ubiquitous Gulaschsuppe (seasoned beef stew) for about DM 6—it's hearty and healthful.

Fraunhofer. Earthy intellectuals socializing over a hearty meal frequent this Gaststätte-cum-culture joint. Try the *Zwei Paar Schweinswürste* (pork sausages; DM 10.80), one of the daily vegetarian dishes (DM 9–DM 18), *Kaiserschmarrn mit Apfelmus* (chopped pancakes with apple sauce; DM 13.50), or a mug of Optimator, a strong dark beer that lives up to its cool name (DM 5.60 per ½ liter). The adjacent **Theater im Fraunhofer** (tel. 089/267850) hosts live music, fantastic improv theater, and poetry readings every night of the summer, much of it free. On Sundays from late October until Easter, come for special dishes and live music. *Fraunhoferstr. 9, tel. 089/266460. U1 or U2 to Fraunhoferstr.*

La Bohème. The tables are covered with white cloths and decked with candles, but you won't feel out of place—the atmosphere is relaxed and perfect for pizza (DM 7–DM 14), omelets (DM 8.50–DM 10.50), and Hofbräu beer (DM 3.90 per liter). *Türkenstr. 79, tel. 089/272–0833. U3 or U6 to Universität. Closed weekends.*

UNDER DM 20 • Möwe. A walk through the door into this sparsely decorated Middle Eastern restaurant is like a trip to the Mediterranean coast. Popular with thirtysomethings, this spot offers live music on Sundays and frequent belly dancing. Try the fresh seafood dishes; grilled octopus with bread and salad goes for DM 17. *Theresienstr. 93, tel. 089/526886. U2 to Theresienstr. Mon.–Thurs. 11 AM–1 AM, weekends 11 AM–3 AM.*

Zum Franziskaner. The "original Bavarian specialties" are excellent and worth the splurge. Pasta and vegetarian dishes run DM 13.50–DM 19.80, wursts are DM 4–DM 6, and other entrées take off from DM 14. Order food to go from the counter just inside for a 30% discount. *Residenzstr. 9, tel. 089/231–8120.*

HAIDHAUSEN

In a quiet corner of Munich, Haidhausen has managed to avoid the tourist restaurant scene. Wander the streets and you'll find ethnically diverse restaurants, laid-back cafés, and a uniquely unspoiled beer garden (*see* Hofbräukeller, *in* Beer Gardens, *below*). Besides serving food, these places provide an upbeat atmosphere for hanging out and drinking.

MICROCOSMIC MUNICH

Since 1996 the Kunstpark Ost—the newest addition to Munich's restaurant and nightlife scene—has defied definition. A huge complex of art galleries, bars, clubs, and intimate concert halls, the Kunstpark promises a "must-see" event each evening. As Germany's Stern magazine recently noted, "Nowhere in Germany do people party as they do in Kunstpark Ost." And this conclusion is based more on fact than opinion. More than 250,000 visitors a month swarm into this cultural mecca to experience concerts, parties, and art exhibits and check out the park's six concert halls, seven discos, 10 music clubs, 11 bars, and five restaurants. From gemütliche (cozy) Bavarian eateries to antique shops to Munich's largest flea market, the 80,000-sq-m Kunstpark is a microcosm of Munich, even catering to fitness-fanatics with Germany's largest volleyball and inline skating halls, as well as Europe's largest indoor rock-climbing facility. "This is where Munich looks the most like New York," beamed a critic at the renowned Frankfurter Allgemeine newspaper. Come in and see why. Grafingerstr. 6 (directly across from the U-bahn stop Ostbahnhof), tel. 089/ 490–4350; www.kunstpark.de.

UNDER DM 20 • Haidhauser Augustiner. This restaurant-bar features a huge menu with tons of salads, pasta, and meat dishes. The rich mahogany walls and black pillars give the interior a classy beer-hall feel—definitely a place to sink into. The *Putenschnitzel* (DM 15.60), a turkey cutlet in paprika cream sauce served with roasted potatoes, is filling and tastes great! *Wörthstr. 34, tel. 089/480–2594. U- or S-Bahn to Ostbahnhof, straight up Wörthstr.*

Kytaro. Although Munich's best-known Greek restaurant isn't cheap, it's always packed, especially on the back terrace during summer. Lots of smoke and the music of live bands (weekends) accompany your meal. Try one of the lamb dishes (DM 14.50–DM 19.50). *Innere Wiener Str. 36, tel. 089/480–1176.*

Lissabon Café/Bar. Musicians and an international crowd frequent this Portuguese café, and a couple of times a week there's live Latin and jazz music free of charge. Try a large glass of *galao,* a creamy Portuguese coffee drink, or the delicious and filling *caldo verde,* a traditional soup. Vegetable dishes (DM 14–DM 16), salads (DM 7–DM 17), and fresh fish (DM 20–DM 23) are what keep this spot on the map. *Breisacher Str. 22, tel. 089/448–2274. U- or S-Bahn to Ostbahnhof, up Wörthstr., right on Breisacher Str.*

Maria Passagne. Black curtains shroud the windows, no sign announces its presence, but press the buzzer marked CLUB PRIVÉ and enter a hidden gem: a dimly lit, intimate whirl of beads, red tapestry, and African statuettes. Despite the Arabic decor, this restaurant has a classic Japanese menu. Popular dishes include maki sushi (DM 9–DM 12), salmon teriyaki (DM 21), and Japanese-style noodle soup (DM 19). Another draw is the menu of exotic cocktails (DM 10–DM 15) and wine (DM 5–DM 8). Reserve ahead. *Steinstr. 42, tel. 089/486167. S-Bahn to Rosenheimer Pl., exit north to Steinstr.*

UNDER DM 35 • El Español. The food in this Spanish restaurant-bar is excellent. Splurge on one of the fresh fish dishes (DM 19–DM 32) or check out the daily specials (DM 10–DM 25). Come Thursdays between 9 and 10 and enjoy Flamenco dancers and other live attractions. *Pariser Str. 46, tel. 089/ 488496. S-Bahn to Rosenheimer Pl., down Balanstr., left on Pariser Str.*

CAFÉS

Many of Munich's cafés double as inexpensive restaurants, and especially on **Leopoldstraße** (*see* After Dark, *below*) as funky evening lairs. Head to the eight computers at the **Internet-Café** (Nymphenburger Str. 145, cnr Landshuter Allee, tel. 089/129–1120) to write jealous friends stuck at home.

Baadercafé. Excellent, inexpensive food (daily early bird special 6 PM–8 PM, DM 9.80), superb coffee, and a diverse, hip, largely bohemian clientele make the Baader one of Munich's baadest. *Baaderstr. 47, tel. 089/201–0638. U1 or U2 to Fraunhoferstr.*

Café Schädel. This small café in Haidhausen is a laid-back hangout for the down-to-earth. Go for a shot of ouzo or to write in your journal. *Preysingstr. 18, tel. 089/448–6559. S-Bahn to Rosenheimer Pl. Closed Mon.*

Glockenspiel. A diverse crowd stamped by a toned-down Schickeria and a healthy gay presence enjoys Weißbier (DM 5.80 per ½ liter), a variety of salads and homemade soups (around DM 15), and an unbeatable setting—an open-air, rooftop terrace five stories above Marienplatz. Heaters will keep you and your friends warm in the evenings. *Marienpl. 28 (enter on Rosenstr.), tel. 089/126–4256.*

Stadtcafé im Stadtmuseum. Armchair anarchists, film types, journalists, and a hip intello crowd chat, read the paper, and write poetry while quaffing cappuccino (DM 4.80) and ordering soup (DM 6.50) that is that made fresh each day. Enjoy a variety of vegetarian and meat entrées (DM 10–DM 16) in Munich's loveliest courtyard beer garden. *St. Jakobspl. 1, in Stadtmuseum, tel. 089/266949.*

Vivo! This bistro is a pleasant break from the quiet that is typical for Haidhausen. This crowded, comfortable café with rustic roots attracts a colorful mix of intellectuals and students as well as the local regulars. The menu features daily specials, a long list of combination sandwiches (DM 10–DM 20), and a choice of exotic coffees (DM 3.80). *Lothringer Str. 11, tel. 089/448–5035. S-Bahn to Rosenheimer Pl.; left on Metzstr. toWeißenburger Pl., right on Lothringer Str.*

BEER GARDENS

To keep their kegs cool during hot summers, brewers used to store them under shady chestnut trees. This practice evolved into the contemporary beer garden, where you share long tables with the rest of the city and lap up liters on those long, hot summer days. At most beer gardens you can bring your own snacks or buy a meal there. One indispensable bit of beer-garden vocabulary is *ein Maß,* the standard measure (about 1 liter) of beer in Bavaria. Note: A beer garden is not the same as a beerhall. For the latter, *see* After Dark, *below.*

Augustinerkeller. Forget the Hofbräuhaus. If you drink one beer in Munich, drink it here. Leafy chestnut trees, a local clientele of all ages, brass bands, and the city's best brew generate a Maß-o-meter rating right off the scale. Your taste buds are uninitiated until you've experienced the matchless Weißbier (DM 5.40 per ½ liter) and superb Edelstoff (Maß, DM 11), literally, "the stuff of nobility." During the summer, complement them with spare ribs (DM 14). *Arnulfstr. 52, west of train station, tel. 089/594393. S-Bahn to Hackerbrücke, right on Arnulfstr. Open daily 10:30 AM–midnight.*

Chinesischer Turm. Along with Seehaus (*see below*), this smaller garden is located in the Englischer Garten and sees lots of tourists taking pictures of one another with their enormous beer steins; a Maß starts at DM 9. On weekends a brass band plays from inside the tower. The party kicks off daily at 10 AM and winds down around 11 or midnight. *From Münchener Freiheit U-Bahn, Bus 54 to Chinesischer Turm, or just wander north from Haus der Kunst.*

Hirschgarten. Munich's largest beer garden (it seats 8,000) is pleasantly situated in a lovely park, perfect for whiling away a summer's day. A Maß costs DM 9.40 and the deer in the park will gladly lap up what you spill. *Hirschgarten 1, tel. 089/172591. S-Bahn to Laim; walk east on Winfriedstr. (which becomes De-la-Paz-Str.), right on Königbauerstr; or, from Schloß Nymphenburg, Hirschgartenallee runs into Hirschgarten.*

Hofbräukeller. If you're disappointed with the Hofbräuhaus (*see* After Dark, *below*), come here to see what real Bavarian beer drinking is like. This small garden in Haidhausen sees mostly regulars and young people downing their recommended daily allowance of liquid bread. A Maß starts at DM 10.20. *Innere Wiener Str. 19, tel. 089/459–9250. U-Bahn to Max-Weber-Pl.*

Max Emanuel Brauerei. You can't bring your own food to this beer garden in the university district, but full meals start at about DM 10.50. Don't miss the hottest, freshest, plumpest pretzels around (DM 4).

WHERE ARE YOU ON THE FOOD CHAIN?

One way to keep costs down in Munich is to eat at one of the city's numerous chain restaurants. Though the term may conjure up ugly visions of Burger King, these places actually offer reasonably priced, tasty full-course meals.

BELLA ITALIA. The food—and prices—are wonderful. This chain is located in all the right spots—near Karlsplatz, by the university (Türkenstr. 50), and in Haidhausen (Weißenburger Str. 2). Pizza and pasta start at about DM 5 and beer is a cheap DM 3.50 per ½ liter. Finish up with a slice of heaven—rich tiramisu—for DM 5.20.

CAFERICHART. This chain pops up in the grooviest of places, including the Viktualienmarkt (Viktualienmarkt 15) and the main pedestrian zone (Neuhauserstr. 53). At the Viktualienmarkt location you can munch on salad (DM 7.80, little plate; DM 12.80, big plate) as you look out over the market.

MUNCHNER SUPPENKUCHE. This cheap, health-conscious chain offers filling soups and sandwiches for prices almost unheard of in Munich. Branches can be found at several locations including Zenetti Str. 11. They're closed on Sundays.

WIENERWALD. These ubiquitous restaurants are more like diners and have the interior and prices to match. The food is tasty and a relative bargain; half a grilled chicken with french fries is DM 9.40. At Bayerstraße 33, enjoy a salad (DM 5.90–DM 7.90) or a Schnitzel with side dishes (DM 16.90) in the adjoining Imbiß. Wienerwalds can be found everywhere, so keep your eyes peeled.

A Maß will set you back DM 10.20. *Adalbertstr. 33, tel. 089/271–5158. U3 or U6 to Universität; walk north on Leopoldstr, left on Adalbertstr.*

Seehaus. Munich's most gorgeous beer garden sits along the Kleinhesseloher See in the middle of the Englischer Garten; it's packed on warm nights and perfect during sunsets. *Bier und Grünzeug,* a large bowl of salad floating in a Maß of beer, isn't sold here (or anywhere, for that matter), but you can buy each separately for DM 10.20. *Tel. 089/381–6130. U3 or U6 to Münchener Freiheit; exit to Feilitzschstr., follow Feilitzschstr. east, left on Biedersteiner Str., right on Liebergesellstr., right over small bridge, then left and around the lake.*

Waldwirtschaft. The WaWi ("vavi"), as this beer garden is affectionately known, was the site of the great Munich Beer Riots of 1994, when 20,000 took to the streets to protest a court order requiring that it close in the early evening. There were certainly grounds for protest—the WaWi serves up terrific suds (Maß DM 10.20), juicy spare ribs (DM 17), and a daily dose of live summer jazz (weekdays noon–2:30 and 4:15–9:30, Sat. noon–9:30, Sun. 11–8), weather permitting. *G.-Kalb-Str. 3, tel. 089/795088. S7 or S27 to Solln, right on Pullacher Str., left on Promenadew.*

EXPLORING MUNICH

The focal point of Munich sightseeing is the shop-lined pedestrian zone that runs from Marienplatz to the Hauptbahnhof. Most of the city's major tourist attractions are concentrated here and are within walking distance of one another. The most effective way to explore Munich is to pick a few sights and wander between them, keeping your eyes open for other things that interest you. You can sometimes find the free *Eyes & Ears,* an excellent guide to activities for English-speakers, in the Hauptbahnhof's Fremdenverkehrsamt (tourist office; *see* Visitor Information, *above*).

MAJOR ATTRACTIONS

ALTE & NEUE PINAKOTHEK

The **Alte Pinakothek** has reopened after four years of renovation and reconstruction. Let your eyes feast on masterpieces by da Vinci, Dürer, Raphael, Rembrandt, and other European masters who were active from the 14th through the 18th centuries. All works are displayed in bright halls that evoke the periods they chronicle. *Barerstr. 27, entrance on Theresienstr., tel. 089/23805-216. U2 to Theresienstr. Admission: DM 7, DM 4 students; free Sun. and holidays. Open Tues.–Sun. 10–5 (Tues. and Thurs. until 8).*

Schwabing is where Munich's jet-set congregates. But not even here do Müncheners stand for the superficial. Schickis—people who value chic appearance over serious content—are indisputably unwelcome.

Directly across from the entrance to the Alte Pinakothek, you'll find the **Neue Pinakothek,** whose accent lies on works produced from the 18th century to the end of the 19th century. Masterpieces include Van Gogh's *Vase of Sunflowers* and Monet's haunting impression of water lillies in the painting of the same name. Look for works by Klimt, Klee, and Caspar David Friedrich. *Barerstr. 29, entrance on Theresienstr., tel. 089/2380–5195. U2 to Theresienstr. Admission: DM 7, DM 4 students; free Sun. and holidays. Open Tues.–Sun. 10–5 (Wed. until 8).*

If you happen to visit these galleries in the second half of the year 2000, you will be greeted by a new addition, the **Pinakothek der Moderne** (Pinakothek of Modern Art), which will house Munich's most ambitious and prestigious collections of 20th-century art. In addition to paintings and sculptures, the Pinakothek will feature photography, lithography, and installations created by the pioneers of 20th-century art. Artists will include Baselitz, Ploke, Picasso, and Palermo, as well as Joseph Beuys. The collections presently housed in three other museums, the Staatsgalerie Moderner Kunst, the Neue Sammlung, and the Architekturmuseum, will relocate to the Pinakothek der Moderne once construction is complete.

ASAMKIRCHE

Known formally as St.-Johann-Nepomuk-Kirche, this extravagant 18th-century church is better known as the Asamkirche because of the two Asam brothers, Cosmas Damian and Egid Quirin, who built it. Open the doors of this modest church to reveal a Baroque vision of paradise on earth—an overwhelming combination of intricate stucco, swirling frescoes, and gilding work. The figure of St. Nepomuk, a 14th-century Bohemian monk who drowned in Prague's Moldau River, is suspended above the entrance. He is immortalized in wax in a glass shrine on the high altar. *Sendlinger Str. 32. U1 or U2 to Sendlinger Tor; or from Marienpl., walk down Rosenstr. (which becomes Sendlinger Str.).*

BAYERISCHES NATIONALMUSEUM

This gigantic, three-story museum, covering the history of Bavarian culture and the influence of the region's European neighbors, is under renovation through much or all of 2000. The wing that houses the museum's Renaissance and Baroque collections has already been completed; at press time, the medieval wing was up next. Fortunately, however, some parts of the museum will be open to the public for the duration. You'll be able to peruse some of its 25,000 items, from the Middle Ages to the 19th century, including medieval and Renaissance wood carvings, tapestries, and armor. The museum features primarily

GOOD FOR WHAT ALES YOU

In Bavaria, you'll find a unique approach to beer. It's cheaper than water, it's thought of as "liquid bread," it's consumed by the liter, and it's brewed by monks and nuns. The world's most ancient food law, unchanged since 1516, ensures its continued quality. As decreed by Duke Wilhelm IV, the Reinheitsgebot specifies the four ingredients—water, hops, yeast, and barley—acceptable for the fine art of beer brewing. Only Weißbier, in which wheat is substituted for barley, is excepted. To order the standard pale beer, ask for a "Helles"; for dark beer, "Dunkles." And don't forget to try the tasty beer-and-lemon soda concoction called Radler. To toast, clink glasses at the base instead of the rim, hit the table with your beer, and look your fellow toasters in the eyes while sipping.

sculptures, but also boasts the world's largest collection of Christmas manger scenes and the largest collection of Tiffany outside the United States. Architect Gabriel von Seidl designed the building so that different genres of art appear in rooms that reflect their period and style. *Prinzregentenstr. 3, tel. 089/211–2401. U4 or U5 to Lehel. Admission: DM 3, DM 2 students; free Sun. Open Tues.–Sun. 9:30–5.*

DEUTSCHES MUSEUM

A German counterpart to the Smithsonian Institute, this science and technology museum—the largest of its kind in the world—is overwhelming in size and scope: It covers 13 acres and six stories. Among the 16,000 items on display are the first Mercedes-Benz, the original airplanes of the Wright brothers, and the first mechanical computer, invented by German entrepreneur Konrad Zuse years before IBM had a clue. Since not all exhibitions have English explanations, visitors planning to stay a while should invest in the 288-page *Guide Through the Collections* (DM 5), sold in the **museum store** (open daily 9–5:30). For a list of demonstrations and a map of the exhibitions, pick up an "Information for Your Visit" leaflet (30 Pf). Afterward, turn the corner to Ludwigsbrücke and enter the **Forum der Technik.** Their IMAX films are impressive. *Museuminsel 1, tel. 089/2177–9433. S-Bahn to Isartor; walk or take Tram 18 to museum. Admission: DM 10, DM 4 students, DM 3 extra for planetarium. Open daily 9–5.*

ENGLISCHER GARTEN

More than 200 years old, the Englischer Garten is the world's largest and oldest recreational city park. Designed along the lines of the rolling parklands popular with the English aristocracy during the 17th century, the garden runs along the Isar River for 5 km and is almost 2 km wide. You'll find four beer gardens, a Japanese tea garden, a lake with ducks and swans, and open space great for naps or playing. On sunny days the park teems with baseball, soccer, and Frisbee games, picnics, cyclists, music groups, and sunbathers. Walk up a small hill, built with the soil excavated to create the Kleinhesseloher See, to reach **Monopteros,** a Greek pavilion in the southern part of the park with a nice view of the Munich cityscape. North of here, the world-famous beer garden at the **Chinesischer Turm** (Chinese Tower) and the **Seehaus,** a chic beer garden beautifully situated by the Kleinhesseloher See, serve local beers on sunny afternoons. Rent a bike to see the park more thoroughly. *U3 or U6 to Münchener Freiheit; walk east on Feilitzschstr.*

FRAUENKIRCHE

Munich's most famous cathedral, the late-Gothic brick Frauenkirche (Church of Our Lady), was begun in 1468 and built in only 20 years. The cathedral underwent a 10-year restoration after suffering severe damage from wartime bombing; workers altered the original design to create a modern interior, which contrasts sharply with the weathered and war-scarred brick exterior. On the church's stone floor is the imprint of a foot, known as *Der Schwarze Tritt* (the Dark Footprint). According to legend, the Devil visited the church immediately after its completion and couldn't see any of the huge 22-m windows from where he was standing. Thinking that a building without windows was useless, he stamped his foot in triumph—leaving the mark—and left. Stand at the footprint and play Satan for a moment, then take a step forward and see how architect Jörg von Halspach outsmarted the Evil One. Even if you don't go inside, you can't miss the two bulbed towers, 109 and 110 m tall, added almost 75 years after the cathedral was completed. The view from the top is definitely worth the climb. *Frauenpl. U- or S-Bahn to Marienpl. Tower admission: DM 4, DM 2 students. Open Apr.–Oct., Mon.–Sat. 10–5. Closed Sun. and holidays.*

HAIDHAUSEN

On the right bank of the Isar, where tourists rarely venture, lies the district of Haidhausen. Once a low-rent, working-class district, it later became a haven for hippies and artists, replacing Schwabing for a time as the chic place to be. Now peaceful Haidhausen has a healthy mix of contrasting personalities. Most of the in-crowd frequents **Weißenburger Platz** and **Pariser Platz.** If you ride the U- or S-Bahn to Ostbahnhof or Rosenheimer Platz, you can take Weißenburger Straße through both squares and get a taste of Haidhausen's unique and mellow atmosphere.

MARIENPLATZ

For good luck, passing Müncheners rub the hand-worn lion snouts on the western facade of the Residenz.

Originally a marketplace for farmers and traders, Marienplatz has been Munich's main square since the city was founded in 1158. The name comes from the 16th-century **Mariensäule,** the gilded statue of the Virgin Mary and Child that stands in the square's center. Originally part of the Frauenkirche's high altar, Mary was hoisted onto the red marble column by Maximilian I after Munich survived the Thirty Years' War relatively unscathed; golden mother and babe have remained perched here since the 17th century.

The **Neues Rathaus** (New Town Hall), a neo-Gothic building constructed between 1867 and 1908, borders Marienplatz to the north. It's probably best known for the **Glockenspiel,** Europe's fourth-largest carillon. Every day at 11 AM and noon (also 5 PM May–Oct.), tourists flock to the square to watch the mechanical figures spin and dance to folk-music chimes. For DM 3, tower enthusiasts can make the 94-m climb weekdays 9–7, weekends 10–7.

The **Altes Rathaus** (Old Town Hall) stands at the eastern corner of the square. Destroyed in World War II, it was reconstructed along the original 15th-century Gothic design. Its tower houses the tiny **Spielzeugmuseum** (Toy Museum), which features 19th-century chemistry sets, centenarian teddy bears, and the first American Barbies. *Tel. 089/294001. U-Bahn to Marienpl. Admission: DM 5. Open daily 10–5:30.*

RESIDENZ

A trip to the 600-year-old home of the Wittelsbach dynasty provides a glimpse into the life of one of Germany's most rich and influential families. Construction on the royal residence began in the late 14th century, when the family decided their place at the Alter Hof (OldCourt) was too small and vulnerable to attack. With the Bavarian monarchy's 1918 demise, the royal residence was transformed into a museum. Though nearly fully destroyed in World War II—of the 23,500 sq m of ceiling, only 50 sq m remained intact—the Residenz was rebuilt, at a cost of DM 93 million.

Official tours might not be the best way to see the palace—they only cover half of the rooms and are in German. An excellent supplement to any tour is the "Residenz Guidebook" (DM 5), available at the entrance. You may wish to visit the **Staatliche Sammlung Ägyptischer Kunst** (State Collection of Egyptian Art) and the **Münzhof** (State Collection of Coins) housed in the palace. Don't miss the gilded **Altes Residenztheater,** dubbed the Cuvilliés-Theater after its architect and deemed the world's most beautiful rococo theater (*see* After Dark, *below*).

RESIDENZMUSEUM • The oldest part of the Residenz palace, the **Neuveste** (New Fortress), burned in 1750, but one of its finest rooms—the **Antiquarium**—survived intact. The largest Renaissance room north of the Alps now houses Duke Albrecht V's collection of classical statuary, and doubles as a reception hall for visiting dignitaries. The rococo **Ahnengalerie** (Gallery of Ancestors) displays portraits of 121 members of the Wittelsbach family, though some, like Charlemagne, are genealogically questionable. Other highlights include the rococo **Reiche Zimmer** (Rich Rooms), designed by François de Cuvilliés, and the **Silberkammer** (Silver Chamber), featuring all 3,500 pieces of the Wittelsbachs' dinnerware.

Entrance at Max-Joseph-Pl. 3, tel. 089/290671. Admission: DM 7, DM 5 students. Open Tues.–Sun. 10–4:30, last entry at 4.

SCHATZKAMMER • You can spend hours marveling at the blinding collection of jeweled crowns, swords, altars, and icons in the Wittelsbach treasury. Most famous is the **Statuette des Ritters St. Georg,** a small Renaissance statue of St. George on horseback, studded with 209 pearls, 406 rubies, and 2,291 diamonds. *Entrance at Max-Joseph-Pl. 3, tel. 089/290671. Admission: DM 7, DM 5 students. Open Tues.–Sun. 10–4:30.*

HOFGARTEN • North of the Residenz is the former royal garden. On its east side, the bombed ruin of the Armeemuseum (Bavarian Army Museum) has been converted into the Bavarian State Chancellery, a project dubbed the Straußoleum (after the late Franz Josef Strauss, the project's principle supporter and long-time Bavarian statesman), and long opposed on the grounds that it would detract from the unique ensemble of the Renaissance-style garden and Residenz. In front of the Chancellery, stairs lead down to the **Kriegerdenkmal** (Tomb of the Unknown Soldier), a sunken crypt that holds the remains of a German soldier from World War I.

SCHLOSS NYMPHENBURG

Prince Ferdinand Maria transformed a small summer villa into a *Schloß* (castle) in 1663 to placate his homesick Italian wife, Henriette. Some features of the complex, including the canals that wind through the grounds (meant to recall Venice for poor Henriette), date from this time. The digs you see today, however, are largely the result of more than 200 years of additional construction. To better understand and find your way through this huge palace, which stretches 800 m from one wing to the other, pick up the English-language guidebook "Nymphenburg" (DM 4) just inside the palace entrance. Notable elements of the Schloß include the **Steinerner Saal** (Stone Hall). The ceiling fresco depicts scantily clad nymphets, a reference to the name of the palace, paying homage to the goddess Flora. Ludwig I's **Schönheiten Galerie** (Gallery of Beauties) displays the most beautiful women in the king's court, including portraits of women from different social classes, even plebes. Helene Sedlmayr, the king's supposed favorite, graces the north wall; the shoemaker's daughter was only 17 when she caught his eye. The infamous Lola Montez, beautiful dancer and former mistress of Franz Liszt and Alexandre Dumas, gazes out from the west wall. Her affair with Ludwig I unleashed the unrest that ultimately led to his forced abdication. The southern wing of the Schloß, once the royal stables, now houses the **Marstallmuseum** (The Carriage Museum), which features Wittelsbach riding equipment and sleighs. Look for the golden coach built for King Ludwig II's wedding, left unused when he cancelled before ascending the altar. Ludwig was also a great riding enthusiast; the remains of his horse are kept in the museum's opposite wing.

The 500-acre **Nymphenburg Park,** a patchwork of gravel paths, shady groves, and tall grass, stretches out behind the Schloß. Impressive pavilions dot the greenery. After a rough round of *Mail-Spiel,* a game similar to golf, the royal court would retire to the two-story **Pagodenburg** for royal tea. The **Badenburg,** Max Emanuel's bathhouse and retreat, houses Europe's first heated indoor pool. Princess Maria Amalia hunted from the roof of the **Amalienburg,** an opulent, rococo hunting lodge designed by François Cuvilliés. The **Botanischer Garten** (Menzinger Str. 63, tel. 089/1786–1310; open daily 9–6, until 4:30 in winter), one of the best in all of Europe, adjoins the park at its north end. DM 3 (DM 2 students) gains access to more than 14,000 plants, from rhododendrons, rice, and alpine flowers to greenhouses (open daily 9–11:45 and 1–6, until 4 in winter) stuffed with cacti and exotic greens. *Schloß Nymphenburg 1, tel. 089/179080. U1 to Rotkreuzpl., then Tram 12 (direction: Amalienburgstr.) to Schloß Nymphenburg. Combined admission to palace, Amalienburg, and Marstallmuseum: DM 8, DM 6 students. Palace and Amalienburg open Apr.–Sept., 9:30–12:30 and 1:30–5; Oct.–Mar., 10–12:30 and 1:30–4. Badenburg and Pagodenburg open Apr.–Sept., 10–12:30 and 1:30–5. Marstallmuseum open Apr.–Sept., 9–noon and 1:30–5; Oct.–Mar., 10–noon and 1–4. All are closed Mon.*

SCHWABING

This legendary artists' quarter, north of the city center and university district, centers around the café-lined **Leopoldstraße,** which begins at the Siegestor arch. You can still find some artists setting up their easels on the boulevard, but for the most part it's full of pubs, restaurants, and outdoor cafés. If you're pinching Pfennige, eat elsewhere—the Bavarian restaurants and chic cafés can be expensive. To reach the quarter, take U3 or U6 to Gieselastraße or Münchener Freiheit.

In the summer Munich is a sea of outdoor picnics. Everywhere are shady beer-gardens where you can quench your thirst and try *Radi,* a large white radish that is cut into spirals and salted.

STAATSGALERIE MODERNER KUNST

The pillared, neoclassical **Haus der Kunst** (House of Art) was designed in the monumental style favored by the Nazi regime and once housed Hitler's exhibit of so-called *entartete Kunst* (degenerate art). Today the State Gallery of Modern Art (in the building's west wing) displays 450 works representing all the major art movements of the 20th century. You can see works by Anselm Kiefer, Lyonel Feininger, Franz Marc, and Paul Klee, as well as entire rooms devoted to Expressionism, Cubism, the Blaue Reiter (Blue Rider) group, Surrealism, Bauhaus, Constructivism, Italian plastic arts, pop art, minimalist art, and chromatic painting. The museum also houses superb temporary exhibits (open Tues.–Fri. 10–10, Sat.–Mon. 10–6; admission DM 8–DM 12). Ask the about special exhibits at the tourist office. *Prinzregentenstr. 1, tel. 089/2112–7137. U4 or U5 to Lehel. Admission: DM 6, DM 3.50 students; free Sun. Open Tues.–Sun. 10–5 (Thurs. until 8).*

THEATINERKIRCHE

Prince Ferdinand Maria commissioned the Theatinerkirche on Odeonsplatz in 1663 to honor the birth of his long-awaited heir, Crown Prince Max Emanuel. Italian architect Agostini Barelli modeled the church after Rome's St. Andrea della Valle and ignited a fascination with the Baroque style. Under the high altar a **crypt** holds the graves of more Wittelsbachs, including Ferdinand Maria, Max Emanuel, and King Maximilian I. *Theatinerstr. 22, tel. 089/210–6960. U-Bahn to Odeonspl., or walk north from Marienpl. Crypt admission: DM 1. Open weekdays 10–1 and 2–4:30, Sat. 10–3.*

During the height of Nazi power, everyone who walked in front of the Feldherrnhalle on Odeonsplatz was required to give the "Heil Hitler" salute. Dissidents used Viscaldistraße to avoid paying homage to the Führer.

TIERPARK HELLABRUNN

Animals in this 90-acre zoo appear to be living in their natural habitats. Indeed, the enclosures are ingeniously engineered; moats and multilevel landscaping minimize artificial barriers between you and the animals. The result is an optical illusion that makes it seem as if you're actually in a forest watching bears climb trees or on a plain with the deer and elk. Don't miss the aquarium (complete with electric eels and venomous lionfish) or the goat and sheep compound, where you can pet billy goats, rams, and European deer. *Tierparkstr. 30, tel. 089/625–0834. U3 to Thalkirchen, walk up ramp, exit on Tierparkstr., follow signs across bridge. Admission: DM 10, DM 7 students. Open Apr.–Sept., daily 8–6; Oct.–Mar., daily 9–5.*

VIKTUALIENMARKT

The colorful Viktualienmarkt, Munich's best-known open-air food market, is held on the square where public executions took place during the Middle Ages. Six fountain-statues of Munich's most popular folk singers and comedians dot the market grounds; the statue of comedian Karl Valentin receives fresh flowers from the market women every morning. The many stands sell high-quality, if slightly pricey fresh fruits, vegetables, flowers, meat, and fish—everything you could possibly need for a picnic on the river. The Viktualienmarkt opens Monday–Saturday at about 7 AM and is particularly vibrant on Saturday morning, when the whole world comes out to shop and socialize. The market stays open until around 7 PM, but closes earlier on Saturday. *From Marienpl., make a right at Spielzeugmuseum.*

CHURCHES AND CHAPELS

Munich's most famous churches—the Frauenkirche, Asamkirche, and Theatinerkirche—stand near the city center and are covered in Major Attractions (*see above*). Michaelskirche and the Bürgersaal are close to one another on the main pedestrian zone, so it doesn't take much effort to find them on your way to other sights. Rotating German-language tours of Munich's churches (DM 4, DM 2 students) run from April to October, Mon.–Sat. 10–5. Closed Sundays and holidays. It's helpful to pick up "Kirchen in München" at the Frauenkirche for info on dates and locations.

Bürgersaal. Originally an assembly hall when built in 1710, the two-story Bürgersaal has been used as a church since 1778. Compared to the richly decorated Baroque upper level, the ground floor is barren—though it does hold the tomb of Rupert Mayer, a famous Jesuit priest and opponent of the Hitler regime. Because of his stand against National Socialism he was arrested and sent to the Kloster Ettal concentration camp, where he remained from 1940 until the end of the war. A glass case on the ground floor contains related pictures and documents. *Neuhauserstr. 48., btw Karlspl. and Marienpl. Open Sun.–Fri until 6 PM.*

THE WHITE ROSE

Many students and professors had entered the ranks of the Nazi party by 1934, the year the University of Munich came entirely under Nazi control. Yet five students and one professor forged an underground resistance movement called Die Weiße Rose and secretly printed leaflets attacking the Nazi regime, calling for passive resistance. On February 18, 1943, Hans and Sophie Scholl let the last copies of their sixth leaflet flutter from the balcony of the university, but a janitor saw them and locked the doors. The Scholls were arrested, tried, and beheaded. Copies of the last pamphlet reached England and were then reprinted and dropped over Germany.

Today the White Rose is cited as an important milestone in the history of the resistance movement. Franz Joseph Müller, one of the group's survivors, formed the White Rose Foundation in memory of those who lost their lives. The university (U3 or U6 to Universität) has also fashioned a memorial to the White Rose located between the Geschwister-Scholl-Platz entrance and the fountain. Here you'll find reproductions of the original pamphlets and photographs of the society's Munich members.

Ludwigskirche. The main attraction of this curious neo-Byzantine/early Renaissance parish church, commissioned by Ludwig I in 1829, is its 18-by-11-m fresco of the Last Judgment, second in size only to Michelangelo's version in Rome's Sistine Chapel. *Ludwigstr. 22.*

Michaelskirche. When the tower of St. Michael's Church collapsed in 1590, only seven years after the building's completion, Duke Wilhelm V interpreted the disaster as a sign from heaven that the church wasn't big enough. During the seven-year reconstruction a great deal of square-footage was added—and the tower removed. Today the Michaelskirche is the largest Renaissance-style church north of the Alps and boasts the second-largest barrel-vaulted roof in the world. The duke rests in the crypt (admission DM 1), along with 41 members of the Wittelsbach family. The most infamous of them—loopy Ludwig II, the castle-building nut—lies here as well. *Neuhauser Str. 52. Crypt open weekdays 10–1 and 3–4:45, Sat. 10–3.*

Peterskirche. St Peter's Church, first erected 100 years before Munich's founding, has since been restored in a variety of architectural styles—today it sports a Baroque interior with a late-Gothic high altar. Labor up to the top of the tower (affectionately dubbed the Alter Peter, or Old Peter) for a view that extends as far as the Alps. On the way down, wave to Saint Munditia, the jeweled skeleton in the glass coffin with hand raised in eternal salutation. *Rindermarkt, just off Marienpl. Tower admission: DM 2.50, DM 1.50 students. Open Mon.–Sat. 9–7, Sun. and holidays 10–7.*

MUSEUMS AND GALLERIES

Munich supports so many diverse collections that it's hard to keep them straight, much less decide which ones to visit. Check your map before you go; a number of museums are clustered together, so you can often plot a convenient museum-hopping route and also see things you wouldn't normally seek out. Of the main attractions, the Neue Pinakothek, Deutsches Museum, Residenz, and Bayerisches Nationalmuseum are discussed in Major Attractions (*see above*). Of Munich's many private galleries, the **Kunsthalle der Hypo-Kulturstiftung** (Theatinerstr. 15, tel. 089/224412; open daily 10–6, Thurs. until 9) hosts world-class temporary exhibits.

BMW Museum. This high-tech museum uses videos, slides, and its gorgeous collection of cars, engines, and cycles to chronicle the technical development, social history, and future plans of the *Bayerische Motoren Werke* (Bavarian Motor Works). You can book a tour of the BMW factory and watch the assembly of BMWs from beginning to end. Free two-hour tours are given three times per week. Book one week ahead. *Petuelring 130, tel. 089/3822–3307. U3 to Olympiazentrum. Admission: DM 5.50, DM 4 students. Open daily 9–5 (last entry at 4).*

Glyptothek. Sit for hours amidst the stupendous collection of Greek and Roman statuary, enjoy an espresso in the Hall of the Sphinx, or bask in the Glyptothek's sunny courtyard as local art students sketch millennia-old antiquities. The Glyptothek and the Staatliche Antikensammlungen (*see below*) together comprise Germany's largest collection of classical art. *Königspl. 3, tel. 089/286100. U2 to Königspl. Admission: DM 6, DM 3.50 students; free Sun. Combination ticket with Staatliche Antikensammlungen: DM 10, DM 6 students. Open Tues.–Sun. 10–4:30, Thurs. 12–8:30. Free admission Sun.*

Jüdisches Museum München. The private Munich Jewish Museum has a wall detailing the search for Raoul Wallenberg, the Swedish diplomat who saved hundreds of Jews during World War II; some of the articles are in English. Also on display are photographs and sketches of prewar Jewish life, religious paraphernalia, and the yellow stars used to mark Jews in areas under Nazi control. *Maximilianstr. 36, tel. 089/297453. Admission free. Open Tues. and Wed. 2–6, Thurs. 2–8.*

Olympic Spirit. You'll get as close as possible to actually experiencing an Olympic event at this interactive center. Participate as a batter, a target shooter, a runner, or an ice-skating judge, or let the simulated rides show you what it's like to kayak, bobsled, or vault yourself over pole. Avoid the jerky rides if you get motion-sickness; get a drink at the Sports Café instead. *Toni-Merkens-Weg 4, tel. 089/3063–8623, fax 089/3063–8670. Admission DM 26, DM 18 students. U3 to Olympiazentrum. Open daily 10–7 (Fri.–Sat. until 10).*

Paläontologisches Museum. A 10-million-year-old skeleton of a mammoth tries to steal center stage at this paleontological and geological collection, but don't let it eclipse the remains of the giant tortoise, cave bears, saber-toothed tigers, and pterodactyls. *Richard-Wagner-Str. 10, tel. 089/520–3361. U2 to Königspl. Admission free. Open Mon.–Thurs. 8–4, Fri. 8–2.*

If you think the quality of a museum is directly proportional to the number of postcards bought in its giftshop, head first to the Lenbachhaus, then to the Glyptothek.

Prähistorische Staatssammlung. The State Prehistorical Collection traces the development of human settlement in Bavaria from the early Stone Age to the early Middle Ages. An especially spine-chilling exhibit features the perfectly preserved body of a young girl ritually sacrificed and recovered centuries later from a peat bog. *Lerchenfeldstr. 2, next to Bayerisches Nationalmuseum, tel. 089/293911. U4 or U5 to Lehel. Admission: DM 5, DM 1 students; free Sun. and holidays. Open Tues.–Sun. 9–4, Thurs. until 8.*

Staatliche Antikensammlungen. King Ludwig I first commissioned the State Collection of Antiquities, an impressive collection of Greek, Roman, and Etruscan art. Also featured are small bronzes, Greek and Etruscan gold jewelry, and pottery from Crete and Mycenae. *Königspl. 1, tel. 089/598359. U2 to Königspl. Admission: DM 6, DM 3.50 students; free Sun. and holidays. Combination ticket with Glyptothek: DM 10, DM 5 students. Open Tues.–Thurs., Sun. 10–5 (Wed. until 8).*

Staatliche Graphische Sammlung. The State Graphic Collection is one of the few free museums in Munich. Its 300,000 drawings and graphics from the 14th through 20th centuries include works by Dürer and Rembrandt, as well as a fine collection of works by lesser known European masters. *Meiserstr. 10, tel. 089/559–1490. U2 to Königspl. Open Tues.–Thurs. 10–1 and 2–4:30 (Thurs. until 6), Fri. 10–12:30.*

Städtische Galerie im Lenbachhaus. Outstanding! Most notably, the Lenbachhaus displays the work of the Blaue Reiter (Blue Rider) group, a German Expressionist circle (1911–1914) centered for some time in Schwabing. You'll find an exhaustive collection of works by group leader Wassily Kandinsky, Paul Klee, Franz Marc, and August Macke, among others. The Lenbachhaus also traces Munich's artistic development from the late Gothic period, through the *Münchner Schule* (Munich School) of the 19th century, Realism, Impressionism, and Jugendstil. Look for rotating exhibits (extra charge) on Munich's contemporary artists and movements. Those without a passion for modern art will enjoy lounging among the fountains and statuary of the mansion's intimate, enclosed Italian Renaissance garden. *Luisenstr. 33, tel. 089/233–0320. U2 to Königspl. Admission: DM 8, DM 4 students. Open Tues.–Sun. 10–6.*

Zentrum für Außergewöhnliche Museen (ZAM). If you're a fan of art and inventions far from the beaten path, you'll love this place. The Center for Unusual Museums includes the world's first exhibits devoted to the pedal car, the chamber pot, the lock, and the Easter Bunny. Other eccentric historical and cultural exhibits come and go; call to inquire about the latest preoccupation on display. *Westenriederstr. 41, tel. 089/290–4121. S-Bahn to Isartor. Admission: DM 8, DM 3 students. Open daily 10–6.*

BAYERN-MÜNCHEN

They are Germany's perennial favorites—the winning team that rivals love to hate. They are Bayern-München (B-M for short), sitting tight atop the throne of Germany's Bundesliga (National Soccer League), record holders for the highest number of goals scored per season (a whopping 101) and the most players to be awarded the "Soccer Player of the Year" award (5). The B-M home-game ritual begins as legions of militant, provincial fans descend on Munich's Olympiastadion (U3 to Olympiazentrum) and souse themselves silly. Tag along, if you dare, into the "Süd-Kurve," a fenced-in cage reserved for the most fanatical pilgrims. Chant along with the crazies, "LO-thaaaar, Ma-TTHÄ-us," in homage to the team's long-time star and demigod. Then, after B-M has pummeled the likes of FC Freiburg into submission, watch as 40,000 Germans drunk with victory pump their right arms and scream over and over and over "Sieg! Sieg! Sieg!" (Victory!) with nary a care in the world. For FC Bayern fans every game is like a Superbowl Sunday. For schedule info and tickets (DM 12–DM 40), call 089/6993–1333 or purchase online at www.bayernmuenchen.de.

CHEAP THRILLS

On a sunny day the **Englischer Garten** provides a glorious haven for broke travelers. You can sunbathe, picnic, stroll, or relax on the huge grassy grounds, and on weekends bands often set up and play here. After you poke your head into the interactive **Olympic Spirit** center (*see* Museums and Galleries, *above*), you might head to the **Theatron** in Olympiapark, site of the 1972 Olympic games, which features free rock concerts almost every Sunday at 4 PM throughout the summer. You can also catch live music, puppet shows, mimes, and other entertaining street performers in the **pedestrian zone,** particularly on Marienplatz and by the Feldherrnhalle monument on Odeonsplatz.

If you have a penchant for classical music, drop by the Konservatorium for *Ladenschlußkonzerte,* dress rehearsals of classical performances for zilcho. Pick up the *Monatsprogramm* at the Fremdenverkehrsamt (tourist office; *see* Visitor Information, *above*) and check for the *Eintritt frei* (free admission) notation. Catch a free **organ concert** every Thursday at 6 PM at the Lukaskirche. To get there, take the S-Bahn to Isartor, go down Zweibrückenstraße toward the Deutsches Museum, and make a left on Steindorfstraße. Check in the *Monatsprogramm* for other free *Orgelkonzerte.*

Collectors and connoisseurs will have a field day at the **flea market,** held every Friday and Saturday 6 AM–4 PM at Munich's old airport, Flughafen Riem. On the last Wednesday of every month, entry to **clubs** like Unterfahrt (*see* After Dark, *below*) is free. State **museums,** like the Neue Pinakothek and Deutsches Museum, are free on Sunday.

FESTIVALS

JANUARY AND FEBRUARY • To prepare for the ascetic period of Lent, Müncheners don masks and indulge in elegant balls and huge parties during the week of **Fasching** (carnival). The main fun begins on Fasching Sunday (the Sunday before Ash Wednesday), when a huge parade rips through the city center. On the morning of Fasching Tuesday, the party continues with dancing in the streets—no matter the weather—and general merriment that lasts the whole day and officially ends at midnight with the onset of Ash Wednesday and the fasting period.

MARCH • Starkbierzeit, the strong-beer season, marks the coming of spring with dark, strong beer. Originally brewed to nourish monks during Lent, this beer is strong in taste and high in alcohol. All the major breweries have their own version, identifiable by the -ator suffix—try Animator, Optimator, and the famous Salvator. The season lasts two weeks, beginning the third Friday after Ash Wednesday. Places to imbibe include **Salvatorkeller** (Hochstr. 77, tel. 089/459–9130) and **Löwenbräukeller** (Nymphenburger Str. 2, tel. 089/526021).

APRIL AND MAY • Auer Dult, a traditional eight-day Bavarian fair known for its antique and collectibles markets, is held three times each year on Mariahilfplatz (in the Au district). The first fair, **Maidult** (May Fair), begins on the last Saturday of April and runs through the first week of May. The **Frühlingsfest,** or Spring Festival, is a smaller version of Oktoberfest that takes place at the end of April at Theresienwiese. On **Corpus Christi,** the second Thursday after Whitsunday, a huge religious procession snakes through the streets, intended to celebrate the miracle of bread and wine being transformed into the body of Christ. Look for it near the Odeonsplatz U-Bahn stop.

JUNE • Castle concerts featuring symphonies, operas, jazz, and folk music are held in several Munich castles in June and July (*see* Classical Music *in* After Dark, *below*). **Filmfest München** has been held annually in June since 1984; the concert and movie hall **Gasteig** (Rosenheimer Str. 5, tel. 089/4895–4053) has info as well as tickets—the films are reasonably priced. Late June also marks the beginning of **Tollwood.** First organized by environmentalists, the two-week fest features free jazz, rock, and blues performances in the Olympiapark; see the Fremdenverkehrsamt for daily offerings. For tickets, visit the *Vorverkaufstelle* (ticket booth; tel. 089/383–8500) in the Marienplatz S-Bahn station.

Mettler (metal-heads) and Gruftis (goths) step aside: Light pop Schlagermusik is back in vogue after a 20-year hiatus. Germany's Schlager kings, Modern Talking, dominate the airways and the disco scene.

JULY AND AUGUST • In mid-July, **Feierwerk** (Hansastr. 39, tel. 089/743–1340, fax 089/769–6932) hosts Munich's annual scene party: one week of nonstop concerts, theater, artisans, and magic, all of it free. **Jakobidult,** a summer festival similar to Auer Dult (*see above*), begins in late July; it features a flea market and plenty of beer tents. The **Sommerfest,** which includes concerts, ballet, and other performances, takes place in July and August.

SEPTEMBER AND OCTOBER • From the middle of September to the first week of October, Munich's world-famous Oktoberfest (*see box,* **Oktoberfest,** *above*) rages for 16 days. The year's last Dult, known as the **Herbst Dult** (Autumn Fair), follows in mid-October.

DECEMBER • During the three weeks before Christmas, the **Christkindlmärkte** (Christmas markets) at Marienplatz, the Frauenkirche, Münchener Freiheit, Rotkreuzplatz, and Weißenburger Platz are filled with the aroma of specially prepared *Glühwein* (mulled wine) and grog as merchants sell their holiday trinkets and ornaments.

AFTER DARK

Schwabing is absolutely packed with chic cafés and bars. For an after-dark overview of its cliquish, touristy scene, stroll down **Leopoldstraße,** crowded with outdoor cafés that can resemble a mix between an ice-cream parlor and a trendy bar. For a more unconventional night out, head to **Türkenstraße** and meet up with young Müncheners who will appreciate your taste for things original. Visit **Haidhausen** or **Isarvorstadt** (btw the Sendlinger Tor and Fraunhoferstr. U-Bahn stops) to experience unadulterated Munich nightlife.

For the fine arts, live concerts, and the jazz scene, the *Monatsprogramm* and *Munich Found* (found in your finer English-language bookstores) are indispensable resources. Though in German, *in München* gives extensive listings of absolutely everything going on. All three can usually be obtained at the Fremdenverkehrsamt (tourist office) in the main train station.

BARS AND BEER HALLS

Café Muffathalle. Completely renovated, yet still wholeheartedly post-modern, the Muffathalle is the city's number-one center for avant-garde art and culture. Its central location on the banks of the Isar

MUNICH'S FINEST GAY BARS

Gay and lesbian nightlife flourishes in Munich and is concentrated between Isartor and Sendlinger Tor, particularly around Gärtnerplatz and on Hans-Sachs-Straße. If you're in town during Oktoberfest, be sure to visit the gay tent—called Bräu-Rösl—on the second day of the fête. For a listing of Munich's gay hot spots, pick up the Rosa Seiten, Munich's "pink pages," at any bar.

FORTUNA MUSIKBAR. *This trendy bar is the main attraction for lesbians in search of a friendly place to drink, dance, and relax with friends. Each night has its own theme—try to swing by on a Thursday, when salsa parties and Latin rhythms transform the bar into a roaring disco. Maximilianpl. 5, tel. 089/554070. From Karlspl. U-bahn stop walk northeast along the Ring. Open Thurs.–Sat. 11 PM–6 AM.*

MORIZZ. *This chic bar with lots of mirrors and wood is reminiscent of a classic club from the 1940s. The menu is equally exotic and features a variety of European and Asian dishes ranging from DM 15 to DM 30 and local beer (DM 5.00–DM 6.50 per ½ liter). Klenzestr. 43, tel. 089/201–6776. U1 or U2 to Fraunhoferstr. Open Sun.–Thurs. 7 PM–2 AM, weekends until 3 AM.*

SOUL CITY. *Practically the entire under-30 gay population shows up here every Saturday after 1 AM—too bad this huge underground dance club (said to be the biggest in the city and surroundings) is too crowded, smoky, and loud to enjoy. Maximilianpl. 5, entrance on Max-Joseph-Str., tel. 089/595272. From Karlspl. U-Bahn stop, walk along north edge of Maximilianpl., left on Max-Joseph-Str. Cover: approximately DM 10.*

SUB. *This groovy, well-lit bar sports a young crowd and a smoke-free second-floor library and lounge area. Relax in the lounge or head down the spiral staircase into the bar to mingle. Müllerstr. 43, near Sendlinger Tor, tel. 089/595272. Open Sun.–Thurs. 7 PM–11 PM, weekends 7 PM–midnight.*

makes it a "must." In the evenings the hall is transformed into a pulsating disco with theme parties ranging from 1970s "retro" to South American salsa. *Zellstr. 4, just north of Ludwigsbrücke, tel. 089/4587–5000. Open Mon.–Sat. 6 PM–4 AM, Sun. 4 PM–1 AM. Beer garden open daily 6 PM–1 AM.*

Café Puck. One of the spiffier bars on Türkenstraße, Puck has a lenient bouncer who won't snub you if you're not dressed to the nines. Inside, a fashionable crowd is enthusiastic and the staff friendly. *Türkenstr. 33, at Schellingstr., tel. 089/280–2280. U3 or U6 to Universität. Open daily 9 AM–1 AM.*

Esco Bar. This Tex-Mex restaurant is housed in surroundings that resemble a run-down Mexican jail—but with humor and niveau. The casual atmosphere makes this a place where you can amble away hours over firey tequila and cocktails (DM 12–DM 16) or plates of enchiladas (DM 17). *Breisacher Str. 19, tel. 089/ 485–137. U- or S-Bahn to Ostbahnhof; straight up Wörthstr., right on Breisacher Str. Open daily 6 PM–1 AM.*

Haus der 111 Biere. Start off your night at the House of 111 Beers with an EKU Doppelbock Kulminator 28 (DM 7 per ½ liter); at 22 proof, it's the strongest beer in the world. This place is dark, cramped, and smoky—everything a German corner bar should be. *Franzstr. 3, tel. 089/331248. From U-Bahn Müchener Freiheit, go down Leopoldstr. (toward city center), left on Franzstr. Open weekdays 4 PM–2 AM, weekends 3–3.*

Hofbräuhaus. Just as tourists feel obliged to pass through the Louvre while in Paris, so they pay homage to the Hofbräuhaus while in Munich. Come and bow to its 400-year-old beer-brewing tradition, try some of the brands yourself, and join the party. Yodeling is often on the agenda, so stop in to experience the look and feel of the Alps in the center of the city. *Am Platzl 9, tel. 089/221676. Open daily 9 AM–midnight.*

Paulaner Bräuhaus. Courses like ¼ duck with cabbage and *Knödel* (dumplings) or *Wurstsalat* (sausage salad) go for just over DM 10; wash it all down with a home-brewed Maß in the beergarden or indoors, where a tiled parquet and thick marble-like columns lend the place an air of authenticity and pride. *Kapuzinerpl. 5, tel. 089/544–6110. U-Bahn to Goetheplatz, Bus 58 to Kapuzinerplatz. Open daily 11 AM–midnight.*

Shamrock. Prepare to be body-slammed by packs of sweaty Irish rugby players. This fun Irish pub serves Munich's best Guinness (DM 7.50 per ½ liter) to travelers from all over, and hosts free, live Irish music every summer night at 9 PM. *Trautenwolfstr. 4, tel. 089/331081. U3 or U6 to Giselastr.; walk north (away from city) on Leopoldstr., right on Trautenwolfstr. Open Sun.–Thurs. until 1 AM, weekends until 3 AM.*

Türkenhof. A relaxed meeting place for artists and intellectuals, this *Kneipe* (bar) attracts open-minded students and professionals for a few of Munich's finest beers. *Türkenstr. 78, near Schellingstr., tel. 089/ 280–0235. U3 or U6 to Universität. Open Sun.–Thurs. 11 AM–1 AM, weekends until 3 AM.*

Welser Kuche. This beer hall and restaurant gives guests a true taste of life in the Middle Ages. All the food is prepared according to recipes created by Philippine Welser, a daughter of Augsburg royalty, some 450 years ago. To make the illusion complete, the staff serves all meals dressed in medieval garb and rents peasant costumes (DM 20) to guests who want to join the festivities. Weekends often feature medieval singing, dancing, and other dinner entertainment. *Residenzstr. 27, tel. 089/296973, www.welser-kuche.de. U-bahn to Odeonspl. Open 7 PM–1 AM.*

Schelling Salon. Reputedly the oldest restaurant in Schwabing, this place is the quintessential Viennese-style café with true Bavarian cusine. The owners don't mind if you spend hours there and invite guests to play billiards (DM 7 for 30 min) or participate in a game of chess, backgammon, or cards with the locals. You can rent the games—just ask. *Schellingstr. 54, at Barer Str., tel. 089/272–0788. U3 or U6 to Universität. Open daily 6:30 AM–1 AM.*

CLUBS

Munich's club scene ranges from tame, teenybopper discos to exclusive clubs for the jet set. If you need to boogie, slip on your least wrinkled outfit and make your way past the bouncer and onto the dance floor.

Backstage. This classic disco draws a huge crowd of fun-loving types who want to dance the night away. Every evening is a theme party and once a month crowds pour in from all over the city to experience "Ring the Alarm" night, an evening of loud but mellow reggae played over an intricate sound system. If you tire of the dancing in the large hall, slip over to the neighboring club to check out the not-so-private parties, or take a stroll in the fresh air at the partially sheltered beer garden. *Helmholtzerstr. 18, tel. 089/ 183330. S-bahn to Donnerbergsbrücke. Cover: DM 5–DM 15.Open Sat.–Wed. 7 PM–3 AM, Thurs. 7 PM–5 AM, weekends 9 PM–5 AM.*

Far Out. Formerly a Hare Krishna hangout, this disco near Marienplatz now fills with teens trying out their new moves. The crowd feels slightly high school, but you won't find any pretentious characters here; people don't just stand around schmoozing, they dance. Funk Thursdays are best. *Am Kosttor 2, near Hofbräuhaus, tel. 089/226661. Cover: DM 5 (DM 10 Fri. and Sat.). Open Wed.–Sun. 10 PM–4 AM.*

Nachtwerk. On nights when the exclusive clubs are having "private parties," come instead to this huge warehouse-turned-disco west of the train station. On Saturdays you'll boogie to a mix of music from the 1950s to the 1990s; on Sundays Schlager rules. Nachtwerk doubles as a live rock venue; check listings to see what's on. Skip on over to the neighboring **Club,** a more modern bi-level dance floor. *Landsberger Str. 185, tel. 089/578–3800. S-Bahn to Donnersbergerbrücke; exit onto bridge, right on Landsberger Str. (10-min walk). Cover: DM 10. Dancing Thurs. 10 PM–4 AM, weekends 10:30 PM–4 AM.*

Park Café. An exclusive interior and an exclusive clientele make this disco one to skip if you're looking for a casual evening. If you think you've got what it takes, join the young and stylish as they move to a mixture of techno and trance beats. *Sophienstr. 7, tel. 089/598313. U2 to Königspl. Cover DM 10. Open Wed.–Thurs. 10:30 PM–4 AM, weekends 10 PM–5 AM.*

Pulverturm. Especially beloved in summer for its beer garden and outdoor dance floor, the Pulverturm leans towards gothic, psychedelic, and independent beats. Sundays are reggae nights—a refreshing break from hard-core music. *Schleißheimer Str. 393, tel. 089/351–9999. U2 to Harthof. Cover: DM 5–DM 10. Open daily 10 PM–4 AM.*

Tilt. Home to most everyone—from hippie to Schicki-Micki—and often packed, Tilt offers a nicely varied program ranging from reggae to house music. Come on Saturday, when this warehouse disco pulsates with its infamous acid-jazz sounds. Covers are under DM 10. *Helmholtzstr. 12, tel. 089/129–7969. S-Bahn to Donnersbergerbrücke; exit north to Helmholtzstr. Open Wed.–Thurs. 9 PM–1 AM; weekends 10 PM–3 AM.*

LIVE MUSIC

For the most up-to-date schedule of concerts, be certain to look at the listings in one of the local magazines, such as *Münchner* (DM 4) or *Munich Found,* an excellent English city magazine with an even better website (www.munichfound.de). You can purchase tickets to shows at the full price (plus 12% service charge) at any kiosk. If you'd like to see a classical music concert—and the show isn't a guaranteed sell-out—wait and buy tickets at the venue (*see* Classical Music, *below*). State-affiliated performances, like those at the Residenz, are only sold at the theater's box office.

ROCK AND JAZZ • Munich's rock and jazz productions are often big and usually expensive. Outdoor arenas and U.S.-style stadiums are unknown to Munich, so there's a good chance this may be one of the few opportunites to see a major band without binoculars. But don't ignore local talent. These groups are legends in their own right—and often playing sets for free at beer halls and jazz cafés (*see* Bars and Beer Halls, *above*).

Kaffee Giesing. Enjoy Sunday brunch over Bach or a relaxed, post-dinner beer (DM 6) over live jazz in this stylish café-bar. The airy space comes complete with an unfinished cellar motif, faux classical statues, and papier-mâché tree roots running through the ceiling. *Bergstr. 5, tel. 089/692059. U1 or U2 to Silberhornstr.; walk up Silberhornstr., left on Bergstr. Open Mon.–Sat. 4 PM–1 AM, Sun. 10 AM–1 AM.*

Oklahoma. More American than America, this country music institution is as popular with crowds as the Grand Ole Opry. Bands from Germany and the U.S. perform live regularly Wednesday–Friday beginning at 8:30, Saturday at 8. The cover varies (usually around DM 10) but is always free on the last Wednesday of the month. *Schäftlarnstr. 156, tel. 089/723–4327. U3 to Thalkirchen; exit at Zennerstr. Open Tues.–Sat. 7 PM–1 AM.*

Unterfahrt. If you have a passion for jazz, then this club is a must. Once dubbed one of the 10 best in Europe, Unterfahrt lives up to its reputation. Every Sunday at 9 PM, the house is packed for DM 5 jam sessions. On other nights, the cover charge can run DM 10–DM 15. *Einsteinstr. 42, tel. 089/448–2794. U-Bahn to Max-Weber-Platz. Closed Mon.*

Wirtshaus zum Isartal. Bop with locals to big band, jazz, and blues in this crowded, high-spirits beer hall. Reservations aren't a bad idea. Cover varies from DM 10 to DM 20, and most shows start by 9 PM. A popular new attraction is the transvestite show every Thursday at 9 PM. *Brudermühlstr. 2, at Schäftlarnstr., tel. 089/772121. U3 to Brudermühlstr. Open weekdays 11 AM–1 AM, weekends 10 AM–1 AM.*

CLASSICAL MUSIC • Get in line an hour before the show to get reasonable seats for reasonable prices. Certain seats are reserved for students—show your ID and cross your fingers. June and early July are filled with concerts—among them the **Schloßkonzerte** (Palace Concert Series), held in Schleißheim, Dachau, Blutenburg, and the Residenz's Brunnenhof. Tickets run anywhere from DM 50 to DM 70 before the student reduction.

Gasteig. This palatial hall is Munich's largest. With several smaller venues, something is always going on. For ticket info, call the box office at 089/5481–8181. Students pay half price. *Rosenheimerstr. 5, tel. 089/480980. S-Bahn to Rosenheimer Pl. Box office open weekdays 9–6, Sat. 10–2.*

Prinzregententheater. Come here to hear the renowned Munich Symphony. The theater also presents contemporary German-language plays. For tickets, contact the National Theater box office (Maximilianstr. 11, tel. 089/221316). *Prinzregentenpl. 12, tel. 089/470–6270. U4 to Prinzregentenpl., or Bus 53 or 54.*

Residenz. The Residenz (*see* Exploring Munich, *above*) houses the Herkulessaal and the Max-Joseph-Saal, both of which feature classical music performances. The Herkulessaal has a full calendar and sells reduced-price tickets one hour before shows; call 089/2906–7263 for ticket info. *Residenzstr. 1, tel. 089/2185–1940. From Marienpl., walk north up Dienerstr. (which turns into Residenzstr.); enter through Hofgarten on Odeonspl.*

THEATER AND OPERA

Munich is well known for its staggering array of small theaters and cabarets that stage German productions—but don't overlook the big venues. Special student rates are usually offered. Act fast if you want to catch the Nationaltheater's annual **Opera Festival** in June and July—shows often sell out months in advance.

Altes Residenztheater. Also known as Cuvilliés-Theater, the old Nationaltheater (*see* Residenz *in* Exploring Munich, *above*) hosts performances of opera and chamber music. The venue—decked in gold and red velvet—is stunning. For ticket info, call 089/225754. *Residenzstr. 1, tel. 089/290671. U-Bahn to Odeonspl.*

Deutsches Theater. Here you'll find smaller musical and ballet productions as well as local debuts. For tickets call Monday–Saturday, 9 AM–8 PM. Tickets run DM 30–DM 100, but there are student discounts just before the show. *Schwanthalerstr. 13, at Sonnenstr., tel. 089/5523–4360. S-Bahn to Karlspl.*

Nationaltheater. Munich's biggest theater venue includes the Bayerische Staatsoper (Bavarian State Opera)—the place to go for world-class opera. For schedules and tickets, call the box office (Maximilianstraße 11, tel. 089/221316). *Max-Joseph-Pl., tel. 089/2185–1920. U-Bahn to Odeonspl.*

Staatstheater am Gärtnerplatz. Built in 1865, this theater now serves as a light opera house; performances include ballet, musicals, operas, and operettas. Tickets cost DM 18–DM 86, but one hour before the show, students can purchase remaining tickets at a considerable discount. *Gärtnerpl. 3, tel. 089/201–6767. U1 or U2 to Fraunhoferstr.*

No trip to Munich is complete without a visit to the archetypal beer hall, the Hofbräuhaus, immortalized in folk songs and rock songs alike. It may not be Munich at its best, but it is undeniably Bavarian.

MOVIE THEATERS

When scanning film posters, look for the designations of "oF" and "OmU," which translate as "original version" and "original with subtitles." Take U1 to Stiglmaierplatz for **Cinema** (Nymphenburger Str. 31, tel. 089/555255), which screens English-language films daily and offers sneak previews Friday nights. Tickets cost DM 11–DM 14 (DM 9.90 students), DM 6.90 until 4:30 PM, DM 7.90 for all films on Monday and Tuesday. **Theater Werkstatt-Kino** (Fraunhoferstr. 9, tel. 089/267850) is one of Munich's better alternative theaters. Take U1 or U2 to Fraunhoferstraße. Other theaters with frequent "oF" and "OmU" films include **Türkendolch** (Türkenstr. 74, tel. 089/271–8844), **Museum-Lichtspiele** (Lilienstr. 2, at Ludwigsbrücke, tel. 089/482403), and **Arri-Kino** (Türkenstr. 91, tel. 089/3819–0450). Last but not least, Munich's annual **film festival** (*see* Festivals, *above*), held in June, screens a thick catalogue of German and foreign films.

NEAR MUNICH

DACHAU

Although the 1,200-year-old town of Dachau was a haven for painters and artists from the mid-19th century until World War I, most people remember it as the site of Nazi Germany's first concentration camp. Opened in 1933, the camp's **Jourhaus,** the front gate, greeted more than 206,000 Jews, political dissidents, clergy, and other "enemies" of the Nazi regime with the promise that ARBEIT MACHT FREI (WORK BRINGS FREEDOM). The camp's watchtowers and walls remain, as do its gas chambers, disguised as showers. Records show that more than 32,000 prisoners perished here before American soldiers stormed the camp in 1945; even after the liberation, many died from disease and the effects of prolonged starvation. Through photographs, letters, and official documents, the **museum** chronicles the rise of the Third Reich as well as the brutal working and living conditions endured by the camp's prisoners (brief English captions accompany most exhibits). A 22-min **film** is shown in English at 11:30 and 3:30 and is sometimes repeated between these two showings. EurAide (*see* Visitor Information, *above*) leads English-language tours of the camp (DM 30 including transportation, DM 23 if you use your rail pass) every Tuesday and Thursday starting in June; inquire at the office in Munich's Hauptbahnhof at least one day in advance. Also ask about weekend tours. *Alte Römerstr. 75, tel. 0813/11741. Admission free. Open Tues.–Sun. 9–5.*

In the center of town above the tourist office (Konrad-Adenauer-Str. 3, tel. 08131/84566), a **Gemäldegalerie** (picture gallery) displays works from the artists' colony that thrived in Dachau until 1920. A short distance from here stands the **Dachauer Burg,** a 16th-century palace partially destroyed in the Napoleonic Wars of 1806–1809. The palace's elaborate hall survived and now hosts classical concerts in summer—call 08131/3604 for tickets and info.

COMING AND GOING

From Munich's city center, take S2 toward Petershausen (20 min) to Dachau. To reach the former concentration camp from the station, take Bus 722 to Gedenkstätte (Memorial). Note: Dachau is one S-Bahn stop out of the Innenraum (inner zone); people without valid tickets are constantly nabbed here and fined DM 60 (*see* Getting Around, *above*). On the strip ticket, cancel two strips for the S-Bahn and two for the bus. If you have a railpass, pay only for the bus (DM 1.70). To reach Dachau's city center from the camp, take Bus 724 or 726 to the Rathaus.

STARNBERGER SEE

Once a favorite summer destination of the Wittelsbach rulers, this 21-km-long lake awoke from its Sleeping-Beauty-sleep in the middle of the 19th century, when a new rail line made transportation to and from Munich easy and quick. These days, Starnberger See is a popular weekend getaway for sunbathers, sailors, windsurfers, swimmers, and hikers, and makes a great stopover between Munich and the Alps.

In 1886 King Ludwig II drowned here (*see box* A Dream Come True, *in* Chapter 6) after he had been deposed and confined to the castle at **Berg,** a small village on the shores of Starnberger See. Ludwig's favorite cousin, Sissi, lived in a castle across the lake; some theorize that the king drowned trying to swim the mile to her home. The castle you see from the ferry on the way to Berg is the genuine article; relatives of Ludwig live there still. Round-trip boat rides from Starnberg to Berg and the neighboring village of Leoni cost DM 10. Three-hour round-trip cruises on the lake cost DM 23.50; a one-hour cruise DM 12.50. Boats run April–October, weather permitting; for tickets and schedules check the **Staatliche Schifffahrt** booth (tel. 08151/8061) next to the boat dock by the Starnberg S-Bahnstop.

After a quick stop in Berg, head to the adjacent **Schloßpark,** the castle park that runs along the lakeshore between Berg and Leoni. Stroll through the park and up to the **Votivkapelle,** a memorial chapel built high above the place where King Ludwig II's body was discovered; a cross marks the spot.

COMING AND GOING

To reach Starnberger See from Munich, hop on S6 toward Tutzing and disembark at Starnberg. The trip takes less than 40 min; cancel four strips on that strip ticket or use your Eurail, InterRail, or DM 20 day pass.

OUTDOOR ACTIVITIES

From the train station, face the lake and walk left along the promenade if you feel like sunbathing or swimming. From the station, head right to rent **boats** powered by electric motors (DM 20 per hr), **paddle boats** (DM 6 per ½ hr), or **rowboats** (DM 8 per hr). Rent windsurfing equipment (DM 50 per day) from **Surf Tools** (Münchner Str., tel. 08151/89333). For more info, visit the helpful, English-speaking **tourist office** (Wittelsbacherstr. 9, tel. 08151/90600), open weekdays 8–6 (July–Sept., also Sat. 9–1 PM); from the S-Bahn station, walk 10–15 min away from the lake on Wittelsbacherstraße. If you're interested in **hiking,** request information about the 6-km trail that eventually intersects with the **König-Ludwig-Weg,** a 100-km path that stretches from Starnberg all the way to Füssen. The office also has biking maps; rent **bikes** at the S-bahn station.

AMMERSEE AND ANDECHS

Smaller and less visited than the Starnberger See, Ammersee (Lake Ammer) and the nearby monastery at Andechs make excellent getaways for water-sport enthusiasts, hikers, and beer connoisseurs. The S-Bahn stop at Herrsching is only minutes from the lake promenade, where you can stop to take in the beauty of the gently stirring water or take a 50-min ferry ride (DM 15) to other lakeside towns. One of the most picturesque, **Dießen,** full of fishermen and artists, is known for its pottery and its Baroque **Marienmünster** (open 8–noon and 2–6); the famous court architect Cuvilliés designed the church's high altar. The ferry to Dießen leaves approximately every 90 min between 9:23 AM and 6:25 PM (buy your ticket on the boat).

To reach the lake from the S-Bahn station, walk through the tunnel under the tracks and follow the gravel path down to the water. As you approach Ammersee, look left to see the **Schlößchen im Kurpark,** a romantic villa built for the artist Ludwig Scheuermann. The villa is now used as a cultural center and summer concert hall; for info call 08152/4250. Veer left at the water and look for the KASSE sign to rent **boats** from Stummbaum (tel. 08152/1375). Paddle boats are DM 6 per ½ hour; rowboats are DM 6 per ½ hour; two-person electric boats are DM 15 per ½ hour; solar-powered boats cost DM 25 per hour. For more info, visit the **tourist office** (Verkehrs-Zentrale; Bahnhofpl. 2, tel. 08152/5227), opposite the tiny Herrsching station. It's open weekdays 8:30–noon and 2–5, Saturday 10–12:30.

To visit an authentic brewery with old world style, take the scenic 3-km trek up Heiliger Berg (Holy Mountain), which ends at the Benedictine monastery-brewery of **Andechs** (tel. 08152/3760). The walk takes about an hour; start up Bahnhofstraße behind the station and continue until you see signs to Andechs. Today people visit mainly to taste the monks' special brews, either in the **beer garden** (open daily 10–9) overlooking rolling farmland, or in the **beer hall.** Before you get too hammered, check out the 15th-century pilgrimage church, the final resting place of Carl Orff, composer of *Carmina Burana.* The church is open daily 8–8 in the summer. If you didn't pack your own picnic, grab a giant pretzel and try the homemade cheese (DM 3. 20); it may stink, but it's surprisingly tasty. A Maß of Andechs beer costs only DM 8—but don't deny yourself the pleasure of a potent *Doppelbock Dunkel* (Maß DM 9.40).

COMING AND GOING

From Munich take S5 to the last stop, Herrsching. The trip takes less than an hour (cancel six strips on a strip ticket). The S-Bahn returns to Munich every 20 min until 11:40 PM. You don't need to pay if you have a valid rail pass or DM 17 day pass. To reach Andechs by bus from Herrsching's S-Bahn station, catch Bus 956 (DM 3) or any private bus displaying an ANDECHS sign in the front window. The last bus to the S-Bahn station leaves the monastery at 6:45 PM.

CHIEMSEE AND SCHLOSS HERRENCHIEMSEE

Nicknamed the "Bavarian Sea," enormous Chiemsee (Lake Chiem) is an outdoorsy person's paradise. Its shores are dotted with resorts for sailing, horseback riding, hiking, and mountaineering. Rent **bikes** at Reischenbök near the Bahnhof (tel. 08051/4631) in the Chiemsee town of Prien. You can also hang glide in nearby **Übersee** or paraglide in **Aschau** (13 km south of the Chiemsee). For info, check at the **tourist office** (open weekdays 12:45–5:45) in Prien's train station. The Chiemsee's main draw, however, is **Schloß Herrenchiemsee,** Ludwig II's copy of the Versailles palace that dominates **Herreninsel** (Men's Island). Don't overlook the idyllic **Fraueninsel** (Women's Island), a tiny cluster of quaint homes and gardens that offers a welcome break from the greater Munich area.

The most relaxing and reasonably priced way to see the Chiemsee islands is to buy a **Tag am Chiemsee** ticket (DM 38), a same-day return ticket that covers all the transportation you need to get to and from the islands from Munich. Tickets can usually be purchased daily May–September at the Reisezentrum in Munich's train station. If you have a Eurail, Interrail, or DB pass, you can get the same package for DM 15 from Munich's EurAide office (*see* Visitor Information, *above*). No matter what you pay, getting to Chiemsee requires an hour-long ride from Munich to the town of Prien. In Prien expect to board a steam train that is the second leg of your journey. After a 5-min ride, the train deposits you in the lakeside town of Stock, where you board the ferry that takes you to Herreninsel and Fraueninsel. The last ship leaves the islands sometime between 7 and 8 PM; check the departure schedules for exact times.

If you plan to stay longer, look into a list of *Privatzimmer* and hotels at the tourist office. A bed at the **HI-Jugendherberge Prien** (Carl-Braun-Str. 66, tel. 08051/68770, fax 08051/687715) costs DM 24. To get there, turn right out of the train station, go under the tracks, and follow the JUGENDHERBERGE signs. Campers should head south from the ferry landing along the main road to **Panorama Camping Harras** (tel. 08051/90460; closed Oct.–Apr.) for a woodsy spot (DM 8 per site plus DM 8.50 per person) on the Chiemsee.

HERRENINSEL

Herreninsel is best known for the unfinished, yet still impressive **Schloß Herrenchiemsee** (tel. 08051/68870), a palace strikingly similar to Versailles in France. A devoted fan of the French "Sun King" (Louis XIV), Ludwig commissioned the palace in the hopes it would allow him to command the same respect and power as did his French idol. Of the 20 rooms open to the public, the spectacular **Spiegelsaal** (Hall of Mirrors) and Ludwig's sumptuous bedroom are the most impressive. The **König Ludwig II Museum** displays the royal robes, Ludwig's death mask, and other objects that shed light on the personal life of this eccentric monarch. As you hike the 20 min through the island's greenery, you'll pass the old **Schloß,** a monastery-turned-castle where West Germany's constitution was written in 1948. *Combined ticket for palace and museum: DM 9, DM 5 students. Both open Apr.–Sept., daily 9–5; Oct.–Mar., daily 10:15–3:45. Closed holidays. Guided tours only (English tours at 10:30, 11:30, 2, 3, and 4).*

FRAUENINSEL

Arriving on this lush, traffic-free isle is a pleasing cap to the beautiful ride across the lake. A former artists' colony, Fraueninsel has a summer-only gallery in the ancient **Torhalle** (tel. 08054/7256; admission DM 3, DM 1.50 students), which used to be the gatehouse to the Frauenwörth convent. The remains of local artists and beloved townspeople rest in the small cemetery at the **Benediktiner Kloster**; next door is the 1,200-year-old **Frauenchiemsee Abbey,** the oldest nunnery in Germany. Stroll through the nuns' colorful *Krautgarten* (herb garden), take a walk around the lake (25 min) and indulge in the tranquillity of the many lovely homes and gardens, then relax in Fritzi's beer garden on the island's west side, and watch the people and the hours go by.

LANDSHUT

If you need a break from the tourist scene, spend an afternoon in the 15th-century town of Landshut, about 75 km northeast of Munich. Lined with pastel-colored Baroque facades, the cobblestone **Altstadt** deserves its reputation as one of Germany's prettiest streets, as does its sister, **Neustadt,** a similar but less bustling avenue. The superlatives continue with the largest brick tower in the world (131 m), attached to **St. Martin's Church.** Inside, don't miss the unusual stained-glass windows, which cast the personages of three Nazi leaders as the torturers of St. Kastulus.

Landshut's treasure is **Burg Trausnitz,** a 13th-century castle sprawled atop a hill overlooking the town, and home to the Wittelsbach dukes until 1503. Today the mazelike complex is overgrown with ivy and wildflowers, creating dozens of picnic-perfect sanctuaries within the castle's ramparts. For those who want to learn about the history of this impressive castle and the battles it has witnessed, there is a 45-min, German-language tour (DM 5, DM 4 students). Tel. 0871/924110. Open daily 9–5.

But Landshut is perhaps best known for *Die Landshuter Hochzeit* (the Landshut Wedding), a celebration that takes place every three years (next one's up in 2002) during the month of May. At this time the city's inhabitants reenact the wedding procession of the last Landshut Duke, Georg, and his bride, Hedwig, the daughter of the King of Poland. When the majestic celebration first took place in 1475, the city was the prosperous capital of Lower Bavaria. Nowadays the day is marked by medieval jousting tournaments and folk dances in the streets—the city is at it merriest and most beautiful.

COMING AND GOING

Trains from Munich make the 45- to 60-min trip to Landshut hourly (DM 20). Landshut is also a convenient and worthwhile stop if you're headed to Passau (*see* Chapter 6). Store your stuff in a locker at the station before heading into town. A *Tageskarte* (DM 2.60, DM 1.60 students) is valid for one day's unlimited use of the bus system. From the station, Buses 1, 2, 3, and 6 take seven min to reach the Altstadt.

WHERE TO SLEEP

Ask at the station's **info office** (tel. 0871/963–7262; closed Sun.) or at the main **tourist office** (Verkehrsverein; Altstadt 315, tel. 0871/922050; open weekdays 9–noon and 1:30–5, Sat. 9–noon) for a list of private rooms and hotels. Within walking distance of the Altstadt, **Hotel Park Café** (Papiererstr. 36, tel. 0871/69339) has singles for DM 50, doubles for DM 95. For a grassy camping spot along the Isar, walk northeast along the river, turn left on Konrad-Adenauer-Straße, then right onto Breslauer Straße, which dead-ends at **Campingplatz der Stadt Landshut** (tel. 0871/53366; closed Oct.–Mar.). Sites are DM 5 plus DM 6 per person.

HI-Jugendherberge Ottonianum lies halfway between the Altstadt and Burg Trausnitz and affords an excellent view of St. Martin's. Beds cost DM 17–DM 20.50; breakfast is an additional DM 6. Men and women can share a double for DM 20.50 each, and there's no curfew if you ask for a key. *Richard-Schirmann-Weg 6, tel. 0871/23449, fax 0871/274947. From Altstadt, walk up Alte Bergstr., turn right before Burghauser Tor (Burghauser Gate), follow bend to Richard-Schirmann-Weg. 120 beds. Reception open daily 8–noon and 5–10, checkout 9:30. Closed Christmas.*

6 BAVARIA

UPDATED BY PEGGY SALZ-TRAUTMAN

Sandwiched between the Danube and the Alpine massif, Bavaria (Bayern) is perhaps the most beautiful and certainly the largest and richest *Land* in Germany. A region of glacial lakes, forested hills, golden fields, and azure skies, Bavaria is renowned for its fairy-tale castles, onion domes, and delightfully preserved villages. Although it is an integral part of Germany, you'll soon sense that Bavaria is also a land apart—note the YOU ARE ENTERING THE FREE STATE OF BAVARIA sign at the border and the nightly playing of the Bavarian national anthem on TV. This fierce devotion to a homegrown style and culture may be protective behavior learned over centuries of successive flag raising. By the time Charlemagne annexed Bavaria to his empire in 788, the territory had already survived its share of Roman and Germanic invasions. Holy Roman Emperor Frederick I (a.k.a. Barbarossa) signed the wealthy duchy over to the Wittelsbach family in 1180; the clan would preside over the land for almost a millennium. In 1806 Napoleon dissolved the Holy Roman Empire and granted Bavaria kingdom status, which ushered in what is nostalgically recalled as Bavaria's Golden Age.

While the Wittelsbach dynasty left its mark on Munich, it is the work of the Golden-Age kings that has come to define much of the Bavarian landscape. King Ludwig I, a dedicated builder, diverted considerable state and personal income to make Munich the showpiece of Bavaria and the cultural center of Europe. His building mania was passed on to his son, and later to his grandson, Ludwig II, who gave Bavaria Neuschwanstein (*see box* A Dream Come True, *below*), the Cinderella-style castle for which Bavaria is best known. But such extravagant building projects have their price; in 1871 Bavaria lost its prized independence when Bismarck rescued the region from bankruptcy and incorporated it into the German Empire. Following World War I, Bavarian soil nurtured brown-shirted Hitlerian thugs, and in the elections of 1932, reactionary Bavarians cast their lot with Hitler in greater proportion than did residents of any other German state.

These days, Munich (*see* Chapter 5) and Nuremberg (*see* Chapter 7) reign as Bavaria's first and second cities. Don't let them eclipse **Regensburg,** an exciting city blessed with Germany's loveliest Altstadt (old town) and hip student flair. Less-touristed towns—Renaissance-style **Augsburg,** Frankenstein's **Ingolstadt,** and watery **Passau,** the "Venice of Bavaria"—generate even more bang for the budget buck. To the east along the Czech border, the **Bavarian Forest** beckons travelers in search of outdoor adventure. To the south, the **Bavarian Alps** are often overrun with waves of summertime visitors. Yet they shelter Germany's most spectacular scenery, and, of course, King Ludwig's magnificent castles.

AUGSBURG

Founded by two stepsons of Roman emperor Augustus in the year 15 BC, Augsburg is and the oldest of Bavaria's cities and the envy of its neighbors. In the 15th century, with the help of beneficiaries like the Fugger clan, Ausburg became the center of attention and Continental high finance. Indeed, the Fuggers were to Augsburg what the Medicis were to Florence; they bankrolled much of the Renaissance-style Altstadt and in 1519 erected the *Fuggerei,* a "town within the town" founded to provide homes for the city's poorer citzens. Today Augsburg has an active cultural life, particularly since its university opened its doors in 1970. The Romantic Road bus, which journeys from the Main Valley via Augsburg to Füssen, spills camera wielders onto Augsburg's streets twice daily from April to October (*see* Romantische Straße *in* Chapter 7).

BASICS

CHANGING MONEY

The post office next to the train station has the best exchange rates but charges DM 6 per traveler's check. Take your Visa to the ATM at **Citibank** (Bahnhofstr. 2, tel. 0821/156061).

MAIL AND PHONES

Make long-distance calls and buy phone cards at the **Hauptpost** (main post office) next to the train station. The postal code is 86150. *Viktoriastr. 3, tel. 0821/3466710. Open weekdays 8 AM–10 PM, Sat. 8–8.*

VISITOR INFORMATION

The **tourist office,** called the Verkehrsverein, is 300 m from the train station. The office stocks the usual free maps and lodging info, and can book you into a private room for a DM 3 fee. *Bahnhofstr. 7, tel. 0821/19433. Open weekdays 9–6.*

The **information office** on Rathausplatz provides still more tourist literature and makes room reservations for a DM 3 fee as well. This is the only place to get the *Radwegkarte,* a free map of bicycle routes, and the indispensable English-language pamphlet "Augsburg and its Sights" (DM 1), which maps out a number of walking tours. *Tel. 0821/502–0724. Open weekdays 9–5, Sat. 10–1 (in summer Sat. 10–4, Sun. 10–1).*

COMING AND GOING

From Augsburg's *Hauptbahnhof* (main train station), frequent **trains** leave for Munich (40 min, DM 16.20) and Regensburg (2½ hrs, DM 38). Make use of the new 24-hour hot line (0180/599–6633) to get information on train departures and prices. Deposit your bags in a locker and head downtown (a 10-min walk): Go east down Bahnhofstraße and veer left onto Annastraße. The **bus** and **tram** system (in operation 5 AM–midnight) is the most practical way to get around. The main tram station is on Halderstraße in front of the Hauptbahnhof; rides cost DM 1.70. Pick up a **bike** at Zweirad Bäumel (Jakoberstr. 70–72, tel. 0821/33621) for DM 10 per day.

Between April 1 and October 31, you can take Deutsche Bahn's **Romantic Road Bus** (free with Eurail or DB pass). The bus stops twice daily in Augsburg, with further stops in Munich and Füssen in one direction, in Rothenburg-ob-der-Tauber, Würzburg, and Frankfurt in the other.

WHERE TO SLEEP

Lodging in Augsburg is moderately priced, with well-located rooms starting at DM 35 for a single, DM 65 for a double. If you'd rather not brave the hostel, book a room through the tourist office or try **Jakoberhof** (Jakoberstr. 39–41, tel. 0821/510030), a simple but cozy guest house near the Fuggerei, about a 10-min walk from the city center. Singles cost DM 50, doubles DM 75 (add DM 25 for private bath). **Lenzhalde** (Thelottstr. 2, tel. 0821/520745), right behind the train station, has singles for DM 42, doubles for DM 78.

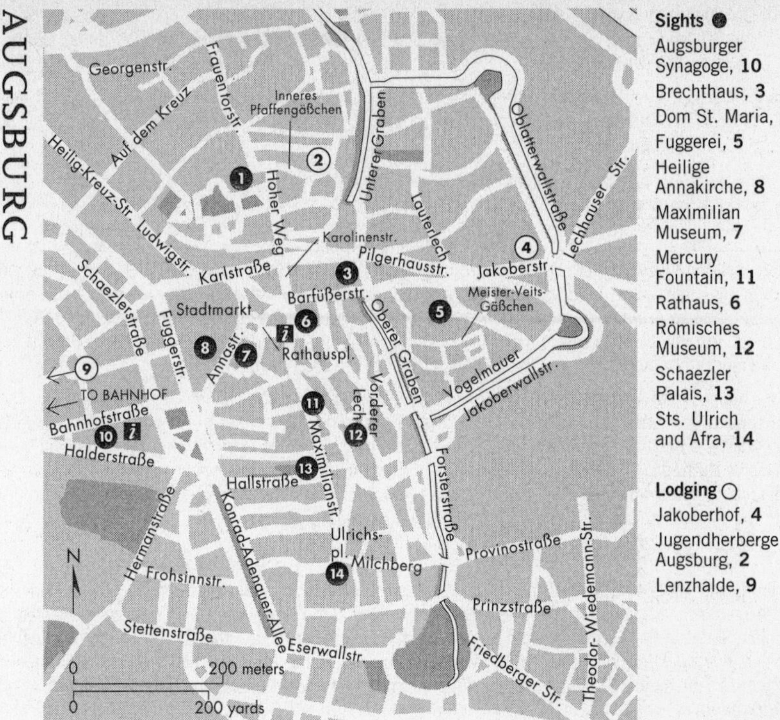

HOSTELS

Jugendherberge Augsburg (HI). Only a three-min walk from the Dom, this is easily the cheapest and most convenient place to crash, and even hostelers over the age of 26 are accommodated if there's room. Space in one of the 132 beds costs DM 18 per night (DM 20.50 over 26) including breakfast and showers. *Beim Pfaffenkeller 3, tel. 0821/33909, fax 0821/151149. From train station, Tram 2 to Stadtwerke; walk toward Dom, right on Inneres Pfaffengäßchen (30 min). Curfew 1 AM. Reception open 2–4 and 8–10, checkout 9 AM. Key deposit (DM 20). Closed Dec. 20–Jan. 20.*

CAMPING

Campingplatz Augusta. Sporting a washing machine, warm showers, and bathrooms, this campground has tent sites for DM 6 plus an additional DM 8 per person or DM 6 per car. *Mühlhauserstr. 54, tel. 0821/707575, fax 0821/705883. From train station, Bus 23 to Hammerschmiede (20 min, DM 4) and then a 30-min walk. 100 sites. Reception open year-round 8 AM–noon and 2 PM–8 PM.*

FOOD

You'll find many an **Imbiß** (snack stand) on the Rathausplatz (the main market square) and on nearby Maximilianstraße. For something more substantial, try **Fuggerkeller** (Maximilianstr. 38, tel. 0821/516260), a traditional Swabian restaurant housed in the cellars of the former Fugger family home. A full dinner runs around DM 20, but the lunch menu has a few selections priced under DM 14. A hearty meal of simple but well-prepared food awaits you at **Zum Ochsen** (Klausenberg 2, tel. 0821/91381) a *gemütlich* (cozy) place to get away from it all. For fresh produce, meats, and cheeses, check out the **Stadtmarkt** (city market), open weekdays 7–6, Saturday 7–noon. Enter the market from Fuggerstraße, Annastraße, or Ernst-Reuter-Platz.

König von Flandern. Given the rarity of all-you-can-eat opportunities in Germany, wise travelers will stop by the King of Flanders for the hunger that comes. Order the daily special *aus der Pfanne* (from the fry-ing pan; DM 9) and take your pick of the unlimited side dishes. The King serves up a respectable salad plate (DM 9.30) and brews an impressive Drei-Keller-Bier (DM 3.50). *Karolinenstr. 12, under Bücher Pustel bookstore, tel. 0821/158050.*

Ristorante Caruso. This fine Italian restaurant features an extensive menu, superb victuals, and reasonable prices. The lunchtime penne special is popular at DM 8; pizzas also start at DM 8. *Karlstr. 9, enter at Karlpassage, tel. 0821/155240.*

WORTH SEEING

Augsburg may be a large city, but its historic Altstadt is compact and easily navigated on foot. English-language **walking tours** (DM 10, DM 7 students) leave from outside the Rathaus daily at 2 PM during the summer; November–April, tours are Saturdays only. If you'd rather strike out on your own, head from the tourist office to Annastraße and the 14th-century **Heilige Annakirche** (St. Anne's Church), Augsburg's most important Protestant church. In 1518 Martin Luther stayed in Room 5 as he met with Cardinal Cajetan, the papal legate sent to convince Luther of the error of his ways.

At the northern end of Annastraße you'll stumble upon Rathausplatz, the historic heart of Augsburg. The **Perlachturm** (open Apr.–Oct., daily 10–6), a tower 86 m in height, dominates the square; the tower's Glockenspiel is played at noon and 5 PM. For DM 2, you can climb to the top of the tower and play bird. The massive **Rathaus** (City Hall), considered one of the finest Renaissance structures north of the Alps, sits adjacent to the tower. Inside, a gallery houses temporary art exhibits; admission is free. Climb the stairs to the third floor for a look at the glittering **Goldener Saal** ballroom.

DOM ST. MARIA

Considering that more than half of Augsburg was destroyed in World War II, it's incredible that Dom St. Maria, Augsburg's largest cathedral, escaped unscathed. After the war, grateful citizens erected a memorial column at the western entrance. On top sits a single pinecone, the symbol of the city. Inside the door is the oldest stained-glass work in central Europe, dating from the 11th century. Don't leave before you see the exquisite altarpieces by Augsburg resident Hans Holbein the Elder. *Open Mon.–Sat. 7–6, Sun. noon–6.*

FUGGEREI

Ten min east of the city center sits the mustard-color Fuggerei, the world's oldest subsidized housing project. Jacob Fugger had the tranquil complex built in 1516 to accommodate the city's poor yet industrious Catholics—if they had become impoverished through no fault of their own. The Fuggerei's 67 homes contain 147 apartments that still serve the same purpose—welfare housing for the city's destitute. There residents of Augsburg can find shelter for a symbolic rent of one "Rheinisch Guilder" per year, set according to 1873 exchange rates at DM 1.72.

Although none of the (private) homes are open for viewing, you can see how people lived during the Fugger era in the **Fuggerei Museum,** an original three-room apartment filled with period furniture. Consider the old bellpulls (precursor to the doorbell), all of which bear different shapes: Prior to the days of street lighting, residents identified their homes in the dark streets by their feel. Feel free to walk the grounds. Admission to the museum is DM 2; it's open daily in summer 9–6, and in winter on weekends only.

MAXIMILIANSTRASSE

A few blocks south of Rathausplatz, this lantern-lined avenue contains dozens of shops and cafés, as well as the **Mercury Fountain,** created in 1599 by the Dutch artist Adrian de Vries. Continue south along Maximilianstraße and you'll soon pass another de Vries fountain, this one depicting Hercules battling the Hydra. Lounge on the steps of the fountains, enjoy the atmosphere, and write a few postcards.

Farther along the street you'll find the 18th-century **Schaezler Palais.** At the time it was built, property tax was levied according to the amount of street frontage; to avoid hefty taxes the palace was built deep and narrow, running far back from Maximilianstraße. Today it contains the **Deutsche Barockgalerie** (German Baroque Gallery), with a large collection of 17th- and 18th-century works. For a glimpse of pure rococo ostentation, make your way to the **Festsaal** (ballroom). *Maximilianstr. 46, tel. 0821/324–2175. Admission: DM 4, DM 2 students. Open Wed.–Sun. 10–4.*

At the southern end of Maximilianstraße, the adjacent churches **St. Ulrich** and **St. Ulrich und Afra** mark the site where St. Afra was buried in AD 304. The joint crypt also holds the tomb of St. Ulrich, a

10th-century bishop. Catholic St. Ulrich und Afra is the older and far larger cathedral, but little Evangelical St. Ulrich is worth the a visit: Look for the organ above the church altar and don't miss the reversible pews, which allow worshippers to see their priest at all times.

MUSEUMS

Augsburg has a wealth of small, unique museums, almost all of which are closed Monday and Tuesday. The **Brechthaus** (Auf dem Rain 7, tel. 0821/324–2779; admission DM 2.50, DM 1.50 students) houses exhibits dedicated to the Augsburg-born dramatist Bertold Brecht (1898–1956), best known for his plays *Mother Courage* and the *Threepenny Opera.* To view relics of Augsburg's past, visit the **Maximilian Museum** (Philippine-Welser-Str. 24, tel. 0821/324–2174), or explore Roman artifacts in the **Römisches Museum** (Dominikanerg. 15, tel. 0821/324–2180). Both museums charge DM 6 (DM 3 students) admission and are open Wednesday–Sunday 10–4. The **Jüdisches Kulturmuseum** (Museum of Jewish Culture; Halderstr. 6–8, tel. 0821/513658), housed in the gorgeous Jugendstil **Augsburger Synagoge,** documents the history of Augsburg's Jewish community. The museum is open Tuesday–Friday 9–6, Sunday 10–5; admission is DM 4, DM 2 students.

AFTER DARK

Once the sun sets, stroll down Maximilianstraße for a taste of Augsburg's lively café scene. For brews, your best bet is the beer garden at **Brauereigasthaus Drei Königinnen** (Meister-Veits-Gäßchen 32, tel. 0821/158405; closed Mon.). The garden closes at 10:30 PM, but the bar doesn't shut down before 1 AM. Augsburg's student pubs are concentrated in the alleys and streets behind the Rathaus. The Irish pub **Fuki's Fuchsbau** (Bei St. Ursula 1, tel. 0821/159–8892) has a mellow patio area in a quiet alley off Maximilianstraße. Heilig-Kreuz-Straße is another good place to explore; here you'll find **Thorbräukeller** (Heilig-Kreuz-Str. 20, tel. 0821/511991), a beer garden and bar favored by locals. Students, artists, and nonconformists head to **Liliom** (Unterer Graben 1, tel. 0821/159–8089). Sculpture graces the leafy beer garden, and black floors, oak furniture, great tunes, and modern art set the tone for the adjacent café-bar. All four are open daily until about 1 AM.

Access to the Fuggerei is controlled by guarded gates that are locked from 10 PM to 5 AM, severely curtailing the social lives of the occupants. Residents who come home after midnight are fined the equivalent of seven months' rent—a whopping DM 1.

INGOLSTADT

Most foreigners have never heard of the walled city of Ingolstadt, home to Bavaria's first university, founded in 1472 by Duke Ludwig the Rich. Yet it was as a medical student in Ingolstadt that the university's most illustrious (if fictional) graduate, Victor Frankenstein, first honed his Promethean powers. It was here, while the town lay blackened in sleep, that *Doktor* Frankenstein forged the awful monster that came to bear his name. And it was here that Duke Wilhelm IV issued the 1516 *Reinheitsgebot,* or beer purity law, ensuring Bavarian party standards for centuries to come. Today, as the official tourist pamphlet likes to point out, "Ingolstadt is in." The town's allure stems from a vigorous café-bar scene catering to local students, an outstanding, eclectic set of museums, an extensive net of bike paths traversing the velvet-green countryside, and a unique series of military fortifications ringing an Altstadt largely untrodden by tourists. Meanwhile, the Danube surges by on its long, long way to the Black Sea.

BASICS

The **tourist office** (Rathauspl. 2, tel. 0841/305–1098; open weekdays 8–5, Sat. 9–noon) hands out free maps and books rooms commission-free. To get there, take Bus 10, 11, 15, 16, or 44 to Rathausplatz (10 min, DM 2.30) in the town center. You can also make the heavily trafficked 30-min trek on foot: Exit right from the train station onto Bahnhofstraße, go right on Münchener Straße, keep going straight across the bridge, and follow Donaustraße into the city center. If you plan to cruise the region via bike, buy a *Radwegkarte* (DM 9.80), with routes already inscribed, at the tourist office. Rent **bikes** for DM 10–DM 20 per day at Stadtrad (Poppenstr. 1, tel. 0841/931–1194; closed Mon.). Frequent **trains** whiz between Ingolstadt and Munich (50 min, DM 22); Eichstätt and the Altmühl Valley await less than 20 min away (DM 10).

WHERE TO SLEEP

If you arrive late, try the computerized "Infoboy Tourist Informations System," an information kiosk on Rathausplatz that lists hotels and pensions. In the city center, **Gaststätte City-Pub Pension** (Kupferstr. 6, tel. 0841/910167) has simple rooms above a bar. At DM 40 for singles and DM 80 for doubles (all with hall showers), it's as cheap as you'll find in this area. Campers should head for the lakeside **Campingplatz Auwaldsee** (tel. 0841/961–1616), a 40-min ride from town. From the Hauptbahnhof, take Bus 10 to the Omnibus depot, then transfer to Bus 60 for Auwaldsee. From the bus stop, walk straight ahead, right around the AUWALDSEE sign. A one-night stay costs DM 8.60 per person, DM 5.90–DM 10.90 for a site.

HOSTELS

Jugendherberge (HI). If you're under 27, consider heading straight to the convenient hostel, near both the Kreuztor and a great café and bar area. The many cyclists passing through in summer rise early and the halls echo like mad, so don't expect to sleep late. With breakfast, a night costs DM 20. *Friedhofstr. 4½, tel. 0841/34177. From city center, walk west on Theresienstr. past Kreuztor. 84 beds. Curfew 11:30. Reception open 7 AM–11:30 PM. Lockers (DM 1 deposit). Closed mid-Dec.–Jan. and every 2nd and 4th weekend Nov.–mid-Dec. and Feb.–mid-Mar.*

FOOD

Ingolstadt eateries dish up plenty of good Bavarian food, as well as Greek and Italian fare. Browse along the pedestrian zone that runs from Theresienstraße to Ludwigstraße to examine your options. An Aldi **supermarket** sells discount groceries at Theresienstraße 7.

Neue Welt. The "New World" serves up a great mix of good food, fine art, and excellent atmosphere. This bistro is frequented by artists and musicians, and local bands perform on Mondays and Tuesdays. Filling pasta dishes start at DM 8, the chili con carne goes for DM 7.50. With Guinness on tap and a choice of over 20 fine whiskeys, it's easy to see why this place remains so popular with the over- and under-thirty crowd. *Griesbadg. 7, tel. 0841/32470. Open daily 7 PM–1 AM (weekends until 2).*

Osteria Italiana. This low-key Italian restaurant has a roomy dark-wood interior, hospitable servers, and relatively cheap food. Pizzas start at DM 8 and top out at DM 10.50 for the special: tuna and onion. Pasta dishes are DM 9–DM 10.50. *Dollstr. 13, just off Rathauspl., tel. 0841/33300. Open daily noon–2:30 and 5–midnight.*

Zum Weissbierbrauer Kuchlbauer. Come here for inexpensive Bavarian fare, including bread served with regional meats, cheeses, and *Schmalz,* a tasty mix of seasoned goose fat and herbs (DM 5.80). There is also also a superb home-brewed beer and, on occassion, live folk music and dancing in the beer garden. Entrées start at DM 8; the *Schweinshaxe* (leg of pork) may cost a bit more (DM 14), but it's well worth it. *Schäffbräustr. 11a, tel. 0841/35512. Open daily 10 AM–1 AM.*

WORTH SEEING

Ingolstadt's most recognizable landmark, the 14th-century **Kreuztor,** is a holdover from the days when Ingolstadt served as Bavaria's military stronghold. Today this stone gate marks the entrance to the Altstadt and its conglomeration of cafés, bars, and shops. Continue through the gate and turn left on Konviktstraße to Ingolstadt's most impressive church, **Maria-de-Victoria-Kirche** (Neubaustr. 1½, tel. 0841/17518). The Asam brothers designed the sublime rococo interior in the 18th century. To appreciate Cosmas Damian's ceiling masterpiece, walk a few steps inside the church and find the faded circle on the floor. From this point the ceiling fresco appears three-dimensional; walk away and it warps flat. The church is open 9–noon and 1–5; admission is DM 2.50, DM 1.50 students. Other churches worth a closer look include **St. Moritz** (Rathauspl.), the oldest in Ingolstadt, and the 15th-century **Liebfrauenmünster** (beyond Kreuztor on the way to Theresienstr.).

MUSEUMS

Ingolstadt has one of the most bizarre collections of museums you'll find in Bavaria, and even better, they're all free on Sundays and holidays.

Bayerisches Armee-Museum. War buffs can rampage through the Bavarian Army Museum, home to Germany's most extensive collection of military artifacts. The museum is housed in the sprawling **Neues Schloß,** which served as the residence of Ludwig the Bearded in the 15th century. Marvel at two-handed swords, chain mail, and full suits of armor from the Thirty Years' War. Admission is DM 5.50 or DM 1 for students; a combo ticket that also gains admittance to the World War I exhibits next door costs DM 5, DM 3.50 for students. *Neues Schloß, Paradepl. 4, tel. 0841/93770. Open Tues.–Sun. 8:45–4:30.*

Deutsches Medizinhistorisches Museum. Housed in the university's former school of medicine, the Museum of Medical History displays everything from pacemakers to voodoo dolls to hacksaws used for early modern surgery. Yet the museum's true gem has to be its collection of manually operated rectum-suckers, crowned by the pièce de résistance, a 19th-century self-service enema machine. Ask for a demo, rely on your highly vivid imagination, or pick up the English-language guidebook for DM 10. *Anatomiestr. 18–20, tel. 0841/305–1860. Admission: DM 4, DM 2 students. Open Tues.–Sun. 10–noon and 2–5.*

Museum für Konkrete Kunst. If you've grown weary of the paintings of the Renaissance masters and their traditional themes, visit Germany's only museum of constructionist art. The movement, tied in Germany to the Bauhaus school, originated as a celebration of earth-shaking industry and fast-paced technology. *Tränktorstr. 6–8, tel. 0841/305–1875. Admission: DM 4, DM 2 students. Open Tues.–Sun. 10–6, Wed. 10–2 and 5–9.*

The nighttime Frankenstein Murder Mystery Tour jaunts through Ingolstadt's dark, dark streets, serves up a "Monster-Menü" dinner, and ends with a farcical Frankenstein musical. Call 0841/1539 for details.

AFTER DARK

Ingolstadt presides over a youthful, dynamic café-bar scene whose boundaries are approximately defined by the Kreuztor, the Liebfrauenmünster, and the Medizinhistorisches Museum. The area is known as the Bermuda Triangle, but looks more like the Bermuda Octagon. A bronzed baritone sax hangs from the ceiling at **Neue Welt** (Griesbadg. 7, tel. 0841/32470; open daily 7 PM–1 AM), a woodsy café with live music and cabaret twice weekly. The beer garden **Glock'n** (Oberer Graben 1, tel. 0841/34990; open daily from 10 AM) is the busiest and best in town. Supplement your *Maß* (1 liter of beer; DM 9.50) with light Bavarian snacks (DM 6.50–DM 13.50). **Goldener Stern** (Griesbadg. 2, tel. 0841/35419) serves cheap beer (DM 5 per ½ liter) to a younger clientele, has a mini–beer garden out front, and is open 7 PM–1 AM daily. Jazz greats drop into town in late October and early November for the annual **Jazz Festival.** Swing by the tourist office for details.

NEAR INGOLSTADT

EICHSTÄTT AND NATURPARK ALTMÜHL

Eichstätt is a serene little university town tucked between verdant hills and majestic cliffs in a valley of the Altmühl River. These days, cyclists, hikers, amateur paleontologists, and sundry nature lovers traverse the terrain where once only beasts roamed, for Eichstätt now serves as the gateway to **Naturpark Altmühl,** Germany's largest nature preserve. Hit the trails as soon as you've covered the town's architectural legacy.

Remnants of the time when that legendary mastodon, the woolly mammoth, trod the earth can be seen at Eichstätt's outstanding **Jura Museum,** housed in the 14th-century **Willibald Schloß.** Highlights of the collection include dinosaur fossils—the sleek *ichthyosaur,* the batlike *rhamphorhynchus,* the flighty *archaeopteryx*—a superb aquarium, and a collection of artifacts dating back to the third century. Also in the Schloß is the **Museum für Ur- und Frühgeschichte,** which displays prehistoric, Celtic, and Roman artifacts. *Tel. 08421/2956. Admission: DM 6, DM 4 students. Open Apr.–Sept., Tues.–Sun. 9–noon and 1–5; Oct.–Mar., 10–noon and 2–4.*

Eichstätt's main cathedral, the **Dom** (Dompl. 10), dates from the 8th century and is now a fascinating mix of architectural styles—Romanesque (the spires), Gothic (the nave, main body, and mortuary), and Baroque (the western facade). Inside, the Pappenheim Altar depicts in stone the scene of the Crucifixion and the grieving masses. At the heart of the Altstadt, Residenzplatz is home to the **Fürstbischöfliche Residenz,** former home of the prince-bishops. Take the required German-language tour (DM 2) and revel in all the rococo splendor. *Residenz: Residenzpl. 1, tel. 08421/700. Tours Mon.–Thurs. at 10, 11, 2, and 3; Fri. at 10 and 11; weekends and holidays every 30 min, 10–11:30 and 2–3:30.*

The cobblestone Marktplatz, north of the Residenz, has numerous markets and shops. Of the many Italian Baroque facades in the colorful square, the **Altes Rathaus** has the finest. In front of the Rathaus stands the **Willibaldsbrunnen,** a bubbling fountain that depicts Bishop Willibald, who founded the town in the 8th century.

BASICS

The park's **information center,** Informationszentrum Naturpark Altmühltal (Notre Dame 1, tel. 08421/98760), is open Monday–Saturday 9–5 and Sunday 10–5. The office stocks a wealth of maps and info on hiking, cycling, boating, climbing, even fossil collecting. Both this office and the adjacent **Eichstätt tourist office** (Karl-Preysing-Pl. 14, tel. 08421/98800; closed weekends) will help you find a place to stay for DM 3. To get to the office, exit right from the train station, cross the bridge (Spitalbrücke), cut through Residenzplatz to Leonrodplatz, pass the church, and go left at Karl-Preysing-Platz.

COMING AND GOING

From Ingolstadt trains make the 30-min trip (DM 7.40) to **Eichstätt Bahnhof,** 20 km out of town. From here you can take one of the frequent trains (DM 3) to Eichstätt's center, **Eichstätt Stadt.** There are no lockers in the station, but you can store your things at the Fahrradgarage (*see* Biking *in* Outdoor Activities, *below*) for DM 3 per day.

WHERE TO SLEEP

Privatzimmer (rooms in private homes), starting at DM 23 per person, are a reasonable lodging option; the information offices have lists. Otherwise, try a larger bed-and-breakfast like **Gasthof zum Griechen** (Westenstr. 17, tel. 08421/2640). Conveniently located just north of Marktplatz, the Greek's 13 rooms go for DM 35 (singles) and DM 70 (doubles); add DM 3 for private showers. Reception is open 11 AM–12:30 AM, but call ahead.

To reach the excellent **HI-Jugendherberge,** go behind the train station and walk halfway up the hill on Burgstraße to Willibaldsburg. One of their 112 beds will cost you DM 24, including breakfast. *Reichenaustr. 15, tel. 08421/980-4190, fax 08421/980415. Curfew 10 PM. Reception open 8–9 and 5–7. Laundry. Closed Dec. and Jan.*

FOOD

The **university cafeteria** (Ostenstr. 28, tel. 08421/930) serves up institutional grub for next to nothing. Bring your ISIC card. A place to lounge and have a snack is **Stadt Café** (Marktpl. 5, tel. 08421/2698), where from 7 to 7 you can choose from a wide menu of local snacks and specialties ranging from DM 5 to DM 10. One spot that lives up to its name is **Café im Paradies** (Marktpl. 9, tel. 08421/3313); your wallet will start a diet for the freshly brewed large coffee (DM 6.20). From Marktplatz, head down Westenstraße to **Minimal** (Westenstr. 42), one of the few grocery stores in the old town.

OUTDOOR ACTIVITIES

As the gateway to the Altmühl nature park, Eichstätt provides an ideal base for outdoor excursions. Your best resources are the stacks of brochures, maps, and guides available at Informationszentrum Naturpark Altmühltal (*see* Basics, *above*), as well as the people who work there.

BIKING • Head to the **Fahrradgarage** (Herzogg. 3, tel. 08421/2110) for your standard two-wheeler (DM 15 per day). Rent a mountain bike for DM 20 at **Sport and Action** (Pfahlstr. 14, tel. 08421/902290); the staff can recommend routes as well. Otherwise, ask at the Informationszentrum for a copy of *Freizeitfibel,* which details the route of a nice four-hour, 42-km ride along the river from Eichstätt to Beilngries.

BOATING • The mossy Altmühl River gurgles through Eichstätt and the surrounding region. **Suttner** (Westenstr. 15, tel. 08421/1899) rents rowboats (DM 5 per half hour) and a paddle boat (DM 6 per half hour). **Heinz Glas** (Industriestr. 18, tel. 08421/3055) rents canoes and kayaks for DM 20–DM 30 per person per day.

HIKING • If you plan to hike, invest in Eichstätt's *Wanderkarte* (DM 4), a trail map available at the tourist office. The Wanderkarte has specifics on more than 140 km of hiking trails through forests and meadows, including a 3½-km nature walk and an 8½-km geological-botanical walk through Eichstätt.

REGENSBURG

The Romans established a fortress on this site in AD 179—dubbed Castra Regina (Fort Regen) after a local tributary of the Danube—as an outpost against marauding German tribes. Yet the Romans grew soft, the Germans persevered, begot and begot, and in subsequent centuries, Regensburg flowered. The city was designated the first capital of Bavaria, a Freie Reichsstadt (free imperial city), and later, the seat of the Holy Roman Reichstag, or imperial diet. Artist Albrecht Altdorfer stamped the city's intellectual life, as did astronomer, astrologer, and imperial mathematician Johannes Kepler. The town's formidable pedigree has bequeathed one of Germany's loveliest Altstädte—a medieval townscape modeled stylistically along lines favored by then-powerful Italian clans, and miraculously spared wartime bombing. If you have only a day, skip the museums and wander aimlessly among Regensburg's stony bridges and byways. By nightfall, however, the turrets and pastel towers of the town's patrician homes mark out a massive party zone for every single one of Regensburg's 15,000 students, and you.

Displays in Ingolstadt's Museum of Medical History are likely to enter your dream life for weeks to come; chairs that look like plush, old-fashioned toilets with convenient handles for that extra effort are actually 18th-century contraptions designed to help women give birth.

BASICS

CHANGING MONEY

The best rates can be found at the main post office (*see below*). Most Regensburg banks take MasterCard for cash advances; if you carry Visa go to **Citibank** (Maximilianstr. 15, tel. 0941/55075). After hours, hit the Citibank **ATM,** which accepts both credit cards.

LAUNDRY

Wasch Center (Winklerg.; open Mon.–Sat. 6 AM–10 PM), at the west end of the Altstadt, charges DM 6 for a wash (detergent included), DM 1.50 for 15 min of drying time.

MAIL

The **Hauptpost** (main post office; Bahnhofstr. 16) charges DM 6 for each traveler's check exchanged, as does the post office on Domplatz. The code for poste restante is 93041.

VISITOR INFORMATION

The friendly **tourist office** has free maps, English-language pamphlets, and a list of Privatzimmer, hotels, and pensions; they also sell tickets for concerts and the Reichstagsmuseum. *Altes Rathaus, tel. 0941/507–4410, fax 0941/507–4419. Open weekdays 8:30–6, Sat. 9–4, Sun. 9:30–4.*

For info on East Bavaria, including the Bavarian Forest, call or visit the **Fremdenverkehrsband Ostbayern.** *Landshuter Str. 13, tel. 0941/585390. Open Mon.–Thurs. 7:30–noon and 1–5, Fri. 7:30–noon.*

RESOURCES FOR GAYS AND LESBIANS • For info on current activities about town, call or stop by **Resi** (Blaue Lilieng. 1, off Goldene-Bären-Str., tel. 0941/51441), Regensburg's gay and lesbian center. They're in Wednesday, Friday, and Saturday 8 PM–1 AM, and Sunday 3 PM–8 PM.

COMING AND GOING

BY TRAIN

Frequent trains run to Munich (1½ hrs, DM 37), Nuremberg (1 hr, DM 27), and Passau (1½ hrs, DM 32). Daily trains also travel to transportation hubs in the Bavarian Forest like Zwiesel (1–2 hrs, DM 29). Regensburg's Hauptbahnhof is south of town; to reach the city center, take Bus 1, 2, 6, or 11, or walk

REGENSBURG

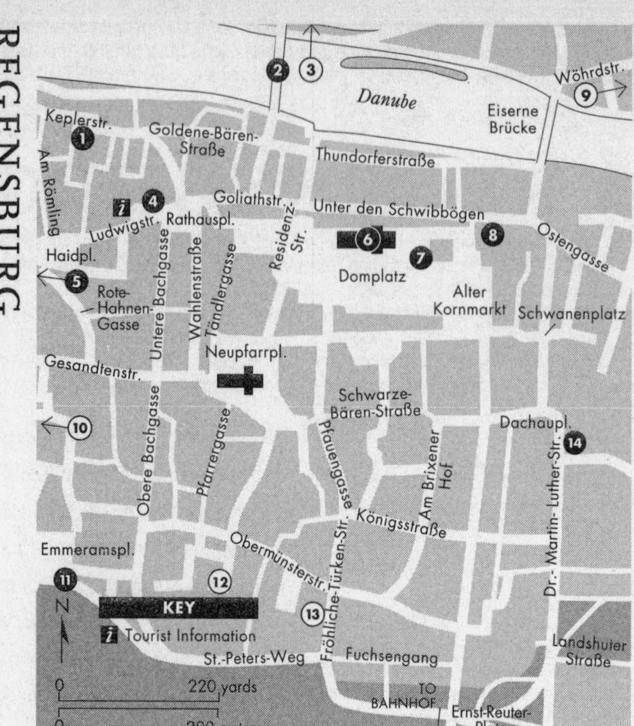

Sights ●
Altes Rathaus, **4**
Diözesanmuseum St. Ulrich, **7**
Dom St. Peter, **6**
Kepler-Gedächtnishaus, **1**
Kreuzgang St. Emmeram and Crypts, **11**
Museum der Stadt Regensburg, **14**
Museum Ostdeutsche Galerie, **5**
Porta Praetoria, **8**
Steinerne Brücke, **2**

Lodging ○
Am Peterstor, **13**
Azur-Camping, **10**
Diözesanzentrum Obermünster, **12**
Jugendherberge Regensburg, **9**
Spitalgarten, **3**

10–15 min up Maximilianstraße. You can rent a **bike** at Feine Räder (Furtmayrstr. 12, tel. 0941/700-0365) for DM 15 per day.

BY BOAT

Set right on the Danube, Regensburg offers several opportunities to cruise the river in style. **Regensburger Personenschifffahrt Klinger** (Werftstr. 8, tel. 0941/55359) offers an hour-long tour of the city (DM 11, DM 7 students) that includes historical info (in German). They also offer a two-hour trip (DM 20, DM 15 students). Another option is to take the Walhalla-Schifffahrt (DM 15, DM 10 students) to Donaustauf, home of the Grecian-columned Walhalla, built between 1830 and 1842 by King Ludwig I as a "Hall of Fame" for Germans. All tours leave from the Steinerne Brücke. For complete information and schedules, grab a brochure at the tourist office.

BY MITFAHRGELEGENHEIT

To arrange rides throughout Germany and Europe, stop by or call **Mitfahrzentrale Regensburg** (Prüfeninger Str. 13, tel. 0941/378–2024) a few days before you want to begin your trip. They're open weekdays 1–6.

WHERE TO SLEEP

Aside from the hostel, *Privatzimmer* (starting at DM 30) are your best option; get a list at the info office. The few cheap places in town are popular, so call ahead. Keep in mind that some hotel reception desks are closed on Sundays or even for the whole weekend; you can't check in on those days, although you can stay through the weekend if you checked in during the week. Call 0941/19414 day or night for info about room vacancies.

Am Peterstor. This hotel right between the train station and city center has undergone a substantial face-lift. Singles are DM 65 and doubles DM 75; breakfasts cost an additional DM 10. *Fröhliche-Türken-Str. 12, tel. 0941/54545, fax 0941/54542. 36 rooms, some with bath.*

Diözesanzentrum Obermünster. In this former monastery, plain but immaculate conceptions, er, singles cost DM 50–DM 55, doubles DM 90, breakfast included. *Obermünsterpl. 7, tel. 0941/59702. 52 rooms, some with bath. Reception open 6:30–noon and 1–5.*

Spitalgarten. The rooms are spartan but serviceable and, thankfully, cheap. The attached beer garden is a perfect spot to meet some fellow travelers. Singles cost DM 40, doubles DM 80. *St. Katharinenpl. 1, just off Stadtamhof directly north of Steinerne Brücke, tel. 0941/84774. 9 rooms, none with bath.*

HOSTELS

Jugendherberge Regensburg (HI). Often teeming with adolescents, Regensburg's hostel rests on an island in the Danube, a short bus ride or a 35-min walk from the train station. Beds cost DM 27, including breakfast. The hostel has a washer and dryer (DM 3 each) and rents bikes at DM 6 per day. Curfew is 1 AM. *Wöhrdstr. 60, tel. 0941/57402, fax 0941/52411. From Hauptbahnhof, Bus 8 to Eisstadion (direction: Keilberg-Grünthal; DM 2.30; last bus 11:30 PM); or, walk up Maximilianstr., cross river at Eiserne Brücke, right on Wöhrdstr. 203 beds. Reception open 6:30 AM–midnight. Closed Nov. 15–Jan. 15.*

CAMPING

Azur-Camping in the Donaupark along the Danube River charges DM 10 per person plus DM 9 per tent. *Weinw. 40, tel. 0941/270025. From Hauptbahnhof, Bus 6 to Hans-Sachs-Str., then head right (Hans-Sachs-Str. turns into Weinw.); last bus (DM 2.30) at 11:30 PM. 200 sites. Kitchen, showers, washer and dryer (DM 5 each).*

FOOD

The cafés and restaurants on and around **Haidplatz** make it one of the better hunting grounds for victuals; in summer colorful tables spill out onto the square. Stop for lunch or snack at the Regensburg institution **Beim Dampfnudel Uli** (Am Watmarkt 4, tel. 0941/53297; closed Sun. and Mon.), housed in the Baumburger Turm. It's frequented by politicans and VIPs, including former president Ronald Reagan. You'll get a good deal on fruits and vegetables at the Saturday morning **Donaumarkt** near Hunnenplatz, on Maximilianstraße between the train station and the Altstadt. Otherwise, try **Tengelmann** (Ernst-Reuter-Pl. 2).

Einhorn. This *gemütlich* (cozy) pub-restaurant with lots of rich, dark timber draws a cosmopolitan crowd of students and locals. Meals range from cold traditional dishes to large salads and vegetarian main courses (DM 7–DM 20). Try the freshly made soup of the day—it's always hearty and never over DM 5. *Wördstr. 31, tel. 0941/52790.*

Hinterhaus. Tucked away in a quiet courtyard, this pub is a *Kneipe* with *Kultur,* and a largely student clientele. Complement your snacks or light meals (DM 5–DM 14) with Portuguese wine or the local Thurn-und-Taxis brand of beer. *Rote-Hahnen-Gasse 2, tel. 0941/54661.*

Historische Wurstkuch'l. This lively riverside beer garden and restaurant has a colorful past that spans more than 850 years. A half-liter brew costs DM 5.20. If you want to eat, you have one option: juicy *Schweinbratenwürste* (small pork sausages; DM 8.20) with sauerkraut. The adjacent **Wirtshaus Salzstadel** has a view of the Steinerne Brücke and offers a wide variety of Bavarian cooking, including homemade sausages that are prepared by the owners. Be certain to try the other specialties, including an assortment of traditional pastries. *Weisse Lammg. 1, tel. 0941/59098.*

Spaghetteria. This restaurant has vaulted ceilings and a lot of atmosphere for an average Italian pizzeria. It serves an assortment of inexpensive, authentic Italian pasta (DM 10–DM 15) and lets customers choose their own noodle and sauce. Other popular items include pizza (DM 13–DM 18) and superb appetizers. *Am Römling 12, tel. 0941/563695.*

WORTH SEEING

Virtually every second building in Regensburg's lovely Altstadt is deemed a cultural treasure. Be sure to explore Regensburg's **patrician houses,** enormous, medieval Italian-style homes built with soaring towers around an inner courtyard. **Haidplatz** and **Scheugäßchen,** just south of the Kepler-Gedächtnishaus, feature particularly good examples. The original northern gate of the Roman fortress, **Porta Praetoria** still stands on Unter den Schwibbögen. Christian businessmen and craftsmen razed Regensburg's Jewish quarter in 1519; see the newly excavated remains of the 11th-century **synagogue** at Neupfarrplatz.

English-language **tours** (DM 8, DM 4 students) of the city leave the tourist office May–September on Wednesday and Saturday at 1:30.

ALTES RATHAUS

The old town hall has been converted into the **Reichstagsmuseum** (tel. 0914/ 507–4411). Though most English-speakers associate the *Reichstag* with Berlin, the term is actually more generic, meaning Imperial Convention. Guided tours show you the **Reichssaal** (Imperial Hall), where the decision-makers of the Holy Roman Empire convened from 1663 to 1806, as well as creative torture devices in the original interrogation room and prison cells found in the dungeon below. Purchase tour tickets from the Rathaus tourist office. Look up at the overhang of the adjacent Rathaus and you'll see the Hebrew inscription on a Jewish gravestone, plundered in 1519 and incorporated into the Rathaus walls. *Required tour: DM 5, DM 2.50 students. English-language tours May–Sept., Mon.–Sat. at 3:15. German tours every 30 min. Mon.–Sat. 9:30–noon and 2–4, Sun. and holidays 10–noon.*

DOM ST. PETER

St. Peter's Cathedral is considered Bavaria's most outstanding example of Gothic architecture. Because it took six centuries to build, you can clearly see the evolution of the Gothic style: Compare the two towers rising from its western end—the older, northern tower is much simpler than its southern counterpart, which features the characteristic late-Gothic double arch and ornate design. Once inside, look toward the apse and you'll see the cathedral's two most famous sculptures: Gabriel, the Laughing Angel, telling Mary of the immaculate conception to come; and the figures of St. Martin and St. George, charged with protecting the church from the darkness outside. To the left side of the west entrance sits the Devil's grandmother, her head covered by a shawl, while on the right sits Satan himself. The Christ figure on the south wall is decorated with real human hair. Legend has it that the Messiah will come once his shaggy mane reaches the floor. The **Domspatzen** (literally, cathedral sparrows), the famous boys' choir, performs during mass every Sunday morning at 9. *Dompl., tel. 0941/57796. Admission free. Open Apr.–Oct., daily 6:30–6; Nov.–Mar., daily 6:30–4. Tours (DM 4, DM 2 students) Nov.–Apr., weekdays at 11 AM, Sun. at noon; May–Oct., weekdays at 10, 11, and 2, Sun. at noon and 2.*

FÜRSTLICHES THURN UND TAXIS'SCHES SCHLOß

The Princes of Thurn und Taxis founded Europe's first large-scale postal service in the 15th century and controlled it until 1867; by 1809 they felt a need to erect a palace worthy of their prominence, and so the Schloß was built on and around the 8th-century St. Emmeram abbey. Today the massive construction is known as the party grounds of spotlight-loving Princess Gloria von Thurn und Taxis (Michael Jackson and Mick Jagger have joined the princess for drinks). While some treasures are on display within the 500-plus-room palace, the true family gem is the **Kreuzgang St. Emmeram** (St. Emmeram Cloister), which dates back to the 8th century. In 1730 Bavaria's favorite church decorators, the infamous Asam brothers, gave the Thurn-und-Taxis family church a Baroque makeover: ostentation. Step inside to admire the **crypts** of Regensburg bishop St. Emmeram (who was martyred the 7th century) and St. Wolfgang, or take a look at the monuments erected to dukes and the nine Regensburg bishops interred here; don't miss the two skeletal remains on either side of the basilica. For DM 12 (DM 10 students) you can catch a guided tour of the palace and cloister from April through October daily at 11, 2, 3, and 4 (weekends more frequently; Nov.–Mar., tours only on weekends); the cloister alone costs DM 6 (DM 5 students) and the palace alone is DM 6 (DM 4 students) from November through March (more with Marstallmuseum, *see* below, from Apr.–Oct.). *Emmeramspl. 5, tel. 0941/504–8133. Basilica and crypts open Mon.–Sat. 10–6 (Wed. 1–6), Sun. noon–6. Palace open daily 11–5 (weekends from 10).*

The palace is also home to the **Marstallmuseum** (Coach House Museum), where you can admire 18th- and 19th-century carriages and sleighs. *Open Apr.–Oct., daily 11–5 (weekends from 10); tours available Nov.–Mar., weekends 11:30 and 2. Admission: DM 4 (DM 3 students), DM 7 (DM 6 students) with guided tour, DM 8 (DM 6 students) with palace Apr.–Oct.*

KEPLER-GEDÄCHTNISHAUS

Johannes Kepler—astronomer, astrologer, optician, mathematician, and man behind the laws of planetary motion—died in Regensburg in 1630. Take the superb tour (available in English) of his deathhouse, and learn how Kepler struggled to prove that planets orbit the sun along elliptical, not circular paths, a discovery that was revolutionary and laid the basis for science to follow. *Keplerstr. 5, tel. 0941/ 507–3442. Admission: DM 4, DM 2 students. Open Tues.–Sat. 10–noon and 2–4, Sun. 10–noon.*

STEINERNE BRÜCKE

Built 1135–46 at the behest of Henry the Proud, the bridge—a 309-m span set on 16 massive pillars sunk deep into the swirling green water—was an engineering miracle in its time, often lauded in medieval chronicles. As the first and only bridge across the Danube for centuries, it helped transform Regensburg into a trading hub; those who controlled the bridge presided over the power of the purse.

MUSEUMS

Diözesanmuseum St. Ulrich. Formerly a parish cathedral, early Gothic St. Ulrich now houses the diocesan museum, which displays nine centuries of ecclesiastic art. Take a look at golden goblets and ornate staffs made from the bones of holy men. *Dompl. 2, tel. 0941/51688. Admission: DM 3, DM 1.50 students. Open Apr.–Oct., Tues.–Sun. 10–4:45.*

Museum der Stadt Regensburg. The 100 rooms that make up Regensburg's municipal museum house an extensive, diverse collection that includes Roman settlements, historic relics related to the city, and paintings by the fastidious Albrecht Altdorfer (1480–1538). *Dachaupl. 2–4, tel. 0941/507–1440. Admission: DM 4, DM 2 students. Open Tues.–Sun. 10–4, Sun. 10–1.*

Museum Ostdeutsche Galerie. This gallery has a unique collection of 19th- and 20th-century paintings, graphic art, and plastic works from artists who were in some way connected to former German settlements in eastern or southeastern Europe. Highlights include works by Lovis Corinth, president of the avant garde Berlin Sezession movement; look for changing exhibits. The museum is in the Stadtpark in the western part of town. *Dr.-Johann-Maier-Str. 5, tel. 0941/297140, fax 0941/297–1433. Admission: DM 4, DM 2 students. Open Tues.–Sun. 10–4.*

As imperial mathematician and astronomer, Kepler composed monthly horoscopes for the emperor and his minions. The author of the first known sci-fi book, Kepler slighted astrology, but his prophecies were deemed reliable.

AFTER DARK

Begin your evening at a beer garden, either under the shady chestnut trees of the **Kneitinger Keller** (Galgenbergstr. 18, tel. 0941/76680) or at the Regensburg institution **Spitalgarten** (*see* Where to Sleep, *above*), which overlooks the Danube from across the Steinerne Brücke. Both are open daily 9 AM–midnight. A highly chic crowd boogies at **Scala** (Gesandtenstr. 6, tel. 0941/52293) Wednesday–Sunday from 11 PM; cover DM 3–DM 7. The equally stylish club **Sudhaus** (Untere Bachg. 8, tel. 0941/51946; closed Wed. and Sun.) preserves the hip quotient of its slightly older crowd via strict door selection. **Irish Harp** (Brückstr. 1, tel. 0941/57268) keeps up its tradition by offering live music—satisfying tunes from rock to folk and everything in between—every night. Stop by any day after 4 PM.

PASSAU

Assembled on a thin spit of earth at the confluence of three rivers—the moss-green Danube, the luminous milk-green Inn, and the murky Ilz—Passau has snatched the title of *das bayerische Venedig,* or the Venice of Bavaria. The beautiful *Dreiflüssestadt* (three-river city) dates back to Roman times, when it served as a colonial outpost from which to ward off unwanted residents: first the Celts and then some bands of maddeningly persistent Germans. A decidedly Italian architectural flair, a perch along the Austrian border, and a kicking nightlife orchestrate their own cultural confluence at this old episcopal city, so don't miss out.

BASICS

CHANGING MONEY

The **post office** (Bahnhofstr. 27; postal code 94032) by the Bahnhof charges DM 6 per traveler's check. You'll find an ATM around the corner. Head to **Citibank** (Heiliggeistg. 5) with your Visa card.

LAUNDRY

Bring your dirty duds and a handful of coins to **Rentwash** (Neuburgerstr. 19; open daily 7 AM–midnight). It costs DM 6 to wash a load and DM 3 to dry it.

VISITOR INFORMATION

The **information office** in the train station has info on the Bavarian Forest and its cycling routes, six of which pass through Passau. Pick up a copy of the orange "Information" pamphlet for concert, theater, festival, and exhibit listings. *Bahnhofstr. 36, tel. 0851/955580. Open mid-Apr.–mid-Oct., weekdays 9–5, weekends 10–2.*

The **main tourist office** makes room reservations (DM 2.50) and has maps and general info, including Danube cruise schedules. *Rathauspl. 3, tel. 0851/955980. Open Apr.–Oct., weekdays 8:30–noon, weekends 10–2; Nov.–Mar., weekdays 8:30–4.*

RESOURCES FOR GAYS AND LESBIANS • Head to the **Schwulenzentrum** (Höllg. 12, tel. 0851/32541), open Monday and Friday from 8 PM, for info on Passau's scene.

COMING AND GOING

BY TRAIN

Passau's Bahnhof has frequent connections to Munich (2 hrs, DM 52), Regensburg (1 hr, DM 32), and the Bavarian Forest, including Bodenmais (2½ hrs, DM 34) and Frauenau (2 hrs, DM 32), both via Zwiesel. The station is equipped with lockers. To reach the Altstadt from the station, follow Bahnhofstraße to the right, cross Ludwigsplatz to Ludwigstraße (the pedestrian zone), and follow it to Domplatz, the central square.

BY BUS

Passau is small enough to explore on foot, so you may be able to avoid taking a bus. For trips to other cities, try the private company **RBO** (tel. 0851/73435), at the Bahnhof; buses to Linz, Austria (DM 30 round-trip) leave from the Hauptbahnhof at 10 AM.

BY FERRY

The **Wurm + Köck** ferry company (Höllg. 26, tel. 0851/929292) offers cruises to Linz, Austria (DM 36, DM 44 round-trip), April 27 through October 20. The ferry leaves at 9 AM and arrives in Linz at 2 PM. March through October, you can also take the 45-min **Dreiflüsse-Rundfahrt** cruise (DM 11) around the peninsula for a great introduction to Passau. For more info, pick up the "Donau-Schifffahrt Passau-Linz" brochure from either tourist office.

BY BIKE

Every summer, Passau plays host to hordes of cyclers cruising the *Donauradweg,* a bike path running along the Danube from its source in the Black Forest through Vienna and beyond. You can rent a bike at the train station or at **Pedalo-Radtours** (Kleine Messerg. 6, tel. 0851/32124), who will even return the bike, your pack, and you from as far as Budapest back to Passau at the end of your tour. Call at least one day in advance. The tourist office sells detailed maps of the route, as do most bookstores.

WHERE TO SLEEP

You may have a hard time finding budget accommodations near Passau's center, but both tourist offices can give you a hotel list or book you a room for a DM 3–DM 5 fee. Privatzimmer, listed in the tourist office pamphlet, start as low as DM 25 per person but are rarely located in the city center. For a mere DM 10 per person, campers can claim a grassy spot along the river at tent-only **Zeltplatz an der Ilz** (Halser Str. 34, tel. 0851/41457; closed Nov.–Apr.), 10 min from the Altstadt. From Exerzierplatz, take Bus 1, 2, 3, or 4 to Ilzbrücke.

Pension Rößner. The cheapest pension in the Altstadt has comfy rooms and an amiable owner—as if that weren't enough, it's right on the Danube. Singles are DM 60, doubles DM 100. Some of the DM 100 doubles can be transformed into three- to five-person rooms for an extra DM 30 per person. All rooms have showers and bath. Reservations are a good idea. *Bräug. 19, tel. 0851/931350, fax 0851/931-3555. From train station, right onto Bahnhofstr., first left to river, right along river, right at Luitpoldbrücke to Bräug. 16 rooms.*

Rotel Inn. Billed as a "Hotel of the Future" and built in the shape of an enormous person lying prone along the Danube (enter through a hole in the skull), the Rotel offers a location just seconds from the train station, modern (but tiny) rooms, and moderate prices. Singles are DM 30, doubles DM 50; showers are in the hall. Breakfast costs an extra DM 8. *Am Hauptbahnhof/Donauufer, tel. 0851/95160, fax 0851/951–6100. 93 rooms. Reception open 24 hrs.*

HOSTELS

If you're prepared to forego the nightlife to make an 11:30 curfew, stay at Passau's **HI-Jugendherberge,** a 30-min uphill hike from town. You will be rewarded: The hostel is housed in a 13th-century castle with great views of the city. Think twice before lugging your backpack up after 5 PM, when the buses stop running and the shortest path is closed. Beds run DM 22. *Veste Oberhaus 125, tel. 0851/41351, fax 0851/43709. From Ludwigspl., Bus 1, 2, or 4 to Ilzbrücke; or from station, face the Danube and follow it right; cross at Luitpoldbrücke, and climb the steps (45 min). 130 beds. Reception open 7 AM–noon, 4 PM–11:30 PM.*

FOOD

Passau is the kind of place that inspires you to dangle your legs over the Danube and enjoy a few freshly made sandwiches. At **Kleine Passauer Markthalle** (closed Sun.) on Ludwigstraße you can find all the right ingredients for an excellent picnic and pleasant afternoon. An alternative is a quick meal for about DM 7 at the ***Stehimbis*** (stand-up snack bar).

A great place to save on a hearty meal of french fries, salad, and a large serving of pan-fried pork is Passau's Café Kowalski during its popular Schnitzel Happy Hour. Prices start at just DM 9.50 from 6 PM to 9 PM. Another popular stop is Café Innsteg (DM 6.50; 11 PM–midnight).

Café Altstadt. White Christmas-tree lights strung from branches give this alleyway eatery a festive feel. The menu includes salads (DM 5.50–DM 13.50), omelets (DM 9–DM 12), and pasta (DM 7.50–DM 10.50). *Schusterg. 11, behind Rathaus, tel. 0851/34833.*

Café Innsteg. This café sits right on the banks of the picturesque Inn River. Join Passau's in-crowd in the bungalow-bar atmosphere—it's ideal for relaxing and listening to music. *Innstr. 15, near Fünferlsteg Brücke, tel. 0851/51257.*

Pizzeria Angelina. Just off the town's main square, this quiet little spot offers students and others hefty, delicious pizza and pasta dishes for DM 7. (The special offers listed on the Studentenkarte are meant for card-carrying Passau University students.) *Brunng. 2, off Ludwigstr., tel. 0851/33203.*

WORTH SEEING

ALTES RATHAUS

Passau's Gothic town hall was a private home until a local uprising in 1298. The giant fresco in the great hall depicts scenes from the *Nibelungenlied,* the great 13th-century Middle High German epic (incorporated by Wagner in his *Ring* cycle), rumored to have been written in Passau. In the building's **tower,** Bavaria's largest Glockenspiel chimes every half hour daily between 10 AM and 5 PM. The *Wasserstand* (water-level) table on the front of the tower shows how high Passau's rivers have risen over the past 500 years. *Enter on Schrottg. From Dompl., east down Steinw. (which becomes Große Messerg.), left on Schrottg. Admission: DM 4, DM 2 students. Open mid-May–Sept., daily 10–5; Apr.–mid-May and Oct., daily 10–4.*

MUSEUM MODERNER KUNST PASSAU

This private museum, opened in 1990, continues to raise eyebrows. Exhibits rotate every three or four months, but the goal remains the same: to display the cutting edge in modern art, from Christo and Jean-Claude to counter-culture videos. After viewing the works take some time to reflect in the adjoining **Café Museum.** *Bräug. 17, east of Dom in Altstadt, tel. 0851/383–8790. Admission: DM 8, DM 5 students. Open Tues.–Sun. 10–6, Thurs. 10–8. Café open Tues.–Sat. 10 AM–midnight, Sun. 10–8 (also summer Mon. 10–8).*

PASSAUER GLASMUSEUM AM RATHAUSPLATZ

This four-story museum houses the world's finest and largest collection of Bohemian glass. A labryinthine display of 16,000 glass objects chronicles Bohemian glassmaking from 1700 to 1950 (yet another 14,000 objects are in storage). A special attraction is the colorful Jugendstil collection—the objects come alive with color and form. Drop by the rooftop terrace café at the end of the circuit. *Rathauspl. 2, tel. 0851/35071. Admission: DM 5, DM 3 students. Open daily 10–4.*

RÖMERMUSEUM CASTELL BOIOTRO

The Römermuseum lets you connect with Passau's turbulent past in an original way: As you inspect the original walls of the Roman fort Boiotro and other archeological treasures, you'll return to the times when the Romans fought back the Celts (the town's original settlers) and held the city against marauding Germanic tribes. The fort's remains were discovered during the construction of a kindergarten in 1974. *Ledererg. 43, tel. 0851/34769. From Dompl., cross Inn River at Innbrücke, right on Ledererg. Admission: DM 3, DM 2 students. Open Mar.–Nov., Tues.–Sun. 10–noon and 2–4; also June–Aug., Tues.–Sun. 1–4.*

STEPHANSDOM

Originally built in the 8th century and later modified in Gothic form, St. Stephan's was rebuilt in its present Baroque style in the 17th century, after two huge fires razed the city. Be sure to study the church's five-man, 17,774-pipe organ, the largest in the world. Attend one of the cathedral-trembling concerts (DM 4, DM 2 students) weekdays at noon from May through October, but arrive early—lines form by 11:30. Evening concerts (DM 10, DM 5 students) are given every Thursday at 7:30 PM from May to mid-November. From the church, enter the great hall of the **Residenz** (where the prince-bishop used to live) to see the **Cathedral and Diocese Treasure Museum.** *Domplatz. Museum: tel. 0851/393374. Admission: DM 2, DM 1 students. Open May–Oct., Mon.–Sat. 10–4.*

AFTER DARK

In Passau's back alleys, especially Innstraße and Ledergasse, a cadre of cool café-bars caters to the town's hip student population. The nighttime version of Café Innsteg (*see* Food, *above*) is perhaps the best bar in town, with great music, company, and views of the River Inn. Further east along the banks of the Inn is **Studio 11** (Innstr. 11, tel. 0851/752211). During the warm months you could swear you're actually in Italy. First there's seating on the 30-m long terrace overlooking the Inn river; second, the menu is packed with Italain specialities, wines, and an assortment of over 30 grappas (Italian schnapps). Close by is **Café Kowalski** (Obere Sandstr. 1, tel. 0851/2487), which was built in 1730 and boasts having served prominent guests such as Mozart, who frequented the café in 1763. The mystique continues to this day—one reason why it draws such a crowd.

If you're looking for a bit more grunge, cross the river and descend into **Joe's Garage** (Ledererg. 38, tel. 0851/31999), where students play cards and turn the day into night. Down the street, a string of pubs including **Café Espresso** (Ledererg. 3) serve beers and snacks to occassional tourists and regulars. All the bars listed above stay open until 1 AM.

THE BAVARIAN FOREST

Nature lovers looking for clean air, low prices, and excellent skiing and hiking opportunities will find the majestic wooded mountains of the *Bayerischer Wald* (Bavarian Forest) the perfect getaway. Twenty thousand acres of this forest—Central Europe's largest—are protected as a national park. You'll encounter few tourists in this wild landscape that stretches from the Austian to the Czech borders, but you probably will happen upon Bavarians engaged in traditional pursuits—like glassblowing—that have occupied their time for centuries. And you'll find the warm Bavarian hospitality you might have thought was only a fairy tale.

COMING AND GOING

With infrequent bus and rail connections, travel through the Bavarian Forest is a test of your resourcefulness. The Reisezentrum or DB ticket window in most train stations can usually help you with schedules and transfers, but fluent English-speakers are rare. To avoid getting stuck somewhere, check the *Abfahrt* (departure) schedule *before* you leave the station. Remember that schedules change frequently—but you'll do fine if you learn to expect the unexpected.

Trains into the forest run from Plattling on the Regensburg (45 min)–Passau (35 min) line. From Plattling, trains head to Bodenmais (1½ hrs, DM 19.40) and Frauenau (1 hr 20 min, DM 16.20), both via Zwiesel. The Bodenmais–Zwiesel–Frauenau stretch costs DM 9 (35 min). NOTE: Neither town is serviced by train from Zwiesel on weekends.

WHERE TO SLEEP

Although the many youth hostels are often rather far from the forest, you will find a surprising number of inexpensive, centrally located guest houses and hotels; rooms run DM 40–DM 60 per night. Many towns have farms where you can stay, usually in a private room, for DM 20–DM 40 per night. You'll find them listed in pamphlets under *Urlaub auf dem Bauernhof* (Holiday on a Farm). For information on where to stay, consult the local tourist offices, which usually have lodging pamphlets and lists. Wherever you stay, be sure to ask for a *Kurkarte* (guest card). Have it stamped at the info office and you'll be entitled to all sorts of freebies and discounts.

OUTDOOR ACTIVITIES

Gorgeous hiking trails run through just about every town in the forest. For invaluable information on trail routes and distances, pick up a *Wanderkarte* (hiking map) at the nearest tourist office. They usually cost DM 10, but it'll be about DM 5 less if you get a Kurkarte from your hotel. Bike paths also run deep into the forest; inquire at a tourist office or bike rental shop about routes. Most of the larger towns in the forest offer mountain-bike rentals for DM 16–DM 26 per day. If your cycling aspirations are more moderate, ask the tourist office or train station if they rent standard two-wheelers—rates are always a bit cheaper.

From the first snowfall in December until the last patches of slush disappear in May, the forest is a haven for German skiers. There are resorts all over the forest, and towns like Bodenmais and Frauenau have especially good downhill and cross-country skiing. Ski rentals run about DM 20–DM 25 per day.

Now that's hospitality! Visitors to Frauenau are welcomed on a regular basis by the local tourist office and treated to a hearty snack: local breads, meats, and cheeses—and a shot of Bärwurz, a traditional liqueur made with selected herbs.

FRAUENAU

A peaceful and pastoral vacation getaway, Frauenau is best known as the "Glass Heart" of the Bavarian Glasstraße (Glass Road), which winds through the region's glassmaking centers. It's a meeting place for international artists who work with glass—and home to museums that chronicle the 2,500-year history of glassmaking. Indeed, Frauenau has cultivated the art of glassmaking for over seven centuries; the tradition lives on at **Glashütte Eisch** (Althüttenstr. 30, tel. 09926/1890), a respected name in modern glass design. For DM 1 you can take an intimate tour of the factory Monday–Thursday 9–11:30 and 1–2:45; Friday and Saturday 9–11:45. During the 25-min German-language tour, over 100 workers will yank white-hot (1250°) balls of molten glass out of their furnaces and fashion them into works of art. **Glashütte Freiherr von Poschinger** (tel. 09926/94010; open weekdays 9:30–5, Sat. 9–noon), the oldest glass factory in the world (since 1568), offers free tours and a wide selection of modern Poschinger glass on sale in the neighboring shop. To get there, walk south down Bahnhofstraße and continue straight along the dirt path. The final stop on Frauenau's glass circuit is the **Glasmuseum** (Am Museumspark 1, tel. 09926/940035; admission DM 3, DM 2.50 students), where you can admire the history of glassmaking—compare Egyptian and Roman artifacts to the today's finest specimens. Don't miss the beautiful contemporary international glass art exhibits to the left of the entrance. The museum's blown stock is on display in summer daily 9–5; 10–4 in winter (closed Nov. and Dec.).

BASICS

The happy staff at Frauenau's **tourist office** (Hauptstr. 12, tel. 09926/710) will give you a map of the village and the *Tierfreigelände* (animal preserve; *see box* Bavarian Forest National Park, *below*), and a booklet listing all accommodations in town. The excellent summer or winter **Wanderkarte** costs DM 10 (DM 5 with Kurkarte; *see* Where to Sleep, *above*)—and is well worth the price as it lists every trail in the area. The office is open weekdays 8–noon and 1:30–5, Saturday 9:30–11:30 AM (closed Sat. in winter). From the train station, turn right on Hauptstraße. The post office is farther up the street.

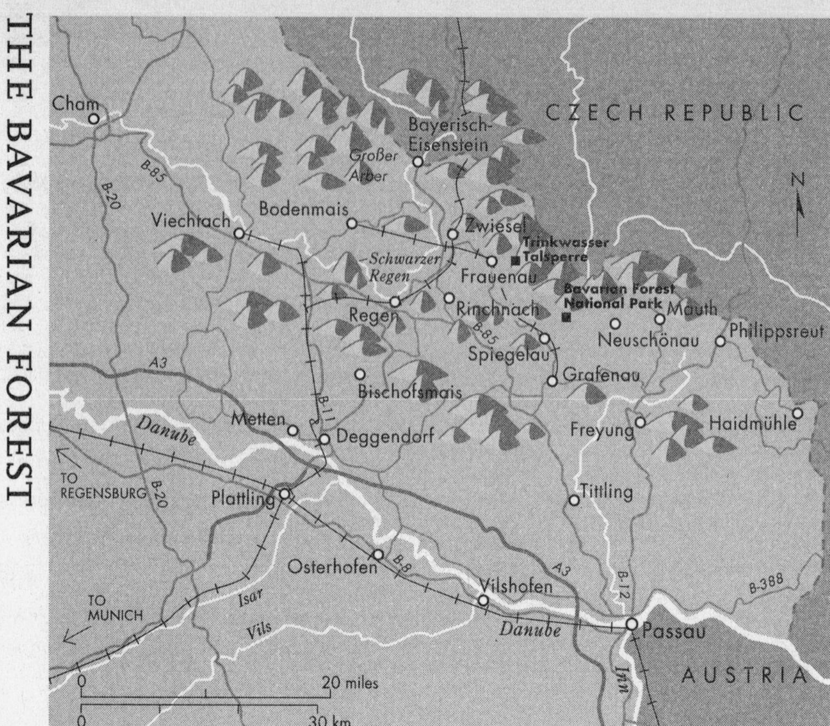

WHERE TO SLEEP

Stay at a pension (DM 25–DM 40) or get a room on a farm (DM 18–DM 25). The tourist office also recommends a stay at the **Pension Waldkristall** (Krebsbachw. 8–9, tel. 09926/293)—and with good reason: Their 20 comfortable rooms await guests who are looking to get away from it all but not willing to do without a few pleasant extras such as hobby rooms, a solarium, and an attentive staff. Singles cost DM 50 and doubles DM 90 without breakfast.

OUTDOOR ACTIVITIES

The tourist office has good maps (DM 5.50) for biking, hiking, and cross-country skiing that cover Frauenau, Zwiesel, and Bodenmais. A good, short (two-hour round-trip) hike runs around the manmade **Trinkwasser Talsperre,** the largest lake in the Bavarian Forest. More adventurous souls will take the six-hour round-trip **Schuchten-Hochmoor** trail, which follows a plateau along the Czech/Bavarian border. Rent a **bike** for DM 10 per day at the tourist office, which leads free guided hikes once a week for those with a Kurkarte. Grab a pair of **cross-country skis** for DM 12 per day from Sport Berndl (Hauptstr. 6, tel. 09926/292).

BODENMAIS

Bavarian hospitality lives in Bodenmais, but you sure have to go deep into the forest to enjoy it. Set at the foot of the imposing Großer Arber mountain, Bodenmais's glorious topography makes it one of the best places to hike in the Bavarian Forest. Despite the crowds, the mood here is relaxed—many of the inhabitants run cozy guest lodges where you're treated like family.

Aside from great hiking and skiing, Bodenmais offers a glimpse at the centuries-old practice of glassmaking. You can visit the workshop at **Austen-Glashütte** (Bahnhofstr. 57–59, tel. 09924/7006) weekdays 10–6, Saturday 9–2. Or enjoy a tour of the Bavarian countryside and a look at the glassmaking process by taking the 15-min walk along Am Wiesengrund (a path just southwest of the train station) to the glassblowing exhibit at **Joska Waldglashütte** (Am Moosbach 1, tel. 09924/7790), open weekdays 9:15–6 and Saturday 9–2. Both exhibits are free.

BASICS

Once you get a place to stay, you'll receive a Kurkarte—have it stamped at the **information office** (tel. 09924/778136; open weekdays 8–6, Sat. 9–1, Sun. 9–noon) at the train station. It entitles you to two free passes for a bus tour of town, an extensive hiking and biking map, and discounts on the Arbersesselbahn chair lift. From the tourist office, head west on Bahnhofstraße to reach the **post office** (tel. 09924/94249), which exchanges currency weekdays 8:30–noon and 2–5, Saturday 8:30–11.

WHERE TO SLEEP

Hotels and pensions line the streets of Bodenmais. Take advantage of the electronic lodging board at the train station, or visit the information office and pick up a free booklet full of lodging options. Especially luxurious is **Pension Königshang** (Unterlohwies 2a, tel. 09924/407), with stylish rooms at DM 40–DM 60 per person.

If you really want something to write home about, pay a visit to Bodenmais's **HI-Jugendherberge** (Chamberhütte 1, tel. 09924/281; beds DM 22, DM 27 over 26), 1,364 m up Mt. Arber. You can reach Germany's highest hostel via two routes. 1) To make the 2–2½-hour hike, get a *Wanderkarte* from the tourist office (DM 10) and start at trailhead "D." Go up Scharebenstraße and follow the "Green 3" trail heading toward the DJH triangle. 2) To take the chair lift, catch a bus (30 min, DM 5) on the west side of the tourist office at the sign marked ARBER. Get off at the Arbersesselbahn stop, hop on the Sesselbahn (DM 6 one-way) and then hike west about an hour to the hostel. The last bus leaves the tourist office at 5:10 PM; the Sesselbahn's last run is at 5:45 PM. The hostel is closed April 20–May 20 and November 8–December 26.

If you're in good shape you can actually ski to Bodenmais's mountain-top hostel from the chair lift. Otherwise it's about 8 km from the city center—a staggering hike that takes at least 1½ hours for the fittest among us.

OUTDOOR ACTIVITIES

Bodenmais is a regular Garden of Eden for hikers and skiers. Pick up the summer or winter trail map from the tourist information office—both are packed with hiking, biking, and cross-country trails. The **Rißlochfälle** (Rißloch Waterfall), a popular destination, is only a one-hour hike from the tourist office. Continue past the falls for another 1½ hours and you'll have conquered the summit. Ski passes on Mt. Arber cost DM 33 per day (DM 20 per half-day), or you can buy a **10-Punkte-Karte** (10-point card), which entitles you to 10 rides for DM 17. Call 09925/245 for a current snow and weather report. Skiing the less popular Silberberg costs DM 20 per day or DM 12 for two hours. Bikers and skiers can rent equipment at **Sporthaus Weinberger** (Jahnstr. 20, tel. 09924/902273); bikes run DM 20 per day, cross-country skis DM 18 per day, downhill skis DM 20 per day.

THE BAVARIAN ALPS

Stretching from the Bodensee (Lake Constance) in the west to Berchtesgaden in the east, the Bavarian Alps have graced the covers of many a tourist brochure, spreading pastoral Alpine scenes worldwide. And the covers don't lie: You really will see milkmaids and meadows and church steeples set against snowy peaks. Inevitably, this tranquility will inspire you to take a hike and see it all for yourself. If that's the case, you couldn't have chosen a better place; around here, sightseeing takes a backseat to hiking, swimming, and skiing (with a few exceptions). Be warned that the weather is totally unpredictable; and on a single hike you may encounter a range of meteorological aberrations.

BAVARIAN FOREST NATIONAL PARK

The Bavarian Forest National Park encompasses 8,000 hectares of forest and shares a 25-km border with the Czech Republic's Bohemian Forest. The two together form one of Europe's largest and most beautiful forested areas. Hiking and skiing—downhill and cross-country—are the big draws here. With good timing you may catch a glimpse of the native deer and rare birds in the Tierfreigelände—a section of forest divided into natural enclosures for different animals. Tours and theme hikes are arranged through Hans-Eisenmann-Haus (Bohmstr. 35, tel. 08558/1300; open daily 9–5) in Neuschönau; the office is closed November to mid-December. The tourist office in Frauenau also provides maps, brochures, and suggestions for exploring the park.

To reach the park, catch one of the infrequent RVO (Regional Verkehr Oberbayern) buses that depart from Passau's bus depot for Grafenau (11/2 hrs, DM 11). From Grafenau, buses travel hourly into the park (20 min, DM 6); the last one leaves at 4 pm. If you're staying in Frauenau, take the train to Spiegelau (20 min), then the bus to the park's Info-Zentrum (25 min). The last bus leaves the Info-Zentrum around 5:20 pm for the trip back to Spiegelau. There's no place to sleep inside the park; if you miss the last bus it's a two-hour hike to the closest hostel—HI-Jugendherberge Waldhäuser (Herbergsw. 2, tel. 08553/6000) in Neuschönau.

BASICS

VISITOR INFORMATION

The **tourist office** (Kurverwaltung or Verkehrsamt) in each town gives lodging suggestions, but they don't make reservations. Some offer guided hikes, and all can give you trail maps. Make sure you get your Kurkarte wherever you're staying; you're most likely already being charged an extra DM 3 for it. The Kurkarte often provides free or reduced admission fees to museums and other sights, and even free local bus transportation in Garmisch-Partenkirchen, Oberstdorf, and other towns.

COMING AND GOING

Trains from Munich can get you to most of the main Alpine towns, but if you want to travel between towns, you must take the **regional buses** or be ready to make about a zillion transfers between trains. **RVO buses** service the area east of Füssen; **RVA buses** service the area to the west. BahnCard holders receive a 50% discount on both. The **trains** take a little longer but are a better deal for travelers with Eurail and InterRail passes, since those passes are not accepted on the buses. Train travel between Alpine towns is tricky, so have a railroad information agent at the station print out a list of the transfers you'll need to make.

WHERE TO SLEEP

Enjoy the peace of a private guest house for DM 30–DM 60 per night. Many places discourage short stays and charge DM 3–DM 5 more if you don't stay for at least three nights. Another note: If you are

THE BAVARIAN ALPS

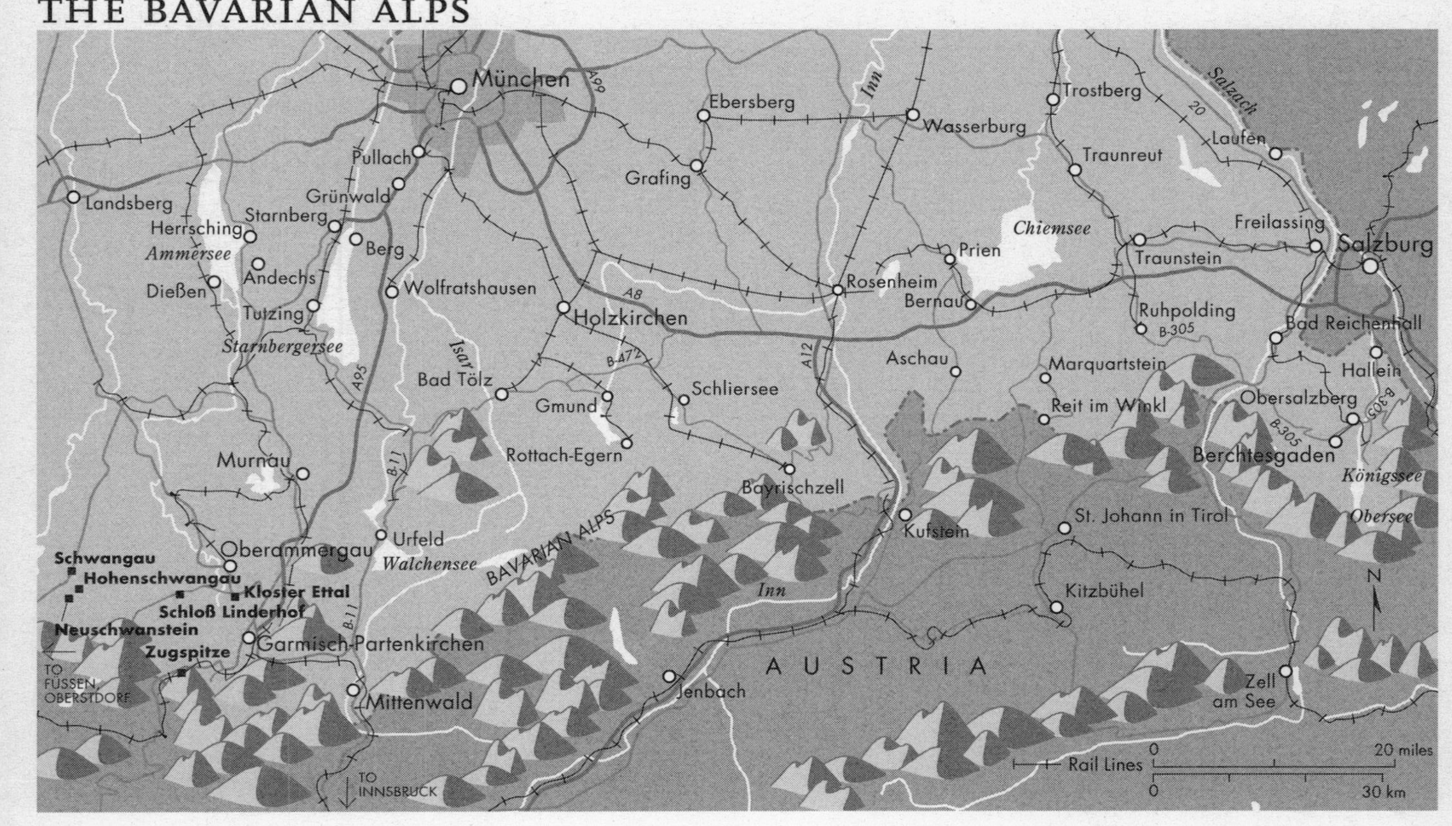

over 26, few hostels will house you, and most will greet nonmembers with a DM 6 surcharge. Campgrounds are cheap and easy to find, but often packed—reservations are in order. Ask the tourist office staff about *Berghütten* (unheated mountain huts), the least utilized, but easily most beautiful option. Prices range from DM 20 to DM 35 for bunk beds, and they'll never turn you away. Bring your own nylon sleep sack.

FÜSSEN

A small Alpine town near the Austrian border, Füssen has several monasteries and an impressive castle, and is surrounded by some incredibly lush countryside. Yet Füssen's greatest appeal is its proximity to Schloß Neuschwanstein, the model for Walt Disney's magnificent palace, and another celebrated castle, Schloß Hohenschwangau (*see* Near Füssen, *below*). Both are postcard-perfect sights that you wouldn't want to miss. Neither castle is connected to the German rail network, and since only Füssen has a youth hostel, most budget travelers stay here while exploring the nearby sights.

Füssen has a few worthwhile attractions of its own. **Hohes Schloß** (Magnuspl. 10) is an imposing late-Gothic castle that's a refreshing contrast to Ludwig's extravagant dwellings. It was built on the site of a Roman fortress designed to guard this section of the Via Claudia, an important trade route that once connected Rome with the Danube. All you can see of the castle's interior is the art-filled **Gemäldegalerie** (open Tues.–Sun. 11–4; admission DM 5, DM 2 students). Füssen's **Rathaus** was built in the 9th century as a Benedictine abbey. A Romanesque crypt in the basement preserves a 10th-century fresco, the oldest in Bavaria. Visit the crypt during tours (Tues. at 4:30, Sat. at 10:30)—the tours are free, but it's polite to tip the guide DM 5. Summer concerts are sometimes held in the Rathaus's **Fürstensaal** (Princes' Hall).

BASICS

The **tourist office, Kurverwaltung Füssen** (Kaiser-Maximilian-Pl. 1, tel. 08362/93850), is in the center of Füssen's Altstadt; it's open weekdays 8–noon and 2–6, Saturday 9–12:30 (July and Aug., also Sun. 10–noon). You can also check the **Informations-Pavilion** (open daily 7 AM–12:30 AM), which provides computerized vacancy listings in front of the tourist office.

COMING AND GOING

Daily **trains** connect Füssen with Augsburg (hourly, 2 hrs, DM 28) and Munich (15 daily via Buchloe, 2 hrs, DM 35). Regional **RVA buses** connect Füssen with Hohenschwangau and Schwangau (both DM 2.30) year-round. Bus 1084 runs to Oberammergau (DM 13) and Garmisch (DM 16). Between April 1 and October 31, Füssen is also the southern hub for Deutsche Bahn's **Romantic Road bus** (*see* Romantische Straße, in Chapter 7). These leave daily from Füssen's Bahnhof at 8 AM and 10:45 AM.

WHERE TO SLEEP

Ask the tourist office staff for information on *Privatzimmer* (private rooms; DM 25–DM 40) in both Füssen and Schwangau, or try the machine in front of the post office. **HI-Jugendherberge** Füssen (Mariahilferstr. 5, tel. 08362/7754, fax 08362/2770) is an easy 10-min walk from the train station (follow the tracks west). Small rooms and bare-bones beds are DM 19 per night, including breakfast. It's closed November 15–December 26. Other options, all on Frauensteinweg, are **Pension Bergkranz** (No. 45, tel. 08362/7216), **Haus Hubertus** (No. 55, tel. 08362/6923), and **Haus Lutz** (No. 54, tel. 08362/6419); all three have rooms for DM 30–DM 50 per person. To reach them from the tourist office (10–15 min), go south down Sebastianstraße, left on Hochstift, right when it becomes Weidachstraße, right on Gernspitzstraße, and left on Frauensteinweg.

FOOD

Gasthaus zum Schwanen (Brotmarkt 4, next to Rathaus, tel. 08362/6174) is a homey restaurant with reasonable prices. The homemade *Maultaschen* (DM 12), the local version of ravioli, is particularly good. The Gasthaus closes Sunday evening and all day Monday. For real Italian fare, try the family-run **Roma-Città** pizzeria (Bahnhofstr. 6, tel. 08362/5444; closed Mon.), which serves filling Italian meals for under DM 11. Stock up on staples at **Kaiser's** grocery (Reichenstr. 26).

OUTDOOR ACTIVITIES

Don't forget that Füssen is near a number of Alpine and lakeside hikes. **Forggensee,** a large teardrop-shaped lake, is only 1 km to the northeast. To get there from the train station, go left down Bahnhofstraße and continue straight to Sebastianstraße, then make a left at the river. Another option is to take Bus 9713 (DM 5) from Füssen's Bahnhof to **Tegelbergbahn.** From there, you can catch the cable car (DM 26 round-trip) to the top of the **Tegelberg,** where the view and the hiking trails will reaffirm your faith in life. The cable car runs daily 8:30–5 (8:45–4:30 in winter). You can also hike the mountain on the 2½-hour trail that begins at the Bahnhof. Bikers can rent wheels at the Bahnhof for DM 10 per day. If **mountain bikes** are more your style, rent one at Radsport Zacherl (Rupprechtstr. 8½, tel. 08362/3292) for DM 20 per day. Serious cyclists should invest in the tourist office's **Radwanderkarte** (DM 3), which shows the bike paths around Füssen, as well as biking directions to the castles.

NEAR FÜSSEN

Füssen is a short hop from two impressive Romantic Road sights: the castles of **Hohenschwangau** and **Neuschwanstein.** Both are within 5 km of Füssen, and when the weather's good, you might consider going there on foot. Otherwise, catch the hourly RVO bus that runs from Füssen's train station to Königschlösser (DM 6 round-trip); it stops right at the steps that lead to Hohenschwangau, a short distance from Neuschwanstein. Keep in mind that roughly one million people pass through the two castles every year, and during summer you can wait in line upwards of two hours before gaining entry. Neuschwanstein is by far the more popular and crowded, so visit early. If you catch the bus at 8:05 AM, you'll arrive just in time to catch a spot at the front of the line when the castle opens. If you'd like to indulge your Cinderella fantasies, take a horse-drawn carriage from Hotel Müller, near the Königschlösser bus stop, up the hill to the castle (DM 8 up, DM 4 down).

HOHENSCHWANGAU

Bavaria's mad King Ludwig II spent his formative years in Hohenschwangau, and it's said that the palace's neo-Gothic atmosphere influenced the fairy-tale king in the design of his romantic masterpiece, Neuschwanstein. Hohenschwangau itself was built by the knights of Schwangau in the 12th century, in a heavy Romanesque style. Between 1832 and 1836, the battle-ravaged castle was completely restored by Ludwig's father and transformed into an elegant palace, one that attracted the notice of composer Richard Wagner. Wagner spent a few summers here at Ludwig's invitation. Their friendship deepened Ludwig's already keen interest in music, theater, and mythology. Come to see the piano Wagner played, as well as the bed he slept in. Other highlights include the dizzying **Festsaal** (festival hall), positively littered with gold statuettes. *Tel. 08362/81127. Admission: DM 12, DM 9 students. Open mid-Mar.–mid-Oct., daily 8:30–5:30; mid-Oct.–Mar., daily 9:30–4:30.*

NEUSCHWANSTEIN

Walk 20 min northeast from Hohenschwangau and it's impossible to miss Ludwig's so-called fairy-tale castle, built between 1869 and 1892. Set atop a hill in the middle of a small forest, Neuschwanstein has towers, gates, battlements, courtyards, gables, lookouts, spiral stairways, and just about everything else a proper castle should have. Most visitors spend the 35-min tour, eyes wide and mouths agape, simply trying to process the opulence of the castle's innards. In September chamber music concerts are sometimes held in the ornate **Minstrel's Hall.** Call Füssen's tourist office (*see above*) for more info. After the tour, be sure to wander through the surrounding forest. Head to the **Marien Brücke** (Mary's Bridge), a span high above the **Pöllat Gorge,** for the Kodak moment of a lifetime with Neuschwanstein in the background. For the Kodak moment of two lifetimes, continue upward to the top of the mountain (2½ hrs). The Tegelbergbahn (*see* Outdoor Activities *in* Füssen, *above*) will get you there as well. *Tel. 08362/81801. Castle admission: DM 12, DM 9 students. Open Apr.–Sept., daily 9–5:30; Oct.–Mar., daily 10–4.*

OBERSTDORF

The little mountain town of Oberstdorf is home to a diverse range of attractions, including the world's longest ski jump *and* the world's largest shoe. The huge shoe, among other articles from the town's history, is housed in the 35-room **Heimatmuseum** (Oststr. 13, tel. 08322/5470; closed Sun. and Mon.). Oberstdorf is as far south as you can get in Germany, and in summer the town fills up with visitors seeking the curative wonders of the numerous health resorts. For this reason, it's probably a better idea to

A DREAM COME TRUE

A somewhat withdrawn and slightly melancholy youth, Ludwig II, grandson of Ludwig I, inherited his grandfather's passion for beauty and building. During his reign as "Dream King" (1864–1886), Ludwig was driven by the maddening desire to create a castle even more magnificent than Versailles. From his childhood home in Hohenschwangau Castle he would look with pride at the construction of his masterpiece across the valley, the fairy-tale castle at Neuschwanstein—prototype for Walt Disney's fanciful landmark. The original plans of this palace were drawn up not by an architect but by a theater director—handpicked by Ludwig II, who was himself a dedicated patron of the arts.

Yet although he began work on this glorious stucture, the mustachioed king would not live to see it finished. The cause of his death at age 41 remains a mystery, fuel for Bavarian lore and legend. Afraid that his lavish expenditures would bankrupt Bavaria, Ludwig's enemies had him declared insane, a first step toward removing him from the throne. Only a few days later Ludwig and his personal physician were found drowned in the Starnberger See. Regardless of whether it was murder or suicide, his admirers still see in charismatic Ludwig the ultimate symbol of Bavarian independence.

aim for the uncrowded hiking paths. The Nebelhorn is a popular spot for mountaineers and hikers. The gondola (tel. 08322/960096) to the peak is open daily 8:15–5 (last ascent 4:30) and costs DM 42 round-trip, less if you get off at one of the intermediary stations. The **Fellhorn** (tel. 08322/3035 for info; gondola DM 38) is a less strenuous alternative, but opt for climbing **Söllereck** if you want a fairly easy hike. The tourist office sells a trail map (DM 9) that shows the main routes. All three of these peaks offer excellent skiing in winter; rent skis for DM 20 per day from **Neue Skischule Oberstdorf** (An der Nebelhornbahn, tel. 08322/2737).

BASICS

Across the street from the train/bus station is **Tourist Information Zimmervermittlung** (tel. 08322/700217), which helps find rooms free of charge. Check the concert information that is often posted outside and have the Kurkarte you receive from your hotel stamped here. The **main tourist office** (tel. 08322/7000) on Marktplatz has free maps and sports info and also helps with accommodations. Both are open weekdays 8:30–noon and 2–6, Saturday 9:30–noon.

COMING AND GOING

Oberstdorf no longer has buses leaving the city for local destinations, so be prepared to use only the train to get around. You can take the **train** from Munich (2½ hrs, DM 46), but you usually have to transfer at Buchloe or Immenstadt. From Oberstdorf trains run to Füssen (hourly, DM 34) and Garmisch-Partenkirchen (every 2 hrs, DM 36). The **train station** (tel. 083221/3092) has the standard selection of lockers and also rents bikes. From the station, walk 10 min south on Hauptstraße to reach the town center.

WHERE TO SLEEP AND EAT

The tourist office lists beds for DM 30–DM 40. The **Berghütte Edmund-Probst-Haus** (Nebelhorn 1, tel. 08322/4795) sits 1,932 m up the Nebelhorn (*see above*), either a 2½-hour walk or five-min cable-car ride away. Beds cost DM 22, a mattress DM 18; bring sheets or a sleeping bag. Down below, cheap guest houses include **Buchenberg** (Lorettostr. 6, tel. 08322/2315), where tiny rooms with shower are DM 32–DM 35 per person (DM 28 without shower), and **Alpenglühn** (Wittelsbacherstr. 4, tel. 08322/4692), where rooms with bath and TV cost DM 38–DM 48. There's a **campground** (tel. 08322/4022) just north of the Bahnhof at Im Steinach 6. Come 7:30–11 or 2–6 to snag a site (DM 4–DM 9 plus DM 9 per person). On Tuesday and Thursday, the **Dampfbierbrauerei** (Bahnhofpl. 6–8, tel. 08322/8908) sells beer at DM 7 per Maß and 1 m of bratwurst with sauerkraut and bread for DM 13. Get groceries at **Feneberg** (Hauptstr., cnr Bachstr.).

HOSTELS • HI-Jugendherberge Kornau has standard dorm beds for DM 22 and a 10 PM curfew. Bonuses include a granola-and-yogurt breakfast and laundry facilities. *Kornau 8, tel. 08322/2225. From train station, take bus (direction: Kleinwalsertal) to Reutte (last bus 8:50 PM); or, take Hauptstraße, turn right on Walserstraße, walk uphill for 40 min, and right on Kornau (45 min total). Reception open 8–noon and 5–8 PM.*

GARMISCH-PARTENKIRCHEN

Since the separate towns of Garmisch and Partenkirchen merged for the 1936 Winter Olympics, tourism has exploded and recreational facilities of all kinds compete for your marks. The biggest high around here, in both price and altitude, is the **Zugspitze,** Germany's tallest mountain (2,963 m). A ride to the top costs DM 75; try to go on a clear day, otherwise it's a waste of money. Weather permitting, the view of the surrounding peaks and lowlands is priceless. Make the ascent on a cogwheel train (1¼ hrs), or take the cable car (a stomach-jarring 10 min). Both leave from Olympia Straße 27 (tel. 08821/7970), just east of the train station.

Other cable cars are cheaper and access heavenly hiking trails and winter ski runs. The **Alpspitze** cable car drops you off at the 2,255-m Osterfelderkopf for DM 25 (DM 36 round-trip); the **Wankbahn** takes you up 1,958 m for DM 18 (DM 26 round-trip); the **Kreuzeckbahn** lifts you 1,484 m for DM 20 (DM 28 round-trip); and the **Eckbauerbahn** carries you 1,377 m high for DM 15 (DM 20 round-trip). The tourist office (*see below*) provides lift hours, hiking maps, and trip descriptions. Hiking enthusiasts who feel they can climb for 9½ hours straight can do the tours without lifts. It's scenic and easy since it requires no special experience; the tourist office is more than happy to print out directions in English. But do make certain you call for **weather conditions** first (tel. 08821/797979).

In winter the ski slopes are incredible. At the Zugspitze Bahnhof, you can rent skis for DM 27 a day (less for multiday rentals). A Zugspitze lift pass costs DM 60 per day. A Wank lift pass costs DM 35, and an Eckbauer lift pass costs DM 31. For DM 145, a **Happy Ski Card** entitles you to three days of skiing in Seefeld, Mittenwald, and Garmisch-Partenkirchen.

If heights frighten you, perhaps you'd feel more secure wandering through the cavernous passageways of the **Partnachklamm gorge** (admission DM 4, DM 2 with Kurkarte), carved over thousands of years by the Partnach River. In the winter bizarre ice formations dangle from the gorge's walls. Get there by taking local Bus 1 or 2 (direction: Kreiskrankenhaus) to Olympic Skistadion; then follow the signs for a 30-min hike to the gorge. For a gorgeous four-hour hike, take the Alpspitze cable car to Osterfelderkopf, descend through the Höllental (Hell's Valley) to the gorge, and finish up in Hammersbach. The Zugspitzbahn brings you back to Garmisch.

If you can pull yourself away from the mountains, take a stroll to see the home of composer Richard Strauss (1864–1949), who spent his last years in the **villa** at the end of Zöppritzstraße (at Feldstr.). The town pays homage to its *Rosenkavalier* and other composers in June during the annual **Richard-Strauss-Tage**; contact the Ticket-Service (tel. 08821/752545, fax 08821/752547) if you'd like to see a performance.

BASICS

To change money, hit the **post office** by the station; it's open weekdays 8–noon and 2–6, Saturday 8–noon, Sunday 10 AM–11 AM. The **information booth** at the train station (open daily 3:50 PM–7:30 PM) books rooms for free and provides general info. The main tourist office (Richard-Strauss-Pl., tel. 08821/180419, open Mon.–Sat. 8–6, Sun. 10–noon) also leads hikes and gives out sports info.

COMING AND GOING

If you're coming from Munich or Augsburg, ask at the train station about a special round-trip train ticket for DM 90 that includes a free ride on the Zugspitze cable car. In winter, the same ticket includes a Zugspitze lift pass for the day. Hourly **trains** head to Munich (1½ hrs, DM 28) and Mittenwald (30 min, DM 7). **RVO buses** (tel. 08821/948274) run to other Alpine villages, such as Oberammergau (40 min, DM 6), Füssen (2 hrs, DM 15 with Tageskarte), and Oberstdorf (4 hrs, DM 30). Rent **bicycles** (DM 20) and **mountain bikes** (DM 35) at Schöch (Ludwigstr. 39, tel. 08821/1230).

The train station separates Garmisch from Partenkirchen. On the western side is **Marienplatz,** the heart of Garmisch; attractions are to the north in the Altstadt. On the east side of the tracks is **Ludwigstraße,** Partenkirchen's main strip; Sonnenbergstraße and Ballergasse are also key places to find restaurants and shops. Since the two halves together comprise an extra-large Alpine town, you should use the **Ortsbus** (DM 3, free with Kurkarte) to shuttle back and forth. The buses run from around 6 AM to 10:30 PM, but only every 30 min at best; bus maps are available at the tourist office.

WHERE TO SLEEP

The tourist office and information booth will help you find a room. If they're closed, 24-hour screens outside the tourist office and above the travel agency in the train station list accommodations. After hours you can also call 08821/19412 for listings. A nice alternative to the hostel, the **Naturfreundeheim** (Schalmeiw. 21, tel. 08821/4322) charges only DM 15 for a bed, DM 5 for sheets, and DM 8 for breakfast. Reservations are vital. From the train station, take Bus 1 or 2 to Ludwigstraße (last bus around 10 PM); backtrack down Ludwigstraße and turn right on Sonnenbergstraße, left on Professor-Michael-Sachs-Straße, and left on Schalmeiweg.

HOSTELS • To reach the **HI-Jugendherberge,** 4 km out of town, take Bus 3, 4, or 5 from the train station to Burgrain. With breakfast, a night at the hostel costs DM 20. Make sure you catch the last bus at 10:30 in order to make the 11:30 curfew. *Jochstr. 10, tel. 08821/2980, fax 08821/58536. 220 beds. Reception open 7 AM–9 AM and 5 PM–midnight. Laundry. Closed Nov.–Christmas.*

CAMPING • Campingplatz Zugspitze (Griesener Str. 4, tel. 08821/3180) is a year-round campground at the foot of the Zugspitze, between Grainau and Garmisch-Partenkirchen. Take the hourly blue bus (DM 3.10; last bus 8 PM) from the stop across the street from the train station. Get off at Schmultz and follow the signs. Tent sites are DM 6 plus DM 12 per person.

FOOD

One reason to travel here is to become familiar with local customs, culture, and cusine—so be ready to circumvent the McDonald's on Marienplatz. If your budget is tight try the **Cafeteria** (Griesstr. 1, tel. 08821/2109), where everything costs less than DM 8.50. Another place with moderate prices is **Charivari** (Sonnenbergstr. 17, tel. 08821/2789) where the menu features a long list of pasta dishes. **Sebastians Stub'n** (Ludwigstr. 93, tel. 08821/78889; closed Sun.) has a delicious plate of *Käsespatz'n* (cheese noodles; DM 9.50) and mongo salads (DM 14). Although you are in the land of over 1,200 different regional beers you can also order imported Guinness in festive company at the **Irish Pub** (Rathauspl. 8, tel. 08221/78798). For picnic supplies, turn left down Bahnhofstraße from the train station and a **Plus** grocery store will be waiting on your left.

OBERAMMERGAU

Oberammergau's ubiquitous, expensive shops crammed with wood carvings reveal a bit about the inhabitants' famed flair: Since the 16th century the town has been a renowned center of wood carving. For DM 4 (DM 2 students), you can view the prized collection of woodcraft at the **Heimatmuseum** (Dorfstr. 8, tel. 08822/32256; closed Mon.). In summer, you can watch wood-carvers doggedly chipping away in the workshop of the **Pilatushaus** (Verlegerg., at Ludwig-Thoma-Str., tel. 08822/1682), open weekdays 1–6. Franz Seraph Zwinck, a renowned fresco painter, painted the house's facade.

Still more distinguished than its wood carving is Oberammergau's **Passionsspiele** (Passion Play), which was first performed in 1634 and has been staged every decade since 1680. When the Black Plague struck Oberammergau during the Thirty Years' War, citizens tried to save themselves by vowing to act out the suffering and death of Christ every 10 years. The 16-act, 5½-hour play features 1,500 locals; it runs May through September of the year 2000 and then again in 2010. If you miss out on tickets (they cost upwards of DM 100 and reservations are made years in advance), you can still visit the open-air

Passionspielhaus (Passion Play Theater) on Passionwiese. The intriguing backstage museum is open daily 9:30–noon and 1:30–4:30; admission is DM 5, DM 3 for students. At press time this theater was under renovation, so be sure to call first.

BASICS

To reach Oberammergau's **tourist office** (Eugen-Papst-Str. 9a, tel. 08822/92310; open weekdays 8:30–6, Sat. 8:30–noon) from the train station, exit onto Bahnhofstraße, cross the Ammer canal, and turn right onto Eugen-Papst-Straße. The staff will help you find rooms (DM 1 charge) and hand you free English-language maps.

COMING AND GOING

Trains between Oberammergau and Munich take less than two hours (15 per day, DM 24.20), but you'll have to transfer at Murnau. **Bus 9606** to and from Garmisch-Partenkirchen departs hourly until 6 or 7 PM (45 min, DM 6), passing through Kloster Ettal (*see* Near Oberammergau, *below*). You can also travel between Oberammergau and Füssen on Bus 1084 (4 per day, 1½ hrs, DM 13). On a nice day, you may want to bike to Schloß Linderhof or Kloster Ettal. Rent **mountain bikes** at Sport-Zentrale Papistock (Bahnhofstr. 6a, tel. 08822/4178) for DM 26 per day.

WHERE TO SLEEP AND EAT

The **HI-Jugendherberge** (Malensteinw. 10, tel. 08822/4114) has beds for DM 20.50, including breakfast. Reception is open 8–noon and 5–7, and the curfew is 10:30 PM. From the train station, take Raisachweg south along the Ammer River, hang a right at König-Ludwig-Straße, then a left on Malensteinw.; it's about a 15-min walk. The hostel is closed November 15–Christmas. Or get a private room (DM 25–DM 35 per person) through the tourist office. For a sit-down meal, try **Alte Post** (Dorfstr. 19, tel. 08822/9100), a 350-year-old inn and beer garden that serves traditional Bavarian specialties for DM 10–DM 20. For groceries head to **Tengelmann** at Bahnhofstraße 9.

If you have a burning desire to see yet another majestic house of worship, head for Kloster Ettal, famous for its 78-m-high dome and the enormous fresco within. Take Bus 9606 (1–2 per hr, 15 min, DM 3) from Oberammergau to Klostergasthof.

NEAR OBERAMMERGAU

SCHLOSS LINDERHOF

If you don't have the time to go castlehopping through Bavaria, snap a few shots of Neuschwanstein and then explore the stunning rococo interior of Schloß Linderhof. The smallest of King Ludwig's castles, Linderhof was his favorite hangout, probably because it was the only one finished during his lifetime. Modeled after the Petit Trianon at Versailles, Linderhof was built between 1874 and 1878 on the former site of a hunting lodge owned by Ludwig's father. The magnificent master bedroom has an 8½-foot bed covered in blue velvet, and a half-ton chandelier.

The immaculate English- and French-style **park** features an illuminated **grotto** constructed for Wagner's operas. Every hour in summer the park's fountains do a little dance of their own. Stained glass, bejeweled peacocks, and potted palms set the stage for the Orientalist **Maurisher Kiosk** (Moorish Pavilion), originally built for the Second World Expo in Paris. RVO Bus 9622 runs the 15 km from Oberammergau to Linderhof seven times daily (20 min, DM 9 round-trip). Don't miss the last return at 5:35 PM or you'll be spending the night at the expensive hotel across the street from the gift shop. *Tel. 08822/3512. Required tour of palace and grotto: DM 10, DM 7 students (in winter DM 7, DM 4 students). Open Apr.–Sept. daily 9–12:15 and 12:45–5:30; Oct.–Mar., daily 10–12:15 and 12:45–4.*

MITTENWALD

If you have only a day or two in the Bavarian Alps, spend your time in Mittenwald. Sandwiched between the Karwendel and Wetterstein mountains, this romantic town is a picture-perfect Alpine village. It's got fresh, snowcapped peaks, blue skies, and lush meadows. The tiny town has also attained international renown as a center for the production of violins. Nevertheless, Mittenwald is often overlooked because of its more famous neighbor, Garmisch-Partenkirchen, only 20 km away.

Take advantage of Mittenwald's gorgeous views and hiking opportunities by taking the cable car that leaves from Alpenkorpsstraße 1 (tel. 08832/8480; DM 29 round-trip) and runs to the **Karwendel summit** (2,244 m). Before you go, call the **weather hot line** (tel. 08823/5396). Once on top, you can take an easy 30-min hike around the summit, or, for a view of the surrounding forest, take the **Sessellift** (chair lift; tel. 08823/1553; DM 10 round-trip) from the northern end of Kranzbergstraße up the Kranzberg. To reach the **Leutaschklamm gorge** and **waterfall** (open summer, daily 9–5:30), walk south on Innsbrucker Straße and veer right onto Am Köberl—it's an easy 25-min walk. A popular swimming destination in summer is the tiny lake **Lautersee,** an easy 40-min walk westward on Laintalstraße, which turns into Laintal. Come winter, the Karwendel boasts Germany's longest downhill ski run (6.5 km). A lift pass costs DM 36 for one day, DM 69 for two. Rent skis at **Skischule Mittenwald** (Bahnhofstr. 6, tel. 08823/8080).

The **Geigenbau und Heimatmuseum mit Schauwerkstatt** (Ballenhausg. 3, tel. 08823/2511) displays violins fashioned by Mittenwald's best; check them out weekdays 10–11:45 and 2–4:45, weekends 10–11:45. To see the violin makers in action, stop by the museum's *Schauwerkstatt* (workshop), open daily in summer and Friday–Sunday in winter. Admission is DM 2, DM 1 students. Next door is the 18th-century church of **St. Peter und Paul,** famous for its Baroque, frescoed tower. Outside the church stands a bronze statue dedicated to master violin maker Matthias Klotz (1653–1743). West of the church extends the oldest part of town, **Im Gries,** great walking territory lined with fruit stands and other markets.

BASICS

The **post office,** across from the train station, exchanges money. The **tourist office** (Kurverwaltung; Dammkarstr. 3, tel. 08823/33981) will help you find a place to stay for no charge and offers excellent hiking and biking maps (DM 5) and sightseeing information. The office is open weekdays 8–noon and 1–7, weekends 10–noon (shorter hrs off-season). If you arrive late, the 24-hour computer screen by the entrance lists available lodging options.

COMING AND GOING

Frequent **trains** connect Mittenwald with Munich (hourly, 2 hrs, DM 32), Innsbruck (hourly, 1 hr, DM 13.80), and Garmisch-Partenkirchen (20 min, DM 7). **RVO buses** also run from Mittenwald to Garmisch-Partenkirchen (30 min, DM 6), but aren't as frequent.

WHERE TO SLEEP AND EAT

Like most Alpine villages, Mittenwald has a number of guest houses that offer rooms for DM 30–DM 50 per person. The 120-bed **HI-Jugendherberge** (Buckelwiesen 7, tel. 08823/1701, fax 08823/2907; closed Nov. and Dec.) is a one-hour hike north from town on the Tonihof-Buckelwiesen trail. Hikers may want to stay at the **Berghütte Dammkarhütte** (1,650 m), a 1½–2-hour hike up the Karwendel. Mattresses cost DM 10. Try to send a postcard (Dammkarhütte, Mittenwald) to let them know you're coming. For private room, call to see if space is available at the centrally located **Haus Antonia** (In der Wasserwiese 14, tel. 08823/8202); at DM 40 per person, including breakfast, it's a bargain. To get there exit right from the station, go right on Dammkarstraße, left on Tiefkarstraße, and right on In der Wasserwiese. The nearest year-round **campground** is at Isarhorn (tel. 08823/5216; DM 8 per space), 3 km north of Mittenwald. Take the Omnibus (DM 4) from the Bahnhof toward Krün to the Campingplatz stop.

Mittenwald has plenty of rather expensive *Gäststätten* (restaurants), but if you're counting pfennige, **Sali's Grill Shop** (Hochstr. 14; closed Wed.) has *Schnitzelburgers* for DM 4.50 or bratwurst with fries for DM 5.30. An attractive but inexpensive version of the **Osteria** Italian food chain stands across the street at Hochstraße 15. Next door, you'll find **HL Markt** to fulfill all your grocery needs.

BERCHTESGADEN

It's not surprising that Berchtesgaden is so popular with tourists; it has some unique sights and it's virtually next door to popular Salzburg. Historically, Berchtesgaden was a salt-mining center, but these days it's probably better remembered as Adolf Hitler's favorite resort and the site of *Kehlsteinhaus* (Eagle's Nest), a former Nazi retreat perched atop a 2,017-m mountain. Two beautiful natural wonders nearby are **Königssee,** Germany's cleanest and arguably most beautiful lake, and the towering **Watzmann** massif, second in height only to the Zugspitze. If you want to avoid the trampled track, take the bus to the neighboring village of Ramsau (DM 4.50, roundtrip DM 8.80); from here it's a one-hour walk westward to peaceful lake **Hintersee.** Another option is the three-hour hike to the **Schellenberg ice cave** (open June–Oct., daily 9–4; required tour DM 9), Germany's largest. From the front of the train station, take Bus 9540 (DM 4) to Markt Schellenberg to reach the ice-cave trailhead. The hike is strenuous, so it might be better to simply take the bus a few stops farther to St. Leonard and spend DM 20 (DM 33 round-trip) on a cable car that drops you off at a trailhead for a 1½-hour hike down to the caves.

BASICS

Because you're so close to the border, many places also accept Austrian Schillings. **Reisebüro ABR** (tel. 08652/5081; closed Sun.) in the train station will solve your travel problems and exchange currency. The **tourist office** (Königsseer Str. 2, tel. 08652/9670), opposite the Hauptbahnhof, is open weekdays 8–6, Saturday 8–5, and Sunday 9–3 (slightly shorter hrs off-season). They can help you find mid-price rooms (DM 35–DM 45 per person) and offer the only English-language tour available for both the Kehlsteinhaus and the Obersalzberg bunkers. The tour costs DM 55, including transportation. The Nationalpark Haus (Franziskanerpl. 7, tel. 08652/64343; open Mon.–Sat. 9–5) offers guided hikes and info about the many hiking trails in **National Park Berchtesgaden,** which covers over 200 sq km from the Königssee to the Austrian border.

COMING AND GOING

Hourly **trains** travel between Berchtesgaden and Salzburg (55 min, DM 12), but the hourly **bus** from the Hauptbahnhof is faster and cheaper (45 min, DM 7). Trains from Munich depart hourly (2½–3 hrs, DM 48), but you may have to transfer at Freilassing. There are 24-hour lockers in the station.

WHERE TO SLEEP

To reach the lakeside **Hotel Königssee-Betriebe** (Seestr. 29, tel. 08652/6580, fax 08652/65849), take Bus 9541 to Königssee and walk 5 min through the souvenir gauntlet. The hotel has squeaky-clean singles (DM 40–DM 60) and doubles (DM 70–DM 100), showers included. The place is decorated with Bavarian charm and some rooms have balconies with a view of the lake. **Hotel zum Türken** (Hintereck 2, tel. 08652/2427), at the entrance to the Obersalzberg and the foot of the road that leads up to Eagle's Nest, is a warm, friendly hotel with a pleasant terrace and a view of the surrounding majestic mountains. Prices are similar to those at Hotel Königssee. Walk 25 min from town, or take the Kehlsteinhaus bus to Hintereck.

HOSTELS • The closest **HI-Jugendherberge** is in nearby Strub. Note that its 370 luxurious beds (DM 20) are usually filled by 14- to 16-year-olds. Take Bus 9539 (DM 2.40) from the train station to Jugendherberge or to Strub Kaserne (a more distant but more frequently serviced stop). *Gebirgsjägerstr. 52, tel. 08652/94370, fax 08652/66328. Curfew 10 PM. Reception open 8–noon and 5–7. Laundry (DM 4). Closed Nov. and Dec.*

CAMPING • You'll see more mobile homes than woodsy creatures at the year-round **Camping Grafenlehen** (tel. and fax 08652/4140), up the Königsseer Fußweg from the Parkplatz Königssee bus stop. On the bright side, Grafenlehen has warm showers and laundry facilities. Tent sites are DM 10; add DM 8.50 per person.

FOOD

For fast food to go, try *Nürnberger Rostbratwürstl* (six tasty little sausages over sauerkraut; DM 8.50) at **Bernds Grillstüberl** (Marktpl. 24, tel. 08652/2123; closed Sun.). They also serve double cheeseburgers (DM 5.70). The **Brotzeitstüberl** (Schloßpl. 3, tel. 08652/64557; closed Sun.) is a gemütlich spot that lets you make your own small salad for DM 4.90. For a more solid meal, **Schwabenwirt** (Königsseer Str. 1, tel. 08652/2022) has Bavarian specialties for DM 10–DM 15, or do it yourself at **Kaiser's grocery store** (Metzgerstr. 5), near the Schloß.

WORTH SEEING

KEHLSTEINHAUS • This extraordinary retreat, perched atop a 2,017-m mountain, was presented to Hitler by the Nazi party for his 50th birthday. The road leading from the Obersalzberg to to the so-called Eagle's Nest is a feat of engineering. In less than 13 months the road was blasted out of solid rock—which makes it unique in the world. The ascension to the building itself is equally spectacular. A stone-lined tunnel leads some 407 feet straight into the side of the mountain—and from there a brass-lined elevator takes the visitor up another 407 feet through the heart of the mountain and into the building within only 41 seconds. Buses leave every 30–45 min from the Berchtesgaden train station for Obersalzberg-Hintereck (DM 7.50 round-trip), from which you ride another bus (2 per hr, 20 min, DM 21) up a steep, coiling road to the parking lot, where you enter the elevator that takes you to the peak. The site is open mid-May–October, daily 8–5; inquire at the tourist office about English-language tours.

KOENIGLICHES SCHLOSS • Wittelsbach treasures, including an impressive collection of fine wood carvings, are displayed in the Renaissance rooms of the Königliches Schloß in the center of town. Take in art and architecture from the Romantic period through the Biedermeier School. *Tel. 08652/2085. Admission: DM 7, DM 3.50 students. Open weekdays 10–1 (last tour at noon) and 2–5 (last tour at 4).*

OBERSALZBERG • Far below the Eagle's Nest lie the former southern headquarters of the Nazi party. Don't expect more than stripped-down walls at the remains of the Berghof bunkers, where Hitler met with foreign dignitaries, including British prime minister Neville Chamberlain, the man who ensured "peace in our time" just prior to World War II. Germans won't go near the place—but foreigners can't be kept from it. You enter the bunkers, which also served as underground air-raid shelters, through Hotel zum Türken (*see* Where to Sleep, *above*). *Admission: DM 5. Open daily 9–5:30.*

SALZBERGWERK BERCHTESGADEN • Organizers of these 1-hr tours provide you with protective clothing and prepare you for the ride of lifetime—reminiscent of a roller coaster into the bowels of the earth. You're carried through this one-of-a-kind tourist extravaganza by four distinct modes of transportation (tram, raft, giant slide, elevator), making you feel as if you've landed in a game of Chutes and Ladders. All tours and informative films are in German, but you can borrow English-language tour tapes for free. *Bergwerkstr. 83, tel. 08652/60020. Bus 9540 from station or walk 15 min from town center. Admission: DM 21. Open May–Oct. 15, daily 8:30–5; Oct. 16–Apr., weekdays 12:30–3:30.*

NUREMBERG AND FRANCONIA

7

UPDATED BY SARAH SLOAT

Though Franconia—Franken, in German—comprises the geographic bulk and northern half of the Bavarian state, the region and its people stand apart. The Danube River demarcates the unofficial cultural border between Bavaria to the south and Franconia to the north, and in local parlance the river is known as the *Weißwurstäquator,* or equator of white sausage. While true-blue Bavarians messily *freß* (feed on) boiled gray Weißwurst dunked in sweet mustard, Franconians prefer the greasy pleasures of ruddy Bratwurst. As for beverages, the rolling farmland of Oberfranken (Upper Franconia) nurtures the hops crucial to a tradition of beer brewing superior even to that of southern Bavaria, while the verdant hills of Lower Franconia yield the grapes that make cities like **Würzburg** favored stops on the German *Weinstraße,* or Wine Road.

In the late Middle Ages, Franconia emerged as a prime example of German *Kleinstaaterei,* a jumble of tiny states, dukedoms, and principalities loosely joined under the authority of the Holy Roman Empire. Only at the turn of the 16th century, when Emperor Maximilian I divvied up the empire with a stroke of the pen, did Franconia's blurry lines sharpen into a recognizable political entity. Soon thereafter, the Protestant Reformation and Counter-Reformation hurled the region into serious religious strife, yet left a stupendous architectural legacy as well, visible today in Franconia's ornate churches and cathedrals. After the Thirty Years' War (1618–48), the region lapsed into poverty and obscurity. More than 150 years later, Napoleon allocated a disgruntled Franconia as war booty to Bavaria, which lent support to the smallish Frenchman in his escapades against England and Austria.

Today Franconia's uncontested metropolis is **Nürnberg** (Nuremberg). This industrial center sports a spectacular medieval *Altstadt* (Old Town) and a young, progressive population, yet for many the city remains inexorably linked to Nazism. Tucked between Würzburg and the Austrian border lie many of the towns along the **Romantische Straße** (Romantic Road), a heavily touristed cluster of medieval fortresses and citadels that deservedly ranks among Europe's star attractions. To the north in Oberfranken await **Bayreuth,** where Richard Wagner wrote many of his ground-breaking operas; the stunning townscape of **Bamberg**; and the outdoor pleasures of the **Fränkische Schweiz** (Franconian Switzerland). An impressive number of *Wanderwege* and *Radwege* (hiking and biking trails) traversing the forests invite you to commune with Mother Earth, and if you're into hiking through the trees but not sleeping in them, budget accommodations await your tired feet in even the most remote forest towns.

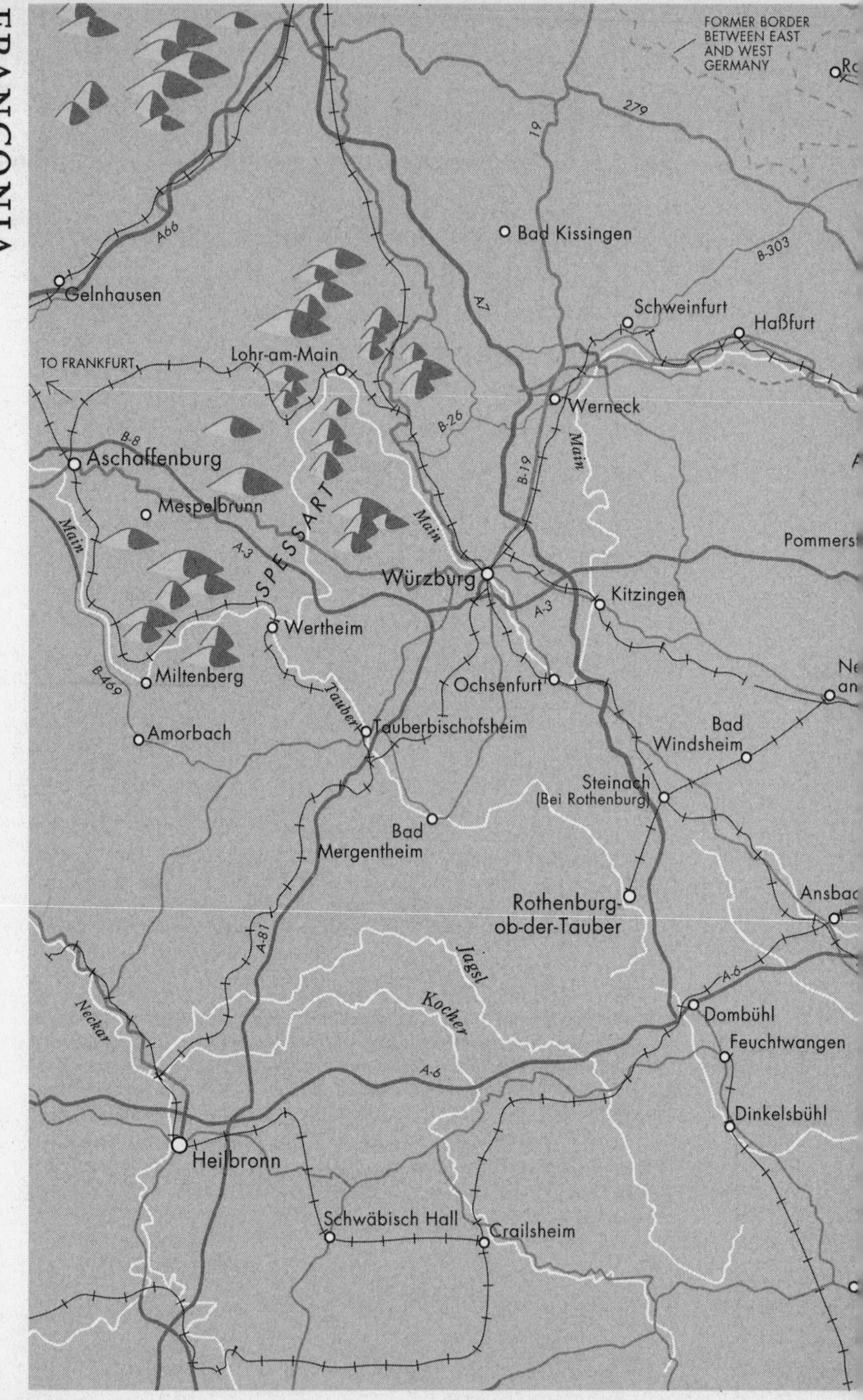
FORMER BORDER BETWEEN EAST AND WEST GERMANY
279
19
A66
Bad Kissingen
B-303
Gelnhausen
A7
Schweinfurt
Haßfurt
TO FRANKFURT
Lohr-am-Main
Werneck
B-26
B-8
Aschaffenburg
Main
B-19
Mespelbrunn
Main
SPESSART
Main
A-3
Würzburg
Kitzingen
A-3
Wertheim
B-469
Miltenberg
Ochsenfurt
Tauber
Amorbach
Tauberbischofsheim
Bad Windsheim
Steinach (Bei Rothenburg)
Bad Mergentheim
Rothenburg-ob-der-Tauber
A-81
Jagst
A-6
Kocher
Neckar
Dombühl
Feuchtwangen
A-6
Dinkelsbühl
Heilbronn
Schwäbisch Hall
Crailsheim

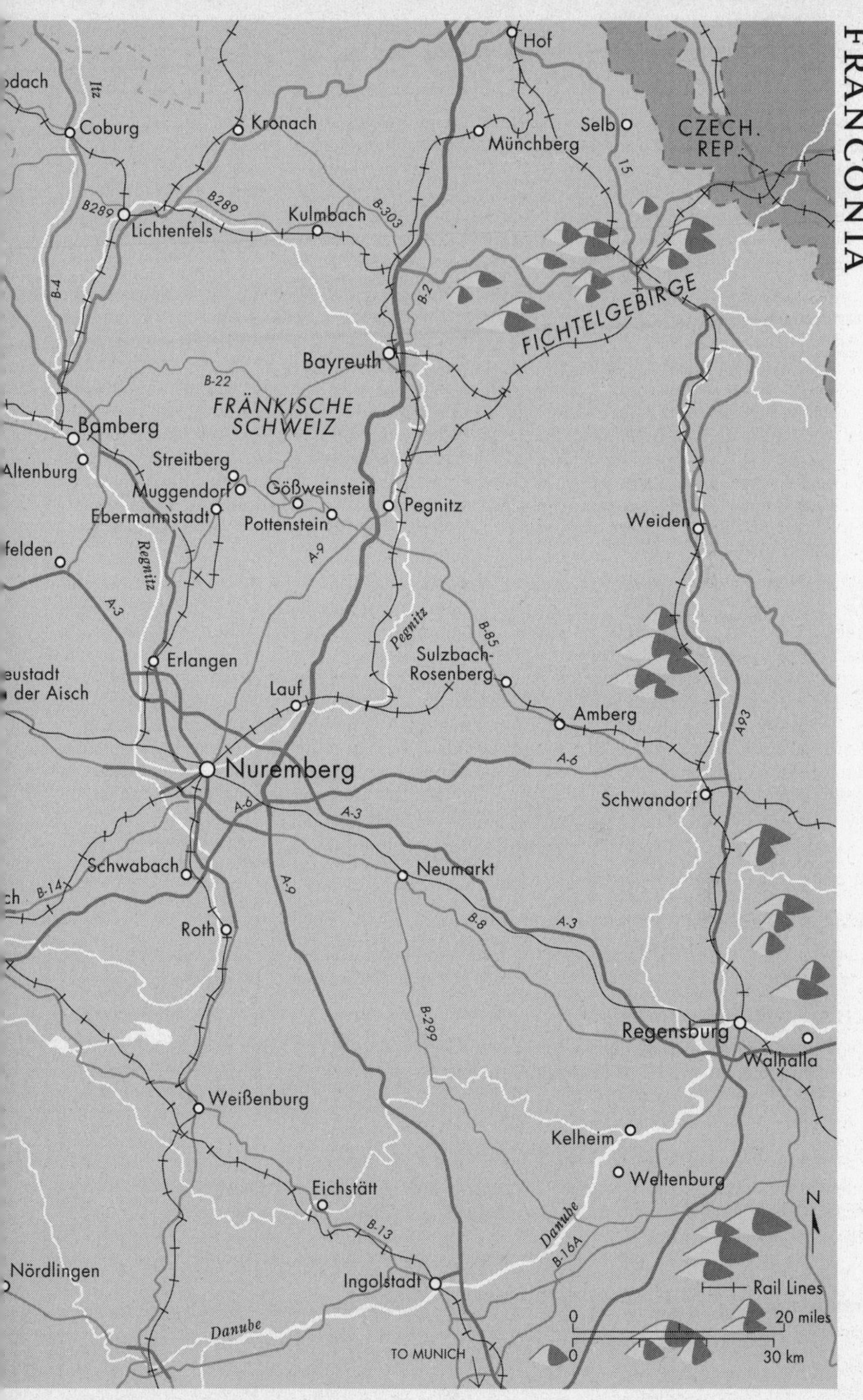
Hof
Selb
CZECH. REP.
Coburg
Kronach
Münchberg
Itz
B-4
B289
Lichtenfels
B289
Kulmbach
B-303
15
B-2
FICHTELGEBIRGE
Bayreuth
B-22
FRÄNKISCHE SCHWEIZ
Bamberg
Altenburg
Streitberg
Muggendorf
Gößweinstein
Pegnitz
Ebermannstadt
Pottenstein
Weiden
Regnitz
A-9
A-3
Pegnitz
B-85
Sulzbach-Rosenberg
Erlangen
Lauf
Amberg
A93
A-6
Nuremberg
Schwandorf
A-6
A-3
Schwabach
Neumarkt
B-14
A-9
B-8
A-3
Roth
B-299
Regensburg
Walhalla
Weißenburg
Kelheim
Weltenburg
Eichstätt
N
B-13
Danube
B-16A
Nördlingen
Ingolstadt
Rail Lines
0
20 miles
Danube
TO MUNICH
0
30 km

FRANCONIA

NUREMBERG

If you head to Franconia's largest city expecting Grimm-Brothers-style gingerbread-type homes, you won't be disappointed. These are sprinkled throughout Nuremberg's medieval Altstadt, split by the sinuous Pegnitz River and a series of tree-lined canals. Yet today, Nuremberg's cosmopolitan mix of students, immigrants, social outcasts, tourists, and regular German townsfolk spills far beyond the old city walls. Modernity, as incarnated in swank boutiques, lively cafés, discos, and sex shops—many located, appropriately enough, on the site of the former *Frauenhaus* (brothel)—is as much a part of northern Bavaria's industrial center as picture-perfect footbridges and fairy-tale lanes.

Nuremberg flowered quickly. In 1050 the first stones were laid on the Kaiserburg, the fortress overlooking the city, and the town emerged over the next few centuries as the unproclaimed capital of the Holy Roman Empire. A magnificent city arose along the banks of the Pegnitz, and all 30 Holy Roman Emperors paid a required visit. Such patronage helped transform Renaissance-era Nuremberg into a center for the arts and sciences. Albrecht Dürer—Germany's genius artist and wood engraver—worked for most of his life in an Altstadt studio, and Nuremberg's craftsmen invented the pocket watch, the clarinet, and the globe. Today Nuremberg's *Hauptmarkt* (central market) teems with street vendors in summer. Toward the end of July it is the focal point of the annual **Bardentreffen,** an internationally renowned festival of songwriters who perform their latest under open skies for free. And from early December until Christmas Day, Nuremberg bustles with the wintry attractions of the **Christkindlesmarkt,** whose two million visitors and many, many kegs of *Glühwein* (mulled wine) make it the largest Christmas bash in Germany, if not the world.

Notwithstanding the city's formidable pedigree, Nuremberg functions in the minds of millions as little more than a synonym for Nazism. Though the city's working-class population leaned heavily to the left during the Weimar Republic, Hitler designated Nuremberg the site of the annual Nazi *Reichsparteitage* (party rallies). Hitler wished to draw on the city's historical centrality in the First Reich (the Holy Roman Empire) to cement the legitimacy of the Third, and he knew he could count on the fervent support of local Nazi leader and rabid anti-Semite Julius Streicher. The Nuremberg Laws were promulgated during the 1935 rally on the Hauptmarkt, at that time known as—what else?—Adolf-Hitler-Platz. The laws defined as a Jew anyone with a Jewish grandparent, deprived Jews of German citizenship, and forbade sexual relations between Jew and "Aryan" under penalty of sterilization or death. Appropriately, the Allies chose Nuremberg as the site of their war-crimes tribunals, where top-ranking Nazis were charged with—and almost without exception convicted of—crimes against humanity.

BASICS

AMERICAN EXPRESS

Bring traveler's checks and foreign currency here for a commission-free exchange; cardholders can pick up their mail. *Adlerstr. 2, tel. 0911/232397. Open weekdays 9:30–5:30, Sat. 9:30–12:30.*

CHANGING MONEY

The **Deutsche Verkehrs-Bank** (open Mon.–Sat. 7:45–7:45, Sun. 9:15–12:30 and 1:30–5:15) in the main train station has an ATM that accepts Visa and AmEx cards. Avoid their high fees by taking checks to AmEx. **Citibank**'s three branches (Hallpl. 23, Ludwigstr. 65–69, and Aufseßpl. 7) have 24-hour ATMs that accept AmEx, MasterCard, Visa, and Cirrus cards.

DISCOUNT TRAVEL AGENCIES

Schüler und Studentenreisen specializes in cheap, last-minute flights and package deals for students. *Beckschlagerg. 6, tel. 0911/586–8650. From Rathauspl., east on Theresienstr. to Innere Laufer Gasse. Open weekdays 9–6, Sat. 10–2.*

LAUNDRY

Pritzl charges DM 6 for a wash, DM 1 to dry for 10 min. *Obstmarkt 6, 1 block east of Rathauspl. Open weekdays 8–6, Sat. 9–1.*

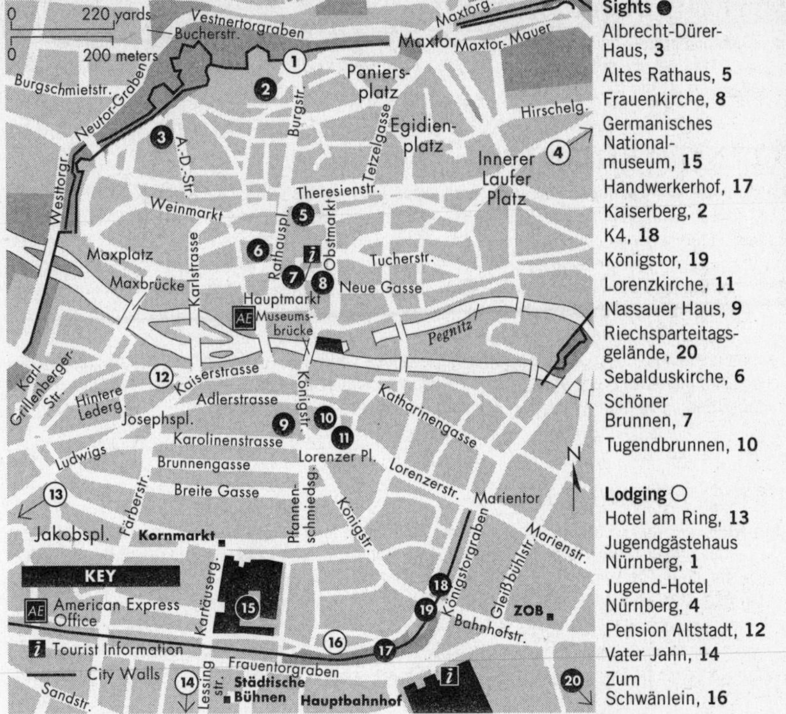

MAIL AND PHONES

At the **Hauptpost** just east of the train station you can send telegrams, make international phone calls, buy stamps and phone cards, and exchange money.

MEDICAL AID

Call 19292 for a **doctor.** For life-or-death emergencies call 19222. For pharmacological items, stop by the **Egidien-Apotheke** (Theresienpl. 2, tel. 0911/203043), a five-min walk from the hostel.

VISITOR INFORMATION

The **Hauptbahnhof** tourist office (tel. 0911/233–6132; open Mon.–Sat. 9–7) has a whole wall of brochures that cost up to DM 1. There's a second tourist office on the **Hauptmarkt** (Hauptmarkt 18, tel. 0911/233–6135, fax 0911/204359), open Monday–Saturday 9–6, Sunday 10–1 and 2–4 (closed Sun. off-season). Either office will help you find a room (DM 5 fee), sell English-language city guides (DM 6–DM 10), or provide you with the free "Hotels" brochure.

COMING AND GOING

BY TRAIN

The **Hauptbahnhof** (main train station; tel. 0911/19419) is at the Altstadt's southeast corner. Inside are a bank, an ATM, luggage lockers and storage, a bookshop with English books and magazines, and a tourist office. Trains head at least once an hour to Bayreuth (1 hr, DM 24.20), Würzburg (1½ hrs, DM 28), Bamberg (40 min, DM 16.20), and Munich (2½ hrs, DM 60); other destinations include Coburg (hourly, DM 31), Frankfurt (hourly, DM 72), and Berlin (every 2 hrs, DM 220 with express ICE train). The station is also the hub for local transit (trams, buses, and the U-Bahn).

BY MITFAHRGELEGENHEIT

Citynetz Mitfahr-Zentrale gets you almost anywhere in Europe. Chances are better of getting a ride (Berlin DM 39, Frankfurt DM 23, Munich DM 21) if you ring ahead. *Willy-Brandt-Pl. 4, tel. 0911/19444. Open weekdays 9–6, Sat. 9–1.*

GETTING AROUND

Nuremberg's Altstadt is almost completely surrounded by the huge stone **city walls.** To orient yourself, remember that the train station perches on the Altstadt's southeast corner, Kaiserburg castle and the youth hostel on the northwest corner. Königstraße, accessed via an underground passage from the train station, runs the entire north–south length of the old town and passes all the main sights. Snaking its way west–east through the old town is the **River Pegnitz,** another good landmark. Its main crossing point is the pedestrian-only **Museumsbrücke** (Museum Bridge), which connects the **Hauptmarkt** in the north with **Lorenzer Platz** in the south. If you keep within the moats, towers, and gates of the Altstadt, public transit is hardly an issue. If you do have the urge to ride a tram or bus, buy a ticket (DM 3.30) onboard or from any street-side *Automat,* ticket machines that also sell U-Bahn tickets. **Taxis** cluster around Hauptmarkt and the train station; you can call a cab by dialing 0911/19410. The meter starts at DM 4.80.

WHERE TO SLEEP

Hotel Am Ring. Though in a slightly sleazy area, this hotel is secure and just one noisy block from pedestrian-only Ludwigstraße. Clean, slightly depressing doubles with sinks run DM 90 (singles DM 50). Rooms with showers and TVs are a world (and DM 20–DM 30) apart. The included breakfast is a nice spread. *Am Plärrer 2, tel. 0911/284530 or 0911/926120, fax 0911/284859. From Bahnhof, U-Bahn to Plärrer. 33 rooms, some with bath. AE, MC, V.*

Pension Altstadt. This friendly, family-run pension is very conveniently located. It's best to book ahead since there are just 12 rooms. Singles cost DM 55, doubles DM 90, including breakfast. *Hintere Lederg. 4, tel. 0911/226102, fax 0911/221806.*

Vater Jahn. You wouldn't guess from the neighborhood or exterior, but this is a cheery, family-run pension. Doubles (DM 75–DM 95) and singles (DM 43–DM 63) are plain but bright, the bathrooms clean. It's quite a deal if you don't mind a 20-min walk to the Altstadt. *Jahnstr. 13, tel. and fax 0911/444507. From Bahnhof, east through Celtis-Unterführung, right on Celtis-Str., left on Jahnstr. 20 rooms, some with bath.*

Zum Schwänlein. This place is cheap, period. The management is less than efficient, the restaurant is mediocre and overpriced, and you may be uncomfortable alone in the surrounding neighborhood at night, but it's close to everything. Singles are DM 40–DM 60, doubles DM 70–DM 90. *Hintere Sterng. 11, tel. 0911/225162, fax 0911/241–9008. 16 rooms, 2 with bath.*

HOSTELS

Jugendgästehaus Nürnberg (HI). High above the city inside the 500-year-old Kaiserburg castle (*see* Worth Seeing, *below*), the hostel has a spectacular view of town. For DM 29, a bunk with red-checkered sheets in the former castle stables plus an early breakfast are all yours. Doubles are available for the same price, but they book up fast in summer, so reserve in advance. Call from the train station before coming up here. *Im Burg 2, tel. 0911/221024, fax 0911/23093611. Curfew 1 AM, 10 PM "silent time." Luggage storage.*

Jugend-Hotel Nürnberg. If the Jugendgästehaus is full and you're pinching pennies, this unofficial hostel is a reasonable alternative. Beds in three- to six-person rooms are DM 25 (DM 22 after first night), but it's a 20-min ride north of town. Either forget nightlife or figure in cab fare. Singles (DM 37) and doubles (DM 58) are also available. Add DM 8 for breakfast. Curfew is 10 PM, but you get a key. *Rathsbergstr. 300, tel. 0911/521–6092, fax 0911/521–6954. From Bahnhof, U2 to Herrnhütte, then Bus 41 (direction: Buchenbühl) to Zum Felsenkeller, and walk straight. Reception open 7 PM–9 PM.*

CAMPING

Campingplatz Nürnberg. Near beautiful Lake Dutzendteich, this 200-site campground has all the fixin's—showers, a restaurant, a store, and even washing machines. Sites run DM 10, plus DM 5 per person. *Hans-Kalb-Str. 56, tel. 0911/811122. From Bahnhof, Tram 9 (direction: Luitpoldhain) to Meis-*

tersingerhalle, then Bus 55 (direction: Langwasser Mitte) to Beuthener Str.; backtrack to Hans-Kalb-Str. and go left. Closed Oct.–Apr.

FOOD

The pedestrian streets around Lorenzer Platz and the streets intersecting the Hauptmarkt boast the thickest concentration of traditional German eateries and elegant riverfront cafés. On sunny days, the setting of **Café Kiosk** (Bleichstr. 5, tel. 0911/269030), on the edge of Rosenau Park, is unbeatable; sip a beer or try one of the daily specials (DM 9–DM 12). If you're pressed for cash, walk a few blocks southeast of Museumsbrücke. *Imbiß* (snack) stands are the norm here, along with student-filled bars. **Roldi,** on the Hauptmarkt, stocks cheap groceries.

Balazzo Brozzi. A large, open eating area, creaky hardwood floors, and rotating art exhibits lend this bistro the feel of a gallery. Local students wolf down pasta and salads (all around DM 10). A bowl o' cappuccino is a steal at DM 3.30. *Hochstr. 2, tel. 0911/288482. From Spittlertor, north to Obere Turnstr., left to Hochstr. Closed first Mon. of each month.*

Star Club. Whether they come in through the window or the door, students fill this grungy dive to drink, play backgammon, or chow down on the legendary baguette sandwiches (at DM 5, the word gets around). Beer and Earl Grey flow into the wee hours, and a pleasant patio awaits out front. *Maxtorgraben 33, tel. 0911/551682. From Äußerer Laufer Pl., north along Maxtorgraben.*

Treibhaus. Artsy types, Harley lovers, and self-professed hipsters come to this popular hangout for breakfast (from DM 4), coffee and tea, and the daily specials of salads and sandwiches (DM 5–DM 9). *Karl-Grillenberger-Str. 28, at Mohrenstr., tel. 0911/22304.*

WORTH SEEING

Large sections of the walls surrounding the Altstadt were seriously damaged during World War II, but the network of moats, gateways, and watchtowers has since been lovingly restored. **Königstor** (King's Gate), opposite the train station, is a typical example of the wall's sturdy, centuries-old fortifications. Nestled behind the gate, the **Handwerkerhof** (closed Sun. and Dec. 24–Mar. 19) is meant to be just like a medieval artisans' courtyard. In other words, glassblowers, weavers, potters, and candle makers dress up in costume and hawk their goods at a heady price. It's worth a quick peek, but don't lose any sleep over it. English-language **walking tours** leave the Hauptmarkt tourist office daily at 2 May–October. The DM 12 fee includes admission to the Kaiserburg.

ALBRECHT-DÜRER-HAUS

This stunning house just west of Kaiserburg castle was formerly home to painter and wood engraver Albrecht Dürer, who is credited with almost singular responsibility for the emergence of German Renaissance art. He lived here from 1509 until his death in 1528, and his three-story pad is one of the best-preserved early modern relics in Nuremberg. The museum has recently added a multimedia show, as well as a number of Dürer's own creations, to the exhibit. *Albrecht-Dürer-Str. 39, tel. 0911/231–2568. Admission: DM 5, DM 2.50 students. Open Mar.–Oct. and during the Christkindlesmarkt, Tues.–Sun. 10–5, Thurs. until 8.*

ALTES RATHAUS

The highlight of Nuremberg's old town hall is the **Lochgefängnisse,** a group of underground dungeons that were hacked from damp rock and used for interrogation and torture from the 14th to the early 19th century; the tools of the trade are on display. Across from the *Rathaus* (town hall) is the 13th-century **Sebalduskirche,** a Gothic creation with a monster organ, and the first stop in Nuremberg for each Holy Roman Emperor. Occasional exhibits lend the place some avant-garde flair. *Lochgefängnisse: Tel. 0911/231–2690. Admission and required tour: DM 4, DM 2 students. Open Apr. 7–Oct. 30, Tues.–Sun. 10–4:30, Nov. 2–27, weekdays 10–4.30, and during the Christkindlesmarkt, daily 10–4:30.*

GERMANISCHES NATIONALMUSEUM

The sprawling Germanic National Museum of Art and Culture is dedicated to all aspects of German culture and history, from Stone Age Nurembergers to why Germans wear Lederhosen and eat salted cabbage and pretzels. Highlights include the German Renaissance exhibit (with works by Dürer and Cranach), the medieval pieces (manuscripts, altarpieces, stained glass, suits of armor), and the exhibit of antique and modern toys. Try to catch the free English tour, given at 2 PM on the first Sunday of every

KOMM INTO SUBCULTURE

Though just across the street from the Handwerkerhof, K4 im Künstlerhaus (short for Kunst, Kultur, Kino, and Kommunikation) stands worlds apart. Formerly known as KOMM, the center provides an alternative meeting place for artists, theatergoers, musicians, and even seniors with its disco, café, bar, and movie theater. It's worth checking out what's going on during your stay in Nuremberg. Drop by to pick up a copy of the K4 Programm, the monthly schedule of activities and showings. Königstr. 93, tel. 0911/223647.

month; otherwise, most of this stuff may remain a mystery to you. *Kornmarkt 1, tel. 0911/13310. Admission: DM 6, DM 3 students. Open Tues.–Sun. 10–5 (Wed. until 9).*

HAUPTMARKT

Nuremberg's central open-air market is a busy and colorful meeting place for old men, brawny fruit sellers, and tourists. In the center of the square look for the **Schöner Brunnen,** an elegant, 20-m-high fountain fashioned at the turn of the 15th century. It's adorned with more than 30 carved figures, including biblical prophets, Julius Caesar, and Alexander the Great. The **Frauenkirche,** which dominates the eastern side of the square, stands on the former site of the Nuremberg Synagogue. After the Jewish quarter was destroyed in a 1349 pogrom, Kaiser Karl IV gave the order to erect this church in its place. Today crowds gather daily at noon to watch the church's 16th-century **Männleinlaufen**—an especially elaborate cuckoo clock—do its thing. A parade of seven prince-bishops glides, spins, and bows to Karl while his musicians play in the background.

KAISERBURG

Towering over the city at the northern end of Burgstraße, this castle complex is comprised of three separate groups of buildings. To the east is the **Kaiserstallung,** the 15th-century imperial stables that now house the youth hostel. The castle itself occupies the westernmost part of the fortress. Inside, the **Doppelkapelle** (Double Chapel) reflects the stratification of medieval society in its two-tiered design. A paltry light filters into the austere lower-level **Margaretenkapelle,** the section reserved for the Great Unwashed, while the upper chapel, designated for privileged personalities, provides good ventilation, a view of the altar, and an entrance to the palace to boot. So much for equality in the eyes of the Lord. In the outer courtyard you'll wait a full five seconds to hear the sound of a drop of water echo back from the 50-m-deep **Tiefer Brunnen,** a 12th-century well shaft hacked into sandstone.

Climb to the top of the **Sinwellturm,** a round tower built right into the rock, for a good view of the site on your way down the hill. The Kaiserburg complex is open around the clock and admission is free, but to enter the castle itself you have to pay DM 6 for the required tour. *Tel. 0911/225726. Open Apr.–Sept., daily 9–noon and 12:45–5; Oct.–March, daily 9:30–noon and 12:45–4.*

LORENZER PLATZ

The **Lorenzkirche** (open Mon.–Sat. 9–5, Sun. 1–4) rises above this square a few blocks south of the Hauptmarkt and the River Pegnitz. Two towers flank the church, and its portal is covered floor to ceiling with ornate carvings. Inside, look for Veit Stoß's 1517 *Engelsgruß* (*Annunciation*), cut on the eve of the Reformation, at the height of the Mary cult in European art. Back on the square, the **Tugendbrunnen** (Fountain of Virtues) is popular for summertime water fights. Nuremberg's oldest dwelling, the **Nassauer Haus** (Lorenzer Pl. 6), is on the square's west side.

REICHSPARTEITAGSGELÄNDE

In the imagination of millions, the Nazi Party rally grounds—immortalized in Leni Riefenstahl's propaganda film *Triumph of the Will*—embody the very essence of evil. As testament to the power of the fascist aesthetic, images of the Reichsparteitage held here have remained an object of collective fascination. By 1938 the gatherings had developed into the most important demonstration of power available to the National Socialist regime—massive rallies of 750,000 participants with an audience of a half million. The grounds were transformed into a sprawling park soon after the war, but if you understand even rudimentary German, you can take the superb tour arranged by **Geschichte für Alle** (tel. 0911/332735). Tours (May–Sept.; DM 8, DM 6 students) meet weekends at 2 PM at Luitpoldhain, the last stop on Tram 9. Otherwise, take U1 or U11 (direction: Langwasser Süd) to Messezentrum and exit east on Otto-Bärnreuther-Straße. Turn left on Karl-Schönleben-Straße and you'll soon reach the southern tip of the **Große Straße** (Great Road), a 2-km-long, 60-m-wide road that points directly at the Kaiserburg, symbolically linking the First Reich with the Third. From the footpath on the right just before the lake, you'll see reflected in the water the New Congress Hall, an unfinished, oversized model of Rome's Colosseum, built with stone quarried by concentration camp prisoners. Continue along the footpath to the crumbling *Haupttribüne* (grandstands) of the Zeppelin field. In back lies the entrance to the exhibit ***Faszination und Gewalt*** (*Fascination and Violence*; admission DM 2, DM 1 students; open May 10–Oct. 31, Tues.–Sun. 10–6), including film clips of the rallies and anti-Semitic posters, flyers, and children's books.

CHEAP THRILLS

Architect Albert Speer designed the Große Straße for military-style marching. The width of the stones was equivalent to exactly two Prussian goose steps.

On sunny weekend afternoons, young teens flock to Albrecht-Dürer-Platz, which serves as a stage for the occasional musician. To join an older, blue-collar crowd, make your way to the beer gardens by the Reichsparteitagsgelände (*see above*). During the warmer months, what could be better than a visit to the ol' watering hole?: The **Naturgartenbad** (Schlegelstr. 20, tel. 0911/592545; admission DM 6, DM 3 students) outdoor swimming pool is *the* place to see and be seen. Before you go, make sure you're pierced in all the right places; **Sin-a-matic** (Ludwigspl. 1a, tel. 0911/230–5986) can do the job.

AFTER DARK

Nuremberg may be known and loved for its romantic Altstadt and historical treasures, but when the sun goes down, a modern university town rears its head. To get a handle on what's shaking, look for a copy of the free monthly *Doppelpunkt* in cafés and bars, or pick up the city magazine *Plärrer* (DM 3.80). Boogie down at **Mach 1** (Kaiserstr. 1–9, tel. 0911/203030; open Thurs.–Sat. 10 PM–4 AM), deemed one of the best clubs in Germany, for DM 8–DM 12. Catch live music—from techno to metal to Queen revival—at **Rockfabrik** (Klingenhofstr. 56; U2 to Herrnhütte). Pick up their bimonthly schedule at the Jugendgästehaus. Gays should head to the bookstore **Männertreu** (Bauerng. 14, tel. 0911/262676) and pick up a copy of the *Magnus Plan,* a map of gay spots in Nuremberg, as well as the *Nürnberger Schwulenpost,* a monthly with info on gay-oriented activities in town.

Café Ruhestörung. Laid-back, hip students and slightly pricey beer mix at the "Disturbance of the Peace." Sit on the patio out front or chill in the plant-filled interior. *Tetzelg. 21, tel. 0911/221921. Open weekdays 7:30 AM–1 AM, weekends 9:30 AM–1 AM.*

Irish Castle Pub. Head downstairs into the cellar for live music, or work your way toward the back for darts and some air. A casual crowd, heavily seasoned with English-speakers, munches pub grub and whoops it up with a pint of stout and a dram of whiskey. *Schleheng. 31, west of Jakobspl., tel. 0911/224878. Open Sun.–Thurs. 7 PM–1 AM, Fri. and Sat. until 2 AM.*

Jazz Studio. This homey jazz club nests in a stone cellar just down the street from the hostel. A mostly student audience soaks up the cool atmosphere, nurses red wine, and grooves. Shows (DM 10–DM 30) are generally on Friday and Saturday. Flash a student ID for a 20%–25% discount. *Paniersp1. 27–29, tel. 0911/224384.*

THEATER

Nuremberg's **Städtische Bühnen** (municipal theaters) include the Opernhaus, the Schauspielhaus, and the Kammerspiele, and between the three they put on everything from Shakespeare and ballet to Handke and Fassbinder. Students get great deals (50% discounts) at the box office one hour before each show. You can also get regular tickets at the record store WOM (Josephspl. 18, tel. 0911/204295).

The theaters are closed from the end of July to October. *Richard-Wagner-Pl. 2–10, tel. 0911/231–3808. Box office open weekdays 9–6, Sat. 9–1.*

ASCHAFFENBURG

There are two major reasons for stopping in Aschaffenburg: to blaze trails in the Spessart forest and to see even more German castles. Though it's now basically a suburb of Frankfurt, Aschaffenburg was once the second residence of the bishop of Mainz. The bishops took off in the 19th century, but their legacy remains in such grand works as the English-style Schönbuschpark garden and *Schlößchen* (little castle) across the Main, and Schloß Johannisburg, indisputably one of the finest examples of Renaissance architecture in Germany. Aschaffenburg is small enough to explore on foot, and you'll notice locals greeting each other on the market square and at bus stops. They'll probably even be friendly to you, especially now that the 8,000 American soldiers once stationed here have moved out.

Aschaffenburg is also a gateway to one of Germany's largest and least spoiled forests, the **Spessart Naturpark.** The forest contains scores of hiking trails, from short strolls to long-distance numbers like the **Eselweg,** a medieval footpath used by miners and their donkeys to transport salt between Miltenberg and Schlüchtern, about 80 km as the crow flies. The **Tourist-Information Spessart-Main-Odenwald** office (Bayernstr. 18, tel. 06021/394271) can help you plan your exploration, and the **Wanderheime des Spessartbundes** (Strickerg. 16a, tel. 06021/15224) sells detailed maps for about DM 13.

BASICS

To the left as you exit the train station, the **post office** has phones, exchanges money, and holds mail. The helpful staff at the **tourist office** (Schloßpl. 1, tel. 06021/395800; open weekdays 9–5, Sat. 10–1) will outfit you with free maps of the city and sells hiking/biking maps (DM 8) for Aschaffenburg and its surroundings. Snag copies of the free *Stadtmagazin* and *Kultur Extra* for comprehensive music and theater listings. **City tours** (DM 4) leave every second Sunday of the month at 2 PM (Apr.–Oct.) from the tourist office, next to Johannisburger Schloß. To get there from the train station, walk up Frohsinnstraße, go left on Weißenburgerstraße, cross the traffic island to Friedrichstraße, and head right on Luitpoldstraße. For answers on the Spessart Naturpark, talk to the park's tourist office (*see above*).

COMING AND GOING

Aschaffenburg's train station has hourly service to Nuremberg (3 hrs, DM 59), Frankfurt (40 min, DM 12), and Würzburg (1 hr, DM 22). The station has lockers and an ATM that accepts credit cards, Plus, and Cirrus.

WHERE TO SLEEP

Gasthof Goldener Karpfen. The Golden Carp may be old (built in 1691), but you'll be a happy little guppy in its clean, comfortable rooms, just a few minutes from the city center. Including breakfast, singles are DM 48, doubles DM 88. Three-bed rooms are available. *Löherstr. 20, tel. and fax 06021/23946. From Hauptbahnhof, Bus 4 to Löherstr.; or up Frohsinnstr., left on Weißenburger Str., cross traffic island to Friedrichstr., right at tower onto Herstallstr. (which turns into Dalbergstr.), left on Löherstr. 18 rooms, some with bath.*

Hotel Pape. Clean, simple singles and doubles run DM 50–DM 90, including breakfast but without private bathroom or shower. Call in advance. *Würzburgerstr. 16, tel. 06021/22673. 10 rooms.*

HOSTELS • The **HI-Jugendherberge,** a quick bus ride from the city center, is in an older house with clean rooms and firm mattresses. Beds go for DM 18, breakfast included. If they have room and it doesn't look like anyone else is likely to drop by, they'll house people over 27 here, but rooms aren't available until 5 PM, unless you've booked in advance. *Becherstr. 47, tel. 06021/930763, fax 06021/970694. From Hauptbahnhof, Bus 15 to Sülzerweg; backtrack to Würzburger Str., turn left, right on Gentilstr., left on Becherstr. 115 beds. Reception open until 10 PM.*

FOOD

The pedestrian zones around Steingasse and Sandgasse harbor a bunch of cheap cafés and restaurants. There's a fresh produce **market** on Schloßplatz Saturday and Wednesday 9–1, and the first floor of **Kaufhalle** (26–38 Herstallstr., at Roßmarkt) has cheap groceries. Locals of all ages congregate at the **Schlappeseppl** (Schloßg. 21, tel. 06021/25531; closed Sun.), a veritable Aschaffenburg institution, for traditional German food at reasonable prices and Schlappeseppl Beer, brewed on the premises. A slightly younger crowd frequents **Pasta al dente** (Treibg. 16, tel. 06021/28535; closed Sun.), which sports a Central American decor and a lively staff. Try gnocchi with gorgonzola cream sauce (DM 11) or *rigatoni arrabiati* (DM 9).

WORTH SEEING

Upon his election as archbishop of Mainz, Johann Schweickard von Kronberg began construction of **Schloß Johannisburg,** erected between 1605 and 1614 in late-Renaissance style. It is said that a few years later, Sweden's Gustavus Adolphus encountered the Woman in White here after conquering the city during the Thirty Years' War (back when the Swedes were still aggressors); a year to the day later, Adolphus met his end in battle. Though largely destroyed in World War II, the Schloß was rebuilt and now houses the **Schloßmuseum.** The museum's principal draw is a collection of masterpieces by Lucas Cranach the Elder and his school. The castle's east tower houses a carillon with 48 bronze bells, rung daily at 9:05, 12:05, and 5:05. On the first weekend in August, legions of renowned carillonneurs descend on the Schloß for the annual **Carillonfest.** *Schloßmuseum: Schloßpl. 4, tel. 06021/330446. Admission: DM 5. Open Tues.–Sun. 9–11:30 and 1–4:30 (in winter, 10–11:30 and 1–3:30).*

Just outside town is the English-style **Schönbusch Park,** first conceived on a whim of Carl Joseph von Erthal, archbishop of Mainz. The **Schlößchen,** a small summer palace built on the grounds in 1778, is open for guided tours. The interior decor has been carefully restored, and in the mirrored ballroom you can see the reflection of Schloß Johannisburg. The rest of the park is peaceful and lush, with towers, temples, and bridges behind every tree, and two lakes where you can rent boats (DM 5 per half hour). *Tel. 06021/221417. From Hauptbahnhof or Schloßpl., Bus 3 (direction: Waldfriedhof) to Schönbusch. Admission: DM 4, DM 3 students. Open mid-Mar.–mid-Oct., Tues.–Sun. 10–12:30 and 1:30–5.*

Stick to your tour guide: Schloß Johannisburg is said to be frequented by the specter of the Weiße Frau (Woman in White), whose appearances throughout Franconia have signaled coming disaster.

NEAR ASCHAFFENBURG

MILTENBERG

Half-timbered houses thickly concentrated between the mountain and the River Main, a handful of family breweries, and a 13th-century castle combine to create a village that is precious beyond measure. Since its founding in 1285, the town has become fairly touristy, but you can still immerse yourself in its half-timbered splendor. To do so, walk straight from the station down Brückenstraße, cross the bridge, go downstairs, and continue straight ahead until you reach the tourist office. Pick up a copy of their English-language booklet "Strolling Through Town" for DM 2, and then head west down Hauptstraße to the **Marktplatz,** with its red sandstone Renaissance fountain and the 16th-century **Weinhaus.** Continue down Haupstraße and you'll encounter Miltenberg's two family breweries: **Brauhaus Faust** (Hauptstr. 219, tel. 09371/97130) and **Kalt-Loch Brauerei** (Hauptstr. 201, tel. 09371/2283). If you manage to cull a group of 10 or more, you can take a tour (in German) of the Faust brewery every Saturday at 10:30 from April through October. It costs DM 8 per person, but included in the price are two glasses of the product for you to sample. If the tour is inconvenient (or your German rusty), you can still peek through the brewery windows at the huge copper vats and the bottle assembly line. If you liked the beer, be sure to stick around until the last week of August, when Miltenberg kicks off its annual **Michaelis Messe,** a lively folk festival marked by Franconian dance and plenty of the aforementioned.

To reach Miltenberg's main attraction, the 13th-century **Mildenburg** fortress, walk back to the Marktplatz, turn right, and go through the tiny passageway at the top of the hill. From here it's a pleasant five-min walk through a lush, peaceful forest to the castle, where you can cruise around the ancient walls and climb the tower's rickety stairs for a knockout view. Although the interior of the castle is temporarily inaccessible, the courtyard remains gloriously overrun by the surrounding forest. *Courtyard admission: DM 2. Open Tues.–Sun. 10:30–5:30.*

BASICS • Trains between Aschaffenburg and Miltenberg (40 min, DM 10) travel seven–eight times per day. The **tourist office** (Engelpl. 69, tel. 09371/404119), open weekdays 9–noon and 2–5 (and Saturdays 9:30–noon from May to Oct.) has a wealth of info about the nearby Spessart and Odenwald national forests and sells excellent hiking and biking maps. Rent **mountain bikes** at Sporthütte Wild (Untere Walldürnerstr. 11, tel. 09371/3154) at DM 27 per day.

WHERE TO SLEEP AND EAT • **Campingplatz Mainwiese** (tel. 09371/3985) is right under the Mainbrücke, across the river from the Altstadt. A grassy spot with a river view runs DM 8 plus DM 7.50 per person. If you want a room with your river view, head to **Hotel Mildenburg** (Mainstr. 77, tel. 09371/2733, fax 09371/80227). Singles start at DM 58, doubles at DM 98; some rooms have a bath; rates are sometimes lower in the off-season. **Café Bauer** (Hauptstr. 41, tel. 09371/2384; closed Mon.) has a shaded outdoor terrace with a fountain and offers *Weizenbier* (wheat beer) for DM 4.60 and baguettes with the works for DM 8.50. The grocery store **HL Markt** is on Brückenstraße between the train station and the bridge.

WÜRZBURG

Leafy vines shoot delicate green tendrils across the latticed hills around Würzburg, located along the banks of the River Main beneath the gaze of the imposing Marienberg fortress. Vines mean grapes, and so it's little surprise that Würzburg has made a name for itself as the heart of Germany's *Rosinenland,* or raisin country. Yet Würzburg's numerous and sizable wineries, and its annual **Weindorf** celebration, are at least equal to raisins, if not superior, as testament to the city's sublime transformative powers vis-à-vis that magical juice-nut known as the grape. Würzburg's 25,000 students supplement Dionysian attractions with a vibrant, eclectic nightlife and cultural scene, while the city's historic role as a seat of Catholic power has bequeathed the architectural wonders that make Würzburg a favored stop on the Romantic Road.

Würzburg's roots twine back to the late 7th century, and its annals are filled with names that together embody centuries of cultural and social trends: The minnesinger Walther von der Vogelweide (1170–1230) is buried behind Neumünster; the late Gothic sculptor Tilman Riemenschneider (1460–1531) served here as mayor and alderman; the masterful Baroque architect Balthasar Neumann (1687–1721) designed the Residenz, whose gilded Imperial Hall and gigantic ceiling above the main staircase were painted by Giovanni Battista Tiepolo (1696–1770); and in 1895 Wilhelm Conrad Röntgen (1845–1923) discovered the x-ray in Würzburg. The city loves cultural celebrations (*see* Festivals, *below*), but know that these draw bullying crowds in the summer, especially during the annual **Mozart Festival** (May 31–July 2, 2000); it's a good idea to make reservations ahead of time.

BASICS

The **ATM** in the train station takes credit cards, Plus, and Cirrus, or try any of the banks between the train station and the Markt, or around the Dom. The **main post office** (Bahnhofspl. 2) is across from the train station.

The **main tourist office** (Pavilion am Hauptbahnhof, tel. 0931/372436; closed Sun. and from mid-Dec. until the end of March) is just outside the train station; a second office (Haus zum Falken, Am Markt, tel. 0931/372398), open weekdays 10–6, weekends 10–2, sits on the central market square. Both stock free city maps, organize guided city tours, and will help you find a room in town for DM 2. For more alternative info, stop by the **Neuer Weg Buchladen** (Sanderg. 23), in the university district. There you can pick up the trendy *Trend!,* a comprehensive list of Würzburg's cultural offerings, and a brochure detailing gay-oriented activities published by the **Würzburger Schwulenzentrum** (Nigglweg 2, tel. 0931/412646).

COMING AND GOING

As the Romantische Straße's major northern hub, Würzburg is extremely easy to reach by train or bus. The local **Mitfahrzentrale** (Bahnhofvorpl. Ost, tel. 0931/19440), next to the Bahnhof, arranges rides to Berlin (DM 46), Munich (DM 30), Frankfurt (DM 15), and other destinations.

BY TRAIN • Würzburg has frequent rail connections to Nuremberg (1 hr, DM 28) and Frankfurt (1 hr 20 min, DM 41). The **Hauptbahnhof** is on the north edge of the Altstadt, a 15-min walk from the Markt, Würzburg's main town square. To reach the Markt and Schönbornstraße, Würzburg's pedestrian-only shopping avenue, walk out of the station and past the fountain, head south down Kaiserstraße, and hang a right on Juliuspromenade. Schönbornstraße is a block farther on the left.

BY BUS • Between April and Oct., Würzburg is serviced by the **Romantische Straße Bus** (also called EB 190; *see* Romantische Straße, *below*). One leaves the bus station (next to the rail depot) daily for Füssen and another heads for Frankfurt. Check at the station for times. No reservations are needed—just hop on the bus with the blue-green racing stripe.

WHERE TO SLEEP

Hotel-Pension Spehnkuch. Close to the train station, the Spehnkuch has tidy rooms with big, fluffy comforters for DM 90 (doubles) and DM 50 (singles), bountiful breakfast included. Ask the friendly proprietor for one of the two rooms with a balcony overlooking the woodsy courtyard. *Röntgenring 7, tel. 0931/54752. From Hauptbahnhof, right on Röntgenring. 7 rooms, none with bath. Reception open daily.*

Pension Siegel. At this pension, a few minutes' walk from the station, clean and simple doubles go for DM 89 (singles DM 46), including breakfast. Someone with artistic pretensions took a brush to the hallway walls and gave the unassuming place some colorful flair. *Reisgrubeng. 7, tel. 0931/52941 or 0931/52964, fax 0931/52967. From Hauptbahnhof, walk straight up Kaiserstr., left on Reisgrubeng. 15 rooms, none with bath. Reception open Mon.–Sat. 7 AM–2 PM and 5 PM–10 PM, Sun. 7 AM–12:30 PM and 6 PM–10 PM.*

HOSTELS • Jugendgästehaus Würzburg (HI). This cavernous hostel is nestled below Festung Marienberg on the Main's west bank. A bed costs DM 29, including breakfast and bed linens. Be sure to catch the last tram around midnight to make the 1 AM curfew. *Burkarderstr. 44, tel. 0931/42590, fax 0931/416862. From Hauptbahnhof, Tram 5 (direction: Heuchelhof) to Löwenbrücke; follow sign down steps, cross the street and go right; hostel is on the left after tunnel. 300 beds. Reception open 10 AM–1 AM. Luggage storage.*

FOOD

Würzburg's central market and the adjacent streets boast the usual concentration of Imbiß stands and tourist-geared beer halls. Cheapish food stands and greasy hole-in-the-wall joints also cluster around the train station and in the maze of streets around Sanderstraße and Münzstraße. The grocery store **Kupsch** is on Domstraße, one block west of the Dom. Würzburg is in the middle of Franconian wine heaven, and two of the area's largest vineyards serve their nectar at restaurants in town. **Juliusspital Weinstuben** (Juliuspromenade 19, tel. 0931/54080; closed Wed.) and **Bürgerspital zum Heiligen Geist** (Theaterstr., tel. 0931/13861; closed Tues.) dish out Franconian specialties for DM 15–DM 35. **Zum Lämmle** (Marienpl. 5, tel. 0931/54748; closed Sun.) serves enormous platters of traditional German fare—Schnitzel, fries, and salad for DM 13—to a diverse clientele seated on a leafy, sprawling patio.

For a cheaper meal in a less touristy atmosphere, follow the Straßenbahn tracks down Augustinerstraße until it becomes Sanderstraße. **Café Haupeltshofer** (Sanderstr., at Tiepolostr., tel. 0931/13417), a big, airy place with a lively crowd, serves lots of breakfast stuff (under DM 12) and hot specials for DM 5–DM 13. For great cheap German casseroles (*Auflauf*), stop by **Auflauf** (Peterpl. 5, tel. 0931/571343). Delicious medium-sized casseroles like broccoli garlic chicken or tomato basil mozzarella go for DM 10.90–DM 15.90.

WORTH SEEING

Stuffed between Würzburg's two main tourist sights, Festung Marienberg and the Residenz palace, are no less than 16 churches, five historic mansions, and a solid handful of galleries. Of the latter, don't miss the **Municipal Art Gallery** (Hofstr. 3, tel. 0931/322250; open Tues.–Fri. 10–5, weekends 10–1, admission free), which displays a good collection of 19th- and 20th-century Franconian art and sculpture—it's one of the few places you can see works by Kirchner and Heckel for free. On the same street is the rotating (and also free) collection of modern art at **Otto-Richter-Halle** (Hofstr. 11, tel. 0931/51552), open Tuesday–Friday 10–1 and 2–5, weekends 9–noon.

If you're going to tackle Würzburg's gaggle of sights, the excellent (and free) English-language walking map available from any tourist office is indispensable. Between April and October, guided **walking tours** in English leave from the Markt tourist office Tuesday–Saturday at 11 AM. The DM 13 (DM 10 students), two-hour tour encompasses nearly every sight in the city and includes admission to the Residenz (*see below*). Or you can go solo by renting a Walkman with tour cassette (DM 10, DM 50 deposit) at the Markt office.

FESTUNG MARIENBERG • Dominating Würzburg's skyline, the Marienberg fortress was home to generations of Würzburg prince-bishops from 1200 until the Residenz (*see below*) was completed in the 18th century (probably after one bright monarch got tired of panting up the hill). If you're pooped, take the bus; otherwise hoof it—half the fun of this place is the hike up the path that starts at St. Burkard (just north of the hostel) and runs up through the castle vineyards. The focal point of the fortress is the 8th-century **Marienkirche,** one of the oldest churches in Germany. The formidable Gustavus II of Sweden conquered the fortress in the Thirty Years' War. Afterwards, the Würzburg princes embarked on a campaign of mas-

NINETEEN MINUTES

On March 16, 1945—six weeks before Nazi Germany would surrender to the Allies—England's Royal Air Force launched a bombing run that nearly annihilated Würzburg. The reason for the attack is unclear; Würzburg had no heavy industry nor any military stationed within the city limits. But the weather conditions that day were brutally perfect, and in no more than 19 minutes 95% of Würzburg was in flames. When the blaze died down, only 7,000 of the town's 103,000 residents remained; the rest were either dead or evacuated. Many of the Residenz's treasures were saved, however, by Würzburgers with the foresight to move tapestries, furniture, and even the wall paneling to bomb shelters. When visiting the Residenz you may notice that the stunning rococo bedroom lacks a bed—they forgot where they buried it.

sive fortification. One major addition, the Armory, now houses the **Mainfränkisches Museum** (Main-Franconian Museum), whose collection includes the oeuvre of Tilman Riemenschneider and works by Tiepolo and Cranach the Elder. Outside, double-fluted staircases and fountains surround the **Berggarten,** chock-full of nothing but red roses and blessed with a sweeping view of the city. *Bus 19 (summer only) from west end of bridge. Museum admission: DM 5, DM 2.50 students. Open Tues.–Sun. 10–5 (off-season until 4). Fortress admission free. Berggarten open Mon. 9–3:30, Tues.–Sun. 9–4:30 (Nov.–Mar. from 10).*

MARKT • People come to Würzburg's central marketplace to soak up the sun on steamy summer days, and street vendors gather here to hawk fresh fruit, tourist trinkets, and an inexplicably large number of kitchen utensils. The square is surrounded by Baroque relics, including the **Haus zum Falken** (now home to a tourist office), whose original 18th-century facade is as rococo as they come. On the site of the former Jewish quarter, leveled in a 1349 pogrom, stands the late-Gothic **Marienkapelle.**

RESIDENZ • As one of the finest examples of Baroque architecture anywhere, the magnificent Würzburger Residenz has been deemed a UNESCO World Heritage Site. The palace is the brainchild of Baroque giant Balthasar Neumann, who designed the marbled, gold-covered, stucco-studded wonderland and began construction in 1720, when Prince-Bishop Johann Phillip Franz von Schönborn decided that the Festung Marienberg was no longer fit as a place from which to rule. One of the most dazzling features of the palace is the ornate **Treppenhaus,** the largest Baroque staircase in the country, which lies under the largest fresco in the world, Giovanni Tiepolo's *The Four Continents* (geography has come a long way since then). The figure of Tiepolo himself actually emerges from the painting, along with other superbly fashioned trompe l'oeils. Behind the palace stretch the manicured **Hofgarten** and the marble-and-stucco **Hofkirche** (palace chapel). *Residenzpl., tel. 0931/3551712. From Dom, east down Hofstr. Admission: DM 8 (tour included), DM 3.50 students; church and garden admission free. Open Apr.–Oct., Tues.–Sun. 9–5; Nov.–Mar., Tues.–Sun. 10–4. English tours available.*

Right below the Residenz is the candlelit **Staatlicher Hofkeller** (Stately Court Cellar; Residenzpl. 3, tel. 0931/305–0923, fax 0931/305–0966), where wines are aged in gigantic oak barrels, bottled in the distinctive *Bocksbeutel* (a flat, flask-like bottle), and served to discriminating palates. Though the Hofkeller survived the bombings of the Second World War unscathed thanks to its massive arched walls (which are covered with a fungus that is desirable in wine cellars), its extensive historic collection of wines was thoroughly looted by soldiers; today's locked-up stash was built up from scratch after the war. You can come by for a 45-min cellar and wine-tasting tour (DM 12); the two-hour tour (DM 32) lets you sample five selected estate wines as you listen to expert wine commentary. The cellar is open Monday–Thursday 7:30–noon and 12:30–4:15, Friday 7:30–noon and 12:30–2.

SCHOENBORNSTRASSE • Würzburg's pedestrian shopping avenue, filled with modern boutiques and cheesy cafés, runs north–south past the Markt. At the southern end of the street tower the twin spires of the 11th-century Romanesque **Dom. Neumünster,** built alongside the Dom, houses the tomb of the Irish missionary St. Killian, martyred in AD 689. Having just arrived in town, Killian promptly informed the ruler of the city, Duke Gosbert, that the duke's recent marriage to his brother's widow wasn't very Christian-like. The highly miffed Duchess hired a group of thugs who, presumably while Killian's angels weren't looking, slit the missionary's throat.

FESTIVALS

Würzburg kicks off summer with the **Weindorf** (late May–early June), when one and all charge hundreds of food and wine stands erected on the Marktplatz. Beginning near the end of May, Würzburg is host to the annual **Mozart Festival,** which lasts about six weeks. Get tickets well in advance (call the tourist office) if you'd like to attend the outdoor events and chamber music concerts. Also in late May, Würzburg jiggles to the rhythms of modern and traditional African tunes during the **Afrika Festival.** The 16-day Catholic holiday **Kilianivolksfest** starts on July 6—it's marked by Franconian music, beer tents, and the macabre practice of parading the bodily remains of poor St. Killian (*see above*) through the streets. In late September Würzburg takes on Munich's Oktoberfest with a little fête of its own: the **Winzerfest.** It's a lot like Munich's infamous bash, but many of the tents erected on Talarera (a meadow northwest of the old town) harbor sumptuous regional wine rather than beer.

AFTER DARK

Believe it or not, even the Romantic Road (*see* Romantische Straße, *below*) supports a decent night scene. If you'd like to go bar-hopping, head to the Sanderstraße, which is lined with a number of lively bars and clubs. Industrial **Standard** (Oberthürstr. 11a, tel. 0931/51140; open daily 10 AM–1 AM), one block east of Theaterstraße, attracts a mellow, funky crowd. Jazz lovers groove to the tunes at **Omnibus** (Theaterstr. 10, tel. 0931/56121), Würzburg's oldest jazz cellar. Anarchists boogie down at the **Autonomes Kulturzentrum Würzburg** (AKW) disco (Frankfurter Str. 87, tel. 0931/417800) Thursday–Saturday (cover up to DM 10), while techno freaks wig out at the legendary **Das Boot** (Veitshöchheimer Str., tel. 0931/14123; closed Mon. and Tues.), just past the Brücke zur deutschen Einheit.

ROMANTISCHE STRAßE

In a stroke of promotional genius, Germany's National Tourism Board designated a collection of medieval villages and scenic southern towns "The Romantic Road" in 1950. Most of these spots have in common beautiful architecture, narrow cobblestone streets, strong folk traditions, and lots of Old World charm. Today, the route has become one of the most heavily traveled regions in Germany. During the summer months, the tour buses start rolling, the hotels raise their prices, the souvenir stands stock up, and the hordes start coming, and coming, and coming. As well they should. Many of the route's destinations rank among the most interesting and beautiful sights in Germany, if not Europe. Beginning in Würzburg, the route encompasses some 30 towns before ending in Füssen along the German-Austrian border. The Franconian section is the route's heart, but skip back to Chapters 5 and 6 to find out about Munich and destinations in southern Bavaria. Tourist offices in Frankfurt, Munich, and Würzburg stock information on the entire road.

COMING AND GOING

Keep in mind that the "road" in "Romantic Road" is a tourist-industry fiction—the route does not cover a single, continuous road, or even a remotely linear path. The Deutsche Bahn (the national rail company) created a bus line that covers the entire route daily from April to October. Called the **Romantische Straße Bus,** or Europabus 190, the bus—easily recognized by the blue-green racing stripe on its side—has scheduled stops at every Romantic Road destination. Every morning one bus heads south from Frankfurt to Munich, with a connection to Füssen, and another heads north from Füssen to Dinkelsbühl, with a connection to Frankfurt; travelers are free to get on and off at any point along the route. In most towns, the bus stops only long enough to pick up new passengers; if you want to explore, you'll have to get off and pick up the bus again the next day. The Romantische Straße Bus works best as a supplement to the trains that actually do exist here (Würzburg, Rothenburg, and Nördlingen are accessible by rail), but trains can take much longer than the buses due to the many, many transfers. For holders of Eurail, Interrail, and Deutsche Bahn passes, the bus is free, free, free! . . . almost. There's a "processing fee" of DM 7 per day, and all passengers must pay DM 3 to store a suitcase underneath the bus. If you're a cyclist and don't feel like pedaling all 480 km of the Romantic Road, you can hook your bike onto the trailer on the back of the bus. For schedules and prices, stop by the tourist office in any Roman-

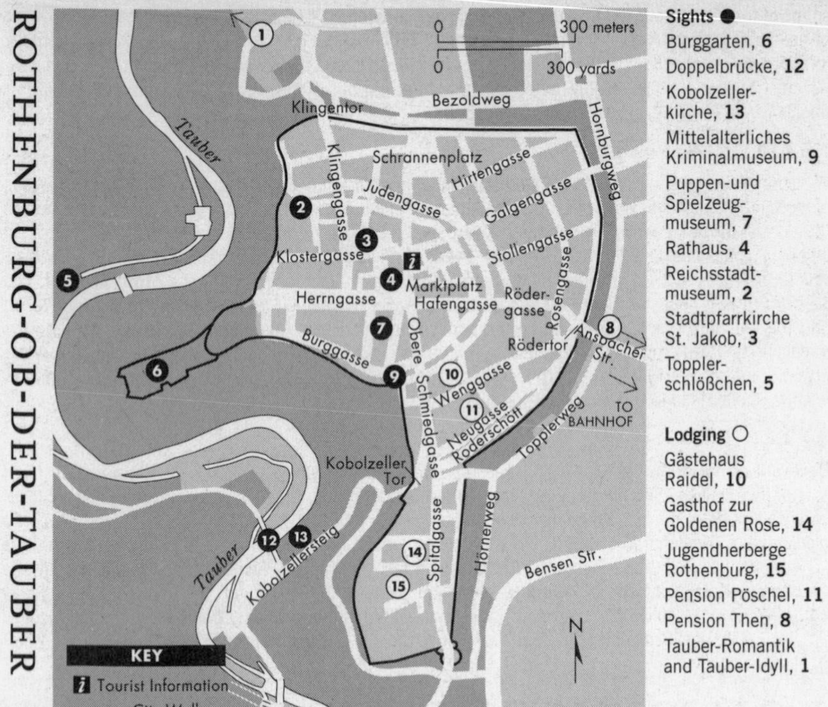

tic Road town, or contact **Deutsche Touring GmbH** (Am Römerhof 17, 60486 Frankfurt, tel. 069/790–3256, fax 069/790–3219).

ROTHENBURG-OB-DER-TAUBER

Tucked along the eastern bank of the Tauber River, Rothenburg-ob-der-Tauber, literally "the red castle on the Tauber," is best known for its compact Altstadt. Preserved inside the stout city wall is, quite simply, the most impressive medieval citadel anywhere. Honest. With not one modern building in the entire Altstadt, Rothenburg is easily the most evocative Romantische Straße destination. After the Thirty Years' War wreaked serious havoc on the region's economic base, Rothenburg foundered for centuries, impoverished and forgotten. Yet by the 1820s, the German romantics had "rediscovered" the town, and over the course of the 19th century, Rothenburg was transformed from a traveler's tip into an outright point of pilgrimage for the romantically inclined. These days, Rothenburg functions as nodal point for legions of sight-hoppers from Osaka, Milan, and Nashville, Tennessee. But if you just smile and accept the kitsch, you'll actually enjoy yourself.

BASICS

The **tourist office** (Marktpl., tel. 09861/40492) dishes out city maps, walking guides, and the useful English-language brochure "Rothenburg: Worth Seeing, Worth Knowing." The office can also arrange private rooms starting around DM 25. Open weekdays from May to October 9–12:30 and 1–6, Saturday and Sunday 10–1. In the off-season, it's open weekdays until 5 and Saturday until 1. You can exchange money at the Altstadt **post office** (Milchmarkt 5) or at the post office across from the train station.

COMING AND GOING

The **Hauptbahnhof** (tel. 09861/2330) is a 10-min walk from the Altstadt. Turn left out of the station, right on Ansbacher Straße, and pass through the 12th-century **Rödertor,** one of the oldest components of the old town wall. Trains go 8–10 times per day to Nuremberg (1½ hrs, DM 22) and Würzburg (1 hr,

DM 16.20). Destinations served by regional **buses,** which depart from the rail depot, include Feuchtwangen (3 daily, 2 hrs, DM 9) and Nuremberg (daily, 2 hrs, DM 10). Between April and October, Rothenburg is also serviced twice daily by the **Romantische Straße Bus** (*see above*).

WHERE TO SLEEP

The cheapest options are private rooms, which you can book at the tourist office. Otherwise try the affordable **Pension Then** (Johanniterg. 8a, tel. 09861/5177, fax 09861/86014), near the train station. Willy and Helene speak fluent English (Willy's V.P. of the local English conversation club), and they eagerly offer advice on what to do in town. With breakfast, doubles start at DM 70, singles at DM 40. An apartment with kitchen for four people costs DM 100 per day (three-day minimum) plus a one-time clean-up fee of DM 50. To get here, turn left from the train station, right on Ansbacher Straße, and right on Johannitergasse.

Within the town walls try **Gästehaus Raidel** (Wengg. 3, tel. 09861/3115), a few blocks south of Marktplatz. Comfortable doubles start at DM 69, singles at DM 35; three- to four-person rooms run DM 130 and DM 150 with bath and shower. Across the street in a 300-year-old house you'll find **Pension Pöschel** (Wengg. 22, tel. 09861/3430). This small inn has doubles with breakfast starting at DM 60 and singles for DM 35. Near the hostel, rooms in the 220-year-old main house of **Gasthof zur Goldenen Rose** (Spitalg. 28, tel. 09861/4638, fax 09861/86417; closed Jan.–Feb.) start at DM 35 for a single the size of a closet, DM 65 for a double, DM 90 for a triple, and DM 190 for a "family apartment" with bath and shower.

HOSTELS • Jugendherberge Rothenburg (HI). The hostel's reception office is located in a 500-year-old *Rossmühle* (horse-powered mill). Combined with the new Spitalhof annex, this thoroughly renovated establishment, conveniently located mere minutes from the Marktplatz, offers 188 beds (DM 22, DM 27 in a double, both with breakfast), no less than three Ping-Pong tables, a disco, and a TV room where you can watch movies for free. Reception hours are 7–midnight. If there's room, they may house those over 26. It's best to call a few days in advance. *Mühlacker 1, tel. 09861/94160, fax 09861/941620. Curfew 11:30 PM. Luggage storage.*

CAMPING • The two campsites closest to Rothenburg are about 1.2 km away in the village of Detwang. Grassy, tree-enclosed **Tauber-Idyll** (tel. 09861/3177) is smaller, cheaper, and better, with sites for DM 6.50 per person and DM 6 per tent. Idyll lies right on the Tauber River (really a creek), while **Tauber-Romantik** (Detwang 39, tel. 09861/6191) is on a fairly busy street. Romantik will set you back DM 7.50 per person and DM 8 per tent, but you get a communal kitchen and washing machines. To reach either campground, exit the Altstadt at Klingentor gate and proceed straight, following the DETWANG signs. Follow the footpath that veers to the left away from the road, cross two major streets, and enter Detwang proper. To reach Romantik, descend the stairs, turn right a few steps *before* the yellow Gasthof Schwarzes Lamm, and continue for 100 m; for Idyll turn right *after* the Gasthof.

Once you've wandered around medieval Creglingen, try to stop by the **Hergottskirche** (Lord's Chapel) to see the 16th-century wooden altar by master carver Tilmann Riemenschneider; you might also poke your head into the town's prized possession across the road from the chapel, the **Fingerhutmuseum** (thimble museum). For more info contact Creglingen's **tourist office** (Klaus Hein, Postfach 20, 97993 Creglingen, tel. and fax 07933/631).

FOOD

The Altstadt contains the best selection of cafés and restaurants, but little within the walls is particularly cheap. For groceries stop by **Kupsch** at the base of the Rödertor. Nearby **Adria Pizzeria-Restaurant** (Röderg. 36, tel. 09861/7478) has Germanized pizza and pasta for less than DM 15. For excellent Franconian wine (DM 5–DM 8), you can go to hell—to **Zur Höll** (Burgg. 8, tel. 09861/4229) that is, where vino is sampled in Rothenburg's oldest house. One of the few places with rock-bottom prices is **Albig's Imbiß** (Hafeng. 2); burgers and fries and Döner Kebab are about DM 10. After the sun sets, leave the city walls behind and make tracks for the **Traumfabrik** (Ansbacher Str. 15, through the tunnel). Industrial decor and a young, hip, local crew make this bar a great place to quaff beer and rest your battered feet until 1 AM (Fri. and Sat. until 2 AM).

WORTH SEEING

Rothenburg is ringed by a **city wall,** which stretches for nearly a mile around the perfectly preserved medieval citadel. Most of the wall dates from 1350–1380, though only two of the remaining 25 towers are original; the others date from the 16th and 17th centuries. For an insightful overview of the city, join one of the tourist office's **walking tours.** Between April and October, German-language tours (DM 5)

HITTING THE HAY IN CREGLINGEN

Technically it's not in Franconia, but the **Heuhotel** *on the outskirts of Creglingen (Baden-Württemberg), just 20 km northwest of Rothenburg on the Romantic Road, is a perfect spot to find out the origin of the expression to hit the hay (see A Roll in the Hay box in Chapter 14). The hospitable Familie Stahl has converted the attic of their 300-year-old farm into a slumber spot for up to 25 nonfussy guests; they'll pick you up in downtown Creglingen, give you sheets and a sleeping bag, and show you to your hay pile. Make sure you even out the hay before you lie down—you'll wake up with a mighty backache otherwise. (Allergic types can find refuge in a downstairs room with a mattress-bed.) In the morning, you'll get a generous farmer's breakfast with homemade bread, cheeses, and sausages; in the evening you might ask for a shot of home-made Zwetschgenschnaps (plum brandy) before you take a walk through the fields. A night (including breakfast) costs DM 28 per person. Ferienbauernhof/Heuhotel Stahl, Weidenhof 1, 97993 Creglingen, tel. 07933/378, fax 07933/7515, e-mail: ferien-heuhotel@t-online.de.*

leave daily from the Marktplatz at 11 and 2, and English-language tours (DM 6) leave daily at 2. Leaving at 8 PM are tours in English led by a night watchman who hobbles through town with a lantern and a bag of stories; the German tour starts an hour later.

BURGGARTEN • At the westernmost point within the city wall, the castle garden marks what was once the site of King Conrad II's imperial castle, erected in 1142. An earthquake in 1356 destroyed all of the castle's buildings except the **Blasiuskapelle,** which remains in the garden today. Step inside to view the tiny chapel's fading 14th-century murals and the 20th-century dedication to Rothenburg's war dead. The park remains relatively quiet, even in summer, and offers stunning views of the town's southern skyline and the picturesque Tauber Valley; consider a picnic along the city wall.

MARKTPLATZ • The 13th-century **Rathaus** dominates Rothenburg's pedestrian-only market square. In the building's basement vaults, the **Historiengewölbe** museum charts the city's history, and houses former torture chambers and prison cells used as air-raid shelters in World War II. Much ado is also made of the so-called *Meistertrunk,* or Master Draught. According to legend, when Protestant Rothenburg was captured by Catholic troops during the Thirty Years' War, the conquering general found he could not down a six-pint tankard of wine, a town tradition. The general offered to spare Rothenburg if any of the captured town councilors could manage the feat. Mayor Nüsch stepped up, downed the full 3.25 liters with a single *Schluck,* burped, and saved the town. The **Meistertrunk clock** on the exterior of the **Ratstrinkstube** (councilor's tavern), on the square's north side, performs a mechanical reenactment of the event every hour 11–3 and 8–10. *Museum admission: DM 3, DM 2 students. Rathaus and museum open May–Sept., daily 9–6; mid-Mar.–Apr. and Oct.–mid-Nov., daily 10–5.*

MITTELALTERLICHES KRIMINALMUSEUM • Rothenburg's criminal museum is dedicated to medieval legal procedures and—the real reason it's so popular—medieval criminal punishment (i.e., torture). There's an impressive array of instruments here, from thumb screws and executioners' axes to spiked whips, masks of shame, and the famed Iron Maiden. Equally fascinating is the extensive collection of public ordinances (which went so far as to regulate the type and cost of gifts to be given at weddings) that marked Germany's emergence as a well-ordered police state. This museum is not to be missed. *Burgg. 3, tel. 09861/5359. Admission: DM 5, DM 4 students. Open Apr.–Oct., daily 10–6; Nov.–Feb., daily 2–4; Mar., daily 9:30–4.*

PUPPEN- UND SPIELZEUGMUSEUM • The famous puppet and toy museum epitomizes Rothenburg's fixation with all things unbearably cute. Inside are antique Legos, octogenarian teddy bears, and little playhouses Barbie would die for. *Hofbronneng. 11–13, tel. 09861/7330. Admission: DM 5, DM 3.50 students. Open Jan–Feb., daily 11–5; Mar.–Dec., daily 9:30–6.*

REICHSSTADTMUSEUM • The Imperial City Museum displays the original tankard used in the Meistertrunk (probability of authenticity: 1%), paintings and church statuary by Rothenburg's finest, and—the frenzied thrill-a-minute pace continues with—Germany's oldest kitchen. Creep down into the cellar and you'll find what is left of Rothenburg's Jewish cemetery, as well as an exhibit on the history of the town's Jewish residents. *Klosterhof 5, tel. 09861/40458. Admission: DM 4, DM 3 students. Open Apr.–Oct., daily 9:30–5:30; Nov.–Mar., daily 1–4.*

STADTPFARRKIRCHE ST. JAKOB • Northwest of Marktplatz, this church looms large on the horizon with its massive Gothic body and towering spires. Construction began in 1311, and during the Middle Ages it became a destination for pilgrims intent on prostrating themselves before the church's reliquary. Of particular note are Tilman Riemenschneider's *Heiliges Blut* (Holy Blood) altar and, above the altar, a crystal capsule said to contain a drop of Christ's blood. *Klingeng. Admission: DM 2.50, DM 1 students. Open Apr.–Oct., daily 9–5:30 (shorter hrs off-season).*

TAUBER VALLEY • If the clicking of tourists' cameras is driving you mad, take leave of the city walls down in the scenic Tauber Valley. Paths lead out from the south side of the Burggarten, the Kobolzeller Tor (right off Plönleinstr.), and behind the criminal museum. At the north end of the valley lies tiny **Toplerschlößchen** (Toppler's Little Castle; admission DM 2), replete with minuscule moat and dinky drawbridge. The Schlößchen served as a summer home for Rothenburg's most beloved mayor, Heinrich Toppler, in the 14th century. Although it's officially open only Friday–Sunday 1–4, give a holler and chances are that Heinz Boaz, whose great-grandfather once owned the place, will hobble out of his garden and give you a personal tour. Unfortunately, Heinz speaks only German, but his cats are still cute. To reach the castle, exit the Burggarten on the south side, keep going to the right and down, cross the bridge, and turn left. To prolong your escape from Rothenburg's surreality, go back over the bridge, turn right, and follow the meandering paths south along the river. You'll find lush greenery and the late-Gothic **Kobolzellerkirche,** which was plundered in 1525 and clearly has yet to recover. Nearby is the 14th-century **Doppelbrücke** (double bridge).

FESTIVALS

Nothing brings Rothenburg's history to life like a performance of *Der Meistertrunk,* staged in the Rathaus daily during Pentecost (the end of May), then once per month June–October. The play reenacts Rothenburg's close call during the Thirty Years' War (*see* Marktplatz, *above*). Also during Pentecost, and on periodic weekends throughout the year, townsfolk don shepherd's garb, parade through the streets, and boogie down on the Marktplatz. The **Schäfertanz,** as it's known, recalls yet another escape from near-certain mass death. It seems that the town's shepherds, endowed in medieval times with particularly spectacular rhythm, stomped, waltzed, and moshed the Black Death right out of Rothenburg. All this merriment comes to a head during the **Imperial City Festival** bonanza, during the first weekend in September. Lucky travelers can witness the *Meistertrunk,* the shepherd dance, and a fireworks show over the Tauber Valley. The **Weihnachtsmarkt** (Christmas market) sprouts four weeks before Christmas and offers what Rothenburg knows best—kitsch and charm. Cute wooden stalls line the dimly lit streets, offering everything from tree ornaments to mulled wine.

DINKELSBÜHL

Completely untouched by the ravages of World War II (unlike Augsburg, Würzburg, and Rothenburg), little Dinkelsbühl harbors medieval streets, fortifications, and houses that haven't changed one iota in centuries. A constant influx of wealthy tourists hasn't marred the town's rural tone either. Dinkelsbühl's main draws are its medieval town wall, complete with 19 towers, and the late-Gothic **Stadtpfarrkirche St. Georg,** on the Marktplatz. Church tower connoisseurs can climb St. Georg's 66-m tower (admission DM 3, DM 1.50 students) for a stunning view of the town's red-tile roofs and the surrounding fortifications. Tower admission hours are irregular but summer weekends are a pretty good bet. Across the street from the church sits the 15th-century **Deutsches Haus** (Marktpl.) and, to the west on Segringer Straße, the Baroque **Neues Rathaus.** Give them a once-over and then devote the rest of your time to getting lost in the town's crooked alleys. If you catch yourself taking centuries-old quaintness for granted, you'll warp right back into the present at Dinkelsbühl's **Museum of Three Dimensions.** Housed in a 15th-century battlement, the museum has four floors of computer-generated optical illusions, interactive 3-D exhibits, and even those old plastic 3-D ViewMasters you thought were the apex of technology as a kid. Save a whopping DM 1 off the steep DM 10 admission by flashing a flyer from the info office or a student ID. *Nördlinger Tor, at end of Nördlinger Str., tel. 09851/6336. Open Apr.–Oct., daily 10–6; Nov.–Mar., weekends only 11–4.*

Dinkelsbühl hosts one of the most interesting and best-known historical festivals in southern Germany, the 10-day **Kinderzeche** (Children's Pageant), held in mid-July. This festival celebrates the deliverance of the town during the Thirty Years' War. According to local legend, when Swedish troops laid siege to Dinkelsbühl, a contingent of the town's children went to ingratiate themselves with the enemy general, who soon decided to spare the town. Festival highlights include a parade of townspeople in costume, historic performances, and an endless flood of beer and food. The kitsch-o-meter will be running high, and visitors will far outnumber residents, but it's worth the trouble.

BASICS

The **tourist office** sells a basic walking guide for 50 Pf, or a more elaborate guide with glossy photos for DM 5. Aimless rambles are free. The staff books rooms for a DM 4 fee, plus an 8% deposit. *Marktpl., tel. 09851/90240. Open Apr.–Oct., weekdays 9–noon and 2–6, Sat. 10–1 and 2–4, Sun. 10–1; Nov.–Mar., weekdays 9–noon and 2–5, Sat. 10–1.*

COMING AND GOING

Between April and October, Dinkelsbühl is serviced by the **Romantische Straße Bus** (*see above*), and regular bus service reaches Nördlingen (40 min, DM 8) and Rothenburg (1 hr 50 min, DM 10). Dinkelsbühl's train depot is serviced irregularly by a slowpoke steam engine that runs to Nördlingen one or two Sundays per month in summer. For info, call 09081/9808 or inquire at the tourist office. If you're of the rustic persuasion, hop into a horse-drawn carriage outside the tourist office (DM 8 per person during the summer).

WHERE TO SLEEP AND EAT

For a small, clean room in the heart of the Altstadt, try **Gasthof Sonne** (Weinmarkt 11, tel. 09851/57670, fax 09851/7548). Doubles start at DM 70, singles at DM 45, breakfast included; expect to pay a bit more should you wish to bathe (DM 89 and DM 65). Housed in the 14th-century Kornhaus, **HI-Jugendherberge Dinkelsbühl** (Koppeng. 10, tel. 09851/9509, fax 09851/4874; closed Nov.–Feb.) charges DM 18 for one of its 148 beds and breakfast. Call to check availability and the mood of the staff. Check-in is only 5 PM–7 PM, but make reservations anytime. To get there from the tourist office, head west down Segringer Straße, right on Bauhofstraße, and left on Koppengasse.

Campers should hike 20 min northeast of the Altstadt to **DCC Campingplatz "Romantische Straße"** (Dürrwanger Str., tel. and fax 09851/7817), which is open all year. Exit the town wall at Wörnitz Tor, cross the two bridges, and then veer left onto the side of Route B 25. After a few minutes, turn right on Dürrwanger Straße, and the campground will be on your right. A site costs DM 16.50 plus DM 7.50 per person. For enormous platters of pasta and pizza for about DM 10 and outstanding tiramisù (DM 4.50), head to **Zum Koppen** (Segringer Str. 38, tel. 09851/9504). The only grocery store in the Altstadt is **Gobi,** on Nördlinger Straße.

NÖRDLINGEN

Like most Romantische Straße destinations, the mid-size town of Nördlingen has its share of half-timbered homes, cobblestoned squares, and an impressive spire-capped church. Unlike its touristy brethren, however, rural Nördlingen remains a mellow farming community where the friendly townsfolk know their local butcher and baker by name. Nördlingen sits in a crater (called the **Ries**) formed 15 million years ago when a meteor 1.2 km in diameter smashed into the earth. A lake filled the crater, later dried up, and left behind mountains of fertile soil—as well as some stark, moonlike stretches. The history of the Ries, quite a few meteorites, and even a moon rock brought back by Apollo 16 are all on display in the **Rieskrater Museum** (Eugene-Shoemakerpl. 1, tel. 09081/273–8220; closed Mon.). Once you've paid the DM 5 (DM 2.50 students) to enter the museum, break out your German dictionary—everything's *auf Deutsch.*

Along with a connection to outer space lacking in most Romantic Road towns, Nördlingen has the only completely intact city wall in Germany. At nightfall sentries make a quick inspection along the wall and then climb to the top of the **Daniel**—St. Georgskirche's 100-m-high tower in the exact center of town—to cry *"So G'sell so"* ("All's well"). They've done this nightly at half-hour intervals between 10 PM and midnight ever since an alert townsperson thwarted the Swedish onslaught during the Thirty Years' War. On a clear day, the view from the top of the Daniel (admission DM 3; open daily Apr.–Oct. 9–8, Nov.–Mar. 9–5) is great. From here, you might be able to discern the boundaries of the Ries.

BASICS

For an English-language walking guide (50 Pf) with detailed information about some of the town's structures, head to the **tourist office** (Marktpl. 2, tel. 09081/84116; open in summer Mon.–Thurs. 9–6, Fri. 9–4:30, Sat. 9:30–1; in winter Mon.–Thurs. 9–5, Fri. 9–4:30, Sat. 9:30–1) behind the Rathaus. German-language **walking tours** (DM 4) leave the office daily at 2 PM in summer. To get here from the train station, exit right and go left on Wemdinger Straße, through the city gate and the following square. Go left on Schrannenstraße, right at the fountain, and keep to your right as you walk through the Marktplatz.

COMING AND GOING

From Nördlingen's **train station** there are daily connections to Stuttgart (2 hrs, DM 31), Nuremberg (2 hrs, DM 34), and Augsburg (1 hr, DM 19.40). Nördlingen is also serviced twice daily by the **Romantische Straße Bus** (*see above*). The Bahnhof has only a few lockers; if they're all taken or you don't feel like donating another DM 4 to the German railroad system, lug your bags to the tourist office (*see above*), where they'll hold them for free. Bikes can be rented for DM 10–DM 15 per day at **Zweirad-Müller** (Gewerbestr. 16, tel. 09081/5675).

When the meteor hit what is now southern Germany, it created an explosion 250,000 times greater than that of the atomic bomb dropped on Hiroshima. The result: a barren, rock-strewn moonscape where NASA trained its astronauts for their landing on that great luminous ball of cheese in the sky.

WHERE TO SLEEP AND EAT

If you're under 27, the cheapest accommodations in town can be found at **HI-Jugendherberge Nördlingen** (Kaiserwiese 1, tel. 09081/271816; closed Nov.–Feb.), just outside the city wall. One of its 104 beds costs DM 18, the reception is open 4:30 PM–7 PM, and curfew is 10 PM. From the Marktplatz, it's a 15-min walk north up Baldinger Straße and through the Baldinger Tor, where you'll see signs directing you to the hostel. One of the best-located hotels in town is **Hotel Altreuter** (Marktpl. 11, tel. 09081/4319, fax 09081/9797), directly across from the Daniel. It offers singles from DM 65 and doubles for DM 98 with private bath and shower. All rooms come with a a breakfast buffet in the elegant café downstairs. Leave your window open at night and listen for the watchman's cry—the signal that you need not fear, at least for now, the dark machinations of those pesky Swedes.

Dine with the locals in the cozy **Sixenbräu-Stüble** (Bergerstr. 17, tel. 09081/3101; closed Mon.), where DM 8–DM 15 exerts a buying power to be reckoned with in the Bavarian food department. For veggie fare, stop by **Ristorante Italia** (Hallg. 2, tel. 09081/1479); pizza and pasta start at around DM 9. For groceries try **Aldi** next to the train station.

OBERFRANKEN

At first glance, Oberfranken (Upper Franconia) may seem little different from its sister regions, Unterfranken and Mittelfranken. Yet Oberfranken does retain a certain distinctiveness. As opposed to their manically engaged neighbors, Oberfrankeners proffer a stance of relaxed equanimity. Nor has Oberfranken sold its soil to the wine-god Bacchus. But worry not: If the Weinstraße ends in Unterfranken's Würzburg, the Bierstraße picks up in Oberfranken's lovely **Bamberg,** and the route continues through tiny **Kulmbach,** whose Doppelbock Kulminator packs the strongest wallop in the world. In Oberfranken you will also find the winding trails and meandering streams of the **Fränkische Schweiz** and the birthplace of modern opera in Richard Wagner's **Bayreuth.** You won't see many foreign tourists here, but in summer you'll share the area with an oppressive number of native fun-seekers, mostly of the walking-stick and wads-of-cash variety. To avoid them, hit the trails, stay away from Wagner festivals, and make detours around the swanky shopping avenues.

BAYREUTH

Depending on your perspective, Bayreuth is blessed or plagued with a yearly Richard Wagner festival, the first of which was held in 1876. During this hoity-toity summer fest, the town's abuzz with opera junkies who reserved their expensive tickets (up to DM 230) literally years in advance. The influx of high-culture fiends means lodging becomes impossible to find, restaurants overflow, and prices rocket into the stratosphere. Other than Wagner's legacy and his music, the town's "excitement" derives from local sports teams, the city's 5,000-student university, and the Maisel Brewery, which cooks up Germany's leading diabetic beer (yuck).

BASICS

Outside the train station, Bahnhofstraße and Luitpoldplatz are loaded with banks, many of which have ATMs. Try **Schmidt Bank** (Luitpoldpl. 15, tel. 0921/23041) unless you're depending on Visa, in which case you should head to the 24-hour ATM outside **Citibank** (Opernstr. 2, tel. 0921/66099). At the **main post office** (Bürgerreuther Str. 1), across from the train station, you can buy stamps, send a telegram, and make international calls.

Gästedienst des Fremdenverkehrsvereins is a travel agency and tourist office that provides free city maps and makes private room reservations for a DM 5 fee. They offer tips on attending performances and Wagner festival events, but don't sell tickets. *Luitpoldpl. 9, tel. 0921/88588, fax 0921/88555. From Hauptbahnhof, left on Bahnhofstr. (which becomes Luitpoldpl.). Open weekdays 9–6, Sat. 9:30–1.*

COMING AND GOING

Bayreuth's **train station** is a 10-min walk from the old town. From the depot, turn left onto Bahnhofstraße (which turns into Luitpoldpl.) and left again when it dead-ends at Opernstraße. From here trains leave hourly for Nuremberg (1 hr, DM 24.20), Bamberg (1 hr 50 min, DM 24.20), Coburg (1 hr 20 min, DM 22), and Munich (3 hrs, DM 94), and six times daily for Berlin (7 hrs, check for current price). Kulmbach is only 40 min (trains run hourly) and DM 9.80 away. Regional buses depart from outside the Hauptbahnhof. Lock your things in a station locker, or leave them in the small lockers at the bus stop on the Markt.

WHERE TO SLEEP

Don't bother coming from mid-July through August unless you've booked months in advance. Unfortunately, private rooms (DM 40–DM 70) are expensive and fairly hard to come by. During summer the hostel sometimes opens its yard to tent campers, but you have to negotiate the price for the use of indoor facilities. Peaceful **Gasthof Kropf** (Tristanstr. 8, tel. 0921/26298) lies in a lush garden minutes from the Festspielhaus. Singles go for DM 40–DM 90, doubles DM 80–DM 140. To get here from the train station, turn right and walk north on Bürgerreuther Straße, right on Gravenreutherstraße, and left on Tristanstraße. A short bus ride from Marktplatz is **Gasthof Zum Brandenburger** (St. Georgen 9, tel. 0921/789060; Bus 1 from Markt to St. Georgen), which sports 20 well-kept rooms and its own beer garden (closed Sat.). Singles cost DM 35–DM 70 and doubles DM 60–DM 130.

HOSTELS • Jugendherberge Bayreuth (HI). "The younger the better" could be the motto here. Luckily, the hostel is sort of within walking distance of the Altstadt (20 min away) and next door to a huge pool and sports complex where you can swim, shoot hoops, or play sand volleyball. For DM 20 you get half of a wooden bunk bed plus breakfast. Grab a key (DM 50 deposit) to beat the 10 PM curfew. *Universitätsstr. 28, tel. 0921/251262. From the Markt, Bus 4 or 18 (direction: Birken/Uni) to Kreuzsteinbad; continue 300 m on Universitätsstr.; hostel is on right just after pool complex. 150 beds. Lockout 9 AM–noon. Kitchen, small lockers. Closed Dec. 20–Feb. 1.*

FOOD

Dozens of street stands litter Bayreuth's Altstadt, especially on Maximilianstraße and Richard-Wagner-Straße. Just off Maximilianstraße is the quiet **Café Florian** (Dammallee 12a, tel. 0921/56757), where students while away quiet hours with newspapers and backgammon boards. Order a sandwich, salad, or meat plate and you won't have to move all day. Fill up on veggie chili (DM 6.60) and a wide range of salads at the comfy **Rosa Rosa** (von-Römer-Str. 2, tel. 0921/68502), or fall in line with Bayreuth's younger population on an evening pilgrimage to the massive beer garden at **Herzogkeller** (Hindenburgstr., tel. 0921/43419). Zee French cuisine for zee backpackeurs? *Mais oui!* The onomatopoetically named **Miamiam-Glouglou** (von-Römer-Str. 28, tel. 0921/65666) offers surprisingly inexpensive French food and candlelit tables to boot. The huge salade Niçoise is well worth the DM 10 price, and the quiche Lorraine is a steal at DM 5. For espresso and ice cream in the Altstadt, head for **Eiscafé Venezia** (Maximilianstr. 49, tel. 0921/65246). All of the above are open daily.

WORTH SEEING

Bayreuth's Altstadt is compact, and all the sights are within easy walking distance of one another. For a quick overview, turn right from the tourist office and left onto Opernstraße; the street passes the opera house and curves to meet Richard-Wagner-Straße on your left and Maximilianstraße on your right. The former leads past some snazzy shops and the Richard Wagner museum; the latter leads toward the Rathaus, Altes Schloß, and the pedestrian alleys around Spitalkirche.

ALTES SCHLOSS EREMITAGE • Not to be confused with the princely *Altes Schloß* (old castle) on Bayreuth's Maximilianstraße, this is a cozy little castle 5 km east of Bayreuth. Soon after it was built in the 18th century, Margravine Wilhelmina—sister of Frederick the Great of Bavaria, wife of the margrave (marquis) of Brandenburg—got her artsy hands on the place and completely redecorated. The bland exterior belies a sumptuous rococo interior, lavished with gilded panels and fluffy, puffy furniture. The surrounding garden and park (with fountains that spout hourly) alone are worth the trip. In summer the on-site **Römisches Theater** presents Shakespeare (in German) and other international works most nights at 8:30. Tickets cost DM 15 (DM 10 students) and are available at the box office. *Eremitage 1, tel. 0921/92561. From the Markt, Bus 2 (direction: St. Johannis) to Eremitage. Admission and required tour: DM 5, DM 4 students. Open Apr.–Sept., Tues.–Sun. 9–11:30 and 1–4:30; Oct. and Mar., 10–11:30 and 1–2:30; Closed Nov.–Apr. 15.*

FESTSPIELHAUS • Wagner designed and largely financed this vast and austere opera house, which held its first public performance in 1876. The spartan look is partly due to Wagner's grim financial state (he was generally on the verge of bankruptcy) and partly due to his desire to achieve perfect acoustics. Nowadays, the theater stands alone on a hill, a temple for the nearly 2,000 tough-bunned Wagner worshipers who endure in their finest finery every July and August a whopping 30 performances of Wagner on unpadded wooden seats. If you haven't bought tickets one to two years in advance, don't even dream of catching a summer show, but the rest of the year, ask the tourist office about tickets. *Auf dem Grünen Hügel, tel. 0921/78780. From the Hauptbahnhof, turn right and walk straight. From the Markt, Bus 7 to Festspielhaus. Admission and required tour: DM 3, DM 1.50 students. Tours Tues.–Sun. at 10, 10:45, 2:15, and 3. Closed during Festspiel and Nov.*

HAUS WAHNFRIED • Wagner owned only one house in his entire life, Bayreuth's Wahnfried (Respite From Delusion) House, which now contains the **Richard Wagner Museum.** Wagner had this squat neoclassical creation, graced by a tree-lined walkway, built in 1874. The composer lived here with his wife, Cosima, daughter of composer Franz Liszt; their graves (and the grave of their dog) are in the backyard. *Richard-Wagner-Str. 48, tel. 0921/757–2816. Admission: DM 4 (DM 5 July and Aug.), DM 2 students. Open daily 9–5, Tues. and Thurs. until 8:30 during the summer.*

MARKGRAEFLICHES OPERNHAUS • From in front of the Neues Schloß (*see below*), you can't help but see Wilhelmina's other great architectural legacy, the 1748 Margrave Opera House. Every nook and cranny is packed with gilded work, ravishing frescoes, and ornate rococo baubles. Wagner originally came to Bayreuth because he felt the sumptuous design and large stage would suit his epic works, and he worked here until the Festspielhaus was built in 1876. Try to catch a performance; tickets (DM 15–DM 65) are sold at the box office, with discounts (5%–30%) for students. *Opernstr. 14, tel. 0921/759–6922. Admission: DM 5, DM 3 students. Open Tues.–Sun. 9–11:30 and 1:30–4:30 (shorter hrs off-season).*

NEUES SCHLOß • The 16th-century Neues Schloß was rebuilt after a fire in the 18th century under the direction of Margravine Wilhelmina, serious fan of rococo embellishment. In renovating the structure—a project that nearly bankrupted the town—she helped to create a wildly ornate palace. Since 1994 the Schloß has housed the **Bayreuther Fayencen-Sammlung,** a display detailing the history of porcelain production in Bayreuth. Directly behind the Schloß is the prim **Hofgarten** (garden). *Ludwigstr. 21, tel. 0921/759–6921. Admission and required tour (in German): DM 4, DM 3 students. Open Tues.–Sun. 10–1 and 1:30–4:20.*

AFTER DARK

Bayreuth caters to highbrow concert-goers with its snazzy Altstadt bars, and to lowbrow students with a handful of clubs. Near the Spitalkirche is **Fledermaus** (Spitalg. 2, just off von-Römer-Str., tel. 0921/

WHAT'S SO GREAT ABOUT WAGNER?

While few artistic geniuses are renowned for their warm, friendly dispositions, Richard Wagner (1813–83) is regularly remembered for his vices: He was stubborn, intolerant, temperamental, exacting . . . you name it. Lucky for Wagner, King Ludwig II of Bavaria—the young and impressionable "dream king"—took a liking to his music and provided him with much-needed financial backing. Ludwig even financed the development of the Festspielhaus, the Bayreuth opera house that was custom-made to suit the spectacular theatricality demanded by Wagner's works.

So what was so terrific about this guy? Well, he revolutionized opera, creating what he called a Gesamtkunstwerk (total art work). Rather than making music the dominant performance element, Wagner treated music, text, and spectacle as equals. With only little formal musical training, Wagner initially demonstrated a remarkable gift for large-scale dramatic opera. Later his "music dramas"—noteworthy for their mythical characters, Leitmotifs (tunes associated with characters, events, emotions, or objects), seemingly never-ending melodies, and intense emotions—took opera goers by storm. The uninitiated should take heed: His marathon-length works are something of an acquired taste.

68333; open daily 7 PM–1 AM), a gorgeous cellar bar. It's often packed by 9, so come early to stake out a spot and order some humongous food (a six-story burger) or pasta dishes with names to yodel (*Nudeldüdeldideldö*).

NEAR BAYREUTH

KULMBACH

Serious beer drinkers should make a pilgrimage to Kulmbach, home to no fewer than five breweries. The best time to visit is during the nine-day **Kulmbach Bierfest,** which begins on the last Saturday in July. The main festival site is a tent that seats 3,500—known as the *Festspülhaus* (Festival Swilling House), a not-so-subtle play on Bayreuth's Festspielhaus.

Kulmbach pumps out more beer per person per year than any other town in Germany (9,000 pints for every man, woman, and child), and the thick aroma of hops virtually assaults your nostrils the moment you step off the train. Hardly surprising, the best way to experience Kulmbach is by touring one of its two most popular breweries: **Kulmbacher Reichelbräu AG** (Lichtenfelser Str. 9, tel. 09221/705225) or **Mönchshof-Bräu GmbH** (Hofer Str. 20, tel. 09221/80519), where for DM 4 (DM 3 students) you can see pictures of kegs bigger than you at the **Bayerisches Brauereimuseum Kulmbach** (tel. 09221/80510; open Tues.–Sun. 10–5). The former is the more popular and offers many free events (all involving beer) on summer weekends.

Once you've sobered up, trek to the **Plassenburg,** the 16th-century castle propped above the city center. Among the reliefs adorning the Plassenburg's arcades (which make the edifice one of the most important Renaissance complexes in Germany), look for the bust of the woman wrapped in snakes. This is the **Weiße Frau** (*see also* Aschaffenburg, *above*), who, as legend has it, murdered her children atop the Plassenburg. The Plassenburg was defeated only once in its long history—in 1554 when the armies of Nuremberg, Bayreuth, and Bamberg ganged up on poor Kulmbach and overran the castle. You might be able to catch a free summer concert in the airy central courtyard; ask the tourist office for a current schedule. Hourly German-language tours (DM 3, DM 2 students) of the castle are offered Tuesday–Sunday. If you ever got a kick out of toy soldiers, the castle's **Zinnfiguren Museum** (admission DM 3, DM 2 students) will blow you away. More than 300,000 of the little pewter guys are on display in the world's most extensive figure museum. To reach Plassenburg from Marktplatz, head southeast down Obere Stadt and turn left at the small shield fountain; follow the signs for a steep 20-min hike to the top.

BASICS • The very modern-looking **Fremdenverkehrsbüro** (Stadthalle Sutte 2, tel. 09221/95880) can fill your pockets with free city maps or book private rooms. The office is open weekdays 9–1 and 1:30–5:30, Sat. 9:30–1 (closed Sat. in winter). To reach the tourist office from the station, walk straight up F.-Hornschuch-Straße, left on Gasfabrikgäßchen, and right on Sutteplatz (10 min total). From Kulmbach's **train station** there are daily connections to Bayreuth (hourly, 35 min, DM 10) and Bamberg (hourly, 45 min, DM 16). Put that annoying travel companion in one of the station's lockers.

WHERE TO SLEEP AND EAT • You can usually find a bare-bones double for under DM 80 at half-timbered **Gasthof Zum Adler** (Dorfberg 7, tel. 09221/1476) or at the more modern **Gasthof Pension Zur Eiche** (Pörbitscherpl. 9, tel. 09221/3873). Cheaper still is **HI-Jugendherberge Kulmbach** (Mangersreuther Str. 43, tel. 09221/7243; closed Dec. 10–Jan. 10 and Aug. 15–Sept. 10), a 90-bed hostel 3 km from the city center. If you're under 27, you can get a bed for DM 18, including breakfast. From the train station, hop on Bus 2 to Mangersreuther Straße. Groceries can be had at **Tengelmann** (Langeg. 16).

Although it sounds like an Arnold Schwarzenegger movie, Doppelbock Kulminator 28 is actually the strongest beer in Germany, brewed only in Kulmbach. Enjoy, but be careful: At 22 proof, this Doppelbock might permanently terminate your beer-drinking days.

COBURG

Every July, legions of Germans descend on Coburg, a small town with a colorful Renaissance and rococo-style Altstadt, to bump and grind to the rhythms of the **Samba festival.** Though now known as Bavaria's "Little Rio," Coburg has belonged officially to Bavaria only since 1920. From the 15th to the 19th century, the dukes of Saxe-Coburg ingeniously secured a power that belied the duchy's Lilliputian proportions and climbed the European social ladder via a series of opportunistic royal marriages. Coburg's Prince Albert hit the jackpot in 1840 when he snared Britain's Queen Victoria, thus establishing the royal lineage of present-day Britain (whose name was quietly anglicized during World War I to the House of Windsor). In 1920, conservative Coburg rejected union with socialist Thüringen and voted to join Bavaria instead, which proved fortuitous on two counts: Coburg avoided inclusion in the GDR following World War II, and Bavaria was obligated to maintain Coburg's cultural treasures "for all time." After the war, Bavaria had to foot the bill for the reconstruction of **Schloß Ehrenburg** (Schloßpl.; admission DM 5, DM 4 students; closed Mon.), longtime residence of the Saxe-Coburg dukes. Prince Albert spent much of his childhood at the Schloß, originally built in the 16th century but reconstructed after a fire gutted the place in 1690. An English neo-Gothic style prevailed; Buckingham Palace in Coburg was the result. Here Queen Victoria had the honor of being the first to perch on a different kind of throne—Germany's first flush toilet, on display next to her guest bed.

The fortress **Veste Coburg,** the town's namesake and principal attraction, lies a taxing but beautiful 30-min walk away from the Markt—follow the FUßWEG ZUR VESTE signs (take Bus 8 if you eschew physical exertion). Along the way you'll go through the weedy **Hofgarten** (Palace Garden) and pass by the **Natur-Museum** (tel. 09561/750689; admission DM 3, DM 2 students, open weekdays 9–1 and 1:30–5, weekends 9–5). The museum houses an extensive collection of stuffed animals—a three-toed romping mountain sloth, yellow-bellied, duck-billed platypi, and an exceptionally cute marmot among them. Also on display is a truly fascinating, if woefully out of place, set of African statuary and ritual costume.

The first brawny buildings of Veste Coburg date back to 1055, but most of what you see today stems from the Gothic and Renaissance eras. Protected by the fortress's thick walls is the **Fürstenbau** (Palace of Princes), which sheltered Martin Luther for six months in 1530 and served as home to Coburg's dukes until World War I. Unfortunately, the Fürstenbau is now closed to visitors. But you can view the

Kunstsammlungen (art collection; admission DM 6, DM 3 students), which houses an eclectic mix of guns, armor, and torture instruments (with how-to pictures), as well as paintings by Dürer, Rembrandt, and Cranach. *Open Apr.–Oct., Tues.–Sun. 9:30–1 and 2–5; Nov.–Mar., Tues.–Sun. 2–5.*

BASICS

For free maps and help with rooms, check with the **tourist office** (Herrng. 4, tel. 09561/74180), open weekdays 9–6:30 (until 5 in winter), Saturday 9–1. To get there, and to the Markt at the center of the Altstadt, exit right from the train station, go left on Mohrenstraße, right on Spitalgasse to the Markt, then left on Herrngasse (a 15-min walk). **Trains** run hourly to Bayreuth (2 hrs, DM 21), Bamberg (35 min, DM 14), and Nuremberg (1¼ hrs, DM 30).

WHERE TO SLEEP

You can't beat the location of **Goldenes Kreuz** (Herrng. 1, tel. 09561/90473, fax 09561/90502), a cute 45-bed guest house right in the thick of things at the Markt. Singles run DM 48.50, doubles between DM 80 and DM 98.50. The rooms are narrow but clean; some have showers or great views of the street scene.

HOSTELS • A large and fairly luxurious **HI-Jugendherberge** occupies Schloß Ketschendorf, a 20-min walk south of the Altstadt. The addition of a modern sleeping facility hasn't diminished the redbrick pseudocastle's charm (the common room still has chandeliers and dark oak paneling). Beds cost DM 22, including breakfast. Curfew is 10 PM. No keys are available. *Parkstr. 2, tel. 09561/15330, fax 09561/28653. From station, Bus 1 to Ketschendorf. Phone reception open 8–noon; phone reception and check-in open 5 PM–6 PM and 8 PM–9:30 PM. Closed mid-Dec.–mid-Jan.*

FOOD

You'll encounter a host of inexpensive restaurants down Spitalgasse and Steinweg from the Markt. Near Ehrenburg castle, **Café-Bistro "Hallo Dolly"** (Rückertstr. 2, tel. 09561/90709; closed Sun.) serves hot and cold sandwiches on family-size baguettes for around DM 7. Italian pizza and pasta goes for about DM 10 at **Macaroni** (Oberer Bürglaß 18, tel. 09561/509660; closed Mon.). The mouthwatering cakes at the ultra-hip **Stadtcafé** (Steinweg 1, tel. 09561/90372; closed Tues.) will ease your bread-and-cheese blues.

BAMBERG

Bamberg is absolutely stunning. The old town, on an island in the Regnitz River with cobbled lanes snaking past colorful and rickety half-timbered houses, looks like it stepped off the pages of some medieval epic. Even the view from afar—a hazy jumble of red-tile roofs, gables, and church towers (Bamberg has 10)—should convince you to visit.

Bamberg originated as a farming village in the late 2nd century AD and was transformed into an elegant seat of power under the guidance of Heinrich II, an 11th-century Holy Roman Emperor. He commissioned the impressive Dom, one of the most stupendous cathedrals in all Germany. The cathedral and Domplatz—and its two lavish Baroque palaces—generate a wonderfully refined, centuries-old air. "Official" sights here could occupy anyone for a day, but in summer stick around for the night. The hilltop beer gardens become respectably bacchanalian, and the nooks tucked along the riverbank are perfect for passing time with a friend or a bottle.

BASICS

Tourist information (Geyerswörthstr. 3, tel. 0951/871161; open weekdays 9–6, Sat. 9–3) doles out a glossy English brochure with a city map for 50 Pf and books hotel rooms for a DM 5 fee (but not private rooms, which don't exist in Bamberg). **Citibank** (Hainstr. 2–4, just off east end of Lange Str., tel. 0951/982460) cashes Visa traveler's checks (they won't accept the American Express variety) free for cardholders; everyone else pays DM 1 per check (DM 7 minimum). The Cirrus ATM outside gives Visa and MasterCard cash advances. Otherwise, plan on a uniform DM 10 charge for exchanging up to $100 worth of traveler's checks at any city-center bank. The **main post office** (Ludwigstr. 25), across from the Hauptbahnhof, also exchanges money and has an ATM, as well as phones aplenty.

COMING AND GOING

From Bamberg's **Hauptbahnhof** (tel. 0951/19419), roughly 1 km northeast of the old town, trains leave hourly for Bayreuth (2 hrs 20 min, DM 24.20), Berlin (5 hrs, DM 103), Coburg (45 min, DM 14), Frankfurt (2 hrs 40 min, DM 71), Kulmbach (45 min, DM 16.20), and Nuremberg (50 min, DM 14.60). You can use the lockers here or at the **ZOB,** which has bus departure points outside the train station and on Promenadestraße, opposite Maxplatz. Buses leave up to five times daily for Bayreuth (1 hr 40 min, DM 12) and Coburg (1½ hrs, DM 9). For regional bus info, call 09561/76009.

To reach the tourist office and the Altstadt, exit the station, go straight on Luitpoldstraße across the Main-Danube canal, and turn right onto Franz-Ludwig-Straße; Maxplatz and Grüner Markt are one block ahead. To reach the tourist office, turn left on Grüner Markt, cross the bridge, and make a U-turn, crossing the bridge to your left and turning right on Geyerswörthstraße. The Altstadt is easily navigated on foot and is traversed by both the Regnitz River and the Main-Danube canal.

WHERE TO SLEEP

Fässla. Best known for its tavern, where deep amber home brews are tapped from kegs with a big wooden hammer, Fässla, only three blocks from the station, doubles as a guest house. Singles cost DM 63, doubles DM 98; all come with shower, TV, and phone. If you already have a place to sleep, stop in for a pint (Obere Königstr. 19, tel. 0951/22998, fax 0951/201989; closed Sun.). Across the street, **Gasthof Spezial** (Obere Königstr. 10, tel. 0951/24304, fax 0951/26330) is a similar tavern–cum–guest house with singles for DM 50 and doubles for DM 90, both with private bath, shower and breakfast included. *From Hauptbahnhof, straight down Luitpoldstr., right on Obere Königstr.*

Bamberg is associated with a few culinary oddities. One is Rauchbier, or smoked beer, a deep amber brew that acquires a unique smoky taste from being filtered through charred beech-wood logs. Also try Bierbrauervesper, a mixed plate of smoked meat, sour-milk cheese, and black bread.

Hospitz. The Hospitz is a plain but pleasant pension near the Promenadestraße ZOB. Many of the singles (DM 50–DM 70) and doubles (DM 80–DM 100) lie over a peaceful courtyard. Some of the 35 rooms have balconies, most have showers, and all have phones. *Promenadestr. 3, tel. 0951/981260, fax 0951/981–2666. From Hauptbahnhof, down Luitpoldstr., cross canal, right on Franz-Ludwig-Str., left on Promenadestr. Reception open until 10 PM.*

Hotel Garni Graupner. The Graupner is great: It's affordable (doubles start at DM 85, singles at DM 55, both with breakfast), it's clean, and it's well located (in the middle of the Altstadt, a short walk from Grüner Markt). Bring your bubble bath and a friend—the enormous, spotless bathtub in the *Etagendusche* (hall shower) is big enough for two. The staff is friendly, speaks English, and will hold your luggage until 10 PM on the day you check out. Reservations strongly advised. *Lange Str. 5, tel. 0951/980400, fax 0951/980–4040. 20 rooms, some with bath.*

Maisel-Bräu-Stübl. This 12-bed guest house is above a don't-bother restaurant, five min from the station and 10 min from the Altstadt. Some rooms are above a quiet courtyard, and the singles (DM 39, none with shower) and doubles (DM 70–DM 80, some with shower) are a deal. All come with fluffy comforters. *Obere Königstr. 38, tel. and fax 0951/25503. From Hauptbahnhof, straight down Luitpoldstr., left on Obere Königstr. Closed Sun. and last two weeks of Aug.*

HOSTELS • Jugendherberge Wolfsschlucht (HI). The hostel is in a large and peaceful mansion by the Regnitz River—a great place if you can stand the petty tyrant manager. Nearby is a miniature golf course and boat rental. Though buses frequently make the 3-km trip from the Altstadt during the day, they stop running at 7 PM; plan on DM 6–DM 10 for a taxi, or take the beautiful but unlighted footpath (20–30 min) that begins just under the east end of the bridge on Wagner Straße and runs along the Regnitz; you'll see the hostel on the other side. Red metal bunk beds squeezed into small rooms are DM 20, including breakfast. There's a 10 PM curfew but there are some keys available. *Oberer Leinritt 70, tel. 0951/56002 or 0951/56344, fax 0951/55211. From ZOB depot, Bus 18 (DM 1.50) to Rodelbahn; walk downhill and left on Oberer Leinritt. 84 beds. Closed mid-Dec.–Jan.*

CAMPING • Campingplatz Insel. Roughly 5 km south of the city center, this beautiful and popular spot along the Regnitz charges DM 6.50–DM 12 (depending on tent size) plus DM 6.50 per person. The camp's cantina is stocked with all kinds of food supplies and there's a small restaurant (closed Tues.). *Am Campingpl. 1, Bamberg-Bug, tel. 0951/56320. From ZOB depot, Bus 18 (20 min, DM 1.50) to Schloßstr., continue 300 m. Reception open 7:30–1 and 3–10.*

FOOD

On summer evenings, Bambergers take to the hills to enjoy Rauchbier *auf'm Keller* (atop the cellar). In the days before refrigeration, breweries burrowed into the city's seven hills to create a suitably chilly spot to store beer; of the many beer gardens that now adorn Bamberg's hills, the **Spezial-Keller** (Oberer Stephansberg 47, tel. 0951/54887; closed Mon.) offers a stunning view and great Rauchbier. Bamberg's Altstadt is littered with cheap Imbiß stands and snazzy tourist-oriented *Gaststätten* (restaurants). The former dominate Maxplatz and the streets immediately south and east. For home-brewed beer and light snacks head to Fässla or Gasthof Spezial (*see* Where to Sleep, *above*), two top-rate taverns that double as guest houses. It's your birthday every day at **Riffelmacher** (Obere Brücke 12, tel. 0951/25815). Open Monday–Saturday 9–6:30, Sunday 10–6, Bamberg's oldest café dishes out delicious homemade cake and ice cream. Pick up groceries at **Tengelmann** (Lange Str. 12–14).

Bistro S'n'S. The bistro sports a pseudo–avant-garde decor heavy on black and white, as well as an electronic dartboard. Food is cheap (pasta DM 8.50–DM 11, salads DM 9–DM 12, hot baguette sandwiches DM 4.50–DM 6.50), and the cappuccinos (DM 3.80) are enormous. *Generalsg. 15, off Lange Str., tel. 0951/203041.*

Café Müller. In the afternoon students pack this place near the university. The dark wood floors and the menu—pasta (from DM 8.50) and veggie quiches (DM 9.50)—lend the place a neo-Italian feel. *Austr. 23, tel. 0951/202943. From Grüner Markt, take Fischstr. to Austr.*

Schlenkerla Brauereigaststätte. Come to the Schlenkerla for authentic Bamberg cuisine. That means pig, pig, pig, in every possible permutation. House specialties run around DM 16, but every day but Sunday you're welcome to bring your own meal and just enjoy the home-brewed Rauchbier (DM 4.20 per ½ liter). *Dominikanerstr. 6, tel. 0951/56060. From Lange Str., cross Untere Brücke onto Dominikanerstr.*

WORTH SEEING

Bamberg's sights occupy a fairly small area—in fact, four are on Domplatz. The tourist office leads **city tours** (in German) Monday–Saturday at 2 PM; stop by to sign up and get tickets (DM 9, DM 5 students). Don't miss out on Bamberg's unofficial sights like **Klein-Venedig** (Little Venice), the riverfront collection of red-roofed and brightly colored homes huddled along the left bank of the Regnitz just north of the Old Rathaus. You could do worse than spend a few hours just staring at the squat, 15th-century **Altes Rathaus,** anchored in the Regnitz. The centuries-old stone bridge **Obere Brücke** runs through the Rathaus.

DOMPLATZ • Domplatz lies in the heart of Bishops' Town a few hundred yards west of the Regnitz River and the Altes Rathaus (look for four closely grouped towers on the skyline; that's Domplatz). Its most impressive landmark is the 13th-century **Dom.** Originally built in 1003 by Heinrich II, who was crowned Holy Roman Emperor here in 1012, the Dom was rebuilt in the 13th century after a fire destroyed it. By far the Dom's best known artwork is the **Bamberger Reiter,** an equestrian statue hewn in 1235. The figure (and its creator) remains unidentified, but this didn't stop the Nazis from appropriating the Reiter as an ideal type of medieval royalty who somehow prefigured National Socialism. The Dom also houses the marble mausoleum of King Heinrich II and his wife, Kunigunde, and the **Nagelkapelle,** with a splinter of wood and a rusted nail reputedly from the one true cross. *Admission to Dom free. Open Apr.–Oct., Mon.–Sat. 8–6, Sun. 1–6; Nov.–Mar. until 5.*

DIOEZESANMUSEUM • Adjoining the Dom, the cathedral museum houses a spectacular array of medieval and early modern statuary (e.g., gargoyles engaged in ejecting smaller creatures from their own gaping orifices), as well as the reputed belt and crown of Queen Kunigunde. *Dompl. 5, tel. 0951/502329. Admission: DM 4, DM 2 students. Open Tues.–Sun. 10–5.*

NEUE RESIDENZ • Across Domplatz from the cathedral, this sprawling Baroque palace was once home to the princes and electors of the Holy Roman Empire. Be sure to locate the monkey perched at the edge of the ceiling fresco in the **Kaisersaal** (Emperor's Hall)—his eyes will follow you wherever you go. Also interesting is the palace's **Staatsbibliothek** (State Library). What started as a small personal collection by Heinrich II has grown into an impressive holding of rare handwritten and illuminated manuscripts. Highlights include manuscripts by painters Cranach and Dürer. *Dompl. 8, tel. 0951/56351. Admission: DM 4, DM 3 students. Neue Residenz open daily 9–noon and 1:30–5 (Oct.–Mar. until 4). Staatsbibliothek: tel. 0951/54016. Open weekdays 9–5, Sat. 9–noon.*

HOFFMANN-HAUS • Ernst Theodor Amadeus Hoffmann, composer and author of dark romantic tales, lived in this small Baroque house between 1808 and 1813. You may be familiar with the opera written about his stories by Jacques Offenbach, *The Tales of Hoffmann.* Even if you aren't, Hoffmann's house is a good example of late-Baroque craftsmanship and contains reams of papers along with personal belongings and—the most popular attraction—the hole in his study floor through which he spoke with his wife below. Unrequited love for a 15-year-old music student led Hoffmann to abandon Bamberg, and the house along with it. *Schillerpl. 26. From east side of Obere Brücke, south on Am Kanal,* *left at Nonnenbrücke. Admission: DM 2, DM 1 students. Open May–Oct., Tues.–Fri. 4–6, weekends 10–noon.*

AFTER DARK

BARS AND CLUBS • The coolest bar this side of the Donau may well be **Torschuster** (Obere Karolinenstr. 10, west of Dompl., tel. 0951/55508). Multicolored lights filter through the sand sprinkled on the floor to create a disco–meets–litter box effect, and the black lighting will make your teeth glow. Crowds descend day and night on **Eulenspiegel** (Obere Brücke 10, tel. 0951/203052), mostly because its outdoor tables are right on the bridge. At the **Absolut/Absurd** (Obere Sandstr., tel. 0951/53603) club/bar combo you can boogie Tuesday, Thursday, Friday, and Saturday or visit the platinum-and-glass bar for drinks poured by Bamberg's reputedly best-looking barkeeps. The music of Led Zeppelin and Guns 'n Roses fills the smoky den of **Soul Food** (Obere Sandstr. 20, tel. 0951/55025), where an early twenties, alternative clientele actually knows (and laughs at) the lyrics. All four are open Tuesday–Friday until 1 AM, until 2 AM on Saturdays.

THEATER • **E. T. A. Hoffman Theater.** The Hoffman company puts on a range of musicals, comedy, and drama, from Büchner to *Dracula—The Musical.* In June and July they leave the theater to perform in the courtyard of the Alte Hofhaltung palace, on Domplatz. Stop by the tourist office or the theater box office for schedules and tickets (DM 17–DM 30; 50% off with student ID), which are discounted an hour before show time. *Schillerpl. 5, tel. 0951/871431. Box office: tel. 0951/871433. Open Tues. 9 AM–11 AM, Wed. 11–1 and 4–6; Thurs. and Fri. 11–1, Sat. 10–1.*

Be on guard! Legend has it that the "Wilder Heer," a band of wild marauders, lurks in these woods, lying in wait for unwary travelers.

FRÄNKISCHE SCHWEIZ

The Fränkische Schweiz (Franconian Switzerland) region is shaped like an upside-down triangle, with Nuremberg forming the tip, Bayreuth and Bamberg the base. There's nothing particularly "Swiss" about the area except, perhaps, the range of low-lying hills that might, after a few dozen brewskies, look vaguely like the mile-high Alps. But over 200 years ago, local residents decided to rename the area, and with a more recent wave of the Marketing Fairy's wand, the whole region got a new lease on life. Fränkische Schweiz is hardly as scenic as Switzerland itself, but its clipped hills, rocky crags, lush meadows, and uncut forests combine to form a rural paradise. During winter snow often blankets the ground, which dampens the crowds, but after the spring thaw, German tourists descend on the area to hike, bike, fish, canoe, rock climb, kayak, spelunk—you get the idea. Plan to pant and sweat along with 'em while you explore ruined castles and dusky forests.

COMING AND GOING

There are only two ways to get into the Fränkische Schweiz: the bus that runs between Bayreuth and Gößweinstein (1 hr, DM 8), or the train from Bamberg (45 min, DM 9) or Nuremberg (1 hr, DM 16) via Forchheim to Ebermannstadt. Once you've arrived, Bus 8418—which runs from Ebermannstadt to Pegnitz (and the reverse) with stops in Streitberg, Muggendorf, and Gößweinstein—and your achin' feet will be your main means of transport. Bus 8418 runs 12 times each weekday, four times per day weekends. Ebermannstadt is a good place to start longer jaunts in the Fränkische Schweiz, as it houses the **Tourismuszentrale** (Oberes Tor 1, tel. 09194/8101, fax 09194/9078; closed weekends), the regional tourist office. They stock topographic hiking maps, will fill you in on the lodging and dining scene, and can help outfit a fishing or biking expedition. However little time you're spending in the Fränkische Schweiz, it is imperative that you pick up a regional bus plan; also ask the tourist office about seven- or 14-day regional bus tickets.

WHERE TO SLEEP

In the Fränkische Schweiz, hostels and surprisingly cheap pensions and hotels abound and almost always provide good breakfasts. Private rooms (which can be arranged through the local tourist offices) are also a great deal—they normally cost DM 25–DM 30 per person. Official camping spots are plentiful, and while *Wildcampen*—simply pitching a tent by the roadside or in an open space—is illegal, many farmers will let you set up camp in their fields, provided you ask nicely. As for the hostels, remember Bavaria's motto—if you're over 26, you're out of luck. Wherever you stay, be sure to pick up a *Kurkarte*, which will entitle you to discounts at various sports facilities in the area.

STREITBERG AND MUGGENDORF

Don't expect more than a few ordinary tunnels at Streitberg's main attraction, the **Binghöhle** caves (required tour DM 4; open Mar. 15–Nov. 10, daily 8–noon and 1–5). Natural wonders like this are pretty much what the two small villages of Streitberg and Muggendorf, just east of Ebermannstadt in the narrow, meadowy Wiesenttal (Wiesent Valley), are all about. Not a big surprise, considering both villages are surrounded by gorgeous wooded hills flanking the quiet Wiesent River. If the great outdoors isn't calling, head for the **Alte Kurhaus Brennerei** (Hans-Hertlein-Str. 1), Streitberg's Schnapps brewery, where you can try their specialty, the Streitberger bitter.

BASICS

Streitberg's **tourist office** (Burgstr. 4, tel. 09196/346), open mid-May–mid-September, weekdays 9–noon and 2–4 (Wed. 9–noon only; shorter hrs in winter), will help with lodging and supply you with hiking and biking maps. The same services can be found at **Muggendorf's tourist office** (in Rathaus, tel. 09196/19433), open Monday–Thursday 8–noon and 2–4 (Wed. 8–noon only), Saturday 10–noon (shorter hrs off-season). On the corner of Wiesentweg and Marktplatz lies Muggendorf's **Raiffeisenbank,** which has an ATM that accepts Visa and MasterCard. You can change money in Streitberg at **Sparkasse Forchheim** (Streitberger Berg 10, tel. 09196/626).

WHERE TO SLEEP

HI-Jugendherberge Streitberg (Am Gailing 6, tel. 09196/288, fax 09196/1543) charges DM 17 for one of its 122 no-frills beds; use of the grill and volleyball court is free. Ask for a "family room" and you may get a bed in a separate bungalow, away from the crowd. Make phone reservations 7:30 AM–9 AM; check-in noon–1 and 5–7. Bypass the 10 PM curfew with a DM 50 key deposit. To get there from the tourist office (a five-min jaunt), walk northwest on Am Bürgerhaus, make a left on Bahnhofstraße, and head uphill on Am Gailing. Another option in Streitberg is the pleasant **Schwarzer Adler** (Dorfpl. 7), with reasonably priced rooms and a great beer garden out back.

In Muggendorf, **Gasthof Kohlmannsgarten** (Lindenberg 2, tel. 09196/201) has singles for DM 43–DM 50, doubles DM 61–DM 81, all with breakfast included. The more expensive rooms have showers and a nice view of the valley, the cheaper ones have drab furniture. At **Pension Seybert** (Oberer Markt 12, tel. 09196/372), singles start at DM 41, doubles at DM 72, and they serve Schnapps from their very own brewery. **Zur Wolfsschlucht** (Wiesentweg 2, tel. 09196/324) rents its singles for DM 48 and doubles with showers for DM 88–DM 96. All rooms have modern furniture and some sport balconies with flower-filled window boxes.

OUTDOOR ACTIVITIES

In Streitberg, the **Schwimmbad** (follow the sign on Dorfstr., tel. 09196/298; admission DM 3) rents canoes and rowboats (mid-May–mid-Sept.) for use on one of a dozen nearby rivers. Boat rental costs DM 6 per half hour, DM 5 with a Kurkarte. One-speed bikes can be rented from Streitberg's friendly Herr Distler (Schauertal 2, tel. 09196/256) for DM 10 per day. In Muggendorf, hit **Rückenwind** (Forchheimer Str. 14, tel. 09196/489), where bikes are DM 20 (mountain bikes DM 30). If you're in town with your significant other, they also rent tandem bikes for DM 60. After a 2½- to 4½-km hike from Muggendorf (depending on which trail you take; pick up both on Lindenberg) you'll reach **DOOS** (tel. 0161/290–7075; 09197/1015 after 8 PM), a kayak rental firm that arranges river expeditions for DM 25–DM 43 from April to September. Another great short hike runs to the **Neideck ruins.** Only 25 min outside of town, this former 12th-century fortress is usually completely deserted—no guides, admission fees, or lines—just the castle, the view, and you. To get there, cross the river from Muggendorf, turn right, and follow the signs.

GÖßWEINSTEIN

Thirteen km east of Ebermannstadt, this hilltop village first sprouted in the Middle Ages. In this case old age is a plus: Gößweinstein offers some historically significant sights to complement the fantastic hiking and fishing found in the area. A trip to the musty castle **Burg Gößweinstein** (open daily 10–6; admission

DM 3) yields a sweeping view of eastern and northwestern Franconian Switzerland, a peek at lots of dusty weapons, and a glimpse of an 11th-century dungeon into which prisoners were lowered by rope. You should definitely check out the frenzied Baroque interior of **Basilika Gößweinstein**; the golden stained glass behind the church's altars creates a heavenly effect on sunny days. **Schumann's Fahrrad Shop** (Burgstr. 20, tel. 09242/7336; open weekdays 10–noon and 1–6, Sat. 9–1) rents bikes (DM 10–DM 15 per day) and mountain bikes (DM 25 per day). **Verkehrsamt Gößweinstein** (Burgstr. 6, tel. 09242/456) can help with a room or sell you hiking and biking maps (DM 7–DM 11). Pick up a copy of the brochure "Erlebniswanderungen mit Pfiff" for details, including maps, on 25 different hikes of various fitness levels. To get there, walk up the hill from the post office and take the first right onto Burgstraße. The office is open weekdays 8–noon and 2–5 (Fri. 8–noon only), Saturday 9–noon (shorter hrs off-season).

WHERE TO SLEEP

HI-Jugendherberge Gößweinstein (Etzdorfer Str. 6, tel. 09242/259; closed mid-Dec.–mid-Jan.) has 129 institutional-grade beds for DM 18 a pop. Reception is open 8–noon (phone reservations) and 5 PM–10 PM (check-in). From the Marktplatz, walk west down Pezoldstraße until it becomes Etzdorfer Straße. Your best bet in town is **Zweck Gunda** (Pezoldstr. 9, tel. 09242/252), with spotless, charming rooms and a bountiful breakfast buffet for DM 28–DM 37 per person. A sunny balcony awaits out back. **Gasthof Frankenland** (Burgstr. 5, tel. 09242/247) charges DM 36 per person, including breakfast, and all rooms come with showers. The friendly staff at **Campingplatz Fränkische Schweiz** (Tüchersfeld 57, tel. 09242/1788, fax 09242/1040; closed Nov.–Easter) will give you a tent site for DM 8.50 (DM 4.50 with Kurkarte) plus DM 7.30 per person. From Gößweinstein walk along B 470 toward Pottenstein; after Tüchersfeld (and a 10-min trek) it'll be on your right.

8

THURINGIA

UPDATED BY CHARLES MONDRY AND DEIKE PETERS

You won't need to take along a history book to appreciate Thuringia's rich and volatile past: An incongrous juxtaposition of architectural styles speaks volumes about the region's heritage. Within lush forests and verdant valleys, medieval villages, castles, and Baroque palaces coexist with impersonal, pre-fab Communist blocks and the swirling cranes of today's building boom. Arguably the most culturally significant *Land* (state) in Germany, Thuringia (Thüringen)—whose name was derived from the pre-Christian kingdom of Toringi—nurtured a host of highly influential Western minds over the centuries. While it lingered in virtual obscurity under East German control, the region has reemerged as a vital cultural hot spot in a reunited Germany.

Much of Thuringia's historic appeal stems from the 18th and 19th centuries, when **Jena, Weimar,** and **Erfurt** transformed the region into the cultural heart of Germany. Because of their small size, the many principalities into which Thuringia had been divided could ignore foreign policy and focus instead on art, science, local politics, and popular culture. During the Enlightenment, Duke Carl August of Saxe-Weimar (1757–1828) sponsored Germany's larger-than-life literary figures, Johann Wolfgang von Goethe and Friedrich Schiller.

Thuringian native and renegade composer Johann Sebastian Bach spent years bouncing around the state from job to job; though forgotten after his death, his music was rediscovered in the 19th century and today resounds throughout Thuringia during the yearly **Thüringer Bachwochen** (Thuringian Bach Weeks festival; Mar. 19–Apr. 25 in 2000). Since the year 2000 marks the 250th anniversary of the Baroque master's death, you won't be surprised to see the *Land* teeming with even more festivals than usual; a state exhibition called *Bach and Thuringia* is scheduled for June–September 2000 at Erfurt's Prediger Church (for info call 0361/562–4888). Arnstadt, Eisenach, Erfurt, Mühlhausen, and Weimar are where most of the festivities will take place. For more information contact the Thuringian tourism office (tel. 0361/37420, fax 0361/3742388) or local tourist offices.

The 20th century has left mixed marks on Thüringen. Architect Walter Gropius continued the region's tradition of cutting-edge cultural innovation by founding his influential Bauhaus school of art and design in Weimar; yet just a few years later, and only 6 km away, the Nazis terrorized thousands of innocent victims at **Buchenwald,** one of Germany's largest concentration camps. Later, while a postwar West Germany eased into the economic miracle, the Stasi (secret police) rose out of the rubble in East Germany and began the reign of suspicion that lasted until the Germanies reunited in 1990.

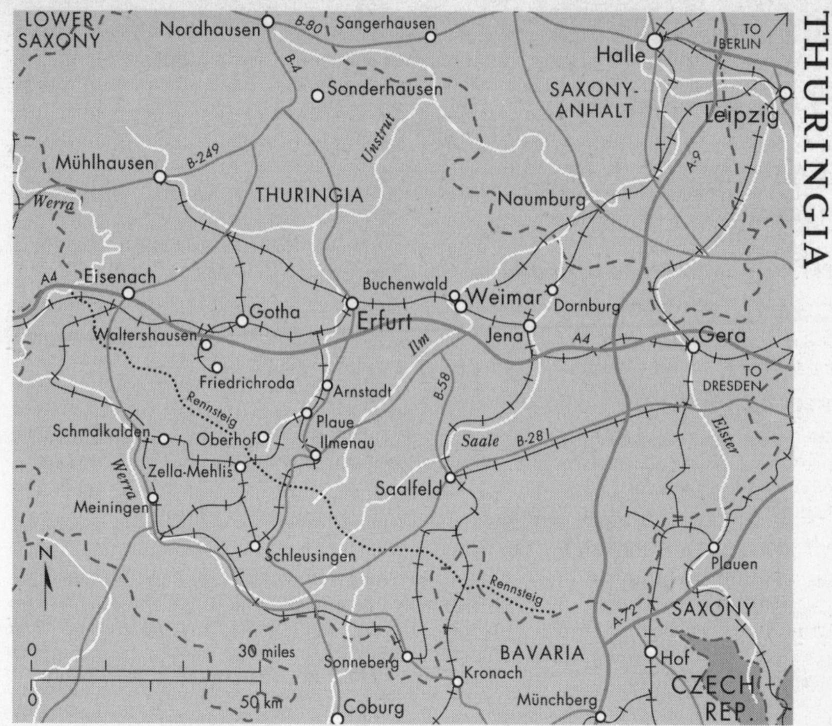

Today, Thuringia is busy rebuilding. Most towns, even a decade after unification, are still in the process of renovating their historic centers and restoring infrastructure neglected during GDR days. Not surprisingly, the infusion of Western cash has led to a proliferation of strip malls, superstores (most being the do-it-yourself home improvement variety), and vast expanses of parking lots all over the city outskirts. There's no need to despair, however: This economic boom is accompanied by widespread open political forums and a theater and art explosion in Weimar, Jena, Erfurt, and Meiningen. If you'd like to escape and commune with nature, head to the pristine **Thüringer Wald** (Thuringian Forest), with its wooded mountain range, miles of hiking, and stunning mountaintop views.

WEIMAR

Weimar's claim as Thuringia's cultural capital is incontestable, largely thanks to just two individuals: Johann Wolfgang von Goethe (1749–1832) and Friedrich Schiller (1759–1805), Germany's literary luminaries. It is here the two remain, side-by-side in simple, wooden caskets in the Weimar Historic Cemetery. Yet the city also nurtured the likes of J. S. Bach, Liszt, Nietzsche, Klee, and Kandinsky. Walter Gropius formed the Bauhaus here in 1919, and that same year the German National Assembly, drawn by Weimar's cultural tradition, met here to declare the founding of Germany's first-ever republic—the troubled, short-lived Weimar Republic (1919–33). The citizens of Weimar, however, saw this as a "communist" defilement of their traditions and elected a Nazi city government as early as 1925. The ultimate irony is that one of Germany's most infamous concentration camps, **Buchenwald** (*see* Near Weimar, *below*), lies just outside the city limits.

Despite its formidable history, Weimar is surprisingly small and welcoming—provincial, if you like. Restoration continues to rejuvenate the *Altstadt* (old town), where you may expect to see literati gathering over coffee and poetry. Throughout the year, Weimar's winding streets are alive with people shopping, strolling, or just hanging out—in parks, at cafés, or on street-side benches. Weimar's designation as European Cultural Capital in 1999 prompted an extension of museum hours and a burgeoning of cultural activity; nevertheless, the small city was not entirely prepared for the sharp increase in the number of tourists. And despite the greater influx of foreign visitors, tours, displays, and information are not always available in English.

BASICS

BIKE RENTAL

In the city center around the corner from the Stadtschloß, **Zweirad Hopf** rents your average machine for DM 30 per day. *Untergraben 2, tel. 03643/202120. Open weekdays 9–1 and 2–6, Sat. 9:30–12:30.*

CHANGING MONEY

A slew of ATM machines dot the city center; almost all accept major credit cards and Cirrus/Plus ATM cards. Try the one at the **Hauptpost** (Goethepl. 7–8; postal code 99423).

EMERGENCIES

The central **Stadt Apotheke** (Frauentorstr. 3, tel. 03643/202093) is right near the Markt. You'll find phone numbers and addresses for all current Bereitschaftsdienste (24-hr on-call duty) clinics, dentists, other emergency services, and pharmacies in the back of the monthly German-language "live–Stadtinformation" booklet, available at the tourist office as well as in many cafés and pensions.

VISITOR INFORMATION

Weimar's very busy **tourist office** books private rooms (*see* Where to Sleep, *below*) and has English-language maps and guides, but is mostly geared toward German-speaking visitors. They also sell the WeimarCard (*see* Worth Seeing, *below*). *Markt 10, tel. 03643/24000, fax 03643/240040. From Goethepl., cross to Wielandstr., left after Theaterpl., and left on Frauentorstr. to Markt. Open Apr.–Oct., weekdays 10–7, Sat.–Sun. 10–4; Nov.–Mar., weekdays 10–6, Sat. 10–1.*

COMING AND GOING

BY TRAIN

Weimar's newly renovated **Hauptbahnhof** (tel. 03643/331–9417 or 903330) is 1½ km north of the city center at the end of Carl-August-Allee. You can catch trains to Berlin (3½ hrs, DM 70), Dresden (2½ hrs, DM 55), Leipzig (½ hr, DM 20), and Erfurt (2 per hr, 30 min, DM 5), as well as many other destinations.

BY BUS

Weimar's **Busbahnhof** is at the southern end of Heinrich-Heine-Straße, two blocks south of Goetheplatz. Bus destinations from Weimar include Jena (50 min, DM 9) and Ilmenau (1½ hrs, DM 15). *Tel. 03643/202822. Information and ticket counter open weekdays 8–noon and 1–5 (Wed. until 3:15).*

GETTING AROUND

Weimar's concentrated Altstadt lies 1½ km south of the train station, a 20-min walk down Carl-August-Allee (turn left after Goethepl.). Otherwise take Bus 7 or 8 (same side of the street) or Bus 1 or 6 (across the street) to **Goetheplatz,** the hub of public transport on the western edge of the old town. Weimar's four main squares are all in the pedestrian-only Altstadt: **Theaterplatz** in the west, **Herderplatz** in the north, **Burgplatz** in the east, and the **Markt** in the south. Down Frauentorstraße from the Markt is **Frauenplan,** the square at the southernmost tip of the Altstadt and site of the Goethehaus (get used to seeing his name).

WHERE TO SLEEP

For DM 5 the tourist office will book you a private room (DM 25–DM 35 per person, add DM 8 for breakfast). The two buildings of **Pension Savina** (Rembrandtw. 13 and Meyerstr. 60, south of train station, tel. 03643/86690, fax 866911) lie about five blocks apart; the newer Meyerstraße location has excellent doubles with bath and kitchenette for DM 120, and singles start at DM 70. In a beautiful hillside home (but in a run-down neighborhood), **Pension Am Kirschberg** (Am Kirschberg 27, tel. 03643/871910, fax 8719116) has singles (DM 75–85 per person), doubles (DM 50–DM 65 per person), and a triple (DM 50–DM 55 per person).

HOSTELS

Hababusch Jugendhostel Weimar e.V. Very informally run by a group of students living on the second floor, this run-down but incredibly central old house is Weimar's funkiest recent addition to the hostel scene, so call ahead to reserve one of their few (8–10) beds. Grab a dorm bed for DM 15 or a double for DM 20; sheets are DM 5, kitchen and laundry facilities are available. Ask about week- or month-long stays. *Geleitstr. 4 (off southeast corner of Goetheplatz), tel. 03643/850737, fax 03643/402615.*

Jugendherberge Am Poseckschen Garten (HI). Only five–10 min by foot from the city center, this hostel fits comfortably into a grand old manor. Beds are DM 24 (DM 29 over 26), including breakfast. *Humboldtstr. 17, tel. and fax 03643/64021. From train station, Bus 6 (direction: Legefeld or Obergrunstedt) to Cranachstr., then backtrack ½ block. 112 beds. Curfew 12:30, lockout 10–2:30. Luggage storage.*

Jugendherberge Germania (HI). A mere two blocks from the Hauptbahnhof, Germania is your typical institutional hostel and nearly always booked. Next door is the fine late-night bar/restaurant Café Szenario (*see* Food, *below*), and you'll find a small market nearby. Beds run DM 24 (DM 29 over 26), including breakfast. *Carl-August-Allee 13, tel. and fax 03643/202076. 121 beds. No curfew (ring bell after 11 PM), lockout weekends 10–2:30. Reception open 3 PM–10 PM. Luggage storage.*

Jugendgästehaus Maxim Gorki (HI). This hostel, a 20-min walk south of the Altstadt, acquired its Russian name because of Gorki's contributions and writings for youth. Beds are DM 24 (DM 28 over 26), breakfast included. *Zum Wilden Graben 12, tel. 03643/ 850750, fax 03643/850749. From train station, Bus 8 (direction Merketal) to Wilder Graben (15 min), then follow signs. 60 beds. No curfew. Check-in after 3 PM. Luggage storage.*

FOOD

Restaurants and cafés are sprinkled about the pedestrian zone between Theaterplatz and the Markt, and near the castle on Burgplatz. You'll find a **supermarket** on Theaterplatz and a handful of quiet, smoky beer halls near Herderplatz.

ACC Café Galerie. It's hard to find a table at this local bohemian favorite, even in winter. Great food (including fresh cakes and yummy casseroles starting at DM 12) and a cool atmosphere make up for slow service. The upstairs gallery displays exhibits by local and international artists. *Burgpl. 1–2, tel. 03643/851161. Gallery: tel. 03643/851261; open Tues.–Sun. noon–6.*

Café Szenario. This chic bar and Italian café offers top-rate pizza from DM 5 and vegetable and seafood pastas from DM 10. If it's nice out, nurse a coffee or beer on the outdoor patio. *Carl-August-Allee, at Meyerstr., tel. 03643/419640. Closed Sun.*

Theater Café. The decor suggests a clubroom rather than a café. Sip a cocktail or sample a do-it-yourself, raclette-like *Heißer Stein* (hot stone), which lets you prepare veggie, fish, or meat selections at the table (from DM 13). *Theaterpl. 1a, tel. 03643/903209.*

WORTH SEEING

The number of museums and cultural attractions squeezed into Weimar's small urban district is truly mind-boggling, even if most major sights are conveniently spread between its five main squares in the Altstadt. Consider taking one of the two-hour self-guided **audio tours** offered by the tourist office to get an overview. Also get the **WeimarCard** (DM 19.99), good for reduced admission to most museums, 72 hours of free bus travel, 25%–30% off city tours, and 10% off tickets for the Deutsches Nationaltheater.

BURGPLATZ

From Burgplatz **you can enter the Stadtschloß,** whose **Schloßmuseum** displays works by Lucas Cranach the Elder, 17th-century Dutch paintings, German Romantic works, and rotating exhibits featuring contemporary German artists. *Stadtschloß, tel. 03643/546160. Admission: DM 6, DM 3 students. Open Apr.–Oct., Tues.–Sun. 10–6, Nov.–Mar., Tues.–Sun. 10–4:30.*

A short walk south of the castle, you'll find the **Herzogin Anna Amalia Bibliothek.** Don't miss the library's central hall, the famous **Rokokosaal,** an oval-shaped, three-story reading room decorated with oak banisters, carved plaster ceilings, and gilded molding—the epitome of rococo embellishment. *Pl. der Demokratie, tel. 03643/545200. Open Apr.–Oct., Mon.–Sat. 11 AM–12:30 PM.*

GOETHE-NATIONALMUSEUM

Goethephiles, rejoice! Goethe lived in **Goethes Wohnhaus** for decades, and he was a pack rat. He moved into this house (a gift from Duke Carl August) in 1782, and lived here almost continuously until his death in 1832. Peruse letters, manuscripts, boring oil paintings of jowly noble types, and Goethe's own furniture. Since the curators' aim is to preserve the house as Goethe might have left it, the museum is devoid of plaques and information. Ask any of the helpful (and passionate) guards to give you some extra insight into Goethe's life or, if your German's not too broken, watch a free film introducing the house. *Am Frauenplan, 1 block south of Markt, tel. 03643/545320. Admission: DM 8, DM 2.50 students. Open Tues.–Sun. 9–5, Wed. and Thurs. until 7 (Nov.–Feb. until 4).*

In the buidling that houses Goethes Wohnhaus, you will also find the **Goethe-Museum,** where you can ogle Goethe memorabilia and some of the collections previously shown in the now closed Literaturmuseum (formerly attached to the Schillerhaus). Also represented are Goethe's close friends, Schiller, Herder, and the poet Christoph Martin Wieland.

For purposes of historic preservation, a maximum of 25 people are allowed to enter **Goethes Hausgarten** (Goethe's garden house) at any one time; as a result, to avoid denying entry to eager Goethe fans, Weimar's cultural planners decided to simply erect an identical copy of the garden 300 yards away. If neither the authentic nor the faux version appeals to you, take a stroll in the surrounding **Park an der Ilm,** Weimar's riverside park (of course landscaped by Goethe himself). *Park an der Ilm, tel. 03643/545102. Admission: DM 4, DM 1 students. Open Wed.–Mon. 9–6 (10–4 in winter).*

HERDERPLATZ

Named after philosopher Johann Gottfried von Herder, who helped lay the basis of German Romanticism, the central Herderplatz features the **Herder statue** and the **Herderkirche,** officially known as the **Stadtkirche St. Peter and Paul** (open Apr.–Nov., Mon.–Sat. 10–12 and 2–4, Sun. 11–12 and 2–3, Nov.–Mar., daily 11–12 and 2–3). The colorful church interior is home to Herder's grave and the **famous triptych *Winged Altar,*** begun by Lucas Cranach the Elder and completed by his son.

HISTORISCHER FRIEDHOF

Goethe and Schiller are laid to rest in the **Fürstengruft** (Princes' Vault) of this spooky, overgrown cemetery. But save yourself the admission, unless you want to see the names of this most famous pair of German writers stenciled on a couple of wood coffins. The small Russian Orthodox chapel in the back of the mausoleum is aesthetically more appealing (and free). *Am Poseckschen Garten, 4 blocks south of Markt. Fürstengruft admission: DM 5, DM 3.50 students. Open Mar.–Oct., Tues.–Fri. 9–1 and 2–6; Nov.–Feb., Tues.–Fri. 10–1 and 2–4. Chapel is open Wed.–Mon. 9–4:45.*

LISZTHAUS

From 1869 until his death in 1886, the Hungarian pianist and composer Franz Liszt spent his summers in this tree-ringed mansion. The house itself, set on the fringe of Ilm Park, is attractive, but inside you'll find only a weary display and period decor. *Marienstr. 17, tel. 03643/62041. From Markt, walk south past Goethes Wohnhaus, veer left at Wieland Pl. onto Marienstr. Admission: DM 4, DM 3 students. Open Tues.–Sun. 9–1 and 2–6 (Nov.–Feb. 10–1 and 2–4).*

MARKT

Weimar's market square dates from 1400, when the city received its first charter. Over the next 200 years it was a venue for knightly tournaments and the occasional bazaar. On the square stand the 18th-century **Neptun Fontäne** (Neptune Fountain) and the **Lucas Cranach Haus** (open Tues.–Fri. 10–6, Sat. 11–3), where the elder Cranach lived out the last years of his life. The building's exquisitely sculpted facade is far more stimulating than the anemic art collection inside. On the south side of the square is the **Hotel Elephant,** which has hosted the notorious and the nefarious, including Goethe (surprise), Napoléon, and Hitler; it's also the setting for Thomas Mann's novel *Lotte in Weimar.*

The **Neues Museum** (New Museum) opened its doors on the first day of 1999 inside a newly restored neo-Renaissance building, which formerly housed the Landesmuseum. Look for works by Keith Haring, Roehr, and other well represented German and Italian artists in this important collection of international contemporary art since the 1960s. *Rathenaupl., at Carl-August-Allee., tel. 03643/546163. Walk north* *from Goethepl. on Karl-Liebknecht-Str. toward Hauptbahnhof. Admission: DM 8, DM 6 students. Open Tues.–Sun. 10–6 (Nov.–Mar. 10–4:30).*

NIETZSCHE ARCHIV

The house in which the influential philosopher spent his fuzzy final three years now houses a *very* small museum. The two living rooms hold various personal belongings, as well as Nietzsche's death mask. *Humboldtstr. 36, tel. 03643/5450. Bus 6 to Hufelandstr. Admission: DM 4, DM 3 students. Open Tues.–Sun. 1–6 (Nov.–Mar. until 4).*

SCHILLERS WOHNHAUS

Schiller bought this Baroque house—where he lived in ill health from 1802 until his death in 1805—on credit from Duke Carl August, and agreed to write one play each year to pay it off; *Wilhelm Tell,* a parable against imperial tyranny, was one of his payments. Although all furnishings are period pieces, only the study and the bed where he died actually belonged to Schiller. Don't expect much in the way of information unless you know German and can ask the knowledgable guards for info. *Schillerstr. 12, off the Altmarkt, tel. 03643/545102. Admission: DM 5, DM 3 students. Open Wed.–Mon. 9–6 (Nov.–Mar. 10–4).*

SCHLOß BELVEDERE

This stately, domed Baroque palace contains the **Rokoko-Museum** (recommended if you appreciate 17th-century glassware, china, and firearms) and a superb **collection of Historical Coaches** (historische Kutschensammlung in German). In summer, the surrounding park itself is worth a visit. *Burgplatz 4. Admission to museum: 5 DM, 3 DM students; coach collection: DM 1, 50 Pf students. Open Tues.–Sun., 10–6, closed Nov.–Mar.*

Many of the romantics admired Goethe but felt his works were only the start of a truly poetic literature. Inspired by the French Revolution, these young authors believed Goethe's aristocratic ties stifled real individual and artistic freedom.

THEATERPLATZ

On the west side of Weimar's largest square looms the neoclassical **Deutsches Nationaltheater,** built in 1798 and inaugurated with a performance of Schiller's *Wallenstein's Camp.* Goethe, who served as the theater's director, helped rebuild the structure after it burned in 1825. In 1919 the National Assembly debated the constitution here, leading to the foundation of the Weimar Republic. Destroyed again in 1945, the theater reopened in its present form in 1948 with a production of Goethe's *Faust. Theaterpl. 2, tel. 03643/755334.*

Not to be missed is the **Bauhaus Museum** opposite the theatre. The Bauhaus was formed in Weimar in 1919 but had to leave for Dessau six years later, after the Nazi Party gained control of Weimar's city council. A relatively small exhibit chronicles the evolution of the school's philosophy; its unification of art and function has been a major influence on modern design and architecture. On display are works by Bauhaus professors like Walter Gropius, László Moholy-Nagy, and Wassily Kandinsky, as well as their students. *Theaterpl., tel. 03643/546161. Admission: DM 5, DM 3 students. Open Tues.–Sun. 10–6.*

The life of Christoph Martin Wieland (1733–1813), who established the literary genre of *Bildungsroman* and whose *Dschinnistan* served as the basis for Mozart's *Magic Flute,* is commemorated in the small **Wieland-Museum,** housed inside the 18th-century **Wittumspalais** on the Theaterplatz. *Theaterpl., tel. 03643/545102. Admission: DM 6, DM 2 students. Open Tues.–Sun. 9–6, winter 10–4.*

AFTER DARK

For thorough listings of evening events, ask at the tourist office or grab the free magazines found in most cafés and bars. The tourist office ticket service number is 03643/20024. Also check the *Weimar Kultur Journal* for complete listings including Erfurt and Jena (available at kiosks, DM 4.50). If you're looking to relax with a beer, the best places in town are the outdoor cafés around Schillerstraße and Theaterplatz. **The Deutsches Nationaltheater** stages performances of everything from Schiller to Shakespeare in a sometimes dauntingly interpretive fashion (picture *The Merchant of Venice* in a Third Reich setting). Tickets cost DM 5–DM 45; students get 50% off. *Theaterpl. 2, tel. 03643/755334; box office open Mon. 2–6, Tues.–Fri. 10–1 and 4–6, Sat. 10–noon and 4–6.*

BARS AND CLUBS

Weimar has a large network of student clubs; check the flyers plastered all over town. For a slightly mellower nighttime atmosphere, head to any of Weimar's cafés (*see* Food, *above*) or simply explore the Altstadt's winding streets.

Jazzkeller der Stadtbücherei Weimar. Jazz lovers and bibliophiles alike will get a kick out of this cellar archive venue in the state library. An irregular schedule of live jazz performances reverberates through the lower stacks, usually Thursday–Saturday at 10 PM. *Steubenstr. 1, no phone. Across and down from Goethehaus. Cover: DM 5–DM 15. Doors open at 9 PM.*

Mon Ami. Listen to live music ranging from rock to jazz in this Goetheplatz club (cover DM 5–DM 15). *Goethepl. 11, tel. 03643/847717.*

Studentenclub Kasseturm. Students have partied in this medieval tower for 30 years. There's beer in the basement, a stage on the second floor, and a dance floor at the top. Covers range from DM 3 (no live band) to DM 15 (live music); there's no cover Monday, Tuesday, or Thursday. *Goethepl., tel. 03643/584955. Open 7 PM–3 AM, beer garden opens at 1 PM. Closed Sun.*

NEAR WEIMAR

BUCHENWALD

The whole point of Buchenwald's continued existence can be summed up in two words: Never forget. At its peak in early 1945, this Nazi concentration camp only 6 km north of Weimar interned 110,000 people, but when inmates overwhelmed the few remaining SS officers in April of that year, only 21,000 remained. All told, 56,000 people were starved, shot, tortured, or worked to death during Buchenwald's eight-year operation (1937–45); about 30,000 other inmates were sent on death marches by the SS. The camp—with its barbed-wire fences, ghostly barracks foundations, crematorium, and iron entry gate reading "Jedem das Seine" ("To Each His Own")—is a powerful reminder of the human capacity for brutality.

Pick up a map (50 Pf) of the camp at the **bookstore** (open Tues.–Sun. 9:30–noon, 12:30–4:30; Oct.–Apr. until 4). For a more detailed history, get yourself an official walking-tour guidebook (available in English), which provides excellent information and routes to points of interest—it's worth the DM 3.50 investment.

In the bookstore building, a 30-min **film** (only in German) shows four times daily, with recollections by camp survivors, American soldiers, and Weimarers forced by American soldiers to view the camp and corpses. A plaque just inside the gate lists the nationalities of all the people the Nazis murdered during their reign. The former storehouse (where prisoners' personal belongings were kept) now houses an impressive **museum** detailing the rise of National Socialism; life, death, and survival at Buchenwald; and the camp's eventual liberation and its use as a detention camp by the Soviet occupation forces, who starved or worked to death another 7,113 people by 1950.

On your way out follow the signs marked MAHNMAL (memorial) to the **Glockenturm** (bell tower), which stands 1 km south of the visitor center. Commissioned in 1954 by the GDR government to "warn against the reestablishment of fascism in any form," the crypt contains ashes of unknown inmates brought from concentration camps throughout Europe. The sculpture at the tower's foot portrays 11 prisoners gazing triumphantly over the valley below. *Gedenkstätte Buchenwald, tel. 03643/4300, fax 03643/430100. From Weimar's Goethepl. or Hauptbahnhof, Bus 6 (direction: Buchenwald) to last stop; bus also stops at Glockenturm. Admission free. Open May–Sept., Tues.–Sun. 9:45–5:15; Oct.–Apr., Tues.–Sun. 8:45–4:15.*

JENA

Goethe called Jena his "beloved, foolish little place." Culturally speaking, Jena is Weimar's sister city. Founded in 1558, its university attracted Goethe and Schiller (who met here), the philosophers Hegel, Feuerbach, and Fichte, and the Jena Romantics—Tieck, Novalis, and the brothers Schlegel, who made the city a major center of the movement that rejected Enlightenment reason to embrace the irrational.

In 1841, another dabbler in (bad) romantic verse received his doctorate in philosophy at Jena—that poetic soul named Karl Marx.

Today the skyline of this quiet little city in the beautiful Saale valley is branded by the soaring **university tower,** visible for miles in every direction. Built in GDR days for the optics giant Zeiss, the swaying tower proved unsuitable for precision fabrication and so was given to the university (which has made little use of it). The legacy of Carl Zeiss and Ernst Abbe, who perfected optics here in the late 19th century, is largely responsible for Jena's growth. Until the unification, about 30,000 people worked for Zeiss Jena; today only 4,000 jobs remain. As tourism goes, the city still sits in the shadow of its smaller neighbor to the west. Jena's "Seven Wonders," for instance, may provoke less wonder than head shaking. But Jena's tiny Altstadt, with its uncomfortable mix of old and ultramodern and a vibrant student life, definitely warrants a visit.

BASICS

Jena's **tourist office** (Johannisstr. 23, tel. 03641/58630; open weekdays 9–6, Sat. 9–2), on the north side of Eichplatz, has English-language walking guides, sells bus tickets, and books private rooms free of charge. They also lead German-language tours (DM 4) on Wednesday and Saturday at 10 AM. The **main post office** is at Engelplatz 8; you can make international calls on pay phones throughout the city.

Buchenwald's camp clock reads 3:15—the time on April 11, 1945, when inmates raided the armory and took control of the camp four days before the arrival of the U.S. Army.

COMING AND GOING

Jena has several train stations, but chances are you'll arrive at **Bahnhof West** (tel. 03641/417342), a small station with luggage lockers and not much else. Destinations include Erfurt (hourly, 50 min, DM 11), Gera (every 1–2 hrs, 50 min, DM 11), and Weimar (hourly, 30 min, DM 7). The **Saalbahnhof** (tel. 03641/426060) lies northeast of town and is the departure point for most long-distance trains, such as those to Berlin (6 per day, 3 hrs, DM 63), Munich (5 per day, 4½ hrs, DM 109), Leipzig (via Naumburg, every 2 hrs, 1 hr, DM 21), and Halle (via Naumburg, hourly, 1½ hrs, DM 19). Note that the Deutsche Bahn threatened a price hike at press time.

WHERE TO SLEEP

The **Internationales Jugendgästehaus** (Am Herrenberge 3, tel. 03641/687230, fax 03641/687202) is in a utilitarian apartment block, but it's cheap (DM 30–DM 34 in dorm-style rooms), and the rooms are clean and decent. You pay DM 10 less starting the second night. From Bahnhof West (walk under tracks and uphill) or downtown, take Bus 11, 12, 40, or 90 to Mühlenstraße, then continue and head right on Mühlenstraße for 10 min. You can't buy tickets on the bus, so get a few (DM 2) from the train station attendant. The central **Pension H&R** (Neugasse 1, 2 blocks south of info office, tel. 03641/615533, fax 03641/615533) has comfortable singles (DM 60) and doubles (DM 90), all with showers. Just kitty-corner, **Altdeutsches Gasthaus Roter Hirsch** (Holzmarkt 10, tel. 03641/443221) has similar prices. You can also ask the tourist office to book you a private room (DM 25–DM 50).

FOOD

Altdeutsches Gasthaus Roter Hirsch (*see* Where to Sleep, *above*; closed Sun.) has a great lunchtime menu, with Schnitzel and such for under DM 10. For an ultracool dining experience, look for the banners and faded graffiti of **Café Immergrün** (Fürstengraben 30, tel. 03641/25470), just uphill from Johannisplatz. Get a filling plate of spaghetti for DM 7, then join in conversation or a board game. **Café Stilbruch** (Wagnergasse 2, near Johannispl., tel. 03641/54777) is a tri-level, candlelit student hangout where German fare goes for DM 10–DM 14.

WORTH SEEING

It's hard to get lost in Jena—just look for that big blue steel piston (the university tower) above the huge, cement-laden **Eichplatz.** In the alley to the left of the tower is the 13th-century Dominican monastery that served as **Collegium Jenense**'s original building. All you can do is peek inside the empty, cobblestone courtyard weekdays during school hours. On the university tower's uphill side is the **Johannistor,** a remnant of the city's original medieval fortifications.

MARKT • Jena's market has survived the bombing and building frenzy of the last 50 years better than much of the town. **Stadtmuseum Göhre** (Markt 7, tel. 03641/423245; open Tues.–Sat. 10–6; winter

10–5) has exhibits on the history of Jena and the university, including an explication of early frat parties; admission is DM 5 (DM 3 students). The twin-roofed Gothic **Rathaus** has a Baroque tower (currently undergoing restoration) whose clock puts on a goofy show—a devil/fool named Schnapphans attempts to catch a golden apple (one of those "wonders"). The **statue** on the Markt honors Duke Hanfried, founder of Jena's university. Directly north of the Markt is **Stadtkirche St. Michael,** a dark and brawny church that contains Martin Luther's original tombstone. (He's actually buried far away in Wittenberg; his tombstone was diverted here because of the Schmalkaldic War.) In summer the cathedral hosts free organ concerts every Wednesday at 10 AM.

OPTISCHES MUSEUM • Explore optical illusions; the history of glasses, cameras, microscopes, and telescopes; and the lives of Carl Zeiss, Ernst Abbe, and Otto Schott (who developed the perfect optical glass for Zeiss and Abbe) in this entertaining museum. *Carl-Zeiss-Pl. 12, 3 blocks west of Eichpl. (through Goethe Galerie), tel. 03641/443165. Open Tues.–Fri. 9–4, Sat. 9–4, Sun. 9:30–1. Admission: DM 8, DM 6 students.*

ZEISS-PLANETARIUM • It may just be a planetarium, but it was the world's first. Consider taking a star tour or having a laserium experience. *Am Planetarium 5, 3 blocks north of Eichpl., tel. 03641/ 885488. Call for showtimes.*

AFTER DARK

In this university town most nighttime activities are student-oriented. **Café Wagner** (Wagnerg. 26, 2 blocks west of Johannispl., tel. 03641/636324) has anything from drinking and dancing to music or films. Covers range from zip to DM 10, and it's open daily until 1 AM. **Doc.Jazz** (Krautg. 20, 1 block west of lower Johannispl., tel. 03641/345–8553) tries to bring as much live jazz as possible into its cozy little bar, open daily until 1 AM. **J. G. Stadtmitte** (Johannisstr. 14, no phone) produces a random selection of blues, reggae, film, and other events. Next door you can boogie to DJ-spun tunes Tuesday and Saturday and live music otherwise at **Rosenkeller** (Johannisstr. 13, tel. 03641/444346; closed Sun. and Mon.).

ERFURT

Now one of the most visited towns in eastern Germany, the capital of Thuringia is still busily renovating its center. You will see entire city blocks of gutted 17th-century houses. But despite the flashy new luxury shops, hotels, and restaurants, Erfurt's Altstadt of winding cobblestone alleys feels like a thriving medieval market town. At the end of the day, the scores of bright red church spires manage to vastly outnumber the dull construction cranes looming over the historical center. Erfurt's been in business for 1¼ millennia and isn't about to slow down.

The city's main squares, lined with beautiful, colorful buildings or hulking Gothic churches, are always filled with people. Erfurt's most curious attraction is the 14th-century Krämerbrücke (Merchant's Bridge), Europe's longest inhabited bridge—it contains 32 half-timbered houses. The Gera underneath can hardly be called a river, but still makes for scenic waterviews. Although Erfurt's old university buildings will only reopen their doors towards the very end of this millennium, small colleges provide a critical mass of young people that makes for a shaking nightlife with a little something for everyone.

BASICS

CHANGING MONEY

The **Reisebank** (Haptbahnhof, tel. 0361/643–8361; open Mon. 8–1 and 1:30–4, Sat. 9–1 and 1:30–4, Tue.–Fri. 8–7:30) exchanges foreign currency and traveler's checks and allows you cash advances, all for standard fees (DM 5 and up). Any branch of **Sparkasse, Deutsche Bank,** or **Dresdner Bank** accepts credit cards and Plus/Cirrus.

LAUNDRY

The **Waschsalon** next to the Hauptbahnhof has self-service washers (about DM 10) and dryers (DM 1 per 10 min). *Bahnhofstr. 22, near overpass, tel. 0361/562–1728. Open weekdays 6 AM–10 PM, weekends 9–8.*

MAIL

The main **post office** is housed in a beautiful steepled clock-tower building at Anger 66. Stamp machines are out front.

VISITOR INFORMATION

Just around the corner from the Krämerbrücke, Erfurt's **tourist office** (Fischmarkt 27, tel. 0361/66400, fax 0361/664–0290, open weekdays 10–7, Sat. 10–4) has small map guides for free and bigger ones for sale. The staff also books private rooms for DM 5 per person. Pick up a free copy of *Erfurt Magazin,* the monthly events guide.

COMING AND GOING

BY TRAIN

Erfurt's **Hauptbahnhof** (central station) was turned into a major construction site in 1999, since the city is scheduled to become a major stop along the new Berlin–Nuremberg ICE route. By 2002, travel time along this route will be reduced from more than 6½ hours to a mere 2½ hours. The new helpful DB service desk in the foyer (open daily 4:50 AM–10:40 PM) is stacked with free schedules for all major destinations. An ATM, the Reisebank, lockers, and a stamp machine are around the corner from the desk. From Erfurt trains leave every two hours for Berlin (3½ hrs, DM 73), Dresden (3 hrs, DM 57), and Leipzig (1½ hrs, DM 28), twice per hour for Eisenach (30 min, DM 13) and Weimar (20 min, DM 5), and hourly for Frankfurt (2½ hrs, DM 68).

BY BUS

On the off-chance that you want to leave Erfurt by bus, you'll find the **Busbahnhof** to the right of the Hauptbahnhof. Ask about exact schedules and buy your tickets from the drivers. Principal regional destinations include Gotha and Weimar.

BY MITFAHRGELEGENHEIT

Tourismus Agentur Otto (Schmidstedter Str. 28, tel. 0361/643–0971), near the Busbahnhof, runs the local ride-share service. It's open weekdays 9–6, Sat. 10–12:30 (unless Otto's on vacation, in which case it's simply closed, no alternatives).

GETTING AROUND

Nearly everything of interest is concentrated in the Altstadt, 10 min north of the Hauptbahnhof; veer left out of the station and turn right on Bahnhofstraße. Dead ahead lie the town's three pedestrian squares—the **Anger, Fischmarkt,** and **Domplatz.** One block east of Fischmarkt, the touristy **Krämerbrücke** straddles the shallow Gera River. The Anger is the center of the public transit system, where an info office (tel. 0361/19449 or 0361/642–1322) sells tickets (DM 5 for a 24-hr *Tageskarte*) weekdays 6 AM–8 PM, weekends 8–6. Tickets are also available from machines at major stops and inside the vehicles. Rent **bikes** at Allgemeiner Deutscher Fahrrad Club (Espachstr. 3a, tel. 0361/642–1634; open weekdays 9–4, Tues. and Wed. until 6) for DM 15 per day (DM 50 deposit). **Taxis** wait on Domplatz, or call 0361/51111 or 0361/666666.

WHERE TO SLEEP

Cheap lodging in the Altstadt is hard to find. There are a handful of less pricey pensions in the quiet southern district of Daberstedt, all within 10 min of a tram line. The tourist office books private rooms (DM 30–DM 50 per person) and can tell you if any of the large hotels are running specials.

Augustinerkloster. The friendly staffmembers who run this center (which is attached to the famous monastery) claim that the 42 guest rooms (single, double, and triple starting at DM 35 per person) are "simple according to monastery life." But don't worry, contrary to the freezing and fasting Luther five centuries before, you will find bright rooms with running water, some with bath, and an ample breakfast buffet. Reservations advised. Couples living in sin also welcome. Don't miss the amazing fresh cakes in the downstairs Klosterstuben café for an equally amazing buck. *Augustinerstr. 10, tel. 0361/576600, fax 0361/576–6099.*

Hotel Garni Daberstedt. It may be in a bland apartment building, but the rooms are nice and the management friendly. Singles run DM 60–DM 90, doubles DM 70–DM 110, DM 10 less on weekends. *Buddestr. 2, tel. 0361/373–1516. Tram 3 or 6 to Tschaikowskistr., then left on Häßlerstr. for 3 blocks. 12 rooms, some with bath.*

Pension Fiege. Run by talkative, young do-it-yourself Monika Fiege, some of this pension's best features are its location (right at a tram stop), the hairdryers in every room, and the menu-style breakfasts. You'll pay DM 50–DM 65 for a single, DM 70–DM 95 for a double, or DM 90–DM 120 for a triple. *Kranichfelder Str. 15, tel. 0361/413839, fax 0361/421–5087. Tram 3 or 6 to Blücherstr. 5 rooms, some with bath.*

Pension Francke. There are only three rooms, starting at DM 40 per person, and the neighborhood's a bit drab, but the pension has a garden and swimming pool, and the tram stops about five min from here. If it's booked, try the estranged daughter's **Pension Kalunov** (Stadtw. 22, tel. 0361/422–2139, cellular 0172/792–2411; doubles DM 70–DM 95) next door. *Stadtw. 21, tel. 0361/669976. Tram 3 or 6 to Blücherstr., then up Blücherstr. and left on Scharnhorststr., which becomes Stadtw.*

Pension Stilbruch. In an unbeatable location right on Domplatz, this quirky place offers a number of rooms each with original furniture from a different period. Bath, TV, and parking available; singles cost DM 50–DM 100, doubles DM 80–DM 160. *Andreasstr. 37, tel. and fax 0361/562–6039. Bookings are made in the café downstairs.*

HOSTELS

Jugendherberge Hochheimer Straße. In a renovated mansion, Erfurt's hostel is close to public transportation and has a pool table. Beds are DM 24 (DM 28 over 26), including an 8 AM breakfast. Lunch (DM 8) and dinner (DM 6–DM 8) are available. *Hochheimer Str. 12, tel. 0361/562–6705. Tram 5 to Steigerstr., then back ½ block to Hochheimer Str. 111 beds. No curfew. Reception open 3–8. Luggage storage.*

FOOD

Erfurt's Altstadt is moderately stocked with *Imbiß* (snack) stands and cheapish cafés. There's a **Rewe** market near the train station; Domplatz has a **Top** grocery store and, on Wednesday, Friday, and Saturday, a **farmers' market.**

double b. This cozy joint serves more of those oh-so-healthy Thuringian meals to young, kick-back Erfurters. Decent-size entrées cost DM 10–DM 18, salads and American-style breakfasts (served all day!) are DM 7–DM 12. At night a student crowd gathers to swill beer (DM 4.50) and play pool. *Marbacher Gasse 10, 2 blocks north of Dompl., tel. 0361/642–1671.*

Zum Augustiner. Traditional German bar? No way—from the decor, it looks more like an antiques store. Musical instruments, coffee mills, and wooden toys line the walls or hang haphazardly from the ceiling. One of Erfurt's few affordable sit-down restaurants is also a mellow candlelit bar. Fish specialties and occasional vegetarian dishes run DM 8–DM 17. If you need something more hard-core, try some of the 230 different "whisk(e)ys" at **Johnny Worker** a few doors down. *Michaelisstr. 32, tel. 0361/562–3830. From Fischmarkt, head toward Krämerbrücke, then left on Michaelisstr.*

WORTH SEEING

With more than 30 churches, nearly 100 historic houses, and an endless supply of bridges and lanes, Erfurt is a sightseer's dream. Unless otherwise noted, museums are open Tuesday–Sunday 10–5, Friday 10–1, and Saturday 1–5. The Krämerbrücke tourist office (*see* Visitor Information, *above*) organizes German-language guided tours (DM 6, DM 3 students), which begin at 1 PM daily (in winter, weekends only). The DM 5 **Tageskarte** (Day Pass) is available at and good for all museums below, except Galerie am Fischmarkt.

ANGER

The Anger is a long pedestrian mall (the plaza exists only because buildings destroyed in World War II were not replaced) and Erfurt's main shopping area. The rather odd mix of facades reflects the different tastes (neo-Baroque, neo-Renaissance, neo-Gothic) of the merchants who built their shops here in the 19th century. At the Anger's eastern end is a statue of Martin Luther in front of the 11th-century **Kaufmannskirche,** where he gave a sermon in 1522. Past the **Angerbrunnen** (fountain) at the other end of the Anger is the red-and-white, half-Renaissance, half-Baroque **Staatskanzlei** (Governor's Palace), where Goethe and Napoléon first met. Napoléon is reported to have said, *"Voilà un homme!"* ("Now there's a man!")

The large yellow building on Bahnhofstraße houses the **Angermuseum,** a first-rate collection of medieval relics—coins, tools, jewelry, and a huge 14th-century crossbow—along with a hodgepodge display of more recent landscape paintings. *Anger 18, tel. 0361/562–3311. Admission: DM 3, DM 2.50 students.*

AUGUSTINERKLOSTER

Martin Luther was a monk at this 13th-century Augustinian monastery from 1505 to 1511. The monks who designed the monastery adhered to a strict code of austerity both in their lives and in their architecture—with one exception: the stunning stained-glass church windows. They were taken down and stored underground during World War II and thus survived the bombings. The old library, however, was completely destroyed, burying all 230 people who had believed the thick walls and ceilings to be safe shelter. Today, the monastery is still the proud home of about 65,000 original books and manuscripts, the majority dating back to the 16th and 17th centuries. Although the monastery was already secularized in the 16th century, it continues to be one of the most important centers of religious life in Germany, frequently serving for interfaith gatherings and meetings. Join an hourly (highly informative, but German-only) guided tour, which covers a small exhibition on Luther's residence here. *Augustinerstr. 10, tel. 0361/576–6010, fax 0361/576-6099. From west end of Krämerbrücke, right up Michaelisstr., right on Augustinerstr. Admission: DM 6, DM 5 students. Open Tues.–Sat. 10–12 and 2–6, Sun. after 10:45 (Nov.–Mar. by appointment).*

Medieval Erfurt produced dye in a foul-smelling process that involved the addition of urine. You can identify old dye houses by the large number of small windows in their roofs, used for ventilation.

DOMPLATZ

Street vendors always fill this vast plaza at the western end of Marktstraße, but it really comes alive on market days (Wed., Fri., and Sat.). As Domplatz opens before you, an awe-inspiring pair of Catholic churches, Mariendom and Severikirche, loom into view. Monstrous enough upon initial completion in 1154, **Mariendom** had a choir added in front in the 14th century. Don't miss the cathedral's stunning cycle of 14th-century stained glass, composed of 20-m-long panels, or the "Wolfram" bronze candelabra (1161). *Tel. 0361/646–1265. Open Mon.–Sat. 10–11:30 and 12:30–4, Sun. 2–4.*

Across the courtyard stands the 13th-century **Severikirche** (Church of St. Severus), whose five equal-height naves make it architecturally unique. The large red sandstone sarcophagus of St. Severus depicts the scene of his promotion to high office in the church. If you're 8 ft tall, you can also see the lid relief, which shows the saint standing aloof between his wife and daughter. (Since saints and women weren't supposed to be compatible, mother and daughter were forced into a nunnery after St. Severus died a natural death.) *Tel. 0361/576960. Admission free. Open weekdays 10–12:30 and 1:30–4.*

FISCHMARKT

Busy Marktstraße leads east from Domplatz and, after a few crooked blocks, funnels onto Fischmarkt. Among the Baroque houses here is **Zum Breiten Herd Haus** (No. 2), which has a 16th-century exterior frieze depicting the five senses—a refreshing change from all the gargoyles and cherubs. The Zum Roten Ochsen Haus (No. 7) houses the excellent **Galerie am Fischmarkt** (tel. 0361/642–2188; open Tues.–Sun. 11–6, Thurs. until 10), a modern-art gallery with rotating exhibitions by young international artists. Admission is DM 4, DM 2 students. A few houses down toward the Anger is **Museum Neue Mühle** (Schlösserstr. 25a, tel. 0361/646–1059). German tours (DM 4, DM 2 students) leave on the hour and show the workings of an operational 19th-century mill.

KRÄMERBRÜCKE

The Krämerbrücke has been home to shops and houses since 1325, when a stone bridge was constructed in place of an earlier wooden one; the current half-timbered structures were built in 1475. During the day, entertain yourself by watching the tourists scamper back and forth between shops and galleries; at dusk, the empty cobblestone street bridge will make you feel like you've been transported back to the 14th century. The bridge is best enjoyed from below; walk through the archway at the far

THE SHADOW EXECUTIVES

For a fascinating peek into recent history, check out Petersberg 19, where East Germany's infamous Stasi (Ministry of State Security) collected secret dossiers on millions of GDR and FRG citizens. Just days after the wall came down in November 1989, thick smoke clouds made their way out of the building's chimney. Some smart Erfurt citizens caught on right away, and the building was seized from the evidence-destroying GDR bureaucrats almost immediately. Today, it houses the special federal investigation office which, upon public request, checks whether certain German figures of public interest were Stasi informants. To get to the unassuming white building, keep walking over the Petersberg and back down through the gate on the other side. Don't miss the exhibits on the second and third floors; entry is free weekdays until 6.

end. The **Ägidienkirche** is randomly open to visitors, especially on sunny days; don't miss the opportunity to climb the church tower for a marvelous view of the city and its surroundings.

MUSEUM FÜR THÜRINGER VOLKSKUNDE

The Thuringian Folklore Museum portrays the history of Thuringia's unwashed masses. Tours are in German, but the guides communicate with *Händen und Füßen* (hands and feet). Special exhibits include wreaths woven from the hair of maidens who died young, and animal-shaped baubles created by throwing molten lead into water to predict the future. The museum also displays such household objects as manacles and shackles that were used to goad women and slaves into working more efficiently. If you're hungry, the attached **Museum Garten Café** serves inexpensive grub. *Juri-Gagarin-Ring 140a, tel. 0361/642–1765. Tram 1 or 6 to Schottenstr., then back and left on Mohrerg., left on Juri-Gagarin-Ring. Admission: DM 3, DM 1.50 students.*

STADTMUSEUM HAUS ZUM STOCKFISCH

Erfurt's excellent city museum documents over 1250 years of history, as well as some archaeological finds from the region's prehistory. City models, pictures, drawings, weapons, and other artifacts illustrate Erfurt's evolution and historical events. An English-language tape recording in the main exhibit room provides a good overview. Special exhibits range from "When Neighbors Became Jews" to "The Magic of Board Games." *Johannesstr. 169, near Futterstr., tel. 0361/562–4888. From Krämerbrücke, east on Futterstr.; or Tram 1 or 6 to Schottenstr. Admission: DM 4, DM 2 students.*

ZITADELLE PETERSBERG

Uphill from the Domplatz, you can explore what's left of Erfurt's fortress—admittedly not much. Built in 1103, the 17th-century star-shaped, thick-walled Citadel sat above deep tunnels, where soldiers listened for digging noises from above—signs that the enemy was packing black powder under the fortress in an attempt to blow it up. Despite such architectural tricks, the citadel was taken by Napoleon in 1806, then destroyed by Austrian and Prussian troops in 1813. Visit the tunnels and the small but free historic exhibit (open Tues.–Sun. 9:30–6, winter until 5) to find out about the early citadel's construction in 1103. Views of the *Domhügel* (Cathedral Hill) and the Erfurt skyline are spectacular—think "perfect picnic spot."

AFTER DARK

Pick up a copy of the monthly *Erfurt Magazin* for recent openings and closings and doings about town. Erfurt's **Jazzkeller** (jazz cellar) was expected to reopen soon after press time; call 0361/5612535 or ask for info at the tourist office. The old student quarter around Michaelisstraße has the heaviest concentration of cool spots.

BARS AND CLUBS

P. 33 is a popular bar that offers live music (no cover–DM 10) ranging from rock to folk to jazz several days a week. *Pergamenterg. 33, 1 block north of Dompl., tel. 0361/210–8714. Open weekdays noon–1 AM, weekends 9 AM–1 AM.*

MAD Discothek. If you're simply in a dancing mood, head on over to this down-to-earth dance joint. *Nordstrand 4, tel. 0361/56500, hot line 0361/525–6914. Open Thurs.–Sat. and before holidays from 9 PM.*

Studentclub Engelsburg. This dark, literally underground club is stuffed with denim- and leather-clad students bopping to a bizarre mix of current alternative music and vinyl rock 'n' roll classics. There's also an outdoor patio and a back room where local bands jam, and a café-bar upstairs. A mellower mid-twenties crowd hangs out across the street at candlelit **Roter Elephant** (Allerheiligenstr. 4, tel. 0361/561–2887). *Allerheiligenstr. 20–21, off Marktstr., tel. 0361/562–9036, hot line 5403234. Cover: DM 5–DM 10. Club open Wed., Fri., and Sat. 9 PM–1 AM, Thurs. 8 PM–midnight. Café open Tues. 7 PM–1 AM, Wed., Fri., and Sat. 7 PM–midnight.*

OPERA AND THEATER

Erfurt's **Schauspielhaus** (Klostergang, btw Neuwerkstr. and Regierungsstr., tel. 0361/223–3300) offers a year-round program of drama, as well as a *Kleinbühne* (small stage) for local productions. Classical-music fans should consider a night at the **Opernhaus** (Theaterstr., Tram 1 or 2 to Brühler Garten, tel. 0361/22330), with its year-round schedule of opera and chamber music. Tickets for either venue cost DM 18–DM 40; students with ID get a 50% break. For tickets, call 03621/223–3155, 223–3156, or 664–0100; or go to the ticket office at Dalbergsweg 2 (open Mon.–Sat. 10–1, Sun. 10–12, and Tues.–Fri. 2–5:30).

Theater Waidspeicher is a children's and puppet theater, but evenings find the stage usurped by "Die Arche," a cabaret troupe that pokes fun at everything from news anchors to disaster preparedness. Tickets (DM 15, DM 10 students except Sat.) are available at the theater or the ticket office (Dompl. 18; open Tues.–Fri. 10–2 and 3–5:30, Sat. 10–1); check the door for the current schedule. *Große Arche, at Mettengasse, tel. 0361/598–2924.*

NEAR ERFURT

MÜHLHAUSEN

With so much to see in Thuringia, few travelers make it to out-of-the-way Mühlhausen. Cradled in the gorgeous Unstut River valley, this 800-year-old city (once important for its trade) is filled with cobblestone streets, church spires, and well-preserved half-timbered houses. From here in 1525, radical preacher Thomas Müntzer (lauded by the GDR as Germany's first revolutionary) led the peasant revolt that would find its brutal and bloody end at nearby Frankenhausen in that same year.

The Gothic **Marienkirche** (open daily 10–4:30; admission DM 3, DM 2 students), just west of the Hauptmarkt, is where Müntzer rallied the masses with his fiery oratory. Inside is a small memorial to the man who considered Martin Luther a sellout, then recanted his own beliefs under torture. Down Ratsstraße you'll pass the **Rathaus** (No. 19)—where the "Eternal Council" talked revolution—on the way to the small **Bauernkriegsmuseum** (Peasants' War Museum; Kornmarktkirche, tel. 03601/870021; open Tues.–Sun. 10–4:30). For DM 2, DM 1 students, you can learn about the peasants' movement and see weapons they used. But there's more to Mühlhausen than just class war. Johann Sebastian Bach was organist at the 14th-century **Divi-Blasii-Kirche** (Untermarkt) 1708–09, when he wrote some of his famous cantatas. Mühlhausen also has an almost totally intact **city wall** (Holzstr.), part of which you can walk along with admission (DM 2, DM 1 students) to the **Rabenturm** (Raven's Tower; open Tues.–Sat. 1–5, Sun. 10–noon and 1–5), at the western end of the Altstadt. The tower affords a majestic view of the town and surrounding countryside and houses a small exhibit on city fortifications and local history.

When not seeing the sights you'll probably find yourself on the **Obermarkt** and Steinweg, the pedestrian zone teeming with shoppers, market-goers, and street musicians.

BASICS

Mühlhausen-Information (Ratsstr. 20, 1 block south of Obermarkt, tel. 03601/452335; open weekdays 9–5, in summer also Sat. 10–noon) has free maps and English-language brochures and will book you a private room (DM 30–DM 40) for DM 2.50. The **post office** on the Obermarkt has pay-after long-distance phones and a credit card ATM, and changes money for DM 6 per check.

COMING AND GOING

Mühlhausen can be reached by **train** from Erfurt (hourly, 1 hr, DM 13) and Gotha (6 per day, 1 hr, DM 9), or by **bus** from Eisenach (2 per day, 1 hr, DM 7). There are a handful of luggage lockers in the train station. From the Bahnhof (tel. 03601/812442), head rightish down Karl-Marx-Straße, cross busy Kiliansgraben, hang a right on Steinweg and you'll bump into the lively **Obermarkt.** From here, Linsenstraße leads left past Kornmarkt to the **Untermarkt.** The **Busbahnhof** (tel. 03601/591700) is just north of the Altstadt; walk down Stätte and turn right on Steinweg.

WHERE TO SLEEP AND EAT

Mühlhausen has several affordable lodging options. **Hotel Stadt Mühlhausen** (Untermarkt 18, tel. 03601/4550, fax 03601/455709) provides almost-budget luxury, including an elevator. Singles cost DM 50–DM 90, doubles DM 80–DM 120. **Pension Schilling** (Erfurter Str. 30, btw Untermarkt and Kiliansgraben, tel. 03601/812883, fax 03601/812233) has singles, doubles, and triples for DM 40–DM 45 per person. The cheaper rooms face the traffic on Erfurter Straße. The local **HI-Jugendherberge** (Auf dem Tonberg 1, tel. 03601/813318; closed 1 week at Christmas) has 78 beds (DM 19, DM 23 over 26) and is a 15-min walk from the city center. From the Bahnhof, take Bus 5 four stops to Pfortenteich, then go right on Schaffentorstraße, left on Tonbergstraße, and take the first right.

There are quite a few sidewalk cafés and Imbiß stands along Stätte and Steinweg near the Obermarkt, also the site of a Tuesday–Sunday **market.** You'll find a **Spar supermarket** on the Untermarkt. **Café-Bistro Swing** (Stätte 1b, tel. 03601/441965; open Sun.–Thurs. 11 AM–1 AM, Fri. and Sat. 11 AM–3 AM) draws a young crowd, but if you're sick of pizza and pasta (DM 7–DM 12), grab some Schnitzel (DM 10) at **Zur Alten Wache** (Untermarkt 14, tel. 03601/812664; open weekdays 11:30–11, Sat. 6–midnight).

GOTHA

Tiny Gotha, situated on the Leine Canal, is a good base for a day trip to Friedrichroda and the Thüringer Wald (*see below*), and its sights and Altstadt make for a relaxing afternoon. After making your way through the crumbling and abandoned buildings surrounding Gotha's city center, you can't help but fall in love with the colorful buildings on **Neumarkt** and **Hauptmarkt,** the two bustling squares. The town's history dates back over 12 centuries; it has been an important trade center (today it produces chemicals, textiles, and precision instruments) and was the summer retreat of the dukes of Saxe-Coburg-Gotha, the ancestors of England's royal house (which changed its name to non-German-sounding Windsor during World War I). Here in 1875 the Social Democratic Workers' Party (formed six years earlier in Eisenach) fused with other leftist groups to form what is now called the Social Democratic Party (SPD), today Germany's oldest political party.

Uphill from the Hauptmarkt, past the cascading 19th-century **Wasserkunst** (tiered fountain), is the largest early Baroque castle in Germany, **Schloß Friedenstein** (tel. 03621/53036; open daily 9–5). Built in the mid-1600s by the dukes of Saxe-Gotha-Altenburg, the castle houses two so-so **museums** (admission DM 8, DM 4 students). The Schloßmuseum's richly decorated rooms—including the Ekhof Theater, Germany's first stationary theater—display period paintings and such oddities as Egyptian mummies and a 17th-century ivory model of a pregnant woman (complete with innards). The Regional History Museum shows local artifacts, including Thuringian porcelain, and a cool collection of weapons through the ages. Behind the castle is the **Museum der Natur** (Parkallee 15, tel. 03621/53167; open daily 9–5), Thuringia's largest museum of natural science, with exhibits on fossils, minerals, and fauna and flora. Admission is DM 4, DM 2 students; a ticket to all three museums is DM 10, DM 5 students. Afterward, stroll the tree-lined walking paths surrounding the Schloß, or meditate on the serene duck pond.

BASICS

Down Hützelgasse from the Hauptmarkt's 16th-century Rathaus, **Gotha Information** (Blumenbachstr. 1–3, tel. 03621/854036, fax 03621/222134) has free English-language brochures and city maps. It is also the main regional tourist office for the Thüringer Wald, and it's open weekdays 9–5, Saturday 9–noon. Change money or use the ATM (credit cards and Plus/Cirrus) at **Deutsche Bank** just west of Neumarkt.

COMING AND GOING

Gotha's **Hauptbahnhof** (tel. 03621/53974) has luggage lockers and stays open all night, but sleeping here is frowned upon. Gotha is connected hourly with Weimar (40 min, DM 11), and twice hourly with Erfurt (20 min, DM 7) and Eisenach (30 min, DM 7). The **Waldbahn** (Tram 4) leaves from in front of the Bahnhof for Friedrichroda. The DM 8 **Touristen Ticket** includes the ride and discounted same-day admission to Gotha's museums and sights around Friedrichroda. Tickets are available at tourist offices or from the Waldbahn driver. To reach town, head straight down Bahnhofstraße (which becomes Friedrichstraße) for six or seven blocks, turn left up the steps at Erfurter Straße, and you'll hit the Neumarkt and, one block later, Hauptmarkt; or take any tram to Huttenstraße.

Local museums still carry an English-language brochure (50 Pf) describing the Peasant Revolt in Marxist terms.

WHERE TO SLEEP AND EAT

The tourist office lists private accommodations (DM 30–DM 45) and books rooms for free. **Am Schloß** (Bergallee 3a, to right of castle, tel. and fax 03621/53206) has only six rooms (doubles DM 70–DM 90), so if it's booked, check out **Regina** (Schwabhäuser Str. 4, tel. 03621/408020, fax 03621/408022; doubles DM 80–DM 130), on a small street between Friedrichstraße and the Hauptmarkt. The **HI-Jugendherberge** (Mozartstr. 1, 2 blocks toward town from station, tel. and fax 03621/54008) is large and cheap (DM 12, DM 16 over 26). Add DM 5 for breakfast, and pick up a key if you'll be out past 10. The busy year-round **open-air markets** in Gotha (Neumarkt or Hauptmarktstr.) proffer fresh fruit, bread, and Wurst. **Gockel Grill** (Hauptmarkt 26, tel. 03621/52955; closed Sun.) serves Hungarian paprikas (DM 7 and up) and traditional German wieners (under DM 5). **Ali Baba** (Arnoldpl. 2, tel. 03621/300137) has tasty sit-down or to-go meals starting at DM 5.

THÜRINGER WALD

The Thüringer Wald (Thuringian Forest), with its tranquil woods, rugged trails, and sleepy villages, is one of eastern Germany's most treasured retreats. The forest stretches from the outskirts of Eisenach to the Czech Republic, and once you breach its border there's nothing but trees, lakes, and spiny peaks—an ideal place for an extended hike. For hiking and nothing but, head to tiny **Oberhof** or **Friedrichroda,** or larger **Ilmenau.** Ignore the industry outside Ilmenau and **Arnstadt** (glass and porcelain production have a long history here)—the cities themselves consist of beautiful old houses and winding streets and lie just on the edge of the forest. **Schmalkalden** is a medieval gem, and **Meiningen** is a Baroque city known for its theater.

BASICS

The **tourist office** in Gotha (*see* Near Erfurt, *above*) is the headquarters for info on amenities and accommodations throughout the Thüringer Wald, though tourist offices in Eisenach and Erfurt stock a comprehensive selection as well. Offices in smaller forest towns often only stock information on the immediate area, and they rarely have detailed hiking guides.

COMING AND GOING

The aptly named **Waldbahn** runs every half hour from Gotha to Friedrichroda (45 min, DM 4). Buy the Touristen Ticket and save (*see* Gotha, *above*). Meiningen can be reached from Eisenach (hourly, 1½ hrs, DM 14) and Erfurt (every 2 hrs, 2 hrs, DM 21). The Erfurt–Meiningen line also passes through Arnstadt and Oberhof. Erfurt is a good jumping-off point for Arnstadt (2 per hr, 30 min, DM 7), Ilmenau (hourly, 1 hr, DM 13), and Oberhof (hourly, 1 hr, DM 13). Schmalkalden is accessible from Eisenach (via Wernshausen, hourly, 1 hr, DM 11) and Erfurt (via Zella-Mehlis, every 2 hrs, 2½ hrs, DM 19).

WHERE TO SLEEP

You can easily make day forays into the woods from Eisenach, Gotha, or Erfurt, but lodging in the forest towns and cities is actually affordable. It's even cheaper *in* the woods. A few youth hostels are scattered along the Rennsteig (*see below*): above Tabarz near Friedrichroda on the **Großer Inselberg** (tel. 036259/2329), above **Schnellbach** (Wanderherberge Weidmans, tel. 03683/604671) near Schmalkalden, and at **Neuhaus am Rennweg** (Apelsbergstr. 54, tel. 03679/722862). Beds are DM 17–DM 23 (DM 21–DM 28 over 26); HI cards may be required. The hostels are closed one week for Christmas. There are also plenty of pensions in the region, where you'll pay around DM 40–DM 50 per person. But on weekends, in summer, and especially on summer weekends, be sure to phone a few days ahead.

OUTDOOR ACTIVITIES

Serious hikers should consider the 168-km **Rennsteig** (Border Way), a ridge-top trail that extends from Hörschel, near Eisenach, to Blankenstein near the Czech border. From there it links up with trails to Budapest, Hungary. The stretch between Eisenach and Oberhof will take you through the most picturesque and sight-rich zone, although it is probably the most taxing, and takes a fit person a good two or three days. The Erfurt–Ilmenau–Schleusingen train stops at an unstaffed depot named Rennsteig, up in the mountains in the middle of nowhere. From here follow signs ¼ km to the trail. Needless to say, long-term hikers will need bad-weather gear, a good topographic map, and a serious sense of adventure. If you don't feel the need to cross a few international borders on foot, plenty of shorter hikes (3–8 hrs) also exist throughout the region.

WINTER SPORTS • In winter the Thüringer Wald is paradise for snow-sport enthusiasts. Certain towns—notably Oberhof, but also Friedrichroda and Ilmenau—attract downhill and cross-country skiers and snowboarders from all over the country. Check with local tourist offices for weather conditions, prices (expensive to very expensive), and lists of facilities (even hiking trails) open to the public.

FRIEDRICHRODA

Friedrichroda has been a resort town since the 1830s and was an extremely popular vacation spot in GDR times. Check out the Jugendstil buildings in the pedestrianized center, then spend the rest of the day wandering in the hills. A number of marked two- to three-hour circular hikes start from town; there are signposts and a map in the park between the Waldbahn station and town. The most popular hike leads to **Marienglashöhle** (An der Marienglashöhle, tel. 03623/30495; open daily 9–5, until 4 in winter), an eerie cavern that claims to have the largest crystal grotto in Europe. From 1775 until 1903, it was worked as a gypsum mine; nowadays you can take a highly recommended guided tour for DM 7 (DM 4 students). Bring a coat, as the white quartz walls are a chilly 46°F. If you're feeling lazy, the Waldbahn stops near the grotto, circumventing the pleasant hike. Another popular hike (again, follow the signs) leads to **Schauenburg Friedrichroda,** an overgrown ruin on the cusp of a forested hill. Formerly home to a cell of Benedictine monks, this crumbly 17th-century fort now makes an ideal picnic spot. On the same trail are signs for the Rennsteig, which runs within 3 km of Friedrichroda.

For a longer trek, follow the signs toward Schloß Reinhardsbrunn (a hotel for petits bourgeois with money to spare), and onward 3 km to **Schloß Tenneberg** (open Tues.–Sun. 10–4; admission DM 3, DM 1.50 students). Built in 1168, the castle houses an interesting puppet museum, as well as a peasant museum that documents everyday life from 1800 to the present. From here the trail meanders through a serene valley and clusters of dense forest before reaching **Waltershausen,** a friendly and relaxed town filled with bakeries, butcher shops, and lively beer halls. The last Waldbahn back to Friedrichroda leaves at 9:45 PM from Waltershausen Wahlwinkel or Waltershausen Gleisdreieck—*not* from the Bahnhof.

The **Touristen Ticket** (*see* Gotha, *above*) gives discounts on the above sights and two **trolleys** that head to nearby mountaintops on the Rennsteig trail: The Thüringer Wald Express leaves six times daily from Marktstraße near the info office for the **Heuberg,** while the Inselberg Express trundles up to the **Inselberg** (and its hostel, *see* Where to Sleep *in* Thüringer Wald, *above*) eight times daily from Tabarz, at the end of the Waldbahn. Both run in summer and cost DM 12 round-trip.

BASICS

From the Waldbahn station, it's a 15-min walk over the hill to town; follow the signs toward the hostel. The **information office** (Marktstr. 13–15, tel. 03623/304575, fax 03623/200694; open Mon.–Thurs. 9–5, Fri. 9–6, Sat. 9–noon) sells detailed hiking maps (DM 7) and books private rooms (DM 30–DM 40).

The **bus** stop for Schmalkalden (1–2 per day, 1 hr, DM 4.50) is three blocks past the upper end of Hauptstraße on the right.

WHERE TO SLEEP AND EAT

The peaceful **HI-Jugendherberge Friedrichroda** (Waldstr. 25, tel. 03623/304410) has beds in spartan rooms for DM 17 (DM 21 over 26), including breakfast. If you can't take the hostel scene, check out **Hotel Thüringer Hof** (Bahnhofstr. 20, tel. and fax 03623/304365). Singles are DM 35, doubles DM 50, including breakfast. **Haus Reinhardsberg** (Burchardtsweg 6, tel. 03623/36300, fax 03623/304304) has singles for DM 45–DM 50, doubles DM 75–DM 90 (call 8–10 or 1–2). For a sit-down meal, stroll Hauptstraße until you find something to your liking. You can restock your trail-mix supply at the **Rewe supermarket** two blocks down Marktstraße from the info office.

SCHMALKALDEN

In a round valley on the southern edge of the Thüringer Wald, Schmalkalden's well-preserved medieval center features scores of half-timbered houses. In 1531 German Reformists and dukes met here to form the Schmalkadic League, which was to defend the new Lutheran churches from attack by Catholic Emperor Charles V. Martin Luther himself came in 1537 to present his "Schmalkaldic Articles," a list of Protestant tenets and ideas. But the Force was not with them. Shortly after Luther's death, the emperor smashed the rebels in the Schmalkaldic War of 1546–47.

During the cold war, the Rennsteig was mostly inaccessible, since it passed along the border with West Germany. The trail has since been repaired and re-marked with a white "R"; prior to 1989, people were always getting lost.

The best way to experience Schmalkalden is by merely wandering its colorful streets and hidden alleys. Then climb up Schloßberg, a cobblestone street that leads directly to **Schloß Wilmhelmsburg,** a beautiful late-Renaissance castle built as a small (by royal standards) summer retreat for the dukes of Hessen-Kassel (to which Schmalkalden belonged at the time). The castle **museum** (tel. 03683/403186; open Feb.–Oct., Tues.–Sun. 9–5; Nov.–Jan. 10–4) houses an exhibit on Luther and the Schmalkaldic League, all in rooms with exquisitely restored frescoes. Inside the gold-fringed **chapel** is one of Europe's oldest still-functioning organs, piping up since the Renaissance. Just down the hill from the Schloß, the Altmarkt's late-Gothic **Stadtkirche St. Georg** (open May–Sept., Mon.–Sat. 10:30–12:30 and 1:30–3:30; Oct.–Apr., Mon.–Sat. 12–12:30 and 1:30–2:30) is where Luther and other League members preached. Take a peek at the hand-carved altar in the sacristy. Down Mohrengasse on Lutherplatz is the **Lutherhaus** (now a bookstore), where Luther stayed during his 1537 visit.

BASICS

Buses to Friedrichroda (1–2 per day, 1 hr, DM 4.50) depart from the Busbahnhof (tel. 03683/604067) across from the train station. Walk down Bahnhofstraße, turn left on Haindorfsgasse, and take the first right to get to the Altmarkt and the **tourist office** (Mohreng. 1, tel. 03683/403182; open Mon.–Fri. 9–1 and 2–6; Oct.–Mar. until 3 and also Sat. 10–1). Besides handing out brochures, city maps, and hiking maps, the staff books private rooms (DM 30 and up per person) for a DM 1 fee.

WHERE TO SLEEP AND EAT

Schmalkalden makes an easy day trip from Eisenach or Meiningen, but if you want to stay, there are two friendly, affordable pensions facing each other across a placid duck pond just outside the Altstadt. **Pension Rau** (Am Neuen Teich 12, tel. 03683/603506) has three singles (DM 45–DM 60) and four doubles (DM 90–DM 110). A great plus: Frau Rau has an extensive collection of maps, brochures, and guides (some in English) of the whole region laid out in her breakfast room. If you speak any German (or Russian), be sure to get some of her fascinating anecdotes on GDR social life. Drawback: B.Y.O.S. (bring your own soap). **Pension Am Neuen Teich** (Am Neuen Teich 13, tel. 03683/3861) has four doubles for DM 80–DM 90. From the station, walk down Bahnhofstraße, turn left on Recklinghäuser Straße, and left on Röthweg, an easily missed small street. With luggage, it is quite a hike from the station to the pond, and it's another 7 min to town.

Market days on the Altmarkt are Wednesday and Saturday; otherwise head to the **Spar** supermarket on Neumarkt. For hearty Thruingian cuisine, try the DM 13–DM 20 dishes at the **Ratskeller** (Altmarkt, tel. 03683/2742), at **Gasthaus Hessischer Hof** (Lutherpl., tel. 03683/3902), or at the **Teichhotel** (Teichstr.

21, near the two pensions, tel. 03683/402661). Also on Altmarkt are the **Thurback** bakery-café and the excellent **Grillstub'n** snack window, whose DM 1.80 Bratwurst is a big hit with locals and tourists alike.

MEININGEN

Under Georg II, known fondly as the "Theater Duke," Meiningen's stage was once the talk of Europe. Today this lively city still offers outstanding theater, as well as a colorful market, lots of cafés and beer halls, and even a few sights. Although Meiningen is too far from the forest proper to be used as a starting point for long-distance hikes, the smart-looking stores that line **Georgstraße** and the adjacent **Markt** are good places to prepare for a week on the trails.

Meiningen's most notable feature is the **Elisabethenburg** (tel. 03693/3641), a small Baroque castle built in 1692 by the duke of Thuringia and used as the ducal residence until the early part of the 20th century. Look for it at the edge of a small wood four blocks northwest of the Markt. Inside are an art gallery devoted to Italian and Dutch masters, lavish period rooms, and an exhibit on the history of theater in Meiningen. You can catch weekly recitals and seasonal concerts (DM 15–DM 18) in the **Schloßkirche** (castle chapel). Admission (DM 6, DM 4 students) to the Elisabethenburg also admits you to the nearby **Baumbachhaus** (Burggasse 22, tel. 03693/502848), an 18th-century timber-frame house that contains a small literature museum, as well as exhibits on Schiller, Ernst Wagner, and Carl Gottlob Cramer, each of whom spent at least one summer working and living in Meiningen. (You have to be seriously into minor German literature to get a kick out of this place.) Tickets for the Baumbachhaus alone are DM 2 (DM 1 for students). The castle and the Baumbachhaus are open Sat.–Thurs. 10–6 (Oct.–Apr. 9–5).

BASICS

To reach the town center, go straight out of the Bahnhof and head for the far left corner of the serene, sculpture-filled Englischer Garten. The **tourist office** (Bernhardstr. 6, tel. 03693/44650), half a block to your right, books private rooms for a DM 3 fee, and stocks maps and German-language walking guides. It's open weekdays 9–6 and Saturday 10–3 (Sept.–Mar., weekdays 9–5). The Altstadt centers around the Markt, four blocks down Georgstraße.

WHERE TO SLEEP AND EAT

Meiningen doesn't have a hostel; the best budget option is to book a private room (DM 30–DM 45) at the tourist office. A 20-min walk from behind the train station, **Pension Monika** (Tiroler Weg 27, tel. 03693/3738) has one single (DM 34) and doubles for DM 86. To get there, walk south on Berliner Straße, which becomes Tiroler Weg. If you want to spoil yourself a bit after all that hiking, **Pension Pelzer** (Georgstr. 8, tel. 03693/44210, fax 03693/442125) has modern rooms in the middle of the Altstadt's pedestrian zone for DM 60–DM 100 per person, breakfast included. For cheap eats, head to "Treffpunkt," a long line of cafés and Imbiß stands on the Markt to the right of the church with the wacky rainbow fish-scale roof. The quieter **Ristorante Italiano** (Schloßpl. 3–5, tel. 03693/470775) has a view of the Elisabethenburg and varied dishes priced DM 8–DM 15. Pick up groceries at the **Konsum supermarket** on Luisenstraße just west of the Markt.

AFTER DARK

Meiningen Theater (Bernhardstr. 5, tel. 03693/4510; box office tel. 03693/451222) produces an extensive and eclectic range of performances in a grand, columned structure built in 1909—after the original theater burned to the ground. The most unusual (and best) shows appear on the smaller stage called **Georgie's Off.** Plays run September–June, with the occasional special event in summer. Tickets are DM 15–DM 50; DM 8 buys a student ticket to any performance at Georgie's Off.

ILMENAU

Ilmenau's claim to fame is its association with Goethe, who spent many summers writing and doing scientific work in the surrounding mountains. In the main square is the **Goethe-Gedenkstätte im Amtshaus** (Markt 1, tel. 03677/202667; admission DM 2, DM 1 students), where Goethe worked for a few years; the only original pieces in the re-created living room and study are his diary and some personal letters. Pop in for a beer at **Gasthaus zum Löwen,** across the street from the tourist office, where Goethe celebrated one of his 82 birthdays. Once you've explored all the Goethe-related attractions of this small, provincial town, mosey on down one of the many beautiful trails leading into the mountains.

Follow Goethe's summer ramblings on the **Goethe-Wanderweg,** a rigorous 19-km trail posted with wood markers bearing the letter "G." It will take you about seven–eight hours from the trail's starting point (at the Amtshaus on the main square) to Stützerbach. An alternate route lets you walk a four–five-hour loop—a great way to experience the forest without having to rough it under the stars in a soggy sleeping bag.

About two hours into the hike you pass the funky rock formation **Großer Hermannstein** (where Goethe took his beloved Charlotte von Stein) and **Goethes Häuschen auf dem Kickelhahn,** where he penned "The Wayfarer's Night Song II." From here a trail leads back to town, but if you continue downhill you'll come to **Jagdhaus Gabelbach** (tel. 03677/202626; mid-Mar.–Nov., Wed.–Sun. 9–5, Nov.–mid-Mar., Wed.–Sun. 10–4). Goethe was a frequent guest here and did much of his scientific work in the restored library, which now houses a museum displaying Goethe's spectacles, research notes, and other memorabilia. Admission is DM 4, DM 3 students.

BASICS

The **Busbahnhof** (tel. 03677/88890), just across from the Hauptbahnhof, has service to Arnstadt (3–5 per day, 30 min, DM 4), Erfurt (3–5 per day, 1 hr, DM 8), and Weimar (3 per day, 1½ hrs, DM 10). To reach the **tourist office** (Lindenstr. 12, tel. 03677/62132 or 202358, fax 03677/202502; open weekdays 9–6, Sat. 9–noon), head down Bahnhofstraße, turn right at Wetzlarer Platz, and walk down pedestrian-only Friedrich-Hoffmann-Straße (which becomes Straße des Friedens and then Lindenstraße). The office stocks city maps and info on hiking and skiing. If your train continues to Schleusingen, get off one stop farther at Ilmenau Ost and you'll be right near the tourist office. Ilmenau's main **post office** (Poststr.) is on Wetzlarer Platz. Many branches of **Dresdner Bank** and **Sparkasse** along Straße des Friedens have ATMs that accept all credit and bank cards.

Meiningen Theater is probably the only playhouse to offer puppet theater, Goethe, and a ballet version of A Clockwork Orange *under the same roof.*

WHERE TO SLEEP AND EAT

HI-Jugendherberge Ilmenau (Stollen 48, tel. 03677/884681; beds DM 22, DM 27 over 26) is a 10-min walk from the Hauptbahnhof—go left as you come out from the station and follow the footpath along the train tracks until you reach the public pool. The hostel is next door; there is an **Aldi supermarket** across the street. **Haus Neuschwander** (Lindenstr. 37, tel. 03677/68080, fax 03677/680818) is right downtown and has six apartment-style rooms for DM 40–DM 90. The tourist office can book a wide variety of private rooms (starting as low as DM 20 for a single) for a DM 2 fee. Most of the town's other hotels and pensions start at DM 60 for a single room.

In the city center, you'll find many restaurants in the DM 10–DM 15 range. Along Straße des Friedens, try **Restaurant Nirsberger** (Str. des Friedens 11, tel. 03677/62156) or **Café Arche** (Str. des Friedens 28, tel. 03677/894711; closed Mon.) for international snacks and Nicaraguan coffee. In the main square (even in winter), there is often an open-air market; right nearby you can pick up groceries at **Edeka supermarket** (Marktstr.).

OBERHOF

High in the mountains, Oberhof is a scenic resort town that's short on history (it's only been around since 1861), but full of activities that vary with the seasons—tennis, swimming, year-round bobsledding (don't worry, the sleds have wheels). The town's proximity to the famous Rennsteig trail, 1 km away, makes it an excellent pit stop for hikers. With the first snowfall, Oberhof becomes ski central, a mecca for families on vacation as well as die-hard skiers, who come for the World Cup ski-jumping events. Take advantage of the numerous downhill and cross-country runs, all reachable via ski shuttle buses.

If you really think you can handle bobsledding down a hill at 90 km per hour, contact **BSR Rennsteig** (Crawinkler 10, tel. 036870/22520, fax 21149). Rent your ski equipment at **Sport Luck** (Gräfenroder Str., tel. 036842/22212) or at the **Skiverleih & Testcenter** (Am Grenzadler, tel. 036842/22357). Full gear starts around DM 20 per day, snowboards at DM 25. Lift tickets for **Rennsteig-Therman** run DM 19. The hot line for information on ski conditions in Oberhof is 036842/20195.

HITLER'S WET FANTASYLAND

Though Ilmenau is flooded with tourists in the summer, nearby Schwarzburg was almost obliterated by a very real deluge. Seems Hitler fancied Schwarzburg castle so much he wanted to live in it. The catch: He wanted the castle, which sits on a hill above town, to be surrounded by water so he could enjoy an island home. Lucky for the townspeople, this mad dream proved an engineering conundrum, and Hitler eventually got distracted (that global conquest thing). Today Schwarzburg is a nice stop, but don't expect a lot. Pick up some trail maps to the castle or book a private room at the tourist office (Hauptstr. 2, tel. 036730/22305).

BASICS

Oberhof's Bahnhof is at the bottom of a steep hill, 6 km south of town. The **bus** up to town (DM 1.10) meets incoming trains (don't dawdle in the station). The **tourist office** (Crawinkler Str. 2, tel. 036842/22143, fax 036842/22332) is permanently located in a makeshift building across from the bus stop. The staff book private rooms (DM 25 and up per person), have info on the Rennsteig and skiing, and organize guided hikes. They're open April–October, weekdays 9–5, Saturday 9–3, and Sunday 1–3 (shorter hrs in winter). A **Sparkasse** branch ATM machine (Zellaerstr. 7), the **post office** (Zellaerstr. 13), and a **pharmacy** near the Rathaus are all located along the town's main drag, Zellaerstraße.

WHERE TO SLEEP AND EAT

If you don't book a room through the **tourist office,** keep your eyes open for ZIMMER FREI (private room) signs in house windows. A few affordable pensions line Crawinkler Straße and Rudolf-Breitscheidstraße. **Haus Immergrün** (Rudolf-Breitscheidstr. 2, tel. 036842/22339) offers kitchen facilities with its single (DM 30) and two doubles (DM 50–DM 70). Take your growling stomach to **Café Luisensitz** (Theo-Neubauer-Str. 25, tel. 036842/22196) for filling meat-and-potato meals (DM 8–DM 17). They also have a respectable selection of goods from the local baker if you just want to nibble, sip coffee, and read.

ARNSTADT

Arnstadt is the oldest town in Thuringia (AD 704) and a cheerful place to visit in summer. Although most people come for the hiking and cross-country trails, Arnstadt is best known for its association with Johann Sebastian Bach; when he was 18 years old, he had his first job as organist at the single-nave, 16th-century **Bachkirche** (Jägerstr., tel. 03628/608822; open Tues., Thurs., and weekends 3–3:45), commonly known as the Neue Kirche (new church). It seems Bach's genius was not appreciated by the traditional worshippers, who thought his sweeping harmonies too fancy for mass. There is some debate as to whether Bach quit or was fired, but in either case, he left the church's employ in 1707 after about three years' service. For a DM 1 admission fee, you can view the organ he played and some of his personal memorabilia.

A better bet for Bach fans is **Haus zum Palmbaum,** with exhibits on Arnstadt's history, Bach's musical legacy, and his residence in town. Standing (well, actually slouching) guard on the Markt out front is a statue of young Bach, looking incredibly relaxed. Amidst the celebration of Bach's 300th birthday, the unconventional depiction of Arnstadt's local hero caused quite a ruckus at its 1985 unveiling. *Markt 3, tel. 03628/602978. Admission: DM 4, DM 2 students. Open weekdays 8:30–noon and 1–5:30, weekends 9:30–4:30.*

Arnstadt's well-preserved shopping lanes radiate from the Markt. Follow Schloßstraße north and you'll dead-end at the **Schloßmuseum mit Puppenstadt,** a 16th-century castle that's been converted into an arts-and-crafts museum. Yes, it sounds woefully dull, but don't miss the intriguing "Mon Plaisir" exhibit (also called the "Puppenstube"). This collection of over 400 handmade dolls set in dioramas (uh, well, dollhouses) was commissioned around 1700 by Princess Augusta Dorothea von Schwarzburg-Arnstadt. *Schloßpl. 1, tel. 03628/602932, fax 03628/640720. Admission: DM 3.50, DM 2.50 students. Open Tues.–Sun. 8:30–noon and 1–5:30 (winter 9:30–4).*

Die-hard train aficionados can check out the **Museum für Dampflokomotiven** (Rehestadter Weg, tel. 03628/602395, ext. 354; admission DM 7, DM 2 students) to catch a glimpse of a traditional steam engine rail operation plant. Call for daily open hours.

BASICS

The city center is a 15-min walk north of the Hauptbahnhof; head left out of the station and turn right on Bahnhofstraße. Once in the Altstadt, turn right to reach the tourist office (Markt 3, tel. 03628/602049, fax 03628/640720; open weekdays 9–noon and 12:30–6, Sat. 9–noon), which has hiking maps and books private rooms (DM 25–DM 30 per person) for a DM 3 fee. The main **post office** (Ritterstr.) is just north of the Schloßmuseum.

The **Busbahnhof** (tel. 03628/01330) to the left of the train station doesn't have an information kiosk; either check the posted schedules and buy a ticket onboard, or get info and tickets at the tourist office. Destinations include Ilmenau (4–8 per day, 1 hr, DM 5.60) and Erfurt (3–6 per day, 30 min, DM 4).

The ponderous commercialization of Goethe is best seen in Ilmenau's Goethe Passage, a monstrous lavender-and-yellow mini-mall brimming with shiny appliance shops and swank boutiques. Follow the big G.'s lead and head for the woods.

WHERE TO SLEEP AND EAT

The hospitable **Pension & Pub Globetrotter** (Rosenstr. 24, 2 blocks NW of Markt, tel. 03628/603779) has a single (DM 60), two doubles (DM 80), and a triple (DM 120). Among the many Altstadt eateries, **Waffelstübchen** (Holzmarkt 1, tel. 03628/602747) is best for light meals (DM 10), while **Bachkeller-Alt-Arnscht** (Ledermarktg., tel. 03628/602013) serves more heavy-duty German meals (DM 10–DM 20). After dinner, grab a beer with the kick-back crowd at **Kulisse** (Holzmarkt 6, tel. 03628/78288), which stays open until midnight every day.

OUTDOOR ACTIVITIES

If you're in Arnstadt to hike, try the flat, six-hour trek to **Die Drei Gleichen,** three ruined castles that sit side by side in a landscape of rolling wheat fields. The castles' name loosely means "three of the same." One explanation is that all three were bombed on the same day during World War II. Nowadays no one tends the grounds, though you'll sometimes find kids scrambling through the skeletal ruins. The tourist office has free route maps, and if you like, you can take the train back from Wandersleben (hourly, 20 min, DM 4.20). Or pack a picnic and grab a bike at Arnstadt's train station or **Zobel's Zweirad Shop** (Zimmerstr. 17, tel. 03628/602432; open weekdays 9–6, Sat. 9–noon). Everything from training wheels to serious cycles goes for DM 11–DM 20 a day.

EISENACH

Once a dilapidated and begrimed industrial town (known primarily as a center of car-production in the former GDR), Eisenach has since recovered much of its medieval charm. The biggest draw is the **Wartburg,** a beautiful 11th-century castle just south of town that serves as an important symbol in German history: It was here that Martin Luther translated the Bible into German, laying the foundation for Protestantism as well as standard written German. In 1817, a group of students met at the castle to call for a unified, democratic Germany, and the castle and its history later inspired Richard Wagner's *Tannhäuser.* But the mobs of tourists you will encounter (especially on long weekends) are entirely Luther's doing.

Don't limit your stay to the Wartburg, however—wander the narrow streets past Baroque facades in Eisenach's Altstadt and visit the local museums, and you'll get a taste of this small city's history. J. S. Bach was born here, as was the German workers' movement. During GDR days, Eisenach was known for the rather box-like car, also known as the "Wartburg," which can still be seen on the streets today (through a thick cloud of black exhaust). When the Wartburg factory went belly-up after unification, Eisenach suffered plenty of layoffs, but has since recouped some of the loss with a new Opel factory. If you want to get away from it all, you're only an hour by train from the Thüringer Wald towns of Meiningen and Schmalkalden (*see above*).

BASICS

CHANGING MONEY

ATMs can be found at the Hauptbahnhof and throughout the Altstadt at branches of **Sparkasse** and **Dresdner** banks (one branch at cnr of Theatrpl. and Querstr.). All credit and bank cards are gladly accepted.

MAIL AND PHONES

There's a small post office with phones to the left of the train station as you exit. The **main post office** (Markt 16; postal code 99817), on the city's main square, has phones and exchanges traveler's checks at fair rates.

PHARMACIES

You won't have to search hard for one of the many pharmacies in the Altstadt (along Karlstr. and Querstr.). Or try the **Ost-Apotheke** (Bahnhofstr. 29, tel. 03691/203242), about halfway between the Hauptbahnhof and Busbahnhof.

VISITOR INFORMATION

Eisenach's **tourist office** (Markt 2, tel. 03691/79230, fax 03691/792320) stocks an English-language walking guide (50 Pf), and books private rooms for free. The office is open Monday 10–6, Tuesday–Friday 9–6, and Saturday 10–2. To get here from the Hauptbahnhof, turn right and continue until you reach the Marktplatz. **Wartburg Information** (Schloßberg 2, behind post office, tel. 03691/77073, fax 03691/77072) has Wartburg- and Luther-specific info.

COMING AND GOING

BY TRAIN

Eisenach's **Hauptbahnhof** (tel. 03691/732744) is east of the city center. To get to the Markt, head right down Bahnhofstraße and through the gate to Karlstraße, a pedestrian street that leads to the square. Destinations from Eisenach include Berlin (9 per day, 4 hrs, DM 83), Frankfurt (hourly, 2 hrs, DM 53), Erfurt (2 per hr, 40 min, DM 12.20), and Leipzig (hourly, 2½ hrs, DM 40). Dump your bags in the station's luggage lockers: a locker will cost you DM 2 (DM 4 for a large locker) per 24-hour period (up to three days).

BY BUS

The **Busbahnhof** (tel. 03691/228844) is to the right of the train station at Müllerstraße. Unless you're headed for the campground or Mühlhausen (6 per day weekdays between 6:30 AM and 5 PM, less on weekends, 1 hr, DM 7), you probably won't find yourself here. For schedules and prices head to the info office (open weekdays 8–4) at the far end of the bus lot. The **Urlauber ticket** (DM 5 for one day, DM 10 for three days) is good for all buses in the Eisenach region. All **city buses** terminate across from the Hauptbahnhof and cost DM 1.50 (DM 1 if you buy your ticket from the machine at the station).

WHERE TO SLEEP

The tourist office books private rooms (DM 25–DM 56 per person). **Haus Hainstein** (Am Hainstein 16, tel. 03691/2420, fax 03691/242109) has singles for DM 70–DM 95, doubles DM 130–DM 150. From the train station, take Bus 3, 10, or 11 to Auto Pavillon, continue down Wartburgallee, and go right on

Barfüßerstraße, which becomes Am Hainstein.

Haus Waldblick. Run by a friendly couple, this hotel offers singles for DM 65–DM 75, doubles for DM 120, and one triple for DM 135; breakfast is included. *Albrechtstr. 1, tel. and fax 03691/732344. Exit rear of station, turn right, continue straight and across bridge, take 1st left, then 1st right (20 min); or Bus 6 to Weimarische Str. (last bus 11:20 PM), cross bridge. 10 rooms, all with bath. Laundry. Reservations advised.*

Villa Elisabeth. The quiet option in town is a 10-min walk from the Altstadt and has three singles (DM 70–DM 100), four doubles (DM 120–DM 140), and a suite (DM 150). All are nonsmoking (a rare find in these parts). Bikes are also available for rent. *Reuterstr. 1, tel. 03691/77052, fax 03691/743652. From Markt, walk east on Karlstr., turn right on Querstr., which turns into Frauenberg and then Marienstr., until you reach Reuterstr. (10 min).*

Villa Kesselring. This grand old manor is in a quiet green neighborhood, just a five-min walk (albeit uphill) from the Markt. You'll spend DM 60 for a single, DM 96–DM 120 for a double. *Hainw. 32, tel. and fax 03691/732049. 6 rooms, some with bath. From Wartburg Information, up Schloßberg and left on Hainw. Reservations strongly advised.*

HOSTELS

Jugendherberge–Mariental. At the foot of Wartburg castle 3½ km southwest of the train depot, the hostel is definitely worth the trek: The mansion is perched in a peaceful forest on the hill. Beds in the two- to eight-bed dorms are DM 22 (DM 26 over 26), sheets run DM 7; lunch and dinner are available for DM 8 each. A taxi from town costs around DM 10. *Mariental 24, tel. 03691/743259, fax 03691/743260. From train station, Bus 3 to Liliengrund (Mariental is 300 m to your right). 102 beds. Be there by 8 PM; get key to avoid the curfew. Reception open 8 AM–10 AM and 4 PM–8 PM. Luggage storage.*

CAMPING

Altenberger See Campingplatz. Off Highway B-19, 9 km south of Eisenach, the camp has showers, toilets, telephones, a snack bar, a lake, and heaps of family-filled motor homes. It can be difficult to reach on weekends, when there are only two buses per day (last bus 5:20 PM); during the week, buses leave hourly (last bus 6 PM). Campsites cost DM 6 per person plus DM 5 per tent and DM 2 per car. *Tel. 03691/215637. 60 sites. From Busbahnhof, Bus 31 (DM 2) to Altenberger See.*

If you're in Eisenach three weeks before Easter, don't miss the Sommergewinn festival, a bash dating back to the Middle Ages that marks summer's triumph over winter in a decidedly pagan manner. There's a bonfire and an enactment on the Markt of "Frau Sunna" giving Old Man Winter the boot.

FOOD

Karlstraße is where you'll find Eisenach's fast food and snack stands. A great place to savor a beer or a glass of wine is the **Brunnenkeller** (Am Markt, tel. 03691/71429.). Set in an old monastery wine cellar across from post office (south of Georgenkirche), this restaurant serves German entrées that go for DM 12–DM 25. For a Greek lunch menu, walk one block south from Karlstraße to **Olympia** (Goldschmiederstr. 28, tel. 03691/77242). Look for **Skyline** (Karlstr.) on the main drag; this trendy, U.S.-inspired café-bar is replete with neon sign and features eclectic, fairly priced cuisine. The bakery-café across Kaufhaus Schwager on Johannisplatz has has cheap (DM 7) potato and pasta dishes for lunch (from here don't miss the great view of the curious 18th-century Narrow House—it's only 1.95 m wide).

WORTH SEEING

Most of Eisenach's sights are concentrated inside the cobbled city center. As you pass through the 12th-century **Nikolaitor,** you first come upon **Karlsplatz** and busy, pedestrian-only **Karlstraße,** which starts at the square's far end. Karlstraße runs into the central Markt and **Georgenkirche.** This modest church is where J. S. Bach was baptized, and where Eisenach's citizens gathered in 1989 to rally for an end to Soviet domination. Perpendicular to Karlstraße, Querstraße runs north to **Theaterplatz** and south to

Frauenplan.

AUTOMOBILBAUMUSEUM

Eisenach's auto factory produced cars for almost 100 years. Its models ranged from the Dixi to the Wartburg; even the very first BMWs were built here. This museum across from the now-defunct plant displays prototypes never put into mass production and a few pristine showroom models. Visit the secondary showroom (Wartburgallee 54, near Barfüßerstr.) to examine a few more models. *Rennbahn 8, tel. 03691/77212, fax 03691/743234. From Karlstr., north on Querstr., under tracks and right. Admission: DM 4, DM 2 students. Open Tues.–Sun. 9–5.*

BACHHAUS

Dedicated to the Bach family legacy and highlighting J. S. as its most accomplished member, this museum also houses a collection of fascinating historical instruments. Every visit concludes with a short live concert played on period instruments. A must-see for Bach fans. *Frauenplan 21, tel. 03691/79340, fax 03691/793424. Admission: DM 5, DM 4 students. Open Apr.–Sept., Mon. 12–5, Tues.–Sun. 9–5:45; Oct.–Mar., Mon. 1–4:45, Tues.–Sun. 9–4:45.*

GOLDENER LÖWE

The Golden Lion Memorial marks the founding site of the Social Democratic Workers' Party (precursor of today's SPD). An exhibit examines the work of August Bebel and Karl Liebknecht, as well as Eisenach's role in their movement. *Marienstr. 57, tel. and fax 03691/75434. Open Mon., Tues., Fri. 9–4, weekends by appointment.*

LUTHERHAUS

Germany's most revered heretic spent three years in this house, arriving in 1498 at age 15 to study in Eisenach. Traditional and interactive multimedia displays (some in English) chronicle Luther's life and work. If you decide to skip the life history, at least catch a peek at the renovated house itself. *Lutherpl. 8, 1 block south of Markt, tel. 03691/29830, fax 03691/298331. Admission: DM 5, DM 2 students. Open May–Sept., daily 9–5; Oct.–Apr., Mon.–Sat. 9–5, Sun. 2–5.*

REUTER-WAGNER MUSEUM

Fritz Reuter, northern Germany's most important *Plattdeutsch* dialect poet, retired to this lovely villa for the last six years of his life. On display are samples of his writing and drawings. The Wagner connection is pure chance: The collection of the composer's artifacts ended up here because the town didn't have anywhere else to put them. *Reuterw. 2, 3 blocks south of Frauenplan, tel. 03691/203971. Admission: DM 4, DM 2 students. Open Tues.–Sun. 10–5.*

WARTBURG

In May 1521, with his arrest for sedition imminent, Martin Luther faked his kidnapping and disappeared into the Wartburg, a medieval fortress long prized by German kings for its strategic location. He grew a beard, disguised himself as a nobleman named Junker Jörg, and, protected by his allies, spent the next 10 months here. During this time he translated the New Testament into German, thereby laying the foundation for standard written German. The main building, a 12th-century Romanesque hall, can only be seen on a **guided tour** (DM 11, DM 6 students). The sometimes drab, sometimes ornate rooms have a fascinating history of their own, predating Luther's visit by almost 500 years—the fortress dates back to 1067. Since then this most German of German castles has played host to the lauded minstrels Walther von der Vogelweide and Wolfram von Eschenbach, as well as Richard Wagner and Goethe. Tour admission includes the **museum** (which can be seen alone, DM 6, DM 4 students) with its Luther exhibit. For a bite while you're here, head to the small restaurant. From the grounds you get a great view of Eisenach below and the Thüringer Wald to the south, but be prepared for *lots* of company—during the high season the wait can be up to two hours. *Tel. 03691/77072. Open Mar.–Oct., daily 8:30–6:30 (last tour at 5); Nov.–Feb., daily 9–5 (last tour at 3:30).*

Getting to the castle involves a short but strenuous climb, even if you drive or take the bus. If you're in the mood to hoof it all the way, steep 30-min hiking trails start at the Wartburg Information office and the foot of Marienstraße near the Reuter-Wagner Museum. Bus 10 (May–Sept. only) is a more laid-back option; it leaves every 20 min from the Hauptbahnhof and the end of Marienstraße. April–October you can catch a shuttle van (DM 4) from the Marienstraße bus stop. If you're driving to the top during high season, know that parking (cars DM 5, motorcycles/mopeds DM 2) is limited.

AFTER DARK

At the **Landestheater** you'll hear classical concerts, see diverse drama, and witness anything from puppet to political theater. Many productions rely on montage and mime, so fluent German is not always a prerequisite. For schedules and ticket prices, stop by the theater's **information office** (Sophienstr. 53, tel. 03691/256232; open weekdays 10–5, Sat. 10–noon). *Theaterpl. 4–7, tel. 03691/256219. Box office open Tues.–Fri. 10–6, weekends 10–noon (also 1½ hrs before performances).*

Bistro-Café Swing. Young and old alike, Eisenachers come here for coffee and ice cream during the day, more substantial fortification at night. This is a great place to relax after sunset, when the scene is mellow and the Nikolaitor, an ancient stone gate, is illuminated. *Karlspl. 10, tel. 03691/213049. Open Mon.–Thurs. 10 AM–1 AM, Fri. and Sat. 10 AM–2 AM, Sun. noon–1 AM.*

Klapsmühle. There are two bars in town that advertise themselves as *verrückt* (crazy): **Klimperkasten** (Alexanderstr. 49, tel. 03691/624752) is a traditional bar with a lively mixed-age crowd, but Klapsmühle was an instant twentysomething favorite when it opened. The decor is "traditional with a touch of kitsch," the musical selection eclectic. *Am Markt, 2nd floor, next to post office, no phone. Open daily from 5 PM.*

What pilgrimage would be complete without donkeys? From Easter to October, people under 60 kilos (132 pounds) can get a four-legged lift (DM 2) to the Wartburg from the bus drop-off point.

SAXONY

9

UPDATED BY CHARLES MONDRY AND DEIKE PETERS

While their *Land* (state) is vying desperately to stake its claim as the new "heart of Europe," Saxony's residents aren't terribly picky about pinpointing themselves on the map. They're as comfortable calling themselves "south Germans" as they are "Ossis" (a nickname for Germans from the East). However you think of them, Saxony's 4.5 million people reside in a region that was indisputably the first German Free State (even before Bavaria, they'll quickly remind you). It was here, not in Berlin, that the first peaceful demonstrations began in 1989, signaling the beginning of the end to the cold war.

As a people, Saxons have long had a reputation for hard work and a love of the outdoors. Behold the state's natural wealth and you'll see why. Just outside Dresden, the Elbe River snakes through the sheer, rugged sandstone cliffs that define the Elbsandstein Mountains of the **Sächsische Schweiz** (Saxon Switzerland). Who could resist a hike through the majestic ore-hills of the **Erzgebirge** (Ore Mountains)? While maintaining their close ties to nature, the hard-working Saxons accelerated the pace of industrialization, which befell Saxony while even the Ruhr Valley was still agrarian, and the region was rapidly built up. To the Saxons' credit, and despite half a century of isolation under East German rule, beautiful and historic **Dresden** and **Leipzig** are today world-class cities of culture and business. If you set aside aesthetics, you'll see that heavily industrialized, socialist-planned **Chemnitz** (known in GDR times as Karl-Marx-Stadt) also testifies to the region's vitality with more than 250 booming firms and factories.

The region's history dates back to the sixth century AD, when the land was settled by Sorbian tribes. Yet it was not until Augustus the Strong (1670–1733), elector of Saxony and king of Poland, took up residence in Dresden that the region began to flourish. He built or enlarged most of the region's ornate castles and palaces and transformed Dresden into a center of European art and culture. Today modern music follows in the footsteps of Richard Wagner and Richard Strauss, both of whom premiered several operas at Dresden's fabulous Semperoper, and Leipzig University continues in the tradition of former students like Friedrich Nietzsche, Gotthold Lessing, and Johann Wolfgang von Goethe. Robert Schumann left his legacy in his native **Zwickau,** a city known today as the home of the Sachsenring factory, creator of that little two-stroke car, the Trabant. As for the decorative arts, the porcelain artists and craftsmen of **Meißen,** the birthplace of European porcelain, are still among the world's finest.

SAXONY

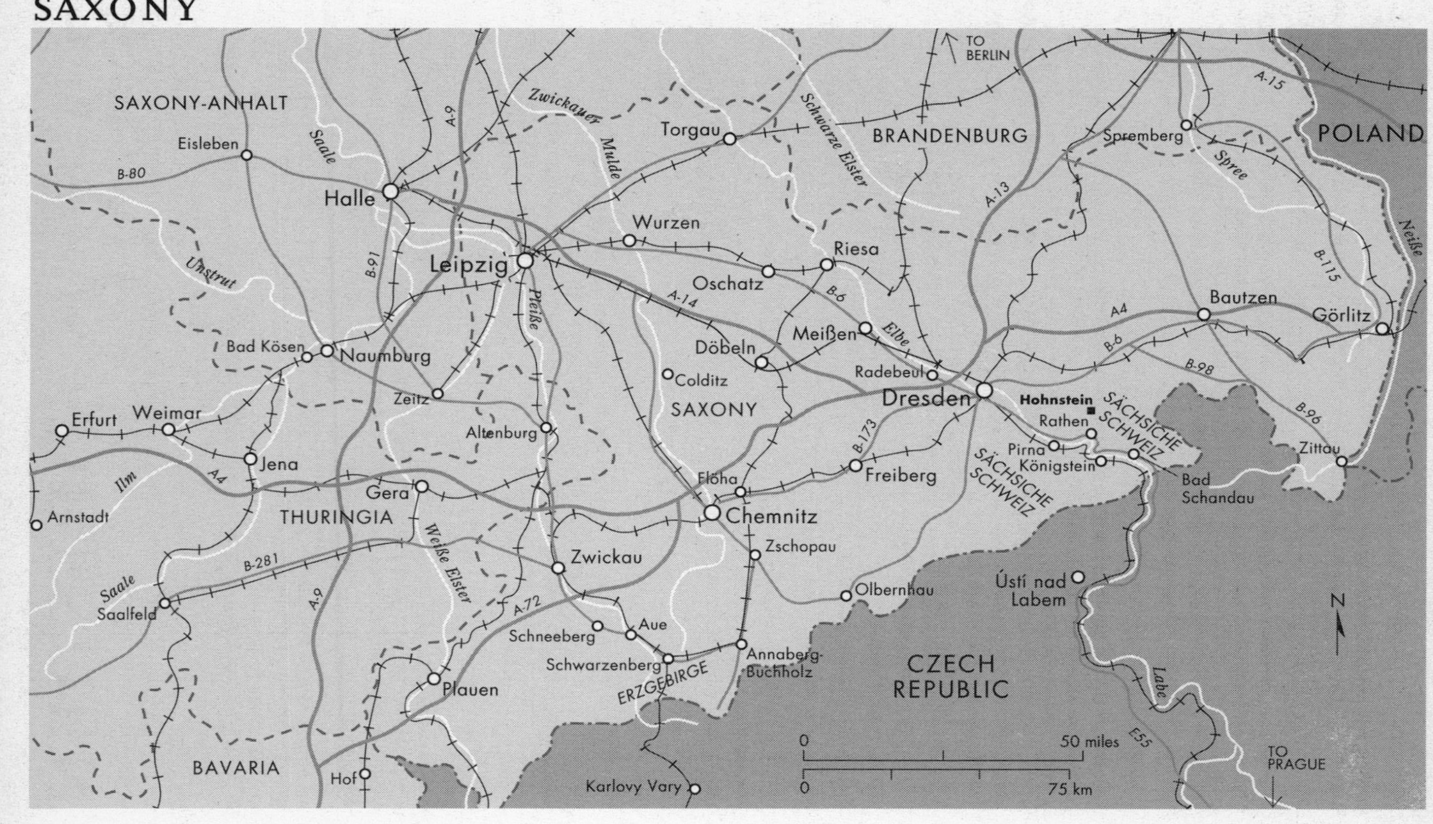
SAXONY-ANHALT
Eisleben
B-80
Saale
Halle
A-9
Zwickauer Mulde
Torgau
Schwarze Elster
BRANDENBURG
TO BERLIN
A-13
A-15
Spremberg
Spree
POLAND
Unstrut
B-91
Leipzig
Wurzen
Riesa
Oschatz
A-14
B-6
Pleiße
Meißen
Elbe
Döbeln
Bad Kösen
Naumburg
Colditz
Radebeul
Dresden
Zeitz
SAXONY
Bautzen
Görlitz
A4
B-6
B-98
B-115
Neiße
B-96
Hohnstein
Rathen
SÄCHSICHE SCHWEIZ
Pirna
Königstein
Bad Schandau
Zittau
Erfurt
Weimar
Altenburg
Jena
Ilm
A4
Gera
Flöha
B-173
Freiberg
Arnstadt
THURINGIA
Chemnitz
Weiße Elster
Zwickau
Zschopau
B-281
Saale
Saalfeld
A-9
A-72
Olbernhau
Ústí nad Labem
Schneeberg
Aue
Schwarzenberg
Annaberg-Buchholz
ERZGEBIRGE
Plauen
CZECH REPUBLIC
N
Labe
E55
BAVARIA
Hof
Karlovy Vary
0 50 miles
0 75 km
TO PRAGUE

DRESDEN

Dresdeners claim they live in the most beautiful city in Germany, quite a bold statement considering the city's almost complete destruction by brutal Allied firebombing on February 13–14, 1945. Dresden was dealt another blow when much of the elegant Baroque city was bleakly rebuilt with factories and cement-block housing, courtesy of the GDR.

Fortunately, with the help of funds from the West, "the pearl of the Elbe" is again becoming the shining jewel it once was. One by one, giant Baroque buildings along the Elbe have begun to reemerge from under scaffolding to again define the cityscape. The construction of these landmark edifices was originally financed during the early 18th century by the elector of Saxony, Augustus the Strong, a passionate patron of art and culture. His son Friedrich Augustus II continued in his father's footsteps, invigorating the city that would eventually entice a trio of brilliant composers: Carl Weber in the 1820s, Richard Wagner in the 1840s, and Richard Strauss at the end of the 19th century. The exquisite collection of works by old and new masters, superb porcelain, sculptures, coins, and jewels in the Zwinger palace prompted philosopher Johann Gottfried von Herder (1744–1803) to christen Dresden "the German Florence."

Modern Dresden is incredibly diverse and cultured; mainstream and experimental opera and theater flourish side by side, and clubs and cultural centers offer film and live music from jazz to hard-core—all this in the city that was mockingly called the "Valley of the Clueless" because its population couldn't receive Western television during GDR days. If you're ready for nature or merely looking for smaller-scale city life, strike out along the Elbe into the beautiful cliff landscape of nearby Sächsische Schweiz or medieval towns like Rathen or Meißen (*see* Near Dresden, *below*).

BASICS

AMERICAN EXPRESS

Dresden's AmEx office issues and cashes traveler's checks, arranges MoneyGrams, and holds customer mail for a month. *Münzg. 4, near Frauenkirche, tel. 0351/494–8114. Open weekdays 10–6 (cashier open 10–1:30 and 2–5:30).*

CHANGING MONEY

Inside the Hauptbahnhof, **Deutsche Verkehrs-Bank** (open weekdays 7:30–7:30, Sat. 8–4, Sun. 9–1) exchanges traveler's checks (commission DM 7.50 under DM 750) and deals with credit cards. Also use your credit card or Plus/Cirrus at any Dresdner Bank, Commerzbank, or Deutsche Bank branch. Deutsche Bank has the best exchange rates (commission DM 5 under DM 300, DM 10 up to DM 1000). There is a Citibank in the back of the UFA cineplex on Prager Straße.

EMERGENCIES AND MEDICAL AID

Apotheke Prager Straße (Prager Str. 3, tel. 0351/495–1320) and **Kronen Apotheke** (Bautzner Str. 15, tel. 0351/802–3146) have elixirs and vitamins for all your ills. The **National Health Emergency Service** (tel. 0351/459–5112) makes house calls 7–7 if you're in a bad way. There is also a Red Cross clinic inside the train station. Women in trouble can call **Frauen in Not** (tel. 0351/281–7788) for counseling and help. English speakers at all the above are a possibility.

LAUNDRY

Malwina e.V. (Louisenstr. 48, at rear of bldg. btw Rothenburger Str. and Martin-Luther-Str., tel. 0351/502–3533, open Mon., Tues., Thurs. 8–7; Wed. and Fri. 8–4) is a Neustadt social service center where self-service laundry costs DM 4–DM 7 plus DM 3 to dry. Stop by or call to sign up for one of the four machines. The **Jugendgästehaus Dresden** (*see* Where to Sleep, *below*) has laundry facilities for guests.

MAIL AND PHONES

Postamt 72 on Prager Straße is only a few doors down from the tourist office. They exchange traveler's checks for a stiff DM 7 per check. *St. Petersburger Str. 26 (entrance on Prager Str.). Postal code: 01069.*

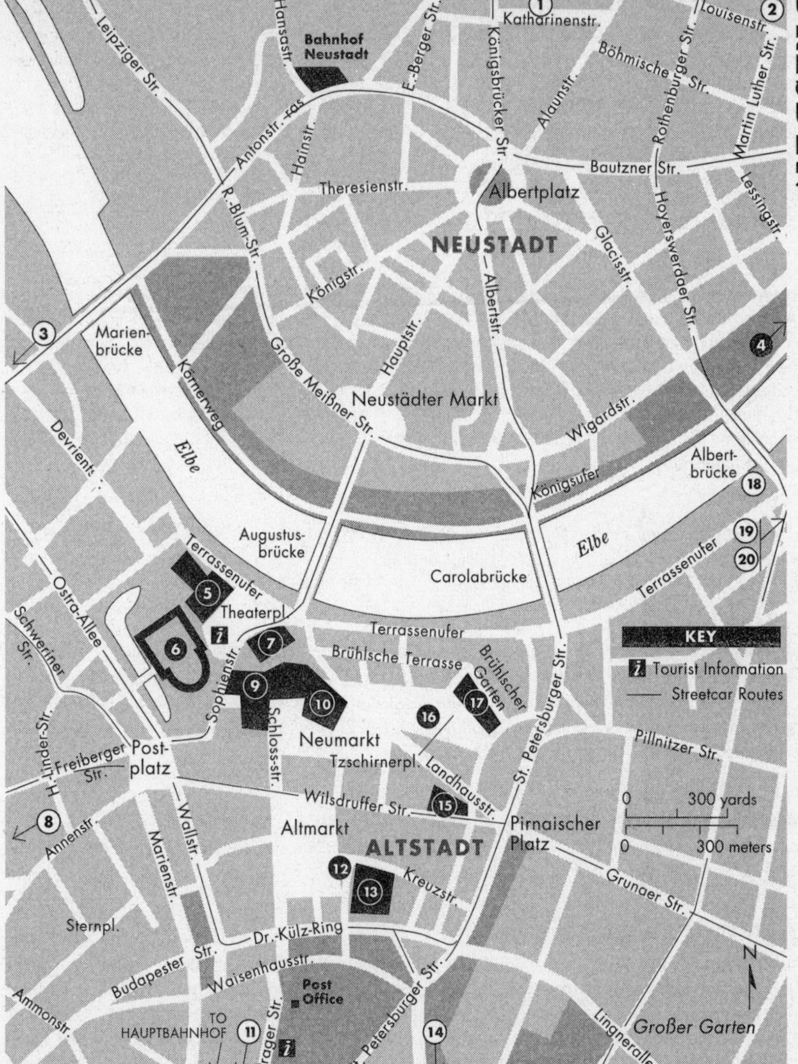

Sights ●
Albertinum, **17**
Dresdner Schloß, **9**
Frauenkirche, **16**
Johanneum, **10**
Katholische Hofkirche, **7**
Kreuzkirche, **12**
Landhaus, **15**
Rathaus, **13**
Schloß Pillnitz, **4**
Semperoper, **5**
Zwinger, **6**

Lodging ○
Camping Wostra, **19**
Campingplatz Mockritz, **14**
Die Boofe, **1**
Hotel Stadt Rendsburg, **2**
Jugendgästehaus Dresden, **8**
Jugendherberge Oberloschwitz, **20**
Jugendherberge Rudi-Arndt, **11**
Pension Omsewitz, **3**
Zum alten Fährhaus, **18**

VISITOR INFORMATION

The friendly but busy **ticket and tourist office** (Schinkelwache/Theaterpl., btw Zwinger and Semperoper, tel. 0351/491920, room finding service 0351/4919–2222) is best equipped to sell theater and concert tickets; only one station handles tourist requests. They'll find you a room for a DM 5 fee; drop by weekdays 10–5 or Saturday 10–1. Ask for the free English "Tourist City Guide," which provides a self-guided walking tour of the old city. At press time the tourist office at Prager Straße 10 was expected to reopen "in the near future."

COMING AND GOING

BY TRAIN

Dresden has two train stations: **Dresden Hauptbahnhof** (tel. 0351/471–0600), on the southern fringe of the Altstadt, and **Dresden Neustadt** (tel. 0351/51185), across the river in the Neustadt. Most trains stop at both, so if you're headed for a Neustadt hotel, find out whether your train stops at Dresden Neustadt. Trains leave the Hauptbahnhof for Berlin (9 per day, 2 hrs, DM 45), Chemnitz (hourly, 1¼ hrs, DM 17), Erfurt (every 2 hrs, 3 hrs, DM 55), and Leipzig (hourly, 1½ hrs, DM 28). Both stations have lockers, a 24-hour left-luggage desk, a credit card ATM, and a small market. S-Bahn S1 and Trams 11 and 26 travel between the stations. To reach the Altstadt from the Hauptbahnhof, exit under Track 19 and walk north up Prager Straße.

BY BUS

The main **Busbahnhof** (info window open weekdays 7–noon and 12:30–3:30) is just east of the Hauptbahnhof. The tourist office also stocks bus schedules. From here there's frequent daily service to Bautzen (50 min, DM 22), Görlitz (1¼ hrs, DM 28), and Leipzig (2 hrs, DM 17).

BY BOAT

Dampfschiffe (steamboats) run by **Sächische Dampfschiffahrt** (tel. 0351/866090) puff up and down the Elbe River, stopping in Pillnitz, the Sächsische Schweiz, and Meißen (*see* Near Dresden, *below*). Boats leave 1–3 times daily (Apr.–Oct.) from the Terrassenufer by the Augustusbrücke. A 90-min tour along the Elbe in Dresden is DM 18, a Jazz Boat tour is DM 26, and a Summer Night Trip is DM 30. Tickets and schedules are available on the dock and at the tourist offices.

BY MITFAHRGELEGENHEIT

ADM Mitfahrzentrale (Königstr. 10, near Albertpl., tel. 0351/19440) has both short- and long-distance listings. Berlin is DM 25, Munich DM 49, Prague DM 16. The office is open weekdays 9–1 and 2–6, Saturday 9–1, Sunday 11–3.

GETTING AROUND

The waters of the Elbe divide Dresden into the **Altstadt** and **Neustadt.** The Altstadt, where you'll find most sights, is easy to spot by the jumble of towers and spires. The Hauptbahnhof is on the Altstadt's southern border; outside the train station, pedestrian-only Prager Straße leads straight to the **Altmarkt** (Old Market). Farther north, **Augustusbrücke** crosses the river to Neustadt; straight ahead is the **Neustädter Markt,** an elegant square at the base of the Hauptstraße pedestrian zone. Neustadt's mix of students and families, drunks and punks is increasingly threatened by creeping yuppification as buildings are renovated and rents soar. Dresden's hippest neighborhood offers nightlife with the edge of Berlin's but without the pretension.

BY S-BAHN

Of Dresden's commuter trains, S1 is the one to know: It travels from Meißen through Radebeul and Dresden's two stations all the way into the Sächsische Schweiz. Tickets must be purchased from machines at the stations and validated in the red machine near the tracks. Check schedules to see from which track your train departs (usually from the upper level in the Hauptbahnhof). The S-Bahn shuts down 11 PM–4 AM.

BY TRAM AND BUS

Buy tickets for all **Dresdner Verkehrsbetrieb** (DVB) vehicles, including the Pillnitz ferry and Loschwitz Schwebebahn (which you'll need for the Oberloschwitz hostel), from the yellow machines at major stops, and validate them in the orange boxes on board. The *Kurzfahrt* ticket (DM 1.60) is good for four stops, the *Stundenfahrt* (DM 2.80) for one hour. A 24-hour ticket costs DM 8. Buses and trams are free for 48 hours with the **Dresden-Card** (*see* Worth Seeing, *below*). Dresden now also offers the 72-hour **Regio-Card** (DM 45), which entitles you to museum discounts, unlimited bus, tram, and S-Bahn (btw Meißen and Königstein) rides, and 50% off on the funky narrow-gauge trains at Weißritztal and Lößnitztal. Pick up a city route map and *Nachtfahrplan* (night schedule) at the booth in front of the Hauptbahnhof. Bus lines run until 8 PM, some until midnight; most trams come at least every hour during the night, every 10–20 minutes during the day.

BY TAXI

Taxis cost DM 3.60 plus about DM 1.50 per km. The main taxi stands are at the Hauptbahnhof and on Dr.-Külz-Ring, but you can also count on them at Bahnhof Neustadt and Theaterplatz. To call a cab, dial 0351/459–8112.

BY BIKE

Biking around Dresden is easy and fun. Pick up the famous Elbe Bike Path at the left bank of Augustus Bridge and go out to Pillnitz—or even all the way into the Sächsische Schweiz (*see below*). If you have a Dresden Regio-Card (*see above*) you can return via S-Bahn for free. **The bike shop AVANTI** (Wallstr.19/21, tel. 0351/4963172, open weekdays 9:30–6:30, Sat. until 4) in the old city rents bikes for DM 15 per day. The **Hilton Hotel** (An der Frauenkirche, near Neumarkt) charges DM 15 for five hours, DM 20 per day. You can also rent bikes at the train stations and from other shops and hotels. You'll find more bikes in the morning, and you usually need a credit card for a deposit.

Though generations of Saxons have been taught to be ashamed of their "Sächseln," the distinctive light, lazy accent is still heard throughout the land.

WHERE TO SLEEP

Hotel prices in Dresden are relatively steep and likely to get worse as renovation costs are passed on to the consumer. Call the tourist office **room-finding service** (tel. 0351/4919–2222, open daily 8 AM–10 PM) to secure accommodations; the staff speaks English. Economical package deals are available through **Dresden Advertising and Tourism** (tel. 0351/4919–2120, fax 0351/4919–2116): A DM 80 deal for people between 16 and 26 includes bed and breakfast, a 48-hour Dresden-Card, and info materials. Ask about deals that entail train fare discounts.

Hotel Stadt Rendsburg. Rooms at this Neustadt hotel (winner, best location award) range from small and basic (and cheap) to large and bright. Singles are DM 65–DM 115, doubles DM 95–DM 165, triples DM 150–DM 270. The friendly Knöfels speak some English and serve a hearty breakfast buffet. *Kamenzer Str. 1, at Louisenstr., tel. 0351/804–1551, fax 0351/802–2586, www.zugast.de/hotel-stadt-rendsburg. From Bahnhof Neustadt, Tram 6 or 11 to Bautzner/Rothenburger Str. 25 rooms, some with bath.*

Pension Omsewitz. With the fields and gardens next door, it's hard to believe this modest house with comfy rooms is in Dresden (okay, 20 min away). Singles are DM 35–DM 80, doubles DM 65–DM 140, including breakfast. *Gompitzer Str. 24, tel. 0351/421–0349, fax 0351/421–0365. From Postpl. or Pirnaischer Pl., Tram 2 or 51 (direction: Gorbitz) to Hebbelpl., then Bus 79 or 80 (direction: Omsewitz) to Lise-Meitner-Str. 18 rooms, all with bath. No credit cards.*

Zum alten Fährhaus. Rooms at this cozy German pension near the Elbe River are often booked in summer—call ahead to reserve a spot. Singles are DM 80–DM 100, doubles DM 100–DM 150; breakfast costs an extra DM 10. *Fährstr. 20, tel. 0351/237–1842, fax 0351/252–3621. From Hauptbahnhof, Tram 4, 6, or 10 to Leubener Str., then toward river on Altlaubegast to Fährstr. 11 rooms, all with bath. No credit cards.*

HOSTELS

Die Boofe. This Neustadt newcomer offers singles at DM 49, doubles at DM 39 per person, and 3–5-bed rooms at DM 26.50 per person in an unbeatable location (for bar-swarming night owls, that is). Sheets are DM 4.50. You can book online at www.my-time.de/boofe or make an old-fashioned phone

TRABI HO!

So you've seen the cute little Trabants putt-putting back and forth for a while and you're wondering what it's like to actually ride in one. You've called Avis, you've checked Hertz, you've considered "borrowing" one, but you've encountered nothing but blank stares and a pesky conscience. Grab some friends (make some, if need be) and call Welcome Tourist (tel. 0351/410–0100, Kesselsdorfer Str. 173a), a tourist and room-finding service that organizes Trabi tours of Dresden. From their list of driver-owners, they'll find someone (even an English-speaking guide, if you like) to chauffeur you wherever you want for a few hours. Three people can ride per car, and for DM 100 (replacement parts ain't cheap), bring along those friends—it's worth every Pfennig.

call. *Louisenstr. 20, tel. 0351/801–3361, fax 0351/801–3362. From Albertspl. head north along Königsbrücker to Louisenstr., turn right.*

Jugendgästehaus Dresden (HI). It's large, bland, and more expensive than other hostels, but you'll save on tram fare and avoid long walks home. Rooms (2–4 beds) in this bright and boxy apartment building are DM 33 (DM 38 over 26) per person. Add about DM 5 for your own bath, DM 15 if you want the room all to yourself. If you don't already have an international youth hostel membership, add another DM 35 to your total. *Maternistr. 22, tel. 0351/492620, fax 0351/492–6299. From Hauptbahnhof, Tram 7, 9, 10, or 26 to Ammon-/Freiberger Str., then right on Freiberger Str., right on Maternistr. 450 beds. No curfew. Check-in 4 PM–10 PM (otherwise call). Laundry, snack and soda machines.*

Jugendherberge Oberloschwitz (HI). It's a long haul to the classy Loschwitz residential area, especially the hike uphill, but there's a backyard patio, and laundry service is around DM 6. The *Schwebebahn* (gondola) runs until 8 PM and is included in your validated transit ticket. Beds run DM 24.50 to 27.50 (DM 29.50–32.50 over 26), including breakfast. *Sierksstr. 33, tel. 0351/268–3672. From Bahnhof Neustadt, Tram 6 (direction: Niedersedlitz) to Schillerpl.; then one block NE, across Elbe to Körnerpl., and follow signs to hostel and Schwebebahn. 51 beds. No curfew, lockout 9–4. Reception open 4–10. 1-day luggage storage. Reservations advised.*

Jugendherberge Rudi-Arndt (HI). In a safe and quiet neighborhood south of the Hauptbahnhof, the hostel is nearly always full, so book in advance. If you can't make the short reception hours (3 PM–6 PM), call ahead. Space in rooms with 3–12 beds costs DM 24 (DM 29 over 26), including an extra-hearty breakfast. *Hübnerstr. 11, tel. 0351/471–0667, fax 0351/472–8959. From Hauptbahnhof, south on Winckelmannstr., right on Schnorrstr., leftish onto Hübnerstr. 81 beds. Curfew 1 AM. Luggage storage.*

CAMPING

Campingplatz Mockritz. It may not be in the woods, but this is the closest campground to Dresden. The site is well-equipped with bathrooms and hot showers; you can even catch German TV in the common room. Campsites cost DM 3 plus DM 4–DM 6 per tent, DM 4 per person, and DM 4 per car; bungalows (reserve in advance) run DM 20–DM 40. *Boderitzer Str. 30, tel. 0351/471–5250. From Hauptbahnhof, Bus 76 (direction Mockritz) to Campingpl. Mockritz. Last bus 8 PM. 85 sites. Open 7 AM–10 PM. Closed Nov.–Mar.*

Camping Wostra. The bad news: It's an unscenic campground 40 min by tram from downtown. The good news: It's cheap and adjacent to a nude swimming area (DM 1 for students) that rents volleyballs for a game in the buff. Sites cost DM 4 per tent, per person, and per car, plus a DM 3 user's fee. Comfortable bungalows are DM 24 a night plus DM 10 per person. *Trieskestr. 100, tel. 0351/201–3254. From Hauptbahnhof, Tram 9 to end in Kleinzschachwitz; then two blocks toward Elbe, right on Wilhelm-Weitling-Str., left on Trieskestr. 60 sites. Check-in 8–10 and 3–8. Gates closed 10 PM–6 AM. Closed Nov.–Mar.*

5 CENTS
CANADA
1978
DIEZ PESOS
LIBERTY
VINGT
FRANCS
FB 747022 T

PASSPORT
US$100
American Express Travelers Cheque
PLEASE READ INSTRUCTIONS ON REVERSE SIDE
U.S.$100

FOOD

Prager Straße, the Altstadt, and the narrow streets along the riverfront are spiked with cafés, ice-cream shops, bakeries, and tourist-oriented restaurants—beware of high prices. For a less touristy take on Dresden's daytime cafés, head to Neustadt's less-scenic (read: ugly) pedestrian-only **Hauptstraße,** above Neustädter Markt. You'll find a Spar **supermarket** on Alaunstraße near Albertplatz in the Neustadt, and a daily **market** on the Altstadt's Altmarkt.

Café aha. Attached to an Altstadt shop that sells developing-world merchandise (masks, voodoo dolls) at fair-trade prices, aha offers vegetarian meals made almost wholly of organic produce from local farmers. Entrees are worth the DM 11–DM 15—you'll be back for more. *Kreuzstr. 7, near Kreuzkirche, tel. 0351/496–0671 or 492–3379. Closed Mon.*

El Perro Borracho. In a funky Kunsthof (artists' courtyard), this Spanish tapas restaurant-bar is no longer a neighborhood secret. Take your meals (DM 13–DM 20) inside or on the terrace. On weekends you can enjoy breakfast as of 10 AM. *Alaunstr. 70, tel. 0351/803–6723.*

Pizzeria Vecchia Napoli. This spot may be the your best Neustadt bet if you actually want to relax and enjoy your meal. Extremely popular, it's as full for lunch as it is for dinner or a late-night meal. A large variety of pizza and pasta goes for DM 8–DM 15, and the excellent mushroom risotto costs DM 14. *Alaunstr. 33, tel. 0351/802–9055.*

Scheunecafé. It's hard to miss Dresden's most popular student hangout—it's in a bright red building set back from the street. The kitchen whips up a large selection of Indian food, including lots of veggie dishes. All meals cost about DM 10. *Alaunstr. 36–40, tel. 0351/804–5532.*

The Neustadt along Hauptstraße was actually the original Dresden settlement. It was named the "new town" after being rebuilt following a 1685 fire.

WORTH SEEING

The Altstadt's main attractions are between the Altmarkt and the Elbe River. Be your own guide with the tourist office's "Tourist City Guide," which shows all the main sights, or consider taking one of the flexible **bus tours** (tel. 0351/899–5650, fax 0351/899–5660, DM 29) that let you get off and on at 12 different stops and explore at your own pace. Museum fans should invest in a **Tageskarte** (Day Pass; DM 14, DM 7 students), good for free admission to the Albertinum, Schloß (except tower), Zwinger (except Salon), and Schloß Pillnitz. Buy the ticket at any museum it covers or the tourist office. The 48-hour **Dresden-Card** (DM 27), worthwhile if you're not a student, is good for free public transit, free admission to the above (except both Gemäldegalerien), discounts at other museums, and DM 3 off the Dresden ferry tour. If you plan on staying three days, consider buying a DM 45 **Regio-Card** (*see* Getting Around by Tram and Bus, *above*).

ALBERTINUM

Named after Saxony's King Albert (1828–1902), this excellent art museum, entered from Brühlsche Terrasse, houses several centuries of art in its three stories. The bottom floor displays classical statues (Greco-Roman he-men and limbless goddesses); upstairs, the **Grünes Gewölbe** (Green Vault) houses Augustus the Strong's collection of goodies, originally kept in the Schloß. (Once the castle is rebuilt—early this century—this collection will move back.) The royal loot contains oodles of gold, silver, ivory, and jewels, including the world's largest green diamond (41 carats). On the top story is the museum's true jewel, the **Gemäldegalerie Neue Meister** (Gallery of Modern Masters), with works by German artists from the Romantic tradition (don't miss the whole room of Caspar David Friedrich's moody landscapes) through the Expressionistic period. Look for works by Fritz Bleyl, Erich Heckel, Ernst Ludwig Kirchner, and Karl Schmidt-Rottluff, who made art history by forming "Die Brücke" (The Bridge) in Dresden's Topflappen district in 1905; Otto Dix himself taught at Dresden's university—don't miss his haunting triptych, *Der Krieg* (War). *Brühlsche Terrasse, tel. 0351/491–4619, fax 0351/491–4616. Admission: DM 7, DM 4 students. Open Fri.–Wed. 10–6.*

The promenade and garden along Brühlsche Terrasse sit atop the only remaining part of Dresden's defensive wall. Besides housing artillery and ammo, these damp, cavernous tunnels (called the *Kasematten*) were used as a laboratory: Augustus the Strong kept alchemist Johann Böttger captive here under orders to make gold. In 1708 he accidentally developed white gold—and Meißen porcelain was born. *Admission: DM 6, DM 4 students. Open Mon.–Sun. 10–5, Nov.–Mar. until 4.*

BRING ON THE KITSCH

In Radebeul, a small suburb 10 km northeast of Dresden, "Villa Bärenfett" houses the curious anachronism that is the Karl-May-Museum. Karl May himself never set foot in America, and yet his books about the Wild West—whose heroes include the Apache warrior Winnetou and palefaces with macho names like Old Surehand—were gobbled up by Germans fascinated with the adventure and freedom associated with the American frontier. This allure continues today, though the totem poles and hitching posts in front of the log cabin are wildly out of place here in the Old World, as is the museum's exhibit of life in pre-Columbian North America. Next door is the home of Karl May himself. Karl-May-Str. 5, tel. 0351/830–2723. Admission: DM 8, DM 5 students. From Radebeul-Ost S-Bahn station, left on Sidonienstr., right on Schildenstr., left on Karl-May-Str. Open Mar.–Oct., 9–6; Nov.–Feb., 10–4; closed Mon.

ALTMARKT

Despite the best efforts of Allied bombers and communist city planners, the colonnaded Altmarkt retains much of its original elegance. On the square's east corner, the **Kreuzkirche** (tower open Mon.–Sat. 10–5:30, Sun. noon–4:30; admission DM 2, DM 1 students) is a lush Baroque creation dating from 1792—though there's been some kind of church here since the 1200s. If you're in the neighborhood on Saturday at 6 PM or for Sunday mass, stop in to hear the regionally famous Kreuzchor boys' choir. Just beyond the Kreuzkirche, check out the newly rebuilt **Rathaus** (town hall).

DRESDNER SCHLOSS

The former residence of Augustus the Strong on Schloßplatz is about half rebuilt. Peruse exhibits of the castle's history, from its medieval origins to its Baroque expansion under Augustus to its destruction and rebuilding, in the **Georgentor** (at the foot of Augustusbrücke). Climb the beautiful **Hausmannsturm** for a spectacular view over the Altstadt (closed Nov.–Mar.). *Georgentor: tel. 0351/49140. Admission DM 5, DM 3 students. Open Tues.–Sun. 10–6.*

KATHOLISCHE HOFKIRCHE

The Katholische Hofkirche (1744) is the largest church in Saxony and thoroughly dominates Dresden's skyline. Inside, look for the 250-year-old organ, said to be one of the finest to come from the Silbermann family's mountain workshop. (Speaking of organs, Augustus the Strong's heart is in an urn in the crypt.) The cavernous interior is filled with organ music Saturdays at 4, May–October (donations accepted). *Admission free. Open Mon.–Thurs. 9–5, Fri. 1–5, Sat. 10:30–4, Sun. noon–4.*

NEUMARKT

A stone's throw north of the Altmarkt is Dresden's other main square, the Neumarkt. Today mostly a parking lot, the Neumarkt is best known for the ruined **Frauenkirche.** Once considered Germany's greatest Baroque cathedral, the ruin has stood for the past 50 years as stark testimony to the horrors of war. Frauenkirche survived the Allied air raid on February 13, 1945, but was ravaged by the subsequent firestorm that leveled most of Dresden. After much controversy, Dresdners decided in 1991 to restore the cathedral and have been busy drumming up money, in part through the sale of souvenirs: A china model of the restored church costs DM 1,500, while a Frauenkirche watch runs DM 85–DM 1,500. Check out the renovation plans daily 10–5 at the trailers on the construction site.

Across from the Frauenkirche stands the 16th-century **Johanneum,** formerly the royal stables. Today it houses the **Verkehrsmuseum** (Museum of Transportation), whose extensive collection of locomotives, cars, bikes, and motorcycles is scattered on ugly, greyish linoleum floors. Spanning the 102-m length of the outer wall along Augustusstraße is the *Kurfürstenzug,* a giant mosaic—composed of 25,000 hand-painted porcelain tiles—depicting Saxon royalty having a jolly good time. *Verkehrsmuseum: Augustusstr. 1, tel. 0351/86440, fax 0351/864–4110. Admission: DM 4, DM 2 students. Open Tues.–Sun. 10–5.*

SCHLOSS PILLNITZ

Far from Dresden's center, Schloß Pillnitz was built 1720–1722 as a summer getaway and all-around pleasure palace for King Augustus the Strong and the Saxon court. Both the **Wasserpalais** (closed Tues.), whose steps lead straight into the Elbe, and the **Bergpalais** (closed Mon.) were built in late Baroque faux-Chinese style, with little pagoda rooftops. Today the two are home to the **Kunstgewerbemuseum Dresden.** An interesting display of modern design, including some Bauhaus pieces, breaks up the usual porcelain and period furniture. On summer Sundays, the Wasserpalais hosts concerts for DM 15–DM 20. If you take a steamboat (DM 15 one-way, DM 21 round-trip) to the palace, along the way you'll pass the Blaue Wunder (Blue Wonder) bridge, so beloved by Dresdeners that two locals risked their lives to cut the wires when the SS wanted to blow up the bridge in 1945. Certain palace rooms may be closed due to ongoing renovations. *Tel. 0351/261–3263. Tram 9 or 14 to Kleinzschachwitz, then continue to river and crossing ferry. Admission to museum: DM 4, DM 2 students. Open 9:30–5:30.*

The daily market on the Altmarkt is not only a good place to gather your comestibles, it also adds a curious small-town feel to busy Dresden.

SEMPEROPER

The opera house bears the name of its creator, architect Gottfried Semper, even though the original burned down only 28 years after its completion in 1841. The second version—built in 1871 by Semper's son, Manfred—was destroyed in the 1945 bombing. The opera house's third incarnation may or may not match its predecessors, since it was based on prewar black-and-white photographs, but the interior is still dazzling. Richard Wagner premiered his operas *Der fliegende Holländer* (*The Flying Dutchman*; 1841) and *Tannhäuser* (1845) here, Richard Strauss his *Salome* (1905) and *Elektra* (1909). You can check out the lavish interior on the guided tour (in German only; DM 8, DM 5 students); check the door for postings listing tour schedules. *Theaterpl. 2, tel. 0351/491–1496.*

STADTMUSEUM DRESDEN IM LANDHAUS

The 18th-century Landhaus contains Dresden's illuminating city history museum, with exhibits showing the extent of the city's destruction in 1945, life for the survivors (there's a wood-burning stove made from an Allied bomb casing), and daily life in the GDR up through unification. Other items on display include a 250-kg American bomb unearthed in 1984 and GDR-era posters of cheery proletarians. *Wilsdruffer Str. 2, at Landhausstr., tel. 0351/498660, fax 0351/495–1288. Admission: DM 3, DM 1.50 students. Open Sat.–Thurs. 10–6.*

ZWINGER

On the south side of Theaterplatz stands the Zwinger palace complex, one of the world's finest Baroque masterpieces. In 1709 the palace construction began with five linked pavilions built onto a section of the *Zwinger,* Dresden's centuries-old fortifications. A century later Gottfried Semper made a few worthy additions, including a sixth pavilion and a serene central courtyard. The central plaza, now filled with pluming fountains, was the scene of spectacular knightly tournaments in the mid-18th century. There are three entrances to the Zwinger complex: from Theaterplatz, Sophienstraße, and through the **Kronentor** (Crown Gate) off Ostra-Allee, northwest of Postplatz. The latter passes over a tree-lined, moatlike waterway called "Zwingerteich." Inside the Glockenspielpavillon (the building with the porcelain bells hanging over the gate) is the **Porzellansammlung** (Porcelain Collection; open Fri.–Wed. 10–6), where you can ogle giant Chinese and Japanese urns and check out an extensive array of porcelain—Meißen porcelain, of course. To the right of the Kronentor is another small museum, the **Mathematisch-Physikalischer Salon** (open Fri.–Wed. 9:30–5), dedicated to scientific toys such as watches, telescopes, and globes. Admission to each is DM 3, DM 1.50 students.

Besides the elaborate architecture, the highlight of the Zwinger is the **Gemäldegalerie Alte Meister** (Gallery of Old Masters) in the *Semperbau* (Semper building) across from the Kronentor. The outstanding collection includes Raphael's *Sistine Madonna,* Cranach's Adam and Eve series, and selections by Botticelli and Rembrandt. Admission includes the **Rüstkammer,** packed with ornate 16th- and 17th-century weapons and armor. *Tel. 0351/491–4619. Admission: DM 7, DM 3.50 students. Open Tues.–Sun. 10–6.*

CHEAP THRILLS

Frequent farmers' and flea **markets** crowd the Altmarkt (especially on weekends), and wine and beer fests often litter the pedestrian zone on Hauptstraße above Neustädter Markt. **Großer Garten Park**—Dresden's largest landscaped park and home to a botanical garden, a zoo, and a popular marionette theater—can be glimpsed from the cars of a **miniature railway** (tickets DM 2, DM 1 students; open Apr.–Oct. 10–6) that circles the huge English garden. Otherwise go for a bike ride or stroll the tended path along the Neustadt bank of the Elbe and enjoy frequent music performances on the lawns between the bridges.

FESTIVALS

In early May a lavish parade of Saxon steamers cruises the Elbe, followed a week or two later by the more jovial **International Dixieland Festival,** with concerts in bars, clubs, and city parks. There's a good bit of merrymaking to consider, and a parade through town to wrap it up. In late June check out the Neustadt locals letting it all hang out during the tongue-in-cheek **Bunte Republik Neustadt**—a post-unification party that pokes fun, as the name suggests, at the reconfigured Bundesrepublik Deutschland. The streets are blocked off, and everything from kiddy parties to street theater rages. In late June and early July, the incredibly popular **Dresdner Elbhangfest** takes place in the area around the Blaue Wunder bridge (technically the Loschwitz Bridge). Dresdeners don costumes from the days of Augustus the Strong and generally kick up their 17th-century heels. July also brings open-air theater to the Elbe for movies and concerts. In August, Dresden celebrates its **City Anniversary.** Germany's oldest Christmas market, the **Dresdner Striezelmarkt,** dates back to 1434; starting in late November, it enlivens the Altmarkt. The tourist office sells tickets to most events.

AFTER DARK

Dresden is the cultural heart of Saxony and is as attractive to the club kid as to the opera lover. The Altstadt is for highbrow cultural events, while Neustadt means bohemian watering holes, raunchy anarchist haunts, and eclectic student clubs. Scheunecafé (*see* Food, *above*) is your best bet for live music, with anything from rock to African tribal percussion. You may encounter your favorite underground band at **Star-Club** (Altbriesnitz 2a, tel. 0351/436693). Check listings before you make the 15-min bus trip: From the Maxstraße or Könneritzstraße tram stop, take Bus 94 (night bus) to Merbitzer Straße and go one block left. For a complete list of what's shakin', pick up a copy of *SAX* or *Dresdner* at any tourist office or kiosk.

BARS AND CLUBS

Alaunstraße and Luisenstraße form your simple "bar-coded" coordinate system for Dresden by night—go explore!

Café Hieronymous. This chic upstairs tavern is a pleasant break from student hangouts. Music is of the Lou Reed/Suzanne Vega variety, the atmosphere cozy and smoke-filled. *Louisenstr. 10, btw Alaunstr. and Königsbrücker Str., tel. 0351/801–1739. Open daily 7 PM–2 AM.*

Die 100. Neustadt hipsters knock 'em back under the cavernous brick arches of this cellar café-bar. The relaxed atmosphere and cheap beer (DM 3–DM 4) make it a great place to hang out and gawk. *Alaunstr. 100, two blocks north of Louisenstr., tel. 0351/801–3957. Open Sun.–Thurs. 7 PM–2 AM, Fri. and Sat. 7 PM–4 AM.*

Jazzclub Tonne. Before you start tapping your foot to the those jazzy tunes, stop by the Jazz-Café (opens daily at 6 PM) for international treats; Sunday is sushi night. The Tonne also houses a small store, where you can pick up a few CDs. *Am Brauhaus 3, tel. 0351/802–6017. Open Mon.–Sun. after 8 PM. Cover: DM 12–DM 20.*

Planwirtschaft. This is an excellent place to round off a night in Neustadt. Relax in the upstairs café (all sorts of munchies are available) or head down to the basement bar. To enter the bar after 1 AM, ring the bell. *Louisenstr. 20, btw Alaunstr. and Königsbrücker Str., tel. 0351/801–3187. Café open daily 8 AM–1 AM; bar open daily 7 PM–3 AM.*

Raskolnikoff. Don't be daunted by the crack house–esque exterior—this is one of the coolest café-bars in Dresden. Black-clad locals perch on makeshift chairs, smoke like chimneys (and ash on the sand-covered floor), and chat over espresso and wine. *Böhmische Str. 34, btw Rothenburger Str. and Martin-Luther-Str., tel. 0351/567–0447. Open Sun.–Thurs. 7 PM–1 AM, Fri. and Sat. 7 PM–2 AM.*

riesa efau. This cultural center in the Friedrichstadt area just west of the Altstadt has occasional movies, performances upstairs, and live music (folk, jazz, hard-core) in the cellar several days a week. The gallery on the second floor is open Friday 5–9 PM and Saturday 2–6 PM. Event or not, there's always something going on in the candlelit bar. *Adlerg. 14, near Schweriner Str., tel. 0351/866–0222 or 866–0211. Tram 2 or 8 to Berliner Str. or Tram 1, 9, or 26 to Könneritzstr., then west on Schweriner Str. Bar open daily 7 PM–1 AM.*

MUSIC AND DANCE

The **Schinkelwache box office** (tel. 0351/491920) in the building on the southeast corner of Theaterplatz sells tickets for the **Semperoper** (very expensive) and for classical music, modern dance, and ballet at **Kleine Szene** (Bautznerstr. 107, tel. 0351/484–2595). Students get a 50% break. For (sometimes drastically reduced) last-minute Semperoper tickets, line up at the main entrance an hour before the performance. Whenever the door opens, an usher usher yells out the number and price of tickets that have become available. The interested person closest in line gets to purchase the tickets.

Two blocks north of the Zwinger is Dresden's most unusual sight: the Yenidze tobacco factory, named after a Turkish tobacco city and modeled after a mosque. It's most impressive at night, when the colorful dome is lit.

THEATER

Several small theater companies put on everything from Shakespeare to Woody Allen. The tourist offices have schedules and tickets. Tickets are available at individual theaters or at the Schauspielhaus (*see* Leipzig, *below*) Monday–Saturday 4–8. See what's playing at Podium (Hauptstr. 11, near Neustädter Markt, tel. 0351/804–3266) and funky **theater 50** (Maternistr. 17, near Jugendgästehaus, tel. 0351/859–0995). Tickets cost DM 15–DM 25; students often get a few marks off.

NEAR DRESDEN

MEIßEN

One-thousand-year-old Meißen thinks of itself as the cradle of Saxony. Relatively untouristy and remarkably well-preserved, the medieval city's colorful market bustles on sunny days with vendors hawking their wares. You can spend all day ambling through the tangled network of narrow cobblestone streets. While Meißen was seized by the Saxon Wettin dynasty from Slavic tribes in the 12th century, the city had entered into a long relationship with fame after Augustus the Strong set up Europe's first porcelain factory here in 1710. It should come as no surprise, then, that the town's buildings are positively drenched in porcelain. The bells of the **Frauenkirche** (Marktpl.), for instance, and the decorative figures in **Nikolaikirche** (Stadtpark) are all made of this coveted material. A tip for shoppers: Make sure the bottom of each porcelain piece is stamped with a pair of blue swords, the sign of authentic Meißen porcelain.

Built in 1525, the spire-tipped **Albrechtsburg** castle and neighboring **Gothic Dom** (which dates back to the Middle Ages) loom over town on top of a steep cliff overlooking the Elbe. Nearly two hundred years after the castle's construction, Augustus the Strong moved his porcelain factory here as a safeguard against corporate spies out to steal his formula. The castle is as beautiful inside as it is out. *Admission: DM 6, DM 3 students. Open daily 10–6, Feb. and Dec. until 5, closed Jan. The Gothic Dom (admission DM 3.50, DM 2.50 students) is best experienced during a live organ concert (May–Oct., Mon.–Sat. at noon).*

The factory in the castle has long closed, but you can still see porcelain makers in action at the work station of **Staatliche Porzellan-Manufaktur,** down the main street from the Altstadt. The site also contains a good museum. The work station and the museum each charge the same (steep) price: DM 7, DM 5 students. *Talstr. 9, tel. 03521/468700. Open daily 10–1 and 1–5 (last entry at 4:30). Tour cassettes available in several languages.*

COMING AND GOING

S1 runs from Dresden every half hour (45 min, DM 5); regular trains cost DM 7. Leipzig (every 2 hrs, 2 hrs, DM 24) is 107 km farther on the same line, though not all these trains stop in Meißen—check the schedules. To reach the Altstadt from the Bahnhof, head diagonally up Bahnhofstraße, cross the bridge, and continue straight. In the mood for a more scenic journey? Take a ferry through the Saxon wine country (weekends only, 2 hrs, DM 16) from Dresden. The steamers will drop you off on the Altstadt side of the river, less than a five-minute walk from the town center.

WHERE TO SLEEP

The **tourist office** (An der Frauenkirche 3, tel. 03521/454470) books private rooms (DM 25–DM 55) for a DM 4 fee. A cheaper option is Meißen's **HI-Jugendherberge,** in the Altstadt at the top of a steep hill. Beds DM 18 (DM 20.50 over 26), including breakfast. *Wilsdruffer Str. 28, tel. 03521/453065. From Bahnhof, down Bahnhofstr., across river, leftish up Gerberg., left on Hahnemannspl. to Plossenw. (which becomes Wilsdruffer Str.—stay left). No curfew. Reception open 5 PM–10 PM. Luggage storage. Closed Nov.–Feb.*

SÄCHSISCHE SCHWEIZ

The name Sächsische Schweiz, which means "Saxon Switzerland," alludes to the low-lying Elbsandstein Mountains that extend from the outskirts of Dresden to the Czech border. Here the rock bed along the Elbe has been eroded over the millennia into curious stone columns and plateaus that protrude out of the forest canopy. Nestled along the river or looking down from on top of steep cliffs are several looming castles and quiet, well-preserved small towns perfect for rejuvenating mind and body after forays along the region's 1,200 km of hiking tails. Today the region that may have served as an inspiration to German Romantics draws the most dedicated of rock climbers and bikers to its unspoiled natural beauty.

OUTDOOR ACTIVITIES

Paved, traffic-free **bike paths** run along the banks of the Elbe all the way from Dresden to the Czech border. The best place to start pedaling is Pirna, 18 km southeast of Dresden; you can pick up a bike at the train station and return it in Bad Schandau. Many trails lead into the hills, through quiet valleys and past raging cliffs—check with the tourist offices below or in Dresden for maps. The Sächsische Schweiz is also famous for its **rock-climbing** opportunities, and enthusiasts from all over the world come to test their skills. To tackle the rock, contact Bernd Arnold's **Bergsportladen** (Obere Str. 25, tel. 035975/246; open weekdays 9–6, Sat. 9–noon) in Hohnstein, above Rathen. Bernd organizes hikes, cycle tours, and rock-climbing expeditions for all skill levels.

COMING AND GOING

Dresden's S1 **S-Bahn** (direction: Schöna) runs along the river every half hour, stopping in Pirna (25 min, DM 4), Kurort Rathen (40 min, DM 5), Königstein (45 min, DM 5), and Bad Schandau (50 min, DM 6). It costs less than DM 3 to hop from one town to the next; purchase *and* validate your ticket before you board. In summer **steamships** are a far more scenic mode of transport. Pick up schedules in Dresden at the tourist office or the pier on Terrassenufer. Ships leave Dresden at 8, 9, and noon for Pirna (3 hrs, DM 16), Rathen (4½ hrs, DM 21), Königstein (5½ hrs, DM 23), and Bad Schandau (6½ hrs, DM 26).

RATHEN

Straddling the Elbe River just 30 km south of Dresden, the popular Kurort (resort town) of Rathen is dwarfed by the 300-m-tall **Bastei,** a grouping of unusually shaped cliffs linked by narrow, arched, wood and sandstone bridges. From Rathen's main drag, the Basteiweg (Bastei path) will take you to a lookout point 193 m above the Elbe, from where you can take in a spectacular view of the region. To reach the Felsenburg (cliff fortress), you'll have to cross the 76.5-m-long, stone Basteibrücke (Bastei bridge), which was built in 1850–51 and hovers 165 m above the Elbe. During the Middle Ages, a wooden drawbridge served as the upper entrance to the stone fortress, which was used intermittently throughout the centuries and as late as the early 19th century; it now stands in ruins high up on a group of sheer rocks. A walking path identifies the main features of the fortress—don't miss the replica of the catapults of yore, used to crush the hulls of vessels plying the river below. The gated path is locked at dusk; a donation box requests a fee to maintain the monument (DM 4, DM 2 students).

If you'd like to spend a summer evening in Rathen, find out about performances at **Felsenbühne Rathen,** a huge open-air theater cut into flaky layers of rock. Pick up a schedule at the tourist office (*see* Where to Sleep and Eat, *below*). Tickets run DM 10–DM 35 (DM 6–DM 28 students). *Felsenbühne, tel. and fax 035024/70496.*

Signs point the way to another popular destination near Rathen: the handsome, red-roofed village of **Hohnstein.** Follow the AMSELSEE signs to the Pionierweg, which winds its way northeast to Hohnstein. The hike takes two hours or less; a horizontal green line marks the trail. The village is dominated by the towering **Burg Hohnstein,** a 14th-century fortress that seems to rise directly out of the cliffs. The fortress was one of Hitler's first prisons; today it serves a less sinister purpose as a converted restaurant and the **HI-Jugendherberge Burg Hohnstein** (Markt 1, tel. 035975/202, fax 035975/203), with beds for DM 21 (DM 25 over 26).

WHERE TO SLEEP AND EAT

Rathen's **tourist office** (Niederrathen 31, tel. 035024/422; open weekdays 8–noon and 2–6, Sat. 9–noon) books rooms and hands out trail info; from the ferry landing, head straight for five minutes. The **HI-Jugendherberge** (Auf den Halden 33, tel. 035024/70425; closed Nov.–Mar.) is 15 min downstream and has beds for DM 21.50 (DM 24 over 26). A ferry shuttles people (DM 1) and bikes (50 Pf) from the train station in Oberrathen to Niederrathen (where the action is, relatively speaking) until 12:45 AM. Stock up on supplies at Rathen's sole **grocery store,** on the main street not far from the dock.

KÖNIGSTEIN

Try to arrive in Königstein by ferry. Drift along the Elbe, between eroded sandstone cliffs and ragged outcroppings that rise from the steep slopes of the riverbanks. As your boat rounds a bend in the Elbe, the magnificent stone **Festung Königstein** appears to dominate the horizon. Built into the rock of a high plateau, this hulking citadel seems to have erupted right out of the mountain itself. Even at the hilltop, its stone walls literally tower above you. The musuems inside may not measure up to the impressive structure itself, but you won't want to miss the view from the battlements, the best vista for miles. In recent history, the Festung held such political prisoners as socialist August Bebel (1840–1913); it later housed art and dissidents captured by the Nazis. Either follow the signs for a very taxing 45-min climb, or take the goofy **Festungs Express** (DM 4, summer only), a toy-like train that leaves from Reißiger Platz. *Tel. 035021/64607. Admission: DM 6, DM 4 students (Nov.–Mar. DM 5, DM 3 students). Open Easter–Sept., daily 9–8; Oct., daily 9–6; Nov.–Mar., daily 9–5.*

WHERE TO SLEEP

The **tourist office** (Am Schreiberberg 2, tel. 035021/68261; open Tues.–Fri. 9–12 and 3–5:30, Sat. 9–10:30 AM) has maps and hiking info and books private rooms. If you've got gear, head to **Camping Königstein** (Schandauer Str. 25e, tel. 035021/224; closed Nov.–Mar.), just 500 m upstream from the train platform, with 114 sites right on the Elbe for DM 10 plus DM 3 per tent. Comfy bungalows run DM 14–DM 20.

BAD SCHANDAU

A pretty, riverside town of cobblestone streets nestled between rolling mountains and the river, Bad Schandau is, unfortunately, a bit of a tourist trap. Its restaurants and hotels cater more to the bed-and-breakfast set than the budget traveler, but the town is an ideal base for a host of hikes in the surrounding regions. Most of these start at the **Lichtenhainer waterfall**—unimpressive if you've ever seen a garden hose on really high. The 7-km path to the falls starts at the intersection of Badallee and Rudolf-Sendig Straße. A quicker (and cooler) option is the **Kirnitzschtalbahn** (follow the signs), a rural tramway (two per hr, 30 min, DM 8 round-trip) that has creaked and jiggled its way to the waterfall since 1898. One of the most popular hikes is the 7.8-km trail from the falls to the ruins of the **Wildenstein** "robber baron" castle, passing through a narrow crack in the plateau by a stone outcropping called Kuhstall Rock—which is where most people give up and have a picnic. Another option for a panoramic view is Rudolf Sendig's **Personenaufzug** (DM 2), a 50-m-high electric elevator, built way back in 1904; follow the signs to Rudolf-Sendig Straße.

return and use "basics" head here? The train station has lockers and rents **bikes** (tel. 035022/44354) for DM 12 per day. One block uphill from the Markt, **Mountain Bike Tours** (Poststr. 14, tel. 035022/42883; open weekdays 9–noon and 2–6, Sat. 9–11) charges about DM 20 per day.

WHERE TO SLEEP AND EAT

Bad Schandau is across and up the river from the train station. The ferry (two per hr, DM 1) will drop you off one block from the **tourist office** (Markt 8, tel. 035022/42412; open weekdays 9–noon and 1–6, Sat. 9–noon; shorter hrs in winter), which has loads of hiking info and books private rooms. Consider stopping by the cheap bakery across the street—dining in this town can burn a hole in your wallet. The hostel, **HI-Jugendherberge Bad Schandau** (Dorfstr. 14, tel. and fax 035022/42408) sits above town in the Ostrau area. Snag one of their 100 beds (DM 22, DM 26 over 26) during the scant reception hours: 7:30 AM–8:30 AM and 4:30 PM–6:30 PM. To get there, take the bus (which runs until 7 PM) to Ostrauer Scheibe, go straight, and then make a left on Dorfstraße. **Campingplatz Kirnitzschtal** (tel. 035022/42742) has 190 sites for DM 12 each and is located along the Kirnitzschtalbahn route (Ostrauer Mühle—last train 10 PM, 9 PM Sun.). Before you hit the trail stop by **Spar** grocery store (Kirchstr. 3), just north of the Markt.

LEIPZIG

Some of Europe's major trade routes once converged at Leipzig, which began to flourish as a center of commerce and cultural diversity in the 12th century. More recently, as the eastern bloc began to crumble, the GDR's second-largest city (after Berlin) was thrust back into the spotlight. Weekly peace prayers at Leipzig's Nikolaikirche grew into *Montagsdemonstrationen* (Monday protests), which attracted thousands of citizens despite GDR laws forbidding unauthorized assembly. October 9, 1989, will be remembered as a kind of turning point: Two days earlier, security forces had violently dispersed a downtown protest, and now 70,000 people were gathered for the Monday prayer. A call for nonviolence was issued and respected by protesters *and* police. In the following weeks more and more people gathered until November 6, three days before the wall came down, when 600,000 people marched peacefully through town. The Leipzig protests were a beacon for others throughout East Germany.

In an effort to resuscitate its pre–cold war traditions, the city that published Germany's first daily newspaper in the 17th century has again become home to major publishing houses, such as Brockhaus, Meyer, and Reclam. As one of Germany's biggest convention sites, the "City of Books" is also home to the spectacular, glass Neue Messe (new convention center).

You can easily explore the small Altstadt (old city) on foot—you may find that it retains more of its medieval character than Dresden's. Once the sun goes down, a vibrant nightlife of cabaret, theater, and concert music awaits you in Leipzig. The opera house is world famous, and J. S. Bach was organist and choir director at the Thomaskirche for the last 27 years of his life. If you want small, not urban, two to three hours south are the beautiful towns of the Erzgebirge. Nearby Zwickau and Chemnitz are more like Leipzig's ugly stepsisters, but a day-trip to Zwickau's Trabi museum or Chemnitz's downtown (a Stalinist cement paradise) can be a diverting and enlightening look into life in the GDR.

BASICS

CHANGING MONEY

The ATM inside the **Hauptbahnhof** accepts Visa, MasterCard, and AmEx. You'll find banks and ATMs in the city center, along **Katherinenstraße** and around the **Markt.** The **American Exchange** office (Dorotheenplatz 2–4, tel. 0341/211–3596) near Thomaskirche is open weekdays 9:30–6, Saturday 9–noon.

CONSULATES

The **American Consulate** (Wilhelm-Seyfferth-Str. 4, near Museum der Bildenden Künste, tel. 0341/213840, fax 0341/213–8417) is open weekdays 8–5. Leave a detailed message on the machine if you're in a pickle after hours.

ENGLISH-LANGUAGE BOOKSTORE

Universitäts-Buchhandlung has a small selection of English-language titles at fair prices. *Grimmaische Str. 30, tel. 0341/216370, fax 0341/217–3711. Open weekdays 9–7, Sat. 10–2.*

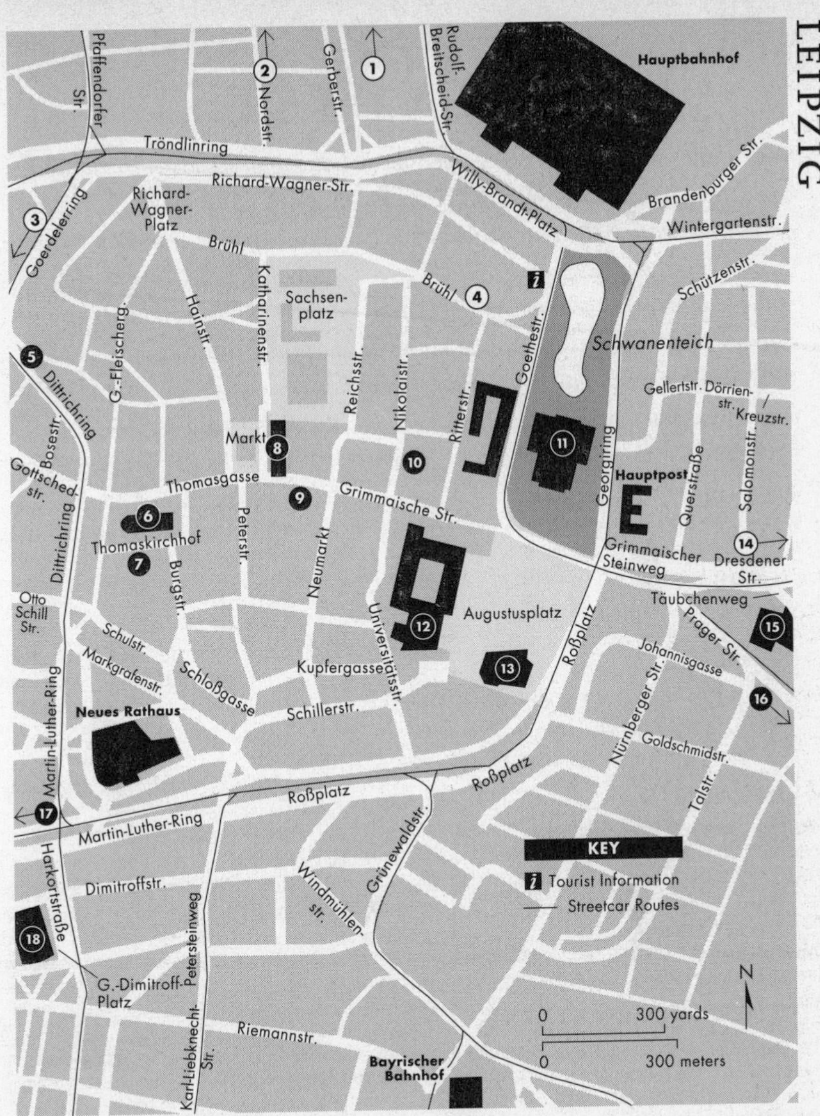

Sights ●

Altes Rathaus, **8**
Bachmuseum, **7**
Gewandhaus, **13**
Grassimuseum, **15**
Johannapark, **17**
Mädlerpassage, **9**
Museum der Bildenen Kuenste, **18**
Museum in der Runden Ecke, **5**
Nikolaikirche, **10**
Opernhaus, **11**
Thomaskirche, **6**
Uni-Turm, **12**
Völkerschlachtdenkmal, **16**

Lodging ○

Campingplatz am Auensee, **1**
Haus Ingeborg, **2**
Hotel IBIS, **4**
Jugendherberge Leipzig-Centrum, **3**
Pension prima, **14**

SQUATTER'S PARADISE

With unification the German government has promised to return property taken from landowners by the GDR. Problem is, many buildings remain unclaimed because the original owner is long dead and the heirs don't know that they own anything. These buildings are usually managed by the city, but many stand empty because no one wants to invest in property that may be claimed by someone else. Because of the patchwork of settled claims, decrepit shells linger next to modern or newly renovated apartment houses and office complexes. Sometimes buildings have become occupied by squats, though these have diminished. Still, until the "rightful owner" can be found, this subsociety continues.

LAUNDRY

Waschcenter charges DM 7 for a wash, DM 1 for 15 minutes of heat. *Str. des 18. Oktober 28a, tel. 0341/221–9391. Tram 12 or 21 (direction Probstheida or Meusdorf) to Johannisallee and right. Open daily 6 AM–10 PM.*

MAIL AND PHONES

Leipzig's massive grey **Hauptpost** (Grimmaische Str., east of Augustuspl.) has rows of phone booths for domestic and international calls. Leipzig's postal code is 04109.

MEDICAL AID

The pharmacists at **Löwenapotheke** (Grimmaische Str. 19, tel. 0341/960–5027 or 960–5028) are at your beck and call 24 hours, though the doors are only open weekdays 8–6, Saturday 9–noon. Call 011500 for a doctor, dentist, or pharmacist at any hour. The **Bereitschaftsdienst** (tel. 19292) sends doctors out on house calls weekdays 7–7, and weekends at any hour. The people at the above may or may not speak English.

Frauen-Notruf (tel. 0341/306–5246) helps women who are victims of rape and sexual abuse weekdays 6 AM–10 PM. On weekends an answering machine picks up.

VISITOR INFORMATION

The highly professional **Leipzig-Information** tourist office has plenty of free info, including bus/tram maps and an English-language map/walking guide. The staff can book you a hotel room free of charge; for a short-term apartment share, however, contact the **Mitfahr- und Wohnzentrale** (*see* By Mitfahrgelegenheit, *below*). Pick up a copy of the free monthly magazine *Blitz* for current theater, concert, and other nightlife listings. *Richard-Wagner Str. 1, tel. 0341/710–4260 or 710–4265, fax 0341/710–4271 or 710–4276. Open weekdays 9–8, Sat. 9–4, Sun. 9–2.*

COMING AND GOING

BY TRAIN

Leipzig's **Hauptbahnhof** (tel. 0341/960–4978 for reservations, 0341/968–3670 for information) is the largest in Europe and one of the most elegant. The gargantuan structure has all the fixings—luggage lockers, ATMs, phones, newsstands, cafeterias, grocery and clothing stores, and bars. (Leipzigers head to the Bahnhof for after-hours shopping—stores are open until 10 PM.) To reach the city center, cross traffic-filled Willy-Brandt-Platz and go straight. From Leipzig there are trains to Berlin (every 2 hrs, 2 hrs,

DM 45), and hourly departures to Dresden (1½ hrs, DM 30), Erfurt (1½ hrs, DM 25), Chemnitz (1½ hrs, DM 20), Magdeburg (1 hr 20 min, DM 30), and Halle (35 min, DM 10).

BY BUS

In the unlikely event that rail transport does not match your plans, call the regional bus information service at 034203/600. The tourist office also gives advice on regional buses.

BY MITFAHRGELEGENHEIT

Mitfahr- und Wohnzentrale (Rudolf-Breitscheid-Str. 39, west of Hauptbahnhof, tel. 0341/19440, fax 0341/980–5001) arranges rides throughout the country daily 9–8. They also arrange short-term stays in apartment shares.

GETTING AROUND

Nearly all of Leipzig's sights are concentrated inside a one-sq-km area surrounded by the "Ring" streets, erstwhile location of the city wall. On the edge of this district are the **Hauptbahnhof** to the northeast, **Augustusplatz** to the east, and **Thomaskirche** to the west. If you get lost, scan the skyline for Leipzig's imposing **university tower** over Augustusplatz.

Though Leipzig's regional flavor is diluted by students from all over Germany, the lilting Saxon accent is strongest in this city, pronounced by the "Saggsen" as "Leipsch."

BY TRAM AND BUS

The only time you'll need public transit is to reach a hostel or pension, or to check out some nightlife outside of downtown—and even then you'll rarely travel more than 10–15 min. With the **Leipzig Card** (*see* Worth Seeing, *below*), bus and tram are free. Pick up a schedule of nighttime routes at the tourist office.

BY TAXI

Leipzig's **taxis** start their meters at DM 3.50 and add DM 1.50 per km. Catch one outside the Hauptbahnhof or at the Markt, or call 0341/4884, 4233, or 982222.

WHERE TO SLEEP

As a major convention city, Leipzig has plenty of rooms in all price categories. During off-season, even centrally located hotels offer unbeatable special rates. Call the Leipzig booking hotline at 0341/710–4260 or 710–4265 for reservations in hotels and *Pensionen.*

Hotel IBIS. Very centrally located, this comfortable chain hotel offers a DM 89 double-room deal (without breakfast) as a last-minute special in winter and July–August. Ask the tourist office for offers at other times or call the hotel directly. Feel like a drink at 5 AM? Visit their 24-hour bar. *Brühl 69, a block behind the tourist office, tel. 0341/21860, fax 0341/218-6222.*

Haus Ingeborg. Eight bright, pleasantly outfitted rooms await you on a quiet street five blocks north of downtown. Singles cost DM 80, doubles DM 80–DM 100, DM 110 with bath. *Nordstr. 58, tel. 041/960–3143, fax 0341/564–9871.*

Pension prima. Only a 20-min walk east of Augustusplatz, prima has spacious, bright doubles for DM 80, smaller but equally nice singles for DM 55. You'll have to share bathrooms, but breakfast is included and there's a restaurant downstairs. *Dresdner Str. 82, tel. 0341/688–3481. From Hauptbahnhof, Tram 4 or 20 (direction: Stötteritz) to Reudnitz Straßenbahnhof, which stops on Dresdner Str. 21 rooms, none with bath.*

HOSTELS

Jugendherberge Leipzig-Centrum (HI). Make a reservation for this hostel RIGHT NOW! You can't get more central for this cheap unless you bed with the winos. This homey place has a TV room, lounge areas, and a dining room with bay windows overlooking the backyard. Beds are DM 24 (DM 29 over 26), including breakfast. *Käthe-Kollwitz-Str. 62–66, tel. 0341/245–7011, fax 0341/245–7012. From Hauptbahnhof, Tram 1 (direction: Lausen) or Tram 2 (direction: Plagwitz) to Marschnerstr. 106 beds. Curfew 1 AM. Check-in 2:30–10. Luggage storage.*

CAMPING

Campingplatz am Auensee. Right by lake Auensee, this campsite has spaces for DM 10 per night. Lean-to tents—little A-frame numbers—are DM 3, trailers DM 7, and bungalows DM 25 (plus DM 4 per person). Hot water is plentiful and there's a little café. *Gustav-Esche-Str. 5, tel. and fax 0341/461–1977. From Hauptbahnhof, Tram 10 or 28 (direction: Wahren) or Tram 11 (direction: Schkeuditz) to Rathaus Wahren; then straight to Linkelstr., right on Rittergutstr. and follow curves.*

FOOD

Fruit, vegetable, and Imbiß stands abound, especially around Sachsenplatz, the Markt, and the pedestrian part of Grimmaische Straße. In addition to the markets in the train station, there's a Tengelmann **grocery store** on Brühl, next to McDonald's.

UNDER DM 15 • academixer-Keller. This cellar restaurant-bar fills with cabaret-goers during intermission, but serves great, inexpensive meals. Nontheater types come for beer and cool-cat tunes (Tom Waits, Nick Cave), and to munch on a wide selection of items for DM 12–DM 18. *Kupferg., off Universitätsstr., tel. 0341/211–4274. No lunch.*

Bagel Brothers. Aching for some fresh NY-style bagels? This is the place to go! Choose from 12 different varieties (including chocolate) and crunchy toppings. If you're headed out into unbageled territory, get a dozen bagels and a pound of cream cheese to go for DM 16.95. Check the free *Fritz* weekly for a "Buy one, get the second one 50% off" coupon. *Nikolaistr. 42, down the street from IBIS Hotel, tel. 0341/980–3330.*

Café Barbakane. This café inside the Moritzbastei (*see* After Dark, *below*) serves cafeteria-style food for under DM 8 to students on break (or skipping class for coffee and a cigarette). *Universitätsstr. 9, behind Uni-Turm, tel. 0341/702590 or 702–5915, fax 0341/702–5959. Closed most Sun.*

Paulaner. Locals and tourists flock to both sections of this centrally located eatery. The café has cheaper entrées, though the main restaurant offers filling specials (DM 12) daily 11–4. *Klosterg. 3, near Thomaskirche, tel. 0341/281985.*

UNDER DM 30 • Auerbachs Keller. This historic restaurant, built in 1530, was a favorite of Goethe's and made an appearance in his *Faust*. Centuries later the Keller cashes in with overpriced entrées (DM 20–DM 40) from Schnitzel to chateaubriand, but you can always come in and enjoy a glass of wine in the large, ambient cellar hall. *Grimmaische Str. 2–4, in Mädlerpassage, tel. 0341/216100.*

WORTH SEEING

Leipzig's small and walkable city center focuses on the Markt and the Thomasgasse/Grimmaische Straße axis. Consider taking the 2½-hour **bus tour** (DM 28) or joining one of the 2-hour **city walks** (DM 12) or combined 1½-hour bus/½-hour walking tours (DM 20). Ask for details at the tourist office or call 0341/710–4280. The **Leipzig Card** (DM 9 one-day, DM 21 three-day) allows you free travel on buses and trams, reduced admission (up to 25%) to all sights below, DM 9 off bus tours, DM 2 off city walks, and DM 5 off the combined option.

AUGUSTUSPLATZ

Towering over Nikolaikirche and everything else around Augustusplatz is the 154-m-tall **Uni-Turm** (University Tower), a rather imposing metal-and-glass creation. In 1968 the GDR government blew up nearby Paulinerkirche so the university faculty wouldn't have to be near a religious monument. A bronze cast of Lenin, surrounded by a group of determined-looking students and workers, hovers over the entrance to the university building that replaced the church. Street performers are common here on summer weekends, and on sunny afternoons local students hang out planning the night's diversions.

To the left, the **Gewandhaus** (Augustuspl. 8, tel. 0341/127–0280), home to Leipzig's symphony orchestra, is actually an aesthetic piece of GDR architecture. The statue of Beethoven at the front entrance won first prize at the 1912 World Art Exhibition. Across the square, the **Opernhaus** (Augustuspl. 12, tel. 0341/126–1261) has the dubious distinction of being the first postwar theater built in East Germany. When you hear the clock on the square strike, look up to the tower to the left—two buff, bronze-cast proletarians swivel to strike the bell with their sledgehammers.

GRASSIMUSEUM

This complex houses three so-so museums. Skip the **Museum of Arts and Crafts** (Tues., Thurs., Fri. 10–6, Wed. 10–8, weekends 10–5) unless there's a special exhibit, but do poke your head into the **Museum of Folklore** (Tues.–Fri. 10–5:30, weekends 10–4, closed Mon.). Then head to the **Musical Instrument Museum** (Tues.–Sat. 10–5, Sun. 10–1, closed Mon.), which features antique violins, flutes, clavichords, and even a few music boxes. Also on display are original scores by Bach and Wagner. Wander the courtyard and the foyers for a free glimpse of some unusual sculptures. A **movie theater** (Täubchenw. 20, tel. 0341/960–4838) in the museum shows the occasional English film. *Johannispl. 5–11, tel. 0341/21420. Admission to each museum: DM 5, DM 2 students.*

MARKT

Parts of the Markt were severely damaged during World War II, but thanks to detailed restoration the square retains its centuries-old appearance. One side is taken up by the 16th-century **Altes Rathaus,** best known for its off-center tower and brilliant blue clock. The tower houses the **Stadtgeschichtliches Museum** (Markt 1, tel. 0341/965130), which explains Leipzig's history with late-medieval ecclesiastic paraphernalia, armor and weapons, and excellent rotating exhibits. The museum is open Tuesday 2–8, Wednesday–Sunday 10–6; admission is DM 5 (DM 2.50 students, free admission every first Sunday of the month). In the city block south of the Rathaus are several narrow glass-roof shopping arcades (read: malls). On Grimmaische Straße is the main entrance to Leipzig's finest arcade, the **Mädlerpassage.** Goethe set a scene of *Faust* in its Auerbachs Keller restaurant (*see* Food, *above*). Do as the other tourists do and rub Dr. Faust's foot for good luck.

The Uni-Turm may resemble the business end of a fountain pen, but it's supposed to represent an open book, as a symbol of learning. Look closely. Go around to the other side. Still don't see it? Join the club.

MUSEUM DER BILDENDEN KÜNSTE

The Museum of Fine Arts is one of Leipzig's best, with an extensive collection of Old German and Dutch painters, including works by Dürer, Cranach, and Caspar David Friedrich, as well as a sizable holding of 20th-century sculpture. The museum will move into a brand-new, glass cube building on Sachsenplatz in 2002. Until then, the bulk of the collection is on display at the interim location in the *Handelshof* at Grimmaische Straße 1–7. *Admission: DM 5, DM 2.50 students. Open Tues., Thurs.–Sun. 10–6, Wed. 1–9:30, closed Mon.*

MUSEUM IN DER RUNDEN ECKE

Going inside the former headquarters of the Stasi (the GDR's infamous secret police) is an eerie and sobering experience. The museum's exhibition, called "Power and Banality," consists of materials Leipzigers discovered here when they took over on the night of December 4, 1989. Even if you can't read German, definitely check out the countless photos of innocent citizens, mountains of seized letters (40 years' worth), and the black-and-white video of demonstrators taken just before the Stasi were ousted from the building. The museum is run as a public service by the Leipzig citizens' committee, formed in those hectic days in 1989, to educate people about life in the GDR. *Dittrichring 24, tel. 0341/961–2443. Admission free. Open Wed.–Sun. 2–6.*

NIKOLAIKIRCHE

In the early 1980s, Leipzig's Nikolaikirche started hosting Monday peace prayers to speak out against the arms race. As the only (relatively) safe realm for public protest, these weekly meetings became the focal point of demonstrations for human rights, environmental issues, and peace; the Monday prayers and community service still continue. The church itself is a modest Baroque creation, but the interior is splendid. The nave columns burst into soft green tendrils that spread across the ceiling, making you feel like Peter Rabbit underneath the turnips in Mr. McGregor's garden. Every Saturday there's an (often free) organ concert at 5 PM. *Nikolaikirchhof 3, tel. 0341/960–5270. Open weekdays 10–6.*

THOMASKIRCHE

J. S. Bach was choirmaster of Thomaskirche for nearly 27 years and wrote dozens of cantatas for the church's famous **Thomanerchor** boys' choir. For info about their fairly frequent concerts, contact the tourist office. Though the choir thrives on Bach's reputation, Bach himself was hardly appreciated during his lifetime. When he died in Leipzig in 1750 he was given only a simple grave in a disreputable cemetery. It wasn't until 1945 that Bach found his final, fitting resting place on the altar platform of Thomaskirche, a church for which he had deep feelings. Across the street is the **Bachmuseum** (Thomaskirchhof 16, tel. 0341/964410; open daily 10–5), whose excellent display of period musical instruments and English-language displays make it a must-see for Bach fans. Admission is DM 4 (DM 2.50 students). Summer Mondays at 7 PM there are free classical music concerts in front of the church. Come about an hour early if you want a seat at the surrounding sidewalk cafés or on one of the few folding chairs set up for the occasion. *Tel. 0341/960–2855. Open daily 10–6, 9–5 in winter.*

VÖLKERSCHLACHTDENKMAL

Built in the 1870s, the Völkerschlachtdenkmal has more to do with German hypernationalism after the founding of the second Reich (Bismarck's unification of Germany in 1871) than the event it actually commemorates: the 1813 Battle of the Nations, in which Russian, Austrian, and Prussian forces combined to "liberate" Leipzig from Napoléon. The whole thing is more than just a bit overdone, from the brawny stone warriors to the Gothic angelic voices echoing off the walls from unseen speakers. For the best view of Leipzig's smoggy skyline, climb the dizzying, narrow staircase 91 m up to the observation platform. *Prager Str., tel. 0341/878–0471. Tram 15 or 21 (direction: Meusdorf) to Völkerschlachtdenkmal. Admission: DM 3.50, DM 2 students. Open daily 10–5 (Nov.–Apr., 9–4).*

CHEAP THRILLS

To escape city pressures, locals head to the green splotches in **Johannapark,** on Karl-Tauchnitzstraße a few blocks west of the Neues Rathaus. On hot summer days, the fountains on **Sachsenplatz** become a spectacle of splashing, pasty white bodies, and the **Markt** fills with beer and wine vendors and street musicians. People-watching on **Peterstraße** below the Markt will never disappoint—stretch out on the lawn with the punks, the grannies, and the sunbathers. Behind the opera house, the tree-lined paths around the **Schwanenteich** (swan pond) also make for a lazy afternoon.

FESTIVALS

You may not call Leipzig "a little Paris," as Goethe did, but the comparison rings a little truer during the city's many festivals. The tourist office can help with details and, if necessary, tickets. The **"Leipzig Is Reading" Book Fair and Literature Festival** draws literary types to the Neue Messe in late March. During the **Easter Fair Spectacle** people in historical costumes celebrate on the market square. The **Bach Festival** brings internationally renowned musicians to town in May (the festival was launched in 1999). The 250th anniversary of Bach's death is the impetus behind the **Bachfest Leipzig 2000,** which will be held from July 21 through July 30, 2000. During May Leipzig is also host to the colorful **Saxonia International Balloon Fiesta** (one of Europe's biggest balloonist meetings), the unique **Wave Gothic Meeting** (your chance to catch up with the Gothic and neo-Romantic scene), and the funky **Honky Tonk International Pub Festival** (advertised as "the largest pub festival in Europe with over 100 bands"). The **Street Music Festival** completes the spring festivities. In summer, the **Leipziger Stadtfest** turns Sachsenplatz and Grimmaische Straße into one big carnival stage. Then, Germany's Music City turns up the volume with the **Richard Wagner Festival** in July, the traditional **Gewandhaustage** in August, and the **Mendelssohn Bartholdy Festival** in October/November. For more contemporary tunes, come in late September/early October, when the city's churches, student-club stages, and opera house are filled with cool beats during the **Leipzig Jazz Festival.** In October, you can amuse yourself at the Leipzig satirical **"Laughter Fair"** or watch movies at the **International Festival for Documentary and Animated Film.** In November, the **euro-scene-leipzig** festival brings cutting-edge contemporary theater to the city. In December follow your nose to the mulled wine and gingerbread at the traditional **Christmas market.**

AFTER DARK

It's hard *not* to find "the scene" in Leipzig, especially on weekends, when throngs take to the streets around the Markt. You'll come across an abundance of hip bars along Klostergasse and Barfußgäßchen, but beware of touristy places like **Zill's Tunnel.** Check out the quieter options at Thomaskirchhof. Even some of the less overtly hip places (like the cabaret bars) are packed. As an alternative, it's a worthwhile 10-min tram ride south to the funky district of Connewitz or west to

Schaubühne Lindenfels (Karl-Heine-Str. 50, tel. 0341/484620; Tram 4 or Bus 52 to Felsenkeller), an alternative theater/movie house with a good café/bar. Catch classical music concerts at the **Bach Museum** (tel. 0341/964410) every Wednesday (Sun. July–Aug., Sat. in Dec.), at the **Thomaskirche** (tel. 0341/984420) on Fridays and Saturdays (except holidays), and at the **Mendelssohnhaus** on Sundays (tel. 0341/127–0294). The free *Fritz* magazine has fairly complete entertainment listings, as does the more generic Leipzig edition of *Blitz*.

BARS AND CLUBS

Conne Island ("Eiskeller"). A young and funky crowd flocks to this hot spot at the far southern end of Connewitz. Some days there's dancing, but generally it's the best place in town to catch shows by local and touring underground bands. *Koburger Str. 3, tel. 0341/311044. Tram 28 or 58 (direction: Markkleeberg-West) to Koburger Brücke. Cover: DM 5–DM 15. Open Tues.–Sun. from 9 PM.*

die naTo. This popular Connewitz bar is anything but pretentious, and it's probably the best introduction to the district (there are a handful of other bars nearby). Best of all is the cinema, which shows new and old films (DM 7) from around the world, all in the original language with subtitles. *Karl-Liebknecht-Str. 46, tel. 0341/391–5539. Tram 11 to Arndtstr. Open daily 7 PM–2:30 AM (Fri. and Sat. until 3:30 AM).*

The Neue Messe, Leipzig's new, architecturally impressive convention center, always has something going on (often open to the public).

Filmcafé Intershop. It might look a little cheesy, but this pink-walled café fills with a casual crowd of students and moviegoers from the theater on Peterstraße. Soak up the kitsch and enjoy a coffee or beer. At night, the bar in back handles the overflow. *Burgstr. 9, at Sporerg. near Thomaskirche, tel. 0341/960–8504. Open daily 2 PM–late.*

Moritzbastei. The "mb" (pronounced *em–bay*) is Leipzig's number-one student night spot. Visit the two music stages, take a seat at one of the heavy wooden tables, or set off down the brick halls in search of Café Barbakane (*see* Food, *above*) for the cheapest coffee and beer in town. Some nights there's live jazz or blues, comedy, readings, or a combination of the above. *Universitätsstr. 9, behind Uni-Turm, tel. 0341/702590 or 702–5915, fax 0341/702–5959. Club cover: DM 2–DM 8. Open Mon.–Sat. (sometimes Sun.) from 7:30 PM.*

Pfeffermühle. Attached to Leipzig's most popular cabaret is a small, cozy bar perfect for conversation or just relaxing. No hipsters here, just candlelight, beer, wine, coffee, and inexpensive café food. *Thomaskirchhof 16, behind Bachhaus (go through door to get to courtyard), tel. 0341/960–2499. Open daily 6 PM–3 AM.*

Spizz. After enjoying a drink and perhaps a snack (filling baguette sandwiches start at DM 5!) in the lively bar, head for the popular jazz cellar downstairs to round off the night. *Am Markt 9, tel. 0341/960–4078.*

MUSIC AND THEATER

Leipzig has an ever-increasing number of cabarets, though you'll need to know German (and Germany) quite well to understand the humor. Check out Pfeffermühle (*see above*), academixer-Keller (*see* Food, *above*), **Gohglmohsch** (Markt 9, in back, tel. 0341/961–5111), or Sanftwut (in the Mädlerpassage, tel. 961–2346). Tickets are DM 15–DM 30, DM 12–DM 25 students. German isn't a prerequisite for traditional opera and ballet performances, which happen on the main stage at **Opernhaus** (Augustuspl. 12, tel. 0341/126–1261), or head to the Opernhaus's **Kellertheater** (cellar theater, tel. 0341/12610) or **Probebühne Mockau** (rehearsal stage; Simon-Bolivar Str. 92, tel. 0341/12680) for more progressive offerings. The box office is open weekdays 10–6, Saturday 10–1; tickets run DM 10–DM 80. There are no student tickets for the **Gewandhaus,** and ticket prices start at a steep DM 54 (Augustusplatz 8, tel. 0341/12700, tickets 0341/127–0280).

Leipzig's main theater, the **Schauspielhaus,** shows traditional drama, contemporary comedy, modern dance, and erotic theater all under the same roof. It also supervises **Neue Szene,** which emphasizes modern, smaller productions. Get tickets (DM 20–DM 50, DM 10–DM 25 students) at the info office, Schauspielhaus, or one hour before show time. *Schauspielhaus: Bosestr. 1, just west of Dittrichring, tel. 0341/12680. Box office open weekdays 10–6, Sat. 10–1. Neue Szene: Gottschedstr. 16, 2 blocks NW of Schauspielhaus, tel. 0341/980–4842.*

NEAR LEIPZIG

CHEMNITZ

An important industrial center since the 19th century, Chemnitz became known the "Saxon Manchester," but the name it officially carried from 1953 to 1990 more accurately describes this concrete monster: Karl-Marx-Stadt. Few cities in the former GDR have been as affected by communist architectural ideology as Chemnitz. Its sprawling cement plazas, overwhelming glass-and-steel-lined avenues, and rows of cinder-block homes for the proletariat stand as a physical manifestation of cultural revolution. Empty lots are currently being filled with the latest in capitalist construction, but much of the postwar architecture (some of it is already under landmark protection) will remain.

Chemnitz's showpiece is Straße der Nationen, also the city center's main artery. On the way downtown, you'll pass **Theaterplatz,** a beautiful (or, if you prefer, bourgeois-aristocratic) reminder of times past. Here you'll find the obligatory Opernhaus, the **Museum für Naturkunde** (Natural Science Museum; Theaterplatz 1, tel. 0371/488–4550) and a small, more worthwhile, rotating collection of works by Rodin, Otto Dix, and local artists in the **Kunstsammlung** (tel. 0371/488–4424; open Tues.–Sun. 11–5). Admission to each is DM 5 (DM 2.50 students). In front of the museum is the **Versteinerter Wald** (Petrified Forest), a group of 250-million-year-old tree stumps. The Straße der Nationen begins here and opens onto a giant plaza dominated by boxy high-rises and the 1970s Hotel Mercure, which dwarf even the Markt's huge neo-Gothic Rathaus.

Lest you think Chemnitz is all modern metropolis, take a short stroll across the Chemnitz River through a pleasant residential quarter and past the Schloßteich lake to the **Schloßbergmuseum** (tel. 0371/488–4501; admission DM 5, DM 2.50 students), housed in an old monastery and castle for the dukes of Saxony. The excellent exhibit details (in German) the city's evolution from medieval trading center to the present. It's open Tuesday–Sunday 10–6 (Oct.–Apr. until 5). You can ride the **mini-train** (DM 3) Tuesday–Saturday around the Küchwaldpark—a placid green knob near Schloßberg.

BASICS

The **tourist and ticket office** (tel. 0371/19433; open weekdays 9–6, Sat. 9–12) recently moved into new offices in the Stadthalle. There is also a **tourist information** across the train station on Bahnhofstraße. They stock city maps, organize walking tours in summer, and have free copies of the regional magazine *Blitz*. The main **post office** (Str. der Nationen 33) is near the Bahnhof.

COMING AND GOING

From the **Hauptbahnhof** (tel. 0371/414257) there are connections to Dresden (hourly, 1¼ hrs, DM 20), Leipzig (hourly, 1½ hrs, DM 22), Berlin (6 per day, 3 hrs, DM 55), and Zwickau (2 per hr, 55 min, DM 14). The station is equipped with lockers and a credit-card ATM. Cross Bahnhofstraße and turn left on Straße der Nationen for the city center. Chemnitz's **Busbahnhof** (tel. 0371/461–3857; info office open weekdays 7–4, Sat. 8:30–noon) is one block straight ahead from the train station. Destinations include Dresden (two per weekday, DM 14) and the Erzgebirge (*see below*). To reach the travel agency–run **Mitfahrzentrale** (Dresdner Str. 181, tel. 0371/446511), take Bus 32 from Straße der Nationen to its end at Dresdner Straße.

WHERE TO SLEEP AND EAT

The tourist office books private rooms (DM 35–DM 50) for a DM 2 fee. The **room-finding service** (tel. 0371/45191; open weekdays 8 AM–10 PM, Sat. 8–2) in the Hauptbahnhof next to the bookstore charges DM 38–DM 50, fee included. For food, stick to the beer halls and Imbiß-style eateries around the Markt and Straße der Nationen, or try the cafés and restaurants in the pleasant pedestrian zone between the Busbahnhof and the lake. If it's liquid nutrition you're after, **Bier Academy** (Rosenhof 2, tel. 0371/611260; open daily) lives up to its name, educating drinkers with a color photo of each of its 25 types of beer.

ZWICKAU

Unlike Chemnitz, Zwickau's city center has been turned into a busy pedestrian area filled with cafés, restaurants, and shops—nothing to go out of the way for, but chances are you're here to pay homage to

Zwickau's hometown hero: the infamous Trabant car first produced here in 1957. The disposable little Trabi looks like it should have a wind-up key, and its two-stroke motor is similar to those in lawn mowers and mopeds. (Though they are ridiculed, many Germans view them as perky little underdogs, as memorialized in the feature film *Go Trabi, Go!*) The city's sole tribute to this lovable, atrocious vehicle is the **Automobilmuseum,** displaying nine decades of Zwickau auto history. *Walther-Rathenau-Str. 51, tel. 0375/205218. Tram 4 to Schlachthofstr., then left down W.-Rathenau-Str. Admission: DM 5, DM 3.50 students. DM 1 extra charge for photos, DM 3 for video. Open Tues. and Thurs. 9–noon and 2–5, weekends 10–5.*

If you're not here for the Trabis, you must be here because of Robert Schumann (if you're here for any other reason, you're in the wrong town). On the city's Hauptmarkt, next to the beautiful neo-Gothic Rathaus and the theater, is the **Robert-Schumann-Haus** (Hauptmarkt 5, tel. 0375/215269). The house where Zwickau's most famous resident was born on June 8, 1810, now serves as a museum and archive, with lots of personal memorabilia on display. The museum is open Tuesday–Saturday 10–5, and admission is DM 5 (DM 3 students). Each year in early June the town celebrates the **Robert Schumann Music Days and Competition,** which features music performances in venues throughout the city. Check your DM 100 bill for a portrait of Schumann's wife, Clara, who also was a composer and an excellent pianist.

BASICS

Tourist Information Zwickau (Hauptstr. 6, at Hauptmarkt, tel. 0375/293713 or 0375/293714), open weekdays 9–4, Saturday 9–noon, books private rooms (DM 30–DM 45) and hotel rooms for free. Zwickau's **post office** is just outside the train station. There is a Laundromat at Leipziger Straße 27.

At Brückenstraße and Straße der Nationen, the four-story-high head of Karl Marx gazes stonily over what was, what is, and what will be.

COMING AND GOING

Zwickau can be reached by train from Chemnitz (2 per hr, 55 min, DM 14) and Leipzig (hourly, 1¼ hrs, DM 20). The **Bahnhof** (tel. 0375/893202) has rows of lockers. It's a 20-min walk to the city center; walk leftish out of the station and onto Bahnhofstraße, or hop on Tram 1 to Georgenplatz and head right down Äußere Plauensche Straße to the Hauptmarkt.

WHERE TO SLEEP AND EAT

There is really no reason to spend more than a few hours in town, but if you insist: **Beherbergungsgewerbe Kretzschmar** has two drab hostel-like pensions, with beds in two- to four-bed rooms for DM 25, and singles and doubles from DM 30 to DM 50. One is a 10-min walk from the Hauptbahnhof (Hilfegottesschachtstr. 3b, at Reichenbacher Str., tel. 0375/215410) in a decrepit area with a nauseating chemical odor; the other is at the north end of town (Leipziger Str. 240, tel. 0375/441–3372) at the Pöblitz end of Tram 4. A few cafés and restaurants are scattered around the Hauptmarkt.

THE ERZGEBIRGE

Rising along the southeastern edge of Saxony, the Erzgebirge (Ore Mountains), best reached from Chemnitz or Zwickau, are named for the rich deposits of minerals and metals mined here from the 1400s. Though some mining continued into the 20th century (most notably uranium, labeled the "ore for peace" by the GDR), the original boom lasted only until the 1700s. Since then, the area has become famous for its crafts. Besides lace, the Erzgebirge towns fashion wooden incense-holder mannequins, Christmas carousels, and *Schwibbogen*—wooden arches decorated to reflect a town's history and personality.

SCHNEEBERG

The tiny mining village of Schneeberg is home to one of the most beautiful of the Erzgebirge traditions, the **Lichtelfest** (Festival of Light). Just before Christmas the entire town lights up their Schwibbogen decorated with the town's symbol: a miner. Schneeberg also offers more than 75 km of hiking trails that meander through the region's meadows and ferny woods and past sheer rock faces. Many of the trails make for great cross-country skiing in winter. Contact the tourist office for maps and info.

Schneeberg is well-connected by **bus** with Zwickau (40 min, DM 7). Buses arrive at Schneeberg's Rathaus, where you'll also find the **tourist office** (tel. 03772/2251; open weekdays 9–5:30, weekends 9–1). They book private rooms free of charge, and have info on nearby hiking trails.

ANNABERG-BUCHHOLZ

Deeper in the mountains lies the small, well-preserved town of Annaberg-Buchholz, created by the union of two mining towns in 1945. The eight-day **Annaberger Kät,** a local folk festival, has been celebrated every June since 1520, though it has evolved into a carnival-type event. The festivities start the second week after *Pfingsten* (Pentecost) and include a parade through town in traditional dress, lots of beer, and a closing fireworks bonanza. If you miss the Kät, don't miss the **Stadtkirche St. Annen** (Große Kirchg., tel. 03733/23190). The bright interior with its twisting ceiling ribs and colorful, intricate carvings will impress even the staunchest agnostic. Across the street, the **Erzgebirgsmuseum** (Große Kirchg. 16, tel. 03733/23497; open Tues.–Sun. 10–5) has an especially good display of mining and local arts, including spinning and bobbin-lace making. Admission is DM 5 (DM 2.50 students). For DM 8 (DM 5 students) you can also tour one of Annaberg's original silver mines, right below the museum.

Trains connect to Dresden (via Flöha, three per day, 2 hrs, DM 29) and Chemnitz (every two hrs, 1½ hrs, DM 15). Get off at the Unterer Bahnhof (the first Annaberg stop); it's a 10-min walk up the footpath to downtown. Buses leave from the **Busbahnhof** (tel. 03733/24875) on Adam-Ries-Straße (down Wolkensteiner Str. from tourist office) for Dresden (two per day, 3 hrs, DM 20), Zwickau (1–2 per day, 1¾ hrs, DM 13), and Chemnitz (hourly weekdays, eight per day weekends, 1 hr, DM 10). The **tourist office** (Markt 1, behind Rathaus, tel. 03733/425139), open weekdays 9–6, Saturday 9–noon, has info on hiking and skiing trails, and books private rooms for a DM 2 fee.

10

SAXONY-ANHALT

UPDATED BY PEGGY SALZ-TRAUTMAN

Saxony-Anhalt (Sachsen-Anhalt) didn't become a *Land* (state) until the end of World War II, when the Soviet military authorities united the Prussian province of Saxony with the tiny duchy of Anhalt. Eliminated by the GDR in 1952, the state was then resurrected after unification. Despite the two regions' diversity—flat, Brandenburg-like plains and a marked Prussian influence in the north, and the gently rolling Harz Mountains and Saxon cheer in the south—this relatively young state remains dedicated to its unity. Defying the region's high rate of unemployment, the residents seem eager to build the state up from the ashes of its now defunct chemical industry.

German companies and foreign investors, as though inspired by the people's resolve, are transforming the state and breathing new life into its outmoded businesses, including tourism. Visitors anxious to see the spectacular nature reserves that were off-limits during GDR times are making a beeline to the **Harz Mountains,** home of the Brocken. The highest mountain in northern Germany, it long served as the chief surveillance point for the GDR and Russian military, but tourists are hardly interested in the ancient facility—except perhaps to visit the restaurant nearby. They come to Saxony-Anhalt to hike, take in the beautiful scenery, and wonder at the centuries-old facades in towns such as **Wernigerode** and **Quedlinburg. Wittenberg,** best known as the city where Martin Luther started the Protestant Reformation, has a quaint charm that contrasts sharply with the cement cityscapes of **Dessau** and **Magdeburg.** But even these cities have their architectural and historical monuments, be they thousand-year-old Gothic cathedrals and Romanesque churches in Magdeburg or minimalist architecture from the Bauhaus school of design, which enjoyed a brief tenure in Dessau. For a taste of contemporary art and theater, visit **Halle,** whose university culture has given rise to a student-flavored café and nightlife scene that complements the city's well-preserved architectural heritage.

HALLE

Saxony-Anhalt's largest city was originally an important center in the salt trade, but since 1694, Halle has been known primarily as a university town, and today its active student population supports a flourishing café scene, offbeat nightlife, and lots of political activity. Though the town was spared during World War II, half a century of architectural neglect followed by half a decade of post-unification reces-

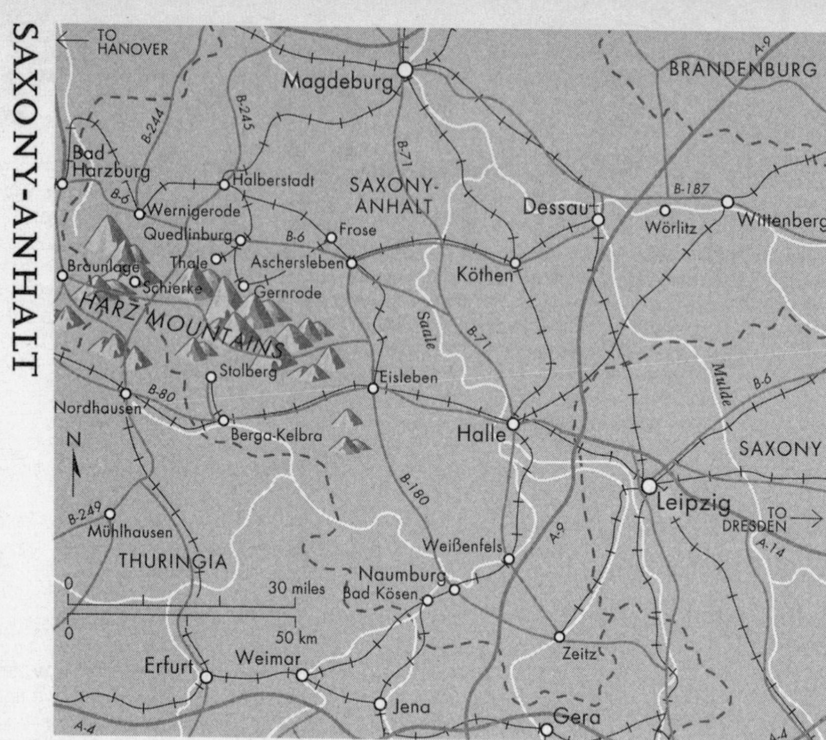

sion have taken their toll. Investors and construction cranes have been rolling in, however, and the town is starting to show signs of progress—measured in jackhammer decibels. Know that Halle is a bit like a pressure cooker of cultures: The extreme left and right have been known to clash on the streets of the Neustadt—and the results have not been pretty. Stick to the *Altstadt* (old town), where you'll find impressive Gothic architecture and the birthplace of native son and composer Georg Friedrich Händel (1685–1759). Although he officially anglicized his name to George Frederic Handel, you'll find his renounced German names alive and well throughout the region.

BASICS

CHANGING MONEY • The **ATM** inside the train station accepts credit cards and Cirrus bank cards. The attached **DVB Bank** gives Visa, MasterCard, and AmEx cash advances and cashes traveler's checks, but the **Deutsche Bank** on the Markt (market square) takes less of a commission.

LAUNDRY • Head to **Waschhaus,** where you can chill at the attached café or wander nearby Reilstraße, a lively street with shops and more cafés. A wash costs DM 5; 15 min of dryer time is DM 1.50. *Richard-Wagner-Str., at Böckstr., tel. 0345/522–0611. Tram 2, 3, 7, or 10 to Reileck. Open weekdays 8 AM–10 PM, Sat. 9 AM–10 PM, Sun. 10–6.*

MAIL • The **post office** is just outside the city center, south of Joliot-Curie-Platz. *Hansering 20, at Große Steinstr. Postal code: 06021. Open weekdays 8–6, Sat. 8–noon.*

VISITOR INFORMATION • The **tourist office,** in the Roter Turm on the Markt, charges DM 5 to book rooms. Pick up the transit schedule, which lists late-night bus routes. *Markt 1, tel. 0345/202–4700, fax 0345/502798. Open weekdays 10–8, weekends 10–2.*

COMING AND GOING

BY TRAIN • Halle's **Hauptbahnhof** (main train station; tel. 0345/215–1901) is near Riebeckplatz, a 10-min walk from the Markt. To reach town, take the main exit, go left through the pedestrian tunnel, and continue down Leipziger Straße. Trains arrive from Berlin (every 2 hrs, 2 hrs, DM 46), Leipzig (3 per hr, 30 min, DM 9.40), Dessau (hourly, 44 min, DM 14.20), Magdeburg (hourly, 1 hr, DM 25), and Erfurt (hourly, 1½ hrs, DM 28). **Taxis** gather at the Hauptbahnhof and the Marktkirche and can take you anywhere within the city center for less than DM 10. To catch a **tram** (DM 2.20, DM 1.40 for 10 min), go upstairs halfway through the second tunnel from the train station. Route maps are available at the transit booth in the Hauptbahnhof.

WHERE TO SLEEP

Privatzimmer (private rooms) run DM 35–DM 50 per person. If you prefer the great outdoors, visit the 20-site **Nordbad Campingplatz** (Pfarrstr., tel. 0345/523–4955; closed Oct.–Apr.). It's 15–20 min by tram (2, 3, 8, or 10 to Nordbad) from town, near the river and Burg Giebichenstein. Spots cost DM 2.20 per person, DM 1.10 per tent, and DM 5.50 per car. Reservations are strongly advised for the friendly **Pension Giebichenstein** (Burgstr. 11, tel. and fax 0345/523–2573 or 0345/202–8408), which offers three singles (DM 60), 10 doubles (DM 90), and a triple (DM 120), none with bath. To get there, take Tram 7 or 8 to Volkspark, then continue one half-block ahead.

HOSTELS • Jugendherberge Halle (HI). One of the cleanest and most modern hostels in Germany and mere blocks from downtown, this place is a mansion—dark wood walls, chandeliers, high ceilings, and well-kept rooms. Rooms cost DM 23 (DM 28.50 over 26). *August-Bebel-Str. 48a, tel. and fax 0345/202–4716. From station, Tram 1, 5, 6 or 7 to J.-Curie-Pl., past fountain and uphill (past theater) to August-Bebel-Str. 72 beds. No curfew (ask for key). Reception open 7 AM–10 AM and 5 PM–11 PM, checkout 9 AM.*

Villa Jühling. A cheap bed and friendly staff await you in this peaceful green alcove 30 min from town by S-Bahn (DM 2.20; trains run around the clock). The Villa, run by a Protestant church, can be crowded at times, so call ahead to see if there's a vacancy. Beds are DM 37. *Semmelweisstr. 6, tel. 0345/551–1698. From Hauptbahnhof, S-Bahn (direction: Dölau) to Heidebahnhof; then over train tracks and turn right. 40 beds. No curfew.*

Around the corner from the Händel-Haus, check out the mural at the corner of Große Klausstraße and Oleariusstraße. Painted in 1987–88, it contained too many references to freedom and was supposed to be removed, but the 1989 revolution saved it.

FOOD

Most of Halle's eateries are pricey *Gaststätten* (restaurants), but lots of *Imbiß* (snack) stands circle the Markt, where you can also nab some fresh produce at the daily **market.** For a **grocery store** head to the Bahnhof. You can get a filling German meal for DM 15 at the three-story (but cozy) restaurant-brewery **Zum Schad** (Reilstr. 10, near Reileck, tel. 0345/523–0366).

Apotheke. The odd decor—like something out of a mad pharmacist's dream—makes you forget that you're in a bland modern building. The lamps are made of doctors' bags, strange-looking jars fill the shelves, and a prosthetic leg hangs from the ceiling. All this with the dark-wood feel of an Irish Pub and tasty snacks (DM 6) and meals (DM 10). *Mühlberg 4a, one block north of Dom, tel. 0345/503118.*

Café Nöö. The local crowd meets here to enjoy good music and good food. Stop by for a cappuccino (DM 3.50) or a beer (DM 4); if you're hungry, go for the weekly pasta specials (meat optional; DM 7). *Große Klausstr. 11, at Domstr., tel. 0345/202–1651.*

WORTH SEEING

Just about anything of interest lies in Halle's compact Altstadt, centered around the well-preserved **Markt.** The marketplace overflows with a daily market, a herd of Imbiß stands, cafés, restaurants, and a fleet of trams zipping back and forth past hapless pedestrians. The four sharply steepled, Gothic-style towers of the **Marktkirche** (open weekdays 10–noon and 3–6, Sat. 9–noon and 3–5) watch over the square. The church is a fusion of two previous churches, whose towers were connected to form today's structure. Luther's death mask lies inside the sacristy, and free organ concerts take place every Tuesday and Thursday at 4:30. The separate fifth tower in the middle of the Markt is the **Roter Turm** (Red Tower), which isn't red; it was built between 1418 and 1506 as a symbol of the local merchants' secular power. The name comes from the bloody executions that used to take place on the Markt. West of the Altstadt are the meandering arms of the Saale River, along which stretch several small parks, perfect for a lazy sunny afternoon. Especially beautiful is the stretch near **Burg Giebichenstein** (open Apr.–Oct., Tues.–Sun. 9–6; admission DM 2, DM 1 students), the ruin of Halle's original fort. Take Tram 7 or 8 to Burg Giebichenstein.

DOM • Halle's cathedral is probably the world's most unusual. Upon being promoted to Dom, the modest Gothic Dominican church was wrapped in Baroque redecorations. Its facades now lack the imposing austerity characteristic of many cathedrals; instead, the Dom sports a birthday-cake look with unadorned white buttresses that separate delicate arched walls. Just south of the Dom stands the palatial Neue Residenz, home to the **Geiseltalmuseum** and its world-famous collection of fossils from the nearby Geisel valley. *Museum: Dompl. 5, tel. 0345/5526–1353. Admission free. Open weekdays 9–noon and 1–5.*

FRANCKESCHE STIFTUNGEN • A definite winner in the weirdness category, the top floor of this museum holds a collection of cultural artifacts, toys, globes, animal skeletons, and pickled embryos, all displayed as they would have been in the 18th century. This odd assortment was used by pietist August Francke to teach the children in his orphanage about the strange world outside. Downstairs are more exhibits on Francke's work. *Franckepl. 1, 3 blocks south of the Markt, tel. 0345/212–7450. Admission: DM 5, DM 3 students. Open Tues.–Sun. 10–5.*

HÄNDEL-HAUS • Halle's star attraction is the Händel-Haus, a quiet spot between the Marktplatz and the Domplatz, where Händel was born. Inside you'll find dozens of original scores and a piano used by the composer himself. The excellent recorded tour (available in 20 languages) not only describes Händel's life and works, but also plays selections from his most famous pieces. The house's instrument collection is on display up the street at the **Musikinstrumentensammlung des Händel-Hauses** (Marktpl. 13, tel. 0345/202–4022; open Wed.–Sun. 1:30–5:30) in the Marktschlößchen (near Marktkirche), a High Renaissance structure that also contains a small modern art gallery. *Große Nikolaistr. 5–6, tel. 0345/500900. Admission: DM 4, DM 2 students (free Thurs.). Open daily 9:30–5:30 (Thurs. until 7).*

MORITZBURG • In the northwest corner of the Altstadt stands the Moritzburg, built for the archbishop of Magdeburg in the late 15th century. Replete with dry moat and four corner towers, the castle now houses the **Staatliche Galerie Moritzburg,** a small but impressive art museum containing Rodin's *The Kiss,* Klimt's *Damenbildniß,* and works by eminent 20th-century painters like Klee and Feininger. *Friedemann-Bach-Pl. 5, tel. 0345/281–2010. Admission: DM 5, DM 3 students (free Tues.). Open Mon. and Wed.–Fri. 10–5:30, Tues. 11–8:30, weekends 10–6.*

AFTER DARK

Thanks in large part to Halle's student population, the nightlife here is the best in Saxony-Anhalt, but it's still pretty tame. Places to meet, drink, and socialize are Apotheke or Café Nöö (*see* Food, *above*), or **Kaffeeschuppen** (Kleine Ulrichstr. 11, tel. 0345/208–0803; open daily 10–midnight, Fri. and Sat. until 1 AM) up the street from Apotheke. Another place worth visiting is the area near Burg Giebichenstein (*see* Worth Seeing, *above*), which hosts events in the evening. For listings, check the free *Fritz* magazine.

Café Unikum. This café is a prime place for cheap but nutritious sandwiches and salads at prices under DM 10. It's also the meeting place for students and activists—just the atmosphere guaranteed to produce lively conversation and political debate. *Universitätsring 23, 0345/ 202–1303. Open weekdays 8 AM–12 AM, Saturdays 6 AM–2 AM and Sundays 6 AM–1 AM.*

Deix. Drinking on Friday night doesn't have to mean shouted conversation over loud music. Those looking for a cozy atmosphere to go with their wine settle in at Deix. *Seebener Str. 175, tel. 0345/522–7161. Tram 8 to Wittekind-Str. Open Mon.–Thurs. 10 AM–1 AM, Fri. and Sat. 10 AM–2 AM.*

Objekt 5. This popular student haunt draws a bohemian crowd for live music, dancing, theater, drinks, and food. For more of the same, head down the street to Burgstraße and check out **Gosenschänke** (Burgstr. 71, tel. 0345/202–4594). *Seebener Str. 5, tel. 0345/770–0443. Tram 7 or 8 (late night Bus 97) to Burg Giebichenstein. Café open Mon.–Thurs. 6 PM–2 AM, Fri.–Sat. 6 PM–5 AM, Sun. 6 PM–2 AM.*

Turm. Enter through Moritzburg's former moat and follow stairs leading underneath the castle to the best *Studentenklub* (student club) in the city. The main room is an old stone congregation chamber with a brick floor; jazz and folk bands play in the alcove several times a week. Coffee is DM 1.50. *Friedemann-Bach-Pl. 7, tel. 0345/202–3737. Open daily from 9 PM. Cover: free–DM 5.*

NEAR HALLE

NAUMBURG

The lovely town of Naumburg overlooks the Saale River about 40 km south of Halle. The **Naumburger Dom** (open Mon.–Sat. 9–6, Sun. noon–6), one of Germany's most important examples of Romanesque architecture, alone makes the town worth a visit. The current structure, built in the 13th and 14th centuries, contains two separate choirs (admission DM 4.50, DM 3 students) plus some impressive stained-glass windows. A few blocks away, Naumburg's picture-perfect **Markt** is surrounded by Renaissance houses and presided over by the 80-m tower of **Stadtkirche St. Wenzel.** Come in early June for Naumburg's **Kirschenfest** (Cherry Festival), held in honor of the local children who saved the town by making peace with a besieging army of Hussites (a rebellious proto-Protestant sect). In gratitude, the townsfolk presented the children with cherries, now a symbol of peace and friendship for Naumburgers. Naumburg is also a good place to bike along the Saale—**Radhaus** (Rosengarten 6, NW of Markt, tel. 03445/203119) rents three-speeds for DM 12 per day, DM 20 per weekend, and has route maps (DM 4). The **tourist office** (Markt 6, tel. 03445/19433; open weekdays 9–6, Sat. 10–4, Sun. 10–2) books private rooms for a DM 2 fee. **Jugendgästehaus Naumburg** (Am Tennispl. 9, tel. and fax 03445/703422) charges DM 21 per night (DM 26 over 26), including breakfast. **Trains** arrive from Halle (1–2 per hr, 45 min, DM 11) and Leipzig (every 2 hrs, 45 min, DM 13). To reach the Dom from the station, head straight, then left at the main street and uphill.

DESSAU

Dessau's postwar architecture may not be quite as impressive as Magdeburg's, but its architectural legacy was bolstered by the renowned Bauhaus school of design, which moved here from Weimar in 1925. Several Bauhaus buildings now stand under landmark protection, a belated honor to the school's short-lived (but influential) tenure in town. By 1932, conservative opposition to what was seen as a radical rejection of "higher" architectural forms had become so strong that Dessau withdrew its welcome. The school then moved to Berlin, where it was promptly shut down by the Nazis. Today, Bauhaus Dessau once again houses a school of art and design, with the addition of a museum containing a good collection of works by some of the original Bauhaus artists.

The theater scene in Halle is exploding is both size and notoriety. You'll find a wide variety of performances—from Schiller's classics to the avant-garde works of homegrown playwrights—near the University and around the Moritzburg Turm.

BASICS

Dessau's **tourist office** (Friedrich-Naumann-Str. 12, tel. 0340/204–1442, fax 0340/215233; open weekdays 10–6, Sat. 9–noon) stocks a guide to Bauhaus sights and books private rooms for a DM 5 fee. Dessau has two **post offices**: the main post office (Kavalierstr. 30–32, at Friedrichstr.; postal code 06844), and a branch next to the train station.

There's an **ATM** at the Hauptbahnhof; **Deutsche Bank** (Kavalierstr., tel. 0340/252050) charges DM 10 or 1% to cash a traveler's check. Pick up tonics at **Fürst-Leopold Apotheke** (pharmacy; Antoinettenstr. 37, tel. 0340/220–2107), near the Hauptbahnhof.

COMING AND GOING

Dessau's **Hauptbahnhof** (main train station; tel. 0340/214064) has hourly arrivals from Berlin (2 hrs, DM 31) Halle (50 min, DM 14.20), Leipzig (1 hr, DM 14.20), and Magdeburg (1 hr, DM 14.20). **Buses** to Wörlitz (DM 4) leave from in front of the station several times a day; purchase tickets from the driver. To reach downtown, walk leftish down Antoinettenstraße, left on Friedrichstraße, right on Kavalierstraße; or take any tram (DM 2) to Museum/Zentrum.

WHERE TO SLEEP

Private rooms cost DM 30–DM 40 per person, but tend to be in out-of-the-way houses. **Zimmervermietung Siewert** (Wilhelm-Müller-Str. 19, tel. 0340/212318) and the nearby **Pension Nord** (Kantstr. 2, same phone) are run by an enthusiastic husband-and-wife tag-team. Siewert has six clean, spacious rooms in a brightly refinished house in a peaceful neighborhood. Singles are DM 40, doubles DM 70. Walk straight out of the Bahnhof, cross Antoinettenstraße to Wolfgangstraße, turn left on Albrechtstraße, and right at Wilhelm-Müller-Straße (10 min total). The drabber Pension Nord has 14 rooms for slightly less.

HOSTELS • Jugendherberge Dessau (HI). This villa, 15 min by foot from the Bauhaus, has 70 beds. Call before you come, because they're sometimes overbooked. Beds DM 21 (DM 26 over 26), breakfast included. *Waldkaterw. 11, tel. and fax 0340/619452. From Bauhaus, cross Bauhauspl., right on Fischereistr., left on Ziebigker Str., left on Waldkaterw.; or Bus A (direction: Kühnau) to Ziebiker Str. No curfew. Reception open 7 AM–10 PM, checkout 9 AM.*

THE EVOLUTION OF BAUHAUS

The Bauhaus concept was, in a nutshell, to do away with the rigid distinction between abstract design (artists) and concrete creation (craftsmen). The instructors at the Bauhaus school of design were mostly abstract painters (contrary to popular belief, Peter Murphy was not a member of Bauhaus), including Paul Klee, Lyonel Feininger, and Wassily Kandinsky, who encouraged students to realize their ideas in physical form to gain an understanding of the properties of building materials. This technique, when combined with the philosophy that the end product should be affordable for the average worker, produced designs that were conducive to industrial and prefab construction—hence the simple, clean lines and predominance of steel, concrete, and glass. After fleeing Nazi persecution, many Bauhaus artists brought the style to the United States, where the sleek cubes and spheres (whose only ornamentation is the form itself) strongly influenced urban design in the 1940s and '50s.

CAMPING • Campers can claim one of 27 spots at **Adria,** set on a beautiful lake to the east of Dessau. Tent sites cost DM 9 per night plus DM 2 per person. *Dessau Mildensee, tel. 0340/216–0945. From Hauptbahnhof, Bus B to Mildensee/Adria (last stop).*

FOOD

There are several bistro-cafés along Zerbster Straße north of the Rathaus. Tuesdays, Thursdays, and Saturdays you'll find a street **market** here. Avid museum-goers and students frequent **Der Klub im Bauhaus** (Gropiusallee 38, tel. 0340/650–8444; open weekdays 8 AM–midnight, Sat. 10 AM–1 AM, Sun. 10—6), in the basement of the Bauhaus. It serves a variety of small meals (the best deal is pasta for DM 8) and is the place to be at night.

WORTH SEEING

There's more to this former *Residenzstadt* (royal capital) than Bauhaus. Known for its English-style gardens, wildlife ponds, and gondola rides, Dessau has also completed extensive renovation on its city center and surroundings. The 40-m tower of Dessau's oldest building, the **Marienkirche** on Schloßplatz, offers a scenic view of the city. Like much of eastern Germany, the region is not overly religious, so it will come as no surprise that the Marienkirche primarily hosts a variety of art exhibits and live theater. Times and admission prices vary, so it's best to check at the tourist office. Just south of the Marienkirche is the one remaining wing of Dessau's old castle, whose cellar also occasionally hosts art exhibits. North of Marienkirche, the turn-of-the-century neo-Renaissance Rathaus was rebuilt after the war. The only downtown Bauhaus building is the 1928 **Arbeitsamt,** a saucer-shaped structure on August-Bebel-Platz. Pick up "Bauhausbauten in Dessau" from the tourist office for a map to other Bauhaus sights.

BAUHAUS DESSAU • The world-famous Bauhaus school's design, concocted by Walter Gropius in 1925, is based on identical interior cubes connected via long rectangular walkways, all encased within a vast facade of glass. Badly damaged during World War II, it was not until 1976 that the building was restored. Today it houses a community college and an excellent **museum** (admission DM 5, DM 3 students). The exhibit features everyday items like coffee pots, chairs, and lamps that may appear unremarkable to your modern eyes but were considered revolutionary when they were first designed. There's also an excellent video guide (in both English and German) to Dessau's other Bauhaus sights.

Gropiusallee 38, tel. 0340/65080. From Hauptbahnhof's Westausgang, right down Schwabestr. and left on Bauhausstr. Building open weekdays 10–6, museum open Tues.–Sun. 10–8.

MEISTERHAEUSER • To showcase their concept of stylish, affordable construction, the Bauhausians built three duplexes and a detached house (for Gropius) a 10-min walk from the Bauhaus. Gropius's house and half of another were destroyed in the war, but the rest still stand, including the **Feininger Haus,** which today houses the **Kurt-Weill-Zentrum,** a small exhibit on the native-born composer of the *Threepenny Opera. Ebertallee 65–71, tel. 0340/619595. From Bauhaus, north on Gropiusallee and left on Ebertallee. Admission: DM 5, DM 3 students. Open Tues.–Fri. 10–5, weekends noon–5.*

SCHLOSS GEORGIUM • Duke Franz's (*see* Wörlitz, *below*) love for all things English knew no bounds. As in Wörlitz, he had this castle's grounds modeled after an English garden, though these are not nearly as impressive as those at Wörlitz. The castle itself may be small and modest, but its collection of works of Lucas Cranach, as well as Dutch and Flemish masters, is awe-inspiring. Also look for paintings of some of their prize pupils. *Puschkinallee 100, tel. 0340/613874. Admission: DM 5, DM 3 students. Open Tues.–Sun. 10–5.*

SCHLOSS MOSIGKAU • If you can't make it to Wörlitz (*see* Near Dessau, *below*), this exquisite 18th-century palace 9 km southwest of Dessau makes a good alternative. Commissioned by Duke Leopold I (grandfather of Wörlitz's Franz) for his favorite daughter, Anna Wilhelmine, the rococo palace/garden ensemble is one of Germany's best preserved. Many of the rooms have been decorated in their original fashion. Only about a third of the palace's rooms can be visited (you must don floor-friendly slippers), including the impressive Baroque **Picture Gallery,** with a swirling rococo ceiling. *Knobelsdorfallee 3, tel. 0340/521181. From Bahnhof, Bus D or L (direction: Mosikgau) to Schloß or Anhalter Str. Mandatory tour: DM 5, DM 3.50 students. Open Apr. and Oct., Tues.–Sun. 10–5; May–Sept., Tues.–Sun. 10–6; Nov.–Mar., Tues.–Fri. 10–4, weekends 11–4.*

An entire subdivision in the district of Törten (Tram 1 to Damaschkestr.) was designed in Bauhaus style in the late 1920s. The two-story row houses strongly resemble a lot of American postwar architecture.

NEAR DESSAU

WÖRLITZ

Duke Franz of Anhalt-Dessau was an "enlightened ruler," a lover of arts and progress, and an avid traveler. On one of his journeys, he fell in love with the English countryside and its royal estates. Short of moving there, he decided to bring England to Dessau. In the late 1760s and early 1770s, he and his architect friend Friedrich Wilhelm von Erdmannsdorff designed a sprawling park on the family's old hunting grounds along the Wörlitzer See, a former arm of the Elbe. Franz's summer retreat, **Schloß Wörlitz** (open May–Sept., Mon. 1–6, Tues.–Sun. 10–6; Apr. and Oct. until 4:30; admission DM 5, DM 2.50 students) was built near the town (instead of in the middle of the park) as a sign of his enlightenment. You have to take the tour (every half hour) to see the lavish rooms, decorated with detailed wall paintings and the trendiest funiture of the time. The yellow structure across the lake is the **Gotisches Haus** (Gothic House; admission DM 5, DM 3 students); it has the same hours as the Schloß and is notable for its collection of Cranach paintings.

If you only have a few hours in Wörlitz, take the opportunity to walk through the park. A seemingly endless maze of trails (okay, keep the map) crisscrosses the park, along canals, past faux ruins, and across more than a dozen small, picturesque bridges. At several points, **ferries** (DM 2.50) cross arms of the lake, and **gondola rides** (DM 7 for 45 min) are available during daylight hours when the weather is warm.

BASICS

The **tourist office** (Neuer Wall 103, tel. 0340/204–1442; open daily 9–6, weekdays 10–6 in winter) is two blocks from the bus stop, near the park entrance. Pick up a map (DM 1) or English-language guide (DM 2.50), or join the tour (DM 10) that leaves from near the Schloß daily (May–Sept.) at 1:30 PM. The office can book you a **private room** (DM 30–DM 40) in sleepy Wörlitz for free. Only occasional **trains**

LUTHER, LEO, AND THE BURNING BULL

Augustinian monk Martin Luther came to Wittenberg University in 1508 to teach philosophy, physics, and the Scriptures. He soon became disillusioned with the Catholic Church, particularly with its practice of selling indulgences (i.e., granting absolution in exchange for payment) to sinners whose only redeeming quality was a bulging coffer. To express his outrage, Luther composed a list of 95 proposed reforms (the famous 95 theses) and nailed it to the door of Wittenberg's Schloßkirche in 1517. The reforms gained popularity both among the masses and among nobles. In 1520 the Pope Leo X issued a bull condemning "the errors of Martin Luther." Luther burned the bull and was promptly excommunicated from the Catholic Church. He remained in Wittenberg preaching his new brand of religion until his death in 1546.

make the trip from Dessau's Wörlitzer Bahnhof (just north of the train station), but frequent **buses** run from Dessau (4–10 per day, 35 min, DM 4) and Wittenberg (4–5 per day, 40 min, DM 4). There is no bus service on weekends from November to April.

WITTENBERG

An anomaly in Saxony-Anhalt, Wittenberg's Altstadt is lined with brightly renovated buildings, and there's not a scaffold in sight. The city draws hundreds of thousands of pilgrims, church groups, and tourists who have come to see the place where the Reformation began its inexorable path of social and political change. Most of Wittenberg's sights center around Luther, yet the town is refreshingly free of Lutheresque commercialism you might expect.

On the way to town from the station is the **Lutherhaus** (Collegienstr. 54, tel. 03491/42030), built 1504–1507 as an Augustinian monastery. Luther arrived as a monk in 1508, stayed on after the building's secularization, and lived here with his family from 1525 until his death. Inside is the **Lutherhalle** museum (open winter daily 10–5, summer daily 9–6; admission DM 7, DM 4 students), which chronicles the reformer's life. A few houses down, the **Melanchthonhaus** (Collegienstr. 60, tel. 03491/403279; open winter daily 10–5, summer daily 9–6; admission DM 7, DM 4 students) is dedicated to Luther's friend and ally, Philipp Melanchthon. The renowned humanist and theologian transformed Wittenberg University into a model Protestant school. Because of his numerous contributions to the development of higher education in Germany, Melanchton is still known as *Praeceptor Germaniae* (Germany's teacher).

Down Collegienstraße is the **Markt,** with its elegant Rathaus and statues of Luther and Melanchthon. Farther down, you'll see the tower of the **Schloßkirche** (tel. 03491/402585; open Mon. 2–5, Tues.–Sat. 10–5, Sun. 11:30–5), the church where Luther posted his 95 theses. The original church doors were destroyed during the Seven Years' War; today's portal is a bronze replica engraved with the theses. Inside are the modest graves of Luther and Melanchthon. For DM 2 (DM 1 students) you can climb the stairs of the 88-m-high tower.

BASICS

Wittenberg's **tourist office** (Schloßpl. 2, tel. 03491/402239; open weekdays 9–6, Sat. 11–2, Sun. 11–3) has an impressive collection of maps, brochures, and Luther paraphernalia, and books rooms for a DM 3 fee. German-language tours leave daily from the Schloßkirche at 2 PM (May–Oct.) for DM 5. Do it yourself with an English-language booklet for DM 4. The **post office** (Friedrichstr., at Fleischerstr.) is two blocks north of Lutherhalle.

COMING AND GOING

Wittenberg's **Hauptbahnhof** (tel. 03491/401132) is about a 15-min walk from the Altstadt; walk straight out of the station for five min, turn right under the tracks, and continue straight. **Trains** arrive in Wittenberg from Dessau (every 1–2 hrs, 35 min, DM 9.40), Halle (8 per day, 45 min, DM 15.60), and Magdeburg (via Rosslau, 14 per day, 1½ hrs, DM 21.20). You'll find lockers for baggage at the train station. **Buses** to Wörlitz leave from the stop on Mauerstraße and Neustraße.

WHERE TO SLEEP AND EAT

Private rooms in Wittenberg cost DM 40–DM 60 per person, about the same as the handful of pensions in the city center. **Glöckner-Stift** (Fleischerstr. 17, tel. 03491/410707) has 10 tidy rooms for DM 30–DM 40 per person. From the station, go straight, turn right under the tracks, right on Friedrichstraße, and left on Fleischerstraße. Wittenberg's **Jugendherberge** is in the tower of Schloß Wittenberg right next to the Schloßkirche; you have to drag yourself up a spiral staircase to reach the dorms. Beds run DM 20 (DM 25 over 26). Avoid the 10 PM curfew with a key (deposit DM 10). *Schloß Wittenberg, tel. and fax 03491/403255. 104 beds. Reception open 6:30 AM–10 AM, 5 PM–10 PM, checkout 9 AM. Reservations advised.*

Wittenberg has plenty of restaurants along the Collegienstraße and the other streets off the Markt. You can choose from pizza (DM 6–DM 12), kebab (DM 4–DM 6), or German meals (DM 9–DM 15); bars offer a casual break from the daily routine. If the weather is nice, pick up picnic supplies at **City Markt** (Collegienstr. 91), and head to the Stadtpark gardens around the Schloß, where students and residents relax or walk their dogs.

MAGDEBURG

Charlemagne founded this city some 1,200 years ago, after which it quickly evolved into an important trade center and bishop's seat. When the entire city was burned to the ground during the Thirty Years' War, Magdeburg quickly picked up its pieces and rebuilt. In 1945 Allied bombers obliterated 90% of the city; unfortunately, urban plastic surgery of the 1950s left much to be desired. Today, restoration of the city's monuments and churches is in progress. The city aims to capitalize on its location between east and west, but a town of this size won't become a cosmopolitan center overnight. To its credit, Magdeburg does have its share of attractions—don't miss the city's lovely Romanesque Kloster Unser Lieben Frauen, and the massive, two-towered cathedral, Germany's first Gothic Dom.

BASICS

Magdeburg's tourist office dispenses city and transit maps, books rooms (DM 3 fee), and leads walking tours. Pick up a copy of *Dates,* a free magazine with events listings, and the *Kultur- und Veranstaltungsführer,* with an indexed city map. *Alter Markt 12, tel. 0391/540–4903 (room hotline: 0391/540–4904), fax 0391/540–4910. From Hauptbahnhof, down Ernst-Reuter-Allee, left on Breiter Weg. Open weekdays 10–6, Sat. 10–1.*

The late-Gothic **post office** (Breiter Weg 203; postal code 39104) is across from the Dom. Change money at **Deutsche Bank** (Otto-von-Bürikestr. 5, tel. 0391/56990) and its ATM (all credit and Plus/Cirrus cards accepted). Get your prescriptions filled at **Rats-Apotheke** (Ernst-Reuter-Allee 33, tel. 0391/53780), between the train station and downtown.

COMING AND GOING

Magdeburg's **Hauptbahnhof** (main train station; tel. 0391/549–5511) is a major hub in the IC/ICE system. Trains arrive from Berlin (1–2 per hr, 1¼ hrs, DM 38), Dessau (hourly, 1 hr, DM 14.20), Halle (hourly, 1 hr, DM 21.20), Hanover (1–2 per hr, 1½ hrs, DM 35.60), and Leipzig (1–2 per hr, 1¾ hrs, DM 32). The station has lockers, and its **DVB Bank** (open weekdays 7–7:30, Sat. 8–noon) exchanges traveler's checks for a DM 5 fee and has a credit-card ATM around the corner. To reach downtown from the train station, head left from the main exit, right on Ernst-Reuter-Allee, and left on Breiter Weg. For a ride share, stop by **ADM Mitfahrbüro** (Otto-von-Guericke-Str. 60, near Hasselbachpl., tel. 0391/19440).

WHERE TO SLEEP

Many of Magdeburg's private rooms (DM 30–DM 50) and pensions are at least a 15-min tram ride outside the city. Housed in a renovated old barn, **Pension Birkenhof** (Buschfeldstr. 20a, tel. 0391/500657) has ten bright rooms that combine rustic charm and modern convenience; singles go for DM 50, doubles for DM 80. The party hall is used on special occassions. Take the S-Bahn to Schule Roten See. **Pension Eberlein** (Letzlinger Str. 6, tel. 0391/561–7397, fax 0391/561–7397) is in a quiet neighborhood near the S-Bahn Neustadt stop (DM 1.80) and the Agnetenstraße tram stop (Lines 1, 8, 9, or 10). Singles are DM 50, doubles DM 90. **Campingplatz Barleber See** is at the S-Bahn or tram (Line 10) stop Barleber See. Spots cost DM 4 per person, DM 5 per tent, and DM 3 per car.

FOOD

The cafés and street stands around the Alter Markt and Breiter Weg have a reasonable selection of reasonably priced restaurants. **Pannekoekenhuis** (Sternstr. 29, tel. 0391/544–0140) is on one of Magdeburg's most beautiful streets, just off Hasselbachplatz at the southern end of Breiter Weg. Delicious and filling pancakes like broccoli-cheese or ham-mushroom cost DM 9–DM 13. **Ristorante Kugelblitze** (Breiter Weg 200, at Leiterstr., tel. 0391/561–8503), next to a cabaret of the same name, has pizza and pasta for DM 8–DM 15. Tuesday–Saturday pick up fresh produce at the Alter Markt's **open-air market.** Just across from the Alter Markt, the gigantic **Karstadt** has a grocery store in the basement.

WORTH SEEING

Most of Magdeburg's sights lie between Breiter Weg and the Elbe, and are best toured via back streets and paths that show the city's more aesthetic face. The heart of town is the **Alter Markt** and its neighboring **Rathaus.** Magdeburg's past is chronicled at the **Kulturhistorisches Museum Magdeburg** (Museum of Cultural History; Otto-von-Guericke-Str. 68–73, tel. 0391/536500; open Tues.–Sun. 10–6). The DM 2 (DM 1 students) admission also gets you into the not-quite-thrilling **Museum für Naturkunde** (Museum of Natural Science).

JOHANNISKIRCHE • Just north of the Alter Markt is Johanniskirche, whose 13th-century Romanesque towers blend well with the 15th-century nave and Baroque cupola. Though its walls are intact, the burned-out interior remains a memorial to the city's destruction. Bit by bit the city continues to rebuild the historic church—with any luck it'll be finished sometime in 2000. In the meantime, the church's gallery, which features moving before-and-after pictures of Magdeburg's bombing, may be closed to the public as well. *Jakobstr., no phone at press time.*

KLOSTER UNSER LIEBEN FRAUEN • Magdeburg's oldest remaining building (from the early 11th century) was painstakingly rebuilt after World War II. The monastery's courtyard seems worlds apart from the noisy city outside, much as it must have felt for generations of monks and nuns. Today, the tranquil café is a good place to relax, and a small museum (admission DM 4, DM 2 students) displays a fascinating selection of mostly early 20th-century sculpture, which contrasts strikingly with the venerable venue. *Regierungsstr. 4–6, halfway btw Dom and Johanniskirche, tel. 0391/565020. Open Tues.–Sun. 10–6.*

LUKASKLAUSE • Otto von Guericke (1602–1686), whose statue stands near the Rathaus, is a local hero because as mayor of Magdeburg he helped rebuild the city after the Thirty Years' War. But few people know that he also discovered the vacuum. In his experiments he joined two cups together, pressed out the air, and tried to get two teams of eight horses to pull them apart—they couldn't. A 10-min walk downstream along the Elbe from the Johanniskirche is this small museum dedicated to the man and his works. *Schleinufer 1, tel. 0391/541–0616. Open Wed.–Sun. 10–6. Admission: DM 1, 50 Pf students.*

MAGDEBURGER DOM • Charlemagne founded the original settlement of Magdeburg on this site. After a fire in 1207 destroyed a previous church, it was rebuilt in the "French" (i.e., Gothic) style—the first of its kind in Germany. Three centuries later the cathedral was finished—just in time for the Reformation. Inside lies the sarcophagus of Kaiser Otto I, who founded the Holy Roman Empire and built Magdeburg up into a frontier settlement. The Dom was a center for the peace prayers that led to the 1989 revolution; today visitors light candles for peace under a 1929 antiwar carving by Ernst Barlach. Behind the Dom (towards the river) is a piece of the city wall, and to the south stretches the city's most elegant promenade, Hegelstraße. *Tel. 0391/541–0436. Open May–Sept., Mon.–Sat. 10–6, Sun. 11:30–6 (Oct.–Apr. until 4).*

AFTER DARK

Although Magdeburg isn't known for its nightlife there are a few places that deserve a second look. **Paternoster** (Sternstr. 31, tel. 0391/543–5753; closed Mon.) is a friendly bar with inexpensive drinks, good food, and a mellow student clientele. Behind a library one block north and west of Alter Markt, all-purpose **Exlibris** (Weitlingstr. 1a, tel. 0391/543–4008; closed Tues. and Wed.) has live jazz and folk, dancing (cover DM 5–DM 15) on weekends, and films Thursday and Sunday. Gay-friendly **Feuerwache** (Halberstädter Str. 140, entrance on Ambrosiuspl., tel. 0391/602809; open Wed.–Sat. until midnight) is a similar nightspot with film showings and jazz performances.

EASTERN HARZ MOUNTAINS

The Harz Mountains are densely forested but gentle, a prime setting for peaceful day hikes and—if you have plenty of time and energy—long-distance treks through Saxony-Anhalt all the way to Lower Saxony (*see* Western Harz Mountains *in* Chapter 14). Gems like **Quedlinburg** and **Wernigerode** draw plenty of visitors with their cobbled plazas and timber-framed homes, and—along with tiny **Thale** and mellow **Stolberg**—make excellent bases for forays into the forest. The best map to pick up is "Der Harz und Kyffhäuser," available for DM 10.80 at any local bookstore or the tourist offices listed below; tourist offices also supply a list of campsites in the Harz. Whether you're here to hike or ski, before heading into the great unknown call the **Harz Hotline** (tel. 05321/20024), which rattles off the latest weather forecast in German.

Oddly enough, the small gold script above the Rathaus door directly behind the statue of Luther reads: "Fear God, honor authority, and do not join the rabble-rousers."

COMING AND GOING

The small town of Halberstadt is the hub for trains coming to the northern Harz from Magdeburg, Halle, and Goslar in Lower Saxony. The Halle–Goslar line passes through Wernigerode, while Magdeburg **trains** continue to Quedlinberg and Thale. Stolberg, just off the Halle–Kassel line, is the farthest regular trains go into the mountains. The only way to cross the Harz is with infrequent, frustrating **bus** service, or with the quaint **Schmalspurbahnen** (steam-powered narrow-gauge railroads) that travel from Wernigerode and Gernrode, near Quedlinburg, through the mountains at a speed of 20 km per hour.

WERNIGERODE

Wernigerode is a historic city with charm and style. The Altstadt is awash with half-timbered homes and the tourists who come to see them. The town was founded in the 10th century, but it wasn't until the early 1900s that its stunning Mühlental location emerged as a draw for visitors in search of a pastoral hideaway. Nowadays thousands frequent the city whose dense jumble of Renaissance-era homes remains almost totally untouched by time—an impression heightened by one of Germany's most beautiful castles looking down over it all.

BASICS

Wernigerode's **tourist office** (Nikolaipl. 1, 1 block east of Rathaus, tel. 03943/633035) stocks free city maps and books *Privatzimmer* free of charge. It's open weekdays 9–6, weekends 9–3. The **post office** (Marktstr. 14; postal code 38855), just south of the Markt, has an international telephone office. Do your banking at the **Deutsche Bank** (Breite Str., at Kohlmarkt), or its ATM (all credit and Plus/Cirrus cards accepted).

COMING AND GOING

Wernigerode's **Bahnhof** (train station; tel. 03943/69680) is a 15-min walk north of the city center and has luggage lockers. To reach the tourist office, turn right from the station and left on Albert-Bartels-Straße. Trains arrive from Halle (every 2 hrs, 1½–2 hrs, DM 30), Halberstadt (hourly, 25 min, DM 10), and Goslar (every 2 hrs, 40 min, DM 15).

BY SCHMALSPURBAHN • Germany's most extensive network of narrow-gauge railroads crisscrosses the Harz. The year 1999 marked the 100th anniversary of the Schmalspurbahnen, but don't think you missed the party. The three old-timer trains, the **Brockenbahn,** the **Selketalbahn,** and the

Harzquerbahn, celebrate holidays such as Easter, Christmas, and Walpurgisnacht—the German answer to Halloween—every year with the same enthusiasm. Organizers decorate the trains and host parties—some with live music and all with local specialities. For info contact the Harzer Schmalspurbahnen GmbH (tel. 03943/558143, fax 03943/558148). Trains leave from the depot (tel. 03943/558160) next to Wernigerode's Bahnhof; a single ticket costs DM 26, roundtrip is DM 42. When you get as far as Drei Annen Hohne (12 per day, 45 min, DM 6), you can choose to follow the trails up to the peak of the Brocken mountain to explore the national park or simply hike back to town. The Harzquerbahn chugs along at 60 km across the hills to Nordhausen (3 times daily, 3 hrs, DM 16). Trains don't run as often in October–May due to the weather; check the tourist office for schedules.

WHERE TO SLEEP

Quite a few hotels (even central ones) have affordable rooms, as long as you don't mind getting one without a shower. Just off the pedestrian zone, **Hotel Zur Tanne** (Breite Str. 57–59, tel. 03943/632554) has singles for DM 40–DM 80, doubles DM 60–DM 145. From the station, go straight up R.-Breitscheid-Straße and right on Breite Straße. The main drawback of the relatively posh **Pension Oberbeck** (Hilleborchstr. 4, tel. 03943/632662; one single DM 60, doubles DM 100) is the short uphill walk south from town (take Marktstr., turn right on Kanzleistr. at post office, and left on Lindenbergstr. to Hilleborchstr.). Otherwise, book a private room (DM 25–DM 50) through the tourist office.

HOSTELS • Jugendgästehaus Wernigerode, 2 km west of the city center, charges DM 22 per person. They sometimes close in the middle of the week if no groups are present, so always call ahead. *Friedrichstr. 53, tel. 03943/632061. From Bahnhof, Bus lines 1 and 4 (DM 1.50) to Kirchstr.; or walk 25 min from Markt down Westernstr. and Friedrichstr. 60 beds. No curfew. Reception open weekdays 6:30 AM–3 PM, 5 PM–7 PM.*

CAMPING • Camping am Brocken sits on the edge of the woods 10 km from town. It's open year-round and has useful amenities, including washers and dryers. Tent spots go for DM 9 plus DM 7 per person. To get here from Wernigerode's Bahnhof, take the bus marked ELBINGERODE (every 1–2 hrs, 25 min, DM 3) and get off at Elbingerode's Markt, and signs point the way. *Elbingerode, tel. 039454/42589. 200 sites. Last bus around 7 PM.*

FOOD

Dozens of cafés and beer halls cluster around the Markt, along with the usual Imbiß stands selling large helpings of Bratwurst and french fries. You'll stumble upon more affordable menus farther away from the Markt; **Harzstube** (Breite Str. 100, tel. 03943/34374) has tasty regional meat-and-potato dishes for DM 10–DM 12. At **Ristorante Pizzeria da Filippo** (Am Markt 9, tel. 03943/32646), pizza and pasta run DM 10–DM 15. Stock up on groceries at **Spar** (Breite Str. 3), near the Markt.

WORTH SEEING

Wernigerode's landmark attraction is the Marktplatz's 16th-century **Rathaus,** with its elegant Gothic towers and exquisite half-timbered construction. Note the dragon-head rain spouts and the figures along the right wall. To the right past the Rathaus is the **Harzmuseum** (Klint 10, tel. 03943/654454; open Mon.–Sat. 10–5), which houses an exhibit on the town's history. Admission is DM 3, DM 2 students.

At the top of Marktstraße huddles the 18th-century **Kleinstes Haus** (Kochstr. 43; open daily 10–5; admission DM 1). Wernigerode's smallest dwelling is only 3.1 m wide and 4.3 m tall, and displays the witches and demons of Harz-related folklore on its two floors. East of the Markt, **Breite Straße** has several good examples of Baroque craftsmanship. The house at No. 95 was built in 1678 and served continuously as the town's smithy until 1975. Today it houses the **Museum Krell'sche Schmiede** (tel. 03943/601772; admission DM 4, DM 3 students), exhibiting the workshop, complete with blacksmith's tools, and kitchen where generations of smiths brewed beer and swapped gossip. Stop by Wed.–Sat. 10 AM–4 PM.

It's hard to miss the 13th-century brick-and-timber **Schloß Wernigerode,** nestled on a tree-covered hill with sweeping views over the town and Brocken mountain. The sumptuous interior (Renaissanced in the 17th century) is not as exciting as the view, but still worth the steep, 15-min climb from town. For DM 3 you can ride the popular **Bimmelbahn** (tel. 03943/34384), a tourist shuttle that leaves every 20 min 9:30–5:50 (shorter hrs in winter) from behind the Rathaus. The last train back to town is at 6:10. *Schloß: Am Schloß 1, tel. 03943/500395. From Markt, 1 block past end of Marktstr., left at river and up Burgberg. Admission: DM 7, DM 6 students. Open May–Oct., daily 10–6; Nov., weekends only; Dec.–Apr., Tues.–Sun. Last entry at 5.*

QUEDLINBURG

Quedlinburg is a beauty. The town is filled with winding streets lined with colorful, centuries-old half-timbered houses (so many that UNESCO has designated Quedlinburg a World Heritage Site). The town centers around the **Markt,** a triangular plaza surrounded by an eclectic mix of Renaissance, Baroque, and neoclassical architecture. The best way to enjoy the city is by simply walking around, or (if you speak German) by taking one of the **walking tours** (DM 6) that leave the tourist office May–October daily at 10 AM and 2 PM. To explore the details of half-timbered (*Fachwerk*) architecture, head to the museum (open Apr.–Sept., Fri.–Wed. 10–5; admission DM 4, DM 2.50 students) in the **Ständerbau** (Wordg. 3, tel. 03946/3828), probably Germany's oldest *Fachwerkhaus.*

Quedlinburg owes its existence to the **Schloßberg** (castle hill)—or, more precisely, to the castle atop the hill. The town was founded in the 10th century by King Heinrich I, who spent a lot of time in his favorite of all the castles he built to ward off Magyar invasions. Today's castle is a Renaissance/Baroque reworking of the original; inside is the **Schloßmuseum** (tel. 03946/2730; open Oct.–Apr., Tues.–Sun. 9–5; May–Sept., Tues.–Sun. 10–6), with a display on Quedlinburg's geology and historical development (fire, reconstruction, war, reconstruction, plague, reconstruction). Admission is DM 5 (DM 3 students). The surrounding rose-filled **Schloßgarten** looks out over miles of red roofs.

The waiting list for weddings at Wernigerode's Rathaus stretches three to six months. In GDR times, it was said that the groom should first sign up, then book a hotel room, and then find a bride.

King Heinrich was buried in the Romanesque **Stiftskirche St. Servatius** (Schloßberg 9, tel. 03946/3552; closed Mon.). Admission to the church is DM 5 (DM 3 students), but his crypt behind the altar can only be seen on the tour at 11, 1, and 3, Sunday at 1 and 3. (Incidentally, the crypt is empty: Heinrich was removed and reinterred. No one knows where.) The dark patch on the back wall marks the spot where Gestapo head Heinrich Himmler had a window with a giant swastika built to commemorate the 1000th anniversary of King Heinrich's death and to glorify Hitler's "Thousand-Year Reich." The **Domschatz** contains the church's medieval artifacts, including bejeweled treasures and ancient books stolen by a U.S. soldier in 1945. After his death, the treasures resurfaced when his family tried to sell them in Switzerland. Years of legal battles, negotiations, and a tidy sum later, the prodigal treasures are back home.

The area below the castle is known as *Finkenherd* (Finch rookery)—Heinrich I was an avid bird-catcher. According to legend, Heinrich (then king of the Saxons) was listening to his birds here when news came that he had been elected the first king of Germany. Nearby, the **Lyonel Feininger Galerie** (Finkenherd 5a, tel. 03946/2238; open Tues.–Sun. 10–noon and 1–6) welcomes you back to the 20th century with Europe's largest collection of works by the American *Bauhäusler* (Bauhaus artist), mostly graphic art, some jagged-line wood-block prints, and airy watercolors. Admission is DM 4, DM 2 students.

BASICS

The knowledgeable staff at Quedlinburg's **tourist office** (Markt 2, tel. and fax 03946/77300) hands out free city maps and brochures (English-language walking guide: DM 2), and books private rooms for free. It's open weekdays 9–8, weekends 9–6 (shorter hrs off-season). Luggage lockers are available at the **train station** (open weekdays 4:50 AM–8 PM, weekends 8–5:30). To reach the Markt, head straight down Bahnhofstraße and make a left at the dead end on Heilige-Geist-Straße (10–15 min). Trains arrive hourly from Halberstadt (20 min, DM 5) and Magdeburg (1 hr, DM 14). The **bus** to Stolberg (2–3 per day, 1½ hrs, DM 7) leaves from the train station.

WHERE TO SLEEP AND EAT

Beauty has its price: Lodgings in town frequently run into triple-digit rates for double rooms. Call ahead to reserve a gorgeous room at **Pension am Dippeplatz** (Breite Str. 16, tel. 03946/4200; doubles: DM 80), in a timber-framed house two blocks past the tourist office. If Dippeplatz is full, get yourself a private room (DM 25–DM 50 per person).

For a variety of potato dishes and hearty local cooking (DM 7–DM 10) in a rustic atmosphere, try **Kartoffelhaus** (Breite Str. 37, near Markt; tel. 03946/708–334, open weekdays 11–7, Sat. 11–3). **Lüdde Bräu** (Blasiistr. 14, tel. 03946/3251) brews its own beer (DM 3–DM 5) and offers traditional, sit-in-your-gut German meals (DM 14–DM 19). After dinner, spoil yourself with a glass of wine (DM 6–DM 8) at the **Weinkeller Theophano** (Markt 13, tel. 03946/96300) in the cellar of the same-named hotel. Wednesday and Saturday, the Markt fills with fruit and vegetable stands; other days head for the Pfannkuch **grocery store** (Heilige-Geist-Str. 4).

SCHIERKE: THE QUIET RESORT TOWN THAT COULD

Isn't it time to treat yourself resort-style? Then Schierke may be the place for you: It has all the advantages of Bavaria—minus the swarms of tourists and the inflated prices. Despite a glowing reputation ensured by the likes of Goethe and Heine in the early 19th century, Schierke, like many towns in eastern Germany, recently struggled to reinvent itself in the face of economic adversity. Today it's clear that the town's transformation into a vacation resort and health spa has been a success, largely thanks to its alpine climate and proximity to the Harz National Park. Although Schierke's bid to host the 2006 Winter Olympics did not bear fruit, you'll find a host of activities (nature tours, hiking, ice skating, skiing) at your fingertips.

True to its haunted history and mystical roots, Schierke is also where rare herbs and plants have been cultivated for over 70 years. Some of them are the ingredients in Schierker Feuerstein (Schierke Fire-Stone), an elixir that is as healthy as it is mysterious. As the town's top export, the liqueur has brought the city worldwide renown—but you can enjoy it locally, in any of Schierke's many authentic bars.

Contact the tourist office (Kurverwaltung Schierke, Brockenstr. 10, tel. 039455/8680) for hiking maps, guides to accommodations, and to reserve a room at one of the moderately priced (DM 40–DM 100 for a double) resorts or hotels. To get to Schierke, take Bus 257 (45 min, DM 4.50) from Wernigerode; it leaves from across from the main train station every half hour.

THALE

Thale is a tiny town, worth visiting because of its location at the opening of the narrow Bodetal (Bode Valley), at the foot of the Harz, whose jagged cliffs, worn granite walls, and rushing rivers make it an essential stop on any nature adventurer's itinerary. Such dramatic beauty has inspired many legends: One holds that, in the time of witches and giants, a knight named Bodo sought the love of the princess Brunhilde. She spurned him and set off on her horse, with Bodo in hot pursuit. As she reached the cliffs, her horse jumped over the valley and they landed safely on the other side, though Brunhilde's crown fell to the bottom. Poor horseless Bodo didn't make it. Today he lies under the river and, changed into a dragon, guards Brunhilde's crown.

A well-marked trail (2.8 km) leads up to the **Hexentanzplatz** (Witches' Dance Floor) plateau, from which Brunhilde made her legendary leap. According to local lore, the Hexentanzplatz was once a sacred site for the worship of forest and mountain goddesses, a tradition that continues today on **Walpurgisnacht** (Witches' Sabbath), a fête on April 30. Thale is positively packed on this day—and with good reason. Visitors from all over Europe gather to watch locals dress up like witches and warlocks, dance and chant around a raging fire, and act out legends, such as the one about a sorceress named Watelinde, who led the the earliest pagan rituals. For information about this evening and the program of festivities contact the Walpurgisverein Thale (tel. 03947/2516). The rest of the year, Hexentanzplatz is a major draw for tourists seeking to experience the otherworldy atmosphere that permeates the woods and hills. The nearby **Walpurgishalle** (tel. 03947/2516, open May–Sept., daily 9–5) is a small museum dedicated to the history and culture of the Harz region. Nearby is the **Harzer Bergtheater,** a stunning outdoor amphitheater that puts on plays, concerts, and opera productions from May through September; tickets (DM 12–DM 25) are sold at the tourist office.

Across the valley is another vista point, at the **Roßtrappe** (Hoof Print), an indentation at the edge of the gorge, left by the lovely Brunhilde's giant steed. A moderate 2.7-km hike leads to the top. You can also take the **Sessellift** (chair lift; DM 4, DM 6 round-trip) from the valley floor. A few meters down, the **Kabinenbahn** (gondola; DM 5, DM 8 round-trip) swings and sways up to the Hexentanzplatz. A day-long ticket for both the gondola and the chair lift costs DM 12, and both are open daily 9:30–6 with shorter hours off-season. Longer trails go 12 km up the Bodetal, where you can hook up with trails through the Harz.

BASICS

There are exactly seven lockers in the train station, because they only need seven lockers in Thale. Beware—the station locks up at 6 PM. **Trains** head hourly to Quedlinburg (10 min, DM 3), Halberstadt (30 min, DM 7), and Magdeburg (1½ hrs, DM 19). Just across the street, Thale's **tourist office** (Rathausstr. 1, tel. 03947/2597 or 03947/2277) stocks trail maps and souvenirs, and will book you a private room (DM 25–DM 40 per person) for free. It's open weekdays 9–6, Saturday 10–3 (shorter hrs off-season). The **post office** (Poststr., off Bahnhofstr.) is a few minutes' walk from the train station.

WHERE TO SLEEP AND EAT

Jugendherberge Thale (HI) (Bodetal Waldkater 1, tel. and fax 03947/2881) is located in the Bode Valley 15 min from the station (follow signs across park) just off trails to the Roßtrappe and Hexentanzplatz. One of its 202 beds costs DM 23 (DM 27 over 26). Check-in is after 3 PM, checkout is 9 AM, and curfew is 10 PM, but you can get a key (DM 20 deposit). If you run out of things to do in Thale, you can always dance the night away in the hostel's Discothek (cover DM 1).

For a cheap snack, stop at any of the Imbiß stands around Hexentanzplatz. If you want scenery with your food, try **Gastatte Altes Boothaus** (Silberbachtal, tel. 0171/836–1242), a family-run restaurant serving tasty local specialties and homemade pastries (under DM 5). The restaurant is right next to a lake where you can rent a boat by the half hour (DM 2). You can also head downtown (across tracks) to **Gaststätte Zum Harz** (Karl-Marx-Str. 3, tel. 03947/2516) for good and affordable local German cuisine; try the Bratwurst Harzer-style (DM 7.80) or Schnitzel with potato salad (DM 10). Buy groceries across the street at **Markendiscounter Spätverkauf.**

STOLBERG

In the southern Harz, at the confluence of three small creeks, the red rooftops of Stolberg line narrow green valleys almost untouched by the modern world. No industry pollutes the gathering of half-timbered houses, nothing but trees and hiking trails inhabit the surrounding hills. As the birthplace of Protestant revolutionary Thomas Müntzer (*see also* Mühlhausen *in* Chapter 8), Stolberg was a proud little bastion of peasant power in the eyes of GDR politicians, and in 1993 Stolberg became the first town elected "Historic City of Europe" by the EU.

Stolberg's rows of houses converge at the **Markt,** where a monument to Müntzer stands. Erected in honor of his 500th birthday, the statue depicts Müntzer with an ambiguous hooded figure standing behind him. Also on the Markt is the **Rathaus,** built in the 15th century, though the detailed sundial and paintings representing Stolberg's craftsmen weren't added until 1724. On the hill behind the Rathaus sits the **Stadtkirche St. Martini** (open Apr.–Oct., daily 11–4), a late-Gothic creation where Martin Luther condemned his former disciple Müntzer in 1525. Müntzer's army was defeated and he himself tortured and executed later that year. Stolberg's **Schloß,** above the church, was once residence for the dukes of Stolberg-Stolberg. Today it is in the process of becoming a luxury hotel.

Stolberg's two museums are small and easy to tour. In the **Altes Bürgerhaus** (Ritterg. 14, tel. 034654/80152; closed Mon.), you can scan 16th-century furnishings and peek into an old cobbler's workshop for DM 1.50 (75 Pf students). The **Heimatmuseum** (Niederg. 19, tel. 034654/80151; closed Mon.) is a former mint showing where you can learn the details of coinage and read about Stolberg's importance as a hub for the industry from the 13th through 19th centuries; one display examines Müntzer's life and accomplishments. Admission is DM 2 (DM 1 students). Follow the street to Müntzer's birthplace and souvenir shop.

BASICS

To reach Stolberg by **train** from Halle (hourly, 1½–2 hrs, DM 23), you'll need to transfer at Berga-Kelbra. Buses to Quedlinburg (2–3 per day, 1 hr, DM 7) leave from the train station and one block past the **tourist office** (Markt 2, tel. 034654/454; open weekdays 9–12:30 and 1–6) from the Markt. The office has hiking maps, a list of Harz campgrounds, and maps. It's an easy 10-min walk from the train station to the Markt.

WHERE TO SLEEP AND EAT

The numerous **private rooms** (DM 25–DM 35 per person) are the best option; the tourist office will reserve you a room for free. Call ahead to reserve a spot at **Harzhof Nerlich** (Niederg. 60, tel. and fax 034654/296) or nearby **Pension Bauernstube** (Hinterg. 17, tel. 034654/389), two tiny pensions (2–3 rooms) with singles for DM 40, doubles DM 60–DM 80. The handful of restaurants almost all serve medium-priced (DM 14 and up) German meals. The **Ratskeller** (Markt 1, tel. 034654/421; closed Thurs.) has a good selection of fish or steak meals in the DM 10–DM 12 range.

OUTDOOR ACTIVITIES

After Thale (*see above*), Stolberg is the best place to go on easy day hikes. A popular option is the 4-km mosey to the **Josephs Kreuz** on top of the nearby Auerberg. Erected in 1896, it's the world's largest iron double cross, with a wonderful view over the Harz. The hill behind Müntzer's birthhouse offers the best view of the castle and the tiny valleys into which the town is wedged. Here stands the **Lutherbuche,** the beech tree from which Luther saw in Stolberg the form of a bird: The castle is its head, the Markt its body, the church its heart, and the three alleys radiating from the Markt the wings and tail. From here, trails crisscross the hills (two even circle the whole town), and connect with trails across the Harz—get maps at the tourist office. In winter there are a few cross-country trails, though the town isn't a big winter-sport center; rent your equipment at the Heimatmuseum.

11 BERLIN

UPDATED BY PEGGY SALZ-TRAUTMAN

As the European Union shifts its focus to Eastern Europe, Berlin is greeting the new millennium not only as the new seat of Germany's parliament, but also as what Chancellor Gerhard Schröder has promoted as the "Berlin Republic," the symbol of a united Germany. A decade after unification, the city is a beehive of activity, radiating with energy and vibrating with the sound of jackhammers as it rebuilds its infrastructure. Roughly 150 international missions are expected to follow the parliament from Bonn to the new capital, and a few museums are scheduled to do the same. While native Berliners might joke that the massive construction projects are destroying many of the buildings that World War II didn't, even they must admit that a new and vibrant Berlin is rising from the rubble. You can feel history in the making—and nowhere else can you have such fun doing it.

Berlin is the quintessential mixing pot of Germany—a cauldron of assorted ethnicities, cultures, mentalities, and lifestyles. But there are also collisions, particularly between the so-called *Wessis* (formerly West Germans) and the *Ossis* (ex-citizens of the former GDR). Many Ossis have seen their living standard drop since West Germany annexed the GDR in 1990; they pin much of the blame for their hardships on West German carpetbaggers, who they feel bought eastern Germany cheap and left them with only the crumbs. It also doesn't help that the lunatic fringe in western Berlin has begun a campaign to rebuild the Berlin Wall. Luckily, no one is taking them seriously. Most agree it will be another generation before Berliners have torn down the mental wall that separates them. To understand Berlin you have to listen to—and visit—both sides.

Berlin has always beeen a magnet for all that is new and daring—by no means a typical German city. Isolated from the rest of Germany by the Berlin Wall, the city reinvented itself and learned to love living on the edge. The virtual island of West Berlin drew squatters, draft dodgers, and other radicals, while East Berlin's dissidents helped bring about the *Wende,* the nonviolent revolution that brought the GDR to its knees. The synthesis of these two halves has created a Berlin that is both extreme and exciting. You can expect to see at least one demonstration each weekend—and you can bet you will be exposed to a counterculture unlike any you've seen before. The city's music scene is pulsating with rhythms ranging from African tribal to techno. Each year millions flock to events such the annual Love Parade, the avant-garde Berlinale Film Festival, and the ever-popular Classic Open Air on the Gendarmenmarkt square. With its famous nightclubs and all-night techno dance parties, a booming gay scene, and affordable avant-garde theater and cinema, Berlin certainly remains on the cutting edge of German popular culture. In every part of this city you'll sense a frenetic energy—a scene both abrasively cool and

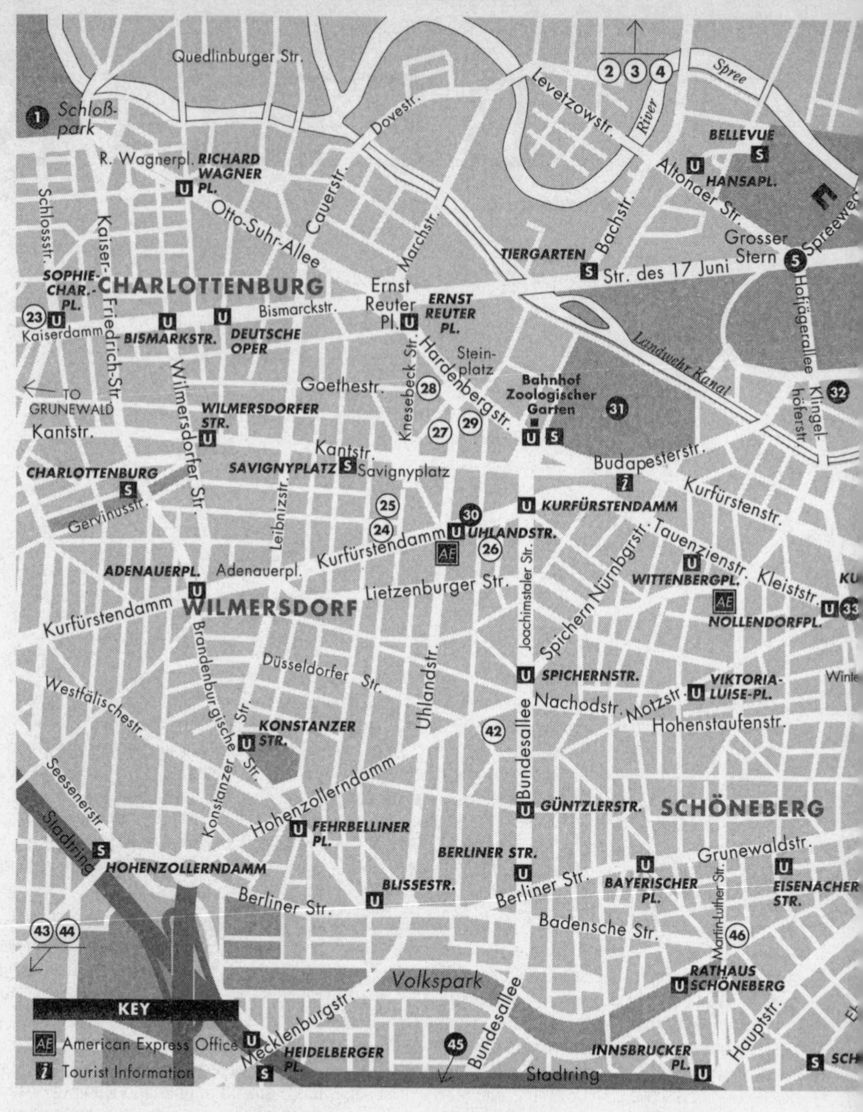

Sights ●

Alexanderplatz, **21**

Bauhaus-Archiv, **32**

Bebelplatz, **16**

Brecht-Weigel-Gedenkstätte, **9**

Brandenburger Tor, **8**

Checkpoint Charlie, **38**

Dahlem Museums, **45**

Deutsches Historisches Museum, **15**

Gendarmenmarkt, **17**

Humboldt University, **14**

Jüdisches Museum, **39**

Kulturforum, **35**

Kurfürstendamm, **30**

Marx-Engels-Platz, **18**

Martin-Gropius-Bau, **37**

Museumsinsel, **13**

Nikolaiviertel, **22**

Nollendorfplatz, **33**

Potsdamer Platz, **36**

Reichstag, **7**

Rotes Rathaus, **20**

Scheunenviertel, **19**

Schloß Charlottenburg, **1**

Siegessäule, **5**

Sowjetisches Ehrenmal, **6**

Zoologischer Garten, **31**

Lodging ○

Artist Hotelpension Die Loge, **11**

Die Fabrik, **41**

Gästehaus der Fürst-Donnersmarck-Siftung, **3**

Gästehaus Luftbrücke, **47**

Hotel Fasanenhaus, **26**

Hotel-Pension Majesty, **24**

Hotel Transit, **51**

Jugendgästehaus am Wannsee, **43**

Jugendgästehaus am Zoo, **29**

Jugendgästehaus Berlin (HI), **34**

Jugendgästehaus Central, **42**

Jugendgästehaus Deutsche Schreberjugend, **40**

Jugendgästehaus Nordufer, **10**

Jugendgästehaus Tegel, **2**

Jugendherberge Ernst Reuter (HI), **4**

Jugendhotel Berlin, **23**

Kladow Camping, **44**

Krossinsee International Camping, **48**

Pension Alexis, **27**

Pension Charlottenburg, **12**

Pension Knesebeck, **28**

Pension Kreuzberg, **50**

Pension Silvia, **25**

Pension Süd-West, **49**

Studentenhotel Berlin, **46**

fascinating. Savignyplatz's gallery crowd and Kreuzberg's anarchists will not be charmed by a foreign visitor, and Mitte's self-consciously hip clubs don't shower travelers with affection. But if you're adventurous and refuse to be intimidated, Berlin's crowded streets will give you a glimpse of the tensions, resentments, hopes, and fears of a city in the throes of change.

Berlin's chaotic present grew out of a tumultuous past. Unlike other German cities dating back to Roman times, Berlin's rise to greatness did not begin until the 17th century, when the ruling Hohenzollerns acquired territories stretching from present-day Russia to the Rhine, and the royal treasury swelled. Many of the finest buildings in the Mitte district date from this triumphant time, when Berlin became the biggest and most powerful city in northern Europe as the capital of the kingdom of Prussia. During the 19th century, Berlin industrialized rapidly and became capital of a newly unified Germany. The city's sprawling new inner *Bezirke* (districts), like Kreuzberg, Prenzlauer Berg, and Friedrichshain, housed a population of over a million, and monumental buildings like the Reichstag demonstrated Germany's imperial might.

World War I and the victory of the Social Democrats in 1918 brought the downfall of the Hohenzollerns and the birth of the Weimar Republic, a kind of golden age for Berlin. Not all was golden in the Weimar period though: Rampant inflation wiped out families' savings, and communists and fascists fought in the streets. The hardship of the Great Depression helped fuel the rise of the Nazis to power in 1933. The Nazis annihilated Berlin's Jewish population, and wartime bombing raids largely obliterated the city's historic center. Berlin's division between the Soviets and the Allies in 1945 added to the woes of a city that had become a ghost of its former self. For more than 40 years, West Berlin lived in a state of siege, surrounded by the authoritarian GDR, whose repressive measures included the building of the Berlin Wall in 1961. Though enclosed by barbed-wire barriers on all sides, West Berlin enjoyed freedoms (and affluence) denied to East Berlin. Finally, in 1989 the Wall fell, and with it the GDR regime. German unification followed, and in 1991 the German Parliament voted to move the capital to Berlin.

Caught between a traumatic past and an unknown future, a new Berlin is being born amid tense anticipation. Decisions made now will determine whether Berlin becomes a city for all of Europe to emulate or the 21st century's first big disaster. Whatever happens, now is your chance to jump into the mix. Whether you're shopping in a busy outdoor market, scamming in a café, enjoying the quiet greenery of the city's parks, or coming home at 4:30 AM from a sweaty club, you'll find many Berlins all simmering in a tasty stew. Come and get it while it's hot.

BASICS

AMERICAN EXPRESS

Bring your passport to exchange money or cash traveler's checks at one of two offices. Mail service is free for cardholders, DM 2 for everyone else. *Main office: Bayreutherstr. 37, tel. 030/21476- 6292. U-Bahn to Wittebergpl. Open weekdays 9–6, Sat. 10–1. Mitte: Friedrichstr. 172, tel. 030/20455721. U6 to Französische Str. Open weekdays 9–6, Sat. 10–1.*

CHANGING MONEY

Most bureaux de change in Berlin charge a DM 2–DM 4 commission to exchange cash or traveler's checks, but no commission to draw money against your MasterCard or Visa. The branches of the **Deutsche Verkehrsbank (DVB)** have longer hours and often marginally better rates. There's one at each of the following train stations: Bahnhof Zoo (tel. 030/881–7117; open Mon.–Sun. 7:30 AM–10 PM, Sun. 8–7), Friedrichstraße S- and U-Bahn station (closed due to construction at press time so check before going there), and the Ostbahnhof (formerly Hauptbahnhof; tel. 030/296–4393; open weekdays 7 AM–7:30 PM, weekends 8–6). At most banks you'll find an ATM for cash advances and/or withdrawals. All **Deutsche Bank** branches have Cirrus and Plus ATMs, including the one opposite **Bahnhof Zoo** (Hardenbergpl. 4–5). The AmEx office also changes money. If it's late at night and everything is closed, luxury hotels change money at rip-off rates. Decadence, decadence!

DISCOUNT TRAVEL AGENCIES

Kilroy is the student and budget travel authority in Berlin. They have branches in Charlottenburg (Hardenbergstr. 9, tel. 030/3100–0444), Dahlem (Takustr. 47, tel. 030/831–1025), and Berlin Mitte (Ecke Georgenstr. and S-Bahnbogen 184, tel. 030/2016–5900).

EMBASSIES

Put your tax money to work by using your embassy. These consulates-in-transition house the people you call from jail . . . as well as travel bulletin boards, medical referrals, and a reasonably current stock of newspapers.

Australia. *Uhlandstr. 181–183, tel. 030/880–0880. West from Bahnhof Zoo on Kantstr. to Uhlandstr.*

Canada. *Friedrichstr. 95, tel. 030/261–1161. U-Bahn or S-Bahn to Friedrichstr.*

United Kingdom. *Unter den Linden 32–34, tel. 030/201840. U6 to Französische Str.*

United States. The embassy (Neustädtische Kirchstr. 4, tel. 030/238–5174) is near the Friedrichstraße S-Bahn, but for most services (8:30 AM–5 PM), head for the old consulate in the city's southwestern outskirts. Hours may change, so call first. *Clayallee 170, tel. 030/832–9233. U1 to Oskar-Helene-Heim.*

EMERGENCIES AND MEDICAL AID

Two central pharmacies are **Europa Apotheke** (Joachimstaler Str. 38, south of Bahnhof Zoo, tel. 030/882–6446), and in eastern Berlin, **Berlin-Apotheke** (Oranienburger Str. 51, tel. 030/283–3530; U6 to Oranienburger Tor). For homeopathic help, try **Roland Apotheke** (Ansbacher Str. 70, tel. 030/218–2276; U4 to Viktoria-Luise-Pl.). If your German is good, dial 1141 for a recorded list of late-night pharmacies. **Berliner AIDS-Hilfe** (tel. 030/19411) provides over-the-phone AIDS counseling. For emergency **rape counseling,** call 030/251–2828; the phones are staffed Tuesday and Thursday 6 PM–9 PM, Sunday noon–2 PM, otherwise leave a message. They *will* call you back. Women (lesbian and straight) can also call **Frauenkrisentelefon** (tel. 030/615–4243).

ENGLISH BOOKS

Along with the embassies, bookstores in the city center stock a small selection of English books and newspapers. The library at **Amerika Haus** (Hardenbergstr. 22–24, tel. 030/311073), one block due west of Bahnhof Zoo, has a good selection of U.S. newspapers and English books, as well as a photocopy machine. Next door is **British Council** (Hardenbergstr. 20, 2nd floor, tel. 030/3110–9930), with its own little reading room. Your best bet for lowbrow used paperbacks is **Books** (Goethestr. 69, tel. 030/313–1233; U2 to Ernst-Reuter-Pl.), where you can unload your old books, too. The most established carrier of English-language books is **Marga Schoeller Bücherstube** (Knesebeckstr. 33, tel. 030/881–1112; S-Bahn to Savignypl.). For English-language magazines, try any **Internationale Press** (in Bahnhof Zoo, a kiosk on Hardenbergpl., the Alexanderpl. S-Bahn station, and the Ostbahnhof), or the **Europa Press Center** (Europa-Center, ground floor, tel. 030/261–3003; open Mon.–Thurs. 9 AM–10 PM, Fri.–Sat. 9 AM–11 PM and Sun. 9 AM–10 PM).

INTERNET RESOURCES

Internet Café Hai Täck (Brünnhilderstr. 8, Wishamstr. 1, tel. 030/8596–1413, fax 030/859–1415, www.haitaeck.de) costs DM 12 per hour online. You can chat at their terminals daily 11 PM–1 AM.

LUGGAGE STORAGE

Berlin's larger train stations all have luggage lockers for DM 2–DM 4 per day. Bahnhof Zoo has row upon row of backpack-size lockers. You should find one empty, but if you don't, the Friedrichstraße and Alexanderplatz S-Bahn stations also have lockers, as do the Ostbahnhof and Bahnhof Lichtenberg. Many lodgings also have luggage storage, but most hostels require that you bring a lock.

MAIL

The **post office** in Bahnhof Zoo, outside the station at Budapesterstr. 42, is the place to come to send packages, telegrams, and faxes, to make international calls, and to pick up mail from home (at the counter labeled POSTLAGERNDE SENDUNGEN). This latter service is free; just show your passport. Letters should be addressed: Hauptpostlagernde Briefe, Postamt 120, Bahnhof Zoo, 10612 Berlin. This office is open Monday–Saturday 8 AM–midnight, Sunday and holidays 10 AM–midnight.

PHONES

Coin-operated phones are going the way of the dinosaurs; invest in a **telephone** card if you plan on making many calls. These are available at most post offices, money-exchange places, and newsstands in DM 12 and DM 50 denominations. Inside the main post office at Bahnhof Zoo are dozens of international phone boxes, some of the "Call Back" variety (*see* Phones *in* Chapter 1).

VISITOR INFORMATION

Berlin Tourism Marketing stocks tourist literature, maps, and bus/train schedules. The main office, at Europa-Center near Bahnhof Zoo, books rooms (DM 5 fee) in hotels, pensions, hostels, private homes, and universities—it's the easiest way to find a bed in sprawling Berlin. Check out their useful "Berlin Magazine" for DM 3.50, or buy the helpful booklet "Berlin for Young People," for DM 7.50. A branch office inside the Brandenburg Tor is open daily 9:30–6. Pick up transit info, including the *Nachtlinienetz* (Night route map) at the **BVG kiosk** (tel. 030/19449; open daily 8 AM–8 PM) on Hardenbergplatz in front of Bahnhof Zoo. For **online Berlin info,** check out www.Berlin.de. *In Europa-Center, Breitscheidpl., entrance on Budapester Str., tel. 030/250025. Open Mon.–Sat. 8 AM–10 PM, Sun. 9–9.*

ARiC (Schumannstr. 5, tel. 030/280–7590, fax 030/280–7591, aric-berlin@ipn-b.comlink.apc.org) is a useful source of information if you have questions about safety or discrimination or want to contact people of color in Berlin. The **Regionale Arbeitstelle für Ausländerfragen** (Schumannstr. 5, tel. 030/282-3079, fax 030/238–4303) is part of a network of support organizations for visible foreigners throughout eastern Germany. To reach their office, take the U6 to Oranienburger Tor.

To get the 411 on women's centers, women's cafés, bars, child-care possibilities, and tips for lesbian travelers visit the combination infothek and magazine publishing offices of the **Lesbenberatung.** This center for lesbian life, which also features books, films, and cultural events, is housed in the same building as the *Siegessäule,* the free magazine for lesbian and gay life in Berlin. All services are free—and the staff is friendly. *Kulmerstr. 20a, tel. 030/215–2000. U8 to Bulowstraße. Magazine office open weekdays 10–6 pm, Lesbenberatung open Wed. and Fri. 2–7.*

Jewish Community Center (Jüdische Gemeinde zu Berlin) offers info and advice to Jewish visitors. They'll also give you a monthly calendar of religious, cultural, and other cool events. *Fasanenstr. 79, tel. 030/880280. From Bahnhof Zoo, west on Kurfürstendamm to Fasanenstr. Open Mon.–Thurs. 8–4, Fri. 9–3.*

Mann-O-Meter gives out all kinds of tips on gay Berlin and can help with accommodations. Pick up "Magnus Map" for nighttime entertainment tips. For online info on gay Berlin, check out http://users.aol.com/pinkpower1/. Schwules Überfall-Telefon (tel. 030/216–3336; open daily 6 PM–9 PM) is a hot line for gays and lesbians to call in case of trouble. *Mann-O-Meter: Motzstr. 5, tel. 030/216–8008. U-Bahn to Nollendorfpl.; ½ block SW on Motzstr. Open Mon.–Sat. 5 PM–10 PM, Sun. 4 PM–10 PM.*

PUBLICATIONS • The tourist offices stock many of the following publications. The biweekly magazines *Zitty* (DM 4) and *Tip* (DM 4.50)—available at any newsstand—are the best way to find out what's going on about town. Though less thorough (no theater listings), *030* is good and free at many clubs and bars, and *Metropolis* (DM 3) can be your English-language security blanket if all this German party-info is too intimidating. *Siegessäule* (for guys) and *Schnepfe* (for gals) are free publications, found in gay spots, with addresses of venues and calendars of events.

COMING AND GOING

BY PLANE

Berlin has two major airports: Flughafen Tegel and Flughafen Schönefeld. Western Berlin's **Flughafen Tegel** (tel. 030/500–0186) has started to compete more aggressively for commercial business and is becoming competitive with Frankfurt (the more traditional point of entry for travelers); however, no American carriers fly directly to this destination. They operate through partners such as Lufthansa, Germany's national airline. **Lufthansa** (tel. 800/645–3880 in U.S., 030/88750 in Berlin) is a partner of United Airlines and offers flights to Tegel from locations around the world—but none of them are nonstop. Eastern Berlin's **Flughafen Schönefeld** (tel. 030/60910) is used mainly by East European and Russian airlines. The former military base at **Tempelhof** (tel. 030/6951–2288) is sometimes used for domestic flights, but it's unlikely you'll end up here.

AIRPORT TRANSIT • Flughafen Tegel is 6 km north of the city center. There's no direct subway link, but airport Buses X9 (express) and 109 (local) zip to Bahnhof Zoo every half hour, daily 5 AM–11:30 PM. The ride takes 35 min and costs DM 3.90. For a more direct connection to Kreuzberg or eastern Berlin, take Bus 128 from the airport and change at Kurt-Schumacher-Platz for the U6 (direction: Alt-Mariendorf) to Friedrichstraße. A taxi between Bahnhof Zoo and Tegel costs around DM 40. **Schönefeld Airport,** 24 km south of the center, is connected to both Alexanderplatz and Bahnhof Zoo via the S9 every half hour or so. If you don't want to wait around for the S9, take any inbound line and make a series of connections to more frequent S-Bahn lines at Schöneweide, Ostkreuz, or Warschauer Straße. You can also take the new Airport Express bus directly to Bahnhof Zoo for DM 3.90. A taxi from Schönefeld costs upward of DM 60.

BY TRAIN

Until the construction of a massive new *Hauptbahnhof* (main train station) at the Lehrter-Stadtbahnhof is complete (around 2004), you'll end up at one of Berlin's three major train stations. If you're coming from the west, odds are you'll end up at **Bahnhof Zoo** (*Zoo* is pronounced "tsoh"), the city's busiest hub. From points north, south, or east, you're likely to end up in eastern Berlin's **Hauptbahnhof** or **Bahnhof Lichtenberg.** All stations are served by Berlin's extensive public transit network. To avoid a big "I've missed my train" headache, pick up a Berlin *Städteverbindungen* timetable at any ticket window. Note that ticket lines can be very long at Bahnhof Zoo and Lichtenberg, especially in summer. You can save time by buying tickets to any German destination from Deutsche Bahn ticket counters in many S-Bahn stations, including Alexanderplatz and Charlottenburg; then take the S-Bahn to your departure point and smile as you cruise past the ticket line directly to the platform. For general rail info call the 24-hour hot line: 01805/996633.

BAHNHOF ZOOLOGISCHER GARTEN • Bahnhof Zoo has direct trains to Frankfurt (hourly, 6 hrs, DM 198), Hamburg (hourly, 2½ hrs, DM 86), Cologne (hourly, 4½ hrs, DM 182), Magdeburg (hourly, 1½ hrs, DM 38), and Munich (hourly, 7½ hrs, DM 190–DM 270, depending on travel times). International destinations include Amsterdam (7 per day, 6½ hrs, DM 200), Paris (5 per day, 9 hrs, DM 310), and Stockholm (2 per day, 14½ hrs, DM 369). The center of western Berlin is right outside; exit onto Hardenbergplatz and head immediately underground for the U-Bahn, or walk two blocks east to reach the tourist info office at Europa-Center. The S-Bahn leaves from the platforms above Bahnhof Zoo's south end. Any eastbound S-Bahn will get you to Alexanderplatz in eastern Berlin.

If you're traveling by taxi from the airports, agree on a fare—or at least get a ballpark figure—before leaving. Airport taxis are notorious for charging too much or driving in circles to jack up the rate.

OSTBAHNHOF • Eastern Berlin's Ostbahnhof (formerly the Hauptbahnhof), in the district of Friedrichshain, has a new name and a new importance as the hub for all destinatations in Eastern Europe. Destinations include Leipzig (every 2 hrs, 2 hrs, DM 54), Frankfurt an der Oder (hourly, 1 hr, DM 21.20), Warsaw (3 per day, 6 hrs, DM 61.40), Prague (every 2 hrs, 5 hrs, DM 97) and Budapest (1 per day, 15½ hrs, DM 277).

BAHNHOF LICHTENBERG • Destinations from Lichtenberg include Dresden (2 per day, 2 hrs, DM 50), Rostock (every 2 hrs, 3 hrs, DM 62), Chemnitz (every 2 hrs, 3 hrs, DM 59), and Breslau (2 per day, 5 hrs, DM 42.80). The station is far east of central Berlin, but the S5, S7, or S75 (direction: Strausberg, Ahrensfelde, or Wartenberg) can get you there.

BY BUS

The **Zentralen Omnibus-Bahnhof (ZOB),** Berlin's main bus depot, is a grimy pit infested with drunks and junkies—not recommended. Yet the ZOB does offer service to most major German cities at fares that are about 10% less than train fares. (Trips take roughly twice the time.) Tourist offices carry timetables and fare info. Otherwise, contact ZOB directly. To get here from Bahnhof Zoo, take Bus 149 straight to Messedamm. *Masurenallee, at Messedamm, tel. 030/301–8028 or 030/302–5294.*

BY MITFAHRGELEGENHEIT

Mitfahrzentrale Zoo (in Zoo U-Bahn station, tel. 030/19440), on the U2 platform (direction: Vinetastr.), is open weekdays 9–8, weekends 10–6. **Mitfahrzentrale Yorckstraße** (Yorckstr. 52, outside Yorckstr. U- and S-Bahn station, tel. 030/19420) is open weekdays 9 AM–8 PM, weekends 10–4. In the same building is the gay- and lesbian-oriented **Mitfahrzentrale für Schwule und Lesben** (tel. 030/216–4020), which has the same hours as Mitfahrzentrale Yorckstraße. **Citynetz** has offices throughout Germany and two in Berlin (Joachimstalerstr. 17, tel. 030/882–7604 or 030/19444; Bergmannstr. 57, tel. 030/693–6095).

HITCHING

Hitching from Berlin is quite easy, though you'll face stiff competition from locals during summer. Heading west or south toward Hanover, Frankfurt, Leipzig, or Munich, hop on the S1, S3, or S7 (direction: Potsdam or Wannsee) to Wannsee; take the rear exit from the station onto Nibelungenstraße, head right, and then walk left (east) against the traffic along the westbound Potsdamer Chaussee. Within a kilometer you'll reach the on-ramps to Autobahn A 115. Stand with your sign at the westbound on-ramp. For northern destinations such as Hamburg and Kiel, take the U6 or S25 to Alt-Tegel and then Bus 224 (direction: Hennigsdorf), and ask the driver to drop you at the *Trampenplatz* (hitching spot). For eastern and southeastern destinations like Dresden, take the S9 or S45 to Altglienicke and stand on busy Am Seegraben at the Autobahn on-ramp, about 100 m beyond the station in the direction the train was traveling.

BERLIN PUBLIC TRANSIT SYSTEM

U2 U-Bahn
S1 S-Bahn

Oranienburg S1
Lehnitz
Borgsdorf
Birkenwerder S10
Hohe Neuendorf
Bergfelde
Schönfliess
Mühlenbeck/Mönchmühle
Frohnau
Hermsdorf S2
Waidmannslust U8
Wittenau
Wilhelmsruh
Rath. Reinickendorf
Karl-Bonnhoeffer-Nervenklinik
Schönholz
Lindauer Allee
Paracelsus-Bad
Residenzstr.
Wollankstr.
Franz-Neumann-Pl.
Osloer Str. U9
Bornh
Alt-Tegel U6
Borsigwerke
Hotzhauser Str.
Seidelstr.
Scharnweberstr.
Kurt-Schumacher-Pl.
Afrikanische Str.
Rehberge
Seestr.
Leopoldpl.
Nauener Pl.
Pankstr.
Gesundbrunnen
Wedding
Humbo
Amrumer Str.
Westhafen
ReinickendorferStr.
Nord
Birkenstr.
Schwartzkopffstr.
Zinnowitzstr.
Oranienburger Tor
Turmstr.
Former location of Berlin Wall
BUS X9
BUS 109
BUS 128
Berlin-Tegel Airport
Beusselstr.
Altstadt Spandau
Zitadelle
Haselhorst
Paulsternstr.
Rohrdamm
Siemensdamm
Halemweg
Jakob-Kaiser-Pl.
Jungfernheide
Rath. Spandau U7
Westend S45 S46
Mierendorffpl.
Ruhleben U2 U12
Olympia-Stadion (Ost)
Neu-Westend
Theodor-Heuss-Pl.
Kaiserdamm
Sophie-Charlotte-Pl.
Rich.-Wagner-Pl.
Deutsche Oper
Bismarckstr.
Ernst-Reuter-Pl.
Tiergarten
Bellevue
Hansapl.
Lehrter Stadtbhf.
U.d.Linden
Zoologischer Garten
S5
Savignypl.
Charlottenburg
Westkreuz S9 S75
Kurfürstendamm
U15
Uhlandstr.
Wittenbergpl.
U4 Nollendorfpl.
Kurfürstenstr.
Mohrenstr.
Stadtm
Potsdamer Pl.
Anhalter Bhf.
Möckernbrücke
Gleisdreieck
Bülowstr.
Adenauerpl.
Augsburger Str.
Grossgörschenstr.
Viktoria-Luise-Pl.
Yorckstr.
Grunewald
Konstanzer Str.
Spichernstr.
Kleistpark
Halensee
Hohenzollernpl.
Güntzelstr.
Bayerischer Pl.
Eisenacher Str.
Hohenzollerndamm
Fehrbelliner Pl.
Rath. Schöneberg
Blissestr.
Berliner Str.
Heidelberger Pl.
Innsbrucker Pl.
Rüdesheimer Pl.
Papestr.
Breitenbachpl.
Bundespl.
U4
Schöneberg
Friedr.-Wilhelm-Pl.
Priesterweg
Podbielskiallee
Dahlem-Dorf
Walther-Schreiber-Pl.
Friedenau
Südende
Oskar-Helene-Heim
Thielplatz
Lankwitz
Attilastr.
Krumme Lanke
Schloßstr.
Feuerbachstr.
Marienfelde
Onkel Toms Hütte
U1
Steglitz
U9 Rath. Steglitz
Lichterfelde Ost
Potsdam Stadt
Babelsberg
Griebnitzsee
Nikolassee
Buckower Chaussee
U6
Schlachtensee
Mexikoplatz
Zehlendorf
Sundgauer Str.
Lichterfelde West
Botanischer Garten
Osdorfer Str.
S25 Lichterfelde Süd
Schichauweg
S3
S7
S1 Wannsee
Lichtenrade
Former location of Berlin Wall
Mahlow
Blankenfelde (Kr. Teltow-Fläming) S2

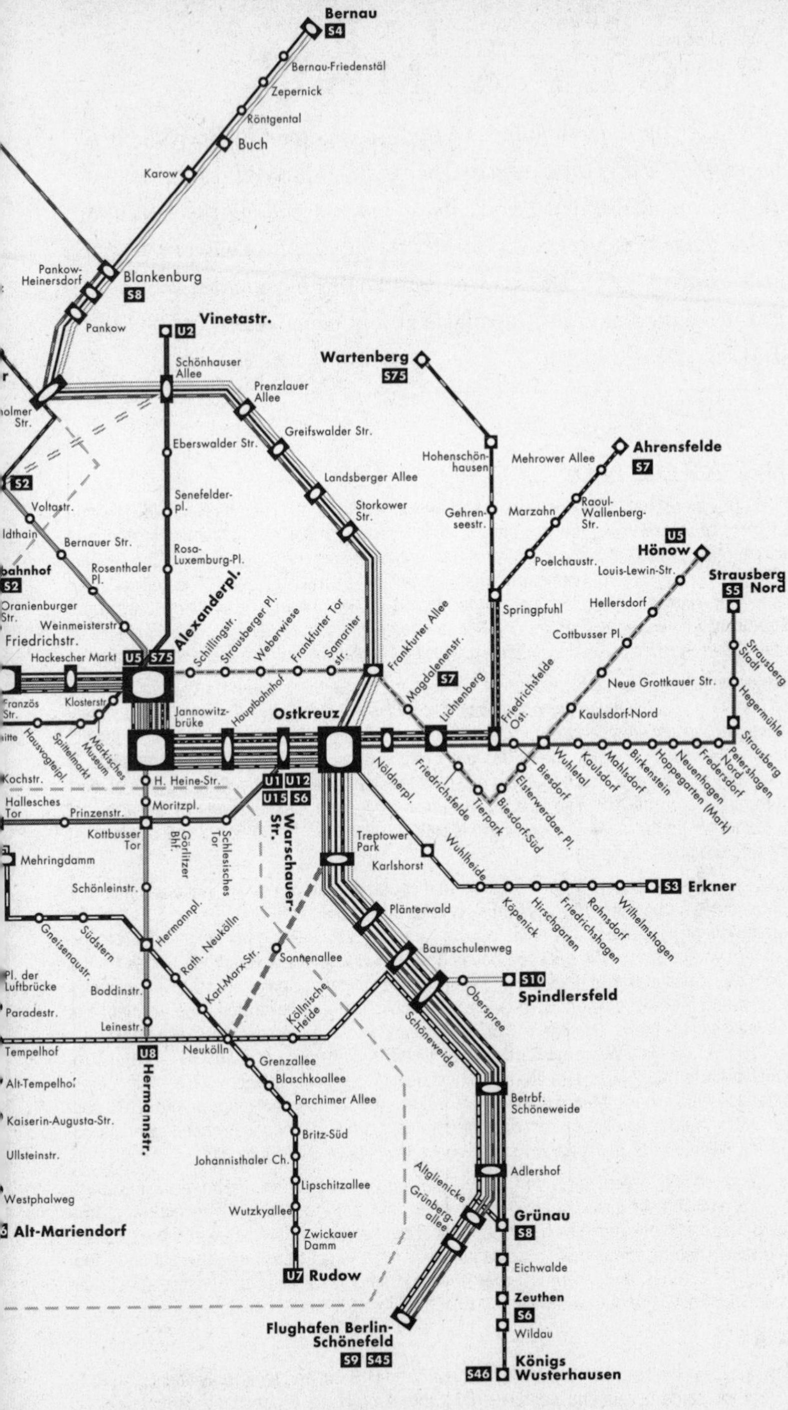
Bernau
S4
Bernau-Friedenstal
Zepernick
Röntgental
Buch
Karow
Pankow-Heinersdorf
Blankenburg
S8
Pankow
Vinetastr.
U2
Schönhauser Allee
Prenzlauer Allee
Wartenberg
S75
Greifswalder Str.
Eberswalder Str.
Landsberger Allee
Hohenschönhausen
Mehrower Allee
Ahrensfelde
S7
Senefelder-pl.
Storkower Str.
Gehrenseestr.
Marzahn
Raoul-Wallenberg-Str.
U5
Hönow
Rosa-Luxemburg-Pl.
Poelchaustr.
Louis-Lewin-Str.
Strausberg Nord
S5
Hellersdorf
Springpfuhl
Cottbusser Pl.
Alexanderpl.
Schillingstr.
Strausberger Pl.
Weberwiese
Frankfurter Tor
Samariterstr.
Frankfurter Allee
Magdalenenstr.
S7
Lichtenberg
Friedrichsfelde Ost
Neue Grottkauer Str.
Strausberg Stadt
Hegermühle
Strausberg
Kaulsdorf-Nord
Voltastr.
Bernauer Str.
Rosenthaler Pl.
S2
Oranienburger Str.
Weinmeisterstr.
Friedrichstr.
Hackescher Markt
U5
S75
Jannowitz-brüke
Hauptbahnhof
Ostkreuz
Klosterstr.
Französ. Str.
Hausvogteipl.
Spittelmarkt
Märkisches Museum
Nöldnerpl.
Friedrichsfelde
Tierpark
Biesdorf-Süd
Elsterwerdaer Pl.
Biesdorf
Wuhletal
Kaulsdorf
Mahlsdorf
Birkenstein
Hoppegarten (Mark)
Neuenhagen
Fredersdorf
Petershagen Nord
Kochstr.
H. Heine-Str.
U1
U12
U15
S6
Moritzpl.
Hallesches Tor
Prinzenstr.
Kottbusser Tor
Görlitzer Bhf.
Schlesisches Tor
Warschauer-Str.
Treptower Park
Karlshorst
Wuhlheide
Mehringdamm
Schönleinstr.
Köpenick
Hirschgarten
Friedrichshagen
Rahnsdorf
Wilhelmshagen
S3
Erkner
Plänterwald
Gneisenaustr.
Südstern
Hermannpl.
Rath. Neukölln
Karl-Marx-Str.
Sonnenallee
Baumschulenweg
Pl. der Luftbrücke
Boddinstr.
S10
Spindlersfeld
Oberspree
Paradestr.
Leinestr.
Köllnische Heide
Schöneweide
Tempelhof
U8
Hermannstr.
Neukölln
Grenzallee
Blaschkoallee
Alt-Tempelhof
Parchimer Allee
Betrbf. Schöneweide
Kaiserin-Augusta-Str.
Britz-Süd
Ullsteinstr.
Johannisthaler Ch.
Adlershof
Lipschitzallee
Altglienicke
Westphalweg
Wutzkyallee
Grünau
S8
Grünbergallee
Alt-Mariendorf
Zwickauer Damm
Eichwalde
U7
Rudow
Zeuthen
S6
Flughafen Berlin-Schönefeld
S9
S45
Wildau
S46
Königs Wusterhausen

GET A LIFE: GET A MAP

You wouldn't tour the Inferno without Virgil, so why tour Berlin without a map? The best map is also the cheapest: The "ViBB Nahverkehrsatlas" covers every single street in Berlin and Brandenburg and even indexes them. It also has a complete guide to public transit. Buy this invaluable (but bulky) resource at any public transit office for DM 5. If you want something handier, your next best bet is a fold-out "Falk Plan," available at any major newsstand or book shop for DM 13.

GETTING AROUND

Berlin's two major hubs are Bahnhof Zoo in the west and Alexanderplatz in the east. **Bahnhof Zoo** is within easy walking distance of several major tourist sights. To reach the city center, exit right onto Hardenbergplatz (by Track 1) and then head left along the busy street; within five min you'll stumble onto the Europa-Center, Breitscheidplatz, and the Kurfürstendamm (known familiarly as the Ku'damm). The station is also near three of the more upscale districts: Charlottenburg and its Savignyplatz lie west on Kantstraße; Wilmersdorf is southwest down the Ku'damm; and Schöneberg centers on Nollendorfplatz, southeast on Tauentzienstraße. The green expanse of the Tiergarten stretches east all the way to the Brandenburger Tor.

Alexanderplatz (known as Alex) is the focal point of the former East Berlin, in the Bezirk known as Mitte (Center). When orienting yourself in Berlin, remember that this is the hub of the whole awkward wheel: Berlin's historic center lies just southwest of Alex, and many of its major streets radiate from this district. Bordering Mitte are Prenzlauer Berg (to the north) and Friedrichshain (to the east), both with a mix of old East Berlin working class and young bohemian hipsters. Western Berlin's subculture centers on east Kreuzberg, south of Mitte on the U8. The best way to cross town from Alex to Zoo is by S-Bahn (the mostly above-ground commuter rail system), which is much faster than the U-Bahn and offers great views of the city and the green Tiergarten.

The Berlin transit system is a complex network of lines that course through all major sections of the city. The city's 150 bus routes and eastern Berlin's trams serve as capillaries to the U-Bahn and S-Bahn and can put you within walking distance of any point in town. One DM 3.90 ticket gives unlimited access to all public transit for two hours; for DM 7.80 you have access for a whole day. Purchase tickets from a bus driver or from machines in transit stations. Tickets must be validated upon entering the system, in the red boxes at station entrances or onboard the tram or bus. Ticket checks aren't too frequent but come when you least expect them. The fine is DM 60, and you won't wriggle out of it. For people on a very short visit, a good choice is a **Welcome Card** (DM 29), valid for 72 hours of unlimited bus and subway travel. A **Wochenkarte** (week pass; DM 40) is the best deal for serious sightseers; it's good for seven days of public transportation thrills. **Monatskarten** (DM 99) are valid for one calendar month. *BVG customer service and info: Hardenbergpl., in front of Bahnhof Zoo, no external phone number. Open Mon.–Sun. 8 AM–8:30 PM. Kleistpark U-Bahn station office: Open Mon.–Sun. 8 AM–8:30 PM.*

In general, the transportation system is prompt, clean, and safe—Berliners are proud of their efficient transit system. Late at night, however, shady figures often lurk around dark S-Bahn platforms and remote bus stops. Stay alert, look mean as hell, and think about hailing a taxi. Women and the disabled can have any U-Bahn announcer call them a cab after 8 PM. You can get transit maps (night ones, too) from tourist offices, BVG offices, and, assuming they haven't run out, in any station from the announcer in the glass booth. You know, the one who yells "Zu-RÜCK-bleiben!" ("Stand back!").

BY SUBWAY

Berlin has two main types of rail transit—the mostly underground **U-Bahn** and the mostly aboveground **S-Bahn.** Both accept the same tickets and operate during the same hours (4 AM–midnight or 1 AM). On weekends, the U12 (Ruhleben–Charlottenburg–Bahnhof Zoo–Kreuzberg–Warschauer Straße), U9 (Rathaus Steglitz–Wilmersdorf–Bahnhof Zoo–Wedding–Osloer Straße), and all S-Bahn lines operate all night. A EurailPass gets you on the S-Bahn for free, but not the U-Bahn, and the S-Bahn tends to cover a larger area, including outlying suburbs and Potsdam, in the neighboring state of Brandenburg (*see* Chapter 12). Berlin's subway systems are subject to delays as construction projects connect the formerly separate eastern and western systems. In addition to the U-Bahn and S-Bahn, a new fleet of modern **trams,** including four night lines, operates in eastern Berlin. Their main hub is the S-Bahn station at Hackescher Markt, and most lines connect with the U-Bahn at Rosenthaler Platz or Rosa-Luxemburg-Platz.

BY BUS

Buses stop in every part of the city that's more than a short walk from a U-Bahn or tram station. Standard operating hours are 4 AM–1 AM daily, but buses marked with an "N" are night owls that run every 30 min all night; "N" bus stops are recognizable by yellow-on-green tabs atop the streetside stands. Pick up a comprehensive day or night route map from one of BVG's offices (*see above*). Many western Berlin buses stop at Bahnhof Zoo. Bus 100 goes between Zoo and Alex through the Tiergarten and past some of Berlin's main sights in Mitte (including the Brandenburg Gate); it runs all night Friday and Saturday.

BY TAXI

BMW and Mercedes taxis—who needs limos? The standard fare is DM 4 plus DM 2.10 per kilometer (DM 2.30 after midnight). Quick trips (less than five min and 2 km) cost DM 5. Cabs line up outside airports, train stations, and in front of many luxury hotels. There are more than 200 listings; some main numbers are 030/69022, 030/261026, 030/210101, or 030/210202.

Don't fear the folks in gray suits and red ties standing around subway maps. They can help you find the right train—and they'll communicate through charades if need be.

BY BIKE

Many locals commute on bikes; paths are everywhere, and many street corners have signal lights specifically for cyclists. In the city center, watch for the red lanes on the sidewalk, where you can legally ride next to pedestrians. Flats are a chronic problem because of broken glass; rental shops are generally good about fixing tires free of charge, but some may charge you DM 10–DM 25. Bicycling is undoubtedly best in the suburbs or in one of Berlin's vast public parks. Both the Tiergarten (*see* Districts *in* Exploring Berlin, *below*) and Grunewald (*see* Parks and Gardens *in* Exploring Berlin, *below*) have bike-only paths that meander through the trees. **Fahrradstation** is the most convenient bike rental place. They have high-quality bikes—road and mountain. Prices are DM 17–DM 25 per day, DM 40–DM 60 per weekend, and DM 80–DM 120 per week. Your passport or DM 100–DM 200 is a deposit. They have five locations in Berlin: in Bahnhof Zoo (tel. 030/2974–9319), in Bahnhof Lichtenberg (tel. 030/2971–2949), in west Kreuzberg (Möckernstr. 92, tel. 030/216–9177), and in Mitte (Rosenthaler Str. 40–41, tel. 030/2859–9895). They're all open weekdays 10–6; the train station branches are also open weekends 10–2. Fahrradstation is convenient, but you'll get better prices and a more interesting experience if you call **Herr Beck** (Goethestr. 7, 4 blocks west of Bahnhof Zoo, tel. 030/312–1925). You'll need to speak some German, and you can call him any day of the week at any reasonable hour. He rents good bikes for only DM 15 per day.

WHERE TO SLEEP

Most hotels cost between DM 110 and DM 160 per person per night—well beyond the reach of budget travelers. Fortunately you can turn to Berlin's collection of pensions, which cost DM 50–DM 70 per person. Hostels are even more affordable, but unfortunately they are almost all located in the western half of the city. Don't let this discourage you from staying in the east: The tourist office at Europa-Center (*see* Visitor Information *in* Basics, *above*) has computerized listings of thousands of rooms in private homes all over the city that start as low as DM 25 per night. Let them know which district you want to stay in, and they'll book you a room for a DM 5 fee. Tourist offices also distribute the free German-English-language pamphlet "*Hotels und Pensionen*" ("Hotels and Pensions"). For DM 1 you can get the brochure "*Jugend Gästehäuser & Camping Plätze*" ("Youth Hostels & Campgrounds") that lists budget accommodations and campgrounds for youth.

ALTERNATIVE CULTURE COMES OF AGE

Germany's largest commune has come a long way since it was set up on an old Ufa film lot as a circus tent full of hippies in sleeping bags. The 18,000-sq-m site at Tempelhof is the hottest place in town for non-mainstream art and culture. Over the years the commune has grown—and so has its range of events, which now includes jazz and dance evenings, cabaret, and theater workshops. Every district in Berlin tries to emulate the Ufa-Factory, but there's only one original. Complete with an open-air cinema, the city's first, this commune takes a pragmatic approach to the ideals of the 1970s—drop by for a delicious mix of culture that isn't too strange to swallow. Ufa-Factory, Viktoriastr. 10–18, tel. 030/755030. Bus 170 and 174, or U6 to Ullsteinstr.

CHARLOTTENBURG

If you're a daytime explorer who wants peace and quiet in the evening, this is the district for you: These places are near the sight-packed Bahnhof Zoo area and far from the raucous nightlife in Kreuzberg, Mitte, and Prenzlauer Berg. Doubles generally run about DM 100, though a few places have rooms for less.

Hotel Fasanenhaus. This elegant family-run pension has combined modern convenience with a style reminiscent of the 1920s. Singles are DM 70 (DM 120 with shower and toilet), and doubles run DM 110 (DM 170 with shower and toilet), breakfast included. *Fasanenstr. 73, tel. 030/881–6713, fax 030/882–3947. 19 rooms, some with bath. No credit cards.*

Hotel-Pension Majesty. Most of the small, comfortable rooms here come with a phone and a safe. Singles start at DM 80 but cost more depending on the season and the view. Doubles start at DM 100, and breakfast is DM 11. *Mommsenstr. 55, off Leibnizstr., tel. 030/323–2061, fax 030/323–2063. 10 rooms, all with shower. No credit cards.*

Pension Alexis. This quiet, family-oriented pension is only 10 min by foot from Bahnhof Zoo. The spacious rooms are comfortable, if a bit grandmotherly (the furniture seems too nice to sit on). So is the owner, a woman who loves Americans and likes to chat with visitors over coffee. Singles run DM 70–DM 75, doubles DM 100–DM 110, breakfast included. *Carmerstr. 15, off Steinpl., tel. 030/312–5144. 7 rooms, none with bath. Reservations advised. No credit cards.*

Pension Charlottenburg. This classy, ornate pad has prices similar to those at more modest pensions. Singles are DM 70 (DM 100 with shower and toilet), and doubles run DM 110 (DM 150 with shower and toilet), breakfast included. The gentleman who runs the place speaks perfect English. *Grolmanstr. 32–33, off Ku'damm, tel. 030/8803–2960, fax 030/883–2407. 15 rooms, some with bath. Reservations advised.*

Pension Knesebeck. Rooms are spacious, and the friendly, oddball staff has been known to give price breaks to poor travelers. Singles run DM 65–DM 95, doubles DM 100 (DM 150 with shower), breakfast included. For a small fee visitors can use the newly installed washing machine and dryer. *Knesebeckstr. 86, 1 block north of Savignypl., tel. 030/312–7255, fax 030/313–9507. 12 rooms, some with bath. Reservations advised.*

Pension Silvia. The most reasonable rooms in this area (singles DM 55 without shower, doubles DM 100 with shower) are housed in an unobtrusive building with a lovely, chandeliered, dark-wood interior. Breakfast is DM 9.50 extra. *Knesebeckstr. 29, 1 block south of Savignypl., tel. 030/881–2129, fax 030/885–0435. 15 rooms, some with bath. No credit cards.*

KREUZBERG AND MITTE

The pick of the litter for the penniless party vampire is a DM 30 dorm bed in Die Fabrik, but all of these places are in fine proximity to some serious night haunts, and prices here tend to be slightly lower than in Charlottenburg.

Artist Hotelpension Die Loge. This pension caters to Berlin's artists and actors, but tourists are welcome as well. The rooms are furnished with honey-colored wood and the whole hotel is decorated in warm, friendly colors. This popular place fills up fast in the summer, so reservations are recommended. The location is central and the clientle fascinating. Singles cost DM 60 (DM 90 with bath and toilet); doubles are DM 100 (DM 130 with bath and toilet). *Friedrichstr. 115, tel. 030/280–7513. U6 to Oranienburger Tor. 14 rooms, half with bath and toilet. No credit cards.*

Die Fabrik. Cool industrial meets art deco (with a touch of kitsch) in this converted factory in east Kreuzberg. This mecca for nonconformists and artists has been recently renovated, leaving just enough rough edges to be interesting—but not annoying. Tidy rooms in the very Bauhaus building cost DM 66 for singles, DM 94 for doubles, DM 120 for triples, and DM 144 for quads. A dorm bed costs DM 30 (no curfew). A couple of cool bars are right downstairs, and it's close to Kreuzberg and Mitte hotspots. *Schlesische Str. 18, tel. 030/611–8254, fax 030/611–2974. U-Bahn to Schlesisches Tor, then SE on Schlesische Str. 105 beds. Reception open 24 hrs, checkout 11 AM. No credit cards.*

Berlin is a surprisingly safe city, but hooligans, from neo-Nazi skinheads to Turkish gangs, can be violent. Everyone should avoid traveling alone at night, especially in outlying districts.

Hotel Transit. This large, friendly, surprisingly upscale pension near Viktoriapark in west Kreuzberg offers comfortable doubles with TVs. This place is run by gay management and welcomes homosexuals. It has a bar, and the clientele is an odd mix of German families and foreign backpackers. Including breakfast, singles are DM 90, doubles are DM 105, and a bed in a dormlike room with six beds is DM 33, but no reservations for single beds are accepted. *Hagelberger Str. 53–54, tel. 030/789–0470, fax 030/7890–4777. U-Bahn to Mehringdamm. 49 rooms, all with bath. Laundry (DM 7, including soap).*

Pension Kreuzberg. This place offers the best of both worlds: It's close to some great clubs but sits on a quiet, tree-lined street in west Kreuzberg. Clean singles go for DM 70, and roomy doubles are DM 95. Some triples are available for DM 42 per person. Prices include breakfast. Sometimes groups pass through, so reservations are a good idea. *Großbeerenstr. 64, off Yorckstr. near Mehringdamm, tel. 030/251–1362, fax 030/251–0638. U-Bahn to Mehringdamm. 12 rooms, none with bath. No credit cards.*

Pension Süd-West. This run-down pension lies in the heart of west Kreuzberg, near the district's many bars and cafés. Typical of Kreuzberg, the rooms are small and a bit damp. Singles are DM 35, doubles DM 90. *Yorckstr. 80a, off Mehringdamm, tel. 030/785–8033. U-Bahn to Mehringdamm. 8 rooms, none with bath. No credit cards.*

HOSTELS

Hostels in Berlin, especially the central ones that don't attract German school groups, fill up fast with backpackers and students looking for friendly conversation with like-minded travelers. Keep in mind that many of Berlin's old and worn youth hostels provide minimum comfort and sometimes dismal facilities. There are two types of hostels: *Jugendgästehäuser* (youth guest houses) and *Jugendherbergen* (youth hostels). The former tend to have higher prices and fewer beds per room, and the latter require an HI membership card, though in the off-season they'll sometimes admit nonmembers for DM 6 extra.

CHARLOTTENBURG AND WILMERSDORF

Jugendgästehaus am Zoo. This popular hostel is just five min on foot west of Bahnhof Zoo. DM 35 gets you a bed in a spacious four- to six-bunk dorm room. There are not enough showers or hot water and the management is rude, but these are some of the cheapest cots in town, and the clientele consists mostly of backpackers and other young vagabonds—not giddy preteens. *Hardenbergstr. 9a, 4th floor, tel. 030/312–9410, fax 030/3125–5430. No curfew, lockout 10–noon. 85 beds. Reception open 24 hrs, checkout 10 AM.*

Jugendgästehaus Central. It's conveniently located five min from Bahnhof Zoo by subway, which means 1) the crowd is diverse and 2) reservations are essential. Beds cost DM 38 (including breakfast), and if you book ahead you may get one of the few small singles. There's a midnight curfew, but the management opens the doors to let you in all night long at the top of the hour. You can avoid the wait completely by getting a key (DM 100 deposit). *Nikolsburger Str. 2–4, off Hohenzollerndamm, tel. 030/873–0188, fax 030/861–3485. U-Bahn to Spichernstr. Curfew 1 AM. Checkout 9 AM.*

Jugendhotel Berlin. A clean, friendly place, this hostel is only a short jaunt from the forests of Spandau and Grunewald. Each three-bed room has its own bathroom and shower. You'll pay DM 44 per night per person (including breakfast), and DM 47 for a small dinner. It's slightly more expensive—and more pleasant—than other hostels. You must be under 27 for the low price, otherwise singles are DM 92, doubles DM 143. *Kaiserdamm 3, tel. 030/322–1011. U2 to Sophie-Charlotte-Pl. No curfew. Reception open 24 hrs, checkout 9 AM.*

SCHÖNEBERG

Gästehaus Luftbrücke. This guest house is in a nice old building in an unpretentious section of Schöneberg, where the mellow pubs and cafés draw a decidedly local crowd. Breakfast and a clean bed (singles or quads) costs DM 45. Note: You must check-in by phone. *Kolonnenstr. 10, entrance on Leberstr., tel. 030/7870–2130. U7 to Kleistpark. No curfew. Check-in by phone 24 hrs, checkout 11 AM.*

Studentenhotel Berlin. At this central student hotel, one block from Rathaus Schöneberg, typical linoleum-floored dorm rooms are DM 40 per person. A bed in a double room is DM 44, but you can have the double room to yourself for DM 60. There's also a communal self-service kitchen. The management is more laid-back than you have any right to expect. *Meininger Str. 10, tel. 030/784–6720, fax 030/788–1523. From Bahnhof Zoo, Bus 146 to Rathaus Schöneberg. 163 beds. No curfew. Reception open 8 AM–noon. Checkout 10:30 AM. Luggage storage.*

TEGEL AND NORTH BERLIN

Gästehaus der Fürst-Donnersmarck-Stiftung. This hostel is a 45-min trek from the city center. There are only seven beds for visitors, so try to reserve ahead, especially since they sometimes book up for months. Beds are DM 32. *Wildkanzelw. 28, tel. 030/406060, fax 030/401–6914. S1 to Frohnau, then Bus 125 (direction: Invalidensiedlung) to Schönfließer Str.; right on Am Pilz, left on Wildkanzelw. No curfew, no lockout. Reception open 24 hrs.*

Jugendgästehaus Nordufer. In the northern district of Wedding, this rustic-looking (from the outside) guest house is about 20 min from Bahnhof Zoo, near the Plötzensee beach, which guests can use for DM 3–DM 5 per day. Beds in singles and doubles cost DM 37.50, breakfast included. All rooms have sinks, and there's a pool table, a Ping-Pong table, and a sundeck with a place to grill in good weather. If you plan to paint the town red, ask for a key. *Nordufer 28, tel. 030/451–7030, fax 030/452–4100. Bus 126 to Dohnagestell, then west on Nordufer (Bus 126 connects to the U7 at Mierendorffpl., the U6 at Seestr., and the U8 and U9 at Osloer Str.). No curfew, no lockout. Reception open 7 AM–midnight.*

Jugendgästhaus Tegel. If you tranquilized all the little kids at this clean hostel, sandwiched between two graveyards, it just might be peaceful enough for a sound night's sleep. As it is, it isn't. On the upside, there's a Ping-Pong table, and you get your own key. Beds are DM 37.50, breakfast and fresh sheets included. *Ziekowstr. 161, tel. 030/433–3046, fax 030/434–5063. S25 to Tegel or U6 to Alt-Tegel; then east on Gorkistr., left on Ziekowstr. 200 beds. No curfew, no lockout. Reception open 7 AM–midnight.*

Jugendherberge Ernst Reuter (HI). This hostel has a helpful staff and clean, comfy facilities, but it's far from the center—45 min from Bahnhof Zoo. Rooms vary in size, and the price is DM 25 (DM 32 over 26), breakfast included. Peaceful Tegel Forest is just across the road. *Hermsdorfer Damm 48–50, tel. 030/404–1610. S25 to Tegel or U6 to Alt-Tegel, then Bus 125 (direction: Invalidensiedlung) to Hermsdorfer Damm. 111 beds. Midnight curfew. Reception open 24 hrs. Key deposit (DM 10).*

TIERGARTEN AND KREUZBERG

Jugendgästehaus Berlin (HI). Due to its prime location in the middle of town near the Tiergarten, this hostel fills up quickly. Reservations are imperative: To book more than two weeks in advance, call 030/262–3024. The hostel itself is your basic no-frills dorm with clean, institutional, multibed rooms. Note that the neighborhood around Potsdamer Straße gets sketchy at night, especially for women. Beds are DM 44, breakfast included. *Kluckstr. 3, tel. 030/261–1097, fax 030/265–0383. From Bahnhof Zoo, head down Joachimstaler Str., cross to the opposite side of the Ku'damm, then Bus 129 (direction: Herrmannpl.) to Kluckstr. 380 beds. Midnight curfew, but the management will open the door every half hour until 3 AM. The reception is open 24 hrs. Key deposit (DM 10).*

Jugendgästehaus Deutsche Schreberjugend. This Kreuzberg guest house combines a central location with pleasant surroundings. Your room may look onto the Schrebergarten, a small plot of land where a few sheep, horses, and other livestock wander quietly—try to ignore the surrounding gray housing projects. Everything's very clean, and there's plenty of hot water. A night costs DM 38.50 including breakfast, DM 41 with dinner. *Franz-Künstler-Str. 4–10, off Alte Jakobstr., tel. 030/615–1007, fax 030/6140–1150. U-Bahn to Hallesches Tor. 280 beds. No curfew. Reception open 24 hrs. Luggage storage, TV room.*

WANNSEE

Jugendgästehaus am Wannsee (HI). This large hostel lies on Lake Wannsee on the outskirts of Berlin, a 10-min S-Bahn ride from Potsdam. The surroundings are perfect for swims and strolls, but it's a 30-min train ride to central Berlin. Because it caters to youth groups, reservations are imperative during summer. Beds DM 34 (DM 42 over 26), including breakfast. *Badew. 1, tel. 030/803–2034. S-Bahn to Nikolassee, then west on Spanische Allee to Kronprinzessinw.; hostel is on the right. 288 beds. No curfew, reception open 24 hrs. Key deposit (DM 20), luggage storage.*

STUDENT HOUSING

Student housing is pretty scarce—so don't get your hopes up that you'll find anything. Once the **Studentenwohnheim Hubertusallee** (Delbrückstr. 24, tel. 030/891–9718, fax 030/892–8698) reopens, though, it'll be one of the best deals in Berlin. Call to see if construction is finished or ask at a tourist office. From Bahnhof Zoo, head down Joachimstaler Str. to Ku'damm, then take Bus 129 (direction: Roseneck) to Delbrückstraße.

If you can, check into pensions on Sunday, when rooms are more apt to be vacant and prices may be lower.

CAMPING

Berlin's campgrounds are all in rural settings far from the city center. As a rule, the sites are quiet and boast clean bathrooms with flush toilets and hot showers. During summer expect to meet lots of families, youth groups, and other travelers. To ensure a spot contact the **Deutscher Camping Club** (Geisbergstr. 11, 10777 Berlin, tel. 030/218–6071, fax 030/213–4416), an organization that will help you find a place in one of its five camping grounds in Berlin free of charge. All campsites cost DM 9.70 per person, tent rentals go for DM 7.20, and larger tents and caravans are DM 12.70. Showers cost 50 Pf–DM 1. Campgrounds are open year-round.

Kladow Camping (Krampnitzer Weg 111, tel. 030/365–2797, fax 030/365–1245), with 300 sites, sits in a forest by a small lake over an hour, all told, from the city center. The most rural of Berlin's campgrounds, Kladow also attracts summertime hordes. It features an on-site bar, restaurant, and food shop, and the nearby Sacrower See offers lovely lakeside hikes. From Bahnhof Zoo, take Bus 149 to Gatower Straße, then Bus 134 to Hottengrundweg; walk right on Hottengrundweg, right on Siebitzer Straße, and left on Krampnitzer Weg (a 25-min walk). In eastern Berlin, **Krossinsee International Camping** (Wernsdorfer Str. 45, tel. 030/675–8687, fax 030/675–9150) lies at the edge of Krossin Lake. The 1,000 sites are scattered around the woods, but definitely within earshot of each other. While you're 90 min from the city center, you're only a 20-min walk from the sleepy village of Schmöckwitz, with grocery stores and a beer hall. Take any S-Bahn to Ostkreuz, then S8 to Grünau, and then Tram 86 (direction: Alt-Schmöckwitz) to the end of the line; walk 30 min east on Wernsdorfer Straße. The last tram leaves around 11 PM.

ROUGHING IT

Sad to say, Berlin is not a good city for roughing it. Junkies and prostitutes often camp out by Bahnhof Zoo, and there are always a few people passed out in Kreuzberg alleyways. **Bahnhof Lichtenberg** is clean and open 24 hours, but we can't promise that you won't be hassled. Crashing in a park at night does not come without its risks, but if you're inconspicuous, you can probably pass a quiet night among trees and spiders in the more remote parts of the Tiergarten (btw Siegessäule and Entlastungsstraße). From July to late August, scrounge up DM 10 and you can stay under a giant tent with hordes of the young and/or desperate in **Internationales Jugendcamp** (Ziekowstr. 161, tel. 030/433–3046; no reservations). You're supposed to be under 26, and the maximum stay is three nights. They don't have lockers, but they have a tent where you can leave your stuff. Otherwise, stash your bags in a locker elsewhere (*see* Luggage Storage *in* Basics, *above*). To reach the Jugendcamp, take the S25 to Tegel or U6 to Alt-Tegel, and then head east on Gorkistraße and left on Ziekowstraße.

LONGER STAYS

If you're staying in Berlin for a week or more, contact one of the city's **Mitwohnzentralen.** These room-finding agencies arrange accommodations in all sorts of places—from apartments and family homes to shared flats and student dorms. Commissions are steep (anywhere from 10% to 20% of the rent for your entire stay up to a year). Most Mitwohnzentralen can provide women-only or wheelchair-accessible apartments. **Mitwohnzentrale Freiraum** (Wiener Str. 14, tel. 030/618–2008, fax 030/618–2006) has fewer short-term listings but tends to serve an interesting, "alternative" Kreuzberg clientele. You can find them near the Görlitzer Bahnhof U-Bahn stop weekdays 10 AM–6 PM. **Home Company Berlin,** formerly the Mitwohnzentrale Kudamm-Eck (Joachimstalerstr. 17, tel. 030/19445, fax 030/882–6694), two blocks south of Bahnhof Zoo, has loads of short-term listings, mostly with folks (often families) who take in travelers to augment their income. They're open weekdays 9–6, Saturday 11–2. **Mitwohnzentrale Wohnwitz** (Holsteinische Str. 55, tel. 030/861–8222, fax 030/861–8272) serves a lot of young professional types. Take the U1 to Hohenzollernplatz; the office is open weekdays 10–7 and Saturday 11–2.

A typical small city-center apartment fetches DM 500–DM 1,000 per month, run-down one-room studios can go for as little as DM 400 per month, and rooms in shared flats run DM 300 and up. Women (lesbian or straight) can also contact Fraueninfothek, and gays can check listings at Mann-O-Meter (for both, *see* Visitor Information *in* Basics, *above*). To avoid Mitwohnzentrale commissions on long-term rentals or shares, arrange for a phone where you can get messages and place an ad in the **classifieds** in the back of *Tip* or *Zitty* magazine, or even better, the triweekly *Zweite Hand.* In Berlin, the person looking for a room, rather than the person hoping to fill a room, generally places the ad. Although your English skills may actually be an asset in finding a share, watch out for roommates who expect you to give them lessons.

FOOD

Berlin is a haven for cheap eating. The *Imbiß* (snack) stand is a very German concept, and you'll still find plenty of stands serving a *Boulette* on a *Schrippe* (a meat patty on a roll) for about DM 3. Wurst aside, the majority of Imbiß stands in Berlin are Turkish (or Arabic). You can always get takeout falafel or kebabs for under DM 7. The immigrant communities dominate the tasty and affordable sit-down market as well, and in many Indian or Middle Eastern restaurants, you can have a filling and tastebud-thrilling meal for DM 10–DM 15. Both traditional German and trendy places (like many "American" or "Mexican" eateries) will suck away at least DM 20. Restaurant staff are paid better here than in the States, but a 5% tip is becoming customary. If you just have a cup of coffee, round it up.

There are supermarkets everywhere; the cheapest are **Aldi, Plus,** and **Penny Markt,** but others (with more selection) include **Kaisers** and **Reichelt.** Also try your luck at Berlin's open-air public markets, where everything is fresh and cheap. For the Istanbul-meets-Berlin experience, head to Neukölln's lively **Türkenmarkt** (Maybachufer, on Landwehrkanal) Tuesdays and Fridays noon–6:30; take the U-Bahn to Kottbusser Tor, then walk down Kottbusser Straße and across the bridge. The **Winterfeldtmarkt** on Winterfeldtplatz is open Wednesday and Saturday 8 AM–2 PM. To get here, take the U-Bahn to Nollendorfplatz and walk down Maaßenstraße. There's an incredible contrast between these two markets: Winterfeldt has a wide and orderly selection of global delicacies and is reasonable but not dirt cheap—while Türkenmarkt is crowded, fragrant, full of Oriental flair, and much cheaper than any other market in Berlin.

CHARLOTTENBURG

Most everything along the Ku'damm is overpriced and geared for tourists, so head instead to **Savignyplatz** (north of the Ku'damm on Kantstraße) and the streets that border it, particularly **Grolmanstraße, Knesebeckstraße,** and **Goethestraße.** These are littered with cheap Indian and Middle Eastern Imbiß stands. One of your best bets is **Café Voltaire** (Stuttgarterpl. 14, tel. 030/324–5028), a friendly and artsy 24-hour bistro that offers as much atmosphere as it does choice on the menu. Warm, hearty breakfasts (DM 6–DM 8) are served from 4 AM to 3 PM—ideal if you've been up all night exploring Berlin. The rest of the day you can choose from warm meals and snacks. Take the U7 to Wilmersdorferstraße.

UNDER DM 10 • Assam. Look for the sandwich-board specials (under DM 10) outside this atmospheric Indian restaurant. Otherwise, stick to appetizers like *samosa* (two vegetable-stuffed pastries; DM 4.50) for a reasonable meal. Chicken or veggie dishes range DM 8–DM 15. The mango *lassi* (yogurt smoothie; DM 3.50) is delicious. *Grolmanstr. 27, just SE of Savignypl. near Zoo, tel. 030/883–4702. Open daily noon–midnight.*

Satyam. The best Indian food in the area (all-vegetarian) is served on Satyam's simulated wood-grain tables. The *palak paneer* (spinach and fresh cheese with rice) is DM 5.50, and their subtly spiced *natur biriyani* (a rice dish with nuts and vegetables) is only DM 6.50. *Goethestr. 5, at Knesebeckstr., tel. 030/312–9079. U-Bahn to Ernst-Reuter-Pl.*

UNDER DM 15 • einhorn. this mainly vegetarian imbiß serves everything from broccoli quiche to vegetarian lasagna (DM 9). Portions aren't huge, but the food is tasty and the grease content low. Most people order to go since there are only a handful of tables inside. *Mommsenstr. 2, south of Savignypl. near Zoo, tel. 030/881–4241. Closed Sun.*

Rogacki. Fish-lovers will be impressed with the choice of over 150 fish dishes to buy or eat on the premises at this delicatessen. You pay for your meal according to its weight. Fresh side dishes complement the fish: Try the potato salad (DM 8) or the hearty soups (DM 6.50). *Wilmersdorferstr. 145, tel. 030/343–8250. U7 to Wilmersdorferstr. Closed Sun.*

SCHÖNEBERG

To get a sense of what's going on in Schöneberg, walk south of Nollendorfplatz along **Maaßenstraße** to **Winterfeldtplatz** and **Goltzstraße.** Eateries around here serve some of the best falafel in Berlin, and you'll find Indian and Thai places spilling into the street. The area's rambunctious nightlife affects both the atmosphere and hours of its restaurants; people eat out to see and be seen, and tiny stand-up places stay open late for the late-night crowd.

UNDER DM 10 • Habibi. Big, fat, lip-smacking homemade falafel for DM 4 make this place an essential stop when you've got the munchies. It stays open into the wee hours to catch the last barhoppers and serves Middle Eastern food in a pleasant, bistro atmosphere. Sit at a table or grab a bite to go. *Goltzstr. 24, tel. 030/215–3332. U-Bahn to Nollendorfpl.*

Rani Indischer Imbiß. This Winterfeldtplatz Imbiß stand-cum-restaurant is popular with just about everyone. Try the *sabzi* (chicken with spinach; DM 8.50) or the Indian vegetarian plate (DM 10), both cooked fresh and served in large portions. On warm nights, seating spills out onto the street along with the brain-numbing aroma of curry. *Goltzstr. 32, tel. 030/215–2673. U-Bahn to Nollendorfpl. or Eisenacher Str.*

UNDER DM 25 • Carib. This is one of the few restaurants in Berlin that specializes in honest-to-goodness Caribbean food (expat Caribs actually come here to hang out and drink). The owner makes everyone feel welcome, even if you just want a splash of rum in your coffee. The food is first-rate: Try the jerk chicken (DM 21) or grilled fish with coconut milk (DM 22). *Motzstr. 30, tel. 030/213–5381. U4 to Viktoria-Luise-Pl.*

KREUZBERG

Because of the fly-by-night nature of Kreuzberg restaurants, don't be surprised if some of the places below are nailed shut by the time you arrive; snoop around for the latest hot spot. East Kreuzberg's main drag, **Oranienstraße** (U-Bahn to Kottbusser Tor), is a good place to start. It's lined with cafés, bars, and thrift stores from Moritzplatz east to Skalitzer Straße, where it becomes the mellower **Wiener Straße.** Down here, cafés, bars, and restaurants cluster around **Spreewaldplatz.** In west Kreuzberg (U7 to Gneisenaustr.), explore **Bergmannstraße** and **Gneisenaustraße,** which are full of affordable eateries.

UNDER DM 10 • Mangla Ashru. This dark, cavernous, fabric-draped Indian restaurant offers good food starting at just DM 1.50 for seasoned, grilled meat or a vegetable *biryani* (a lightly seasoned rice dish) for just DM 6.50, so you might as well spring for a mango lassi (DM 3.50). *Lausitzer Str. 6, tel. 030/612–4201. U-Bahn to Görlitzer Bahnhof.*

Rissani. Everything about healthy, vegetarian Rissani—floor seating on small mats under palms, fresh orange and carrot juices, crispy falafel—is a notch above what you've come to expect. Except the prices. Fresh pita stuffed with outstanding falafel and salad is only DM 5; you may as well splurge for a huge combination plate (DM 8–DM 10 depending on the combination). *Spreewaldpl. 4–6, tel. 030/612–4529. U-Bahn to Görlitzer Bahnhof.*

UNDER DM 15 • Chandra Kumari. Even the most adventurous palates are often unfamiliar with the delicate, soothing flavors of Sri Lankan cuisine. With any of the spicy curries here you can try *appe* (rice flour, wheat, and coconut-milk pancakes; DM 8–DM 12). Also worth trying are string hoppers—steamed rice noodles, only available weekends and evenings. *Gneisenaustr. 4, tel. 030/694–3056. U-Bahn to Mehringdamm.*

China Imbiss. Missing Chinese fast food? Get your fix at this authentic eatery in Kreuzberg. Chicken fried rice is DM 8, and chop suey with tofu and vegetables runs DM 8.50. Or try the tasty China Minirolls (7 for DM 3.50). *Gneisenaustr. 62, tel. 030/691–7177. U7 to Gneisenaustr.*

MITTE

Once an alternative oasis, Mitte's funky dives are slowly succumbing to expensive, yuppie eateries. Fortunately there are always plenty of Imbiß stands clustered on **Oranienburger Straße** (S1 or S2) and **Alexanderplatz.** There's an overpriced restaurant in the Sputnik-like ball atop Alexanderplatz's 365-m-tall television tower, but come only if you enjoy that sort of thing.

UNDER DM 15 • Beth Café. This small kosher restaurant is run by the congregation of the Adass Jisroel Synagogue. The hummus, baba ghanoush, and tabouleh plate (DM 10.80) makes a substantial meal. *Tucholskystr. 40, near Oranienburger Str., tel. 030/281–3135. S-Bahn to Oranienburger Str. Closed Sat.*

Freßco. Next door to Obst und Gemüse (*see* After Dark, *below*), this café-eatery serves inexpensive Italian dishes to hungry hepcats. Snarf a homemade broccoli-ricotta calzone with yogurt or tomato sauce (DM 3), or a range of 23 baguettes with avocado cream and eggs (DM 7). There's a DM 2 *Pfand* (deposit) on drink glasses in the summer. *Oranienburger Str. 49, tel. 030/281–3128. U6 to Oranienburger Tor.*

UNDER DM 20 • Zur Nolle. The arched ceilings under the S-Bahn go a long way in helping Zur Nolle grasp an elegant, carefree, '20s feel—have a drink and let the jazz standards take you back. Veggie lasagne is just DM 12.80, but things can get much more expensive. Zur Nolle is near the Museumsinsel and major Mitte sights. *S-Bahnbogen 203 (Georgenstr.), tel. 030/208–2655. U- or S-Bahn to Friedrichstr.*

UNDER DM 30 • Kellerrestaurant im Brecht-Haus. This restaurant, in Bertolt Brecht's former house, features the recipes of Helene Weigel, Brecht's wife and partner. For the echt-Brecht experience, order his favorite—veal with apricot sauce and apple horseradish (DM 26.50). *Chausseestr. 125, tel. 030/282–3843. U6 to Oranienburger Tor.*

PRENZLAUER BERG

New places to eat and drink pop up constantly on Prenzlauer Berg's wide streets. Things remain spread out, but many restaurants are clustered around **Kollwitzplatz** and the **Wasserturm** off Knaackstraße. Imbiß stands sell all things fried for under DM 6; they tend to cluster near late-night hangouts and around the U2 stops at Senefelderplatz and Eberswalder Straße.

Little Shop of Food. This casual vegetarian and vegan Imbiß stand offers simply outstanding fresh food from a menu that changes daily. Recently remodeled, the spot seats about 25 and lets you order to go. Meals are filling and cheap at between DM 10 and DM 12. Indulge in the chicory with melted cheese in a fresh rosemary-and-tomato sauce (DM 12.50). *Kollwitzstr. 88/90, tel. 030/4405–6444. U2 to Senefelderpl.*

Pasternak. You'll have to decipher the Cyrillic sign, but you don't find much Russian cuisine these days in Berlin, so this place is a treat. Try the *blini* (pancakes) for DM 19 or the *soljanka* (thick meat and veggie soup) for DM 9.50. After dinner you'll probably notice one more plus: Pasternak is surrounded by hip bars. *Knaackstr. 22–24, at Rykestr., tel. 030/441–3399. U-Bahn to Senefelderpl.*

CAFÉS AND COFFEEHOUSES

Berlin is inundated with cafés—the city's social and artistic crucibles, the meeting places for ideologues and poets, politicians and philosophers. The unique coffeehouses in eastern Berlin are irreverent spots that cater to Berlin's alternative crowd—places with thrift-shop decor and tattoo-covered servers who don't mind if you nurse a lonely cappuccino for hours. If you find this alienating or passé, there are swarms of neon-lit cafés on and around the Ku'damm, and cafés with an older, more subdued crowd around Savignyplatz.

CHARLOTTENBURG AND WILMERSDORF

Café Hardenberg. Reminiscent of a Vienna coffeehouse, this subdued café-eatery is a popular student hangout. Someone here will speak fluent English, because the café is right by the popular Jugendgästehaus am Zoo. Coffee starts at DM 2.50, pastries and snacks at DM 5. *Hardenbergstr. 10, near Zoo, tel. 030/312–3330.*

Café Savigny. The tiny tables at this stylish café remain the place to be cultured and fashionable near Savignyplatz—definitely not a place for the not-trendy. *Grolmanstr. 53–54, near Zoo, tel. 030/312–8195. Open daily 9 AM–1 AM.*

KREUZBERG

Barcomi's. If you've been traveling a while, the fresh roasted coffee, bagels, great homemade brownies, and Celestial Seasonings teas (hot or iced DM 3.50) in this cozy café taste like home. Read *The New Yorker* while you sip your latte and talk cultural crossover with the German sharing your table. *Bergmannstr. 21, tel. 030/694–8138. U7 to Gneisenaustr.*

Café Elephant. Exactly what a café should be: dark, smoky, and full of serious-looking idealists engaged in heated dialogues. Potent coffee costs DM 2.50, and a beer runs about DM 5. If you prefer a more publike atmosphere, check out the larger **Die Rote Harfe** next door. *Oranienstr. 12, tel. 030/612–3013. U-Bahn to Kottbusser Tor.*

Ex. Run by the Mehringhof Collective—along with their bookshop, theater, center for Turkish residents, and concert space—Ex is a mellow and friendly place to kick back with a beer (DM 3.50), coffee (DM 2), or a light meal (DM 3–DM 10). *Gneisenaustr. 2a, in back, tel. 030/693–5800. U-Bahn to Mehringdamm.*

Shocko Café. This women's café is a part of the popular women's center, Schocko Fabrik (Naunynstr. 72) around the corner. Customers are relaxed and happy, especially when they've just enjoyed the center's Hamam Turkish Baths. *Mariannenstr. 6, tel. 030/615–1561. U-Bahn to Kottbusser Tor. Café and baths open Tues.–Sun. 1 PM–midnight.*

MITTE

Café CC. This café (CC means "Café Cinema") doubles as a gallery space and a meeting place for young Mitte residents and local art students. Art without affectation is the general theme; it's a relief to be here. Next door is the very hip Chamäleon Varieté performance space. *Rosenthaler Str. 39, tel. 030/280–6415. S-Bahn to Hackescher Markt.*

Hackbarths. The dark wood of this unpretentious, student-filled Mitte café lets you know you're in Germany. Offerings are cheap and good; expect to share a table. *Auguststr. 49a, tel. 030/282–7706. U8 to Weinmeisterstr.*

PRENZLAUER BERG

Café November. This is a comfy, gay-friendly, and unpretentious spot for watching life on restored Husemannstraße. Sitting outside is nice, but the interior is refreshingly light and no one seems to mind that it's not a hotbed of artistic creativity. *Husemannstr. 15, tel. 030/442–8425. U2 to Eberswalder Str.*

SCHÖNEBERG

M. The "M" is more of a neon squiggle, but this is currently Schöneberg's hot spot. You can watch an "in" crowd of eccentric dressers and leather lovers come and go for snacks of light Italian food and *Milchkaffee* (café au lait; DM 4). At night revolving red lights create a bizarre atmosphere, and booze catches up with coffee as the drink of choice. *Goltzstr. 33, tel. 030/215–4230. U-Bahn to Nollendorfpl. or Eisenacher Str.*

EXPLORING BERLIN

Because of Berlin's size and the sheer number of sights, your best strategy is to target and explore a particular district before moving on. When you hop from one "don't-miss" attraction to the next, Berlin's vastness translates into incoherence. Time spent wandering the districts one by one gives you insights into the city's diversity and rich history. The most exciting way to experience Berlin is to walk around and

THE BERLIN WALL

Throughout the 1950s nearly 20,000 East Germans were fleeing to West Berlin every month. To stem the flow, the GDR, faced with a worsening labor shortage, decided to seal the border completely. At 1 AM on August 13, 1961, more than 25,000 GDR workmen wiped the sleep from their eyes and built a wire-and-mortar barrier—the Berlin Wall—along the entire length of the border, demolishing houses and bisecting streets when necessary. East of the Wall lay a "no-man's-land," a death strip vigilantly patrolled by troops who shot those who tried to escape to the West. Having survived the city's destruction in World War II, Berliners now had to cope with a bitter division between two opposed social orders—a division that glared in physical, public terms. Today the Wall may be down, but cultural barriers are harder to erase.

let it happen to you. If you're in a hurry, it is possible to see Berlin's major attractions (*see below*) at a frenzied pace, but, if at all possible, slow down and enjoy one or two districts a day, or pick the handful of sights or neighborhoods that interest you most and leave the rest for another visit. Generally the S- and U-Bahn are useful for getting from one district to another, but not for transport from sight to sight within a district. Buses help in sprawling districts like Kreuzberg, but plan on a lot of walking.

Be warned that construction and consolidation mean museum collections are moving and changing, and buildings may close for renovation. Many of Berlin's museums belong to the **Staatliche Museen Preußischer Kulturbesitz (SMPK)** and most can be visited individually for DM 4 (DM 2 students), or with a one-day combination ticket for DM 8 (DM 4 students). Some major SMPK museums, like the Pergamon, require a DM 8 ticket.

For an overview (especially if you're in a hurry), consider a guided tour. For excellent tours entirely in English, try Berlin Walks (Harbig Str. 26, tel 030/301–9194). Itineraries include "Infamous Third Reich Sites" (Tues., Thurs., and Sat. at 10 AM), "Jewish Life in Berlin" (Wed. at 10 AM), and "Discover Berlin" (daily at 10 AM and 2:30 PM). The tours (DM 15, DM 12 under 26) meet by the taxi stand in front of Bahnhof Zoo; look for someone with a "Berlin Walks" badge. To see Berlin from the comfort of a cushy bus, hop on one of the popular tours offered by Stadtrundfahrtbüro Berlin (Europa-Center, near Bahnhof Zoo, tel. 030/261–2001). Buses leave daily from Europa-Center and cost DM 19–DM 29; for a few extra marks you can add on a boat ride or special request. Pick up a program at any tourist office. Your regular transit ticket or pass lets you take Bus 100 from Bahnhof Zoo to Alexanderplatz. On the way you'll pass sights like the Siegessäule, the Reichstag, Brandenburger Tor, and everything on Unter den Linden itself (*see* Mitte *in* Districts, *below*).

It's not Venice, but you can also see Berlin from its canals for around DM 11. The best company is Reederei Heinz Riedel (Planufer 78, tel. 030/693–4646). For a three-hour tour of the city (and the sites are worth it), take the DM 21 tour that leaves from Kottbusser Brücke in Kreuzberg (U-Bahn to Kottbusser Tor). Tours of the huge lakes west of the city are offered by Stern- und Kreisschiffahrt (tel. 030/536–3600), whose cruises through watery wilds cost DM 15–DM 25 and leave from Wannsee (S1, S3, or S7) or Alt-Tegel (S25 or U6).

MAJOR ATTRACTIONS

BRANDENBURGER TOR

If you watched the Berlin Wall crumble in 1989, you will certainly recognize the Brandenburger Tor (Brandenburg Gate), perhaps the most vivid symbol of German unification. On the night of November 9, 1989, after the first holes had been hammered in the Wall, thousands of Berliners from East and West embraced and staged an impromptu party under the gate. Today, the gate opens onto an open-air flea market, where sidewalk merchants peddle postcards and little chunks of the Wall (some wall, anyway). If you want to see an extant part of the *Mauer* (wall), head over to Friedrichshain (*see* Friedrichshain and Treptow *in* Districts, *below*).

The Brandenburg Gate, built in 1791 for King Friedrich Wilhelm II by architect Carl Gotthard Langhans, was once part of an older wall that encircled Berlin until 1861, when it was torn down because the city grew too big for it. The Brandenburger Tor was one of 14 other gates once part of this wall, some of them memorialized as names of U-Bahn stops, like Hallesches Tor, Kottbusser Tor, and Oranienburger Tor. The gate is topped by the **Quadriga,** a chariot drawn by four horses and driven by Irene, the goddess of peace. Ironically, the peace goddess was destroyed during World War II, but the original molds were discovered in West Berlin in 1957 and a new Quadriga was cast. The Gate is on the border between the Tiergarten and Mitte (*see* Districts, *below*). The most spectacular approach is from **Straße des 17. Juni,** a 2-km-long avenue that cuts through the Tiergarten's center. *Bus 100 from Bahnhof Zoo.*

CHECKPOINT CHARLIE

Between 1961 and 1989, Checkpoint Charlie (Kochstr. and Friedrichstr.) was the most (in)famous crossing point between East and West Berlin. You can still take a snapshot of the famous cold war–era sign posted at the checkpoint, reading: YOU ARE NOW LEAVING THE AMERICAN SECTOR. The checkpoint itself, a wooden guard hut, was removed shortly after the Wall came down in 1989. Remaining are a grim, skeletal watchtower and a somber memorial slab dedicated to those killed in escape attempts. Also remaining is a red-and-white cement barrier formerly used to guard against vehicles rushing the checkpoint—a favorite scenario in Hollywood spy movies.

Although the checkpoint has been dismantled, you can trace its history at the nearby **Haus am Checkpoint Charlie.** This small but packed museum has hundreds of cold war–era photographs, loads of provocative antifascist paintings and sculptures, and a fascinating exhibit on ingenious escape attempts. Look for the miniature submarine that safely brought one East German across the Spree, a "find-the-hidden-easterner" escape car, and photos of tunnels dug under the Wall during the 1970s. There are also short biographies of some of the East Germans killed during escape attempts (more than 100 people were killed, the last one in 1989 . . . three months before the Wall came down). The museum's gift desk sells numerous books about the Wall, many in English. *Friedrichstr. 43, tel. 030/253–7250. U6 to Kochstr. Admission: DM 8, DM 5 students. Open daily 9 AM–10 PM.*

DAHLEM MUSEUMS

Suburban Dahlem, 20 min by subway southwest of the city center, is a quiet enclave of tree-lined streets and sleepy pubs, and also home to the Freie Universität, one of Berlin's three universities. The neighborhood is best known for the Dahlem Museum Complex, made up of seven internationally acclaimed museums. The main complex, at Lansstraße and Arnimallee, is home to a world-class collection that could take at least two head-spinning days to see. Go slowly. If you get hungry, there's a café in the complex and Imbiß stands around the U-Bahn stop. *Lansstr. 8 and Arnimallee 23–27, tel. 030/830–1465. U2 to Dahlem-Dorf; right on Königin-Luise-Str., then a soft left on Iltisstr., and left on Lansstr. Admission: DM 4, DM 2 students; SMPK ticket accepted. Open Tues.–Fri. 10–6, weekends 11–6.*

The **Gemäldegalerie** on Arnimallee is home to Germany's foremost collection of 13th- through 18th-century European painting. The rooms dedicated to Dürer, Cranach, and Holbein are organized chronologically to show each painter's development. Other rooms are organized by region, including the Italian masters room, with a solid collection of works by Botticelli, Titian, Giotto, and Raphael; and the Dutch room, with works by van Eyck, Bosch, Breughel, and van Dyck. On the second floor is the huge collection of Rembrandt oil canvases.

On the same street is the **Museum für Spätantike und Byzantische Kunst** (Museum of Late-Ancient and Byzantine Art), with a sampling of Byzantine and European sculpture; most of the collection has been relocated to the Pergamon on Museumsinsel (*see below*). The **Skulpturensammlung** (Sculpture Collection) displays mostly medieval sculpture. Its best pieces are those from Italy, including Donatello's *Madonna and Child,* sculpted in 1422. The Holy Virgin may need a change-of-address form—much of this collection has relocated to the Bodemuseum, which is closed for construction until sometime in 2002.

On the Lansstraße side, the **Museum für Völkerkunde** has famous ethnographic holdings, including large sections on Asia, Africa, the Pacific Islands, and the Americas. Also on Lansstraße, the **Museum für Islamische Kunst** (Islamic Art Museum), the **Museum für Ostasiatische Kunst** (East Asian Art Museum), and the **Museum für Indische Kunst** (Indian Art Museum) together constitute the best collection of Asian art in Germany, notably the Turfan frescos, which illustrate Buddhist lore. Besides these major museums, there's the **Museum für Volkskunde** (Im Winkel 6–8), a folklore museum north across Königin-Luise-Straße. At press time this museum was closed for construction.

Also in Dahlem, but not part of the complex, the **Brücke-Museum** houses pre–World War I examples of Berlin's expressionist movement, including works by Erich Heckel and Ernst Kirchner. Although the Brücke is a 25-min walk from the Dahlem Complex (use your map), it's worth the trip. *Bussardsteig 9, tel. 030/831–2029. U-Bahn to Fehrbelliner Pl., then Bus 115 (direction: Potsdamer Chaussee or Neuruppiner Str.) to Pücklerstr.; right on Pücklerstr., left on Fohlenw., and right on Bussardsteig. Admission: DM 4.50, DM 3 students. Open Wed.–Mon. 11–5.*

KULTURFORUM

The task of unifying art collections divided since 1945, not to mention reduced Government subsidies, has forced Berlin's art world to cope with some consolidation. To solve the problem, the government has opted to shuffle much of Berlin's vast art collection into the already impressive Kulturforum, located near the Tiergarten. For general info, call 030/266–2666.

The Kulturforum's finest attraction is the **Neue Nationalgalerie,** housed in a delicate glass-and-steel structure designed by Bauhaus hero Mies van der Rohe in 1966. The upper floor houses rotating exhibits of mostly contemporary art. The ground-floor gallery is dedicated to 20th-century European and American work. Offerings here include expressionist masterworks by Grosz and Dix. A new collection includes 20th-century works formerly held by the Alte Nationalgalerie in eastern Berlin, from fawning socialist realism to the grim satire of 1970s "conflict painters." This collection illustrates problems specific to making art in an authoritarian society. An adjoining gallery houses works by Klee, Bacon, and Johns. *Potsdamer Str. 50, tel. 030/266–2651. U-Bahn to Wittenbergpl., then Bus 129 (direction: Herrmannpl.) to Potsdamer Brücke; the museum's across the bridge. Admission: DM 8, DM 4 students; SMPK ticket accepted. Open Tues.–Fri. 10–6, weekends 11–6.*

Directly across from the Neue Nationalgalerie is the **Staatsbibliothek** (Potsdamer Str. 33, tel. 030/2660; open weekdays 9–9, Sat. 9–5), known to the many students who practically live there as the Stabi, one of the largest public libraries in Europe, with more than four million volumes. The building itself, designed by Berlin architect Hans Scharoun, appeared in the Wim Wenders film *Der Himmel über Berlin* (*Wings of Desire*). Inside is a peaceful foyer stocked with English-language newspapers, and a cheap cafeteria filled with chain-smoking students. Diagonally across Potsdamer Straße is the impressive **Kunstgewerbemuseum** (Matthäikirchpl., tel. 030/266–2902; open Tues.–Fri. 10–6, weekends 11–6) with a collection of European arts and crafts. Exhibits range from the technical (the innards of antique clocks) to the purely decorative (handcrafted jewelry). In the basement there's a good collection of art deco and Bauhaus pieces. *Admission: DM 4, DM 2 students; SMPK ticket accepted.*

Also on Matthäikirchplatz, the **Kupferstichkabinett** (tel. 030/266–2002) features engravings and woodcuts from the 15th century through the present. The rotating exhibits may show charcoal sketches by Rembrandt, pen-and-ink studies by Dürer, sketches by Käthe Kollwitz, or works by contemporary artists. If you are a serious art freak, you can make an appointment to view items not currently on exhibit. The museum is housed next to the Philharmonie, Berlin's space-age concert hall designed by Scharoun, and admission is free.

MUSEUMSINSEL

Bordered on either side by the Spree, the **Museumsinsel** (Museum Island), one of the best museum complexes in Europe, is located in Mitte, a short walk north of Marx-Engels-Platz at the east end of Unter den Linden. As collections are shifted from Dahlem to the island, the complex will become even more impressive. The following museums cost DM 4 (DM 2 students) each, except the Pergamon, which costs DM 8 (DM 4 students). Combination tickets (DM 8, DM 4 students) entitle you to admission to all these and other SMPK museums for the day. All Museumsinsel museums are open Tuesday–Sunday 9–5. The Pergamonmuseum (*see below*) houses the main information center for the entire Museumsinsel.

The first museum you encounter as you walk north through the Lustgarten is the **Altes Museum** (Bodestr. 1–3, tel. 030/203550), worth a peek for its excellent rotating exhibits on various periods and themes in German art. The **Bodemuseum,** at the northern end of the island, is closed for renovations until sometime in 2002, and most of its holdings are temporarily on display at the **Ägyptisches Museum** (*see* Schloß Charlottenburg, *below*). **The Alte Nationalgalerie** (Bodestr. 1–3, tel. 030/209050) contains Berlin's largest collection of 18th- and 19th-century paintings. The museum is closed for construction but should open its doors again in 2001. Repetitive landscape and portrait work dominates the collection, but the French impressionist room (2nd floor, Room 14) includes pieces by Monet, Cézanne, and

Renoir; in the next room (Room 13), Arnold Böcklin's spooky *Toteninsel* (Death Island) is worth a stare. *S-Bahn to Hackescher Markt; exit left from station, under railway bridge onto Burgstr., then right across bridge onto Bodestr.*

With one of the world's best collections of Hellenic, Egyptian, and Mesopotamian art, the **Pergamonmuseum** falls directly into the don't-miss category. The museum is named for its principal display, the Pergamon Altar, a dazzling 2nd-century BC Greek temple that was moved block by block from a mountaintop in Turkey; today it stands as a monument to the 19th-century German archaeologists who ceaselessly roamed the world for plunder. Equally remarkable is the Babylonian Processional Highway and, in the Asia Minor section, the Ishtar Gate, both of which date from the 6th-century BC reign of Nebuchadnezzar II. *Am Kupfergraben, tel. 030/2090–5555. From Bodestraße, continue west across the canal, turn right on Am Kupfergraben, and right again over the footbridge. Open Tues.–Sun. 10–6. Admission: DM 8, DM 4 students; free admission on the first Sunday of each month.*

REICHSTAG

Just west of the Brandenburger Tor, the imposing *Reichstag* (Imperial Parliament) shines like the beacon of a unified, united Germany—replacing a Reichstag that was primarily the symbol of failed democracy. The interior of the redesigned building, the work of the British architect Sir Norman Foster, boasts a harmony of art, function, and ergonomics. Without doubt the main attraction is the parliament's roof, a stunning dome of steel and glass where visitors can walk up a spiral ramp to a 50-m-high viewing platform. From here the panorama of Berlin is breathtaking. The new government quarters isn't everybody's cup of tea, however: Some still long for the simplicity and warmth of the old Bundestag, which was originally a school gymnasium. Gone are the wooden lockers and plain furniture. In their place is the glitz and glamour of a steel and glass palace. Others like the modern touch, and still others complain it's hard to tell the difference between the Reichstag and a Hauptbahnhof. See it for yourself and decide.

Berlin's motto seems to be "If you build it, they will come." With this kind of massive public outlay in a time of national belt-tightening, they'd better.

The Reichstag's chronicle mirrors that of the German people like no other structure. The new home of the German Parliament, which moved here from Bonn in April 1999, was originally built in 1891 for the parliament of a fiercely nationalistic and expansionist empire. The Reichstag also represents the failure of Germany's first democracy: On February 28, 1933, as Germany struggled with a broken economy and the Weimar Republic's warring ideologies, the Reichstag was set ablaze under mysterious circumstances. The Nazis swiftly blamed the Communists (though the man accused was found innocent and evidence indicates that Nazis may actually have torched it themselves) and used the fire as a pretext for Hitler's appointment as chancellor and the suspension of the constitution. In May 1945, Soviet soldiers raised their flag above the Reichstag, signaling Germany's imminent surrender. *Pl. der Republik, tel. 030/2270. From Bahnhof Zoo, Bus 100 to front steps. Admission free.*

SCHLOß CHARLOTTENBURG

Prior to its incorporation into greater Berlin in 1920, Charlottenburg was one of Prussia's wealthiest cities—largely because King Friedrich I, the flamboyant Prussian monarch, took up residence here at the end of the 17th century. In 1695, at the request of his future queen, Sophie Charlotte, he renamed the area Charlottenburg (it was previously a village known as Lützow) and embarked on a massive building campaign. The showpiece was Schloß Charlottenburg, a lavish country palace graced by gardens and lakes. Friedrich II (a.k.a. Frederick the Great) was so enamored of the site that he commissioned a number of stately additions, including the gold-plated dome and rococo wings.

Over the centuries, the complex continued to evolve under the direction of each new ruler and is now representative of nearly every major stylistic trend ever to pass through Germany, including Baroque, rococo, and even Bauhaus. Entering the grounds on foot, you'll first notice the prim **Court of Honor** (dominated by an equestrian statue of Elector Joachim of Brandenburg, ancestor of the kings of Prussia) and the 52-m domed **tower** that marks the palace's main entrance. Inside, on the **ground floor** (separate admission DM 8, DM 4 students), are the lavish chambers of Friedrich and Sophie. Take the tour to see other highlights, such as the ground-floor **Oak Gallery,** with a solid collection of 18th- and 19th-century landscape paintings, and the **New Wing,** housing works by Dürer and the 19th-century master Caspar David Friedrich, one of the founders of Germany's Romantic movement.

Unfortunately, most of the palace can only be seen on a German-language guided tour. These leave every hour, on the hour, from 9 to 5. If the weather's good, spend some time exploring the large palace

RENAISSANCE OF JEWISH HISTORY

Reinvigorated by a huge influx of Jews from the former Soviet Union and energized by the vitality of a new generation, Jewish Berlin is larger and more vibrant than it has been in 50 years. The number of Jews in the city has almost doubled in the last decade to about 11,000, a lively presence that is reflected in a number of Jewish and Israeli restaurants and cafés, kosher grocery stores, and cultural events. Today Berlin boasts seven synogogues that offer services from Reform to rigorously Orthodox. The umbrella group for much of this activity is the Jewish Community of Berlin (Fasanenstr. 79–80, tel. 030/880280); another important congregation is that of Orthodox Adass Yisroel (Tucholskystr. 40). For more information, including contact info, about the history of the city and its Jewish spirit, leaf through the recent Goldapple Guide to Jewish Berlin, available in bookshops throughout the city or directly from the publisher (Goldapple Publishing, Eylauer Str. 3, tel. 030/785–1255). To meet with Berlin's Jewish community in a more social atmosphere, try one of the many new restaurants and bistros popping up around Berlin:

ARCHE NOAH. The ark is the perfect spot for old-fashioned kosher food. Fasanenstr. 79–80, tel. 030/882–6138.

CAFEUND RESTAURANT OREN. Go for the fish, pasta, and Middle Eastern specialties. Oranienburger Str. 28, tel. 030/282–8228.

RIMON RESTAURANT. Dig into latkes, gefilte fisch, and other Eastern European and Middle Eastern fare at this mid-priced, two-story restaurant in the new Jewish Communication Center. Oranienburger Str. 26, tel. 030/2838–4032.

SALAMON BAGELS. This bright, friendly snack bar serves up handmade bagels. Joachimstalerstr. 13, tel. 030/821–0404.

grounds. Along with the lake and shaded walking paths, check out the 18th-century **Belvedere House** (admission DM 3, DM 2 students) overlooking the river. Today it contains a reasonably priced tea shop. Just beyond this is the **Schinkel Pavillion** (admission DM 3, DM 2 students), housing paintings by Caspar David Friedrich and some fin-de-siècle furniture. Slightly farther on is the **Charlottenburg Mausoleum,** containing the tombs of King Wilhelm II and his wife, Queen Louise. *Schloß Charlottenburg: Luisenpl., tel. 030/320911. U-Bahn or S-Bahn to Bahnhof Zoo, then Bus 145 to Schloß Charlottenburg. Tour and admission to palace and grounds: DM 15, DM 10 students. Palace open Tues.–Fri. 9–5, weekends 10–5; grounds open daily sunrise–sunset.*

Just opposite the Schloß is Berlin's fabulous **Ägyptisches Museum** (Egyptian Museum), with the somewhat dubiously dated but *very* stunning bust of Nefertiti (thought to be 3,300 years old). *Schloßstr. 70,* *tel. 030/320911. Admission: DM 8, DM 4 students; SMPK ticket accepted. Open Tues.–Fri. 10–6, weekends 11–6.*

DISTRICTS

Twenty-three Bezirke make up the city of Berlin. Twelve belonged to West Berlin, 11 to East Berlin, and each has its own town hall and district council. Every district in Berlin offers something of interest, be it a massive Soviet war memorial or an impressive nighttime leather scene. The most intriguing districts are those in the historic center of Berlin, namely Prenzlauer Berg, Mitte, and Kreuzberg.

CHARLOTTENBURG

Charlottenburg is a huge and disparate expanse, stretching all the way from Tiergarten in the east almost to Tegel Airport in the north and the Ku'damm in the south. As such, exploring the area on foot is next to impossible. Instead, spend a day at the sprawling Schloß Charlottenburg and its museums (*see* Major Attractions, *above*), then concentrate on more central sights. While in Charlottenburg, don't miss the **Käthe Kollwitz Museum** (Fasanenstr. 24, near Zoo, tel. 030/882–5210), open Wednesday–Monday 11–6. Admission DM 8, DM 4 students. Best known for her moving sculptures depicting motherhood and lithographs on social issues, Kollwitz (1867–1945) won Prussia's highest art prize and is considered one of Germany's greatest artists. Her work was vetoed by both the Kaiser, who considered her proletarian subject matter "gutter art," and later by the Nazis, who didn't approve of the socialist and antiwar sentiments expressed in much of her art.

Berlin's lively Turkish community—the largest outside of Turkey—is centered in Kreuzberg. The atmosphere they've created keeps the neighborhood from getting too grim and gray.

KURFÜRSTENDAMM • The Kurfürstendamm, western Berlin's most famous thoroughfare, was built during the 16th century by Elector Joachim II of Brandenburg (Kurfürstendamm means "elector's causeway"—causeway because so much of Berlin was once sandy or muddy marshland) to connect his Berlin palace with his hunting lodge in Grunewald (*see* Parks and Gardens, *below*). In the 19th century, Chancellor Bismarck had it widened to give Berlin a stately avenue befitting Germany's growing power, something like Paris's Champs-Elysées. Nearly half of the Ku'damm's Bismarck-era buildings were flattened by Allied bombs and replaced by the gaudy cafés and ugly mid-rises you see today.

In its entirety, the Ku'damm stretches for 3½ km. Its liveliest section is just south of Bahnhof Zoo, near the Europa-Center. Here you'll find a sampling of Berlin's commercial side, from upscale boutiques to seedy sex shops. On **Breitscheidplatz,** immediately opposite Europa-Center, a crowd—evenly divided between middle-class Berliners, tourists (and the people who fleece them), and junkies—carouses and browses and souses at all hours of the day. This is probably the most amusing and gawk-worthy section of the Ku'damm, and if you don't hear someone singing "O Sole Mio," you'll probably see a demonstration to help the Kurds.

The Ku'damm's most famous landmark is the **Kaiser-Wilhelm-Gedächtniskirche,** opposite Europa-Center on Breitscheidplatz. The church remains in its war-scarred state as a memorial, and houses an exhibit of pre- and postwar photos that document the church's history. On one side of the neo-Romanesque bell tower stands a new glass-and-concrete chapel, designed by Edgar Eiermann. *Breitscheidpl. Admission free. Open Tues.–Sat. 10–4.*

SAVIGNYPLATZ • Savignyplatz and the surrounding neighborhood host a crowd of students and stylish professionals slacking off in cafés or vegetarian restaurants, plus more respectable types buying antiques. Savignyplatz's side streets are home to dozens of bars and cafés, and once the clubs open at night, the area can get quite lively. This is a good place to come for cheap food; try one of the Imbiß stands or bargain restaurants that surround the square. During the day Savignyplatz itself is pretty in a quiet sort of way, with benches under ivy-covered arches. The streets around it, including **Goethestraße, Kantstraße, Bleibtreustraße, Knesebeckstraße,** and **Grolmanstraße,** feature loads of bars, bookstores, and restaurants, as well as both upscale clothing shops and thrift stores. Although the area's bars are liveliest after dark, you'll find students, budding journalist types, and the fashion-conscious around at all hours.

SCHÖNEBERG

East of Charlottenburg lies the fun-loving district of Schöneberg, where residents enjoy the good life without too much pretension. Though the district is short on conventional "sights," it's a fun place to hang out and

BERLIN AT THE BARRICADES

Berliners have always had an uneasy relationship with their rulers. With the rest of Europe, Berliners called for democracy (and German unity) in 1848—barricades and all. When Otto von Bismarck orchestrated unification without democracy in 1871, Berliners largely supported the young Social Democratic Party, which was then banned by Bismarck. In 1918 Berlin was the focal point of the revolution that deposed the Hohenzollern Kaisers. And Berlin did not take to Hitler (the Nazis got only ⅓ of the vote here in 1933), who in turn certainly didn't like city that openly embraced everyone from cross-dressing queers to intellectual Jews. Today the May Day Riots (traditionally in Kreuzberg but increasingly in Prenzlauer Berg as well), when anarchists burst out of their squats and clash with police, carry on the Berlin tradition of resisting authority.

has a booming gay scene. At the heart of Schöneberg lies **Nollendorfplatz,** and the streets south and west of here feature the area's crowded markets, dusty bookshops, and lively bars and cafés. At the Nollendorfplatz U-Bahn station is a plaque dedicated to homosexuals murdered in Nazi concentration camps. (Gays in Nazi Germany were forced to wear the pink triangle and an estimated 100,000 were killed in camps.) Though the entire area is mixed, **Motzstraße,** which runs southwest from Nollendorf, is a center for gay nightlife. Walking along **Maaßenstraße** past cafés and shops, you reach **Winterfeldtplatz,** with its open-air market (*see* Food, *above*) and used bookstores, and the street life continues south down **Goltzstraße.**

KREUZBERG

Kreuzberg is one of Berlin's liveliest quarters, home to an odd mix of progressive youth, Turkish immigrants, yuppies, and blue-collar types. It's an excellent place for cheap dives and basement cafés. The district is divided into two distinct sections: more middle-class **west Kreuzberg,** which is most interesting along Gneisenaustraße and Bergmannstraße between Marheinekeplatz and Mehringdamm; and the wilder, scruffier **east Kreuzberg,** between Oranienplatz in the west and Spreewaldplatz or Schlesisches Tor in the east. For west Kreuzberg, take the U-Bahn to Mehringdamm or Gneisenaustraße. For east Kreuzberg, take the U-Bahn to Kottbusser Tor.

EAST KREUZBERG • East Kreuzberg has always harbored Berlin's downtrodden. This includes Turkish immigrants who moved here as *Gastarbeiter* (guest workers) during the '60s and '70s in search of factory work. It also includes radicals, draft dodgers, and others living cheaply in squats. As a result, the area has evolved into one of western Berlin's most offbeat quarters, which makes it the place to visit for an alternative take on the city. You'll see posters supporting Turkish revolutionaries, international record stores, Turkish bakeries, radical bookstores, and co-op art galleries. Not surprisingly, east Kreuzberg has a pretty wild nightlife. Women should be cautious about visiting this area alone at night; stick to the busier streets.

From Kottbusser Tor, make your way north on any of the small sidestreets. Soon you'll reach **Oranienstraße,** the district's main drag, loaded with bars and cafés. This street continues east of the Görlitzer Bahnhof U-Bahn stop as **Wiener Straße,** loaded day and night with small, hopping bars and Imbiß stands. North of here across Skalitzer Straße and west of the **Schlesisches Tor** U-Bahn station is a neighborhood undergoing gentrification, where working-class pubs are giving way to moderately upscale restaurants. A walk south from any of these U-Bahn stations brings you to the Landwehrkanal (where the police disposed of the revolutionary Rosa Luxemburg's body after murdering her). Walk along its banks to find quiet parks, *Kneipen* (bars), and ivy-covered cafés.

WEST KREUZBERG • While east Kreuzberg has the best clubs and dive bars and the best streets for rambling walks, west Kreuzberg has a mellower feel, with lots of restaurants and cafés. The tree-lined streets and inviting squares of west Kreuzberg are cozily shared by vegetarian student types, old men playing chess, and once-radical baby boomers whose interests have shifted from revolution to karma and cabernet.

West Kreuzberg runs from Checkpoint Charlie in the north to Viktoriapark and Tempelhof Airport in the south. The northern part is generally a bore, but near Checkpoint Charlie look for the impressive **Martin-Gropius-Bau** (Stresemannstr. 110, tel. 030/254860), built in 1822 by Martin Gropius, uncle to Bauhaus founder Walter Gropius. At press time the building was closed for construction. Behind the Martin-Gropius-Bau is the excellent **Topographie des Terrors** (Stresemannstr. 110, tel. 030/2548–6703; admission free, open daily 10–8), an outdoor museum on the site of the former Gestapo, S.S., and S.A. headquarters. They give you a free booklet (there's one in English) explaining the history of the site—sobering, to say the least. To reach either, take the S-Bahn to Anhalter Bahnhof and walk up Stresemannstraße; or take the U6 to Kochstraße and walk two blocks west.

Kreuzberg, which literally means "cross hill," is named after the hilltop iron cross designed by Schinkel; a memorial to those who died in the Napoleonic Wars, it is enveloped by peaceful **Viktoriapark.** There's a good view of sprawling central Berlin from the top. This shady hill is bordered by cafés and a few decent restaurants; it's a good place to come on a clear night when **Golgotha,** an outdoor disco, rocks the hill. It's also the site of occasional Sunday afternoon food and music festivals (keep your eyes and ears open). **Mehringdamm,** to the east of the park, is a well-kept shopping street. Running east from Mehringdamm are **Gneisenaustraße** and **Bergmannstraße,** both home to some of the city's best cafés, bars, restaurants, and thrift shops.

From Kreuzberg Hill, look out over Tempelhof Airport. At the height of the Berlin Airlift in 1948, Allied planes landed here every minute with desperately needed supplies for blockaded West Berlin.

The new **Jüdisches Museum** (Jewish Museum) is expected to open its first permanent exhibit of documents and art in October 2000. Housed within architect Daniel Liebeskind's jagged new building, the pedagogic exhibit will illustrate the history of German-speaking Jews from Roman times to the present, with a focus on the relationship between German Jews and non-Jews. If you're here before October 2000, call 030/2839–7444 to join a 90-min guided tour (DM 8; English tours Sat. 1:30 and Sun. 11:30). *Lindenstr. 14, tel. 030/2599–3410. U6, U15 to Hallesches Tor.*

TIERGARTEN

The Tiergarten extends from the Brandenburger Tor in the east to Bahnhof Zoo in the west—a peaceful expanse of forest and lake smack in the middle of urban Berlin. Rising above it is the **Siegessäule** (Victory Column), built between 1865 and 1873 to celebrate Prussia's military might. A long, 285-step climb leads to the **observation deck** (admission DM 2, DM 1 students; open Mon. 1–6, Tues.–Sun. 9–6) atop the 70-m-tall monument. It's worth a quick look, but don't go out of your way to get here.

South of the column, just outside the park, is the **Bauhaus-Archiv** (Klingelhöferstr. 14, tel. 030/254–0020; open Wed.–Mon. 10–5), in a structure designed by Walter Gropius. It features his designs and models along with those of Mies von der Rohe and works by the likes of Paul Klee, Laszlo Moholy-Nagy, and Wassily Kandinsky. All exhibits date from the Berlin workshop days, 1919–1933. Admission is DM 5 (DM 2.50 students), and the museum is a short walk north of the Nollendorfplatz U-Bahn stop. East of here, the **Haus der Kulturen der Welt** (House of World Cultures; John-Foster-Dulles-Allee 10, tel. 030/397870), in an odd building dubbed "the pregnant oyster" by Berliners, offers diverse treats, including anything from Tanzanian sculpture to Klezmer concerts to workshops by Indian flutists; check listings for evening performances. The building is open Tuesday–Sunday noon–8, and daytime admission is free. Take Bus 100 to Kongreßhalle.

Don't leave the Tiergarten without visiting Berlin's tremendous zoo, the **Zoologischer Garten** (*see* Parks and Gardens, *below*), and the Brandenburger Tor (*see* Major Attractions, *above*). Following the southeastern edge of the Tiergarten funnels you into **Potsdamer Platz,** the busiest intersection in Europe and the heart of Berlin during the 1920s. Following World War II, which reduced it to rubble, it became a deserted patch of no-man's-land along the Berlin Wall. Today, building cranes are hard at work creating the new corporate headquarters of multinational and local firms. Already settled in are the headquarters of Daimler-Benz, and Sony's offices are scheduled for completion in 2001.

JUST WHERE IS PRUSSIA, ANYWAY?

Okay, so Berlin was once the capital of Prussia. But where is Prussia, you ask? Originally the name referred to a Baltic coast region conquered by Germans in the Middle Ages and divided between Poland and Russia after World War II, when its name disappeared from the map. The Hohenzollern dynasty—the Electors of Brandenburg—who ruled Berlin and the surrounding region, married their way into control of Prussia in the 17th century. Elector Friedrich decided around 1700 that he was too important for a piddling title like elector—he wanted to be KING. But Brandenburg was part of the Holy Roman Empire, and Fred's archrivals, the Hapsburg emperors, refused to designate Brandenburg a kingdom. Since Prussia was outside the Empire, Fred named himself King Friedrich I of Prussia, and from then on the name referred to the entire area ruled by the Hohenzollerns from their capital in Berlin.

MITTE

Mitte (Center) is Berlin's old core, the Prussian royal capital, and, more recently, the seat of the GDR's government. The most important sights are in the 3-km stretch between the Brandenburger Tor and Alexanderplatz, on or near **Unter den Linden** (the haughty, stolid Prussian promenade). Along the way, you'll pass the Museumsinsel (*see* Major Attractions, *above*). To the north, the **Scheunenviertel** houses infamous squats, avant-garde cultural centers, and the scant remains of Berlin's sizable prewar Jewish community.

At night Mitte embraces the "Entertain me *now*" attitude of former Mitte residents like Bertolt Brecht and cabaret-star/bisexual-heroine Anita Berber, a kind of scandalous 1920s prototype for Madonna who danced naked and attended every major sporting event with a coterie of hoodlums. Today's Mitte offers everything from 20th-century opera in bombed-out department stores to cooperative bars with tiny dance floors. If you're not up for the scene, there are as many mellow *Kneipen* (pubs) in Mitte as anywhere else. For info on the joys Mitte has to offer, grab some flyers and the magazine *Auf Einen Blick* at **Kulturhaus Mitte** (Rosenthaler Str. 51, near Hackescher Markt S-Bahn stop, tel. 030/282–7393). Despite modest resources, the Kulturhaus runs two galleries, publishes the magazine, and sponsors local shows. Just east of the Oranienburger Tor U-Bahn stop is a weekend **flea market** (cnr of Oranienburger Str. and Auguststr.) surrounded by Imbiß stands and bars.

UNTER DEN LINDEN • This shop-jammed, 1½-km-long thoroughfare is something like a snobby cousin of Rodeo Drive, while the Ku'damm is akin to the Sunset Strip. It stretches from Brandenburg Gate in the west to Marx-Engels-Platz in the east. On it you'll find fin-de-siècle mansions and embassies—the sort of imperial architecture that gives eastern Berlin its stately, majestic feel.

Around 1700, Friedrich I designed the thoroughfare as a centerpiece for the new capital, establishing a modern geometric grid more appropriate for powerful Prussia than medieval Berlin across the Spree. Soon after, palaces began to appear along the promenade, and in the 1760s Friedrich II (the Great) decided to build an opera house, a library, and a second palace nearby. By the 20th century Unter den Linden had become Berlin's most famous boulevard, with all the best clubs, dance halls, cafés, and whorehouses. It was the city's social and cultural focus, embodying all that Germany could offer. Ravaged by the war and sealed off from its affluent clientele by the Berlin Wall, the boulevard declined under Communist rule. In the years since unification, it's had a dramatic revival.

The best way to appreciate Unter den Linden is on foot, roughly a two-hour undertaking. For bipeds, the traditional starting point is **Pariser Platz** (Bus 100 or S-Bahn to Unter den Linden), just east of Brandenburger Tor. Continuing east, you'll pass a collection of bulky, worn buildings that once housed GDR ministries. The Russian embassy is recognizable by its tricolor flag and the bust of Lenin, now somewhat pathetically concealed in a handmade wooden box, leftover from the days when it was the Soviet embassy. Farther east is the **Altes Palais,** former abode of Kaiser Wilhelm I. Across from the palace, in the middle of the street, is an equestrian statue (1851) of Friedrich II (Frederick the Great). The sculptor, Rauch, took a few liberties by incorporating the heads of Gotthold Lessing and Immanuel Kant, two of the emperor's harshest critics, on the horse's rear end, right below the tail. Continuing past the horse, you'll reach **Humboldt University,** originally built in the 18th century as a palace for Friedrich II's brother, and recognizable by the statues of Wilhelm and Alexander von Humboldt, the university's founders. Humboldt's students and faculty have included Marx, Engels, Hegel, Einstein, the brothers Grimm, and Max Planck. Adjacent to Humboldt U is the neoclassical **Neue Wache** (New Guardhouse), designed by Schinkel as a war memorial. Its stately Roman columns were restored by the GDR and rededicated in 1960 as the Memorial for Victims of Fascism and Militarism, guarded by goose-stepping GDR soldiers. Inside is the poignant Käthe Kollwitz statue, *Mother with Dead Son,* and outside is a plaque with a more recent rededication to the "Victims of War and Authoritarianism," controversial for its shift of focus away from fascism. The moving passage is translated and well worth reading.

Tiergarten's Straße des 17. Juni commemorates an East German workers' revolt on June 17, 1955. The GDR ("the farmers' and workers' state"), with Soviet help, suppressed the workers and killed at least 350.

If you crave still more German history, zip over to the **Deutsches Historisches Museum** next door at the **Zeughaus,** built in 1706. Once the armory, reflecting the military glory of Prussia, the Zeughaus now houses a quirky permanent collection (including Panzer tanks, Bismarck's cane, and one of Karl Marx's flower vases), as well as an art gallery and a movie house (tickets DM 5) that shows history flicks. The gallery's rotating exhibits are generally fantastic. *Unter den Linden 2, tel. 030/203040. S-Bahn or U-Bahn to Friedrichstr. Admission free. Open Thurs.–Tues. 10–6.*

The plaza just southeast of the university is known as **Bebelplatz,** a pleasant square bordered by linden trees. Bebelplatz was the site of the 1933 *Bücherverbrennung* (book burning) orchestrated by Hitler. Thrown into the fire were works considered too "dangerous" for public consumption; banned authors included Thomas Mann, Hegel, Benjamin Franklin, and Dostoevsky. On the square's east side is Berlin's main opera house, the **Deutsche Staatsoper** (Unter den Linden 7, tel. 030/2035–4555); stop by the box office (open weekdays 10–6) for a schedule. The current structure was built in the 1840s in a neoclassical style by Karl Langhans. The lush interior is famed for its period decor and ceiling murals and is definitely worth a peek. If you can't convince someone to let you in during the day (a smile and an obvious camera may help), you can get opera tickets for less than DM 30.

Following Unter den Linden across Schinkel's statue-festooned Schloßbrücke (Palace Bridge) brings you to **Marx-Engels-Platz,** the former site of the 15th-century Berliner Schloß (Berlin Palace), headquarters of the Prussian kings and German Kaisers. The Schloß was bombed by the Allies and finished off by the GDR in the 1950s, with the **Palast der Republik** as a replacement. This '70s, futuristic, copper-tinted space capsule, known by locals as Palazzo Prozzo (Show-off Palace), housed the GDR's Peoples' Chamber. Today it's fenced off and condemned (ostensibly because of asbestos, though buildings with comparable amounts of asbestos remain open), but remains untouched because some people believe it is now historic and worthy of preservation. Others want to demolish it and rebuild the Berliner Schloß in a return to royalist fantasyland. Think about that while touring the **Schloß-Museum** (Marx-Engels-Pl. 1; admission DM 9, DM 3 students; open daily 9–9).

Just north of the Palast der Republik, facing the leafy Lustgarten, is the flamboyant 19th-century **Berliner Dom,** one of Berlin's most impressive churches mainly for its gaudy, over-the-top feel—par for the course under the reign of pompous Kaiser Wilhelm II. Part of the structure was destroyed in the war, but recent renovations have restored it, particularly the vaulted nave and mosaic-covered dome. To get a better view, climb up to the second-story balcony via a set of ornately carved stairs. *Marx-Engels-Pl., tel. 030/202090. S-Bahn to Hackescher Markt. Admission: DM 5, DM 3 students. Open daily 9–7.*

GENDARMENMARKT • Formerly known as Platz der Akademie, this graceful square southwest of Bebelplatz, perhaps the loveliest in the city, is home to a trio of stately historical buildings: the Deutscher Dom, the Schauspielhaus, and the Französischer Dom. The 18th-century **Deutscher Dom** (admission

THE POOR MAN'S RENAISSANCE

The Scheunenviertel—the fringes of the Spandauer Vorstadt (the area in and around the Auguststr.)—sparkles with a new energy as run-down tenements and the remnants of a poorer past are being revitalized or razed. Cafés and art shows are benefiting from the boost, and the recent building activity has even brought on a renaissance for some old-fashioned survivors—including Berlin's oldest dance hall, which dates back to 1913. Yet the old character of the Scheunenviertel—a traditional center of avant-garde art and the heart of the Jewish community—is also fading as gentrification transforms the low-rent quarter into a high-rent yuppie haven. Go see the following art houses and galleries while the artists and curators can still afford them: Jochen Hemple (Dogenhaus Galerie, Auguststr. 63), Friedrich Loock (Galerie Wohnmaschine, Auguststr. 34–36), and Gerd Harry Lybke (Galerie Eigen & Art, Auguststr. 26). U6 to Oranienburger Tor, head up Oranienburger Straße, and veer left onto Auguststr.

free; open Tues.–Sun. 10–6, in summer until 7) is recognized by its broad steps and massive cupola. Inside is a plaque dedicated to the church's Lutheran founders, and a small but colorful cycle of stained glass. On the opposite side of the square, beyond the statue of Friedrich von Schiller, is the neoclassical **Schauspielhaus,** one of the greatest works by Berlin architect Karl Schinkel. Completing the trio is the **Französischer Dom,** one block north. It was built in 1708 by French Protestant Huguenots fleeing persecution, and its design is based on the Huguenots' original cathedral in Charenton, France. Inside is the Huguenot museum (admission DM 3, DM 2 students; open Wed.–Sat. 12–5, Sun. 11–5). *Gendarmenmarkt. U-Bahn to Stadtmitte or Französische Str.*

A short walk east, the **Schinkel-Museum** is in the Friedrichswerdersche Kirche, also designed by Karl Schinkel, the guy who seemingly built Berlin all by himself. Inside is a permanent show dedicated to his life and work. *Werderscher Markt, tel. 030/208–1323. U2 to Hausvogteipl. Admission: DM 4, DM 2 students; free Sun. Open Tues.–Sun. 10–6.*

NORTH MITTE • If you walk north up Friedrichstraße from the Friedrichstraße S- or U-Bahn station toward Oranienburger Tor, you'll notice new stores and snazzed-up hotels. Continue north on Friedrichstraße (which becomes Chausseestraße) for the **Brecht-Weigel-Gedenkstätte** (Chausseestr. 125, tel. 030/282–9916; U-Bahn to Oranienburger Tor), where Brecht and his wife and partner Helene Weigel worked and lived. Tours are given in German every half hour, Tuesday–Friday 10 AM–11:30 AM (also Thurs. 5 PM–6:30 PM) and Saturday 9:30–1:30. Admission is DM 4, DM 2 students. Next door is the **Städtischer Kirchhof,** the cemetery where Brecht and Weigel are buried along with such luminaries as Schinkel and Hegel.

SCHEUNENVIERTEL • Traditionally both a Jewish neighborhood and a stronghold of Berlin's underworld, the Scheunenviertel section of Mitte is still a good neighborhood for "alternative" cafés and cultural centers. Although there are few Jews left in the Scheunenviertel, it developed a reputation as the shtetl of Berlin during the late 19th century, when thousands of Eastern European Jews sought refuge here from pogroms. By 1942 the neighborhood's Jews had been deported; most were killed. Today the quarter is vibrantly artistic, with many galleries and cafés and some very creative talent on display (*see box,* The Poor Man's Renaissance, *above*).

Take the S-Bahn to Hackescher Markt and walk north along Rosenthaler Straße. From here, head left up Sophienstraße, a beautifully restored street housing the serene 18th-century **Sophienkirche** and the interesting **Heimatmuseum Mitte.** The museum's collection on the history of the neighborhood is good, but the real draws are the temporary exhibitions on topics such as "Kneipen, Beer, and Politics." *Sophienstr. 23, tel. 030/282–0376. Admission free. Open Mon.–Thurs. 10–noon and 1–5, Sun. 1–6.*

At the heart of today's modest Jewish community is the synagogue for Congregation Addass Jisroel (Tucholskystr. 40) and a neighboring kosher café—just head west on Auguststraße and turn onto Tucholskystraße. For a glimpse of vibrant, prewar Jewish Berlin, check out the huge, mosquelike **Neue Synagoge.** The original building was torched in the pogrom of Kristallnacht in 1938 and flattened by bombs in 1943. Today the reconstructed synagogue houses a **gallery** (tel. 030/2840–1250; open Mon.–Thurs. 10–6, Fri. 10–2) and a **library** (open Mon.–Thurs. 10–4). Next door, hepcat Jews and goyim converge at **Café Oren,** a gallery/café/hip-hop dance hall. *Neue Synagoge: Oranienburger Str. 28–30, tel. 030/2840–1250. Info desk open Mon.–Thurs. 10–6, Fri. 10–2.*

NIKOLAIVIERTEL • The Nikolaiviertel is bordered by Alexanderplatz to the north and the Spree River to the south. Much of the neighborhood was reduced to rubble during World War II, but for a change the GDR boldly attempted to re-create Nikolaiviertel's prewar appearance, including exact replicas of the quarter's famous historical buildings. Modern Nikolaiviertel does indeed feel like the old and refined "heart of Berlin," dominated by Baroque facades. Although you can often detect that it's a reproduction (e.g., columns are cement rather than marble), for the most part the quarter really does look as if it's stuck in the 19th century. Nikolaiviertel starts at Spandauer Straße; from Alexanderplatz, walk south down Rathausstraße, past tourist shops, swank modern restaurants, and the brick *Rathaus* (city hall). Turn left on Spandauer Straße for the quarter's four main alleys, each packed with taverns, cafés, and sidewalk food stands. To reach the area by U-Bahn, take the U2 to Klosterstraße, then head west.

The Mitte you see got its feel during the early 19th century. Von Humboldt founded the university in 1809, and by 1815, Karl Schinkel was redesigning the area in the neoclassical style that survives today.

The district is dominated by **Nikolaikirche** (tel. 030/238–0900; admission DM 3, DM 1 students), the oldest building in Berlin (1230). Be sure to stay a while to hear the unique play of 41 bells. Opposite the church is the **Knoblauch-Haus** (Poststr. 23, tel. 030/240020; admission DM 4, DM 2 students, Wed. free), a detailed replica of a 17th-century merchant house. The museum inside traces the life of Christian Knoblauch, a wealthy silk merchant who lived here. The Haus is open Tuesday–Sunday 10–6. **Zum Nußbaum,** across from Nikolaikirche at the corner of Propststraße, is a re-creation of Berlin's oldest inn. It still serves a hearty tankard of beer (DM 5) along with pricey German meals.

A stone's throw south is Berlin's most lavish rococo house, the **Ephraim-Palais,** originally built in 1766 for Veitel Ephraim, court jeweler to Friedrich II. Because Veitel was Jewish, the Nazis razed the structure and plundered its collection of rare stones in 1933. Fortunately, pieces of the original rococo facade were discovered in West Berlin after the war and later incorporated into the reconstruction you see today. Inside is a privately owned art gallery and a small, posh restaurant. *Poststr. 16, tel. 030/240020. Admission: DM 5, DM 2.50 students, Wed. free. Open Tues.–Sun. 10–6.*

ALEXANDERPLATZ • Alexanderplatz is *echt* (genuine) eastern Berlin in transition. Bright neon lights and murals exist alongside the peeling paint of dull GDR-era buildings. Dominating the square, the hard-to-believe **Fernsehturm** (television tower) is a good reference point if you get lost, but, aesthetically speaking, it's a freak show—a blend of cement, gaudy gold-plating, and poor taste. But that's Alex in a nutshell: a rich history and not much to show for it, except perhaps immortalization in Alfred Döblin's novel, *Berlin Alexanderplatz* (not to mention Rainer Fassbinder's majestic 15½-hour screen adaptation).

Revolutionaries have congregated here en masse since the square's beginning, occupying official buildings, demonstrating, and doing all the things that revolutionaries like to do. Since 1989, it's become the domain of street musicians from all over, as well as small markets and Imbiß stands. Grab a Wurst and a beer and walk southwest past the tower toward Spandauer Straße and the 13th-century brick **Marienkirche,** miraculously undamaged by World War II bombing. Step in for a quiet moment, a free organ concert (daily 3:30–4), or a look at the 18th-century carved pulpit and the excellent late-Gothic *Totentanz* fresco, in which Death democratically dances with everyone from peasant to king. Outside the church, to your left, is the immense **Rotes Rathaus** (Red City Hall), built in the 1860s as the seat of Berlin's *Oberbürgermeister* (mayor). Partly destroyed in World War II, it was rebuilt from 1951 to 1956, and since 1990 has resumed its role as the seat of the head of state. To the right of the Rathaus is an out-of-control fountain of Neptune and his foxy courtiers, and slightly south is the **Marx-Engels Forum,** featuring statues of the two troublemakers looking grimly into the future of socialism. Also check out the nearby graffiti-covered columns honoring communists.

On the opposite side of Alex are two stylish prewar buildings, **Alexander-Haus** and **Berolina-Haus,** designed in the 1930s by Peter Behrens, an early modernist who employed the young Walter Gropius and Mies van der Rohe, founders of the Bauhaus movement. While everything else on Alex was flattened during World War II, these two buildings somehow survived. At the opposite end of the square, near Karl-Liebknecht-Straße, is the **Berliner Markthalle,** an informal produce market. If you can bear the cheesiness, have a surprisingly tasty microbrew in **Alexanderbräu.**

FRIEDRICHSHAIN AND TREPTOW

Friedrichshain is a gritty working-class residential neighborhood without many sights other than some of the best-preserved remnants of the Berlin Wall remaining in the city—namely a km-long section along the river, across from Kreuzberg. The **East Side Gallery** lines the Spree along Mühlenstraße. The art here is on the Wall's east side and dates from 1990, just after the border opened. Until then, the east side of the Wall, guarded by the death strip, remained grafitti-free. Unfortunately, most of the art is now crumbling, and no one knows if it would be better to restore it or let it decay. From the Hauptbahnhof, walk southwest on Straße der Pariser Kommune to Mühlenstraße. Look to your left. Admission is free and it's always open.

If you have a bit more time and are nostalgic for the Stalinist architecture of yore, head over to Treptower Park's humongous **Sowjetisches Ehrenmal** (Soviet War Memorial). Although 5,000 of the 300,000 Red Army soldiers killed in the Battle of Berlin lie here, the future of this memorial is uncertain—see it while you can. There's a giant statue of a victorious Soviet soldier (he's holding a baby and smashing a swastika), a mosaic of a Russian funeral procession, and frescoes with scenes from the Battle of Berlin. *Pushkin Allee. S-Bahn to Treptower Park. Open daily 10–7.*

PRENZLAUER BERG AND WEISSENSEE

Prenzlauer Berg is noted for its working-class history, for the squatters and East German artists who made their homes here, and, in contemporary terms, for being a focus of unified Berlin's counterculture. Weißensee, just east of Prenzlauer Berg, is more staid and middle class; its main point of interest is its vast Jewish cemetery. Though Prenzlauer Berg was a part of the GDR, you won't find bland apartment blocks here, but rather 19th-century neo-baroque tenements that are elegant in a dilapidated sort of way. One by one they are being beautifully restored, and bullet-scarred, crumbling facades are often right next to brightly colored, solid-looking contemporaries. The contrast is fabulous. Throughout Prenzlauer Berg you can still see 1920s advertisements painted on faded walls, some of which are still pockmarked by shrapnel from the war. Fringe dwellers now share the neighborhood with chic shops and restaurants, and political intrigue has been replaced with artistic energy and hedonism. Head to one of the district's mellow cafés, most of which don't have that swank art-deco feel that plagues cafés and bars elsewhere in Berlin. Once you're caffeinated, search out a no-name disco or a basement bar, one of the short-lived, bacchanalian places that make Prenzlberg the hub of Berlin's offbeat nightlife.

The best way to reach Prenzlauer Berg is by subway: Take the U2 to Senefelderplatz or Eberswalder Straße, both of which empty onto the district's main western artery, **Schönhauser Allee,** a shopping street lined with grand prewar buildings. From Senefelderplatz, head east across the grassy patch behind the tenements and left on Kollwitzstraße to reach the graceful **Kollwitzplatz,** named for the famous artist born only a few blocks away (*see* Charlottenburg, *above*). At the square's center is a prim, Parisian-style park, which is sometimes trashed in the May Day riots (*see box,* Berlin at the Barricades, *above*); in it stands Kollwitz's sculpture *Die Mutter* (*The Mother*).

Leading north from Kollwitzplatz is one of eastern Berlin's most remarkable streets, **Husemannstraße.** Following the war, poverty forced many landlords to neglect their once stately 19th-century buildings, sometimes even to abandon them to the government. In 1986 the GDR decided it was time to beautify; it commissioned a troop of workers to restore the buildings, creating a glorious street scene from turn-of-the-century Berlin, including wrought-iron street lamps, a tobacco shop, and old-time bars. Two excellent free museums also lie on Husemannstraße. The first is the odd **Friseurmuseum** (Husemannstr. 8), ostensibly the world's first and only hairdressing museum. Inside are replicas of turn-of-the-century barber shops, a display of early safety razors, and snippets of hair from Goethe and Bismarck. Two doors down is the **Museum Berliner Arbeiterleben um 1900** (Husemannstr. 14, tel. 030/448–5675; open Tues.–Sat. 10–5, Fri. 10–3), documenting working-class Berlin from 1870 to

1910. Exhibits include photos, period furniture and clothing, and faded ads and magazines. Take a right on Sredzkistraße and another on Rykestraße and you'll pass **Friedenstempel,** a synagogue whose 24-hour guard belies its name (Temple of Peace). Continue to Knaackstraße and, past Kollwitzplatz at its intersection with Dimitroffstraße, take a break at the **Kulturbrauerei** (tel. 030/443–9382), an old brewery turned gallery and performance space. Any street off Danziger (in particular Pappelallee and Lychener Straße) will take you north to more cafés, bars, and record stores.

One way to grasp the enormity of the annihilation of Berlin's Jews is to visit the city's main 20th-century **Jüdischer Friedhof** (Jewish Cemetery). While only a tiny Jewish community inhabits present-day Berlin, the cemetery is vast, as Berlin's Jewish population once was. If you spend time here wandering among the hundreds of thousands of graves, you will probably get lost, and you will certainly be shocked by the scale of the human loss. Many people murdered in concentration camps are buried here, and the dates and epitaphs are a moving testimony to the crimes the Nazis committed. *Herbert-Baum-Str., no phone. S-Bahn to Hackescher Markt, then Tram 2, 3, or 4 to Pistoriusstr; backtrack 1 block on Berliner Allee, then left on Herbert-Baum-Str. for 4 blocks. Admission free but donation requested. Open Tues.–Sun. 8–5.*

PARKS AND GARDENS

Berlin has dozens of parkland escapes. In fact, more than 30% of Berlin is covered by woodland and public parks. The most accessible is the centrally located **Tiergarten** (*see* Districts, *above*), particularly the tree-lined area just east of Bahnhof Zoo that contains Berlin's zoo and dozens of lakeside trails. On the western edge of town is the vast **Grunewald,** complemented in eastern Berlin by the state forest surrounding **Großer Müggelsee.** A visit to these last two parks may require advance planning because of their remoteness. You can obtain trail maps at a tourist office, or use the detailed ViBB map (*see box,* Get a Life: Get a Map, *above*).

GRUNEWALD

This is western Berlin's most popular weekend retreat, a 32-sq-km expanse of horse trails, bike paths, beaches, and trees, trees, trees. The Havel River and Großer Wannsee lake entice thousands of swimmers and sun worshipers on warm days. **Großer Wannsee** is especially popular for its long stretch of powdery beach: With sand imported from the Baltic, it's known in Berlin as "the poor man's Riviera." Take the S-Bahn to Nikolassee and follow the STRANDBAD WANNSEE signs. If you're in the mood to walk, follow the signs to **Jagdschloß Grunewald** (Hüttenw. 100, tel. 030/813–3597; open weekends 10–4), a 16th-century royal hunting lodge on the Grunewaldsee that now houses a privately owned (and boring) art gallery. Another popular excursion is to **Pfaueninsel** (Peacock Island), set in a wide arm of the Havel River. The island is noted for its lush gardens—home to hundreds of wild peacocks—and the white marble faux-ruin, **Schloß Pfaueninsel** (tel. 030/805–3042; admission DM 2, DM 1 students). The island is about the only place in Berlin that doesn't allow cars, dogs, or smoking. From the Wannsee S-Bahn, take Bus 216 or 316 to the ferry. In the park's northeastern corner, the top of the **Teufelsberg** is green and breezy, with excellent views and even kite flying. The highest point in the city, this hill is actually a mound of rubble cleared from Berlin after World War II.

ZOOLOGISCHER GARTEN

Berlin's zoo is located at the southwest corner of the Tiergarten, a two-min walk from Bahnhof Zoo. Founded in 1841, the zoo boasts the world's largest variety of animals—more than 11,000 cuddly, noisy, slimy creatures representing some 1,600 different species. The fact that World War II left fewer than 100 animals alive makes the zoo's accomplishments even more amazing. You'll need a full day to cover the expanse in detail. Don't miss the cats, caged very close to the walkway (notice their lip-licking as you pass). It's also worth the extra money to check out the massive aquarium complex. Most signs are in German, so pick up a free English-language guidebook when you enter. *Entrances at Hardenbergpl. and Budapester Str., tel. 030/254010. Zoo admission: DM 13, DM 6.50 students. Combined aquarium and zoo admission: DM 21, DM 14 students. Open daily 9–5.*

CHEAP THRILLS

The city itself is the greatest cheap thrill around. Just wandering the neighborhoods you'll find loads of interesting people to watch from a shady park bench or over a slow cup of coffee. If you go for street performers—from unicycle-riding knife jugglers to one-man guitar, harmonica, and drum bands—try the busiest tourist spots like the Ku'damm's **Breitscheidplatz, Tauentzienstraße,** or the large square surrounding the **Brandenburger Tor.** The latter hosts a daily flea market where people gather to hawk junky antiques, tacky postcards, communist memorabilia, and mostly fake pieces of the Wall. Or head to Mitte's **Oranienburger Straße,** for impromptu art galleries and no-name bars filled with artsy dropouts seeking a remedy for urban ennui. Many of these venues—and most of the "art"—have grown out of what used to be vacant, trash-filled lots. On weekends jazz and blues musicians often play informal gigs along the avenue.

The city's countless markets—like those on **Winterfeldtplatz** and Kreuzberg's **Türkenmarkt** (*see* Food, *above*)—are entertaining and, if you restrain yourself, cheap. For a lively glimpse of working-class Berlin, check out the weekend market on **Gustav-Meyer-Allee** in Wedding. Take the S-Bahn or U-Bahn to Gesundbrunnen, then walk south over the bridge and along the edge of Humboldthain park. The park itself, with a fragrant rose garden and a hill with a view, is a nice hangout, as are Berlin's many other parks (*see* Parks and Gardens, *above*). On sunny days, escape to one of Berlin's many free lakeside beaches, with your swimsuit or without.

FESTIVALS

A complete list of Berlin festivals would fill a book larger than the one you're holding. For details, ask at the tourist office in Europa-Center (*see* Visitor Information *in* Basics, *above*). Periodicals like *Zitty, Tip,* and *Berlin Programm* also have major festival listings, as does the hefty German-language publication *Multikulturelles Berlin* (DM 20), useful even to those with just a smattering of German.

JANUARY • At the end of the month, a small **Opera Festival** is held in venues throughout the city center.

FEBRUARY • The **Internationale Filmfestspiele,** Berlin's International Film Festival, rivals those in Cannes and Venice. It features new works from international filmmakers as well as remastered classics. Cinemas all over Berlin are co-opted for the event, and admission runs anywhere from DM 6 to DM 50. For tickets and more info, contact Filmfestspiele Berlin (Budapester Str. 50, tel. 030/254890).

MAY • The **Berlin Drama Festival** is Berlin's largest theater extravaganza, featuring mostly German plays in a variety of venues. Many performances are of the puppet/experimental/music type, so fluent German isn't always a prerequisite. Prices vary according to the performance, but expect to pay around DM 15.

JUNE • **Jazz in the Garten** brings local and international talent to the Neue Nationalgalerie for four consecutive Fridays in June. The music is first-rate and, best of all, free. Weather permitting, many of the sessions are held outside in the gallery's lush gardens. This festival is passionately recommended. Because of the influx of musicians, Berlin's jazz clubs are particularly lively in June.

JULY • In recent years **Jazz in Juli** has become Berlin's premier jazz event, attracting big-name stars from the States and Britain for the first two to three weeks of the month. It's sponsored by the Quasimodo Club (*see* Live Music *in* After Dark, *below*), which is the festival's main venue. Tickets, usually DM 10–DM 25, should be purchased well in advance. July also hosts Berlin's most popular classical music festival, the **Classic Open Air** on the Gendarmenmarkt. Tickets range from DM 40 to DM 150 and must be ordered in advance; contact the organizers (tel. 030/3157–5413, email mom£snx.de) for info.

AUGUST • **Deutsch-Amerikanisches Volksfest** is a big late-August shindig at Truman Plaza celebrating the "bonds of friendship" between Germany and America. Bring money for gambling in the casinos erected for the event and the phone numbers of your friends back home: At the front end of a massive line, there's a "friendship phone" for free minute-long calls to the United States.

Berliner Festwochen, which run August–October, combine a wide range of music, opera, ballet, and theater in venues throughout the city. The tourist office has complete listings and ticket info. A festival pass, good for entrance to all major events, costs more than DM 110.

SEPTEMBER • **Kreuzberger Festliche Tage,** Kreuzberg's largest festival, includes street musicians, open-air markets, and lots of beer. Come here for good deals on local art and offbeat antiques. The festival usually falls on the last weekend of September, though exact dates change from year to year.

DECEMBER • Berlin celebrates Christmas with its annual **Weihnachtsmarkt,** an outdoor market held on the Ku'damm's Breitscheidplatz. Besides mobile food and drink stalls, look for handcrafted jewelry and clothing along with the obligatory overpriced stocking stuffers. **New Year's Eve** is celebrated wildly throughout Berlin, with the largest crowds at the Brandenburger Tor, along the Ku'damm, and on Kreuzberg's Oranienstraße. Watch out for the hail of firecrackers!

AFTER DARK

Berlin's many nighttime districts are impossible to typecast. Kreuzberg, Schöneberg, Mitte, and Prenzlauer Berg all have every kind of bar and club and every kind of clientele imaginable. In each you'll find well-dressed yuppies, young punks, ravers, and a queer crowd, though one group or another may be more prevalent. If you want to go clubbing, it's best to check out the mags *Zitty, Tip,* or *030* for current listings, since offerings vary wildly at most venues. Keep your *Nachtliniennetz* (night-bus route map) handy, but remember that Berlin's most serious night owls use the night buses only to start their evening: By the time they go home, regular transit is up and running again.

BARS

Berlin supposedly has more bars per square km than any other city in the world (over 5,000 total), and that's not including cafés, beer gardens, and liquor shops. Berlin's bars are notoriously short-lived, especially those in Kreuzberg and Prenzlauer Berg. To avoid disappointment, you should probably target an area rather than a name. Most bars open around 6 PM or 7 PM at the latest and close around 4 AM, maybe an hour later if customers linger. Police don't mind people drinking in the streets, but noise outside after 10 PM is frowned upon. Distinctions in Berlin tend to blur, and many of the city's cafés are popular bars late into the night, particularly in Charlottenburg, Schöneberg, Kreuzberg, and Prenzlauer Berg (*see* Food, *above*).

Nightlife is a Berlin strong point but beer is not. Beware of these two prevalent brews: Schultheis and Berliner Kindl. They're horrible.

CHARLOTTENBURG AND WILMERSDORF

Charlottenburg is the most established realm of BMWs and tourists (who hit the Ku'damm's nauseating rhinestone discos). **Savignyplatz** has well-scrubbed, fun cafés and bars run by people who were once hippies but have undergone the metamorphosis into left-leaning entrepreneurs.

Dicke Wirtin. A warm, Irish-pub atmosphere makes this unassuming watering hole a choice spot for a tasty Guinness on tap (DM 5.80) or a shot of Bailey's (DM 2.80). *Carmerstr. 9, between Savignypl. and Steinpl., tel. 030/312–4952. Open noon–morning.*

Khan. Located on Wilmersdorf's Pariser Straße amongst other fashionable new bars, Khan sports a hip, clean clientele, cool bartenders, and up-to-date music. The scene stirs on weekends. Beer is DM 5, coffee DM 3. *Pariser Str. 20, tel. 030/262–0421. U7 to Adenauerpl. Open weekdays until 2 AM, weekends until 4 AM.*

Luisen-Bräu. This microbrewery serves homebrews for DM 2.80 and has good German meals for under DM 10. The drinking area overlooks vats and a hopper; the front door faces Schloß Charlottenburg. Warning: If you don't cover your empty glass with a coaster, you'll soon get a full-price refill. *Luisenpl. 1, tel. 030/341–9388. Bus 145 from Bahnhof Zoo. Open daily 11 AM–1 AM, weekends until 2 AM.*

SCHÖNEBERG

The streets around **Winterfeldtplatz** stay crowded late as people hit the bars and refuel in the good, cheap eateries. **Motzstraße** and surrounding streets host Schöneberg's very busy gay male scene.

Anderes Ufer. This extremely popular lesbian and gay bar offers a small menu of light meals, and a fun, diverse crowd. *Hauptstr. 157, tel. 030/7870–3800. U7 to Kleistpark. Open weekdays 11 AM–1 AM and weekends 11 AM—2 AM.*

Hafen. If the fervent gay men's cruising at Tom's (*see below*) gets too intense, Hafen provides a hip, gay, mellow place to unwind. *Motzstr. 19, tel. 030/211–4118. U-Bahn to Nollendorfpl. Open daily 8 PM–4 AM.*

Mutter. It means "mother," but also "nut" (as in "and bolts"), and it is packed and chaotic weekend nights with a mostly het crowd. Once you've had a few, visit the toilet for a dramatic little journey. *Hohenstaufenstr. 4, tel. 030/216–4990. Open daily 9 AM–4 AM.*

Tom's Bar. If you're looking for serious gay action, come here. Be aware, though, that people here are often intersted in more than a friendly get-to-know-you flirt. *Motzstr. 19. U-Bahn to Nollendorfpl. Open daily 10 PM–morning.*

SEE AND BE SCENE

In 1989, 150 brightly dressed house and techno fans got together and staged a little love parade—bringing people together with a pounding beat. That began Berlin's rapid rise to the top of the techno scene. The Love Parade shakes annually on the first or second Saturday in July and grooves from Ernst-Reuter-Platz to the Brandenburger Tor and back to the Siegessäule. Fashion and music notwithstanding, the most common comparisons are with Woodstock. In 1998, it drew more than one million fluorescent flower children from all over Europe and the world, and Deutsche Bahn rolled ravers to town on 30 special Love Trains. This is not just a parade, it's a citywide celebration that got top coverage on CNN. The party pumps all weekend long in the streets and countless clubs (check Zitty, Tip, or 030). So get clubby, get jumpy, get something bright green, come see and be seen. It's all the rave.

Village. Tribal masks cover the walls of this new bar, which pulsates with African and Latin beats and entrancing lighting effects. *Frankenstr. 13, tel. 030/216–2635. U7 to Eisenacher Str., north through Barbarossapl. Open 6 PM–1 AM.*

KREUZBERG

Check out **Oranienstraße** and **Wiener Straße** in east Kreuzberg, which have lots of loud bars, some evening cafés, and a remaining alternative collective or two. In west Kreuzberg, **Bergmannstraße** and **Gneisenaustraße** offer a quieter scene, with live shows, glitzy cafés, and dark, catacomb-like bars.

Kit Kat Klub. A spot known for cult parties and erotica, this Klub is not a place for people with sexual inhibitions—but don't expect action either: It's strictly look and don't touch. Depending on the event, admission can cost DM 10–DM 15. *Glogauer Str. 2 , tel. 030/611–3838. U-Bahn to Görlitzer Bahnhof. Open Mon.–Sat. 5 PM–morning.*

Madonna. For raucous and grimy fun in Kreuzberg, come to Madonna, which puts the grunge back in grungy. You might not engage in intimate conversation in this dirty little hole—but you'll have a rowdy good time. *Wiener Str. 22, tel. 030/611–6943. U-Bahn to Görlitzer Bahnhof. Open daily noon–3 AM.*

Milchbar. This alternative rock bar sports loud music, an oceanic decor, a hip staff, and a mid-20s crowd. *Manteuffelstr. 41, off Oranienstr., tel. 030/611–7006. U-Bahn to Görlitzer Bahnhof. Open daily from 7 PM.*

Niagra. A cult pub for musicians and artists—and wanna-bes. The music is loud and independent, and the accent is on fun. Most weekends feature live concerts—some for free. *Gneisenaustr. 58, tel. 030/692617. U-Bahn to Šdstern. Open daily from 8 PM.*

Die Rote Harfe. This *Kneipe* (pub) offers a nice mix of coffee and cake in the afternoons and beer and other beverages in the evenings. Once the ruins of a Kreuzberg haven for anarchists and social unrest, this two-story pub now caters to a mixed crowd of regulars and tourists. *Oranienstr. 13, tel. 030/618–4446. U-Bahn to Görlitzer Bahnhof. Open daily 10 AM–whenever.*

MITTE

The closer you get to Friedrichstraße along Mitte's **Oranienburger Straße,** the thicker the crowds of tourists get. The bars are crowded and fun here, but locals head down Auguststraße or out to **Rosenthaler Straße** and **Rosenthaler Platz.** Definitely check out **Tacheles,** an anarchist squat where you can down a beer and watch the freak show in the *Skulpturenpark.* Across the street, **Obst und Gemüse** (Oranienburger Str. 48, U6 to Oranienburger Tor), once a fruit and vegetable store, is now a packed, no-frills hipster hangout.

Oscar Wilde. This Irish pub serves as a meeting place and informal office for blue-collar Irishmen and Londoners looking for work. Grab a Guinness (DM 5.80) after 7 PM, when everyone stops by to drink with their chums, talk politics, listen to drunken poets reciting impassioned verse, and party into the night. *Oranienburger Str. 28, tel. 030/280–8029. U-Bahn to Oranienburger Tor.*

Zosch. This is the kind of dive that makes you feel at home. Live music—from speed metal to tango—is quite likely on weekend nights. Next door, **AKS** draws a similar mellow, punk-tinged, twenty-something crowd. *Tucholskystr. 30, tel. 030/280–7664. S-Bahn to Oranienburger Str. or U-Bahn to Oranienburger Tor.*

PRENZLAUER BERG

Due to changing economics, the Prenzlberg scene is a bit ephemeral; bars come and go rapidly, but **Kollwitzplatz** and **Schönhauser Allee** always have an assortment of hip hangouts.

Doors. Not only does it sometimes play the Doors, this funky old pub is decorated completely in doors. Join the lively mixed crowd of mixed ages. *Knaackstr. 94, tel.030/442–7847. U-Bahn to Senefelderpl. Open daily 7 PM–2 AM (at least).*

Duncker. A mecca for the revived dark-wave scene that is just as apocalyptic as it is avant-garde. If there is a concert, and there often is, then expect to pay DM 5–DM 10 cover. *Dunckerstr. 64, no phone. Open daily 10 PM–morning.*

Kommandantur. Look like you belong when you invade this tiny bar full of loyal, politically active locals. *Knaackstr. 20, no phone. U2 to Eberswalder Str. Open daily 2 PM–morning.*

Nostalghia. Next to a small studio that presents plays and foreign films, this mellow spot has a romatic Russian touch. The crowd is subdued and there are few tourists. *Knaackstr. 43, 030/4400–8596. U-Bahn to Senefelderpl. Open daily 8 PM–1 AM.*

Schall und Rauch. Named after Max Reinhardt's famous Weimar-era cabaret, this blue-lit bar is a stylish gay and lesbian hangout and is open for breakfast on weekends. Be sure to note the electrifying interior—it's won design awards. *Gleimstr. 23, tel. 030/448–0770. U-Bahn to Schönhauser Allee.*

DANCE CLUBS

Excluding the flashy clubs along the Ku'damm, many discos and dance clubs have free admission or covers under DM 10. Beers inside average DM 7, so get liquored up elsewhere. Clubhopping is easy on most streets; most clubs open around 10 PM and don't close until the beer's gone or the last patron has left, often after dawn. The music changes by day (if not by hour). Check the "Dancing" sections in *Zitty* or *Tip* to see which clubs are playing which kind of music on which night. Many clubs will alternate music styles and host diverse theme nights—from drag to '70s disco to leather and whips. If you like raves, you're lucky: Berlin is in a constant state of rave.

Boudoir. The Mitte cultural scene gets sexy here on weekends. Parties vary (check listings)—it may be jazzy, it may be house. Monday through Thursday the Boudoir is a stylish bar; there may be a cover charge depending on the event. *Brunnenstr. 192, no phone. U8 to Rosenthaler Pl. Open daily 10 PM–3 AM.*

Drama. A plush, pumping, popular gay bar/club with a tiny dance floor and people spilling onto the street weekend nights—where do they put the DJs? Across the street, the collective **T.E.K.** (No. 36) may still exist; if it does, look for their tremendous, unadvertised, mixed-crowd parties. *Oranienstr. 169, tel. 030/614–8501. U-Bahn to Kottbusser Tor. Open daily 8 PM–5 AM. No cover.*

E-Werk. This is *the* headquarters for Berlin's techno-jungle scene—a massive club in the old electric works. You get several bars and nonstop beats, but it'll cost you. Don't bother coming before 1 AM, later on Saturdays. *Wilhelmstr. 43, tel. 030/252–2012. U2 to Mohrenstr. Cover: DM 15. Open Thurs.–Sat. 9 PM–morning.*

Knaack. Prenzlauer Berg's Knaack has three floors for nonstop dancing to '70s funk and heavy house. Some nights there are live gigs. *Greifswalder Str. 224, tel. 030/442-7060. S-Bahn to Hackescher Markt, then Tram 2, 3, or 4 to Marienburger Str. Open Wed.–Sat. 8 PM–4 AM.*

Madow. A sign on the door reads A CLUB FOR PLAYERS; inside you'll find one of Berlin's busiest dance clubs, popular with all types and ages. The music is eclectic, but always very danceable. Drinks are DM 5–DM 8; the kitchen is open until midnight. *Pariser Str. 23, tel. 030/883–9260. U1 to Hohenzollernpl. Cover: DM 8. Open Wed.–Sun. until the last person leaves.*

Manson. Live DJs and passionate music are what this club is known for. On techno nights students and young people frolic to tribal beats. *Schliemannstr. 37, tel. 030/440–9869. U2 to Eberwalderstr. Open daily 7 PM–morning.*

SchwuZ. This is the favorite weekend place for young gay men in Kreuzberg (women are also welcome). Music ranges from techno to retro. *Mehringdamm 61, enter through Café Sundstör, tel. 030/693–7025. U-Bahn to Mehringdamm. Open Fri.–Sat. 10 PM–6 AM, Sat. disco gets going at 2 AM.*

SO 36. Whether you're gay, straight, or neuter, SO 36 is a good place to dance into the wee hours with a friendly, happy, Kreuzberg crowd. *Oranienstr. 190, tel. 030/6140–1306. U-Bahn to Görlitzer Bahnhof. Open Wed.–Sat. from 10 PM, Sun. 5 PM–11 PM.*

LIVE MUSIC

Berlin's live-music scene is excellent and diverse, whether it's punk or jazz or classical or simply strange. For dirt-cheap classical concerts, poke your nose in any church. **Gethsemanekirche** (Gethsemanestr. 9; U2 to Schönhauser Allee), **Petruskirche** (Oberhofer Pl. 2; S25 to Lichterfelde Ost), and **Lindenkirche** (Johannisberger Str. 15a; U1 to Rüdesheimer Pl.) all feature world music from the Mediterranean to the Caribbean to the South Pacific. Lacking medium-sized venues, many live gigs happen in cafés, bars, and unmarked basements throughout Berlin. Look for flyers and posters, or flip through the magazines *Tip* and *Zitty* for current listings. Tickets for major events can be purchased at the door or, for a DM 3 fee, at the massive **KaDeWe** department store (Tauentzienstr. 21–24, tel. 030/21210) on Wittenbergplatz.

ROCK, INDIE, AND POP

Emitaay. A boiling mix of rock and percussion, this club offers more than dance music. Some nights the feature is film and others a live poetry reading—so check first to be sure of the program. *Potsdamer Str. 157, tel. 030/2175–6750. U7 to Kleistpark. Open daily from 9 PM.*

KulturBrauerei. Galleries, practice rooms, and performance spaces share this extensive complex in Prenzlauer Berg. The music in this one-time brewery ranges from Czech riot-grrrl stuff to jazz poetry. *Knaackstr. 97, tel. 030/441–9269. U2 to Eberswalder Str.*

Metropol. The disco, housed in a beautifully restored art deco theater, is touristy and full of teenyboppers, but live performances in the **Loft,** its concert space, feature the best of those about to make it big. Maybe. *Nollendorfpl. 5, tel. 030/217–3680. Box office open weekdays 11 AM–6 PM, Sat. 9:30–2, most shows start after 8 PM.*

Miles—The Club. The booker has eclectic tastes, from avant-garde klezmer to psycho-funk. Every night there's a concert and every night it's something else. Admission costs DM 12–DM 15. *Greifswalderstr. 212–213, tel. 030/4400–8140. U-Bahn to Greifswalderstr. All concerts start at 10:30 PM.*

Pfefferberg. Housed behind a yellow, fortresslike wall, this Prenzlauer Berg concert hall/cultural complex is a wonderful space, day or night. Among others, many African and world-beat bands play at Pfefferberg. *Schönhauser Allee 176, tel. 030/449–6534. U2 to Senefelder Pl.*

Tempodrom. When big-name international bands roll through Berlin, they play here in the Tiergarten, next to the Haus der Kulturen der Welt (*see* Tiergarten *in* Districts, *above*). With ticket prices at DM 20–DM 40, you should only come if you know who's playing. *In den Zelten, tel. 030/394–4045. From Bahnhof Zoo or Alexanderpl., Bus 100 to Kongresshalle. All concerts start at 8 PM.*

Wild at Heart. Small local bands blast several nights a week for a house full of twenty-somethings. A sassy, grinning bar staff serves DM 5 ½ liters in this dim, red bar—it's like the inside of a very dark heart. *Wiener Str. 20, tel. 030/611–7010. U-Bahn to Görlitzer Bahnhof. Cover: DM 5. Open daily from 8 PM.*

JAZZ

Berlin's jazz scene is second to none. Jazz performances usually start around 9 PM and often continue until 3 AM or later, and cover charges vary from DM 2 to DM 20. In June and July, Berlin hosts two world-class jazz festivals (*see* Festivals, *above*). The tourist office sells passes for DM 95 or so, which get you into all major festival events.

Blues Café. Seedy and intimate, in a sketchy neighborhood, Blues Café features local talent and the occasional big-name act. It's the place to come if you enjoy the dive jazz scene but aren't necessarily interested in flawless music. *Körnerstr. 11, tel. 030/261–3698. U-Bahn to Kurfürstenstr.*

Junction Bar. Just the kind of dark, small, intimate, and rough-edged club every city needs more of. The music is mostly jazz, but expect anything from Afro-rhythm nights to piano jams. DJs spin dance tunes after the show Tuesday–Saturday nights until 5 AM. *Gneisenaustr. 18, tel. 030/694–6602. Cover DM 5–DM 10. U7 to Gneisenaustr. Most shows start 10 PM or later.*

Flöz. It looks the way a blues joint ought to—dark and smoky. Local and big-name bands play pre-1950s jazz, Dixieland, and swing. Very bohemian. *Nassauische Str. 37, tel. 030/861–1000. U-Bahn to Berliner Str. Shows start 9 PM.*

Quasimodo. Largely responsible for Berlin's recent jazz renaissance, Quasimodo brings in the biggest international names and hosts most of Jazz in Juli (*see* Festivals, *above*). It's one of the few clubs with a website: www.quasimodo.de. *Kantstr. 12a, near Savignypl., tel. 030/312–8086. Cover: DM 5–DM 20. Open 5 PM–1 AM.*

CLASSICAL AND OPERA

World-famous classical music is found at Berlin's **Philharmonie und Kammermusiksaal** (Matthäikirchstr. 1, tel. 030/2548–8132 or 030/2548–8232), northwest on Bellevue Straße from Potsdamer Platz. Catch world-class opera at **Deutsche Oper** (Bismarckstr. 34–37, tel. 030/343–8401; U-Bahn to Deutsche Oper) in the west and **Staatsoper Unter den Linden** (Unter den Linden 7, tel. 030/2035–4555; U- or S-Bahn to Friedrichstr.) in the east. Tickets usually start at DM 25 (DM 15 students). More eclectic (and cheaper) shows can be found at smaller venues like **Metropol-Theater** (Friedrichstr. 101–102, tel. 0180/523–7454; U- or S-Bahn to Friedrichstr.) or **Urania** (An der Urania 17, tel. 030/218–9091; U-Bahn to Wittenbergpl.). Metropol is known for its comical, offbeat productions of opera and dance; Urania hosts smaller orchestras and chamber groups. Many venues offer student discounts, particularly for same-day performances. Check the biweeklies *Zitty* or *Tip* for listings of current performances. **Last Minute Theaterkasse** (Friedrichstr. 95, near U- and S-Bahn station, tel. 030/2096–2233) has 50% discounts on some same-day shows. They're open daily 4 PM–7:30 PM.

CABARET

With its combination of spectacle and smart-ass political commentary, cabaret has been central to Berlin's musical theater for 100 years. Contemporary cabaret and variety shows include touristy extravaganzas like the **Wintergarten-Varieté** (Potsdamer Str. 96, tel. 030/2308–8230; U-Bahn to Kurfürstenstr.), but your money is better spent on the less glitzy, more inventive, edgier cabarets, which cost DM 15–DM 30 per person. In Mitte, try **Chamäleon-Varieté** (Rosenthaler Str. 40–41, tel. 030/282–7118; S-Bahn to Hackescher Markt); in Prenzlauer Berg there's **Schlot** (Kastanienallee 29, tel. 030/448-2160; U2 to Eberswalder Str.). In Friedrichshain **Theater Schmales Handtuch** (Marchlewskistr. 6, tel. 030/426–6636) has recently broadened its repertoire to include music and an open stage for theatrical groups that have plays but no producers. Very cutting edge. Admission is DM 16, DM 12 for students. Take the U- or S-Bahn to Frankfurter Allee.

THEATER

Berlin is far and away the center of German-language theater—from mainstream to the incredibly creative alternative stages that Berliners call "Off Theater." English-language theater has some devout followers, who get their fix at **Friends of the Italian Opera** (Fidicinstr. 40, tel. 030/691–1211; U6 to Pl. der Luftbrücke), which despite its name is an all-English stage. One venue that shows performances in English, German, and other languages is **Stükke** (Hasenheide 54, tel. 030/6940–9869; U7 to Südstern). Excellent German venues include **The Berliner Ensemble** (Bertolt-Brecht-Pl. 101, tel. 030/2840–8155; U- or S-Bahn to Friedrichstr.) and the **Volksbühne** (Rosa-Luxemburg-Pl., tel. 030/247–6772), both major civic theaters. Catch a show by Theater Kreatur at the **Theater am Ufer** (Tempelhofer Ufer 10, tel. 030/251–3116; U-Bahn to Hallesches Tor). For all of these and other venues, check the listings in *Zitty* or *Tip*. Prices vary, but expect to pay DM 15–DM 35; if you're a student, ask about an *Ermäßigung* (discount).

MOVIE THEATERS

You can enjoy mainstream movies in Berlin even if you don't speak German. Check the listings carefully and look for one of the following symbols: "OmU" for original language with subtitles, "OV" or "OF" for original language. Otherwise the film will be dubbed in German. Tickets in large theaters cost DM 12–DM 16, except Wednesdays when they're DM 7. Small theaters often charge less than DM 10.

THE SPICE OF LIFE

There's no point in trying to classify the productions mounted at the following venues. They encompass every performance medium, from explorations of Afro-German identity to Büchner puppet pieces. Whatever your opinion of lesbian jazz poetry and black-light theater, these spaces offer a chance to experience cutting-edge Berlin. Check local publications, or call directly, to see what's cookin'.

NEUKÖLLNER OPER: Karl-Marx-Str. 131–133, tel. 030/688–90777. U7 to Karl-Marx-Str.

PODEWIL: Klosterstr. 68–70, tel. 030/247496. U2 to Klosterstr.

TACHELES: Oranienburger Str. 53–56, tel. 030/282–6185. U6 to Oranienburger Tor.

THEATER AM HALLESCHEN UFER: Hallesches Ufer 32, tel. 030/251–0941. U-Bahn to Möckernbrücke.

UFA-FABRIK: Viktoriastr. 10–18, tel. 030/755030. U6 to Ullsteinstr.

The **Odeon** (Hauptstr. 116, tel. 030/787040; U-Bahn to Rathaus Schöneberg) shows Hollywood films in English. The **Eiszeit** (Zeughofstr. 20, tel. 030/611–6016; U-Bahn to Schlesisches Tor) runs art films, sometimes in English. **Amerika Haus** (Hardenbergstr. 22–24, near Bahnhof Zoo, tel. 030/3100–0122) shows oldies from the States; next door, the **British Council Film Club** (Hardenbergstr. 20, tel. 030/3110–9910) shows classics made in the United Kingdom. Eastern Berlin's most popular art house is **Babylon Mitte** (Rosa-Luxemburg-Str. 30, near Alexanderpl., tel. 030/242–5076), which features American and European classics in their original languages. **Arsenal** (Welserstr. 25, tel. 030/219–0010; U-Bahn to Wittenbergpl.) is a repertory cinema with eclectic taste. **Babylon** (Dresdnerstr. 126, tel. 030/6160–9693; U-Bahn to Kottbusser Tor) shows recent art movies and blockbusters in their original language. **Checkpoint** (Leipziger Str. 55, tel. 030/208–2995; U2 to Spittelmarkt) screens everything from John Waters to Shakespearean epics. Shows at **fsk** (Segitzdamm 2, tel. 030/614–2464; U-Bahn to Prinzenstr.) aren't always in English, but the obscure experimental films unite the entire multinational audience in confusion.

12 BRANDENBURG AND THE BALTIC COAST

UPDATED BY GARRETT HERING

At first glance, the two German *Länder* (states) of Brandenburg, just outside Berlin, and Mecklenburg-Vorpommern, on the Baltic coast to the north, look a lot alike. Both are flat, low-lying, and mostly rural regions. Both share a Slavic past and a history of conquest by German princes in the early Middle Ages, and both suffered economically from the collapse of the GDR. Though Mecklenburg-Vorpommern is, today, even poorer than Brandenburg, it looks back to a prosperous past as part of the Hanseatic League from the 14th through the 17th century. The region looks forward to a future as a seaside resort, and though few foreigners have discovered the beauty of its beaches, oodles of Germans flock to the Baltic coast in summer. Rural Brandenburg surrounds Berlin but lives perpetually in its shadow, and Brandenburgers have a love-hate relationship with the monster in their midst. Historically, though, Berlin owes its greatness to this now humble region, which formed the core of mighty Prussia. Generations of Brandenburgers served as cannon fodder for Prussia's imperial ambitions, and the palaces of its nobility in towns like Potsdam serve as evidence of its former power.

Aside from history, the main draw for both states is their natural beauty: Bike tours are extremely popular, as are boat rides on the lazy canals of Brandenburg's Spreewald or basking on the white sands of remote Baltic island beaches. The absence of heavy tourism means fewer crowds, but it can also mean a lack of affordable accommodations. Because of their years of isolation in the GDR, few people in either region speak English, and travelers may have difficulty if they can't speak a few words of German. Visitors who don't look German may also encounter racist or xenophobic hostility, especially in suburban and rural areas, and should exercise caution about traveling alone outside city centers. On the other hand, both regions offer an escape from big, modern cities like Hamburg and Berlin and a glimpse of a slower-paced, more traditional Germany.

BRANDENBURG

Obscured by boisterous Berlin at its center and by decades of virtual inaccessibility in the GDR, the open spaces, lakes, and rivers of rural Brandenburg await discovery by foreign travelers. The striking contrast between gritty, chaotic Berlin and serene, elegant towns like Potsdam or quiet lakeside villages like

Buckow makes travel here all the more inviting. The region was settled as early as the 7th century AD by the Slavic Wends, and their descendants, the Sorbs, still live in southern Brandenburg's Spreewald. In the 12th century, German princes finally defeated the Wends and the *Mark Brandenburg* (March of Brandenburg) became the Holy Roman Empire's eastern frontier. The electors of Brandenburg eventually became the kings of far-flung Prussia. Their royal palaces still stand in Potsdam, and Prussian leaders, such as Kaiser Wilhelm I and his chancellor, Otto von Bismarck, united Germany about 130 years ago through a series of brutal wars and clever diplomacy that pulled the *Länder* together.

Brandenburg is extremely biker- and hiker-friendly—woodsy, lakeside trails are everywhere. If you want to take a bike on the train, be sure to purchase a special pass (DM 10–DM 15) *before* boarding. Local tourist offices can provide biking tips and hiking info. If the woods and waterways—the hilly, green Märkische Schweiz, the narrow canals of the Spreewald—seem untouched by the ages, the larger towns are an architectural clash of the centuries. Ornate Baroque and stately neoclassical palaces share the streets with medieval churches and the GDR's square, concrete "urban renewal" projects. Everywhere Brandenburg is busily renovating and reconstructing, urgently trying to recapture its pre-20th-century identity while forging a new 21st-century one.

POTSDAM

Potsdam is the jewel in Brandenburg's crown. Frederick the Great, the powerful 18th-century king of Prussia, built the extravagant rococo **Schloß Sanssouci** here, and its flamboyant architecture alone is reason to visit. The town center is also quite picturesque: Along Friedrich-Ebert-Straße, Brandenburger Straße, and Platz der Einheit you'll find a colorful Baroque quarter, redbrick 18th-century houses, and tree-lined parks set along the shores of the lakes that surround the city.

BASICS

Potsdam's **tourist office** provides guidebooks and maps (DM 1) and distributes *Potz* (DM 2.50), a monthly events magazine. For DM 29, the **Welcome Card** covers three days worth of local bus and city rail transportation for Berlin and Potsdam, and gets you 50% off at museums. After 1 PM the tourist office can book you into a private room (DM 15–DM 30) for a DM 5 fee, or call the *Zimmervermittlung* (room-finding service; tel. 0331/293385), located in this office. *Friedrich-Ebert-Str. 5, tel. 0331/275580. From station, up the access road and right across Lange Brücke; keep right for Friedrich-Ebert-Str. Open Apr.–Oct., weekdays 9–8, weekends 9–6; Nov.–Mar., weekdays 10–6, weekends 10–2.*

COMING AND GOING

The best way to reach Potsdam from Berlin is by the S3 or S7 to Potsdam Stadt **station** (40 min, DM 4). Direct trains also leave Potsdam Stadt for Brandenburg (every 30 min, 30 min, DM 9.40), Cottbus (6 per day, 2 hrs, DM 39), and Hanover (every 2 hrs, 2½ hrs, DM 49–DM 81). To get to other parts of Brandenburg, your best bet is to take the S-Bahn to the appropriate station in Berlin and transfer for your ultimate destination; buy a through ticket in Potsdam. Both the S3 and S7 run to Berlin's Bahnhof Zoo and Friedrichstraße; the S3 continues to Berlin-Hauptbahnhof (for trains to Frankfurt an der Oder); the S7 runs to Berlin-Lichtenberg, with connections to most other parts of Brandenburg. Store your belongings in the station's **lockers** or luggage storage (open Mon.–Sat. 8–5, Sun. 10–4). Outside the station, rent **bikes** from City Rad (DM 20 for 24 hrs, DM 14 students). Another option is a scenic approach on the ferries run by **Weiße Flotte** (tel. 0331/275-9230), which leave hourly 10–5 from the dock across from the Wannsee S-Bahn station (1½ hrs, DM 8–DM 15) or **Havel Dampfschifffahrt Postdam** (tel. 0171/544-6140), a steam engine ferry that leaves from Lange Brücke (2 hrs, DM 10–DM 17).

To reach the city center from the train station walk up the access road and right across Lange Brücke; keep right for Friedrich-Ebert-Straße into the center (15 min total). At the top of the access road there's also a tram stop. Any tram heading to the right will take you to Platz der Einheit in the city center; Trams 91, 96, and 98 continue to Luisenplatz near Schloß Sanssouci and neighboring palaces. Public transit in Potsdam costs DM 2.40 (30-min trip) or DM 4.10 (2-hr trip), including transfers, or DM 7.80 for 24 hours.

WHERE TO SLEEP

Potsdam is somewhat lacking in budget lodging, though the selection is increasing as the city welcomes more and more tourists each year. If the tourist office has run out of *Privatzimmer* (private rooms), try the nearby **HI-Jugendgästehaus am Wannsee** (*see* Where to Sleep *in* Chapter 11) or the centrally located **Jugendgästehaus Siebenschläfer** (Lotte-Pulewka-Str. 41, tel. 0331/741125), where you'll find

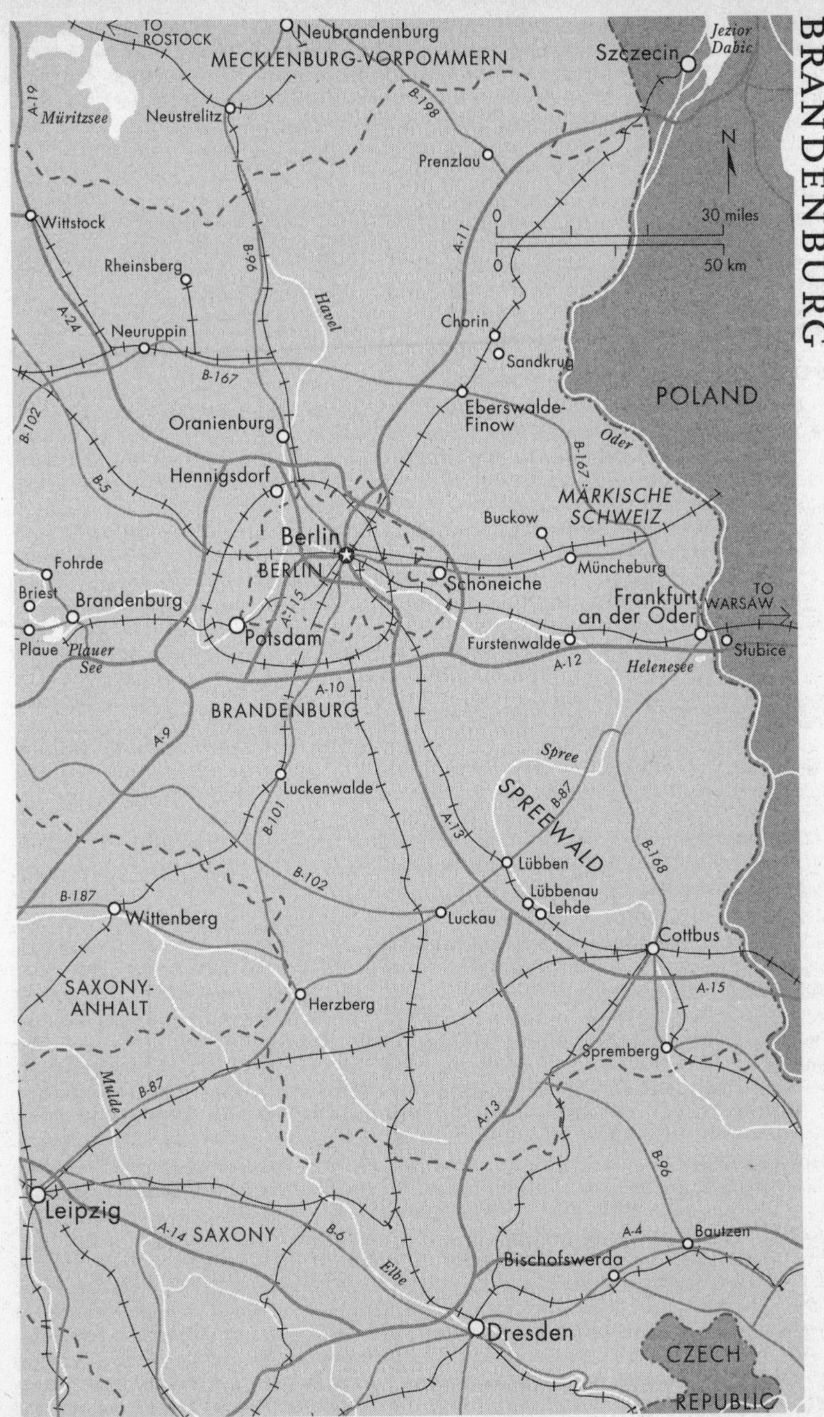
BRANDENBURG
TO ROSTOCK
Neubrandenburg
MECKLENBURG-VORPOMMERN
Szczecin
Jezior Dabic
Müritzsee
Neustrelitz
Prenzlau
Wittstock
0
30 miles
0
50 km
Rheinsberg
Havel
Chorin
Neuruppin
Sandkrug
POLAND
Eberswalde-Finow
Oranienburg
Oder
Hennigsdorf
MÄRKISCHE SCHWEIZ
Buckow
Berlin
Fohrde
BERLIN
Müncheberg
Schöneiche
Briest
Brandenburg
Frankfurt an der Oder
TO WARSAW
Potsdam
Plaue
Plauer See
Fürstenwalde
Słubice
Helenesee
BRANDENBURG
Spree
SPREEWALD
Luckenwalde
Lübben
Lübbenau
Lehde
Wittenberg
Luckau
Cottbus
SAXONY-ANHALT
Herzberg
Spremberg
Mulde
Leipzig
SAXONY
Elbe
Bautzen
Bischofswerda
Dresden
CZECH REPUBLIC
A-19
A-24
B-96
B-198
A-11
B-167
B-102
B-5
A-115
A-10
A-12
A-9
B-101
A-13
B-87
B-168
B-102
B-187
A-15
B-87
A-13
B-96
A-14
B-6
A-4

clean doubles for DM 55, singles for DM 37, or dorm beds for DM 25 (add DM 8 if you're over 26), breakfast included. You can also try the elegant, yet affordable **Hotel Babelsberg** (Stahndorfer Str. 68, tel. 0331/749010), where singles go for DM 40–DM 100 and doubles for DM 90–DM 130. Add DM 10 for breakfast. If you like to camp, try woodsy **Kohlhasenbrück** (Neue Kreisstr. 36, tel. 030/805–1737). A spot costs DM 5.50, plus DM 7.50 per person. From Griebnitzsee S-Bahn station, head east on R.-Breitscheid-Straße.

FOOD

Potsdam's Brandenburger Straße has a good selection of cafés and cheap restaurants. Try **Am Stadttor** (Brandenburger Str. 1–3), which serves a variety of traditional German dishes for under DM 15. A more elegant option is **Minsk-Nationalitätengaststätte** (Max-Planck-Str. 10, tel. 0331/293636), overlooking the Havel River near Potsdam's S-Bahn station. The view of the city is superb, as are the Russian and Belorussian dishes (around DM 20). For inviting light fare, stop by **La Leander** (Benkerstr. 1, tel. 0331/270–6576), a hip bar/restaurant that serves sandwiches and salads for DM 7–DM 10.

WORTH SEEING

On **Alter Markt** (Old Market Square), behind the tourist office, check out the **Nikolaikirche** (1724) and the colorful facade of the **Rathaus** (1755), curiously topped by the gilded figure of Atlas supporting the world. West of the tourist office is the 18th-century Neustadt, and Yorkstraße and the surrounding streets retain their Baroque flavor. At the south end of Neuer Markt on Breite Straße you'll find the **Marstall** (royal stables). These are all that remain of the 17th-century Royal Palace; they now house Potsdam's excellent **Filmmuseum** (tel. 0331/271–8114; open Tues.–Sun. 10 AM–6 PM), which documents German cinema since 1895. Particularly interesting are Nazi-era propaganda films. Admission is DM 6–DM 12. If your hunger for film is not yet satiated, take the five-min S-bahn ride (S-7) to Bahnhof Babelsberg and tour Germany's largest and most legendary film studio, **Filmpark Babelsberg** (August-Bebel-Str. 26–53, tel. 0331/721–2737). This film fun-park reveals sets, editing techniques, and themes of innovative Expressionist psycho-thrillers such as *Nosferatu* and *Dr. Caligari,* as well as of other Weimar-period notables, such as Fritz Lang's *Metropolis.* For tours in English, call ahead. North of the Neustadt is the **Baroque quarter,** now Potsdam's city center, focused on pedestrian-only **Brandenburger Straße.** At the west end of the boutique- and café-lined strip is Potsdam's own Brandenburger Tor. From the east end of Brandenburger Straße, Friedrich-Ebert-Straße leads north to the **Holländisches Viertel,** the "Dutch Quarter." It was designed in 1732 by King Friedrich Wilhelm I, who hoped to induce Dutch artisans to settle in the city. Few Dutch ever came, but the quarter's gabled, redbrick homes give it a very un-German feel. North past Nauener Tor, an 18th-century city gate, is the **Alexandrowka** district, a dense jumble of Russian-style wood houses built in the 19th century for Russian singers brought back by Prussia during the Napoleonic Wars. The Russian church **Kapelle des Heiligen Alexander** sits on top of the hill.

SCHLOSS CECILIENHOF • If you head up Friedrich-Ebert-Straße and turn right on Alleestraße, you'll hit the **Neuer Garten** (New Garden), a sprawling, tree-lined park with some excellent lakeside walking trails. Inside the park stands Schloß Cecilienhof, the 1913 manor house that hosted the 1945 Potsdam Conference, where Truman, Churchill (and then Attlee), and Stalin met to divvy up postwar Germany. Nowadays the Schloß is a luxury hotel, but you can still see the conference room—adorned with historical memorabilia—and the participants' personal studies. Nearby stands the two-story **Marmorpalais** (Marble Palace), built by King Friedrich Wilhelm II in 1792. Once home to a military museum, the palace recently underwent extensive renovations and is now as stunning as ever. *Tel. 0331/969–4244. Admission: DM 5, DM 3.50 students. Open daily 9–5. Closed 2nd and 4th Mon. each month. Park and gardens open daily sunrise–sunset.*

PARK SANSSOUCI • Frederick (*Friedrich*) the Great had the park's main attraction, 18th-century **Schloß Sanssouci,** built in a rococo style that leaves no part of the facade unadorned. You can practically smell the expense of this palace in Friedrich's cedar-paneled bedroom, his gilded and heavily carved study, and in the circular central library, where Friedrich was tutored by Voltaire. Another highlight is the palace's music chamber, considered one of Germany's finest rococo interiors. Here, Friedrich and C.P.E. Bach would sometimes play duets on the harpsichord. You can only view the palace interior on one of the guided tours (make sure to pick up the English supplement) that leave every 30 min and come with the price of admission. On the ground floor, the Park Sanssouci **information center** (tel. 0331/969–4200) stocks maps of the park. *Walk down Brandenburger Str. (or take Trams 91, 96, or 98 from the station) to Luisenpl., just outside Brandenburger Tor; cross the square and keep right from the Tor to Allee nach Sanssouci, leading to the sprawling park; continue up the tree-lined path and turn right* *toward the bridge to Schloß Sanssouci. Admission: DM 10, DM 5 students. Open Apr.–mid-Oct., daily 9–5; mid-Oct.–Jan., daily 9–3; Feb.–Mar., daily 9–4. Closed 1st and 3rd Mon. each month.*

East of the palace, the **Bildergalerie** (Picture Gallery; admission DM 4, DM 2 students), built in 1755, displays Friedrich's impressive collection of 17th-century Italian, Flemish, and Dutch paintings. Friedrich made history when he opened this gallery to the public in 1785 as Germany's first public museum; it has once again opened after lengthy renovations. To the southwest of the palace is the bizarre **Chinese Teahouse,** a relic of the 18th-century fascination with things "Oriental." If you head west along the broad Hauptallee that cuts through the park, you'll discover Friedrich's second palace, the heavy Baroque **Neues Palais.** Friedrich built it after the Seven Years' War to prove that his treasury was not empty—a typically extravagant gesture. Highlights include a collection of antique musical instruments on the second floor, and paintings by 17th-century Italian masters in the upper gallery. German-language tours (DM 2) are given whenever there's enough interest. *Admission to Neues Palais: DM 8, DM 4 students. Same hours as Schloß Sanssoucci. Closed 2nd and 4th Mon. each month.*

After Frederick the Great's death in 1786, another Prussian king, Friedrich Wilhelm III, made additions to Sanssouci Park. The most famous is **Schloß Charlottenhof,** designed in an austere neoclassical style by Karl Schinkel and located near the southern tip of the park. The exterior is spartan, but inside Schinkel went a bit wild, especially with the "tent room." Inspired by Roman tents, it's decorated with canvas hanging from the walls and ceiling. *Tel. 0331/969–4228. From Sanssoucci, west along Hauptallee, then follow signs south (1 km). Admission: DM 6, DM 3 students for mandatory tour. Open mid-May–mid-Oct., daily 9–12:30 and 1–5. Closed 4th Mon. each month.*

Brandenburg's residents recently nixed a proposal to fuse their rural state with Berlin. Apparently, they take a "This Land is my Land, that Land is your Land" attitude.

BRANDENBURG

Brandenburg is one of the region's finest Baroque towns, with a mix of half-timbered houses, old-style storefronts, and relaxed, open-air squares. Until they moved to Berlin and—after many a conquest—became kings of Prussia, the medieval margraves of Brandenburg had their seat in this town, which gave its name to the surrounding region. The winding Havel River splits Brandenburg into sections crisscrossed by bridges, canals, and riverside paths. The city suffered damage during World War II and is still being restored today; you'll see bullet holes and tank blasts on many city-center facades.

BASICS

To reach the **tourist office,** take Tram 2 or 6 from the Hauptbahnhof to Neustädtischer Markt, and head up Hauptstraße. They book Privatzimmer and provide maps, bus and train schedules, and info on cultural events. *Hauptstr. 51, tel. 03381/19433. Open weekdays 9–7 (Thurs. until 8), Sat. 9–2.*

COMING AND GOING

Trains run every two hours from Brandenburg to Berlin's Bahnhof Zoo (1 hr, DM 16), and every half hour to Potsdam Stadt (30 min, DM 9). The last train back to Berlin leaves at 10:15 PM. Brandenburg's **Hauptbahnhof** (main train station) is 1½ km from Neustädtischer Markt; Trams 2 and 6 (DM 2.20) make the trip every 10 min or so. To return to the station from here, take Tram 1 or 9. The **bus station** (tel. 03381/5340) is adjacent to the train depot. You can rent **bikes** at the Hauptbahnhof (DM 15–DM 30 per day), where you'll also find **luggage lockers.**

WHERE TO SLEEP

Brandenburg's cheapest hotels cost at least DM 90 per room in winter and DM 110 or more in summer. Luckily, the tourist office can book you into a comfortable Privatzimmer for DM 25–DM 40 per person; ask for a place in the city center. Another option is **Pension Engel** (Große Gartenstr. 37, tel. 03381/200393), right in the center of town in a modestly attractive house with friendly staff. Singles start at DM 55, doubles at DM 90. Add DM 10–DM 20 for shower and bath. Otherwise, it's youth-hostel time. Get a bed and breakfast for a mere DM 18–DM 23 (add DM 8 if you're over 26) at **Jugendherberge Brandenburg** (HI; Hevellerstr. 7, tel. 03381/521040. From Neustädtischer Markt walk down Mühlendamm, by the Dom, right on Hevellerstr. 80 beds. Midnight curfew, lockout 9–2. Reception open 7–9 and 5–7 or by arrangement). The large, informal hostel squats on the central but deserted Dominsel (*see* Worth Seeing, *below*) and fills up quickly during the summer. Although you might consider it grimy, noisy (the entire management leaves at 7 PM, the curfew is barely enforced), and unsettling (renovations are underway), you'll appreciate the low rates.

FOOD

If you walk west from the Markt along Hauptstraße, Brandenburg's pedestrian shopping zone, you'll pass a horde of cafés, bakeries, restaurants, *Imbiß* (snack) stands, and even a few smart-looking bars. In summer good food can be found at the **farmers' market,** held outside of **Katharinenkirche** (*see below*) daily until about 6 (a bit earlier on Sunday). The fruit is luscious, the cheese and breads fresh and local. Just off the Markt, you'll find **Pizzeria No. 31** (Steinstr. 31, tel. 03381/224473), which fills bellies for under DM 10. There's also a **Spar** market at Hauptstraße 31–33.

WORTH SEEING

Brandenburg's three main districts are the **Altstadt** (Old City), **Neustadt** (New City), and **Dominsel** (Cathedral Island). The Altstadt, which hugs the banks of the Havel on the west side of town, was founded by German merchants in the 10th century. South across the Havel is the "new" city, settled more recently . . . in 1250. Oldest of all is in fact the Dominsel, site of the original Slavic settlement founded in the 6th century AD; the island was later conquered by the Germans. On the island, the Gothic 12th-century **Dom St. Peter und Paul** (open Mon.–Sat. 9–6) looms heavily over the river. Inside, take a look at the unusual relief of a fox in monk's clothing. Oddly enough, he's spreading the Word to a congregation of geese. Also of interest is the cathedral's collection of 13th-century stained glass, particularly the ornate cycle that crowns the altar.

From the Dominsel, a walk south along atmospheric Mühlendamm brings you to the Neustadt's **Markt** (market square), now the site of a major archaeological dig. Watch through a chainlink fence as students dig, scrape, dust, and label various artifacts. The next sight to jump out at you is the Gothic **St. Katharinenkirche,** open daily 10–6. It's noted for its redbrick facade and towering, ornately decorated spire. Although much of the structure was badly damaged during World War II, the stained-glass windows were, thankfully, hidden by church priests and thus preserved. Many of its windows originally stood in the now ruined **Klosterkirche,** a 12th-century monastery whose skeletal remains stand on nearby Paulikirchplatz.

Walk west down touristy, attractive Hauptstraße, and you'll cross the Havel River to Ritterstraße, in the Altstadt. Immediately you'll notice the late-Gothic **St. Johanniskirche,** built in the 15th century. Made of weathered brick and surrounded by a handful of half-timbered buildings, the ruined church looks impressively old—a bulky but respectable outcast in the Baroque district. To the north is the lean, redbrick **Altstädtisches Rathaus** (Old Town Hall), guarded by an 8-m-high statue of Roland, who strikes a heroic, macho pose. Inside the Rathaus is an expensive restaurant and beer garden. Farther north (pass the Rathaus and turn right) is **St. Gotthardtkirche** (Gotthardtkirchpl.; open daily 10–6), another embellished Gothic creation well worth a look inside.

EASTERN BRANDENBURG

The eastern part of Brandenburg stretches from the outskirts of Berlin through the undulating, lake-dotted forests of the **Märkische Schweiz** to the Oder river, where the border town of **Frankfurt an der Oder** has been an outpost of German culture since the Middle Ages. The region offers a refreshing escape from the hustle and bustle of the metropolis to the west. It is also refreshingly free of the crowds of tourists that fill other picturesque parts of Germany.

MÄRKISCHE SCHWEIZ (BUCKOW)

So the Love Parade—or any old weekend in Berlin—just ended and you need to treat your aching mind and body with some peace and quiet. Well, blissfully serene Buckow—at the heart of the hilly, wooded **Märkische Schweiz**—is just a charming train ride away. Buckow's quiet streets lie between four little ponds and the expansive Schermützelsee, where you can swim, boat, and fish. Both Theodor Fontane and Bertolt Brecht found inspiration here—Brecht even preferred living here to Berlin. The **Brecht-Weigel-Haus** (Bertolt-Brecht-Str. 29, tel. 033433/467) is the beautiful house where he and his collaborator and lover Helene Weigel lived during the '50s. It's now a museum on their life and Buckow, open Tuesday–Saturday 1–5, admission DM 3. To sample the region's natural beauty, ask at the tourist office for trail maps and other hiking info. The lovely **Poetensteig** trail inspired Fontane and other writers—start out by walking east along another trail (like the Hopfenweg) to Pritzhagener Mühle at the far end of the Poetensteig. Return along the Poetensteig and you'll get great views to the west over the lake and surrounding hills (8 km or 3 hours total). Wandering through these woods, you may just find your muse, too.

BASICS

Trains run hourly from Berlin-Lichtenberg (55 min, DM 10–DM 14) with a transfer in Müncheberg. Just riding the wobbly narrow-gauge train the final leg to Buckow is worth the trip. From the station walk 15 min straight up Hauptstraße to reach the Markt and **tourist office** (Wriezener Str. 1a, tel. 033433/65981). They have plenty of maps and will book you a room (DM 2 fee). The tiny free map shows trails and is surprisingly good, but if you want to hike between towns pick up the huge "Märkische Schweiz Reisegebiet" map (DM 6). Along the lake on Wriezener Straße you'll find boat excursions, rowboat rentals, and a sandy beach (admission DM 3.50). The Stadtsparkasse (Wriezener Str. 2) has a Plus and Cirrus **ATM** and is next to a **supermarket.**

WHERE TO SLEEP AND EAT

You can practically ring doorbells at random and find a Privatzimmer for the night. The competition keeps prices as low as DM 25 per person. Cheaper still is the **HI-Jugendherberge Buckow** (Berliner Str. 36, tel. 033433/286), which sits among the trees along a footpath to town south of the tiny Weißer See. It's eight to a room in bungalows or four in the main building, but the beds cost only DM 20 (DM 25 over 26) including breakfast, and there's no curfew. To reach the hostel from the station, head briefly down Hauptstraße, make a sharp left on Berliner Straße, and walk 15 min. Eating options are less appealing, though cafés like **Café Berendy** (Werderstr. 30, at Wriezener Str., no phone) will fill you with coffee and pastry, and a couple of Imbiß stands grace the Markt.

FRANKFURT AN DER ODER

The "other" Frankfurt sits on the far eastern side of Germany, about 90 km east of Berlin and quite literally just a short walk over the Oder River from Poland. The city is visually dull despite its few surviving Baroque buildings; more interesting is the cultural mixing of Poles and Germans who function in two languages on a daily basis. Frankfurt, a commercial center since Hanseatic League times, was basically unscathed by World War II until May 1945, *after* the Third Reich had already surrendered. The Werewolves (a Nazi guerrilla group) had a hard time accepting defeat and began attacking Polish forces. The clash between the Werewolves and Poles quickly degenerated into house-to-house warfare, sparking a ferocious fire that consumed 90% of the town within days. Today there is residual tension between the Poles and Germans, but you probably won't notice it.

BASICS

Get your maps and brochures at the **tourist office** (Karl-Marx-Str. 8a, tel. 0335/325216), open weekdays 10–noon and 12:30–6, weekends 10–12:30; the staff can book you a private room for DM 5 and provide you with a free list of food and lodging options. South of the tourist office across Heilbronner Straße, the **Deutsche Bank** (Zehmepl. 12) exchanges money at competitive rates and has a networked ATM.

COMING AND GOING

Trains for Frankfurt (hourly, 1¼ hrs, DM 21) depart Berlin's Hauptbahnhof. Frankfurt can also be reached from Cottbus (hourly, 1¼ hrs, DM 21) and Leipzig (5 per day, 3 hrs, DM 49–DM 68). If you want to get farther into Poland, several trains per day run to Warsaw (5 hrs, DM 26), and other Polish cities. From the station, walk away from the tunnel on Bahnhofstraße, then right on Heilbronner Straße and left on Karl-Marx-Straße to reach the tourist office and city center. **Bikes** can be rented at the Hauptbahnhof for DM 9 per day, DM 7 with a train ticket.

WHERE TO SLEEP

The tourist office books rooms (DM 5 fee) starting around DM 30 per person. **Gästehaus des Bildungszentrums** (Heinrich-Hildebrand-Str. 20a, tel. 0335/535828) offers very well kept rooms in the guest house of an organization for educational development. Singles start at DM 35, doubles at DM 85; there's a shared bath. **Freizeit- und Campingpark Helenesee** (closed Oct.–Mar.) is a hip resort with 2,000 lakeside sites perfect for water sports (including skinny dipping) and long walks in the woods. Bungalows cost DM 10–DM 40 per person depending on the season and category. From the Hauptbahnhof take Bus H (DM 2.80) to Helenesee and follow the signs.

FOOD

Broilereck (Tunnelstr. 48, just through Bahnhofstr. tunnel, tel. 0335/27991) is a local joint that serves salads (DM 4–DM 10) and *Hähnchen* (chicken) for under DM 10. **Cultur-Café Calliope** (Lindenstr. 5, tel. 0335/680–3906) serves pizza and pasta in the Haus der Künste (House of Art). Mix and mingle at courtyard tables with artsy types who haven't yet moved to Berlin. Imbiß stands in the city center offer a variety of Wursts and kebabs for under DM 5.

WORTH SEEING

The area south of Rosa-Luxemburg-Straße, east of Karl-Marx-Straße, and north of Logenstraße contains Frankfurt's remaining sights. First constructed in 1253, the **Rathaus** (Town Hall, Bischofstr. 11) underwent numerous renovations and redecorations throughout the centuries; its imposing 17th-century Baroque facade oversees the heart of the city. Behind the Rathaus is the world's only museum dedicated to Frankfurt native Heinrich von Kleist, considered one of the greatest Romantic dramatists and novelists. You can learn about him, his influence on contemporaries like Goethe, and his bizarre suicide (in a pact with his lover in Berlin) at age 34 at the **Kleist-Museum** (Faberstr. 7, tel. 0335/531155; closed Mon.). The dark, gloomy remains of **St. Marienkirche** (Große Scharrnstr., tel. 0335/22442), built from 1253 to 1524, have been undergoing restoration since 1979. This largest Gothic brick church in northern Germany was reduced to rubble in April 1945 and left in ruins for 39 years. The **Carl Philipp Emanuel Bach Konzerthalle** (Collegienstr. 8, tel. 0335/663–8823), named after the son of J.S. Bach, was first built on the Oder in 1270, then rebuit into its current Gothic brick manifestation in 1525. It contains the oldest functional organ in Germany. Tickets for classical music performances (DM 12–DM 20) can be purchased at the tourist office (*see* Basics, *above*), which publishes a free schedule of events.

SOUTHERN BRANDENBURG

About 75 km southeast of Berlin, the formerly smooth Spree River fragments into countless small tributaries. Slavic **Sorbian** tribes settled this marshland in the 6th century AD and have preserved their ethnic identity despite German expansion and settlement in the Middle Ages and Nazi efforts to erase them as a people. Sorbian communities are still scattered throughout the marshland and forest, and you'll see street signs and railroad placards in both German and Sorbian. The region's unofficial capital, the small city of **Cottbus,** has its own 18th-century charm. Or for a boat ride on the Spree and a glimpse of the **Spreewald** wetlands, join thousands of Berlin day trippers in **Lübbenau,** which also offers an enchanting glimpse of modern-day German kitsch.

COTTBUS (CHOSÉBUZ)

Cottbus, the second-largest city in Brandenburg, is the cultural center of eastern Germany's ancient Slavic minority, the Sorbs. The town is graced with a ribbon of parks and gardens and preserves a charming Altstadt centered around the Baroque **Altmarkt.** The old market square and nearby streets are full of Imbiß stands, beer halls, and snazzy tourist restaurants. A few blocks east of the Altmarkt squats the brick **Oberkirche,** a 17th-century church that looks out of place among the apartment complexes that line the adjacent streets. Inside its white-walled interior you'll find an impressive 11-m-high Baroque altarpiece, built in 1680, depicting scenes from the Crucifixion and Resurrection. Just north of the Altmarkt by the youth hostel is a Gothic brick church, the **Klosterkirche,** built in 1303. **Schillerplatz,** west of the Altmarkt, boasts a few cafés, beer-hallish restaurants, and the **Staatstheater** (Karl-Liebknecht-Str. 23, tel. 0355/78240), seasonal home to opera, dance, and drama. Tickets can cost as little as DM 8 for students.

In late June, Cottbus celebrates its Sorbian culture with the **Domowina** ("homeland") festival. For more information on Spreewald's Sorbs, contact **Sorbische Kulturinformation "Lodka"** (August-Bebel-Str. 82, tel. 0355/791110), which stocks information about Sorbian cultural history in the area and houses a library of German and Sorbian texts, newspapers, audio recordings, and videos that chronicle Sorbian life. The center is open weekdays 10–4:30 and closed the first Monday of the month.

BASICS

The **tourist office** (Karl-Marx-Str. 68, at Berliner Str., tel. 0355/24254) has maps and will book you a room (DM 5, tel. 0355/24255) weekdays 9–6, Saturday 9–1. Getting to Cottbus is a snap from Berlin (hourly from Berlin-Schöneweide, every 2 hrs from Berlin-Lichtenberg, both 1½ hrs, DM 33), Potsdam Stadt (6 per day, 2 hrs, DM 37), or Dresden (every 1–2 hrs, 2¼ hrs, DM 38). To get to town on foot exit the rear of the station (follow AUSGANG WILHELM-KÜLZ-STR. signs) and head up Schillerstraße. Turn right at the appropriate street to reach the tourist office or Sorbian info center. Tram 1 also runs from the front of the station into town; from the Stadthalle stop, the tourist office is a brief walk down on Berliner Straße.

WHERE TO SLEEP

Privatzimmer start around DM 30 per person, but your best bet is the excellent **Jugendherberge am Klosterplatz (HI)** in the courtyard around the Klosterkirche. A night in one of the bright four-bed rooms costs DM 20 (DM 25 over 26, DM 30 nonmembers), and cozy, hardwood-floored doubles in the half-timbered pension (just across the courtyard) start at DM 80. *Klosterpl. 2–3, tel. 0355/22558, fax 0355/23798. Tram 1 to Stadthalle; walk east on Berliner Str. and follow the signs left to Klosterkirche. 40 beds (hostel). No curfew or lockout. Reception open 7 AM–4 PM and 7 PM–9 PM.*

FOOD

Gaststatte Paulaner (Sandower Str. 57, just east of Berliner Str., tel. 0355/22994) serves Bavarian meals for about DM 10. If piles of pork turn you off, stick to something simple like *Ofenkartoffeln mit Kräuterquark* (baked potatoes with herb cream) for DM 4.50. Come here to sip the best Hefeweizen on the planet, Munich's Paulaner *Hefe Weiß* (DM 4.50). **Kebab-Haus** (Weinberg 4, tel. 0355/472048), to your right on Neumarkt as you walk toward Altmarkt on Berliner Straße, serves up tasty, oversized *Döner* (spit-roasted lamb on Turkish bread; DM 3) and falafel (DM 3) to take-out types, or complete Middle-Eastern meals inside for around DM 10. For a sizable dose of absurdity, check out the ludicrously decorated, hopping party bar, **Pflaumenbaum—Total Unmögliches Gasthaus** ("The Totally Impossible Inn"; Schloßkirchpl. 1, tel. 0355/25663).

Is Poland exerting a pull on you? Just walk down Rosa-Luxemburg-Straße, cross the Oder bridge, and, with the flash of a passport, you can gain entry to Frankfurt's Polish suburb of Słubice.

SPREEWALD (LÜBBENAU)

Lübbenau (Lubnjow in Sorbian), 25 km northwest of Cottbus, is the gateway to the **Spreewald.** As you walk along Dammstraße, the main promenade, you're greeted by leafy tree branches, melodic bird calls, the river itself, and thousands of German tourists, most on day trips from Berlin. At least 600,000 tourists visit tiny Lübbenau every year, and a massive industry provides them with the oompah bands, plastic souvenirs, ice cream, and beer that they crave. Conduct your own ethnography of German kitsch, or head for the more tranquil countryside beyond the town.

The most popular excursion is the footpath 2 km east to the small village of Lehde (Ledy), with a more rustic version of Lübbenau's beer-garden kitsch. Here you'll also find a re-creation of traditional Sorbian life at the open-air **Spreewaldmuseum** (Schloßbezirk, tel. 03542/2472), open daily 10–6; admission is DM 3, DM 2 for students. Another popular pastime in Lübbenau is a boat ride on a **Kahn** or punt, the local version of a gondola. Follow signs to either the *Kleiner Hafen* (little harbor) or *Großer Hafen* (big harbor) and ride a punt with aging East Germans (DM 5 per hr at Kleiner Hafen, minimum 2 hrs). For more exercise and independence, you can also rent your own boat. From the Kleiner Hafen walk left over and along the waterway to reach **Bootsverleih Hanemann** (Am Wasserl, tel. 03542/3647; open daily 9–7), one of several boat rental outfits listed at the tourist office, where you can rent kayaks (2 people, DM 31 per day) and canoes (3 people, DM 38 per day). Prices drop considerably off-season. If you want to hike or bike through the Spreewald pick up the topographic map "Oberspreewald" for DM 9.50. Otherwise the tourist office has decent free maps, and trails (more than 800 km of them) are well marked.

BASICS

For trail maps or lodging info, head to the **tourist office** (Ehm-Welk-Str. 15, tel. 03542/3668; open weekdays 9–6, weekends 9–4), near the church on the Markt. Rent a bike at the train station, or at **Kowalsky's** (Poststr. 6, tel. 03542/2835) for DM 10 per day. Hourly trains arrive from Berlin-Schöneweide (1 hr, DM 18); hourly trains also run to Cottbus (25 min, DM 6). Lübbenau's center is so small that you can't get lost. In any case, signs from the Hauptbahnhof send you to the Markt—just follow Poststraße northeast from the station.

WHERE TO SLEEP

The tourist office books rooms for DM 5. **Pension Am Stadtgraben** (Bergstr. 9, tel. 03542/3532), popular with backpackers, has doubles for DM 75. Next door is **Pension im Spreewald** (Bergstr. 11, tel. 03542/2661), which offers doubles for DM 70–DM 85. Camping is possible in any old field, but if you'd rather be safe than sorry, head to **Am Schloßpark Camping** (tel. 03542/3533; closed Nov.–Feb.), about halfway to the village of Lehde (follow the signs), where spots are DM 6 per person, DM 5 per tent. Facilities include showers, bathrooms, a little canteen, and boat rentals.

BALTIC COAST

Germany's forgotten northeastern corner has repeatedly fallen by history's wayside. The state of Mecklenburg-Vorpommern, stretching along Germany's eastern Baltic coast, lacks the bustle and sophistication of wealthier and more modern parts of Germany, but its timeless simplicity is part of its appeal. Conquered by German princes from Slavic tribes during the Middle Ages, the Baltic coast prospered as part of the Hanseatic League from the 13th to the 17th century. The region's ports, Wismar, Rostock, and Stralsund, preserve reminders of these glory days in their *Backsteingotik,* northern Germany's distinctive Gothic brick architecture. Swedish occupation after the Thirty Years' War (1618–1648) destroyed the League and with it the region's prosperity. Mecklenburg (the coast west of Darß and most of the interior) was divided into minor duchies, and Vorpommern (including Stralsund and most of the coastal islands), became first a Swedish territory and then a minor Prussian possession. As a result the region remained in a state of suspended animation while the rest of Germany industrialized; its cities retained their historical character, and the countryside remained unspoiled. Industry really only arrived after World War II, when the GDR, in dire need of a world-class harbor, built shipping facilities, especially in Rostock, where ugly Stalinist blocks now mingle with delicate Gothic brick remnants. Crippled economically by the collapse of the GDR, the region may face yet another battle with historic obscurity, yet a stroll through some of Mecklenburg-Vorpommern's Baltic Sea ports will allow you a glimpse of bygone eras.

While its cities offer aged architectural gems, Mecklenburg-Vorpommern's real beauty lies in its countryside, an ensemble of lonely, windswept beaches and yellow fields not often visited by foreigners. Few people speak English, and non-Europeans may experience uncomfortable stares outside of city centers. For those who persevere, this is a lazy, quiet place, ideal for people who appreciate kilometer-wide views over rolling fields and long, drawn-out sunsets over the sea. Germans (mostly easterners) flock to the coast in summer, and finding a room then on the islands of Rügen and Usedom can be difficult—it pays to plan ahead, even if you want to stay in hostels. Outside of the main season, the visitors are gone, and the gray, blustery Baltic can be eerily beautiful.

SCHWERIN

A real estate agent's fantasy, Schwerin can lay claim to three essential attributes: location, location, and location. The capital of Mecklenburg-Vorpommern sits right on the southeastern shore of the big Schweriner See, whose scenery has always drawn 'em in—from the dukes who established their residence here to the Slavic tribes who named this place *Zuarin,* or "rich in forest and animals." Today the only wild animals here are in the zoo—but the forested lake, a picture-perfect island castle, and a pretty (though run-down) Altstadt still beckon. For a state capital, the city (population 120,000) is a bit of a backwater, so don't expect much nightlife.

BASICS

Schwerin's **tourist office** (Am Markt 10, tel. 0385/592–5213, fax 0385/83081; open weekdays 10–6, Sat. 10–4, Sun. 10–2, closed Sun. in off-season) has maps and brochures and can reserve you a room (call 0385/565123). The **post office** (Mecklenburgstr. 4–6) also has a pay-later phone booth. **BFG Bank** (Am Markt 7) has a networked ATM.

COMING AND GOING

Schwerin can be reached by train from Berlin (8 per day, 3 hrs, DM 49), Hamburg (every 2 hrs, 1¾ hrs, DM 33), Lübeck (hourly, 1½ hrs, DM 21), and Rostock (every 2 hrs, 1¼ hrs, DM 20). The **station** (tel.

THE BALTIC COAST

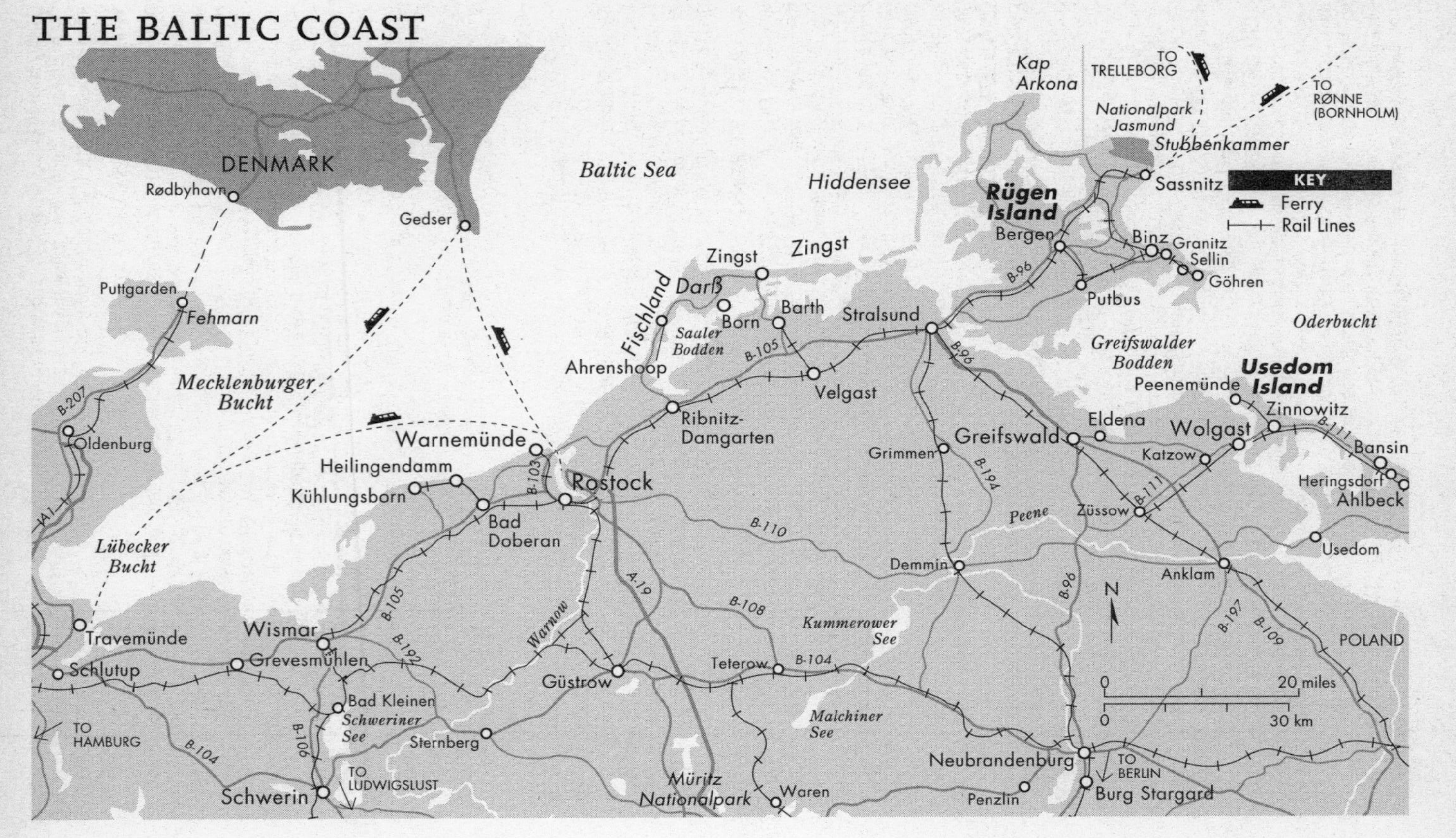

0385/750–5491) has lockers. To go downtown, head across the plaza, down Zum Bahnhof, right along the Pfaffenteich (pond), then follow the shore to the left on Arsenalstraße, keep right for Friedrichstraße, and the Markt is one block down on the right.

WHERE TO SLEEP

Privatzimmer (DM 30–DM 45) through the tourist office (no fee) tend to be outside the city center. The very central and very small **Pension Wilk** (Buschstr. 13, tel. 0385/550–7024) has three doubles for DM 90, including breakfast. From the Markt, head up Schmiedestraße to Buschstraße. **Hotel Zur Traube** (Ferdinand-Schultz-Str. 20, tel. 0385/512417) lies on the eastern edge of the Schelfstadt (*see* Worth Seeing, *below*) and has two singles (DM 85), five doubles (DM 98), and one triple (DM 115); breakfast is included. From the train station, head to the Pfaffenteich, cross on the ferry (DM 1) or walk around to Gaußstraße, then continue straight, past the church. **Campingplatz Seehof** (Seehof, tel. and fax 0385/512540) charges DM 4–DM 6 per tent plus DM 7 per person on the shores of the Schweriner See 6 km north of town. From the station, take the hourly Bus 8 (DM 2) to Seehof and continue five min on foot. The last bus leaves at 10:50 PM (Sun. 9:25 PM).

HOSTELS • Jugendherberge Schwerin (HI). Ah, the joys of hosteling! Remember that you're paying a mere DM 21 (DM 26 if you're over 26) when you trek from downtown into the woods, only to settle into those plain, multibed rooms. Oh, stop whining. *Waldschulenw. 3, tel. 0385/213005. From station, Bus 15 to Zoo, then 100 m straight ahead. Last bus 10:13 PM. 91 beds. No curfew (get key), lockout 9–4. Reception open 4 PM–10 PM.*

FOOD

The streets of the Altstadt offer plenty of cafés and Imbiß stands where a nibble won't cost too much. The Schlachtenmarkt behind the Rathaus is home to a **farmer's market** Tuesday–Sunday. A few blocks down, **Eiscafé Mexikana** (Großer Moor 32, tel. 0385/565352) has decent German food and sorry attempts at Mexican food for DM 10–DM 12. Another good deal is happy hour (3 PM–5 PM daily) at **Friesenhof** (Mecklenburgstr. 2, near Pfaffenteich, tel. 0385/557–0155), when fish and steak platters cost DM 10–DM 14. At night, sleepy Schwerin's faint heartbeat pulses on at **Boomerang** (Mecklenburgstr. 35, tel. 0385/557–4971), an Australian-themed indoor/outdoor hangout that serves Foster's on tap.

WORTH SEEING

Schwerin's **Altstadt** was once an island—the narrow divide to the mainland was filled in long ago, and the only bit of water left now forms the Pfaffenteich, a duck pond at the city center's northern edge. In the midst of it all is the **Marktplatz,** Schwerin's old marketplace, with its *Rathaus* (town hall), built in an unfortunate mock-Tudor style. Much more interesting is Schwerin's beautiful **Dom** (open Mon–Sat. 10–noon and 1–5, Sun. 2–4). The Gothic cathedral's bronze baptismal font dates from the 14th century, the altar from 1440. Huff and puff your way up the 219 steps of the church's 117-m-high **tower** (admission DM 1; open Tues.–Sat. 11–1 and 2–5, Mon. until 4; Sun. noon–5) for sweeping views of Schwerin and its lakes. East of the pond and just north of the Altstadt is the **Schelfstadt,** once an independent city. Years of extensive renovation revived the beauty of this picturesque neighborhood of little 16th–17th-century houses.

Opposite the Schloß is the **Alter Garten,** once the royal gardens, now used for outdoor concerts and the like. The majestic **Mecklenburgisches Staatstheater** (tel. 0385/530–0126 for tickets) here offers a mix of opera, classical music, and mostly German-language drama. Check the notice board for current performance schedules; cheap student tickets are available for most shows. To the right, the **Staatliches Museum Schwerin** (Alter Garten 3, tel. 0385/592400; open Tues. 10–8, Wed.–Sun. 10–6; Oct.–Apr. until 5) houses a solid collection of Flemish and Dutch masters, and works by 19th-century German artists like Max Liebermann and Lovis Corinth. Rotating exhibits display contemporary art, often by local artists. Admission is DM 7 (DM 3.50 students). **Lake cruises** (May–Sept. every 30 min, Apr. and Oct. 3–5 per day, DM 12.40) leave from the nearby docks. Call ahead to reserve tickets for a two-hour sunset cruise (tel. 0385/581–1596; June–Aug. 7:30 PM; DM 18) with smooching German couples.

SCHLOß SCHWERIN • The opulent Schloß Schwerin was built by the Mecklenburg royal family in 1857, but some form of castle has stood on this island off the Altstadt since medieval times. The Slavs, knowing a good site when they saw one, used the island for defensive purposes, but to no avail. In 1160 the German Heinrich der Löwe (Henry the Lion) defeated their last king, Niklot, near Schwerin. A huge equestrian statue high on the castle's facade honors Niklot—some of whose descendants would later form the Mecklenburg royal family. Inside the castle's 80 rooms you'll find pristine antiques, silk tapestries, carved wood floors, and ornate walls. Locals claim the Schloß is haunted by Petermännchen (Little Man Peter), a friendly ghost with the politics of Robin Hood. When your tired feet demand a rest, plop down in the castle café or catch one of the free summer concerts. Optional DM 3 tours leave at 11:30 and 1:30. *Lennéstr. 1, tel. 0385/565738. Admission: DM 6, DM 3 students. Open Tues.–Sun. 10–6.*

NEAR SCHWERIN

WISMAR

Thanks to its rich Hanseatic past—and, paradoxically, its economic marginality since the League's passing—Wismar is one of Mecklenburg's most attractive towns. The beautifully preserved old merchants' homes wind along Wismar's cobbled streets much as they have for centuries. The wealth generated by Hanseatic merchants is still conspicuous in Wismar, particularly in the ornate, gabled houses that front the Marktplatz—the biggest and most colorful in northern Germany. Dominating the square are the Rathaus and the 16th-century Dutch Renaissance **Wasserkunst,** an ornate pumping station that supplied the town's water until 1897. One of the city's oldest houses is the Gothic brick **Alter Schwede** (1380) on the Marktplatz. Its name commemorates the years 1648–1803, when Wismar was Swedish territory. (Sweden took control after Thirty Years' War.) Above the doorway is a **Schwedenkopf** (Swedish head). No one knows their exact origin, but such heads used to sit on top of harbor pylons.

As you pedal through the Spreewald, stop for lunch at one of the quiet roadside stands, where friendly farmers sell local delicacies such as pickles, fresh honey, and eels.

If you found the Alter Schwede's brick construction impressive, the late-Gothic **Nikolaikirche** (open Mon.–Sat. 8–noon and 1–6, Sun. 1–6), a few blocks north of the Marktplatz, will leave you speechless. Its 37-m-high interior arches create an experience that is . . . well, spiritual. Across the canal is the **Schabbelhaus** (Schweinsbrücke 8, tel. 03841/282350; closed Mon.), built from 1569 to 1571, which houses a local history museum and Hanseatic nautical exhibits; a developed sense of morbidity may help you appreciate the bony, leather-skinned severed hand of a pre–16th-century murder victim presented as evidence in court (*corpus delicti,* for all you budding lawyers). Admission is DM 3 (DM 1.50 students). Two more Gothic brick churches (parts of them, at least) stand west of the Marktplatz. Both were heavily damaged in World War II—only the 83-m tower of the **Marienkirche** (Kellerstr.) remains, its bells intact (listen for a carillon tune at noon, 3, and 5). One block west, the **Fürstenhof** (Bliedenstr.) was home to the dukes of Mecklenburg. Across the street, Europe's largest Gothic World War II ruin, the **Georgenkirche,** is slowly being rebuilt.

BASICS • The **tourist office** (Am Markt 11, tel. and fax 03841/19433 or 251815; open daily 9–6) has free maps, ferry and train tickets, and can book you a room (DM 5). Wismar's **train station** (tel. 03841/282394) has a handful of lockers. Trains leave hourly for Rostock (1¼ hrs, DM 14.20), Lübeck (1½ hrs., DM 19.40), and Schwerin (30 min, DM 9.40). It's a 10-min walk to the city center: Head straight across the square and up Mühlengrube, left over the canal on Schweinsbrücke, continue straight a few blocks, then right on Hinter dem Rathaus, and left onto the Markt.

WHERE TO SLEEP AND EAT • Privatzimmer (DM 28–DM 38 per person) are the only real budget option, since Wismar doesn't have a hostel. Consider staying in Schwerin's hostel and visiting on a day trip. The most affordable downtown hotel, **Hotel Reingard** (Weberstr. 18, tel. 03841/213497), has comfortable singles (DM 79–DM 120) and doubles (DM 99–DM 159). After crossing Schweinsbrücke on your way from the station (*see above*), walk straight one block, then left on Weberstraße. Sniff out restaurants, cafés, and markets on Lübsche Straße and Krämerstraße, the main pedestrian drags. **Fischgaststätte Seehase** (Altböterstr. 6, tel. 03841/282134) is popular with locals for its Mecklenburg *Fischsuppe* (fish soup) and *Pannfisch* (fried fish)—local specialties both under DM 15. Near the harbor on Am Lohberg are several pleasant cafés perfect for a sunny afternoon. Need a drink? Stop by **Schlauch Irish Pub** (Lübsche Str. 18, tel. 03841/282960) after 8 PM; if you're lucky, you might even catch some live music.

ROSTOCK

Rostock, the largest city in Mecklenburg-Vorpommern and the home of northern Germany's oldest university, has had its ups and downs. Once a thriving member of the Hanseatic League, in the 1950s Rostock regained some of its old prosperity when the GDR, lacking a decent seaport, spent millions developing a shipbuilding and shipping industry for East Germany's "Gateway to the World." With the fall of the GDR, however, the industry collapsed, and a shaky Rostock had a frightening resurgence of right-wing activity: In 1992, television pictures beamed throughout the world showed young neo-Nazis torching a home for refugees in the district of Lichtenhagen, while locals stood by—sometimes cheering on the hooligans.

In the intervening years, Rostock has regained its footing and polished its tarnished image, and neo-Nazi activity has all but disappeared, though people who don't look German should still avoid low-income suburbs like Lichtenhagen. Harbor activity is back to 90% of its pre-1989 volume and the city center bustles with shoppers, visitors, and students attending Rostock's university, a center of tolerant leftist thought. Visitors from around the world come in early July to see the start of a Windjammer race around the Baltic, and the coastal resort of Warnemünde draws crowds the week before with a wacky summer festival featuring the *Waschzuberrennen,* where anything and everything that floats competes in a wild, fun-filled race through the harbor. Beyond summer excitement, Rostock's students provide for decent nightlife and hip hangouts year-round.

BASICS

Citibank (Kröpeliner Str. 62–63, near Kröpeliner Tor) does credit-card advances and has a Plus/Cirrus ATM, but it only exchanges Visa traveler's checks. At the Warnemünde S-Bahn station, **DVB Bank** charges a 1% *or* DM 7.50 commission. **Ratsapotheke** (Neuer Markt 13, tel. 0381/493–4747) is a standard pharmacy. The **post office** (Neuer Markt; closed Sun.; postal code 18055), in a gabled building across from the Rathaus, has play-then-pay telephones.

Rostock's **tourist office** (Schnickmannstr. 13–14, off Lange Str., tel. 0381/497990; open weekdays 10–6, weekends 10–2:30) stocks city maps (including a free English-language walking guide), info on cultural events, and books private rooms (DM 5). **Rat-und-Tat** (Gerberbruch 13–15, tel. 0381/453156; open Mon. and Thurs. 10–noon and 1–6, Tues. 2–6) is a gay and lesbian center whose friendly staff and café (open Tues.–Sat. 7 PM–2 AM, Tues. women only) will help you get introduced to the local scene. Take trams 1, 2, 4, or 5 to Gerberbruch.

COMING AND GOING

Trains arrive at the **Hauptbahnhof** (tel. 0381/19419) from Berlin (8 per day, 2½ hrs, DM 49–DM 61), Schwerin (hourly, 1¼ hrs, DM 19.40), Stralsund (hourly, 1 hr, DM 17), and Lübeck (hourly, 2¼ hrs, DM 35.40). Rostock's Überseehafen (S-Bahn to Seehafen Nord) sends **ferries** year-round to Trelleborg, Sweden (5 per day, 3 hrs, DM 35–DM 52), and Gedser, Denmark (6–9 per day, 2 hrs, DM 16.50–DM 30). If you want to catch a cheap ride, Rostock has a **Mitfahrzentrale** (Am Kabutzenhof 21, tel. 0381/19440; open weekdays 4 PM to 8 PM, Sat. 12 PM to 2 PM), on tram lines 2, 5, and 12 west of the center. Call ahead.

GETTING AROUND

Most of Rostock's sights are concentrated in the Altstadt, about 2 km north of the Hauptbahnhof. The Altstadt focuses on the **Neuer Markt,** and its two main streets, **Lange Straße** and **Kröpeliner Straße,** run parallel west from Neuer Markt. To the north of the Altstadt is the **Unterwarnow,** Rostock's harbor. The seaside suburb of Warnemünde lies at the harbor's mouth, 10 km north. Rostock's integrated S-Bahn, tram, and bus system costs DM 2.40 for two hours, DM 4.20 for a *Tageskarte* valid from 9 AM to 3 AM. To Warnemünde or the harbor, get an interzone (*Gesamtnetz*) ticket for DM 3 or DM 5.50. Most lines run until around midnight. Trams 11 and 12 take you from the Hauptbahnhof to the city center and tourist office; get off at Lange Straße. The S-Bahn connects the Hauptbahnhof with Warnemünde and other suburbs.

WHERE TO SLEEP

Rostock's lodging scene stinks like the Unterwarnow on a bad-algae day. Pull yourself out of the slime with a **Privatzimmer** (DM 30–DM 60 per person, through the tourist office). One block from the Hauptbahnhof (walk right down Herweghstraße), **Pension Nielsen** (Lindenbergstr. 10, tel. 0381/490–8818, fax 0381/27425) has seven small rooms on a quiet street for DM 75 (singles) and DM 120–DM 135 (doubles). **Pension Zum Alten Strom** (Alexandrinenstr. 128, tel. 0381/51616, fax 0381/51617) in Warnemünde offers singles for DM 80–DM 90, doubles DM 100–DM 120, triples DM 125–DM 150, and a four-bed room for DM 160–DM 180. When staying more than one night in Warnemünde, a *Kurtax* of DM 3.50 (DM 2 students) is added to your bill, but you get a nifty booklet with useless coupons in exchange.

HOSTELS • Jugendherberge Warnemünde (HI). This ugly gray box is, thankfully, right across from the (clothing-optional) beach. Beds run DM 21 (DM 26 over 26). *Parkstr. 46, tel. 0381/548–1700, fax 0381/5481–7023. S-Bahn to Warnemünde-Werft, then Bus 36 or 37 to Warnemünde Strand (last bus 1 AM). 74 beds. No curfew (get key), no lockout. Reception open 10 AM–7:30 PM.*

Jugendgästeschiff Rostock (HI). Yes, this comfortable, well-run hostel is on a ship, but don't get too excited: It lies anchored at the edge of a marsh halfway up the Unterwarnow. There's a small beach with harbor view, and onboard you'll find a café, a bar, and a museum on shipbuilding, whose only real interest lies in the peek at the engine room. A bed will cost you DM 23 (DM 31 if you're over 26). *Tel. 0381/716202 or 0381/716224, fax 0381/714014. S-Bahn to Lütten-Klein, then walk 20 min to the right. 85 beds. No curfew, no lockout. Reception open 3 PM–6 PM.*

FOOD

There's no lack of snack stands and produce vendors on and around Kröpeliner Straße, and a Spar **supermarket** (Kröpeliner Str. 38, near Kröpeliner Tor) helps battle the lack of affordable restaurants. Monday through Saturday there's a small **farmer's market** on Glatter Aal, a small square one block south of Kröpeliner Straße. **Raedel's Boulevard-Garten** (Universitätspl., no phone) is an Imbiß–cum–beer garden in the middle of Kröpeliner Straße. Steak is DM 7, daily pan-fried specials are DM 8–DM 13. You'll taste the freshness as you bite into a fish sandwich prepared on one of Warnemünde's floating Imbiß stands; starting at DM 2.50, they're a steal. **Café Am Strom** (Am Strom 61, on Warnemünde's harbor, tel. 0381/548230) offers the catch of the day, be it *Matjes* (marinated herring; DM 10), *Aal* (eel; DM 18), or a vegetarian platter (DM 13).

Hop on one of the rowboats or pedal boats by the castle for a one-hour putt-putt across the pond (DM 10).

WORTH SEEING

Though Rostock proper includes vast expanses of hideous GDR-era concrete blocks, the historic city center is fairly compact and appealing. The center of downtown hustle and bustle is the pedestrian-only **Kröpeliner Straße,** affectionately known as *Kröpi.* At its center is Rostock's university, whose main building presides over the western edge of **Universitätsplatz.** Next to the university is the entrance to **Kloster Zum Heiligen Kreuz** (Klosterhof, tel. 0381/455913), a former Cistercian nunnery that now houses a museum with works by Ernst Barlach (1870–1939) and paintings of Rostock over the ages. Your admission stub gives you half-off entry to the **Kröpeliner Tor** at the far end of Kröpeliner Straße. Once one of 22 city gates (part of the city wall still stands nearby), the 54-m tower shows rotating exhibits on Rostock's history. Admission to either the Kloster or the Tor is DM 4 (DM 2 students), and both are open Tuesday–Sunday 10–6. At the other end of Kröpi is the **Neuer Markt,** with a collection of gabled houses including the 13th-century **Rathaus,** whose seven slender towers were fronted by a Baroque facade in the 18th century, then bookended with a not-so-Baroque addition after World War II.

Just off the Neuer Markt, Rostock's 13th-century Gothic brick **Marienkirche** (Lange Str.; open Mon.–Sat. 10–5, Sun. 11:15–noon) is a result of what psychologists call "church envy." Rostock's merchants, feeling underendowed and put to shame by Lübeck's newly erected Marienkirche, set out to build a monument befitting their egos. The spacious interior houses a 3-m-high astronomical clock, Germany's oldest (1472). At noon, apostles prance out, greet Jesus, get blessed, and pass through the heavenly gates (which slam in Judas's face). Admission is DM 2 (DM 1 students). The eastern Altstadt behind the Rathaus is a maze of hills and narrow lanes that feels more like a medieval town than part of a modern port. Head down Große Wasserstraße, turn left on An der Viergelindenbrücke (which becomes Am Wendländer Schilde), and you'll come to the modest **Nikolaikirche.** Wander to your left down Altschmiedestraße, past many small houses that are turning into tourist-trapping restaurants and shops, until you reach the Alter Markt. Here you can enjoy the tranquillity as you poke around the hilltop site of Rostock's founding, the **Petrikirche** (tel. 0381/455951), whose tower you can climb (DM 2.50) for a picturesque view over the town. Take a look at the church's new west portal, whose bronze and copper door displays biblical scenes that reflect seafaring motifs (a tribute to Rostock's traditional role as a harbor town). The church is open weekdays 9–5 (Dec.–Mar., 10–noon and 1–4), weekends 11–5.

Rostock has a few lesser-known attractions worth a quick look. The tallest building on August-Bebel-Straße, between the Altstadt and Hauptbahnhof southwest of the Neuer Markt, used to be the headquarters of the local **Stasi,** the GDR's secret police. If ships really turn you on, don't miss the **Schifffahrtsmuseum** (August-Bebel-Str. 1, tel. 0381/492–2697; open Tues.–Sun. 9–5), which traces the history of Baltic shipping. Admission is DM 4, DM 2 for students. From the Neuer Markt, head down Steinstraße just past the Steintor.

Though it's within the city limits, residents will vehemently deny that the seaside suburb of **Warnemünde** is part of Rostock, and the narrow streets, small fishermen's houses, fishing boats, and beautiful sandy beaches are indeed a world apart from the "big" city. Though popular with Germans seeking that Mallorca bronze without having to leave the country, Warnemünde manages to retain its small-town atmosphere. For DM 3, climb the white **Leuchtturm** (lighthouse tower) near the end of the harbor for a view of the town and the sea. The most scenic way to reach Warnemünde from Rostock is by **ferry** (5 per day, 1 hr, DM 10) from the Stadthafen near the downtown Rostock tourist office. The S-Bahn takes 20 min and gives you a tour of Rostock's high-rise housing developments.

AFTER DARK

A visit to a local club generally entails plenty of cheap beer, good tunes, and people eager to practice their English. For nighttime listings pick up the monthly magazine *Mecks* (DM 1.80). For a peek at the student scene, check out the **Studentenkeller** (Universitätspl., tel. 0381/455928; closed Sun.), a daytime café with nighttime activities ranging from drinking to live music and dancing. You'll find tribal wall art and a mellow thirty-something crowd at **Crocodil** (Friedhofsw., at Feldstr., tel. 0381/490–2121; open daily 7 PM–1 AM), the best of the small cluster of pubs near Doberaner Platz, just west of downtown. From the Kröpeliner Tor, continue straight across Lange Straße and walk right into Gertrudenplatz—Doberaner Platz (also on Tram lines 1, 2, 5, 11, and 12) is straight ahead; keep left for Wismarsche Straße, and turn left on Feldstraße to Crocodil. Live concerts and dance nights (DM 5–DM 15) also rock the **MS Stubnitz** (Stadthafen, tel. 0381/492–3143), a ship anchored near the center. Just to prove there's nightlife downtown, Rostock's young gay scene gathers at fun and friendly **Aalglatt** (Kistenmacherstr. 17, tel. 0381/493–4214; closed Sun.), in a little hovel behind Kröpeliner Straße.

FISCHLAND, DARß, AND ZINGST

Shaped like a crooked finger pointing east from the coast between Rostock and Stralsund, Fischland, Darß, and Zingst were once distinct islands; over the centuries, drifting sand joined the islands to each other and the mainland. Today they are home to tiny former fishing villages popular with eastern Germans as a quiet vacation retreat. Though vacation homes outnumber the traditional thatched-roof houses of fishermen, the landscape is relatively unspoiled, thanks in large part to the **Nationalpark Vorpommersche Boddenlandschaft,** which protects the *Bodden* (shallow tidal lagoons) between Rügen and Darß for migratory birds. Large parts of Darß and Zingst fall within the park and are therefore car-free zones. Even near the towns, it's easy to escape to empty, unspoiled beaches with only the sun and the wind as companions.

COMING AND GOING • Hop on the hourly Rostock–Stralsund train and get off at **Ribnitz-Damgarten West** or make your way to **Barth.** Ribnitz-Damgarten West is easily reached from both Rostock (25 min, DM 7.40) and Stralsund (50 min, DM 11.80). There are five direct trains daily to Barth from Stralsund (40 min, DM 8.80), but you'll have to transfer at Velgast when coming from Rostock (2 hrs, DM 17). A bus runs hourly (weekdays) or five times per day (weekends) from Barth down the peninsula to Ribnitz-Damgarten (and vice-versa). From Ribnitz-Damgarten West the bus runs to Wustrow (25 min, DM 5.80), Ahrenshoop (30 min, DM 6.50), Born-Ibenhorst (40 min, DM 8.20), Prerow (1 hr, DM 9.80), Zingst (1¼ hrs, DM 12.20), and Barth (1½ hrs, DM 16.80); from Barth the bus makes the same stops back to Damgarten-Ribnitz—subtract travel times and prices from the listing above. Getting around by bike is a good alternative; for rental info, *see* Outdoor Activities, *below.*

WHERE TO SLEEP AND EAT • Privatzimmer (DM 25–DM 40 per person) abound, though it would be wise to reserve through the local tourist office a few weeks (even months) ahead for the high season (June–September). **Pensions** are also plentiful and affordable, but the best options are the region's youth hostels and campgrounds, many of them a stone's throw from the beach. Most towns charge a lodging tax (DM 2–DM 4 per day), though students can get a 25%–50% discount. Restaurants are expensive and few, and the lack of mass tourism means Imbiß stands are rare, too. Stock up instead at grocery stores (Zingst is your best bet), or go for the full room and board deal if your hostel or pension offers it.

OUTDOOR ACTIVITIES • This stretch of coast is one of the best areas for bicycling on the Baltic. A well-paved trail runs atop the protective dike and hugs almost the entire coastline, with a short stretch of forest on Darß. Rent a bike to cover as long or short a stretch as you like. **Fahrradvermietung Luft** (tel. and fax 038232/80143) is based in Zingst, with five outlets, including one at Campingplatz Am Freesenbruch (*see below*) and at the kiosk (open daily 7–6) on the road toward the campground. Three- or five-speeds cost DM 10 per day (DM 60 per week), and you can drop the bike off at franchises throughout the region: in Ahrenshoop at the Spar-Markt (Grenzw. 17, tel. 038220/389), in Dierhagen at Campingplatz An den Dünen, and in Barth at VW-Autohaus Neu (Am Mastw., tel. 038231/2721; open weekdays 7–6, Sat. 9–noon), a 15-min walk west of the train station.

FISCHLAND

A sunset over the Baltic, a campfire on the long white beach . . . Welcome to Fish Country. As long as tourist agencies overlook this stunning stretch of the Baltic coastline, yours will be among the few footprints that dot this long, narrow spit. In less than 10 min you can walk right across Fischland, from its long sandy beach to the marshy shores of the Saaler Bodden. Its tiny towns, with fishermen's homes and modest vacation houses, offer a few sights, but generally this is a place to enjoy the out-of-doors. Tiny **Wustrow** and **Ahrenshoop** offer pensions and private rooms; contact the local tourist office for reservations. At the narrowest point on Fischland, Wustrow is a quiet bicoastal town with easy access to both marsh and ocean. Its town center is known for its traditional thatched-roof houses, some dating from fishing times. Walk toward the beach from the bus stop to reach Wustrow's **tourist office** (Strandstraße 10, tel. 038220/251; open weekdays 9–4, weekends 9–3). Just north of Wustrow, Ahrenshoop is even smaller, occupying a long, narrow strip along the coast. Here, the beach-and-dune terrain rises to a steep coastal cliffscape that, along with the wide sky and sea, has attracted artists for over a century. In 1889, German artist Paul Müller-Kaempf fell in love with Ahrenshoop and, shortly after, founded a small artists' colony. Today artists continue to seek inspiration from the Nordic landscape and peaceful countryside. Founded in 1909, Ahrenshoop's **KunstKaten** (Strandw. 2, tel. 038220/80308; open daily 10–1 and 2–6) exhibits work by local artists, past and present, as do **Kunsthaus Guttenberg** (Feldw. 3, tel. 038220/80726) and **Haus Lukas** (Dorfstr. 35, tel. 038220/80633). The **tourist office** (Kirchnersgang 2, tel. 038220/234; open Mon., Wed., and Fri., 9–4, Tues. and Thurs. 9–noon, weekends 9–3) is one block west of the bus stop.

According to legend, the bronze snake on the Rathaus's left-most column was a test of Rostocker citizenship: In lieu of a passport, residents mentioned the shiny serpent.

DARß

The largest landmass in this triad of connected islands, Darß falls almost entirely within the **Nationalpark Vorpommersche Boddenlandschaft** and is therefore home to beautiful forest and unspoiled beaches accessible only by hiking or biking across the forest. The park is a breeding and feeding ground for cranes and other migratory birds, as well as frogs, salamanders, and other little critters. The region's largest town, **Prerow,** is depressingly quiet and far from the beach. To be close to the forest trails, get off the bus at Ibenhorst and follow the signs to the **HI-Jugendherberge** (Im Darßer Wald, tel. and fax 038234/229), where beds cost DM 24 (DM 28 over 26). From the same stop, it's a short hike to **Campingplatz Am Bodden** (Born, tel. and fax 038234/244), with sites for DM 8–DM 9 plus DM 6 per person and a DM 2 (DM 1.50 students) tax. Take the first right off the main road and walk about 20 min. Otherwise call to see if the comparably priced **Regenbogen Camp** (038233/276) still has spots. If you really want to stay in Prerow, contact the **tourist office,** which books Privatzimmer for free (Gemeindepl. 1, tel. 038233/551).

ZINGST

The town of Zingst is a veritable metropolis compared to the other little villages, and it makes a good introduction or base for exploring the region. Not only does it have a long, white-sand beach where you can escape the crowds, but it is well-equipped with tourist services like bike rental (*see above*) and near both Darß and the Zingst peninsula (also within the Nationalpark). Zingst's **tourist office** (Klosterstr. 21, tel. 038232/81525, fax 038232/633) has info on the entire region and can book you a room or pension. About 1 km west of the tourist office along the beach, you can camp at **Campingplatz Am Freesenbruch** (Seestr., tel. 038232/786) for DM 7 per person, DM 5–DM 7 per tent, and DM 3 per car. The **HI-Jugendherberge Zingst** (Glebbe 14, tel. 038232/465) is one of the cleanest, most modern youth hostels around; the bicyclists and budget-oriented nature lovers who stay here bring the average age into the over-18 category (in the rest of town the age averages around 50). Beds cost DM 23 (DM 28 over 26).

NECESSITY IS THE MOTHER OF INVENTION

When German princes conquered the Slavic territories to the east in the Middle Ages, they brought Gothic architecture with them—Christianization was, after all, the supposed reason for their land grab. However, the lack of stone quarries in Mecklenburg forced them to switch to a different material for their imposing monuments—brick. So was born Backsteingotik (Gothic brick architecture), a unique and beautiful style marked by austere yet playful facades and a somber severity befitting the gray skies of the German north. Among the most famous examples of this architecture are the Stralsund Rathaus and the Alter Schwede in Wismar, but examples are found throughout Mecklenburg-Vorpommern.

STRALSUND

Stralsund, founded in 1234 as a member of the illustrious Hanseatic League, has seen better days. But after centuries of decline, the town is dusting off and sprucing up its historic Altstadt, one of the least altered in all Germany—including a fabulous Rathaus, one of the most impressive Gothic brick structures ever built. Though a bit run-down, the old houses, mostly late Gothic, Renaissance, and Baroque, share the streets with only a few modern ugly ducklings. As of yet, tourism has not begun to approach the scale of that other Gothic brick paradise, Lübeck (*see* Chapter 13), and Stralsund is a good place to experience a fairly intact, if down-at-the-heels Hanseatic town. As a gateway to Rügen (*see below*), the city makes a good base for day-long excursions, though the island is best experienced at a more leisurely pace. In early June, Stralsund hosts its annual sailing festival, the **Stralsunder Segelwoche.** Head to the port for the spectacle of hundreds of sailboats parading and racing across the harbor.

BASICS

The **tourist office** (Ossenreyerstr. 1–2, at Alter Markt, tel. 03831/24690, fax 03831/246949) books rooms (DM 5) and has free maps. It's open weekdays 9–6:30, weekends 9–1 (shorter hrs off-season). At the **Hauptbahnhof** (tel. 03834/19419), trains run to Berlin (1–2 per hr, 2¾ hrs, DM 49–DM 59), Rostock (hourly, 1¼ hrs, DM 17.80), Wolgast (every 2 hrs, 1¼ hrs, DM 15.80), and Rügen (*see below*). To reach the tourist office from the Hauptbahnhof, walk right along Tribseer Damm, continue on Tribseer Straße, left on Mönchstraße at Neuer Markt, right on Apollonienmarkt, and left down Ossenreyerstraße to Alter Markt.

WHERE TO SLEEP

Privatzimmer are in the DM 30–DM 40 range; affordable pensions are few. **Pension Regenbogen** (Richtenberger Chaussee 2a, tel. 03831/497674, fax 03831/494846) is a small, pleasant place to stay near the Hauptbahnhof (walk left 4 blocks) with one single (DM 50–DM 70), five doubles (DM 70–DM 90), and a triple (DM 90–DM 120), though the neighborhood is a bit drab, to say the least. The labyrinthine **HI-Jugendherberge Stralsund** (Am Kütertor 1, tel. 03831/292160, fax 03831/297676) is housed in a section of the old town wall. Climb a maze of stairs to reach your dorm bed (DM 22, DM 26 over 26). To reach the hostel, walk right up Tribseer Damm and turn left on Knieperwall (15 min). The more remote **HI-Jugendherberge Stralsund-Devin** (Sandstr. 21, tel. 03831/270358) has beds for DM 18 (DM 26 over 26) and is a 20-min ride from the Hauptbahnhof on Bus 3 (direction: Devin). Reception opens at 4 PM. Call ahead, as both hostels are often booked and close for a few weeks around Christmas.

FOOD

Along Ossenreyerstraße, you'll find an **Ihre Kette** grocery store before hitting produce-and-Imbiß heaven at the corner of Badenstraße (weekdays, anyway). Darn good—and affordable—are the fish filet (DM 11) and Schnitzel (DM 15) at **Nr. 10–Die Wirtschaft** (Tribseer Str. 10, off Neuer Markt, tel. 0383/280139; open daily from 6 PM), a friendly traditional restaurant/bar with occasional live Irish folk or oldies music. For cheaper, less atmospheric fare, try **Nur Fisch** (Heiliggeiststr. 92, at Mönchstr.; closed Sun.). Treat your palate to the *Soljanka* (fish stew; DM 4.30) or the calamari with roasted potatoes (DM 11.50). **Galerie-Café Art** (Badenstr. 44, tel. 03831/290765; closed Sun.) offers small meals (soups, sandwiches; DM 5–DM 7) in a relaxed arty atmosphere. **Speicher-Café** (*see* After Dark, *below*) has a DM 4.50 lunch at 11:30, when you can chow down, cafeteria-style.

WORTH SEEING

After being attacked by a fleet from Lübeck in 1249, Stralsund erected a brawny defensive wall (bits of which remain) to protect the town, which centered on the impressive **Alter Markt,** flanked by dozens of Renaissance and Gothic brick merchant houses. The square's highlight is the flamboyant 13th-century **Rathaus,** considered the finest example of secular Gothic brick architecture in northern Germany. Its gables, added in the early 1300s, are the crowning glory of this style. Each column represents a separate Hanseatic town with its town logo. Across from the Rathaus, the **Wulflamhaus** was built as a smaller copy by the vain Mayor Wulflam, who wanted to show the town council that he was something, too. The council restricted his house's height: It had to be smaller than the Rathaus. Over the square stands the steeple-less tower of the **Nikolaikirche** (open Mon.–Sat. 10–5, Sun. 11–noon and 2–4). Inside are some of the most colorful church wall paintings in Germany and one of the world's oldest astronomical clocks. One block north of the Alter Markt is the former monastery **Johanniskloster** (Schillstr., tel. 03831/294265; open May–Oct., Tues.–Sun. 10–6). Founded in 1254, it was destroyed by bombs in 1944; today a replica of Ernst Barlach's sculpture *Mother with Dead Soldier* (the Nazis destroyed the original) sits among the ruins. The monastery's museum (admission DM 3, DM 2 students) is worth a peek to see the beautiful Baroque library and the *Räucherboden* (smokehouse), whose wooden beams were preserved by the chimney smoke that gathered here over the centuries.

Stralsund belonged to Sweden from the 17th to the 19th centuries, and some jokesters have suggested petitioning Sweden for reunification.

If you head down **Ossenreyerstraße,** the main pedestrian and commercial street, you'll pass through the quiet Apollonienmarkt (turn right) before butting into the **Katharinenkloster,** a former monastery dating from the mid-1200s. Inside, the **Meeresmuseum** (Katharinenberg 14–20, tel. 03831/295135; admission DM 7, DM 3.50 students) displays anything and everything related to the sea. Saturday at 11 AM is shark-feeding time; Sunday you can watch the octopuses crunch 'n' munch. The museum is open daily 10–5; July–August 9–6; November–April closed Monday. Next door, the **Kulturhistorisches Museum** (Mönchstr. 25–27, tel. 03831/292180; open Tues.–Sun. 10–5) exhibits all that Viking jewelry you've been dying to see. Admission is DM 5 (DM 2.50 students). If organs inspire you, walk down Mönchstraße to Neuer Markt and the redbrick **Marienkirche.** The colossal 17th-century Stellwagen organ here is played daily at 11 AM except Thursday and Sunday. Climb the 104-m tower (DM 2) for a breathtaking—literally (cough, wheeze)—view of Rügen and Hiddensee.

AFTER DARK

There's not much to do here at night, but Stralsund does have one aesthetically brilliant place to hang out—**Benn gunn bar** (Fährstr. 27, no phone; open daily 6 PM–1 AM), a basement swillery popular with college-age locals that looks like a cross between an Irish pub and a mineshaft. Be sure to try the thumbs-up hometown Pilsner, Stralsunder. Or drink beer with a more alternative crowd at **Speicher-Café** (Katharinenberg 34, no phone; open daily from 9 PM), three blocks behind the Katharinenkloster; dance to live music on weekends (cover DM 8) in the multilevel converted warehouse.

RÜGEN ISLAND

The island of Rügen is a don't-miss attraction—the high point of a trip to the Baltic coast. During the 1920s and '30s Rügen's main towns—**Bergen, Sassnitz,** and **Putbus**—became popular holiday resorts, and Rügen continues to balance its natural wonders with the less wonderful creations of modern soci-

THE COLOSSUS OF PRORA

The Koloß von Prora, a huge concrete structure stretching 3½ km along Rügen's east coast, wasn't just built for mass tourism. It was built for the masses—20,000 of them, to be exact. Begun in the '30s but left uncompleted, the complex was meant to provide fun and sun for the German worker in Hitler's "Kraft durch Freude" ("Strength Through Happiness") program. Other KdF projects included the VW ("Volkswagen" means "Car of the People").

ety (tourist shops, bars, and some stern communist-era hotels). People don't come here for the architecture or nightlife; they come for the incredible mix of simple and natural sights: from villages like **Putgarten** and **Vitt** full of thatched-roof cottages to km-long windswept beaches surrounded by dramatic chalk cliffs and lighthouses. The jewel of Rügen is the Wittow peninsula around **Kap Arkona,** a peaceful stretch of tiny villages and unspoiled coast. The weather here is mild, but it's always, *always* windy.

COMING AND GOING • From Stralsund, hourly trains travel to the Rügen towns of Bergen (30 min, DM 8) and Sassnitz (1 hr, DM 14.40), and via Bergen to Binz (1 hr total, DM 14.40) and Putbus (50 min total, DM 12.80). No trip is complete without a ride on the romantic, narrow-gauge **Rasender Roland** (Racing Roland), a steam train that starts in Putbus (*see below*), though buses are a cheaper way to get from town to town. For a taste of Rügen without the hassle, hop on a **Weiße Flotte** (Fährstr. 16, tel. 03831/268119) cruise boat. These leave from Stralsund's harbor every few hours for Sassnitz and Hiddensee (DM 20 round-trip) and let you take in a few of Rügen's sights, walk the coast, have some lunch, and return to Stralsund by nightfall.

WHERE TO SLEEP AND EAT • Your best bet is to settle down somewhere and take day trips to the nooks and crannies. It's possible to explore Rügen from Stralsund, but staying on Rügen makes it easier to enjoy the island's pleasures. Note, however, that budget lodging is EXTREMELY scarce between June and September, and you should book weeks or even months ahead to prevent getting stranded. That said, there are 18 campgrounds on Rügen and a slew of private houses that rent space for DM 30–DM 45 per person; check with the tourist offices around the island. To book a private room anywhere on Rügen, call **Touristik Service Rügen** (tel. 038306/6160, fax 038306/61666, toll-free within Germany 0800/846–8357) or **Tourismusverband Rügen** (Am Markt 4, tel 03831/80770). When hungry, avoid the overpriced boardwalk and oceanside diners and relish the omnipresent Imbiß stands (though they have fewer veggie options) and the true poor wanderer's gift from the poverty god: the market.

OUTDOOR ACTIVITIES • Like the entire Baltic coast, Rügen is popular for long-distance bike treks, though day-long rides can be equally rewarding, since they let you get away from the very well-beaten path. Consult tourist offices and bike rental shops about the countless trails through forests and hills and to beaches. If possible, rent a bike with gears (DM 8–DM 15 per day), as Rügen has its ups and downs. After a long, strenuous ride or a long, strenuous day of lounging around, a dip in the cool Baltic waters is icing on the cake.

BERGEN

The main reason to come to Bergen, the island's central city and nominal capital, is to transfer to a Putbus- or Binz-bound train or to visit **Touristinformation Bergen** (Marktpl. 11, tel. 03838/811206; open weekdays 10–8, Sat. 10–2; weekdays 10–6 in off-season) for info on the whole island, including hiking, biking, and camping facilities. The office is in the city center, a 15-min walk uphill from the Bahnhof (left, then right on Bahnhofstraße and left on Marktstraße). On Kirchplatz, near Marktplatz, do a bit of sightseeing in the odd 14th-century brick **Marienkirche.** The faded frescoes on the walls and ceilings were painted with a strange mixture of pigment and sour milk. Particularly interesting are those on either side of the altar, showing heaven (left) and hell (right). At the back of the church stands the **Totenuhr** (Clock of the Dead), which has not ticked for more than 100 years (ever since, rumor has it, a woman died of fright after looking at the skeleton above the clock).

BINZ AND ENVIRONS

On Rügen's east coast, Binz is the island's largest seaside resort and has little to offer except its beachfront location and a youth hostel. Take a quick look at the town's principal sight—the 3½-km-long boardwalk—then rent a bike and explore the surrounding sights. Five km south is **Jagdschloß Granitz** (admission DM 4.50, DM 2 students), a fairy-tale creation resembling an overgrown sand castle. Check out the elaborate ceilings of the castle's restored rooms, and on the way out, climb 125 steps to the top of the adjacent watchtower for a view of the coast. To hike to the Schloß, start at Parkplatz Klünderberg (a parking lot at the south end of Heinrich-Heine-Straße) and follow the signs up the trail. If you don't feel like straining yourself, you'll have to surrender your dignity to a 45-min ride to the castle on a choo-choo car (yes, a car disguised as a train) from the intersection of Binz's Hauptstraße and Strandpromenade; pay when you get on. The **Jagdschloßexpress** runs hourly and costs DM 8 round-trip. An excellent bike trail runs from Binz through forested hills to **Sellin,** a smaller resort and the gateway to the Mönchgut Peninsula—a less-crowded part of Rügen—6 km to the southeast. North of Binz is the **Koloß von Prora** (Colossus of Prora), Albert Speer's monstrous cement creation that has to be seen to be believed (*see box,* The Colossus of Prora, *below*). When the East German government attempted to blow it up, the massive building actually survived unscathed. You can inquire about tours at the youth hostel. About 15 min past the **Jugendherberge Prora** (*see below*) inside the Koloß is the low-budget but inspired **Museum Zum Anfassen** (tel. 038393/32640; open daily 10–6; admission DM 4.50), a hands-on science and technology exhibit that also tells the Colossus's history.

BASICS • Binz's **tourist offices,** one near the HI hostel (Schillerstr. 15, tel. 038393/2215 or 038393/2782; closed Sun.), the other with longer hours (Heinrich-Heine Str. 7, tel. 038393/37421; open weekdays 9–6, Sat. 9–noon), both book private rooms and have the usual info. **HI-Jugendherberge Binz** (Strandpromenade 35, tel. 038393/32597, fax 038393/32596) is right on the beachfront promenade (head straight from the station and right at the beach). Try for a room overlooking the sea. There's almost always a bed free at the seaside **Jugendherberge Prora** (Prora, tel. 0383939/32844, fax 0383939/32845), one short train stop away at Prora-Ost inside the massive Nazi-era Koloß. In such a monstrous building, how could there not be room? Its 360 beds actually use only a fraction of the Koloß. Both hostels cost DM 22 (DM 26 over 26). Rent a **bike** at the train station (pick up 10–noon, return 5–6) for DM 12–DM 30 per day, depending on how many gears you want, or at the Prora hostel (pick up 8 AM–9 AM, return 5 PM) for DM 8. Binz's main **station** is at the west end of town—Roland (*see below*) stops at a smaller station 2 km south on the main road.

PUTBUS

The tiny town of Putbus is best known for its neoclassical architecture. GDR textbooks say that the Schloß here, once the local princes' residence, was torn down in 1962 to rid the town of a "decadent stigma," but locals say the castle fell due to lack of funds. Console yourself with the **Circus,** Putbus's unique central circle, dominated by odd geometric designs and orderly white plazas. Nearby August-Bebel-Straße contains the best examples of Putbus's small, one-story merchant houses. **Park zu Putbus,** with almost 75 varieties of exotic trees, makes for a cool walk. Stop by **Putbus Information** (August-Bebel-Strasße 1, tel. 038301/431) to get tourist info or buy city and park maps. Regular trains arrive hourly from Bergen (15 min, DM 3.50), but much more jolly is the ride to Binz on **Rasender Roland,** the narrow-gauge train that puffs seven times daily from Putbus via Binz (30 min, DM 9) to Göhren (1¼ hrs, DM 13.80), a village on the southeastern tip of Rügen surrounded by sandy beaches and cliffs. Ask for Roland timetables at any tourist office or train station.

SASSNITZ

"A visit to Rügen is a visit to Sassnitz," wrote Theodor Fontane in the late 19th century. Today, as Sassnitz clings to a weathered collection of hotels and buildings on the northeast coast of the island, the nearby Nationalpark Jasmund radiates as a haven of natural beauty. Convenient **bus connections** can take you to the park's Stubbenkammer (hourly, 15 min, DM 2.50), Altenkirchen near Kap Arkona (every 1–2 hrs, 40 min, DM 7.40), and Binz (hourly, 20 min, DM 2.50). Rent a **bike** (DM 10 per day) from **Fahrradhaus** (Birkenw. 12, near Bahnhof, tel. 038392/35075). The **tourist office** (Seestrasße 1, tel. 038392/5160; open Apr.–Oct., weekdays 8–7, weekends 3–7, shorter hrs in off-season) has maps, brochures, and info on lodging. From the Sassnitz harbor, **Hansa-Ferry** (tel. 038392/33233) sends ships to Rønne, on the Danish island of Bornholm (1–2 per day; 2½ hrs, DM 20–DM 30) and Trelleborg, Sweden (4–5 per day, 3¾ hrs, DM 20–DM 30), with rail connections onward to Stockholm and other cities. Sassnitz also has the only **DVB** bank in Rügen (Trelleborger Str. 16, near harbor; closed Sun.), which changes traveler's checks for DM 7.50 and has an ATM. Stock up at the **Plus** market at the Bahnhof.

NATIONALPARK JASMUND

The indisputable high point of Rügen is Nationalpark Jasmund, with a variety of terrains from deserted rock beaches to eerie, silvery forests. The seaside nature reserve contains six clearly marked trails that run along beaches and cliffs. A short path leads from Sassnitz to **Wissower Klinken,** a group of rugged chalk cliffs exalted by the painter Caspar David Friedrich (1774–1840). Farther north is the equally famous **Königstuhl** (King's Chair), which towers 120 m above the sea. It got its name (according to legend) from a footrace held each year by the Ranen, an ancient tribe of Slavs: The first runner to reach the cliff top was crowned king. Hike down (10 min) to Victoriasicht for a spectacular view of the cliffs themselves. The park's true jewels are the twin chalk cliffs of the **Stubbenkammer** at the northern end of the park. Bone-white, they tower majestically over the greenish sea, inspiring Romantics like Friedrich. Today, they draw a suffocating number of German tourists. It's difficult to appreciate the cliffs from land, so consider a **boat tour** from Sassnitz's Stadthafen (from the station, head down Bahnhofstraße, left on Hauptstraße, right on Seestraße, and right on H.-Bebert-Straße). The **MS-Nordwind** (5 per day, 2 hrs, DM 13, DM 7 students) is the best deal. You can also take the Sassnitz–Stubbenkammer bus (hourly, 15 min, DM 2) or, even better, make the 3½-hour hike through Nationalpark Jasmund.

The Nationalpark has two **information offices** (tel. 038393/2425), one in the kiosk at the end of Sassnitz's Weddingstraße (from the station, head down Bahnhofstr., left on Hauptstr., and continue straight for 20 min) and one near the Stubbenkammer, but you can pick up trail maps in tourist offices all over Rügen. Bring your food, as everything in and around the park is overpriced. Camping is possible in the park, otherwise shack up in Sassnitz. The tourist office there has details on camping all around Rügen. The only official spot in the park, **Camping Nipmerow** (Nipmerow, tel. 038302/9244; closed Nov.–Mar.), 3 km west of Königsstuhl just outside the little village of Nipmerow, costs DM 14 per night.

KAP ARKONA

Kap Arkona, perched on the storm-battered tip of Rügen, is the northernmost point in Mecklenburg-Vorpommern and the quietest corner of Rügen. In typical GDR paranoia, the cape was jealously guarded because it was a mere 77 km from Sweden. Well known for rugged cliffs, sweeping views of the horizon, tiny thatched-roof fishing villages, and vast yellow rapeseed fields, the cape itself is, like Stubbenkammer, so popular it had to be made car-free; nevertheless, the surrounding area is notably lacking in mass tourism. **Vitt,** on the coast 1 km south of the cape, consists of 45 thatched houses protected by UNESCO as a World Heritage Site. Sing sad songs of your far-off homeland while standing dead center in the small, white, octagonal church—the acoustics are exceptional. To reach the cape from Sassnitz, ride your bike (about 30 km), or take a bus (direction: Wiek or Borkenberg) to Altenkirchen (hourly, 1 hr, DM 7.40), then take a second bus 6 km to Putgarden, 1 km west of the cape. The island's best campground is probably **Camping-Park Altenkirchen** (Drewoldke, tel. and fax 038391/12484; closed Nov.–Feb.) between Juliusruh and Altenkirchen. Get off the Altenkirchen bus at Drewoldke for shady spots near the beach. Sites are DM 6.50 per car, DM 7 per person, and DM 8 per tent. The campground has 300 spots but is more spread out and has fewer motor homes than other sites. You can rent bikes here for a tour around the cape and the windswept countryside for DM 10–DM 30 per day.

HIDDENSEE

If you're really adventurous, consider an excursion to Hiddensee, a 17-km-long island off the west coast of Rügen. Known in local dialect as *"dat söte Länneken"* ("the sweet little island"), the only two cars on the island belong to the post office and fire department. The island's "no cars" rule keeps away those windshield tourists, with their noise and fumes. On remote Hiddensee, the languid rhythms of nature prevail: Animals lazily graze, stillness surrounds you, and Ricardo Montalban calls out "Smiles everyone, smiles!" every day at noon. Tattoo had to leave his golf cart at home, so bring your hiking shoes or rent a **bike** (DM 12–DM 35 per day) in any of the ferry villages and pedal through the rolling terrain. Ferries operated by **Weiße Flotte** (tel. 03831/268116) run daily to the village of Neuendorf from Stralsund (3 per day, 2 hrs, DM 13.80, DM 26 round-trip) and from Schaprode on the west coast of Rügen (every 1–2 hrs, 30 min, DM 11, DM 19 round-trip). Similar service will connect you to Vitte and Kloster farther north on Hiddensee; travel times are slightly longer, fares slightly higher. There are no hostels or campgrounds, but the local **tourist office** (Norderende 162, Vitte, tel. 038300/64225) can book you a room (DM 20–DM 50 per person).

USEDOM ISLAND

Locals say that no matter where you are on this narrow, 40-km-long island, you can always hear waves crashing. More than 85% of Usedom is a protected nature area, and the whole island may eventually be turned into a national park; in other words, Usedom is devoid of cement-and-steel structures, gruesome factories, and toxic muck. Here you find only vast stretches of sand, sea, and endless horizon. Stay in the small resort towns of **Bansin, Ahlbeck,** or **Heringsdorf** (known as "The Imperial Three"), and then strike out into the placid natural wonderland of Usedom by day. Most of the island belongs to Germany, but the eastern part has been Polish territory since 1945. A few words about Usedom's beaches: You won't be surfing here, not even a little bit—waves are nonexistent. And if you're not used to swimming with jellyfish, you will be (don't worry, the tiny little buggers aren't vicious; the scariest creatures by far are the naked old people).

BASICS • Usedom's tourist offices all have camping, biking, and hiking info for the entire island. The office in **Ahlbeck** (Dünenstr. 45, tel. 038378/24414 or 24416) books rooms in Bansin, Ahlbeck, or Heringsdorf. Heringsdorf, Usedom's nicest (and most popular) town, has a **tourist office** (Kulmstr. 33, in complex just off pier, tel. 038378/22234) with more information but without a room-booking service. Both are open weekdays 9–noon and 12:30–6, Saturday until 4, and Sunday only until noon.

GDR-era bunkers aren't the only fortifications on Kap Arkona. The Slavic Ranen also feared a Scandinavian invasion—rightly so. In 1168, the Danes, determined to Christianize the Slavs, destroyed the fortress dedicated to the Slavic god Svantevit. Only its protective wall remains.

COMING AND GOING • Rail tickets are sold directly to destinations on Usedom, but getting here always involves a transfer at **Wolgast.** Trains arrive at the Wolgast Hafen station (usually with a transfer at Züssow) from Berlin (hourly, 2¼ hrs, DM 49–DM 59) and Stralsund (every 2 hrs, 1¼ hrs, DM 17.50). From Wolgast Hafen, cross the bridge (follow the crowd) to the Wolgaster Fähre station and jump on the Usedom-Bäderbahn, which runs at least hourly to Peenemünde (via Zinnowitz, 35 min, DM 9), Ückeritz (40 min, DM 10), Bansin (50 min, DM 12), Heringsdorf (1 hr, DM 14), and Ahlbeck (1¼ hrs, DM 15.80).

WHERE TO SLEEP • If the hostel is booked solid, you may be able to find reasonable doubles in Privatzimmer, but make reservations months in advance or you're looking at more than DM 60 per person. In tiny Ückeritz, 10 km west of Heringsdorf, **Campingplatz Ückeritz** (Bäderstr. 4, tel. 03875/20265) has 700 beautiful sites between the woods and beach for DM 4.50 per person, DM 4–DM 6 per tent, and DM 4 per car. You can rent a bike here for DM 10 per day. From Ückeritz's Bahnhof head north for about 15 min.

HI-Jugendherberge Heringsdorf. This 167-bed hostel, in a squeaky-clean building near the nude beach, is usually as packed as a hard-rock concert (same crowd, too). Definitely reserve ahead, or phone the hostel between 8 AM and 9 AM the day you arrive. A bed will cost you DM 22 (DM 26 over 26), including breakfast. *Puschkinstr. 7–9, tel. 038378/22325, fax 038378/224761. From Heringsdorf station, follow sign down Friedenstr., turn right and right again on Delbrückstr., left on Eichenw. Midnight curfew. Reception open 8–9, noon–1, 5–6, and sporadically 7–9:30. Closed mid-Dec.–Jan.*

OUTDOOR ACTIVITIES • Just about every Thor, Dirk, and Heinrich seems to have a **bike** for rent. You can get one right off the train at Bahnhof Heringsdorf for DM 10–DM 25 per day. In Ückeritz on Usedom's southern Bodden coast (walk south on Hauptstraße from the station), **Segel- und Surfschule Ückeritz** (tel. 038375/20641) rents windsurf boards for DM 19–DM 28 per hour.

PEENEMÜNDE

Neil Armstrong probably wouldn't have made it to the moon if it hadn't been for Peenemünde's top-secret testing range, where Wernher von Braun designed the V-1 and V-2 rockets for the Nazis before following the shifting winds of opportunity to the U.S. space program. Entering the former test site is an eerie experience: The quiet forest surrounding Peenemünde (which was, until a few years ago, off-limits to visitors) seems to want to hide something and the occasional guard tower still rises from the trees. The **Historisch-technisches Informationszentrum Peenemünde** (Bahnhofstr. 28, tel. 03837/20573; open Tues.–Sun. 10–6) in the former test bunker is big on the technological details and back-patting cradle-of-space-flight tra-la-la, but manages to fit in a discussion of the rockets' victims in London and the Netherlands. Admission is DM 6 (DM 4 students). The museum is a five-min walk from the Peenemünde train station.

BANSIN, AHLBECK, AND HERINGSDORF

Die drei Kaiserlichen (The Imperial Three)—Bansin, Heringsdorf, and Ahlbeck—are 19th-century bathing resorts and the local tourist industry's raison d'être. **Bansin** is the westernmost, smallest, and quietest of the three, and the resorts' clientele of retirees gives a whole new meaning to the word "sleepy." Just east, you'll stumble into **Heringsdorf,** the oldest resort on the island. Kaiser Wilhelm II built a villa here, and Russian playwright Maxim Gorky spent the summer of 1922 strolling the promenade. The beach is packed, but as you wander away from town, the crowds (and clothes) seem to decrease. If you're dying to get naked, look for the FKK signs *and* make sure other people are doing it first. **Ahlbeck** is the easternmost of The Imperial Three, a hop, skip, and a jump (actually 2 km) from Poland's border. It's famous for its wooden pier adorned with four towers—the only one of its kind in Germany. The nearby beachfront promenade is lined with late-19th-century villas whose rooms are sometimes rented to visitors; look for ZIMMER FREI signs and haggle away.

13 HAMBURG AND SCHLESWIG-HOLSTEIN

UPDATED BY GARRETT HERING

As Germany's second largest city (Berlin is the first), Hamburg stands in bustling contrast to the quiet towns of its neighboring regions. Known for its sex trade, the city is admittedly flavored by its Reeperbahn brothels and strip clubs, but it has *a lot* more to offer. Come here and you'll find an open-minded, cosmopolitan city with diverse neighborhoods, and a cultural scene that is very much alive and kicking.

North of Hamburg, Schleswig-Holstein is a state shaped by its proximity to the sea. Located on the neck of land connecting Germany to Denmark, the area draws German tourists who come in droves to pamper themselves with sandy beaches and seaside vistas, injecting needed revenue into local port-based economies. Schleswig-Holstein's cities are for the most part small and relaxed, but their many architectural and cultural treasures are a reminder of the region's grandiose past as a mighty trade center from the 13th to the 17th centuries. The acclaimed progressiveness of Northerners is often attributed to Schleswig-Holstein's history of independence: It was not until 1937 that Lübeck lost its status as an independent city-state, and Hamburg remains its own *Land* (state) to this day. Together with Hamburg, Schleswig-Hostein is a part of Germany too often left off travelers' itineraries.

HAMBURG

When travelers learn that Hamburg is Germany's largest port, they conjure up images of heavy industry, cranes, oil-soaked waters, and sleazy bars. While they're right about the sleazy bars, most travelers are surprised by how green and elegant Hamburg is. In fact, the metropolis is home to the greatest share of nature preserves enclosed within any German state. That's not to say that Hamburg is quaint or charming, because it's not. If you want cozy, go to Bavaria—Hamburg is too busy making money to bother with such niceties. The city isn't too picky about how it makes its money, either. A lot of gray-suited commerce types earn it the old-fashioned way, but another segment of the population makes its living in an even older fashion. Prostitution, pornography, and sex shows have given Hamburg a reputation (not altogether deserved) as the European capital of hedonism.

Much of Hamburg burned in the Great Fire of 1842, and between 1940 and 1944, huge sections of the city were once again annihilated. Yet you'd be hard-pressed to find evidence of this devastation today,

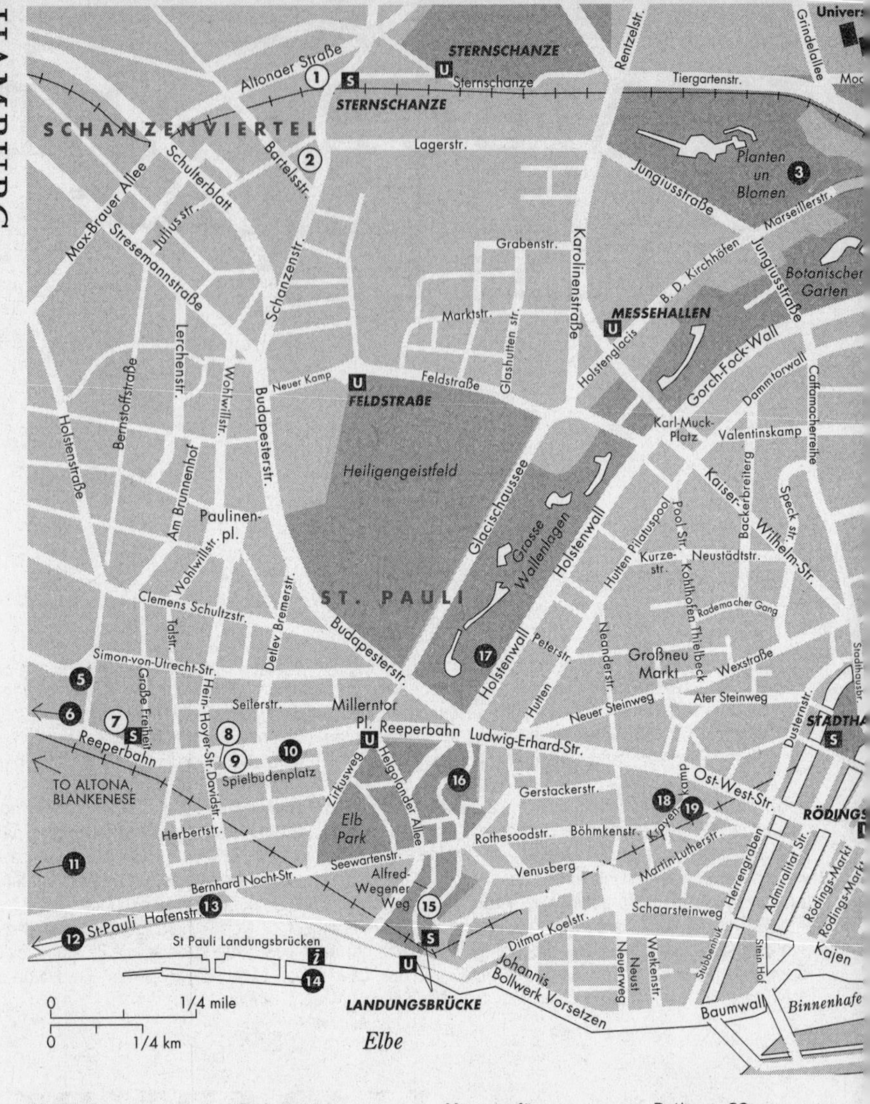

Sights ●

Alsterarkaden, **24**

Bismarck-Denkmal, **16**

Deichstraße, **20**

Deichtorhallen, **39**

Ernst-Barlach-Haus, **11**

Erotic Art Museum, **5**

Fischmarkt, **12**

Gedenkstätte Janusz-Korczak Schule, **40**

Hafenstraße, **13**

Hamburger Kunsthalle, **28**

Jakobikirche, **26**

Jüdischer Friedhof, **6**

Krameramtswohnungen, **19**

Michaeliskirche, **18**

Museum für Hamburgische Geschichte, **17**

Museum für Kunst und Gewerbe, **38**

Museumschiff *Rickmer Rickmers*, **14**

Petrikirche, **25**

Planten un Blomen, **3**

Platz der Jüdischen Deportieren, **4**

Rathaus, **23**

Reeperbahn, **10**

Speicherstadt, **22**

Speicherstadt-museum, **27**

Turmruine St. Nikolai, **21**

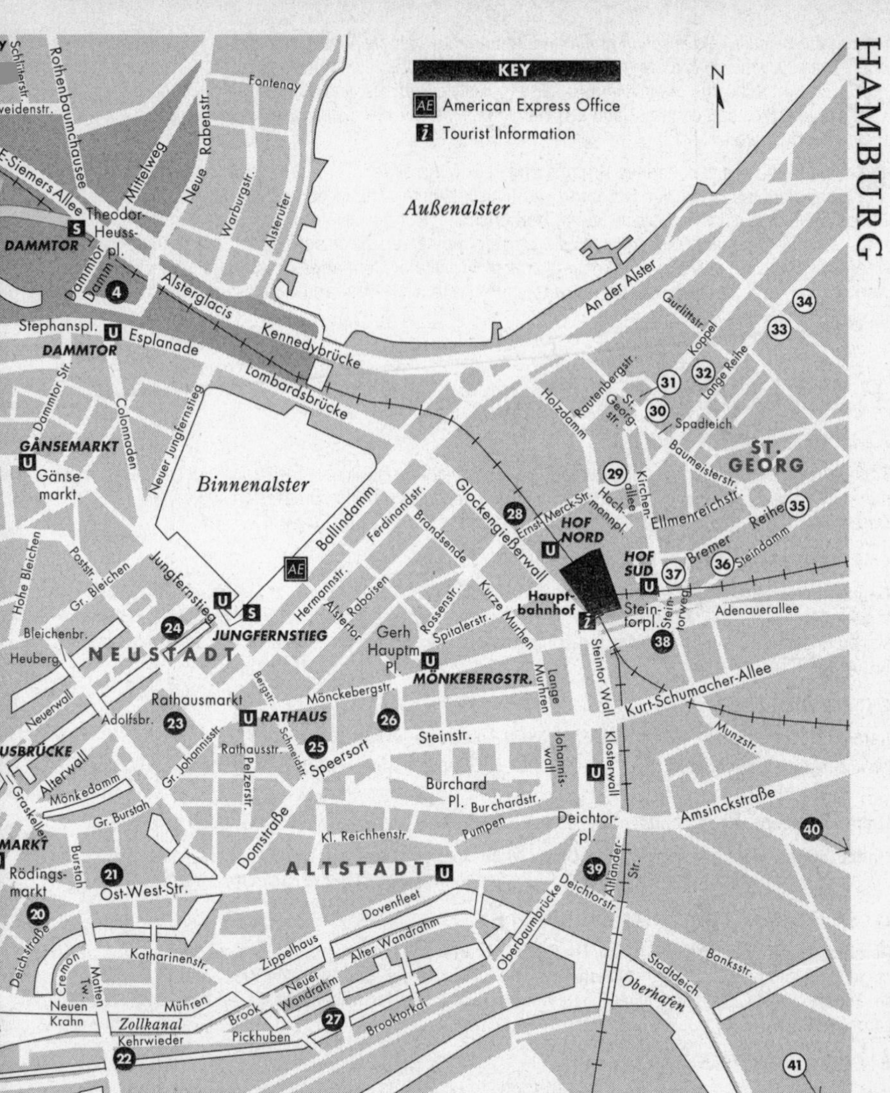

Lodging ○

Auto-Hotel "Am Hafen," **8**

Hotel Alt Nürnberg, **37**

Hotel Florida, **9**

Hotel-Pension Alpha, **30**

Hotel-Pension Annenhof, **32**

Hotel-Pension Köhler, **31**

Hotel-Pension von Blumfeld, **34**

Hotel St. Georg, **29**

Hotel Stern, **7**

Hotel-Sternschanze, **1**

Hotel Terminus, **36**

Hotel Wikinger Hof, **35**

Jugendgästehaus Hamburg "Auf dem Stintfang," **15**

Jugendgästehaus Hamburg "Horner Rennbahn," **41**

Künstlerpension Sarah Petersen, **33**

Schanzenstern, **2**

with all the beautiful expanses of green and innumerable canals. Water, in fact, still dominates the layout of the city, which has more than 2,400 bridges—more than London, Amsterdam, and Venice combined. Elegant villas, the magnificent Renaissance-style Rathaus, and many department stores line the banks of the lakes and canals. Water also dominates the city in a meteorological sense: Baltic rains saturate Hamburg life for much of the year.

Today the birthplace of Johannes Brahms and Felix Mendelssohn is best known for the flashing lights and brash store fronts that line Hamburg's hedonistic quarter. The most notorious attraction may be the Reeperbahn and its infamous side street, Herbertstraße. But the city has much more to offer. Hamburg houses many top-notch museums, hosts an astounding variety of performances, ranging from the bizarre to classical, and lays legitimate claims to the title of Germany's music capital. Hamburg is a worldly city—at once bustling and down-to-earth—with a diversity and richness of culture not to be missed.

BASICS

AMERICAN EXPRESS

This office books hotel rooms and airplane and train tickets, and will hold mail up to four weeks for cardmembers. They also cash traveler's checks and change cash for no commission. *Ballindamm 39, tel. 040/309080. U-Bahn to Jungfernsteig. Open weekdays 9–5:30, Sat. 10 AM–1 PM.*

CHANGING MONEY

Deutsche Verkehrs-Bank (Hauptbahnhof, tel. 040/323483), open daily 7:30 AM–10 PM, charges DM 1 to change cash and DM 3 for traveler's checks. For late-night emergencies, try the machines in the train station or at the various banks around Jungfernsteig; they accept Visa, MasterCard, and cards on the Cirrus and Plus networks.

CONSULATES

Ireland. *Feldbrunnenstr. 33, tel. 040/4418–6213. Open weekdays 9–1.*

New Zealand. *Heimhuderstr. 56, tel. 040/442–5550. Open Mon.–Thurs. 9–noon and 1–5:30, Fri. 9–noon and 1–4:30.*

United Kingdom. *Harvestehuder Weg 8a, tel. 040/448–0320. Open weekdays 9–noon and 2–4.*

United States. Known by locals as the "little White House," the American Consulate General overlooks the Alster. *Alsterufer 27–28, tel. 040/411710, after hours 040/4117–1211. Open weekdays 9–noon.*

DISCOUNT TRAVEL AGENCIES

Rainbow Tours (Johanniswall 4c, tel. 040/336217) arranges European bus tours geared to young people looking for cheap fun. Both **Akzent-Touristik** (Grindelallee 28, tel. 040/443061) and **STA** (Rentzelstr. 16, tel. 040/442363) specialize in student trips and cheap last-minute flights, and they also sell ISIC cards (DM 18).

EMERGENCIES

Police: tel. 110. **Fire**: tel. 112. **Ambulance**: tel. 112. **Medical assistance**: tel. 228022. **Foreigner Legal Service**: Cremon 11, tel. 040/366534. All hospitals and even the emergency telephone operators speak English. The **Opferhilfe Beratungstelle** (Paul-Nevermann-Pl. 2–4, tel. 040/381993), open weekdays 10–1 (also Tues.–Thurs. 2–5) is a help center for victims of crime. Hamburg's **Rape Crisis Line** (tel. 040/255566) has someone answering the phones Monday and Thursday 10–1 and 3–7, Tuesday 10–1 and 3–4, and Wednesday 3–4; the 24-hour answering machine is checked daily.

ENGLISH-LANGUAGE BOOKS

Amerika Zentrum (Tesdorpfstr. 1, tel. 040/450–1040; open weekday afternoons; closed weekends) and **British Council** (Rothenbaumchaussee 34, tel. 040/446057; open weekday afternoons; closed weekends) have reading libraries open to the public. **English Books** (Stessemanstr. 169, tel. 040/8514478; open weekdays 9:30–6:30, Sat 10–4) has a diverse selection of used books at fair prices. The extensive collection of English books at **Frensche-International** (Spitalerstr. 26e, tel. 040/327585; closed Sun.) covers everything from romance to politics. For gay-oriented books, go to **Männerschwarm Buchladen** (Neuer Pferdemarkt 32, tel. 040/436093).

INTERNET RESOURCES

FunClub Internetcafé, a 10-min walk from the Altona rail station (Fischers Allee 78, tel. 040/3990–1009; www.icafe-funclub.de; open 2 PM–1 AM daily), costs DM 10 per hour and offers friendly service in a comfortable environment. While surfing you should visit the following Hamburg homepage addresses for insider tips in English and German: **Szene Hamburg,** a city events magazine for the culturally keen, at www.szeneonline.germanscene.de; **Hamburg Magazine,** an electronic city magazine created especially for tourists, at www.hamburg-magazine.de; and **Tourismus-Zentrale,** the mothership of all tourist agencies in Germany, which offers useful information at www.hamburg-tourism.de.

LAUNDRY

Münzwaschsalon, on a side street off the Reeperbahn, has instructions in English. Bring change for the washers (DM 7, including soap), dryers (DM 1 for 10 min), and pinball machines. *Hein-Hoyer-Str. 12, no phone. Open Mon.–Sat. 7 AM–10 PM, Sun. 10–10.*

LUGGAGE STORAGE

The Hauptbahnhof, the Hamburg-Altona train station, and many S-Bahn stations have 24-hour **lockers** for DM 2–DM 4, depending on size. The Hauptbahnhof also has a **luggage check** (open daily 6:15 AM–11 PM), which charges DM 4 per piece per day.

Germany's second-largest city has been an autonomous city-state since 1189 and its long-ruling Social Democrats have created Germany's most liberal laws concerning homosexuality and drug use.

MAIL AND PHONES

Called the *Hühnerposten* (chicken coop) by locals, the **Hauptpost** is across from the Hauptbahnhof. They deal with mail and telephones, but won't exchange money or sell eggs. *Hühnerposten 12. Postal code: 20997. Open weekdays 8–6, Sat. 8–noon.*

The branch in the **Hauptbahnhof** offers the usual services downstairs; upstairs you'll find a telephone center that includes a credit card phone (No. 19) that accepts American Express, MasterCard, and Visa. *Hachmannpl. 13, Kirchenallee exit, tel. 040/23950. Open weekdays 8–8, Sat. 9–6, Sun. 10–6.*

MEDICAL AID

Senator Apotheke am Hauptbahnhof (Hachmannpl. 14, on the northern side of the station, tel. 040/327527) takes the big three credit cards and has a friendly English-speaking staff that will assist you weekdays 8–6:30 (Thurs. until 7:30), Saturday 9–2.

VISITOR INFORMATION

Hamburg's two tourist offices offer identical services, including an English-speaking staff, ticket sales, maps, public transit ticket machines, and a room-booking service (DM 7 fee). The offices also sell the **Hamburg-CARD,** which gives you free access to public transport (inquire about time restrictions), free or reduced admission to 11 museums, and up to 30% discounts on city tours and harbor cruises. A one-day card costs DM 12.50 (group card good for up to four adults and three children, DM 24); a three-day card is DM 26 (group card DM 42). Be sure to pick up "The Hamburger," a monthly pamphlet with important addresses and events. Every other month the **Amt für Kirchenmusik** publishes a calendar, available in churches and tourist offices, that lists all free organ concerts.

Harbor: *St. Pauli-Landungsbrücken, btw Piers 4 and 5, tel. 040/3005–1203. Open daily 10 AM–7 PM.*

Hauptbahnhof: *Kirchenallee exit, tel. 040/3005–1201 or 3005–1202. Open daily 7 AM–11 PM.*

RESOURCES FOR GAYS AND LESBIANS • Gay male travelers should contact **Hein und Fiete** (Kleiner Pulverteich 21, near Hauptbahnhof, tel. 040/240333), which gives out info and runs a gay room-finding service weekdays 4–9, Saturday 3–6. For gay and lesbian information and help of various kinds, try **Magnus-Hirschfeld Centrum** (Borgw. 8, U3 to Borgw., tel. 040/279–0069). They have counseling services, legal and medical help, and an on-site café (open weekdays 5 PM–11:30 PM); Wednesday 3–7 is women's night. The office is open Mondays, Tuesdays, and Thursdays noon–8 PM. The university's **Frauenlesben-Rat,** in the AStA student office (Von-Melle-Park 5, S-Bahn to Dammtor, tel. 040/4502–0438), has lots of info on lesbian Hamburg; it's open Tuesday 11 AM–1 PM, Wednesday noon–2, Thursday 2–5, and Friday noon–2. Ask for *Lesben Piste,* a weekly publication that lists lesbian events with addresses and prices. *Hinnerk, Du und Ich,* and *Gay Express* have similar info for gay men.

LET THE HEADS ROLL!

From the nearby island of Helgoland, the perfidious pirate Klaus Störtebeker jeopardized late-14th-century trade between Hamburg and England. By 1401 an ailing Hamburg was determined to squash her enemy: The city's fleet captured Störtebeker and his crew and returned them to Hamburg's Grasbrook (in today's Speicherstadt), site of many a pirate's beheading. Störtebeker's last wish was for his crew to be set free if he marched past them after his decapitation; legend holds that he submitted to the henchman's sword and that his headless body walked past the 71 men (in reality they were all beheaded, for which the henchman earned 12 marks). Today, at the corner of Magdeburger Brücke, you can gaze at a bronze version of the proud pirate; statues of his captors guard the red Kersten-Miles-Brücke, which runs across the Helgoländer Allee.

COMING AND GOING

BY PLANE

Hamburg's **Flughafen Fuhlsbüttel** (Paul-Bäumer-Pl., tel. 040/50750; www.ham.airport.de) is about 10 km north of downtown. The spanking-new terminals have banks, a post office, and an American Express ATM. You can store your luggage for DM 4 per piece per day at the *Gepäckaufbewahrung* (luggage check), open 4 AM–midnight. To reach the city center, take the **Airport Express** (# 110) to the Ohlsdorf stop, and then the S-Bahn or U-Bahn into town. Otherwise, the **Airport City Bus** makes the 30-min trip (DM 8.50) between the Hauptbahnhof and the airport every 20 min.

BY TRAIN

All trains, except those heading north to destinations like Sylt, stop at the **Hauptbahnhof** in central Hamburg. Nine daily trains run to Berlin (3–5 hrs, DM 49–DM 76); two per hour head to Bremen (1–2 hrs, DM 32–DM 39), Hanover (1½–2½ hrs, DM 49–DM 64), and Frankfurt (3½–5 hrs, DM 69–DM 182); less frequent trains go to Lübeck (1–2 per hour, 45 min, DM 16.20) and Copenhagen (every 2 hrs, 5 hrs, DM 117.40). Ask for specials. If you have time to spare, are short on cash, and like to take the paths less traveled, inquire about the **Wochenende Ticket** (weekend ticket), which will allow you to travel to any destination in Germany on weekends for DM 35, albeit in twice the normal duration. The station itself sits between the aesthetically challenging and somewhat drug-infested neighborhood of St. Georg and the elegant shopping promenades on Mönckebergstraße and Spitalerstraße. Northbound trains depart the **Hamburg-Altona** station (Max-Brauer-Allee), in a formerly independent suburb west of downtown. The S-Bahn connects the two stations.

BY BUS

ZOB, across from the Hauptbahnhof, is the central station for a bunch of bus companies that offer service all over Germany and Europe. **Eurolines** (tel. 040/245310) sells tickets to cities like Paris (DM 102) and Amsterdam (DM 72). Students under 26 get 10% off . The station has lockers for DM 2.50. *Adenauerallee 78, tel. 040/247576. Open daily 5 AM–9 PM.*

If you don't find anything at ZOB, try nearby **Berbig,** which offers reasonably priced bus trips to cities like Berlin (DM 27) and Paris (DM 77). *Lange Reihe 36, tel. 040/280–3464. Open weekdays 9–noon and 2–6, Sat. 9–noon.*

HAMBURG PUBLIC TRANSIT SYSTEM

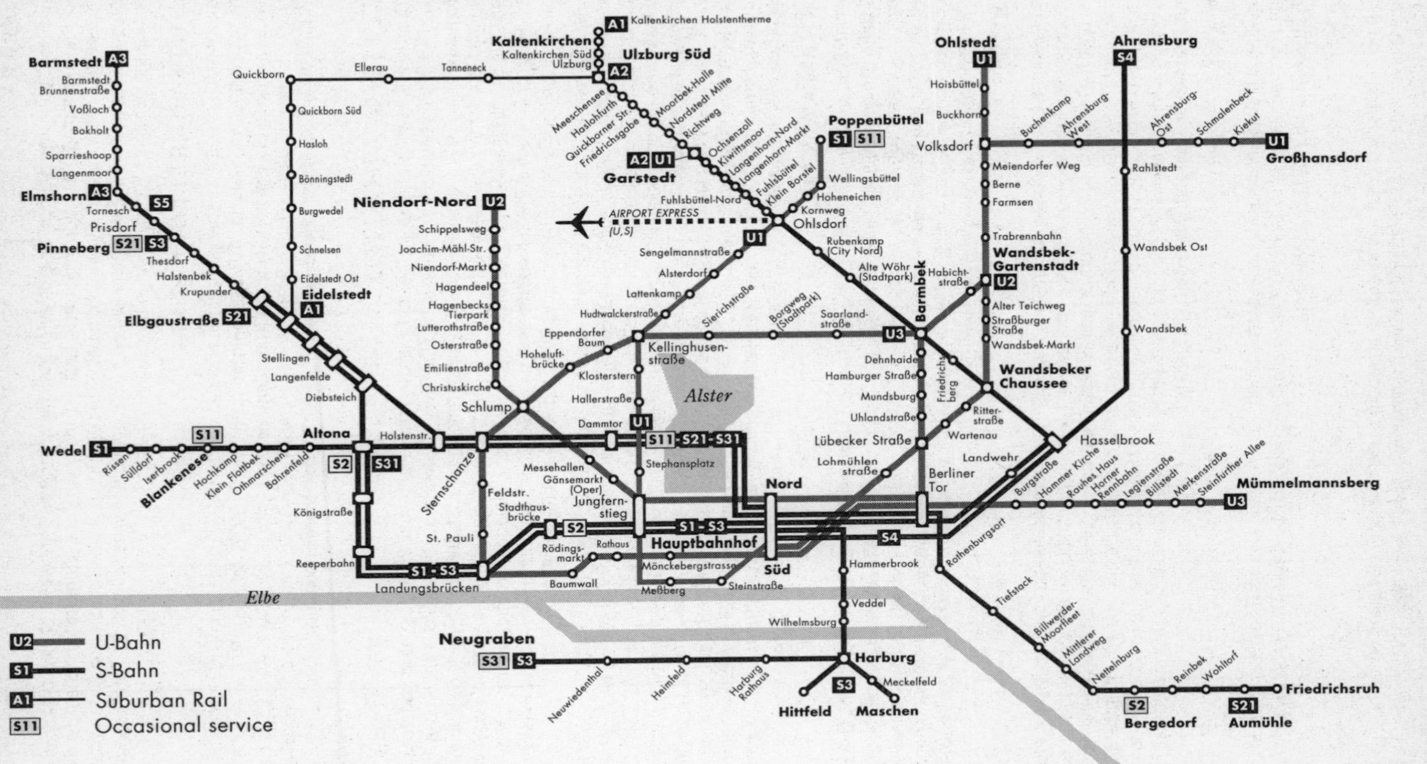

BY FERRY

The *MS Hamburg,* operated by **Scandinavian Seaways** (Van-der-Smissen-Str. 4, tel. 040/389030), makes the mammoth 20-hour trip to Harwich, England, every other day; from Harwich there's a direct train connection to London. Prices range from DM 97 to DM 490, depending on day, season, and cabin. Students and passengers under 26 regularly get a 25% break. All ferries sail from St. Pauli-Landungsbrücken at the harbor (U-Bahn/S-Bahn to Landungsbrücken).

BY MITFAHRGELEGENHEIT

Hamburg's ride-share offices offer competitive prices to Berlin (DM 31) and Cologne (DM 34); call the offices two or three days ahead. **ADM Mitfahrbüro** (Ernst-Merck-Str. 8, tel. 040/19440; S1 or S3 to Altona) is open daily 8 AM–9 PM; **Citynetz Mitfahr-Zentrale** (Gotenstr. 19, tel. 040/19444; S3 to Hammerbrock) is open daily from 9 to 7. At the University, **AStA** (Von-Melle-Park 5) offers a free service. Check their big bulletin board labeled MITFAHRGELEGENHEIT for ride-share opportunities.

GETTING AROUND

Hamburg is a sprawling metropolis, but most of the major sights and interesting neighborhoods are sandwiched in the walkable area between the Elbe River and two lakes, Binnenalster and Außenalster. The **Rathaus** (Town Hall) is the central point in the downtown area. **St. Georg,** the seedy neighborhood behind the Hauptbahnhof, is home to the bulk of cheap, decent lodging and is the center of Hamburg's gay life. The **St. Pauli** area, west of downtown near the harbor, includes Hamburg's famous red-light district. North of St. Pauli is the **Schanzenviertel,** a diverse, liberal residential area. The **university district** sits north of the city center between the Schanzenviertel and the Außenalster.

If you want to reach St. Pauli from the station or are tired of walking, make use of Hamburg's excellent public transit system. **HVV** (tel. 040/19449) operates an extensive network of buses, as well as the U-Bahn and S-Bahn. The system is complicated, so grab a map. One-way tickets (DM 2.70–DM 4.20), good on all forms of transit (including city ferries) are available at the orange ticket-dispensing machines in stations and at most bus stops. The all-day **Tageskarte** (DM 9.50) is good for all forms of public transit except night buses and first-class travel on the S-Bahn. A *Gruppenkarte* (DM 13.80) works like the Tageskarte but is good for up to five adults. The best deal is the **Hamburg-CARD** (*see* Visitor Information, *above*). **Ferries** to Blankenese (*see* Near Hamburg, *below*) leave every half hour from Landungsbrücken (free with Tageskarte, DM 7 otherwise).

BY SUBWAY/RAIL

Deciphering the subway system can give even the most weathered traveler a headache. The **U-Bahn** and **S-Bahn** can be used interchangeably to get around the city; the **A-Bahn,** Hamburg's suburban rail, connects the distant suburbs. Trains run every five, 10, or 20 min until about 12:30 AM; bikes are allowed on the U-Bahn and S-Bahn except during weekday rush hours. Because there is no regular ticket control, *Schwarzfahren* (riding without a ticket) is not uncommon. Do so only if you're feeling lucky: If inspectors do check tickets, you're out DM 60.

BY BUS

The rail system is generally easier and more efficient than the complicated bus system. Lawless types often board buses from the rear entrance so they don't have to pay, although at night all passengers have to board in front and show the driver their tickets. **Night buses** (Lines 600–640) serve the downtown area after the subway closes at 12:30 AM. Buses leave the Rathausmarkt and the Hauptbahnhof every half hour all night long for limited destinations; maps at the stops outline the routes. Pick up the *Bus-Fahrplan Nacht* at any HVV office for schedules and routes. For more bus information call the **Hamburg Passenger Transport Board** (tel. 040/322911).

BY TAXI

You can always find cream-color Mercedes taxis at stands near the train stations. The meter starts at DM 4.80, and every additional km is DM 2.40. Calling a taxi (tel. 040/211211, 040/441011, 040/656–2011, 040/661166, or 040/611061) costs the same.

BY BIKE

Unless it rains, biking is a great way to explore Hamburg's neighborhoods. Excellent paved bike paths circle the Binnenalster and Außenalster lakes. Rent a newer mountain bike or elegant 1920s street bike near the Hauptbahnhof from **Fahrradladen St. Georg** (Schmilinskystr. 6, tel. 040/243908; open daily 10–6) for DM 15–DM 30 per day.

WHERE TO SLEEP

Unless you were born with a silver room key in your mouth, Hamburg's lodging scene can break your budget. The two large hostels, easily accessible by the U-Bahn, are your best bet. The cheapest hotels (aside from those that rent by the hour) start at DM 50 for singles, DM 80 for doubles, and most of these are in the city's more adventurous neighborhoods. The hotels themselves are generally clean and the neighborhoods safe, but always ask to see a room before taking it. If you are planning to be in Hamburg for more than one night, **Zimmerfrei Hamburg** (Semper 16, tel. 040/2787–7777, fax 040/2787–7779) finds singles from DM 45 and doubles for DM 75–DM 100. They charge a flat fee of DM 10 per person. The tourist office will also book hotel rooms for a DM 6 fee. **Hein und Fiete** (*see* Resources for Gays and Lesbians, *above*) has a free room-finding service for gay male travelers.

ST. GEORG

St. Georg's proximity to the Hauptbahnhof and ZOB makes it a convenient and affordable place to stay, and the hotels tend to be small, friendly establishments with a down-to-earth atmosphere. Still it's not the best neighborhood: The main streets are relatively safe, but the drug scene here is fairly prominent, and you may see the occasional prostitute. Walk down **Bremer Reihe,** loaded with budget options, but be wary of hotels where the man greeting you at the reception is dressed in a suit—you may end up paying for your room by the hour.

UNDER DM 85 • Hotel-Pension Alpha. The big-hearted woman at the door and the large clean rooms (all with private showers) make this pension the best value in the area. Singles are DM 50 and doubles DM 80 (for breakfast add DM 10); all rooms have coffee makers, plates, and cutlery, and most have a fridge. *Koppel 6, tel. 040/245365, fax 040/243794. 12 rooms. No credit cards.*

Hotel-Pension Annenhof. This small and atmospheric pension offers clean rooms outfitted with new pine furniture and simple decor. The friendly owners rent out singles for DM 48, doubles for DM 82 (DM 100 with bath), and breakfast is DM 8. Call ahead to let them know you're coming. *Lange Reihe 23, tel. 040/243426. 15 rooms. No credit cards.*

UNDER DM 95 • Hotel Alt Nürnberg. A respectable establishment on an otherwise seedy street, this hotel dates from the first half of the 19th century. It has a beautiful wood-panelled reception area and clean rooms, each enhanced with medieval-style furniture and the "coat-of-arms" of a different city on the door. Singles start at DM 60, doubles at DM 90, including breakfast. *Steintorw. 15, tel. 040/246023, fax 040/280–4634. 16 rooms, some with private bath. Luggage storage. Closed Christmas–New Year's. No credit cards.*

Hotel-Pension Köhler. The roly-poly manager of this quiet, homey hotel proffers a famous guest list, real Oriental carpets, and a cabinet full of gifts from satisfied guests. DM 65 will get you a single, DM 90 a double, none with private shower. Prices include one "normal-length" shower per day. *St. Georgstr. 6, tel. 040/249065, fax 040/280–1846. 5 rooms. No credit cards.*

Hotel-Pension von Blumfeld. If quaint exists in Hamburg, it is possibly here at this family-owned-and-run diamond in the rough. Herr and Frau Malchow will treat you like their own. Singles cost DM 60 (DM 90 with bath), doubles are DM 80 (DM 110 with bath), and breakfast is included. *Lange Reihe 54, tel. 040/245860. 14 rooms. No credit cards.*

Hotel Wikinger Hof. With newly renovated rooms, a friendly staff, and a great buffet breakfast, the Wikinger will reward you for venturing up the street. You'll pay DM 50–DM 80 for a single, DM 80–DM 120 for a double. *Steindamm 53, tel. 040/243834. 20 rooms, some with private bath and shower.*

UNDER DM 115 • Hotel Terminus. The conscientious management of this recently refurbished hotel rents out singles for DM 80, doubles for DM 110–DM 160, three-bed rooms for DM 150–DM 170, and four-bed rooms for DM 180; all rooms come with TV, telephone, and breakfast. *Steindamm 5, tel. 040/280–3144, fax 040/241518. 20 rooms, none with bath. Reception open 24 hrs.*

Künstlerpension Sarah Petersen. This small, primarily gay pension is almost always booked. Call eccentric artist/owner Sarah Petersen ahead of time to claim one of the six comfy rooms in this 200-year-old building. Temporary art exhibits line the walls of the breakfast room and entryway. Singles go for DM 80–DM 120, doubles DM 110, triples DM 160, quads DM 190, including a scrumptious breakfast. *Lange Reihe 50, tel. 040/249826. 6 rooms, 2 with bath and shower facilities. Laundry facilities. Reception open 8 AM–midnight. No credit cards.*

Hotel St. Georg. Every room in this hotel is unique. The owner runs the place as a hobby and changes the decor whenever he feels like it: If you're lucky, you may end up in a room with a cheesy landscape mural over the bed. Singles with breakfast are DM 65–DM 110, doubles DM 115–DM 165. Reservations are recommended. *Kirchenallee 23, behind Hauptbahnhof, tel. 040/241141, fax 040/280–3370. 26 rooms, some with bath. Luggage storage.*

ST. PAULI

Your mom probably wouldn't be very happy to know you're spending nights on the Reeperbahn, a.k.a. "the world's most sinful mile," but it can't be beat for cheap accommodations. Don't expect a peaceful night's sleep, though—sex and throbbing nightclubs are this district's raisons d'être. The area frequented by tourists is fairly safe, but stay alert when venturing off into the side streets. To reach the Reeperbahn take U3 to St. Pauli, or S1 or S3 to Reeperbahn.

UNDER DM 80 • Auto-Hotel "Am Hafen." This clean and well-kept hotel is more respectable than its St. Pauli counterparts. Prices for singles (DM 65–DM 110) and doubles (DM 95–DM 125) don't include breakfast (an extra DM 10–DM 13), but the pricier rooms are outfitted with a private bath. *Spielbudenpl. 11, tel. 040/316631, fax 040/319–2922. U-Bahn to St. Pauli. 21 rooms, some with bath. No credit cards.*

UNDER DM 100 • Hotel Florida. This predominantly gay hotel has clean, large, and relatively quiet rooms. In fine Reeperbahn tradition, there are even condom machines conveniently located outside the rooms. Equally convenient, the hotel's reception desk doubles as the bar. Singles run DM 55, doubles DM 95, and triples DM 135, all with breakfast. *Spielbudenpl. 22, tel. 040/314393. U3 to St. Pauli. 18 rooms, none with bath. No credit cards.*

Hotel Stern. Popular with groups, this gigantic hotel has both old and newly refurbished rooms. An extra DM 10 gets you a new, sterile-smelling room with TV and private shower. Singles cost DM 60, doubles DM 100. *Reeperbahn 154–166, near Reeperbahn station, tel. 040/3176–9990, fax 040/312052. 208 rooms, some with bath. Luggage storage.*

SCHANZENVIERTEL

North of St. Pauli, the Schanzenviertel has a liberal atmosphere that attracts students, immigrants, gays and lesbians, and an occasional tourist. The area offers a host of second-hand shops, ethnic grocery stores, lively pubs, and exciting clubs to satiate your desire for eccentricities. To reach the Schanzenviertel, take the U3, S21, or S31 to Sternschanze, or walk from St. Pauli or downtown.

Hotel Sternschanze. Once you squeeze out of the narrow hallways and into your clean, bright room, you can relax in a relatively quiet atmosphere. Singles go for DM 50, doubles for DM 70, not including breakfast. *Schanzenstr. 101, across from Sternschanze station, tel. 040/433389, fax 040/430–5165. 20 rooms, none with bath. Reception open daily 8 AM–10 PM. Luggage storage. No credit cards.*

Schanzenstern. Located in a former Mont Blanc pen factory, this alternative hotel offers bright singles, doubles, and quads decorated with natural-wood furniture. The hotel shares the building with a movie theater, a school, a drug-counseling center, and a café. Singles cost DM 71, doubles DM 112–DM 122, and quads DM 140. *Bartelsstr. 12, tel. 040/439–8441, www.info-schanzenstern.de. From Sternschanze, 5-min walk west. 50 beds, some with bath. Luggage storage. Closed last week of Dec. No credit cards.*

HOSTELS

Jugendgästehaus Hamburg "Auf dem Stintfang" (HI). Overlooking Hamburg's lively harbor, this huge hostel's eight-bed dorms are almost always full. Call ahead or come before 6 PM. The 1 AM curfew puts a damper on exploring Hamburg's nearby naughtiness. Beds cost DM 26 (DM 32 over 26); HI cards are mandatory. The hostel offers discounts of up to 50% on harbor tours. *Alfred-Wegener-Weg 5, entrance around building, tel. 040/313488, fax 040/315407. U3, S1, or S3 to Landungsbrücken; follow Jugendherberge signs up the hill. 362 beds. Lockout 9–noon. Reception open 12:30 PM–1 AM. Luggage storage. Closed Feb. No credit cards.*

Jugendgästehaus Hamburg "Horner Rennbahn" (HI). A bit removed from downtown but quickly accessible by public transportation, this hostel offers high-quality rooms for the correspondingly high price of DM 32 (DM 37 over 26), including an appealing buffet breakfast. The neighborhood derby may disturb your siesta if you happen to be here during the races. Try calling ahead or come early to snag a bed. *Rennbahnstr. 100, tel. 040/651–1671. U3 to Horner Rennbahn, then 10-min walk north. 277 beds. Curfew 1 AM. Reception open 1–1. Luggage storage. Closed Feb. No credit cards.*

CAMPING

Campingplatz Buchholz. Buchholz is a small campground right off Kieler Straße. Although your tent will sit on cool green grass, it's tough to ignore the traffic streaming by. Make reservations a week in advance during the crowded summer months. Sites run DM 14.50, plus DM 7 per person. *Kieler Str. 374, tel. 040/540–4532. U2 to Schlump, then Bus 182 to Basselw.; walk 200 m further on right-hand side of street. 75 sites. Reception open 8 AM–11 AM and 6 PM–8 PM. Showers.*

City Camp Tourist. Four times as big as Buchholz, this high-security, highly organized campground also lies just off Kieler Straße, so don't expect to hear the birds singing. Sites are DM 7 per person and DM 12–DM 18 per tent, showers included. *Kieler Str. 650, tel. 040/570–4498. U2 to Schlump, then Bus 182 to Reichbahnstr.; walk 100 m. 150 sites. Grocery store, laundry.*

FOOD

With more than 4,000 restaurants, bars, and cafés, Hamburg offers everything from high-priced exotic cuisine to greasy Imbiß grub. Here "Imbiß" doesn't necessarily mean Bratwurst—you're just as likely to see stands selling seafood, in particular Maatje's Filets (breaded, deep-fried baby herring), a welcome change from sausage—if you like fish. Local Hamburg specialties make use of several sea beasts, but the most celebrated is the eel, which comes smoked (*Räucheraal*) or in a soup (*Aalsuppe*). Every restaurant serves Northern Germany's luscious local dessert, *Rote Grütze,* a red berry dish served with vanilla sauce. Hamburg's only after-hours specialty, *Alsterwasser,* is a combination of beer and lemon soda.

INNENSTADT

Hamburg's central hub, the Innenstadt, lies within the area originally enclosed by the city walls. Here you'll find most of the main tourist attractions, the train station, and very few affordable restaurants.

UNDER DM 10 • bon appétit. This busy stand-up café behind Mönckebergstraße serves local business people who know a good lunch when they eat one. Don't be put off by the long lines—they move quickly. A changing menu of meat-and-potato dishes costs less than DM 10, but the *Bauernfrühstück* (farmer's breakfast; DM 7.90) and the salad bar are the best deals. *Rathausstr. 4, tel. 040/324570. Closed weekends.*

UNDER DM 15 • Café-Bar Wien. Make your finest entrance into this exeptionally hip Hamburgean try at a late-19th-century Viennese coffee house, where moderately priced yet filling meals (DM 9–DM 12.50) come with a great view of the Inner Alster. Ask for a mélange, relax, and absorb. *Ballindamm/Binnenalster, tel. 040/336342.*

Gestern & Heute Treff. Open 24 hours a day (a true anomaly in Germany), this restaurant is a favorite with Hamburgers. Among the cheap, decent menu items: scampi (DM 11), rump steak (DM 11–DM 17), pizza (DM 9), and an eclectic selection of sandwiches (DM 6–DM 14). *Kaiser-Wilhelm-Str. 55, tel. 040/344998.*

Picasso. Just around the corner from the Petrikirche, this Spanish restaurant is a family-owned establishment that gets crowded with loyal customers come mealtime. Some seafood dishes are pricey, but even the cheapest dishes are good. Try one of their pasta dishes (DM 14), fish dishes (DM 15), steaks (DM 20), or a Spanish tortilla with salad (DM 13). *Rathausstr. 14, tel. 040/326548. Closed Sun.*

ST. GEORG

Despite St. Georg's proximity to the train station, restaurants here manage to avoid tourist prices. Check out Lange Reihe for an abundant selection.

Café Gnosa. Among the best gay cafés in Germany, this beautiful Kaffeehaus is the place to check out the gay scene and enjoy fantastic meals. Try the vegetarian *Auflauf* (DM 12), a casserole of zucchini, cauliflower, carrots, and cheese. Gnosa also serves a mean piece of homemade cake. *Lange Reihe 93, tel. 040/243034.*

Café Koppel. Housed inside an art complex, this yuppie vegetarian café serves salads and quiches (DM 10–DM 15) and specializes in unusual teas and coffees. On Sunday afternoons a jazz combo sets the mellow mood. *Lange Reihe 75, tel. 040/249235.*

Max & Consorten. Conversation buzzes over the low music as local students and the occasional tourist gather in this smoky joint for a quick beer (DM 4) or a cheap meal. In summer sit outside and sample their delicious salads (DM 8–DM 13). *Spadenteich 7, tel. 040/245617.*

ST. PAULI

Filled with curious tourists, the St. Pauli district is a haven for quick eating. Imbiß snacks on the Reeperbahn are relatively expensive (and after sauntering along this strip of debauchery for about 15 min you may not feel much like eating). Two supermarkets are located at the intersection of the Reeperbahn and Holstenstraße: **Spar** (Reeperbahn 157) and **Safeway** (Nobistor 27).

Medusa. This family-run Italian restaurant features lasagna, tortellini, or fettuccine for DM 10–DM 13; broccoli *überbacken* (baked with cheese on top) is DM 7.50. Culinary voyeurs can even watch their meal being made through a small window that opens onto the kitchen. *Spielbudenpl. 21, tel. 040/313503.*

Schindlers. Just off the Reeperbahn, this pub-restaurant has good food and a down-to-earth atmosphere with an edge. Pasta and casseroles (try spinach noodles with gorgonzola sauce) go for DM 10–DM 15 and good breakfasts (around DM 7) are served on weekend mornings. *Taubenstr. 23, tel. 040/315092.*

Zorba the Buddha. This vegetarian restaurant occupies a beautiful courtyard in northern St. Pauli. The meditation center upstairs sets the serene tone here; dining is especially peaceful outside in the garden. Dishes like tofu with spinach and goat cheese run about DM 17. *Karolinenstr. 7–9, tel. 040/439–4762. U2 to Messehallen; across from Gnadenkirche down a small alley.*

SCHANZENVIERTEL

The Schanzenviertel's large immigrant and student population has created a demand for and nurtured a wide variety of reasonably priced restaurants serving everything from Greek to Chinese. Wander down **Schulterblatt** or **Schanzenstraße** for more Turkish Imbiß stands than you'll find in Istanbul.

Krümel. This restaurant/bar/café offers a broad selection of international dishes, including Greek salad (DM 11.50) and broccoli casserole (DM 10) in a cozy, laid-back environment. Cake and coffee goes for a mere DM 3.90 from 3 PM to 6 PM. You can also shoot some pool on their table and read up on local events in the mags and flyers lying around the place. *Neuer Pferdemarkt 15–16, tel. 040/430–1421.*

La Famille. If you're in the mood for a sandwich, salad, or crepe, head for this popular, funkily decorated hole-in-the-wall, where a huge variety of the above (DM 5–DM 10) is served up with attitude. Get a cheap beer (DM 1.80–DM 2.50) to go down with it. *Shulterblatt 62, tel. 040/435384.*

noodles & mehr. Not many tourists have discovered this modern restaurant, where scrumptious, ample pasta dishes cost around DM 10. Try the tortellini in a rich cream sauce with spinach and walnuts. This place really knows how to use *Knobi* (garlic). *Schanzenstr. 2–4, tel. 040/439–2840.*

UNIVERSITY DISTRICT

The streets around the University of Hamburg will do you right when it comes to inexpensive delights and a hip environment. Wander down **Grindelallee** or **Grindelhof** to find a good restaurant or bar or to observe the university crowd doing the same thing. Take the S-Bahn to Dammtor, then walk up Edmund-Siemers-Allee to Grindelallee.

DIRT CHEAP • Café Neumann (Grindelhof 11, tel. 040/538–6322). This colorful and popular hole-in-the-wall serves great fresh-baked *Kuchen* (cake) and damn cheap coffee (DM 1).

UNDER DM 15 • Hindukusch. This moderately priced and softly decorated restaurant offers a host of rice-based specialties from Afghanistan at DM 10–DM 25. Vegetarian dishes are in the plenty and on the less expensive side. *Grindelhof 15, tel. 040/418164. Reservations recommended.*

Limerick. Colorful posters, music, and dark wood set the scene in this restaurant near the university. Students take advantage of the reasonable prices and unusual pizzas—choose toppings like artichoke, eggplant, or broccoli—for DM 9–DM 15. Also try the fresh salads (DM 6–DM 13) or pasta (DM 8–DM 15). A lot of students come here just to hang out on the patio and drink a beer or two. *Grindelallee 18, tel. 040/447836.*

Roxie. This is another popular student hangout with a welcoming atmosphere. Delight in dishes such as eggplant in tomato sauce (DM 11) or macaroni with spinach in cream sauce (DM 12) inside or out back in the garden (open until 10 PM during summer). *Rentzelstr. 6, tel. 040/451770.*

UNDER DM 20 • Balutschi. Best to call and make reservations on weekend nights for this immensely popular, gorgeously decorated Pakistani restaurant. The delicious offerings (entrées run DM 15–DM 20) include many veggie options, and the cook uses whole grains and natural products. *Grindelallee 33, tel. 040/452479.*

Dwaraka. If you're willing to shell out some extra bucks, come here for great Indian food and incredible service. Vegetarian dishes such as curried mushroom and potatoes start at DM 15; meat dishes are DM 20–DM 25. The portions are large, and if you're still hungry, just ask for more saffron rice—it's included with all meals. *Rentzelstr. 38, tel. 040/453237.*

EXPLORING HAMBURG

It will take you at least a couple days to familiarize yourself with Hamburg's diverse corners on your own; if you're in a hurry, consider taking one of the many sightseeing tours that give you a quick, if superficial, overview. Tourist offices organize English-language **bus tours** that last 1–1½ hours and cost DM 23 (DM 16.50 with Hamburg-CARD). Tours start at the harbor near Landungbrücken. **Harbor tours** let you check out large cargo ships in the labyrinthine canals. Call or stop by the tourist office for the lowdown on bus and harbor tours, or to get information on any of the alternative city tours covering the history of Nazism in Hamburg.

Local Hamburg specialties include Birnen, Bohnen, und Speck (pears, beans, and bacon) and Labskaus, a stew made from pickled meats, potatoes, and herring, garnished with a fried egg, sour pickles, and lots of beets. Mmm.

ALTSTADT

Although one third of the old city was destroyed in the Great Fire of 1842, and more than half of the city was again reduced to rubble during World War II, you can still visit the restored Rathaus, churches, and a few historic streets with houses that survived both catastrophes. Walking between sights is definitely doable, even though they are spread throughout the Altstadt. To reach the area's heart, take U3 to Rathaus or U1, U2, S1, or S3 to Jungfernstieg.

BINNENALSTER AND AUSSENALSTER

Once an insignificant waterway, the Alster was dammed during the 18th century to form an artificial lake in the middle of Hamburg. Stately hotels, department stores, fine shops, and cafés now line the Binnenalster (Inner Alster); the Aussenalster (Outer Alster) is framed by spacious parks and set against a background of private mansions. In winter the Alster lakes sometimes freeze over, and the pure white stretches of snow-covered ice are dotted with residents in vibrantly colored snowsuits, mittens, and caps. From late spring into fall you'll see sailboats and windsurfers skimming across the surface of the Aussenalster, narrowly missing passenger steamships. Take a walk over to the **Alsterarkaden,** a white neo-Renaissance arcade designed in 1843 by Alexis de Chateauneuf; filled with interesting shops, it sits on the Inner Alster between Jungfernstieg and the Rathaus, offering a great view of the Alster swans. Rent a paddleboat or rowboat for about DM 20 per hour for two people at **Alfred Seebeck** (tel. 040/247652) or **Segelschule Pieper** (tel. 040/247578), just across from the Hotel Atlantic.

DEICHSTRAßE

For over 600 years, people have lived on Deichstraße, a genuinely charming and peaceful residential street that runs along one of Hamburg's oldest canals. Although many Deichstraße residences were destroyed in the Great Fire of 1842, a number of homes date from the 17th century. Many others have been restored, giving the street a pleasant uniformity of style. Among the oldest structures are No. 27, a warehouse dating from 1780, and No. 39, whose Baroque facade dates from 1700. *U3 to Rödingsmarkt, then down Rödingsmarkt, 1st left to Deichstr.*

JACOBIKIRCHE

This 14th-century church was rebuilt after being severely damaged during World War II. The reconstructed interior is rather uninspired, but some of the church's treasures—including three Gothic altars and a unique 1693 Baroque organ supposedly played by Johann Sebastian Bach—remain intact. Summer organ concerts (DM 5) are held every Wednesday at 5:15 PM. *Jacobikirchhof 22, tel. 040/327744. U3 to Mönckebergstr; or, from Rathaus, east on Mönckebergstr. Open daily 10–5.*

HAMBURGER KUNSTHALLE

The 3,000 paintings, 400 sculptures, and coin and medal collections in the Kunsthalle present a remarkably diverse picture of European artistic life from the 14th century to the present. The collections amassed here are among Europe's most treasured, particularly noted for a fine stock of Rembrandts and works by 19th-century German Romantic greats, including Caspar David Friedrich and Philipp Otto Runge. In the Kunsthalle's new building, **Galerie der Gegenwart** (Modern Art Gallery), you'll find masterpieces by German Impressionist Max Liebermann, Expressionists Edvard Munch and Wassily Kandinsky, and pop art deities Andy Warhol and Roy Lichtenstein. Find out about the rotating exhibits from other top European and American modern art museums. *Glockengießerwall 1, near Hauptbahnhof, tel. 040/2486–2612. Admission: DM 8, DM 6 students; DM 2 with Hamburg-CARD. Open Tues.–Sun. 10–6 (Thurs. until 9).*

PETRIKIRCHE

Considered the oldest church in Hamburg, this early 13th-century building fell victim to the Great Fire of 1842 and was rebuilt shortly afterward. It contains a number of attractions, including a Gothic pulpit and various votive panels. At 5 PM on the first Sunday of every month, they hold a Lutheran service in English. *Speersort 10, 2 blocks east of Rathaus, tel. 040/324438. U3 to Rathaus. Open weekdays 9–6, Sat. 9–5, Sun. 9–noon and 1–5.*

RATHAUS

The *Rathaus* (Town Hall) presides impressively over the city-state of Hamburg, sheltering legislators and tourists alike in its neo-Renaissance elegance. Construction of the sandstone structure began in 1866, when 4,000 oak trunks were sunk into the moist soil to provide stability for its mighty bulk. When neither city council nor the state government is in session here, you can tour the Rathaus's tortuous hallways. Especially opulent and rather tragic is the intricately carved **Orphan's Room,** chiseled by 80 orphan carvers between the ages of eight and 14. Near the Rathaus is a work by **Ernst Barlach,** depicting a sorrowful mother hugging a child. The Nazis deemed the artwork's message improper and replaced it with an eagle, meant to represent Germany's strength and power. Later, the Barlach piece was reconstructed as a warning against war. *Rathausmarkt, tel. 040/3681–2470. U3 to Rathaus. Tours (DM 2, some in English) every 30 min, Mon.–Thurs. 10–3:15, Fri.–Sun. 10–1:15.*

SPEICHERSTADT

Warehouses generally don't elicit oohs and aahs for their architecture, but you have to admit this 19th-century collection of warehouses for the port of Hamburg includes some mighty fine storage sheds. Take time to wander along some of the enormous, Gothic-influenced brick structures, some of which are loaded with carpets, bags of coffee, oats, and rivets. Gain entry into one of these warehouses at the **Speicherstadtmuseum** (St. Annenufer 2; closed Mon.), where you can see antique equipment used in the early days of the quarter's existence. *U1 to Meßberg, then west along water and across Mattentwiete bridge; or, from Deichstr., south to water, then left and across bridge.*

TURMRUINE ST. NIKOLAI

After this 19th-century neo-Gothic church was partially destroyed in World War II, the remaining 162-m tower (Hamburg's tallest), the outside walls, and the interior bells were left as a monument to those killed and persecuted during the war. For a detailed look at the history and architecture of the building, visit the exhibit next door. *Hopfenmarkt. U3 to Rödingsmarkt, then east on Ost-West-Str. to Hopfenmarkt; or, from Rathaus, west on Johannisstr., left on Hahntrapp. Admission free. Exhibit open Mon., Wed., Fri. 10–6, Tues. and Thurs. 10–2.*

ST. PAULI

St. Pauli is the place to see Hamburg's gritty but contemporary side. Besides checking out that renowned pleasure quarter, the Reeperbahn (S1 or S3 to Reeperbahn), you can head down to the harbor (U3, S1, or S3 to Landungsbrücken).

FISCHMARKT

Every Sunday morning, eager early risers and late-night party-goers congregate at the Fischmarkt, Hamburg's most famous market, which opens at 5 AM (7 AM in winter) and runs until 10 AM. If you can manage to get up, you can get fresh fish, rabbits, birds, flowers, veggies, knickknacks, souvenirs, and just about anything else you can imagine. A bag filled with all the fish or fruit you can carry (haphazardly packed by screaming grocers) costs DM 10. Prices go down at about 9:30, when the market begins to wind down. Listen to free jazz or rock until noon in the **Fischauktionshalle,** where hundreds of rowdy, drunk Germans down a few pints to prepare for happy hour. Try very, very hard not to miss this quintessential Hamburg experience, even if it means forcing yourself to stay up all night. *U3, S1, S2, or S3 to Landungsbrücken and follow the signs.*

HAFEN

With 33 individual docks and 500 berths, Hamburg's *Hafen* (harbor) is one of the largest and most efficient in the world (it's the second largest in Europe) and will send ship aficionados into raptures. Even if modern shipping isn't your gig, the harbor has a number of neat old ships along its docks. **Museumschiff** *Rickmer RickmersBIBIBI* (Pier 1, tel. 040/319–5959; open daily 10–5:30) is a beautiful 19th-century East Indies Windjammer that has become a museum with a temporary exhibition hall. Admission is DM 4, DM 3 for students. Many companies offer harbor tours; try **HADAG** (St. Pauli Fischmarkt 28, tel. 040/311–70724). Tours leave from Bridge 2 at Landungsbrücken, last one hour, and cost DM 16 (DM 8.50 students). A cheaper way to see the harbor is to take a city ferry, free with a Day Transit Pass or Hamburg-CARD. Ferries leave every half hour from Landungsbrücken for destinations such as Blankenese (*see* Near Hamburg, *below*).

In the park north of the harbor stands Hamburg's largest monument, the 38-m-high **Bismarck-Denkmal.** Otto von Bismarck, the former chancellor, impressed citizens with his devotion to a reunited Germany; now he impresses visitors with his giant, 6-m head.

KRAEMERAMTSWOHNUNGEN

This cluster of courtyard houses in the shadow of the Michaeliskirche dates from the 1620s, when they were built to house shopkeepers' widows. Nowadays the tiny old structures—a real rarity in bombed-to-ashes Hamburg—are home to eclectic antiques stores as well as a **museum** that replicates the setup of a typical house—minus the widow. *Krayenkamp 10–11, tel. 040/321–0130. S1, S2, or S3 to Stadthausbrücke. Museum admission: DM 1. Open Tues.–Sun. 10–5.*

MICHAELISKIRCHE

Hamburg's most famous and best-loved landmark, the Michaeliskirche (St. Michael's Church, popularly known as "Michel"), stands guard over the city. Its copper-covered spire makes a distinct mark on Hamburg's already stately skyline, while the restored interior reflects its original 18th-century elegance. In the vault you can see a presentation on the church's history (DM 5, DM 3.50 students), as well as the graves of three famous composers: Hamburg-born Johannes Brahms, Georg Telemann, and Carl Phillip Emanuel Bach (Johann Sebastian's son), who was the musical director of Hamburg's five major churches for 20 years. As if all this weren't enough, Michel's distinctive 132-m brick-and-iron tower, home to the largest clock in Germany, is open for climbing (DM 4, DM 3 students). Twice daily, at 10 AM and 9 PM (Sunday at noon only), a watchman plays a trumpet solo from the tower platform. *Krayenkamp 4c, tel. 040/376780. S1, S2, or S3 to Stadthausbrücke. Open summer, Mon.–Sat. 10–6, Sun. 12:30–5; winter, daily 10–5. Organ concerts (DM 10, DM 5 students) Easter–Aug., Sat. at 5 PM.*

REEPERBAHN

Stretching from the Reeperbahn S-Bahn station to the St. Pauli U-Bahn station, this strip has a well-deserved reputation as "the wickedest mile in the world." Picture Las Vegas's gaudiness, Amsterdam's prostitution, and Berlin's nightclubs all sharing the same space, and you've got a good idea what the Reeperbahn is like. During the day, the area looks like any large dirty street, so wait until night to check it out. If sex clubs turn you on, you'll have no problem finding one to fit specific "needs." Both the Reeperbahn and the side streets are overloaded with straight and gay clubs, specializing in just about everything. *And* they all take credit cards. Hamburg's legalized prostitution strip, **Herbertstraße,** which is off-limits to women and children, has window after window of prostitutes, who are regulated by the government and tested regularly for sexually transmitted diseases. The same cannot be said for the dozens of prostitutes who line Davidstraße and other side streets. The whole scene becomes really depressing really quickly.

For a more mature look into the material and psychological origins of Hamburg's sinful side, head to the **Erotic Art Museum,** which displays one of the largest collections of erotic art in Europe. Sculptures, sketches, and paintings dating back five centuries provide historical commentary on humankind's passions and taboos. You might catch a rotating photography exhibit. *Nobistor 10a, tel. 040/3178410. S1*

HAMBURG'S DISTURBING HISTORY

Until the Third Reich, Hamburg housed a thriving Jewish community that numbered nearly 25,000. Today you can remember them at Platz der Jüdischen Deportierten (Moorweiderstr.). In the 1940s this simple, peaceful park just north of S-Bahn Dammtor was the site of deportation to concentration camps for Hamburg Jews. Plaques on each edge of the park and a small statue remind visitors of the ghastly events that took place here just decades ago. Another place to reflect upon the fate of the Jewish community is the Jüdische Friedhof, Hamburg's old Jewish cemetery, five minutes west of the Reeperbahn S-Bahn station. The first permanent guest arrived in 1666, and the last grave was laid in 1942. Don't just show up here; you must contact the Jewish Community Center (Schäferkampsallee 27, tel. 040/440944) to get the key to this beautiful place. They'll also direct you to other Jewish groups and organizations.

or S3 to Reeperbahn. Admission: DM 15, DM 10 students and with Hamburg-CARD. Open Sun.–Thurs. 10 AM–midnight, Fri.–Sat. 10 AM–1 AM.

If you're looking for the perfect Hamburg souvenir, **Condomerie** (Spielbudenpl. 18, tel. 040/319–3100) has a huge selection of condoms: scented ones, flavored ones, textured ones, musical ones, and even very, very big ones—more than 100,000 condoms in all. Every 10th customer gets a free one. The condom that causes the most titillation and idle speculation is a custom-made, 5-inch-wide superrubber. Any man who can fill this puppy up wins DM 100; on-site proof required. Viagra test mandatory for serious contenders. The manager says two men have already succeeded. Guys can give it a go 24 hours a day.

MUSEUMS AND GALLERIES

In addition to its fabulous Kunsthalle (*see* Altstadt, *above*), Hamburg has more than 100 art galleries and more than 30 museums, ranging from the ridiculous to the highbrow. Pick up *The Museums*—which includes a helpful map—at a tourist office or a museum. The **Hamburg-CARD** (*see* Visitor Information, *above*) gets you discounts at 11 of Hamburg's museums.

Deichtorhallen. This large old building near the Hauptbahnhof used to be a vegetable-and-flower market, but it now displays changing modern art exhibits in its airy rooms. Don't mistake the simple sculpture outside the entrance for archaic remains or garbage—it's a work by artist Richard Serra. *Altländer Str., near Hauptbahnhof, tel. 040/323730. Admission: DM 14, DM 10 students. Open Tues.–Sun. 11–6.*

Ernst-Barlach-Haus. This museum dedicated to one of Germany's most influential Expressionist sculptors contains a mighty collection of the artist's works, including 116 sculptures and more than 300 drawings, prints, and documents on his work and life. Barlach was born in nearby Wedel and, like many other modern artists, was declared a degenerate by the Nazis in the 1930s. *Baron-Voght-Str. 50a, in Jenisch-Park, tel. 040/826085. S1 to Klein Flottbek. Admission: DM 6, DM 4 students. Open Tues.–Sun. 11–5.*

Gedenkstätte Janusz-Korczak-Schule. Located outside the city center, this memorial reminds visitors of the brutal murder of 40 Jewish children and teenagers just hours before the Allies liberated the neighborhood. One exhibit recounts Nazi medical experimentation on prisoners. Try to arrange a visit to the memorial rose garden and plant a flower of your own. *Bullenhuser Damm 92, tel. 040/783295. S21 to*

Rothenburgsort; then 5-min walk north across the canal on Auschläger Billdeich. Open weekdays 9–5, Sun. 10–5. Admission to museum and guided tours free. For tours, contact Joachim Lietke (tel. 040/553–2230).

Museum für Hamburgische Geschichte. This museum traces the history of Hamburg from its origins in the 9th century to the present day. Exhibits include a medieval merchant's house, a model of the harbor, and a 250-sq-m model train set showing Hamburg's rail lines. Also inside is the **Historic Emigration Office** (tel. 040/3005–1282), with microfilm records of the names of the almost five million people who left the port of Hamburg for the promise of a better life in the New World. *Holstenwall 24, tel. 040/3504–2380. U3 to St. Pauli. Admission: DM 6, DM 2 students. Open Tues.–Sat. 10–5, Wed. 10–9, Sun. 10–6.*

Museum für Kunst und Gewerbe. Built in 1876 as a combo museum and school, the Arts and Crafts Museum now contains an impressive collection of crafts from ancient Egypt, Greece, Japan, and China, as well as applied European arts from the Middle Ages through the present. *Steintorpl. 1, tel. 040/2486–2630. Admission: DM 12, DM 6 students. Open Tues.–Sun. 10–6 (Thurs. until 9).*

CHEAP THRILLS

The **Außenalster** is usually dotted with colorful sailboats and sailboarders, and sunbathers line the banks in summer—it's legal to go topless in Hamburg. In winter, entrepreneurial types erect stands around the Alster lakes, selling mulled wine, candy, and corn on the cob. There's a popular **beach** (Am Schulberg; open Apr.–Sept., daily 1–11) on the Elbe River where people picnic, drink, and just have a good time when the sun manages to peek through. Don't be fooled into thinking you can actually swim in the polluted water. From Reeperbahn, take Bus 36 toward Blankenese to Liebermann Straße. Thursday–Sunday nights in July and August, the **Freiluftkino auf dem Rathausmarkt** shows movies on a big screen in front of the Rathaus. Admission is free, and there are usually a couple of films in English with German subtitles. Pick up a flyer at the tourist office or at clubs and theaters.

The controversial Nazi-era war monument between Stephansplatz and Dammtor contains an inscription that states: "Deutschland muß leben auch wenn wir sterben müssen" ("Germany must live, even if we must die").

Harry's Hamburger Hafenbasar is a spectacular 2,400-sq-m bazaar that occupies a total of five houses and is owned by the bearded Harry Rosenberg, a collector of anything and everything for the last 37 years. The highlight of the collection is a young girl's shrunken head, found in Brazil. Rosenberg charges DM 2.50 for a peek. *Bernhard-Nocht-Str. 63, 3 blocks south of Reeperbahn, tel. 040/312482. Admission: DM 4, but admission price subtracted from purchases of more than DM 10; free entrance on your birthday. Open daily 9–6.*

The **Isemarkt,** on Isestraße near the Hoheluftbrücke, is considered the best and most beautiful market in the city; about 300 stalls sell produce, fish, clothing, and toys. The market is held Tuesday and Friday 8:30–2 under the U-Bahn tracks in a residential district. Unlike the over-the-top Fischmarkt, this market is primarily for locals intent on their haggling. *U3 to Hoheluftbrücke or Eppendorfer Baum.*

Opened in 1877, **Friedhof Ohlsdorf** (Ohlsdorf Cemetery) is the largest graveyard in the world. More than 1.3 million souls rest in peace here, and the living can keep an eye on them from more than 2,800 benches. Hamburgers come here to commune with the dead, walk, make out, and have picnics. City Buses 170 and 270 run right through the cemetery. *Fuhlsbüttler Str. 756, tel. 040/593880. Entrance outside U- and S-Bahn station Ohlsdorf. Open daily 8 AM–9 PM.*

Although **"Planten un Blomen"** technically refers to one garden within the larger Alter Botanischer Garten, everyone just refers to the whole thing as Planten un Blomen (Low German for Plants and Flowers). Meander the ubiquitous flower-surrounded pathways and green expanses, regress at the many playgrounds, check out summer concerts at the open-air stage, lounge near the lake, or partake in a tea ceremony at the Japanese garden. There's also a **greenhouse** full of tropical plants. At 10 PM from May to September, crowds gather to watch a free water-and-light show accompanied by classical music. The nearby **TV Tower** (Lagerstr. 2, tel. 040/438024) affords a great view of the city for DM 6. *U-Bahn to Stephanspl. or S-Bahn to Dammtor. Gardens open weekdays 7 AM–11 PM, weekends 10 AM–11 PM.*

FESTIVALS

MARCH • Every year from late March to late April thousands of fun-seekers visit the **Frühlingsdom** (Spring Festival) at the Heiligengeistfeld, near the Reeperbahn. Germany's biggest fun fair traces its history to the 10th century, and the modern version features a giant amusement park with roller coasters, food booths, beer tents, stuffed animals, and the world's biggest transportable Ferris wheel. Rides are expensive (DM 3–DM 10), but prices go down every Wednesday (family day). There's a free fireworks show on Friday. *U2 to Messehallen or U3 to St. Pauli or Feldstr. Open Mon.–Thurs. and Sun. 3–11, Fri. and Sat. 3–midnight.*

MAY • On May 6 and 7 Hamburg's 800-year-old harbor comes alive when hordes of people gather to celebrate the **Hafengeburtstag** (Harbor Birthday). Back in 1189, Kaiser Friedrich Barbarossa signed a charter on May 7 declaring Hamburg a duty-free state. The celebration has evolved into a spectacle of historic ships, food booths, and loud music.

JULY–AUGUST • The **Schleswig-Holstein Musik Festival** is a summer-long series of classical concerts (starting at the end of June and running through August) featuring international musicians. Founded by acclaimed pianist Justus Frantz, the festival makes regular stops in Hamburg. Tickets are available at major ticket outlets; try the **Theaterkasse Central** (Gerhart-Hauptmann-Pl. 48, tel. 040/324312), in the Landesbank-Galerie, a covered mall.

A repeat of the Frühlingsdom (*see above*), the summer festival, known as the **Hummelfest,** takes place July–August at the Heiligengeistfeld.

AUGUST–SEPTEMBER • In the last week of August, street theater, vendors, food booths, and musicians crowd the streets around the Alster for the **Alstervergnügen** (Alster Enjoyment). Fireworks and music also highlight this festival, held on different dates in September every year.

NOVEMBER–DECEMBER • Around the end of November and the beginning of December, Hamburg celebrates the holiday season at many Hanseatic **Weihnachtsmärkte.** The best of these Christmas markets are the Rathausmarkt and the Gänsemarkt. Don your mittens and earmuffs, and browse through the booths lining the streets for the perfect Christmas gift. You can get hot cider and *Glühwein* (mulled wine) to warm your spirits.

AFTER DARK

Hamburg's nightlife spans the spectrum from live sex shows to performances of John Neumeier's renowned ballet company. Pick up tickets to the city's theater and music productions at most tourist-information offices. Try getting same-day tickets at the particular theater's *Abendkasse* (box office) or at **Last-Minute im Hanse-Viertel** (Poststr., entrance at Groß Bleichen, tel. 040/353565), which sells half-price tickets for that day's performances 3 PM–6:30 PM. Young Hamburgers usually have a couple of beers in a pub until 11:30 PM or midnight, then head to the disco until dawn. *Prinz* (DM 5), *Szene* (DM 5), and *OK-Pur* (free at tourist office) have good listings of pubs, discos, and other nighttime fun (the free monthly magazine *Hinnerk* has listings of gay activities). Although you'll find downtown activity around Valentinskamp, most nightlife is concentrated in two areas: the Schanzenviertel, particularly Feldstraße, and (no surprise) the Reeperbahn. If you venture onto the Reeperbahn at night, be prepared to be approached or even harassed, regardless of your gender.

BARS

ST. PAULI • **Hans Albers Eck.** This disco/bar just off the Reeperbahn is named after a famous German actor buried in nearby Ohlsdorf. Large crowds of rowdy students and locals come for the cheap cover, dim lights, and a slightly seedy ambience. *Friedrichstr. 26, at Davidstr., tel. 040/317–5960. Cover: DM 6–DM 10. Open Tues.–Sat. 10 PM–3 AM.*

Purgatory. With an endless string of kitschy lights and saints' pictures, this tacky but fun bar is the place to atone for your sins (or accumulate a few more). DJs play progressive house and trance; industrial bands occasionally take the stage. *Friedrichstr. 8, off Reeperbahn, tel. 040/315807. Open Thurs.–Sat. until 5 AM.*

SCHANZENVIERTEL • **Frauenkneipe.** If you've had enough of Herbertstraße's men-only sleaze, come to this bar exclusively for women. The clientele is mainly lesbian, and the environment may be intimidating for many. *Stresemannstr. 60, tel. 040/436377. U3 to Feldstr. Fri. disco cover: DM 6. Open weekdays 8 PM–1 AM, Sat. 9 PM–3 AM, Sun. 2 PM–1 AM.*

Kir. Rotating theme parties, diverse dance music (independent, soul, and pop), and a devoted crowd of locals make this club a must visit for boogie enthusiasts. *Max-Brauer Allee 241, tel. 040/438041. Open weekdays 10 PM–3 AM, weekends 11 PM–4 AM. Cover DM 5–DM 15.*

Logo. Located just east of the Schanzenviertel, in the university district, this late-night club/bar offers some of the best of Hamburg's local alternative music scene and a broad selection of cocktails in a smoky, candlelit atmosphere. *Grindelallee 5, tel. 040/362622. From Dammtor Station, walk up Edmund-Siemers-Allee to 4-way intersection. Open weekdays 8 PM–2 AM, weekends 10 PM–3 AM.*

Shamrock. A mixed crowd, including lots of English-speaking international students, meets in this dark pub for Irish music and Guinness. *Feldstr. 40, tel. 040/439–7678. Open daily 5 PM–2 AM.*

CLUBS AND LIVE MUSIC

Many pubs have great live music ranging from Irish folk to funk. And it's true that Hamburg is *the* city for jazz. Check individual listings (*see below*) or pick up one of the many magazines that list concerts.

INNENSTADT • Cotton Club. The oldest jazz club in Hamburg plays cool blues, Dixieland, big band, and hot jazz every night (except Sunday) starting at 8 PM. *Alter Steinw. 10, tel. 040/343878. S1 or S3 to Stadthausbrücke. Cover varies.*

Madhouse. Disco-goers consistently crowd this club to shake down to a supreme selection of music. Prince (when he still went by that name) rented it twice for after-concert celebrations. *Valentinskamp 47, tel. 040/344193. Cover: DM 6–DM 12; women enter free.*

ST. PAULI • Docks und Prinzenbar. This club hosts a wide variety of events including a *Tanzpalast* (dance palace) with two DJs (Sat.), watergame parties (Thurs.), indie music (Thurs.), and films. Cover varies, and, as you can imagine, the crowd varies, too. *Spielbudenpl. 19–20, tel. 040/3178–8311. Call 040/433039 for tickets. Open daily from 9 PM.*

Women who aren't prostitutes are not welcome on Herbertstraße and should be prepared to have a glass of water tossed in their faces by one of the street guards if they try to venture in.

Finnegans Wake. A lively English-speaking crowd gathers here for live blues and Irish folk music. Pub grub is served from 11 AM until 9 PM. *Börsenbrücke 4, near Rathaus, tel. 040/374–3433. Cover: DM 3–DM 5. Open weekdays until 1 AM, weekends until 4 AM.*

Kaiserkeller. In the basement of the Große Freiheit 36 complex north of the Reeperbahn, this dark, cavernous club has seen some pretty big names—The Beatles, for instance—and continues to draw rock celebrities. Make an appearance of your own at the Keller's disco, held after live shows and every other night of the week. *Große Freiheit 36, tel. 040/319–3649. Disco cover: DM 6–DM 15.*

Mojo Club. Formerly a bowling alley, this club now hosts modern jazz in the large front room; later in the evening the back room converts into one of Hamburg's most popular discos. Come Thursday evenings to listen to free jam sessions. *Reeperbahn 1, tel. 040/435232. Open Tue.–Sun. Live music cover: DM 8–DM 20. Disco cover: DM 10.*

SCHANZENVIERTEL • Entrée. For live music and "jazz food," swing on by this vibrant jazz club. Mainstream jazz and blues (Mon.–Sat. at around 8 PM) bring the Miles Davis and Billie Holiday posters on the walls to life. Check any entertainment magazine for schedules. *Juliusstr. 13–15, tel. 040/430–4042. U3, S21, or S31 to Sternschanze, then south on Schanzenstr., right on Susannenstr. (which becomes Juliusstr.). Cover: DM 7–DM 10. Closed Sun.*

Fabrik. This old converted factory in Altona has been a cultural center for 25 years, presenting offbeat performers, musicians, and dancers. Some of the most interesting performances in Hamburg are staged here. Call or stop by for tickets (DM 10–DM 40). Saturdays are gay/lesbian dance nights (cover DM 15). Call Hein und Fiete (tel. 040/240333) for tickets. Fifteen minutes before the performance, the box office sells discounted rush tickets. *Barnerstr. 36, tel. 040/391070. S1, S3, or S31 to Altona, then north on Präsident-Krahn-Str., left on Julius-Leber-Str. to Barnerstr.*

CLASSICAL MUSIC

Hamburg's three symphony orchestras—the Philharmonische Staatsorchester, the Sinfonieorchester des Norddeutschen Rundfunks (NDR), and the Hamburger Symphoniker—perform regularly in Hamburg's most important concert hall, the neo-Baroque **Musikhalle** (Karl-Muck-Pl., tel. 040/357–6660). Call the tourist office or check entertainment magazines for schedules and ticket information. The **Hamburgische Staatsoper** (Dammtorstr. 28, tel. 040/351721) is one of the most beautiful theaters in the country and the leading north German venue for top-notch opera and ballet. Tickets can be purchased up to two weeks in advance by phone or in person at the Staatsoper box office, open weekdays 10–2 and 4–6:30, Saturday 10–2 (also 1½ hours before the performance). The **Operettenhaus** (Spielbudenpl. 1, tel. 040/311170) puts on light opera and popular musicals. The box office sells tickets weekdays 11–7, weekends 11–2 and 3–7. Student discounts are available for weekday performances.

MOVIE THEATERS

Going to see a flick in Hamburg can be pretty expensive—ranging between DM 10 and DM 15. Prices sink a bit for matinees and on "movie days" (usually Tues. or Wed.), and are sometimes cheaper for students with ID. When you're scanning the movie listings, check for the notations OF and OmU, which refer to "original language" and "original language with subtitles," respectively. The **Abaton** (Allendepl. 3, tel. 040/4132–0321), near the university, is an enormously popular alternative cinema. Even if you can't understand the film, the café-restaurant one level up will keep you entertained. Many movie theaters sporadically show popular American films in English, but you can *always* count on **Streits** (Jungfernstieg 38, tel. 040/346051) to show one or two American films per week (late Wednesday night and/or early Sunday morning). **City-Kino** (Steindamm 9, tel. 040/244463), near the Hauptbahnhof, now shows exclusively English films and is a good place to meet English-speaking foreigners and Germans.

THEATER

Although some theaters take a summer break, Hamburg has a good variety of year-round theater productions, most of which are staged in German. The **Deutsche Schauspielhaus** (Kirchenallee 39, tel. 040/248713), in all its restored 19th-century opulence, is now the most important venue in Hamburg for classical and modern theater, including American musicals. The box office is open for ticket sales weekdays 10–6, Saturday 10–3, Sunday 10–1. Some student and last-minute tickets are available. The **English Theatre** (Lerchenfeld 14, tel. 040/227–7089) has reasonably priced tickets (usually about DM 10) for funny, whimsical productions in English. Hit **Schmidt** (Spielbudenpl. 24, tel. 040/317–7880) or **Schmidts Tivoli** (Spielbudenpl. 27–28, tel. 040/3177–8899) for cabaret shows and variety numbers that you should be able to understand regardless of linguistic ability—slipping on a banana peel is international. Tickets are available at the theater daily noon–7 PM or over the phone. Check out **Pulverfaß** (Pulverfeich 12, tel. 040/249791 or 040/247878) for one of the better local drag shows. Tickets run about DM 28.

NEAR HAMBURG

ALTES LAND

This fertile, fruit-growing region extends 30 km west from Hamburg along the south bank of the Elbe, making for some blissful wanderings. Take a day hike or picnic among the canals, half-timbered farmhouses, and fruit trees (you can even buy fresh fruit from local farmers for dessert). Some of the prettiest walks take you along the dikes running next to the Este and Lühe rivers. May, when the apple and cherry trees bloom pink and white, is especially beautiful. To reach the area, take S1, S2, or S3 to Landungsbrücken, then the HAPAG lines ship (2 per day, DM 24.50 round-trip) from Brücke 3 to Altes Land (Cranz or Lühe).

BLANKENESE

Although this waterside area 15 km west of Hamburg is now one of the city's wealthiest neighborhoods, it still manages to preserve some of its fishing-village ambience. The 58 lanes that wind through town are dotted with villas—the perfect place to lose yourself for an afternoon. Wander through **Hirschpark** and check out the enclosure with reindeer and peacocks. To reach Blankenese, take a ferry from Landungsbrücken, or S1 to Blankenese. Perhaps the best route back to Hamburg is the trail that starts west of town near Kösterbergstraße and winds through rolling green heaths to the Sülldorf S-Bahn station.

KZ-GEDENKSTÄTTE NEUENGAMME

It's frightening to stand on this peaceful overgrown land and realize that just over half a century ago the Nazis murdered more than 55,000 people here. National Socialists interned more than 100,000 victims at the Neuengamme concentration camp, in operation between 1938 and 1945. Upon entering the camp, you'll come across a memorial wall and a building housing death records and banners chronologically listing the names of all those the Nazis killed here. An exhibition whose information panels run clear across the camp opened in 1995 for the 50th anniversary of the camp's liberation. The museum, located in the Walther-Werke factory (a private rifle and weapons company that put prisoners to work) chronicles the horrors of daily camp life. Much of the accompanying text is in English. Call ahead to find out about the museum's Sunday afternoon lecture series (in German). *Jean-Dolidier-Weg 39, Neuengamme, tel. 040/723–1031. S21 to Bergedorf, then Bus 227 (leaves hourly on the half hour, DM 9.20 round-trip) toward Neuengamme to Jean-Dolidier-Weg. Admission free. Open Oct.–Mar., Tues.–Sun. 10–5; Apr.–Sept., weekends 10–6.*

SCHLESWIG-HOLSTEIN

After a few nights in Hamburg you'll quite likely need some time to regain your senses. Consider the sandy beaches and remote fishing villages of Schleswig-Holstein. Although today the region's towns, cities, and cow-covered flatlands are among the most serene in Germany, Schleswig-Holstein has a history as one of the most powerful trading centers in Europe. Its cities' wealth began to grow in the days of the Hanseatic League (12th–17th centuries), when merchants amassed large new fortunes through trade, and challenged the nobles' privileged role as the only moneyed class. It was with the league that **Lübeck,** still a busy harbor, became one of northern Europe's richest, most magnificent cities. Here and in other cities such as **Schleswig** and **Flensburg,** fabulous old mercantile buildings, churches, and residences still attest to those bustling glory days. The region gradually fell under Danish control during the Middle Ages, remaining a Danish province until German troops seized it in 1864. To this day, Schleswig-Holstein's architecture and landscape are reminiscent of neighboring Denmark, and a small Danish minority still inhabits the region around Flensburg.

Very few foreign tourists come to the North Sea's shores, but Germans flock here in the summer to revive themselves with the fresh ocean air. The North Frisian island of **Sylt** is Germany's most popular (and most expensive) resort. During summer, you're bound to run into regional festivals during which the resorts and local villages come alive. A bit more upscale is Schleswig-Holstein's **Music Festival** (*see* Festivals *in* Hamburg, *above*), a world-renowned classical music event running from the end of June through August. Every city hosts concerts, with most tickets starting at DM 16. Pick up a schedule or info at any tourist office. If you want a flood of material, contact the t**ourist office** (Fremdenverkehrsverband Schleswig-Holstein; Niemannsw. 31, 23109 Kiel, tel. 0431/5600–2526), open Monday–Thursday 9–5, Friday 9–3.

LÜBECK

With more than 1,100 monuments, the port of Lübeck is a museum in itself. Hordes of tourists visit the city's compact and highly walkable *Altstadt* to get an eyeful of the city's numerous treasures. Lübeck's ancient core—the area surrounding its impressive *Marktplatz* (marketplace)—was founded by Henry the Lion in 1159. Nowadays, Lübeck's Altstadt is protected as a UNESCO World Heritage Site, placing it in the same league as the Great Wall of China, the Acropolis, and Venice. From the train you'll see the endless spires that dot the sky above town, and walking in from the station, you can't help but be impressed by the **Holstentor** (the gate formerly pictured on the DM 50 note), welcoming you to the Altstadt with a pair of pointy towers. Lübeck's young people are surprisingly hip and politically active. Their amusements, though few, are well publicized and easily accessible. Needless to say, you'll want a couple of days to explore the Altstadt's medieval lanes, Gothic and Baroque churches, cobblestone courtyards, centuries-old canals, and waterside promenades.

BASICS

Lübeck's four **tourist offices** have a myriad of brochures, pamphlets, and ferry/bus schedules, but by and large the staffs are woefully unhelpful. The most helpful office, Amt für Lübeck-Werburg und Tourismus (Beckergrube 95, tel. 0451/122–8109; open weekdays 8–4), specializes in Lübeck and Lübeck alone. You might also try the Tourismus-Zentrale, which offers information via the internet at www.lue-

THAT AIN'T GERMAN

Plattdeutsch (Low German), a dialect common in Schleswig-Holstein, Hamburg, and Mecklenburg-Vorpommern on the Baltic coast, is still spoken in small villages, especially by older folks. Sylt has a newspaper with a section called "Dit und Dat" (This and That), and you might hear people calling one another a Döshaddel (idiot). Recently, there's been a movement to preserve Plattdeutsch in local schools, much to the chagrin of city slickers who view it as hick-town drawl. Some words that have found their way from Plattdeutsch into High German are "Moin" (hi), "Tschüß" (bye), and "so ein Scheit" (what shit).

beck.de. Log on to the web and e-mail under plastic palm trees at **Key West Cocktail and Internet Café** (Mühlenstr. 39, tel. 0451/705690).

The main **post office** (Königstr. 44–46; postal code 23552), a block north of the Rathaus, sells stamps and phone cards, and changes money. You can also change money at **Deutsche Bank Lübeck** (Kohlmarkt 7, tel. 0451/1490), which has good rates and a 24-hour ATM that takes American Express, MasterCard, Visa, and cards on the Plus and Cirrus networks.

COMING AND GOING

Lübeck is easy to reach from all over Germany and Scandinavia. The **Hauptbahnhof** (central train station; Am Bahnhof, tel. 0451/19419) features a tourist office, lockers, a grocery store, and a 24-hour ATM machine connected to the various networks. Lübeck is well-connected to Hamburg (2 per hr, 40 min, DM 16–DM 25) and Kiel (hourly, 1¼ hrs, DM 21). Trains also run five times daily to Copenhagen (3½–5 hrs, DM 123) and hourly to Schwerin (1½ hrs, DM 19–DM 28). To reach the Altstadt, exit the station and walk toward the Holstentor.

BY FERRY • For assistance, advice, and many brochures on international ferries, hit the tourist office on Beckergrube. Ferries leave from the nearby port city of **Travemünde.** Trains and Bus A (both DM 2.80) travel regularly from Lübeck to Travemünde's **Skandinavienkai** station. Ferries to Sweden and Finland leave from Skandinavienkai, and ferries to Denmark, Rostock, and Wismar leave from **Ostpreußkai** (near Skandinavienkai). For prices and departure times, call **Seltouristik** (tel. 04502/6411) or FRS (Vorderreihe 40a, tel. 04502/6411).

GETTING AROUND

Although Lübeck is the most walkable city in Schleswig-Holstein, a bike or bus may make getting around a little bit easier. Rent the former at **Leihcycle** (Schwartauer Allee 39, near Bahnhof, tel. 0451/42660) for DM 15 per day. Local buses (DM 2.80) run throughout the Altstadt and to nearby suburbs. Buy tickets from the driver.

WHERE TO SLEEP

Lübeck brims with clean, fun, centrally located hostels and hostel-like hotels—the best places to crash. Otherwise, a number of cheap pensions (DM 40–DM 50 singles, DM 80–DM 100 doubles) are located right outside of the Altstadt, and any tourist office can book you a room for a DM 5 fee plus 10% of the room price.

CVJM-Haus. Ignore the mildly Christian overtones—it won't affect your sleep in this quiet YMCA in a beautiful old house in the heart of the Altstadt. Doubles are DM 20 per person (DM 30 with kitchen and bath), and large dorms are DM 15 per person. *Große Petersgrube 11, next to Petrikirche, tel. 0451/71920. 200 beds. Curfew 10 PM (ask for key). Reception closed noon–5. Breakfast (DM 5).*

Hotel Rucksack. Call ahead to reserve a spot in this very hip and *umweltfreundlich* (environmentally friendly) hotel/hostel. Toilets use collected rainwater, and the building runs mostly on gas. The hotel is part of the Werkhof Community, a leftist cultural center that houses a weaving workshop, a natural foods

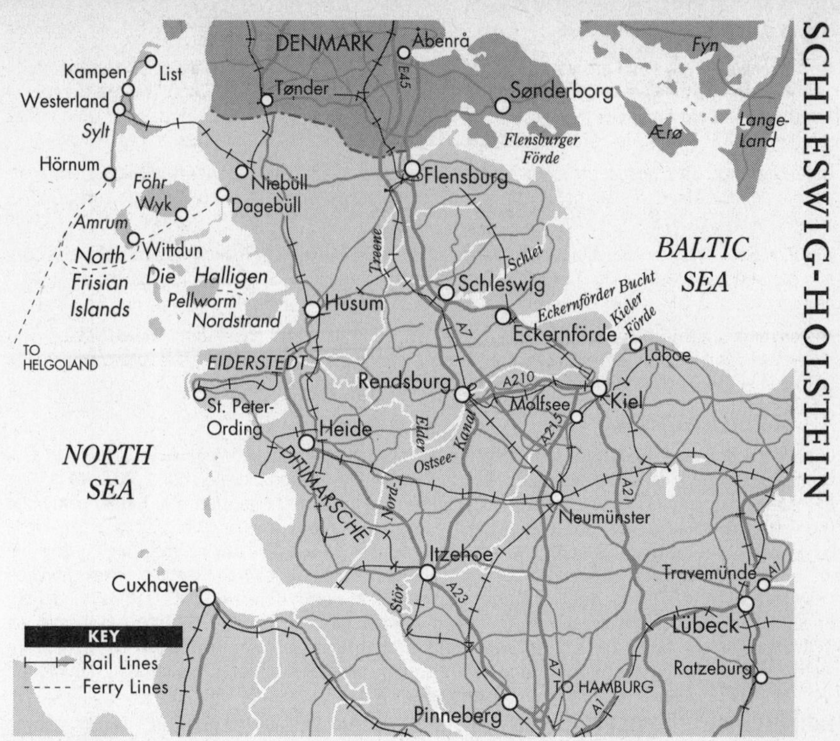

store, and the only all-veggie restaurant in town (*see* Food, *below*). Dorm beds in pleasant but small rooms go for DM 24–DM 34; two- and four-bed rooms with private bath cost DM 35–DM 40 per person. *Kanalstr. 70, at Glockengießerstr., tel. 0451/706892. From Bahnhof, walk past Holstentor into town, left on Königstr., right on Glockengießerstr. (25 min total). 28 beds. Kitchen facilities.*

Hotel Stadtpark. Located just outside the Altstadt, this medium-sized, well-kept, and friendly hotel has clean, cozy rooms at good prices. Singles go for DM 55–DM 80, doubles for DM 90–DM 125, including a buffet-style breakfast. Reserve ahead. *Roeckstr. 9, tel. 0451/34555, fax 0451/34555. From station, straight through ZoBaud, across Holstenbrücke, left on Königstr. 20 rooms, some with bath. Reception open 9–8.*

HOSTELS • Jugendgästehaus (HI). Down the street from the Mann brothers' house, this clean hostel has singles and doubles (DM 35–DM 38, DM 37–DM 40 over 26) as well as three- and four-person rooms (DM 28.50, DM 30.50 over 26). HI membership is required. *Mengstr. 33, tel. 0451/702–0399, fax 0451/77012. From Bahnhof, walk past Holstentor, left on An der Untertrave, right on Mengstr. 71 beds. Midnight curfew. Reception open 1 PM–6 PM and 7 PM–11 PM. Breakfast included.*

Jugendherberge (HI). The only hostel not in the Altstadt features exceptionally charmless rooms at exceptionally low prices. Make this your back-up. Beds DM 26 (DM 32 over 26) including breakfast; HI membership required. Send a postcard to reserve a spot. *Am Gertrudenkirchhof 4, tel. 0451/33433, fax 0451/34540. From Bahnhof, Bus 1, 3, 11, or 12 to Gustav-Radbruch Pl. (just after Burgertor), walk down Travemünder-Allee, left on Am Gertrudenkirchhof. 208 beds. Reception open after 11:30 AM. Midnight curfew.*

CAMPING • Campingplatz Lübeck-Schönböcken. This 70-spot campsite charges DM 8–DM 12 per tent and DM 8 per person. Facilities include washing machines (DM 4), hot and cold water, cooking facilities, and a small food store. *Steinrader Damm 12, tel. 0451/893090 or 0451/892287. From Bahnhof, Bus 7 or 8 (direction: Dombreite) to Bauernw., then walk 2 min along Steinrader Damm. Closed Nov.–Mar.*

FOOD

No matter where you stand in the Altstadt, odds are a cheap eatery is less than a block away. After dark, wander to the northeastern side (Fleischhauerstraße and Hüxstraße are good bets), where a number of café/bars like **Café Amadeus** (Königstr. 26, tel. 0451/705357) serve up pizza, pasta, and sandwiches for DM 6–DM 9. To stock up on groceries, head to **Coop** (Sandstr., at Schmiedestr.).

Café Affenbrot. This veggie restaurant serves soy burgers, salads, and assorted sandwiches like goat-cheese and tomato. Come sip herbal tea with Lübeck's leftists. Prices (and portions) are small. *Kanalstr. 70, tel. 0451/72193.*

Heinrich Böll. This place plays up its location in a 200-year-old house by making its atmosphere as cozy and old world as possible. Don't miss the back garden, a perfect place to chow Tamm's pasta, Auflauf, and pizza (DM 8–DM 13). *Beckergrube 65, tel. 0451/74494.*

Hieronymus. This 15th-century house is a great place for pizza and pasta (both DM 8–DM 12) and cheap beer. All types come to enjoy the pre-industrial atmosphere and the lunch specials, which are the best deal in town. *Fleischhauerstr. 81, 2 blocks beyond Rathaus, tel. 0451/151117.*

WORTH SEEING

Lübeck's skyline is marked by tile roofs, brick towers, and seven imposing church spires. The enormous **Dom** (end of Parade) was founded and built in 1173 by Henry the Lion. Severely damaged in World War II, the white-washed interior still contains some impressive pieces of religous art. The **Katharinenkirche** (Königstr.; closed Nov.–Mar.) was completed in 1370 and is now a museum housing various exhibits along with 13th-century paintings and a huge statue of St. George slaying the dragon. Still not impressed? **Jakobikirche** (Breitestr., across from Heiligen-Geist-Hospital) is one of the oldest churches in town (built in 1227). Its magnificent organ is shown off at weekly concerts (DM 10, DM 5 students), Fridays at 8 PM. Last but not least on the holy hunt, **Petrikirche** (Kolk, just off Holstenstr.), built from the 13th to the 16th centuries, has a 50-m tower (DM 3 to climb) with great views of the city. The white, bare interior houses rotating art exhibits. To feel the awesome silence of a tourist-free church, slip into the 14th-century **St. Aegidien Kirche** on Aegidienstraße.

HEILIGEN-GEIST HOSPITAL • Prepare to be stunned by the stained glass and paintings in the main room of one of the oldest hospices in Europe. For more than 700 years, this building has housed the elderly and ailing in times of need. While the tiny rooms in back re-create the living quarters of centuries ago, the surrounding buildings are still home to some of Lübeck's older folks. Feel free to wander through the 300-year-old gardens, but keep quiet or a resident will tell you to shut up and leave. *Große Burgstr. 9. Open Tues.–Sun. 10–5.*

MARIENKIRCHE • Looming ominous and Gothic over the Marktplatz, Germany's third-largest church, built 1260–1350, can best be appreciated by staring up at the huge vaulted ceiling. Original paintings and an ornate astronomical clock decorate the walls. Though carefully rebuilt after a World War II air raid, the church bells remain embedded in the floor, exactly where they fell in 1942. Every Saturday at 6:30 PM, the four-tiered organ (the largest mechanical organ in the world) plays to an awed assemblage. Tickets are DM 8 (DM 5 students). In summer 30-min concerts (DM 4, DM 2 students) are held Tuesdays and Saturdays at 6:30 PM, Thursdays at 8 PM. *Open daily 10–6 (except during services).*

RATHAUS • One of the oldest town halls in Germany, Lübeck's Rathaus stands impressively in the Marktplatz in front of the Marienkirche. Completed in 1240 and added onto during the 15th and 16th centuries, the town hall is an aesthetically tantalizing mishmash of styles from Gothic to Renaissance with numerous small pointy turrets, red, black, and white brickwork, ornate archways, and a beautifully carved stone stairway added onto the Breite Straße wing of the building in 1594.

MUSEUMS • Lübeck's city museums all have the same opening hours: Tuesday–Sunday 10–4, until 5 PM September to April. Admission is DM 6 (DM 3 students), free on Fridays (except for Holstentor). If you plan to hit four or more, buy a **Lübeck Card** (DM 10 for one day, DM 20 for three days), which allows you free bus rides and a train ride to Travemünde as well as reduced admission (usually 40% off) to museums and city tours. Check out Lübeck's history (or at least its city models, ship displays, armor, and old photographs) at **Museum Holstentor** (Holstentorpl., tel. 0451/122–4129), inside the most famous city gate in Germany. The art and culture of 14th- to 18th-century Lübeck is displayed inside a medieval Augustinian cloister at **St. Annen Museum** (St. Annen Str. 15, tel. 0451/122–4137), with golden altars and an exhibit on porcelain.

Heinrich und Thomas Mann Zentrum. Inside the Buddenbrookhaus, Lübeck's newest museum is heaven for Mann fans, with enough letters, photographs, and exhibits to send a German-literature fan into a frenzy. The average tourist may just yawn. *Mengstr. 4, tel. 0451/1220. Open daily 10 AM–5 PM.*

Museum Behnhaus/Drägerhaus. This 18th-century home, a relic of Lübeck's former wealth, has a surprisingly strong 19th- and 20th-century art collection with such notables as Edvard Munch, Caspar David Friedrich, and Max Beckmann. *Königstr. 9–11, tel. 0451/122–4148. Open Tues.–Sun. 9–5.*

Museum für Puppentheater. This museum claims that it has the largest private puppet and marionette collection in Germany. After seeing the myriad puppets from Europe, Asia, and Africa, you'll probably believe it. Check their schedule for the marionette theater across the street. *Kolk 16, tel. 0451/78626. Admission free (donations welcome). Open daily 9:30–6:30. Call in advance to arrange an English-language tour.*

Völkerkunde-Sammlung. This small collection has changing anthropological exhibits on such varied topics as racism in Germany and culture in former Soviet Central Asia. *Parade 10, in the Zeughaus, tel. 0451/122–4342. Open Tues.–Sun. 9–5.*

AFTER DARK

When the sun goes down, Lübeck either goes to bed or hangs out in cafés and bars. Some clubs do host late-night dancing; check free local rags like *Szene Journal, Piste,* or *Ultimo.* Lübek's younger crowd throngs **Body and Soul** (Kanalstr. 78, tel. 0451/73936; cover DM 5–DM 10). Monday the club features hip-hop and reggae, Tuesday is rock, and the other nights are a mixed bag. Dance haven **Hüx** (Hüxterdamm 14, tel. 0451/76633; cover up to DM 7) heats up on weekends with an upscale, trendy crowd. Tracks are mostly house and techno, varying with the DJ's mood. **Stern Schuppe** (Fleischhauerstr. 68, tel. 0451/65960) is a hole-in-the-wall student pub with night-blue walls, stars on the ceiling, and a welcoming atmosphere just perfect for sitting, guzzling a few, and chatting.

Summer here is generally sunny and warmish with the occasional bout of windy rain. During winter, however, the weather is bone-chillingly cold and wet, wet, wet.

NEAR LÜBECK

RATZEBURG

On an island in a lake 25 km south of Lübeck, the tiny town of Ratzeburg is linked to the mainland by three marsh-enveloped causeways. Although it's small (population 12,200), Ratzeburg has an overwhelming number of sights. Foremost among them is the **Dom,** dating from 1220. In the courtyard look for Ernst Barlach's bronze statue *Bettler auf Krücken* (*Beggar on Crutches*). See more Barlach at the **Ernst Barlach Museum "Altes Vaterhaus"** (Barlachpl. 3, tel. 04541/3789), the half-timbered house in which Barlach spent his youth. It's open Tuesday–Sunday 10–noon and 3–6; admission is DM 4 (DM 2 students).

Don't miss the **A. Paul Weber-Haus** (Domhof 5, tel. 04541/888326; admission DM 2.50, DM 1.50 students), which exhibits political artist Weber's lithographs, drawings, and paintings—stinging satires on politics, pollution, and militarism that got him in trouble with the Nazis. To culture yourself silly, purchase the **Ratzeburg Museum Gemeinschaftskarte** (DM 6, DM 3 students). This pass is available at any city museum and gets you into them all, including the **Kreis Museum** of local history (Domhof, tel. 04541/8880), and **Haus Mecklenburg** (Domhof 41, tel. 04541/83668), which exhibits typical regional furnishings and clothing. Admission to these two museums is DM 2 (DM 1 students). All the museums above are open Tuesday–Sunday 10–1 and 2–5.

BASICS • Ratzeburg's **tourist office** (Schloßwiese 7, tel. 04541/19433) sells brochures and town maps and can book you a room; it's open weekdays 9–5 (Thurs. and Fri. until 6) and weekends 10–4. Ratzeburg doesn't draw many overnight visitors, but you can sleep cheaply in the local **HI-Jugendherberge** (Fischerstr. 20, Am Küchensee, tel. 04541/3707). One of its 142 beds goes for DM 21 per night (DM 26 over 26). The reception is open 8–noon and 4–9. To reach Ratzeburg from Lübeck, take **Bus** 1806 or 1810 towards Hamburg (40 min, DM 7) or the hourly **train** (20 min, DM 7) toward Lüneburg. Daily **ferry** connections to Ratzeburg leave from the distant Moltkebrücke dock at Lübeck's northern edge. The trip is long (3½ hrs, DM 20 round-trip), and you have to transfer at Rothenhusen, but it makes for a beautiful day on Lake Ratzeburg.

KIEL

Even locals consider Kiel a *Landeshauptdorf* (capital village) because they don't think it's exciting enough to be called the capital city of Schleswig-Holstein. And truly, in relation to the nearby European cultural hot-spots of Hamburg and Copenhagen, Kiel may feel remote and chilly. Since 80 percent of the city was destroyed during Allied bombings, not much of its history from 1233 to 1945 can be seen from the street and much green space was replaced with concrete. The surrounding marine views, however, as well as a sufficient amount of engaging architecture from past and present, make Kiel a fine place to stop on your way up the peninsula. With 30,000 students spilling over from the 335-year-old university, the town does have a vibrant side. As the eastern anchor of the **Nord-Ostsee Kanal**—the busiest artificial waterway in the world—Kiel *does* have the unique privilege of being the only harbor with access to both the North and Baltic Seas. And if you're interested, a free ferry will take you from the canal observation platform through the locks and on to a free museum on the canal's construction.

The annual **Kieler Woche** sailing regatta in late June gets much hype in the local press. Not all for nothing either. The festival is the largest boat race in the world, attracting over 4,000 yachts of all shapes and sizes. While the regatta's popularity makes the city a tight fit for a couple weeks, the races can be very exciting to watch. If you're interested in older sail- or motorboats, it's certainly worth the visit from June 15 to July 1. For information on the event (or to pick up a town map), head to the **Tourist Information Kiel** (Sophienblatt 30, tel. 0431/67910) across from the train station.

COMING AND GOING

Frequent trains leave the **Hauptbahnhof** (central station; Sophienblatt 32, south end of the Kieler Fjord, tel. 0431/6011) for Lübeck (hourly, 1¼–2 hrs, DM 21–DM 34), Copenhagen (5 per day, 5 hrs, DM 92), and Hamburg (hourly, 1¼–2 hrs, DM 28–DM 37). Dump your bags in one of the station's lockers. Across from the Hauptbahnhof is the main bus station, **ZOB** (tel. 0431/666366), which offers service to Berlin (DM 40) and Hamburg's airport (DM 24). From either station, walk straight up Sophienblatt to reach Kiel's center.

From Kiel, ferries go to Oslo, Stockholm, and St. Petersburg, among other ports. **Color Line** (tel. 0431/73000) sails daily to Oslo. Prices are DM 160–DM 675 and students get a 50% discount during the off-season (after August 18).

WHERE TO SLEEP

For a cheap private room, try the tourist office. **Hotel Runge** (Elisabethstr. 16, tel. and fax 0431/731992) charges DM 60–DM 90 for singles and DM 100–DM 135 for doubles—at least they take American Express. Kiel offers two budget hotel options: **Hotel Rendsburger Hof** (Rendsburger Landstr. 363, tel. 0431/690131), where clean and simple singles start at DM 53, doubles at DM 90. From the Hauptbahnhof, take Bus 15 to Rutkamp. **Dom-Hotel** (Domziegelhof 6, tel. 0431/24313), in an attractive 19th-centrury building with courtyard and bicycle rental, charges DM 56–DM 81 for singles and DM 92–DM 106 for doubles.

HOSTELS • Ask for one of the renovated rooms at the **HI-Jugendherberge.** Beds cost DM 26 (DM 31 over 26), including breakfast. HI membership required. Send a postcard to reserve a spot. *Johannesstr. 1, tel. 0431/731488, fax 0431/735723. From train station, Bus 4 to Kiel Str., backtrack 1 block, then left on Johannesstr. 265 beds. Curfew 1 AM. Reception open 7 AM–10 PM.*

FOOD

The Alter Markt has a number of cheap cafés and pubs serving Germanized Italian food. On the German side of things, **Klosterbrauerei** (Alter Markt 9, tel. 0431/906290) is a typically robust German beer hall that charges about DM 12 (depending on the weight of your plate) for a buffet-style meal of wieners, cabbagey things, and dumplings. **Forstbaumschule** (Düvelsbeker Weg 46, tel. 0431/333496) is popular for its forested outdoor beer garden, and for green salads, pizzas, and pasta dishes (all under DM 12). Even cheaper eats are available near the university on Knooper Weg and Holtenauer Straße.

WORTH SEEING

St. Nikolai Kirche (open weekdays 10–1 and 2–6, Sat. 10–1), a late-medieval brick church with a beautiful, intricate altar, stands on Kiel's clean and modern Alter Markt, which is a stone's throw from the water. Right outside, Ernst Barlach's *Geistkämpfer* (*Fighter for the Spirit*) guards the church. At the south end of the Markt you can shop on **Holstenstraße,** reputedly the nation's first pedestrian zone. A few blocks away on Kleiner Kiel (a small artificial lake) is the **Rathaus,** whose 117-m tower dominates Kiel's skyline. Climb the tower for DM 1 and ponder the sweeping view of Kiel and the Kieler Fjord. The **Kunsthalle** (Düsternbrooker Weg 1–3, tel. 597–3756; Tues.–Sun. 10 AM–5 PM) has a mighty collection of 19th- and 20th-century German and international art. Admission is DM 10 (DM 6 students). The **Aquarium des Instituts für Meereskunde** (Kiellinie, tel. 0431/597–3857; open daily 10 AM–5 PM) has 31 aquariums filled with Baltic Sea creatures and is home to some playful seals. Admission is DM 3 (DM 2 students).

NEAR KIEL

LABOE

This windy beach resort 20 km from Kiel is popular with locals as a convenient seaside getaway. There is, alas, a DM 6 *Kurtax* (day-use fee). The primary tourist draw is the **Marine-Ehrenmal** (Ostseebad Laboe, tel. 04343/42700), a naval museum/memorial with exhibits and models of great moments in naval history. The 95-m-high monument itself honors sailors lost in the World Wars. From the top you get a good view of the fjord and Kiel, and, on clear days, Denmark. It's open daily 9:30–6 (until 4 in off-season; admission DM 5, DM 3 students). Next door to the memorial sits *U-995,* the submarine used in the German film *Das Boot.* Its cinematic career over, *U-995* now acts as a small submarine museum; admission is DM 4 (DM 2.50 students). To reach Laboe from Kiel's Bahnhof, take Bus 4 or 54 or the hourly ferry (DM 7.50).

Herring will haunt you after too much time in Schleswig-Holstein. Herring specialties like fillets, creamed herring, baked potato with herring, or herring salad are found on every menu.

SCHLESWIG

Schleswig is a medium-size town at the tip of the **Schlei,** an arm of the Baltic Sea that reaches some 40 km inland. With both seafront location and access to the state's rural heart, Schleswig has long been a strategic trading post. In the early 8th century, the Vikings established a settlement here called Haithabu, and the area became a major center for sea-roving pirates—a fact that really excites the staff at the tourist office. In late July, the town celebrates its Nordic heritage with **Wikingertage** (Viking Days), a weekend festival complete with near ridiculous Viking revelry, better-than-average jazz concerts, good beer, and general merrymaking (albeit slightly kitschy). Beyond a proud Viking past, Schleswig's beautiful harbor, quiet streets, and exceptional museums (for a town its size) make it a great stop in the oft-forgotten North.

BASICS

The **tourist information office** (Städtische Touristinformation; Plessenstr. 7, tel. 04621/24878, room hotline 04621/24832), open weekdays 9–12:30 and 1:30–5, Saturday 9–noon, has plenty of brochures and city maps. The staff will book rooms free of charge, and they even speak English. Just north of the Altstadt on the pedestrianized Stadtweg, the **post office** (Stadtw. 53–55; postal code 24837) will change your traveler's checks (DM 3.80 per check) or cash. About 150 m straight down Bahnhofstraße, **Fahrradhandel Ute Peters** (Bahnhofstr. 14a, tel. 04621/37688) rents bikes for DM 12–DM 20 a day.

COMING AND GOING

The train station (Bahnhofstr., tel. 04621/32109) has luggage lockers and is 2 km south of Schloß Gottorf, a long, long way from the Altstadt. To get here take Bus 1, 2, 4, or 5 to **ZOB** (Königstr. 1), the central bus station in the heart of the downtown area. Trains run from Schleswig to Flensburg (hourly, 30 min, DM 12–DM 20), Kiel (every 2 hrs, 1½ hrs, DM 16–DM 24), Husum (hourly, 30 min, DM 8–DM 15), and Hamburg (every 2 hrs, 1½–2½ hrs, DM 35–DM 41). Sights here are spread out, so use the bus (DM 2.10) or rent a bike.

WHERE TO SLEEP

The tourist office, in addition to booking rooms, distributes two helpful leaflets: "Gastgeberverzeichnis" has loads of info on hotel listings, bike rentals, etc; their town map has a street index to help you navigate. **Hotel Skandia** (Lollfuß 89, tel. 04621/24190) offers large singles at DM 76, doubles at DM 117. From the Bahnhof, take Bus 1, 2, or 4 to Skandia, and turn left. **Hotel zum Weissen Schwan** (Gottorf-str. 1 and 7, tel. 04621/93930) has singles from DM 83, doubles from DM 115. Take Bus 1, 2, 4, or 5 to Oberlandesgericht and it's on your right.

HOSTELS • The **HI-Jugendherberge** has a few singles and doubles, which you should reserve in advance. Otherwise, you'll be sleeping in cramped six- to eight-person rooms not unlike renovated jail cells. Beds are DM 25 (DM 30 over 26), including breakfast. *Spielkoppel 1, tel. 04621/23893. From train station, Bus 1 or 2 to Stadttheater, cross street, hike up huge flight of stairs, and keep straight. Curfew 11 PM. Reception open 7:30–1 and 5–8.*

CAMPING • Camp next to the Wikinger Museum at **Camping Haddeby,** 3½ km from the train station and about 8 km from the Altstadt. It's overcrowded, and sites cost DM 13.50 plus DM 7.50 per person. *Tel. 04621/32450. From Bahnhof or ZOB, any regional bus (direction Kiel) to Haddeby. Open Mar.–Oct.*

FOOD

The best street for cheap student dives and alternative-type bars is Lollfuß, which runs parallel to the Schlei between Schloß Gottorf and Schleswig's northside residential areas. Many places here double as bars and/or cafés at night. The cozy two-story **Patio** (Lollfuß 3, tel. 04621/29999) has an outdoor terrace and is Schleswig's most popular pub among young people. Pizza, pasta, and rice dishes run DM 7–DM 18. For reinvented German dishes with untranslatable names (DM 8–DM 17), try **Anna's** (Lollfuß 79, tel. 04621/26072; closed Sun.–Mon.). Near the ZOB, **Panorama** (Plessenstr. 15, tel. 04621/24580) offers a wide selection of vegetarian entrées for DM 7–DM 16, and pizza starting at DM 8.50.

WORTH SEEING

As in any good God-fearing town, Schleswig's sights center around the Dom. Those not within a few blocks lie along the bus route to the train station.

HOLM • From the Dom it's only a short walk east to this tiny fishing village, Schleswig's oldest district. Narrow lanes and quiet walkways meander through a maze of rose-bedecked half-timbered houses, most dating from the 1700s. Explore Holm's white **Lilliputian Chapel** and adjacent cemetery. The ocean has given Holm its livelihood and flavor, and tough-skinned fishermen still gather on the waterfront to spin yarns about the big one that got away.

LANDESMUSEUM SCHLOSS GOTTORF • With colorful, informative exhibits covering 2,000 years of history and art, this is by far the best museum in Schleswig-Holstein. In the **Nydamhalle,** check out a 1,600-year-old Anglo-Saxon rowboat and the collection of *Moorleichen,* the eerie corpses of hapless people who, 2,000 years after falling (or being thrown) into peat bogs, remain remarkably well preserved. You can ponder German Expressionist and other 20th-century art at the **Kreuzstall.** The **Reithalle** houses first-rate temporary exhibits. *Schloßinsel, tel. 04621/813222. Bus 1, 2, 4, 5 to Oberlandesgericht. Admission: DM 8, DM 4 students; extra for special exhibits. Tours (in German; DM 2 extra) daily in summer at 11, 1:30, 3. Open Mar.–Oct., daily 9–5; Nov.–Feb., Tues.–Sun. 9:30–4.*

ST. PETRI DOM • While the facade of St. Petri is less than half a century old, some parts of this cathedral date back 1,000 years. Since its construction by Otto the Great in 948, the Dom has seen overhaul after overhaul, and is now an impressive confusion of styles. The most beautiful and unique addition was made in 1521, when Hans Brüggermann completed the awesomely intricate **Bordesholm Altar,** one of Europe's most celebrated pieces of wood carving. According to legend, poor Hans was blinded by his patron, the greedy duke of Gottorf, to ensure that this masterpiece remained unique. Concerts are currently held in the cathedral Wednesdays at 8 PM June–September. Tickets cost DM 13 (DM 8.50 students). Free noontime organ concerts are held Saturdays, May through September. *Süderdomstr. 13, 2 blocks west of Marktpl., tel. 04621/963054. Open May–Sept., Mon.–Sat. 9–5 (Fri. until 3), Sun. 1–5; Oct.–Apr., Mon.–Sat. 10–4 (Fri. until 3), Sun. 1–4. Tours (DM 2) Sat.–Thurs. at 2.*

STÄDTISCHES MUSEUM • See the city's 1,200-year history displayed in art, sculpture, maps, and furniture in this 17th-century building. The halls display changing art exhibits from throughout Europe, and the attached printing press house shows a brief history of printing. *Friedrichstr. 7–11, tel. 04621/93680. Halfway between Bahnhof and Schloß Gottorf; or Bus 5 to Kleinberg. Admission: DM 6.50 (DM 3 students). Open Tues.–Sun. 10–5.*

WIKINGER MUSEUM HAITHABU • Once upon a time, Haithabu was a center of trade for northern Europe. Relics in the museum include a Viking ship, exhibits on Viking trade and religious practices, and archaeological finds from the Haithabu site. A definite don't-miss. *Tel. 04621/813300. From Bahnhof or ZOB, any regional bus (direction Kiel) to Haddeby. In summer, special ferries (DM 9 round-trip) leave from Altstadt harbor. Admission: DM 10.80 (DM 5 students). Open Mar.–Oct., daily 9–5; Nov.–Feb., Tues.–Sun. 9:30–5.*

FLENSBURG

Danish flags and the occasional Danish street sign decorate this city on the Danish border. The heart of Flensburg is wrapped around the Flensburger Fjord, which juts in from the Baltic Sea, giving Flensburg its brisk ocean breezes and distinct port-city flavor. A mellow, relaxing town, Flensburg is dotted with the old buildings and *Handelshöfe* (trade courtyards) remaining from the days when merchants here capitalized on its prime location. Among Germans the town is famous as the home of Beate Uhse, proprietor of one of the country's largest sex-shop chains. Flensburg is also known as the home of the wacky comic book character Werner, once infamous for his incessant guzzling of the incredibly popular local beer, Flensburger Pils. The brewery owner didn't appreciate the publicity, though, so Werner now drinks Bölkstoff. Speaking of potables, Flensburg produces its own brand of rum. Sample some during the International Rum Regatta, held at the end of May.

BASICS

Pick up *Information Flensburg,* an invaluable guide to the main sights, at the **tourist office.** A decent map costs DM 4. *Speicherlinie 40, tel. 0461/23090 or 0461/25901. From ZOB bus station, north on Bahnhofstr., right on Fredrich-Ebert-Str. (which becomes Füderhofenden and then Norderhofenden), left on Speicherlinie. Open weekdays 9–1 and 3–6.*

COMING AND GOING

The Flensburg **Bahnhof** (Am Bundesbahnhof, tel. 0461/861301) offers hourly connections to Hamburg (2–3 hrs, DM 49–DM 69), Kiel (1–2 hrs, DM 27–DM 35), and Schleswig (30–40 min, DM 10–DM 18). Walk up Bahnhofstraße and veer right to reach Flensburg's downtown, centered around **Große Straße.** Avoid the 20-min walk by taking any bus marked ZOB; it'll take you to the central bus station, which handles regional buses to places like Niebüll (1 hr, DM 16). The city center is two blocks to the left as you leave the ZOB.

WHERE TO SLEEP

Lodging in Flensburg is pretty grim. In either building of **Pension Annegret Ziesemer** (Wilhelmstr. 2, right behind ZOB, tel. 0461/25164; or Augustastr. 8, down Wilhelmstr. and left, tel. 0461/23770), singles are DM 41–DM 65; doubles start at DM 80. Sadly, the low price and the cable TV are offset by the management's hostility. Nearby **Hotel Handwerkerhaus** (Augustastr. 2, tel. 0461/144800) offers slightly older singles for DM 50–DM 90, doubles DM 84–DM 135, including a great breakfast. For cheaper sleeps, take Bus 7 from ZOB to Stadion for the **HI-Jugendherberge** (Fichtestr. 16, tel. 0461/37742, fax 0461/312952). One of its 220 dorm beds costs DM 21 (DM 26 over 26).

FOOD

Food and fun in Flensburg center on Große Staße. The **Nordermarkt,** at the north end of Große Straße, has a large cluster of cafés and bars for licking ice cream or guzzling beer. A five-minute walk out of the city center, **Kontraste** (Heinrich Str. 5, tel. 0461/13477) is a restaurant lauded by locals for its good, cheap food and homey atmosphere. They have a huge variety of wood-oven-baked pizzas (DM 5.50–DM 13), pasta dishes (DM 8–DM 12), and other dishes like *Zucchinipfanne* (zucchini and other goodies) for around DM 12. **Croquedile** (Schiffbrücke 14, tel. 0461/23019; closed Mon.) serves up delicious and absolutely massive (one large feeds two hungry people) croque sandwiches in a cozy, funky environment. Join a hip crowd at **Pierrot** (Toosbüystr. 11, tel. 0461/13366), a little, many-tiered pub/restaurant. Sip a Hefeweizen (DM 4) and eat some good food (try the stuffed peppers for DM 13.50) at one of their candlelit tables.

WORTH SEEING

Packed between Nordertor and Südermarkt (at the north and south ends of the pedestrian zone), nearly all of Flensburg's sights can be seen in an afternoon. It's hard to miss the town's two historic avenues: **Rote Straße**—with cutesy houses and beautifully landscaped *Kaufmannshöfe* (merchants' courtyards)—lies just southwest of Südermarkt, while the stoically weathered Baroque-era facades of **Kompagniestraße** are just off Nordermarkt. The sugar and rum merchants who erected their homes, warehouses, and stores around these *Höfe* benefited greatly by being within walking distance of the port. The oldest *Hof,* dating from the 16th century, is on Holm at No. 19–20.

Built in 1602 as a sailor's guildhall, the stout **Kompagnietor** looms over Kompagniestraße, harkening back to Flensburg's glory days as a great Baltic shipping center. The imposing **St. Nikolaikirche** (built in 1390), with its flamboyant rococo altar, hosts Saturday morning concerts for the entire Südermarkt. The less dramatic **Marienkirche** on Nordermarkt has beautiful stained-glass windows. On the hill overlooking the old city, the **Städtisches Museum** (Museumsberg 1, tel. 0461/852956) houses local artists' work, an impressive furniture collection, and regional history exhibits. Admission is DM 3 (DM 1.50 students, free Sun., closed Mon.).

NIEBÜLL

This small, beautifully tended town 16 km west of Flensburg and 11 km from the Danish border is the main transportation hub for the North Frisian Islands (*see below*). Niebüll's **train station** (Bahnhofstr., tel. 04661/4233) is a short walk down Rathausstraße from the tourist office and town center. The **bus station** is on the Marktplatz (from Rathaus Str. walk north on Böhmes Str.). All trains to Sylt (hourly, 30 min, DM 7–DM 10) and Dagebüll (the ferry port for Amrum and Föhr; DM 10–DM 15), and buses to and from Flensburg (15 per day, DM 10) pass through here. Trains to Hamburg (2–3 hrs, DM 49–DM 69) pass through Niebüll every two hours. Consider visiting Niebüll's two museums. The **Richard-Haizmann-Museum** (Rathauspl., tel. 04661/1010; closed Mon.) displays works by this local painter-sculptor who was exiled in 1934 to what the Nazis considered the most remote spot in Germany—Niebüll. Admission is DM 4 (DM 2 students). The **Friesisches Heimatmuseum** (Osterw. 76, tel. 04661/3656) has exhibits that introduce you to the pre-flush-toilet living standards of the 17th and 18th centuries. Admission is DM 4 (DM 2 students) and it's open daily 2 PM–4 PM.

The cows grazing in the backyard of the **tourist office** (Rathaus, tel. 0466/60190; open weekdays 9–noon and 3–6, Sat. 10–1) won't stop munching as you gather info on local events or ask the cheerful local staff to book you a room (it's free). The **HI-Jugendherberge** (Deezbüll Deich 2, tel. 04661/8762) is in a century-old thatched-roof house, an atmospheric place to spend the night. Beds are DM 21 (DM 26 over 26) and membership is required. To get here, turn right out of the Bahnhof and left on Rathausstraße, walk past the Rathaus, and keep going straight down Hauptstraße (which becomes Deezbüll). Check out Hauptstraße for grocery stores, cafés, and restaurants. **Rustikal** (Deezbüller Str. 2, tel. 04661/8899) serves up pizzas and pastas for DM 7–DM 13. Don't leave town before you try the spinach–potato Auflauf (DM 11).

NORTH FRISIAN ISLANDS

Off Schleswig-Holstein's west coast you can sometimes see the flat outline of the North Frisian Islands (*Nordfriesische Inseln*)—a scattered group of sandy, flat islands that seem in danger of being submerged whenever the weather gets rough. **Sylt,** the most popular beach resort in all of Germany, attracts thousands of wealthy Germans to its easily accessible shores (trains get here over reinforced sandbars). The other islands in the group—including **Amrum, Föhr,** and **Pellworm**—are honest-to-goodness islands, accessible only by ferry.

The islands are part of the **Nationalpark Schleswig-Holsteinisches Wattenmeer,** the biggest national park in Europe. With any luck, your ferry will cruise by one of the many sandbars, where it's not uncommon to see a pack of seals sunning themselves. The *Watt,* sticky mud that appears after the tide pulls out, teems with birds and aquatic life. Ask any tourist office about guided tours—the Watt is extremely dangerous, and amateurs can't tell where the mud will hold a person's weight. Don't go alone. Tours are nice alternatives to beach-bumming (for which local authorities often charge a "beach-sitting" tax of DM 3–DM 6). There's nothing wrong with lounging in the sand, however, and the islands offer some of the nicest beaches in northern Europe. *Freikörper* (nude) beaches are sometimes marked FKK.

WHERE TO SLEEP

Call tourist offices in advance to arrange for private rooms (the only cheap option), since everyone and their grandmother (literally) visits these islands. Hotels are way overpriced and the hostels are a bit inaccessible or inhospitable. They tend to book school groups months ahead of time, so unless you can reserve a spot in advance, you *may* get in by calling/showing up and begging.

SYLT

This long (40 km) and skinny (3 km) island is a playground for Germany's wealthy. Every other car here is an out-of-town Mercedes, BMW, or Porsche, and come nightfall, the island's swank restaurants are filled with loaded yuppies having a good, expensive time. Windsurfers, too, flock to Sylt in summer, when the island's population surges from 21,000 to 110,000. In September the island hosts the **Wind Surfing World Cup,** and more hordes of tourists. Sylt has beaches to fit everyone's personality—nude beaches, beaches crowded with families, dog beaches, and distant quiet beaches. With beaches, however, comes the day-use fee of DM 6, collected at each beach entrance. Apart from sand, Sylt also offers fishing, surfing, sailing, and other water-related sports. Yet Sylt's cheapest activity will always be lying on the sand, sipping a drink, and watching the world go by. Farther north, in the nature preserve area of Sylt, you can wander among the sand dunes for hours without seeing a single soul.

You'll have a hard time finding a room in the island's train hub, **Westerland,** home to tourist resources and nighttime fun. Markets—like **Kaiser's** on Friederichstraße—have long summer hours to help you avoid expensive restaurants. Just outside the train station, the **tourist office** (tel. 04651/9980) is open weekdays 9–12:30 and 2–5, weekends 9–12:30 (closed weekends in off-season). They book private rooms or pensions, provide nature info, and list other tourist offices on the island. The train station rents **bikes** daily 8:30–6:30 for DM 10–DM 15 per day.

Visitors often take advantage of Flensburg's location to hop across the Danish border, usually to Sønderborg (which has a fascinating medieval castle). Buses (DM 28 round-trip) leave Flensburg's ZOB almost every hour.

Outside of Westerland things get quiet quickly. The rest of the island defers to rolling dunes, thatched-roof houses, endless beaches, and tranquil resortdom. Two hostels are at Sylt's northern and southern ends. Near List in the north, **HI-Jugendherberge-List** (Mövenberg, tel. 04651/870397) has beds for DM 21 (DM 26 over 26) in former Nazi barracks. Unfortunately, the peace of the surrounding nature preserve is shattered when screaming kids take over. From Westerland, take any bus toward List—the bus will stop at the Jugendherberge in summer; otherwise it's a 15-min walk from List. To reach **HI-Jugendherberge-Hörnum** (Friesenpl. 2, tel. 04651/870397), a standard hostel with wooden-bunked dorm rooms, take any bus from Westerland ZOB (direction: Hörnum) to Hörnum-Nord and continue for about 200 m. Beds are DM 24 (DM 31 over 26); reception is open 5 PM–10 PM.

COMING AND GOING

Trains connect Westerland with Niebüll (2 per hr, DM 10), and ferries from **Hörnum,** at the southern tip of Sylt, go to Amrum and Föhr. Trains run to Hamburg (2½–3 hrs, DM 49–DM 67), and Sylt is also accessible by frequent trains from other large northern German cities.

AMRUM AND FÖHR

Windswept and storm-battered Amrum and Föhr give you a sense of how generations have eked out a difficult living from the ocean. Many of Föhr's residents (mostly old fishermen on the remote west coast) still speak *Föhringer,* a dialect of Frisian. Tiny Amrum, located to the west of Föhr, is less than half its neighbor's size and features dunes and sandy beaches. Oval-shaped Föhr is characterized by its large areas of marshland and lush greenery; both islands attract a sparser, less affluent group of tourists than those on Sylt. Amrum and Föhr are ideal for bike rides, hikes across sand dunes and through small forests, swimming, and surf fishing. If you're searching for peace, quiet, and magnificent ocean views, look no further.

Wyk is the largest village on Föhr. It attracts the bulk—okay, the small handful—of island day-trippers because of its few shops and eateries. The **tourist office** (Kurverwaltung Wyk auf Föhr; Hafenstr. 23, tel. 04681/3052), open weekdays 8–7, weekends 10–noon, provides info, lists Watt tours, and has a computerized listing of all the available rooms in town (call 04681/3040 for room reservations). At the 162-bed **HI-Jugendherberge** (Fehrstieg 41, tel. 04681/2355) room and board costs DM 35.50 (DM 40.50 over 26). Send a postcard to reserve, as the hostel is booked from May to September almost a year in advance. To get here from the harbor, follow the beach left for about 40 min, then make a right onto Fehrstieg. Wyk has some overpriced restaurants, bunches of ice cream stores, bike rental shops on every corner, and even a disco, the **Olympic** (Koogskuhl 6, tel. 04681/3744). To rent a two-wheeler, try

Deichgraf (Hafenstr. 5, tel. 04681/2487), near the harbor, which rents out bikes for DM 7–DM 15 per day.

Wittdün, the largest village on Amrum, has a 212-bed **HI-Jugendherberge** (Mittelstr. 1, tel. 04682/2010, fax 04682/1747; closed Dec.). On the beach about 300 m from the ferry port, the hostel charges DM 24.50 (DM 31 over 26), including breakfast. If the hostel doesn't appeal to you, call the **Kurverwaltung Wittdün** (Mittelstr. 34, tel. 04682/891, room reservations 04682/864), which is open weekdays 9–5, Saturday 9:30–2, and Sunday 9:30–noon. They can set you up in a private room and load you with info about Watt tours. Rent bikes at **Siebert** (Am Fähranleger, tel. 04682/2084; open daily 9–6) for DM 8–DM 10.

COMING AND GOING

From Niebüll, **NVAG-Bahn** (in conjunction with the DB) offers train/ferry service; the full Niebüll–Dagebüll–Wyk–Wittdün trek takes 2½ hours. To Wyk you'll pay DM 31; to Wittdün it's DM 37.50. There are up to 12 island connections daily. From Hörnum on Sylt's southern tip, ferries run by **Adler-Schiffe** (tel. 04651/24520) leave for Amrum and Föhr at around 10 AM; the return ferry leaves Amrum around 3 and Föhr around 4:30. Exact times depend on the tides.

PELLWORM

With its untroubled pastureland and lazy villages, Pellworm is spiritually much closer to Amrum and Föhr than Sylt. Bike riding, walking, and surf combing (there aren't any proper beaches on Pellworm, only grassy strands that buffer the sea) are the norm here. This serene environment attracts an older, low-key crowd. If you happen to visit on a rainy day, duck inside one of Pellworm's two churches, the **Alte Kirche** (Old Church), whose original cornerstone was laid in 1095, or the not-so-*neu* **Neue Kirche,** built in 1528. **Reederei NPDG** (tel. 04844/753) runs ferries directly from Husum to Pellworm via Nordstrand (DM 16.80 one-way, DM 34 round-trip). **Kurverwaltung Pellworm** (Uthlandestr. 2, tel. 04844/18943; room reservations 04844/18940) has maps and ferry schedules; they're open weekdays 8–noon and 2–4:30, weekends 10–noon (shorter hrs off-season). To rent a bike, try **Momme von Holdt's** (Uthlandestr. 4, tel. 04844/348) near the ferry landing, which rents wheels for DM 6.50–DM 14 per day.

HUSUM

German author Theodor Storm (1817–1888) called his birthplace, Husum, *"die graue Stadt am Meer"* ("the gray city on the sea"). During the suffocatingly long winter, Husum is indeed battered by fierce, relentless gales. But in April, when millions of irises bloom and cast a light purple haze around the city, Husum is emphatically ungloomy. Spring's effulgence is particularly noticeable in the Schloßgarten around **Schloß vor Husum** (tel. 04841/89730), in the middle of the city. The rather dull castle was built by the Gottorf dukes in the 16th century; these days it houses art exhibits (admission DM 8, DM 3 students) and a concert hall. The castle is open April–October, Tuesday–Sunday 11–5, and the garden is open daily 8–6. When the flowers aren't in bloom, the only memorable thing about Husum is its harbor, where modern trawlers and rough-hewn fishing skiffs scurry to get in and out during the six hours each day when high tide allows it.

Surrounded by a stoic collection of half-timbered and Baroque facades, the central **Markt** has a bunch of shops and pleasant cafés. Cultural attractions include the **Nissenhaus** (Herzog-Adolf-Str. 25, tel. 04841/2545; closed Sat.), documenting the northern Frisian landscape and the area's culture and history. It's open daily 10–5 (Nov.–Mar., daily 10–4), and admission is DM 5.50 (DM 3 students). A worthwhile trip for Theodor Storm aficionados (but probably not for anyone else) is the **Storm-Haus** (Wasserreihe 31, tel. 04841/666270), where the Realist poet and novelist lived and wrote from 1866 to 1880. Admission to see original furnishings and a collection of Storm artifacts is DM 2.80 (DM 1.50 students). In the middle of May, Husum hosts **Amerikanische Woche** (American Week), a festival dedicated to locals who emigrated to America.

BASICS

The **tourist office** (Rathaus, tel. 04841/66991; open weekdays 9–6, Sat. 10–1, Sun. 10–noon) has the usual city maps, brochures, and a free room-finding service (tel. 04841/89870). Pick up the English-language pamphlet "Husum: A Stroll Through the Town." Just to the west is the **post office** (Großstr.). If you're planning a trip to any of the islands, stop by the **Nördseebäderverband** (Parkstr. 7, tel. 04841/

897510), with more brochures and pamphlets (all in German) than anyone could possibly read. Stop in weekdays 8–5 (Fri. until 12:30). **Service Center** (Schulstr. 4, tel. 04841/4465) rents bikes for DM 12 per day.

COMING AND GOING

The **Bahnhof** (train station; Poggenburgstr., tel. 04841/4074), 10 min south of the town center, has connections to St. Peter-Ording (every 2 hrs, 1 hr, DM 14.50), Sylt's Westerland (hourly, 1 hr, DM 23), Kiel (hourly, 1½ hrs, DM 26.50), and Hamburg (hourly, 1½ hrs, DM 49). **Buses** run frequently to Nordstrand. **Autokraft GmbH** (Ringstr. 3–9, tel. 04841/3634) is a long-distance bus network you can use in the unlikely event the train doesn't go in your direction.

WHERE TO SLEEP AND EAT

The tourist office lists private rooms (about DM 35 per person). The pension **Rödekrog** (Wilhelm Str. 10, tel. 04841/3771), with a sunny patio, breakfast buffet, and 14 rooms near the train station, is a relative steal for the area at DM 51 for a single, DM 87 for a double (cheaper if you stay longer). Reservations are recommended. Hostelers should take Bus 51 from the ZOB (across the river from the Bahnhof) to the town of Westerkampweg (DM 2, last bus at 5 PM) or walk (30 min) to the clean and spacious **Theodor Storm Jugendherberge (HI)** (Schobüller Str. 34, tel. 04841/2714). Dorm beds are DM 23 (DM 29 over 26). Reception is open from 4 until 10, when the dreaded curfew goes into effect (ask nicely to get a key). **Campingplatz Dockkoog** (Dockkoog 17, tel. 04841/61911) is near the beach at Dockkoog, a 20-min walk east of the harbor. It's open from the end of March through September and charges DM 7–DM 15 per site, plus DM 7.50 per person.

North Frisians have much in common with their eastern brethren (see East Frisian Islands, in Chapter 14), right down to the last "Moin!" Northerners distinguish themselves by pointing out their superior weather (three weeks of sun, instead of just two).

Sample the local specialty, *Krabben Brötchen* (little shrimp sandwiches), for about DM 5 at any of the zillion Imbiß stands along the harbor. **Peter Pub** (Schiffbrücke 5, tel. 04841/2050) serves pizza, pasta, and salads, all for DM 10.50–DM 16.90. Locals line up for helpings of *Bauernfrühstück mit Schinken* (farmer's breakfast with ham, DM 9) in the always-packed **Gaststätte "Treffpunkt Am Zob"** (Süderstr. 2, tel. 04841/477).

NEAR HUSUM

ST. PETER-ORDING

St. Peter-Ording is a semiupscale resort town on the Eider peninsula, 41 km southwest of Husum. The most notable attraction here is the beach—a 12-km-long strip of plush sand that looks out over the North Sea. St. Peter-Ording attracts sun-loving vacationers in summer, and a few adventurous sorts come out year-round to experience the favorite local pastime, *Strandsegeln* (beach sailing). Take a sporty go-cart, a sail, a strong wind, and a love of plowing face-first into the sand at high speed (when you crash), and you've got gosh-darn fun. To learn beach sailing, rent gear, or find a room, contact **Kurverwaltung St. Peter-Ording** (tel. 04863/9990 or 04863/999155 for lodging). If you just want to lounge on the beach, don't forget about the day-use fee (DM 5, DM 2.50 students). Hourly **trains** connect St. Peter-Ording (often listed as Bad St. Peter-Ording) and Husum; the trip takes one hour and costs DM 17.50.

14

LOWER SAXONY

UPDATED BY HELEN SOMMERVILLE

hile Lower Saxony (*Niedersachsen*) may lack the glitz and sparkle generated by other German regions, its special north Germanic flair and its stretches of charming countryside will handsomely repay your patience. The region, one of the least densely populated of the German *Länder* (states), is especially suited to nature enthusiasts: The **Harz Mountains** provide hilly terrain perfect for hiking and cross-country skiing; the rolling heaths of the **Lüneburger Heide** bloom purple in August; and East Friesland's coastal mud flats support thousands of specially adapted critters. With their unspoiled beaches and wind-raked dunes, the **East Frisian Islands,** just off the North Sea coast, serve as a popular getaway resort for vacationing Germans. Yet, even at high season, the islands' km-long beaches offer solitude to the sea-lover. Proud of its heavily rural makeup, the state offers vacationers *Urlaub auf dem Land,* a holiday in the country (or on a farm), complete with comfortable accommodations in tastefully renovated barns.

Even if frolicking in the wild gratifies all your vacation needs, try not to miss out on Lower Saxony's city life; sprawling **Hanover,** mellow **Hildesheim,** and student-filled **Göttingen,** along with lively **Bremen,** an independent city and state in the middle of Lower Saxony, have impressively reconstructed *Altstädte* (old towns) and nurture high-energy cultural and café scenes. Although Lower Saxony itself is a postwar creation, many of its cities were unified as members of the powerful Hanseatic League, a medieval trade alliance. Much of the region also stood under the centuries-long rule of the Guelph family, a dynasty whose claim here dates back to Henry the Lion's 12th-century move to **Braunschweig,** today an industrial center. Although the traces of royal residence are fainter in larger cities due to massive bombing in World War II, signs of the region's medieval and early modern heyday can still be seen in colorful, half-timbered Weser Renaissance buildings and Gothic to Baroque castles and cathedrals in towns throughout the state.

HANOVER

Hanover (Hannover), the capital of Lower Saxony, prepared for the World Exposition, **Expo 2000** (*see* Festivals, *below*), by undergoing a facelift to give its low-grade image a bit of a boost. Centrally located on major rail lines and highways, Hanover is more of a business travel center (there are huge conventions here in spring and fall) than a tourist destination. Yet thanks to a lively student population and alter-

LOWER SAXONY

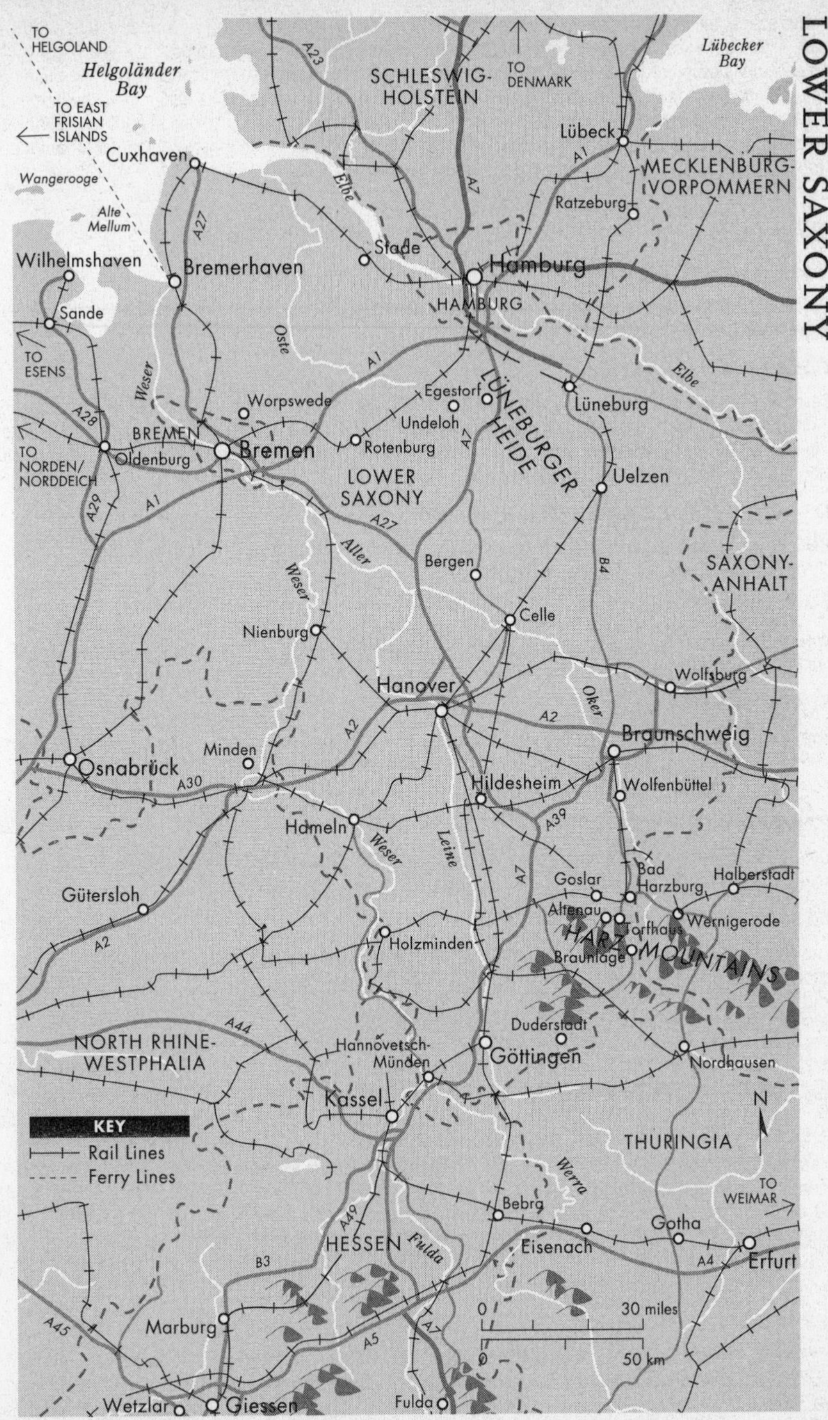

native scene, this modern city offers travelers world-class museums, a thriving café culture, and a throbbing nightlife. In keeping with its image enhancement, Hanover plays de facto host to a yearly convention of punks from around the country, the *Chaos-Tage* (Chaos Days; usually in August). While building its reputation as a forward-thinking place, Hanover holds on to reminders of its past role as the home of the Hanoverian princes, members of the mighty Guelph dynasty who ruled the region and, for a century, an island across the Channel. The royal gardens of Queen Sophia are the most spectacular inheritance from the noble ones, and are worth the trek from the train station.

BASICS

AMERICAN EXPRESS

Come for currency exchange and to pick up mail. *Georgstr. 54, tel. 0511/363428. Open weekdays 9–6, Sat. 10–1.*

CHANGING MONEY

Several banks line the streets between the train station and the central plaza, Kröpcke. Many of them, including one in the train station and **Sparkasse** (Bahnhofstr. 13–14), will take your ATM card. Inside the station, **Deutsche Verkehrs-Bank** (open weekdays 7:30–7, weekends until 5) has good rates, albeit with a DM 2 commission per traveler's check.

DISCOUNT TRAVEL AGENCIES

RDS Reisedienst sells train tickets and specializes in last-minute and student flights. *Hahnenstr. 8, tel. 0511/702454. Open weekdays 9–12:45 and 2–6.*

LAUNDRY

Wasch-Salon, near Raschplatz, charges DM 6 for 6 kg of grunge, DM 1 for 15 min drying time. *Friesenstr. 47, at Eichstr. Open daily 6 AM–11 PM.*

MAIL AND PHONES

The **Hauptpost,** right next to the train station, has a poste restante counter, currency exchange, and fax service. *Ernst-August-Pl. 2. Postal code: 30159. Open weekdays 7 AM–8 PM, Sat. 8–6, Sun. 10–3; limited service (stamps and phones) weekdays 7 PM–8 PM and weekends.*

PHARMACIES

Take care of those unexpected holiday ailments at **Ernst-August Apotheke,** a pharmacy that even accepts credit cards. *Bahnhofstr. 8, tel. 0511/363432. Open weekdays 8–6:30, Sat. 8–2.*

VISITOR INFORMATION

The efficient **tourist office** (Verkehrsbüro Hannover), inside the post office, has tons of pamphlets and books private and hotel rooms for DM 5. Snag the city map that appears in the "Hotels" brochure. Gays and lesbians can pick up *Magnus Plan,* a guide to the local scene. *Ernst-August-Pl. 2, tel. 0511/301420, 301421, or 301422, fax 0511/301414. Open weekdays 9–7, Sat. 9:30–3.*

COMING AND GOING

BY TRAIN

Hanover's **Hauptbahnhof** (main train station) has frequent service to Berlin (hourly, 2 hrs, DM 96), Bremen (hourly, 1 hr, DM 47), Göttingen (1–3 per hr, 30 min, DM 48), Hameln (every 2 hrs, 45 min, DM 14.60), Frankfurt (1–2 per hr, 2½ hrs, DM 134), and Hamburg (1–2 per hr, 1½ hrs, DM 64). The information stand is open 24 hours. Lockers at the train station are accessible around the clock, but those at the Kröpcke underground station are cleaned out at 1 AM. **Buses** to small regional towns leave from behind the station.

BY PLANE

Hanover's airport, **Flughafen Hannover** (tel. 0511/977–1899), has service to most major European cities. Bus 60 (DM 10) runs from the airport to the rear of the Hauptbahnhof every 20–30 min 5 AM–10:30 PM.

BY MITFAHRGELEGENHEIT

Citynetz Mitfahr-Zentrale can hook you up with cheap long-distance rides (sample rates: Berlin DM 32, Bremen DM 17). To reach the office, pass under the train station and exit at Weißekreuzplatz. Call ahead for the best arrangement—they speak English. *Weißekreuzstr. 18, tel. 0511/19444. Open weekdays 9–6, Sat. 9–1, Sun. noon–3.*

GETTING AROUND

Huge and sprawling, Hanover is tough to negotiate on foot, but very bike-accessible. **Toursport** (Lavesstr. 71, tel. 0511/322378) rents basic wheels (DM 25 a day) weekdays 9–6, Saturday 9–2. The center of Hanover life and public transit is **Kröpcke,** a large plaza 200 m in front of the train station. Just to the southwest lies the reconstructed **Altstadt,** where you'll find most museums and historical sights. Ten min south of that, across the very wide street Friedrichswall, lies the man-made **Maschsee,** stomping grounds for local picnickers and festival-goers. The multi-ethnic **Linden** district, home to Hanover's hipsters and the better bars and clubs, is about 3 km west of the city center.

BY PUBLIC TRANSIT

The *Stadtbahn* (trams; partially underground) and buses use the same tickets, and some lines run as late as 2:30 AM. However, the DM 3 price (good for one hour) quickly adds up. Drop by **ÜSTRA** (entrance to Kröpcke underground station) for a strip of six tickets (DM 16), a 24-hour ticket (DM 9), or a students-only, week-long ticket (DM 17 plus photo), as well as a public transit map. You can purchase bus tickets as you board, but tram tickets must be bought in advance at underground stops; dispensers are located by the turnstiles. To activate your ticket, stick it in one of the green boxes located in tram stations and on buses. Public transit is free with the **HannoverCard** (*see* Worth Seeing, *below*).

BY TAXI

Given the price of mass-transit tickets, taxis are actually cheaper for groups of three or more within central Hanover. Hail a cab in front of the Hauptbahnhof or the Steintor (Caution: This is the red-light district), or call **Taxi** (tel. 0511/2143) or **Hallo Taxi** (tel. 0511/8484).

WHERE TO SLEEP

Sleeping in Hanover is pricey, and during the *Messen* (business conventions) and festivals, it can be nearly impossible to find a bed—call in advance to avoid bedlessness or bankruptcy. Hanover's **Mitwohnzentrale** shares an office with the Mitfahr-Zentrale (*see* Coming and Going, *above*) and will help you find a private room for a DM 5 fee plus commission (20% of one night's rent) if you call ahead. If you've nowhere else to turn, the **Bahnhofhospiz** (Joachimstr. 2, tel. 0511/324297), run by the church, has singles starting at DM 55, doubles at DM 95.

Hotel Flora. Hanover's cheapest hotel is only a 10-min walk from the station and has plain, cramped singles for DM 50–DM 85, doubles for DM 95–DM 140, and triples for DM 140–DM 170, some with bath. *Heinrichstr. 36, tel. 0511/342334, fax 0511/345899. From Hauptbahnhof, left down Joachimstr., left under tracks at Thielenpl. onto Königstr., follow park left to Heinrichstr. 23 rooms. Reservations strongly recommended.*

Hotel Gildehof. As its 43 rather drab rooms are often full, this place should probably be your last option. Singles start at DM 75, doubles at DM 110; add about DM 20 for private bath. *Joachimstr. 6, tel. 0511/363680, fax 0511/306644. From Hauptbahnhof, left on Joachimstr.*

HOSTELS

Jugendgästehaus. This luxurious hostel has immaculate rooms with views of the neighboring tree-lined Leine River. Unfortunately, the trip from the station can take an hour. Singles are DM 45, doubles, triples, or quads DM 34 per person. Third-story doubles are DM 80. *Wilkenburgerstr. 40, tel. 0511/864440, fax 0511/863230. Tram 1 (direction: Sarstedt) or Tram 2 (direction: Rethen) to Am Brabrinke (last tram around 2 AM); follow tracks back 10 min to Wilkenburgerstr. and turn left. 65 beds. No curfew. Reception open 8–8.*

Jugendherberge Hannover (HI). The trip from town takes about 30 min, but for your trouble you get a renovated canal-side room with a great view. One of the 350 beds costs DM 27 (DM 32 over 27). *Ferdinand-Wilhelm-Fricke-Weg 1, tel. 0511/131–7674, fax 0511/18555. Tram 3 or 7 (direction: Mühlen-*

WANTED: PROTESTANT MONARCH FOR BRITAIN. NO ENGLISH REQUIRED.

It's always been difficult to get good help. In 1701 the British Parliament, in need of a Protestant monarch for the throne, chose Queen Sophia of Hanover, granddaughter of James I. At birth she had been 54th in line to the throne, but by 1701 the other 53 were all either dead or Catholic. In 1714 her son George I began the House of Hanover's five-generation reign over both Hanover and England. Hanoverian monarchs included George I, who ruled England for 13 years without ever learning English, and George III, notable for having lost control of several small colonies across the Atlantic. The German wives of these kings introduced to the English-speaking world what had previously been a uniquely German tradition—the Christmas tree. Because of different laws of succession, the union between Britain and Hanover died with William IV in 1837.

berg) to Fischerhof/Fachhochschule; backtrack 10 m to intersection, follow signs right and across bridge, and turn right. Curfew 11:30 PM. Reception open 1–8. Reservations advised.

Naturfreundehaus Stadtheim. This quiet hostel, among rows of community gardens on the edge of Eilenriede Park 20–30 min from town, offers misanthropes and lovebirds the cheapest private rooms around: Prices start at DM 34.80 per person. And for this, you can expect to spot the odd rabbit bobbing about on the big lawn out back. *Hermann-Bahlsen-Allee 8, tel. 0511/691493. Tram 3 (direction: Lahe) or Tram 7 (direction: Fasanenkrug) to Spannhagengarten (last trams around 2 AM); backtrack to intersection, left on H.-Bahlsen-Allee, walk 10 min and look for sign on right. 76 beds. No curfew. Reception open 8 AM–10 PM.*

FOOD

If Hanover's overpriced hotels have emptied your pockets, follow Karmarschstraße south from Kröpcke to Leinstraße and the **Markthalle** (open weekdays 7–6, Sat. 7–1), a raucous indoor market where meals go for around DM 5. There's also a **Co-op** supermarket in the underground Passarelle mall, below Kröpcke.

Backöfle. This traditional German restaurant has a friendly feel and a cozy little beer garden. Entrées start at DM 14—this is the place to try some Hanoverian *Bratkartoffeln* (home fries). *Mittelstr. 11, tel. 0511/18524. Tram 3, 7, or 9 to Waterloo, then right on Mittelstr.*

Hiller. This vegetarian spot is one of the few in Hanover—they even have some vegan choices. Specialties include fresh whole-grain bread and gourmet vegetable and pasta combos (DM 13–DM 25). *Blumenstr. 3, tel. 0511/321288. From Hauptbahnhof, down Joachimstr., right on Blumenstr. Closed Sun.*

Masa. Tucked away in an alley off Georgstraße is this small hangout for Hanover's intellectuals and smart shoppers. Sit on the floor Japanese-style or grab a seat outside. Afghan dishes like baked eggplant in garlic sauce run DM 8–DM 15. *Georgstr., near Windmühlenstr., tel. 0511/363-1376. From Kröpcke, head up Georgstr. past opera house. Closed Wed.–Thurs.*

Safari. Once you've made sure someone fed the snakes who slither about in their terrarium near your table, you can select internationally flavored sandwiches, soups, salads, and beers and head on over to the dart board for a game or two. A young crowd comes to this bamboo-ceilinged, palm-tree-dotted spot for breakfast, Happy Hour (5–7), and late-night dining (on weekends). *Siemensstr. 4–6, tel. 0511/880180. From Gilde Brauerei U-Bahn stop, walk north on Hildesheimer Str., turn left on Siemensstr.*

CAFÉS

The funky Linden-Nord district has oodles of cafés and bars. Artsy **Doko's Café Deli** (Limmerstr. 58, near Leinaustr., tel. 0511/455231) serves stark espresso (DM 2.50) and lunches for around DM 8–DM 10. Also come to find out about gay and lesbian events. For a nighttime café-bar scene, join a hip, college-age crowd at **Café Izarro** (Ahlemer Str. 5, no phone). Both **Café Safran** (Königsworther Str. 39, tel. 0511/131–7936) and **Café Übü** (Elisenstr. 35, tel. 0511/442929) attract older, more intellectual types for cheap coffee and pub food (DM 8–DM 14). Across from the opera, **Georgxx** (Georgenpl. 3, tel. 0511/306183) serves hearty and delicious lunches, as well as a number of salads. A window seat in **Mezzo** (Lister Meile 4, tel. 0511/314966) is the perfect spot for lingering over coffee or a Schneider Weiße beer (DM 5) with a newspaper. In the evening, the café becomes *the* meeting place for Hanover's preclubbers, who head for the Raschplatz and Weißekreuzplatz clubs after a few drinks.

To combat a flooding Leine River and the fierce unemployment of the 1930s, the government gathered workers to dig out what is now the Maschsee. Today it's the perfect place for a leisurely boat ride or a lakeside picnic.

WORTH SEEING

Allied bombing leveled much of Hanover's historical and architectural heritage; follow the 4-km red line painted on the sidewalk from one of the city's surviving attractions to the next. If you're short on time (or patience), head straight for the truly magnificent Herrenhausen Gardens and invigorating Sprengel Museum; if you're planning a sightseeing extravaganza, buy a **HannoverCard** (DM 14 for 1 day, DM 22 for 3 days), which offers free entrance to the bigger museums and unlimited free travel on public transit. Find it at the tourist office, ÜSTRA, and Jugendherberge Hannover.

ALTSTADT

Hanover's quaint, largely rebuilt Altstadt huddles around Ballhofstraße, Knochenhauerstraße, and Kramerstraße. The 14th-century **Marktkirche** (the city's unofficial emblem) and the 15th-century brick **Altes Rathaus** (Old Town Hall) face each other across the Marktplatz. On nearby Holzmarkt is the reconstructed Baroque facade of the **Leibnizhaus.** Gottfried Wilhelm Leibniz (1646–1716), the renowned mathematical and philosophical genius, was an adviser to Queen Sophia of Hanover while he lived in this house. Highlights of the **Historisches Museum** (Burgstr., at Kramerstr., tel. 0511/168–3052; admission DM 4, DM 2 students), next door to the Leibnizhaus, include several horse-drawn coaches of the House of Hanover and a 1928 two-seat prototype car dubbed the *Kommissbrot* (army loaf). It's open Tuesday 10–8, Wednesday–Friday 10–4, and weekends 10–6. On Saturday mornings the area behind the museum, flanking both sides of the river, is home to the **Flohmarkt,** Lower Saxony's largest flea market. Dedicated foragers have until 2 PM to browse through rows of stalls selling everything from antique picture frames to costume jewelry. To the south, across Friedrichswall, stands Hanover's most impressive structure, the elaborate **Neues Rathaus** (Trammpl.; open daily 10–5). For DM 2 (DM 1 students), an elevator hoists you to the top of its enormous dome for a great view of the city. Inside the Rathaus, four fascinating dioramas replicate the Hanover of 1689, 1939, 1945, and today.

HERRENHAUSEN GARTEN

If you do nothing else in Hanover, make the trip out to the royal gardens northwest of downtown. Of the three main gardens, laid out between 1666 and 1720, the **Großer Garten** (Great Garden) is the most famous and Queen Sophia's dream come true. Giant swaths of flowers curve in precise swirls around elaborate fountains and statues of lascivious gods and licentious nymphs. From May through September, the garden fountains shoot water high into the air weekdays 11–noon and 2–4, weekends 11–noon and 2–5. For DM 4 you can also see the fountains lit up at dusk Wednesday–Sunday. The tourist office has an invaluable map of the whole layout (50 Pf), as well as a list of classical concerts and plays performed at the **Galerie** and outdoors in the garden theater. Tickets run DM 12–DM 40. *Tram 4 or 5 to Herrenhäuser-Gärten. Admission: DM 3 (free Oct.–Apr.). Open May–Sept., daily 8–8; Oct.–Apr., daily 8–4:30.*

THOSE DARN KIDS

Imagine Shel Silverstein writing about a pair of hellish pranksters—a cross between Dennis the Menace and Beavis and Butthead—and you come pretty close to "Max und Moritz," by famed storyteller Wilhelm Busch. In seven rhyming, illustrated chapters, this devilish duo does everything from murdering a widow's chicken to placing gunpowder in their teacher's smoking pipe. In the end they get what's coming to them: They're thrown in a mill and end up as bird feed. So much for your benign, G-rated children's story. Find out more about Busch (and other famous cartoonists) at the popular Wilhelm-Busch-Museum in the Georgengarten. (Georgengarten, tel. 0511/714076. Tram 4 or 5 [direction: Stöcken] to Schneiderberg/Wilhelm-Busch-Museum. Admission: DM 6, DM 3 students, DM 2 children. Open Tues.–Sat. 10–5, Sun. 10–6.)

In the northwest corner of the Großer Garten, the **Herrenhausen-Museum** replicates the posh 1665 summer palace of the Guelph dynasty (*see box, above*). Period furniture and art fill the rooms, though the most interesting feature is the collection of royal portraits—including every George who ever reigned. Don't miss Gainsborough's portraits of mad king George III and his Sophia in the lobby. *Fürstenhaus, Alte Herrenhäuser Str. 14, tel. 0511/750947. Admission: DM 6, DM 3.50 students. Open Tues.–Sun. 10–6 (Oct.–Mar. until 5).*

The two other gardens worth strolling through are the Berggarten and Georgengarten (admission to both free). The **Berggarten,** across Herrenhäuser Straße from the Großer Garten, displays oodles of exotic greenhouse flora, including rare orchids, cacti, and a riotous rhododendron stand. At the far end of the garden is the neoclassical **mausoleum** of the House of Hanover. Just west of the Großer Garten is the **Georgengarten,** an English garden designed to look wild, where you can wander along the 2-km Herrenhäuser Allee, lined by more than 1,300 lime trees. Get off the tram two or three stops early (try Universität or Schneiderberg), then amble along the meandering paths.

LANDESMUSEUM

Just up the street from the Sprengel Museum, the Landesmuseum houses large collections of medieval and 17th-century art, natural history, archaeological exhibits on the area (including a corpse found preserved in a peat bog), and an aquarium. *Am Maschpark 5, tel. 0511/883051. Admission free. Open Tues.–Sun. 10–5 (Thurs. until 7).*

SPRENGEL MUSEUM

This superb modern-art museum displays works by Beckmann, Ernst, Klee, Picasso, and a slew of other artists. Go early to avoid a long line for the highly recommended **James Turrell room,** a psychedelic interactive exhibit near the museum entrance that's guaranteed to trigger quite a few sensory nerves. Hanover's homegrown hero, Kurt Schwitters, gets several rooms for his efforts at making art out of discarded scraps. *Kurt-Schwitters-Pl., northern tip of Maschsee, tel. 0511/168–3875. Admission: DM 6, DM 3 students. Open Tues. 10–10, Wed.–Sun. 10–6.*

FESTIVALS

The tourist office has a list of all the great parties that Hanover throws. Most notable are the **Schützenfest** in early July, a 10-day shooting festival with flamboyant floats and fireworks, eased along by an endless flow of beer; the **Maschseefest,** two weeks of lakeside merriment in early August; and the **Altstadtfest,** a weekend of music and madness at the end of August. On several spring and autumn

Sundays, thousands of people stroll the shopping district during the **Schorsenbummel,** with street vendors, jazz music around the opera house, and the best of the Wurst.

Spearheading **Expo 2000**'s marketing strategy, Twipsy the mascot carelessly waves his disfigured arm on Hanover's trams and buses, countless T-shirts, posters, and postcards, and throughout the immense World Expo grounds. If Twipsy's done his job well, and you happen to be in the area between June and October 2000, you'll probably spend a day or two perusing some of the high-tech and ecologically sound Expo pavilions erected by over 150 nations. If you do, don't miss a walk along United Trees Avenue, which is lined by 400 different trees. Japan's pavilion is made entirely of paper (with a textile roof), Nepal's entirely of wood; the Netherlands is showcasing a "stay-put landscaped" multi-level construction of dunes, forests, and windmills. If you have a taste for misalliance, try to get tickets to the concert featuring the Berlin Philharmonic with the Scorpions; if you understand German, consider the 17-hour production of *Faust.* Surf on over to www.expo2000.de or call the hotline at 0/2000 to buy tickets (DM 15–DM 120 per day, same-day tix available) or to get a room at the home of one of the *Messemuttis* (convention moms) for DM 50–DM 60. If you're coming from another city, the ICE train will drop you off right at the Expo entrance hall.

AFTER DARK

Hipsters and alternative types will find the best bar-hunting grounds around Limmerstraße in Linden, while the Altstadt provides a more mainstream scene. To find out what's happening in town, pick up one of the entertainment freebies at the tourist office. The monthly *Magascene* is a guide to music, film, and theater. *Hannover Vorschau* and *Kultur! News* are two other free listings of cultural events and activities. *Prinz* (DM 4.50) can point you to gay and lesbian clubs; *Schädelspalter* (DM 5) has the lowdown on all of Hanover's events. The tourist office can book tickets for Hanover's various and wonderful theater and music productions, from opera to classical concerts to experimental theater.

Activities in the Royal Gardens are practically endless: Get dizzy in the hedge maze, arrange a romantic tryst in the shrub gardens, or stay till dusk for the light display.

Summertime brings out the beer gardens in this self-proclaimed green city. The best are at opposite ends of town: **Turmgarten** (Am Lindener Berge 29a, tel. 0551/446139) is in Linden, atop the Lindener Berg. **Leo's Biergarten am Zoo** (Adenauerallee 3c, tel. 0511/813060) is at the zoo, on the eastern edge of the city. Close to the Jugendherberge are Backöfle (*see* Food, *above*) and **Waterloo** (Waterloostr., tel. 0511/15643), more good places to quaff outdoors.

BARS AND CLUBS

Bad. This former swimming-pool complex now hosts a veritable smorgasbord of local and touring bands from ska to folk to thrash-metal-hard core. On Friday and Saturday, there's dancing in the basement. *Am Großen Garten 60, tel. 0511/703404. Tram 4 or 5 to Herrenhäuser Gärten, then take free shuttle. Cover: DM 6–DM 30.*

Café Glocksee. On the edge of the Linden district, Glocksee brings underground/experimental music and theater to a subculture-loving crowd. Duck into the popular café-bar next door or come Fridays at 10 for DJ dancing. *Glockseestr. 35, tel. 0511/161–4712. Tram 10 to Glocksee, then through park. Cover: DM 5–DM 13.*

Café International. The students who run this cheap cellar dive recently got in hot water with authorities for housing illegal aliens from Nigeria (who were promptly deported). Nowadays they continue to sell cheap drinks, and they'll let you sell home-cooked food as long as you don't charge an arm and a leg. Sometimes live bands provide funky music. *Cellar of the Hanover University AStA (student union) building, Theodor Lessing Haus, Welfengarten 2c, tel. 0511/762–5061 (AStA info). From University bus stop, cross Nienburger Str., turn right on Welfengarten.*

Irish Pub. The heavily Eired crowd at the Irish Pub has been known to break into song on a good night. The same MacGowans that run this place have opened up another pub, **Irish Harp** on Schwarzer Bär (Bär 1, tel. 0511/447070)—it even has a beer garden. *Brüderstr. 4, at Odeonstr., tel. 0511/14589. From info office, up K.-Schumacher-Str., right on Odeonstr.*

Men's Factory. A mixed crowd boogies at this gay techno club in Nordstadt on Fridays. There's also a bar in the back for mingling. Cover is DM 10. *Engelbosteler Damm 7, tel. 0511/702487. From Kröpcke, Tram 6 or 11 to Christuskirche. Open Fri. and Sat. 10 PM–late.*

Palo Palo. Of the cluster of clubs on Raschplatz, this is the coolest, hosting live jazz one night (DM 8–DM 20), dancing to funk, soul, and hip-hop the rest of the week. *Raschpl. 8a, behind train station, tel. 0511/331073. Cover: DM 6–DM 8.*

Pindopp. Graduate students and professionals play pool or darts and listen to live blues and country music twice a month at this large Südstadt spot. Have a beer with your mamma mia–size Italian fare, or stop by for a cheapo breakfast (DM 5–DM 9). *Altenbekener Damm 9, tel. 0511/806523. From Gilde Brauerai U-Bahn stop, walk north on Hildesheimer Str., make a first right onto Altenbekener Damm.*

NEAR HANOVER

HAMELN

The name sounds familiar? It should: Hameln (anglicized as Hamelin) is the site of the *Rattenfänger* (Pied Piper) fairy tale. According to the legend, a mysterious musician rid the town of rats by luring the musically inclined rodents out of town with his piping. When the town bigwigs didn't pay for his services, the peeved piper used his music to similar effect on their children, who were, alas, never seen again. The stricken parents made the best of the situation and turned tragedy into tourism: Rat-shaped pastries and rodent-inspired knickknacks abound in Hameln's shops, and Sundays at noon (May–Sept.) there's a reenactment of the Rattenfänger story in front of the stone Hochzeitshaus. Even **Museum Hameln** includes a Pied Piper display among exhibits on Hameln's history—the piper's visit was recorded in a 14th-century chronicle. *Osterstr. 8–9, tel. 05151/202215. Admission: DM 3, DM 1 students. Open Tues.–Sun. 10–4:30.*

But wait! The Piper isn't the town's only claim to fame. Along with Hann-Münden and Duderstadt, Hameln is the place to scope out Weser Renaissance houses. Hameln's collection is small but includes some of the most energetically whimsical work around, like the houses on pedestrian-only **Osterstraße** and **Bäckerstraße,** as well as narrow **Wendenstraße.** Most Weser-style houses are also cafés or restaurants—*Kaffee und Kuchen* (coffee and cake) can provide essential sightseeing fuel.

BASICS

The **tourist office** (Verkehrsverein; Deisterallee 3, at Bürgergarten, tel. 05151/202617) stocks English brochures and is open May–Sept., weekdays 9–1 and 2–6, Saturday 9:30–12:30 and 2–4, and Sunday 9:30–12:30; Oct.–Apr., weekdays 9–1 and 2–5. The unusually large **post office** is on the corner of Baustraße and Sedanstraße.

COMING AND GOING

Trains travel once or twice an hour to Hanover (40 min, DM 14) and Hildesheim (50 min, DM 12). The Bahnhof has lockers, but requires an out-of-town trek; to reach the town proper, walk straight out of the station, turn right on Bahnhofstraße and left on Deisterstraße. The tourist office is ahead on the right, next to the flower-filled Bürgergarten.

WHERE TO SLEEP AND EAT

The **HI-Jugendherberge** (Fischbeckerstr. 33, tel. 05151/3425; closed late Dec.–early Jan.) sits on the edge of the tranquil Weser River. Beds cost DM 20 (DM 24.50 over 26); reception is open from 5 PM until the 10 PM curfew. From the Bahnhof, take Bus 2 to Wehler Weg; continue west on Fischbeckerstraße toward the river, and turn left onto the riverside path; or make the lovely 10-min walk north along the river on the Weserpromenade. Across the river is **Campingplatz zum Fährhaus** (Uferstr. 80, tel. 05151/61167) with an 11 PM curfew. It's DM 10 for a tent site plus DM 5 per person. In town, the cozy **Kaffee-Stube Pfannkuchen** (Hummenstr. 12, tel. 05151/41378) serves a plethora of pancake dishes, stuffed with everything from mushrooms and cheese (DM 9.50) to chili con carne (DM 13.50). Wednesday and Saturday until 1 PM are **open-air market** days at Kastanienwall and Sedanstraße. Stock up on groceries at **Plus Market** (Bahnhofstr. 31–33).

HILDESHEIM

Hildesheim was little more than a medieval truck stop until, as legend has it, the 9th-century emperor Ludwig the Pious hung his religious relics on a rosebush here one summer's night and found them frozen the next morning. In celebration of this divine message, he ordered a chapel built on the spot. This thousand-year-old rosebush still blooms today and as long as it does, according to legend, so will Hildesheim. When a World War II bombing raid left 80 percent of the town in cinders, the roses inspired the townspeople to rebuild. Though much of the postwar building is sterile and nondescript, there are some magnificent reconstructions—notably the breathtaking Marktplatz—which perfectly render a sense of Hildesheim's premodern history, and Hildesheim's student population lends the town a spirited edge. Hildesheim is hosting **YouthCamp 2000** in July and August; if you'd like to join 1,200 young people from around the globe in a city of tents, participate in workshops that focus on the theme "Man, Nature, Technology," and take advantage of musical, cultural, and sports events, call 05121/301649 or visit the website www.youthcamp2000.org for more info. Know that the hosts are members of Christian organizations.

BASICS

Hildesheim's **tourist office** (Verkehrsverein) has various maps and brochures, including a 50-page English-language walking guide (DM 2), and books rooms (DM 5 fee). *Markt 3, tel. 05121/301395, fax 05121/17988. From Bahnhof, up Bernwardstr. (which becomes Almsstr.), left on Markstr., to the Markt (15 min total). Open weekdays 9–6, Sat. 9–1.*

If it's money you need, stop at **Citibank** (Scheelenstr. 12), around the corner from the tourist office. It has a 24-hour ATM that accepts bank and credit cards. The **post office** (postal code 31134), outside the Bahnhof, slaps a DM 3 commission on traveler's checks. Cleanse your grimy clothes for DM 6 at **Waschcenter** (Bahnhofsallee 10), open weekdays 6 AM–11 PM.

COMING AND GOING

Frequent **trains** link Hildesheim to Braunschweig (hourly, 30 min, DM 21), Göttingen (10 per day, 30 min, DM 37), Hameln (8 per day, 50 min, DM 12), and Hanover (1–2 per hr, 30 min, DM 10). The station closes daily 1 AM–4:30 AM and has lockers. To reach the city center, follow Bernwardstraße (which becomes Almstraße) all the way—it's a 15-min walk to the Rathaus. **Buses** leave from right outside the train station for nearby rinky-dink towns.

Hildesheim's English-savvy **Mitfahrzentrale** can hook you up with long-distance rides. They also book cheap last-minute seats on international flights. *Annenstr. 15, tel. 05121/39051. From Rathaus, east up Rathausstr., right on Gartenstr., right on Braunschweiger Str., left on Annenstr. Open weekdays 10–6, Sat. 10–1.*

WHERE TO SLEEP

Lodging in Hildesheim falls into two mutually exclusive categories: cheap and convenient. In the budget category are a pair of family-run hotel-restaurants, across from each other on the northern outskirts of town. The larger and less friendly **Hotel Meyer** (Peiner Landstr. 185, tel. 05121/53179) offers impersonal singles for DM 50–DM 90, doubles with shower from DM 90, and triples DM 190–DM 220. Flower-strewn **Hotel Marheineke** (Peiner Landstr. 189, tel. 05121/52667) has singles for DM 48–DM 70, doubles for DM 120, and triples for DM 145. To get there, take Bus 1 (direction: Drispenstedt) to Ehrlicherstraße; backtrack to the highway, and go under the overpass. The hotels are on the first small side street on the right; neither accepts credit cards.

Hotel Weißer Schwan. After Pension Kurth, this is the next best downtown option. It costs more, but they have all the accoutrements, from a TV, phone, and shower in each room to the chocolate mints on the pillow. Unfortunately, the hotel is on a busy street—some rooms are noisy. Singles cost DM 60–DM 75, doubles DM 110–DM 130. *Schuhstr. 29, tel. 05121/16780, fax 05121/39112. From Bahnhof, walk down pedestrian zone for 15 min, right on Schuhstr. 36 rooms, some with bath.*

Pension Kurth. This pension has clean, light-filled rooms and plush feather beds and is the only affordable place near the Altstadt. Call a few days in advance to ensure yourself a room. Singles run DM 35, doubles DM 70. *Küsthardtstr. 4, tel. 05121/36272. From Bahnhof, down pedestrian zone for 15 min, left on Schuhstr., right on Zingel, left on Braunschweiger Str., then first left (look for the doorbell under the GAST ZUR POST sign). No credit cards.*

HOSTEL • Jugendherberge (HI). Although low prices and a woodsy, quiet location make this a great budget option, you'll have to embark on your own personal odyssey to get here—it's a 45-min trek (uphill) from town. Rooms are clean—some have a view of Hildesheim at the foot of the hill—and the basement is equipped with a piano (in the smoking area) and a rec room. A bed will cost you DM 23 (DM 28 over 27). Call ahead. *Schirrmannw. 4, tel. 05121/42717, fax 0512/47847. From Hauptbahnhof, Bus 1 to Am Dammtor, then Bus 4 to Triftstr.; cross street, turn left, and follow sign up long slope for 15 min. Flexible 10 PM curfew. 104 beds. Reception open 9 AM–10 PM.*

CAMPING • Campingplatz am Müggelsee. It isn't exactly secluded, but it's pleasant enough and has its own swimming lake. You can even rent a very basic rowboat for DM 5. Tent sites cost DM 8 per person. *Am Müggelsee 4, tel. 05121/53131. From Hauptbahnhof, left down Butterborn, under and then across bridge, then north for 25 min. Reception open 7 AM–10 PM. Closed mid-Sept.–Mar.*

FOOD

Hildesheim's large student population supports a galaxy of good café-bars, clustered on Friesenstraße and Hindenburgplatz. An **open-air market** is held outside the Rathaus every Wednesday and Saturday until 1 PM. During May, the Markt's Weinfest calls for wine tastings, music, and wurst-eating. Otherwise, do your shopping at **Plus Market** (Wallstr. 3–5).

The restaurant in the **Knochenhauer Amtshaus** (Am Markt, tel. 05121/32323) serves reasonably priced German cuisine and has a café with a great Marktplatz view. Hildesheim's intellectuals gather at **Gastwirtschaft Café Schärling** (Burgstr. 2, across from Roemer- und Pelizaeus-Museum, tel. 05121/134494), where the slogan is *Zeitgeist der Welt* (the Global Spirit). Greek salads are DM 13.50, baked camembert DM 8.50, and ground-meat stew DM 7. Don't leave Hildesheim without seeing Lower Saxony's oldest wine parlor, the **Historische Weinstube "Bürgermeisterkapelle"** (Rathausstr. 8, tel. 05121/33632; closed Sun.), which dates from 1562. The low, vaulted ceilings, tin-plate-adorned fireplace, and art-covered walls will convince you to sit down with a quality wine. **Schlegels Weinstuben** (Am Steine 4–6, tel. 05121/33133; closed Sun.), with its beamed ceilings, walls lined with wine bottles, and shady walled garden, is *the* place for a romantic evening. *Eintöpfe* (soups and stews) cost up to DM 8.50, entrées DM 18–DM 36.

WORTH SEEING

Hildesheim's sights lie within easy walking distance of one another; follow the white roses spray-painted on the sidewalk for a 5-km tour of all the biggies. The tour takes you through Hildesheim's southern parts, into narrow alleyways, and to the old city wall and a riverside park. Besides the major sights, worth visiting is the **Roemer- und Pelizaeus-Museum** (Am Steine 1–2; closed Mon.), with extensive exhibits on ancient Egyptian, Chinese, and Peruvian civilizations (to name a few). South of the Altstadt, on the former site of Hildesheim's synagogue, is the **Mahnmal am Lappenberg** (Am Lappenberg, at Weinberg Str.), erected in 1988 on the 50th anniversary of the synagogue's destruction. Each side of this metallic cube represents a different aspect of Judaism. The east side represents predestination; the west, persecution and the Holocaust; the south, the legal code; and the north, worship.

HILDESHEIMER DOM • The exterior reconstruction may be unspectacular, but the cathedral's appeal lies in its impressive accessories: the crypt and its gold shrine, the enormous wheel-shaped chandelier (1060), the bronze column of Christ (early 11th century), and the giant bronze doors (1015), on which major biblical scenes are depicted in relief. For a mere 50 Pf (30 Pf students), you can check out the legendary **Tausendjähriger Rosenstock** (1,000-year-old rosebush), but the small white blooms appear for only two weeks in early June. *Am Domhof. Admission: DM 4, DM 1.50 students. Dom open Tues.–Sat. 10–5, Sun. noon–5. Rosenstock open Mon.–Sat. 9:30–5, Sun. noon–5.*

MARKTPLATZ • Give yourself plenty of time to treasure all the captivating details of this gracious square, restored in the 1980s. The magnificent **Knochenhaueramtshaus** (Butchers' Guildhouse), a massive 16th-century timber-framed building, looms in the northwest corner. Leveled in World War II and replaced by a hotel, it was reconstructed in 1987 using traditional techniques: The structure is held together only with wooden pegs, no nails. The building now houses a café and the **Stadtmuseum,** which displays tankards, halberds, and other shards from Hildesheim's past. Look up at the tiers of the Guildhouse's east side to see several artists' daunting interpretations of theme of War and Peace. The adjacent **Bäckeramtshaus** (Bakers' Guildhouse) forms the other part of this half-timbered duo. Crusaders' memories of Middle Eastern architecture may have inspired the bizarre, 15th-century **Tempelhaus**; its name comes from the medieval Jewish synagogue that supposedly stood at the site. *Stadtmuseum: tel. 05121/301163. Admission: DM 3, DM 1 students. Open Tues.–Sun. 10–6.*

MICHAELISKIRCHE • St. Michael's was founded by Bernward, Hanover's bishop from 993 to 1022. Unesco was prompted to claim the church as a World Heritage Site thanks to its painted wood ceiling, which shows various biblical scenes involving trees (the church's relic was a fragment of the true cross). Because the ceiling was removed for protection during World War II, you can actually see the 13th-century original. (Push the mirror cart along the nave to see the depictions without breaking your neck.) When the church turned Protestant with the Reformation, the crypt remained Catholic, since it contains Bernward's remains. *From Marktpl., 1 km west on Michaelisstr. Admission free. Open Apr.–Sept., Mon.–Sat. 8–6, Sun. 11:30 or 1–6; Oct.–Mar., Mon.–Sat. 9–4, Sun. 11:30–4.*

SCHLOSS MARIENBURG • This stately fairy-tale castle dominates the Leine Valley from atop a forested ridge 12 km west of Hildesheim. The castle, a neo-Gothic beauty, was built in the 1860s as a residence for Hanoverian Queen Marie—a birthday gift from her husband, King George V. The guided tour takes you through the richly decorated interior and provides a glimpse into the personal life of the Hanover royals. To get here, take the hourly train to Nordstemmen (7 min, DM 5), then make the half-hour trek across the river and uphill. *Tel. 05069/535. Admission: DM 8, DM 3.50 students. Open Tues.–Sat. 10–noon and 1—5, Sun. 10–5; Dec.–Feb., weekends only. Call ahead for English tour.*

AFTER DARK

Head to the tourist office to pick up the free monthly *Public,* which clues you in to the entertainment scene, or *Hildesheim Aktuell,* with the lowdown on cultural events. **Kulturfabrik** (Langer Garten 1, tel. 05121/55376) sponsors cultural bashes and hosts musical acts and dance parties. For live punk on Friday and Saturday nights, zip through the tunnel outside the train station to **BeBop** (Steuerwalder Str. 60, tel. 05121/515153; open Wed., Fri., and Sat. 10 PM–3 AM). **Thav** (Güntherstr. 21, tel. 05121/132829; open weekdays 7 PM–2 AM, weekends until 3 AM), in a big garage set back from the street, has a sleek bar and dance floor and is as hip as Hildesheim gets. From Hindenburgplatz, walk down Zingel past the post office, turn left on Braunschweiger Straße, right on Annenstraße, and right on Günterstraße.

A few times a week, the huge **Vier Linden** cultural center stages theater and live music from pop to jazz to reggae. Tickets are DM 15–DM 40. Dance nights (check listings) draw an alternative crowd after 10 PM, and the restaurant serves "new" (healthier, less meaty) German fare. *Alfelder Str. 55b, tel. 05121/25255. From Hauptbahnhof, Bus 1 to Dammtor, then Bus 5 (direction: Ochtersum) 2 stops to Vier Linden (last bus back 11 PM). Open Tues.–Sat. 6 PM–midnight, closed Sun.–Mon.*

NEAR HILDESHEIM

BRAUNSCHWEIG

Ignore the characterless office buildings you'll see as you exit the train station, and strike a path for Braunschweig's Altstadt, suspended on an island in the Oker River. Accessible from the North Sea, Braunschweig (Brunswick) enjoys a strategic location that earned it a special place in the hearts of German rulers. Heinrich der Löwe, one of the original Guelphs, established his court here in 1166, and his lion is the city's (and the family's) symbol. The Dom and the castle he built are reminders of the courtly culture that thrived in medieval Braunschweig. The town's later role as an industrial center made it a target for heavy Allied bombing in the war and a sprawling postwar building boom. Today, this regional center's unique island-Altstadt and lively nightlife merit a day (or evening) trip.

The most impressive sights center around **Burgplatz,** a cobblestone square presided over by Heinrich's bronze lion. The square is dominated by **Dom St. Blasius** (open daily 10–1 and 3–5), a magnificent early Gothic cathedral with a 20-ft candelabra, a 12th-century wooden crucifix, and a dark association with the Nazis, who used the Dom as an assembly hall. For DM 2, visit the Dom's **crypt,** which holds the remains of the beloved Heinrich. Also on Burgplatz, the massive stone **Burg Dankwarderode** was Heinrich's residence. Today the fortress houses the medieval-art branch of the **Herzog Anton Ulrich Museum.** The main museum (Museumstr. 1, tel. 0531/482400) features a large collection of works by Vermeer, Van Dyck, Rembrandt, and Rubens, as well as the largest exhibit of porcelain in Germany. Admission is DM 5; the museum is open Tuesday–Sunday 10–5 (Wed. until 8).

Braunschweig has a number of other good museums. The **Jewish Museum** (Hinter Ägidien, tel. 0531/484–2630) has one of the oldest collections of Jewish antiquities in Germany and a reconstructed synagogue interior. Learn all about the history of the region at Braunschweig's **Landesmuseum** (Burgpl. 1, tel. 0531/484–2602). Both are open Tuesday–Sunday 10–5; admission to each is DM 5, DM 3 students.

For DM 3 (DM 2 students) you can check out the small, quirky **Museum für Photographie** (Helmstedter Str. 1, tel. 0531/75000; open Tues.–Fri. 1–6, weekends 2–6), in the Steintorhaus, featuring work by some of the best-known photographers in Germany.

BASICS

The two **tourist offices** have maps and book rooms for a DM 3 fee. Verkehrsbüro Hauptbahnhof (tel. 0531/273550; open weekdays 8:30–5, Sat. 9–noon) is just outside the train station; Verkehrsbüro Bohlweg (Pavillon Bohlw., tel. 0531/79237; open weekdays 9:30–6, Sat. 9:30–12:30) is one block west of the Rathaus. Braunschweig's main **post office** (Berliner Pl., across from Bahnhof) has phones for both local and international calls. The friendly student staff at **Studentenwerk AStA** (Katharinenstr. 1, tel. 0531/337851; open weekdays 10 AM–2 PM) provides info on restaurants, nightlife, gay and lesbian events—just about anything. They rent **bikes** to students for as low as DM 2.50 per day, and rarely check IDs.

COMING AND GOING

Trains leave Braunschweig's **Hauptbahnhof** for Göttingen (hourly, 1 hr, DM 46), Hanover (3 per hr, 40 min, DM 16.20), Hildesheim (hourly, 30 min, DM 21), and Wolfenbüttel (2 per hr, 15 min, DM 5). It's a 20-min walk to town from the station; cross Berliner Platz, head straight down Kurt-Schumacher-Straße to John-F.-Kennedy-Platz, and turn right on Auguststraße. Or take Tram 1 to the Bohlweg tourist office. **ADM Mitfahrzentrale** (Bohlmarkt 3, at Katharinekirche, tel. 0531/14041) arranges rides weekdays 10–6, Sat. 10–2.

WHERE TO SLEEP

Finding budget lodging here can be a headache; your best bet might be to book private rooms at one of the tourist offices. Close to the university, **Hotel Meyer** (Wendenring 18, tel. 0531/340363, fax 0531/336867; no credit cards) has flowery doubles for DM 80–DM 90. To get there, take Bohlweg north (it changes names twice) to Schubertstraße and turn left, then veer right onto Bammelsburger Straße and cross the river to Wendenring. Though it's much cheaper, Braunschweig's downbeat **HI-Jugendgästehaus** (Salzdahlumer Str. 170, tel. 0531/264320, fax 0531/2640–3270) is inconveniently located. Its 160 beds go for DM 19–DM 39; add DM 7 for breakfast. Get a key (DM 30 deposit) to beat the 10 PM curfew. From the train station, head left on H.-Büssing-Ring, then left on Salzdahlumer Straße (20 min total).

FOOD

In the Altstadt, cheap eateries can be found on Bohlweg; near the university try Konstantin-Uhde-Straße and Bültenweg. You get industrial meals for as low as DM 1.60 at the university's **Mensa** (Katharinenstr. 1). **Café L'Etage Restaurant** (Münzstr. 2, off Ägidienpl., tel. 0531/41497) offers good plain German cuisine for DM 10–DM 15. **Dialog** (Rebenring 48, at Bültenw., tel. 0531/331455) serves calzones and pizzas in a hip student environment.

AFTER DARK

For the latest entertainment listings, pick up a free copy of *Cocktail* or *Das Programm* at the tourist office or the university. Near the university, at **Liro Dando** (Kalenwall 3, at Friedrich-Wilhelm-Pl., tel. 0531/15709), you'll find loud music and even louder conversation daily until 1 AM. The quaint Magni quarter (Magniviertel), whose main drag is Ölschlägern, is dotted with cute cafés and chic bars. **Brunsviga** (Karlstr. 35, tel. 0531/238040) hosts everything from theater to dancing.

WOLFENBÜTTEL

If authentic Old World spots exert a pull on you, sidestep Braunschweig and let Wolfenbüttel draw you in. Unscathed by World War II, this placid town consists of scads of half-timbered homes gathered around picturesque squares and canals. The other big draw is the giant **Herzog August Bibliothek,** a library begun by Duke August in the late 16th century (he collected books for 80 years). Academics from around the world come to peruse over half a million works, including 16th-century maps, illuminated manuscripts, and psalm books covered with Martin Luther's margin notes. Henry the Lion's 12th-century illuminated gospel book is on display in the library's museum rooms a few weeks a year. Casanova left his carnal pursuits to come here for a week of reading, and philosopher Gottfried Leibniz and classical dramatist Gotthold Ephraim Lessing both spent time as librarians here. Admission to the Bibliothek also gives you access to the **Lessinghaus** (just across Lessingpl.); Lessing spent the last 11 years of his life here and wrote his most famous play, *Nathan der Weise* (*Nathan the Wise*), during his Wolfenbüttel residence. *Library: Lessingpl. 1, tel. 05331/8080. Admission: DM 5, DM 3 students. Library and Lessinghaus: open Tues.–Sun. 10–5.*

Though its origins lie in the 1100s, the 18th-century appearance of Wolfenbüttel's **Schloß** (Schloßpl., tel. 05331/5713; open Tues.–Sat. 10–5, Sun. 10–1) can be attributed to damage sustained in the Schmalkaldic and Thirty Years' wars (religion, religion), and to renovations made by Prince August Wilhelm. As you enter, note his motto on the lintel: *Parta Tueri* (Keep What You Have Obtained). Shell out DM 3 of what you have obtained to visit the castle's **museum,** which re-creates Braunschweig-Lüneburg (part of that now-familiar Guelph dynasty) court culture.

A key church in the establishment of the Protestant Reformation, the 1608 **Hauptkirche Beatae Mariae Virginis** (Kornpl., open Tues.–Fri. 10–12:30 and 2–5, Sun. 10–12:30 and 2–4) weds Gothic vaults to Baroque light and adornment. Jägermeister enthusiasts initiating a different kind of pilgrimage—to the *Kräuterlikör* (herbal liqueur) mecca—will have to get organized (which may be hard if you're a major fan of the infamous inebriant). Free tours happen twice a week at the **Jägermeister Distillery** (Jägermeisterstr. 7–15, tel. 05331/810), but they often book up a year in advance. Call the number above or write to Jägermeister, Postfach 1663, 38299 Wolfenbüttel to reserve a place or to ask about tours in English.

Although locals call Wolfenbüttel's library the "Eighth Wonder of the World," the town is home to another wonder—that distilled herbal drink with the cough-syrup taste known as Jägermeister.

COMING AND GOING

Wolfenbüttel is easily reached from Braunschweig by train (2 per hr, 12 min, DM 5) or by Bus 20 or 20S (1–3 per hr, 30 min, DM 3). To reach the city center from the train station, go left down Bahnhofstraße and continue through the passageway to the Stadtmarkt, where you'll find the super-friendly **tourist office** (Stadtmarkt 9, tel. 05331/86487), open weekdays 9–12:30 and 2–4, Saturday 9–1.

WHERE TO SLEEP

The centrally located **Jugendgästehaus** (Jägerstr. 17, tel. 05331/27189) has beds in four-bunk rooms for DM 24.50 (DM 30 over 26). Reception is open 9–6 and there's no curfew. The idyllic **Campingplatz** (next to Stadtbad, tel. 05331/298728; closed Oct.–Apr.), with trees, a canal, and a swimming pool, costs DM 6.50 per person and DM 6.50 for a tent spot.

FOOD

Kartoffelhaus (Komißstr. 10, tel. 05331/88040) is a local favorite for all kinds of potato (and meat and potato) dishes for DM 6–DM 20. **Alter Fritz** (Großer Zimmerhof 20, tel. 05331/26989) is a lively pub on an Altstadt corner that serves German fare. For fresh fruit and veggies, head to the **market** on the Altstadtmarkt on Wednesday and Saturday mornings.

GÖTTINGEN

When George Augustus (1683–1760), king of England and *Kurfürst* (elector) of Hanover, decided to immortalize himself by founding a university, folks were skeptical about his choice of venue—in 1734 Göttingen, on the southern edge of the Harz, wasn't much of a town. The city had enjoyed prosperity during the later Middle Ages as a member of the powerful Hanseatic League, but it gambled and lost because of its membership in the 16th-century Protestant Schmalkaldic League, crushed by Catholic Emperor Karl V, and was finally milked dry during the Thirty Years' War. But Georg August University students have been infusing the town with intellectual, social, and political energy for more than 200 years, and they don't show any indication of letting up. Göttingen's half-timbered houses and winding streets are enticing, and the astounding number of cultural events—and pubs—the small city has to offer may warrant an extended stay. Maybe some of the genius Göttingen has housed (think Max Planck, Werner Heisenberg, and over 30 other Nobel Prize winners) will rub off on you.

BASICS

AMERICAN EXPRESS

This branch just 2 blocks from the Hauptbahnhof exchanges money and AmEx traveler's checks (no fee) and provides standard travel services. *Goetheallee 4a, tel. 0551/522070. Open weekdays 9–6, Sat. 9:30–12:30.*

CHANGING MONEY

The most convenient place to change money is the main post office, next to the Bahnhof. One block from the Marktplatz tourist office, **Deutsche Bank** (Gotmarstr., at Johannisstr.) has good rates and an ATM that accepts Cirrus cards as well as MasterCard and Visa.

LAUNDRY

Dump your clothes at Göttingen's **Waschcenter** (Ritterplan 3), across from the Städtisches Museum (*see* Worth Seeing, *below*). The laundry is open weekdays 7 AM–10 PM and charges DM 6 to wash 7 kilos.

MAIL AND PHONES

The **Hauptpost,** just outside the train station, has a bureau de change and international phones. *Berliner Str. Postal code: 37073. Open weekdays 8 AM–6:30 PM, Sat. 8 AM–1 PM*

VISITOR INFORMATION

Tourist Office am Bahnhof (tel. 0551/56000) is open weekdays 10–1 and 2–6, Saturday 10–1. The larger and extremely helpful **Fremdenverkehrsverein Altes Rathaus** (Marktpl., tel. 0551/54000; open May–Sept., weekdays 9:30–6, Sat. 10–1; Apr.–Oct., weekdays 1–6, weekends 10–4) sells hostel cards, and has an extensive walking-tour brochure. From April through October, guided tours (DM 7) leave the office weekdays at 11:30 AM.

RESOURCES FOR GAYS AND LESBIANS • Schwulenzentrum (Immanuel-Kant-Str. 1, tel. 0551/770–1100), Göttingen's gay and lesbian center, has a café and local info on help lines, clubs, and meetings.

COMING AND GOING

BY TRAIN

Trains leave Göttingen's **Hauptbahnhof,** just west of the city center, for Hanover (1–3 per hr, 30 min, DM 48), Hildesheim (10 per day, 30 min, DM 37), and Kassel (1–3 per hr, 20 mins, DM 22). Lockers are accessible anytime but 1 AM–4:30 AM, when the station closes. Tickets for **city buses** (DM 2.60) are good for one hour after purchase. To get to the Marktplatz from the train station, cross Berliner Straße, head straight down Goetheallee (which becomes Prinzenstr.), and turn right on Weender Straße.

BY MITFAHRGELEGENHEIT

Göttingen's two ride-share offices are **Citynetz Mitfahr-Zentrale** (Burgstr. 122, tel. 0551/19444; open weekdays 9:30–6, weekends 7–1) and **Cheltenham House** (Friedrichstr. 1, tel. 0551/485988; open weekdays 10–6, Sat. 10–1:30).

WHERE TO SLEEP

Anything in the Altstadt will cost you, but there are a few cheap options on and near Weender Landstraße, across from the university campus.

Hotel Central. The name speaks for itself—stay here and you're in the heart of the Altstadt. You do, of course, pay for this luxury, but not dearly: A baroque-meets-the-1970s single with shower runs DM 95, a double with shower DM 130. The friendly staff serves a huge breakfast. *Jüdenstr. 12, tel. 0551/57157, fax 0551/57105. From Marktpl., up Barfüßerstr., left on Jüdenstr. 38 rooms, some with bathrooms.*

Landgasthaus Lockemann. If you like to hike and walk, consider this half-timbered lodge at the edge of the Stadtwald. Locals descend on the friendly, country-style hotel-restaurant for hearty German cooking.

Small, airy singles are DM 45, doubles DM 70 (without bath), breakfast included. *Im Beeke 1, tel. 0551/209020, fax 0551/209–0250. From Omnibusbahnhof, Bus 10 (direction: Herberhausen) to last stop, then left on Im Beeke (20 min total). 18 rooms, some with bath. Reception open Tues.–Sun. 4–midnight.*

HOSTEL

Jugendherberge (HI). This large, modern hostel up in the hills has a few doubles, singles, and rooms with private bath—call in advance to reserve. Beds in six-person dorms run DM 23 (DM 28 over 27), breakfast included. *Habichtsw. 2, tel. 0551/57622, fax 0551/43887. From Hauptbahnhof, Bus 1 to Hermann-Föge Weg and follow signs (10–15 min); or Bus 6 from Jüdenstr. to Jugendherberge. Last bus 11 PM. 161 beds. Curfew midnight; lockout 9–11:30. Reception open 6:30 AM–midnight; checkout 9 AM.*

FOOD

Göttingen's pedestrian walkways are full of international eateries that cater to the city's student population. Try Groner-Tor-Straße and Wilhelmsplatz for cheap eats around DM 6. **Plus market** (Prinzenstr., at Stumpfelbiel) stocks groceries aplenty.

Diwan. This upscale Turkish restaurant serves delicious Anatolian cuisine. Vegetarian appetizers and main dishes—such as Imam Bayildi (a delicately seasoned baked eggplant)—cost DM 12–DM 16; meat dishes are more, so consider splitting a large entrée with a friend if you're feeling carnivorous. *Rote Str. 11, tel. 0551/56085.*

Nudelhaus. A few doors up from Diwan, this popular pasta restaurant serves *Auflauf* (baked dishes), *Grüne Bandnudeln* (spinach linguine), and a "surprise plate for two" (DM 30). Dishes average DM 13. *Rote Str. 13, tel. 0551/44263.*

Troublemakers like Otto von Bismarck landed in a one-room cell in the old university Karzer (student prison) in the Aula on Wilhelmsplatz. Their offenses? Public drunkenness, dueling, gambling, and smoking.

Pfannkuchenhaus. More than 20 different kinds of stuffed German pancakes are served in a maze of dark, timbered rooms. Favorites include No. 24 (fresh mushrooms and cream sauce garnished with a Greek salad; DM 11.50) and No. 19 (vanilla ice cream, hot cherries, and Kirschwasser; DM 11). *Speckstr. 10, tel. 0551/41870. From Rathaus, up Barfüßerstr., left on Jüdenstr., right on Speckstr.*

WORTH SEEING

Göttingen is a great place to just hang out and imbibe the atmosphere unique to old German student towns. When your lounging needs are satisfied, grab the camera and focus on medieval churches. North of the Altes Rathaus, pay tribute to your patron saint, **St. Jacobi,** protector of travelers; the church has an ornate 15th-century altar. Just west of the Markt, **St. Johannis** shoulders two mismatched towers (one of which is inhabited by students; *see* Cheap Thrills, *below*).

ALTES RATHAUS

Snatch a brochure at the tourist office and take time to explore the interior of the 13th-century Old Town Hall on the Markt. A reminder of Göttingen's late-medieval glory days, the lobby is decorated with *Wappen* (coats of arms) of Göttingen's fellow Hanseatic League members, northern cities stretching from the Weser to the Elbe. On your way out, look for the unassuming lion door knocker, which dates from 1300.

BISMARCKHAUS

Like many medieval towns, Göttingen's Altstadt is encircled by an earth-and-brick wall, originally designed to ward off marauders. A wide walkway runs along the top of the wall and makes for perfect afternoon strolls. Just outside the wall, at the southern end of town, is the Bismarckhaus. Otto von Bismarck, who unified Germany in 1871 and became its first chancellor, lived in this small stone cottage during his swinging student days. *Admission free. Open Tues. 10–1, Wed., Thurs., and Sat. 3–5; shorter hrs off-season.*

STÄDTISCHES MUSEUM

This small museum gives great local perspective on Germany's history. Göttingen's prehistory, medieval heyday, university life, and its darker Third Reich days are on display. There's even a room focusing on

THE LITTLE GOOSE GIRL

On the Markt stands Göttingen's symbol, the Gänseliesel statue, the "little goose girl" in the Grimms' fairy tale. Traditionally, graduates of the university kiss this cold hunk of metal on the lips when they receive their doctoral degree. Since completion in 1901, she's become the most kissed girl in Germany, despite a 1926 city council resolution banning the practice. Göttingen's students still throw caution to the wind to get a little action from the bronze babe.

Jewish life and religion in the area. *Ritterplan 7–8, tel. 0551/400–2843. From Rathaus, up Weender Str., right on Jüdenstr., right on Ritterplan. Admission: DM 3, DM 1 students. Open Tues.–Fri. 10–5, weekends 11–5.*

FESTIVALS

Göttingen's **Altstadtfest,** held around the last weekend in August, is billed as the biggest outdoor party in Lower Saxony. Festivities consume the pedestrian zone and include alcohol, live music, and the usual culinary delights. In late May/early June, the **Händelfest** draws international music groups for a celebration of Handel's music. The performances aren't cheap; try for student tickets at the tourist office. The city also hosts the obligatory Lower Saxon **Schützenfest** (*see* Hanover, *above*) in July, and a reputedly groovy two-day **Jazz festival** in early November.

CHEAP THRILLS

The woodsy hills south of Göttingen make a great place to get away from it all; take Hainholzweg uphill until you reach the **Schillerwiese,** a meadow/park, then cross the road and take a trail into the woods. For a fine view, climb the **Bismarckturm** (DM 1), one of a whole slew of monuments in Lower Saxony (and beyond) dedicated to the first chancellor. Then trek another five–10 min uphill until you reach the **Kehr,** a wildlife sanctuary that is home to wild pigs (don't worry, they're contained) and deer. Stop for coffee or lunch at the **Hainholz-Kehr Hotel-Restaurant Café** (Borheckstr. 66, tel. 0551/75008), and if you can't bear to leave the pigs, the room rates aren't bad. Bus A runs back to town a few times a day. Back in town, you can climb the **watchtower** at St. Johannis (*see* Worth Seeing, *above*). If you go on Saturday afternoon (2 PM–4 PM) and schlepp some water up to the students who live there rent-free and plumbing-free, you'll get in (and up) for free; otherwise it's DM 2.

AFTER DARK

The free monthly brochure "Universitätsstadt Göttingen Informationsheft," available at the Rathaus tourist office, has schedules of cultural events. Göttingen's theater scene is well-known and student tickets are only DM 11. The **Deutsches Theater** (Theaterpl. 11, tel. 0551/55123) and the somewhat more experimental **Junges Theater** (Hospitalstr. 6, tel. 0551/55123) stage canonical German works as well as newer pieces. If you get stuck somewhere after dark, taxis congregate around the Rathaus. The cheapest taxi service is **Puk** (tel. 0551/484848). **Hallo Taxi** (tel. 0551/34034) is just for women.

CAFÉS

At Göttingen's mellow student cafés, the crowd tends to enjoy conversation more than downing their next beer. Cozy **Café Kabale** (Geismarlandstr. 19, tel. 0551/485830) serves as Göttingen's lesbian café. Next door, the cinema **Lumiere** (tel. 0551/484523; tickets DM 8) shows films in their original language. Sophisticated types listen to jazz until 1 AM daily at **Café Kadenz** (Jüdenstr. 17, off Barfüßerstr., tel. 0551/47208). In the shadow of St. Nikolaikirche, **Café Protz** (Nikolaikirchhofstr. 11, tel. 0551/57699), open daily until 2 or 3 AM, is frequented by gays, lesbians, and anyone looking for a liberal environment.

BARS AND CLUBS

The Altstadt has plenty of student pubs to crawl through—just work your way around. Nikolaistraße (especially between Turmstr. and Hospitalstr.) is a hip place to be on Saturday night; hop from the handful of bars to **Die Oper** (Nikolaistr. 1b, no phone), a club where the lively crowd spills out onto the street.

Blue Note. Once a week during the school year (Oct.–Jun.) this basement bar hosts live jazz and blues, in addition to Tuesday-night reggae, Wednesday-night salsa, and African and Caribbean music on Friday nights. The club throws various DJ dance parties as well—check the schedule posted at the entrance. *Wilhelmspl. 3, tel. 0551/46907. From Rathaus, up Weender Str., right on Barfüßerstr., right on Wilhelmspl. Cover: DM 10–DM 12. Open Sun.–Thurs. 8 PM–2 AM, Fri. and Sat. 8 PM–3 AM.*

Irish Pub. If you're dying to order a drink in English and can't sleep until you hear a bar rendition of "Piano Man," this jam-packed pub has live music nightly and (surprise) Guinness on tap. *Mühlenstr. 4a, tel. 0551/45664. From Bahnhof, up Goetheallee, left on Am Leinekanal, right on Mühlenstr. Open daily 4 PM–2 or 3 AM.*

KAZ. All of Göttingen gathers outside on warm summer nights for beer. In winter, mingle inside the pub with the theater crowd or head downstairs with black-clad anarchist types. *Hospitalstr. 6, tel. 0551/53062. From Rathaus, down Kurze Str., left on Hospitalstr. Open Mon.–Thurs. noon–2 AM, Fri. noon–3 AM, weekends 11 AM–2 AM.*

Trou. This place is for the romantic streak in all of us; it's in an old wine cellar in the remains of a 15th-century cloister. Thick stone walls, candles, and the smell of *Glühwein* (mulled wine) make you feel like not much has changed in the last 500 years. *Burgstr. 20, no phone. From Weender Str., up Theaterstr., left on Burgstr. Open daily 7:30 PM–2 AM.*

The Markt's "other" statue, that of Göttingen's beloved 17th-century physicist G. C. Lichtenberg, is life-size; the poor guy was a bit short, and he doesn't get kissed much these days.

NEAR GÖTTINGEN

HANNOVERSCH-MÜNDEN

Usually referred to as "Hann. Münden," this small town, with its collection of 700 half-timbered houses, sits pretty at the confluence of the Fulda and Werra rivers. Hann. Münden is a popular stop along the "Fairy Tale Road" (one of many themed paths invented by the German tourist industry). At noon, 3, and 5, those curious about 18th-century medicine can congregate in front of the 14th-century **Rathaus** to witness the town's **Glockenspiel** in action. As bells chime, the legendary doctor **Johann Andreas Eisenbart** (1663–1727) pries a tooth from a struggling patient. The doctor was considered a quack by his fellow townsfolk (no wonder—his dental treatment apparently also involved pistols), but went down in history as a medical pioneer of sorts. His story is acted out on the Marktplatz every Sunday June–September.

Hann. Münden offers eager travelers more than *Fachwerk* (half-timbered construction) and medicine; at the mouth of the Weser River, it is the starting point of the **Weser Bike Trail.** You can rent a bike at the hostel (*see* Where to Sleep, *below*) for DM 6 per day or DM 3 per half day and pedal up the Weser, visiting other Weser Renaissance-style towns, and return (if you're exhausted) by train; similar biking paths also weave through the scenic Werra and Fulda valleys. Cruising up the river is another option (get info at the tourist office), or you can take matters into your own hands and row while you enjoy the view. **Weserbootsverleih** (tel. 05541/818), at the campground (*see* Where to Sleep, *below*), rents boats for DM 18–DM 28 per person.

BASICS

The **tourist office** (tel. 05541/75313; open weekdays 8:30–5, Sat. 8:30–12:30; shorter hrs off-season) is tucked away on one side of the Rathaus. Information about biking and boating is available here, as are maps and guides to the Weser and Werra bike routes. The staff charges 15% commission to book rooms. In the same building, the **Auskunftschalter** (info desk) gives advice daily until 8 PM.

COMING AND GOING

Trains to Göttingen (40 min, DM 12) and Kassel (20 min, DM 8) stop here every hour. To reach the Rathaus and tourist office from the station, follow the INNENSTADT signs down Bahnhofstraße, and turn right on Lange Straße. A whopping seven luggage lockers await you on Platform 1 outside the station.

WHERE TO SLEEP

The **Gasthaus im Anker** (Bremer Schlagd 18, tel. 05541/4923; no credit cards) is a creaky pension overlooking the Fulda. Doubles and singles are DM 45 per person; so the walls may be a little crooked—just try to appreciate the *Fachwerk* workmanship you're sleeping in. **HI-Jugendherberge Münden** (Prof.-Oelkers-Str. 10, tel. 05541/8853; closed Dec.), by the banks of the Weser, has beds for DM 20 (DM 24.50 over 26), breakfast included. The hostel is 30 min from the station: Go down Beethovenstraße, turn left on Wallstraße, cross the bridge, then turn right on Veckerhäger Straße. Otherwise, take the hourly Bus 35 from the station. The crowded but scenic **Campingplatz Münden** (Oberer Tanzwerder, tel. 05541/12257; closed Nov.–Feb.), on an island in the Fulda, charges DM 3.50 for a tent site and DM 8.50 per person. From the Markt, take Tanzwerderstraße west and cross the bridge.

FOOD

There is an inordinate number of Greek restaurants here. Try **Samos** (Mühlenstr. 12, tel. 05541/2300) on the Fulda side of town for reasonable prices and the culture clash (or hybridity) of downing the complimentary ouzo shot while staring out at half-timbered buildings. Head to **Plus Market** (Ziegelstr. 20) for cold cuts, veggies, and other groceries if you miss the **open-air market** in front of the Rathaus (Wed. and Sat. until 1 PM).

DUDERSTADT

Only 30 km east of Göttingen, Duderstadt stands on the old border between East and West Germany. If you'd like to spend a quiet afternoon wandering medieval streets, take a day trip out here. The town's 500 half-timbered buildings, though not as numerous as Hann. Münden's, are also impressive: Carved facades on **Apothekenstraße** and **Hinterstraße** carry prayers, sayings, and intricate gargoyles. Also check out the supporting figures on the building that faces the Gothic **St. Cyriakus** church, at the end of Marktstraße. Behind the church, pick up the 3.5-km **wooded trail** that follows the route of the old walls around Duderstadt. Duderstadt's **tourist office** (Marktstr. 66, tel. 05527/841200; open weekdays 9–4:30, Thurs. until 7, weekends 9:30–12:30, and Apr.–Oct., 2:30–4:30), in the basement of the split-level Rathaus, has a booklet with the scuttlebutt on this and other longer walks.

From Göttingen, Duderstadt is accessible only by bus. Several make the trip, but only Bus 170 (6–8 per day, 1 hr, DM 9) stops at **Ebergötzen.** This sleepy hamlet is home to the **Wilhelm-Busch Mühle,** the house-cum-museum where Busch, creator of the twisted "Max und Moritz" stories (*see box* Those Darn Kids, *above*), spent his later years with his lover Erich Bachmann. *Mühlengasse 8, tel. 05507/7181. Admission: DM 5, DM 3 students. Open Mon.–Sat. 9–1 and 2–5, Sun. 10–1 and 2–5.*

WHERE TO SLEEP

The tourist office provides a free list of private rooms that go for roughly DM 25. A bed in one of the spanking-clean and spacious doubles at the friendly **HI-Jugendgästehaus Duderstadt** (Mühlhäuser Str. 27, tel. 05527/98470) is yours for DM 26.50 (DM 31 over 26), and you can cook in the communal kitchen. To get there, walk east along Marktstraße (it changes names twice) and follow the sign to the right; it's about a 15-min walk.

WESTERN HARZ MOUNTAINS

The Harz Mountains sit in the heart of Germany and occupy an equally central space in German folklore, from *Walpurgisnacht* (the witches' sabbath; *see box* Escape From Witch Mountain, *below*) to fairy tales. This densely forested and relatively gentle range is popular with those who thrive on a good 17-km hike before breakfast and with nature enthusiasts who believe in the healing powers of mountain air. Historic towns *am Harz* (at the foot of the range)—half-timbered **Goslar** being the biggest and most famous—are better for warm-weather visits, while towns *im Harz* (in the mountains)—scenic **Altenau** and touristy **Braulage,** for instance—are year-round favorites. In winter, budget travelers face haphazard transit schedules, seasonal price-gouging, and hordes of ski-lovers, though the excellent downhill and cross-country facilities make it worth it—almost. Come spring, there are hikes aplenty, including trails that lead all the way to Saxony-Anhalt (*see* Eastern Harz Mountains *in* Chapter 10). A string of thoughtfully placed hostels makes longer hikes a snap. Even so, square one for any expedition is the knowledgeable **tourist office,** Goslar's Harzer Verkehrsverband (*see below*), with stacks of pamphlets on sights, hotels, and campgrounds. Tourist offices all over the Harz sell the guide *Grüner Faden.* It's well worth DM 3 for listings on local bike, ski, and sailboat rentals, chairlifts, and more. The **Harz Hotline** (tel. 05321/20024) rattles off the latest weather forecast in German.

COMING AND GOING

The Harz is easily reached by train; the restored rail connection between East and West makes negotiating the region simpler and cheaper. Trains travel frequently from Goslar to Hanover (1 hr 20 min, DM 29) and to Wernigerode (20–30 min, DM 12); both stop in Bad Harzburg (15 min, DM 5). Buses are, however, still the main mode of transportation (other than your feet) within the mountains. The historic and pricey scenic narrow-gauge railway based in Wernigerode makes hiking the famous Brocken and other longer hikes more appealing to the dilettante—hike up, ride down (or vice-versa).

GOSLAR

Embraced by the northern arms of the Harz, Goslar extracted silver from the same mine for more than 1,000 years, and the resultingly rich Altstadt boasts some strikingly unique timber-framed houses, mercifully untouched by Allied bombs. In 1992, UNESCO put Goslar on the World Heritage list—you'll see why as you amble along the town's cobblestone lanes.

BASICS

Goslar's often swamped **tourist office** (Markt 7, tel. 05321/78060), across the Marktplatz from the Rathaus, books rooms for a small fee. They're open weekdays 9–6, Saturday 9:30–4, Sunday until 2 (shorter hrs Nov.–Apr.). In the old Bäckergildehaus, **Harzer Verkehrsverband** (Marktstr. 45, tel. 05321/20031), open Monday–Thursday 8–5 and Friday 8–1, brims with info on the Harz. On your way from the Bahnhof to the Altstadt, stop at **Citibank Goslar** (Rosentorstr. 14) to change money or use the ATM, which takes Plus cards, Visa, and MasterCard. The **post office** (Klubgartenstr. 10; postal code 38640) is near the train station. Rent a mountain bike (DM 15 per day) at **Harz Bike** (Bornhardstr. 3–5, tel. 05321/82011).

COMING AND GOING

Buses leave the Hauptbahnhof for towns such as Altenau, Torfhaus, Braunlage, and Halberstadt. Local buses stop running around 6 PM. To reach the Altstadt, walk south down Rosentorstraße for 10 min.

WHERE TO SLEEP

Rooms in Goslar often fill up, so call ahead. The genuinely friendly **Gästehaus Möller** (Schieferw. 6, tel. 05321/23098) has homey, bright singles with TVs for DM 40–DM 60, doubles for DM 80–DM 110. From the Hauptbahnhof, go right down Klubgartenstraße, cross Von Garßen Straße, and turn right on Schieferweg (10 min). If you plan to whoop it up at an Altstadt pub, you can stumble home to the central **Gästehaus Schmitz** (Kornstr. 1, tel. 05321/23445). Large rooms with bath, TV, and phone are DM 55 (single) and DM 70 (double). Neither hotel accepts credit cards.

HOSTELS • Jugendherberge Goslar (HI). Surrounded by woods, this hostel perches on the Rammelsberg, with a great view over town. Beds DM 21 (DM 26 over 26). *Rammelsbergerstr. 25, tel. 05321/22240, fax 05321/41376. From Hauptbahnhof, Bus D to Theresienhof or Bus A to Rammelsbergerstr., then follow signs uphill for 10–15 min. 170 beds. Reception open 8:30–2:30 and 3–10.*

CAMPING • Campingplatz Sennhütte. This standard campground is clean and cheap and only 10 min from town, but right on the edge of Route B 241. From the train station, take the Clausthal-Zellerfeld bus to Sennhütte. Sites are DM 4 plus DM 5 per person. *Clausthaler Str. 28, tel. 05321/22498. Closed in winter.*

FOOD

Imbiß stands and fast-food restaurants line the streets of the Altstadt, serving cheap Greek and Turkish fare. Try the local favorite, **Paulaner an der Lohmühle** (An der Lohmühle, tel. 05321/26070), for smaller Bavarian-style meals like *Käse Spätzle* (cheese noodles) and salads that will fill you up for DM 8.50–DM 13.50. They also have a lovely beer garden overlooking an old mill, just across the river from the city's museum. An **open-air market** fills the Marktplatz Tuesday and Friday until 1 PM. The place to socialize after dark is the Brauhof courtyard, surrounded by a few bars and cafés. The anchor and old standby is, naturally, the **Brauhaus** (Marstalstr. 2, tel. 05321/22155). From the Marktplatz, go down Marktstraße, right on Marstalstraße, then right again at the small parking lot, and you're there.

WORTH SEEING

Goslar has hundreds of pre-17th-century houses to ogle. The 16th-century **Brusttuch Haus** (Hoher Weg, behind Marktkirche), now a hotel, is the best known and adorns many a postcard. A handful of gorgeous buildings cluster near the corner of Bergstraße and Schreiberstraße, where vibrantly painted houses contrast with the **Siemenshaus,** the large brick-and-black-wood edifice at the intersection. For all the details on the town's buildings, pick up the self-guided tour brochure at the tourist office, or take one of the **tours** (Mon., Wed., and Sat. at 2 PM) for DM 6.

KAISERPFALZ • The 12th-century imperial palace (reconstructed in the 19th century) sports an imposing facade and Romanesque windows. In St. Ulrich's chapel, you can tiptoe over the heart of Emperor Heinrich III, which rests in a gilded octagonal vessel under a memorial slab (his body was buried in Speyer). Goslar's cathedral once stood at the bottom of the palace's front yard. Destroyed in 1822, it has been replaced by a parking lot for tourist buses, though the preserved antechamber and 11th-century imperial throne still stand. Come up here to relax on the expansive lawn, enjoy the view of town, and admire Henry Moore's *Goslar Warrior*—an unusual sculpture of a fallen warrior whose shield is rolling away. For the guided tours at 10:30, 12:30 and 2:30, call 05321/757810. *From Marktpl., left on Hoher Weg. Admission: DM 2.50. Open daily 9–2:30.*

MARKTPLATZ • Several old edifices line this lovely little square; the sober **Rathaus** and gray-and-slate-hued building to the south offset the jovial red facade of the Kaiserworth Hotel and the central fountain's imperial eagle. The **Huldigungssaal** (Hall of Honor) in the Rathaus is painted with splendid, newly restored 16th-century murals; it was closed for restoration at press time, but is scheduled to reopen in June 2000. Behind the Rathaus is the ornate **Marktkirche,** whose two spires are stunningly incongruous. A Glockenspiel depicts Goslar's mining history at 9, noon, 3, and 6.

MUSEUMS • The Mönchehaus (Mönchestr. 3, at Jakobistr., tel. 05321/29570) shows modern art in a wood-beamed 16th-century artisan's house with sculptures out back. Admission is DM 3.50, DM 2 students (Sundays free); the house is open Tuesday–Saturday 10–1 and 3–5, Sunday 10–1. DM 5 gets you into the **Musikinstrumente und Puppenmuseum** (Hoher Weg 5, tel. 05321/26945; open daily 11–5); among the Nordic dolls and musical instruments is a Brazilian xarango, with an armadillo for a sounding board. Put on a hard hat and take an interactive tour of **Rammelsberger Bergbaumuseum** (Bergtal 19, tel. 05321/2891; open daily 9–6). Two one-hour tours are offered: One puts you in a mine train for a view of contemporary mining techniques and explosions (DM 13.50); the other takes you down, down, down into an old mine shaft (DM 9) for a fascinating look at mining in centuries past. To get there, take Bus C to Rammelsberg.

NEAR GOSLAR

ALTENAU

The most scenic of the larger Western Harz resorts, the former mining town of Altenau has plenty of beer halls (it even has its own brewery, the only one in the Harz) and pensions, and its well-groomed streets brim with vacationing families in summer. For hikers Altenau's most important feature is its location, at the foot of three very challenging trails, which start on or near Schultal. The first is the 28-km **Bruchberg,** which winds its way through dense forest before cresting on the Bruchberg Summit (1,011 m), after which it's an easy descent into Torfhaus (*see* Near Bad Harzburg, *below*). The **Polsterberger** is a 15-km hike that skirts dozens of teardrop lakes before reaching the village of Clausthal-Zellerfeld. From here you can take Bus 408 back to Altenau (last bus 6 PM), or stop over at Clausthal-Zellerfeld's **HI-Jugendherberge** (Altenauer Str. 55, tel. 05323/84293) for DM 21 (DM 26 over 27) a night. Finally, there's the **St. Andreasberg trail,** a path that leads 19 km to the remote village of St. Andreasberg. Instead of hiking back, you can hop on Bus 432 to Altenau, which stops running around 6 PM.

Less-athletic types can take **Magdeburger Weg,** a more moderate 8-km hike that begins at Altenau's Marktplatz and leads straight to Torfhaus. Before heading out on any of these hikes, pick up a detailed topographical map from Altenau's **tourist office** (Kurverwaltung, Hüttenstr. 9, tel. 05328/80222; open weekdays 8–5), 150 m east of the bus depot on the Torfhaus/Bad Harzburg road. Bus 432 to Goslar (40 min) runs nearly every hour.

WHERE TO SLEEP • Altenau's **HI-Jugendherberge** (Auf der Rose 11, tel. 05328/361) has beds for DM 21 per person (half-board DM 30, full-board DM 36.50) and a 10:30 PM curfew. They also rent ski equipment for around DM 20. To get there, turn left as you exit the bus depot, go left again on Marktstraße, and continue south; the road's name changes four times before becoming Auf der Rose—it's about a 10-min walk uphill. A more comfortable option is **Haus Ebeling** (Bergstr. 22, tel. 05328/1220; no credit cards), a family-owned hotel with rooms for DM 30 per person.

BAD HARZBURG

A spa town primarily geared to those convalescing (especially the elderly), Bad Harzburg is expensive and slightly snobby. The **Bummelallee,** Bad Harzburg's version of a smart Parisian-style street, is crowded with jewelers and exorbitant clothing stores, and the adjacent Herzog-Wilhelm-Straße brims with tourist shops and outrageously priced restaurants. Bad Harzburg is also the closest major town to the mountains, so stock up on food, money, and "civilization" before heading into the wilderness.

One of the few cheap things to do here is to ride the 1-km-long **Bergbahn** (DM 6), a gondola that connects the Kurpark lodge with the undemanding peak of **Groß Burgberg** (482 m). From the tourist office, turn left on Am Stadtpark and follow the signs. The peak serves as the trailhead for hikes back to Bad Harzburg, on to Torfhaus (*see below*), and beyond; the trails double as ski runs in winter. For info on ski rentals and lift tickets, contact the **Skizentrum** (An der Kirche 20, tel. 05322/2275).

Those with a penchant for the unusual (nay, perverse) may appreciate Goslar's exotically adorned Fachwerkhäuser. Don't miss the "Ducatenscheißer" (gold-coin shitter) on the corner of the Kaiserworth Hotel.

BASICS

The **Kurverwaltung** (Herzog-Wilhelm-Str. 86, tel. 05322/75300; open weekdays 7–8, Sat. 9–4) has tourist and hiking information; they'll also find you a room for free. To get there from the train station, head 1 km south on Herzog-Wilhelm-Straße and turn right at the **post office** (Herzog-Wilhelm-Str. 80), which has an international phone desk. Get basic info at the smaller tourist office (Am Bahnhofspl., tel. 05322/2927) outside the station.

COMING AND GOING

Most **buses** headed into the Harz leave from the Bahnhof. Bus destinations from Bad Harzburg include Braunlage (6 per day, 40 min, DM 7) and Torfhaus (12 per day, 20 min, DM 4). To reach the city center, head straight out of the station and walk to the end of Herzog-Wilhelm-Straße, which turns into Bummelallee.

WHERE TO SLEEP AND EAT

Haus Diana (Golfstr. 17, tel. 05322/1549) offers comfy singles with TV for DM 50, doubles for DM 90—call ahead. The understaffed hostel **HI-Braunschweiger Haus** (Waldstr. 5, tel. 05322/4582, fax 05322/1867) lies on the edge of town, 2 km from the station; beds are DM 31, there's no curfew, and reception is open sporadically. From the Bahnhof, take Bus 73 to Lärchenweg, then go left on Waldstraße. Your *Kurkarte* (guest card) is good for a free bus ride. Just west of town, **Harzer Campingplatz Göttingerode** (tel. 05322/81215) has clean sites (DM 9 per tent, DM 7 per person), a market, pool, sauna, and restaurant. To get here, take Goslar-bound Bus 407 to Göttingerode; the campground is across the street.

For outstanding but overpriced coffee and rotating art exhibits, head to **Palmen-Café** (Im Badepark, 2 blocks east of Bummelallee, tel. 05322/4805). Or treat your tastebuds to an eggplant or artichoke-heart pizza (DM 9–DM 13) at **Pizza Treff** (Herzog-Julius-Str. 54, tel. 05322/1551). A **Mini-Mal** supermarket is across the street from the station.

NEAR BAD HARZBURG

BRAUNLAGE

Braunlage, 26 km south of Bad Harzburg, is one of the region's principal tourist resorts and a well-known *Kurort,* or spa. Braunlage has all the amenities of a large town—budget pensions, beer halls, restaurants, and gift shops—mixed with first-rate scenery and alpine trails. Nevertheless, the town's lack of character makes its popularity as a ski resort and spa all the more obvious. Braunlage's three ski areas are carved out of the **Wurmberg** (971 m), one of the region's tallest peaks. Behind the Rathaus,

ESCAPE FROM WITCH MOUNTAIN

According to legend, the world's witches gather on the summit of the Brocken on Walpurgisnacht (April 30) to brew up a little mischief. (This explains the little flying witches hanging in many a window in the Harz.) A version of the story appears in Goethe's Faust; Goethe himself was an avid walker who spent many summers in the area. Don't expect to see any witches on the Goetheweg, an idyllic and manageable trail that gently winds its way 8 km to the Brocken summit. You can either return to Torfhaus on foot or pay a hefty DM 30–DM 40 to ride the Brockenbahn, a narrow-gauge railway, down to charming Wernigerode (see Chapter 10).

three lifts lead to some novice slopes (lift passes DM 25 per day, DM 15 per half day). Otherwise, ride the **Wurmberg Seilbahn** (cable car) to the top for DM 8, DM 6 students. The Seilbahn parking lot serves as the jumping-off point for several *Langlauf* (cross-country) trails. Rent ski equipment on central Herzog-Wilhelm-Straße for DM 20–DM 25 a day. The **tourist office** (Elbingeröder Str. 17, tel. 05520/93070), one block off the main strip, is open weekdays 7:30–noon and 2–5, Saturday 9:30–noon. The **Busbahnhof,** on Bahnhofstraße, is ½ km south of the village center; ask for the central "Am Brunnen" stop when arriving by bus from Bad Harzburg.

After the spring thaw, Braunlage makes a good hiking base. The village is split by the lazy Warme Bode River; if you follow it south 7 km you'll end up in the remote, picture-perfect village of **Tanne.** Another good hike is to the village of **St. Andreasberg,** 8 km to the west. Stop by the tourist office for detailed maps. For travelers looking for a shorter hike, hit the **Wurmberg summit** itself: You can take the cable car to the mountaintop Bergstation and return to Braunlage via one of a dozen well-marked trails. The most scenic trek is the 3-km **Bärenbrücke**; the most demanding is the 13-km **Dreieckiger Pfahl** to Torfhaus, with good views of the nearby Brocken mountain.

WHERE TO SLEEP • A display outside the tourist office shows every hotel, its price, features, and whether it has vacancies. Conveniently located **Hotel Parkblick** (Elbingeröder Str. 13, tel. 05520/1237; no credit cards) has singles for DM 35, doubles for DM 70–DM 90; if you have nothing against taxidermy, you'll be happy here. A favorite sleepover for school kids, **HI-Jugendherberge** (Von-Langen-Str. 28, tel. 05520/2238; closed Dec.) is a 20-min walk uphill and into the woods from Herzog-Wilhelm-Straße. Beds run DM 21 (DM 26 over 26), with half-board costing DM 30 and full-board DM 36.50, as well as special rates for multiple nights; curfew is 10 PM. Braunlage's **campground** (Rte. B 27, tel. 05520/413), complete with Harz view and highway noise, is 1½ km west of the bus station and hard to find: Turn right onto Bahnhofstraße, left on Wiesen Straße, and left on Lauterberger Straße; when the sidewalk ends, head left onto the hiking trail, walk past the cemetery, under the B 4/Bad Harzburg overpass, and veer right at the sign 100 m ahead. Sites are DM 5.50 plus DM 8 per person.

TORFHAUS

Torfhaus, halfway between Bad Harzburg and Braunlage, consists of little more than a few hotels and an **HI-Jugendherberge** (Torfhaus Str. 3, tel. 05320/242; closed Dec.). With beds at DM 20 per night (DM 25 over 26) and few amenities, this hostel is preferred for its strategic kick-off point for hiking and skiing. It sits 100 m down the small road to Altenau, just opposite the tiny **tourist office** (tel. 05320/258). Head in any direction from this mountaintop burg and you'll find yourself surrounded by lush forests and rolling hills. The most famous trail, the **Goetheweg** (*see box* Escape from Witch Mountain, *above*), begins right next to the tourist office. Also try the marked **Bruchberg** trek (*see* Altenau, *above*), connecting Torfhaus with Altenau; there's a sign for the trailhead by the hostel. Buses connect Bad Harzburg, Braunlage, and Altenau with Torfhaus year-round; the bus stop is on Route B 4, near the large parking lot.

LÜNEBURGER HEIDE

Anchored by the towns of Lüneburg to the north and Celle to the south, the Lüneburger Heide encompasses a national park, famous for vast expanses of heathland covered in heather and crisscrossed by a maze of hiking, biking, and riding trails. The heather, kept knee-high by the nibblings of the long-haired Heidschnucken sheep, blooms vibrant purple in August and early September. Even if you miss the blooms, the region always offers a landscape of rolling grasslands and dense fir. Scattered throughout this countryside are small, backwater villages, which supply cheap lodging and a glimpse of rural German life. You can even travel from farm to farm (or barn to barn), spending your nights with the livestock (*see box* A Roll in the Hay, *below*). For the traveler seeking civilization, Lüneburg and Celle are lively, historically rich cities worth a short visit. The Lüneburger Heide also bears witness to the horrifying side of German history: Bergen-Belsen concentration camp is in the countryside northwest of Celle.

BASICS

Get all the regional info you need from Lüneburg's **tourist office,** the Fremdenverkehrsverband Lüneburger Heide. The place overflows with pamphlets and info on everything from campgrounds and "hay hotels" to bike-rental places and swimming spots. The helpful staff provides directions and bus info, but they don't book rooms. Pick up *Lüneburger Heide Gastgeberverzeichnis,* a guide to accommodations throughout the region. *Barckhausenstr. 35, tel. 04131/73730, fax 04131/42606. From Am Sande, left down Rote Str., which becomes Barckhausenstr.; office is in the unassuming building on the right. Open Mon.–Thurs. 8–4:30, Fri. 8–1.*

COMING AND GOING

Reaching the heath is a snap—Lüneburg and Celle are connected on the Hanover–Hamburg rail line. From Celle, trains go hourly to Hanover (30–50 min, DM 12). Lüneburg has frequent connections to Hamburg (45 min–1 hr, DM 12). Hourly trains between Lüneburg and Celle (40 min) cost DM 22. To get to smaller Lüneburger Heide towns, you'll have to rely on the bus.

LÜNEBURG

The stately brick facades lining the streets and squares of Lüneburg distinguish it from its southern neighbors and tell the city's history as a rich *Hansestadt* (Hanseatic city). These minor architectural wonders were built on the wealth of the nearby salt mines (closed since 1980), which supplied northern Germany and Scandinavia back when salt was as good as gold. Lüneburg's nightlife is surprisingly abuzz for a town this size—but explained by the town's 8,000-student university.

BASICS

Buses to smaller Lüneburger Heide towns leave from the Bahnhof or Am Sande, the town's central square. To reach the **tourist office** (Am Markt, tel. 04131/309593; open weekdays 9–6, weekends 9–1) from the train station, head downhill, go left on Lünertorstraße, and left on Bardowicker Straße. In the yellow Rathaus, the office charges DM 5 to find you a room, and gives out free walking guides, maps of Lüneburg, and the local guide to cultural events, *21 zwanzig.* For anything else, head to the **tourist office** (*see above*).

Bike rentals at Laden 25 (Am Werder 25, off Lünertorstr., tel. 04131/37960) cost DM 12 per day, DM 25 per weekend (three days). Lüneburg's main **post office** (Bahnhofstr. 14; postal code 21337) is near the train station. Collect hard cash at **Citibank** (Rosenstr., one block east of the Markt); its ATM accepts credit and bank cards. **Waschcenter** (cnr Rote Str. and Wallstr.; open Mon.–Sat. 6 AM–10 PM) charges DM 6 for a 6-kilo load, 50 Pf to dry for 10 min.

WHERE TO SLEEP

Lüneburg's surprisingly expensive hotels fill to the bursting point in August—call ahead if you plan to visit then. The closest hotel to the train station is **Hotel Lübecker Hof** (Lünertorstr. 12, tel. 04131/51420, fax 04131/53952), with small, clean singles for DM 45–DM 80, doubles DM 70–DM 105. **Hotel Stadt**

A ROLL IN THE HAY

Lower Saxony's most offbeat sleeping innovation is the Heu-Hotel, a barn or farm outbuilding where, from May to October, you can spread your sleeping bag out on a pile of fresh hay for DM 17. It's remarkably comfortable, but definitely not for the squeamish: Your sleeping bag will smell strongly of hay, mice are common bed partners, there's no heating, and most barns are mixed (everybody rolls in the same hay). In return, you get astounding hospitality, the cheapest lodging around, and huge, delicious breakfasts, often made with fresh produce from the farm. Many of the farms also offer private rooms in the house, in case you chicken out (so to speak). Most Heu-Hotels lie in the countryside near Lüneburg, Celle, Hameln, and Norden; get more info at the tourist offices in these towns or call 04231/96650 or fax 04231/96653 to get details and advice for planning a Heu-Hotel tour.

Hamburg (Am Sande 25, tel. 04131/44438; no credit cards) is a pleasantly rambling and historic hotel with neat, spacious singles (from DM 55) and doubles (from DM 100) right in the center of Lüneburg.

HOSTELS • Jugendherberge (HI). The 104 beds (DM 21, DM 26 over 27) in this standard hostel often fill in summer. You can avoid the 40-min walk by taking the bus from the train station. Although the 10 PM curfew is for real, you can get a key. *Soltauer Str. 133, tel. 04131/41864, fax 04131/45747. From Bahnhof, south and right on Altenbrückertorstr., through Am Sande, left on Rote Str., right on Lindenstr., left on Soltauer Str.; or Bus 11 from Am Sande to Scharnhornstr. Reception open 5 PM–10 PM.*

CAMPING • Campingplatz Rote Schleuse. This campground lies an hour's walk south of town, on the left side of Route B 4. To get here faster, take the hourly Bus 1977 from Am Sande toward Deutsche Evern to Rote Schleuse (last bus around 5 PM). Tent sites are DM 3 plus DM 5.50 per person. *Rote Schleuse 4, tel. 04131/791500. Closed Nov.–Feb.*

FOOD

Lüneburg's cafés and restaurants escape the wurst-and-sauerkraut rut with delicious vegetarian and Italian meals at decent prices. University students chow down pizza, pasta, and traditional pan-fried German dishes (DM 5–DM 15) in the brick-and-wood interior of **Camus** (Am Sande 30, tel. 04131/42820). The popular **Schröder** (Schröderstr. 5, tel. 04131/47777) serves the best breakfast buffet in town. Salads and veggie dishes like baked pasta with spinach and feta start at DM 9. Lüneburg's **open-air market** on Marktplatz bursts with fresh goods from nearby farms on Wednesday and Saturday mornings.

WORTH SEEING

Pick up the tourist office's "Walk through Lüneburg" brochure for a do-it-yourself tour of Lüneburg's brick beauties. The area by the Ilmenau River, with a 14th-century crane, water tower, and waterfall, is especially picturesque. For a view of Lüneburg's signature red rooftops, climb the **Kalkberg,** a modest hill west of town.

On the west side of the Marktplatz stands the well-preserved medieval **Rathaus,** built in 1230. The incredible 15th-century stained-glass windows, wall paintings, and intricate ceilings can be seen on hourly tours (DM 5, DM 3.50 students) between 10 and 4 daily. The 14th-century **St. Johanniskirche** (Am Sande) is most famous for its massive pipe organ, cobbled together with parts dating from the 16th century. In the western part of town, the Gothic **Michaeliskirche** (J.-S.-Bach-Pl.) was built of brick on sinking ground; as a result, the steeple now leans drunkenly to one side. Stand in the nave and look back to get the gist. The church is open Monday–Saturday 10–noon and 2–5 (until 4 in winter).

BRAUEREIMUSEUM • You can learn how that hangover-inducing German beer is made at the 500-year-old Kronen Brewery. The self-guided tour takes the beer fan through the entire process; there's also an exhibit of historical drinking vessels. Afterward, try the brewery's own Moravia Pils in the beer garden. The pricey restaurant (entrées DM 15–DM 30) is a good place to go for local seasonal specialties like Heidschnucken liver (yum). *Heiligengeiststr. 39–41, tel. 04131/41021. Admission free. Open Tues.–Sun. 1 PM–4:40 PM.*

KLOSTER LÜNE • Two km north of town stands the 15th-century Lüne monastery, comprised of idyllic brick-and-timber houses. Be sure to check out the Kloster's church and its 16th-century carved-wood altar. *Am Domänenhof, at Lünetorbrucke, tel. 04131/52318. Admission: DM 5. From Am Sande, Bus 15 or 16 to Kloster Lüne. Open Apr.–mid-Oct., Mon.–Sat. 10–12:30 and 2:30–5, Sun. 12:30–5.*

SALZMUSEUM • Delve into the saline secrets of the town's biggest attraction at this exceptionally detailed salt museum. The exhibits explain everything you ever wanted to know about the salt industry and then some. *Sülfmeisterstr. 1, tel. 04131/45065. From Am Sande, Rote Str. to Wallstr., then right to Lambertipl. (museum ahead on left). Admission: DM 6.50, DM 4 students; with tour DM 8, DM 5 students. Open May–Sept., weekdays 9–5, weekends 10–5; Oct.–Apr., weekdays 10–5.*

Heide delicacies include anything made from the meat of Heidschnucken, the long-horned, straggly-haired sheep that graze the heath. Industrious heath bees also produce loads of honey.

AFTER DARK

The riverside bars on **Am Stintmarkt** host throngs of happily hammered college students. **Dialog** (Am Stintmarkt 12, tel. 04131/391139) changes from a relaxed, lunchtime restaurant to a boisterous student bar every night. Lüneburg's gay bar, **Pit's Bierbar** (Obere Schrangenstr. 9, south of Marktpl., tel. 04131/45967), is open daily until 2 AM and has info on other gay activities in town. Students pack into **Garage** (Auf der Hude 72, tel. 04131/35879), a techno/house dance club, on Wednesday, Friday, and Saturday 10 PM–4 AM. There's no cover before 11; after that it's DM 6.

NEAR LÜNEBURG

Dozens of parks and nature preserves are scattered across the region from Celle to Lüneburg, but the best—and most visited—spots lie 35 km west of Lüneburg in **Naturschutzpark Lüneburger Heide.** In August and September, large fields of heather bloom on low hills freckled with sparse pine and birch. Happily, the park is car-free, so if you're looking to meander or bike along lazy country lanes, this is the place. Several small towns offer bike rental or rides in horse-drawn carriages, and you can find pensions starting at around DM 30 per person; get a list at the local tourist office or at the Fremdenverkehrsverband Lüneburger Heide in Lüneburg. There are two Heu-Hotels (*see box* A Roll in the Hay, *above*) in **Bispingen,** 25 km south of Egestorf. One is at Grevenhof 6 (tel. 05194/1294); the other is at Volkwardingen 1 (tel. 05194/7237). There is also an **HI-hostel** (Töpinger Str. 42, tel. 05194/2375) here, with beds for DM 21 (DM 26 over 27). Bus 7 from Lüneburg leaves for Bispingen a painful once a day at 2:30 PM.

Bus 1910 from Lüneburg runs to **Egestorf** (45 min, DM 8) seven times every weekday, three times on Saturday, and twice on Sunday. All of the weekend buses, but only two of the weekday buses (at 8 AM and 3 PM), continue to **Undeloh** (1 hr, DM 11). Check schedules *carefully.*

UNDELOH

Tiny Undeloh is great for short forays or extended bike rides into the nature park, a scant 4 km away. Climb the 186-m **Wilseder Berg** and look out over the heath, then visit the gorgeous, juniper-strewn **Totengrund Valley,** both a one-hour walk from town. Many places on Wilseder Straße rent bikes for about DM 6 for three hours, DM 10 per day. You can hire a horse-drawn carriage (DM 10 per person for groups of 4 or more, otherwise about DM 60 per trip) for a 2½-hour ride through the heath; just look for the parked carriages. Undeloh's **Verkehrsverein** (Zur Dorfeiche, tel. 04189/333; open Mon., Tues., Thurs., Fri. 10–noon and 3–5, Sat. 10–noon), near Radenbachweg, books rooms in pensions from DM 25.

EGESTORF

So you missed the early bus to Undeloh? No need to panic. You can still catch an afternoon bus to Egestorf, the equally pretty town about 7 km east of Undeloh. You'll be close to the park, and the bike ride between Egestorf and Undeloh passes through a lovely stretch of heath. The **tourist office** (Verkehrsverein; Barkhof 1b, tel. 04175/1516; open weekdays 10–noon and 3–6) is across from the St. Stephanus church. Rent **bikes** at Hotel zu den acht Linden (Alte Dorfstr. 1, tel. 04175/84330) for DM 6 for two hours, DM 12 per day. On the road to nearby Garlstorf, **Freizeit Camp Garlstorfer Forst** (Egestorfer Landstr. 50, tel. 04172/7556) is the nearest campground to the park.

CELLE

A popular stop on the *Fachwerkstraße* (Half-Timbered Road) tourist trail, Celle is chock-full of bus-trippers during the afternoon, but come evening the local color shines through the kitsch. Celle became the merrily decorated city it is thanks to the dukes of Braunschweig-Lüneburg, who established a residence here. For those weary of the Guelphs and Old World architecture, Celle offers some quirkier sights and elegant parks. Celle also makes a good base for exploring the surrounding countryside, including the Bergen-Belsen concentration camp site (*see* Near Celle, *below*).

BASICS

The charming staff at the sleek, modern **tourist office** (Markt 6, tel. 05141/1212) will shower you with brochures; they also find rooms for DM 2. The office is open weekdays 9–6, Saturday 8:30–6 and 10–2 (shorter hrs off-season). To reach town from the train station, walk down Bahnhofstraße and head left when you see the cobblestone pedestrian zone. From the train station, turn right on Bahnhofstraße and go straight for about five min to 2-Rad-Meier (Neustadtstr. 42a, tel. 05141/41369), which rents **bikes** for DM 15 a day. To reach Bergen-Belsen, take Bus 2 from the Bahnhof to Bergen-Celler Straße, then Bus 9 to Gedenkstätte Bergen-Belsen. This bus line only runs two or three times a day—check the schedule carefully. You can also make it there by bike; it's about a 1½-hr ride.

WHERE TO SLEEP

Roll in the hay at Celle's **Heu-Hotel** (Lachtehäuser Str. 28, tel. 05141/34002); take Bus 2 or 5 to Langenhagen, a small village 4 km away. Celle's big black **HI-Jugendherberge** (Weghausstr. 2, tel. 05141/53208; closed early Jan.), adjacent to horse pastures, has its own inescapable scent. It's DM 21 (DM 26 over 27) for bed and breakfast; curfew is promptly at 10 PM. From the Bahnhof, take Bus 3 to Jugendherberge; or exit left, follow the tracks, cross over tracks (left) on Bremer Weg, and go right at the sign on Petersburgstraße (about 15 min). **Am Landgestüt** (Landgestütstr. 1, 05141/217219; no credit cards) has bright singles for DM 45–DM 60, doubles DM 90–DM 110. From the Bahnhof, take Bahnhofstraße left, turn right on Hannoversche Straße, then right on Spörckenstraße, just past the police station.

FOOD

Stock up on picnic fixings at the **market** that floods the streets between Brandplatz and the Rathaus Wednesday and Saturday mornings. **Ronitz bakery** (Großer Plan 5a, tel. 05141/22421) has big loaves of pesto bread for DM 5. For nighttime dining, head to Zöllnerstraße or Neue Straße and take your pick of the many outdoor tables. **Santa Lucia** (Zöllnerstr. 35) serves pizza and pasta (DM 9–DM 11) to an animated crowd.

WORTH SEEING

Among the more interesting and ornately detailed 16th-century buildings in town are the **Hoppenerhaus** (Rundestr., at Poststr.); the **Löwenapotheke,** an old pharmacy on Stechbahn; and the Weser-Renaissance **Rathaus,** with its 14th-century pub. You can view the Baroque interior of the **Stadtkirche** (open Tues.–Sat. 9–12:30 and 3–6; Sun. 9–2) gratis; DM 2 lets you climb the 234 steps to the tower for a great view. The 250-year-old **synagogue** (Im Kreise 24; open Tues.–Thurs. 3–5, Fri. 9–11, Sun. 11–1) is one of Germany's oldest; the interior decoration was destroyed on Kristallnacht, but the building escaped being burned and the rabbi saved the Torah (ask to see it). Pack a picnic and stroll over to the **Französischer Garten** (French Garden)—green, manicured, and very French.

At the end of Stechbahn and across Schloßplatz is . . . you guessed it: the **Schloß.** Check out its Renaissance period rooms, which display an older style than most castles and residences in the region; this

Schloß is the real thing—no reconstruction necessary. Hourly tours leave Tuesday–Sunday 10–4 and cost DM 5, DM 2.50 students. For more noble-type fun, head across the Fuhse River on Spörckenstraße to the **Niedersächsisches Landgestüt** (Stud Farm), where 200 superb stallions live to propagate their oh-so-expensive genes. The studs are shown at the popular **Hengstparade** (Stallion Parade) in late September and October. Tickets must be bought months in advance, but the stables are open to the public mid-July–mid-February (weekdays 8:30–11:30 and 3–4:30, Sat. 8:30–11:30).

NEAR CELLE

BERGEN-BELSEN

The site of the Bergen-Belsen concentration camp, about 25 km northwest of Celle, is a disturbing reminder of incomprehensible inhumanity set in the middle of Lower Saxon normalcy. The Nazis first used the camp as an *Aufenthaltslager* (holding camp) for Jews they then ransomed to Switzerland and Allied nations in exchange for German POWs. In the last year of the war, Bergen-Belsen became an all-out death camp. The Nazis brought prisoners from Auschwitz and other camps on both fronts to Bergen-Belsen and starved them to death; many inmates were killed by disease caused by the overcrowding. Even as the camp was liberated in April 1945, Nazi troops tried to hide the horror, forcing emaciated prisoners to deposit the dead in mass graves. British troops burned the barracks after liberation out of fear of a typhus outbreak, but documented on film what they saw; clips from this film are shown a few times a day inside the museum, which has a display chronicling the history of Bergen-Belsen and the Holocaust. The camp can be visited daily 9 AM–6 PM. From Celle, take Bus 2 from the Bahnhof to Bergen-Celler Straße, and change to Bus 9 to Gedenkstätte.

The Nazis created such barbarous conditions that 100,000 (primarily female) victims of Bergen-Belsen died only months before the war's end. One of the victims was 15-year-old Anne Frank.

BREMEN

In the Brothers' Grimm version of the famous fairy tale, the Bremen musicians never actually make it to Bremen: With their raucous music, the donkey, dog, cat, and rooster scare a band of thieves from their forest hideout and decide to stay there instead. Once a Hanseatic League leader, Bremen carries a thousand-year legacy of successful mercantile trade and industry—seen today in major names like Beck's beer and Eduscho coffee—but this modern city isn't all steel and glass. Bremen boasts not only one of the stateliest market squares in Germany, but also great neighborhoods perfect for lazy exploration or a long *Kaffeeklatsch.* The Schnoor quarter's medieval roofs shelter artisans' shops and excellent restaurants, stores peep out from art nouveau brick whimsies on Böttcherstraße, and Vor dem Steintor is as close as a German street gets to Haight-Ashbury.

BASICS

AMERICAN EXPRESS

Come to change money, pick up mail, and get advice on discos. *Am Wall 138, tel. 0421/14171. Open weekdays 9–5:30, Sat. 9–noon.*

CHANGING MONEY

Change money at the **post office** next to the train station. An **ATM** in the station accepts bank and credit cards.

DISCOUNT TRAVEL AGENCIES

Hapag-Lloyd Reisebüro (travel agency) has discount airline and train tickets. *Bahnhofspl. 17, next to Hauptbahnhof, tel. 0421/350065. Open weekdays 9:15–6, Sat. 9:30–12:30.*

ENGLISH BOOKS

Germany's answer to Barnes and Noble, the two-story **Strom** bookstore comes complete with reading tables and ceiling-high shelves. English-language books are in back on the ground floor. *Langenstr. 10, off Marktpl., tel. 0421/321523.*

MAIL AND PHONES

The **post office,** to the left of the Bahnhof, has a do-it-yourself fax, plenty of phones, poste restante service (postal code 28195), and competitive exchange rates. *An der Weide, at Löningstr. Open weekdays 8–6, Sat. 9–1, Sun. 9 AM–10 AM.*

VISITOR INFORMATION

The large, friendly **tourist office** has an extensive range of maps and brochures, as well as *Lokal Spezial,* a great free guide to hotels, restaurants, and clubs. They also book hotel rooms free of charge. *Hillmannpl. 6, at Bahnhofpl., tel. 0421/308000, fax 0421/308–0030. Open weekdays 9:30–6:30 (Thurs.–Fri. until 8), Sat. 9:30–4, Sun. 9:30–4.*

RESOURCES FOR GAYS AND LESBIANS • The best place to get a handle on the scene is Café Homolulu (*see* After Dark, *below*). Call **Rat und Tat Zentrum** (Theodor-Körner-Str. 1, tel. 0421/704170), in the Ostertor district, on weekdays for info on gay and lesbian services and events and a list of counseling services.

COMING AND GOING

BY TRAIN

Bremen's neoclassical **Hauptbahnhof,** just north of the city center, is one of those great European train stations that will make you want to arrange a romantic reunion or parting on its premises. Trains leave every hour for Bremerhaven (1 hr, DM 16.20), Göttingen (2 hrs, DM 85), Hamburg (1 hr, DM 39), and Hanover (1 hr, DM 47), and several times a day to Cologne (3 hrs, DM 97). The station is open 24 hours and has an **info office** (open daily 5:50 AM–10 PM) and lockers. Buses to nearby towns like Worpswede (every 2 hrs, 50 min, DM 5) leave from in front of the Hauptbahnhof.

BY FERRY

Schreiber Reederei ferries (Schlachte 2, tel. 0421/321229) sail for Bremerhaven (3½ hrs, DM 22) from the dock at the end of Böttcherstraße. **Harbor tours** (DM 13, DM 9.50 students) are available two or three times a day March–September.

BY MITFAHRGELEGENHEIT

Bremen's **Mitfahrbüro** (Körnerwall 1, off Sielwall, tel. 0421/19440), open weekdays 10–6, weekends 10–2, lists rides and runs a student-oriented travel agency.

GETTING AROUND

Bremen centers on the Weser, with everything of interest just north of the river. The Schnoor district is just southeast of the Altstadt, and Ostertor is a stone's throw to the east. The tram and bus lines are confusing, but most pass by the Bahnhof or the **Domsheide,** a plaza between the cathedral and the river. Buy DM 3.30 tickets, good for one hour of travel within the city center, from the driver. **Bremen Kärtchen** (DM 10) all-inclusive passes are available at the booth outside the Bahnhof. **For extensive sightseeing, buy the TouristCard** (DM 9.50 for 1 day for two adults, DM 19.50 for 2 days, DM 26 for 3 days), which offers reductions to the bigger museums and theaters as well as unlimited free travel on public transit. Find it at the tourist office and the Bahnhof. For a **taxi,** call 0421/14141 or 0421/14014. Bremen is a very bikeable city: **Fahrrad Station** (open Mon. and Wed.–Fri. 10–5; Jun.–Sept., also weekends 10–noon), to the left of the Bahnhof, rents one-speeds for DM 15 per day, DM 35 for 3 days; deposit is DM 50. To reach the Markt from the station, walk south down Bahnhofstraße and Herdentor onto pedestrian-only Sögestraße.

WHERE TO SLEEP

Strained welcomes, few vacancies, and steep prices mark the Bremen hotel scene—call a day or two ahead. If you're stuck, try the hostel in Worpswede (*see* Near Bremen, *below*), an hour's bus ride north.

The **Mitwohnzentrale Rolf Poppe** (Humboldtstr. 28, tel. 0421/19445) can help you find private rooms for a DM 5 membership fee plus 28% of one night's rent; call in advance to arrange even a one-night stay. One warning: Women should be wary walking alone in the central Ostertor district at night, especially on side streets.

OSTERTOR DISTRICT

Pension Garni Weidmann. There are only five rooms in this small and friendly pension, but it has just about the most luxurious bath you'll find (of course, you do have to share). The rooms even have TVs. Rates are DM 50 per person (DM 40 excluding breakfast). *Am Schwarzen Meer 35, tel. 0421/498–4455. Tram 2 or 3 (from Markt), or Tram 10 (from Bahnhof) to St.-Jürgen-Str., then straight ahead.*

Pension Kosch. This pension offers neat, wood-paneled rooms on a quiet side street near the river. Singles cost DM 50, doubles DM 75–DM 100. Reception hours are sporadic, so call ahead. *Celler Str. 4, tel. 0421/447101. Tram 2 or 3 (from Markt), or Tram 10 (from Bahnhof); to St.-Jürgen-Str., then right on Lüneburger Str., left on Celler Str. 7 rooms, none with bath.*

SOUTH OF THE WESER

Gästehaus Walter. An officious staff manages this frequently full hotel. Basic singles cost DM 45, doubles DM 75, breakfast included. An extra DM 30–DM 40 gets you a larger pad with TV, phone, shower, and toilet. *Buntentorsteinw. 86, tel. 0421/558027. Across Wilhelm-Kaisen bridge and left on Buntentorsteinw.; or Tram 1 to Rotes-Kreuz Krankenhaus. 12 rooms. Reservations strongly advised.*

Hotel Enzenspenger. Small, lace-curtained rooms, usually filled by travelers who've reserved in advance, perch above a restaurant near the river. Singles start at DM 45, doubles at DM 70, including breakfast; add DM 5–DM 13 for private showers. Check in at the downstairs bar. *Brautstr. 9, tel. 0421/503224. Across Wilhelm-Kaisen bridge, right on Osterstr., right on Brautstr. 10 rooms. No credit cards.*

Bremen, along with its deep-water harbor at Bremerhaven, is the smallest Land (state) in Germany. Its government, one of the most liberal in the country, lends to the city's open, alternative atmosphere.

Hotel-Pension Haus Neustadt. Institutional singles start at DM 55–DM 89, doubles DM 95–DM 110, including breakfast. Bathrooms are in the corridor. The hotel is a 25-min walk from the station. *Graudenzer Str. 33, tel. 0421/551749, fax 0421/553294. Across Wilhelm-Kaisen bridge, left on Kornstr., right on Graudenzer Str. 14 rooms. Reception closed Sun. noon–8.*

HOSTELS

Freizeit-und Tagesstätte "Haus Hugel." To get one of the 26 rooms in this hostel, you'll have to head out of town, to Bremen North. A single room will cost you DM 27–DM 69, a double DM 46–DM 96. Renovations will bring showers, TVs, and new furnishings to rooms by April 2000. *Auf dem Krümpel 95, tel. 0421/623311, fax 0421/623342. Take 20-min local train ride (direction: Schönebeck) from Hauptbahnhof, then a 15-min walk to the hostel.*

Jugendgästehaus Bremen (HI). The hostel is the cheapest and most central (though not the most peaceful) of Bremen's lodging options. Beer lovers will swoon over the view of the Beck's brewery across the river; for others, the heavy brewery smell may need some getting used to. The hip young staff does sell bottles in the cafeteria for DM 1.50. Best of all, it's a painless 20-min walk from the train station. One of the 172 beds, including breakfast, costs DM 29–DM 34 (DM 44 over 27). *Kalkstr. 6, tel. 0421/171369, fax 0421/171102. From Hauptbahnhof, straight down Bahnhofstr. to Herdentorsteinw., right on Am Wall, left on Bürgermeister-Schmidt-Str., right along riverbank; or Tram 6 or Bus 26 to Am Brill and follow riverbank to right. No curfew. Reception open noon–10. Luggage storage.*

CAMPING

Campingplatz Bremen. This distant campground snuggles into a bend in a canal. Sites are DM 7.50 per person and DM 16 per tent. *Am Stadtwaldsee 1, tel. 0421/212002, fax 0421/212002. Tram 5 to Kulenkampfallee, then Bus 22 or 23 to Munte; continue down Kuhgrabenw., left on Hochschulring.*

FOOD

Markets brighten up the cathedral area on Tuesday and Saturday until 2 PM, and cheap international cuisine is available in **Ostertor.** If you're willing to shell out DM 50 for a fantastic meal in an intensely romantic atmosphere, stroll through the Schnoor quarter after dark and pick a likely spot. Head to **Katzencafé** (Schnoor 38, tel. 0421/326621) for fish specialties and dining on the huge, secluded patio. With one of the largest wine cellars in Germany, the pricey and historic **Bremer Ratskeller** (Am Markt, tel. 0421/321676) has a special menu of light fare to go along with your vino.

Engel. This stylish café-restaurant-bar in the heart of Ostertor serves high-quality fare in the DM 13–DM 19 range. Excellent lunch deals will fill your tummy for about DM 12. *Ostertorsteinw. 31–33, tel. 0421/76615.*

Kleiner Ratskeller. Subdued lights, dark green tables, and the hubbub of old friends catching up on all the news—a true Ratskeller experience. The traditional German menu changes daily, but bratwurst and beef goulash are sure to appear. Most dishes cost DM 9.50–DM 15. *Hinter dem Schütting 11, near Böttcherstr. entrance, tel. 0421/326168. Closed Sun.*

Schröter's. Spoil yourself at this Schnoor restaurant, favored by tourists and locals alike for its "new" German cuisine and excellent fish dishes. Entrées run DM 16–DM 35. *Schnoor 13, tel. 0421/326677.*

CAFÉS

Bremen has a lively café scene that centers around Ostertor and the Altstadt. **Café Knigge** (Sögestr. 42–44, tel. 0421/13068) purveys generous slices of various cakes and tortes—it's the traditional favorite for *Kaffee und Kuchen.* **Café Tölke** (Am Landherrnamt 1, tel. 0421/324330), a Viennese-style coffee house in the Schnoor quarter, is elegant in a down-at-the-heels sort of way. Cognac and coffee is only one of the 17 caffeinated concoctions at **Wall Café** (Am Wall 164, off Herdentorsteinweg, tel. 0421/324878), an artsy hangout for Bremen's young intellectuals.

WORTH SEEING

Touring Bremen is largely a matter of soaking up the atmosphere of various neighborhoods, notably the **Schnoorviertel,** a cobblestone patchwork of narrow lanes and steep-roofed medieval dwellings. Originally the haunt of fishermen and tradespeople, the quarter now boasts a wealth of enticing restaurants and artisan shops that make for entertaining (and labyrinthine) strolls. The tourist office gives two-hour English **tours** of the Schnoor and city center for DM 9. Bremen's excellent modern-art **Kunsthalle** (Am Wall 207, tel. 0421/329080) is open daily Wed.–Sun. 10–6 (Tues. until 9); admission is DM 8, students DM 4.

BÖTTCHERSTRASSE

In the 1920s, local coffee nabob Ludwig Roselius transformed this short, narrow alley south of the Marktplatz—originally a barrel makers' street—into a jumble of playful brick constructions, now occupied by shops and galleries. The 14th-century edifice at No. 6, renamed the **Roselius Haus,** holds a small museum of art. The DM 8 entrance fee (DM 4 students) also lets you see the adjacent exhibition of works by Worpswede artist Paula Modersohn-Becker. Both galleries are open Tuesday–Sunday 11–6.

MARKTPLATZ

This is one of the most impressive market squares in Europe, bordered by the imposing 900-year-old Rathaus, a 16th-century guild hall, and a modern glass-and-steel parliament building. The ancient **Rathaus** is worth checking out for its opulent interior; various artists, including Worpswede big shot Heinrich Vogeler, have worked on it intermittently since the 15th century. You can tour the building weekdays at 11, noon, 3, and 4 (also Sunday at 11 and noon) for DM 5 (DM 2.50 students). At the northwest corner of the Rathaus stands Gerhard Marck's bronze statue of the **Bremer Stadtmusikanten** (Musicians of Bremen). Also on the square stands the famous stone statue of **Roland,** erected in 1400. Three times larger than life, the statue serves as Bremen's good-luck piece and symbol of freedom. Legend says that if the statue is knocked down, Bremen will lose its independence.

Ogle the great doors before entering the ocher-, sandstone-, and slate-colored interior of **St. Petri Dom**; inside, a museum (admission DM 3, DM 2 students) exhibits flotsam and jetsam from the church's past. In the southeast corner, the **Bleikeller** (lead cellar; admission DM 2) morbidly displays a set of blackened, though well-preserved, corpses, buried here and then mummified by the mysterious gases in the vault. Pick up the "Kirchenmusik" brochure at the tourist office for listings of roof-rattling pipe organ concerts. *Dom open weekdays 10–5 (Nov.–Apr. 11–4), Sat. 10–1, Sun. 2–5.*

OSTERTOR

This colorful street wails a distinctly alternative tune to the Altstadt's more sedate melodies. Litter-filled sidewalks lead past innumerable cafés, student snack places, and clothing stores specializing in leather.

Browse through the bookstores across from Engel (*see* Food, *above*) for the best selection of gay literature. For info on Bremen's political underground, cross to Post Straße and check out **BBA Buch- und Infoladen** (tel. 0421/700144; open Mon., Wed., Fri. 4–7). This neighborhood really lights up at night, though the side streets can get a bit dicey, especially skanky, prostitute-lined, men-only Helenenstraße.

AFTER DARK

Bremen's **Ostertorsteinweg** is packed with pub-hopping partyers. Join the crowd, or pick up *Mix,* a free monthly with exhaustive lists of theater, film, music, and literary events, at the tourist office. Unless you're planning to move here, you won't need the monthly *Bremer* (DM 4.50 at newsstands), a very detailed resource.

Ostertor and the area just to the northeast form the center of Bremen's gay nightlife. **Café Homolulu** (Theodor-Körner-Str. 1, off Ostertorsteinw., tel. 0421/700007), closed Thursday and Monday, is a popular gay and lesbian café with a mellow neighborhood atmosphere. The most popular gay disco, **Tom's** (Außer der Schliefmühle 49, tel. 0421/323534), opens Wednesday and Friday–Sunday at 10:30 PM and charges a DM 8 cover.

An older crowd frequents **Theater im Schnoor** (Wüste Stätte 11, tel. 0421/326054) for cabaret and underground theater. In the same building, **Theatrium** (tel. 0421/326813) is a puppet theater that does productions ranging from *Dr. Faustus* to Woody Allen. If your German is good, check out the outstanding productions of the Bremer Shakespeare Company at **Theater am Leibnitzplatz** (Friedrich-Ebert-Str., at Leibnitzpl., tel. 0421/500333). Tickets are DM 25; get DM 15 student tickets at the box office or tourist office.

BARS AND CLUBS

Achims Beck Haus. Things at Achims Beck Haus are pretty simple: Sit at a table and drink. The younger crowd here doesn't get going until late, but once it does, it's unstoppable. *Carl-Ronning-Str. 1, just east of Sögestr., tel. 0421/15555. Open weekdays 10 AM–11 PM, Fri. and Sat. until 1 AM.*

Delight. The dancing venue for Bremen's young and beautiful is conveniently located in the city center, "six feet under" the Liebfrauenkirchhof. The music is great (hip-hop, house), despite some ill-conceived party-night themes. *Am Liebfrauenkirchhof 23, tel. 0421/328622. Cover: DM 10. Open Thurs. from 10 PM, Fri. and Sat. from 11 PM until the wee hours.*

Modernes. This multipurpose hangout has second-run movies (DM 8–DM 12) during the week, and rock concerts on Friday. On Saturday come for DJ dancing—the DM 8 cover gets you two drinks and all the reggae, hip-hop, or techno you could ever want. *Neustadtwall 28, south of Weser, tel. 0421/505553. Cross Wilhelm-Kaisen bridge to Friedrich-Ebert-Str., turn right on Neustadtwall.*

Schüttinger Brauerei. Bremen's oldest microbrewery, tucked away off Böttcherstraße, has a cavernous drinking room, bar grub, and heavy German stuff to accompany your beer. Choose your poison. *Hinter dem Schütting 13. Open Mon.–Thurs. until 1 AM, Fri. and Sat. until 2 AM, Sun. until 11 PM.*

NEAR BREMEN

BREMERHAVEN

Built as Bremen's deep-water harbor when the Weser started to silt up in the 19th century, Bremerhaven's industrial docks handle cargo from around the world. (One of the main imports, apparently, is tourists.) The **Deutsches Schifffahrtsmuseum** (German Maritime Museum) explores every facet of humanity's relationship with the sea. The museum is jammed with models and figureheads, but the best part is the pool full of drive-it-yourself model ships. Admission includes access to the real ships moored outside. *Van-Ronzelen-Str., tel. 0471/482070. Admission: DM 6, DM 2.50 students. Book ahead for tours in English. Open Tues.–Sun. 10–6.*

Moored nearby is the claustrophobic *Wilhelm-Bauer,* a World War II U-boat (admission DM 3, DM 2 students). If you thought youth hostel dorms were cramped, check out the berths here. In the building marked STRANDHALLE is the **Zoo am Meer** (Weserdeich, tel. 0471/42071), literally "zoo by the sea"—another way of saying "aquarium." Admission is DM 4, DM 2 students, and it's open daily 8–4:30, until 6:30 in summer.

BASICS • Bremerhaven's two **tourist offices** lie within 200 m of each other; both have brochures and will find you a room. The more accessible (and busier) tourist office (tel. 0471/43000) is on the top floor of the Columbus Center, a shopping center near the Schifffahrtsmuseum, and is open weekdays 9:30–

6 (Thurs. and Fri. until 8), Sat. 9:30–4; the Verkehrsamt (Van-Ronzelen-Str. 2, tel. 0471/42095, open Mon–Wed. 8–4:30, until 4 on Thurs. and 3:30 on Fri.) is just south of the museum. From the Bahnhof, take Bus 2, 5, 6, 8, or 9 to Theodor-Heuss-Platz, or walk 25 min down Friedrich-Ebert-Straße (it curves left and then crosses a bridge) and make for the unsightly blue-and-white high-rises.

COMING AND GOING • Trains leave every hour for Bremen (1 hr, DM 16.20). **Ferries** sail to Bremen (3½ hrs, DM 20 one-way, DM 32 round-trip) on Wednesday, Thursday, and Saturday mid-May–early September. You can also catch the daily ferry to Helgoland (4 hrs, DM 55; *see* Friesland and East Frisian Islands, *below*). The ferry terminal is at the Strandhalle, by the aquarium.

WHERE TO SLEEP • Call ahead before taking Bus 2, 6, or 9 (DM 3.20) from the train station to Gesundheitsamt and the town's **HI-Jugendgästehaus** (Gaußstr. 54–56, at Eckernfeldstr., tel. 0471/590-2533), a big place with beds for DM 25 (DM 30 over 27). **Hotel Elbinger Platz** (Georgstr. 2–4, tel. 0471/21640) offers centrally located singles at DM 40–DM 50, doubles DM 65–DM 80.

WORPSWEDE

Tiny Worpswede offers a forested, tranquil landscape, complete with thatched-roof houses and secluded pathways—an hour here is enough to send anyone into moments of artistic introspection. The town has been a big artists' colony ever since an extraordinary group of late-19th-century artists established a commune here. They came to paint powerful, reflective landscapes and peasant portraits—colorful, sometimes dreamlike, sometimes harshly realistic. The group was led by Heinrich Vogeler and Otto Modersohn (Modersohn's wife, Paula Modersohn-Becker, wasn't acknowledged as the group's real genius until after her death). The **Große Kunstschau** (Lindenallee 1–3, tel. 04792/1302; open daily 10–6) has Modersohn-Becker's portraits of peasants and local girls, as well as a range of Vogeler's stuff. The postcard counter, over 300 cards strong, is astounding. Admission is DM 5, DM 3 students. Follow the signs past thatched-roof farmhouses and sun-dappled folds of forest to Heinrich Vogeler's old house, **Barkenhoff** (Ostendorfer Str. 10, tel. 04792/3968; open daily 10–6), which contains the former owner's works. Poet Rainer Maria Rilke, who hung with the Worpswede group, visited here often. Admission is DM 3, DM 2 students. After their divorce, Heinrich's wife Martha lived in the nearby brick-and-timber **Haus im Schluh** (Im Schluh 35–37, tel. 04792/7160; open daily 2–6). For DM 4 you can see more of Heinrich's works, plus the joyful *Lovelife in Nature,* painted by the entire original group. Martha's daughter lives here now and runs a pension with singles for DM 45–DM 70, doubles for DM 80.

BASICS • If Worpswede enchants you (moors are always enchanting), ask at the **tourist office** (Verkehrsamt; Bergstr. 13, tel. 04792/1477) for info about outdoor activities in town. It has excellent English-language brochures, and is open weekdays 9:30–12:30 and 2:30–5 (also Sat. 10–2 in summer). To reach Worpswede, take Bus 140 (45 min, DM 5), which leaves almost every hour from Bremen's Bahnhof, to the Worpswede-Insel stop in the center of town. The info office is 30 m back and up the hill.

WHERE TO SLEEP AND EAT • On the bus from Bremen, ask to stop at the **HI-Jugendherberge** (Hammew. 2, at Findorffstr., tel. 04792/1360), a sloped-roof affair overlooking fields of corn. The rambunctious owner opens the reception desk sporadically 8–12:30 and 3–4:45, and again 9:45–10, when curfew strikes. Beds are DM 21 (DM 34 over 26), breakfast included. **Café Central** (Bergstr. 11, tel. 04792/7085) is known as the local youth-and-artist watering hole and is a great place to spend a quiet afternoon. Stock up at the **Spar** supermarket (Osterweder Str., at Sophie-Bötjer-Weg).

FRIESLAND AND EAST FRISIAN ISLANDS

Jutting out into the North Sea near the Netherlands, Ostfriesland is a windy and flat peninsula where the weather can be rather dreary. If you thrive on wind, an occasional shower, and the sea, splash on up without delay. The long, narrow islands that lie off the coast are famous for their long sandy beaches, which provide beauty and isolation, at least off-season. The islands' southern coasts bog down in gluey *Watten* (mud flats), notable for their therapeutic effect on those who dare traverse them barefoot. Don't try it alone—the Watten can be extremely dangerous; stick to one of the trail-blazing *Wattführer,* who lead tours, giving detailed lessons on the clams, worms, and other critters that inhabit the mud.

Just as they determinedly reclaimed much of the land they live on from the sea, Frisians have managed to hold on to their own culture, which includes a strong maritime bent and the whispery *Plattdeutsch.* East Frisians also delight in their idiosyncratic and massive tea consumption. Local blends, brewed strong, are poured over *Klöntjes* (big sugar crystals) and drunk unstirred.

BASICS

Most tourist offices in the region only have ferry schedules to nearby islands, but the helpful folks at Norddeich's **Kurverwaltung** (Dörper Weg 22, tel. 04931/98602) have thick pamphlets (DM 1 apiece) on every island. Train station staffs can tell you about connecting ferries, and the stations in Oldenburg, Wilhelmshaven, and Norden have ferry and bus schedules for all islands. For general info about the region, contact the **National Park administration** (tel. 0421/408288) in Wilhelmshaven.

COMING AND GOING

You have little choice but to come via **Oldenburg,** accessible by hourly trains from Bremen (2 hrs, DM 12). From Oldenburg, Germany's local and regional trains push north through Emden to Norden and Norddeich for the western islands, through Sande to Esens for the eastern islands. If you decide to stay in Oldenburg, **Hotel Hegeler** (Donnerschweerstr. 27, tel. 0441/87561) offers clean, quiet singles from DM 50, doubles from DM 70. Oldenburg's friendly **HI-Jugendherberge** (Alexanderstr. 65, tel. 0441/87135) opens its doors at 5 PM and closes them at 11:30. Beds are DM 23.20 (DM 28.20 over 27). No credit cards.

Along the coast, the **Bäderbus** connects Norden and Esens to the eastern harbor towns of Bensersiel, Neuharlingersiel, and Harlesiel for DM 4–DM 10. Ferries cruise over to the islands from the mainland at different times every day. Ferry departure times may appear erratic; timetables change every day because ships have to time their trips for the high tide in order to pass through the channels in the Watten. Most ferries offer *Tagesrückfahrkarten* (one-day excursion passes) that are cheaper than regular round-trip tickets. Rail passes will get you nothing in the way of discounts or perks.

WHERE TO SLEEP

Norddeich and the islands are inundated with German tourists May–November, and the few empty beds are expensive. The islands' tourist offices arrange private rooms, but in high season they tend to require a three-night minimum stay. If you're just there for a night during peak season, you may have difficulties finding affordable accommodations. Always call to make arrangements before planning to spend a night on any island. You can also expect to pay the daily DM 3 **Kurtax** between March and October to walk on the beaches. Many of the region's excellent hostels also have camping spots on the grounds, but guests are *required* to call ahead. Full board is usually obligatory in hostels, and all island hostels close November–February.

WESTERN ISLANDS

The popular western islands are best reached from the tiny mainland towns of **Norden** and **Norddeich.** Just off the coast, Norden is itself worth a visit for its unique tree-filled Marktplatz, home to the brick Ludgerikirche and the ineffectual **tourist office** (Verkehrsbüro; tel. 04931/172201), which has bus and ferry schedules but little else. Norden's pretty, funky **Hotel zur Post** (Am Markt 3, tel. 04931/2787; no credit cards) has beds for DM 40–DM 45 per person and live jazz in the downstairs bar. As a second option, **Hotel Müller** (Uffenstr. 9, tel. 04931/2008; no credit cards) offers rooms with private bath for DM 45–DM 50 per person. The **Bäderbus** leaves from Norden's Bahnhof.

The ferry port for the popular islands of Juist and Norderney is nearby Norddeich, a characterless town full of brick, bunkerlike buildings—don't stay here for atmosphere. Ferries run by **Reederei Norden-Frisia** (tel. 04931/9870) leave from across the Norddeich-Mole train station, a few hundred meters past Norddeich's main stop. The town's **tourist office** (Kurverwaltung, Dörper Weg 22, off Badestr., tel. 04931/98602) is only open Monday–Thursday until 4:30 (Fri. and Sat. until 4), but they have stacks of facts about all the islands. Norddeich's small **HI-Jugendherberge** (Strandstr. 1, tel. 04931/8064; reception open 5 PM–8 PM) has beds for DM 19.10 (DM 23.10 over 26) and tent spots out back for DM 14.50. Head west from the main station on Badestraße and turn left at the signs on Strandstraße. A few doors down, **Hotel-Restaurant Seeblick** (Badestr. 11, tel. 04931/8086; no credit cards) has rooms for DM 35 a head. Local specialties at the adjoining restaurant start at DM 8.50.

NORDERNEY

This glitzy resort packs several casinos, a sizable shopping district, and a handful of bars and discos into its limited space. Head east to Norderney's nature preserve to see the less commercial side of the island. Buses connect the harbor with the town and the eastern part of the island, but bikes are definitely the most popular form of transport; they're also an easy way to reach the beautiful nude beaches in the east. **Fahrrad Verleih** (tel. 04932/1326), up Hafenstraße from the harbor, rents bikes for DM 10 per day, DM 6 per half day. For mud rather than sand, take a tour of the **Watten,** the tidal region that teems with birds and marine life. Tour schedules are available at the National Park Center at the docks, or at the information office.

COMING AND GOING • Ferries leave Norddeich hourly between 7 AM and 6 PM, later in summer. Round-trip tickets are DM 22.50, plus DM 10 per bike. The private ferry MS *Wappen von Norderney* sails from Norderney to a different island each day; these trips are one-day excursions—you pay round-trip fare. For info contact **Reederei Cassen Eils** (Marienstr. 20, tel. 04932/2802).

WHERE TO SLEEP • The **Verkehrsbüro/Zimmervermittlung** (Bülowallee 5, tel. 04932/91850) finds rooms for a DM 7.50 fee weekdays 9–12:30 and 2:30–6, Saturday 10–12:30. The closest **HI-Jugendherberge** (tel. 04932/2451) is at Südstraße 1; from the harbor, go right on Deichstraße, then left on Südstraße. You pay DM 22.20 (DM 25.70 over 26) for the first night, DM 31.90 (DM 35.40 over 26) after that, all meals included. Reception is open daily 5:15 PM–7 PM. The "other" **HI-Jugendherberge** (Am Dünensender 3, tel. 04932/2574) is an hour-long walk east on Karl-Rieger-Weg (look for a low building entirely hidden by wind-sculpted trees), or take the eastbound bus from the dock or rent a bike. Campsites are DM 11 a head; beds cost DM 19.20 (DM 23.20 over 26).

JUIST

Juist (pronounced "youst") is occasionally overcrowded, but its ban on cars and its large nature preserves give it more of a natural, isolated feel than its cosmopolitan eastern neighbor. Juist is also harder to reach due to less frequent ferry service. The north coast is one uninterrupted 17-km-long beach, and all the gabled brick houses with white trim create a sedate, maritime mood. Don't just stay in town, though; escape to the low, wind-raked preserves at the west end. Bike-rental places dot the ferry port, with bikes for DM 2–DM 3 per hour, DM 10 per day. Rides in horse-drawn carriages, the primary means of cargo transport on this carless island, start at DM 7 per head.

Because it draws in a multitude of vacationing Germans, Juist offers few budget options. The **Kurverwaltung** (Friesenstr., at Warmbad Str., tel. 04935/809222) can find you space in a pension for DM 40 and up. They're open weekdays 8:30–noon and 3–5, Saturday 9–11. You can also try for one of the 350 coveted beds at the **HI-Jugendherberge** (Loogster Pad 20, tel. 04935/1094). The obligatory full-board deal costs DM 28.50 (DM 31.20 over 26). From the harbor it's a half-hour trek inland and then left along Billstraße, at the northern foot of the dike.

COMING AND GOING • One or two ferries leave daily from Norddeich (1 hr 25 min, DM 30). Check the schedules carefully, since you get a one-day excursion ticket that, depending on the ferry, may limit you to four hours on the island. Avoid this pitfall with a round-trip, four-day ticket (DM 40) or an open-ended round-trip ticket (DM 42). Either way, it costs DM 16 to transport bikes.

BALTRUM

Baltrum, the smallest island, is extremely nature-conscious. Cars are forbidden, and even bikes are discouraged. Baltrum's beaches and fine nature preserve make a great day trip, but it could get boring pretty quickly—you can walk all the way around the island in three hours. There's no youth hostel, and you need permission from the **Kurverwaltung** (tel. 04939/800) before heading to the campground. Synchronized relays of buses and ferries take you from Norden's Bahnhof to the coastal town of Neßmersiel, then across the waves to Baltrum; call 04939/91300 for info. Round-trip tickets cost DM 38, one-day excursion tickets DM 26. Three boats run in the summer, but if you take the last boat out, you're spending the night.

EASTERN ISLANDS

It's more difficult to get to the eastern than western islands, but you're rewarded for your efforts with smaller crowds and unspoiled nature. Boats to each island leave from different ferry ports, all of which can be reached by regular bus or the Bäderbus from Norden. The Bäderbus also stops in the tiny town of

Esens, worth a stop for its unique sights. The tiny **August-Gottschalk Haus** (Burgstr. 8, tel. 04971/2101), dedicated to Jewish culture, is open Tuesday, Thursday, and Sunday 3–6, Saturday 10–noon. The groovy **Holarium** (Kirchpl., tel. 04971/4392; admission DM 3.50), dedicated to (what else?) holograms, is open daily 10–noon and 2–6. Esens is connected by train to Oldenburg (10 per day, via Sande, DM 18).

Esens's **tourist office** (Kirchpl., tel. 04971/91511) will find you a room free of charge and help you with ferry schedules and island info. Stop in weekdays 8:30–1 and 2–5, Saturday 9–12:30. It's a 25-min walk to the very large, very modern **HI-Jugendherberge** (Grashauser Flage 2, tel. 04971/3717): From the Bahnhof, go west on Bahnhofstraße, veer left onto Siebert-Attena-Straße, then left on Bensersiel Straße. Beds here cost DM 25.30. The reception is open 5 PM–9:45 PM.

LANGEOOG

Germans love Langeoog (the name means "long island") because it affords them guaranteed *Ruhe und Erholung* (peace and relaxation). Endless, shell-laden beaches stretch along the north coast, allowing limitless frolicking when the sun is out. Rolling dunes temper the fierce winds and separate the North Sea from pasture and grazing land. Though touristed (there's even a train from the harbor that covers the mile to town), the island feels more like a nature preserve than a resort. Eight ferries a day (3 per day off-season, 45 min) travel to Langeoog from Bensersiel; tickets are DM 34 round-trip, DM 31 for a round-trip good for four days, and DM 30 for a one-day excursion pass.

To get an idea of how different Juist and Norderney are, look out across the sea from Norddeich. Juist is the green and sandy isle to the left, Norderney is the one with the high-rise buildings on the right.

Since Langeoog's **tourist office** (Hauptstr. 28, tel. 04972/6930) is far from useful, head straight to the helpful staff at the **Zimmervermittlung** (Fährhusw. 7, tel. 04972/69392; open weekdays 9–7, Sat. 10–7, Sun. 10–noon and 3–7) near the Bahnhof for maps and island advice. They'll find you a room in a pension for under DM 35 per person, or check their short list of affordable pensions that take one-night guests. The **HI-Jugendherberge** (Domäne Melkhörn, tel. 04972/276; closed Nov.–mid-Apr.), an old farmhouse settled amid the dunes, is a solid hour out of town; obligatory room-and-board jacks up the price to DM 33.25 (DM 37.75 over 26). Youth groups monopolize the place: Reserve a week to two months in advance, or, in a pinch, brave the wind in the adjacent campground for DM 28 a head. Bike-rental shops dot the island, with rentals starting around DM 2 per hour, DM 9 per day.

SPIEKEROOG

Spiekeroog, the least developed of the islands, flaunts its isolation and considerable backwardness. Come for peace and quiet, and nothing else. Spiekeroog can be reached twice daily (sometimes thrice daily) via ferry from Neuharlingersiel. You'll pay DM 36 for a round-trip ticket, DM 28 for a one-day excursion pass. The **tourist office** (Noorderpad 25, tel. 04976/170) can help in finding private rooms on the island. The office is open weekdays 9–noon and 2–4, Saturday 9–noon (closed Fri. and Sat. off-season). Spiekeroog's 55-bed **HI-Jugendherberge** (Bid' Utkiek 1, tel. 04976/329) lies near the town center. Room and board cost DM 40.

WANGEROOGE

In addition to the usual island goodies—endless grassy dunes, scads of birds and other animals, and a nude beach—little Wangerooge adds a small train and a lighthouse. The **tourist office** (tel. 04469/375) kicks back on the Strandpromenade. The **Westturm,** an old stone tower, houses the remarkable **HI-Jugendherberge** (tel. 04469/439; closed Oct.–Apr.). Full room-and-board runs DM 34, though you can pay DM 18.50 (DM 22.50 over 26) for simple bed-and-breakfast service. The views from the hostel tower are great, but don't compare with those from the nearby lighthouse. A small train chugs ferry passengers into the main village from the harbor, but if you're hostel-bound, it's easier to walk. To reach Wangerooge, take the bus from Norden, Esens, or Sande to Harlesiel; from here you catch one of two daily ferries to Wangerooge (DM 45 round-trip).

HELGOLAND

Helgoland's strategic location—on a plateau of red cliffs way out in the North Sea—has sparked numerous battles over its possession. Though Helgoland's military significance has waned, the cliffs are still occupied by a formidable force: hordes of shop-happy tourists. If the island's serrated precipices cast their spell on you, try reserving a bed in the **HI-Jugendherberge** (tel. 04725/341). Ferries for Helgoland leave from Bremerhaven (*see* Near Bremen, *above*), as well as from Wilhelmshaven and several ports in Schleswig-Holstein (*see* Chapter 12). From Bremerhaven, the ferry costs DM 68 round-trip, DM 55 for a day trip.

15 NORTH RHINE-WESTPHALIA

UPDATED BY MICHAEL WOODHEAD

There was a time when North Rhine-Westphalia (*Nordrhein-Westfalen*) was without question the most important economic and cultural center in Germany. The booming modern art and media industries of **Cologne,** the glass-walled corporate headquarters of prosperous **Düsseldorf,** the bureaucratic and political heft of **Bonn,** the industrial power of the **Ruhrgebiet,** and world-class universities, like that in **Münster,** all combined to make the region Germany's powerhouse. With nearly 18 million residents, the state is by far the most populous in Germany; one out of five Germans lives here. Yet North Rhine-Westphalia's vitality has fallen prey to a series of adversities: Parts of the region are terribly depressed, factories have closed, and unemployment is persistently high, even by European standards. In an effort to resuscitate some of the old verve, the city of Oberhausen (where Hitler chose to build the first European highway) erected Europe's largest shopping mall, the "Centro," right on the site of an old steel factory. The monstrosity comes replete with a movie complex, a Hard Rock Café, a jazz hall, waterways, adventure playgrounds, and shops galore.

What is today North Rhine-Westphalia entered history when the Romans arrived and built cities like Cologne, whose location at the heart of Europe made it one of the cradles of German culture during the Middle Ages. With its massive Gothic cathedral, Cologne was the largest city in the German-speaking world during the Middle Ages. The gritty Ruhrgebiet developed during Germany's 19th-century industrial revolution around a jumble of coal mines and steel mills. Though it's supposedly experiencing a post-industrial rebirth, the area is still a sprawl of people, factories, mills, and mines. Westphalia, stretching across the rolling countryside to the east, remained more focused on agriculture than trade, though its smaller cities, like Münster and Detmold, developed a charm and architectural richness of their own.

The state has more to offer than just business and industry. Avant-garde museums and galleries, picturesque historical towns, and hip student culture in the region's university cities will keep you from getting too serious. Throughout the state, you will find two things in abundance: Beer (from Cologne's Kölsch, to Düsseldorf's Alt, to Dortmund's six massive breweries) and good cheer. It's easy to meet locals ready to share with you their good fortune, local history, or theories on economic recovery. Their state, they'll tell you, has all the art and history, all the nightlife and culture, all the problems and possibilities, and all the beauty (natural and man-made) that you'll need in Germany. Well . . . that's how friendly Rhinelanders are by nature. They are also changing their habits. Even beer, whose price has shot up while breweries experience a crisis, is shifting to the back seat: It is becoming more fashionable to drink foreign wines and cocktails (behavior for which you would have been shown the door just 10 years ago).

COLOGNE

Wading through the punks, transients, tourists, performers, and protesters as you leave the *Hauptbahnhof* (main train station) and enter the shadow of the magnificent *Dom* (cathedral), it suddenly hits you: Cologne (*Köln*) is a big, diverse city. Aside from the architectural wonders, excellent museums, and renowned local brew, Kölsch, visitors here are drawn by the city's open-minded, irreverent, fun-loving spirit. Cologne defies German stereotypes with its wild **Karneval,** a sort of northern Mardi Gras that takes place every February. Busy locals seem happy with what they're doing and are always ready to share secrets about the hippest gallery or the newest hedonistic nightclub. While full of monuments dating back to the time of Charlemagne, Cologne is modern Germany's media hub, producing many of the country's popular TV series. And as a center for contemporary art, Cologne can hold its own.

Cologne's prominence began when Emperor Claudius made the settlement—birthplace of his wife and niece, Julia Agrippina—a full colony with the status of a Roman city (called *Colonia Agrippinensis,* from which the city's modern name derives). With accolades from Charlemagne, who made Cologne an archbishopric, and the acquisition of the alleged relics of the three magi (or wise men) in the 12th century, Cologne became a major pilgrim destination, and construction on the Dom began. Beyond all this, its position on trade routes has kept Cologne economically powerful and culturally diverse. This rich legacy lives on in Cologne's modern-art scene and nightlife, which rival those in Munich and Berlin.

BASICS

AMERICAN EXPRESS

You can change money and AmEx traveler's checks and pick up mail at this dinky branch. There's a 24-hour AmEx ATM outside. *Burgmauerstr. 14, across from Dom, tel. 0221/925–9010. Open weekdays 9–5:30, Sat. 9–noon.*

BIKE RENTAL

For a big city, Cologne has plenty of bike routes. The best deals for rentals are at **Cycles Herriger,** where a day costs DM 10, a week DM 55. *Venloer Str. 26, tel. 0221/550–4813. U-Bahn to Friesenpl., then walk down Venloer Str. Open weekdays 10–6, Sat. 10–1.*

CHANGING MONEY

The **DVB** (open daily 7 AM–9 PM) in the Hauptbahnhof is a convenient place to get your funds rolling again. You can find Cirrus and Plus ATMs at **Deutsche Bank** and **Stadtsparkasse Köln** branches throughout the city.

DISCOUNT TRAVEL AGENCIES

For your budget travel needs, consult **STA Travel.** *Zülpicher Str. 178, tel. 0221/422011.*

LAUNDRY

Öko Express. Wash your duds here for DM 6 (soap included) and spin 'em dry for DM 1 per 10 min. *Cnr of Händelstr. and Richard-Wagner-Str., near Rudolfpl. U-Bahn or tram to Rudolfpl., walk left around the Holiday Inn to Richard-Wagner-Str. Closed Sun.*

MAIL AND PHONES

The **Hauptpost** is just down Dompropst-Ketzer-Straße from the station. The office changes money at good rates (weekdays 8–6, Sat. 8–1), handles poste restante, lets you make long-distance phone calls, and sends and receives faxes. Cologne's postal code is 50668. *An den Dominikanern 4. Open weekdays 7 AM–9 PM, weekends 11–8.*

MEDICAL AID

The **University Clinic** (Joseph-Stelzmann-Str. 9, tel. 0221/4780) gives medical advice in English over the phone or in person. The pharmacy closest to the Hauptbahnhof is **Dom-Apotheke** (Komödienstr. 5, tel. 0221/257–6754; open weekdays 8–6:30, Sat. 8–2), around the corner from the tourist office.

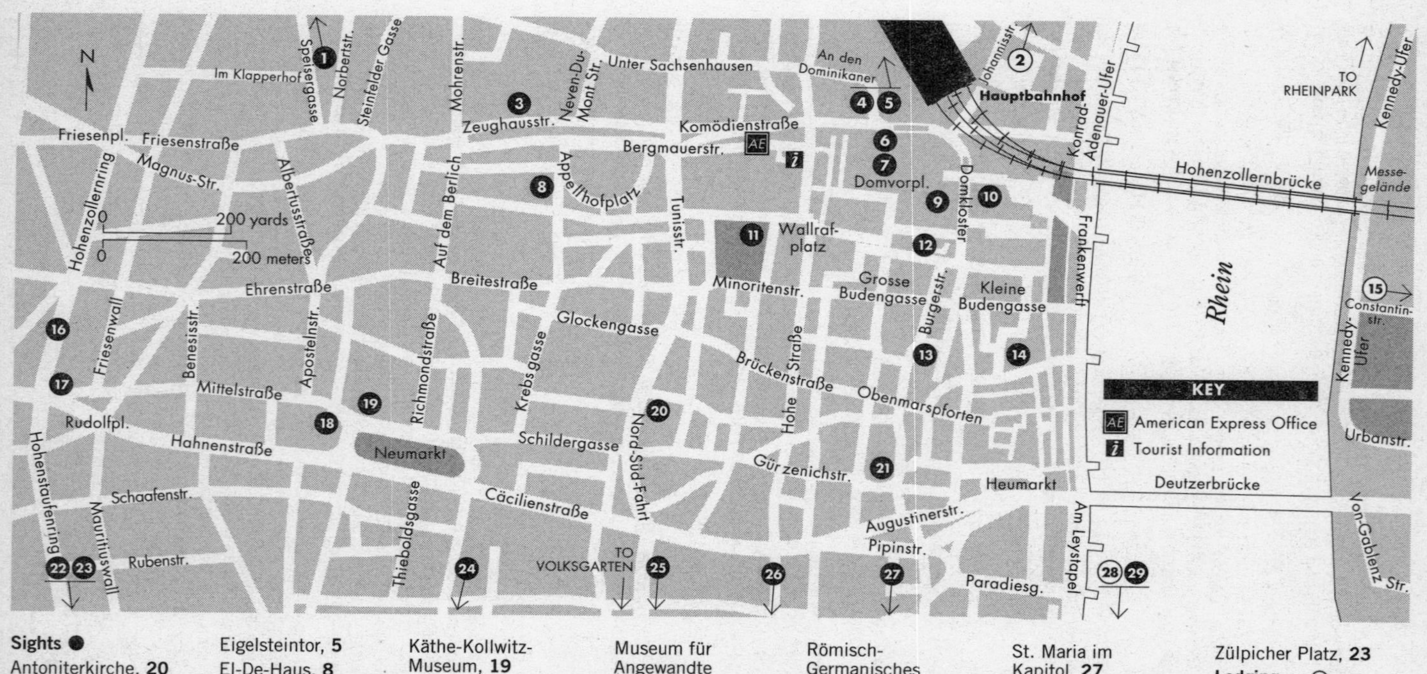

Sights ●
Antoniterkirche, **20**
Beatles Museum, **22**
Chlodwig Platz, **26**
Diözesan-museum, **12**
Dom, **7**
Eigelsteintor, **5**
El-De-Haus, **8**
Groß St. Martin, **14**
Hahnentor, **17**
Imhoff-Stollwerck-Museum, **29**
Käthe-Kollwitz-Museum, **19**
Kölnisches Stadtmuseum, **3**
Medieval City Wall, **16**
Museum für Angewandte Kunst, **11**
Rathaus, **13**
Roman North Gate, **6**
Römisch-Germanisches Museum, **9**
Severinstor, **25**
St. Alban, **21**
St. Aposteln, **18**
St. Gereon, **1**
St. Maria im Kapitol, **27**
St. Pantaleon, **24**
St. Ursula, **4**
Wallraf-Richartz-Museum/Museum Ludwig/AGFA, **10**
Zülpicher Platz, **23**

Lodging ○
Campingplatz Poll, **28**
Jugendgästehaus Köln-Riehl, **2**
Jugendgästehaus Köln-Deutz, **15**

COLOGNE

VISITOR INFORMATION

The **tourist office,** across the street from the Dom, is well staffed with English speakers. They are eager not to waste resources, so if you want good museum info (like the booklet on current exhibitions) or a list of galleries, *ask.* Lame city maps are free, but pay DM 1 for the decent one. They charge DM 5 to book a room. *Unter Fettenhennen 19, tel. 0221/2212–3345, fax 0221/2212–3320. Open Apr.–Oct., Mon.–Sat. 8 AM–10:30 PM, Sun. 9 AM–10:30 PM; Nov.–Mar., Mon.–Sat. 8 AM–9 PM, Sun. 9:30–7.*

RESOURCES FOR GAYS AND LESBIANS • The English-capable information center **Checkpoint** (Pipinstr. 7, tel. 0221/9257–6869; open daily 5 PM–1 AM) can provide info on Cologne's booming gay scene. **Schulz** (Kartäuserwall 18, tel. 0221/9318–8080; open weekdays 6 PM–12:30 AM, weekends from 4 PM) is a community center with a bar, café, and movie theater for lesbians and gays. It's a great place for getting info and meeting people. Take the tram or U-Bahn to Chlodwigplatz and walk down Kartäuserwall.

COMING AND GOING

BY TRAIN

More than 1,000 trains per day pass through Cologne's cavernous **Hauptbahnhof** (main train station; tel. 0221/19419), in the center of town by the Dom. Ongoing reconstruction has transformed the station into a trap for masses of commuters and travelers, so give yourself some extra time to catch that train or get your stuff from the lockers. The S6 leaves every 20 min for Düsseldorf (30 min, DM 11), and regular trains leave every 30 min for Aachen (1 hr, DM 19.60), hourly for Frankfurt (2½ hrs, DM 68), and several times daily for Berlin (6 hrs, DM 165), Brussels (2½ hrs, DM 58), Paris (6 hrs, DM 128), and Amsterdam (2½ hrs, DM 70.20).

BY MITFAHRGELEGENHEIT

The harried, English-speaking staff at **Mitfahrbüro** can generally get you to any major city in Germany if you give them at least a day's notice. Sample fares: Frankfurt DM 22, Berlin DM 50. *Saarstr. 22, tel. 0221/19444. U-Bahn or tram to Eifelpl.; walk north on Am Duffesbach, left on Saarstr. Open weekdays 9–7, Sat. 9–4.*

BY BUS

The **Busbahnhof** is behind the Hauptbahnhof and serves smaller towns in the region. The *Bussteige* (platforms) are confusing, so check with the **RVK** office (in the orange building on the square) or call 0221/124412 for info on regional routes.

BY PLANE

The **Flughafen Köln-Bonn** (tel. 02203/404001) isn't as big as Frankfurt's or Düsseldorf's, but it has direct service to many destinations, including some U.S. cities, London, and Berlin. Bus 170 (20 min, DM 8) makes the trek between the airport and town every 20 min 6 AM–11 PM. Catch it from the Busbahnhof or the airport's lower-level main entrance.

BY BOAT

Cologne is the northernmost point on the Rhine for **Köln-Düsseldorfer,** a fleet of passenger ferries that runs as far south (upstream) as Mainz. Eurail and German (DB) rail passes get you a free trip. Otherwise, you'll pay DM 82 from Cologne to Koblenz and another DM 82 from Koblenz to Mainz (*see* Coming and Going, *in* Chapter 16). Call 0221/208–8318 for info or pick up a pamphlet at the tourist office.

HITCHING

Hitching from Cologne requires a decent map, as the road system is complicated. Hitchers headed north toward Amsterdam, Hamburg, or Berlin stand at the traffic light at Innere Kanalstraße and Lentstraße, next to the Eis- und Schwimmstadion. The road bridges the Rhine, then meets the Autobahn cloverleaf for the northbound A 3 (direction: Oberhausen and Amsterdam), which connects to the A 1 (direction: Wuppertal) toward Hamburg and Berlin. To get here, take the U-Bahn to Reichensperger Platz and walk up Merlostraße, which becomes Lentstraße. For points south and west, try the Verteilerkreis Köln, at the end of Bonner Straße south of the city. This puts you on the A 4, which crosses the Rhine to the east (direction: Köln-Heumar) to connect with the southbound A 3 to Frankfurt, or leads west toward Aachen, Belgium, and France. To get to the Verteilerkreis, take the tram or U-Bahn to Chlodwigplatz and catch the southbound Bus 132 to Heidekaul.

GETTING AROUND

Only the *Innenstadt* (city center, including the museums and sights right around the Dom) and Cologne's main pedestrian zones, **Hohe Straße** and **Schildergasse,** are accessible by foot from the train station. But if you stick to this commercial and touristy center, you'll miss most of Cologne. The city's larger *Altstadt* (old town) actually stretches from Ebertplatz in the north to Chlodwigplatz in the south. On your map (the one you bought at the tourist office, remember?) you'll see that these are the northern and southern ends of the Ring, following the course of 13th-century fortifications. Exploring the city's diverse neighborhoods is easy once you figure out the very extensive subway and tram system.

Most of Cologne's **U-Bahn** (subway and tram) and **S-Bahn** (commuter rail) lines pass beneath the **Hauptbahnhof.** The blue lines are for the U-Bahn, the orange for the S-Bahn, and the green for the Deutsche Bahn (regular German Rail) lines. As you travel beyond the city center, the U-Bahn trains tend to rise to the surface and metamorphose into streetcars. To avoid confusion, pick up a public transit map at the tourist office or from the ticket window downstairs in the Hauptbahnhof, and always know your line's final destination (so that you don't go in the wrong direction). Buy tickets from the large red machines located at some stops and on all buses and subway cars. You'll find a list of every destination with a price code next to it (a letter such as "K"). Press the appropriate letter to find out how many marks (coins only) you need to feed the machine. For DM 10.50, you can buy a ticket that is good for one person for 24 hours; it beats single fares (DM 3) or multiple-ride strips (DM 2.80 per ride). Three-day cards (DM 21) are also available. Validate your ticket immediately in the red machines on the bus or subway car—plainclothes checkers come through (unpredictably) to slap DM 60 fines on rule-breakers. Except for a few night buses and trams, public transit shuts down between 1 AM and 5:15 AM. For a **taxi,** call 0221/2882 or 0221/19410.

WHERE TO SLEEP

Inside the Hauptbahnhof hang ominous, green KÖLN-MESSE (COLOGNE CONVENTION) signs. Messen are a mess for travelers because even the dingiest of pensions finds it easy to fill up. In summer, both hostels are often full, so call way ahead. Once here, consider coughing up the DM 5 for tourist office bookings. Tell them your price range and an area you'd like (the Südstadt, Univiertel, or Belgisches Viertel would be nice). You may get lucky. If you want to go at it alone, a gaggle of nondescript hotels lines **Brandenburger Straße,** a five-min walk from the rear entrance of the Hauptbahnhof. If the ones below aren't available, try **Brandenburger Hof** (Brandenburger Str. 2–4, tel. 0221/122889, fax 0221/135304) or **Hotel Tourist Thielen** (Brandenburger Str. 1–5, tel. 0221/123333, fax 0021/121292), both of which charge DM 65 for singles, DM 85 for doubles. The **Mitwohnzentrale** (An der Bottmühle 16, tel. 0221/327084, fax 0021/325556; closed weekends) is a room-finding agency that can get you an inexpensive sublet (from DM 20 per day) if you stay at least two days.

UNDER DM 90 • Hotel Im Kupferkessel. If you miss *The Waltons,* you'll love this hotel, about 15 min from the Hauptbahnhof. A spiral staircase leads right to the kitchen, where guests breakfast together. Quite elegant considering the price: singles DM 54 (DM 92 with bath), doubles from DM 120, breakfast included. *Probsteig. 6, tel. 0221/135338, fax 0221/125121. From Hauptbahnhof, follow Dompropst-Ketzer-Str., which becomes Gereonsstr. and Christophstr., turn right on Probsteig. 13 rooms, some with bath.*

Pension Jansen and **Pension Kirchener.** Because these two pensions are great bargains, they sell out quickly—call ahead. Both are located in an apartment building, and you get a key to come and go as you please. The rooms are comfortable, funkily decorated, and small. At both hotels, singles are DM 65, doubles DM 145, breakfast included. *Richard-Wagner-Str. 18, Jansen: tel. 0221/251875, Kirchener: tel. 0221/252977. From Hauptbahnhof, U-Bahn to Neumarkt, transfer upstairs to Tram 1 (direction: Junkersdorf) or Tram 2 (direction: Benzelrath) to Rudolfpl., and go left around Holiday Inn to Richard-Wagner-Str. 20 rooms, none with bath.*

UNDER DM 100 • Hotel Berg. This place stands out from its Brandenburger Straße neighbors with slightly cheaper rates: DM 52–DM 90 for a single, DM 90–DM 150 for a double. The breakfast and decor are bland, but you might get a room with a nice view of the Dom. *Brandenburger Str. 6, tel. 0221/121124, fax 0221/132591. Exit rear of Hauptbahnhof, cross to Johannisstr., left on Brandenburger Str. 20 rooms, some with bath.*

Rhein-Hotel St. Martin. This is the only reasonable option in the hotel-strewn area south of the station, about 10 min by foot from the Dom. Some of its antiseptic rooms have a view of the Rhine. Singles from DM 62 to DM 85, doubles from DM 105 to DM 150. *Frankenwerft 31–33, tel. 0221/257–7955, fax 0221/257–7875. From Hauptbahnhof, follow signs to Dom, turn left toward river, right on Frankenwerft. 50 rooms, all with bath. Breakfast included.*

Tagungs- und Gästehaus St. Georg. Run by Cologne's Boy Scouts, this recently refurbished Gästehaus is one of the best bargains in town. There's no curfew or lack of privacy, you'll meet a lot of youngish people, and you'll enjoy the great café and gallery, BiPi's (*see* Worth Seeing, *below*). The surrounding neighborhood is a blast. Singles DM 52–DM 80, doubles DM 96–DM 140. *Rolandstr. 61, tel. 0221/9370–2020, fax 0221/9370–2011. From Hauptbahnhof, U16 (direction: Hersel/Bonn) to Chlodwigpl.; turn right on Merowingerstr., left on Maria-Hilf-Str. to Rolandstr. 33 rooms, some with bath.*

HOSTELS

Jugendgästehaus Köln-Riehl (HI). This monstrosity—the biggest youth hostel in Germany—is clean, functional, efficient, and within 15 min of the train station by U-Bahn. To break the sanitized monotony, rap with the staff, who are friendly and know the city well. Bed, breakfast, and sheets are included in the DM 38.50 price. *An der Schanz 14, tel. 0221/767081, fax 0221/761555. From Hauptbahnhof, U16 (direction: Wiener Pl.) to Boltensternstr.; walk 100 m in same direction as train. 400 beds. No curfew. 24-hr reception. Luggage storage.*

Jugendherberge Köln-Deutz (HI). This hostel, across the river from the Altstadt, is more central and a little cheaper (beds DM 32, DM 37 if you're over 26, including breakfast) than its huge counterpart; it's also a little dirtier and a little louder. The laundry room is free for guests. *Siegesstr. 5a, tel. 0221/814711, fax 0221/884425. From Hauptbahnhof, cross bridge over Rhine to Ottopl. (15 min total on foot); or, take S-Bahn 1 stop to Bahnhof Deutz; cross Ottopl. to Neuhöflerstr., and turn right on Sieggesstr. Curfew 12:30. 24-hr reception. Closed 1 week at Christmas.*

CAMPING

Campingplatz Poll. This manicured field next to the Rhine is easy to reach, but it's not for nature lovers—car campers predominate. Spots cost DM 5 per tent, DM 5.50 per person. *Weidenw., tel. 0221/831966. From Hauptbahnhof, U16 (direction: Hersel/Bonn) to Marienburg, then cross Rodenkirchener bridge and follow signs.*

FOOD

If you're fed up with living off bread and cheese or spending DM 20 on a not-so-appetizing German meal, Cologne may seem like heaven. Around the university near **Zülpicher Straße,** in the **Südstadt** (around Chlodwigplatz), and in the area around Rudolfplatz and Friesenplatz (called the **Belgisches Viertel**), you'll find zillions of inexpensive southern European restaurants, as well as German cafés that serve lighter, more healthful German food. The best places to go for everyday Kölner food are the breweries (*see below*). For some of that bread and cheese, stroll along Hohe Straße and Schildergasse.

UNDER DM 10 • Borsalino. This Italian restaurant in the busy university quarter serves hearty portions at student prices. The capricciosa salad (with tuna, egg, tomatoes, and olives; DM 8.50) or the tortellini with spinach (DM 11) will satisfy. Pizzas run DM 7–DM 10.50. *Zülpicher Str. 7, tel. 0221/248852. U-Bahn or tram to Zülpicher Pl.; alight and continue 1 block down Zülpicher Str. Closed Sun.*

Café Duddel. Among the students and well-thumbed newspapers and magazines at the rickety tables in this café, you'll find good coffee and a couple of things to eat. Müsli with fruit (DM 4.50) is standard, but there will also be a soup or meal of the day (DM 5–DM 8). *Zülpicher Wall 8, no phone. U7 (direction: Sülz) to Dasselstr.; continue under rail crossing on Zülpicher Str. to Zülpicher Wall. 1 block. Closed weekends and Aug.*

Osho's Place. If you come here and admit that you haven't heard of Osho the Bhagwan and his Oregon commune, no one will believe you. (They will be happy to fill you in, though.) Located next to a sunny, plant-filled courtyard, this café and self-service vegetarian restaurant has acquired some of the peaceful vibes from the "Institute for Spiritual Therapy and Meditation" behind it. There's a rotating lunch and dinner menu (DM 12) and a number of smaller choices, such as fresh soups (DM 4.50) and an eclectic salad bar. Sunday brunch is served 11–3. *Venloer Str. 5–7, tel. 0221/574–0745. U-Bahn to Friesenpl.; turn onto Venloer Str.*

SIZE ISN'T EVERYTHING

Cologne is hardly shy about its attractive qualities. One treasure in particular draws the reverence of locals, but the heckles of other Germans: Kölsch. The crisp, hoppy brew is indeed refreshing, and it's proudly produced only by breweries in or near the city. If it is so obviously popular, why do other Germans (especially Bavarians) turn up their noses at Kölsch's bitter aroma? Quite simply, it's not the beer, it's the glass. Slender, delicate, and holding a paltry 0.2 liters, the "Stange" your Kölsch comes in is, well, in the words of one disappointed and eloquent American tourist, "puny." Kölners counter that unlike the warm, flat, sludgy mixture of spit and beer at the bottom of a Bavarian "Maß," your Kölsch, fresh from the tap, is tasty from beginning to end. They have a point. With Kölsch, no one can drink just one, but at about DM 2.50 a pop, no one has to.

UNDER DM 15 • Alcazar. This place is constantly packed with university students and post-college twentysomethings. Crowds form at about 4 PM for beer and coffee, grow for dinner, and remain into the night. The food is outstanding and healthy (they have tons of salad and creative pasta dishes). Expect to pay DM 12–DM 15 for a meal. *Bismarckstr. 39, tel. 0221/515733. U-Bahn to Friesenpl.; walk down Venloer Str., turn left on Bismarckstr.*

Lokal in der Alten Feuerwache. The active members of this social-work organization—housed in an abandoned fire station—address the gamut of social ills. In the attached beer garden you can munch on healthful, yummy, and often-veggie noodle dishes and salads for less than DM 15. Live music (DM 10–DM 15) rolls through several nights a week. *Melchiorstr. 3, tel. 0221/737393. U-Bahn to Ebertpl.; take Sudermanstr. to Sudermanpl., then walk down Melchiorstr.*

BREWERIES AND BEER GARDENS

Kölners pride themselves on their "Rhineland joviality," and Kölsch is at the heart of it. To get a good dose of it yourself, go to one of the many traditional breweries. If the weather is good, Cologne's beer gardens rival almost any Munich spot for sun and relaxation.

Päffgen. There are two Päffgen *Brauhäuser* (brewhouses) in Cologne's Altstadt, serving undistinguished food and plenty of Kölsch: one near the Dom (Am Heumarkt 62, tel. 0221/257–7765), and this one, the youngest and liveliest. *Friesenstr. 66, tel. 0221/135461. U-Bahn to Friesenpl. Open daily 10 AM–midnight.*

Stadtgarten. A beer garden as beer gardens should be. In warm weather, the rows of picnic-style tables in the huge outside seating area get packed with as many as 500 rowdies drinking Gilden Kölsch. Pizza (DM 7–DM 12) and salads (DM 5–DM 12) abound. The outdoor stage features young, innovative jazz musicians Wednesday–Saturday. *Venloer Str. 40, tel. 0221/516037. U-Bahn to Friesenpl.; then walk down Venloer Str. Open daily; live music Wed.–Sat. from 10 PM.*

WORTH SEEING

Cologne is a city of art and history, as evidenced by its large and varied museums. If you're planning lots of sightseeing, the **Köln Bonbon** (DM 26) is a tasty three-day pass that gets you admission to seven museums' permanent collections, a bilingual bus tour (normally DM 23 by itself), discounts on Rhine boat trips, and more. There's also a low-cal version (DM 15) *sans* bus tour. You can buy the Bonbon in the Dom Hotel on Domplatz and at other more upper-crust hotels. Between March and August, **Stadt Reisen Köln** (Hansaring 135, tel. 0221/732–5133) offers cool German-language walking tours. College students lead many of the tours, which include topics like Cologne in 1968 (think Dylan, the Beatles, love, and rebellion) or gay and lesbian life in Cologne 1945–1970. Most tours cost DM 12.

Looking at a city map (get one), you'll see a road forming a half circle around the Dom. This broad, busy street, generically called the **Ring,** marks the path of the town's 13th-century fortifications. Within the Ring are all of Cologne's Romanesque churches and most of its museums. A walk from the northernmost part of the Ring (Ebertplatz) to the southernmost part (Chlodwigplatz) takes at least an hour. This helps you appreciate the size of medieval Cologne, the largest city in Germany until the 17th century. A walk from the Dom to Friesenplatz or Rudolfplatz, whether on a sight-seeing or beer-drinking tour, is a good way to explore the city center.

DOM

This house of God should inspire some awe in even the most fanatical heathens. Construction on this immense archetype of Gothic cathedrals began more than seven centuries ago, and it wasn't completed until 1880. Repairing and refurbishing the Dom, scarred by bombs in World War II and eroded even now by acid rain, is a permanent endeavor. Behind the altar is the 13th-century Shrine of the Three Magi, which looks like the Ark of the Covenant from *Raiders of the Lost Ark.* This shrine is the raison d'être for the Dom; without the Magi, the archbishop would not have authorized the building of a bigger, badder cathedral in 1248.

Climb the 509 steps of the Dom's **Südturm** (south tower; admission DM 3, DM 1.50 students) for a great view of the Rhine. More spectacular, however, is the **Glockenstube,** housing the Dom's nine bells, including the Petriglocke—the world's heaviest working bell. To see the cathedral's treasures, pay DM 3 to enter the **Domschatzkammer** (cathedral treasury) or visit the **Diözesanmuseum** (admission free; open Fri.–Wed. 10–5) across the plaza. They both house art, rings, scepters, funny hats, and everything else you might expect.

Cologne's waiters are famous throughout Germany for the round trays they carry, specially designed to secure the maximum number of .2-liter Kölsch glasses.

MEDIEVAL CITY WALL

Three large, fortified city gates remain, marking the northern, western, and southern ends of Cologne's old wall. (The eastern edge of the medieval city was the Rhine.) Take the U-Bahn to Ebertplatz to check out the **Eigelsteintor,** on the old city's northern border. The western gate, **Hahnentor,** is just off Rudolfplatz, a short U-Bahn trip from Ebertplatz. The southern gate, **Severinstor,** is just a block north of Chlodwigplatz, also accessible by tram and U-Bahn.

ROMAN CITY WALL

Long before the Middle Ages, Cologne was a Roman city, and you can check out the ruins of its walls in a few places. The old stone archway on Domvorplatz, beside the Dom, is part of the original **Roman North Gate.** Continue west from Domvorplatz down Komödienstraße to Tunisstraße to see restored sections of the wall from the 1st century AD. Even the parking lot under the Dom has some relics in it. For more Roman remnants, follow Am Hof, next to the Diözesanmuseum, to find a reconstructed street made with original Roman paving stones, and check out the Römisch-Germanisches Museum (*see below*).

CHURCHES

Cologne is famous for its garland of 12 Romanesque churches. Off busy Neumarkt is **St. Aposteln,** whose bright, cloverleaf nave centers on a giant hanging lantern. Consecrated in AD 980, **St. Pantaleon** (Am Pantaleonsberg, just south of the Poststr. U-Bahn station) is the oldest Romanesque church in Cologne. It has an austere feel, with simple, gray arches like those in the Roman ruins under the Rathaus. Toward the Rhine, south of the Dom, is **Groß St. Martin,** which has the most impressive of Cologne's Romanesque towers. For centuries it, not the Dom's spires, defined Cologne's skyline. The unique golden chamber of **St. Ursula** (Ursulapl., NW of the Hauptbahnhof) is a tribute to a virgin who, legend has it, was killed by Huns along with 11,000 virginal consorts. Their bones are said to lie buried beneath the building. North of Marienplatz, the intricate wooden doors of **St. Maria im Kapitol** open to reveal an elaborate carved wood ceiling. One of the most unusual and decadent interiors you'll see is the golden orange dome of **St. Gereon,** on Gereonshof just east of the Ring. Step off the busy shopping corner of Schildergasse and Nord-Süd-Fahrt into **Antoniterkirche,** and silence will hit you like air-conditioning on a summer day. Floating peacefully in the nave is the smiling, hanging statue of *Der Schwebende Engel* (the suspended angel), created by the sculptor Ernst Barlach (1870–1938) for the victims of wars. On Gürzenichstraße near the Rathaus stands the grass-covered, roofless ruin of **St. Alban,** left in memory of World War II and its victims; step inside to see a copy of Käthe Kollwitz's poignant statue, *Mourning Parents.* Ask the tourist office for a schedule of organ and chamber-music performances in the Romanesque churches.

MUSEUMS

BEATLES MUSEUM • Real fans must make the trip to this tiny museum, a shrine crammed with Beatles dolls, photos, newspaper clippings, and autographs. *Heinsbergstr. 13, tel. 0221/212598. U-Bahn or tram to Zülpicher Pl.; walk down Zülpicher Str., right on Heinsbergstr. Admission: DM 5 (includes coffee). Open Wed.–Fri. 10–2 and 3–7; closed Aug.*

EL-DE-HAUS • Seized from the original Jewish owner in 1935, this building served as headquarters for Cologne's Gestapo, who committed hundreds of atrocities in the basement. Today, it is a museum devoted to the memory of Holocaust victims and a tribute to Nazi-era resistance groups. *Appellhofpl. 23–25, tel. 0221/2212–6331. U-Bahn to Appellhofpl. Admission free. Open weekdays 8–noon.*

IMHOFF-STOLLWERCK-MUSEUM • Stollwerck, the owner of a local chocolate company of the same name, has created a Charlie-and-the-Chocolate-Factory experience with a chocolate fountain (free tastings!), greenhouses where cocoa is grown, demonstrations on production, and, of course, a gift shop at the end. *Rheinauhafen 1a, tel. 0221/931–8880. U-Bahn to Heumarkt, cross Pipinstr. and head down Paradiesg. to the riverfront; turn right on Am Leistapei, and cross drawbridge just past the tower. Admission: DM 10, DM 5 students. Open weekdays 10–6, weekends 11–7.*

KÄTHE-KOLLWITZ-MUSEUM • This museum displays work by one of Germany's better-known 20th-century artists, including sculptures, drawings, and lithographs—all expressing her anger at the death and suffering caused by war. The museum also features regular displays of other modern artists. *Neumarkt 18–24, on 2nd floor of the Neumarkt-Passage, tel. 0221/227–2363. U-Bahn or tram to Neumarkt. Admission: DM 5, DM 2.50 students. Open Tues.–Fri. 10–4, weekends 11–4.*

KÖLNISCHES STADTMUSEUM • Housed in Cologne's 16th-century armory, this museum, just off Appellhofplatz, picks up the city's history where the Römisch-Germanisches Museum leaves off (about AD 750). There are lots of Dom photographs, 16th-century armor, displays on Cologne's Karneval, and a curt chapter on the Nazi era. A 1913 city model gives you a good idea of what Cologne was like before World War I. Those who don't speak German will get less out of this. *Zeughausstr. 1–3, tel. 0221/2212–5789. U-Bahn to Appellhofpl. Admission: DM 5, DM 3 students. Open Tues.–Sun. 10–5.*

MUSEUM FÜR ANGEWANDTE KUNST • About 200 m southwest of the Dom, this museum features applied arts from around Europe, including jewelry, furniture, glass, and weapons. *An der Rechtsschule, tel. 0221/2212–6714. From Domvorpl., walk up Unter Fettenhennen and right on An der Rechtsschule. Admission: DM 5, DM 2.50 students. Open Tues.–Fri. 11–5, weekends noon–5.*

RÖMISCH-GERMANISCHES MUSEUM • Documenting Roman life, especially in Cologne, this museum has a very, very old preserved mosaic floor (AD 220) and the restored tomb of Poblicius, a Roman soldier who died in AD 40. Underneath the museum, you can walk through excavated ruins. *Roncallipl. 4, behind Dom, tel. 0221/2212–2304. Admission: DM 7, DM 4 students. Open Tues.–Fri. 10–4, weekends 11–4.*

WALLRAF-RICHARTZ-MUSEUM • The Wallraf, right behind the Dom, has a huge collection of medieval and Renaissance paintings. On the floors above is the **Museum Ludwig** (tel. 0221/2212–2372) and its massive collection of 20th-century art. One of the more notable pieces is Dwayne Kienhulz's *The Portable War Memorial,* a critique of American patriotism complete with "God Bless America" rasping out from underneath an overturned trash can. Don't leave without seeing Gerhard Richter's 48 portraits of European artists and philosophers. In the same building, the **AGFA Foto-Historama** (tel. 0221/2212–2411) documents the history of photography and the history of Cologne through photographs. All three have interesting special exhibits, which often cost extra. *Bischofsgartenstr. 1, next to Dom, tel. 0221/2212–2372. All museums open Tues.–Fri. 10–6, weekends 11–6. Combined admission: DM 10, DM 5 students.*

GALLERIES

With well over 100 venues, Cologne's art scene is formidable, to say the least. Here are a few galleries worth visiting; ask the tourist office for a list of 100 others. Near the Dom is a spare, serious space at **Galerie Karsten Greve** (Wallrafpl. 3, tel. 0221/257–1012). Behind the Museum für angewandte Kunst is the more commercial **Galerie Boisserée** (Drususg. 7–11, tel. 0221/257–8519). Near Chlodwigplatz you can sit in the bistro after looking through **BiPi's Kulturgalerie** (Rolandstr. 61, tel. 0221/937–0200) and then visit the stark, often fluorescent displays in **Philomene Magers** (Maria-Hilf-Str. 18, tel. 0221/9373–18843). There is also a huge concentration of galleries north and east of Breite Straße at Albertusstraße.

CHEAP THRILLS

Enjoy hefty glasses of Kölsch beer (a .4-liter glass for DM 5) amid the peaceful and funky atmosphere of the **Volksgarten Biergarten,** where students and young people come to drink, smoke funny cigarettes, and watch ducks and paddle boaters on the lake. Take the U-Bahn or tram to Ulrepforte, and then walk south on Vorgebirgstraße or Kleingedankstraße to the park. Some of the most obvious cheap thrills hit you immediately. The Altstadt, especially near the Dom, is filled with musicians, performers, and artists creating incredible, temporary masterpieces in chalk. You'll see numerous protesters at work saving the planet or freeing Leonard Pelletier.

FESTIVALS

Cologne's **Karneval** isn't for everyone. In fact, Kölners who don't enjoy being crushed by fun-loving crowds tend to stay away from the Karneval's procession and gathering areas. Officially, the carnival season starts on the 11th day of the 11th month, but the corks don't really start popping until the Thursday prior to the seventh Sunday before Easter (got it?). Three days of debauchery follow, climaxing in the *Rosenmontagszug* (Rose Monday Parade). Come prepared to be showered with popcorn, chocolate, and the beer of that guy next to you. Spilled beer aside, it's *definitely* worth experiencing. The tourist office will give you a brochure outlining all the events and the history behind each step of the ritual.

Cologne's churches are even more impressive when you realize that almost all were bombed out by the end of World War II. Many churches display photos showing the extent of the devastation.

AFTER DARK

Cologne is a party town, but dance clubs don't start hopping until midnight. You can find out what's happening in the monthly *Stadt Revue* (DM 4.50) or in a copy of the pricey but thorough *Kölner* (DM 7). *Kölner* comes in three varieties: one for dining and nightlife, one for culture, and one for shopping. Also look in the "Tips und Termine" section of Friday's *Kölner Stadt-Anzeiger* and on bulletin boards at bars and cafés. For a fun night out, head to the Ring area and the areas just outside it, like the slightly yuppie but still offbeat **Südstadt** that radiates south from Chlodwigplatz. The student-dominated **Univiertel** (university quarter) centers on Zülpicher Straße and Kyffhäuserstraße. Between Venloer Straße and Aachener Straße is the funky, multicultural **Belgisches Viertel** (Belgian quarter). Typical talk topics in each neighborhood? Südstadt—cars and Kölsch; Univiertel—classes and Kölsch; the Belgisches Viertel—karma and Kölsch.

Hallmackenreuthur. Lots of bars shun the cheesy art of the late '60s and early '70s, but this place embraces it (lava lamps and TVs that look like space helmets). The strictly student crowd dresses to match the funky decor. *Brüsseler Pl. 9, tel. 0221/517970. U-Bahn to Friesenpl.; then Hohenzollernring south toward Rudolfpl., right on Maastrichter Str. to Brüsseler Pl. Open daily 11 AM–1 AM.*

Hotelux. Come here if you like vodka (DM 4)—there are about 25 to choose from. The black curtain in the doorway lets you into a crowded little room with red stars and hard metal tables. The packed restaurant serves expensive (DM 25–DM 35) but excellent dishes from the states of the former Soviet Union. Squeeze into the beer garden if all you want is alcohol. *Rathenaupl. 21, tel. 0221/241139. U-Bahn or tram to Zülpicher Pl.; 1 block west on Zülpicher Str., right on Roonstr., left on Rathenaupl. Open daily 6 PM–1 AM.*

Museum. How can a bar go wrong providing 10-liter mini-kegs of Kölsch outdoors under the protection of a two-story tall dinosaur? It can't, and the studenty crowd loves every inch of that reptile. *Zülpicher Pl. 9, tel. 0221/232098. U-Bahn or tram to Zülpicher Pl. Open Sun.–Thurs. 4 PM–1 AM, Fri. 4 PM–3 AM, Sat. 7 PM–3 AM.*

Wojtyla. If you can take Christianity with a grain of salt, this one-of-a-kind bar/restaurant is a kick. Listen to technofied Latin chants in a decor heavy on stained glass and glowing plastic crosses. The menu, with entrées like Fruits of Circumcision (fried calamari), is somewhat pricey (DM 15–DM 20), but drinks are affordable and many poor sinners order only the latter. *Bismarckstr. 53, tel. 0221/510–4352. U-Bahn to Friesenpl.; walk down Venloer Str., left on Bismarckstr. Open Sun.–Thurs. 7 PM–1 AM, Fri. and Sat. until 3 AM.*

OUT AT NIGHT

Cologne is an open-minded city, and straight Kölners are usually accepting of gay men and lesbians. A number of bars and discos cater to a queer crowd, and areas like Heumarkt and Schaafenstraße near Rudolfplatz draw Dorothy-friendly crowds. Schulz (see Visitor Information, above) holds its own disco Fridays from 10 PM to midnight. It's a good place to begin your evening. The Gloria (Apostelnstr. 11, tel. 0221/254433), a café and disco in an old movie theater, attracts well-dressed dancers and drinkers of both sexes. The cozy, comfortable, popular Vampire (Rathenauer Pl. 5, tel. 0221/240–1211) is a mostly lesbian bar. Mainly males party at Corner (Schaafenstr. 57–59, tel. 0221/249061), which also offers a hearty Sunday brunch at noon. On Friday night, the disco at Osho's (see Music and Dancing, below) becomes the queer disco Pink Triangle. Schampanja (Mauritiuswall 43, tel. 0221/244294) also sizzles with a mostly male crowd.

MUSIC AND DANCING

Das Ding. Much smaller but no less packed than the E-Werk (*see below*), this place lets you sweat with young students to mainstream music. Come weekdays for good deals on drinks. *Hohenstaufenring 30–32, tel. 0221/246348. U-Bahn or tram to Zülpicher Pl. and walk north. Cover: DM 5. Closed Tues. and Sun.*

E-Werk. This gigantic club in the former *Elektrizitätswerk* (power plant), in Mülheim across the Rhine, has two floors, multiple bars, and a quiet café for cooling off. Pumpy-jumpy techno increasingly gives way here to live music, as bands like the Butthole Surfers roll through with DM 20 cover charges. *Schanzenstr. 28, tel. 0221/962–7910 bus service infoline. U-Bahn to Wiener Pl.; walk up Clevischer Ring to Keupstr., turn right, then left on Schanzenstr. Cover: DM 15 (2 drinks included). Open Fri. and Sat. 10 PM–5 AM.*

Luxor. This popular club books wonderfully odd local (and even some international) bands. Whether there's a gig or not, there's usually dancing. Weekday admission is free unless there's live music. Weekend admission is usually DM 15. *Luxemburger Str. 40, tel. 0221/219503. U-Bahn or tram to Barbarossapl. and head down Luxemburger Str. Open nightly 8–3 concert nights, 10–3 otherwise.*

Osho's. This is one of Cologne's best discos. The **One World** disco upstairs complements the **Petit Prince** (tel. 0221/122520) downstairs. In One World, a tiny eatery with stand-up tables sells good food at low prices—all vegetarian and all fresh. Both places have covers (DM 5–DM 12). The Prince's musical theme varies: jazz on Monday, reggae on Friday, and salsa or other Latin music most other nights. On Friday night One World becomes the **Pink Triangle** (*see box* Out at Night, *above*), a gay-and-lesbian club. *Hohenzollernring 90, north of Friesenpl., tel. 0221/574–9725. U-Bahn to Friesenpl. Open weeknights 9–2, Fri. and Sat. from 10.*

Underground. A good concert venue, this club features regular live shows (cover DM 5–DM 18) by creative young bands, and dancing most nights. *Vogelsanger Str. 200, tel. 0221/544376. U-Bahn to Venloer Str./Gürtel; south on Ehrenfeldgürtel, right on Vogelsanger Str. Open nightly from 9 PM.*

NEAR COLOGNE

Cologne sits at the center of one of Germany's densest urban regions, well served by a network of frequent rail connections. In addition to **Bad Münstereifel** (*see below*), other nearby cities like **Bonn, Aachen,** and **Düsseldorf** (*see* North Rhine, *below*) make easy day trips from Cologne.

BAD MÜNSTEREIFEL

At the eastern edge of the Eifel range sits Bad Münstereifel, quaint and confident. The quaintness comes from being a walled, medieval German city with historic monuments and cobblestone, café-laden streets. This, along with curative spas, brings a steady stream of tourists and money. The confidence, however, comes from knowing that should the Nikon-wielding hordes ever threaten to take over, the city's **Stadtmauer** (city wall) and four medieval gates are intact. The 13th-century gates are open to you, though. As you walk south through the **Werthertor** (Werther Gate), enjoy the sensation of time travel: The 20th-century asphalt of Kölner Straße becomes the 13th-century cobblestone of Wertherstraße, the city's pedestrian zone. Continuing south through the carefully restored buildings leads you to the small *Markt* (market square), bordered on the left by the looming yellow facade of St. Michael, a 17th-century Jesuit school. Continue south, and you'll exit the protected town through **Orchheimer Tor.** Turn west (right) from the Markt and walk down Marktstraße to reach the severely red, late-Gothic **Rathaus** (town hall; finished in 1470). A neck-sized manacle still dangles from the facade—jaywalk here and you may end up on public display for small blond children to poke and taunt. West of the Rathaus, at Heisterbacher Straße, stairs lead up to the **ramparts.** Looking west, you see the main city spa, with gardens, waterfalls, and doubles from DM 198. You can continue south along the ramparts to **Heisterbacher Tor.** All along the way are stunning views over the city to the **Johannistor** and **Burg** (castle; now a restaurant) in the east and the hills rising all around.

North of the Rathaus, off Kirchplatz, the **Chrysanthus-und-Daria-Stiftskirche** presides grandly over the town. Both Roman martyrs' remains are in the crypt (it was possession of their relics that brought 9th-century Münstereifel to prominence). On the north side of the church, across Klosterplatz, is the stone **Romanisches Haus** (1167), one of the oldest surviving structures in the region. Inside is the **Heimatmuseum** (tel. 02253/8027), with a sparse collection of local artifacts, open Tuesday–Friday 9–noon, Wednesday also 2–4, and weekends 1–4 for DM 1.

The mountains surrounding Bad Münstereifel are full of hiking opportunities. In the peaceful forests you can find **Waldkapellen** (forest chapels), Roman relics, and gorgeous views through the pines. Though there are some 200 km of trails around here, they can be hard to find from town. The tourist office and youth hostel (*see below*) can help.

BASICS

The **train station** is just north of town; exit it onto Kölner Straße, which continues straight through Werthertor. Ticket agents staff the station weekdays 9–1 and 2–6:30 and Saturday 9–12:30, but there's also a ticket machine (coins only). Direct trains connect Bad Münstereifel almost hourly with Euskirchen, where you can make a quick connection to Cologne (1¼ hrs total, DM 25) or continue directly to Bonn (2–6 daily, 1 hr, DM 30).

The **tourist office** (Langenhecke 2, tel. 02253/505182) is just south of the Romanisches Haus. From Werthertor, walk west along Wallgasse and turn left on Langenhecke. It's open weekdays 9–5, Saturday 10–noon and 2–4, and Sunday 10:30–12:30. Staff members hand out a booklet with a good map and a list of all hotels and *Privatzimmer* (private rooms). These are your best in-town options at about DM 30 per person. If you read some German, you can decipher the detailed instructions for various hikes in the free booklet, "Wanderungen um Bad Münstereifel." The office also lists group hikes that meet most Sundays, and they sell a high-quality topographic map for DM 10. The **post office** (Wertherstr. 40) is next to Werthertor.

WHERE TO SLEEP AND EAT

The hotels in town cater to a DM 150-per-night crowd. Almost any of them would be a nice splurge, but to spare your budget you may want to stay in one of the many private rooms listed at the tourist office. The **Jugendherberge (HI)** (Herbergsw. 1–5, tel. 02253/7438, fax 02253/7483) is a demanding but pleasant 2-km trek from town. Follow signs from the Markt, near St. Michael, through Johannistor and up, up, up. Beds with breakfast are DM 21.50. The rooms are clean and fairly spacious (6–10 beds), and the hostel is near good hiking. Check in any time between 8 and 6; curfew is 10:30. The world may look to Germany for quaint, but the Germans look to the Italians for coffee. Numerous *italienische Eiscafés* (Italian ice-cream cafés) line Wertherstraße, the Markt, and Orchheimer Straße, where you'll also find bakeries and restaurants. You can get picnic food at **Spar** (Wertherstr. 71) or at the fruit stands lining Wertherstraße until about 3 PM.

NORTH RHINE

Centered on the banks of the massive Rhine, this region prides itself on a history of prosperity and cultural achievement. Its wealth dates back to the early days of the Holy Roman Empire, when Charlemagne made **Aachen** his capital, and centuries of art, architecture, and culture were the result. Modern times have meant modern pursuits (high fashion, avant-garde art, finance) and the creation of modern cities, like **Düsseldorf,** the glitzy, well-dressed capital of North Rhine-Westphalia. Düsseldorf is also the front office for the industrial powerhouse of the **Ruhrgebiet,** which straddles the border between the North Rhine region and Westphalia to the east. Visiting the Ruhr gives you a sense of where modern western nations found their prosperity, but now that mines have closed and industry is struggling, the Ruhr is a bit grim, and you may just want to stick to the good life along sunnier stretches of the Rhine.

BONN

Welcome to the former capital of Germany. In 1991 following the heady days of unification, the German Bundestag narrowly approved the decision to move to Berlin. Now with the old chancellor Helmut Kohl (a Rhinelander himself) out of office, the move to Berlin has taken on a special urgency. Soon Bonn will reassume its unofficial role of a small town in Germany, but the turns of Bonn's bureaucratic fortunes should have little impact on your visit.

Best known as the birthplace of Beethoven and stronghold of the ruling Bishop-Electors of Cologne, Bonn need not fear for its historical value. Meanwhile, since it became capital of West Germany in 1949, the city has eagerly absorbed the art, dining, and nightlife that grew up around its newer populations of journalists, diplomats, immigrants, and even more students than before. Bonn has become a place that sophisticated locals enjoy—a small city in beautiful surroundings with quiet streets and a cultured flair. Capital or not, Bonn has excellent museums and a lively university scene. Spend a night or two, or come on a day trip from Cologne, just a 40-min tram ride away.

BASICS

The English-speaking staff at the orderly **tourist office** (Münsterstr. 20, in Cassius-Passage, tel. 0228/773466; open weekdays 9–6:30, Sat. 9–5, Sun. 10–2) will pass you free city maps and brochures through slots in their windows or book you a room for DM 3. From the Hauptbahnhof, follow STADTMITTE signs onto Poststraße, and go left on Münsterstraße. The **main post office** (Münsterpl. 17; open weekdays 7 AM–7:30 PM, Sat. 7–4, Sun. 10–noon) has a bureau de change that's open until midnight, as well as metered and card-operated phones.

COMING AND GOING

The best way to reach Bonn is usually on a **train** headed toward nearby Cologne, since many trains stop in Bonn on their way to or from there. Traveling between Bonn and Cologne is simple, as the cities share a transit system. From downstairs at either Hauptbahnhof (follow the blue "U" signs), the U16 and U18 trams make the 40-min trip every 20 min or so (DM 8). If you want to use your EurailPass or German Rail Pass, take the train (not the tram) between Cologne and Bonn; they run a few times every hour (20 min, DM 16). You can also catch trains from Bonn to Frankfurt (hourly, 2 hrs, DM 54) and Koblenz (2 per hr, 30 min, DM 14). It can be hard to find an available locker in the station, since spaces are often occupied by homeless people's belongings. If you happen to arrive by air at the tiny **Flughafen Köln-Bonn** (airport; tel. 02203/404001), you can catch Bus 670 to Bonn's **Busbahnhof** (bus station), directly behind the train station.

GETTING AROUND

Bonn's U-Bahn lines continue Cologne's massive system and require the same tickets. Hence, ticket buying, costs, and hours are the same (*see* Getting Around *in* Cologne, *above*). Bonn also has an extensive network of bus lines. Bonn's historic center is where most restaurants, bars, hotels, and major tourist sights are located, and is easy to cover on foot, though you'll need the U-Bahn to get to the newer museums and government buildings. If it's taxi time, **Funk Taxi** (tel. 0228/555555) awaits you. If you're here for a day, buy the BonnCard (DM 12), which gives you 24-hour transit access plus admission to all museums. For DM 21 you can buy a three-day transit pass.

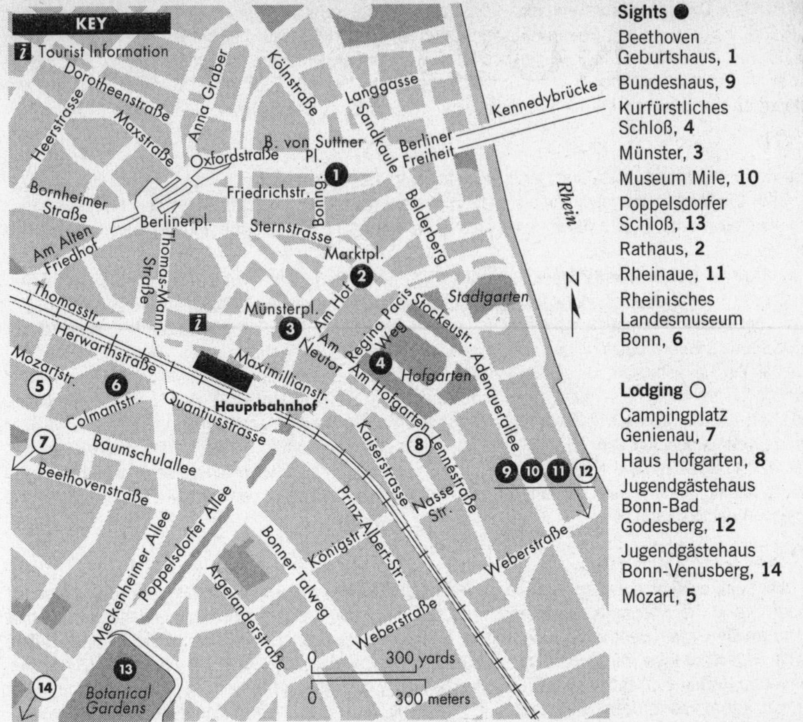

As you exit the Hauptbahnhof, turn right to find the Busbahnhof, where you can get a bus to the hostels; the U-Bahn also stops at the station. Four new night buses make it easy to get home no matter where you sleep. Cycling around the city is also a cinch on the well-marked bike paths in and around Bonn (there's a bike trail as far as Koblenz). Along with BMWs (for slightly higher prices), **Autovermietung Kurscheid** (Römerstr. 4, tel. 0228/631433) rents bikes for DM 15 per day.

WHERE TO SLEEP

Though Bonn gets more than its fair share of tourists, its budget accommodations rarely fill up: Diplomats don't stay in hostels. Things get a little tight during summer, but a call from the train station will usually find you a space. The best lodging deals are in suburban Beuel across the Rhine or Bad Godesberg south of the city, both served daily by regular transit until around midnight, and by night buses (N4 and N3 respectively) on weekends, so you can get a little night action in Bonn before heading back. The tourist office will happily provide info on suburban pensions. Breakfast is included everywhere below.

You'll feel that you're betraying backpackers everywhere at either the elegant **Mozart** (Mozartstr. 1, tel. 0228/659071, fax 0228/659075), off Bachstraße behind the train station, or the almost stately **Haus Hofgarten** (Fritz-Tillmann-Str. 7, tel. 0228/223472, fax 0228/293102), off Kaiserstraße near the university. Both have singles around DM 70 and doubles with bath starting at DM 150. Twenty min from town by Bus 624, 843, or 844, in suburban Röttgen, is **Gästehaus Iris** (Fichtenw. 8, tel. 0228/252332) with cute, fully equipped doubles for DM 80.

HOSTELS • Jugendgästehaus Bonn-Venusberg (HI). This place, poised at the edge of the lush Kottenforst (*see* Near Bonn, *below*), should be the poster child for *Better Youth Hostels and Gardens.* The rooms are small and comfortable two- or four-bedders. The small bistro in the lobby serves beer and pizza. Beds are DM 35 per night. *Haager Weg 42, tel. 0228/289970, fax 0228/289–9714. From Busbahnhof platform A2, Bus 621 to Jugendherberge. Last bus leaves at 12:25 AM. 249 beds. Curfew 1 AM. Reception open 7:30 AM–midnight. Laundry facilities.*

CAMPING • Campingplatz Genienau. The closest campground to Bonn is in a suburban area along the Rhine, a 30- to 45-min trek from town. You can try calling ahead, but the managers don't always pick up the phone. Sites DM 9.50 per person, DM 3 per car, DM 6 per small tent. *Tel. 0228/344949. U63 or U16 to Bad Godesberg, then Bus 613 (direction: Mehlem Süd) to last stop (last bus at 1 AM); follow signs towards the Rhine.*

FOOD

Along with a disproportionate number of tourists, Bonn has an excessive number of good places to eat and drink. On **Marktplatz** you'll find a sea of umbrella-topped fruit, vegetable, cheese, and meat stands open weekdays until 6. The vendors are constantly trying to undersell one another, and you reap the benefits.

Try your luck at the **University Mensa** (Nassestr. 11, no phone), where five cafeterias serve five different (at least one vegetarian) meals for lunch (11:30–2) and dinner (5:30–8). Meals are only DM 4 (DM 8 if you get snagged without a student ID). You can always find a bite at **Imperatore** (Kaiserpl. 18, tel. 0228/634644), where pasta dishes are DM 9–DM 12 but you can get a pizza or "mini" dish for DM 6. Downstairs is the restaurant's lively café/bar (beer DM 3–DM 5); escape the salmon-colored interior and sit under the trees on Kaiserplatz. Grab a quick falafel (DM 3) at **Uni Grill** (Am Neutor 8, tel. 0228/695153), near the Münster. Though the spotless Uni Grill also serves good gyros, the best in town (DM 6) are at **Schmecklecker Grill** (Wenzelg. 40, off Friedrichstr., tel. 0228/632885). **Blau** (Franziskanerstr. 5, tel. 0228/650717), near Koblenzer Tor, under the university's castle wall, is a café/restaurant full of students talking, reading, and studying. The food is healthful and good; nosh on green salad (DM 4) and penne with pesto (DM 6.50).

WORTH SEEING

The dark spire of Bonn's elegant Romanesque **Münster** (abbey church; open daily 7–7) dominates the Altstadt, while the interior is bright and breathtaking. Near the cathedral, on Münsterplatz, is the **Beethoven-Denkmal** (Beethoven Monument), a stoic tribute financed in 1832 by Franz Liszt. Before musical sentiment tugs you to Beethoven's birthplace (*see below*) check out the very pink, very ornate, very rococo **Rathaus** on the Markt. On the first Saturday of every month from noon to 4, you can enter the reception rooms for free. To reach the government center and the new **Museum Mile** (*see below*), take U16 or U63 south toward Rheinallee/Bad Godesberg and get off at Heussallee/Bundeshaus.

Two blocks north of the Rathaus in the Altstadt, the **Beethoven-Haus** (Bonng. 20, tel. 0228/635188; open Mon.–Sat. 10–4, Apr.–Sept. until 5, Sun. 10–1), where Beethoven was born in 1770, now houses a museum in his honor. Displays (including instruments, manuscripts, and most poignantly, the ear trumpets Beethoven used to fight advancing deafness) are sparse and effective. Though he left Bonn at age 22, this museum illustrates his entire intense and tormented life. Admission is DM 8 (DM 5 students). South of the Rathaus, follow Stockenstraße out of Marktplatz to Regina-Pacis-Weg and the **Kurfürstliches Schloß,** a squat castle once the seat of the Bishop-Electors and now a university administration hall. Behind the Schloß are the **Hofgarten** and **Stadtgarten,** two parks filled with students, sunbathers, punks, bums, and lots of trash. Continue past the Schloß through Kaiserplatz and across the railroad tracks until you reach the paths that line Poppelsdorfer Allee. The grassy patch down the middle is a prelude to the **Botanical Gardens** (Meckenheimer Allee 171, behind the 18th-century Poppelsdorfer Schloß, tel. 0228/732259). The gardens' best exhibit is the mammoth Amazon water lilies, which can support up to 80 kilos. Free 90-min tours leave from the Lyrabecken Sundays at 10 AM, April–September. The gardens are open weekdays 9–6 and Sundays 9–1 (shorter hrs Oct.–Mar.). Admission is free except Sundays (DM 1).

From the Heussallee/Bundeshaus U-Bahn station, walk down Heussallee towards the Rhine and make a left on Görrestraße for the **Bundeshaus** (tel. 0228/162–2152; open weekdays 9–4, weekends 10–4), home of the **Bundestag** until April 1999, when the 664-member Parliament that makes most of Germany's laws and elects the chancellor and president moved to Berlin. The crystalline glass and steel building was finished in 1992, and no one wants to talk about what will become of it now that the Bundestag has skipped town. Call ahead for a spot on the mandatory 30-min tour of the dramatic plenary chamber, with explanations of the German political process. Tuesdays at noon the tour's in English (call ahead for hours).

MUSEUMS • Two km south of the Altstadt, near the Bundeshaus, is the **Museum Mile,** a collection of museums all opened, curiously, within three years of the decision to move the government to Berlin. The enormous, concrete, rough-edged **Kunst- und Ausstellungshalle der Bundesrepublik Deutschland** (Friedrich-Ebert-Allee 4, tel. 0228/917–1200) rotates its exhibits frequently to uphold its reputation as the best in the contemporary art scene. Its neighbor, the **Kunstmuseum Bonn** (Friedrich-Ebert-Allee 2, tel. 0228/776260), also goes off on some strange but enjoyable modern art tangents. Though both offer some of the best exhibitions around, they tend to have sparse English-language resources at best. Combined admission to the museums is DM 10 (DM 5 students). Both are open Tuesday–Sunday 10–7. The **Haus der Geschichte der Bundesrepublik Deutschland** (Adenauerallee 250, tel. 0228/91650; open Tues.–Sun. 9–7), just north of the art museums, celebrates and documents the Federal Republic (as West Germany and since reunification). If you're into this period of German history, the thorough and periodically updated coverage here requires most of a day, especially if you read German. If not, you can rent English-language cassette tours, or simply let the audiovisual exhibits enlighten you about everything from concentration camps to 1960s German soap operas. Admission is free except for special exhibits. To reach the Museum Mile, take the U-Bahn to Heussallee/Bundeshaus.

The **Museum Alexander König** (Adenauerallee 160, tel. 0228/91220; closed Mon.), just north of the Museum Mile, is a fine natural history museum noted for its spectacular butterfly exhibits. Unfortunately, explanations are in German only. Admission is DM 4 (DM 2 students). In a nondescript building behind the train station, the **Rheinisches Landesmuseum Bonn** (Colmanstr. 14–16, tel. 0228/72941; closed Mon.) has interesting exhibits on how industry and commerce functioned in the Roman period, with exhibits on recent archaeological findings. Explanations are in German only, and admission is DM 4 (DM 2 students).

CHEAP THRILLS

The biggest, cheapest thrill in Bonn is the **Rheinaue,** a 3-km-long stretch of mostly man-made lakes, hills, and gardens. Aside from general sunbathing and cavorting on both sides of the Rhine (the Rheinaue extends from each end of Konrad-Adenauer-Brücke), you can also catch an all-day **flea market** the third Saturday of every month. In early May, the **Rhein in Flammen** (Rhine in Flames) festival is celebrated in the Rheinaue with drinking, roller coaster riding, and a procession of barges on the Rhine, all lit up in red. If you'd rather do a little urban meandering, don't miss the picturesque **Südstadt** area, a student hangout just east of the Botanical Gardens. The university's **Kino-Club** (tel. 0228/469721) organizes free, nightly (9 PM), original-version films (most in English) in the courtyard of the university *Hauptgebäude* (main building) during the last two weeks of August.

AFTER DARK

The real action is in Cologne, but Bonn has a surprisingly colorful nightlife. You'll find music and dancing, but also some creative cabaret and theater, as well as a decent selection of films. The monthlies *Schnüss* and *Bonner Illustrierte* (both DM 3.50) have current listings.

There are several dark, quirky bars north of the Altstadt. **Pawlow** (Heerstr. 64, at Dorotheenstr., tel. 0228/653603) has an acid-flashback flavored interior and some tables on the street corner. The crowd may look hard, but they're mostly just overeducated and underworked, and hence into piercings and tattoos. Local political thrash bands frequent **Bla** (Bornheimer Str. 20, tel. 0228/637140), which is in a cluster of clubs in case things get too blah. Toward the Rhine is **Jazz Galerie** (Oxfordstr. 24, tel. 0228/639324), where you can hear good, live jazz (DM 6–DM 20) several nights a week below the linoleum-lined stairs. Other nights feature DJ dancing. Among the many quirky, interesting bars is **Zur Kerze** (Königstr. 25, tel. 0228/210769), a labyrinth of candlelit tables open daily 7 PM–5 AM. Along with fun and good music, they serve pricey, delicious Italian food to a happy late-night crowd. If you must have the Greek-system-in-Germany experience, the best spot is **Rheinlust** (Rheinaustr. 134, Beuel, by Kennedybrücke, tel. 0228/469860). Aside from a scenic setting on the river, their best feature may be the daily breakfast buffet (DM 7). Back by the university is **Zebulon** (Stockenstr. 19, no phone), a dark bar with occasional reggae performances.

Some of the most interesting evening activity in Bonn happens in bar/café/performance spaces. These include **Brotfabrik** (Kreuzstr. 16, tel. 0228/475424) in Beuel, which also shows films; **Pantheon** (Bundeskanzlerpl., tel. 0228/212521); **Pauke** (Endenicher Str. 43, tel. 0228/696672); and **Biskuithalle** (Siemensstr. 12, tel. 0228/612044). At any of these spots you can see theater, cabarets, and musical performances, or just have a drink. Covers vary; check *Schnüss* for listings.

NEAR BONN

DRACHENFELS

Don't end your visit to Bonn without traveling a few km south to see the **Siebengebirge** (Seven Mountains) and **Drachenfels** (Dragon Rock), that holy site where Germans claim the legend of the Nibelungen took place. The story that Wagner made famous in his opera, *The Nibelungen Ring,* is enshrined in the **Nibelungenhalle** (admission DM 5), a small, cultish-looking building on the ascent up the Drachenfels. Poorly lit oil paintings of Siegfried slaying the dragon and Siegmund's body in the shape of the Siebengebirge fill the hall. In the back are a den of caged, ferocious iguanas and a large concrete dragon. Continue uphill to the Drachenfels ruins, where Siegfried did the deed and where you'll find an amazing view of Bonn. All told, the hike takes about 45 min. There's a train (DM 12) that goes up to the ruins from Königswinter, a small wine-making town at the foot of the hill. *Drachenfels Str. 53, tel. 02223/22556. From Hauptbahnhof Bonn, U66 (direction: Bad Honnef) to Königswinter Fähre; up Drachenfelsstr. to Drachenfels railway. Trains run May–Sept. every 30 min; fewer trains off-season.*

KOTTENFORST

Bonn has one huge advantage over Cologne: the Kottenforst, a huge forest just a 30-min walk southwest of Bonn. You can take beautiful hikes on the well-marked trails or tour the region by bike (*see* Getting Around *in* Bonn, *above*). Before you set out, head to Bonn's tourist office and pick up a free *Fahrradroutenplan Bonn,* which clearly marks the major trails and their access routes from town, or buy a bigger, more detailed map at a bookstore.

AACHEN

You will certainly notice the countless school groups roving about in this city's labyrinthine Altstadt. But they won't bother you. There is enough to marvel at in this city to keep the kids, their teachers, and you occupied and happy. Aachen rightly sees itself as a gateway, nested as it is near the borders of Belgium and the Netherlands. Known and visited mostly for its unique history as the first capital of the Holy Roman Empire and its rejuvenating hot springs, Aachen is also home to a fun and eclectic student population and a dizzying array of bars and cafés.

From the moment Charlemagne (*Karl der Große*) set up shop here in the late 8th century, Aachen was destined for greatness. Indeed, 32 Holy Roman emperors were crowned in the capital's Dom, a breathtaking structure of symmetry and order. Even in the days of the Holy Roman Empire, Aachen's position as Rome's successor was somewhat overblown and its power largely symbolic. No longer a seat of power, Aachen has become an artistic, cosmopolitan city ready to feed your mind, raise your spirits, and destroy your liver.

Aachen's Cathedral is where the Charlemagne Prize Society awards the coveted *Internationaler Karlspreis* (Charlemagne Prize) to a promoter of European unity every year. In 1999 they gave it to British Prime Minister Tony Blair for his efforts to drag the British into the Single European Currency. All a bit premature, as Tony had not actually put the issue to a national referendum, and had not really gotten around to asking the Brits to vote yes. He says he will do that in 2002, kind of, maybe. The telling dispute over the prize's name—the Germans call it the Karlspreis, the French and British call it the Charlemagne Prize—harks back to the age-old argument over whether the first Holy Roman Emperor is Karl or Charlemagne. What hope is there, you might ask, for a United States of Europe?

BASICS

Aachen's **tourist office** (Friedrich-Wilhelm-Pl. 4, in Elisenbrunnen Atrium, tel. 0241/180–2960; open weekdays 9–6:30, Sat. 9–1), on the Grabenring east of the Dom, has city and transit maps, books rooms (DM 3), and answers questions very nicely. Ask them about current offerings in Aachen's impressive theater and gallery scenes. There is a Cirrus and Plus **ATM** near the train station entrance, and **American Express** (Kleinmarschierstr. 68, tel. 0241/470850), in the Altstadt near the Dom, will change your money weekdays 9–6 and Saturday 10–1. The **main post office** (Kapuzinergraben) is on the Grabenring, south of the Dom.

COMING AND GOING

Aachen's **Hauptbahnhof** (tel. 0241/11531) is just south of the center, a 10-min walk from the main square. Trains leave every half hour for Cologne (1 hr, DM 19) and Düsseldorf (1½ hrs, DM 23), hourly for Brussels (2 hrs, DM 34), and several times daily for Paris (4 hrs, DM 85) and London (8–9 hrs, via Oostende, DM 110). Give the city's **Mitfahrzentrale** (Roermonder Str. 4, tel. 0241/19440; open weekdays 10–6, Sat. until 2) a day or two's notice to arrange a ride share.

GETTING AROUND

Though small and manageable, Aachen is organized like a drunken spider's web. It can be confusing. The heart of the Altstadt is encircled by an inner ring of roads called the Grabenring where the early medieval wall lay. An outer ring, called the Alleenring, follows the course of later fortifications and is marked by the Bahnhof, Kaiserplatz, and the Ponttor. To walk from the station to the Elisenbrunnen (site of the tourist office), cross Bahnhofplatz, head up Bahnhofstraße, turn left on Theaterstraße, and right at Theaterplatz to Friedrich-Wilhelm-Platz.

Since in Aachen there is no such thing as a straight line between two points, get a map. Getting around by bus is easy (with a map), and several major lines stop outside the train station. Bus shelters have maps in them, but you can get one at the tourist office. Individual rides are DM 2.80, so you'll almost definitely get your money's worth with a 24-hour ticket (DM 8), which works for up to four people. If you don't mind some hills and cobblestones, Aachen is a great city for biking. Try **Hobbit Fahrräder** (Beeberstr. 1–3, tel. 0241/49475), where bikes cost DM 15 per day.

WHERE TO SLEEP

For the most part, Aachen is priced beyond budget range. Fortunately, a few places near the Hauptbahnhof are exceptions. One block from the station try **Hotel Dusa** (Lagerhausstr. 5, tel. 0241/403135), with clean rooms over the noisy street from DM 50 (single) and DM 90 (double). If you threw a baseball from in front of the station you'd probably break a window at **Hotel am Bahnhof** (Bahnhofpl. 8, tel. 0241/35449). Generic doubles start at DM 80, singles DM 50, here and at Am Bahnhof's nameless sister hotel (Leydelstr. 10, same phone), which is farther from the buses and above a quiet bar. Prices include breakfast.

HOSTEL • Jugendherberge Aachen-Colynshof (HI). This hostel is perched on a hill in a beautiful neighborhood above Aachen, a nice walk (30 min) from town, but take the bus with your pack unless you want to sweat. The hostel recently emerged from renovations with two- and four-bed rooms. One night costs DM 28.50 (no age limit), including breakfast. *Maria-Theresia-Allee 280, tel. 0241/71101, fax 0241/708219. From Hauptbahnhof, any bus west 1 stop to Finanzamt; at opposite bus stop, either Bus 2 to Ronheide or Bus 12 to Colynshof/Jugendherberge. 160 beds. No curfew. Reception open 7:30 AM–1 AM, but call ahead. Small lockers.*

FOOD

You certainly won't go hungry or thirsty in Aachen. The Altstadt is lined with restaurants that almost all feature outdoor seating among the city's beautiful monuments. Pontstraße, north of the Altstadt, is lined with restaurants, cafés, and *Imbiß* (snack) stands that get more interesting (less touristy) as you move farther from the Altstadt. For picnic supplies, visit **Plus** (Bahnhofstr. 18–20), the nearby bakery **Tappe** (Bahnhofstr. 22), or the produce market **Jansen** (Bahnhofstr. 2), which might be more appetizing. Get a list of Aachen's rotating daily **markets** at the tourist office.

Crowded with young locals, the mouth-watering **Café Lokma** (Kaiserpl. 25, tel. 0241/25827), on the east side of the Alleenring, serves Turkish and Mediterranean specialties. Among the many veggie options are stuffed eggplant (DM 10.50) and vegetarian soup (DM 5). A huge salad with yogurt dressing can be added to any entrée for DM 5. Occupying the ground floor of the college student center, **Chico Mendez** (Pontstr. 74–76, tel. 0241/47000), an exclusively vegetarian restaurant and bar is always packed, with every game imaginable for you to play (well, except Twister). Enjoy a game of *Monopol* over a veggie pizza (DM 7), or salad (DM 4–DM 6). Check for nightlife postings, especially for the attached disco. If you're on the Markt by the Rathaus and feel suddenly drawn toward those golden arches, stop! Just around the corner you can get all the grease you crave in a Vietnamese way at **Nam Phat** (Großkölnstr. 6, tel. 0241/402628). Veggie spring rolls are only DM 1.50 each, mixed plates of flavored specialties run DM 6–DM 12.50, and the batter-fried jumbo shrimp beat any sort of McNugget.

WORTH SEEING

Exploring Aachen's Altstadt is a delight. Even with your map you'll get disoriented as you stumble across yet another fountain (there are 18). Look for the **Puppenbrunnen** with its movable figures or the elaborate **Elisenbrunnen** on the Grabenring. On the Markt sits the 14th-century **Rathaus,** whose stately chambers can be visited daily 10–1 and 2–5 for DM 3 (students DM 1.50). East of the market square is the **Altes Kurhaus** (Old Spa; Komphausbadstr. 19), an ornate 18th-century building. To the north down Pontstraße is the **Ponttor,** all that remains of Aachen's defensive wall. Just outside the Alleenring to the northeast is the famous **Casino** (Monheimsallee), gorgeous to look at and, in proper attire, probably fun to gamble in. Next door, however, you *can* mix with the jet set (well, at least the Cessna set) in **Kurbad Quellenhof** (Monheimsallee 52, tel. 0241/180–2922), where a two-hour soak in their elegant spa costs DM 16. Behind the Casino and Quellenhof arc the rolling hills of Aachen's **Stadtgarten,** where walks and picnics are relaxing (and free).

DOM AND DOMSCHATZKAMMER • If you come to Aachen just to see the Dom, it will be worth it. The original eight-sided *Pfalzkapelle* (chapel) was built during Charlemagne's time, and the dome's ceiling is a stunning mosaic. From here you can see into the Gothic **chancel** constructed after Charlemagne's canonization in the 12th century. To visit the gilded **Shrine of Charlemagne** (which places him and other Holy Roman emperors in the positions usually reserved for Jesus and the 12 apostles) or **Charlemagne's** (so-called) **throne,** you must join one of the guided tours (DM 5) that leave from the **Schatzkammer** (cathedral treasury), a block west. These are in German except when arranged in advance (minimum 10 people). However, if one has been arranged, you can join it; ask at the Schatzkammer. The treasury (admission DM 5, DM 3 students) houses an astonishing array of riches, including the jewel-encrusted Lothar's cross and an ivory diptych from Charlemagne's time. *Dom: open Mon.–Sat. 11–7, Sun. 1–7. Schatzkammer: on Klosterg., tel. 0241/4770–9127. Open Mon. 10–1, Tues.–Sun. 10–6:30, Thurs. until 9.*

MUSEUMS • The **Couven-Museum** (Hühnermarkt 17, tel. 0241/432–4421; closed Mon.) houses a collection of bourgeois artifacts from 18th-century Aachen. Admission is DM 2 (DM 1 students). In the house where Reuter began his news agency is the **Internationales Zeitungsmuseum** (Pontstr. 13, tel. 0241/432–4508; open Tues.–Sat. 9:30–1, Thurs. and Fri. also 2:30–5), with a fascinating collection of press stories from the last 150 years. Admission is free. The **Suermondt Ludwig Museum** (Wilhelmstr. 18, tel. 0241/479800; closed Mon.) has excellent medieval European sculpture on display. Admission is DM 6 (DM 3 students). The **Ludwig Forum für Internationale Kunst** (Jülicher Str. 97–109, tel. 0241/18070; closed Mon.) is dedicated to all forms of art, including performance and film. Admission is DM 6 (DM 3 students).

AFTER DARK

Even if you didn't come here to party, Aachen's bustling nightlife calls to you. While the Altstadt sizzles, you can get equally packed in pubs along Pontstraße. Try **Guinness House** (Neupforte 6, tel. 0241/402211) in the Altstadt, which captures the unique feel—dark yet cheerful—of an Irish pub on two levels with a rooftop beer garden. Guinness on tap is available evenings after 6. You can boogie at **Katakomb** (attached to Chico Mendez, *see* Food, *above*) or **Odeon** (Pontstr. 135, tel. 0241/48874) from about 10 PM for DM 7–DM 10. For the scoop pick up *Klenkes* (DM 3.50) at any newsstand.

DÜSSELDORF

In Düsseldorf you'll see women and men with chiseled jaws and prominent cheekbones wearing tortoiseshell glasses and driving BMWs—but they probably won't see you. They are members the new German class of entrepreneur: Highly educated and multilingual, they work in offices of appropriately polished metal and cut glass. Düsseldorf is Germany's second-largest financial center (following Frankfurt), and it acts as the banking and headquarters city for the **Ruhrgebiet** (*see below*), the big industrial region northeast of the city. It is also the capital of the mighty state of North Rhine-Westphalia. State presidents have a reputation of defending their own against the federal government no matter what party is in power. Ironically, while Düsseldorfers are considered snobby because of their wealth, the city is also written off as a dumping ground for partying blue-collar workers from the Ruhrgebiet. Once you pound the neglected pavement away from the showcase financial center, you may notice that all is not as it once was: Düsseldorf plunges into seediness.

The city, at the intersection of the Rhine and the Düssel rivers, has humble origins as a fishing town. As a city, it is brand-new by European standards. It began to grow only after Napoleon made it the capital of the surrounding region in 1806. As such, it benefited from the industrial revolution that ensued in the nearby Ruhr region, and the city became a force not only in finance and fashion, but also in art—particularly the avant-garde. Düsseldorf has a well-preserved and extensive Altstadt, food that is surprisingly inexpensive, art museums and galleries worthy of any major city, and a diverse nightlife.

BASICS

The **Amex office** (Heinrich-Heine-Allee 14, tel. 0211/82200; open weekdays 10–5:30, Sat. 9–noon) will cash your American Express checks for free and offers the usual services. Take the U-Bahn to Heinrich-Heine-Allee. The **DVB** (tel. 0211/364878) in the Hauptbahnhof is open Monday–Saturday 7 AM–9 PM, Sunday 8 AM–9 PM and has a 24-hour ATM. **Deutsche Bank** branches throughout the city have Cirrus and Plus ATMs. Make phone calls at the **Post** at the back of the Hauptbahnhof; it's open daily and has longer hours than the main post office on Konrad-Adenauer-Platz. The **British Consulate** (Yorckstr. 19, tel. 0211/94480; open weekdays 8–noon) can help its citizens with things like lost passports, but call first. The tiny **Waschsalon** (Wallstr. 2; open Mon.–Sat.) is hard to find, but it's in the Altstadt and costs DM 9 per wash, including soap, and DM 1 for 10 min of drying. Take the U-Bahn to Heinrich-Heine-Allee, veer left (toward Altstadt), and keep alert for Wallstraße.

VISITOR INFORMATION • Düsseldorf's **tourist office** (Verkehrsverein; Immermannstr. 65b, tel. 0211/172020, fax 0211/161071), across from Hauptbahnhof to the right, is surely one of the best-staffed in Europe. The English-speaking employees are happy to make hotel reservations (DM 5), give you free maps, tell you how to get somewhere, or tell you what special events are going on. It's open weekdays 8:30–6, Saturdays 9–12:30, and rooms are reserved Monday–Saturday 8–8, Sunday 4–8.

The average annual income of Düsseldorfers is 25% higher than that of the average German.

Düsseldorf's **lesbian and gay center,** LuSZD (Kronenstr. 76, at Bachstr., tel. 0211/330292, fax 0221/934–5037), has a nice café/bar and a library and is a good place to pick up *Facette,* the bimonthly queer rag. They'll also have postings about **Rosa Mond** (*see* After Dark, *below*). The center is a block west of Trams 707 and 708 and two blocks from the Bilk stop on the S-Bahn.

COMING AND GOING

The **Düsseldorf Hauptbahnhof** is like a small, self-contained city, where you can get money, have coffee or beer, and buy anything from an apricot to a condom. Trains leave four times an hour for Cologne (25 min, DM 12.20) and hourly for Frankfurt (2½ hrs, DM 72), Hanover (2½ hrs, DM 95), and Berlin (5½ hrs, DM 181). Düsseldorf's Hauptbahnhof sits at the hub of an extensive system of S-Bahn lines, serving every major city within an hour of Düsseldorf, including Cologne, Wuppertal, and the entire Ruhrgebiet. S-Bahn tickets for these shorter trips are cheaper than Deutsche Bahn tickets (or you can use your EurailPass), but the S-Bahn is slower than regular trains. To reach the S-Bahn platforms, follow the green "S" signs. **Citynetz Mitfahrzentrale** (Kruppstr. 102, tel. 0211/19444) is open weekdays 9–7, Saturday 9–4, and Sunday (telephone only) 11–5. The English-speaking operators can usually help you get to Munich (DM 53), Berlin (DM 51), or elsewhere with as little as 24 hours' notice. Take S6 or S7 to Volksgarten.

BY PLANE • **Düsseldorf International Airport** is connected to the Hauptbahnhof via the S21 and S7 (3 per hr, 20 min, DM 3.50) daily between 5:20 AM and midnight. The airport serves Munich, Berlin, London, and Paris hourly and has two daily nonstops to New York. Call 0211/421–2223 between 6 AM and midnight for info.

GETTING AROUND

Most of the Altstadt is bordered by Königsallee on the east, the Rhine on the west, Hofgarten on the north, and Haroldstraße on the south. To reach Heinrich-Heine-Allee in the Altstadt by sneaker from the train station, simply head down Friedrich-Ebert-Straße, which becomes Steinstraße, and take a right on Breite Straße, which becomes Heinrich-Heine-Allee.

For a quicker connection, use the **U-Bahn.** Getting around in Düsseldorf might seem intimidating—there are a lot of options, symbols, and numbers—but every U-Bahn line runs from the Hauptbahnhof to Heinrich-Heine-Allee, **tram** and U-Bahn lines run through every neighborhood, and S-Bahn lines offer speedy connections to more far-flung parts of the city. Get maps at the tourist office. The U-Bahn network converges on the Hauptbahnhof's lower level; trams and buses leave from in front of the station. Tickets are valid for a limited time (from validation). Generally the shortest (rate "K," 40 min) is enough, but if in doubt, find your destination on the list. Single rides are DM 3.20, but a "Yes" ticket (for four rides) costs only DM 6. A *Tagesticket* (DM 10.80) lets you, four friends, and one dog party on public transit all day (until 3:30 AM). Buy individual tickets from bus and tram drivers, or from machines in U-Bahn stations. For a **taxi,** call 0211/33333.

WHERE TO SLEEP

When you get off the train in Düsseldorf, you'll probably notice that next to the large DÜSSELDORF HAUPTBAHNHOF signs hang equally large (and considerably more ominous) signs that read IHRE MESSESTADT (YOUR CONVENTION CITY). Conventions bring droves that fill hotels and raise the prices of rooms by DM 20–DM 40. Don't turn the page yet—there's a bright side. When there's no Messe, the prices become reasonable, especially with a little bargaining, and you'll find cheap lodging a few min from the train station.

Christlicher Verein Junger Menschen (CVJM). It's the German equivalent of the YMCA, but with spacious, comfy rooms. Its convenient location near the train station also means the neighborhood can be a little sketchy late at night. Singles DM 65–DM 75, doubles from DM 111, breakfast not included. *Graf-Adolf-Str. 102, tel. 0211/172850, fax 0211/361–3160. From Hauptbahnhof, left on Graf-Adolf-Str. 27 rooms, some with bath.*

Diana. If a Messe hasn't filled this place, the small rooms with adjoining bathrooms are comfortable, if somberly furnished. The Altstadt is a 15-min walk away. Singles start at DM 60, doubles are DM 90 (DM 120 with shower), breakfast included. *Jahnstr. 31, tel. 0211/375071, fax 0211/364943. From Hauptbahnhof, left on Graf-Adolf-Str., left on Pionierstr., right on Luisenstr., left on Jahnstr. 20 rooms, some with bath.*

Haus Hillesheim. This recently renovated place is sort of a family affair, with some rooms in the back garden overlooking a swingset. The friendly owner makes deals for students, especially during slow periods. They'll move a roll-away bed into your room for an extra DM 20. All rooms have a TV and phone. Singles run DM 70–DM 180, doubles DM 80 and up, all including breakfast. *Jahnstr. 19, tel. 0211/371940, fax 0211/384–9151. From Hauptbahnhof, left on Graf-Adolf-Str., left on Pionierstr., right on Luisenstr., left on Jahnstr. 18 rooms, some with bath. No credit cards.*

Komet. This is probably your best budget bet. Modern, black-accented rooms are competitively priced, the location can't be beat, and the huge windows make the rooms comfortable and airy. Singles start at DM 65, doubles at DM 90. Private showers cost DM 10 extra. *Bismarckstr. 93, tel. 0211/178790, fax 0211/178–7950. Left out of Hauptbahnhof, right on Bismarckstr. 18 rooms, some with bath. Breakfast included.*

HOSTEL • Jugendherberge und Jugendgästehaus Düsseldorf (HI). In the posh neighborhood of Oberkassel right along the Rhine, this hostel remains spotless despite nightly abuse by drunken guests. When you hopelessly stumble home after the 1 AM curfew, you need only wait till the next hour tolls to be let in. Beds, with sheets and breakfast in the morning, cost DM 28.50 (DM 32.50 over 27). *Düsseldorfer Str. 1, tel. 0211/557319, fax 0211/492505. From Hauptbahnhof, U70, U74, U75, U76, or U77 (direction: Krefeld, Am Seestern, or Neuss) to Luegpl.; south on Kaiser-Wilhelm-Ring to foot of Rheinkniebrücke (Rhine Bridge). 280 beds. Reception open 7:15 AM–10:30 PM. Laundry (DM 9), luggage storage. Closed 2 weeks at Christmas.*

CAMPING • Campingplatz Lörick. Be prepared for coal barges churning through murky waters. You'll be sharing this scenic spot with car campers. Sites DM 5 per person, DM 8 per tent, DM 2 per car. *Niederkasseler Deich 305, tel. 0211/591401. U-Bahn to Belsenpl., then Bus 828 to Strandbad Lörick; follow path on the levee to site. Closed sometimes Oct.–Mar. due to nasty weather.*

FOOD

The traditional breweries strewn about the Altstadt are great for eating (as well as drinking) in a relaxed, even inexpensive, atmosphere, even though they're only blocks away from snobby, expensive Königsallee. You can find lots of cheap restaurants and Imbiß offerings around Bolkerstraße and Hunsrückenstraße. The Bahnhof area, around Graf-Adolf-Straße in particular, is also a gold mine. To put your own meal together, head for the open-air market on **Karlplatz,** just south of the Altstadt, held weekdays 8–6 and Saturday 8–2. Or try a grocery store like **Plus** (Kölner Str. 26, tel. 0211/352128), just up Worringer Straße from the station.

Anadolu. This shiny, modern Altstadt place serves traditional Turkish fare. Enjoy stuffed pastries for only DM 3–DM 4.50, or dive into daily specials like curried lamb kebab (DM 8.50). There are always vegetarian options. *Mertensg. 10, tel. 0211/329335. U-Bahn to Heinrich-Heine-Allee, then Bolkerstr. to Mertensg.*

Hot-la-Cucina. At the coolest place near the youth hostel, you can join the dressed-to-kill Oberkassel crowd for fresh, creative Italian fare. The tiny restaurant is packed nightly for its pasta and pizzas like *Temperamente* (with fresh peppers, mushrooms, and garlic; DM 12). *Dominikanerstr. 14, near Barbarossapl. U-Bahn, tel. 0211/556418. From hostel, head down Düsseldorfer Str., right on Dominikanerstr.*

Im Golden Kessel Brauerei. Tradition in Düsseldorf mandates that while standing or sitting around the long tables at this place, you drink plenty of Alt, take plenty of flak from the blue-apron-clad waiters, and eat plenty of pork. If you want to dabble in local cuisine, try the aggressive artery clogger *Rheinischer Sauerbraten* (stewed pickled beef; DM 20), or bratwurst, potatoes, and salad for DM 15.50. *Bolkerstr. 44, tel. 0211/326007. U-Bahn to Heinrich-Heine-Pl.; west on Bolkerstr. Closed Tues.–Thurs.*

Zur Uel. A nontraditional brew house, the "Uel" teems with college-age eaters and drinkers who seem a bit tense and frayed. The food—mainly salads, soups, and pastas for DM 9–DM 15—is down-to-earth, and the portions are generous. Every cultural and political event in the city is advertised on at least one of the posters in the entry hall. *Ratinger Str. 16, tel. 0211/325369. U-Bahn to Tonhalle; SE on Hofgartenrampe, right on Ratinger Str.*

WORTH SEEING

Bordered by the serene Hofgarten park to the north and east and by the Rhine to the west, the **Altstadt**'s maze of small streets and alleys is home to more than 200 bars and restaurants, as well as to the major art museums. Get a map from the tourist office and be prepared to use it. Sleek and straight is **Königsallee,** "the essence of Düsseldorf." Enjoy an afternoon stroll along the canal, surrounded by swans, dramatic statues of Neptune, art-nouveau-esque street lamps, and smartly clad middle-aged shoppers staring vapidly over dangling cigarettes. For DM 5, you can get a broader view of the sprawling city from the top of the **Rheinturm** (Stromstr. 20; open daily 10 AM–midnight), a 770-foot TV tower that Düsseldorf considers a sign of being "an important city." To reach the tower, take Bus 725 (direction: Lausward) from the Hauptbahnhof, or hoof it south along the river from the Altstadt. The **Hofgarten**'s (U-Bahn to Jan-Wellen-Pl.) grassy knolls, trees, sandy walking paths, and lake form the northern and northeastern edge of the Altstadt. Düsseldorfers come here to stroll, sunbathe in their Gianni Versace bikinis, bike, or just have a beer. There are no pooper-scooper laws in the Hofgarten, but there are plenty of dogs. Watch your step.

One brochure calls the 80-room rococo **Schloß Benrath** (Benrather Schloßallee 102–104, tel. 0211/899–7271; open Tues.–Sun. 11–5) a "complete work of art," in which the palace's architecture, sculpture, painting, and garden are interwoven. We call it gaudy. The best parts are the benches, flowers, tree-canopied footpaths, and reflecting pools in the extensive gardens. Admission is DM 6 (DM 3 students); tours leave every 30 min. Take Tram 701 to Schloß Benrath (about 20 min). The display text at the ultramodern **Löbbecke-Museum und Aquazoo** (Kaiserswerther Str. 380, tel. 0211/899–6150; open daily 10–6) is in German, but whatever language you speak, you can enjoy the seals, penguins, sharks, turtles, and alligators, as well as some incredibly huge catfish. Admission is DM 8 (DM 4 students). Take the U-Bahn to Nordpark/Aquazoo. Farther north, weeds and vines blanket the ruins of **Kaiserpfalz,** a fortress north of the present-day suburb of Kaiserswerth. The grounds of the fort, built in 1184 by Holy Roman Emperor Frederick Barbarossa, are now just a park. Next door, the **Wintergarten** beer garden (Burgallee 1, behind Burghof restaurant, tel. 0211/401423) is loaded with drinkers, especially on sunny afternoons. Take the U79 (direction: Duisburg) to Klemensplatz; cross the tracks, follow Klemensplatz to Kaisers Werther Markt, and turn left at the Rhine (45-min walk). The park is open sunrise–7 PM.

MUSEUMS • The dark and shiny **Kunstsammlung Nordrhein-Westfalen** (Grabbepl. 5, tel. 0211/83810; open Tues.–Sun. 10–6), a block north of the Heinrich-Heine-Allee U-Bahn stop in the Altstadt, focuses on individual modern artists, with works by Picasso, Matisse, Pollack, and Marc Chagall. It also has one of the finest Paul Klee exhibits anywhere. (Klee lived and taught in Düsseldorf for a few years.) Admission is DM 8 (DM 4 students). Across the street from the Kunstsammlung are the **Städtische Kunsthalle** (Grabbepl. 4, tel. 0211/131469) and **Kunstverein für die Rheinlande und Westfalen** (tel. 0211/327023). Sharing the same building, they feature modern art, photography, and sculpture and complement the Kunstsammlung with a very strong Paul Klee collection. They share hours, too: Tuesday and Thursday–Sunday 11–6, Wednesday 11–8. Enter both halls for DM 5 (DM 2.50 students). The **Kunstmuseum** (Ehrenhof 5, tel. 0211/899–2460; open Tues.–Sun. 11–6) is noted for its collection of paintings from the Middle Ages and exhibits on European arts and crafts. Admission is DM 5 (DM 2.50 students). From the Tonhalle U-Bahn stop, cross the street and walk across the park past the large Picasso sculpture. The **Heinrich-Heine-Institut** (Bilker Str. 12–14, tel. 0211/899–5571; open Wed.–Sat. 10–5), south of the Altstadt, won't do much for you if you don't read German; the man's opera glasses and desk hardly evoke the brave writer exiled for his criticism of Prussian militarism and social inequality. Admission is DM 4 (DM 2 students). A similar fate awaits the German-illiterate at the **Goethe-Museum** (Jacobistr. 2, tel. 0211/899–6262; closed Mon.), northeast of the Altstadt in the posh, gilded Schloß Jägerhof. If you do read German, you may get a kick out of the letters written to Goethe by his friends. Admission is DM 4, DM 2 students.

AFTER DARK

Some Düsseldorfers don't like the rough-edged partyers who flock here from the Ruhrgebiet, but they still shed their glossy facades and join the crowds that cram the bars in the Altstadt. Take a look at the monthly *Überblick* (DM 4.50), *Prinz* (DM 5), *Coolibri* (free), or the local newspaper, the *Rheinische Post.* All of these have fairly good, diverse listings, though you'll find more (especially reviews) in the expensive ones. **Uerige** (Berger Str. 1, at Rheinstr., tel. 0211/866990; open daily until midnight) lives up to its name—old and traditional. Never order a Pils—Alt's the word in beer here. For the occasional Irish band and a rowdy good time, try **Sutton's Irish Pub** (Hunsrückenstr. 13, tel. 0211/133181) daily 7 PM–2 AM. Plenty of dance clubs also dot the Altstadt. For techno-funk go to the **Ratinger Hof** (Ratinger Str. 10, tel. 0211/32877), where the indecent cover of DM 18 gets you an industrial-meets-India decor and mostly straight, ultramodern-styled patrons. An entirely different crowd shakes it at the grungy **Purple Haze** (Lieferstr. 7, tel. 0211/328220). With black-and-whites of Jimi Hendrix and Pete Townsend on the walls, the message is clear—this place is hard and loud. Doors open at 10 for live music, and the cover is DM 10; with DJs, the cover is DM 7. These clubs hop until 5 AM on Friday and Saturday nights, and both are closed Monday and Tuesday. Queer nightlife in Düsseldorf centers on the **Café Rosa Mond** (Oberbilker Allee 310, tel. 0211/775242; open nightly from 8 PM), in an inconspicuous courtyard. Every night there's a different theme (lesbian pub, moon dance, disco) or program (support groups, performances). To see what's up, drop by, or visit LuSZD (*see* Visitor Information, *above*). To reach the café, take the U-Bahn, S-Bahn, or tram to Oberbilk.

NEAR DÜSSELDORF

XANTEN

This comfortable country town sprang up just south of the abandoned Roman colony *Ulpia Traiana.* As Xanten grew, the Roman settlement provided a convenient quarry and soon vanished. Today's Xanten survived wartime bombings and retains much of its medieval character. From a distance, the Romanesque facade of the mostly Gothic **Dom** stands out. Located in a raised courtyard just off the **Markt,** the Dom is an architectural hodgepodge with a cluttered, interesting interior. Much of the 14th-century **city wall** remains, but the north section is the most interesting. The **Klever Tor** (built in 1392) is one of the oldest surviving double gateways in the region. Both the Klever Tor and the more modest **Rundturm** on the west wall have been converted into guest quarters.

Xanten's biggest draw, though, is its **Archaeological Park.** The Romans built *Colonia Ulpia Traiana* as a northern stronghold, but as the empire fell back from its frontiers, the colony was abandoned. In the 1970s (after most of the area had been excavated and the important discoveries housed in Bonn) a controversial idea was proposed: to create life-size re-creations of the town's structures. The result is a somewhat unhappy compromise—most of the park is made up of beautifully groomed gardens and shady lanes, with the city wall and the partially reconstructed temple and amphitheater standing out. Scattered about are examples of early Roman technology (building cranes and mills) and feats of civil engineering (streets, the sewers, and water conduits). It would have been more powerful (and even more controversial) to do further reconstructions or to simply leave the excavation sites open for visitors. But bring a picnic and enjoy a day here; it's an interesting blend of city park and historical wonder. The single most horrifying aspect is the *Taverna,* where Roman dishes are served. *Tel. 02801/37298. From Markt, walk north on Karthaus, which becomes Rheinstr., then take Wardter Str. across highway; the park is on your left. Admission: DM 7, DM 4 students. Open daily 9–6; Jan. and Feb., daily 10–4.*

BASICS • From the station, signs clearly send you down Hagenbaschstraße or Bahnhofstraße right into the pedestrian zone in the Altstadt. When you enter the Markt, you will see the Rathaus, which houses the **tourist office** (Karthaus 2, tel. 02801/37238), open weekdays 10–4:30, weekends until 5. Here you can get a map and book a room. A great way to get around Xanten and its wide-open countryside is by bike. Rent one at **Zweiräder** (Marsstr. 19, tel. 02801/1474) near the Markt at DM 12 per day.

To get to Xanten by train, you must go through Duisburg. You can get from Düsseldorf to Duisburg by the S1 (every 20 min, 30 min) or frequent regular trains (15 min). Trains leave Duisburg for Xanten hourly (50 min). The last train back to Duisburg (with a connection to Düsseldorf) leaves Xanten at 10 PM daily. Total fare one-way is DM 15.

WHERE TO SLEEP AND EAT • Hotels here are either pricey or out of the way, but Privatzimmer, available through the tourist office, are a steal at DM 25–DM 40 per person, including breakfast. There are also several camping grounds including **Campingplatz Bremer** (Urseler Str. 25, tel. 02801/4730) about 3 km west of town, where sites cost DM 6 per person, and DM 4 per tent; again, you'll have to hike, bike, or cab it. From the station, head down Bahnhofstraße, left on Am Langacker to Eprather Weg, left on Trajanstraße, and right on Urseler Straße for 2 km. You can get picnic supplies at a bakery on Marsstraße or at the **supermarket** (on the Markt). The Altstadt's several nice cafés are pricey. **Römer Grill** (Marsstraße 12; closed Sat.–Mon.) has french fries for DM 1.50 and wurst starting at DM 2.30. Salads are DM 3 (small) or DM 6 (large).

WUPPERTAL

You might get confused when you arrive in sprawling Wuppertal, which is really a conglomeration of little cities that coalesced through population and industrial growth. Wuppertal's foci are **Elberfeld,** where you'll probably arrive by train, and **Barmen,** which has a youth hostel. Together, they are considered the birthplace of Germany's industrial revolution. The entire valley is connected by the **Schwebebahn,** Wuppertal's "world-famous" suspension railway. Ride up by the driver to fully experience the thrill of traveling 50 feet above the rambling Wupper River and swaying violently back and forth. You'll be dying to share your excitement with the all-too-blasé local riders. You can't really blame them, though, since the monorail's been trundling along its 13-km course for more than 80 years and carries as many as 50,000 commuters each day. (The railway suffered its first fatal accident in April 1999, when three people died as the monorail plunged into the river; a piece of metal left hanging from the track after repair work was the cause of the accident, not a train defect.) For you, though, the levitating petrified worm is a must-ride. Catch it below the Hauptbahnhof.

Analogies used to describe the Schwebebahn include: the slithering orange millipede, the meandering metal dragon, the floating iron snake, the city's steel backbone, and the big zipper. Suffice it to say that it puts the fun back into mass transit.

Aside from the Schwebebahn, Wuppertal prides itself on being surprisingly cultured. The **Von der Heydt-Museum** (Turmhof 8, tel. 0202/563–2223; open Tues.–Sun. 10–5, Thurs. until 9) in Elberfeld, renowned as one of the nation's foremost art collections, will still surprise you: It's even better than its reputation. It is focused on an interesting local artist, von Marées, but is home to many French Impressionists, including Monet, as well as artists like Dix, Kirchner, and Munch. Admission is DM 5 (DM 2.50 students). To get here, walk down from the Hauptbahnhof past the Schwebebahn and across the river onto Alte Freiheit, and turn left on Turmhof. There is always plenty of theater happening (a current list is available at the tourist office). Much of it finds a home in the newly renovated (and renamed) **Schillertheater** (Bundesallee 260, tel. 0202/563–9444), which is also the venue of world-famous choreographer Pina Bausch's **Tanztheater.** Bausch also organizes frequent dance festivals in Wuppertal; ask the tourist office (*see below*) for details. You'll find the Schillertheater a few blocks east of the Hauptbahnhof.

As industrialization advanced, young Barmen native Friedrich Engels, son of a factory owner, helped found the labor movement. The **Historisches Zentrum,** in the very bourgeois **Engels-Haus** where Engels was born, holds fascinating documents on the man (as well as on Marx and other early socialists) and a museum on early industrialism. Old machines, looms, and photos demonstrate how the region was thrust into the Industrial Age. *Engelsstr. 10, tel. 0202/563–6498. Schwebebahn (direction: Barmen) to Adlerbrücke; from Friedrich-Engels-Allee turn right on Engelsstr. Admission: DM 3. Open Tues.–Sun. 10–1 and 3–5.*

BASICS • Just outside the Wuppertal Hauptbahnhof, the **tourist office** (Pavillon am Döppersberg, tel. 0202/563–2180; open weekdays 9–6, Sat. 9–1) has DM 1 maps that make more sense of the region and the Schwebebahn system. They also have a list of Privatzimmer (from DM 30). Exit the station through the long underground passage and you'll come out beneath the office. The S8 and S11 connect Wuppertal and Düsseldorf (30 min, DM 5) every 20 min. **Trains** also run twice hourly to Cologne (45 min, DM 12). Feeling hungry? There are lots of affordable places to eat in Elberfeld's pedestrian zone or Barmen's Markt.

WHERE TO SLEEP • If you want a room to yourself, ask at the tourist office (*see above*) about Privatzimmer. You'll experience the lush greenery of the valley best if you stay in the **Jugendherberge (HI),** above a park in the hills over Barmen. The hostel isn't in tip-top shape, but the setting is peaceful and the management friendly. Beds cost DM 26 (DM 31 over 26), and breakfast is included. *Obere Lichtenplatzer Str. 70, tel. 0202/552372, fax 0202/557354. S-Bahn to Barmen Bahnhof; or, Schwebebahn from Eberfeld to Barmen (Alter Markt), then Bus 640 (direction: Ronsdorf) to Jugendherberge (DM 2.80 total). Curfew 10:30.*

THE RUHRGEBIET

Germany's industrial core sits along the quiet Ruhr river, on both sides of the (former) border between the Rhineland and Westphalia. The industrial revolution exploited the area's vast coal reserves, built tremendous steel and manufacturing industries, and quickly made the Ruhr Europe's most populous urban region. Today the land, traumatized by mines, mills, and factories, is recovering, but it's the industrial legacy that remains the region's most interesting feature. Museums in **Bochum** and **Dortmund** document the region's past, from mining to tremendous beer production (yes, it's an industry). Today, with plenty of people and not enough work, the landscape is marked by abandoned factories and magnificent graffiti—art or vandalism depending on your perspective—symbolic of the unemployed, for whom museums mean very little.

ESSEN

This is the biggest, baddest industrial town in Europe. At the hands of Alfred Krupp, Essen became the coal-mining capital of Germany, the Ruhrgebiet became Germany's (and Europe's) industrial heartland, and consequently, the Krupp dynasty became hugely rich and powerful. Essen's coal legacy ended when the last mine closed in 1986, but try as it might, Essen cannot shake the fact that its industrial past is the most interesting thing it has to offer. Today the dreary city center has the feel of a modern mall (and all the big-name retailers to go with it). Still the sixth-largest city in Germany, Essen boasts a number of museums and churches and has more lodging opportunities than most parts of the Ruhrgebiet. But it still shouldn't be on your top-10 list of things to see in Germany. Check out the history—some buildings and fine museums—then move along and leave the machinery churning.

Krupp didn't just produce coffeemakers and alarm clocks; he consolidated the economic might of his company in the 19th century by feeding Europe's military conflicts with new and improved killing machines. By World War I this arms trade was so successful that despite Germany's loss, Krupp came out stronger than ever. Alfred Krupp's **Villa Hügel** (tel. 0201/188–4823) shows just how far he went in terms of houses. It's monstrous. The **museum** (admission DM 1.50; open Tues.–Sun. 10–6) details the history of the Krupp dynasty. Recently the company provoked a national outcry when it cheekily attempted to take over its much larger rival, Thyssen. Germans have yet to feel comfortable with American-style corporate battles to the death. Interestingly, once the fuss had died down, the "merger" went ahead anyway. To get to the villa from the Hauptbahnhof, take the S6 (direction: Köln) to Hügel.

Krupp's villa is not the only architectural attraction in Essen. The pale green dome of the **Alte Synagoge** (Steeler Str. 29, tel. 0201/884–5128; open Tues.–Sun. 10–6) was destroyed twice, once during Kristallnacht in 1938 and again by bombs during the war. It's disturbing, to say the least, that the city council was reluctant to turn the synagogue into a memorial, as local Jews requested; scarier still was the text on the stone coffin that stood outside the synagogue from 1949 through 1981 (when it was finally removed), explaining why Jewish victims of the Nazi genocide "had to lose their lives." Today the synagogue houses a collection on Jewish life in Germany before and during World War II. Admission is free. From the Hauptbahnhof, head north across the square to Kettwiger Straße, right on I. Delbrügge, left on Schützenbahn, and across the busy street to the corner of Steeler Straße. Construction on the **Münster** (Burgpl., up Kettwiger Str. from the station) began in the 9th century. The plain Romanesque church remained until 14th-century Gothic additions (notably the spire) embellished it. It houses a statue of the Virgin Mary, **Goldene Madonna,** the oldest such work in western Europe. Other treasures are in the Münster's **Domschatzkammer** (treasury; admission DM 2; open Tues.–Sat. 10–5, Sun. 12:30–5).

For an industrial town, Essen has a pretty hip troika of museums as well. The list of 19th- and 20th-century German and French painters shown at the **Museum Folkwang** (in the Museumszentrum, Goethestr. 41, tel. 0201/884–5300; open Tues.–Sun. 10–6, Thurs. until 9) reads like the starting lineup for the modern-art all-stars: Gauguin, Kandinsky, Monet, Renoir, and Van Gogh, to name a few. It costs DM 5 to get in. Exit the Hauptbahnhof to the south onto Huyssenallee, which becomes Rüttenscheider Straße, turn right on Folkwangstraße, and cross Bismarckstraße to the Museumszentrum. Also in the Museumszentrum, the **Fotographische Sammlung** contains 20,000 photographs covering the history and development of artistic, documentary, and journalistic photography. The posters in the **Deutsches Plakatmuseum** (Rathenaustr. 2, Theaterpassage, tel. 0201/884–5108; open Tues.–Sun. noon–8) come from all over Europe—from Poland to England—and show that even mainstream ads (like circus announcements) can be artistic. Admission is DM 2. From the Hauptbahnhof, head up the left side of Willy-Brandt-Platz to Rathenaustraße.

Near the youth hostel in the suburb of **Werden,** one stop past the Villa Hügel on the S6, are the oldest parish churches north of the Alps: the 8th-century **Luciuskirche** (Heckstr.) and **Basilika St. Ludgerus,** the former *Reichsabteikirche* (Holy Roman imperial abbey). The Romanesque Lucius has been restored to its original 8th-century form, while the Basilika (Brückstr. 54), in the town's quiet Altstadt, has had a Gothic facelift. Its **Schatzkammer** (tel. 0201/491565; open Tues.–Sun. 10–noon and 3–5) preserves religious relics dating back to the 6th century. From the Werden S-Bahn station, cross the bridge over the Ruhr River and keep left for the Werdener Markt; where it meets Brückstraße stands the Basilika. For the Luciuskirche, head up the Werdener Markt from the bridge and turn left on Heckstraße, then right on Dückerstraße.

BASICS

The folks at the **tourist office** just across from the Hauptbahnhof in the Essener Reisebüro (Haus der Technik, tel. 0201/235427, fax 0201/226692) provide maps and lists of Privatzimmer and book hotel rooms. They're open weekdays 9–6, Saturday 10–12:30. Call the **Messe- und Kongreß-Service** (tel. 0201/724–4401; open Mon.–Thurs. 8:30–1 and 2–3:30, Fri. 8:30–noon and 1:30–2:30) if you want your room booked for you for free. Essen is connected every 15–20 min to Düsseldorf by the S1 and S6 (45 min, DM 11); the S6 continues on to Cologne (1½ hrs, DM 15), also accessible by frequent express trains (50 min, DM 25). You can change money in the train station at the **DVB,** or head to the Plus and Cirrus ATM by Track 12. The **Mitfahrzentrale** (Hauptbahnhof, south entrance, tel. 0201/19440; open daily 9–7) can arrange inexpensive shared rides.

WHERE TO SLEEP

Because most of Essen's visitors are here on business, hotel rates run high. You can find Privatzimmer starting around DM 40 through Tourist-Information (*see above*), which can also book you into one of Essen's cheaper hotels. At the homey **Zum Deutschen Haus** (Kastanienallee 16, tel. 0201/232989, fax 0201/230692), with singles from DM 80, doubles from DM 90, the jolly people hanging out in the restaurant/bar downstairs will probably buy you a beer.

The nearest hostel is in the suburb of Werden, where you may enjoy the beautiful hills over the Ruhr River more than Essen. To get here, hop the S6 (every 15 min until 11 PM, 10 min, DM 3) to Werden. Then take Bus 190 (direction: Ruhrlandklinik) to the Jugendherberge stop, or follow directions to the Basilika (*see above*), but turn right from the Werdener Markt onto Klemensborn, trudge up a steep hill for 20 min, and follow the signs to the **Jugendherberge (HI)** (Pastoratsberg 2, tel. 0201/491163, fax 0201/492505). Beds cost DM 26 (DM 31 over 26), breakfast included. Curfew is at 11:30 PM and reception is open until 10 PM, with a lockout 9 AM–11:30 AM.

BOCHUM

Fifteen km east of Essen, the town of Bochum has cleaner streets, well-dressed students, and—though it's also a big shopping area—a lot more charm. The **Deutsches Bergbaumuseum** (German Mining Museum; Am Bergbaumuseum 28, tel. 0234/58770) is the main reason to visit. Underneath the dramatic, 68-m-high pithead tower, the museum captures the changing economics and identity of the Ruhrgebiet. The hourly tour (in German) of the working "demonstration pit" takes you into the bowels of a coal mine as you learn about the history of mining in the region. Given the changes in the Ruhr, this exhibit is a fascinating memorial to an industry in its death throes, and even if you don't speak German, the tour is pretty impressive. Admission is DM 5, and the museum is open Tuesday–Friday 8:30–5, weekends 10–4. From the Hauptbahnhof, take the U35 (direction: Herne/Schloß Strünkede) to Bergbaumuseum. The **Eisenbahnmuseum** (Railway Museum; Dr.-C.-Otto-Str. 191, tel. 0234/992516; open Wed. and Fri. 10–5, Sun. 10–12:45), south of town, has displays from the Deutsche Bahn's past, including a turntable and switching equipment, as well as railcars and locomotives. To get here, take the U-Bahn from Bochum-Hauptbahnhof to Bochum-Dahlhausen, walk about 15 min down Dr.-C.-Otto-Straße. Admission is DM 7 (DM 4, students).

BASICS

In Bochum, inquire at the **tourist office** (in the Hauptbahnhof, tel. 0234/13031; open weekdays 9–5:30, Sat. 10–1) about hotels and sights in the city and be sure to scam a free map. They can also book you a room. Every 15–20 min, the S1 connects Bochum with Essen (15 min, DM 5) and Dortmund (20 min, DM 5).

WHERE TO SLEEP AND EAT

Unfortunately, there are no Privatzimmer in Bochum. One inexpensive hotel is **Kolpinghaus** (Maximilian Kolbe-Str. 14–18, tel. 0234/60190, fax 0234/65852), with singles from DM 45, doubles from DM 74. Head west from the Hauptbahnhof on Südring and walk left on Humboldtstraße to Maximilan-Kolbe-Straße. The best places to eat are on Kortumstraße, just off Südring west of the Hauptbahnhof. Try **Café Konkret** (Kortumstr. 21 at Kerkw., no phone), whose student crowd imbibes coffee, cola, cigarettes, and fresh, hot food like vegetarian stuffed *Fladenbrot* (a thick, flat, round white bread).

At the very modern (lots of steel and glass) **Ruhr-Universität-Bochum** (U35 towards Heustadt to Universität), you can meet students in the **Mensa** (head onto the campus and walk straight through, past the crashed-spaceship auditorium), where meals are only DM 4 (DM 6 for nonstudents), and visit the **Botanical Gardens** (south of the Mensa, tel. 0234/700–3098), open daily 9–6.

DORTMUND

Emerging from the Hauptbahnhof, you immediately notice the contrasts of Dortmund: The 14th-century Gothic Petrikirche and acres of parkland stand out amid the trappings of a modern, industrial city. Try as they might, Dortmund's historic sights, green parks, and tourist representatives can't quite obscure the industrial essence. The city's real calling is **beer,** which has been brewed here since the 15th century. Dortmund is second only to Milwaukee in beer production, according to the tourist office (*see below*), whose staff will let you know that the city brews more than 600 million liters and 25 different varieties of beer each year. If you don't like beer, don't bother visiting.

If you do visit, catch the U-Bahn to Markgrafenstraße and walk east down Landgrafenstraße to the **Brauerei-Museum** (Märkische Str. 85, tel. 0231/502–4856; open Tues.–Sun. 10–6) in a working Kronen brewery. You can smell this museum even before you see the chimney, towers, and well-stocked trucks. Inside, three hands-on levels take you through every step—from the field to your lips in the attached pub. Even if you don't read German, the exhibits are fascinating (for a beer lover). Admission is free. Of the Altstadt's four major churches, the **Petrikirche** (Westenhellw.) is worth a visit for its incredible **Antwerp Altar,** which depicts Christ's life but also opens out (in winter only) to reveal intricate carvings. The **Reinoldikirche** (Ostenhellw. near the Markt) boasts wooden statues of Reinold (the church's patron saint) and (most likely) Charlemagne that flank the chancel. On a more modern note, the very '70s **Museum am Ostwall** (Ostwall 7, tel. 0231/502–3247; closed Mon.), in the Altstadt, holds excellent, very '90s displays of Expressionist works by Macke, Beuys, and others, as well as impressive rotating exhibitions. Combined admission is a steep DM 12 (DM 8 students). The Altstadt's **Museum für Kunst und Kulturgeschichte** (Hansastr. 3, tel. 0231/502–5522; closed Mon.) has works by local artists; admission is DM 4.

BASICS

Dortmund is connected to Essen by the frequent S1 (40 min, DM 5) or by regular trains (every 30 min, 25 min, DM 5); express trains run every half hour to Düsseldorf (50 min, DM 20) and Cologne (1¼ hrs, DM 36); and local trains run hourly to Münster (50 min, DM 14). The **tourist office** (Königswall 20, tel. 0231/140341; open weekdays 9–6, Sat. 9–1), across from the station, has excellent maps for DM 1 and nifty brochures.

Most of Dortmund's sights lie within the circular area that was once the Altstadt, surrounded by streets whose names end in "-wall" and follow the course of the medieval wall. The Altstadt is bisected by the north–south **Hansastraße** and the east–west **Hellweg** (called Westenhellweg to the west of Hansastraße, Ostenhellweg to the east). The Markt is just east of their intersection, and the Hauptbahnhof is just northwest of the Altstadt across Königswall.

WHERE TO SLEEP AND EAT

Dortmund doesn't have a youth hostel or nearby campgrounds, so you're better off staying in Essen (*see above*). If you really want to stay here, **Pension Fritz** (Reinoldistr. 6, tel. 0231/571523), in the Altstadt just north of the Reinoldikirche (*see above*), has decent singles for DM 50 and doubles for DM 90. You can sample Dortmund's brewed concoctions on the **Markt,** where at least four major breweries have beer halls. They all serve food, of course, but if you're dying to try yummy Thüringer Wurst, join the line outside **Der Thüringer** (Markt 4) for the eponymous sausage (just DM 3.50) and other inexpensive specialties (like french fries topped with traditional sauces). Loads of cheap food from Chinese to Italian can be found along **Brückstraße** to the north. If you're around in the evening and want to escape the traditional Altstadt, many interesting bars lie near the Museum am Ostwall. Try either **Zum Schwarzen Schaf** (Olpe 37) or **Lux** (Olpe 45), where customers can send each other "Flirtbriefs" (flirt letters). Both face the museum and are open nightly from 7.

WESTPHALIA

As you head east from the Ruhrgebiet into bucolic Westphalia, urban grit gives way to gently rolling fields and forests. While the North Rhine has commanded mighty trade routes and rubbed elbows with cosmopolitan Belgium and Holland for centuries, Westphalia is more inward-looking, remaining focused on farming. Most non-Germans know Westphalia only as the name on a Volkswagen camper top, and the region remains relatively unspoiled by mass tourism—an attractive quality. Though it technically includes half of the Ruhrgebiet, including Bochum and Dortmund, Westphalia is defined by its countryside, like the lost-in-time **Teutoburg Forest** near Detmold. The surprisingly vibrant, historically majestic university town of **Münster** gives a dose of political activism and all-night partying to a region otherwise best for easy bike trips, long hikes, or rediscovering the Renaissance among the half-timbered houses and castles of **Detmold** and **Lemgo.**

MÜNSTER

If you don't get hit by a cyclist, you may have a close call while walking the winding streets of Münster. The stressful, sometimes hostile encounters on street corners among cyclists, pedestrians, and cars give you an idea of the hyperactive energy flowing through this city. Home to the immense Wilhelms Universität, the third-largest in Germany, Münster teems with nearly 60,000 mostly left-leaning students whose presence pervades protests, rallies, and the mass of bars and cafés in the **Kuhviertel** (*see* After Dark, *below*). If you don't read German, look for the word *gegen* on walls and posters; it means "against" and is a crucial part of the Münster student's vocabulary. Ironically, this liberalism runs rampant in a conservative town steeped in tradition. Assigned its own bishop in 805 after Charlemagne's missionary, Ludgeri, successfully converted the local Saxons to Christianity, Münster takes its name from the monastery he established. The university maintains its conservative heritage with well-bred, elitist professors and administrators who contrast with the students. These elders join Münster's old-guard in maintaining a decidedly conservative city. However, the constant clash of very conservative and very liberal doesn't gridlock Münster in anger and resentment, but forces the two sides to acknowledge each other.

BASICS

The **Stadtwerbung und Touristik** (Klemensstr. 9, tel. 0251/492–2710; open weekdays 9–6, Sat. 9–1) books rooms for free and has indexed color maps for DM 1. These are easier to decipher than the free, gray, one-page maps. From the Hauptbahnhof, head up Windthorststraße (which becomes Stubengasse) and left on Klemensstraße. The friendly employees at **Deutsche Verkehrskreditbank** (Bahnhofstr. 9, near Bahnhof, tel. 0251/58068) change money (DM 3), and there are several 24-hour ATMs on Windthorststraße. The **post office** (Berliner Pl. 37; open weekdays 8–6, Thurs. until 8:30, Sat. 8–1, Sun. 9–noon) is just to the left of the Hauptbahnhof. To make collect and credit-card international calls, try the phones out front. The postal code is 48143.

COMING AND GOING

Hourly trains from the **Hauptbahnhof** link Münster with Frankfurt (4 hrs, DM 90), Cologne (1¾ hrs, DM 44), and Bremen (1¼ hrs, DM 47), and trains run every two hours via Osnabrück to Hanover (1½ hrs, DM 57). The **Münster/Osnabrück Airport** (tel. 02571/943360) serves Berlin, Frankfurt, and Munich daily, and London and Paris on weekdays. Shuttle Buses 50 and 51 make the 30-min trip between the airport and Platform A2 of the **Busbahnhof** (in front of the train station) every 30 min. Münster also offers a zillion buses to everywhere in or near the city. The bus information kiosk (tel. 0251/694732) in the parking lot in front of the Hauptbahnhof has schedules and is open weekdays 7–7, Saturdays 7–2. Unfortunately, no one here speaks English very well. If you're not getting anywhere, go to the main office (Syndikatg. 9, tel. 0251/2835), open weekdays 8:45–4:30.

With so many students looking for rides, Münster's four Mitfahrzentralen, including **Citynetz** (Aegidiistr. 20a, tel. 0251/40400; open weekdays 10–6, Sat. 10–2, Sun. 11–2), are alive and kicking. Two popular destinations are Berlin (DM 45) and Hanover (DM 30). As usual, the more advance notice, the better your chances.

GETTING AROUND

On a map, Münster looks like a seen-better-days bicycle wheel, with the Dom at the center of it all. From there, spoke streets like Königsstraße and Tibusstraße radiate out to support the wheel of the park-fringed ring. For a bike to call your own, the **Deutsche Bahn Vermietung** counter (tel. 0251/691320; open daily 7 AM–10 PM) in the Hauptbahnhof rents rickety bikes that add some excitement to your ride for DM 11 (DM 7 with a train pass). You can also rent bikes at **ADFC** (at Westfalen gas station, Sentruper Str. 169, tel. 0251/81112) in the west end of town, or at the youth hostel (*see* Where to Sleep, *below*) if you're a guest. Remember: Bike bells are not kiddie toys in Münster. Use yours. Or make use of Münster's extensive **bus system** with a DM 7.50 ticket good for 24 hours during the week (or from Saturday through Sunday evening). Regular tickets cost DM 2.70. Friday and Saturday nights, when the system goes beddie-bye around 12:30 AM, call the night shuttle **Nacht AST** (tel. 0251/666605) a half hour or more before you want to get home from designated points such as Ludgeriplatz (Platform A1). It'll cost you DM 5.70 per person. For a regular **taxi** call 0251/60011.

WHERE TO SLEEP

Although finding a hotel in Münster is easy—there are plenty near the Hauptbahnhof—finding a cheap one is next to impossible. Stay at the youth hostel, which is within walking distance of downtown, or else rent a bike or buy a bus pass and get out of the city center. The tourist office will call around for you before you venture off to the outskirts.

Bockhorn. This place looks like it hasn't been redecorated since it opened in 1956, but it's the only cheap option near the station. Call ahead, as it's often full. Singles DM 58, doubles DM 98, including breakfast. *Bremer Str. 24, tel. 0251/65510. Left from Hauptbahnhof, left on Hafenstr., under tracks, left on Bremer Str. 35 rooms.*

Haus vom Guten Hirten. The church group that runs the House of the Good Shepherd has kindly put *die Bibel* on every table and a Gothic picture of the Lord on every wall. Think twice before doing anything sinful. Singles DM 56, doubles DM 92, including breakfast. *Mauritz-Lindenw. 61, tel. 0251/37870, fax 0251/374549. From Hauptbahnhof, Bus 10 or 2 to Dechaneistr.; south to Mauritz-Lindenw.*

Zur Krone. This tiny place, run by a woman who'll remind you of your grandma, boasts a can't-get-any-more-German-than-this restaurant downstairs. Rooms run DM 50 per person, breakfast included. *Hammer Str. 67, tel. and fax 0251/73868. From Hauptbahnhof, head left, then right on Schorlemerstr., left on Hammer Str. at Ludgeripl. 5 rooms, none with bath.*

HOSTEL • Jugendgästehaus Aasee (HI). This place is so new, so efficient, and so clean that the super-professional staff feels comfortable being bossy and short-tempered with guests. But the hostel is also so well-placed, in a student quarter overlooking the shores of the Aasee, that you won't notice. You'll pay a whopping DM 39.50 for space in a four-bed dorm or DM 49.50 for space in a double, breakfast, towels, and sheets included. All rooms have their own shower, toilet, and sink. *Bismarckallee 31, tel. 0251/532470, fax 0251/521271. From Hauptbahnhof, Bus 10 (Platform C3) or 34 (Platform D1) to Hoppendamm. 208 beds. Curfew 1 AM. Reception open 7 AM–1 AM, check-in until 11 PM, checkout 9:30. Bike rental (DM 10 per day), game room, laundry, lockers, luggage storage. Reservations recommended.*

CAMPING • A 20-min bus ride from town, the RV-filled **Campingplatz Münster** (Laerer Werseufer 7, tel. 0251/311982) charges DM 6 per person and per tent and offers grill pits and mini-golf. From the Hauptbahnhof, take Bus 320 or 330 (direction: Wolbeck), get out at Freibad Stapelskotten, and follow the signs.

FOOD

If it's a Wednesday or Saturday morning, head toward Domplatz for the **farmer's market,** where the prices are low. Tuesday through Friday from 11:30 to 2, the **Mensa am Aasee** (Bismarckallee 11, near the hostel) offers hearty lunches and vegetarian meals for under DM 5. The decorator of **Cadaques** (Ludgeristr. 62, tel. 0251/43028) had a somewhat loose grip on the would-be Catalonian theme, but the cook makes an excellent paella (DM 12) that is tough for one person to finish. Nearby, the swank, chic **Café del Arte** (Königstr. 45, tel. 0251/511029) is surprisingly affordable. Try the tortellini (DM 10) or

Pizza Hawaii (DM 12) with your drink of choice. Sunday–Tuesday they dish it up until 1 AM; the rest of the week, Del Arte draws a crowd until 5 AM with its basement disco. A favorite among students is friendly, bustling **Coco Loco** (Hindenburgpl. 20, tel. 0251/45453) near the Schloß. They serve tasty approximations of Mexican food like empanadas (DM 5.50) to loud, "studying" students by day and loud, partying students by night (until 1 AM). Serving delicious homemade noodle dishes for DM 7–DM 9, the gingerbread-house-turned-pub **Das Blaue Haus** (Kreuzstr. 19, in the Kuhviertel, tel. 0251/42151) draws crowds daily 7 PM–1 AM.

WORTH SEEING

To get an idea of just how long a night it was in the Altstadt when the bombs fell on Münster in 1943, check out the sobering photographs in the entryway of the 13th-century **Dom St. Paulus** (alias Münster, open daily 6–6). In the massive 13th-century hall is the amazing **astronomical clock,** which will track time and the stars, sun, and moon until 2071. At noon its carillon plays to tourist hordes. You'll find a more religious blast from the past in the **Domkammer** (tel. 0251/42471; open Tues.–Sat. 10–noon and 2–6, Sun. 2–6), full of church relics, artwork, and liturgical robes. It costs a mere DM 1. The treaty ending the Thirty Years' War was signed in 1648 in the Gothic **Friedenssaal** (Peace Hall) of the Rathaus (Prinzipalmarkt, tel. 0251/492–2724; open weekdays 9–5, Sat. 9–4, Sun. 10–1), but nowadays you'll find no peace within—a recording explains every inch of the room down to the last tedious detail. Gloriously silent pamphlets are available in English. Admission is DM 2 (DM 1 students).

When in Münsterland, be sure to get your tastebuds deeply involved in an Altbierbowle, a Sangrialike concoction made with Altbier in lieu of vino.

Don't leave Münster's beautiful Altstadt without glancing up at the three cages hanging from the graceful spire of **St. Lambert's** church, off the Prinzipalmarkt. In the 16th century, the victorious Catholic bishop's troops left the corpses of three Anabaptist rebels in the cages to rot. The free **Stadtmuseum** (Salzstr. 28, tel. 0251/492–4502; open Tues.–Sun. 10–6) reveals more about Münster's past than you'll ever want to know. For DM 7 (DM 4 students) you can wander from an 18th-century windmill to a 19th-century school at the open-air museum, **Mühlenhof Freilichtmuseum** (Sentruper Str. 223, tel. 0251/82074; open daily 10–6, Nov.–Mar. 11–4). Take Bus 14 toward the Zoo. For more fresh air, take that picnic and your new hostel sweetheart to the peaceful gardens behind the spectacularly Baroque brick-and-sandstone **Schloß** (off Hindenburgpl. on west side of Altstadt), now a university building. The shores of the **Aasee** are also a popular hangout. You may want to test your rented two-wheeler by taking a lap around it before tackling Münster's crowded downtown.

AFTER DARK

To find out everything about Münster's nightlife, pick up a copy of *Na Dann* or *Uni-Gig,* two alternative magazines available in cafés and bars all over town. *Na Dann* comes out Wednesday and is so popular that it's usually gone by Thursday morning. Much of the nightlife in Münster centers on the always-crowded cafés and bars in the studenty **Kuhviertel,** although things can be a little slow during summer break (July–Sept.). To get here, just head to the northwest corner of the Altstadt between Hindenburgplatz and Münzstraße. Be warned that the offerings here are good, but bars are going to cost you. Many clubs are farther away, and though you need never be bored in Münster, it's hard to get home at night. Be prepared to take a taxi or walk (unless you have a designated rider for that bike).

Destille (Kuhstr. 10 at Jüdefelderstr., tel. 0251/43726; open nightly 7–1) in the Kuhviertel is the "old student jazz club"; it's dark, packed, and loud. Live music every Tuesday (jazz and blues) and some other nights is always free. Also in the Kuhviertel, **Malik** (Frauenstr. 14., tel. 0251/44210; open Mon.–Sat. 9 AM–1 AM) is the place for intellectual and muse-ical inspiration. Newspapers lie on racks and poetry adorns the menu. Even the food and drink have a poetic ring, such as *Der gefallene Engel* (The Fallen Angel; DM 5), a scoop of lemon ice cream floating in champagne. **Jovel** (Grevener Str. 91, tel. 0251/201070; open Wed., Fri., and Sat. 9 PM–5 AM), a large, popular dance club a few blocks north of the Kuhviertel, sports random decor, including an automobile slice above the DJ's head and ferns aglow with neon. Wednesday nights are retro; every Friday has a different theme. Cover is DM 8. Next door to and affiliated with the JIB youth center, **Gleis 22** (Hafenstr. 34, tel. 0251/525941; open Mon. noon–3 PM, Tues.–Sat. noon–3 AM), off Ludgeriplatz south of the Altstadt, is where you'll find one of the highest per capita tattoo-and-nose-ring ratios west of Berlin. Catch live bands (usually in the independent, punk vein) Wednesday at 10 (cover DM 10–DM 15), or shake that thang on weekend nights (cover DM 4). Every weekday there's a different vegetarian meal for lunch (DM 5).

DETMOLD

Capital of the tiny principality of Lippe until Germany was unified in 1871 under Otto von Bismarck, Detmold still has the feel of a small but important Renaissance city. Before merging with North Rhine-Westphalia, Lippe was one of Germany's smallest states. Today the streets swell with (German) tourists eating ice cream. Yet if you let your gaze wander a bit, you'll notice the incredible number of restored 16th-century buildings in the walkable Altstadt. The town itself deserves a day of attention, and it is an excellent base for exploring the **Teutoburg Forest,** a vast green expanse with reminders of an ancient Germanic past. From Detmold you can also make an easy day trip to nearby and picturesque **Lemgo.**

BASICS

Detmold's **tourist office** (Rathaus am Markt, tel. 05231/977328) is well stocked with cheesy pamphlets in English and free but inadequate maps. If you're planning any biking or hiking in the area, invest in either the Detmold *Stadtplan* (city map; DM 6.50) or the topographical *Hermannsland* map (DM 10), which covers trails throughout the region. The tourist office will also call around to book you a hotel or one of the few city-center Privatzimmer. The **post office** (Paulinenstr. 52, at Bismarckstr.) is open weekdays 8–6 and Saturday 8–1. It changes money and is close to a **Deutsche Bank** (Bismarckstr. 3) with a Cirrus and Plus ATM.

COMING AND GOING

You will most likely arrive in Detmold on a train from Bielefeld (every 30 min, 1 hr, DM 10). Trains from Bielefeld to Hanover (50 min, DM 30), Cologne (2 hrs, DM 56), and Düsseldorf (1½ hrs, DM 44) leave hourly. There are also direct connections from Detmold to Münster (12 per day, 2½ hrs, DM 32) and hourly connections to Altenbeken, on the Dortmund–Kassel line. To reach the Marktplatz from the station, take Hermannstraße and turn right on Gerichtsstraße (which becomes Bruchstraße), left on Lange Straße. The Altstadt, which radiates from the Marktplatz, is completely walkable, and even outlying sites can be reached by foot. If you're weary, a bus (within the city) is DM 2.70, or DM 7.50 for the whole day. The main **Busbahnhof** is just outside the train station.

WHERE TO SLEEP

Lodgings in Detmold are sparse, and the few real hotels are expensive. Privatzimmer run around DM 30, though only two places in the city center offer them. Ask the tourist office. You'll be comfy in the large, roomy house of **Gästehaus Herrmann** (Woldemarstr. 17, tel. 05231/22527), just east of the Altstadt, where the rooms (DM 48 per person) have large windows overlooking lush green trees (which conveniently hide the railroad tracks). Across from the station, **Brechmann** (Bahnhofstr. 9, tel. 05231/25655, fax 0521/31795) has singles for DM 60, doubles for DM 110.

HOSTEL • This friendly, family-run **Jugendherberge (HI)** is in the foothills above the city. Along with children running around, you'll hear chickens and a friendly donkey. Beds, including breakfast, cost DM 27.60 (DM 26.60 over 26). The hostel is an easy starting point for hikes to Hermannsdenkmal and beyond, and it's just a short walk (15 min) to the Freilichtmuseum (*see below*). *Schirrmannstr. 49, tel. 05231/24739, fax 05231/28927. From station, take Hermannstr., then right on Bielefelder Str., left on Hans-Hinrichs-Str., left on Steinstoß, and left on Schirrmannstr. (30 min total). 60 beds. Curfew 10 PM (ask for a house key), lockout 9:30–11:30. Reception open 8:30–6:30 (knock), checkout 9:30.*

FOOD

Near the bank is a **Spar** market (Bismarckstr. 13) for staples. Along with countless cafés filled with kids and adults eating ice cream creations, Lange Straße and the pedestrian zone in the Altstadt have many bakeries and a few fruit stalls. **Grabbe Café** (Unter der Wehme 7, tel. 05231/24372) has more personality than most of the Eiscafés along Lange Straße. It serves sumptuous desserts in a dark, 17th-century atmosphere that suits the lovely building in which Christian Dietrich Grabbe, a 19th-century German author, spent his last days. Most joints in Detmold are in historically significant buildings, and **Aladin** (Bruckstr. 9, tel. 05231/34822) is no exception. The food here has only become significant in recent German history: typical *Döner* (grilled lamb in Turkish bread; DM 5.50) and many Near Eastern veggie options, like grilled feta and salad (DM 5) or moussaka (DM 8). **Eis und Pizza bei Daniele** (Bruchstr. 14, tel. 05231/23363) has a personal touch usually unknown to stand-up/take-out pizza joints.

WORTH SEEING

Just walking around Detmold's Altstadt gives you a feel of 16th–17th-century Europe—if you leave the heavily touristed stretches, that is. The best streets for seeing these restored half-timbered homes are **Meierstraße,** tiny **Adolfstraße,** and unfortunately busy **Krumme Straße.** The principality of Lippe was ruled from the 16th-century **Residenzschloß** (Schloßpl., tel. 05231/22507) until Germany united in 1871. Inside, the **Roter Saal** (Red Hall) will overwhelm you with gilded mirrors, ruby lamps, porcelain figures, and, well, red. Admission is DM 6, which includes tours (hourly 10–noon and 2–5) and a booklet in English that tells you more than you want to know about the palace's lavish rooms. The Schloß is open daily 10–5 (certain parts are accessible only on tours), but you can explore the peaceful gardens until 9 PM. Detmold's **Lippisches Landesmuseum** (Ameide 4, tel. 05231/25232; admission DM 2) occupies three buildings behind the Schloß and covers all aspects of life and history in the little principality. It's open Tuesday–Friday 10–12:30 and 2–5:30, weekends 10–5:30.

With over 100 preserved buildings, the **Westfälisches Freilichtmuseum** (Westphalian Open-Air Museum) is the best place to get a sense of the state's architectural and cultural heritage. It features interesting crafts demonstrations daily and thorough, thoughtfully constructed exhibits. The 1837 schoolhouse still has its abacus, and livestock run around a model agricultural village. *Krummes Haus, tel. 05231/706150. Bus 355, 701, 703, 782, 792 to Freilichtmuseum; or, walk on Path 1 south of the Altstadt along the left side of Allee (30 min total). Admission DM 7, DM 4 students. Open Apr.–Oct., Tues.–Sun. 9–6 only.*

If you're in the area a while, check out the hundreds of exotic birds at the **Vogelpark** (just off Denkmalstr., tel. 05231/47439), in the outlying village of Heiligenkirche, 6 km south of Detmold. The Vogelpark is open daily 9–6, costs DM 7, and is easily reached by Bus 782. At the **Adlerwarte** (Adlerw. 3–5, tel. 05231/47171; admission DM 7), more than 80 birds of prey take flight daily at 11 and 2. (Otherwise they live in spacious cages—but cages nonetheless.) The Adlerwarte is 8 km south of town in the village of Berlebeck (take Bus 701) and open March–November, daily 8:30–6, with shorter hours in the off-season.

NEAR DETMOLD

TEUTOBURG FOREST

The wooded rolling hills of this forest, known in German as the *Teutoburger Wald,* have sheltered encampments of pagan worshippers, Roman soldiers, and German nature lovers throughout time. Detmold offers an excellent base for following in their footsteps, either on foot or by bike, or if you're lazy, by bus. Anybody planning to hike or bike extensively around Detmold should pick up maps at the tourist office (*see above*). There aren't many tall mountains or steep hills in the forest, so hikers, backpackers, and cyclists can get around easily. By far the most popular destination is the **Hermannsdenkmal** (admission DM 2; open daily 9–6), which towers above the forest and surrounding countryside. Climb the dizzying spiral staircase and stand on the pedestal for an unparalleled view of the patchwork quilt of the Westphalian landscape: dark green woods, golden fields, light green meadows, and bright red village rooftops. To the south and west, you can see along and almost over the narrow Teutoberger Wald. Above you, Hermann gazes victoriously westward. In 9 AD Arminius (known to Germans as Hermann), leader of the Germanic Cherusci tribe, defeated the invading troops of Roman Quintillius Varus. The massive statue, completed in 1875 just after Germany's first unification, is a tribute to Hermann, to German nationalism, and to Germany's then-recent victory over France. You can walk here from the city along **Cheruskerweg** (trail marked X3). The trail starts just south of Detmold's Altstadt from the Allee on the right bank of the canal. Bus 792 runs to the Denkmal twice a day.

LEMGO

Virtually every building in Lemgo's Altstadt is bursting with history, and just looking at the inscriptions, carvings, and ornamentation could take a day—except you'd strain your neck. The elaborate Rathaus alone merits a visit. Today a peaceful little town, Lemgo really came into its own after Count Simon VI of Lippe took up residence in the late 16th century. Lemgo had a fiery history during the post-Reformation years—the Lutheran townsfolk often rose up against the Calvinist counts, and until the late 17th century the city vigorously persecuted "witches." After the 16th century, the counts of Lippe fled hostile Lemgo for friendlier Detmold, and Lemgo faded into relative insignificance. As a result, the town remains largely unchanged from the days when it was the regional capital, and it is one of the best places to check out the architecture of the local Weser Renaissance style.

ROAMIN' LIKE THE ROMANS

A narrow strip of wooded hills, extending 150 km northwest to southeast across eastern Westphalia, the Teutoburg Forest can seem like an endless, ancient forest—if you go lengthwise. The forest is hardly untouched, but nevertheless, this is the kind of place where you lose track of what century it is. Not much has changed here since Germans first stood against Romans centuries ago: THEY charged through the forest on the winding footpaths; YOU charge through the forests on the winding footpaths. After a hard day, THEY drank wine; after any kind of day, YOU drink wine (or beer or whatever). If you're up for a more serious hike, you can continue 11 km from the Hermannsdenkmal southeast along the Hermannsweg *(marked H), a 170-km-long trail that runs along the spine of the forest to the* Externsteine. *The large, fractured sandstone outcropping rises out of the ground like a bad set of teeth. It was a place of pagan worship for millennia, but a 13th-century carving of Christ at the base served to co-opt the stones into Christianity so that the faithful could visit without burning at the stake. Today, New Age pagans frequent the stones in an effort to revive the old faith. The Externsteine are open daily 9–6, and it costs DM 1.50 to scramble around. After such a long walk, you'll want to catch the bus back (or hitch). Bus 782 runs between the Holzhausen Externsteine stop and Detmold eight times a day. As the last one back is at 4 PM, a better option might be to take the bus out in the morning and hike back to Detmold. Cyclists (and hikers) can also take Radweg 1 (marked R1) from Detmold.*

BASICS • Even Lemgo's **tourist office** (Papenstr. 7, tel. 05261/213347) is in a 16th-century merchant's carriage house. They can provide maps and book rooms for free, weekdays 10–3 and Saturday 10–1. The office is in the middle of the Altstadt; to get here from the Bahnhof, turn right down Paulinenstraße, left on Breite Straße, and right on Papenstraße. The **post office** is on Bismarckstraße just east of the Altstadt. Bus 790 (20 min, DM 5) runs every hour to Detmold's Busbahnhof. There is no direct train service to Detmold, but hourly **trains** connect Lemgo with Bielefeld (weekdays until 6, Sat. until 2 PM; 1 hr, DM 8), where you can make a connection to Detmold (*see* Coming and Going *in* Detmold, *above*).

WHERE TO SLEEP AND EAT • Finding a room in Lemgo is not so easy, and if you visit from Detmold, not so necessary. The tourist office will book Privatzimmer and hotels for free. The only somewhat affordable hotel in the city center is **Hotel Bahnhofswagge** (Am Bahnhof, tel. 05261/3525), by the station, which charges DM 45 per person. **Campingplatz Regenstor** (Regenstor, tel. 05261/14858) is full of RVs and car campers but relatively quiet. Sites cost DM 5 per tent, DM 7.50 per person. From the Bahnhof, walk right down Paulinenstraße, go left over the river, then right onto Lindenwall. Turn right on Regenstorstraße and you'll see signs pointing down a path to the campground and Schloß.

There are plenty of bakeries in the pedestrian zone for picnic supplies. The **Meffert Café** (Mittelstr. 178, tel. 05261/4043) mixes 16th-century half-timber with 1990s art gallery. Everything is tasty and inexpensive, like the veggie lasagne (DM 5). Surprisingly, the requisite café by the Schloß, **Café Schloßmühle**

(Schloß Brake, tel. 05261/13915), is worth visiting if (and only if) you can get a seat on their tiny beer garden deck. Enjoy an Alt (DM 3.40) right below one of the locks on the castle's moat system.

WORTH SEEING • Even more than in Detmold, Renaissance-era houses fill the streets of Lemgo. During the 16th century, the town thrived as the residence of the counts of Lippe, and the ornate Renaissance **Rathaus** (am Markt) is a testament to this prosperity. The Markt as a whole is a good sampling of architecture in the local **Weser Renaissance** style, which is generally less flowery than the design of the Dutch-influenced Rathaus. From the Lindenwall (formerly part of the wall encircling the town) in 1609, the Lutheran townsfolk turned cannons on **Schloß Brake** (Schloßstr. 18), where the Calvinist count resided. Count Simon VI, who made the castle his residence in 1587, lost his life at the hands of the townsfolk in 1613 because they didn't like his religion. Between the castle's moat and square tower, you'll find the **Weserrenaissance-Museum** (tel. 05261/94500), documenting art and culture between the Reformation and the Thirty Years' War. It's also your best look inside the castle, as the rest of the building (tower and all) holds offices. Visit Tuesday–Sunday 10–6 for DM 4. On your way to the Schloß, check out the **Ölmühle,** the town's waterwheel-powered grindstone.

On Heustraße is the **Marienkirche,** with an astonishing organ said to be one of the best in Europe. Try to catch performances year-round or especially during the June music festival. Right behind the church is the **Hexenbürgermeisterhaus** (Breite Str. 19, tel. 05261/213276), which houses the city museum and devotes lots of space to the torture devices and trial techniques of the witch-hunting days. It costs DM 1.50 and is open Tuesday–Sunday 10–12:30 and 1:30–5. If you're willing to trek down Hamelner Straße, a 10-min walk east of the Altstadt, check out the ridiculously ornate carvings on the **Junkerhaus** (Hamelner Str. 36, tel. 05261/213347; closed Mon. and also Dec.–Mar.), architect Karl Junker's (1850–1912) half-timbered masterpiece.

On Ostwall at Hirtstraße is the tiny, hard-to-find **Alter Jüdischer Friedhof** (Old Jewish Cemetery). A dozen or so 19th-century tombstones here mourn the passing of Jewish citizens in German and Hebrew. Jews lived in Lemgo for centuries, and the cemetery, as well as other city sites, documents this. To discover the Jewish history of Lemgo, visit the **Frenkel Haus** (Echternstr. 70, tel. 05261/213276; admission free), open Tuesday–Sunday 10–12:30 and 1:30–5, where one of Lemgo's last four Jewish families lived until Nazis deported them in 1942 to the death camps. Of these 22 people, only three survived in 1945.

16 THE RHINE AND MOSEL VALLEYS

UPDATED BY MICHAEL WOODHEAD

Germany is crisscrossed by mighty rivers—the Elbe, the Danube, the Oder, and the Main, to name a few—but the Rhine is the undisputed king. Often called *Vater Rhein* (Father Rhine), the river flows 1,355 km from the Swiss Alps through the borders of tiny Liechtenstein, Austria, France, Germany, and Holland on its way to North Sea. It would take weeks to follow its entire course, and your enjoyment would be hit-or-miss, as much of the valley is heavily industrial. This chapter focuses on the most glorious stretch of the Rhine, between **Mainz** and **Koblenz,** and on its beautiful tributary, the **Mosel River.**

The only thing here that might turn you off is the massive scale of tourism. Bubbly tour guides and self-consciously cute towns threaten to turn a national treasure into a staged event. To avoid the worst, try to visit outside the summer months. If you can't manage that, at least get your act together before mid-morning, when tour buses start disgorging their loads. Tour groups tend to flee small towns after lunchtime, so it's possible to have a beautiful town to yourself on a warm summer evening.

If you're short on time, don't try to "do" both the Rhine and Mosel valleys—choose one or the other. The Rhine is a willful, major waterway that over the years has carved a dramatically beautiful valley. The Mosel is the quiet sibling, and the hills around it roll gently off into the green distance. If you stick to the larger towns, such as Worms, Mainz, Koblenz and Trier, you will run into higher prices and larger crowds, but these cities still preserve some old-world charm and reminders of a rich culture and history. Trier, in particular, deserves a visit for its balanced mixture of Roman cultural and architectural remains and hip modern-day life. Visiting smaller, less central towns has different rewards: Here you will feel closer to the rivers and get to hike past castles and vineyards nestled in the hills.

GETTING AROUND

You will need to vary your modes of transport to get the most out of the Rhine and Mosel valleys. The train can get you there, but if you want to take the time to experience the rivers up close or visit some of the smaller towns, you will need to travel by boat, bus, bicycle, or some combination of these. Though rail lines run along both sides of the Rhine, the views from the west side are better. Because of the Mosel Valley's peculiar geography, trains often bypass smaller towns. Buses are cheap, will take you almost anywhere, and offer great views, but they're hot in summer and always bumpy and slow. Slower still—but also more peaceful and scenic—is travel by boat, the best way to see the Rhine Gorge.

BY BIKE • Bicycles are a good way to travel at your own pace along the Rhine and Mosel, and to stop as you please at villages, castles, and vineyards along the way. Take advantage of paved and well-marked trails and stow your wheels on boats or trains when the road gets too long or busy. The Mosel Valley is especially well suited to bikes, as traffic is lighter and many of the sights are hard to reach by public transportation. Rentals can be a problem, though, since you must always return your bike to your initial starting point and some towns don't have rental shops—call ahead to the tourist office of any prospective town to be sure. Probably your best bet is to bring your own bike with you (*see box* Bikes *in* Flight, *in* Chapter 1).

BY FERRY • The major ferry operator is **Köln-Düsseldorfer Deutsche Rheinschifffahrt** (tel. 0221/258–3011, fax 0221/208–8238), known as the KD Rhine Line. An advantage to KD service is that you can use your EurailPass or Deutsche Bahn (DB) pass. InterRail will get you a 50% reduction. If you don't have a pass, check out KD's combined river-rail tickets, which allow you to break your river trip at any place the boats stop and continue onward by train. The trip from Mainz to Koblenz costs DM 72; pick up detailed info and schedules at tourist offices in Mainz, Koblenz, Bingen, or at any KD booth, located at all the docks. No bridges cross the river along the stretch between Mainz and Koblenz, but you can always hop on a ferry if you want to visit the other side. KD also operates ferries between Koblenz and Cochem on the Mosel—just keep in mind that it will take 4½ hours (as opposed to 30 min by express train).

THE RHINE VALLEY

Culture and history buffs have been making pilgrimages to the Rhine Valley since the 18th century, when aristocratic Englishmen first sailed the Rhine and waxed romantic over its lush beauty, blush wines, and plush estates. Nowadays, visitors pack the tour boats and drift with the barges along the famous **Rhine Gorge.** On this stretch of river between Mainz and Koblenz, quaint towns—most surrounded by rocky cliffs and hillside vineyards—follow one another in quick succession. Castles are equally common and have been ever since robber barons first began exacting tolls from passing boats and barges along the 80-km-long gorge.

Though the most popular parts of the Rhine Valley are the villages and vineyards of the Rhine Gorge, it would be a mistake to bypass the region's principal cities, if you can hack the high cost of lodging. Worms, Mainz, and Koblenz witnessed some of the watershed events in German and European history, and these days they still play important roles in the country's cultural and economic life. If you're short on time or money, consider visiting the Rhine Valley as a day trip: Mainz is a short hop from Frankfurt and Wiesbaden (*see* Chapter 2), and Worms is close to Heidelberg and Mannheim. For info about cities farther upstream, like Mannheim or Karlsruhe, *see* Chapter 3.

WORMS

Located upstream from its bigger, brasher neighbors, Mainz and Koblenz, ancient Worms is nowadays a walkable, mellow city steeped in a rich history. Founded by the Romans, the town's heyday came and went in the 16th century, when it served as a major center for the Holy Roman Empire. Here, in 1521, Emperor Charles V and the Imperial Diet heard the then-heretical teachings of Martin Luther. When Martin refused to denounce his shocking ideas, the imperial bigwigs outlawed him and launched the enduring conflict between Protestantism and Catholicism.

Unlike other cities along the Rhine, where postwar modernity and tourism overwhelm historical remnants, Worms manages to balance these elements, and offers a refreshing day trip or overnight from nearby cities such as Mainz, Mannheim, or even Heidelberg. Although there's nothing glitzy or gigantic about it (or maybe because of this), Worms is a good place to soak it all in and hang with the hip at a café or two.

BASICS

You can always get a city map/hotel list (50 Pf each) from the machine in front of the **tourist office** (Neumarkt 14, across from the Dom, tel. 06241/25045), open weekdays 9–noon and 2–5, Sat. 10–noon (May–Oct., also Sun. 3–5). Make local and long-distance calls from the **Hauptpost** (main post office; Kämmererstr. 44) on Ludwigsplatz.

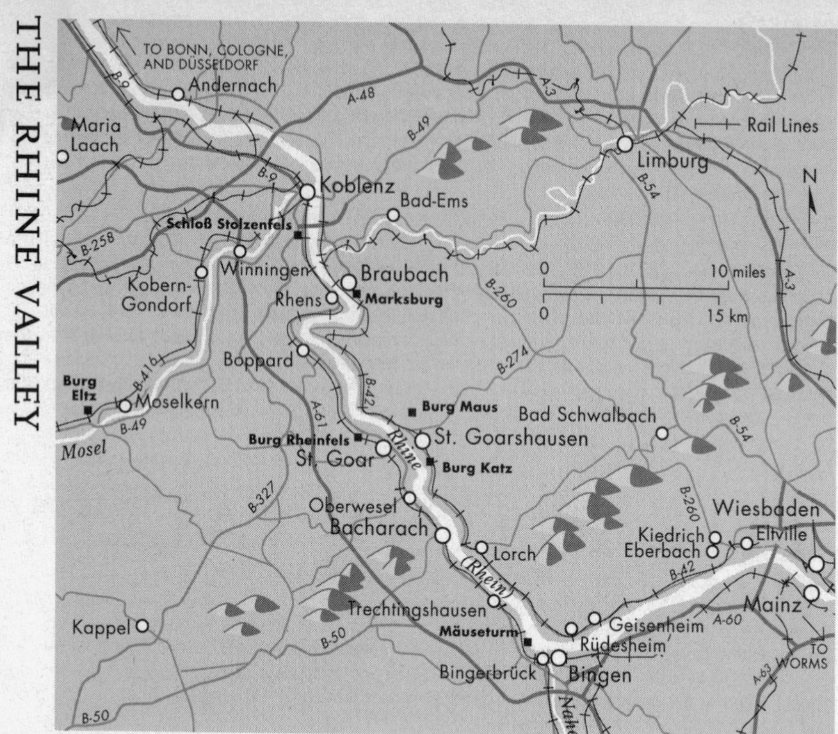

COMING AND GOING

Trains run roughly hourly between Mainz and Worms (40 min, DM 12). Frequent trains also connect Worms to Mannheim (25 min, DM 7), with frequent connections to nearby Heidelberg. Once here, the *Altstadt* (old town) is only minutes from the *Hauptbahnhof* (main train station) down Wilhelm-Leuschner-Straße, one of Worms's major *Fußgängerzonen* (pedestrian zones); the other is Kämmerer-straße, inside the Altstadt. The Hauptbahnhof's lockers are available 5 AM–midnight.

WHERE TO SLEEP

What sets **Hotel Boos** (Mainzer Str. 5, tel. 06241/947639, fax 06241/947638) apart from its cheaper neighbors is a tall glass of orange juice in the morning and a television in every room. If you have a travel partner, take advantage of the firm queen-size beds. Singles start at DM 57, doubles at DM 84, both with breakfast. To get there from the station, head up Siegfriedstraße to Mainzer Straße. With reasonable prices (singles from DM 38, doubles from DM 68, breakfast included) and clean rooms, **Weinhaus Weis** (Färberg. 19, tel. 06241/23500) is your best budget bet—and it's only 15 min by foot from the Hauptbahnhof. The bad news: It's small, it fills up fast, and the managers have been known to take extended vacations in late July.

CAMPING • Campingplatz Nibelungenbrücke. This campground right on the Rhine sports a restaurant, mini-shop, laundry, and lots of young people. It costs DM 7 per person, DM 4.50 per tent, DM 10 per car, and DM 1.50 per bicycle. *An der Nibelungenbrücke, tel. 06241/24355. From town center, walk down Rheinstr. to bridge across Rhine, then follow signs right and under street (30 min total). Reception open 8–1 and 3–10. Closed Nov.–Mar.*

HOSTELS • Jugendgästehaus Worms (HI). This hostel shares the pious, dead-quiet atmosphere of its neighbors—tiny Magnuskirche and enormous Dom St. Peter. Though it has a musty, hamster-cage smell, it's clean, cheap, and rarely full. Bed and breakfast costs DM 25.50, and the 11:30 curfew can sometimes be thwarted with a key. *Dechaneistr. 1, tel. 06241/25780, fax 06241/27394. 138 beds. Reception open 7 AM–11:30 PM.*

FOOD

For cheap eats grab a kebab from one of the Turkish fast-food stands along Wilhelm-Leuschner-Straße and Kämmererstraße. If you want a more substantial meal, seat yourself at an outside table at **La Carbonara Ristorante** (Adenauerring 4, tel. 06241/28220) and choose from a wide selection of pastas and pizzas priced under DM 12. If you're looking for simple groceries, **Plus Markt** (Siegfriedstr.) is just two min from the station.

Worms makes up for its mediocre food with some outstanding ice cream. **Eis Simoni** (Karmeliterstr. 1a, tel. 06241/28393), one block from the train station, has delectable lickables from DM 1. The cavernous **Cafehaus-Dom Regenbogen** (Weckerlingpl. 6, tel. 06241/28883)—where students hold meetings and concerts—is another rare find for coffee and conversation, open weekdays noon–1 AM, Sat. 2–2, Sun. 2–1. Watch out for the free-flying parrots here: They may want to share. From the cathedral's main entrance, walk straight down Dechaneistraße until you hit Weckerlingplatz.

WORTH SEEING

The 11th-century **Dom St. Peter** (Dompl.; open 9–5:45 daily except during services) is a huge, early Gothic cathedral with Baroque highlights that looks somewhat burned-out (the telltale sign of pollution and acid rain). For 20 Pf you can tour the **crypt.** A few hundred yards from the Dom, the **Magnuskirche** (Dechaneistr.) is one of the oldest Protestant churches in Germany and looks like something out of colonial New England. With witch-hat steeples poking up among industrial chimneys, the **Liebfrauenkirche** (Liebfrauenring) at the edge of town looks like something out of Dr. Seuss's *The Lorax.* There's not much to see here, but the walk is pleasant, and you could find worse places for a picnic—buy a cheap bottle of Liebfraumilch (Blue Nun), once Germany's most renowned export wine, at the vineyard next to the church.

Be it a long journey on the KD Rhine Line—free for holders of Eurail and Deutsche Bahn (DB) passes—or a simple ferry crossing from St. Goar to St. Goarshausen, you must take a boat ride to fully appreciate the rivers.

The **Kunsthaus Heylshof,** in the tiny, manicured Heylshof garden, contains the only "serious" art in Worms—a dark, dank collection of Gothic and Renaissance art, starring Peter Paul Rubens's *Madonna with Child.* It was on this site that Martin Luther—after nailing his 95 religious theses to a church door in Wittenberg—declared before the Imperial Diet: "Here I stand. I can do no different. God help me. Amen." *Im Heylshofgarten, 06241/22000. Admission: DM 3, DM 2 students. Open Tues.–Sun. 10–5; Oct.–Apr., Tues.–Sun. 2–4.*

Jewish Worms isn't some Semitic delicacy but rather the title of the cheesy video (in German and English) shown at the **Raschi-Haus Museum** (Hintere Judeng. 6, tel. 06241/853345 and 06241/853370; closed Mon.). The museum's displays are few, but they manage to convey the traumatic history of Worms's once-thriving Jewish community. Admission is DM 3 (students DM 2). Next to the museum stands the simple 11th-century synagogue, the oldest in Germany, where the famous Rabbi Rashi taught. This poor old building has been clobbered time and again, especially in 1938 on Kristallnacht, when the Nazis burned synagogues all over the country. Leading up to the synagogue is Judengasse (Jewish Lane), with replicas of the buildings of Worms's former Jewish quarter. Stained, dilapidated headstones stand among overgrown vines and weeds at the 900-year-old **Judenfriedhof** (Jewish cemetery; Willy-Brandt-Ring at Andreasstr.), also Germany's oldest. Surprisingly, the graveyard escaped the violence of the Nazi era; full of stacked, crooked gravestones, it looks like it hasn't been disturbed in centuries.

NEAR WORMS

OPPENHEIM

Wine, wine, wine. Midway between Worms and Mainz, Oppenheim is one of the most famous wine towns in Germany. It's small, well preserved, filled with middle-aged German tourists, and crammed with wine shops and cafés. Trains from Worms leave every hour for Oppenheim (20 min, DM 3); once here, you can sample the wines (as Charlemagne once did) or stroll around Oppenheim's old *Marktplatz* (market square) and climb the long staircase to **Katharinenkirche.** Behind the church, the Michaeliskapelle's **Beinhaus** (Charnel House) contains the bones of more than 15,000 former townspeople.

While here, plan to live on wine alone: The international restaurants on the town's main square charge prices that'll turn your stomach. Get a list of wine cellars that offer tastings, a map of the town, and a hotel list weekdays 8–noon at Oppenheim's **tourist office** (Merianstr. 2, tel. 06133/70699) in the Rathaus.

MAINZ

As the business center of the Rheinhessen region and the capital of Rhineland-Palatinate, Mainz has plenty of modern office space and a shortage of budget lodgings. Unlike nearby Frankfurt, however, Mainz hasn't let this element get the better of it, and still retains some reminders of its glory days as the seat of one of Germany's most powerful archbishops and the home of printing pioneer Johannes Gutenberg. On Tuesdays, Fridays, and weekends, locals sell their wares on the **Marktplatz** (8–2), the center of a pedestrian zone decorated with plazas and fountains and lined with churches and museums. To avoid the high cost of lodging in Mainz, you may want to visit on a day trip from nearby Frankfurt, Wiesbaden (*see* Chapter 2), or Bingen (*see* The Rhine Gorge, *below*).

BASICS

The helpful and knowledgeable staff at Mainz's **tourist office** (Bahnhofstr. 15, tel. 06131/286210; open weekdays 9–6, Sat. 9–1) gives out free maps and lists of accommodations and charges DM 5 for making hotel reservations. The **Deutsche Verkehrs Bank** (Hauptbahnhof, tel. 06131/238616) offers decent rates on traveler's checks and ATM machines. It's open weekdays 7:30–7, except for Wednesday (and Saturday), when it's open 7:30–noon and 12:30–3. The **Hauptpost** (Bahnhofstr. 2; open weekdays 7:30–6:30, Sat. 7:30–1, Sun. 10:30–noon) has a roomful of phones and exchanges money at rates that may be a bit better than the bank's.

COMING AND GOING

Trains leave at least hourly for Worms (40 min, DM 12), Cologne (1¾ hrs, DM 48), and Koblenz (50 min, DM 23). The S-Bahn (line S8) runs to Frankfurt (40 min, DM 10) and Wiesbaden (15 min, DM 4) every half hour. Store your *Kram* (stuff) in the station's lockers. As the gateway to the most beautiful part of the Rhine, Mainz is an excellent place to start a boat tour. **Deutsche Rheinschiffahrt KD** (tel. 06131/224511) boats leave from the docks in front of the Rathaus on Rheinstraße. For more info about Rhine boat trips, *see* chapter introduction, *above*.

GETTING AROUND

From the Hauptbahnhof, **Kaiserstraße** runs northeast to the Rhine, and **Bahnhofstraße** (which becomes Schillerstraße) runs southeast. The heart of Mainz lies in this rather large (but walkable) triangle between the station and the river. To reach the Dom and *Markt* (market square) at the center of the Altstadt from the Bahnhof, walk down Bahnhofstraße to Schillerstraße and take a left on Ludwigstraße, which leads to the Markt. Rides around the city center on Mainz's buses and streetcars cost DM 3.20, day passes DM 8.50, and you can get a transit map at the tourist office.

WHERE TO SLEEP

Sad to say, the only cheap option in Mainz is the youth hostel, unless you (prudently) stay in a private room in Bingen (*see* The Rhine Gorge, *below*) or in nearby Wiesbaden or Frankfurt (*see* Chapter 2) a few km away. If you're bent on sleeping in Mainz, try the **Terminus Hotel** (Alicestr. 4, tel. 06131/229876, fax 06131/227408) or **Pfeil Continental** (Bahnhofstr. 15, tel. 06131/232179, fax 06131/286–2155). Both have decent singles without showers for DM 75, doubles for DM 100–DM 120. If you've got a tent on hand, pitch it at **Campingplatz Rheinufer** (Rheinufer, tel. 06131/86852; reception open 3:30 PM–9 PM). Regardless of what equipment or vehicle you show up with, it'll cost DM 10 per person. From the station, take Bus 21 (30 min, last bus around 10 PM) to the Laubenheim stop, turn right and walk 1½ km along the Rhine.

HOSTELS • Jugendgästehaus (HI). This hostel is one of the most rundown and seedy in the Rhine Valley, and its location on the outskirts atop a hill doesn't even offer a redeeming view. But if you want a cheap bed (DM 21, including breakfast) in Mainz, you don't have much choice. *Otto-Brunfels-Schneise 4, tel. 06131/85332, fax 06131/82422. From Bahnhofpl., Bus 1 (direction: Laubenheim) to Jugendherberge stop; follow signs right up hill (last bus weekdays and Sun. at 11:15 PM, Sat. at 12:15 AM). 172 beds. Midnight curfew. Reception open 5 PM–10 PM.*

FOOD

For a budget meal in Mainz, head to the pedestrian streets, **Augustinerstraße,** in particular. From the Markt, walk behind the Dom and across Leichhof to reach Augustinerstraße. Another good budget bet is the **Markthalle,** a collection of specialty food stands in the cellar of the huge Kaufhof department store (from Markt, walk one block up Schusterstr. to the corner of Stadthausstr.). It's open weekdays 9–6:30 (Thurs. until 8:30), Saturday 10–2. While there's no lack of kebab houses in Mainz, **Nemrut** (Heiliggrabg. 12, at Augustinerstr., tel. 06131/223915) has the biggest, tastiest, and freshest kebabs and salads for DM 4–DM 7, all in a *Lawrence of Arabia* setting.

Altstadt Café. Have a beer or coffee, muesli with fruit and cream (DM 6.50), or a croque monsieur (DM 5). There's definitely something groovy about throbbing house music on a quiet medieval corner. *Schönbornstr. 9a. From Augustinerstr., head away from the Dom, turn right on Kartäuserstr., right on Schönbornstr.*

Pizza Pepé. This place serves some tasty pizza and is always packed. You can order anything from a cheese pie (DM 8) to one topped with tuna and egg (DM 10), as well as a limited selection of pastas. *Augustinerstr. 21, tel. 06131/229986.*

WORTH SEEING

CHURCHES • As the center of one of Germany's most powerful archbishoprics before its conquest by Napoleon 200 years ago, Mainz boasts some impressive religious architecture. The mammoth Martinsdom cathedral dominates the Marktplatz and is a great navigational aid within the Altstadt. Since its foundation stone was first laid in 1009, the Dom has undergone the ravages of five fires, one flood, and a lot of pollution; amazingly, it has kept its pale rosy hue. On sunny days the massive stained-glass windows bathe the interior with colorful light. The free **Dom- und Diözesanmuseum** (Cathedral and Diocesan Museum) houses glitzy ecclesiastical objects and some relics from the Holy Roman Empire. *Domstr. 3, off Markt, tel. 06131/253344. Admission free. Cathedral and museum open weekdays 10–4 (Thurs. until 8), Sat. 10–2.*

Worms was home to one of the earliest and largest Jewish communities in Germany. The Judenfriedhof (Jewish Cemetery) and synagogue remain, and their caretakers are practically the only Jews left.

In 1973, Father Klaus Meyer asked Marc Chagall to design windows for the church of **St. Stephan** (Kleine Weissg. 12; open daily 10–noon and 2–5 except for Sun. morning services) as a "symbol of Franco-German rapprochement, international understanding, and Jewish-Christian unity." The result is a dreamy wash of biblical tales, a beautiful, blue fishbowl for you to plunge into. From the Markt, head up Ludwigstraße to Schillerplatz, turn left on Gaustraße, and left on Stefansberg. Although it's dwarfed by the Martinsdom's immensity and the fame of the church of St. Stephan windows, the **Augustinerkirche** (Augustinerstr. 34, 1 block south of Dom; open Mon.–Sat. 8–5, Sun. 10–5) sports a sumptuous rococo interior that you just gotta love—notice the chandeliers hanging from the ceiling. Built in the 13th century, the church and its decor have remained unscathed by bombs and fires since 1768.

MUSEUMS • Gutenberg-Museum. Mainz's most popular museum, dominated by displays on the town's local printing hero, has also crowned itself the International Museum of the Art of Printing. Woodcuts, lithographs, early presses, and a fairly tacky replica of the Mainz master's 15th-century workshop do their best to glamorize the potentially boring history of printing. If you come at all, don't leave without looking at the 550-year-old Gutenberg Bible, the first book printed in Europe using movable type. If you want a more hands-on printing experience, check out the schedule of demonstrations at the museum's **Druckladen** (print shop; open weekdays 10–5), across the street. *Liebfrauenpl. 5, tel. 06131/122640. Across from Dom just off Markt. Admission: DM 5, DM 2.50 students. Open Tues.–Sat. 10–6, Sun. 10–1.*

Römisch-Germanisches Museum. Have a coffee before you tackle this tremendous display of prehistoric and Roman artifacts. Because it's primarily a research institution, the exhibits are stark and professional. Even so, the collections are as impressive as the setting: The museum is housed in the **Kurfürstliches Schloß,** the restored Baroque digs of the archbishop-prince. *Große Bleiche, tel. 06131/232231. From Markt, head up Schusterstr., which turns into Flachsmarktstr., and turn right on Große Bleiche. Admission free. Open Tues.–Sun. 10–6.*

THE RHINE GORGE

People may look at you funny if you go all the way to Germany and don't visit the Rhine Gorge. It's that big a deal. You already know what it looks like—the castles, clinging to vine-covered hillsides over the Rhine, have covered German tourist brochures since Gutenberg cranked up his press. You may also know that every tourist from Phoenix to Kathmandu will be right here beside you, especially if you arrive in the peak summer season. Such is life. The Rhine Gorge stretches 140 km from Mainz to Bonn, but

OBERWESEL: A HOSTELER'S PARADISE

Oberwesel, on the Rhine midway between Bacharach and St. Goar, is another of the Rhine Valley's more genuine wine towns. Sixteen of its original 21 medieval towers still keep watch over the town. Towering above it all are the remains of the 1,000-year-old Schönburg castle, a stone's throw from Oberwesel's superb Jugendgästehaus (HI). No kidding—once you make the 20-min uphill climb from the Bahnhof (just follow the signs), you may never want to leave. Facilities include a free indoor pool, a café where you can order dinner or lounge with a glass of beer or wine, and a barbecue where you can brat your own wurst. Beds DM 26, including breakfast. Auf dem Schönberg, tel. 06744/93330, fax 06744/7446.

it's at its finest between Bingen, just north of Mainz, and Koblenz, at the confluence of the Rhine and Mosel rivers. With its spectacular castles, hillside wineries, and river scenes, the gorge has enthralled poets, painters, and artists for centuries. Goethe couldn't forget the place and J. M. W. Turner painted sunsets here.

During summer, plan ahead if you want more than just a short boat ride, since longer cruises (and area hotels) are often booked far in advance. Hotels set their prices according to the area's excessive popularity, and the only bargains are private rooms and youth hostels. Fortunately, the Rhine Gorge has some of Germany's best hostels—often in or next to a castle with magnificent views. Reaching these often means a steep trek, but you can leave your pack in a train station locker and enjoy the Rhineland air.

BINGEN

Bingen and its western outskirt, Bingerbrück (a short walk away), straddle the Nahe, a tributary that meets the Rhine 25 km downstream from Mainz. Bingen feels relatively remote and is less touristed than some of its neighbors, probably due to the fact that it offers few sights worth printing up in a glossy brochure. This makes for a tranquil and authentic town that still affords beautiful views of Father Rhine. If you're exploring Mainz, consider making this nearby town your home base; private rooms here cost less than half as much as hotel rooms in Mainz. Trains run between Mainz and Bingen every hour (30 min, DM 10); the last train returns to Bingen at 11:45 PM.

BASICS

You can leave your bags in lockers at the **Bingen Stadtbahnhof** or the Bingen Hauptbahnhof, one stop further from Mainz. The two are only a 15-min walk apart—although the Hauptbahnhof is closer to the Jugendherberge, the Stadtbahnhof is closer to everything you'll want to see and do—so pick one and go with it. To reach the **tourist office** (Rheinkai 21, tel. 06721/184205; closed Sun.) from the Hauptbahnhof, cross the Bingerbrücker Straße bridge, head down Fruchtmarktstraße (which becomes Vorstadtstraße), left on Hospitalstraße, and right on Rheinkai. From the Stadtbahnhof, follow the signs opposite the station. The map-giving staff will merrily book you into a hotel room (DM 3 fee), but private rooms (about DM 35) are a better bet. Ask the office for a list.

WHERE TO SLEEP AND EAT

If you're dying to shake it at Palazzo (*see below*), you'll have to ask really nicely for a key at the members-only **Jugendherberge Bingen-Bingerbrück (HI)** to avoid the 10 PM curfew. After the 20-min uphill hike it takes to get here, look past the somewhat primitive sleeping quarters to the beautiful view of the two rivers below. Beds are DM 19. *Herterstr. 51, tel. 06721/32163. From the Hauptbahnhof, cross bridge over the tracks and follow signs. 176 beds. Reception open 4 PM–9 PM.*

As far as restaurants go in Bingen, budget options are limited. The pedestrian zone around **Speisemarkt** and **Basilikastraße,** a couple of blocks up from the Stadtbahnhof and parallel to the river, is home to a slew of bakeries and delis, and **Karstadt** (at the corner of Basilikastr. and Amstr.) has a restaurant upstairs with its usual low prices (DM 6–DM 10). Or, invent a feast of your own with goods from **Plus** (Mainzer Str. 19). From the Stadtbahnhof, go straight up Bahnhofstraße, right on Mainzer Straße. If nightlife's your thing, Bingen's **Palazzo** (Rheinanlage, tel. 06721/10032) along the Rhine pumps house and techno for people from as far away as Mainz on Friday and Saturday 9 PM–5 AM. Cover runs from DM 10 to DM 20.

WORTH SEEING

Burg Klopp. In Bingen you'll notice this sturdy castle, known as "Burg Klopp the Invincible." The castle's owners, the Archbishopric of Mainz, repaired the damage inflicted by Louis XIV and his French soldiers way back in 1689, only to get paranoid and destroy the castle themselves in 1875 so that it would never fall into enemy hands. The town bought the castle in 1897, restored it, and moved the town hall and folk museum into the brick structure. The castle's exterior is its most interesting feature: The museum inside probably isn't worth the uphill climb.

At the confluence of the Nahe and Rhine rivers on a tiny offshore island stands the 13th-century **Mäuseturm** (Mice Tower). Legend has it that a greedy old bishop built the tower to levy tolls on river travelers. The townspeople hated the place and the bishop so much that they wouldn't let him come to shore safely. Stuck in his creation, so the legend goes, he was devoured by mice. Today, the treacherous Mäuseturm remains closed to visitors.

During Worms's Backfischfest (Baked-Fish Festival), held in late August and early September, locals drink wine, eat baked fish, and engage in Fischerstechen (drunken jousts) by the riverside.

BACHARACH

A few km downstream from Bingen, Bacharach is named for Bacchus, the Roman god of wine and harvests, i.e., lasciviousness and wild parties. While you don't get much of the latter in modern Bacharach, you do get 18 wineries wedged between the river and steep, grapevine-covered hills. You also get clustered medieval dwellings, cobblestone streets, a network of 14th-century defensive walls, and plenty of wineries offering tastings; for a complete list stop by the **tourist office** (Oberstr. 1, in Rathaus, tel. 06743/2968). From the **Bahnhof,** which has hourly service to Bingen (15 min, DM 5) and Koblenz (40 min, DM 12) and lockers, head right down Mainzer Straße (which becomes Oberstraße). Foodwise, get groceries and local vino at the **Spar** supermarket (Koblenzer Str. 66).

WHERE TO SLEEP

Avoid the HI hostel if you're not the hiking type, and head to **Haus Dettmar** (Oberstr. 8, tel. 06743/2661), a clean, basic pension with friendly owners and friendlier prices. Including breakfast, doubles cost DM 50–DM 60. Otherwise, the tourist office books private rooms that run as little as DM 30. Even cheaper is **Campingplatz Sonnenstrand** (Strandbadw., tel. 06743/1752), a 10-min walk south of central Bacharach along the Rhine. You pay DM 5 per car, DM 5 per tent, and DM 7 per person (including showers). The site has a market and restaurant, and swimming is allowed from the beach.

HOSTELS • Since 1925, the 12th-century **Burg Stahleck (HI)** has served as an idyllic alternative to the average youth hostel. Although the 20-min uphill hike is a pain, the views and majestic setting are worth it. Beds are DM 21, breakfast included, and dinner is DM 9. Reservations recommended. *Burg Stahleck, tel. 06743/1266, fax 06743/2684. From Bahnhof, right on Mainzer Str. and follow BURG CASTLE signs up steep switch-back stairs (which lead left at the church). Curfew 10 PM.*

ST. GOARSHAUSEN

Near St. Goarshausen—a little more than halfway from Mainz to Koblenz—the Rhine narrows, deepens, and quickens around treacherous rocks. Perhaps the most famous Rhine legends concern the craggy Loreley, which towers 132 m over a bend in the river south of St. Goarshausen. Legend has it that a beautiful maiden (or a spirit, or a group of maidens, depending on who's spinning the tale) sat upon the

Loreley rock entrancing sailors with golden locks, good looks, and an enchanting voice. When the breeze wafted her sweet melodies toward passing ships, captains and crew would take leave of their senses (and their helms) and dash their ships against the rocks. See where testosterone gets you? If you take a ride on one of the touristy ferries, you'll even hear the now-famous Loreley song, a tune set to a poem by Heinrich Heine. You can climb up to the Loreley for a good view of the river: From St. Goarshausen's Hauptbahnhof, walk south on Rheinstraße for about 3 km, then climb the steep staircase. On the way, check out the **Loreley statue,** a seductively posed iron woman sitting on a rock near the shore.

You'll notice two castles on either side of St. Goarshausen. Slightly upstream (to the south) is **Burg Katz,** built in 1371 by Count Wilhelm II von Katzenellbogen (cat's elbow). The competition for Rhine tolls and duties was so intense between Wilhelm II and his rival in the castle to the north, that the downstream neighbor was eventually dubbed **Burg Maus** (Mouse Castle—get it? Katz and Maus). On the Burg Maus grounds is the **Adler und Falkenhof** (tel. 06771/7669), a kind of bird zoo with eagles and falcons galore. Some of them take to the air daily at 11, 2:30, and 4:30—which is all you get to see at this closed castle. To reach the Burg from the Hauptbahnhof, walk outside and turn right, turn right again on Nastätterstraße, walk about a half km, and climb the path to the left.

BASICS

Stop by the **tourist office** (Bahnhofstr. 8, tel. 06771/91011; closed Sun.), near the Hauptbahnhof, to book a room (no fee) and grab a free city map, which lists the town's hotels and shows the routes to the Loreley and the youth hostel. Trains run hourly through St. Goarshausen from Koblenz (30 min, DM 10) and Wiesbaden (1 hr, DM 15). The KD ferry also stops here on its trek between Mainz (3¾ hrs, DM 47) and Koblenz (2 hrs, DM 28).

WHERE TO SLEEP

If you're here mainly to see the Loreley, consider staying at **Gasthaus Winzerschänke** (Forstbachstr. 38, tel. 06771/337), hidden among the trees on the trail to the Loreley. You can enjoy wine and the proprietress's homemade goulash and dumplings in the restaurant. Singles are DM 40, doubles range from DM 70 to DM 90, including breakfast. From the ferry landing, turn right on Bahnhofstraße (which becomes Rheinstraße) and left on Forstbachstraße.

Turner- und Jugendheim Loreley (Auf der Loreley, tel. 06771/2619, fax 06771/8158) is a non-HI hostel with beds for DM 11 (DM 12 over 26) and breakfast for DM 6.50. Reception is open 5 PM–6 PM, officially, and dinner is available for DM 8. If you borrow a key, the 10 PM curfew can be escaped. Otherwise, you can camp at **Campingplatz auf der Loreley** (An der Wiese, tel. 06771/430; closed Nov.–Mar.); just follow the signs to the Loreley. It'll cost you DM 7 per person, DM 6 per tent and DM 5 per car to stay.

ST. GOAR

St. Goar sits on the Rhine opposite St. Goarshausen and is worth checking out mostly because the ferry ride can be entertaining. If you're here on Easter Monday, bring an Easter egg for the captain and ride for free as part of the **Fest der Fliegenden Brücke.** Get more info about this festival and fall wine wackiness at the tourist office (Heerstr. 86, tel. 06741/383; closed weekends), which also books rooms for free. St. Goar is a kitschy tourist town, having lost much of the excitement and all of the danger that came with its centuries of military activity. Most notably, its **Stiftskirche** (Collegiate Church) was the site of a legendary shot by a marksman named Kretsch, who pegged a French general and demoralized his shipbound troops, ending their siege during the Thirty Years' War. A few km north of town are the ruins of **Burg Rheinfels,** yet another medieval castle with sweeping views of the river valley and stones to scramble up. The walk is nice, especially if you've reserved a bed at **Jugendherberge St. Goar (HI)** (Bismarckw. 17, tel. 06741/388) just west of the fortress. The hostel offers still more serene Rhine views for DM 19, breakfast included. Call before you come.

COMING AND GOING

From in front of St. Goarshausen's tourist office there are frequent, daily ferries to St. Goar depending on demand; the 10-min trip costs DM 3.50 round-trip. From St. Goar's **Hauptbahnhof,** trains run at least hourly to Mainz (50 min, DM 14), Koblenz (30 min, DM 10), and Bacharach (10 min, DM 5). You can rent a bike at **Golf Pavilion** (tel. 06741/1360) for about DM 13 per day.

BRAUBACH

Braubach, best seen on a day trip from Koblenz or one of the other Rhine Valley towns, is home to **Marksburg,** one of the last castles along the river on your way to Koblenz. Classic in its impenetrable defenses and layout, it's the only fortress on the Rhine that remains untouched—no one ever blew it up, ripped it down, or captured it. If you think life is cruel today, take a look at the "brattice," a wide chute from which the castle's defenders poured hot tar and oil on attackers; an armory showing the development of weapons from 600 BC to AD 1500; and, grimmest of all, a stable full of torture devices. The mandatory, one-hour castle tour is in German, supplemented with an English-language pamphlet. *Tel. 02627/206. Open Easter–late Oct., daily 10–5; Nov.–Easter, daily 11–4. Admission: DM 7, DM 5 students.*

COMING AND GOING

To reach Braubach, take the Wiesbaden–Koblenz rail line up the Rhine's east bank. Once in Braubach, exit the Hauptbahnhof on the "Stadt" (city) side, turn right, and pick up the green-and-yellow tram labeled MARKSBURG EXPRESS across from the post office. The round-trip journey costs DM 5. If you'd rather walk, exit the Hauptbahnhof and continue straight uphill, following signs for 40 min along the trail to the Marksburg. Trains run here from Koblenz (15 min, DM 5) or St. Goarshausen (20 min, DM 7) at least hourly.

In case you're easily disoriented, Mainzers have come up with a clever guiding system: Streets parallel to the Rhine are marked with blue signs, streets perpendicular to the Rhine with red signs.

KOBLENZ

Looking down on Koblenz from **Festung Ehrenbreitstein,** a castle perched on a hill across the river, you'll see a modern city scattered with a few old buildings at the majestic confluence of the Rhine and Mosel. When the Romans founded this town in AD 9 they named it *Castrum ad Confluentes* (Camp at the Confluence). The name evolved to Koblenz, and the town became powerful because of its strategic location. The Allies were well aware of this and pulverized 85% of the city in World War II. After the war, Koblenzers built today's modern city around the few historical remnants. If you just walk from one historic sight to the next, you'll get the feeling that the old Koblenz doesn't quite fit in with the new. Koblenz's modern self is definitely off the map-guided tour. Not too pretty, yet oddly charming, Koblenz is sorta like the **Schängelbrunnen** (Scalawag Fountain), a bronze fountain with a statue of a young boy who spits water every three min or so at unsuspecting passersby. You might like it. You might not. At any rate, its central location makes it a good base for exploring the Rhine and Mosel valleys.

BASICS

The main **tourist office** (Bahnhofpl., tel. 0261/31304; open weekdays 8:30–6, Sat. 11:30–6; shorter hrs off-season), across from the Hauptbahnhof, provides hotel listings, makes reservations for a DM 2 fee, and stocks free boat schedules and city maps—all in decent English. The seasonal **branch office** on Konrad-Adenauer Ufer at Rheinstraße (tel. 0261/129–1630; open summer only, Tues.–Sun. noon–6:25), where the ferry arrives, provides roughly the same services. The Hauptbahnhof doesn't have a bank, so head to **Sparkasse** (Emil-Schüller-Str. 22, tel. 0261/393331; open Mon.–Wed. 8–1 and 2:30–4, Thurs. until 5), just to your left as you exit the station, which charges DM 2 per traveler's check and has a 24-hour ATM. When it's closed, use the **Hauptpost** (open weekdays 7 AM–8 PM, Sat. 7–4, Sun. 10–1), to the right as you exit the Hauptbahnhof, which has metered phones and exchanges money. The postal code is 56068.

COMING AND GOING

You can take a KD ferry from anywhere along the Rhine, but trains are the most efficient way to reach Koblenz. From the **Hauptbahnhof**—the subject of general rebuilding at press time—there are trains at least hourly to Gießen (1½ hrs, DM 32) and other Lahn Valley points (*see* Chapter 2), Cologne (1 hr, DM 24.60), Mainz (50 min, DM 24.60), and Trier (1½ hrs, DM 30). You can stash your stuff in the station's lockers. From the **Busbahnhof,** across from the train station, buses connect nearby towns with Koblenz. The tourist office has schedules and you can buy tickets on board or contact the **Rhein-Mosel Verkehrsgesellschaft** (Neverstr. 5, tel. 0261/17383) at the Busbahnhof.

GETTING AROUND

Unless German suburbia fascinates you, most everything worth seeing lies in the area between the station and the two rivers. If you face the plaza from the station, the Rhine is six blocks ahead (though you

KOBLENZ

Sights ●
Basilika St. Kastor, **6**
Deutsches Eck, **2**
Festung Ehrenbreitstein and Landesmuseum, **4**
Liebfrauenkirche, **7**
Ludwigsmuseum, **5**
Plan, **8**
Residenzschloß, **11**
Schängelbrunnen, **9**
Weindorf, **13**

Lodging ○
Campingplatz Rhein-Mosel, **1**
Jugendherberge (HI), **3**
Hotel Jan van Werth, **12**
Hotel Mäckler, **10**

can't see it), and the Mosel is 2 km to your left (you can't see that, either). Taking a bus within the city center costs DM 2, but you'll probably only use the bus to go across the Rhine to Festung Ehrenbreitstein (*see below*), which costs DM 3. Ferries across the Rhine also cost DM 3 round-trip. You can also get a day pass for DM 8.50. Note that most buses run only once an hour after 7 PM and that the last ferry leaves by 7 PM (6 PM on Saturday).

WHERE TO SLEEP

Although Koblenz's location makes it a convenient place to spend the night, there are few bargains aside from the nice but tough-to-reach hostel. Between April and mid-October, you can always camp at waterside **Campingplatz Rhein-Mosel** (Schartwiesenw. 6, tel. 0261/802489) for DM 5 per person, DM 4 per tent, DM 4 per car. To get here, take the ferry across the Mosel from Deutsches Eck.

The clean, tastefully decorated **Hotel Jan van Werth** (Van Werth Str. 9, tel. 0261/36500, fax 0261/36506), a mere five-min walk from the train station (left on Bahnhofstraße, right on Van-Werth-Straße), is relatively cheap (singles DM 40, doubles DM 85, DM 120 with shower), and prices include a sumptuous buffet breakfast. Reservations are advised. If the youth hostel is full, the nearby **Hotel Mäckler** (Helfensteinstr. 63–65, tel. 0261/73725) is your next cheapest option (singles DM 30, doubles DM 50, including breakfast). Sure, the decor is cheesy and the facilities a little worn at this humble establishment, but everything works, the management is friendly, and it's affordable. Follow directions for Festung Ehrenbreitstein (*see below*) to Charlottenstraße, and walk one block up to Helfensteinstraße.

HOSTELS • The spic-and-span **Jugendherberge (HI)** is inside Festung Ehrenbreitstein with great hilltop views of the Rhine and the Mosel and an on-site bar. Call ahead for vacancies and leave your bags in a station locker if possible; the hike up is a doozy. When walking up from the bus stop, stick to the path; the woods around the Burg have a reputation for criminal activity. Or—if you don't mind swinging 50 ft above rocks and prickly plants—take the *Sesselbahn* (chair lift; *see* directions for Festung Ehrenbreitstein, *below*), which offers discounts to hostelers and lets you off right at the hostel's door. Beds DM 21, DM 51 for a double (buffet breakfast included). *Auf der Festung, tel. 0261/73737, fax 0261/972–8730. Curfew 11:30 PM.*

FOOD

On and around Eltzerhofstraße there's a cluster of hip cafés where young student types hang out. If you're suffering from bratwurst overload, graze at **Salat Garten** (Gymnasialstr. 14, tel. 0261/36455; closed Sun. and Tues.). The atmosphere is a bit sterile, but this *Vollwert* (whole food) restaurant's impressive salad/veggie bar (100 grams for DM 2.35), wide array of pastas and soups, and daily specials like spinach-noodle casserole (DM 7.50) may just hit the spot. For some good German eatin', try **Brasserie Faustus** (Eltzerhofstr. 13, tel. 0261/17991), which has an outdoor patio and books and rags to read while you eat potato soup (DM 7.50) or salad with lamb fillet (DM 17). Another option is Sole (Firmungstr. 32b, tel. 0261/33380). Lunch specials include a salad plus a pasta dish and start at DM 12, or try one of the pizzas (around DM 13) at this modern, well-lit joint.

WORTH SEEING

The focus of Koblenz's photogenic Altstadt is the small square, **Plan,** dominated by the spitting Schängelbrunnen fountain and the bulky Romanesque **Liebfrauenkirche** (Church of Our Lady), which marks the Altstadt's focal point. The nearby streets, with names like Gemüsegasse (Vegetable Alley) and Mehlgasse (Flour Alley), are lined with touristy pubs and wine bars. Toward the Rhine to the southeast is the stately **Residenzschloß,** built in 1786 as the ruling archbishop's palace and now the home of city government. Just south along the river is **Weindorf** (Wine Village), a major Disney-style tourist attraction constructed to simulate a Rhine or Mosel wine village. If you go upstream a bit, you can see real ones. For a dose of more authentic Koblenz river culture, check out the crowd on the **Rheinanlagen** behind the Weindorf. Take your shoes off, grab a beer, and join the sprawlers on the grass.

In 1998 the head of the German Wine Growers' Association shot himself in his castle. He had ruined the family business by trying to persuade Germans to graduate from their traditional sweet wines to something a bit dryer.

DEUTSCHES ECK • The "German Corner" is a pointed, cobbled protrusion that juts into the water where the Mosel meets the Rhine. A bombastic statue of Kaiser Wilhelm I—the ruler of the newly united Germany in 1871—was unveiled here in 1897. Like most German cultural monuments, it was blasted away during World War II, and only the sturdy base remained. In the summer of 1993, the city decided that a huge, bare podium was no longer an appropriate emblem for German unity, and ordered the reconstruction of the original statue. A mighty row ensued: Citizens were divided over whether they should pay for the restoration of a chunk of their Imperial past. Both sides forgot their principles when a local businessman said he would pay for the Kaiser and his horse to be replaced. There was no such argument over the erection of two drab slabs of the Berlin Wall on the river bank as a modern memorial to a united Germany. Behind the monument is the lovely **Basilika St. Kastor,** a Romanesque church built around 1300 and remodeled since—notice the Gothic floral patterns on the ceiling.

FESTUNG EHRENBREITSTEIN • As you glance across the Rhine from the Deutsches Eck, you can't miss this huge castle with its 130-m-high tower. It's clear why Trier's archbishops first built a fortress here in the 16th century: With such a commanding view of both the Rhine and Mosel, anyone could rule with a firm hand. The Prussian army built the current structure around 1830 after Napoleon destroyed the original. New to the fortress is the **Landesmuseum,** with an interesting exhibit of artifacts explained only *auf Deutsch.* To reach the castle, take Bus 7 or 8 to Bahnhof Ehrenbreitstein or Bus 9 or 10 to Charlottenstraße, and then walk uphill for 20 min, or take a ferry across the Rhine, then the *Sesselbahn* (chair lift) to the top for DM 7 (DM 10 round-trip). The lift runs daily 10–5 (until 6 in summer). *Tel. 0261/97030. Castle admission free; museum DM 3. Open Mar.–mid-Nov., daily 9–12:30 and 1–5.*

LUDWIGSMUSEUM • On the Rhine behind the Deutsches Eck is Koblenz's new modern art museum (the house itself dates from the 13th century). With a focus mainly on contemporary French art, the Ludwigsmuseum stays up to date by rotating its exhibits every four months. *Danziger Freiheit 1, tel. 0261/304040. Admission: DM 5, DM 3 students. Open Tues.–Sat. 11–5 (Thurs. until 8), Sun. 11–6.*

AFTER DARK

For listings, pick up a copy of *Picture,* the Middle Rhine's "Kultur Magazin," at any café on Eltzerhofstraße. **Mephisto** (Eltzerhofstr. 3, tel. 0261/31735) draws a lively twentysomething crowd daily 7 PM–1 AM (Fri. and Sat. until 2). Just across the street from Mephisto is **Café Knoch** (Görrestr. 12, tel. 0261/37691; open daily 10 AM–1 AM), which serves innumerable cocktail concoctions such as the "Ernest Hemingway Spezial," all for around DM 9, and has a daily special to boot. Another fun spot near the foot of the Mosel bridge and not far from the river is **Irish Pub No Name** (Florinsmarkt, tel. 0261/36100), also open daily 7 AM–1 AM (Fri. and Sat. until 2). If you wanna boogie, **Blaue Biwel** (Entenpfuhl 9, tel. 0261/35577; open Wed.–Sat. 10 PM–1 AM), just off Am Plan, turns into a dance club in the summer, and also hosts music and comedy acts.

NEAR KOBLENZ

MARIA LAACH

The trip to Maria Laach may not be hassle-free (you'll need a train and a bus), but it's well worth the effort. Considered the finest example of Romanesque architecture anywhere, even architectural ignoramuses will be able to appreciate the beauty and serenity of Maria Laach's **Benedictine Abbey** at the wooded edge of the tranquil **Laacher See,** a water-filled volcanic crater. The **Klosterkirche** (monastery church) was built from the 11th through the 13th century. Its two-toned, balanced exterior and intricate yet restrained interior may stun you into downright reverence, while its isolated setting helps preserve the ancient feel of the place. Entrance is free, and you are welcome to sit in on services, which take place throughout the day. The **information center** (Benedikterabtei, tel. 02652/590), open weekdays 9:30–11 and 1–4:30, Sunday 1–4:30, has literature in German and English for sale, and shows a free 20-min video in German on modern cloistered life—60 monks still reside here today. To avoid the high prices of Maria Laach's only hotel, come on a day trip, or pitch your tent at **Campingplatz Laacher See** (tel. 02636/2485), where a night will cost you DM 8 per person, DM 6 per tent, and DM 6.50 per vehicle. From the monastery, head straight for the Laacher See, turn left and walk 20 min along the lake.

COMING AND GOING • The best connection to Maria Laach is from Andernach, which is easily accessible from Koblenz (trains run several times hourly, 15 min, DM 6). From Andernach, take Bus 6031. From the station walk straight on Kurfürstendamm, take Bahnhofstraße under the bridge to the right, then turn on Breitenstraße; buses stop on the left. Buses travel the route to Maria Laach (50 min, DM 6 each way) just twice daily in each direction. Ask at the Busbahnhof in Koblenz (*see above*), or call the Rhein-Mosel Verkehrsgesellschaft (0261/17383) for the current schedule.

THE MOSEL VALLEY

The Rhine's most famous tributary has its source in the Vosges Mountains of France, but most of its 545 km wind through Germany before it meets the Rhine in Koblenz. Like Vater Rhein, the Mosel is lined with castles, vineyards, and tourists. But unlike the Rhine, the Mosel has no cities larger than Trier, with a population of about 100,000. And while the Rhine conjures images of rough, rocky cliffs and swift-moving water, the Mosel is a calm, quiet river, and the valleys surrounding it are equally mellow. Past Cochem, the Mosel twists and bends so much that large boats can't navigate it, and trains don't bother with the tiny towns that fill the nooks and crannies like cookie crumbs. Tour buses are *not* deterred, yet Mosel towns share a timeless, almost mystical feel that you won't find along the Rhine.

BURG ELTZ

No castle on either the Mosel or the Rhine possesses the grandeur of this monstrous château. Undisturbed for 800 years, Burg Eltz sits on a crag above the village of **Moselkern,** its lookout posts and turrets still intact. An arduous 3-km uphill trek through serene forest will get you to the fortress from Moselkern's train station or KD ferry dock. If you're out of breath, a bus from a parking lot below the castle will drive you the last 10 min for DM 1.50. The castle is open to gazers on mandatory tours (in English) April–October, daily 9:30–5:30. *Tel. 02672/1300. Admission: DM 8, DM 5.50 students.*

COCHEM

Cochem is known for its wine, its picture-perfect Altstadt, and the **Reichsburg,** a turreted castle on a vineyard-covered hill—a 25-min walk from town. As you dodge swarms of middle-aged tourists and navigate your way through touristy shops and restaurants, you can almost see Louis XIV's French hordes scrambling up the curving paths to destroy the castle in 1689. Two hundred years later, a Berlin merchant bought the place and compulsively restored it. From the castle, you'll have a panoramic view of the valley. Inside you'll see wood furnishings as delicate as the torture devices are gruesome. *From sta-*

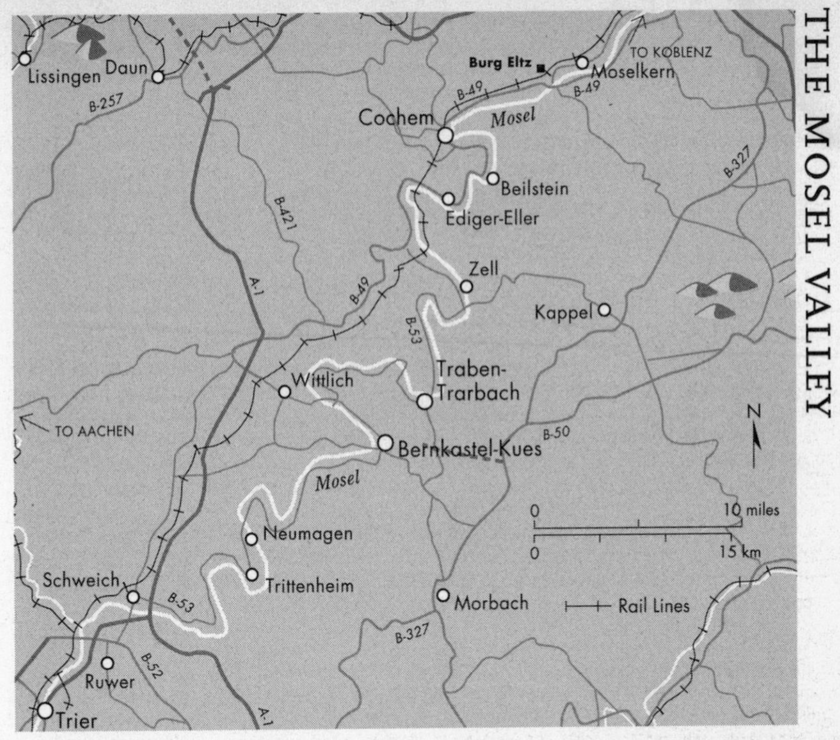

tion, walk south along river on Moselpromenade and turn right on Schloßstr. Mandatory German-language tours (with English pamphlet): DM 6, DM 4 students. Open mid-Mar. to mid-Oct., daily 9–5.

The town itself is a bit Disneyesque, but worth a visit for the Reichsburg or as a base for exploring the surrounding valley. Cochem is a major wine town, with plenty of wine tastings and festivals, notably the **Mosel Wine Week** around the beginning of June and the **Cochem Wine Festival,** a four-day shindig on the last weekend of August. If you'd rather not face the crowds, wine cellars open their doors at **Winzerhoffeste** or **Straßenweinfeste,** more casual weekend street fairs during August and September.

BASICS

The **tourist office** can be a big help—if the crowds don't scare you away. Stop in for free maps and room bookings. *Am Endertpl., tel. 02671/3971. From station, right on Ravenéstr., left into bus station at Endertpl. Open June–Oct., weekdays 10–1 and 2–5, Fri. until 6:30, Sat. 10–3, Sun. 10–noon; Nov.–May, closed Sun.*

COMING AND GOING

Express trains arrive hourly in Cochem from Koblenz (35 min, DM 12) and Trier (1 hr, DM 16). The KD and Hölzenbein ferry companies run daily between Cochem and Koblenz (4½ hrs, DM 30–DM 40) and several smaller companies float between Cochem and nearby tiny towns along the Mosel. For info on water travel, visit the tourist office, or better yet, visit the cluster of company stands located on the station side of the river near the Moselbrücke. Cochem's regional bus system runs from the train station to nearby towns like Bullay (50 min, DM 9) and Zell (1 hr, DM 9). For more info contact the **Rhein-Mosel Verkehrsgesellschaft** (Bahnhof Cochem, tel. 02671/8976).

WHERE TO SLEEP

Cochem has an abundance of private rooms (DM 28–DM 35) and is a good town to crash in; make reservations at the tourist office or, if your German is good, get their list and call for yourself. Most hotels are relatively reasonable and easily accessible: The friendly owners of the cheesy but spacious and convenient **Hotel Zum Landsknecht** (Moselpromenade 28, tel. 02671/7030) on the river have doubles for

DM 35. At **Campingplatz am Freizeitzentrum** (Klottener Str. 17, tel. 02671/1212, fax 02671/8234), along the Mosel next to a swimming-pool complex (offering discounts for campsite patrons), it'll cost you DM 6.50 per person, DM 10 per spot, and DM 3.50 per car per night. RVs abound, but so do little extras like trees and laundry facilities. From the station, head toward the Mosel and bear left across the Nordbrücke, then left again on Klottener Straße.

HOSTELS • Jugendherberge Cochem (HI) is a 10-min walk from the Hauptbahnhof (*see* Campingplatz, *above,* for directions, but turn right at Klottener Straße). For once, it's not on a hill but on the bank of the river in a clean, modern building. Reserve ahead for June through August. Beds are DM 19.50, breakfast included. *Klottener Str. 9, tel. 02671/8633, fax 02671/8568. Curfew 10 PM (key available). Reception open 8 AM–10 PM.*

TRABEN-TRARBACH

Wine came easy to Trarbach. Perched on the sloped, vine-friendly bank of the Mosel, Trarbach is the older sister of Traben, whose position on flat land made it the more convenient building site as the two grew together. Trarbach's Altstadt boasts the always-enchanting array of half-timbered houses, with Jugendstil elements and the explorable ruins of **Schloß Grevenburg** to boot. Cross the river via the twin-towered guardhouse, **Brüchentor,** to Traben's immense **Mont Royal.** Built by Louis XIV in 1687, this palace also lies in ruins. If all the wreckage has you wrecked, try out the **Kurmittelhaus** (Wildbadstr. 203, tel. 05541/4955), a spa where you can be massaged (DM 27) and soaked in various steams and bubbles (DM 36 and up). If your raisined body has got you thinking about grapes, consider sticking around for the annual **Weinfest,** held the second week of July. Hikers can make the two-hour, 7-km hike from Traben-Trarbach to Bernkastel (*see below*). It's mostly uphill, so stow your pack. To access the path from Traben, cross the Moselbrücke, turn right on Brückenstraße (which becomes Wildbadstraße), and follow the signs.

BASICS

The **tourist office** (Verkehrsamt; Bahnhofstr. 22, tel. 06541/83980, fax 06541/839839), three blocks from the station, provides free lodging listings and a useful map of the area, and books rooms at no charge. They're open weekdays 8–5 (Fri. until 6) and Saturdays 2–5. You can rent **bikes** at Egon Wagner (Alte Marktstr. 4, tel. 06541/1649) for DM 10 per day.

COMING AND GOING

Traben-Trarbach is one of the few small places accessible by rail. From Trier (1 hr, DM 16.40) or Koblenz (1½ hrs, DM 19.60), take one of the hourly trains to Bullay, and then transfer to a waiting S-Bahn, which takes you to Traben-Trarbach. Ask for a through ticket. If you're looking for someplace to keep those wine bottles, lockers are available in the station.

WHERE TO SLEEP

Gasthaus Germania (Kirchstr. 101, tel. 06541/9398) charges DM 30 per person for clean, humble rooms, and usually has space. Behind the station, turn right on Bismarckstraße, left on Schulstraße, and right on Kirchstraße. Otherwise camp at **Campingplatz Rißbach** (Rißbacherstr. 165, tel. 06541/3111) for DM 7.50 per head, DM 10 per car and tent. Follow Bahnstraße (which becomes Rißbacherstraße) south from the station.

HOSTELS • The **Jugendherberge (HI)** is 20 min by foot uphill from the station on the same side of the river. Bed down in doubles (DM 28.70 per person) or quads (DM 23.70 per person), all with attached bath. Prices include breakfast and sheets. Call ahead. *Am Hirtenpfädchen, tel. 06541/9278, fax 06541/3759. From the station, take a right on Bismarckstr., left on Laug., left on Am Laubloch, and left on Am Hirtenpfädchen. 175 beds. Midnight curfew, or ask for key. Reception open 7 AM–midnight. Lunch (DM 9.20), dinner (DM 8.50), laundry (DM 6).*

BERNKASTEL-KUES

Though Bernkastel-Kues—about 7 km south of Traben-Trarbach as the crow flies but a winding 25 km by road—doesn't look different from other Mosel spots, its remote location makes it a true find. You feel more isolated here despite the presence of tour buses. Bernkastel, on the north bank, centers on its Marktplatz, and no matter how many cobblestone squares you've seen, this one is still pretty cool. **Michaelsbrunnen** (Michael's Fountain), in the town square, used to spout wine; today water is the fountain's liquid of choice—even during September's **Weinfest** (wine festival). It's a 20-min ascent to **Burg**

Landshut, an evil-looking castle that has loomed over the town since the 13th century. Today, flowers grow among its ruins (visit anytime), and a café serves overpriced food (as well as Bernkasteler Doktor, the town's famous brand of wine).

Across the river in Kues, the outshone half of the duo, sits the 16th-century **St. Nikolaus Hospital** (Cusanusstr. 2). Also known as the Cusanusstift, this home for the aged and downtrodden owes its beginnings to Cardinal Nikolaus Cusanus, who had the foresight to install a vineyard in front of the hospital. You can sample the local vino here. Perhaps more intriguing is Kues's romantic manor-lined river promenade.

BASICS

The **tourist office** (Am Gestude 5, tel. 06531/4023; open weekdays 8:30–12:30 and 1–5, Sat. 10–4), across from the bus station and docks, distributes maps and books rooms for free. More importantly, you can leave your pack here during the day. Rent **bicycles** from Funbiketeam (Schanzstr. 22, tel. 06531/94024) at DM 12 per day for a three-speed, and DM 13.50 for a mountain bike.

COMING AND GOING

Buses to Bernkastel-Kues make the bumpy trek once an hour from both Traben-Trarbach (40 min, DM 7) and Trier (1½ hrs, DM 13). A ferry ride to Bernkastel-Kues from Traben involves two long hours on a small boat with a soundtrack of German folk songs. At least the scenery is nice. Ferries operated by **Moselpersonenschifffahrt** (Goldbachstr. 52, Bernkastel, tel. 06531/8222, fax 06531/7603) charge DM 12 (DM 19 round-trip).

Someone once said Eltz is to castles what Eiffel is to towers and what Fenway is to ballparks.

WHERE TO SLEEP

Kues's clean, simple **Pension Esslinger** (Nachtigallenw. 7, tel. 06531/3131) charges DM 40 per person. Also on the Kues side, try your luck at **Haus Lotti** (Brüningstr. 12–14, tel. 06531/6565), which has lots of charm but few rooms (DM 35–DM 40 per person). **Campingplatz Kueser Werth** (Am Hafen 2, tel. 06531/8200; open Apr.–Oct.), a shady, grassy site on a peninsula, has showers, a market, and a small restaurant. They charge DM 7 per person, DM 5 per tent, and DM 3 per car. From the bus station go south (upriver), then cross the bridge to Kues. Take a left on Saarallee, then another left on Am Hafen.

HOSTELS • Jugendherberge (HI). Situated on top of a hill above Burg Landshut, this 96-bed hostel charges DM 19.50 for a very standard hostel bed. Reserve ahead. *Jugendherbergsstr. 1, tel. 06531/2395. From Bernkastel, walk up through market, right on Karlstr., and follow signs for Burg Landshut. Curfew 10 PM, or ask for key. Reception open 5 PM–7 PM.*

TRIER

At the *Hauptmarkt* (main square) in Trier stands a red house bearing an inscription that translates as "Trier existed 1,300 years before Rome. May it continue to exist and to enjoy an eternal peace." Peace was definitely disturbed during both world wars, when bombs fell and enemies focused on Trier. Still, there is plenty left to see in this relaxed, walkable city, and the Altstadt and Roman antiquities are too impressive to pass up. Once you've seen them, you can always escape to Trier's hip hangouts and happening street life.

Through the millennia, this ancient city has weathered quite a bit. Legend holds that Trier's strategic location led a mythic Celtic prince named Trebeta to establish a settlement here in 2000 BC named after himself. In the 1st century BC, Julius Caesar's Rhine brigade found Trier a handy place to hang out while waging war on the Teutons, and began the transformation of Trier into Roma Secunda, a second Rome north of the Alps. Art, commerce, and bureaucracy developed here so impressively that many Roman bigwigs, including Augustus and Claudius, made Trier their second home. In the early 4th century, when Constantine lived here, the town had its moment of glory as capital of the Western Empire. Such honor brought many civic adornments to Trier, including baths, palaces, barracks, an amphitheater, and plenty of churches. Through the Middle Ages, Trier prospered as the seat of a powerful archbishop. Later Karl Marx's childhood home, Trier is now a mellow college town and a center for trade with nearby France and Luxembourg. If you want to soak up the "new Europe," whose borders no longer exist and whose currency is interchangeable, then Trier is the best place to do it.

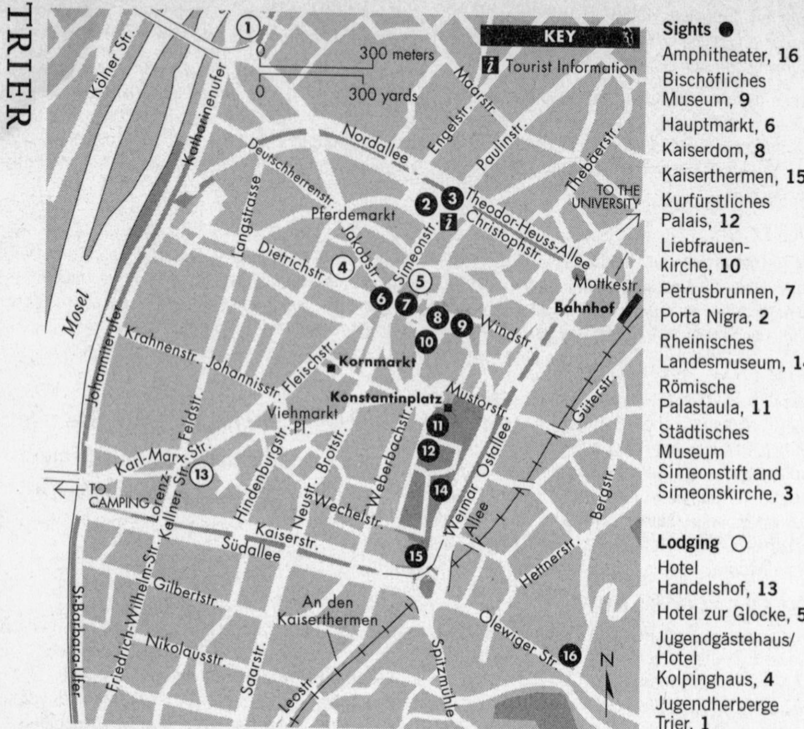

BASICS

The **tourist office** at the Porta Nigra (tel. 0651/978080; open Apr.–Oct., Mon.–Sat. 9–6:30, Sun. 9–3:30; shorter hrs off-season) has free maps and lodging lists, sells biking and hiking maps, and will book rooms for free. It also offers various city tours. A *Trier-Card* (DM 17) will get you into all of the attractions Trier has to offer. The **DVB** bank (tel. 0651/74721; open weekdays 9–noon and 1–5, Sat. 9–noon and 1–2, Sun. 10:30–1) in the train station has better rates and hours than banks in the Altstadt. You can also get a cash advance on your credit card here. Buy stamps or use the metered phones at the **Hauptpost** (Moltkestr. 21), just northeast of the train station. You can rent **bikes** from Tina Fahrrad Verleih at either the train station (tel. 0651/148856; open daily 9–7) or the courtyard of the Jugendgästehaus Kolpinghaus (*see below*), Monday–Saturday 9–noon. DM 8 will get you a clunker, DM 15 a mountain bike.

COMING AND GOING

Ferries don't go all the way to Trier, and buses are aggravatingly slow, so take the train. There's rail service at least hourly from Koblenz (1½ hrs, DM 30) and Cologne (2½ hrs, DM 49), and most trains continue on to Luxembourg (DM 15.60), only 40 min away. Stow your stuff in the **Hauptbahnhof**'s lockers. To reach the Altstadt from the Hauptbahnhof, head straight down Theodor-Heuss-Allee and turn left at the large black gate, the Porta Nigra. For a cheaper alternative to trains, call the **Mitfahrzentrale** (Kaiserstr. 13, tel. 0651/19440) to arrange rides with drivers to various destinations.

WHERE TO SLEEP

At the decent, clean **Hotel zur Glocke** (Glockenstr. 12, tel. 0651/73109), just off Simeonstraße between the Hauptmarkt and Porta Nigra, you can get singles for DM 40 and doubles for DM 70–DM 80 (some with shower). The equally plain and rather austere **Hotel Handelshof** (Lorenz-Kellner-Str. 1, tel. 0651/73933) offers singles for DM 40, doubles for DM 80 (both including breakfast), none with bath, and is a 10-min walk from the Hauptmarkt.

HOSTELS • Jugendgästehaus Kolpinghaus und Hotel Kolpinghaus. This joint hostel-hotel just one block from the Hauptmarkt is the best Trier's got for the price. Beds in the Jugendgästehaus cost DM 25; quads, doubles, and a few singles (DM 35 per person) are available in the hotel; all prices include breakfast. There are no showers in the rooms, but there's no curfew either. *Dietrichstr. 42, tel. 0651/975250, fax 0651/975–2540. 135 beds. Reception open 8 AM–11 PM, checkout 10 AM. Bike rental.*

Jugendherberge Trier (HI). This better-than-average hostel has beds in doubles (DM 39.90) and quads (DM 26.60) with attached showers, including sheets and breakfast. Reservations are a good idea but only possible if you write or fax ahead. *An der Jugendherberge 4, tel. 0651/29292, fax 0651/24080. From Hauptbahnhof, walk down Theodor-Heuss-Allee, right on Paulinstr., left on Maarstr., which becomes An der Jugendherberge (30 min by foot). 242 beds. Midnight curfew, lockout 9:30–1. Phone reception open 7 AM–midnight, check-in 1–6. Bike rental (guests only).*

CAMPING • Campingpark Trier-City, only a 20-min walk from town, has a restaurant and tents for rent. Rates are DM 7 per person, DM 4 per tent, and DM 4 per car. *Luxemburger Str. 81, tel. 0651/86921. From Porta Nigra, head left down Simeonstr. through Hauptmarkt, then down Fleischstr. (which becomes Brückenstr., then Karl-Marx-Str.), cross Mosel at Römerbrücke, turn left on Luxemburger Str.*

FOOD

In Trier's Altstadt, expensive restaurants rub shoulders with *Imbiß* (snack) stands and fast-food joints. The super-touristy **Zum Domstein** (Am Hauptmarkt 5, tel. 0651/74490) serves regional dishes such as *Eifeler Wildragout* (Eifel-style venison ragout with creamy wild mushrooms, served with dumplings and stewed fruit; DM 19.80). Pricey, but they don't serve this stuff in Ohio. You're more likely to meet locals at **Astarix** (Karl Marx Str. 11, tel. 0651/72239), a cool, studenty bar/bistro that hosts concerts, poetry readings, and the like, and serves pizzas, pastas, and salads from DM 6. Centrally located **Plus Markt** (Brotstr. 53) offers the raw ingredients for a self-made feast.

To exercise your brain as well as your brawn, have a go at the enormous chess set along Cochem's Moselpromenade; there's plenty of grass for adoring spectators, too.

WORTH SEEING

Of the many centuries-old structures surrounding Trier's **Hauptmarkt,** the most notable is the 16th-century **Petrusbrunnen** (St. Peter's Fountain) on the southeast corner. One of Trier's famous Renaissance architects, Ruprecht Hoffman, designed it with four allegorical statues of the principal virtues: Justice, Fortitude, Temperance, and Prudence.

Just down Stirnstraße from the Hauptmarkt is Trier's beautiful **Dom** (open daily 6–6; shorter hrs off-season). Its wide arches create a light, airy environment that Romanesque architecture rarely achieves. Constantine began construction in AD 326, and since then the Dom has picked up odds and ends from just about every era. Behind the front altar you can peek through locked doors at the eerily encased *Tunica Christi* (Robe of Christ), supposedly the garment worn by J.C. at his trial by Pontius Pilate. It is so highly valued and delicate that Dom bigwigs bring it out for public display only every 30 years. Next viewing: AD 2019. Next to the Dom on Windstraße, where the second half of Constantine's enormous double church complex once stood, is the 13th-century **Liebfrauenkirche,** one of the best examples of high Gothic architecture. Its constrained rose shape (symbol of the Virgin) and darkened corners contrast nicely with the Dom's brightness. From the little black flagstone halfway down the main aisle, you can see every one of the 12 disciples and the pillars they're on, symbolically and literally helping to support the holy place.

South of the Dom down Konstantinstraße is the basilica Constantine built in AD 300. Today the **Römische Palastaula** serves as Trier's major Protestant church, and resembles a warehouse more than a place of worship. Next door, seemingly attached to the basilica, is the **Kurfürstliches Palais,** former residence of the ruling archbishops of Trier and still home to bureaucrats. Paths lead through the regal, yet low-key *Palastgarten* (Palace Garden) to the **Rheinisches Landesmuseum** (Weimarer Allee 1, tel. 0651/97740) on its eastern edge. The archaeological museum houses the largest collection of Roman antiquities in Germany, including hundreds of podiums, busts, and stone reliefs. Don't miss the Egyptian casket and mummy. The museum is open Tuesday–Friday 9:30–5:30, weekends 10:30–5, and admission is free. Next to the Porta Nigra (*see below*) stands the Romanesque **Simeonskirche,** built in the ruins of the Roman fortifications in the 11th century. The church now holds the **Städtisches Museum Simeonstift** (Simeonstiftpl., tel. 0651/718–2449), containing religious art and lots of city history and artifacts. Admission is DM 3, DM 1.50 for students, and the museum is closed Sunday.

ROMAN TRIER • Greeting you as you enter Trier from the station is **Porta Nigra** (Black Gate), which formed part of the mighty 2nd-century Roman wall that once encircled the city. If you look closely at the seams of the blocks, you'll notice the scars made by Franks who scraped them for precious metals. The gate's name comes from centuries of soot that have turned it black. Trier's **Kaiserthermen** (Imperial Baths; admission DM 4, DM 2 students; open daily), on Kaiserstraße, were once the third-largest in the Roman Empire. All that's left now is the wall of a bath and some underground walkways. Still, it's worth a quick look. Just east of the Kaiserthermen are the remains of the **Amphitheater** (Olewigerstr.; admission DM 4, DM 2 students; open daily), which was built around AD 100 and qualifies as Trier's oldest Roman ruin. You can climb down to the cellars beneath the arena to see what's left of the machines used to change the scenery; in the walls are the cells where they kept the lions before releasing them to devour maidens and folks who got on the emperor's bad side.

AFTER DARK

The good news is that Trier is a university town; the bad news is that most students go home for summer break, leaving lots of retirees and teenage tourists. It's not impossible to find fun, just a bit of a challenge. If you read German, the monthly mag *Katz* (DM 3.50) gives the lowdown on everything from movies to concerts. A popular student nightspot is **Zapotex** (Pferdemarkt 1a, tel. 0651/75822; open daily). Located on a lively square, **In Flagrante** (Viehmarktpl. 13, tel. 0651/40148; open daily until 2 AM) is also a good choice, with a large, hip crowd on weekends, and cheap bistro food to go with its libations. For live jazz try **Mintons Playhouse,** a block from the Hauptmarkt (Jakobstr. 13, tel. 0651/49132), which draws a mellow, friendly twentysomething crowd on weekends. It's open daily from 10 AM to 1 AM, later on weekends. Call for show dates, times, and possible cover charges.

GERMAN GLOSSARY

PRONUNCIATION

German is a relatively phonetic language: What you see is generally what you say, as long as you memorize a few rules. Being able to get by in German will probably come in handy in the the eastern and rural areas of Germany; in urban settings you are likely to encounter English-speaking Germans. For a crash course in German, consider picking up a set of Living Language™ tapes and books (tel. 800/733–3000 in U.S.).

VOWELS

A is usually pronounced like the **a** in ah. **E** varies between the long **a** sound in ray (without the y sound) and the short **u** sound in mutt: Regen (rain) is pronounced ra(y)- gun. A long **i** is like the **ee** sound in beet; a short **i** is like the **i** in mitt. An **o** can sound like the **o** cobra (long) or the **o** in ocular (short). A **u** can sound like the **u** in rule (long) or the **oo** in foot (short). A **y** is pronounced like a **ü** (*see below*).

An **h** after a vowel makes the preceding vowel long. A double vowel (aa, ee) also makes the vowel sound long. An **e** after a vowel acts like an umlaut (ae = ä, oe = ö, ue = ü).

UMLAUTS AND DIPHTHONGS

When it's long, **ä** is like the **a** in nave, but without the y sound after the a; when it's short, **ä** is like the **e** in met. An **ö** is like the **y** in myrrh. The long **ü** is like the French **ue** in rue; a short **ü** is closer to the **i** sound in mitt.

Ai is like the **i** in night. **Au** is like the **ow** in now**. Äu** is like the **oi** in voice. **Ei** is like the **i** in night. **Eu** is like the **oi** in voice. **Ie** is like the **ee** in knee.

CONSONANTS

The harsh **ch** sound is made by breathing through the space between the soft palate and the back of the tongue: Bu**ch** (book), au**ch** (also). To make the softer **ch**, breathe out as you press the front of your tongue close to the hard palate while keeping the tip of the tongue behind your lower teeth: **ich** (I), Bü**ch**er (books). **Sch** is pronounced like **sh** in shoe. An **ß** is like the **ss** in mess. **Sp** is pronounced **shp**; **st** is pronounced **sht. V** is usually pronounced like the **f** in fish; **w** is like the **v** in vase. A **z** is pronounced **ts**.

English	*German*	*Pronunciation*
BASICS		
Yes/no	ja/nein	yah/nine
Hello	Guten Tag	**goo**-ten tahk
Goodbye	Auf Wiedersehen	ouf **vee**-der-zehn
Good morning	Guten Morgen	**goo**-ten **mor**-gen
Good evening	Guten Abend	**goo**-ten **ah**-bent
Good night	Gute Nacht	**goo**-tuh nakht
How are you?	Wie geht es Ihnen?	vee ga(y)t ess **een**-en
I'm fine, thanks.	Danke, gut.	dahnk-uh goot

Excuse me.	Entschuldigung	ent-**shool-**dee-goong
My name is . . .	Ich heiße . . .	ikh **high-**suh
I'm from the United States.	Ich bin Amerikaner(in)	ikh bin ah-meh-ree-**kah**-ner(-in)
I'm Australian.	Ich bin Australier(in)	ikh bin ous-**tra**-lee-ur(-in)
I'm Canadian.	Ich bin Kanadier(in)	ikh bin ka-**na**-dyur(-in)
I'm English.	Ich bin Engländer(in)	ikh bin **ehng**-glenn-der(-in)
I'm Scottish.	Ich bin Schotte/Schottin	ikh bin **shott**-uh/**shott**-in
Kiss me, I'm Irish.	Küß mich, ich bin Ire/Irin	ikh bin **eer**-uh/**eer**- in
Do you speak English?	Sprechen Sie Englisch?	**shprehk-**en zee **eng-**lish?
I don't speak German.	Ich spreche kein Deutsch.	ikh **shprehk-**uh kine doych
I don't understand.	Ich verstehe nicht.	ikh fehr-**shteh**-huh nikht
How do you say . . . ?	Wie sagt man . . . ?	vee zahgt mahn . . . ?
More slowly, please.	Langsamer, bitte.	**lahng**-sahm-er **bitt**-uh
What did you say?	Wie, bitte?	vee **bih-**tuh?
I don't know.	Ich weiß nicht.	ikh vice nikht
Thank you	Danke	**dahn-**kuh
Please	Bitte	**bih-**tuh
You're welcome.	Bitte/Nichts zu danken.	bitt-uh/nikhts tsoo dahnk-un
Are there . . . ?	Gibt es . . . ?	gipt ess . . . ?
Where is/are . . . ?	Wo ist/sind . . . ?	**vo** isst/zind
The bank	Die Bank	dee **bahnk**
The bathroom	Die Toilette	dee twah-**let-**uh
Backpack	Rucksack	rook-zuck
The post office	Die Post	dee **pohst**
Long-distance phone calls	Ferngespräche	fern-guh-**shpra(y)**-khe
Phone card	Telefon(wert)karte	teh-leh-**fohn**-kahr-tuh
Laundromat	Waschsalon	**vahsh**-zah-long
Open	offen	**o-**fen
Closed	geschlossen	guh-**shloss-**en
Yesterday	gestern	**guess**-tern
Today	heute	**hoy**-tuh
Tomorrow	morgen	**mohr**-gun
This morning	heute morgen	**hoy**-tuh **mohr**-gun
This evening	heute abend	**hoy**-tuh **ah**-bent
Tonight	heute nacht	**hoy**-tuh nakht
What time is it?	Wieviel Uhr ist es?	**vee-**feel oor ist ess?
Entrance	Eingang	**ine**-gahng
Exit	Ausgang	**ous**-gahng
Floor/story	Stock	shtok
Neighborhood	Nachbarschaft/Umgebung	**nakh**-bar-shahft/oom-**ga(y)**-boong
How much is this/it?	Wieviel kostet das/es?	vee-**feel koss**-tet dass?
Cheap	billig	bill-ikh
Expensive	teuer	**toy**-uh

EMERGENCIES AND MEDICAL AID

I am sick.	Ich bin krank.	ikh bin krahnk
Help!	Hilfe!	**hill**-fuh
Go away!	Geh weg!	ga(y) vehk
Police	Polizei	po-lee-**tsigh**
Hospital	Krankenhaus	**krahnk**-un-house
I need a doctor.	Ich brauche einen Arzt.	ikh **brow**-khe **ine**-un ahrtst
I have a headache.	Ich habe Kopfschmerzen.	ikh **hah**-buh **kopf**-shmerts-un
I have a stomachache.	Ich habe Bauchschmerzen.	ikh **hah**-buh **bowkh**-shmerts-un
Fever	Fieber	**fee**-beh
Prescription	Verordnung	fer-**ord**-nung

Medicine	Medizin	meh-dee-**tseen**
Aspirin	Aspirin	ahs-pee-**reen**
Condom	Kondom/Präservativ	kon-dohm/preh-zehr-vah-teef

COMING AND GOING

The train station	Der Bahnhof	dare **bahn-**hof
The subway station	Die U-Bahn Station	dee **oo**-bahn shtah-**tsyohn**
The bus stop	Die Bushaltestelle	dee **booss**-hahlt-uh-shtel-uh
Arrival/departure	Ankommen/Abfahrt	**ahn**-kohm-en/**ahb**-fahrt
One-way ticket	Einfache Fahrkarte	**ein**-fah-khuh **fahr**-car-tuh
Round-trip ticket	Rückfahrtkarte	**ruek**-fart-car-tuh
First/second class	Erste/Zweite Klasse	**air**-stuh/**tsvigh**-tuh **klah**-suh
Discount	Ermäßigung	ehr-**ma(y)**-see-goong
Left/right	Links/rechts	links/rekhts

WHERE TO SLEEP

Youth hostel	Jugendherberge	**you**-gint-hair-bear-guh
A room . . .	Ein Zimmer . . .	ein tsim-er
. . . for one person	. . . für eine Person	fuer **ein**-uh pair-**zone**
. . . for two people	. . . für zwei Personen	fuer tsvai pair-**zone**-un
The key	Der Schlüssel	dare **shlue**-sul
A bed	Ein Bett	ine bet
With/without bath	Mit/ohne Bad	mit/**ohn**-eh baht
Breakfast	Frühstück	**frue**-shtik

FOOD

I'd like to have . . .	Ich hätte gerne . . .	ikh **het**-uh **gairn**-uh
The menu	Die Speisekarte	dee **shpy**-zuh-car-tuh
The bill/check	Die Rechnung	dee **rekh**-noong
Bread	Brot	broht
Cheese	Käse	**ka(y)**-zuh
(without) Meat	(ohne) Fleisch	(**ohn**-uh) flishe
How much is it?	Wieviel kostet das?	vee-**feel cos**-tet dahs
I am a vegetarian.	Ich bin Vegetarier(in).	ikh bin veh-guh-**tah**-ree-ah(-rin)
I am diabetic.	Ich bin Diabetiker(in).	ikh bin dee-uh-**ba(y)**-tee- kah (-rin)
Made to order	auf Bestellung	owf buh-**shtel**-oong
Side dishes	Beilagen	**by**-lah-gun
Extra charge	Extraaufschlag	**eks**-tra-**owf**-shlahg
appetizers	Vorspeisen	**for**-shpy-zen
Entrées	Hauptspeisen	**howpt**-shpy-zen
Homemade	hausgemacht	**house**-guh-makht
(not) included	(nicht) inbegriffen	(nikht) **in**-buh-griff-un
local specialties	Lokalspezialitäten	loh-**kahl** shpeh-tsyahl-ee-**teh**-tun
set menu	Menü	muh-**new**
lunch menu	Mittagskarte	**mit**-tahks-car-tuh
desserts	Nachspeisen	**nakh**-shpy-zen
service included	inklusive Bedienung	in-kloo-**zee**-vuh buh-**dee**- noong
specialty of the house	Spezialität des Hauses	shpeh-tsyah-lee-**teht** dess **how**-zes
soup of the day	Tagessuppe	**tah**-guess-zoop-uh
is served from . . . to . . .	wird von . . . bis . . . serviert	virt fon . . . biss . . . zer-**veert**
bread	Brot	broht
butter	Butter	**boot**-tuh
eggs	Eier	**ah**-yah

hot	heiß	hice
cold	kalt	kahlt
jam	Konfitüre	kon-fee-**tue**-ruh
milk	Milch	milkh
organge juice	Orangensaft	o-**rawn**-zhun-zahft
scrambled eggs	Rühreier	**ruer**-ah-yah
bacon	Speck	shpek
sunny-side up eggs	Spiegeleier	**shpee**-gul-ah-yah
shrimp	Garnelen	gar-**na(y)**-lun
salmon	Lachs	lahx
mussels	Muscheln	**moosh**-uln
mushrooms	Pilze	**pill**-tsuh
smoked . . .	Rächer . . .	**roy**-khuh . . .
ham	Schinken	**shing**-kun
asparagus	Spargel	**shpahr**-gul
stew	Eintopf	**ine**-topf
tomato soup	Tomatensuppe	toh-**mah**-ten-zoop-puh
onion soup	Zwiebelsuppe	**tsvee**-bel-zoop-puh
baked	gebacken	guh-**bahk**-un
fried	gebraten	guh-**brah**-tun
steamed	gedämpft	guh-**dempft**
grilled	gegrillt	guh-**grillt**
boiled	gekocht	guh-**kokht**
breaded	paniert	pah-**neert**
raw	roh	roh
(The English words rare, medium, and well done are used and understood in Germany.)		
lamb	Lamm	lahm
beef	Rind	rint
pork	Schwein	shvine
duck	Ente	enn-tuh
eel	Aal	ahl
trout	Forelle	fo-**rell**-uh
herring	Hering	**heh**-ring
lobster	Hummer	**hoom**-uh
cod	Kabeljau	**kah**-bel-yow
crab	Krabbe	**crub**-buh
sole	Seezunge	**za(y)**-tsoong-uh
tuna	Thunfisch	**toon**-fish
eggplant	Aubergine	oh-ber-**zheen**-uh
red cabbage	Rotkohl	**roht**-kohl
beans	Bohnen	**boan**-un
onions	Zwiebel	**tsvee**-bul
potato	Kartoffel	car-**toff**-ul
potato pancakes	Kartoffelpuffer	car-toff-ul-**poof**-uh
french fries	Pommes (frites)	**pom**-muss (freet)
rice	Reis	rice
pasta	Nudeln	**noo**-duln
vinegar	Essig	**ess**-ick
garlic	Knoblauch	**knoa**-blawkh
herbs	Kräuter	**croy**-ter
horseradish	Meerrettich	**mehr**-rett-ikh
oil	Öl	u(r)l
mustard	Senf	zenf
salt	Salz	zalts
pepper	Pfeffer	**pfef**-uh
non-alcoholic	alkoholfrei	al-koh-**hohl**-fry

dark beer	ein Dunkles	ine **doonk**-lus
light beer	ein Helles	ine **hell**-us
a mug (one quart)	ein Maß	ine mahs
draught	vom Faß	fomm fass
dark, bitter, high hops content	Altbier	**alt**-beer
strong, high alcohol content	Bockbier (Doppelbock, Märzen)	**bok**-beer (dop-pul-beer, mehr-tsen)
wheat beer with yeast	Hefeweizen	**heh**-fuh-vigh-tsen
light beer, strong hops aroma	Pilsner	**pils**-ner
wheat beer	Weizenbier	**vite**-sen-beer
light beer and lemonade	Radler	**rahd**-ler
red wine	Rotwein	**roht**-vine
white wine	Weißwein	**vice**-vine
sparkling wine	Sekt	zekt
coffee	Kaffee	**kah**-fa(y)
decaffeinated	koffeinfrei	kof-feh-**een**-fry
with milk/sugar	mit Milch/Zucker	mit milkh/**tsoo**-ker
with artificial sweetener	mit Süßstoff	mit **sues**-shtof
black	Schwarz	shvarts
mineral water	Mineralwasser	mi-neh-**rahl**-vas-er
(hot) chocolate	(heiße) Schokolade	(**high**-suh) shoh-koh-**lah**-duh
tea	Tee	teh
with lemon	mit Zitrone	mit tsee-**tro**-nuh

OTHER USEFUL PHRASES

Cheers!	Prost!	prohst
I'm plastered.	Ich bin besoffen.	ikh bin buh-**zoff**-un
I love you.	Ich liebe dich.	ikh **lee**-buh dikh

NUMBERS

One	eins	eints
Two	zwei	tsvigh
Three	drei	dry
Four	vier	fea(r)
Five	fünf	fimf
Six	sechs	zex
Seven	sieben	**zee**-ben
Eight	acht	ahkt
Nine	neun	noyn
Ten	zehn	tsane
Eleven	elf	elf
Twelve	zwölf	tsvuhlf
Thirteen	dreizehn	**dry**-tsane
Fourteen	vierzehn	**fur**-tsane
Fifteen	fünfzehn	**fimf**-tsane
Sixteen	sechzehn	**zekh**-tsane
Seventeen	siebzehn	**zeeb**-tsane
Eighteen	achtzehn	**akht**-tsane
Nineteen	neunzehn	**noyn**-tsane
Twenty	zwanzig	**tsvahn**-tsick
Thirty	dreißig	**dry**-sick
Forty	vierzig	**feer**-tsick
Fifty	fünfzig	**fimf**-tsig
Sixty	sechzig	**sekh**-tsick
Seventy	siebzig	**zeep**-tsick
Eighty	achtzig	**akht**-tsick

Ninety	neunzig	**noyn**-tsick
One hundred	hundert	**hoon**-dert
One thousand	tausend	**tao**-zund

DAYS OF THE WEEK AND MONTHS

Sunday	Sonntag	**zon**-tahk
Monday	Montag	**mohn**-tahk
Tuesday	Dienstag	**deens**-tahk
Wednesday	Mittwoch	**mitt**-vokh
Thursday	Donnerstag	**don**-ners-tahk
Friday	Freitag	**fry**-tahk
Saturday	Samstag	**zahms**-tahk
January	Januar	**jah**-noo-ahr
February	Februar	**feh**-broo-ahr
March	März	mehrts
April	April	ah-**pril**
May	Mai	my
June	Juni	**yoo**-nee
July	Juli	**yoo**-lee
August	August	ow-**goost**
September	September	zep-**tem**-buh
October	Oktober	okk-**toe**-buh
November	November	noh-**vem**-buh
December	Dezember	deh-**tsem**-buh

INDEX

N

O

P